D0205990

JAMES FENIMORE COOPER

James Fenimore Cooper

THE LEATHERSTOCKING TALES

VOLUME II

The Pathfinder: or, The Inland Sea

The Deerslayer: or, The First War-Path

THE LIBRARY OF AMERICA

Distributed to the trade in the United States
and Canada by the Viking Press.

Published outside North America by the Press Syndicate
of the University of Cambridge,
The Pitt Building, Trumpington Street, Cambridge CB2 1RP, England.
ISBN 0 521 30095 9

Library of Congress Catalog Card Number: 84–25060
For Cataloging in Publication Data, see end of *Notes* section.
ISBN 0–940450–21–6

First Printing

Manufactured in the United States of America

BLAKE NEVIUS

WROTE THE NOTES AND SELECTED THE TEXTS FOR THIS VOLUME

The texts in this volume are from The Writings of James Fenimore Cooper, edited by James Franklin Beard, Editor-in-Chief, and James P. Elliott, Chief Textual Editor, sponsored by Clark University and the American Antiquarian Society, and published by the State University of New York Press. The text of The Pathfinder was edited by Richard Dilworth Rust, and the text of The Deerslayer was edited by Lance Schachterle, Kent P. Ljungquist, and James A. Kilby.

Grateful acknowledgement is made to the National Endowment for the Humanities and the Ford Foundation for their generous financial support of this series.

Contents

Readers who wish to follow the chronological order of Natty Bumppo's career should read The Leatherstocking Tales in the following sequence: The Deerslayer, The Last of the Mohicans, The Pathfinder, The Pioneers, and The Prairie.

THE PATHFINDER

or, The Inland Sea

——Here the heart
May give a useful lesson to the head,
And Learning wiser grow without his books.
Cowper, *The Task*, VI, ll. 86–88.

Preface

THE PLAN of this tale suggested itself to the writer, many years since, though the details are altogether of recent invention. The idea of associating seamen and savages, in incidents that might be supposed characteristic of the Great Lakes, having been mentioned to a publisher, the latter obtained something like a pledge from the author to carry out the design, at some future day, which pledge is now tardily and imperfectly redeemed.

The reader may recognize an old friend, under new circumstances, in the principal character of this legend. If the exhibition made of this old acquaintance, in the novel circumstances in which he now appears, should be found not to lessen his favor with the public, it will be a source of extreme gratification to the writer, since he has an interest in the individual in question, that falls little short of reality. It is not an easy task, however, to reproduce the same character in four separate works, and to maintain the peculiarities that are indispensable to identity, without incurring a risk of fatiguing the reader with sameness, and the present experiment has been so long delayed, quite as much from doubts of its success, as from any other cause. In this, as in every other undertaking, it must be the "end" that will "crown the work."

The Indian character has so little variety, that it has been my object to avoid dwelling on it too much, on the present occasion. Its association with the sailor, too, it is feared, will be found to have more novelty than interest.

It may strike the novice as an anachronism, to place vessels on Ontario, in the middle of the eighteenth century, but, in this particular, facts will fully bear out all the licence of the fiction. Although the precise vessels mentioned in these pages may never have existed on that water, or anywhere else, others so nearly resembling them are known to have navigated that inland sea, even at a period much earlier than the one just mentioned, as to form a sufficient authority for their introduction into a work of fiction. It is a fact not generally remembered, however well known it may be, that there are isolated spots, along the line of the great lakes that date, as settlements, as far back, as many of the oldest American towns, and which were the seats of a species of civilization, long before the greater portion of even the original states was rescued from the wilderness.

Ontario, in our own times, has been the scene of important naval evolutions. Fleets have manœuvred on those waters, which, half a century ago, were as near desert as waters well can be, and the day is not distant, when the whole of that vast range of lakes will become the seat of empire, and fraught with all the interests of human society. A passing glimpse, even though it be in a work of fiction, of what that vast region so lately was, may help to make up the sum of knowledge by which alone, a just appreciation can be formed of the wonderful means by which Providence is clearing the way for the advancement of civilization across the whole American continent.

DECEMBER, 1839.

Preface

FOLLOWING THE ORDER of events, this book should be the third in the Series of the Leather-Stocking Tales. In the Deerslayer, Natty Bumppo, under the *Sobriquet* which forms the title of that work, is represented as a youth, just commencing his forest career as a warrior; having for several years been a hunter so celebrated, as already to have gained the honorable appellation he then bore. In the Last of the Mohicans he appears as Hawkeye, and is present at the death of young Uncas; while in this tale, he re-appears in the same war of '56, in company with his Mohican friend, still in the vigor of manhood, and young enough to feel that master passion to which all conditions of men, all tempers, and we might almost say all ages, submit, under circumstances that are incited to call it into existence.

The Pathfinder did not originally appear for several years after the publication of the Prairie, the work in which the leading character of both had closed his career by death. It was, perhaps, a too hazardous experiment to recall to life, in this manner, and after so long an interval, a character that was somewhat a favorite with the reading world, and which had been regularly consigned to his grave, like any living man. It is probably owing to this severe ordeal that the work, like its successor, the Deerslayer, has been so little noticed; scarce one in ten of those who know all about the three earliest books of the series having even a knowledge of the existence of the last at all. That this caprice in taste and favor is in no way dependent on merit, the writer feels certain; for, though the world will ever maintain that an author is always the worst judge of his own productions, one who has written much, and regards all his literary progeny with more or less of a paternal eye, must have a reasonably accurate knowledge of what he has been about the greater part of his life. Such a man may form too high an estimate of his relative merits, as relates to others; but it is not easy to see why he should fall into this error, more than another, as relates to himself. His general standard may be raised too high by means of self-love; but, unless he be disposed to maintain the equal perfection of what he has done, as probably no man was ever yet fool enough to do, he may very well have shrewd conjectures as to the comparative merits and defects of his own productions.

This work, on its appearance, was rudely and maliciously assailed by certain individuals out of pure personal malignancy. It is scarcely worth the author's while, nor would it have any interest for the reader, to expose the motives and frauds of these individuals, who have pretty effectually vindicated the writer by their own subsequent conduct. But even the falsest of men pay so much homage to truth, as to strive to seem its votaries. In attacking the Pathfinder, the persons alluded to pointed out faults, that the author, for the first time, has now ascertained to be real; and much to his surprise, as of most of them he is entirely innocent. They are purely errors of the press, unless, indeed, the writer can justly be accused of having been a careless proof reader. A single instance of the mistakes he means may be given in explanation of the manner in which the book was originally got up.

The heroine of this tale was at first called "Agnes." In the fifth or sixth chapter this name was changed to "Mabel," and the manuscript was altered accordingly. Owing to inadvertency, however, the original appellation stood in several places, and the principal female character of the book, until now, has had the advantage of going by two names! Many other typographical errors exist in the earlier editions, most of which, it is believed, are corrected in this.

There are a few discrepancies in the facts of this work, as connected with the facts of the different books of the series. They are not material, and it was thought fairer to let them stand as proof of the manner in which the books were originally written, than to make any changes in the text.

In youth, when belonging to the navy, the writer of this book served for some time on the great Western lakes. He was, indeed, one of those who first carried the cockade of the republic, on those inland seas. This was pretty early in the present century, when the navigation was still confined to the employment of a few ships and schooners. Since that day, light may be said to have broken into the wilderness, and the rays of the sun have penetrated to tens of thousands of beautiful valleys and plains, that then lay in "grateful shade." Towns have been built along the whole of the extended line of coasts, and the traveller now stops at many a place of ten or fifteen, and at one of even fifty, thousand inhabitants, where a few huts then marked the natural sites of future marts. In a word, though the scenes of this book are believed to have once been as nearly accurate as is required by the laws which govern fiction, they are so no longer. Oswego is a large and thriving town; Toronto and Kingston, on the other side of the lake, compete with it; while Buffalo, Detroit, Cleveland, Milwaukie, and Chicago, on the upper lakes, to say nothing of a hundred places of lesser note, are fast advancing to the level of commercial places of great local importance. In these changes, the energy of youth and abundance is quite as much apparent as anything else; and it is ardently to be hoped that the fruits of the gifts of a most bountiful Providence may not be mistaken for any peculiar qualities in those who have been their beneficiaries. A just appreciation of the first of these facts will render us grateful and meek; while the vain-glorious, who are so apt to ascribe all to themselves, will be certain to live long enough to ascertain the magnitude of their error. That great results are intended to be produced by means of these wonderful changes, we firmly believe; but that they will prove to be the precise results now so generally anticipated, in consulting the experience of the past, and taking the nature of man into the account, the reflecting and intelligent may be permitted to doubt.

It may strike the novice as an anachronism, to place vessels on Ontario in the middle of the eighteenth century; but, in this particular, facts will fully bear out all the license of the fiction. Although the precise vessels mentioned in these pages may never have existed on that water, or anywhere else, others so nearly resembling them as to form a sufficient authority for their introduction into a work of fiction, are known to have navigated that inland sea, even at a period much earlier than the one just mentioned. It is a fact not generally remembered, however well known it may be, that there are isolated spots, along the line of the great lakes, that date, as settlements, as far back as many of the oldest American towns, and which were the seats of a species of civilization, long before the greater portion of even the original states was rescued from the wilderness.

Ontario, in our own times, has been the scene of important naval evolutions. Fleets have manœuvred on those waters, which, half a century since, were desert wastes; and the day is not distant, when the whole of that vast range of lakes will become the seat of empire, and fraught with all the interests of human society. A passing glimpse, even though it be in a work of fiction, of what that vast region so lately was, may help to make up the sum of knowledge by which alone a just appreciation can be formed of the wonderful means by which Providence is clearing the way for the advancement of civilization across the whole American continent.

Chapter 1

"The turf shall be my fragrant shrine;
My temple, Lord! that arch of thine;
My censer's breath the mountain airs,
And silent thoughts my only prayers."
Moore, "The Turf Shall Be My
Fragrant Shrine," ll. 1–4.

THE SUBLIMITY connected with vastness, is familiar to every eye. The most abstruse, the most far-reaching, perhaps the most chastened of the poet's thoughts, crowd on the imagination as he gazes into the depths of the illimitable void; the expanse of the ocean is seldom seen by the novice, with indifference, and the mind, even in the obscurity of night, finds a parallel to that grandeur, which seems inseparable from images that the senses cannot compass. With feelings akin to this admiration and awe, the offspring of sublimity, were the different characters with which the action of this tale must open, gazing on the scene before them. Four persons in all, two of each sex, they had managed to ascend a pile of trees, that had been uptorn by a tempest, to catch a view of the objects that surrounded them. It is still the practice of the country to call these spots wind-rows. By letting in the light of heaven upon the dark and damp recesses of the woods, they form a sort of oases in the solemn obscurity of the virgin forests of America. The particular wind-row of which we are writing lay on the brow of a gentle acclivity, and it had opened the way for an extended view, to those who might occupy its upper margins, a rare occurrence to the traveller in the woods. As usual, the spot was small, but owing to the circumstance of its lying on the low acclivity mentioned, and that of the opening's extending downward, it offered more than common advantages to the eye. Philosophy has not yet determined the nature of the power that so often lays desolate spots of this description, some ascribing it to the whirlwinds that produce water-spouts on the ocean, while others again impute it to sudden and violent passages of streams of the electric fluid; but the effects in the woods are familiar to all. On the upper margin of the opening, to which there is allusion, the viewless influence had piled tree on tree, in such a manner as had not only enabled the two males of the party to ascend to an elevation of some thirty feet above the level of the earth, but, with a little care and encouragement, to induce their more timid companions to accompany them. The vast trunks, that had been broken and riven by the force of the gust, lay blended like jack-straws, while their branches, still exhaling the fragrance of wilted leaves, were interlaced in a manner to afford sufficient support to the hands. One tree had been completely uprooted, and its lower end, filled with earth, had been cast uppermost, in a way to supply a sort of staging for the four adventurers, when they had gained the desired distance from the ground.

The reader is to anticipate none of the appliances of people of refinement, in the description of the personal appearances of the group in question. They were all way-farers in the wilderness, and had they not been, neither their previous habits, nor their actual social positions would have accustomed them to many of the luxuries of rank. Two of the party, indeed, a male and a female, belonged to the native owners of the soil, being Indians of the well known tribe of the Tuscaroras, while their companions were a man, who bore about him the peculiarities of one who had passed his days on the ocean, and that, too, in a station little if any above that of a common mariner, while his female associate was a maiden of a class, in no great degree superior to his own, though her youth, sweetness of countenance, and a modest but spirited mien, lent that character of intellect and refinement, which adds so much to the charm of beauty, in the sex. On the present occasion, her full blue eye reflected the feeling of sublimity that the scene excited, and her pleasant face was beaming with the pensive expression, with which all deep emotions, even though they bring the most grateful pleasure, shadow the countenances of the ingenuous and thoughtful.

And, truly, the scene was of a nature, deeply to impress the imagination of the beholder. Towards the west, in which direction the faces of the party were turned, and in which alone could much be seen, the eye ranged over an ocean of leaves, glorious and rich in the varied but lively verdure of a generous vegetation, and shaded by the luxuriant tints that belong to the forty second degree of latitude. The elm, with its graceful and weeping top, the rich varieties of the maple, most of the noble oaks of the American forest, with the broad leafed linden, known in the parlance of the country as the basswood, mingled their uppermost branches, forming one broad and seemingly interminable carpet of foliage, that stretched away towards the setting sun, until it bounded the horizon, by blending with the clouds, as the waves and sky meet at the base of the vault of Heaven. Here and there, by some accident of the tempests, or by a caprice of nature, a trifling opening among these giant members of the forest, permitted an inferior tree to struggle upward toward the light, and to lift its modest head nearly to a level with the surrounding surface of verdure. Of this class were the birch, a tree of some account, in regions less favored, the quivering aspen, various generous nut-woods, and divers others, that resembled the ignoble and vulgar, thrown by circumstances, into the presence of the stately and great. Here and there, too, the tall, straight trunk of the pine, pierced the vast field, rising high above it, like some grand monument reared by art on the plain of leaves.

It was the vastness of the view, the nearly unbroken surface of verdure, that contained the principle of grandeur. The beauty was to be traced in the delicate tints, relieved by gradations of light and shadow, while the solemn repose, induced a feeling allied to awe.

"Uncle," said the wondering but pleased girl, addressing her male companion, whose arm she rather touched than leaned on, to steady her own light but firm footing—"this is like a view of the ocean you so much love!"

"So much for ignorance, and a girl's fancy, Magnet"—a term of affection, the sailor often used in allusion to his niece's personal attractions—"No one but a child would think of likening this handful of leaves, to a look at the real Atlantic. You might stop all these tree-tops to Neptune's jacket, and they would make no more than a nosegay in his bosom."

"More fanciful than true, I think, uncle. Look, thither; it must be miles on miles, and yet we see nothing but leaves! What more could one behold, if looking at the ocean?"

"More!" returned the uncle, giving an impatient gesture

with the elbow the other touched, for his arms were crossed, and the hands were thrust into the bosom of a vest of red cloth, a fashion of the times, "More, Magnet; say, rather, what less. Where are your combing-seas, your blue-water, your rollers, your breakers, your whales, or your water-spouts and your endless motion, in this bit of a forest, child?"

"And where are your tree-tops, your solemn silence, your fragrant leaves and your beautiful green, uncle, on the ocean?"

"Tut, Magnet; if you understood the thing, you would know that green water is a sailor's bane. He scarcely relishes a green horn, less."

"But green trees are a different thing. Hist! that sound is the air breathing among the leaves!"

"You should hear a nor-wester breathe, girl, if you fancy noise aloft. Now where are your gales, and hurricanes, and trades, and Levanters and such like incidents in this bit of a forest, and what fishes have you swimming beneath yonder tame surface?"

"That there have been tempests here, these signs around us plainly show, and beasts, if not fishes, are beneath these leaves."

"I do not know that—" returned the uncle, with a sailor's dogmatism. "They told us many stories, at Albany, of the wild animals we should fall in with, and yet we have seen nothing to frighten a seal. I doubt any of your inland animals, will compare with a low latitude shark."

"See!" exclaimed the niece, who was more occupied with the sublimity and beauty of the "boundless wood," than with her uncle's arguments, "yonder is a smoke curling over the tops of the trees—can it come from a house?"

"Ay—ay—there is a look of humanity in that smoke," returned the old seaman, "which is worth a thousand trees. I must show it to Arrowhead, who may be running past a port without knowing it. It is a probable there is a camboose, where there is a smoke."

As he concluded, the uncle drew a hand from his bosom, touched the male Indian, who was standing near him, lightly on the shoulder, and pointed out a thin line of vapor, that was stealing slowly out of the wilderness of leaves, at a distance of about a mile, and was diffusing itself in almost imperceptible threads of humidity, in the quivering atmosphere. The Tuscarora was one of those noble-looking warriors that were oftener met with among the aborigines of this continent a century since, than to day, and, while he had mingled sufficiently with the colonists to be familiar with their habits, and even with their language, he had lost little, if any, of the wild grandeur, and simple dignity of a chief. Between him and the old seaman the intercourse had been friendly, but distant, for the Indian had been too much accustomed to mingle with the officers of the different military posts he had frequented, not to understand that his present companion was only a subordinate. So imposing indeed, had been the quiet superiority of the Tuscarora's reserve, that Charles Cap, for so was the seaman named, in his most dogmatical or facetious moments had not ventured on familiarity, in an intercourse that had now lasted more than a week. The sight of the curling smoke, however, had struck the latter like the sudden appearance of a sail at sea, and, for the first time since they met, he ventured to touch the warrior, as has been related.

The quick eye of the Tuscarora instantly caught a sight of the smoke, and for quite a minute, he stood, slightly raised on tiptoe, with distended nostrils, like the buck that scents a taint in the air, and a gaze as riveted as that of the trained pointer, while he waits his master's aim. Then falling back on his feet, a low exclamation, in the soft tones that form so singular a contrast to its harsher cries, in the Indian warrior's voice, was barely audible. Otherwise he was undisturbed. His countenance was calm, and his quick, dark, eagle eye moved over the leafy panorama, as if to take in at a glance every circumstance that might enlighten his mind.

That the long journey they had attempted to make through a broad belt of wilderness, was necessarily attended with danger, both uncle and niece well knew, though neither could at once determine whether the sign that others were in their vicinity, was the harbinger of good, or evil.

"There must be Oneidas, or Tuscaroras, near us, Arrowhead," said Cap, addressing his Indian companion by his conventional English name; "will it not be well to join company with them, and get a comfortable berth for the night in their wigwam?"

"No wigwam there," Arrowhead answered in his unmoved manner—"too much tree."

"But Indians must be there; perhaps some old mess-mates of your own, Master Arrowhead."

"No Tuscarora—no Oneida—no Mohawk—pale-face fire."

"The devil it is! Well, Magnet, this surpasses a seaman's philosophy—we old sea-dogs can tell a soldier's from a sailor's quid, or a lubber's nest from a mate's hammock, but I do not think the oldest admiral in His Majesty's Fleet can tell a King's smoke from a collier's!"

The idea that human beings were in their vicinity in that ocean of wilderness, had deepened the flush on the blooming cheek, and brightened the eye of the fair creature at his side, but she now turned with a look of surprise to her relative, and said hesitatingly,—for both had often admired the Tuscarora's knowledge, or we might almost say, instinct—

"A pale face's fire! Surely, uncle, he cannot know *that*!"

"Ten days since, child, I would have sworn to it; but, now, I hardly know what to believe. May I take the liberty of asking, Arrowhead, why you fancy that smoke, now, a pale face's smoke, and not a red skin's?"

"Wet wood—" returned the warrior, with the calmness with which the pedagogue might point out an arithmetical demonstration to his puzzled pupil. "Much wet—much smoke—much water, black smoke."

"But, begging your pardon, Master Arrowhead, the smoke is not black, nor is there much of it. To my eye, now, it is as light and fanciful a smoke as ever rose from a captain's tea kettle, when nothing was left to make the fire, but a few chips from the dunnage."

"Too much water—" returned Arrowhead, with a slight nod of the head. "Tuscarora too cunning to make fire with water; pale face too much book and burn anything. Much book, little know."

"Well, that's reasonable, I allow," said Cap, who was no devotee of learning. "He means that as a hit at your reading, Magnet, for the chief has sensible notions of things, in his own way. How far, now, Arrowhead, do you make us by your calculation, from the bit of a pond, that you call the Great Lake, and towards which we have been so many days shaping our course?"

The Tuscarora looked at the seaman with quiet superiority, as he answered.

"Ontario like heaven; one sun, and the great traveller know it."

"Well, I have been a great traveller, I cannot deny, but of all my v'y'ges this has been the longest, the least profitable, and the farthest inland. If this body of fresh water is so nigh, Arrowhead, and at the same time so large, one might think a pair of good eyes would find it out, for apparently, every thing within thirty miles, is to be seen from this look out."

"Look," said Arrowhead, stretching an arm before him, with quiet grace; "Ontario!"

"Uncle, you are accustomed to cry 'land ho,' but not 'water ho,' and you do not see it," cried the niece, laughing as girls will laugh at their own idle conceits.

"How now, Magnet, dost suppose that I shouldn't know my native element, if it were in sight?"

"But Ontario is not your native element, dear uncle, for you come from the salt water, while this is fresh."

"That might make some difference to your young mariner, but none in the world to the old ones. I should know water, child, were I to see it in China."

"Ontario—" repeated the Arrowhead, with emphasis, again stretching his hand towards the North West.

Cap looked at the Tuscarora, for the first time since their acquaintance, with something like an air of contempt, though he did not fail to follow the direction of the chief's eye and arm, both of which were pointing, to all appearance, toward a vacant spot in the heavens, a short distance above the plain of leaves.

"Ay, ay; this is much as I expected, when I left the coast to come in search of a fresh-water pond," resumed Cap, shrugging his shoulders like one whose mind was made up, and who thought no more need be said. "Ontario may be there, or, for that matter, it may be in my pocket. Well I suppose there will be room enough, when we reach it, to work our canoe. But, Arrowhead, if there be pale faces in our neighborhood, I confess I should like to get within hail of them."

The Tuscarora now gave a quiet inclination of his head, and the whole party descended from the roots of the uptorn tree, in silence. When they had reached the ground, Arrowhead intimated his intention to go towards the fire, and ascertain who had lighted it, while he advised his wife, and the two others to proceed to a canoe, which they had left in the adjacent stream, and await his return.

"Why, chief, this might do on soundings, and in an offing where one knew the channel," returned old Cap, "but in an unknown region like this, I think it unsafe to trust the pilot alone too far from the ship, so, with your leave, we will not part company."

"What my brother want?" asked the Indian gravely, though without taking offence at a distrust that was sufficiently plain.

"Your company, Master Arrowhead, and no more. I will go with you, and speak these strangers."

The Tuscarora assented without difficulty, and again he directed his patient and submissive little wife, who seldom turned her full rich black eye on him, but to express equally her respect, her dread, and her love, to proceed to the boat. But, here, Magnet raised a difficulty. Although spirited, and of unusual energy under circumstances of trial, she was but woman, and the idea of being entirely deserted by her two male protectors, in the midst of a wilderness, that her senses had just told her was seemingly illimitable, became so keenly painful that she expressed a wish to accompany her uncle.

"The exercise will be a relief, dear sir, after sitting so long in the canoe," she added, as the rich blood slowly returned to a cheek that had paled, in spite of her effort to be calm, "and there may be females, with the strangers."

"Come, then, child—it is but a cable's length, and we shall return an hour before the sun sets."

With this permission, the girl, whose real name was Mabel Dunham, prepared to be of the party, while the Dew-of-June, as the wife of Arrowhead was called, passively went her way towards the canoe, too much accustomed to obedience, solitude, and the gloom of the forest, to feel apprehension.

The three who remained in the wind-row, now picked their way around its tangled maze, and gained the margin of the woods, in the necessary direction. A few glances of the eye sufficed for Arrowhead, but old Cap, deliberately set the smoke by a pocket compass, before he trusted himself within the shadows of the trees.

"This steering by the nose, Magnet, may do well enough for an Indian, but your thorough-bred knows the virtue of the needle," said the uncle, as he trudged at the heels of the light stepping Tuscarora. "America would never have been discovered, take my word for it, if Columbus had been nothing but nostrils. Friend Arrowhead, didst ever see a machine like this?"

The Indian turned, cast a glance at the compass, which Cap held in a way to direct his course, and gravely answered—

"A pale face eye. The Tuscarora see in his head. The salt water (for so the Indian styled his companion) all eye—now; no tongue."

"He means, uncle, that we had needs be silent; perhaps he distrusts the persons we are about to meet."

"Ay—'tis an Indian's fashion of going to quarters. You perceive he has examined the priming of his rifle, and it may be as well, if I look to that of my own pistols."

Without betraying alarm at these preparations, to which she had become accustomed by her long journey in the wilderness, Mabel followed with a step as light and elastic as that of the Indian, keeping close in the rear of her companions. For the first half mile, no other caution, beyond a rigid silence was observed, but as the party drew nearer to the spot, where the fire was known to be, much greater care became necessary.

The forest, as usual, had little to intercept the view, below the branches, but the tall straight trunks of trees. Every thing, belonging to vegetation, had struggled towards the light, and beneath the leafy canopy one walked, as it might be, through a vast natural vault, that was upheld by myriads of rustic columns. These columns, or trees, however, often served to conceal the adventurer, the hunter, or the foe, and as Arrowhead swiftly approached the spot where his practised and unerring senses told him the strangers ought to be, his footstep gradually became lighter, his eye more vigilant, and his person was more carefully concealed.

"See, Salt-Water," he said exultingly, pointing at the same time through the vista of trees, "pale-face fire!"

"By the Lord, the fellow is right!" muttered Cap. "There they are, sure enough, and eating their grub as quietly as if they were in the cabin of a three decker."

"Arrowhead is but half right," whispered Mabel, "for there are two Indians and only one white man."

"Pale face," said the Tuscarora, holding up two fingers; "red man" holding up one.

"Well," rejoined Cap, "it is hard to say, which is right and which is wrong. One is certainly white; and a comely, fine lad he is, with an air of life and respectability about him; one is a red skin as plain as paint and nature can make him; but the third chap is half-rigged; being neither brig, nor schooner."

"Pale-face," repeated Arrowhead, again raising two fingers; "red-man," showing but one.

"He must be right, uncle, for his eye seems never to fail. But it is now urgent to know whether we meet as friends, or foes. They may be French."

"One hail will soon satisfy us, on that head," returned Cap. "Stand you, behind this tree, Magnet, lest the knaves take it into their heads to fire a broadside, without a parley, and I will soon learn what colours they sail under."

The uncle had placed his two hands to his mouth, to form a trumpet, and was about to give the promised hail, when a rapid movement from Arrowhead defeated the intention, by deranging the instrument.

"Red man, Mohican," said the Tuscarora; "good; pale-face, Yengeese."

"These are heavenly tidings," murmured Mabel, who little relished the prospect of a deadly fray in that remote wilderness. "Let us approach at once, dear uncle, and proclaim ourselves friends."

"Good—" said the Tuscarora—"red man cool, and know; pale-face hurried, and fire. Let squaw go."

"What," said Cap, in astonishment; "send little Magnet ahead, as a look out, while two lubbers like you and me, lie-to, to see what sort of a land-fall she will make! If I do, I——"

"It is wisest, uncle," interrupted the generous girl, "and I have no fear. No christian, seeing a woman approach alone, would fire upon her, and my presence will be a pledge of peace. Let me go forward, as Arrowhead wishes, and all will be well. We are, as yet, unseen and the surprise of the strangers will not partake of alarm."

"Good—" returned Arrowhead, who did not conceal his approbation of Mabel's spirit.

"It has an unseaman like look," answered Cap, "but, being in the woods, no one will know it. If you think, Mabel—"

"Uncle, I know. There is no cause to fear for me, and you are always nigh to protect me."

"Well, take one of the pistols, then—"

"Nay, I had better rely on my youth and feebleness," said the girl, smiling while her colour heightened under her feelings—"Among christian men, a woman's best guard is her claim to their protection. I know nothing of arms, and wish to live in ignorance of them."

The uncle desisted, and, after receiving a few cautious instructions from the Tuscarora, Mabel rallied all her spirit, and advanced alone towards the group seated near the fire. Although the heart of the girl beat quick, her step was firm and her movements, seemingly, were without reluctance. A death-like silence reigned in the forest, for they towards whom she approached, were too much occupied in appeasing that great natural appetite, hunger, to avert their looks, for an instant, from the important business in which they were all engaged. When Mabel, however, had got within a hundred feet of the fire, she trod upon a dried stick, and the trifling noise that was produced by her light footstep caused the Mohican, as Arrowhead had pronounced the Indian to be, and his companion whose character had been thought so equivocal, to rise to their feet, as quick as thought. Both glanced at the rifles that leaned against a tree, and then each stood without stretching out an arm, as his eyes fell on the form of the girl. The Indian uttered a few words to his companion, and resumed his seat and his meal, as calmly as if no interruption had occurred. On the contrary, the white man, left the fire, and came forward to meet Mabel.

The latter saw, as the stranger approached, that she was

about to be addressed by one of her own colour, though his dress was so strange a mixture of the habits of the two races, that it required a near look to be certain of the fact. He was of middle age, but there was an open honesty, a total absence of guile, in his face, which otherwise would not have been thought handsome, that at once assured Magnet she was in no danger. Still she paused, in obedience to a law of her habits, if not of nature, which rendered her averse to the appearance of advancing too freely to meet one of the other sex, under the circumstances in which she was placed.

"Fear nothing, young woman," said the hunter, for such his attire would indicate him to be, "you have met christian men, in the wilderness, and such as know how to treat all kindly that are disposed to peace and justice. I'm a man well known in all these parts, and perhaps one of my names may have reached your ears. By the Frenchers, and the red-skins on the other side of the Big Lakes, I am called la Longue Carabine; by the Mohicans, a just-minded and upright tribe, what is left of them, Hawk Eye; while the troops and rangers along this side of the water call me Pathfinder, inasmuch as I have never been known to miss one end of the trail, when there was a Mingo, or a friend, who stood in need of me, at the other."

This was not uttered boastfully, but with the honest confidence of one, who well knew that by whatever name others might have heard of him, he had no reason to blush at the reports. The effect on Mabel was instantaneous. The moment she heard the last *soubriquet* she clasped her hands eagerly and repeated the word.

"Pathfinder!"

"So they call me, young woman, and many a great lord has got a title that he did not half so well merit, though, if truth be said, I rather pride myself in finding my way, where there is no path, than in finding it where there is. But the regular troops be by no means particular, and half the time they don't know the difference atween a trail and a path, though one is a matter for the eye, while the other is little more than scent."

"Then you are the friend, my father promised to send to meet us!"

"If you are Sarjeant Dunham's daughter, the Great Prophet of the Delawares never uttered a plainer truth."

"I am Mabel, and yonder, hid by the trees, are my uncle, whose name is Cap, and a Tuscarora called Arrowhead. We did not hope to meet you until we had nearly reached the shores of the Lake."

"I wish a juster-minded Indian had been your guide," said Pathfinder, "for I am no lover of the Tuscaroras, who have travelled too far from the graves of their fathers always to remember the Great Spirit, and Arrowhead is an ambitious chief. Is the Dew of June with him?"

"His wife accompanies us, and a humble and mild creature she is."

"Ay, and true-hearted, which is more than any who know him will say of Arrowhead. Well, we must take the fare that Providence bestows, while we follow the trail of life. I suppose worse guides might have been found than the Tuscarora, though he has too much Mingo blood, for one who consorts altogether with the Delawares."

"It is then, perhaps, fortunate we have met—" said Mabel.

"It is not misfortinate, at any rate, for I promised the Sarjeant I would see his child safe to the garrison, though I died for it. We expected to meet you before you reached the falls; where we have left our own canoe, while we thought it might do no harm to come up, a few miles, in order to be of sarvice if wanted. It's lucky we did, for I doubt if Arrowhead be the man to shoot the current."

"Here come my uncle and the Tuscarora, and our parties can now join."

As Mabel concluded Cap and Arrowhead, who saw that the conference was amicable, drew nigh, and a few words sufficed to let them know as much, as the girl herself had learned from the stranger. As soon as this was done, the party proceeded towards the two who still remained near the fire.

Chapter II

"Yea! long as Nature's humblest Child
Hath kept her temple undefiled
By sinful sacrifice,
Earth's fairest scenes are all his own,
He is a Monarch, and his Throne
Is built amid the skies!"

Wilson, "Lines Written in a Highland Glen," ll. 31–36.

THE MOHICAN continued to eat, though the second white man rose, and courteously took off his cap to Mabel Dunham. He was young, healthful and manly in appearance, and wore a dress, which, while it was less rigidly professional than that of the uncle, also denoted one accustomed to the water. In that age, real seamen were a class entirely apart from the rest of mankind, their ideas, ordinary language, and attire being as strongly indicative of their calling, as the opinions, speech and dress of a Turk denote a Mussulman. Although the Pathfinder was scarcely in the prime of life, Mabel had met him with a steadiness that may have been the consequence of having braced her nerves for the interview, but when her eyes encountered those of the young man at the fire, they fell before the gaze of admiration, with which she saw, or fancied she saw, he greeted her. Each, in truth, felt that interest in the other, which similarity of age, condition, mutual comeliness and their novel situation would be likely to inspire in the young and ingenuous.

"Here," said Pathfinder, with an honest smile bestowed on Mabel—"are the friends your worthy father has sent to meet you. This is a great Delaware; and one that has had honors as well as trouble, in his day. He has an Injin name fit for a chief, but as the language is not always easy for the inexperienced to pronounce, we nat'rally turn it into English, and call him the Big Sarpent. You are not to suppose, howsever, that by this name we wish to say that he is treacherous, beyond what is lawful in a red skin, but that he is wise, and has the cunning that becomes a warrior. Arrowhead, there, knows what I mean."

While the Pathfinder was delivering this address, the two Indians gazed on each other steadily, and then the Tuscarora advanced and spoke to the other, in an apparently friendly manner.

"I like to see this," continued Pathfinder; "the salutes of two red-skins, in the woods, Master Cap, are like the hailing of friendly vessels on the ocean. But, speaking of water, it reminds me of my young friend Jasper Western, here, who can claim to know something of these matters, seeing that he has passed his days on Ontario."

"I am glad to see you, friend," said Cap, giving the young fresh-water sailor, a cordial gripe, "though you must have something still to learn, considering the school to which you have been sent. This is my niece Mabel—I call her Magnet, for a reason she never dreams of, though you may possibly have education enough to guess at it, having some pretensions to understand the compass, I suppose."

"The reason is easily comprehended," said the young man, involuntarily fastening his keen dark eye, at the same time, on the suffused face of the girl; "and I feel sure that the sailor who steers by your Magnet, will never make a bad land-fall."

"Ha—you do make use of some of the terms, I find, and that with propriety and understanding. Though, on the whole, I fear you have seen more green than blue water!"

"It is not surprising that we should get some of the phrases that belong to the land, for we are seldom out of sight of it, twenty four hours at a time."

"More's the pity, boy; more's the pity. A very little land ought to go a great way, with a seafaring man. Now, if the truth were known, Master Western, I suppose there is more or less land all round your lake."

"And, uncle, is there not more or less land all round the ocean—" said Magnet quickly, for she dreaded a premature display of the old seaman's peculiar dogmatism, not to say pedantry.

"No, child, there is more or less ocean all round the land. That's what I tell the people ashore, youngster; they are living, as it might be, in the midst of the sea, without knowing it; by sufferance, as it were; the water being so much the more powerful, and the largest. But there is no end to conceit in this world, for a fellow who never saw salt water often fancies he knows more than one who has gone round the Horn. No—no—this earth is pretty much an island, and all that can be truly said not to be so, is water."

Young Western had a profound deference for a mariner of the ocean, on which he had often pined to sail, but he had, also, a natural regard for the broad sheet on which he had passed his life and which was not without its beauties, in his eyes.

"What you say, sir," he answered modestly, "may be true, as to the Atlantic, but we have a respect for the land, up here on Ontario."

"That is because you are always land-locked," returned Cap, laughing heartily: "but yonder is the Pathfinder, as they call him, with some smoking platters, inviting us to share in his mess, and I will confess that one gets no venison at sea. Master Western, civility to girls at your time of life, comes as easy as taking in the slack of the ensign halyards, and if you will just keep an eye to her kid and can, while I join the mess of the Pathfinder and our Indian friends, I make no doubt she will remember it."

Master Cap uttered more than he was aware of, at the time. Jasper Western did look to the wants of Mabel, and she long remembered the kind manly attentions of the young sailor, at this their first interview. He placed the end of a log for a seat, obtained for her a delicious morsel of the venison, gave her a draught of pure water from the spring, and as he sat near, and opposite to her, fast won his way to her esteem, by his gentle, but frank, manner of manifesting his care; a homage that woman always wishes to receive, but which is never so flattering or so agreeable, as when it comes from the young to those of their own age; from the manly to the gentle. Like most of those who pass their time excluded from the society of the softer sex, young Western was earnest, sincere and kind in his attentions, which, though they wanted a conventional refinement that perhaps Mabel never missed, had those winning qualities that prove more efficient as substitutes. Leaving these two inexperienced and unsophisticated young people, to become acquainted through their feelings rather than their expressed thoughts, we will turn to the group, in which the uncle, with a facility of taking care of himself that never deserted him, had already become a principal actor.

The party had taken their places around a platter of venison steaks, which served for the common use, and the discourse naturally partook of the characters of the different individuals that composed it. The Indians were silent and industrious, the appetite of the Aboriginal American for venison, being seemingly inappeasable, while the two white men, were communicative and discursive, each of the latter being garrulous and opinionated in his way. But as the dialogue will serve to put the reader in possession of certain facts that may render the succeeding narrative more clear, it will be well to record it.

"There must be satisfaction in this life of yours, no doubt, Master Pathfinder," continued Cap, when the hunger of the travellers was so far appeased that they began to pick and choose, among the savory morsels; "it has some of the chances and luck that we seamen love, and if ours is all water, yours is all land."

"Nay, we have water too, in our journeyings and marches," returned his white companion. "We border men, handle the paddle and the spear, almost as much as the rifle and the hunting knife."

"Ay, but do you handle the brace and the bow line; the wheel and the lead-line; the reef-point and the top-rope? The paddle is a good thing, out of doubt, in a canoe, but of what use is it in the ship?"

"Nay, I respect all men in their callings, and I can believe the things you mention have their uses. One, who has lived, like myself, in company with many tribes, understands the differences in usages. The paint of a Mingo, is not the paint of a Delaware; and he who should expect to see a warrior in the dress of a squaw, might be disapp'inted. I'm not very old, but I have lived in the woods, and have some acquaintance with human natur'. I never believed much in the larning of them that dwell in towns, for I never yet met with one that had an eye for a rifle, or a trail."

"That's my manner of reasoning, Master Pathfinder, to a yarn. Walking about streets, going to church of Sundays, and hearing rumours never yet made a man of a human being. Send the boy out upon the broad ocean, if you wish to open his eyes, and let him look upon foreign nations, or, what I call the face of natur', if you wish him to understand his own character. Now, there is my brother-in-law, the Serjeant, he is as good a fellow as ever broke a biscuit, in his own way; but what is he, after all; why nothing but a soger. A serjeant, to be sure, but that is a sort of a soger, you know. When he wished to marry poor Bridget, my sister, I told the girl what he was, as in duty bound, and what she might expect from such a husband, but you know how it is with girls when their minds are jammed by an inclination. It is true, the Serjeant has risen in his calling, and they say he is an important man at the fort, but his poor wife has not lived to see it all, for she has now been dead these fourteen years."

"A soldier's calling is an honorable calling, provided he has fit only on the side of right," returned the Pathfinder; "and as the Frenchers are always wrong, and His Sacred Majesty and these colonies are always right, I take it the sarjeant has a quiet conscience, as well as a good character. I have never slept more sweetly than when I have fit the Mingos, though it is a law with me to fight always like a white man, and never like an Injin. The Sarpent, here, has his fashions and I have mine; and yet have we fou't, side by side, these many years, without either's thinking a hard thought consarning the other's ways. I tell him there is but one heaven and one hell, notwithstanding his traditions, though there are many paths to both."

"That is rational, and he is bound to believe you, though I fancy most of the roads to the last, are on dry land. The sea is what my poor sister Bridget used to call a 'purifying place,' and one is out of the way of temptation when out of sight of land. I doubt if as much can be said in favor of your lakes, up hereaway."

"That towns and settlements lead to sin, I will allow, but our lakes are bordered by the forests, and one is every day called upon to worship God, in such a temple. That men are not always the same, even in the wilderness, I must admit, for the difference atween a Mingo and a Delaware, is as plain to be seen as the difference atween the sun and the moon. I am glad, friend Cap, that we have met, howsever, if it be only that you may tell the Big Sarpent, here, that there be lakes in which the water is salt. We have been pretty much of one mind, since our acquaintance began, and if the Mohican has only half the faith in me that I have in him, he believes all that I have told him, touching the white men's ways and natur's laws; but, it has always seemed to me that none of the red skins have given as free a belief, as an honest man likes, to the accounts of the Big Salt Lakes, and to that of there being rivers that flow up stream."

"This comes of getting things wrong end foremost," answered Cap, with a condescending nod. "You have thought of your lakes and rifts, as the ship, and of the ocean and the tides, as the boat. Neither Arrowhead nor the Serpent need doubt what you have said concerning both, though I confess myself, to some difficulty in swallowing the tale about there being inland seas, at all, and still more that there is any sea of fresh water. I have come this long journey, as much to satisfy my own eyes and palate concerning these facts, as to oblige the Serjeant and Magnet, though the first was my sister's husband, and I love the last like a child."

"You are wrong—you are wrong, friend Cap, very wrong to distrust the power of God, in any thing," returned Pathfinder, earnestly. "Them that live in the settlements and the towns get to have confined and unjust opinions consarning the might of His hand, but we who pass our time, in his very presence, as it might be, see things differently—I mean such of us as have white natur's. A red skin has his notions, and it is right that it should be so, and if they are not exactly the same as a Christian white man's, there is no harm in it. Still there are matters that belong altogether to the ordering of God's Providence, and these salt and fresh water lakes are some of them. I do not pretend to account for these things, but I think it the duty of all to believe in them. For my part, I am one of them who think that the same hand which made the sweet water, can make the salt."

"Hold on there, Master Pathfinder—" interrupted Cap, not without some heat; "in the way of a proper and manly faith, I will turn my back on no one, ashore or afloat. Although more accustomed to make all snug aloft, and to show the proper canvass than to pray, when the hurricane comes, I know that we are but helpless mortals, at times, and I hope I pay reverence where reverence is due. All I mean to say, and that is rather insiniated than said, is this; which is, as you all know, simply an intimation that being accustomed to see waters in large bodies salt, I should like to taste it, before I can believe it to be fresh."

"God has given the salt licks to the deer, and he has given to man, red skin and white, the delicious spring at which to slake his thirst. It is onreasonable to think that he may not have given lakes of pure water to the west, and lakes of impure water to the east."

Cap was awed, in spite of his overweening dogmatism, by the earnest simplicity of the Pathfinder, though he did not relish the idea of believing a fact which, for many years, he had pertinaciously insisted could not be true. Unwilling to give up the point, and, at the same time, unable to maintain it against a reasoning to which he was unaccustomed, and which possessed equally the force of truth, faith and probability, he was glad to get rid of the subject by evasion.

"Well, well, friend Pathfinder," he said, "we will nipper the argument where it is, and, as the serjeant has sent you to give us pilotage to this same lake, we can only try the water when we reach it—only mark my words, I do not say that it may not be fresh on the surface; the Atlantic is sometimes fresh on the surface, near the mouths of great rivers; but, rely on it, I shall show you a way of tasting the water many fathoms deep, of which you never dreamed; and then we shall know more about it."

The guide seemed content to let the matter rest, and the conversation changed.

"We are not over-consated consarning our gifts," observed the Pathfinder after a short pause, "and well know that such as live in the towns, and near the sea—"

"On the sea," interrupted Cap.

"On the sea, if you wish it, friend, have opportunities that do not befall us of the wilderness. Still, we know our own callings, and they are what I consider nat'ral callings, and are not parvarted by vanity and wantonness. Now, my gifts are with the rifle, and on a trail, and in the way of game and scoutin', for, though I can use the spear and the paddle, I pride not myself on either. The youth, Jasper there, who is discoursing with the sarjeant's daughter, is a different creatur', for he may be said to breathe the water, as it might be, like a fish. The Indians and Frenchers of the north shore, call him Eau douce, on account of his gifts, in this particular. He is better at the oar and the rope-tie, than in making fires on a trail."

"There must be something about these gifts of which you speak after all," said Cap. "Now this fire, I will acknowledge, has overlaid all my seamanship. Arrowhead, there, said the smoke came from a pale-face's fire, and that is a piece of philosophy that I hold to be equal to steering in a dark night by the edges of the scud."

"It's no great secret—it's no great secret," returned Pathfinder, laughing with great inward glee, though habitual caution prevented the emission of any noise. "Nothing is easier to us who pass our time in the great school of Providence than to l'arn its lessons. We should be as useless on a trail, or in carrying tidings through the wilderness, as so many woodchucks, did we not soon come to a knowledge of these niceties. Eau douce, as we call him, is so fond of the water that he gathered a damp stick or two for our fire, and there be plenty of them, as well as those that are thoroughly dried, lying scattered about, and wet will bring dark smoke, as I suppose even you followers of the sea must know. It's no great secret—it's no great secret—though all is mystery to such as does'n't study the Lord and his mighty ways, with humility and thankfulness."

"That must be a keen eye of Arrowhead's, to see so slight a difference."

"He would be but a poor Injin if he did'n't! No—no—it is war-time, and no red-skin is outlying without using his senses. Every skin has its own natur', and every natur' has its own laws, as well as its own skin. It was many years afore I could master all them higher branches of a forest edication, for red-skin knowledge does'n't come as easy to white skin natur', as what I suppose is intended to be white skin knowledge; though I have but little of the latter, having passed most of my time in the wilderness."

"You have been a ready scholar, Master Pathfinder, as is seen by your understanding these things so well. I suppose it would be no great matter, for a man regularly brought up to the sea, to catch these trifles, if he could only bring his mind fairly to bear upon them."

"I don't know that—The white man has his difficulties in getting red skin habits, quite as much as the Injin in getting white skin ways. As for the raal natur', it is my opinion that neither can actually get that of the other."

"And yet we sailors, who run about the world so much, say there is but one nature, whether it be in the Chinaman, or a Dutchman. For my own part, I am much of that way of thinking, too, for I have generally found that all nations like gold and silver, and most men relish tobacco."

"Then you sea-faring men know little of the red-skins. Have you ever known any of your China-men who could sing their death songs, with their flesh torn with splinters, and cut with knives, the fire raging around their naked bodies, and death staring them in the face? Until you can find me a China-man, or a Christian-man that can do all this, you cannot find a man with a red-skin natur', let him look ever so valiant, or know how to read all the books that were ever printed."

"It is the Savages, only, that play each other such hellish tricks," said Master Cap, glancing his eyes about him, uneasily, at the apparently endless arches of the forest; "no white man is ever condemned to undergo these trials."

"Nay, therein, you are ag'in mistaken," returned the Pathfinder, coolly selecting a delicate morsel of the venison, as his *bonne bouche*; "for though these torments belong only to the red-skin natur', in the way of bearing them like braves, white-skin natur', may be, and often has been agonized by them."

"Happily," said Cap, with an effort to clear his throat, "none of His Majesty's allies, will be likely to attempt such damnable cruelties, on any of His Majesty's loyal subjects. I have not served much in the royal navy, it is true, but I have served—and that is something; and, in the way of privateering and worrying the enemy in his ships and cargoes, I've done my full share. But I trust there are no French savages on this side of the lake, and I think you said that Ontario is a broad sheet of water?"

"Nay, it is broad in our eyes," returned Pathfinder, not

caring to conceal the smile which lighted a face, that had been burnt by exposure to a bright red, "though I mistrust that some may think it narrow; and narrow it is, if you wish it to keep off the foe. Ontario has two inds, and the inimy that is afraid to cross it, will be sartain to come round it."

"Ah! that comes of your d——d fresh water ponds!" growled Cap, hemming so loud, as to cause him instantly to repent the indiscretion. "No man, now, ever heard of a pirate's, or a thief's getting round an end of the Atlantic!"

"Mayhap the ocean has no inds?"

"That it has'n't; nor sides, nor bottom. The nation that is snugly moored on one of its coasts need fear nothing from the one anchored abeam, let it be ever so savage, unless it possesses the art of ship-building. No—no—the people who live on the shores of the Atlantic need fear but little for their skins, or their scalps. A man may lie down at night, in those regions, in the hope of finding the hair on his head in the morning, unless he wears a wig."

"It is'n't so here. I don't wish to flurry the young woman, and therefore I will be no way particular—though she seems pretty much listening to Eau douce, as we call him—but without the edication I have received, I should think it, at this very moment, a risky journey to go over the very ground that lies atween us and the garrison, in the present state of this frontier. There are about as many Iroquois on this side of Ontario, as there be on the other. It is for this very reason, friend Cap, that the sarjeant has engaged us to come out and show you the path."

"What!—do the knaves dare to cruise so near the guns of one of His Majesty's works?"

"Do not the ravens resort near the carcase of the deer, though the fowler is at hand? They come this-a-way, as it might be nat'rally. There are more or less whites passing atween the forts and the settlements, and they are sure to be on their trails. The Sarpent has come up one side of the river, and I have come up the other, in order to scout for the outlying rascals, while Jasper brought up the canoe, like a bold-hearted sailor, as he is. The Sarjeant told him, with tears in his eyes, all about his child, and how his heart yearned for her, and how gentle and obedient she was, until I think the lad would have dashed into a Mingo camp, single handed, rather than not acome."

"We thank him—we thank him; and shall think the better of him for his readiness, though I suppose the boy has run no great risk, after all."

"Only the risk of being shot from a cover, as he forced the canoe up a swift rift, or turned an elbow in the stream, with his eyes fastened on the eddies. Of all risky journeys, that on an ambushed river, is the most risky, in my judgment, and that risk has Jasper run."

"And why the devil, has the serjeant sent for me to travel a hundred and fifty miles, in this outlandish manner! Give me an offing, and the enemy in sight, and I'll play with him in his own fashion, as long as he pleases, long bows, or close quarters; but to be shot like a turtle asleep, is not to my humour. If it were not for little Magnet, there, I would tack ship this instant, make the best of my way back to York, and let Ontario take care of itself, salt water or fresh water."

"That would'n't mend the matter much, friend mariner, as the road to return is much longer, and almost as bad as the road to go on. Trust to us, and we will carry you through safe, or lose our scalps."

Cap wore a tight solid cue, done up in eel-skin, while the top of his head was nearly bald; and he mechanically passed his hand over both, as if to make certain that each was in its right place. He was at the bottom, however, a brave man, and had often faced death with coolness, though never in the frightful forms in which it presented itself, under the brief but graphic pictures of his companion. It was too late to retreat, and he determined to put the best face on the matter, though he could not avoid muttering inwardly a few curses on the indifference and indiscretion with which his brother-in-law, the serjeant, had led him into his present dilemma.

"I make no doubt, Master Pathfinder," he answered, when these thoughts had found time to glance through his mind, "that we shall reach port in safety. What distance may we now be from the fort?"

"Little more than fifteen miles; and swift miles too, as the river runs, if the Mingos let us go clear."

"And I suppose the woods will stretch along, starboard and larboard, as heretofore?"

"Anan?"

"I mean that we shall have to pick our way, through these damned trees!"

"Nay, nay, you will go in the canoe, and the Oswego has been cleared of its flood-wood by the troops. It will be floating down stream, and that, too, with a swift current."

"And what the devil is to prevent these Minks, of which you speak, from shooting us as we double a head-land, or are busy in steering clear of the rocks."

"The Lord!—He who has so often helped others, in greater difficulties. Many and many is the time that my head would have been stripped of hair, skin and all, had'n't the Lord fit of my side. I never go into a skrimmage, friend mariner, without thinking of this great ally, who can do more in battle, than all the battalions of the 60th, were they brought into a single line."

"Ay—ay—this may do well enough for a scouter, but we seamen like our offing, and to go into action with nothing on our minds, but the business before us—plain broadside and broadside work, and no trees, or rocks, to thicken the water."

"And no Lord, too, I dare to say, if the truth were known! Take my word for it, Master Cap, that no battle is the worse fou't, for having the Lord on your side. Look at the head of the Big Sarpent, there; you can see the mark of a knife, all along there by his left ear; now, nothing but a bullet from this long rifle of mine, saved his scalp that day, for it had fairly started, and half a minute more would have left him without the war-lock. When the Mohican squeezes my hand, and intermates that I befriended him in that matter, I tell him, no; it was the Lord, who led me to the only spot where execution could be done, or his necessity be made known, on account of the smoke. Sartain when I got the right position, I finished the affair of my own accord, for a friend under the tomahawk is apt to make a man think quick and act at once, as was my case, or the Sarpent's spirit would be hunting in the happy land of his people, at this very moment."

"Come, come, Pathfinder, this palaver is worse than being skinned from stem to stern; we have but a few hours of sun, and had better be drifting down this said current of yours, while we may. Magnet, dear, are you not ready to get under way?"

Magnet started, blushed brightly, and made her preparations, for an immediate departure. Not a syllable of the discourse just related, had she heard, for Eau douce, as young Jasper was oftener called than any thing else, had been filling her ears with a description of the yet distant post towards which she was journeying, with accounts of her father, whom she had not seen since a child, and with the manner of life of those who lived in the frontier garrisons. Unconsciously, she had become deeply interested, and her thoughts had been too intently directed to these interesting matters, to allow any of the less agreeable subject, discussed by those so near to reach her ears. The bustle of departure put an end to the conversation entirely, and the baggage of the scouts, or guides, being trifling, in a few minutes, the whole party was ready to proceed. As they were about to quit the spot, however, to the surprise of even his fellow guides, Pathfinder collected a quantity of branches, and threw them upon the embers of the fire, taking care even to see that some of the wood was damp, in order to raise as dark and dense a smoke as possible.

"When you can hide your trail, Jasper," he said, "a smoke at leaving an encampment may do good, instead of harm. If there are a dozen Mingos within ten miles of us, some of 'em, are on the heights, or in the trees, looking out for smokes; let them see this, and much good may it do them. They are welcome to our leavings."

"But may they not strike, and follow on our trail?" asked the youth, whose interest in the hazards of his situation had much increased, since the meeting with Magnet. "We shall leave a broad path to the river."

"The broader the better; when there, it will surpass Mingo cunning, even, to say which way the canoe has gone; up stream, or down. Water is the only thing in natur' that will thoroughly wash out a trail, and even water will not always do it, when the scent is strong. Do you not see, Eau douce, that if any Mingos have seen our path below the falls, they will strike off towards this smoke, and that they will nat'rally conclude they who began by going up stream, will ind by going up stream. If they know any thing, they now know a party is out from the fort, and it will exceed even Mingo wit, to fancy that we have come up here, just for the pleasure of going back again, and that, too, the same day, and at the risk of our scalps."

"Certainly," added Jasper, who was talking apart with the Pathfinder, as they moved towards the wind-row, "they cannot know any thing, about the serjeant's daughter, for the greatest secrecy has been observed, on her account."

"And they will larn nothing, here," returned Pathfinder, causing his companion to see that he trod with the utmost care, on the impressions left on the leaves, by the little foot of Mabel, "unless this old salt-water fish, has been trotting his niece about in the wind-row, like a fa'n playing by the side of the old doe."

"Buck, you mean, Pathfinder."

"Isn't he a queerity!—Now, I can consort with such a sailor as yourself, Eau douce, and find nothing very contrary, in our gifts, though yourn belong to the lakes and mine to the woods. Harkee, Jasper—" continued the scout, laughing in his noiseless manner; "suppose we try the temper of his blade, and run him over the falls?"

"And what would be done with the pretty niece, in the mean while?"

"Nay—nay—no harm shall come to her; she must walk round the portage, at any rate, but you and I can try this Atlantic Oceaner, and then all parties will become better acquainted. We shall find out, whether his flint will strike fire, and he may come to know something of frontier tricks."

Young Jasper smiled, for he was not averse to fun, and had been a little touched by Cap's superciliousness, but Mabel's fair face, light agile form, and winning smiles, stood like a shield, between her uncle and the intended experiment.

"Perhaps the serjeant's daughter will be frightened," he said.

"Not she, if she has any of the sarjeant's spirit in her. She does'n't look like a skeary thing, at all. Leave it to me, Eau douce, and I will manage the affair alone."

"Not you, Pathfinder; you would only drown both. If the canoe goes over, I must go in it."

"Well have it so, then; shall we smoke the pipe of agreement on the bargain."

Jasper laughed, nodded his head, by way of consent, and the subject was dropped, for the party had reached the canoe, so often mentioned, and fewer words had determined much graver things between the parties.

Chapter III

"Before these fields were shorn and tilled,
Full to the brim our rivers flowed;
The melody of waters filled
The fresh and boundless wood;
And torrents dashed, and rivulets played,
And fountains spouted in the shade."

Bryant, "An Indian at the Burial Place of His Fathers," ll. 67–72.

It is generally known, that the waters which flow into the southern side of Ontario, are, in general, narrow, sluggish and deep. There are some exceptions to this rule, for many of the rivers have rapids, or as they are termed in the language of the region, rifts, and some have falls. Among the latter was the particular stream on which our adventurers were now journeying. The Oswego is formed by the junction of the Oneida and the Onondaga, both of which flow from lakes, and it pursues its way, through a gently undulating country, a few miles, until it reaches the margin of a sort of natural terrace, down which it tumbles some ten or fifteen feet, to another level, across which it glides, or glances, or pursues its course with the silent stealthy progress of deep water, until it throws its tribute into the broad receptacle of Ontario. The canoe, in which Cap and his party had travelled from Fort Stanwix, the last military station on the Mohawk, lay by the side of this river, and into it the whole party now entered, with the exception of the Pathfinder, who remained on the land, in order to shove the light vessel off.

"Let her starn drift down stream, Jasper," said the man of the woods, to the young mariner of the lake, who had dispossessed Arrowhead of his paddle, and taken his own station as steersman, "let it go down with the current. Should any of them infarnals, the Mingos, strike our trail, or follow it to this point, they will not fail to look for the signs in the mud, and if they discover that we have left the shore, with the nose of the canoe up stream, it is a nat'ral belief to think we went that-a-way."

This direction was followed, and giving a vigorous shove, the Pathfinder, who was in the flower of his strength and activity, made a leap, landing lightly, and without disturbing its equilibrium, in the bows of the canoe. As soon as it had reached the centre of the river, or the strength of the current, the boat was turned, and it began to glide noiselessly down the stream.

The vessel in which Cap and his niece had embarked for their long and adventurous journey, was one of the canoes of bark, which the Indians are in the habit of constructing, and which, by their exceeding lightness and the ease with which they are propelled, are admirably adapted to a navigation, in which shoals, flood-wood, and other similar obstructions so often occur. The two men who composed its original crew had several times carried it, when emptied of its luggage, many hundred yards; and it would not have exceeded the strength of a single man to lift its weight. Still it was long, and for a canoe, wide, a want of steadiness being its principal defect, in the eyes of the uninitiated. A few hours practice, however, in a great measure remedied this evil, and both Mabel and her uncle had learned so far to humour its movements, that they now maintained their places with perfect composure. Nor did the additional weight of the three guides tax its powers, in any particular degree, the breadth of the rounded bottom allowing the necessary quantity of water to be displaced, without bringing the gunwale very sensibly nearer to the surface of the stream. Its workmanship was neat, the timbers were small and secured by thongs, and the whole fabric, though it was so slight and precarious to the eye, was probably capable of conveying double the number of persons, that it now contained.

Cap was seated on a low thwart, in the centre of the canoe; the Big Serpent knelt near him; Arrowhead and his wife occupied places forward of both, the former having relinquished his post aft; Mabel was half-reclining on some of her own effects, behind her uncle, while the Pathfinder and Eau douce stood erect, the one in the bows, and the other in the stern, each using a paddle with a long, steady, noiseless sweep. The conversation was carried on in low tones, all of the party beginning to feel the necessity of prudence, as they drew nearer to the outskirts of the fort, and had no longer the cover of the woods.

The Oswego just at that place was a deep, dark stream, of no great width, its still gloomy looking current winding its way, among overhanging trees, that, in particular spots, almost shut out the light of the heavens. Here and there some half fallen giant of the forest, lay nearly across its surface, rendering care necessary to avoid the limbs, and most of the distance, the lower branches and leaves of the trees of smaller growth were laved by its waters. The picture which has been so beautifully described by our own admirable poet, and which we have placed at the head of this chapter, as an epigraph, was here realized, the earth fattened by the decayed vegetation of centuries, and black with loam, the stream that filled the banks nearly to overflowing, and the "fresh and boundless wood," being all as visible to the eye, as the pen of Bryant has elsewhere vividly presented them to the imagination. In short, the entire scene was one of a rich and benevolent nature, before it has been subjected to the uses and desires of man; luxuriant, wild, full of promise, and not without the charm of the picturesque, even in its rudest state. It will be remembered that this was in the year 175–, or long before even speculation had brought any portion of Western New-York, within the bounds of civilization, or the projects of the adventurous. At that distant day, there were two great channels of military communications, between the inhabited portions of the colony of New-York, and the frontiers that lay adjacent to the Canadas; that by Lakes Champlain and George, and that by means of the Mohawk, Wood Creek, the Oneida, and the rivers we have been describing. Along both these lines of communications military posts had been established, though there existed a blank space of a hundred miles, between the last fort at the head of the Mohawk, and the outlet of the Oswego, which embraced most of the distance that Cap and Mabel had journeyed under the protection of Arrowhead.

"I sometimes wish for peace, again," said the Pathfinder, "when one can range the forest, without s'arching for any other inimy than the beasts and fishes. Ah's! me; many is the day that the Sarpent, there, and I have passed happily among the streams, living on venison, salmon and trout, without thought of a Mingo, or a scalp! I sometimes wish that them blessed days might come back, for it is not my raal gift to slay my own kind. I'm sartain the sarjeant's daughter, don't think me a wretch that takes pleasure in preying on human natur'?"

At this remark, a sort of half interrogatory, Pathfinder looked behind him, and, though the most partial friend could scarcely term his sunburnt and hard features handsome, even Mabel thought his smile attractive, by its simple ingenuousness, and the uprightness that beamed in every lineament of his honest countenance.

"I do not think my father would have sent one like those you mention, to see his daughter through the wilderness," the young woman answered, returning the smile as frankly as it was given, and much more sweetly.

"That he would'n't, that he would'n't; the sarjeant is a man of feelin', and many is the march and the fight that we have stood shoulder to shoulder in, as *he* would call it, though I always keep my limbs free, when near a Frencher, or a Mingo."

"You are then the young friend of whom my father has spoken so often in his letters?"

"His *young* friend—the sarjeant has the advantage of me by thirty years; yes, he is thirty years my senior, and as many my better."

"Not in the eyes of the daughter, perhaps, friend Pathfinder—" put in Cap, whose spirits began to revive, when he found the water once more flowing around him. "The thirty years that you mention, are not often thought to be an advantage in the eyes of girls of nineteen."

Mabel coloured, and in turning aside her face, to avoid the looks of those in the bows of the canoe, she encountered the admiring gaze of the young man in the stern. As a last resource her spirited, but soft blue eyes, sought refuge in the water. Just at this moment, a dull heavy sound swept up the avenue formed by the trees, borne along by a light air that hardly produced a ripple on the water.

"That sounds pleasantly," said Cap, pricking up his ears like a dog that hears a distant baying; "it is the surf on the shores of your lake, I suppose?"

"Not so—not so—" answered the Pathfinder—"it is merely this river tumbling over some rocks, half a mile below us."

"Is there a fall in this stream?" demanded Mabel, a still brighter flush glowing on her face.

"The Devil! Master Pathfinder—or you, Mr. Oh! the-deuce (for so Cap began to style Jasper, by way of entering cordially into the border usages) had you not better give the canoe a sheer, and get nearer to the shore. These water-falls have generally rapids above them, and one might as well get into the Maelstrom, at once, as to run into their suction."

"Trust to us—trust to us, friend Cap," answered Pathfinder; " we are but fresh-water sailors, it is true, and I cannot boast of being much even of that, but we understand rifts and rapids and cataracts, and, in going down these, we shall do our endivours, not to disgrace our edication."

"In going down!" exclaimed Cap—"the devil, man! you do not dream of going down a water-fall, in this egg-shell of bark!"

"Sartain; the path lies over the falls, and it is much easier to shoot them, than to unload the canoe, and to carry that, and all it contains, around a portage of a mile, by hand."

Mabel turned her pallid countenance towards the young man in the stern of the canoe, for just at that moment a fresh roar of the fall, was borne to her ears, by a new current of the air, and it really sounded terrific, now that the cause was understood.

"We thought, that by landing the females, and the two Indians," Jasper quietly observed, " we three white men, all of whom are used to the water, might carry the canoe over in safety, for we often shoot these falls."

"And we counted on you, friend mariner, as a mainstay;" said Pathfinder, winking at Jasper over his shoulder, "for you are accustomed to see waves tumbling about, and without some one to steady the cargo, all the finery of the sarjeant's daughter might be washed into the river, and be lost."

Cap was puzzled. The idea of going over a water-fall was perhaps more serious, in his eyes, than it would have been in those of one totally ignorant of all that pertained to boats, for he understood the power of the element, and the total feebleness of man when exposed to its fury. Still, his pride revolted at the thought of deserting the boat, while others not only courageously, but coolly, proposed to continue in it. Notwithstanding the latter feeling, and his innate as well as acquired steadiness in danger, he would probably have deserted his post, had not the images of Indians tearing scalps from the human head taken so strong hold of his fancy, as to induce him to imagine the canoe a sort of sanctuary.

"What is to be done with Magnet," he demanded, affection for his niece raising another qualm in his conscience. "We cannot allow Magnet to land if there are enemy's Indians near?"

"Nay—no Mingo will be near the portage, for that is a spot too public for their deviltries," answered the Pathfinder, confidently. "Natur' is natur', and it is an Injin's natur' to be found where he is least expected. No fear of him, on a beaten path, for he wishes to come upon you, when unprepared to meet him, and the fiery villains make it a point to deceive you, one way or another. Sheer in, Eau douce, and we will land the sarjeant's daughter, on the end of that log, where she can reach the shore with a dry foot."

The injunction was obeyed, and in a few minutes the whole party had left the canoe, with the exception of Pathfinder and the two sailors. Notwithstanding his professional pride, Cap would have gladly followed, but he did not like to exhibit so unequivocal a weakness in the presence of a fresh-water sailor.

"I call all hands to witness," he said, as those who had landed moved away, "that I do not look on this affair, as any thing more than canoeing in the woods. There is no seamanship in tumbling over a water-fall, which is a feat the greatest lubber can perform, as well as the oldest mariner."

"Nay, nay, you need'n't despise the Oswego Falls, neither," put in Pathfinder, "for though they may not be Niagara, nor the Genessee, nor the Cahoos, nor Glenn's, nor them on the Canada, they are narvous enough, for a new beginner. Let the sarjeant's daughter stand on yonder rock, and she will see the manner in which we ignorant back-woodsmen get over a difficulty that we can't get under. Now, Eau douce, a steady hand and a true eye, for all rests on you, seeing that we can count Master Cap for no more than a passenger."

The canoe was leaving the shore, as he concluded, while Mabel went hurriedly and trembling to the rock that had been pointed out, talking to her companions of the danger her uncle so unnecessarily ran, while her eyes were riveted on the agile and vigorous form of Eau douce, as he stood erect in the stern of the light boat, governing its movements. As soon, however, as she reached a point where she got a view of the fall, she gave an involuntary but suppressed scream, and covered her eyes. At the next instant, the latter were again free, and the entranced girl stood, immovable as a statue, a scarcely breathing observer of all that passed. The two Indians seated themselves passively on a log, hardly looking towards the stream, while the wife of Arrowhead came near Mabel, and appeared to watch the motions of the canoe, with some such interest as a child regards the leaps of a tumbler.

As soon as the boat was in the stream, Pathfinder sunk on his knees, continuing to use the paddle though it was slowly, and in a manner not to interfere with the efforts of his companion. The latter still stood erect, and, as he kept his eye on some object beyond the fall, it was evident that he was carefully looking for the spot proper for their passage.

"Farther west, boy; farther west—" muttered Pathfinder; "there, where you see the water foam. Bring the top of the dead oak in a line with the stem of the blasted hemlock."

Eau douce made no answer, for the canoe was in the centre of the stream, with its head pointed towards the fall, and it had already begun to quicken its motion, by the increased force of the current. At that moment, Cap would cheerfully have renounced every claim to glory that could possibly be acquired by the feat, to have been safe again, on the shore. He heard the roar of the water, thundering as it might be behind a screen, but, becoming more and more distinct, louder and louder, and before him he saw its line cutting the forest below, along which the green and angry element seemed stretched and shining, as if the particles were about to lose their principle of cohesion.

"Down with your helm—down with your helm, man!" he exclaimed, unable any longer to suppress his anxiety, as the canoe glided towards the edge of the fall.

"Ay—ay—down it is, sure enough," answered Pathfinder, looking behind him for a single instant, with his silent joyous laugh—"down we go, of a sartainty! Heave her starn up, boy; farther up with her starn!"

The rest was like the passage of the viewless wind. Eau douce gave the required sweep with his paddle, the canoe glanced into the channel, and for a few seconds, it seemed to Cap, that he was tossing in a cauldron. He felt the bows of the canoe tip, saw the raging, foaming water, careering madly by his side, was sensible that the light fabric in which he floated was tossed about like an egg shell, and then, not less to his great joy than to his surprise, he discovered that it was gliding across the basin of still water, below the fall, under the steady impulse of Jasper's paddle.

The Pathfinder continued to laugh, but he arose from his knees, and searching for a tin pot and a horn spoon, he began deliberately to measure the water that had been taken in, in the passage.

"Fourteen spoonsfull, Eau douce; fourteen fairly measured spoonsfull. I have you must acknowledge known you go down with only ten."

"Master Cap leaned so hard up stream," returned Jasper seriously, "that I had difficulty in trimming the canoe."

"It may be so—it may be so; no doubt it *was* so, since you say it; but I have known you go over with only ten!"

Cap now gave a tremendous hem, felt for his cue, as if to ascertain its safety, and then looked back, in order to examine the danger he had gone through. His impunity is easily explained. Most of the river fell perpendicularly, ten or twelve feet, but near its centre, the force of the current had so far worn away the rock, as to permit the water to shoot through a narrow passage at an angle of about forty, or forty five degrees. Down this ticklish descent the canoe had glanced, amid fragments of broken rock, whirlpools, foam, and furious tossings of the element, which an uninstructed eye would believe menaced inevitable destruction to an object so fragile. But the very lightness of the canoe had favored its descent, for, borne on the crests of the waves, and directed by a steady eye and an arm full of muscle, it had passed like a feather, from one pile of foam to another, scarcely permitting its glossy side to be wetted. There were a few rocks to be avoided, the proper direction was to be rigidly observed, and the fierce current did the rest.*

To say that Cap was astonished, would not be expressing half his feelings. He felt awed, for the profound dread of rocks, which most seamen entertain, came in aid of his admiration of the boldness of the exploit. Still he was indisposed to express all he felt, lest it might be conceding too much in favor of fresh water and inland navigation, and no sooner had he cleared his throat, with the aforesaid hem, than he loosened his tongue, in the usual strain of superiority.

"I do not gainsay your knowledge of the channel, Master Oh! the deuce, (for such he religiously believed to be Jasper's *soubriquet*) and, after all, to know the channel, in such a place is the main point. I have had cockswains with me, who could come down that shoot too, if they only knew the channel."

"It is'n't enough to know the channel, friend Mariner," said Pathfinder; "it needs narves and skill to keep the canoe straight, and to keep her clear of the rocks too. There is'n't another boatman in all this region that can shoot the Oswego, but Eau douce, there, with any sartainty, though, now and then, one has blundered through. I can't do it myself, unless by means of Providence, and it needs Jasper's hand, and Jasper's eye, to make sure of a dry passage. Fourteen spoonsfull, after all, are no great matter, though I wish it had been but ten, seeing that the Sarjeant's daughter was a looker on!"

"And yet you conned the canoe; you told him how to head, and how to sheer."

"Human frailty, Master Mariner; that was a little of white-skin natur'. Now, had the Sarpent, yonder, been in the boat, not a word would he have spoken, or thought would he have given to the public. An Injin knows how to hold his tongue, but we white folk fancy we are always wiser than our fellows. I'm curing myself fast of the weakness, but it needs time, to root up the tree that has been growing more than thirty years."

*Lest the reader suppose we are dealing purely in fiction, the writer will add that he has known a long thirty two pounder carried over these same falls, in perfect safety.

"I think little of this affair, sir; nothing at all, to speak my mind freely. It's a mere wash of spray to shooting London Bridge, which is done every day by hundreds of persons, and often by the most delicate ladies in the land. The King's Majesty has shot the bridge, in his royal person."

"Well I want no delicate ladies or king's majesties, (God bless 'em), in the canoe, in going over these falls, for a boat's breadth, either way, may make a drowning matter of it. Eau douce, we shall have to carry the sarjeant's brother over Niagara, yet, to show him what may be done on a frontier!"

"The devil! Master Pathfinder, you must be joking, now! Surely it is not possible for a bark canoe to go over that mighty cataract!"

"You never were more mistaken, Master Cap, in your life. Nothing is easier, and many is the canoe I have seen go over it, with my own eyes, and, if we both live, I hope to satisfy you that the feat can be done. For my part, I think the largest ship that ever sailed on the ocean might be carried over, could she once get into the rapids."

Cap did not perceive the wink which Pathfinder exchanged with Eau douce, and he remained silent some time; for, sooth to say, he had never suspected the possibility of going down Niagara, feasible as the thing must appear to every one, on a second thought, the real difficulty existing in going up it.

By this time, the party had reached the place, where Jasper had left his own canoe, concealed in the bushes, and they all re-embarked; Cap, Jasper and his niece, in one boat, and Pathfinder, Arrowhead and the wife of the latter, in the other. The Mohican had already passed down the banks of the river by land, looking cautiously and with the skill of his people for the signs of an enemy.

The cheek of Mabel did not recover all its bloom, until the canoe was again in the current, down which it floated swiftly, occasionally impelled by the paddle of Jasper. She witnessed the descent of the falls, with a degree of terror that had rendered her mute, but her fright had not been so great as to prevent admiration of the steadiness of the youth, who directed the movement, from blending with the passing terror. In truth, one much less quick and sensitive, might have had her feelings awakened by the cool and gallant air with which Eau douce had accomplished this clever exploit. He had stood firmly erect, notwithstanding the plunge, and to those who were on the shore, it was evident that by a timely application of his skill and strength, the canoe had received a sheer that alone carried it clear of a rock, over which the boiling water was leaping in *jets d'eau*, now leaving the brown stone visible, and now covering it with a limpid sheet, as if machinery controlled the play of the element. The tongue cannot always express what the eyes view, but Mabel saw enough, even in that moment of fear, to blend forever in her mind, the pictures presented by the plunging canoe, and the unmoved steersman. She admitted that insidious sentiment which binds woman so strongly to man, by feeling additional security in finding herself under his care, and for the first time since leaving Fort Stanwix, she was entirely at her ease in the frail bark, in which she travelled. As the other canoe kept quite near her own, however, and the Pathfinder, by floating at her side was most in view, the conversation was principally maintained with that person, Jasper seldom speaking unless addressed, and constantly exhibiting a wariness in the management of his own boat, that might have been remarked by one accustomed to his ordinary, confident, careless manner, had such an observer been present to rate what was passing.

"We know too well, a woman's gifts, to think of carrying the sarjeant's daughter over the falls," said Pathfinder, looking at Mabel, while he addressed her uncle, "though I've been acquainted with some of her sex, in these regions, that would think but little of doing the thing."

"Mabel is faint-hearted like her mother," returned Cap, "and you did well, friend, to humour her weakness. You will remember the child has never been at sea."

"No—no—it was easy to discover that, by your own fearlessness—any one might have seen how little you cared about the matter! I went over once, with a raw hand, and he jumped out of the canoe, just as it tipped, and you may judge what a time he had of it!"

"What became of the poor fellow?" asked Cap, scarce knowing how to take the other's manner, which was so dry, while it was so simple, that a less obtuse subject than the old sailor might well have suspected its sincerity. "One who has passed the place knows how to feel for him."

"He was a *poor* fellow, as you say; and a poor frontier man, too, though he came out to show his skill among us ignoranters. What became of him?—why he went down the falls, topsy turvey like, as would have happened to a court-house or a fort."

"If it should jump out of a canoe—" interrupted Jasper, smiling, though he was evidently more disposed than his friend to let the passage of the falls be forgotten.

"The boy is right—" rejoined Pathfinder laughing in Mabel's face, the canoes being now so near that they almost touched; "he is sartainly right. But you have not told us what you think of the leap we took?"

"It was perilous and bold," said Mabel; " while looking at it, I could have wished it had not been attempted, though, now it is over, I can admire its boldness, and the steadiness with which it was made."

"Now, do not think that we did this thing, to set ourselves off in female eyes. It may be pleasant to the young to win each other's good opinions, by doing things that may seem praiseworthy and bold, but neither Eau douce, nor myself, am of that race. My natur', though perhaps the Sarpent would be a better witness, has few turns in it, and is a straight natur', nor would it be likely to lead me into a vanity of this sort, while out on duty. As for Jasper, he would sooner go over the Oswego falls, without a looker on, than do it before a hundred pair of eyes. I know the lad well, from use and much consorting, and I am sure he is not boastful or vainglorious."

Mabel rewarded the scout with a smile, that served to keep the canoes together some time longer, for the sight of youth and beauty was so rare on that remote frontier, that even the rebuked and self mortified feelings of this wanderer of the forest, were sensibly touched by the blooming loveliness of the girl.

"We did it for the best," Pathfinder continued; " 'twas all for the best. Had we waited to carry the canoe across the portage, time would have been lost, and nothing is so precious as time, when you are mistrustful of Mingos."

"But we can have little to fear, now! The canoes move swiftly, and two hours, you have said, will carry us down to the fort."

"It shall be a cunning Iroquois who hurts a hair of your head, pretty one, for all here are bound to the sarjeant, and most I think to yourself, to see you safe from harm. Ha! Eau douce; what is that in the river, at the lower turn—yonder beneath the bushes, I mean standing on the rock?"

"'Tis the Big Serpent, Pathfinder; he is making signs to us, in a way I don't understand."

"'Tis the Sarpent, as sure as I'm a white man, and he wishes us to drop in nearer to his shore. Mischief is brewin', or one of his deliberation and steadiness would never take this trouble. Courage, all; we are men, and must meet deviltry as becomes our colour, and our callings. Ah! I never knew good come of boastin', and here, just as I was vauntin' of our safety comes danger to give me the lie!"

Chapter IV

"——Art, stryving to compare
With nature, did an arber greene dispred,
Framed of wanton yvie flowring fayre,
Through which the fragrant eglantine did spred—"
Spenser, *The Faerie Queene*, II.v.29.1–4.

THE OSWEGO, below the falls, is a more rapid, unequal stream, than it is above them. There are places where the river flows in the quiet stillness of deep water, but many shoals and rapids occur, and, at that distant day, when every thing was in its natural state, some of the passes were not altogether without hazard. Very little exertion was required on the part of those who managed the canoes, except in those places where the swiftness of the current, and the presence of the rocks required care, when, indeed, not only vigilance, but great coolness, readiness and strength of arm became necessary, in order to avoid the dangers. Of all this the Mohican was aware, and he had judiciously selected a spot, where the river flowed tranquilly, to intercept the canoes, in order to make his communication without hazard to those he wished to speak.

The Pathfinder had no sooner recognised the form of his red friend, than, with a strong sweep of his paddle he threw the head of his own canoe towards the shore, motioning for Jasper to follow. In a minute, both boats were silently drifting down the stream, within reach of the bushes that overhung the water, all observing a profound silence; some from alarm, and others from habitual caution. As the travellers drew nearer the Indian, he made a sign for them to stop, and then he and Pathfinder had a short but earnest conference, in the language of the Delawares.

"The chief is not apt to see enemies in a dead log," observed the white man, to his red associate; "why does he tell us to stop?"

"Mingos are in the woods."

"That, we have believed these two days; does the chief know it?"

The Mohican quietly held up the head of a pipe, formed of stone.

"It lay on a fresh trail that led towards the garrison"—for so it was the usage of that frontier to term a military work whether it was occupied or not.

"That may be the bowl of a pipe belonging to a soldier. Many use the red skin pipes."

"See," said the Big Serpent, again holding the thing he had found up to the view of his friend.

The bowl of the pipe was of soap stone, and it had been carved with great care, and with a very respectable degree of skill. In its centre was a small Latin cross, made with an accuracy that permitted no doubt of its meaning.

"That does foretell deviltry and wickedness," said the Pathfinder, who had all the provincial horror of the holy symbol in question, that then pervaded the country, and which became so incorporated with its prejudices, by confounding men with things, as to have left its traces strong enough on the moral feeling of the community to be discovered even at the present hour; "no Injin who had not been parvarted by the cunning priests of the Canadas would dream of carving a thing like that on his pipe! I'll warrant ye, the knave prays to the image every time he wishes to sarcumvent the innocent, and work his fearful wickednesses. It looks fresh, too, Chingachgook?"

"The tobacco was burning when I found it."

"That is close work, chief—where was the trail?"

The Mohican pointed to a spot not a hundred yards distant from that where they stood.

The matter now began to look very serious, and the two principal guides conferred apart for several minutes, when both ascended the bank, approached the indicated spot, and examined the trail with the utmost care. After this investigation had lasted a quarter of an hour, the white man returned alone, his red friend having disappeared in the forest.

The ordinary expression of the countenance of the Pathfinder was that of simplicity, integrity and sincerity, blended in an air of self reliance, that usually gave great confidence to those who found themselves under his care, but now a look of concern cast a shade over his honest face, that struck the whole party.

"What cheer, Master Pathfinder?" demanded Cap, permitting a voice that was usually deep, loud and confident to sink into the cautious tones that better suited the dangers of the wilderness; "has the enemy got between us and our port?"

"Anan?"

"Have any of these painted scaramouches anchored off the harbor towards which we are running, with the hope of cutting us off in entering?"

"It may be all as you say, friend Cap, but I am none the wiser for your words, and in ticklish times the plainer a man makes his English, the easier he is understood. I know nothing of ports and anchors, but there is a direful Mingo trail, within a hundred yards of this very spot, and as fresh as venison without salt. If one of the fiery devils has passed, so have a dozen; and what is worse, they have gone down towards the garrison, and not a soul crosses the clearing around it, that some of their piercing eyes will not discover, when sartain bullets will follow."

"Cannot this said fort, deliver a broadside, and clear every thing within the sweep of its hawse?"

"Nay, the forts this-a-way, are not like forts in the settlements, and two, or three light cannon are all they have down at the mouth of the river; and then broadsides fired at a dozen outlying Mingos, lying behind logs and in a forest, would be powder spent in vain. We have but one course, and that is a very nice one. We are judgematically placed here, both canoes being hid by the high bank and the bushes, from all eyes except them of any lurker directly opposite. Here, then, we may stay, without much present fear; but how to get the blood thirsty devils up the stream again?—Ha—I have it—I have it—If it does no good, it can do no harm. Do you see the wide-top chestnut, here, Jasper, at the last turn in the river? On our own side of the stream, I mean."

"That near the fallen pine?"

"The very same. Take the flint and tinder box, creep along the bank and light a fire at that spot. Maybe the smoke will draw them above us. In the mean while, we will drop the canoes carefully down beyond the point below, and find another shelter. Bushes are plenty, and covers are easily to be had, in this region, as witness the many ambushments."

"I will do it, Pathfinder," said Jasper springing to the shore. "In ten minutes the fire shall be lighted."

"And, Eau douce; use plenty of damp wood, this time," half whispered the other, laughing heartily, in his own peculiar manner. "When smoke is wanted, water helps to thicken it."

The young man, who too well understood his duty to delay unnecessarily, was soon off, making his way rapidly towards the desired point. A slight attempt of Mabel to object to the risk was disregarded, and the party immediately prepared to change its position, as it could be seen from the place where Jasper intended to light his fire. The movement did not require haste, and it was made leisurely and with care. The canoes were got clear of the bushes, then suffered to drop down with the stream, until they reached the spot, where the chestnut, at the foot of which Jasper was to light the fire, was almost shut out from view, when they stopped, and every eye was turned in the direction of the adventurer.

"There goes the smoke!" exclaimed the Pathfinder, as a current of air whirled a little column of the vapor from the land, allowing it to rise spirally above the bed of the river. "A good flint, a small bit of steel, and plenty of dry leaves make a quick fire! I hope Eau douce will have the wit to bethink him of the damp wood, now, when it may sarve us all a good turn."

"Too much smoke—too much cunning," said Arrowhead, sententiously.

"That is gospel truth, Tuscarora, if the Mingos did'n't know that they are near soldiers; but soldiers commonly think more of their dinners, at a halt, than of their wisdom and danger. No—no—let the boy pile on his logs, and smother them well too; it will all be laid to the stupidity of some Scotch, or Irish blunderer, who is thinking more of his oatmeal, or his potatoes, than of Injin sarcumventions, or Injin rifles."

"And, yet, I should think, from all we have heard in the towns, that the soldiers on this frontier are used to the artifices of their enemies," said Mabel, "and have got to be almost as wily as the red men, themselves."

"Not they—not they. Exper'ence makes them but little wiser, and they wheel, and platoon, and battalion it about, here, in the forest, just as they did in their parks, at home, of which they are all so fond of talking. One red skin has more cunning in his natur', than a whole rigiment from the other side of the water—that is what I call cunning of the woods. But there is smoke enough, of all conscience, and we had better drop into another cover. The lad has thrown the river on his fire, and there is danger that the Mingos will believe a whole rigiment is out."

While speaking the Pathfinder permitted his canoe to drift away from the bush by which it had been retained, and in a couple of minutes the bend in the river concealed the smoke and the tree. Fortunately, a small indentation in the shore presented itself, within a few yards of the point they had just passed, and the two canoes glided into it, under the impulsion of the paddles.

A better spot could not have been found for the purpose of the travellers, than the one they now occupied. The bushes were thick, and they overhung the water, forming a complete canopy of leaves. There was a small gravelly strand, at the bottom of the little bay, where most of the party landed to be more at their ease, and the only position from which they could possibly be seen, was a point on the river directly opposite. There was little danger, however, of discovery from that quarter, as the thicket there was even denser than common, and the land beyond it, was so wet and marshy, as to render it difficult to be trodden.

"This is a safe cover," said the Pathfinder, after he had taken a scrutinizing survey of his position; "but it may be necessary to make it safer. Master Cap, I ask nothing of you, but silence and a quieting of such gifts as you may have got at sea, while the Tuscarora and I make provision for the evil hour."

The guide then went a short distance into the bushes, accompanied by the Indian, where the two cut off the larger stems of several alders and other bushes, using the utmost care not to make a noise. The ends of these little trees, for such in fact they were, were forced into the mud, outside of the canoes, the depth of the water being very trifling, and in the course of ten minutes a very effectual screen was interposed between them and the point of principal danger. Much ingenuity and readiness were manifested in making this simple arrangement, in which the two workmen were essentially favored by the natural formation of the bank, the indentation in the shore, the shallowness of the water and the manner in which the tangled bushes dipped into the stream. The Pathfinder had the address to look for bushes that had curved stems, things easily found in such a place, and by cutting them some distance beneath the bend, and permitting the latter to touch the water, the artificial little thicket had not the appearance of growing in the stream, which might have excited suspicion, but, one passing it, would have thought, that the bushes shot out horizontally from the bank before they inclined upwards towards the light. In short, the shelter was so cunningly devised, and so artfully prepared, that none but an unusually distrustful eye, would have been turned for an instant towards the spot, in quest of a hiding place.

"This is the best cover, I ever yet got into," said the Pathfinder, with his quiet laugh, after having been on the outside to reconnoitre; "the leaves of our new trees fairly touch the bushes over our heads, and even the painter who has been in the garrison, of late, could not tell which belong to Providence and which are ourn. Hist!—yonder comes Eau douce, wading like a sensible boy, as he is, to lose his trail, in the water, and we shall soon see, whether our cover is good for any thing or not."

Jasper had, indeed, returned from his duty above, and missing the canoes, he at once inferred that they had dropped round the next bend in the river, in order to get out of sight of the fire. His habits of caution immediately suggested the expediency of stepping into the water, in order that there might exist no visible communication between the marks left by the party, on the shore, and the place where he believed them to have taken refuge below. Should the Canadian Indians return on their own trail, and discover that made by the Pathfinder and the Serpent, in their ascent from, and descent to, the river, the clue to their movements would cease at the shore, water leaving no prints of footsteps. The young man had, therefore, waded, knee-deep, as far as the point, and was now seen making his way slowly down the margin of the stream, searching curiously for the spot, in which the canoes were hid.

It was in the power of those behind the bushes, by placing their eyes near the leaves, to find many places to look through, while one at a little distance lost this advantage, or, even, did his sight happen to fall on some small opening, the bank and the shadows beyond prevented him from detecting forms and outlines of sufficient dimensions, to expose the fugitives. It was evident to those who watched his motions, from behind their cover, and they were all in the canoes, that Jasper was totally at a loss to imagine, where the Pathfinder had secreted himself. When fairly round the curvature in the shore, and out of sight of the fire he had lighted above, the young man stopped and began examining the bank deliberately, and with great care. Occasionally, he advanced eight or ten paces, and then halted again, to renew the search. The water being much shoaler than common, he stepped aside, in order to walk with greater ease to himself, and came so near the artificial plantation that he might have touched it with his hand. Still he detected nothing, and was actually passing the spot, when Pathfinder made an opening beneath the branches, and called to him, in a low voice, to enter.

"This is pretty well," said the Pathfinder, laughing; "though pale-face eyes, and red-skin eyes are as different as human spyglasses. I would wager, with the sarjeant's daughter here, a horn of powder agin a wampum belt for her girdle, that her father's rigiment should march by this ambushment of ourn, and never find out the fraud! But, if the Mingos actilly get down into the bed of the river, where Jasper passed, I should tremble for the plantation. It will do, for their eyes, even, across the stream, howsever, and will not be without its use."

"Don't you think, Master Pathfinder, that it would be wisest, after all," said Cap, "to get under way, at once, and carry sail hard down stream, as soon as we are satisfied these rascals are fairly astern of us. We seamen call a stern chase, a long chase."

"I would'n't move from this spot, until we hear from the Sarpent, with the sarjeant's pretty da'ter, here, in our company, for all the powder in the magazine of the fort, below! Sartain captivity, or sartain death would follow. If a tender fa'n, such as the maiden we have in charge, could thread the forest like old deer, it might, indeed, do to quit the canoes, for by making a circuit, we could reach the garrison afore morning."

"Then let it be done," said Mabel, springing to her feet, under the sudden impulse of awakened energy; "I am young, active, used to exercise, and could easily out-walk my dear uncle. Let no one think me a hindrance. I cannot bear that all your lives should be exposed on my account."

"No—no—pretty one; we think you any thing but a hindrance, or any thing that is onbecoming, and would willingly run twice this risk to do you and the honest sarjeant a sarvice. Do I not speak your mind, Eau douce?"

"To do *her* a service," said Jasper, with emphasis. "Nothing shall tempt me to desert Mabel Dunham, until she is safe in her father's arms."

"Well said, lad; bravely and honestly said, too; and I join in it, heart and hand. No—no, you are not the first of your sex I have led through the wilderness, and never but once did any harm befal any of them. That was a sad day, sartainly; but its like may never come again."

Mabel looked from one of her protectors to the other, and her fine eyes swam in tears. Frankly placing a hand in that of each, she answered them, though at first her voice was choked,

"I have no right to expose you, on my account. My dear father will thank you—I thank you. God will reward you—but let there be no unnecessary risk. I can walk far, and have often gone miles, on some girlish fancy; why not now exert myself, for my life—nay, for your precious lives."

"She is a true dove, Jasper," said the Pathfinder, neither relinquishing the hand he held until the girl herself, in native modesty, saw fit to withdraw it, "and wonderfully winning! We get to be rough, and sometimes even hard hearted in the woods, Mabel, but the sight of one like you, brings us back agin to our young feelin's, and does us good for the remainder of our days. I dare say, Jasper, here, will tell you the same; for, like me in the forest, the lad sees but few such as yourself, on Ontario, to soften his heart, and remind him of love for his kind. Speak out, now, Jasper, and say if it is not so."

"I question if many like Mabel Dunham are to be found anywhere," returned the young man gallantly, an honest sincerity glowing in his face, that spoke more eloquently than his tongue; "you need not mention woods and lakes, to challenge her equals, but I would go into the settlements and towns."

"We had better leave the canoes," Mabel hurriedly rejoined, "for I feel it is no longer safe to be here."

"You can never do it; you can never do it. It would be a march of more than twenty miles, and that, too, of tramping over brush and roots, and through swamps, in the dark; the trail of such a party would be wide, and we might have to fight our way into the garrison, a'ter all. We will wait for the Mohican."

Such appearing to be the decision of him to whom all, in their present strait, looked up for counsel, no more was said on the subject. The whole party now broke up into groups, Arrowhead and his wife, sitting apart under the bushes, conversing in a low tone, though the man spoke sternly and the woman answered with the subdued mildness that marks the degraded condition of a savage's wife. Pathfinder and Cap occupied one canoe, chatting of their different adventures, by sea and land, while Jasper and Mabel sat in the other, making greater progress in intimacy in a single hour than might have been effected under other circumstances, in a twelvemonth. Notwithstanding their situation, as regards the enemy, the time flew by swiftly, and the young people, in particular, were astonished when Cap informed them how long they had been thus occupied.

"If one could smoke, Master Pathfinder," observed the old sailor, "this berth would be snug enough, for, to give the devil his due, you have got the canoes handsomely landlocked, and into moorings that would defy a monsoon. The only hardship is the denial of the pipe."

"The scent of the tobacco would betray us, and where is the use of taking all these precautions against the Mingos' eyes, if we are to tell them where the cover is to be found through the nose. No—no—deny your appetites; deny your appetites, and l'arn one virtue from a red skin, who will pass a week without eating even, to get a single scalp.—Did you hear nothing, Jasper?"

"The Serpent is coming."

"Then let us see if Mohican eyes are better than them of a lad who follows the water."

The Mohican made his appearance in the same direction as that by which Jasper had rejoined his friends. Instead of coming directly on, however, no sooner did he pass the bend, where he was concealed from any who might be higher up stream, than he moved close under the bank, and, using the utmost caution, got a position where he could look back, with his person sufficiently concealed by the bushes, to prevent its being seen by any in that quarter.

"The Sarpent sees the knaves!" whispered Pathfinder—"as I'm a christian white man they have bit at the bait, and have ambushed the smoke!"

Here a hearty, but silent, laugh, interrupted his words, and nudging Cap with his elbow, they all continued to watch the movements of Chingachgook, in profound stillness. The Mohican remained stationary as the rock on which he stood, fully ten minutes, and then it was apparent that something of interest had occurred within his view, for he drew back with a hurried manner, looked anxiously and keenly along the margin of the stream, and moved quickly down it, taking care to lose his trail in the shallow water. He was evidently in a hurry and concerned, now looking behind him, and then casting eager glances towards every spot on the shore, where he thought a canoe might be concealed.

"Call him in," whispered Jasper, scarce able to restrain his impatience—"call him in, or it will be too late. See, he is actually passing us."

"Not so—not so, lad; nothing presses, depend on it—" returned his companion, "nothing presses, or the Sarpent would begin to creep. The Lord help us, and teach us wisdom! I *do* believe even Chingachgook, whose sight is as faithful as the hound's scent, overlooks us, and will not find out the ambushment we have made!"

This exultation was untimely, for the words were no sooner spoken, than the Indian, who had actually got several feet lower down the stream than the artificial cover, suddenly stopped, fastened a keen riveted glance, among the transplanted bushes, made a few hasty steps backward, and, bending his body and carefully separating the branches, he appeared among them.

"The accursed Mingos!" said Pathfinder, as soon as his friend was near enough to be addressed with prudence.

"Iroquois;" returned the sententious Indian.

"No matter—no matter—Iroquois—devil—Mingo, Mengwe, or furies—all are pretty much the same. I call all rascals, Mingos. Come hither, chief, and let us convarse rationally."

The two then stepped aside and conversed earnestly in the dialect of the Delawares. When their private communication was over, Pathfinder rejoined the rest, and made them acquainted with all he had learned.

The Mohican had followed the trail of their enemies, some distance towards the fort, until the latter caught a sight of the smoke of Jasper's fire, when they instantly retraced their steps. It now became necessary for Chingachgook, who ran the greatest risk of detection, to find a cover where he could secrete himself, until the party might pass. It was perhaps fortunate for him, that the savages were so intent on their recent discovery that they did not bestow the ordinary attention on the signs of the forest. At all events, they passed him swiftly, fifteen in number, treading lightly in each other's footsteps, and he was enabled again to get into their rear. After proceeding to the place where the footsteps of Pathfinder and the Mohican joined the principal trail, the Iroquois had struck off to the river, which they reached just as Jasper disappeared behind the bend below. The smoke being now in plain view, the savages plunged into the woods, and endeavored to approach the fire unseen. Chingachgook profited by this occasion to descend to the water, and to gain the bend in the river also, which he thought had been effected undiscovered. Here he paused, as has been stated, until he saw his enemies at the fire, where their stay, however, was very short.

Of the motives of the Iroquois the Mohican could judge only by their acts. He thought they had detected the artifice of the fire, and were aware that it had been kindled with a view to mislead them; for, after a hasty examination of the spot, they separated, some plunging again into the woods, while six or eight followed the footsteps of Jasper along the shore, and came down the stream towards the place where the canoes had landed. What course they might take on reaching that spot, was only to be conjectured, for the Serpent had felt the emergency to be too pressing to delay looking for his friends any longer. From some indications that were to be gathered from their gestures, however, he thought it probable that their enemies might follow down on the margin of the stream, but could not be certain.

As the Pathfinder related these facts to his companions, the professional feelings of the two other white men came uppermost, and both naturally reverted to their habits, in quest of the means of escape.

"Let us run out the canoes, at once," said Jasper, eagerly; "the current is strong, and by using the paddles vigorously we shall soon be beyond the reach of these scoundrels!"

"And this poor flower, that first blossomed in the clearin's; shall it wither in this forest?" objected his friend, with a poetry that he had unconsciously imbibed by his long association with the Delawares.

"We must all die first," answered the youth, a generous colour mounting to his temples; "Mabel, and Arrowhead's wife may lie down in the canoes, while we do our duty, like men, on our feet."

"Ay, you are actyve at the paddle and the oar, Eau douce, I will allow, but an accursed Mingo is more actyve, at his mischief; the canoes are swift, but a rifle bullet is swifter."

"It is the business of men, engaged by a confiding father as we have been, to run this risk—"

"But it is not their business to overlook prudence."

"Prudence! A man may carry his prudence so far as to forget his courage."

The group was standing on the narrow strand, the Pathfinder leaning on his rifle, the butt of which rested on the gravelly beach, while both his hands clasped the barrel, at the height of his own shoulders. As Jasper threw out this severe and unmerited imputation, the deep red of his comrade's face, maintained its hue unchanged, though the young man perceived that the fingers grasped the iron of the gun with the tenacity of a vice. Here all betrayal of emotion ceased.

"You are young, and hot-headed," returned Pathfinder, with a dignity that impressed his listeners with a keen sense of his moral superiority; "but my life has been passed among dangers of this sort, and my exper'ence and gifts are not to be mastered by the impatience of a boy. As for courage, Jasper, I will not send back an angry and unmeaning word, to meet an angry and an unmeaning word, for I know that you are true, in your station and according to your knowledge, but take the advice of one who faced the Mingos when you were a child, and know that their cunning is easier sarcumvented by prudence, than outwitted by foolishness."

"I ask your pardon, Pathfinder," said the repentant Jasper, eagerly grasping the hands that the other permitted him to seize. "I ask your pardon, humbly and sincerely. 'Twas a foolish, as well as wicked thing to hint of a man whose heart, in a good cause, is as firm as the rocks on the lake shore."

For the first time, the colour deepened on the cheek of the Pathfinder, and the solemn dignity that he had assumed, under a purely natural impulse, disappeared in the expression of the earnest simplicity that was inherent in all his feelings. He met the grasp of his young friend, with a squeeze as cordial, as if no chord had jarred between them, and a slight sternness that had gathered about his eye disappeared in a look of natural kindness.

"'Tis well, Jasper, 'tis well," he answered, laughing. "I bear no ill will, nor shall any one in my behalf. My natur' is that of a white man, and that is to bear no malice. It might have been ticklish work to have said half as much to the Sarpent here, though he is a Delaware, for colour will have its way—"

A touch on his shoulder caused the speaker to cease. Mabel was standing erect in the canoe, her light, but swelling form, bent forward in an attitude of graceful earnestness, her finger on her lips, her head averted, the spirited eyes riveted on an opening in the bushes, and one arm extended with a fishing-rod, the end of which had touched the Pathfinder. The latter bowed his head to a level with a look-out, near which he had intentionally kept himself, and then whispered to Jasper—

"The accursed Mingos! Stand to your arms, my men, but lay quiet as the corpses of dead trees!"

Jasper advanced rapidly, but noiselessly, to the canoe, and with a gentle violence induced Mabel to place herself in such an attitude as concealed her entire body, though it would have probably exceeded his means to induce the girl so far to lower her head that she could not keep her gaze fastened on their enemies. He then took his own post near her, with his rifle cocked and poised, in readiness to fire. Arrowhead and Chingachgook crawled to the cover, and lay in wait like snakes, with their arms prepared for service, while the wife of the former bowed her head between her knees, covered it with her calicoe robe, and remained passive and immovable. Cap loosened both his pistols, in their belt, but seemed quite at a loss what course to pursue. The Pathfinder did not stir. He had originally got a position where he might aim with deadly effect through the leaves, and whence he could watch the movements of his enemies, and he was far too steady to be disconcerted at a moment so critical.

It was truly an alarming instant. Just as Mabel touched the shoulder of her guide, three of the Iroquois appeared in the water, at the bend of the river, within a hundred yards of the cover, and halted to examine the stream below. They were all naked to the waist, armed for an expedition against their foes, and in their war paint. It was apparent, that they were undecided as to the course they ought to pursue, in order to find the fugitives. One pointed down the river, a second up the stream, and the third towards the opposite bank.

Chapter V

"Death is here, and death is there,
Death is busy every where."
Shelley, "Death," ll. 1–2.

IT WAS a breathless moment. The only clue the fugitives possessed to the intentions of their pursuers, was in their gestures, and the indications that escaped them in the fury of disappointment. That a party had returned, already, on their own footsteps, by land, was pretty certain, and all the benefit expected from the artifice of the fire was necessarily lost. But that consideration became of little moment, just then, for the secreted were menaced with an immediate discovery, by those who had kept on a level with the river. All the facts presented themselves clearly, and as it might be by intuition, to the mind of Pathfinder, who perceived the necessity of immediate decision, and of being in readiness to act in concert. Without making any noise therefore, he managed to get the two Indians and Jasper near him, when he opened his communications in a whisper.

"We must be ready—we must be ready," he said. "There are but three of the scalping devils, and we are five, four of whom may be set down as manful warriors for such a skrimmage. Eau douce, do you take the fellow that is painted like death; Chingachgook, I give you the chief, and Arrowhead must keep his eye on the young one. There must be no mistake; for two bullets in the same body would be a sinful waste, with one like the sarjeant's daughter in danger. I shall hold myself in resarve ag'in accidents, lest a fourth riptyle appear, for one of your hands may prove unsteady. By no means fire until I give the word; we must not let the crack of the rifle be heard except in the last resort, since all the rest of the miscreants are still within its hearing. Jasper, boy, in case of any movement behind us, on the bank, I trust to you to run out the canoe, with the sarjeant's daughter, and to pull for the garrison, by God's leave."

The Pathfinder had no sooner given these directions than the near approach of their enemies, rendered profound silence necessary. The Iroquois in the river were slowly descending the stream, keeping of necessity near the bushes that overhung the water, while the rustling of leaves, and the snapping of twigs soon gave fearful evidence that another party was moving along the bank at an equally graduated pace, and directly abreast of them. In consequence of the distance between the bushes planted by the fugitives and the true shore, the two parties became visible to each other, when opposite that precise point. Both stopped, and a conversation ensued, that may be said to have passed directly over the heads of those who were concealed. Indeed nothing sheltered the travellers, but the branches and leaves of plants so pliant, that they yielded to every current of air, and which a puff of wind, a little stronger than common, would have blown away. Fortunately the line of sight, carried the eyes of the two parties of savages, whether they stood in the water, or on the land, above the bushes, and the leaves appeared blended in a way to excite no suspicion. Perhaps the very boldness of the expedient prevented an exposure. The conversation that took place, was conducted earnestly, but in guarded tones, as if those who spoke wished to defeat the intentions of any listeners. It was in a dialect that both the Indian warriors beneath, as well as the Pathfinder, understood. Even Jasper comprehended a portion of what was said.

"The trail is washed away by the water!" said one from below, who stood so near the artificial cover of the fugitives, that he might have been struck by the salmon spear that lay in the bottom of Jasper's canoe. "Water has washed it so clean, that a Yengeese hound could not follow."

"The pale faces have left the shore, in their canoes," answered the speaker on the bank.

"It cannot be. The rifles of our warriors below, are certain."

The Pathfinder gave a significant glance at Jasper, and he clenched his teeth in order to suppress the sound of his own breathing.

"Let my young men look as if their eyes were eagles'," said the eldest warrior among those who were wading in the river. "We have been a whole moon on the war-path, and have found but one scalp. There is a maiden among them, and some of our braves want wives."

Happily these words were lost on Mabel, but Jasper's frown became deeper, and his face fiercely flushed.

The savages now ceased speaking, and the party that was concealed, heard the slow and guarded movements of those who were on the bank, as they pushed the bushes aside in their wary progress. It was soon evident that the latter had passed the cover, but the group in the water still remained, scanning the shore, with eyes that glared through their war-paint, like coals of living fire. After a pause of two or three minutes, these three began, also, to descend the stream, though it was step by step, as men move who look for an object that has been lost. In this manner, they passed the artificial screen, and Pathfinder opened his mouth, in that hearty but noiseless laugh, that nature and habit had contributed to render a peculiarity of the man. His triumph, however, was premature; for the last of the retiring party, just at this moment casting a look behind him, suddenly stopped, and his fixed attitude and steady gaze, at once betrayed the appalling fact that some neglected bush had awakened his suspicions.

It was perhaps fortunate for the concealed that the warrior who manifested these fearful signs of distrust was young, and had still a reputation to acquire. He knew the importance of discretion and modesty in one of his years, and most of all did he dread the ridicule and contempt that would certainly follow a false alarm. Without recalling any of his companions, therefore, he turned on his own footsteps, and while the others continued to descend the river, he cautiously approached the bushes, on which his looks were still fastened, as by a charm. Some of the leaves, which were exposed to the sun, had drooped a little, and this slight departure from the usual natural laws, had caught the quick eyes of the Indian, for so practised and acute do the senses of the savage become, more especially when he is on the war-path, that trifles apparently of the most insignificant sort, often prove to be clues to lead him to his object.

The trifling nature of the change which had aroused the suspicion of this youth, was an additional motive for not acquainting his companions with his discovery. Should he really detect any thing, his glory would be the greater for being unshared, and should he not, he might hope to escape that derision which the young Indian so much dreads. Then there were the dangers of an ambush and a surprise, to which every warrior of the woods is ever keenly alive, to render his approach slow and cautious. In consequence of the delay that proceeded from these combined causes, the two parties had descended some fifty, or sixty yards before the young savage was again near enough to the bushes of the Pathfinder to touch them with his hand.

Notwithstanding their critical situation, the whole party behind the cover, had their eyes fastened on the working countenance of the young Iroquois, who was agitated by conflicting feelings. First came the eager hope of obtaining success where some of the most experienced of his tribe had failed, and with it a degree of glory that had seldom fallen to the share of one of his years, or a brave on his first war-path; then followed doubts, as the drooping leaves seemed to rise again, and to revive in the currents of air; and distrust of hidden danger lent its exciting feeling to keep the eloquent features in play. So very slight, however, had been the alteration produced by the heat on bushes, of which the stems were in the water, that when the Iroquois actually laid his hand on the leaves, he fancied that he had been deceived. As no man ever distrusts strongly, without using all convenient means of satisfying his doubts, however, the young warrior cautiously pushed aside the branches, and advanced a step within the hiding place, when the forms of the concealed party met his gaze, resembling so many breathing statutes. The low exclamation, the slight start, and the glaring eye, were hardly seen and heard, before the arm of Chingachgook was raised, and the tomahawk of the Delaware descended on the shaven head of his foe. The Iroquois raised his hands, frantically bounded backward, and fell into the water, at a spot where the current swept the body away, the struggling limbs still tossing and writhing in the agony of death. The Delaware made a vigorous but unsuccessful attempt to seize an arm, with the hope of securing the scalp, but the blood-stained waters whirled down their current, carrying with them their quivering burthen.

All this passed in less than a minute, and the events were

so sudden and unexpected, that men less accustomed to forest warfare than the Pathfinder and his associates, would have been at a loss how to act.

"There is not a moment to lose," said Jasper, tearing aside the bushes, as he spoke earnestly, but in a suppressed voice. "Do as I do, Master Cap, if you would save your niece, and you, Mabel, lie at your length in the canoe."

The words were scarcely uttered, when seizing the bow of the light bark, he dragged it along the shore, wading himself while Cap aided behind, keeping so near the bank as to avoid being seen by the savages below, and striving to gain the turn in the river above him, which would effectually conceal the party from the enemy. The Pathfinder's canoe lay nearest to the bank, and it was necessarily the last to quit the shore. The Delaware leaped on the narrow strand, and plunged into the forest, it being his assigned duty to watch the foe, in that quarter, while Arrowhead motioned to his white companion to seize the bow of the boat, and to follow Jasper. All this was the work of an instant. But when the Pathfinder reached the current, that was sweeping round the turn, he felt a sudden change in the weight he was dragging, and looking back he found that both the Tuscarora and his wife had deserted him. The thought of treachery flashed upon his mind, but there was no time to pause, for the wailing shout that arose from the party below, proclaimed that the body of the young Iroquois had floated as low as the spot reached by his friends. The report of a rifle followed, and then the guide saw that Jasper, having doubled the bend in the river, was crossing the stream, standing erect, in the stern of the canoe, while Cap was seated forward, both propelling the light boat with vigorous strokes of the paddles. A glance, a thought, and an expedient followed each other quickly, in one so trained in the vicissitudes of the frontier warfare. Springing into the stern of his own canoe, he urged it by a vigorous shove into the current, and commenced crossing the stream himself, at a point so much lower than that of his companions, as to offer his own person for a target to the enemy, well knowing that their keen desire to secure a scalp would control all other feelings.

"Keep well up the current, Jasper," shouted the gallant

guide, as he swept the water with long, steady, vigorous strokes of the paddle—"keep well up the current, and push for the alder bushes opposite. Presarve the sarjeant's daughter, before all things, and leave these Mingo knaves to the Sarpent and me."

Jasper flourished his paddle, as a signal of understanding, while shot succeeded shot in quick succession, all now being aimed at the solitary man in the nearest canoe.

"Ay, empty your rifles, like simpletons as you be," said the Pathfinder, who had acquired a habit of speaking when alone, from passing so much of his time in the solitude of the forest; "empty your rifles, with an onsteady aim, and give me time to put yard upon yard of river atween us. I will not revile you, like a Delaware, or a Mohican, for my gifts are a white man's gifts, and not an Injin's; and boasting in battle is no part of a christian warrior; but I may say, here, all alone by myself, that you are little better than so many men from the town, shooting at robins in the orchards! That was well meant—" throwing back his head, as a rifle bullet cut a lock of hair from his temple—"but the lead that misses by an inch, is as useless as the lead that never quits the barrel. Bravely done, Jasper! The Sarjeant's sweet child must be saved, even if we go in without our own scalps."

By this time the Pathfinder was in the centre of the river, and almost abreast of his enemies, while the other canoe, impelled by the vigorous arms of Cap and Jasper, had nearly gained the opposite shore, at the precise spot that had been pointed out to them. The old mariner now played his part manfully, for he was on his proper element, loved his niece sincerely, had a proper regard for his own person, and was not unused to fire, though his experience certainly lay in a very different species of warfare. A few strokes of the paddles were given, and the canoe shot into the bushes, Mabel was hurried to the land by Jasper, and, for the present, all three of the fugitives were safe.

Not so with the Pathfinder. His hardy self-devotion had brought him into a situation of unusual exposure, the hazards of which were much increased, by the fact that just as he drifted nearest to the enemy, the party on the shore rushed down the bank, and joined their friends who still stood in the water. The Oswego was about a cable's length in width at this point, and the canoe being in the centre, the object was only a hundred yards from the rifles, that were constantly discharged at it; or, at the usual target distance for that weapon.

In this extremity the steadiness and skill of the Pathfinder did him good service. He knew that his safety depended altogether on keeping in motion, for a stationary object, at that distance, would have been hit nearly every shot. Nor was motion of itself sufficient, for accustomed to kill the bounding deer, his enemies probably knew how to vary the line of aim, so as to strike him, should he continue to move in any one direction. He was consequently compelled to change the course of the canoe, at one moment shooting down with the current, with the swiftness of an arrow, and at the next checking its progress in that direction, to glance athwart the stream. Luckily the Iroquois could not reload their pieces in the water, and the bushes that everywhere fringed the shore, rendered it difficult to keep the fugitive in view, when on the land. Aided by these circumstances, and having received the fire of all his foes, the Pathfinder was gaining fast in distance, both downwards and across the current, when a new danger suddenly, if not unexpectedly presented itself, by the appearance of the party that had been left in ambush below, with a view to watch the river.

These were the savages alluded to in the short dialogue that has been already related. They were no less than ten in number, and understanding all the advantages of their bloody occupation, they had posted themselves at a spot, where the water dashed among rocks and over shallows, in a way to form a rapid, which in the language of the country, is called a rift. The Pathfinder saw that if he entered this rift, he should be compelled to approach a point where the Iroquois had posted themselves, for the current was irresistible, and the rocks allowed no other safe passage, while death or captivity would be the probable result of the attempt. All his efforts, therefore, were turned towards reaching the western shore, the foe being all on the eastern side of the river. But the exploit surpassed human power, and to attempt to stem the stream, would at once have so far diminished the motion of the canoe, as to render aim certain. In this exigency the guide came to a decision with his usual, cool, promptitude, making his preparations accordingly. Instead of endeavouring to gain the channel, he steered towards the shallowest part of the stream, on reaching which, he seized his rifle and pack, leaped into the water, and began to wade from rock to rock, taking the direction of the western shore. The canoe whirled about in the furious current, now rolling over some slippery stone, now filling, and then emptying itself, until it lodged on the strand, within a few yards of the spot where the Iroquois had posted themselves.

In the meanwhile the Pathfinder was far from being out of danger. For the first minute, admiration of his promptitude and daring, which are high virtues in the mind of an Indian, kept his enemies motionless, but the desire of revenge, and the cravings for the much prized trophy, soon overcame this transient feeling, and aroused them from their stupor. Rifle flashed after rifle, and the bullets whistled around the head of the fugitive, amid the roar of the waters. Still he proceeded like one who bore a charmed life, for while his rude, frontier garments were more than once cut, his skin was not razed.

As the Pathfinder, in several instances, was compelled to wade in water that rose nearly to his arms, while he kept his rifle and ammunition elevated above the raging current, the toil soon fatigued him, and he was glad to stop at a large stone, or small rock, which rose so high above the river, that its upper surface was dry. On this stone he placed his powder-horn, getting behind it himself, so as to have the advantage of a partial cover for his body. The western shore was only fifty feet distant, but the quiet, swift, dark current that glanced through the interval, sufficiently showed that here he would be compelled to swim.

A short cessation in the firing now took place on the part of the Indians, who gathered about the canoe, and, having found the paddles, were preparing to cross the river.

"Pathfinder," called a voice from among the bushes, at the point nearest to the person addressed, on the western shore.

"What would you have, Jasper?"

"Be of good heart—Friends are at hand, and not a single

Mingo shall cross without suffering for his boldness. Had you not better leave the rifle on the rock, and swim to us before the rascals can get afloat?"

"A true woodsman never quits his piece, while he has any powder in his horn, or a bullet in his pouch. I have not drawn a trigger this day, Eau douce, and should'n't relish the idea of parting with them riptyles, without causing them to remember my name. A little water will not harm my legs, and I see that blackguard, Arrowhead, among the scamps, and wish to send him the wages he has so faithfully earned. You have not brought the Sarjeant's daughter down here in a range with their bullets, I hope, Jasper!"

"She is safe, for the present at least, though all depends on our keeping the river between us and the enemy. They must know our weakness, now, and should they cross, no doubt some of their party will be left on the other side."

"This canoeing touches your gifts rather than mine, boy, though I will handle a paddle with the best Mingo that ever struck a salmon. If they cross below the rift, why can't we cross in the still water above, and keep playing at dodge and turn with the wolves?"

"Because, as I have said, they will leave a party on the other shore—and, then, Pathfinder, would you expose Mabel, to the rifles of the Iroquois!"

"The Sarjeant's daughter must be saved," returned the guide with calm energy. "You are right, Jasper, she has no gift to authorize her in offering her sweet face and tender body, to a Mingo rifle. What can be done then? They must be kept from crossing for an hour or two, if possible, when we must do our best in the darkness."

"I agree with you, Pathfinder, if it can be effected; but are we strong enough for such a purpose?"

"The Lord is with us, boy; the Lord is with us; and it is onreasonable to suppose that one like the Sarjeant's daughter will be altogether abandoned by Providence, in such a strait. There is not a boat between the falls and the garrison, except these two canoes, to my sartain knowledge, and I think it will go beyond red-skin gifts to cross in the face of two rifles, like these of yourn' and mine. I will not vaunt, Jasper, but it is well known on all this frontier that Killdeer seldom fails!"

"Your skill is admitted by all, far and near, Pathfinder, but a rifle takes time to be loaded; nor are you on the land, aided by a good cover, where you can work to the advantage you are used to. If you had our canoe, might you not pass to the shore, with a dry rifle?"

"Can an eagle fly, Jasper?" returned the other laughing, in his usual manner, and looking back as he spoke. "But it would be onwise to expose yourself on the water, for them miscreants are beginning to bethink them again of powder and bullets."

"It can be done without any such chances. Master Cap has gone up to the canoe, and will cast the branch of a tree into the river to try the current, which sets from the point above in the direction of your rock. See, there it comes already; if it float fairly, you must raise your arm, when the canoe will follow. At all events, if the boat should pass you, the eddy below will bring it up, and I can recover it."

While Jasper was still speaking the floating branch came in sight, and quickening its progress with the increasing velocity of the current, it swept swiftly down towards the Pathfinder, who seized it as it was passing, and held it in the air, as a sign of success. Cap understood the signal, and presently the canoe was launched into the stream, with a caution and an intelligence that the habits of the mariner fitted him to observe. It floated in the same direction as the branch, and in a minute was arrested by the Pathfinder.

"This has been done with a frontier man's judgment, Jasper," said the guide laughing; "but you have your gifts, which incline most to the water, as mine incline to the woods. Now, let them Mingo knaves cock their rifles and get rests, for this is the last chance they are likely to have at a man without a cover."

"Nay, shove the canoe towards the shore, quartering the current, and throw yourself into it, as it goes off," said Jasper eagerly; "there is little use in running any risk."

"I like to stand up face to face, with my inimies like a man, while they set me the example," returned the Pathfinder, proudly. "I am not a red skin born, and it is more a white man's gifts to fight openly, than to lie in ambushment."

"And Mabel?"

"True, boy, true—the Sarjeant's daughter must be saved; and, as you say, foolish risks only become boys. Think you, that you can catch the canoe, where you stand?"

"There can be no doubt, if you give a vigorous push."

Pathfinder made the necessary effort, the light bark shot across the intervening space, and Jasper seized it, as it came to land. To secure the canoe, and to take proper positions in the cover, occupied the friends but a moment, when they shook hands cordially, like those who had met after a long separation.

"Now, Jasper, we shall see if a Mingo of them all dare cross the Oswego in the teeth of Killdeer. You are handier with the oar and the paddle and the sail, than with the rifle, perhaps, but you have a stout heart and a steady hand, and them are things that count, in a fight."

"Mabel will find me between her and her enemies," said Jasper, calmly.

"Yes, yes, the Sarjeant's daughter must be protected. I like you, boy, on your own account, but I like you all the better that you think of one so feeble, at a moment when there is need for all our manhood. See, Jasper; three of the knaves are actually getting into the canoe! They must believe we have fled, or they would not surely ventur' so much, directly in the very face of Killdeer!"

Sure enough, the Iroquois did appear bent on venturing across the stream, for, as the Pathfinder and his friends, now kept their persons strictly concealed, their enemies began to think that the latter had taken to flight. The course was that which most white men would have followed, but Mabel was under the care of those who were much too well skilled in forest warfare, to neglect to defend the only pass, that, in truth, now offered even a probable chance for protection.

As the Pathfinder had said, three warriors were in the canoe, two holding their rifles at a poise, kneeling in readiness to aim the deadly weapons; the other standing erect in the stern to wield the paddle. In this manner they left the shore, having had the precaution to haul the canoe, previously to entering it, so far up stream, as to get into the comparatively still water above the rift. It was apparent, at a glance, that the savage who guided the boat was skilled in the art, for the long steady sweep of his paddle sent the light bark over the glassy surface of the tranquil river, as if it were a feather floating in air.

"Shall I fire?" demanded Jasper in a whisper, trembling with eagerness to engage.

"Not yet, boy; not yet. There are but three of them, and if Master Cap, yonder, knows how to use the pop-guns he carries in his belt, we may even let them land, and then we shall recover the canoe."

"But Mabel?—"

"No fear for the Sarjeant's daughter. She is safe, in the hollow stump you say, with the opening judgematically hid by brambles. If what you tell me of the manner in which you concealed the trail be true, the sweet-one might lie there a month, and laugh at the Mingos."

"We are never certain—I wish we had brought her nearer to our own cover!"

"What for, Eau douce?—To place her pretty little head and leaping heart among flying bullets. No—no—she is better where she is, because she is safer."

"We are never certain—we thought ourselves safe, behind the bushes, and yet you saw that we were discovered."

"And the Mingo imp paid for his cur'osity, as them knaves are about to do—"

At that instant, the sharp report of a rifle was heard, when the Indian in the stern of the canoe leaped high into the air, and fell into the water holding the paddle in his hand. A small wreath of smoke floated out from among the bushes of the eastern shore, and was soon absorbed by the atmosphere.

"That is the Sarpent hissing!" exclaimed the Pathfinder, exultingly. "A bolder or a truer heart never beat in the breast of a Delaware. I am sorry that he interfered, but he could not have known our condition—he could not have known our condition."

The canoe no sooner lost its guide, than it floated with the stream, and was soon sucked into the rapids of the rift. Perfectly helpless, the two remaining savages gazed wildly about them, but could offer no resistance to the power of the element. It was perhaps fortunate for Chingachgook that the attention of most of the Iroquois was intently given to the situation of those in the boat, else would his escape have been to the last degree difficult, if not totally impracticable. But not a foe moved, except to conceal his person behind some cover, and every eye was riveted on the two remaining adventurers. In less time than has been necessary to record these occurrences, the canoe was whirling and tossing in the rift, while both the savages had stretched themselves in its bottom, as the only means of preserving the equilibrium. This natural expedient soon failed them, for striking a rock the light craft rolled over, and the two warriors were thrown into the river. The water is seldom deep on a rift, except in particular places where it may have worn channels, and there was little to be apprehended from drowning, though their arms were lost, and the two savages were fain to make the best of their way to the friendly shore, swimming and wading as circumstances required. The canoe itself lodged on a rock, in the centre of the stream, where, for the moment, it became useless to both parties.

"Now is our time, Pathfinder," cried Jasper, as the two Iroquois exposed most of their persons, while wading in the shallowest part of the rapids—"The fellow up stream is mine, and you can take the lower."

So excited had the young man become, by all the incidents of the stirring scene, that the bullet sped from his rifle as he spoke, but uselessly as it would seem, for both the fugitives tossed their arms in disdain. The Pathfinder did not fire.

"No—no—Eau douce," he answered—"I do not seek blood without a cause, and my bullet is well leathered and carefully driven down, for the time of need. I love no Mingo, as is just, seeing how much I have consorted with the Delawares, who are their mortal and nat'ral inimies, but I pull no trigger on one of the miscreants, unless it be plain that his death will lead to some good ind. The deer never leaped, that fell by my hand wantonly. By living much alone with God in the wilderness, a man gets to feel the justice of such opinions. One life is sufficient for our present wants, and there may yet be occasion to use Killdeer in behalf of the Sarpent, who has done an untimorsome thing to let them rampant devils so plainly know that he is in their neighborhood. As I'm a wicked sinner, there is one of them prowling along the bank, this very moment, like one of the boys of the garrison skulking behind a fallen tree to get a shot at a squirrel!"

As the Pathfinder pointed with his finger, while speaking, the quick eye of Jasper soon caught the object towards which it was directed. One of the young warriors of the enemy, burning with a desire to distinguish himself, had stolen from his party towards the cover in which Chingachgook had concealed himself, and as the latter was deceived by the apparent apathy of his foes, as well as engaged in some further preparations of his own, he had evidently obtained a position where he got a sight of the Delaware. This circumstance was apparent by the arrangements the Iroquois was making to fire, for Chingachgook himself was not visible from the western side of the river. The rift was at a bend in the Oswego, and, the sweep of the eastern shore formed a curve so wide that Chingachgook was quite near to his enemies in a straight direction, though separated by several hundred feet on the land, owing to which fact, air lines brought both parties nearly equidistant from the Pathfinder and Jasper. The general width of the river being a little less than two hundred yards, such necessarily was about the distance between his two observers and the skulking Iroquois.

"The Sarpent must be thereabouts," observed Pathfinder, who never turned his eye for an instant from the young warrior, "and yet he must be strangely off his guard to allow a Mingo devil to get his stand so near, with manifest signs of bloodshed in his heart."

"See," interrupted Jasper—"there is the body of the Indian, the Delaware shot! It has drifted on a rock, and the current has forced the head and face above the water."

"Quite likely, boy; quite likely. Human natur' is little better than a log of drift wood, when the life that was breathed into its nostrils has departed. That Iroquois will never harm any one more, but yonder skulking savage is bent on taking the scalp of my best and most tried friend——"

The Pathfinder suddenly interrupted himself, by raising his rifle, a weapon of unusual length, with admirable precision, and firing the instant it had got its level. The Iroquois, on the opposite shore, was in the act of aiming when the fatal messenger from Killdeer arrived. His rifle was discharged it is true, but it was with the muzzle in the air, while the man himself plunged into the bushes, quite evidently hurt, if not slain.

"The skulking reptyle brought it on himself," muttered Pathfinder, sternly, as dropping the breech of his rifle, he carefully commenced re-loading it. "Chingachgook and I have consorted togither since we were boys, and have fou't in company, on the Horican, the Mohawk, the Ontario, and all the other bloody passes between the country of the Frenchers and our own; and did the foolish knave believe that I would stand by and see my best friend cut off in an ambushment!"

"We have served the Serpent as good a turn, as he served us. Those rascals are troubled, Pathfinder, and are falling back into their covers, since they find we can reach them across the river!"

"The shot is no great matter, Jasper; no great matter. Ask any of the 60th, and they can tell you, what Killdeer can do, and has done, and that too when the bullets were flying about our heads like hail-stones. No—no—this is no great matter, and the onthoughtful vagabond drew it down on himself."

"Is that a dog or a deer, swimming towards this shore?"

Pathfinder started, for, sure enough, an object was crossing the stream, above the rift, towards which, however, it was gradually setting by the force of the current. A second look satisfied both the observers that it was a man and an Indian, though so concealed as, at first, to render it doubtful. Some stratagem was apprehended, and the closest attention was given to the movements of the stranger.

"He is pushing something before him, as he swims, and his head resembles a drifting bush!" said Jasper.

"'Tis Injin deviltry, boy; but christian honesty shall sarcumvent their arts."

As the man slowly approached, the observers began to doubt the accuracy of their first impressions, and it was only when two thirds of the stream was passed, that the truth was really known.

"The Big Sarpent, as I live!" exclaimed Pathfinder, looking at his companion, and laughing until the tears came into his eyes, with pure delight at the success of the artifice. "He has tied bushes to his head, so as to hide it, put the horn on top, lashed the rifle to that bit of log he is pushing afore him, and has come over to join his friends. Ah's! me. The times, and times, that he and I have cut such pranks, right in the teeth of Mingos raging for our blood, in the great thoroughfare round and about Ty!"

"It may not be the Serpent, after all, Pathfinder—I can see no feature that I remember."

"Featur'! Who looks for featur's in an Injin?—No—no—boy; 'tis the paint that speaks, and none but a Delaware would wear that paint. Them are his colours, Jasper, just as your craft on the lake wears St. George's Cross, and the Frenchers set their table cloths to fluttering in the wind, with all the stains of fish bones and venison steaks upon them. Now, you see the eye, lad, and it is the eye of a chief. But, Eau douce, fierce as it is, in battle, and glaring as it looks from among the leaves—" here the Pathfinder laid his finger lightly but impressively on his companion's arm—"I have seen it shed tears like rain. There is a soul and a heart, under that red skin, rely on it, although they are a soul and a heart with gifts different from our own."

"No one, who is acquainted with the chief, ever doubted that."

"I *know* it," returned the other proudly, "for I have consorted with him in sorrow and in joy; in one I have found him a man, however stricken; in the other a chief who knows that the women of his tribe are the most seemly in light merriment. But, hist! It is too much like the people of the settlements to pour soft speeches into another's ear, and the Sarpent has keen senses. He knows I love him, and that I speak well of him behind his back, but a Delaware has modesty in his inmost natur', though he will brag like a sinner when tied to a stake."

The Serpent now reached the shore, directly in the front of his two comrades, with whose precise position he must have been acquainted before leaving the eastern side of the river, and rising from the water he shook himself like a dog, and made the usual exclamation—

"Hugh!"

Chapter VI

"These, as they change, Almighty Father, these
Are but the varied God."
Thomson, "A Hymn on the Seasons," ll. 1–2.

AS THE CHIEF LANDED he was met by the Pathfinder, who addressed him in the language of the warrior's people.

"Was it well done, Chingachgook," he said reproachfully, "to ambush a dozen Mingos, alone! Killdeer seldom fails me, it is true, but the Oswego makes a distant mark, and that miscreant showed little more than his head and shoulders above the bushes, and an onpractysed hand and eye might have failed. You should have thought of this, chief; you should have thought of this!"

"The Great Serpent is a Mohican warrior—he sees only his enemies, when he is on the war-path, and his fathers have struck the Mingos from behind, since the waters began to run!"

"I know your gifts—I know your gifts, and respect them, too. No man shall hear me complain that a red skin obsarved red skin natur', but prudence as much becomes a warriour as valour; and had not the Iroquois devils been looking after their friends who were in the water, a hot trail they would have made of yourn!"

"What is the Delaware about to do?" exclaimed Jasper, who observed, at that moment, that the chief suddenly left the Pathfinder, and advanced to the water's edge, apparently with an intention of again entering the river. "He will not be so mad as to return to the other shore, for any trifle he may have forgotten!"

"Not he—not he; he is as prudent as he is brave, in the main, though so forgetful of himself in the late ambushment. Harkee, Jasper," leading the other a little aside, just as they heard the Indian's plunge into the water—"Harkee, lad; Chingachgook is not a christian white man like ourselves, but a Mohican chief, who has his gifts and traditions to tell him what he ought to do; and he who consorts with them that are not strictly and altogether of his own kind, had better leave natur' and use to govern his comrades. A king's soldier will swear, and he will drink, and it is of little use to try to prevent him; a gentleman likes his delicacies, and a lady her feathers, and it does not avail much to struggle ag'in either; whereas an Indian's natur' and gifts are much stronger than these, and no doubt were bestowed by the Lord for wise inds, though neither you, nor me, can follow them in all their windings."

"What does this mean?—See, the Delaware is swimming towards the body that is lodged on the rock. Why does he risk this?"

"For honor, and glory, and renown, as great gentlemen quit their quiet homes, beyond seas, where as they tell me, heart has nothing left to wish for, that is such hearts as can be satisfied in a clearin', to come hither to live on game and fight the Frenchers."

"I understand you—your friend has gone to secure the scalp."

"'Tis his gift, and let him enjoy it. We are white men, and cannot mangle a dead enemy, but it is honor in the eyes of a red skin to do so. It may seem singular to you, Eau douce, but I've known white men of great name and character manifest as remarkable idees consarning their honor, I have."

"A savage will be a savage, Pathfinder, let him keep what company he may."

"It is well for us to say so, lad, but, as I tell you, white honor will not always conform to reason, or to the will of God. I have passed days thinking of them matters, out in the silent woods, and I have come to the opinion, boy, that, as Providence rules all things, no gift is bestowed without some wise and reasonable ind. If Injins are of no use, Injins would not have been created, and I do suppose, could one dive to the bottom of things, it would be found that even the Mingo tribes were produced for some rational and proper purpose, though I confess it surpasses my means to say what it is."

"The Serpent greatly exposes himself to the enemy, in order to get his scalp!—This may lose us the day."

"Not in his mind, Jasper. That one scalp has more honor in it, according to the Sarpent's notions of warfare, than a field covered with slain, that kept the hair on their heads.

Now, there was the fine young captain of the 60th that threw away his life, in trying to bring off a three-pounder from among the Frenchers, in the last skrimmage we had; he thought he was sarving honor; and I have known a young ensign wrap himself up in his colours, and go to sleep in his blood, fancying that he was lying on something softer even than buffaloe skins!"

"Yes, yes; one can understand the merit of not hauling down an ensign—."

"And these are Chingachgook's colours—he will keep them to show his children's children—" here the Pathfinder interrupted himself, shook his head in melancholy, and slowly added—"Ah's! me! no shoot of the old Mohican stem remains! He has no children to delight with his trophies; no tribe to honor by his deeds; he is a lone man in this world, and yet he stands true to his training and his gifts! There is something honest and respectable in that, you must allow, Jasper; yes, there is something decent in that."

Here a great outcry from among the Iroquois, was succeeded by the quick reports of their rifles, and so eager did the enemy become, in the desire to drive the Delaware back from his victim, that a dozen rushed into the river, several of whom even advanced near a hundred feet into the foaming current, as if they actually meditated a serious sortie. But Chingachgook continued as unmoved, as he remained unhurt by the missiles, accomplishing his task with the dexterity of long habit. Flourishing his reeking trophy, he gave the war-whoop in its most frightful intonations, and for a minute the arches of the silent woods, and the deep vista formed by the course of the river, echoed with cries so terrific that Mabel bowed her head, in irrepressible fear, while her uncle, for a single instant, actually meditated flight.

"This surpasses all I have heard from the wretches," Jasper exclaimed, stopping his ears, equally in horror and disgust.

"'Tis their music, boy; their drum and fife; their trumpets and clarions. No doubt they love them sounds, for they stir up in them, fierce feelings, and a desire for blood," returned the Pathfinder, totally unmoved. "I thought them rather frightful when a mere youngster, but they have got to be like the whistle of the whip-poor-will, or the song of the cat-bird in my ear, now. All the screeching riptyles that could stand atween the Falls and the garrison, would have no effect on my narves, at this time of day. I say it not in boasting, Jasper, for the man that lets in cowardice through the ears, must have but a weak heart, at the best; sounds and outcries being more intended to alarm women and children, than such as scout the forest, and face the foe. I hope the Sarpent is now satisfied, for here he comes with the scalp at his belt."

Jasper turned away his head as the Delaware rose from the water, in pure disgust at his late errand, but the Pathfinder regarded his friend with the philosophical coolness of one who had made up his mind to be indifferent to things he deemed immaterial. As the Delaware passed deeper into the bushes, with a view to wring his trifling calicoe dress, and to prepare his rifle for service, he gave one glance of triumph at his companions, and then all emotion connected with the recent exploit seemed to cease.

"Jasper," resumed the guide—"step down to the station of Master Cap, and ask him to join us. We have little time for a council, and yet our plans must be laid quickly, for it will not be long before them Mingos will be plotting our ruin."

The young man complied, and in a few minutes, the four were assembled near the shore, completely concealed from the view of their enemies, while they kept a vigilant watch over the proceedings of the latter, in order to consult on their own future movements. By this time, the day had so far advanced, as to leave but a few minutes between the passing light, and an obscurity that promised to be even deeper than common. The sun had already set, and the twilight of a low latitude would soon pass into the darkness of deep night. Most of the hopes of the party rested on this favorable circumstance, though it was not without its dangers, also, as the very obscurity which would favor their escape would be as likely to conceal the movements of their wily enemies.

"The moment has come, men," Pathfinder commenced, "when our plans must be coolly laid, in order that we may act together, and with a right understanding of our errand and gifts. In an hour's time, these woods will be as dark as midnight, and if we are ever to gain the garrison, it must be done under favor of this advantage. What say you, Master

Cap; for though none of the most exper'enced in combats and retreats in the woods, your years entitle you to speak first, in a matter like this, and in a council."

"And my near relationship to Mabel, Pathfinder, ought to count for something—"

"I don't know that—I don't know that. Regard is regard, and liking, liking, whether it be a gift of natur', or come from one's own judgment and inclinations. I will say nothing for the Sarpent, who is past placing his mind on the women, but as for Jasper and myself, we are as ready to stand atween the Sarjeant's daughter and the Mingos, as her own brave father, himself, could be. Do I say more than the truth, lad?"

"Mabel may count on me, to the last drop of my blood," said Jasper, speaking low, but with intense feeling.

"Well, well," rejoined the uncle, "we will not discuss this matter, as all seem willing to serve the girl, and deeds are better than words. In my judgment, all we have to do, is to go on board the canoe, when it gets to be so dark the enemy's look-outs ca'n't see us, and run for the haven, as wind and tide will allow."

"That is easily said, but not so easily done," returned the guide. "We shall be more exposed in the river than by following the woods, and then there is the Oswego rift below us, and I am far from sartain that Jasper, himself, can carry a boat safely through it, in the dark. What say you, lad, as to your own skill and judgment?"

"I am of Master Cap's opinion about using the canoe. Mabel is too tender to walk through swamps, and among roots of trees, on such a night as this promises to be, and then I always feel myself stouter of heart, and truer of eye, when afloat, than when ashore."

"Stout of heart, you always be, lad, and I think tolerably true of eye, for one who has lived so much in broad sunshine, and so little in the woods. Ah's! me, the Ontario has no trees, or it would be a plain to delight a hunter's heart! As to your opinion, friends, there is much for, and much ag'inst it. For it, it may be said water leaves no trail—"

"What do you call the wake?" interrupted the pertinacious and dogmatical Cap.

"Anan!"

"Go on," said Jasper. "Master Cap thinks he is on the Ocean—Water leaves no trail—"

"It leaves none, Eau douce, hereaway, though I do not pretend to say what it may leave on the sea. Then a canoe is both swift and easy, when it floats with the current, and the tender limbs of the Sarjeant's daughter will be favored by its motion. But, on the other hand, the river will have no cover but the clouds in the heavens, the rift is a ticklish spot for a bark to venture into even by day-light, and it is six fairly measured miles by water, from this spot to the garrison. Then a trail on land, is not easy to be found in the dark. I am troubled, Jasper, to say which way we ought to counsel and advise."

"If the Serpent and myself could swim into the river, and bring off the other canoe," the young sailor replied, "it would seem to me, that our safest course would be the water."

"If, indeed! and yet it might easily be done, as soon as it is a little darker. Well, well, considering the Sarjeant's daughter, and her gifts, I am not sartain it will not be the best. Though were we only a party of men, it would be like a hunt to the lusty and brave, to play at hide and seek with yonder miscreants, on the other shore. Jasper," continued the guide, into whose character there entered no ingredient that belonged to vain display, or theatrical effect, " will you undertake to bring in the canoe?"

"I will undertake any thing that will serve and protect Mabel, Pathfinder."

"That is an upright feeling, and I suppose it is natur'. The Sarpent, who is nearly naked already, can help you, and that will be cutting off, one of the means of them devils, to work their harm."

This material point being settled, the different members of the party, prepared themselves to put the project into execution. The shades of evening fell fast upon the forest, and by the time all was ready for the attempt, it was found impossible to discern objects on the opposite shore. Time now pressed, for Indian cunning could devise so many expedients for passing so narrow a stream, that the Pathfinder was getting impatient to quit the spot. While Jasper and his companion entered the river, armed with nothing but their knives and the Delaware's tomahawk, observing the greatest caution not to betray their movements, the guide brought Mabel from her place of concealment, and bidding her and Cap proceed along the shore to the foot of the rapids, he got into the canoe that remained in his possession, in order to carry it to the same place.

This was easily effected. The canoe was laid against the bank, and Mabel and her uncle entered it, taking their seats as usual, while the Pathfinder, erect in the stern, held by a bush, in order to prevent the swift stream from sweeping them down its current. Several minutes of intense and breathless expectation followed, while they awaited the result of the bold attempt of their comrades.

It will be understood that the two adventurers were compelled to swim, across a deep and rapid channel, ere they could reach a part of the rift that admitted of wading. This portion of the enterprize was soon effected, and Jasper and the Serpent struck the bottom, side by side, at the same instant. Having secured firm footing, they took hold of each other's hands, and waded slowly and with extreme caution, in the supposed direction of the canoe. But the darkness was already so deep, that they soon ascertained they were to be but little aided by the sense of sight, and that their search must be conducted on that species of instinct which enables the woodsman to find his way, when the sun is hid, no stars appear, and all would seem chaos to one less accustomed to the mazes of the forest. Under these circumstances Jasper submitted to be guided by the Delaware, whose habits best fitted him to take the lead. Still it was no easy matter to wade amid the roaring element, at that hour, and retain a clear recollection of the localities. By the time they believed themselves to be in the centre of the stream, the two shores were discernible merely by masses of obscurity denser than common, the outlines against the clouds being barely distinguishable by the ragged tops of the trees. Once or twice the wanderers altered their course in consequence of unexpectedly stepping into deep water, for they knew that the boat had lodged on the shallowest part of the rift. In short, with this fact for their compass, Jasper and his companion wandered about in the water, for near a quarter of an hour, and at the end of that period, which began to appear interminable to the young man, they found themselves apparently no nearer the object of their search than they had been at its commencement. Just as the Delaware was about to stop, in order to inform his associate that they would do well to return to the land, in order to take a fresh departure, he saw the form of a man, moving about in the water, almost within reach of his arm. Jasper was at his side, and he at once understood that the Iroquois were engaged in the same errand as he was himself.

"Mingo!" he uttered in Jasper's ear—"The Serpent will show his brother how to be cunning."

The young sailor caught a glimpse of the figure, at that instant, and the startling truth also flashed on his mind. Understanding the necessity of trusting all to the Delaware chief, he kept back, while his friend moved cautiously in the direction in which the strange form had vanished. In another moment, it was seen again evidently moving towards themselves. The waters made such an uproar, that little was to be apprehended from ordinary sounds, and the Indian, turning his head, hastily said—

"Leave it to the cunning of the Great Serpent."

"Hugh!" exclaimed the strange savage, adding in the language of his people—"The canoe is found, but there were none to help me. Come; let us raise it from the rock."

"Willingly," answered Chingachgook, who understood the dialect—"Lead; we will follow."

The stranger, unable to distinguish between voices and accents, amid the raging of the rapid, led the way in the necessary direction, and, the two others keeping close at his heels, all three speedily reached the canoe. The Iroquois laid hold of one end, Chingachgook placed himself in the centre, and Jasper went to the opposite extremity, as it was important that the stranger should not detect the presence of a pale-face, a discovery that might be made, by the parts of the dress the young man still wore, as well as by the general appearance of his head.

"Lift—" said the Iroquois in the sententious manner of his race; and by a trifling effort, the canoe was raised from the rock, held a moment in the air to empty it, and then placed carefully on the water, in its proper position. All three held it firmly, lest it should escape from their hands, under the pressure of the violent current, while the Iroquois who led of course, being at the upper end of the boat, took the direction of the eastern shore, or towards the spot where his friends waited his return.

As the Delaware and Jasper well knew there must be several more of the Iroquois on the rift, from the circumstance that their own appearance had occasioned no surprise in the individual they had met, both felt the necessity of extreme caution. Men less bold and determined would have thought that they were incurring too great a risk, by thus venturing into the midst of their enemies, but these hardy borderers were unacquainted with fear, were accustomed to hazards, and so well understood the necessity of at least preventing their foes from getting the boat, that they would have cheerfully encountered even greater risks to secure their object. So all-important to the safety of Mabel, indeed, did Jasper deem the possession, or the destruction of this canoe, that he had drawn his knife and stood ready to rip up the bark, in order to render the boat temporarily unserviceable, should any thing occur to compel the Delaware and himself to abandon their prize.

In the mean time, the Iroquois who led the way proceeded slowly, through the water, in the direction of his own party, still grasping the canoe, and dragging his reluctant followers in his train. Once, Chingachgook raised his tomahawk, and was about to bury it in the brain of his confiding and unsuspicious neighbor, but the probability that the death-cry, or the floating body might give the alarm, induced that wary chief to change his purpose. At the next moment, he regretted this indecision, for the three who clung to the canoe, suddenly found themselves in the centre of a party of no less than four others who were in quest of it.

After the usual, brief, characteristic, exclamations of satisfaction, the savages eagerly laid hold of the canoe, for all seemed impressed with the necessity of securing this important boat, the one side in order to assail their foes, and the other to secure their retreat. The addition to the party, however, was so unlooked for, and so completely gave the enemy the superiority, that, for a few moments, the ingenuity and address of even the Delaware were at fault. The five Iroquois, who seemed perfectly to understand their errand, pressed forward towards their own shore, without pausing to converse, their object being in truth to obtain the paddles, which they had previously secured, and to embark three or four warriors, with all the rifles and powder-horns, the want of which had alone prevented their crossing the river, by swimming, as soon as it was dark.

In this manner, the body of friends and foes united reached the margin of the eastern channel, where, as in the case of the western, the river was too deep to be waded. Here a short pause succeeded, it being necessary to determine the manner in which the canoe was to be carried across. One of the four who had just reached the boat, was a chief, and the habitual deference which the American Indian pays to merit, experience and station, kept the others silent, until this individual had spoken.

The halt greatly added to the danger of discovering the presence of Jasper, in particular, who however had the precaution to throw the cap he wore, into the bottom of the canoe. Being without his jacket and shirt, the outline of his figure, in the obscurity, would now be less likely to attract observation. His position, too, at the stern of the canoe, a little favored his concealment, the Iroquois naturally keeping their looks directed the other way. Not so, with Chingachgook. This warrior was literally in the midst of his most deadly foes, and he could scarcely stir without touching one of them. Yet he was apparently unmoved, though he kept all his senses on the alert, in readiness to escape, or to strike a blow, at the proper moment. By carefully abstaining from looking towards those behind him, he lessened the chances of discovery, and waited with the indomitable patience of an Indian for the instant when he should be required to act.

"Let all my young men, but two, one at each end of the canoe, cross and get their arms," said the Iroquois chief—, "let the two push over the boat."

The Indians quietly obeyed, leaving Jasper at the stern, and the Iroquois who had found the canoe, at the bows of the light craft, Chingachgook burying himself so deep in the river, as to be passed by the others without detection. The splashing in the water, the tossing arms and the calls of one to another, soon announced that the four who had last joined the party, were already swimming. As soon as this fact was certain, the Delaware rose, resumed his former station, and began to think the moment for action was come.

One less habitually under self-restraint, than this warrior, would probably have now aimed his meditated blow, but Chingachgook knew there were more Iroquois behind him on the rift, and he was a warrior much too trained and experienced to risk any thing unnecessarily. He suffered the Indian at the bow of the canoe to push off into the deep water, and then all three were swimming in the direction of the eastern shore. Instead, however, of helping the canoe across the swift current, no sooner did the Delaware and Jasper find themselves within the influence of its greatest force, than both began to swim in a way to check their further progress across the stream. Nor was this done suddenly, or in the incautious manner in which a civilized man would have been apt to attempt the artifice, but warily, and so gradually that the Iroquois at the bow, fancied at first he was merely struggling against the strength of the current. Of course, while acted on by these opposing efforts, the canoe drifted down stream, and in about a minute it was floating in still deeper water at the foot of the rift. Here, however, the Iroquois was not slow in finding that something unusual retarded their advance, and looking back he first learned that he was resisted by the efforts of his companions.

That second nature, which grows up through habit, instantly told the young Iroquois that he was alone with enemies. Dashing the water aside, he sprang at the throat of Chingachgook, and the two Indians relinquishing their hold of the canoe, seized each other, like tigers. In the midst of the darkness of that gloomy night, and floating in an element so dangerous to man, when engaged in deadly strife, they appeared to forget every thing but their fell animosity, and their mutual desire to conquer.

Jasper had now complete command of the canoe, which flew off, like a feather impelled by the breath, under the violent reaction of the struggles of the two combatants. The first impulse of the youth was to swim to the aid of the Delaware, but the importance of securing the boat presented itself with ten fold force, while he listened to the heavy breathings of the warriors as they throttled each other, and he proceeded as fast as possible towards the western shore. This he soon reached, and, after a short search, he succeeded in discovering the remainder of the party, and in procuring his clothes. A few words sufficed to explain the situation in which he had left the Delaware, and the manner in which the canoe had been obtained.

When those who had been left behind had heard the explanations of Jasper, a profound stillness reigned among them, each listening intently, in the vain hope of catching some clue to the result of the fearful struggle that had just taken place, if it were not still going on in the water. Nothing was audible, beyond the steady roar of the rushing river, it being a part of the policy of their enemies on the opposite shore, to observe the most death-like stillness.

"Take this paddle, Jasper," said Pathfinder, calmly, though the listeners thought his voice sounded more melancholy than usual; "and follow with your own canoe. It is unsafe for us to remain here longer."

"But the Serpent?"

"The Great Sarpent is in the hands of his own Deity, and will live, or die, according to the intentions of Providence. We can do him no good, and may risk too much by remaining here, in idleness, like women talking over their distresses. This darkness is very precious—"

A loud, long, piercing yell arose from the other shore, and cut short the words of the guide.

"What is the meaning of that uproar, Master Pathfinder?—" demanded Cap. "It sounds more like the outcries of devils, than any thing that can come from the throats of christians and men."

"Christians they are not, and do not pretend to be, and do not wish to be, and in calling them devils, you have scarcely misnamed them. That yell is one of rejoicing, and it is, as conquerors they have given it. The body of the Sarpent, no doubt, dead or alive, is in their power!"

"And we!—" exclaimed Jasper, who felt a pang of generous regret, as the idea that he might have averted the calamity presented itself to his mind, had he not deserted his comrade.

"We can do the chief no good, lad, and must quit this spot as fast as possible."

"Without one attempt to rescue him!—Without even knowing whether he be dead or living."

"Jasper is right—" said Mabel, who could speak, though her voice sounded husky and smothered. "I have no fears, uncle, and will stay here until we know what has become of our friend."

"This seems reasonable, Pathfinder," put in Cap. "Your true seaman cannot well desert a messmate, and I am glad to find that notions so correct exist among these fresh-water people."

"Tut—tut—" returned the impatient guide, forcing the canoe into the stream as he spoke, "ye know nothing, and ye fear nothing. If ye value your lives, think of reaching the garrison, and leave the Delaware in the hands of Providence. Ah's! me. The deer that goes too often to the lick meets the hunter at last!"

Chapter VII

"And is this—Yarrow?—this the stream
Of which my fancy cherished,
So faithfully a waking dream?
An image that hath perished?
O that some minstrel's harp were near,
To utter notes of gladness,
And chase this silence from the air,
That fills my heart with sadness."
Wordsworth, "Yarrow Visited," ll. 1–8.

THE SCENE was not without its sublimity, and the ardent, generous-minded Mabel felt her blood thrill in her veins, and her cheeks flush, as the canoe shot into the strength of the stream to quit the spot. The darkness of the night had lessened, by the dispersion of the clouds, but the overhanging woods rendered the shores so obscure, that the boats floated down the current in a belt of gloom that effectually secured them from detection. Still, there was necessarily a strong feeling of insecurity in all on board them, and even Jasper, who by this time began to tremble in behalf of the girl, at every unusual sound that arose from the forest, kept casting uneasy glances around him, as he drifted on, in company. The paddle was used lightly, and only with exceeding care, for the slightest sound in the breathing stillness of that hour and place, might apprise the watchful ears of the Iroquois of their position.

All these accessaries added to the impressive grandeur of her situation, and contributed to render the moment much the most exciting that had ever occurred in the brief existence of Mabel Dunham. Spirited, accustomed to self-reliance, and sustained by the pride of considering herself a soldier's daughter, she could hardly be said to be under the influence of fear, yet her heart often beat quicker than common, her fine blue eye lighted with an exhibition of resolution that was wasted in the darkness, and her quickened feelings came in aid of the real sublimity that belonged to the scene, and to the incidents of the night.

"Mabel!" said the suppressed voice of Jasper, as the two

canoes floated so near each other that the hand of the young man held them together, "you have no dread. You trust freely to our care, and willingness to protect you?"

"I am a soldier's daughter, as you know, Jasper Western, and ought to be ashamed to confess fear."

"Rely on me—on us all. Your uncle, Pathfinder, the Delaware, were the poor fellow here, I myself, will risk every thing rather than harm should reach you."

"I believe you, Jasper," returned the girl, her hand unconsciously playing in the water. "I know that my uncle loves me, and will never think of himself until he has first thought of me; and I believe you are all my father's friends and would willingly assist his child. But I am not so feeble and weak-minded as you may think, for though only a girl from the towns, and like most of that class, a little disposed to see danger where there is none, I promise you, Jasper, no foolish fears of mine shall stand in the way of your doing your duty."

"The Sarjeant's daughter is right, and she is worthy of being honest Thomas Dunham's child," put in the Pathfinder. "Ah's! me! pretty one, many is the time that your father and I, have scouted and marched together on the flanks and rear of the inimy, in nights darker than this, and that too, when we did not know, but the next moment would lead us into a bloody ambushment. I was at his side, when he got the wound in his shoulder, and the honest fellow will tell you, when you meet, the manner in which we contrived to cross the river that lay in our rear, in order to save his scalp."

"He *has* told me," said Mabel, with more energy perhaps than her situation rendered prudent. "I have his letters, in which he has mentioned all that, and, I thank you from the bottom of my heart, for the service. God will remember it, Pathfinder, and there is no gratitude that you can ask of the daughter, which she will not cheerfully pay for her father's life."

"Ay, that is the way, with all you gentle and pure hearted creatur's! I have seen some of you afore, and have heard of others! The Sarjeant, himself, has talked to me of his own young days; and of your mother; and of the manner in which he courted her, and of all the crossings and disapp'intments, until he succeeded at last."

"My mother did not live long to repay him for what he did to win her," said Mabel with a trembling lip.

"So he tells me. The honest Sarjeant has kept nothing back, for being so many years my senior, he has looked on me, in our many scoutings together, as a sort of son."

"Perhaps, Pathfinder," observed Jasper, with a huskiness in his voice that defeated the attempt at pleasantry, "he would be glad to have you for one, in reality."

"And if he did, Eau douce, where would be the sin of it? He knows what I am on a trail, or a scout, and he has seen me often, face to face, with the Frenchers. I have sometimes thought, lad, that we all ought to seek for wives, for the man that lives altogether in the woods, and in company with his inimies, or his prey, gets to lose some of the feelin' of kind, in the ind."

"From the specimens I have seen," observed Mabel, "I should say that they who live much in the forest, forget to learn many of the deceits and vices of the towns."

"It is not easy, Mabel, to dwell always in the presence of God, and not feel the power of his goodness. I have attended church-sarvice in the garrisons, and tried hard, as becomes a true soldier, to join in the prayers; for though no enlisted sarvant of the King, I fight his battles and sarve his cause, and so I have endivoured to worship garrison-fashion, but never could raise within me, the solemn feelings and true affection, that I feel when alone with God, in the forest. There I seem to stand face to face, with my master; all around me is fresh and beautiful, as it came from his hand, and there is no nicety, or doctrine, to chill the feelin's. No—no—the woods are the true temple a'ter all, for there the thoughts are free to mount higher even than the clouds."

"You speak the truth, Master Pathfinder," said Cap, "and a truth that all who live much in solitude know. What, for instance, is the reason that sea-faring men, in general, are so religious and conscientious in all they do, but the fact that they are so often alone with Providence, and have so little to do with the wickedness of the land. Many, and many is the time, that I have stood my watch, under the equator perhaps, or in the Southern Ocean, when the nights are lighted up with the fires of heaven, and that is the time, I can tell you, my hearties, to bring a man to his bearings, in the way of his sins. I have rattled down mine, again and again, under such circumstances, until the shrouds and lanyards of conscience have fairly creaked with the strain. I agree with you, Master Pathfinder, therefore, in saying if you want a truly religious man, go to sea, or go into the woods."

"Uncle, I thought seamen had little credit, generally, for their respect for religion."

"All d——d slander, girl. Ask your sea-faring man what his real, private opinion is of your landsmen, parsons and all, and you will hear the other side of the question. I know no class of men, who have been so belied as sea-faring men, in this particular, and it is all because they do not stay at home to defend themselves, and pay the clergy. They have'n't as much doctrine, perhaps, as some ashore, but as for all the essentials of christianity, the seaman beats the landsman, hand over hand."

"I will not answer for all this, Master Cap," returned Pathfinder, "but, I dare say, some of it may be true. I want no thunder and lightening to remind me of my God, nor am I as apt to bethink me most of all his goodness, in trouble and tribulations, as on a calm, solemn, quiet day, in the forest, when his voice is heard in the creaking of a dead branch, or in the song of a bird, as much in my ears at least, as it is ever heard in uproar and gales. How is it with you, Eau douce; you face the tempests as well as Master Cap, and ought to know something of the feelin's of storms?"

"I fear that I am too young, and too inexperienced to be able to say much on such a subject," modestly answered Jasper.

"But you have your feelings!" said Mabel quickly. "You cannot—no one can live among such scenes without feeling how much they ought to trust in God!"

"I shall not belie my training so much as to say I do not sometimes think of these things, but I fear it is not as often, or as much, as I ought."

"Fresh water!" resumed Cap pithily; "you are not to expect too much of the young man, Mabel. I think they call you, sometimes, by a name which would insinuate all this. Eau-de-vie, is it not?"

"Eau douce," quietly replied Jasper, who from sailing on the lake had acquired a knowledge of French, as well as of several of the Indian dialects. "It is a name the Iroquois have given me to distinguish me, from some of my companions who once sailed upon the sea, and are fond of filling the ears of the natives, with stories of their great salt-water lakes."

"And why should'n't they! I dare say they do the savages no harm. They may not civilize them, but they will not make them greater barbarians than they are. Ay—ay—Oh! the deuce, that must mean the white brandy, which is no great matter after all, and may well enough be called the deuce, for deuced stuff it is!"

"The signification of Eau douce is sweet-water, or water that can be drunk, and it is the manner in which the French express fresh-water," rejoined Jasper, a little nettled at the distinctions made by Cap; although the latter was the uncle of Mabel.

"And how the devil do they make water out of Oh! the deuce, when it means brandy in Eau-de-vie? This may be the French used, hereaway, but it is not that they use in Burdux, and other French ports; besides, among seamen Eau always means brandy, and Eau-de-vie, brandy of a high proof. I think nothing of your ignorance, young man, for it is natural to your situation, and cannot be helped. If you will return with me, and make a v'y'ge or two, on the Atlantic, it will serve you a good turn the remainder of your days, and, Mabel there, and all the other young women, near the coast, will think all the better of you, should you live to be as old as one of the trees in this forest."

"Nay, nay," interrupted the single hearted and generous guide, "Jasper wants not for friends, in this region, I can assure you; and though seeing the world, according to his habits, may do him good, as well as another, we shall think none the worse of him, if he never quits us. Eau douce, or Eau-de-vie, he is a brave, true-hearted youth, and I always sleep as sound, when he is on the watch as if I was up and stirring myself; ay, and for that matter, sounder too. The Sarjeant's daughter, here, does'n't believe it necessary for the lad to go to sea, in order to make a man of him, or one, who is worthy to be respected and esteemed."

Mabel made no reply to this appeal, and she even looked towards the eastern shore, although the darkness rendered the natural movement unnecessary to conceal her face. But, Jasper felt that there was a necessity for his saying something, the pride of youth and manhood revolting at the idea of his being in a condition not to command the respect of his fellows, or the smiles of his equals of the other sex. Still he was unwilling to utter aught that might be considered harsh, to the uncle of Mabel, and his self command was, perhaps, more creditable than his modesty and spirit.

"I pretend not to things I do'n't possess," he said, "and lay no claim to any knowledge of the ocean, or of navigation. We steer by the stars, and the compass on these lakes, running from head-land to head-land, and, having little need of figures and calculations make no use of them. But, we have our claims, notwithstanding, as I have often heard from those who have passed years on the ocean. In the first place we have always the land aboard, and much of the time on a lee-shore, and that I have frequently heard makes hardy sailors. Our gales are sudden and severe, and we are compelled to run for our ports at all hours—"

"You have your leads—" interrupted Cap.

"They are of little use, and are seldom cast."

"The deep-seas—"

"I have heard of such things, but confess I never saw one."

"Oh! the deuce, with a vengeance. A trader and no deep sea! Why, boy, you cannot pretend to be any thing of a mariner. Who the devil ever heard of a seaman without his deep-sea!"

"I do not pretend to any particular skill, Master Cap—"

"Except in shooting falls, Jasper; except in shooting falls and rifts," said Pathfinder, coming to the rescue; "in which business, even you, Master Cap, must allow he has some handiness. In my judgment, every man is to be esteemed or condemned according to his gifts, and if Master Cap is useless in running the Oswego falls, I try to remember that he is useful when out of sight of land; and if Jasper be useless when out of sight of land, I do not forget that he has a true eye and steady hand when running the falls."

"But Jasper is not useless—would not be useless when out

of sight of land," said Mabel with a spirit and energy that caused her clear sweet voice to be startling amid the solemn stillness of that extraordinary scene. "No one can be useless there, who can do so much here, is what I mean; though I dare say, he is not as well acquainted with ships as my uncle."

"Ay, bolster each other up in your ignorance," returned Cap, with a sneer. "We seamen are so much outnumbered when ashore, that it is seldom we get our dues, but when your coast is to be defended, or trade is to be carried on, there is outcry enough for us."

"But, uncle, landsmen do not come to attack our coasts, so that seamen only meet seamen."

"So much for ignorance!—Where are all the armies that have landed in this country, French and English, let me inquire, miss?"

"Sure enough, where are they!" ejaculated Pathfinder. "None can tell better than we who dwell in the woods, Master Cap. I have often followed their line of march by bones bleaching in the rain, and have found their trail by graves, years after they and their pride had vanished together. Generals and privates, they lay scattered throughout the land, so many proofs of what men are when led on by their love of great names, and the wish to be more than their fellows."

"I must say, Master Pathfinder, that you sometimes utter opinions that are a little remarkable, for a man who lives by the rifle; seldom snuffing the air but he smells gunpowder, or turning out of his berth, but to bear down on an enemy."

"If you think I pass my days in warfare against my kind, you know neither me, nor my history. The man that lives in the woods, and on the frontiers, must take the chances of the things among which he dwells. For this I am not accountable, being but a humble and powerless hunter and scout and guide. My real calling is to hunt for the army, on its marches, and in times of peace, although I am more especially engaged in the sarvice of one officer, who is now absent in the settlements, where I never follow him. No—no—bloodshed and warfare are not my real gifts, but peace and marcy. Still, I must face the inimy as well as another, and as for a Mingo, I look upon him, as man looks on a snake, a creatur' to be put beneath the heel, whenever a fitting occasion offers."

"Well—well—I have mistaken your calling, which I had thought as regularly warlike as that of the ship's gunner. There is my brother-in-law, now; he has been a soldier since he was sixteen, and he looks upon his trade as every way as respectable as that of a sea-faring man, which is a point I hardly think it worth while to dispute with him."

"My father has been taught to believe that it is honorable to carry arms," said Mabel, "for his father was a soldier before him."

"Yes, yes—" resumed the guide—"Most of the Sarjeant's gifts are martial, and he looks at most things in this world, over the barrel of his musket. One of his notions now, is to prefar a King's piece to a regular double-sighted long-barreled rifle! Such consaits will come over men, from long habit, and prejudyce is perhaps the commonest failing of human natur'."

"Ashore, I grant you," said Cap. "I never return from a v'y'ge, but I make the very same remark. Now, the last time I came in, I found scarcely a man in all York, who would think of matters and things in general, as I thought about them myself. Every man I met, appeared to have bowsed all his idees up into the wind's eye, and when he did fall off a little from his one-sided notions, it was commonly to ware short round on his heel, and to lay up as close as ever, on the other tack."

"Do you understand this, Jasper?—" the smiling Mabel half whispered to the young man who still kept his own canoe so near, as to be close at her side.

"There is not so much difference between salt and fresh water, that we who pass our time on them cannot comprehend each other. It is no great merit, Mabel, to understand the language of our trade."

"Even religion," continued Cap, "is'n't moored in exactly the same place it was, in my young days. They veer and haul upon it, ashore, as they do on all other things, and it is no wonder if, now and then, they get jammed. Every thing seems to change but the compass, and even that has its variations."

"Well," returned the Pathfinder, "I thought Christianity and the compass both pretty stationary."

"So they are, afloat, bating the variations. Religion at sea, is just the same thing to day, that it was when I first put my hand into the tar-bucket. No one will dispute it, who has the fear of God before his eyes. I can see no difference between the state of religion on board ship, now, and what it was when I was a younker. But it is not so ashore, by any means. Take my word for it, Master Pathfinder, it is a difficult thing to find a man—I mean a landsman—who views these matters, to-day exactly as he looked at them, forty years ago."

"And yet God is unchanged—his works are unchanged—his holy word is unchanged—and all that ought to bless and honor his name should be unchanged too!"

"Not ashore. That is the worst of the land, it is all the while in motion, I tell you, though it looks so solid. If you plant a tree, and leave it, on your return from a three years' v'y'ge you do'n't find it, at all, the sort of thing you left it. The towns grow, and new streets spring up, the wharves are altered, and the whole face of the earth undergoes change. Now a ship comes back from an India v'y'ge just the thing she sailed, bating the want of paint, wear and tear, and the accidents of the sea."

"That is too true, Master Cap, and more's the pity. Ah's! me—the things they call improvements and betterments are undermining and defacing the land! The glorious works of God are daily cut down and destroyed, and the hand of man seems to be upraised in contempt of his mighty will. They tell me there are fearful signs of what we may all come to, to be met with, west and south of the great lakes, though I have never yet visited that region."

"What do you mean, Pathfinder?" modestly enquired Jasper.

"I mean the spots marked by the vengeance of Heaven, or which perhaps have been raised up as solemn warnings to the thoughtless and wasteful, hereaways. They call them Prairies, and I have heard as honest Delawares as I ever knew, declare that the finger of God has been laid so heavily on them, that they are altogether without trees. This is an awful visitation to befal innocent 'arth, and can only mean to show to what frightful consequences a heedless desire to destroy may lead."

"And yet I have seen settlers, who have much fancied those

open spots, because they saved them the toil of clearing. You relish your bread, Pathfinder, and yet wheat will not ripen in the shade."

"But honesty will, and simple wishes, and a love of God, Jasper. Even Master Cap will tell you a treeless plain must resemble a desert island."

"Why that as it may be," put in Cap. "Desert islands, too, have their uses, for they serve to correct the reckonings by. If my taste is consulted, I shall never quarrel with a plain for wanting trees. As nature has given a man eyes to look about with, and a sun to shine, were it not for ship-building, and now and then a house, I can see no great use in a tree; especially one that don't bear monkies or fruit."

To this remark the guide made no answer, beyond a low sound, intended to enjoin silence on his companions. While the desultory conversation just related had been carried on in subdued voices, the canoes were dropping slowly down with the current, within the deep shadows of the western shore, the paddles being used merely to preserve the desired direction, and proper positions. The strength of the stream varied materially, the water being seemingly still in places, while in other reaches it flowed at a rate exceeding two, or even three miles, in the hour. On the rifts it even dashed forward with a velocity that was appalling to the unpractised eye. Jasper was of opinion that they might drift down with the current to the mouth of the river, in two hours from the time they left the shore, and he and the Pathfinder had agreed on the expediency of suffering the canoes to float of themselves, for a time, or, at least, until they had passed the first dangers of their new movement. The dialogue had been carried on in voices guardedly low, for though the quiet of deep solitude reigned in that vast and nearly boundless forest, nature was speaking with her thousand tongues, in the eloquent language of night in a wilderness. The air sighed through ten thousand trees, the water rippled, and at places, even roared along the shores, and now and then was heard the creaking of a branch, or a trunk, as it rubbed against some object similar to itself, under the vibrations of a nicely balanced body. All living sounds had ceased. Once, it is true, the Pathfinder fancied he heard the howl of a distant wolf, of which a few prowled through those woods, but it was a transient and doubtful cry, that might possibly have been attributed to the imagination. When he desired his companions, however, to cease talking in the manner just mentioned, his vigilant ear had caught the peculiar sound that is made by the parting of a dried branch of a tree, and which, if his senses did not deceive him, came from the western shore. All who are accustomed to that particular sound will understand how readily the ear receives it, and how easy it is to distinguish the tread which breaks the branch, from every other noise of the forest.

"There is the footstep of a man on the bank," said Pathfinder to Jasper, speaking in neither a whisper, nor yet in a voice loud enough to be heard at any distance. "Can the accursed Iroquois have crossed the river, already, with their arms, and without a boat!"

"It may be the Delaware! He would follow us of course down this bank, and would know where to look for us. Let me draw closer in to the shore, and reconnoitre."

"Go, boy, but be light with the paddle, and, on no account, venture ashore on an onsartainty."

"Is this prudent?" demanded Mabel, with an impetuosity that rendered her incautious in modulating her sweet voice.

"Very imprudent, if you speak so loud, fair one. I like your voice, which is soft and pleasing, after listening so long to the tones of men, but it must not be heard too much, or too freely, just now. Your father, the honest Sarjeant, will tell you, when you meet him, that silence is a double virtue on a trail. Go, Jasper, and do justice to your own character for prudence."

Ten anxious minutes succeeded the disappearance of the canoe of Jasper, which glided away from that of the Pathfinder, so noiselessly that it had been swallowed up in the gloom, before Mabel allowed herself to believe the young man would really venture alone, on a service that struck her imagination as singularly dangerous. During this time, the party continued to float with the current, no one speaking, and it might almost be said no one breathing, so strong was the general desire to catch the minutest sound that should come from the shore. But the same solemn, we might indeed say sublime quiet, reigned as before, the washing of the water, as it piled up against some slight obstruction, and the sighing of the trees alone interrupting the slumbers of the forest. At the end of the period mentioned, the snapping of dried branches was again faintly heard, and the Pathfinder fancied that the sound of smothered voices reached him.

"I may be mistaken," he said, "for the thoughts often fancy what the heart wishes, but them were notes like the low tones of the Delawares."

"Do the dead of the savages ever walk?" demanded Cap.

"Ay, and run, too, in their happy hunting grounds, but nowhere else. A red skin finishes with the 'arth, after the breath quits the body. It is not one of his gifts to linger around his wigwam, when his hour has passed."

"I see some object on the water—" whispered Mabel, whose eye had not ceased to dwell on the body of gloom, with close intensity, since the disappearance of Jasper.

"It is the canoe!" returned the guide, greatly relieved. "All must be safe, or we should have heard from the lad."

In another minute the two canoes, which became visible to those they carried, only as they drew near each other, again floated side by side, and the form of Jasper was recognised at the stern of his own boat. The figure of a second man was seated in the bow, and as the young sailor so wielded his paddle, as to bring the face of his companion near the eyes of the Pathfinder and Mabel, they both recognised the person of the Delaware.

"Chingachgook—my brother!" said the guide in the dialect of the other's people, a tremor shaking his voice that betrayed the strength of his feelings—"Chief of the Mohicans! my heart is very glad. Often have we passed through blood and strife together, but I was afraid it was never to be so again."

"Hugh! Mingos——Squaws! Three of their scalps hang at my girdle. They do not know how to strike the Great Serpent of the Delawares. Their hearts have no blood, and their thoughts are on their return path, across the waters of the Great Lake."

"Have you been among them, chief?—and what has become of the warrior who was in the river?"

"He has turned into a fish, and lies at the bottom with the

eels! Let his brothers bait their hooks for him. Pathfinder, I have counted the enemy, and have touched their rifles."

"Ah! I thought he would be venturesome," exclaimed the guide in English. "The risky fellow has been in the midst of them, and has brought us back their whole history. Speak, Chingachgook, and I will make our friends as knowing as ourselves."

The Delaware now related in a low earnest manner, the substance of all his discoveries since he was last seen struggling with his foe, in the river. Of the fate of his antagonist he said no more, it not being usual for a warrior to boast in his more direct and useful narratives. As soon as he had conquered in that fearful strife, however, he swam to the eastern shore, landed with caution, and wound his way in amongst the Iroquois, concealed by the darkness, undetected and, in the main, even unsuspected. Once, indeed, he had been questioned, but answering that he was Arrowhead, no further inquiries were made. By the passing remarks, he soon ascertained that the party was out expressly to intercept Mabel and her uncle, concerning whose rank, however, they had evidently been deceived. He also ascertained enough to justify the suspicion that Arrowhead had betrayed them to their enemies, from some motive that it was not now easy to reach, as he had not yet received the reward of his services.

Pathfinder communicated no more of this intelligence to his companions, than he thought might relieve their apprehensions, intimating, at the same time, that now was the moment for exertion, the Iroquois not having yet entirely recovered from the confusion created by their losses.

"We shall find them at the rift, I make no manner of doubt," he continued, "and there it will be our fate, to pass them, or to fall into their hands. The distance to the garrison will then be so short, that I have been thinking of the plan of landing with Mabel, myself, that I may take her in, by some of the by-ways, and leave the canoes to their chances in the rapids."

"It will never succeed, Pathfinder," eagerly interrupted Jasper; "Mabel is not strong enough to tramp the woods, in a night like this. Put her in my skiff, and I will lose my life or carry her through the rift safely, dark as it is."

"No doubt you will, lad; no one doubts your willingness to do any thing to sarve the Sarjeant's daughter, but it must be the eye of Providence and not your own, that will take you safely through the Oswego rift, in a night like this."

"And who will lead her safely to the garrison if she land? Is not the night as dark on shore, as on the water, or, do you think I know less of my calling, than you know of yours?"

"Spiritedly said, lad, but if I should lose my way in the dark, and I believe no man can say truly that such a thing ever yet happened to me—but, if I *should* lose my way, no other harm would come of it, than to pass a night in the forest, whereas a false turn of the paddle, or a broad sheer of the canoe, would put you and the young woman into the river, out of which it is more than probable the Sarjeant's daughter would never come alive."

"I will leave it to Mabel, herself; I am certain that she will feel more secure in the canoe."

"I have great confidence in you both," answered the girl, "and have no doubts that either will do all he can to prove to my father how much he values him, but, I confess I should not like to quit the canoe, with the certainty we have of there being enemies like those we have seen, in the forest. But, my uncle can decide for me, in this matter."

"I have no liking for the woods," said Cap, " while one has a clear drift like this on the river. Besides, Master Pathfinder, to say nothing of the savages, you overlook the sharks."

"Sharks! Who ever heard of sharks in the wilderness?"

"Ay sharks, or bears, or wolves—no matter what you call a thing so it has the mind and the power to bite."

"Lord, lord, man; do you dread any creatur' that is to be found in the American forest! A catamount is a skeary animal, I will allow, but then it is nothing in the hands of a practysed hunter. Talk of the Mingos, and their deviltries, if you will; but do not raise a false alarm, about bears and wolves."

"Ay, ay, Master Pathfinder, this is all well enough for you, who probably know the name of every creature you would meet. Use is every thing, and it makes a man bold, when he might otherwise be bashful. I have known seamen in the low latitudes, swim for hours at a time, among sharks fifteen, or twenty feet long, and think no more of what they were doing, than a countryman thinks of whom he is amongst, when he comes out of a church door of a Sunday afternoon."

"This is extraordinary!" exclaimed Jasper, who, in good sooth, had not yet acquired that material part of his trade, the ability to spin a yarn—"I have always heard that it was certain death to venture in the water, among sharks!"

"I forgot to say, that the lads always took capstan-bars, or gunners' handspikes, or crows with them, to rap the beasts over the noses if they got to be troublesome. No—no—I have no liking for bears and wolves, though a whale, in my eye, is very much the same sort of fish as a red-herring, after it is dried and salted. Mabel and I, had better stick to the canoe."

"Mabel would do well to change canoes," added Jasper. "This of mine is empty, and even Pathfinder will allow that my eye is surer than his own, on the water."

"That I will cheerfully, boy. The water belongs to your gifts, and no one will deny that you have improved them to the utmost. You are right enough in believing that the Sarjeant's daughter will be safer in your canoe than in this, and, though I would gladly keep her near myself, I have her welfare too much at heart, not to give her honest advice. Bring your canoe close alongside, Jasper, and I will give you what you must consider as a very precious treasure."

"I do so consider it—" returned the youth, not losing a moment in complying with the request, when Mabel passed from one canoe to the other, taking her seat on the effects which had hitherto composed its sole cargo.

As soon as this arrangement was made, the canoes separated a short distance, and the paddles were used, though with great care to avoid making any noise. The conversation gradually ceased, and as the dreaded rift was approached, all became impressed with the gravity of the moment. That their enemies would endeavor to reach this point before them, was almost certain, and it seemed so little probable any one should attempt to pass it, in the profound obscurity which reigned, that Pathfinder was confident parties were on both sides of the river, in the hope of intercepting them when they might land. He would not have made the proposal he did, had he not felt sure of his own ability to convert this very anticipation of success, into a means of defeating the plans of the Iroquois. As the arrangement now stood, however, every thing depended on the skill of those who guided the canoes, for should either hit a rock, if not split asunder, it would almost certainly be upset, and then would come not only all the hazards of the river itself but, for Mabel, the certainty of falling into the hands of her pursuers. The utmost circumspection consequently became necessary, and each one was too much engrossed with his own thoughts, to feel a disposition to utter more than was called for, by the exigencies of the case.

As the canoes stole silently along, the roar of the rift became audible, and it required all the fortitude of Cap, to keep his seat, while these boding sounds were approached, amid a darkness that scarcely permitted a view of the outlines of the wooded shore, and of the gloomy vault above his head. He retained a vivid impression of the Falls, and his imagination was not now idle, in swelling the dangers of the rift to a level with those of the headlong descent he had that day made, and even to increase them, under the influence of doubt and uncertainty. In this, however, the old mariner was mistaken, for the Oswego rift, and the Oswego Falls are very different in their characters and violence, the former being no more than a rapid, that glances among shallows and rocks, while the latter really deserved the name it bore, as has been already shown.

Mabel certainly felt distrust and apprehension, but her entire situation was so novel, and her reliance on her guides so great, that she retained a self-command that might not have existed had she clearer perceptions of the truth, or been better acquainted with the helplessness of man, when placed in opposition to the power and majesty of nature.

"That is the spot you have mentioned?" she said to Jasper, when the roar of the rift first came fresh and distinct on her ear.

"It is; and I beg you to have confidence in me. We are not old acquaintances, Mabel, but we live many days in one, in this wilderness. I think, already, that I have known you years."

"And I do not feel as if you were a stranger to me, Jasper.

I have every reliance on your skill, as well as on your disposition to serve me."

"We shall see—we shall see. Pathfinder is striking the rapids too near the centre of the river. The best of the water is closer to the eastern shore; but I cannot make him hear me, now. Hold firmly to the canoe, Mabel, and fear nothing."

At the next moment, the swift current sucked them into the rift, and for three or four minutes, the awe-struck, rather than the alarmed, girl, saw nothing around her but sheets of glancing foam; heard nothing but the roar of waters. Twenty times did the canoe appear about to dash against some curling and bright wave, that showed itself even amid that obscurity, and as often did it glide away, again, unharmed; impelled by the vigorous arm of him who governed its movements. Once, and once only, did Jasper seem to lose command of his frail bark, during which brief space it fairly whirled entirely round, but, by a desperate effort, he brought it again under control, recovered the lost channel, and was soon rewarded for all his anxiety by finding himself floating quietly in the deep water below the rapids, secure from every danger, and without having taken in enough of the element to serve for a draught.

"All is over, Mabel," the young man cheerfully cried. "The danger is past, and you may now, indeed, hope to meet your father, this very night."

"God be praised! Jasper, we shall owe this great happiness to you!"

"The Pathfinder may claim a full share in the merit—but what has become of the other canoe?"

"I see something near us on the water—Is it not the boat of our friends?"

A few strokes of the paddle brought Jasper to the side of the object in question. It was the other canoe, empty and bottom upwards. No sooner did the young man ascertain this fact, than he began to search for the swimmers, and to his great joy, Cap was soon discovered drifting down with the current, the old seaman preferring the chances of drowning, to those of landing among savages. He was hauled into the canoe, though not without difficulty, and then the search ended; for Jasper was persuaded that the Pathfinder would wade to the shore, the water being shallow, in preference to abandoning his beloved rifle.

The remainder of the passage was short, though made amid darkness and doubt. After a short pause, a dull roaring sound was heard, which at times resembled the mutterings of distant thunder, and then again brought with it the washing of waters. Jasper announced to his companions that they now heard the surf of the lake. Low, curved spits of land lay before them, into the bay formed by one of which the canoe glided, and then it shot up noiselessly upon a gravelly beach. The transition that followed was so hurried and great, that Mabel scarce knew what passed. In the course of a few minutes, however, sentinels had been passed, a gate was opened, and the agitated girl found herself in the arms of a parent who was almost a stranger to her.

Chapter VIII

> "A land of love, and a land of light,
> Withouten sun; or moon, or night:
> Where the river swa'd a living stream,
> And the light a pure celestial beam:
> The land of vision it would seem,
> A still, an everlasting dream."
>
> Hogg, *The Queen's Wake*,
> "Kilmeny," ll. 46–51.

THE REST that succeeds fatigue, and which attends a newly awakened sense of security, is generally sweet and deep. Such was the fact with Mabel, who did not rise from her humble pallet, such a bed as a serjeant's daughter might claim in a remote frontier post, until long after the garrison had obeyed the usual summons of the drum, and had assembled at the early parade. Serjeant Dunham, on whose shoulders fell the task of attending to these ordinary and daily duties, had got through all his morning avocations, and was beginning to think of his breakfast, ere his child left her room and came into the fresh air, equally bewildered, delighted, and grateful, at the novelty and security of her new situation.

At the time of which we are writing, Oswego was one of the extreme frontier posts of the British possessions on this continent. It had not been long occupied, and was garrisoned by a battalion of a regiment that had been originally Scotch, but into which many Americans had been received, since its arrival in this country, an innovation that had led the way to Mabel's father filling the humble but responsible situation of the oldest serjeant. A few young officers also, who were natives of the Colonies, were to be found in this corps. The fort, itself, like most works of that character, was better adapted to resist an attack of savages, than to withstand a regular siege, but the great difficulty of transporting heavy artillery and other necessaries, rendered the occurrence of the latter a probability so remote, as scarcely to enter into the estimate of the engineers who had planned the defences. These were bastions of earth and logs, a dry ditch, a stockade, a parade of considerable extent, and barracks of logs, that answered the double purpose of dwellings and fortifications. A few light field-pieces stood in the area of the fort, ready to be conveyed to any point where they might be wanted, and one or two heavy iron guns looked out from the summits of the advanced angles, so many admonitions to the audacious to respect their power.

When Mabel, quitting the convenient, but comparatively retired hut where her father had been permitted to place her, issued into the pure air of the morning, she found herself at the foot of a bastion, that lay invitingly before her, with a promise of giving a coup d'œil of all that had been concealed in the darkness of the preceding night. Tripping up the grassy ascent, the light-hearted as well as light-footed girl found herself, at once, on a point where the sight, at a few changing glances, could take in all the external novelties of her new situation.

To the southward lay the forest through which she had been journeying so many weary days, and which had proved so full of danger. It was separated from the stockade, by a belt of open land, that had been principally cleared of its wood, to form the massive constructions around her. This glacis, for such in fact was its military uses, might have covered a hundred acres, but with it every sign of civilization ceased. All beyond was forest, that dense, interminable forest that Mabel could now picture to herself, through her recollections, with its hidden, glassy lakes, its dark, rolling streams, and its world of nature!

Turning from this view, our heroine felt her cheek fanned by a fresh and grateful breeze such as she had not experienced since quitting the far-distant coast. Here a new scene presented itself. Although expected, it was not without a start, and a low exclamation indicative of pleasure, that the eager eyes of the girl drank in its beauties. To the north and east, and west, in every direction, in short, over one entire half of the novel panorama lay a field of rolling waters. The element was neither of that glassy green which distinguishes the American waters in general, nor yet of the deep blue of the ocean; the colour being of a slightly amber hue, that scarcely affected its limpidity. No land was to be seen, with the exception of the adjacent coast, which stretched to the right and left, in an unbroken outline of forest, with wide bays, and low head-lands, or points. Still, much of the shore was rocky, and into its caverns the sluggish waters occasionally rolled, producing a hollow sound, that resembled the concussions of a distant gun. No sail whitened the surface, no whale, or other fish gambolled on its bosom, no sign of use, or service, rewarded the longest and most minute gaze, at its boundless expanse. It was a scene, on one side, of apparently endless forest while a waste of seemingly interminable water spread itself on the other. Nature had appeared to delight in producing grand effects, by setting two of her principal agents in bold relief to each other, neglecting details; the eye turning from the broad carpet of leaves, to the still broader field of fluid, from the endless but gentle heavings of the lake, to the holy calm, and poetical solitude of the forest, with wonder and delight.

Mabel Dunham, though unsophisticated, like most of her countrywomen of that period, and ingenuous and frank as any warm-hearted and sincere-minded girl well could be, was not altogether without a feeling for the poetry of this beautiful earth of ours. Though she could scarcely be said to be educated at all, for few of her sex at that day, and in this country, received much more than the rudiments of plain English instruction, still she had been taught much more than was usual for young women in her own station in life, and, in one sense certainly, she did credit to her teaching. The widow of a Field Officer, who formerly belonged to the same regiment as her father, had taken the child in charge, at the death of its mother, and under the care of this lady, Mabel had acquired some tastes, and many ideas, which otherwise might always have remained strangers to her. Her situation in the family had been less that of a domestic, than of a humble companion, and the results were quite apparent, in her attire, her language, her sentiments, and even in her feelings; though neither perhaps rose to the level of those which would properly characterize a lady. She had lost the coarser and less refined habits and manners of one in her original position, without having quite reached a point that disqualified her for the situation in life that the accidents of birth and fortune would probably compel her to fill. All else that was distinctive and peculiar in her, belonged to natural character.

With such antecedents, it will occasion the reader no wonder, if he learns that Mabel viewed the novel scene before her, with a pleasure far superior to that produced by vulgar surprise. She felt its ordinary beauties, as most would have felt them, but she had also a feeling for its sublimity; for that softened solitude, that calm grandeur, and eloquent repose that ever pervades broad views of natural objects which are yet undisturbed by the labors and uneasy struggles of man.

"How beautiful!" she exclaimed, unconscious of speaking, as she stood on the solitary bastion, facing the air from the lake, and experiencing the genial influence of its freshness pervading both her body and her mind. "How very beautiful; and yet how singular!"

The words, and the train of her ideas, were interrupted by a touch of a finger on her shoulder, and turning, in the expectation of seeing her father, Mabel found Pathfinder at her side. He was leaning quietly on his long rifle, and laughing in his quiet manner, while with an outstretched arm, he swept over the whole panorama of land and water.

"Here you have both our domains," he said, "Jasper's and mine. The lake is for him, and the woods are for me. The lad sometimes boasts of the breadth of his dominions, but I tell him my trees make as broad a plain on the face of this 'arth, as all his water. Well, Mabel, you are fit for either, for I do not see that fear of the Mingos, or night marches can destroy your pretty looks."

"It is a new character for the Pathfinder to appear in, to compliment a silly girl."

"Not silly, Mabel; no, not in the least silly. The Sarjeant's daughter would do discredit to her worthy father were she to do, or say, any thing that, in common honesty, could be called silly."

"Then she must take care and not put too much faith, in treacherous, flattering words. But, Pathfinder, I rejoice to see you among us again, for, though Jasper did not seem to feel much uneasiness, I was afraid some accident might have happened to you, and your friend, on that frightful rift."

"The lad knows us both, and was sartain that we should not drown, which is scarcely one of my gifts. It would have been hard swimming, of a sartainty, with a long-barrelled rifle in the hands, and what between the game, and the savages, and the French, Killdeer and I have gone through too much in company, to part very easily. No—no—we waded ashore, the rift being shallow enough for that, with small exceptions, and we landed with our arms in our hands. We had to take our time for it, on account of the Iroquois, I will own, but, as soon as the skulking vagabonds saw the lights, that the sarjeant sent down to your canoe, we well understood they would decamp, since a visit might have been expected from some of the garrison. So it was only sitting patiently on the stones, for an hour, and all the danger was over. Patience is the greatest of virtues in a woodsman."

"I rejoice to hear this, for fatigue itself could scarcely make me sleep, for thinking of what might befal you."

"Lord bless your tender little heart, Mabel! But this is the way, with all you gentle ones. I must say, on my part, howsever, that I was right glad to see the lanterns come down to the water side, which I knew to be a sure sign of *your* safety. We hunters and guides are rude beings, but we have our feelin's, and our idees, as well as any giniral in the army. Both Jasper and I would have died, before you should have come to harm, we would!"

"I thank you for all you did for me, Pathfinder; from the bottom of my heart, I thank you, and depend on it my father shall know it. I have already told him much, but have still a duty to perform, on this subject."

"Tush, Mabel, the Sarjeant knows what the woods be, and what men—true, real men be, too. There is little need to tell him any thing about it. Well, now you have met your father, do you find the honest old soldier, the sort of person you expected to find?"

"He is my own dear father, and received me as a soldier and a father should receive a child. Have you known him long, Pathfinder?"

"That is as people count time. I was just twelve when the sarjeant took me on my first scouting, and that is now more than twenty years ago. We had a tramping time of it, and as it was before your day, you would have had no father, had not the rifle been one of my nat'ral gifts."

"Explain yourself."

"It is too simple for many words. We were ambushed, and the sarjeant got a bad hurt, and would have lost his scalp, but for a sort of inbred turn I took to the weapon. We brought him off, howsever, and a handsomer head of hair, for his time of life, is not to be found in the rigiment, than the Sarjeant carries about with him, this blessed day."

"You saved my father's life, Pathfinder!" exclaimed Mabel, unconsciously, though warmly, taking one of his hard sinewy hands into both her own. "God bless you for this, too, among your other good acts."

"Nay, I did not say that much, though I believe I did save his scalp. A man might live without a scalp, and so I cannot say I saved his life. Jasper may say that much consarning you for without his eye and arm the canoe would never have passed the rift in safety, on a night like the last. The gifts of the lad are for the water, while mine are for the hunt and the trail. He is yonder in the cove, there, looking after the canoes, and keeping an eye on his beloved little craft. To my eye, there is no likelier youth, in these parts, than Jasper Western."

For the first time since she had left her room, Mabel now turned her eyes beneath her, and got a view of what might be called the fore-ground of the remarkable picture she had been studying with so much pleasure. The Oswego threw its dark waters into the lake, between banks of some height; that on its eastern side, being bolder and projecting farther north, than that on its western. The fort was on the latter, and immediately beneath it, were a few huts of logs, which, as they could not interfere with the defence of the place, had been erected along the strand for the purpose of receiving and containing such stores, as were landed, or were intended to be embarked, in the communications between the different posts on the shores of Ontario. There were two low, curved gravelly points, that had been formed with surprising regularity by the counteracting forces of the northerly winds and the swift current, and which, inclining from the storms of the lake, formed two coves within the river. That on the western side was the most deeply indented, and as it also had the most water, it formed a sort of picturesque little port, for the post. It was along the narrow strand that lay between the low height of the fort and the water of this cove, that the rude buildings just mentioned, had been erected.

Several skiffs, batteaux and canoes were hauled upon the shore, and in the cove itself lay the little craft, from which Jasper obtained his claim to be considered a sailor. She was cutter-rigged, might have been of forty tons burthen, was so neatly constructed and painted as to have something of the air of a vessel of war, though entirely without quarters, and rigged and sparred with so scrupulous a regard to proportions and beauty, as well as fitness and judgment, as to give her an appearance that even Mabel at once distinguished to be gallant and trim. Her mould was admirable, for a wright of great skill had sent her drafts from England at the express request of the officer who had caused her to be constructed; her paint dark, warlike and neat, and the long coach-whip pennant that she wore, at once proclaimed her to be the property of the king. Her name was the Scud.

"That, then, is the vessel of Jasper!" said Mabel, who associated the master of the little craft quite naturally with the cutter itself. "Are there many others on this lake?"

"The Frenchers have three; one of which they tell me is a real ship, such as are used on the ocean, another a brig, and a third is a cutter, like the Scud, here, which they call the Squirrel, in their own tongue howsever, and which seems to have a nat'ral hatred of our own pretty boat, for Jasper seldom goes out that the Squirrel is not at his heels."

"And is Jasper one to run from a Frenchman though he appear in the shape of a squirrel, and that, too, on the water!"

"Of what use would valor be without the means of turning it to account? Jasper is a brave boy, as all on this frontier know, but he has no gun except a little howitzer, and then his crew consists only of two men besides himself and a boy. I was with him in one of his trampooses, and the youngster was risky enough, for he brought us so near the inimy that rifles began to talk, but the Frenchers carry cannon, and ports, and never show their faces outside of Frontenac, without having some twenty men, besides their Squirrel, in their cutter. No—no—this Scud was built for flying, and the Major says he will not put her in a fighting humour, by giving her men and arms lest she should take him at his word, and get her wings clipped. I know little of these things, for my gifts are not at all, in that way, but I see the reason of the thing—I see its reason, though Jasper does not."

"Ah! here is my uncle, none the worse for his swim, coming to look at this inland sea."

Sure enough Cap, who had announced his approach by a couple of lusty hems, now made his appearance on the bastion, where, after nodding to his niece and her companion, he made a deliberate survey of the expanse of water before him. In order to effect this at his ease, the mariner mounted on one of the old iron guns, folded his arms across his breast, and balanced his body, as if he felt the motion of a vessel. To complete the picture he had a short pipe in his mouth.

"Well, Master Cap," asked the Pathfinder innocently, for he did not detect the expression of contempt that was gradually settling on the features of the other—"is it not a beautiful sheet, and fit to be named a sea?"

"This, then, is what you call your lake?" demanded Cap, sweeping the northern horizon with his pipe. "I say, is this, really, your lake."

"Sartain; and if the judgment of one who has lived on the shores of many others can be taken, a very good lake it is."

"Just as I expected! A pond in dimensions, and a scuttlebutt in taste. It is all in vain to travel inland, in the hope of seeing any thing either full-grown, or useful. I knew it would turn out just in this way."

"What is the matter with Ontario, Master Cap? It is large, and fair to look at, and pleasant enough to drink, for those who ca'n't get at the waters of the spring."

"Do you call this large?" asked Cap, again sweeping the air with the pipe. "I will just ask you what there is large about it? Did'n't Jasper himself confess that it was only some twenty leagues from shore to shore, hereaway?"

"But, uncle," interposed Mabel, "no land is to be seen, except here on our own coast. To me it looks exactly like the ocean."

"This bit of a pool look like the ocean! Well, Magnet, that from a girl who has had real seamen in her family is downright nonsense. What is there about it pray, that has even the outline of a sea on it?"

"Why, there is water—water—water—nothing but water, for miles on miles—far as the eye can see."

"And is'n't there water—water—water—nothing but water for miles on miles, in your rivers, that you have been canoeing through, too; ay, and 'as far as the eye can see,' in the bargain?"

"Yes, uncle, but the rivers have their banks, and there are trees along them, and they are narrow."

"And is'n't this a bank where we stand—do'n't these soldiers call this the bank of the lake, and ar'n't there trees in thousands, and ar'n't twenty leagues narrow enough of all conscience? Who the devil ever heard of the banks of the ocean, unless it might be the banks that are under water?"

"But, uncle, we cannot see across this lake, as we can see across a river."

"There you are out, Magnet. Ar'n't the Amazon, and Oronoco, and La Plata rivers, and can you see across them? Harkee, Pathfinder, I very much doubt if this stripe of water here, be even a lake; for to me it appears to be only a river. You are by no means particular about your geography, I find, up here in the woods."

"There *you* are out, Master Cap. There is a river, and a noble one too, at each end of it, but this is old Ontario before you, and, though it is not my gift to live on a lake, to my judgment there are few better than this."

"And, uncle, if we stood on the beach at Rockaway, what more should we see, than we now behold? There is a shore on one side, or banks there, and trees, too, as well as those which are here."

"This is perverseness, Magnet, and young girls should steer clear of any thing like obstinacy. In the first place, the ocean has coasts, but no banks, except the Grand Banks, as I tell you, which are out of sight of land; and you will not pretend that this bank is out of sight of land, or even under water?"

As Mabel could not very plausibly set up this extravagant opinion, Cap pursued the subject, his countenance beginning to discover the triumph of a successful disputant.

"And then the trees bear no comparison to these trees. The coasts of the ocean have farms, and cities, and country seats, and, in some parts of the world, castles and monasteries, and light-houses—ay—ay—light-houses in particular on them; not one of all which things is to be seen here. No—no—Master Pathfinder, I never heard of an ocean that had'n't more or less light-houses on it, whereas, hereaway, there is not even a beacon."

"There is what is better—there's what is better, a forest and noble trees, a fit temple of God."

"Ay, your forest may do for a lake, but of what use would an ocean be, if the earth all around it were forest. Ships would be unnecessary, as timber might be floated in rafts, and there would be an end of trade, and what would a world be without trade. I am of that philosopher's opinion, who says human nature was invented for the purposes of trade. Magnet, I am astonished that you should think this water even looks like sea-water! Now, I dare say, that there is'n't such a thing as a whale, in all your lake, Master Pathfinder?"

"I never heard of one, I will confess, but I am no judge of animals that live in the water, unless it be the fishes of the rivers and the brooks."

"Nor a grampus, nor a porpoise even; not so much as a poor devil of a shark?"

"I will not take it on myself to say there is either. My gifts are not in that way, I tell you, Master Cap."

"Nor herring, nor albatross, nor flying-fish—" continued Cap, who kept his eye fastened on the guide, in order to see how far he might venture. "No such thing as a fish that can fly, I dare say?"

"A fish that can fly! Master Cap—Master Cap do not think, because we are mere borderers, that we have no idees of natur', and what she has been pleased to do. I know there are squirrels that can fly—"

"A squirrel fly!—the d——l, Master Pathfinder. Do you

suppose that you have got a boy on his first v'y'ge, up here among you?"

"I know nothing of your v'y'ges, Master Cap, though I suppose them to have been many; but, as for what belongs to natur' in the woods, what I have seen I may tell, and not fear the face of man."

"And do you wish me to understand that you have seen a squirrel fly?"

"If you wish to understand the power of God, Master Cap, you will do well to believe that, and many other things of a like natur', for you may be quite sartain it is true."

"And yet, Pathfinder—" said Mabel, looking so pretty and sweet even while she played with the guide's infirmity, that he forgave her in his heart—"you, who speak so reverently of the power of the Deity, appear to doubt that a fish can fly?"

"I have not said it—I have not said it, and if Master Cap is ready to testify to the fact, unlikely as it seems, I am willing to try to think it true. I think it every man's duty to believe in the power of God, however difficult it may be."

"And why is'n't my fish as likely to have wings, as your squirrel?" demanded Cap, with more logic than was his wont. "That fishes do and can fly is as true as it is reasonable—"

"Nay, that is the only difficulty in believing the story," rejoined the guide. "It seems onreasonable to give an animal that lives in the water wings, which seemingly can be of no use to them."

"And do you suppose that the fishes are such asses as to fly about under water, when they are once fairly fitted out with wings?"

"Nay, I know nothing of the matter, but that fish should fly in the air seems more contrary to natur' still, than that they should fly in their own quarters; that, in which they were born and brought up, as one might say."

"So much for contracted ideas, Magnet. The fish fly out of water, to run away from their enemies under water, and there you see not only the fact, but the reason for it."

"Then I suppose it must be true," said the guide, quietly. "How long are their flights?"

"Not quite as far as those of pigeons, perhaps, but far

enough to make an offing. As for those squirrels of yours, we'll say no more about them, friend Pathfinder, as I suppose they were mentioned just as a make-weight to the fish, in favor of the woods—But what is this thing, anchored here under the hill."

"That is the cutter of Jasper, uncle," said Mabel, hurriedly—"and a very pretty vessel, I think it is. Its name, too, is the Scud."

"Ay, it will do well enough for a lake, perhaps, but it's no great affair. The lad has got a standing bowsprit, and who ever saw a cutter with a standing bowsprit, before!"

"But may there not be some good reason for it, on a lake like this, uncle?"

"Sure enough—I must remember this is not the ocean, though it does look so much like it."

"Ah! uncle, then Ontario *does* look like the ocean, after all!"

"In your eyes, I mean, and those of Pathfinder; not, in the least, in mine, Magnet. Now you might set me down, out yonder, in the middle of this bit of a pond, and that, too, in the darkest night that ever fell from the heavens, and in the smallest canoe, and I could tell you it was only a lake. For that matter, the Dorothy (the name of his vessel) would find it out as quick as I could myself. I do not believe that brig would make more than a couple of short stretches at the most, before she would perceive the difference between Ontario and the old Atlantic. I once took her down into one of the large South American bays, and she behaved herself as awkwardly as a booby would in a church, with the congregation in a hurry. And Jasper sails that boat? I must have a cruise with the lad, Magnet, before I quit you, just for the name of the thing. It would never do to say I got in sight of this pond, and went away without taking a trip on it."

"Well, well, you need'n't wait long for that," returned Pathfinder—"for the sarjeant is about to embark with a party, to relieve a post among the Thousand Islands, and, as I heard him say, he intended that Mabel should go along, you can join company too."

"Is this true, Magnet?"

"I believe it is," returned the girl, a flush so imperceptible as to escape the observation of her companions, glowing on her cheeks, "though I have had so little opportunity to talk with my dear father, that I am not quite certain. Here he comes, however, and you can inquire of himself."

Notwithstanding his humble rank, there was something in the mien and character of Serjeant Dunham that commanded respect. Of a tall imposing figure, grave and saturnine disposition, and accurate and precise in his acts and manner of thinking, even Cap, dogmatical and supercilious as he usually was with landsmen, did not presume to take the same liberties with the old soldier, as he did with his other friends. It was often remarked that Serjeant Dunham received more true respect from Duncan of Lundie, the Scotch Laird who commanded the post, than most of the subalterns, for experience and tried services were of quite as much value in the eyes of the veteran Major, as birth and money. While the serjeant never even hoped to rise any higher, he so far respected himself and his present station, as always to act in a way to command attention, and the habit of mixing so much with inferiors, whose passions and dispositions he felt it necessary to restrain by distance and dignity, had so far coloured his whole deportment, that few were altogether free from its influence. While the captains treated him kindly, and as an old comrade, the lieutenants seldom ventured to dissent from his military opinions, and the ensigns, it was remarked, actually manifested a species of respect, that amounted to something very like deference. It is no wonder then, that the announcement of Mabel put a sudden termination to the singular dialogue we have just related, though it had been often observed that the Pathfinder was the only man, on that frontier, beneath the condition of a gentleman, who presumed to treat the Serjeant at all as an equal, or even with the cordial familiarity of a friend.

"Good morrow, Brother Cap," said the Serjeant, giving the military salute, as he walked, in a grave, stately manner on the bastion. "My morning duty has made me seem forgetful of you and Mabel, but we have now an hour or two to spare, and to get acquainted. Do you not perceive, brother, a strong likeness in the girl, to her we have so long lost?"

"Mabel is the image of her mother, serjeant, as I have always said, with a little of your firmer figure; though, for that matter, the Caps were never wanting in spring and activity."

Mabel cast a timid glance at the stern, rigid countenance of her father, of whom she had ever thought as the warm-hearted dwell on the affection of their absent parents, and, as she saw that the muscles of his face were working, notwithstanding the stiffness and method of his manner, her very heart yearned to throw herself on his bosom, and to weep at will. But he was so much colder in externals, so much more formal and distant than she had expected to find him, that she would not have dared to hazard the freedom, even had they been alone.

"You have taken a long and troublesome journey, brother, on my account, and we will try to make you comfortable, while you stay among us."

"I hear you are likely to receive orders to lift your anchor, serjeant, and to shift your berth into a part of the world where they say there are a thousand islands?"

"Pathfinder, this is some of your forgetfulness?—"

"Nay, nay, sarjeant; I forgot nothing, but it did not seem to me necessary to hide your intentions so very closely from your own flesh and blood."

"All military movements ought to be made with as little conversation as possible," returned the Serjeant, tapping the guide's shoulder, in a friendly but reproachful manner. "You have passed too much of your life in front of the French, not to know the value of silence. But, no matter. The thing must soon be known, and there is no great use in trying, now, to conceal it. We shall embark a relief party, shortly, for a post on the lake, though I do not say it is for the Thousand Islands, and I may have to go with it; in which case, I intend to take Mabel, to make my broth for me, and I hope, brother, you will not despise a soldier's fare, for a month or so."

"That will depend on the manner of marching. I have no love for woods and swamps."

"We shall sail in the Scud, and, indeed, the whole service, which is no stranger to us, is likely enough to please one accustomed to the water."

"Ay, to salt-water, if you will, but not to lake-water. If you have no person to handle that bit of a cutter for you, I have no objection to ship for the v'y'ge, notwithstanding, though I shall look on the whole affair as so much time thrown away, for I consider it an imposition to call sailing about this pond, going to sea."

"Jasper is every way able to manage the Scud, Brother Cap, and in that light I cannot say that we have need of your services, though we shall be glad of your company. You cannot return to the settlements until a party is sent in, and that is not likely to happen until after my return. Well, Pathfinder, this is the first time I ever knew men on the trail of the Mingos, and you not at their head!"

"To be honest with you, Sarjeant," returned the guide, not without a little awkwardness of manner, and a perceptible difference in the hue of a face that had become so uniformly red by exposure, "I have not felt that it was my gift, this morning. In the first place, I very well know that the soldiers of the fifty fifth are not the lads to overtake Iroquois in the woods, and the knaves did not wait to be surrounded, when they knew that Jasper had reached the garrison. Then, a man may take a little rest, after a summer of hard work, and no impeachment of his good will. Besides, the Sarpent is out with them, and if the miscreants are to be found at all, you may trust to his inmity and sight; the first being stronger, and the last nearly if not quite as good as my own. He loves the skulking vagabonds as little as myself, and, for that matter, I may say that my own feelin's towards a Mingo, are not much more than the gifts of a Delaware grafted on a christian stock. No—no—I thought I would leave the honor, this time, if honor there is to be, to the young ensign that commands, who, if he do'n't lose his scalp, may boast of his campaign in his letters to his mother, when he gets in. I thought I would play idler once in my life."

"And no one has a better right, if long and faithful service entitles a man to a furlough," returned the Serjeant, kindly. "Mabel will think none the worse of you, for preferring her company to the trail of the savages, and I dare say will be happy to give you a part of her breakfast, if you are inclined to eat. You must not think, however, girl, that the Pathfinder is in the habit of letting prowlers around the fort, beat a retreat without hearing the crack of his rifle."

"If I thought she did, Sarjeant, though not much given to showy and parade evolutions, I would shoulder Killdeer, and quit the garrison before her pretty eyes had time to frown. No—no—Mabel, knows me better, though we are but new acquaintances, for there has been no want of Mingos to enliven the short march we have already made in company."

"It would need a great deal of testimony, Pathfinder, to make me think ill of you, in any way, and more than all in the way you mention;" returned Mabel, colouring with the sincere earnestness with which she endeavored to remove any suspicions to the contrary, from his mind. "Both father and daughter, I believe, even owe you their lives, and believe me that neither will ever forget it."

"Thank you, Mabel, thank you with all my heart. But I will not take advantage of your ignorance neither, girl, and therefore shall say I do not think the Mingos would have hurt a hair of your head, had they succeeded by their deviltries and contrivances, in getting you into their hands. My scalp, and Jasper's, and Master Cap's, there, and the Sarpent's, too, would sartainly have been smoked, but as for the Sarjeant's daughter, I do not think they would have hurt a hair of her head!"

"And why should I suppose that enemies known to spare neither women nor children would have shown more mercy to me than to another. I feel, Pathfinder, that I owe you my life."

"I say nay, Mabel, they would'n't have had the heart to hurt you. No, not even a fiery Mingo devil, would have had the heart to hurt a hair of your head! Bad as I suspect the vampires to be, I do not suspect them of anything so wicked as that. They might have wished you—nay forced you to become the wife of one of their chiefs, and that would be torment enough to a christian young woman, but beyond that I do not think even the Mingos themselves would have gone."

"Well, then, I shall owe my escape from this great misfortune to you," said Mabel, taking his hard hand into her own, frankly and cordially, and certainly in a way to delight the honest guide. "To me it would be a lighter evil to be killed, than to become the wife of an Indian."

"That is her gift, sarjeant," exclaimed Pathfinder, turning to his old comrade with gratification written on every lineament of his honest countenance, "and it will have its way. I tell the Sarpent, that no christianizing will ever make even a Delaware a white man; nor any whooping and yelling convart a pale face into a red skin. That is the gift of a young woman born of christian parents, and it ought to be maintained."

"You are right, Pathfinder, and so far as Mabel Dunham is concerned, it *shall* be maintained. But, it is time to break your fasts, and if you will follow me, Brother Cap, I will show you how we poor soldiers live, here on a distant frontier."

Chapter IX

"Now my co-mates and partners in exile,
Hath not old custom made this life more sweet
Than that of painted pomp? Are not these woods
More free from peril than the envious court?
Here feel we but the penalty of Adam—"

As You Like It, II.i.1–5.

SERJEANT DUNHAM made no empty vaunt, when he gave the promise, conveyed in the closing words of the last chapter. Notwithstanding the remote frontier position of the post, they who lived at it, enjoyed a table that, in many respects, kings and princes might have envied. At the period of our tale, and, indeed, for half a century later, the whole of that vast region, which has been called the west, or the new countries, since the war of the revolution, lay a comparatively unpeopled desert, teeming with all the living productions of nature, that properly belonged to the climate, man and the domestic animals excepted. The few Indians that roamed its forests then could produce no visible effects on the abundance of the game, and the scattered garrisons, or occasional hunters, that here and there were to be met with on that vast surface, had no other influence, than the bee on the buckwheat field, or the humming-bird on the flower.

The marvels that have descended to our own times, in the way of tradition, concerning the quantities of beasts, birds and fishes that were then to be met with, on the shores of the great lakes in particular, are known to be sustained by the experience of living men, else might we hesitate about relating them, but having been eye-witnesses of some of these prodigies, our office shall be discharged with the confidence that certainty can impart. Oswego was particularly well placed to keep the larder of an epicure amply supplied. Fish, of various sorts, abounded in its river, and the sportsman had only to cast his line to haul in a bass, or some other member of the finny tribe, which then peopled the waters, as the air above the swamps of this fruitful latitude is known to be filled with insects. Among others, was the salmon of the lakes, a variety of that well-known species, that is scarcely inferior to the delicious salmon of Northern Europe. Of the different migratory birds that frequent forests and waters, there was the same affluence, hundreds of acres of geese and ducks being often seen, at a time, in the great bays that indented the shores of the lake. Deer, bears, rabbits and squirrels, with divers other quadrupeds, among which was sometimes included the elk, or moose, helped to complete the sum of the natural supplies, on which all the posts depended more or less, to relieve the unavoidable privations of their remote frontier positions.

In a place where viands, that would elsewhere be deemed great luxuries, were so abundant, no one was excluded from their enjoyment. The meanest individual at Oswego habitually feasted on game that would have formed the boast of a Parisian table, and it was no more than a healthful commentary on the caprices of taste, and of the waywardness of human desires, that the very diet, which in other scenes would have been deemed the subject of envy and repinings, got to pall on the appetites. The coarse and regular food of the army, which it became necessary to husband on account of the difficulty of transportation, rose in the estimation of the common soldier, and, at any time, he would cheerfully desert his venison, and ducks, and pigeons, and salmon, to banquet on the sweets of pickled pork, stringy turnips and half-cooked cabbage.

The table of Serjeant Dunham, as a matter of course, partook of the abundance and luxuries of the frontier, as well as of its privations. A delicious broiled salmon smoked on a homely platter, hot venison steaks sent up their appetizing odours and several dishes of cold meats, all of which were composed of game, had been set before the guests, in honor of the newly-arrived visiters, and in vindication of the old soldier's hospitality.

"You do not seem to be on short allowance, in this quarter of the world, serjeant," said Cap, after he had got fairly initiated into the mysteries of the different dishes: "your salmon might satisfy a Scotsman."

"It fails to do it, notwithstanding, brother Cap, for, among two or three hundred of the fellows, that we have in this garrison, there are not half a dozen, who will not swear that fish is unfit to be eaten. Even some of the lads, who never tasted venison except as poachers at home, turn up their noses at the fattest haunches that we get here."

"Ay, that is christian natur'," put in the Pathfinder, "and I must say it is none to its credit. Now, a redskin never repines, but is always thankful for the food he gets, whether it be fat, or lean; venison, or bear; wild turkey's breast, or wild goose's wing. To the shame of us white men be it said, that we look upon blessings without satisfaction, and consider trifling evils as matters of great account."

"It is so with the 55th, as I can answer, though I cannot say as much for their christianity;" returned the Serjeant. "Even the Major, himself, old Duncan of Lundie, will sometimes swear an oat-meal cake is better fare than the Oswego bass, and sigh for a swallow of Highland water, when, if so minded, he has the whole of Ontario to quench his thirst in."

"Has Major Duncan a wife and children?" asked Mabel, whose thoughts naturally turned towards her own sex, in her new situation.

"Not he, girl, though they do say that he has a betrothed, at home. The lady, it seems, is willing to wait, rather than suffer the hardships of service, in this wild region, all of which, brother Cap, is not according to my notions of a woman's duties. Your sister thought differently, and had it pleased God to spare her, would have been sitting, at this moment, on the very camp stool that her daughter so well becomes."

"I hope, Serjeant, you do not think of Mabel, for a soldier's wife," returned Cap, gravely. "Our family has done its share, in that way already, and it's high time that the sea was again remembered."

"I do not think of finding a husband for the girl in the 55th, or any other regiment, I can promise you, brother, though I do think it getting to be time that the child were respectably married."

"Father!"

"'Tis not their gifts, Sarjeant, to talk of these matters in so open a manner," said the guide, "for I've seen it verified by exper'ence, that he who would follow the trail of a virgin's good-will, must not go shouting out his thoughts behind her. So; if you please we will talk of something else."

"Well, then, brother Cap, I hope that bit of cold roasted pig is to your mind; you seem to fancy the food."

"Ay, ay, give me civilized grub, if I must eat," returned the pertinacious seaman. "Venison is well enough for your inland sailors, but we of the ocean like a little of that which we understand."

Here Pathfinder laid down his knife and fork, and indulged in a hearty laugh, though always in his silent manner. Then he asked, with a little curiosity in his manner—

"Do'n't you miss the skin, Master Cap; do'n't you miss the skin?"

"It would have been better for its jacket, I think myself, Pathfinder, but I suppose it is a fashion of the woods to serve up shoats, in this style."

"Well, well, a man may go round the 'arth and not know every thing! If you had had the skinning of that pig, Master Cap, it would have left you sore hands. The creatur' is a hedge-hog!"

"Blast me, if I thought it wholesome natural pork, either;" returned Cap. "But then I believed even a pig might lose some of its good qualities, up, hereaway, in the woods. It seemed no more than reason that a fresh-water hog, should not be altogether as good as a salt-water hog. I suppose, serjeant, by this time, it is all the same to you?"

"If the skinning of it, brother, does not fall to my duty. Pathfinder, I hope you did'n't find Mabel disobedient on the march?"

"Not she—not she. If Mabel is only half as well satisfied with Jasper and the Pathfinder, as the Pathfinder and Jasper are satisfied with her, sarjeant, we shall be friends for the remainder of our days."

As the guide spoke, he turned his eyes towards the blushing girl, with a sort of innocent desire to know her opinion, and then with an inborn delicacy that proved he was far superior to the vulgar desire to invade the sanctity of feminine feeling, he looked at his plate, and seemed to regret his own boldness.

"Well, well, we must remember that women are not men,

my friend," resumed the serjeant, "and make proper allowances for nature and education. A recruit is not a veteran. Any man knows that it takes longer to make a good soldier, than it takes to make any thing else, and it ought to require unusual time to make a good soldier's daughter."

"This is new doctrine, serjeant," said Cap, with some spirit. "We old seamen are apt to think that six soldiers, ay, and capital soldiers too, might be made, while one sailor is getting his education."

"Ay, brother Cap, I've seen something of the opinions which sea-faring men have of themselves," returned the brother-in-law, with a smile as bland as comported with his saturnine features; "for I was many years one of the garrison in a sea-port. You and I have conversed on the subject before, and I'm afraid we shall never agree. But if you wish to know what the difference is, between a real soldier, and man in what I should call a state of nature, you have only to look at a battalion of the 55th, on parade this afternoon, and then, when you get back to York, to examine one of the militia regiments making its greatest efforts."

"Well, to my eye, serjeant, there is very little difference—not more than you'll find between a brig and a snow. To me they seem alike; all scarlet, and feathers, and powder, and pipe clay."

"So much, sir, for the judgment of a sailor," returned the serjeant with dignity; "but perhaps you are not aware that it requires a year to teach a true soldier how to eat."

"So much the worse for him! The militia know how to eat at starting, for I have often heard, that, on their marches, they commonly eat all before them, even if they do nothing else."

"They have their gifts, I suppose, like other men," observed Pathfinder, with a view to preserve the peace, which was evidently in some danger of being broken, by the obstinate predilection of each of the disputants in favor of his own calling; "and when a man has his gift from Providence it is commonly idle to endivor to bear up ag'in it. The 55th, sarjeant, is a judicious rigiment, in the way of eating, as I know from having been so long in its Company, though I dare say militia corps could be found that would outdo them in feats of that natur', too."

"Uncle," said Mabel, "if you have breakfasted, I will thank you to go out upon the bastion with me, again. We have neither of us, half seen the lake, and it would be hardly seemly for a young woman to be walking about the fort, the first day of her arrival, quite alone."

Cap understood the motive of Mabel, and having, at the bottom, a hearty friendship for his brother-in-law, he was willing enough to defer the argument until they had been longer together, for the idea of abandoning it altogether, never crossed the mind of one so dogmatical and obstinate. He accordingly accompanied his niece, leaving Serjeant Dunham and his friend the Pathfinder, alone, together. As soon as his adversary had beaten a retreat, the serjeant, who did not quite so well understand the manœuvre of his daughter, turned to his companion, and with a smile that was not without triumph, he remarked—

"The army, Pathfinder, has never yet done itself justice; and, though modesty becomes a man, whether he is in a red coat or a black one, or for that matter, in his shirt-sleeves, I don't like to let a good opportunity slip of saying a word in its behalf. Well, my friend," laying his own hand, on one of the Pathfinder's, and giving it a hearty squeeze—"how do you like the girl?"

"You have reason to be proud of her, sarjeant; you have great reason to be proud at finding yourself the father of so handsome and well mannered a young woman. I have seen many of her sex, and some that were great and beautiful, but never before did I meet with one, in whom I thought Providence had so well balanced the different gifts."

"And the good opinion, I can tell you, Pathfinder, is mutual. She told me last night all about your coolness, and spirit, and kindness—particularly the last; for kindness counts for more than half with females, my friend—and the first inspection seems to give satisfaction on both sides. Brush up the uniform, and pay a little more attention to the outside, Pathfinder, and you will have the girl, heart and hand."

"Nay, nay, sarjeant, I've forgotten nothing that you have told me, and grudge no reasonable pains to make myself as pleasant in the eyes of Mabel, as she is getting to be in mine. I cleaned and brightened up Killdeer, this morning, as soon as the sun rose, and, in my judgment, the piece never looked better than it does at this very moment."

"That is according to your hunting notions, Pathfinder, but firearms should sparkle and glitter in the sun, and I never yet could see any beauty in a clouded barrel."

"Lord Howe thought otherwise, sarjeant, and he was accounted a good soldier!"

"Very true—his Lordship had all the barrels of his regiment darkened, and what good came of it? You can see his 'scutcheon hanging in the English Church at Albany! No—no, my worthy friend, a soldier should be a soldier, and at no time ought he to be ashamed, or afraid, to carry about him the signs and symbols of his honorable trade. Had you much discourse with Mabel, Pathfinder, as you came along in the canoe?"

"There was not much opportunity, sarjeant, and then I found myself so much beneath her in idees, that I was afraid to speak of much beyond what belonged to my own gifts."

"Therein, you are partly right, and partly wrong, my friend. Women love trifling discourse, though they like to have most of it to themselves. Now, you know, I'm a man that do not loosen my tongue at every giddy thought, and yet there were days when I could see that Mabel's mother thought none the worse of me, because I descended a little from my manhood. It is true, I was twenty two years younger then, than I am to day, and, moreover, instead of being the oldest serjeant in the regiment, I was the youngest. Dignity is commanding and useful, and there is no getting on without it, as respects the men, but if you would be thoroughly esteemed by a woman, it is necessary to condescend a little, on occasions."

"Ah's! me, sarjeant; I sometimes fear it will never do!"

"Why do you think so discouragingly of a matter on which I thought both our minds were made up?"

"We did agree that if Mabel should prove what you told me she was, and if the girl could fancy a rude hunter and guide, that I would quit some of my wandering ways, and try to humanize my mind down to a wife and children. But since I have seen the girl, I will own that many misgivin's have come over me!"

"How's this!" interrupted the serjeant, sternly—"Did I not understand you to say that you were pleased?—And is Mabel a young woman to disappoint expectation?"

"Ah! sarjeant, it is not Mabel that I distrust, but myself. I am but a poor ignorant woodsman, after all, and perhaps I'm not, in truth, as good as even you and I may think me!"

"If you doubt your own judgment of yourself, Pathfinder, I beg you will not doubt mine. Am I not accustomed to judge men's characters?—Is it not my especial duty, and am I often deceived? Ask Major Duncan, sir, if you desire any assurances in this particular."

"But, sarjeant, we have long been friends; have fou't side by side, a dozen times, and have done each other many sarvices. When this is the case, men are apt to think overkindly of each other, and I fear me that the daughter may not be so likely to view a plain, ignorant hunter as favorably as the father does."

"Tut—tut—Pathfinder—you do'n't know yourself, man, and may put all faith in my judgment. In the first place, you have experience, and as all girls must want that, no prudent young woman would overlook such a qualification. Then you are not one of the coxcombs that strut about when they first join a regiment, but a man who has seen service, and who carries the marks of it on his person and countenance. I dare say you have been under fire, some thirty or forty times, counting all the skirmishes and ambushes that you've seen."

"All of that, sarjeant, all of that, but what will it avail, in gaining the good will of a tender-hearted young female?"

"It will gain the day. Experience in the field is as good in love, as in war. But you are as honest-hearted, and as loyal a subject, as the King can boast of, God bless him!"

"That may be too—that may be too; but I'm afeard I'm too rude, and too old, and too wild like, to suit the fancy of such a young and delicate girl, as Mabel, who has been unused to our wilderness ways, and may think the settlements better suited to her gifts and inclinations."

"These are new misgivings for you, my friend, and I wonder they were never paraded before."

"Because I never knew my own worthlessness, perhaps, until I saw Mabel. I have travelled with some as fair, and have guided them through the forest, and seen them in their perils and in their gladness, but they were always too much above me, to make me think of them, as more than so many feeble ones I was bound to protect and defend. The case is now different. Mabel and I are so nearly alike, that I feel weighed down with a load that is hard to bear, at finding us so unlike. I do wish, sarjeant, that I was ten years younger, more comely to look at, and better suited to please a handsome young woman's fancy!"

"Cheer up, my brave friend, and trust to a father's knowledge of womankind. Mabel half loves you already, and a fortnight's intercourse and kindnesses, down among the islands yonder, will close ranks with the other half. The girl as much as told me this herself, last night."

"Can this be so, sarjeant!" said the guide, whose meek and modest nature shrunk from viewing himself in colours so favorable. "Can this be truly so! I am but a poor hunter, and Mabel, I see, is fit to be an officer's lady. Do you think the gal will consent to quit all her beloved settlement usages, and her visitin's, and church-goin's to dwell with a plain guide and hunter, up, hereaway, in the woods? Will she not in the ind crave her old ways, and a better man?"

"A better man, Pathfinder, would be hard to find," returned the father. "As for town usages, they are soon forgotten in the freedom of the forest, and Mabel has just spirit enough to dwell on a frontier. I've not planned this marriage, my friend, without thinking it over, as a general does his campaign. At first I thought of bringing you into the regiment, that you might succeed me when I retire, which must be sooner, or later, but on reflection, Pathfinder, I think you are scarcely fitted for the office. Still if not a soldier, in all the meanings of the word, you are a soldier in its best meaning, and I know that you have the good will of every officer in the corps. As long as I live, Mabel can dwell with me, and you will always have a home, when you return from your scoutings and marches."

"This is very pleasant to think of, sarjeant, if the girl can only come into our wishes with good will. But, Ah's! me, it does not seem that one like myself, can ever be agreeable in her handsome eyes! If I were younger, and more comely, now, as Jasper Western is, for instance, there might be a chance—yes, then, indeed, there might be some chance."

"That, for Jasper Eau douce, and every younker of them in, or about the fort!" returned the Serjeant snapping his fingers—"If not actually a younger, you are a younger looking, ay and a better looking man than the Scud's master——"

"Anan!" said Pathfinder, looking up at his companion, with an expression of doubt, as if he did not understand his meaning.

"I say, if not actually younger in days and years, you look more hardy and like whip-cord, than Jasper, or any of them, and there will be more of you, thirty years hence, than of all of them put together. A good conscience will keep one like you a mere boy, all his life."

"Jasper has as clear a conscience as any youth, I know, Sarjeant!—And is as likely to wear, on that account, as any young man in the colony."

"Then you are my friend," squeezing the other's hand—"my tried, sworn and constant friend."

"Yes, we have been friends, sarjeant, near twenty years. Before Mabel was born."

"True enough; before Mabel was born, we were well-tried friends, and the hussy would never dream of refusing to marry a man who was her father's friend before she was born!"

"We do'n't know, sarjeant, we do'n't know. Like loves like. The young prefar the young for companions, and the old the old."

"Not for wives, Pathfinder; I never knew an old man, now, who had an objection to a young wife. Then you are respected and esteemed by every officer in the fort, as I have said already, and it will please her fancy to like a man that every one else likes."

"I hope I have no inimies but the Mingos," returned the guide, stroking down his hair meekly, and speaking thoughtfully. "I've *tried* to do right, and that ought to make friends, though it sometimes fails."

"And you may be said to keep the best company, for even old Duncan of Lundie is glad to see you, and you pass hours in his society. Of all the guides, he confides most in you."

"Ay, even greater than he is, have marched by my side for days, and have convarsed with me as if I were their brother; but, sarjeant, I have never been puffed up by their company, for I know that the woods often bring men to a level, who would not be so in the settlements."

"And you are known to be the greatest rifle shot that ever pulled trigger in all this region."

"If Mabel could fancy a man for that, I might have no great reason to despair; and, yet, sarjeant, I sometimes think that it is all as much owing to Killdeer, as to any skill of my own. It is sartainly a wonderful piece, and might do as much in the hands of another!"

"That is your own humble opinion of yourself, Pathfinder, but we have seen too many fail with the same weapon, and you succeed too often with the rifles of other men, to allow me to agree with you. We will get up a shooting match, in a day or two, when you can show your skill, and then Mabel will form some judgment concerning your true character."

"Will that be fair, sarjeant? Every body knows that Killdeer seldom misses, and ought we to make a trial of this sort, when we all know what must be the result?"

"Tut—tut, man; I foresee I must do half this courting for you. For one who is always inside of the smoke, in a skirmish, you are the faintest-hearted suitor I ever met with. Remember Mabel comes of a bold stock, and the girl will be as likely to admire a man, as her mother was before her."

Here the serjeant arose, and proceeded to attend to his never ceasing duties, without apology, the terms on which the guide stood with all in the garrison, rendering this freedom quite a matter of course.

The reader will have gathered from the conversation just related one of the plans that Serjeant Dunham had in view, in causing his daughter to be brought to the frontier. Although necessarily much weaned from the caresses and blandishments that had rendered his child so dear to him, during the first year or two of his widower-hood, he had still a strong, but somewhat latent, love for her. Accustomed to command and to obey, without being questioned himself, or questioning others concerning the reasonableness of the mandates, he was perhaps too much disposed to believe that his daughter would marry the man he might select, while he was far from being disposed to do violence to her wishes. The fact was, few knew the Pathfinder intimately, without secretly coming to believe him to be one of extraordinary qualities. Ever the same, simple-minded, faithful, utterly without fear and yet prudent, foremost in all warrantable enterprises, or what the opinion of the day considered as such, and never engaged in any thing to call a blush to his cheek, or censure on his acts, it was not possible to live much with this being, who in his peculiar way, was a sort of type of what Adam might have been supposed to be before the fall, though certainly not without sin, and not feel a respect and admiration for him, that had no reference to his position in life. It was remarked that no officer passed him, without saluting him as if he had been his equal, no common man without addressing him with the confidence and freedom of a comrade. The most surprising peculiarity about the man himself, was the entire indifference with which he regarded all distinctions that did not depend on personal merit. He was respectful to his superiors from habit, but had often been known to correct their mistakes and to reprove their vices, with a fearlessness that proved how essentially he regarded the more material points, and with a natural discrimination that appeared to set education at defiance. In short, a disbeliever in the ability of man to distinguish between good and evil, without the aid of instruction, would have been staggered by the character of this extraordinary inhabitant of the frontier. His feelings appeared to possess the freshness and nature of the forests in which he passed so much of his time, and no casuist could have made clearer decisions in matters relating to right and wrong; and, yet, he was not without his prejudices, which, though few and coloured by the character and usages of the individual, were deep-rooted, and had almost got to form a part of his nature. But the most striking feature about the moral organization of Pathfinder was his beautiful and unerring sense of justice. This noble trait, and without it no man can be truly great, with it no man other than respectable, probably had its unseen influence on all who associated with him, for the common, rude and unprincipled brawler of the camp had been known to return from an expedition made in his company, rebuked by his sentiments, softened by his language and improved by his example. As might have been expected with so elevated a quality, his fidelity was like the immoveable rock. Treachery in him was classed among the things that are impossible, and as he seldom retired before his enemies, so was he never known, under any circumstances that admitted of an alternative, to abandon a friend. The affinities of such a character were, as a matter of course, those of like for like. His associates and intimates, though more or less determined by chance, were generally of the higher order as to moral propensities, for he appeared to possess a species of instinctive discrimination that led him, insensibly to himself most probably, to cling closest to those, whose characters would best reward his friendship. In short, it was said of the Pathfinder, by one accustomed to study his fellows, that he was a fair example of what a just-minded and pure man might be, while untempted by unruly or ambitious desires, and left to follow the bias of his feelings, amid the solitary grandeur and ennobling influences of a sublime nature; neither led aside by the inducements which influence all to do evil amid the incentives of civilization, nor forgetful of the Almighty Being whose spirit pervades the wilderness as well as the town.

Such was the man whom Serjeant Dunham had selected as the husband of Mabel. In making this choice he had not been as much governed by a clear and judicious view of the merits of the individual, perhaps, as by his own likings; still no one knew the Pathfinder as intimately as himself, without always conceding to the honest guide a high place in his esteem, on account of these very virtues. That his daughter could find any serious objections to the match, the old soldier did not apprehend, while, on the other hand, he saw many advantages to himself, in dim perspective, that were connected with the decline of his days, and an evening of life passed among descendants, who were equally dear to him through both parents. He first made the proposition to his friend, who had listened to it kindly, but who, the serjeant was now pleased to find, already betrayed a willingness to come into his own views, that was proportioned to the doubts and misgivings proceeding from his humble distrust of himself.

Chapter X

"Think not I love him, though I ask for him;
'Tis but a peevish boy:—yet he talks well;—
But what care I for words?—"

As You Like It, III.v.109–11.

A WEEK PASSED in the usual routine of a garrison. Mabel was becoming used to a situation that, at first, she had found not only novel, but a little irksome, and the officers and men, in their turn, gradually familiarized to the presence of a young and blooming girl, whose attire and carriage had that air of modest gentility about them, which she had obtained in the family of her patroness, annoyed her less by their ill concealed admiration, while they gratified her by the respect which, she was fain to think, they paid her on account of her father; but which, in truth, was more to be attributed to her own modest, but spirited deportment, than to any deference for the worthy serjeant.

Acquaintances made in a forest, or in any circumstances of unusual excitement, soon attain their limits. Mabel found one week's residence at Oswego, sufficient to determine her, as to those with whom she might be intimate, and those whom she ought to avoid. The sort of neutral position occupied by her father, who was not an officer while he was so much more than a common soldier, by keeping her aloof from the two great classes of military life, lessened the number of those whom she was compelled to know, and made the duty of decision comparatively easy. Still she soon discovered that there were a few, even among those that could aspire to a seat at the commandant's table, who were disposed to overlook the halbert, for the novelty of a well turned figure and of a pretty, winning face, and by the end of the first two or three days, she had admirers even among the gentlemen. The quarter-master, in particular, a middle aged soldier, who had more than once tried the blessings of matrimony, but was now a widower, was evidently disposed to increase his intimacy with the Serjeant, though their duties often brought them together, and the youngsters among his messmates did not fail to note that this man of method, who was a Scotchman of the name of Muir, was much more frequent in his visits to the quarters of his subordinate than had formerly been his wont. A laugh, or a joke, in honor of the "Serjeant's daughter," however, limited their strictures, though "Mabel Dunham" was soon a toast that even the ensign or the lieutenant did not disdain to give.

At the end of a week, Duncan of Lundie sent for Serjeant Dunham, after evening roll call, on business of a nature that, it was understood, required a personal conference. The old veteran dwelt in a moveable hut, which being placed on trucks, he could order to be wheeled about at pleasure, sometimes living in one part of the area within the fort, and sometimes in another.* On the present occasion, he had made a halt near the centre, and there he was found by his subordinate, who was admitted to his presence without any delay, or dancing attendance in an ante-chamber. In point of fact, there was very little difference in the quality of the accommodations given to the officers and those allowed to the men, the former being merely granted the most room, and Mabel and her father were lodged nearly, if not quite as well, as the commandant of the place, himself.

"Walk in, serjeant, walk in, my good friend," said old Lundie, heartily, as his inferior, stood in a respectful attitude at the door of a sort of library and bed-room into which he had been ushered; "walk in, and take a seat on that stool. I have sent for you, man, to discuss any thing but rosters and payrolls, this evening. It is now many years since we have been comrades, and 'auld lang syne' should count for something, even between a Major and his orderly, a Scot and a Yankee. Sit ye down, man, and just put yourself at your ease. It has been a fine day, serjeant?"

"It has indeed, Major Duncan," returned the other, who, though he complied so far as to take the seat, was much too practised not to understand the degree of respect it was necessary to maintain in his manner; "a very fine day, sir, it has been, and we may look for more of them, at this season."

"I hope so, with all my heart. The crops look well, as it is,

*This circumstance is a real incident, taken from the "American Lady" of Mrs. Grant, of Laggan.

man, and you'll be finding that the 55th make almost as good farmers as soldiers. I never saw better potatoes in Scotland, than we are likely to have, in that new patch, of ours."

"They promise a good yield, Major Duncan, and, in that light, a more comfortable winter than the last."

"Life is progressive, serjeant, in its comforts, as well as in its need of them. We grow old, and I begin to think it time to retire and settle in life. I feel that my working days are nearly over."

"The King, God bless him, sir, has much good service, in your honor, yet."

"It may be so, Serjeant Dunham, especially if he should happen to have a spare Lt-Colonelcy left."

"The 55th will be honored the day that commission is given to Duncan of Lundie, sir."

"And Duncan of Lundie will be honored the day he receives it. But, serjeant, if you have never had a Lt-Colonelcy you have had a good wife, and that is the next thing to rank, in making a man happy."

"I have been married, Major Duncan, but it is now a long time since I have had no drawback on the love I bear His Majesty and my duty."

"What, man, not even the love you bear that active, little, round-limbed, rosy-cheeked daughter, that I have seen in the fort, these last few days! Out upon you, serjeant! old fellow as I am, I could almost love that little lassie, myself, and send the Lt-Colonelcy to the devil."

"We all know where Major Duncan's heart is, and that is in Scotland, where a beautiful lady is ready and willing to make him happy, as soon as his own sense of duty shall permit."

"Ay, hope is ever a far off thing, serjeant," returned the superior, a shade of melancholy passing over his hard Scottish features as he spoke; "and bonny Scotland is a far off country. Well, if we have no heather, and oat-meal in this region, we have venison for the killing it, and salmon as plenty as at Berwick upon Tweed. Is it true, serjeant, that the men complain of having been over-venisoned, and over-pigeoned of late?"

"Not for some weeks, Major Duncan, for neither deer nor birds are so plenty at this season as they have been. They begin to throw their remarks about concerning the salmon, but I trust we shall get through the summer without any serious disturbance on the score of food. The Scotch in the battalion do, indeed, talk more than is prudent of their want of oat-meal, grumbling occasionally of our wheaten bread."

"Ah! that is human nature, serjeant, pure unadulterated Scotch human nature. A cake, man, to say the truth is an agreeable morsel, and I often see the time, when I pine for a bite, myself."

"If the feeling gets to be troublesome, Major Duncan—in the men I mean, sir; for I would not think of saying so disrespectful a thing to your honor—but if the men ever pine seriously for their natural food, I would humbly recommend that some oat-meal be imported, or prepared in this country for them, and I think we shall hear no more of it. A very little would answer for a cure, sir."

"You are a wag, serjeant, but hang me if I am sure you are not right. There may be sweeter things in this world, after all, than oat-meal. You have a sweet daughter, Dunham, for one."

"The girl is like her mother, Major Duncan, and will pass inspection," said the serjeant proudly. "Neither was brought up on any thing better than good American flour. The girl will pass inspection, sir!"

"That would she, I'll answer for it. Well, I may as well come to the point at once, man, and bring up my reserve into the front of the battle. Here is Davy Muir, the quarter-master, disposed to make your daughter his wife, and he has just got me to open the matter to you, being fearful of compromitting his own dignity—and I may as well add, that half the youngsters in the fort toast her, and talk of her from morning till night."

"She is much honored, sir," returned the father, stiffly, "but I trust the gentlemen will find something more worthy of them to talk about, ere long. I hope to see her the wife of an honest man before many weeks, sir."

"Yes, Davy is an honest man, and that is more than can be said for all in the Quarter-Master's department, I'm thinking, serjeant," returned Lundie, with a slight smile. "Well, then, may I tell the Cupid-stricken youth, that the matter is as good as settled?"

"I thank your honor, but Mabel is betrothed to another."

"The devil she is! That will produce a stir in the fort, though I'm not sorry to hear it, either, for to be frank with you, serjeant, I'm no great admirer of unequal matches."

"I think, with your honor, and have no desire to see my daughter an officer's lady. If she can get as high as her mother was before her, it ought to satisfy any reasonable woman."

"And may I ask, serjeant, who is the lucky man that you intend to call son-in-law?"

"The Pathfinder, your honor."

"Pathfinder!"

"The same, Major Duncan, and in naming him to you, I give you his whole history. No one is better known on this frontier, than my honest, brave, true-hearted friend."

"All that is true enough, but is he, after all, the sort of person to make a girl of twenty happy."

"Why not, your honor; the man is at the head of his calling. There is no other guide, or scout, connected with the army that has half the reputation of Pathfinder, or who deserves to have it, half as well."

"Very true, serjeant, but is the reputation of a scout, exactly the sort of renown to captivate a girl's fancy."

"Talking of girls' fancies, sir, is, in my humble opinion, much like talking of a recruit's judgment. If we were to take the notions of the awkward squad, sir, as a guide, we should never form a decent line, in battalion, Major Duncan."

"But your daughter has nothing awkward about her, for a genteeler girl of her class, could not be found in old Albin itself. Is she of your way of thinking, in this matter, though, I suppose she must be, as you say she is betrothed."

"We have not yet conversed on the subject, your honor, but I consider her mind as good as made up, from several little circumstances that might be named."

"And what are these circumstances, Serjeant?" asked the Major, who began to take more interest than he had at first felt, in the subject. "I confess a little curiosity to learn something about a woman's mind, being, as you know, a bachelor myself."

"Why, your honor, when I speak of the Pathfinder to the girl, she always looks me full in the face; chimes in with every thing I say in his favor, and has a frank open way with her, which says as much as if she half considered him, already, as a husband."

"Hum—and these signs you think, Dunham, are faithful tokens of your daughter's feelings?"

"I do, your honor, for they strike me as natural. When I find a man, sir, who looks me full in the face, while he praises an officer—for, begging your honor's pardon, the men will sometimes pass their strictures on their betters—and when I find a man looking me in the eyes, as he praises his captain, I always set it down that the fellow is honest, and means what he says."

"Is there not some material difference in the age of the intended bridegroom, and that of his pretty bride, serjeant?"

"You are quite right, sir; Pathfinder is well advanced towards forty, and Mabel has every prospect of happiness that a young woman can derive from the certainty of possessing an experienced husband. I was quite forty myself, your honor, when I married her mother."

"But, will your daughter be as likely to admire a green hunting shirt, such as that our worthy guide wears, with a fox-skin cap, as the smart uniform of the 55th?"

"Perhaps not, sir, and therefore she will have the merit of self-denial, which always makes a young woman wiser and better."

"And are you not afraid that she may be left a widow while still a young woman?—What between wild beasts, and wilder savages, Pathfinder may be said to carry his life in his hand."

" 'Every bullet has its billet,' Lundie," for so the Major was fond of being called, in his moments of condescension, and when not engaged in military affairs, "and no man in the 55th can call himself beyond, or above, the chances of sudden death. In that particular, Mabel would gain nothing by a change. Besides, sir, if I may speak freely on such a subject, I much doubt if ever Pathfinder dies in battle, or by any of the sudden chances of the wilderness."

"And why so, Serjeant?" asked the Major, looking at his inferior, with the sort of reverence which a Scot of his day, was more apt than at present to entertain for mysterious agencies. "He is a soldier, so far as danger is concerned, and one that is much more than usually exposed, and, being free of his person, why should he expect to escape, when others do not?"

"I do not believe, your honor, that the Pathfinder considers his own chances, better than any one's else, but the man will never die by a bullet. I have seen him so often, handling his rifle with as much composure as if it were a shepherd's crook, in the midst of the heaviest showers of bullets, and under so many extraordinary circumstances, that I do not think Providence means he should ever fall in that manner. And, yet, if there be a man in His Majesty's dominions who really deserves such a death, it is Pathfinder!"

"We never know, serjeant," returned Lundie, with a countenance that was grave with thought, "and the less we say about it, perhaps, the better. But, will your daughter—Mabel, I think, you call her—will Mabel be as willing to accept one, who, after all, is a mere hanger-on of the army, as to take one from the service itself. There is no hope of promotion for the guide, serjeant!"

"He is at the head of his corps, already, your honor. In short, Mabel has made up her mind on this subject, and as your honor has had the condescension to speak to me about Mr. Muir, I trust you will be kind enough to say that the girl is as good as billeted for life."

"Well, well, this is your own matter, and, now,—Serjeant Dunham!"

"Your honor," said the other rising, and giving the customary salute.

"You have been told it is my intention to send you down among the Thousand Islands, for the next month. All the old subalterns have had their tours of duty in that quarter—all that I like to trust, at least, and it has, at length, come to your turn. Lt. Muir, it is true, claims his right, but being the Quarter Master, I do not like to break up well established arrangements. Are the men drafted?"

"Every thing is ready, your honor. The draft is made, and I understood that the canoe, which got in, last night, brought a message to say that the party already below, is looking out for the relief."

"It did, and you must sail the day after to-morrow, if not to-morrow night. It will be wise, perhaps, to sail in the dark."

"So Jasper thinks, Major Duncan, and I know no one more to be depended on, in such an affair, than young Jasper Western."

"Young Jasper Eau douce!" said Lundie, a slight smile gathering around his usually stern mouth. "Will that lad be of your party, Serjeant?"

"Your honor will remember that the Scud never quits port without him."

"True, but all general rules have their exceptions. Have I not seen a seafaring person about the fort within the last few days?"

"No doubt, your honor; it is Master Cap, a brother-in-law of mine, who brought my daughter from below."

"Why not put him in the Scud for this cruise, serjeant, and leave Jasper behind. Your brother-in-law would like the variety of a fresh water cruise, and you would enjoy more of his company."

"I intended to ask your honor's permission to take him along, but he must go as a volunteer. Jasper is too brave a lad to be turned out of his command without a reason, Major Duncan, and I'm afraid Brother Cap despises fresh water too much to do duty on it."

"Quite right, serjeant, and I leave all this to your own discretion. Eau douce must retain his command, on second thoughts—You intend that Pathfinder shall also be of the party?"

"If your honor approves of it. There will be service for both the guides, the Indian as well as the white man."

"I think you are right. Well, serjeant, I wish you good luck in the enterprise, and remember the post is to be destroyed and abandoned when your command is withdrawn. It will have done its work by that time or we shall have failed entirely, and it is too ticklish a position to be maintained unnecessarily. You can retire."

Serjeant Dunham gave the customary salute, turned on his heels, as if they had been pivots, and had got the door nearly drawn-to after him, when he was suddenly recalled.

"I had forgotten, serjeant, the younger officers have begged for a shooting match, and to-morrow has been named for the day. All competitors will be admitted, and the prizes will be a silver mounted powder horn, a leathern flask, ditto," reading from a piece of paper, "as I see by the professional jargon of this bill, and a silk calash, for a lady. The latter is to enable the victor to show his gallantry, by making an offering of it to her he best loves."

"All very agreeable, your honor, at least to him that succeeds. Is the Pathfinder to be permitted to enter?"

"I do not well see how he can be excluded, if he choose to come forward. Latterly, I have observed that he takes no share in these sports, probably from a conviction of his own unequalled skill."

"That's it, Major Duncan; the honest fellow knows there is not a man on the frontier who can equal him, and he does not wish to spoil the pleasure of others. I think we may trust to his delicacy, in any thing, sir. Perhaps it may be as well, to let him have his own way."

"In this instance, we must, serjeant. Whether he will be as successful in all others, remains to be seen. I wish you good evening, Dunham."

The serjeant now withdrew, leaving Duncan of Lundie to his own thoughts. That they were not altogether disagreeable was to be inferred from the smiles which occasionally crossed a countenance that was hard and martial in its usual expression, though there were moments in which all its severe sobriety prevailed. Half an hour might have passed when a tap at the door, was answered by a direction to enter. A middle-aged man, in the dress of an officer but whose uniform wanted the usual smartness of the profession, made his appearance, and was saluted as "Mr. Muir."

"I have come, sir, at your bidding to know my fortune," said the Quarter Master, in a strong Scotch accent, as soon as he had taken the seat which was proffered to him. "To say the truth to you, Major Duncan, this girl is making as much havoc in the garrison, as the French did before Ty; I never witnessed so general a rout, in so short a time!"

"Surely, Davy, you don't mean to persuade me that your young and unsophisticated heart, is in such a flame, after one week's ignition! Why, man, this is worse than the affair in

Scotland, where it was said the heat within was so intense that it just burnt a hole through your own precious body, and left a place for all the lassies to peer in at, to see what the combustible material was worth."

"Ye'll have your own way, Major Duncan, and your father and mother would have theirs before ye even if the enemy were in the camp. I see nothing so extraordinar' in young people's following the bent of their inclinations and wishes."

"But you've followed yours so often, Davy, that I should think, by this time, it had lost the edge of novelty. Including that informal affair in Scotland, when you were a lad, you've been married four times, already."

"Only three, Major, as I hope to get another wife! I've not yet had my number; no—no—only three."

"I'm thinking, Davy, you don't include the first affair, I mentioned; that, in which there was no parson."

"And why should I, Major? The courts decided that it was no marriage, and what more could a man want! The woman took advantage of a slight amorous propensity, that may be a weakness in my disposition, perhaps, and inveigled me into a contract that was found to be illegal."

"If I remember right, Muir, there were thought to be two sides to that question, in the time of it!"

"It would be but an indifferent question, my dear Major, that had'n't two sides to it; and I've know many that had three. But the poor woman's dead, and there was no issue, so nothing came of it, after all. Then I was particularly unfortunate with my second wife—I say second, Major, out of deference to you, and on the mere supposition that the first was a marriage at all—but first, or second, I was particularly unfortunate with Jeannie Graham, who died in the first lustrum, leaving neither chick nor chiel behind her. I do think if Jeannie had survived I never should have turned my thoughts towards another wife."

"But as she did not, you married twice after her death, and are desirous of doing so a third time."

"The truth can never justly be gainsayed, Major Duncan, and I am always ready to avow it. I'm thinking, Lundie, you are melancholar', this fine evening?"

"No, Muir, not melancholy absolutely, but a little thoughtful, I confess. I was looking back to our boyish days, when I, the Laird's son, and you the parson's, roamed about our native hills, happy and careless boys, taking little heed to the future, and then have followed some thoughts, that may be a little painful, concerning that future, as it has turned out to be."

"Surely, Lundie, ye do not complain of your portion of it. You've risen to be a Major, and will soon be a Lt.-Colonel, if letters tell the truth, while I am just one step higher than when your honored father gave me my first commission, and a poor deevil of a Quarter Master!"

"And, the four wives."

"Three, Lundie; three only that were legal, even under our own liberal and sanctified laws."

"Well, then, let it be three. Ye know, Davy," said Major Duncan, insensibly dropping into the pronunciation and dialect of his youth, as is much the practice with educated Scotchmen, as they warm with a subject that comes near the heart,—"Ye know, Davy, that my own choice has long been made, and in how anxious and hope-wearied a manner, I've waited for that happy hour when I can call the woman I've so long loved a wife; and, here, have you, without fortune, name, birth, or merit—I mean particular merit—"

"Na—na—dinna say that, Lundie—the Muirs are of gude bluid."

"Well then, without aught but bluid, ye've wived four times—"

"I tall ye, but thrice, Lundie. Ye'll weaken auld frindship, if ye call it four."

"Put it at ye'r own number, Davy, and its far more than ye'r share. Our lives have been very different on the score of matrimony, at least; you must allow that, my old friend."

"And which do you think has been the gainer, Major, speaking as frankly the'gither, as we did when lads."

"Nay, I've nothing to conceal. My days have passed, in hope deferred, while yours have passed in—"

"Not in hope realized, I give you my honor, Major Duncan," interrupted the Quarter Master. "Each new experiment I have thought might prove an advantage, but disappointment seems the lot of man. Ah! this is a vain world of ours,

Lundie, it must be owned, and in nothing vainer than in matrimony."

"And yet you are ready to put your neck into the noose for the fifth time!"

"I desire to say, it will be but the fourth, Major Duncan," said the Quarter Master, positively; then instantly changing the expression of his face to one of boyish rapture, he added—"But this Mabel Dunham, is a rara avis! Our Scotch lassies are fair and pleasant, but it must be owned these colonials are of surpassing comeliness."

"You will do well to recollect your commission and blood, Davy; I believe all four of your wives—"

"I wish my dear Lundie, ye'd be more accurate in your arithmetick—three times one, make three."

"All three, then, were what might be termed gentlewomen."

"That's just it, Major. Three were gentlewomen, as you say, and the connections were suitable."

"And the fourth being the daughter of my father's gardener, the connection was unsuitable. But have you no fear that marrying the child of a non-commissioned officer, who is in the same corps with yourself, will have the effect to lessen your consequence in the regiment?"

"That's just been my weakness through life, Major Duncan; for I've always married without regard to consequences. Every man has his besetting sin, and matrimony, I fear is mine. And, now, that we have discussed what may be called the principles of the connection, I will just ask, if you did me the favor to speak to the Serjeant on the trifling affair?"

"I did, David, and am sorry to say for your hopes, that I see no great chances of your succeeding."

"Not succeeding!—An officer, and a Quarter Master, in the bargain, and not succeed with a serjeant's daughter."

"It's just that, Davy."

"And why not, Lundie?—Will you have the goodness to answer, just that?"

"The girl is betrothed. Hand plighted, word passed, love pledged—no, hang me if I believe that either, but she is betrothed."

"Well that's an obstacle, it must be avowed, Major, though it counts for little, if the heart is free."

"Quite true, and I think it probable the heart is free, in this case, for the intended husband appears to be the choice of the father, rather than of the daughter."

"And who may it be, Major," asked the Quarter Master, who viewed the whole matter, with the philosophy and coolness that are acquired by use. "I do not recollect any plausible suitor, that is likely to stand in my way."

"No, *you* are the only *plausible* suitor on the frontier, Davy. The happy man is Pathfinder."

"Pathfinder, Major Duncan!"

"No more, nor any less, David Muir. Pathfinder is the man, but it may relieve your jealousy a little, to know that, in my judgment at least, it is a match of the father's, rather than of the daughter's seeking."

"I thought as much!" exclaimed the Quarter Master, drawing a long breath, like one who felt relieved; "it's quite impossible, that with my experience in human nature,—"

"Particularly hu-woman's nature, David!"

"Ye will have yer joke, Lundie, lat who will suffer! But I did not think it possible I could be deceived as to the young woman's inclinations, which I think I may boldly pronounce to be altogether above the condition of Pathfinder. As for the individual himself, why time will show."

"Now, tell me frankly, Davy Muir," said Lundie, stopping short in his walk, and looking the other earnestly in the face, with a comical expression of surprise, that rendered the veteran's countenance ludicrously earnest—"do you really suppose, a girl like the daughter of Serjeant Dunham, can take a serious fancy to a man of your years, and appearance, and experience, I might add?"

"Hout, awa', Lundie, ye dinna know the sax, and that's the reason yer unmarried in yer forty fifth year. It's a fearfu' time ye've been a bachelor, Major!"

"And what may be *your* age, Lt. Muir, if I may presume to ask so delicate a question?"

"Forty seven, I'll no deny it, Lundie, and if I get Mabel, there'll be just a wife for every twa lustrums! But I did'na think Serjeant Dunham would be so humble-minded, as to dream of giving that sweet lass of his to one like the Pathfinder!"

"There's no dream about it, Davy; the man is as serious as a soldier about to be flogged."

"Well, well, Major, we are auld friends—" both ran into the Scotch, or avoided it, as they approached or drew away from their younger days, in the dialogue, "and ought to know how to take and give a joke off duty. It is possible the worthy man has not understood my hints, or he never would have thought of such a thing. The difference between an officer's consort, and a guide's woman is as vast, as that between the antiquity of Scotland and the antiquity of America. I'm auld bluid, too, Lundie."

"Take my word for it, Davy, your antiquity will do you no good, in this affair, and as for your blood it is not older than your bones. Well, well, man, ye know the Serjeant's answer, and so you perceive that my influence, on which you counted so much, can do nought for ye.—Let us take a glass the'gither Davy, for auld acquaintance sake, and then ye'll be doing well to remember the party that marches the morrow, and to forget Mabel Dunham as fast as ever you can."

"Ah! Major, I have always found it easier to forget a wife, than to forget a sweetheart! When a couple are fairly married, all is settled but the death, as one may say, which must finally part us all, and it seems to me awfu' irreverent to disturb the departed; whereas, there is so much anxiety, and hope, and felicity in expectation, like, with the lassie, that it keeps thought alive."

"That is just my idea of your situation, Davy, for I never supposed you expected any more felicity with either of your wives. Now, I've heard of fellows who were so stupid as to look forward to happiness with their wives, even beyond the grave. I drink to your success, or to your speedy recovery from this attack, Lieutenant, and admonish you to be more cautious in the future, as some of these violent cases may yet carry you off."

"Many thanks, my dear Major, and a speedy termination to an old courtship, of which I know something. This is real Mountain Dew, Lundie, and it warms the heart, like a gleam of bonny Scotland. As for the men you've just mentioned, they could have had but one wife apiece, for where there are several, the deeds of the women, themselves, may carry them different ways. I think a reasonable husband ought to be satisfied with passing his allotted time with any particular wife, in this world, and not to go about moping for things unattainable. I'm infinitely obliged to you, Major Duncan, for this and all your other acts of friendship, and if you could but add another, I should think you had not altogether forgotten the play-fellow of your boyhood."

"Well, Davy, if the request be reasonable, and such as a superior ought to grant, out with it, man."

"If ye could only contrive a little service for me, down among the Thousand Isles, for a fortnight, or so, I think this matter might be settled to the satisfaction of all parties. Just remember, Lundie, the lassie is the only marriageable white female on this frontier!"

"There is always duty for one in your line at a post however small, but this below can be done by the Serjeant as well as by the Quarter Master General, and better too."

"But not better than by a regimental officer. There is great waste, in common, among the orderlies."

"I'll think of it, Muir," said the Major laughing, "and you shall have my answer in the morning. Here will be a fine occasion, man, the morrow, to show yourself off before the lady; you are expert with the rifle, and prizes are to be won. Make up your mind to display your skill, and who knows what may yet happen before the Scud sails."

"I'm thinking most of the young men will try their hands in this sport, Major."

"That will they, and some of the old ones, too, if you appear. To keep you in countenance, I'll try a shot or two myself, Davy, and you know I have some name that way."

"It might, indeed, do good! The female heart, Major Duncan, is susceptible in many different modes, and sometimes in a way that the rules of philosophy might reject. Some require a suitor to sit down before them, as it might be in a regular siege, and only capitulate when the place can hold out no longer; others again like to be carried by storm, while there are hussies who can only be caught by leading them into an ambush. The former is the most creditable and officer-like process, perhaps, but I must say I think the last the most pleasing."

"An opinion formed from experience, out of all question. And what of the storming parties?"

"They may do for younger men, Lundie," returned the Quarter Master, rising and winking, a liberty that he often took with his commanding officer, on the score of a long intimacy; "every period of life has its necessities, and at forty seven it's just as well to trust a little to the head. I wish you a verry good even, Major Duncan, and freedom from gout, with a sweet and refreshing sleep."

"The same to yourself, Mr. Muir, with many thanks. Remember the passage of arms for the morrow."

The Quarter Master withdrew, leaving Lundie in his library to reflect on what had just passed. Use had so accustomed Major Duncan to Lt. Muir, and all his traits and humours, that the conduct of the latter did not strike the former with the same force, as it will probably strike the reader. In truth, while all men act under one common law that is termed human nature, the varieties in their dispositions, modes of judging, feelings and selfishness are infinite.

Chapter XI

"Compel the hawke, to sit that is unmann'd,
Or make the hound, untaught to draw the deere,
Or bring the free, against his will in band,
Or move the sad, a pleasant tale to heere,
Your time is lost, and you no whit the neere!
So love ne learnes, of force the heart to knit:
She serves but those, that feel sweet fancies fit."

Churchyard, *A Mirror for Magistrates*,
"Shore's Wife," ll. 127–33.

IT IS NOT OFTEN that hope is rewarded by fruition, as completely as the wishes of the young men of the garrison were met by the state of the weather, on the succeeding day. It may be no more than the ordinary waywardness of man, but the Americans are a little accustomed to taking pride in things, that the means of intelligent comparisons would probably show, were in reality of a very inferior quality, while they overlook, or undervalue advantages that place them certainly on a level with, if not above most of their fellow creatures. Among the latter is the climate, which, as a whole, though far from perfect, is infinitely more agreeable, and quite as healthy, as those of most of the countries which are loudest in their denunciations of it. The heats of summer were little felt at Oswego, at the period of which we are writing, for the shade of the forest added to the refreshing breezes from the lake, so far reduced the influence of the sun, as to render the nights always cool, and the days seldom oppressive.

It was now September, a month in which the strong gales of the coast often appear to force themselves across the country as far as the great lakes, where the inland sailor sometimes feels that genial influence which characterizes the winds of the ocean, invigorating his frame, cheering his spirits, and arousing his moral force. Such a day was that on which the garrison of Oswego assembled, to witness what its commander had jocularly called a "passage of arms." Lundie was a scholar, in military matters at least, and it was one of his sources of honest pride to direct the reading and thoughts of the young men under his orders, to the more intellectual parts of their profession. For one in his situation, his library was both good and extensive, and its books were freely lent to all who desired to use them. Among other whims that had found their way into the garrison, through these means, was a relish for the sort of amusement in which it was now about to indulge, and around which, some chronicles of the days of chivalry had induced them to throw a parade and romance, that were not unsuited to the characters and habits of soldiers, or to the insulated and wild post, occupied by this particular garrison. While so earnestly bent on pleasure, however, they on whom that duty devolved, did not neglect the safety of the garrison. One standing on the ramparts of the fort, and gazing on the waste of glittering water that bounded the view all along the northern horizon, and on the slumbering and seemingly boundless forest, that filled the other half of the panorama, would have fancied the spot the very abode of peacefulness and security; but Duncan of Lundie too well knew that the woods might at any moment give up their hundreds bent on the destruction of the fort and all it contained, and that even the treacherous lake offered a highway of easy approach, by which his more civilized, and scarcely less wily foes, the French, could come upon him, at an unwelcome and unguarded moment. Parties were sent out, under old and vigilant officers, men who cared little for the sports of the day, to scour the forest, and one entire company held the fort, under arms, with orders to maintain a vigilance as strict as if an enemy of superior force was known to be near. With these precautions, the remainder of the officers and men abandoned themselves, without apprehension, to the business of the morning.

The spot selected for the sports, was a sort of esplanade a little west of the fort, and on the immediate bank of the lake. It had been cleared of its trees and stumps, that it might answer the purpose of a parade ground, as it possessed the advantage of having its rear protected by the water, and one of its flanks by the works. Men drilling on it, could be attacked, consequently, on two sides only, and as the cleared space beyond it, in the direction of the west and south, was large, any assailants would be compelled to quit the cover of the woods, before they could make an approach sufficiently near to render them dangerous.

Although the regular arms of the regiment were muskets, some fifty rifles were produced on the present occasion. Every officer had one, as a part of his private provision for amusement, many belonged to the scouts and friendly Indians, of whom more or less were always hanging about the post, and there was a public provision of them, for the use of those who followed the game with the express object of obtaining supplies. Among those who carried the weapon were some five or six, who had reputations for knowing how to use it particularly well—so well indeed as to have given them a celebrity on the frontier—twice that number who were believed to be much better than common, and many who would have been thought expert, in almost any situation, but the precise one in which they now happened to be placed.

The distance was a hundred yards, and the weapon was to be used without a rest. The target a board, with the customary circular lines in white paint, having the bull's eye in the centre. The first trials in skill commenced with challenges among the more ignoble of the competitors, to display their steadiness and dexterity in idle competition. None but the common men, engaged in this strife, which had little to interest the spectators, among whom no officer had yet appeared.

Most of the soldiers were Scotch, the regiment having been raised at Stirling and its vicinity, not many years before, though, as in the case of Serjeant Dunham, many Americans had joined it since its arrival in the colonies. As a matter of course, the provincials were generally the most expert marksmen, and after a desultory trial of half an hour, it was necessarily conceded that a youth, who had been born in the colony of New York, and who, coming of Dutch extraction, bore the euphonious name of Van Valtenburg, but was familiarly called Follock, was the most expert of all who had yet tried their skill. It was just as this opinion prevailed, that the oldest captain, accompanied by most of the gentlemen and ladies of the fort, appeared on the parade. A train of some twenty females of humbler condition followed, among whom was seen the well turned form, intelligent, blooming, animated countenance, and neat, becoming attire of Mabel Dunham.

Of females who were officially recognised as belonging to the class of ladies, there were but three in the fort, all of whom were officers' wives; staid matronly women, with the simplicity of the habits of middle life, singularly mixed in their deportment, with their notions of professional superiority, the rights and duties of caste, and the etiquette of rank. The other women were the wives of non-commissioned officers and privates, Mabel being strictly, as had been stated by the Quarter Master, the only real candidate for matrimony among her sex. There were a dozen other girls it is true, but they were still classed among the children, none of them being yet of an age to elevate them into objects of legitimate admiration.

Some little preparation had been made for the proper reception of the females, who were placed on a low staging of planks, near the immediate bank of the lake. In their vicinity the prizes were suspended from a post. Great care was taken to reserve the front seat of the stage, for the three ladies and their children, while Mabel, and those who belonged to the non-commissioned officers of the regiment, occupied the second. The wives and daughters of the privates, were huddled together in the rear, some standing and some sitting as they could find room. Mabel, who had already been admitted to the society of the officers' wives, on the footing of a humble companion, was a good deal noticed by the ladies in front, who had a proper appreciation of modest self-respect and gentle refinement, though they were all fully aware of the value of rank, more particularly in a garrison.

As soon as this important portion of the spectators had got into their places, Lundie gave orders for the trial of skill to proceed, in the manner that had been prescribed in his previous orders. Some eight or ten of the best marksmen of the garrison now took possession of the stand, and began to fire in succession. Among them were officers and men, indiscriminately placed, nor were the casual visiters in the fort excluded from the competition. As might have been expected, of men, whose amusements and comfortable subsistence equally depended on skill in the use of their weapons, it was soon found that they were all sufficiently expert to hit the bull's eye, or the white spot in the centre of the target. Others, who succeeded them, it is true were less sure, their bullets striking in the different circles that surrounded the centre of the target, without touching it.

According to the rules of the day, none could proceed to the second trial who had failed in the first, and the adjutant of the place, who acted as master of the ceremonies or marshal of the day, called upon the successful adventurers by name, to get ready for the next effort, while he gave notice that those who failed to present themselves for the shot at the bull's eye, would necessarily be excluded from all the higher trials. Just at this moment, Lundie, the Quarter Master, and Jasper Eau douce appeared in the group at the stand, while the Pathfinder walked leisurely on the ground, without his beloved rifle, for him a measure so unusual as to be understood by all present, as a proof that he did not consider himself a competitor for the honors of the day. All made way as he approached the stand, for Major Duncan, who, in a good-humoured way took his station, levelled his rifle carelessly and fired. The bullet missed the required mark by several inches.

"Major Duncan is excluded from the other trials!" proclaimed the adjutant, in a voice so strong and confident, that all the elder officers and the serjeants, well understood that this failure was preconcerted, while all the younger gentlemen and the privates felt new encouragement to proceed, on account of the evident impartiality with which the laws of the sports were administered, nothing being so attractive to the unsophisticated as the appearance of rigorous justice; and nothing so rare as its actual administration.

"Now, Master Eau douce, comes your turn," said Muir, "and if you do no beat the Major, I shall say that your hand is better skilled with the oar, than with the rifle."

Jasper's handsome face flushed, he stepped upon the stand, cast a hasty glance at Mabel, whose pretty form he ascertained was bending eagerly forward, as if to note the result, dropped the barrel of his rifle, with but little apparent care into the palm of his left hand, raised the muzzle for a single instant with exceeding steadiness, and fired. The bullet passed directly through the centre of the bull's eye, much the best shot of the morning, since the others had merely touched the paint.

"Wall performed, Master Jasper," said Muir, as soon as the result was declared; "and a shot that might have done credit to an older head and a more experienced eye. I'm thinking, notwithstanding, there was some of a youngster's luck in it, for ye were no partic'lar in the aim ye took. Ye may be quick, Eau douce, in the movement, but ye'r not philosophic, nor scientifick in ye'r management of the weepon. Now, Serjeant Dunham, I'll thank you to request the ladies to give a closer attention than common, for I'm about to make that use of the rifle which may be called the intellectual. Jasper's would have killed, I allow, but then there would not have been half the satisfaction in receiving such a shot, as in receiving one that is discharged scientifically."

All this time, the Quarter Master was preparing himself for the scientifick trial, but he delayed his aim until he saw that the eye of Mabel, in common with those of her companions, was fastened on him in curiosity. As the others left him room, out of respect to his rank, no one stood near the competitor but his commanding officer, to whom he now said, in his familiar manner—

"Ye see, Lundie, that something is to be gained by exciting a female's curiosity. It's an active sentiment, is curiosity, and properly improved may lead to gentler inclinations in the end."

"Very true, Davy, but ye keep us all waiting while ye make your preparations, and here is Pathfinder drawing near to catch a lesson, from your greater experience."

"Wall, Pathfinder, and so *you* have come to get an idea, too, concerning the philosophy of shooting! I do not wish to hide my light under a bushel, and ye'r welcome to all ye'll learn. Do ye no mean to try a shot, yersel', man?"

"Why should I, Quarter Master—why should I? I want none of the prizes, and as for honor, I have had enough of that, if it's any honor to shoot better than yourself. I'm not a woman to wear a calash."

"Very true, but ye might find a woman that is precious in your eyes to wear it for ye as—"

"Come, Davy—" interrupted the Major—"your shot, or a retreat. The adjutant is getting to be impatient."

"The quarter-master's department, and the adjutant's department, are seldom compliable, Lundie, but I'm ready—stand a little aside, Pathfinder, and give the ladies an opportunity—"

Lt. Muir now took his attitude with a great deal of studied elegance, raised his rifle slowly, lowered it, raised it again, repeated the manœuvres, and fired.

"Missed the target altogether!" shouted the man whose duty it was to mark the bullets, and who had little relish for the Quarter Master's tedious science—"Missed the target!"

"It cannot be," cried Muir, his face flushing equally with indignation and shame; "it cannot be, adjutant, for I never did so awkward a thing in my life. I appeal to the ladies for a juster judgment."

"The ladies shut their eyes when you fired," exclaimed the regimental wag—"Your preparations alarmed them."

"I will na believe such a calumny of the leddies, nor sic' a reproach on my own skill," returned the Quarter Master, growing more and more Scotch, as he warmed with his feelings; "it's a conspiracy to rob a meritorious man of his dues."

"It's a dead miss, Muir," said the laughing Lundie, "and ye'll just sit down quietly with the disgrace."

"No—no—Major," Pathfinder at length observed—"the Quarter Master *is* a good shot, for a slow one, and a measured distance, though nothing extr'ornary, for raal sarvice. He has covered Jasper's bullet, as will be seen, if any one will take the trouble to examine the target."

The respect for Pathfinder's skill, and for his quickness and accuracy of sight, was so profound and general, that the instant he made this declaration, the spectators began to distrust their own opinions, and a dozen rushed to the target, in order to ascertain the fact. There, sure enough, it was found that the Quarter Master's bullet had gone through the hole made by Jasper's, and that, too, so accurately as to require a minute examination to be certain of the circumstance; which, however, was soon clearly established by discovering one bullet over the other, in the stump against which the target was placed.

"I told ye, ladies, ye were about to witness the influence of science on gunnery," said the Quarter Master, advancing towards the staging occupied by the females. "Major Duncan derides the idea of mathematics entering into target shooting, but I tell him, philosophy colours, and enlarges, and improves, and dilates, and explains every thing that belongs to human life, whather it be a shooting match or a sermon. In a word philosophy is philosophy, and that is saying all that the subject requires."

"I trust you exclude love from the catalogue," observed the wife of a captain, who knew the history of the Quarter Master's marriages, and who had a woman's malice against the monopolizer of her sex—"it seems that philosophy has little in common with love."

"You would'n't say that, madam, if your heart had experienced many trials. It's the man, or the woman that has had many occasions to improve the affections, that can best speak of such matters, and, believe me, of all love, philosophical is the most lasting, as it is the most rational."

"You would then recommend experience as an improvement on the passion?"

"Your quick mind has conceived the idea at a glance. The happiest marriages are those in which youth, and beauty, and confidence, on one side, rely on the sagacity, moderation and prudence of years—middle age, I mean, madam, for I'll no deny that there is such a thing as a husband's being too old for a wife. Here is Serjeant Dunham's charming daughter, now, to approve of such sentiments, I'm certain, her character for discretion being already well established in the garrison, short as has been her residence among us."

"Serjeant Dunham's daughter, is scarcely a fitting interlocutor in a discourse between you and me, Lt. Muir," rejoined the captain's lady, with a careful respect for her own dignity, "and yonder is the Pathfinder about to take his chance, by way of changing the subject."

"I protest. Major Duncan, I protest—" cried Muir, hurrying back towards the stand, with both arms elevated by way of enforcing his words—"I protest in the strongest terms, gentlemen, against Pathfinder's being admitted into these sports with Killdeer, which is a piece, to say nothing of long habit, that is altogether out of proportion, for a trial of skill against government rifles."

"Killdeer is taking its rest, Quarter Master," returned Pathfinder, calmly, "and no one here thinks of disturbing it. I did not think, myself, of pulling a trigger to day, but Sarjeant Dunham has been persuading me that I shall not do proper honor to his handsome daughter, who came in under my care, if I am backward on such an occasion. I'm using Jasper's rifle, Quarter Master, as you may see, and that is no better than your own."

Lt. Muir was now obliged to acquiesce, and every eye turned towards the Pathfinder, as he took the required station. The air and attitude of this celebrated guide and hunter were extremely fine, as he raised his tall form, and levelled the piece, showing perfect self-command, and a thorough knowledge of the power of the human frame, as well as of the weapon. Pathfinder was not what is usually termed a handsome man, though his appearance excited so much confidence and commanded respect. Tall, and even muscular, his frame might have been esteemed nearly perfect, were it not for the total absence of every thing like flesh. Whip-cord was scarcely more rigid than his arms and legs, or, at need, more pliable; but the outlines of his person were rather too angular for the proportions that the eye most approves. Still, his motions being natural were graceful, and being calm and regulated, they gave him an air of dignity that associated well with the idea that was so prevalent, of his services and peculiar merits. His honest, open features were burnt to a bright red, that comported well with the notion of exposure and hardships, while his sinewy hands denoted force and a species of use that was removed from the stiffening and deforming effects of labor. Although no one perceived any of those gentler, or more insinuating qualities, which are apt to win upon a woman's affections, as he poised his rifle, not a female eye was fastened on him, without a silent approbation of the freedom of his movements, and the manliness of his air. Thought was scarcely quicker than his aim, and, as the smoke floated above his head, the breech of the rifle was seen on the ground, the hand of the Pathfinder was leaning on the barrel, and his honest countenance was illuminated by his usual silent, hearty laugh.

"If one dared to hint at such a thing," cried Major Duncan, "I should say that the Pathfinder had also missed the target!"

"No—no—Major," returned the guide, confidently. "That *would* be a risky declaration. I did'n't load the piece, and can't say what was in it; but if it was lead, you will find the bullet driving down those of the Quarter Master's and Jasper's; else is not my name, Pathfinder."

A shout from the target announced the truth of this assertion.

"That's not all—that's not all, boys," called out the guide, who was now slowly advancing towards the stage occupied by the females—"if you find the target touched at all, I'll own to a miss. The Quarter Master cut the wood, but you'll find no wood cut, by that last messenger."

"Very true, Pathfinder, very true," answered Muir, who was lingering near Mabel, though ashamed to address her particularly, in the presence of the officers' wives. "The Quarter Master did cut the wood, and by that means he opened a passage for your bullet, which went through the hole he had made."

"Well, Quarter Master, there goes the nail, and we'll see who can drive it closest, you or I; for, though I did not think of showing what a rifle can do to day, now my hand is in, I'll turn my back to no man that carries King George's commission. Chingachgook is outlying, or he might force me into some of the niceties of the art, but as for you, Quarter Master, if the nail don't stop you, the potatoe will."

"You're over boastful this morning, Pathfinder, but you'll find you've no green boy, fresh from the settlements and the towns, to deal with, I will assure ye!"

"I know that well, Quarter Master; I know that well, and shall not deny your experience. You've lived many years on the frontiers, and I've heard of you, in the colonies, and among the Injins, too, quite a human life ago."

"Na—na—" interrupted Muir, in his broadest Scotch, "this is injustice, man. I've no lived so very long, neither."

"I'll do you justice, lieutenant, even if you get the best in the potatoe trial. I say you've passed a good human life, for a soldier, in places where the rifle is daily used, and I know you are a creditable and ingenious marksman; but then you are not a true rifle shooter. As for boasting, I hope I'm not a vain talker about my own exploits, but a man's gifts are his gifts, and it's flying in the face of Providence to deny them. The sarjeant's daughter, here, shall judge atween us, if you have the stomach to submit to so pretty a judge."

The Pathfinder had named Mabel as the arbiter, because he admired her, and because, in his eyes, rank had little or no value, but Lt. Muir shrunk at such a reference in the presence of the wives of officers. He would gladly keep himself constantly before the eyes and the imagination of the object of his wishes, but he was still too much under the influence of old prejudices, and perhaps too wary, to appear openly as her suitor, unless he saw something very like a certainty of success. On the discretion of Major Duncan he had a full reliance; and he apprehended no betrayal from that quarter; but he was quite aware, should it ever get abroad that he had been refused by the child of a non-commissioned officer, he would find great difficulty in making his approaches to any other woman of a condition to which he might reasonably aspire. Notwithstanding these doubts and misgivings, Mabel looked so prettily, blushed so charmingly, smiled so sweetly, and altogether presented so winning a picture of youth, spirit, modesty and beauty, that he found it exceedingly tempting to be kept so prominently before her imagination, and to be able to address her freely.

"You shall have it your own way, Pathfinder," he answered as soon as his doubts had settled down into determination—"Let the Serjeant's daughter—his charming daughter, I should have termed her—be the umpire then, and to her we will both dedicate the prize, that one or the other must certainly win. Pathfinder must be humored, ladies, as you perceive, else, no doubt, we should have had the honor to submit ourselves to one of your charming society."

A call for the competitors, now drew the Quarter Master and his adversary away, and in a few moments the second trial of skill commenced. A common wrought nail was driven lightly into the target, its head having been first touched with paint, and the marksman was required to hit it, or he lost his chances in the succeeding trials. No one was permitted to enter, on this occasion, who had already failed in the essay against the bull's eye.

There might have been half a dozen aspirants for the honors of this trial, one or two who had barely succeeded in touching the spot of paint, in the previous strife, preferring to rest their reputations there, feeling certain that they could not succeed, in the greater effort that was now exacted of them. The three first adventurers failed, all coming quite near the mark, but neither touching it. The fourth person who presented himself was the Quarter Master, who, after going through his usual attitudes, so far succeeded as to carry away a small portion of the head of the nail, planting his bullet by the side of its point. This was not considered an extraordinary shot, though it brought the adventurer within the category.

"You've saved your bacon, Quarter Master, as they say in the settlements of their creatur's," cried Pathfinder laughing, "but it would take a long time to build a house with a hammer no better than yourn. Jasper, here, will show you how a nail is to be started, or the lad has lost some of his steadiness of hand, and sartainty of eye. You would have done better yourself, Lieutenant, had you not been so much bent on so'gerizing your figure. Shooting is a nat'ral gift, and is to be exercised in a nat'ral way."

"We shall see, Pathfinder; I call that a pretty attempt at a nail, and I doubt if the 55th has another hammer, as you call it, that can do just the same thing, over again."

"Jasper is not in the 55th, but there goes his rap!"

As the Pathfinder spoke, the bullet of Eau douce hit the nail square, and drove it into the target, within an inch of the head.

"Be all ready to clench it, boys," cried out Pathfinder, stepping into his friend's tracks the instant they were vacant. "Never mind a new nail; I can see that, though the paint is gone, and what I can see, I can hit at a hundred yards, though it were only a mosquitoe's eye. Be ready to clench!"

The rifle cracked, the bullet sped its way, and the head of the nail was buried in the wood, covered by the piece of flattened lead.

"Well, Jasper, lad," continued Pathfinder, dropping the breech of his rifle to the ground, and resuming the discourse, as if he thought nothing of his own exploit, "you improve daily. A few more tramps on land, in my company, and the best marksman on the frontiers will have occasion to look keenly, when he takes his stand ag'in you. The Quarter Master is respectable, but he will never get any farther, whereas you, Jasper, have the gift, and may one day defy any who pull trigger."

"Hoot—hoot!" exclaimed Muir, "do you call hitting the head of a nail respectable only, when it's the perfection of the art! Any one, in the least refined and elevated in sentiment, knows that the delicate touches denote the master, whereas your sledge-hammer blows come from the rude and uninstructed. If 'a miss is as good as a mile,' a hit ought to be better, Pathfinder, whether it wound or kill."

"The surest way of settling this rivalry, will be to make another trial," observed Lundie; "and that will be of the potatoe. You're Scotch, Mr. Muir, and might fare better were it a cake or a thistle, but frontier law has declared for the American fruit, and the potatoe, it shall be."

As Major Duncan manifested some impatience of manner, Muir had too much tact to delay the sports any longer, with his discursive remarks, but judiciously prepared himself for the next appeal. To say the truth, the Quarter Master had little, or no faith in his own success in the trial of skill that was to follow, nor would he have been so free in presenting himself as a competitor, at all, had he anticipated it would have been made, but Major Duncan, who was somewhat of a humorist, in his own quiet Scotch way, had secretly ordered it to be introduced, expressly to mortify him; for, a Laird himself, Lundie did not relish the notion that one who might claim to be a gentleman, should bring discredit on his caste by forming an unequal alliance. As soon as every thing was prepared, Muir was summoned to the stand, and the potatoe was held in readiness to be thrown. As the sort of feat we are about to offer to the reader, however, may be new to him, a word in explanation will render the matter more clear. A potatoe of large size was selected, and given to one, who stood at the distance of twenty yards from the stand. At the word "heave," which was given by the marksman, the vegetable was thrown, with a gentle toss, into the air, and it was the business of the adventurer to cause a ball to pass through it, before it reached the ground.

The Quarter Master, in a hundred experiments, had once succeeded in accomplishing this difficult feat, but he now essayed to perform it again, with a sort of blind hope, that was fated to be disappointed. The potatoe was thrown in the usual manner, the rifle was discharged, but the flying target was untouched.

"To the right-about, and fall out, Quarter Master," said Lundie, smiling at the success of his own artifice—"The honor of the silken calash will lie between Jasper Eau douce and Pathfinder."

"And how is the trial to end, Major?" enquired the latter. "Are we to have the two potatoe trial, or is it to be settled by centre and skin?"

"By centre and skin, if there is any perceptible difference; otherwise the double shot must follow."

"This is an awful moment to me, Pathfinder," observed Jasper, as he moved towards the stand, his face actually losing its colour in intensity of feeling.

Pathfinder gazed earnestly at the young man, and then begging Major Duncan to have patience for a moment he led his friend out of the hearing of all near him, before he spoke.

"You seem to take this matter to heart, Jasper?" the hunter remarked keeping his eyes fastened on those of the youth.

"I must own, Pathfinder, that my feelings were never before so much bound up in success."

"And do you so much crave to outdo me, an old and tried friend, and, that, as it might be, in my own way? Shooting is my gift, boy, and no common hand can equal mine!"

"I know it—I know it, Pathfinder—but—yet—"

"But what, Jasper, boy;—speak freely; you talk to a friend."

The young man compressed his lips, dashed a hand across his eye, and flushed and paled, alternately like a girl, confessing her love. Then squeezing the other's hand he said calmly, like one whose manhood has overcome all other sensations—

"I would lose an arm, Pathfinder, to be able to make an offering of that calash to Mabel Dunham."

The hunter dropped his eyes to the ground, and as he

walked slowly back towards the stand, he seemed to ponder deeply on what he had just heard.

"You never could succeed in the double trial, Jasper?" he suddenly remarked.

"Of that I am certain, and it troubles me."

"What a creatur' is mortal man! He pines for things which are not of his gift, and treats the bounties of Providence lightly. No matter—no matter. Take your station, Jasper, for the Major is waiting—and, harkee, lad—I must touch the skin, for I could not show my face in the garrison with less than that."

"I suppose I must submit to my fate," returned Jasper, flushing and losing his colour, as before, "but I will make the effort, if I die."

"What a thing is mortal man!" repeated Pathfinder, falling back to allow his friend room to take his aim—"he overlooks his own gifts, and craves them of another!"

The potatoe was thrown, Jasper fired, and the shout that followed preceded the announcement of the fact, that he had driven his bullet through its centre, or so nearly so, as to merit that award.

"Here is a competitor worthy of you, Pathfinder," cried Major Duncan with delight, as the former took his station, "and we may look to some fine shooting, in the double trial."

"What a thing is mortal man!" repeated the hunter, scarce seeming to notice what was passing around him, so much were his thoughts absorbed in his own reflections—"Toss."

The potatoe was tossed, the rifle cracked, it was remarked just as the little black ball seemed stationary in the air, for the marksman evidently took unusual heed to his aim, and then a look of disappointment and wonder succeeded among those who caught the falling target.

"Two holes in one?" called out the Major.

"The skin—the skin—" was the answer—"only the skin!"

"How's this, Pathfinder! Is Jasper Eau douce to carry off the honors of the day!"

"The calash is hisn," returned the other, shaking his head, and walking quietly away from the stand. "What a creatur' is a mortal man! Never satisfied with his own gifts, but forever craving that which Providence denies!"

As Pathfinder had not buried his bullet in the potatoe, but had cut through the skin, the prize was immediately adjudged to Jasper. The calash was in the hands of the latter, when the Quarter Master approached, and with a politic air of cordiality, he wished his successful rival, joy for his victory.

"But now you've got the calash, lad, it's of no use to you," he added; "it will never make a sail, nor even an ensign. I'm thinking, Eau douce, you'd no be sorry to see its value in good siller of the King?"

"Money cannot buy it, Lieutenant," returned Jasper, whose eye lighted up with all the fire of success and joy. "I would rather have won this calash, than have obtained fifty new suits of sails for the Scud!"

"Hoot—hoot—lad; you are going mad, like all the rest of them. I'd even venture to offer half a guinea for the trifle, rather than it should lie kicking about in the cabin of your cutter, and, in the end, become an ornament for the head of a squaw."

Although Jasper did not know that the wary Quarter Master had not offered half the actual cost of the prize, he heard the proposition with indifference. Shaking his head in the negative, he advanced towards the stage, where his approach excited a little commotion, the officers' ladies, one and all, having determined to accept the present should the gallantry of the young sailor induce him to offer it. But Jasper's diffidence, no less than admiration for another, would have prevented him from aspiring to the honor of complimenting any whom he thought so much his superiors.

"Mabel," he said, "this prize is for you, unless—"

"Unless, what, Jasper—" answered the girl, losing her own bashfulness, in the natural and generous wish to relieve his embarrassment, though both reddened in a way to betray strong feeling.

"Unless you may think too indifferently of it, because it is offered by one who may have no right to believe his gift will be accepted."

"I do accept it, Jasper, and it shall be a sign of the danger I have passed in your company, and of the gratitude I feel for your care of me—your care and that of the Pathfinder."

"Never mind me, never mind me," exclaimed the latter; "this is Jasper's luck and Jasper's gift, give him full credit for both. My turn may come another day; mine and the Quarter Master's, who seems to grudge the boy the calash, though what *he* can want of it, I cannot understand, for he has no wife."

"And has Jasper Eau douce a wife? Or have you a wife, yoursel', Pathfinder? I may want it to help get a wife, or as a memorial that I have had a wife, or as a proof how much I admire the sex, or because it is a female garment, or for some other equally respectable motive. It's not the unreflecting that are the most prized by the thoughtful, and there is no surer sign that a man made a good husband to his first consort, let me tell ye all, than to see him speedily looking round for a competent successor. The affections are good gifts from Providence, and they that have loved one faithfully, prove how much of this bounty has been lavished upon them, by loving another as soon as possible."

"It may be so—it may be so. I am no practitioner in such things, and cannot gainsay it. But Mabel, here, the sarjeant's daughter, will give you full credit for the words. Come, Jasper, although our hands are out, let us see what the other lads can do with the rifle."

Pathfinder and his companions retired, for the sports were about to proceed. The ladies, however, were not so much engrossed with rifle shooting as to neglect the calash. It passed from hand to hand; the silk was felt, the fashion criticised and the work examined, and divers opinions were privately ventured concerning the fitness of so handsome a thing's passing into the possession of a non-commissioned officer's child.

"Perhaps you will be disposed to sell that calash, Mabel, when it has been a short time in your possession?" inquired the captain's lady—"Wear it, I should think, you never can."

"I may not wear it, madam," returned our heroine modestly, "but I should not like to part with it, either."

"I dare say Serjeant Dunham keeps you above the necessity of selling your clothes, child, but, at the same time, it is money thrown away to keep an article of dress you can never wear."

"I should be unwilling to part with the gift of a friend."

"But the young man himself, will think all the better of you, for your prudence, after the triumph of the day is forgotten. It is a pretty and a becoming calash, and ought not to be thrown away."

"I've no intention to throw it away, ma'am, and, if you please, would rather keep it."

"As you will child; girls of your age often overlook their real advantages. Remember, however, if you do determine to dispose of the thing, that it is bespoke, and that I will not take it, if you ever even put it on your own head."

"Yes, ma'am," said Mabel, in the meekest voice imaginable, though her eyes looked like diamonds and her cheeks reddened to the tints of two roses, as she placed the forbidden garment over her well turned shoulders, where she kept it a minute, as if to try its fitness, and then quietly removed it, again.

The remainder of the sports offered nothing of interest. The shooting was reasonably good, but the trials were all of a scale lower than those related, and the competitors were soon left to themselves. The ladies, and most of the officers withdrew, and the remainder of the females soon followed their example. Mabel was returning along the low flat rocks that line the shore of the lake, dangling her pretty calash from a prettier finger, when Pathfinder met her. He carried the rifle which he had used that day, but his manner had less of the frank ease of the hunter about it, than usual, while his eye seemed roving and uneasy. After a few unmeaning words concerning the noble sheet of water before them, he turned towards his companion with strong interest in his countenance, and said—

"Jasper earned that calash for you, Mabel, without much trial of his gifts."

"It was fairly done, Pathfinder."

"No doubt—no doubt. The bullet passed neatly through the potatoe, and no man could have done more; though others might have done as much."

"But no one did as much!" exclaimed Mabel with an animation that she instantly regretted, for she saw by the pained look of the guide that he was mortified equally by the remark, and by the feeling with which it was uttered.

"It is true—it is true, Mabel, no one did as much there, but—yes, there is no reason I should deny my gifts which come from Providence—yes, yes; no one did as much there, but you shall know what *can* be done here. Do you observe the gulls that are flying over our heads?"

"Certainly, Pathfinder—there are too many to escape notice."

"Here, where they cross each other, in sailing about—" he added, cocking and raising his rifle—"the two—the two—now look!"

The piece was presented quick as thought, as two of the birds came in a line, though distant from each other many yards, the report followed, and the bullet passed through the bodies of both the victims. No sooner had the gulls fallen into the lake, than Pathfinder dropped the breech of the rifle, and laughed in his own peculiar manner, every shade of dissatisfaction and mortified pride having left his honest face.

"That is something, Mabel, that is something; although I've no calash to give you! But ask Jasper, himself; I'll leave it all to Jasper, for a truer tongue and heart, are not in America."

"Then it was not Jasper's fault that he gained the prize!"

"Not it. He did his best, and he did well. For one that has water gifts, rather than land gifts, Jasper is oncommonly expart, and a better backer no one need wish, ashore or afloat. But it was my fault, Mabel, that he got the calash; though it makes no difference—it makes no difference, for the thing has gone to the right person."

"I believe I understand you, Pathfinder," said Mabel, blushing in spite of herself, "and I look upon the calash as the joint gift of yourself and Jasper."

"That would not be doing justice to the lad, neither. He won the garment, and had a right to give it away. The most you may think, Mabel, is to believe that had I won it, it would have gone to the same person."

"I will remember that, Pathfinder, and take care that others know your skill, as it has been proved upon the poor gulls, in my presence."

"Lord bless you, Mabel, there is no more need of your talking in favor of my shooting, on this frontier, than of your talking about the water in the lake, or the sun in the heavens. Every body knows what I can do in that way, and your words would be thrown away, as much as French would be thrown away on an American bear."

"Then you think that Jasper knew you were giving him this advantage, of which he has so unhandsomely availed himself?" said Mabel, the colour which had imparted so much lustre to her eyes gradually leaving her face, which became grave and thoughtful.

"I do not say that, but very far from it. We all forget things that we have known, when eager after our wishes. Jasper is satisfied that I can pass one bullet through two potatoes, as I sent my bullet through the gulls, and he knows no other man on the frontier can do the same thing. But with the calash before his eyes, and the hope of giving it to you, the lad was inclined to think better of himself, just at that moment, perhaps, than he ought. No—no—there's nothing mean or distrustful about Jasper Eau douce, though it is a gift nat'ral to all young men to wish to appear well in the eyes of handsome young women."

"I'll try to forget all, but the kindness you've both shown to a poor motherless girl," said Mabel, struggling to keep down emotions that she scarcely knew how to account for, herself. "Believe me, Pathfinder, I can never forget all you have already done for me—you and Jasper—and this new proof of your regard is not thrown away. Here—here is a brooch that is of silver, and I offer it as a token that I owe you life, or liberty."

"What shall I do with this, Mabel?" asked the bewildered hunter, holding the simple trinket in his hand. "I have neither buckle nor button about me, for I wear nothing but leathern strings and them of good deer-skins. It's pretty to the eye, but it is prettier far on the spot it came from, than it can be about me."

"Nay put it in your hunting shirt; it will become it well. Remember, Pathfinder, that it is a token of friendship between us, and a sign that I can never forget you or your services."

Mabel then smiled an adieu, and bounding up the bank, she was soon lost to view behind the mounds of the fort.

Chapter XII

"Lo! dusky masses steal in dubious sight,
Along the leaguer'd wall, and bristling bank
Of the arm'd river; while with straggling light,
The stars peep through the vapour, dim and dank."
Byron, *Don Juan*, VII.LXXXVI.683–86.

A FEW HOURS LATER, Mabel Dunham was on the bastion that overlooked the river and the lake, seemingly in deep thought. The evening was calm and soft, and the question had arisen whether the party for the Thousand Islands would be able to get out that night, or not, on account of the total absence of wind. The stores, arms and ammunition were already shipped, and even Mabel's effects were on board, but the small draft of men that was to go was still ashore, there being no apparent prospect of the cutter's getting under way. Jasper had warped the Scud out of the cove, and so far up the stream as to enable him to pass through the outlet of the river whenever he chose, but there he still lay, riding at single anchor. The drafted men were lounging about the shore of the cove, undecided whether or not to pull off.

The sports of the morning had left a quiet in the garrison that was in harmony with the whole of the beautiful scene, and Mabel felt its influence on her feelings, though probably too little accustomed to speculate on such sensations, to be aware of the cause. Every thing near appeared lovely and soothing, while the solemn grandeur of the silent forest and placid expanse of the lake, lent a sublimity that other scenes might have wanted. For the first time, Mabel felt the hold that the towns and civilization had gained on her habits sensibly weakened, and the warm-hearted girl began to think that a life passed amid objects such as these around her, might be happy. How far the experience of the last ten days came in aid of that calm and holy even-tide, and contributed towards producing that young conviction, may be suspected, rather than affirmed, in this early portion of our legend.

"A charming sunset, Mabel," said the hearty voice of her uncle, so close to the ear of our heroine as to cause her to start—"a charming sunset, girl, for a fresh water concern, though we should think but little of it at sea."

"And is not nature the same, on shore, or at sea; on a lake like this, or on the ocean? Does not the sun shine on all alike, dear uncle, and can we not feel gratitude for the blessings of Providence as strongly on this remote frontier, as in our own Manhattan?"

"The girl has fallen in with some of her mother's books!—Though I should think the serjeant would scarcely make a second march with such trumpery among his baggage. Is not nature the same, indeed!—Now, Mabel, do you imagine that the nature of a soldier is the same as that of a sea-faring man?—You've relations in both callings, and ought to be able to answer."

"But, uncle, I mean human nature—"

"So do I, girl; the human nature of a seaman, and the human nature of one of these fellows of the 55th, not even excepting your own father. Here have they had a shooting match—target firing I should call it—this day, and what a different thing has it been from a target firing afloat. There we should have sprung our broadside, sported with round shot, at an object half a mile off, at the very nearest, and the potatoes, if there happened to be any on board, as quite likely would not have been the case, would have been left in the cook's coppers. It may be an honorable calling, that of a soldier, Mabel, but an experienced hand sees many follies and weaknesses in one of these forts. As for that bit of a lake, you know my opinion of it, already, and I wish to disparage nothing. No real sea-farer disparages any thing; but d——e, if I regard this here Ontario, as they call it, as more than so much water in a ship's scuttle-butt. Now, look you here, Mabel, if you wish to understand the difference between the ocean and a lake, I can make you comprehend it, with a single look. This is what one may call a calm, seeing that there is no wind, though, to own the truth, I do not think the calms are as calm as them we get outside—"

"Uncle, there is not a breath of air! I do not think it possible for the leaves to be more immoveably still than those of the entire forest are, at this very moment."

"Leaves! what are leaves, child; there are no leaves at sea.

If you wish to know whether it is a dead calm, or not, try a mould candle—your dips flaring too much—and then you may be certain whether there is, or is not, any wind. If you were in a latitude where the air was so still that you found a difficulty in stirring it to draw it in, in breathing, you might fancy it a calm. People are often on a short allowance of air, in the calm latitudes. Here, again, look at that water!—It is like milk in a pan, with no more motion than there is in a full hogshead before the bung is started. Now, on the ocean the water is never still, let the air be as quiet as it may."

"The water of the ocean never still, uncle Cap!—Not even in a calm!"

"Bless your heart, no, child. The ocean breathes like a living being, and its bosom is always heaving, as the poetizers call it, though there be no more air than is to be found in a syphon. No man ever saw the ocean still, like this lake, but it heaves and sets, as if it had lungs."

"And this lake is not absolutely still, for you perceive there is a little ripple on the shore, and you may even hear the surf, plunging, at moments, against the rocks."

"All d——d poetry! One may call a bubble a ripple, if he will, and washing decks a surf, but Lake Ontario is no more the Atlantic, than a Powles Hook periagua is a first rate. That Jasper, notwithstanding, is a fine lad, and wants instruction only to make a man of him!"

"Do you think him ignorant, uncle," answered Mabel, prettily adjusting her hair, in order to do which she was obliged, or fancied she was obliged, to turn away her face—"To me, Jasper Eau douce appears to know more than most of the young men of his class. He has read but little, for books are not plenty in this part of the world, but he has thought much; at least, so it seems to me, for one so young."

"He is ignorant, he is ignorant, as all must be who navigate an inland water, like this. He can make a flat knot and a timber hitch, it is true, but he has no more notion of crowning a cable, now, or of a carrick bend, than you have of catting an anchor. No—no—Mabel; we both owe something to Jasper and the Pathfinder, and I have been thinking how I can best serve them, for I hold ingratitude to be the vice of a hog. Some people say it is the vice of a king; but I say it is the failing of a hog, for treat the animal to your own dinner, and he would eat you for the dessert."

"Very true, dear uncle, and we ought indeed, to do all we can to express our proper sense of the services of both these brave men."

"Spoken like your mother's daughter, girl, and in a way to do credit to the Cap family. Now, I've hit upon a traverse, that will just suit all parties, and as soon as we get back from this little expedition down the lake, among them there thousand islands, and I am ready to return, it is my intention to propose it."

"Dearest uncle! this is so considerate in you, and will be so just! May I ask what your intentions are?"

"I see no reason for keeping them a secret from you, Mabel, though nothing need be said to your father about them, for the serjeant has his prejudices, and might throw difficulties in the way. Neither Jasper, nor his friend, Pathfinder, can ever make any thing hereabouts, and I propose to take both with me, down to the coast, and get them fairly afloat. Jasper would find his sea legs in a fortnight, and a twelvemonth's v'y'ge would make him a man. Although Pathfinder might take more time, or never get to be rated able, yet one could make something of him, too, particularly as a look-out, for he has unusually good eyes."

"Uncle, do you think either would consent to this!" said Mabel smiling.

"Do I suppose them simpletons! What rational being would neglect his own advancement. Let Jasper alone to push his way, and the lad may yet die the master of some square rigged craft."

"And would he be any the happier for it, dear uncle? How much better is it to be the master of a square rigged craft, than to be master of a round rigged craft?"

"Pooh—Pooh, Magnet, you do'n't know what you are talking about; you are just fit to read lectures about ships before some hysterical society. Leave these things to me, and they'll be properly managed. Ah! here is the Pathfinder himself, and I may just as well drop him a hint of my benevolent intentions, as regards himself. Hope is a great encourager of our exertions."

Cap nodded his head, and then ceased to speak, while the hunter approached, not with his usual frank and easy manner, but in a way to show that he was slightly embarrassed, if not distrustful of his reception.

"Uncle and niece make a family party," said Pathfinder, when near the two—"and a stranger may not prove a welcome companion?"

"You are no stranger, Master Pathfinder," returned Cap, "and no one can be more welcome than yourself. We were talking of you, but a moment ago, and when friends speak of an absent man, he can guess what they have said."

"I ask no secrets—I ask no secrets. Every man has his inimies, and I have mine, though I count neither you, Master Cap, nor pretty Mabel, here, among the number. As for the Mingos, I will say nothing, though they have no just cause to hate me."

"That I'll answer for, Pathfinder, for, you strike my fancy as being well disposed and upright. There is a method, however, of getting away from the enmity of even these Mingos, and if you choose to take it, no one will more willingly point it out, than myself, without a charge for my advice either."

"I wish no inimies, Saltwater," for so the Pathfinder had begun to call Cap, having insensibly to himself adopted the term by translating the name given him by the Indians, in and about the fort, "I wish no inimies. I'm as ready to bury the hatchet with the Mingos as with the French, though you know that it depends on one greater than either of us, so to turn the heart, as to leave a man without inimies."

"By lifting your anchor, and accompanying me down to the coast, friend Pathfinder, when we get back from this short cruise on which we are bound, you will find yourself beyond the sound of the war-whoop, and safe enough from any Indian bullet."

"And what should I do on the salt-water? Hunt in your towns!—Follow the trails of people going and coming from market, and ambush dogs and poultry. You are no friend to my happiness, Master Cap, if you would lead me out of the shade of the woods, to put me in the sun of the clearin's!"

"I did not propose to leave you in the settlements, Pathfinder, but to carry you out to sea, where only a man can be said to breathe freely. Mabel will tell you that such was my intention, before a word was said on the subject."

"And what does Mabel think would come of such a change? She knows that a man has his gifts, and that it is as useless to pretend to others, as to withstand them that come from Providence. I am a hunter, and a scout, or a guide, Saltwater, and it is not in me to fly so much in the face of Heaven, as to try to become any thing else. Am I right Mabel, or are you so much a woman as to wish to see a natur' altered?"

"I would wish to see no change in you, Pathfinder," Mabel answered with a cordial sincerity and frankness that went directly to the hunter's heart; "and much as my uncle admires the sea, and great as is all the good that he thinks may come of it, I could not wish to see the best and noblest hunter of the woods transformed into an admiral. Remain what you are, my brave friend, and you need fear nothing, short of the anger of God."

"Do you hear this, Saltwater?—Do you hear what the Sarjeant's daughter is saying, and she is much too upright and fair-minded, and pretty, not to think what she says. So long as she is satisfied with me as I am, I shall not fly in the face of the gifts of Providence, by striving to become any thing else. I may seem useless, here, in a garrison, but when we get down among the Thousand Islands, there may be an opportunity to prove that a sure rifle is sometimes a God-send."

"You are then to be of our party?" said Mabel, smiling so frankly and so sweetly on the guide, that he would have followed her to the end of the earth. "I shall be the only female, with the exception of one soldier's wife, and shall feel none the less secure, Pathfinder, because you will be among our protectors."

"The sarjeant would do that, Mabel; the sarjeant would do that, though you were not of his kin. No one will overlook you. I should think your uncle, here, would like an expedition of this sort, where we shall go with sails, and have a look at our inland sea?"

"Your inland sea is no great matter, Master Pathfinder, and I expect nothing from it. I confess, however, I should like to know the object of the cruise, for one does not wish to be idle, and my brother-in-law, the serjeant, is as close-mouthed as a free mason. Do you know, Mabel, what all this means?"

"Not in the least, uncle. I dare not ask my father any questions about his duty, for he thinks it is not a woman's business, and all I can say is that we are to sail as soon as the wind will permit, and that we are to be absent a month."

"Perhaps, Master Pathfinder can give me a useful hint, for a v'y'ge without an object is never pleasant to an old sailor."

"There is no great secret, Saltwater, consarning our post and object, though it is forbidden to talk much about either in the garrison. I am no soldier, howsever, and can use my tongue as I please, though as little given as another to idle conversation I hope; still, as we sail so soon, and you are both to be of the party, you may as well be told where you are to be carried. You know that there are such things as the Thousand Islands, I suppose, Master Cap?"

"Ay, what are so called, hereaway, though I take it for granted that they are not real islands, such as we fall in with on the ocean, and that the Thousand means some such matter as two or three, like the killed and wounded of a great battle."

"My eyes are good, and yet have I often been foiled in trying to count them very islands."

"Ay—ay—I've known people who could'n't count beyond a certain number. Your real land birds never know their own roosts, even, in a land fall at sea. They are what I call 'all things to all men.' How many times have I seen the beach, and houses and churches, when the passengers have not been able to see any thing but water. I have no idea that a man can get fairly out of sight of land, on fresh water. The thing appears to me to be irrational and impossible."

"You don't know the lakes, Master Cap, or you would not say that. Before we get to the Thousand Islands, you will have other notions of what natur' has done in this wilderness."

"I have my doubts whether you have such a thing as a real island in all this region. To my notion, fresh water can't make a bony fidy island; not what *I* call an island."

"We'll show you hundreds of them—not exactly a thousand, perhaps, but so many that eye cannot see them all, or tongue count them."

"And what sort of things may they be?"

"Land with water entirely around them."

"Ay, but what sort of land, and what sort of water? I'll engage, when the truth comes to be known, they'll turn out to be nothing but peninsulas, or promontories, or continents, though these are matters, I dare say, of which you know little or nothing. But islands, or no islands, what is the object of the cruise, Master Pathfinder?"

"Why as you are the sarjeant's brother, and pretty Mabel here, is his da'hter, and we are all to be of the party, there can be no harm in giving you some idea of what we are going to do. Being so old a sailor, Master Cap, you've heard, no doubt, of such a port as Frontenac?"

"Who has'n't? I will not say I've ever been inside the harbor, but I've frequently been off the place."

"Then you are about to go upon ground with which you are acquainted, though how you could ever have got there, from the ocean, I do not understand. These great lakes, you must know, make a chain, the water passing out of one into the other, until it reaches Erie, which is a sheet off here to the westward, as large as Ontario itself. Well, out of Erie the water comes, until it reaches a low mountain like, over the edge of which it passes—"

"I should like to know how the devil it can do that?"

"Why easy enough, Master Cap," returned Pathfinder laughing, "seeing that it has only to fall down hill. Had I said the water went *up* the mountain, there would have been natur' ag'in it; but we hold it no great matter for water to run down hill—that is *fresh* water."

"Ay ay—but you speak of the water of a lake's coming down the side of a mountain; it's in the teeth of reason, if reason has any teeth."

"Well—well—we will not dispute the point, but what I've seen, I've seen: as for reason's having any teeth, I'll say nothing, but conscience has, and sharp ones too. After getting into Ontario, all the water of *all* the lakes passes down into the sea, by a river, and in the narrow part of the sheet where it is neither river nor lake, lie the islands spoken of. Now, Frontenac is a post of the Frenchers above these same islands, and as they hold the garrisons below, their stores and ammunition are sent up the river to Frontenac, to be forwarded along the shores of this and the other lakes, in order to enable the inimy to play his deviltries among the savages, and to take christian scalps."

"And will our presence prevent these horrible acts?" demanded Mabel with interest.

"It may, or it may not, as Providence wills. Lundie, as they call him, he who commands this garrison, sent a party down to take a station among the islands, to cut off some of the French boats, and this expedition of ours will be the second relief. As yet they've not done much, though two batteaux loaded with Indian goods have been taken; but a runner came in, last week, and brought such tidings that the Major is about to make a last effort to sarcumvent the knaves, Jasper knows the way, and we shall be in good hands, for the Sarjeant is prudent, and of the first quality at an ambushment—yes, he is both prudent, and alert."

"Is this all!" said Cap, contemptuously—"by the preparations and equipments, I had thought there was a forced trade in the wind, and that an honest penny might be turned, by taking an adventure. I suppose there are no shares in your fresh water prize money?"

"Anan?"

"I take it for granted the King gets all, in these so'gering parties and ambushments, as you call them?"

"I know nothing about that, Master Cap. I take my share of the lead and powder, if any falls into our hands, and say nothing to the King about it. If any one fares better, it is not I—though it is time I did begin to think of a house, and furniture, and a home."

Although the Pathfinder did not dare to look at Mabel, while he made this direct allusion to his change of life, he would have given the world to know whether she were listening, and what was the expression of her countenance. Mabel little suspected the nature of the allusion, however, and her countenance was perfectly unembarrassed, as she turned her eyes towards the river, where the appearance of some movement on board the Scud, began to be visible.

"Jasper is bringing the cutter out," observed the guide, whose look was drawn in the same direction, by the fall of some heavy article on the deck. "The lad sees the signs of wind no doubt and wishes to be ready for it."

"Ay, now we shall have an opportunity of learning seamanship—" returned Cap, with a sneer. "There is a nicety in getting a craft under her canvass, that shows the thorough-bred mariner as much as any thing else. It's like a so'ger buttoning his coat, and one can see whether he begins at the top, or the bottom."

"I will not say that Jasper is equal to your seafarers below," observed Pathfinder, across whose upright mind an unworthy feeling of envy, or of jealousy never passed, "but he is a bold boy, and manages his cutter as skilfully as any man can desire, on this lake at least. You did'n't find him backward at the Oswego Falls, Master Cap, where fresh water contrives to tumble down hill, with little difficulty."

Cap made no other answer than a dissatisfied ejaculation, and then a general silence followed, all on the bastion studying the movements of the cutter, with the interest that was natural to their own future connection with the vessel. It was still a dead calm, the surface of the lake literally glittering with the last rays of the sun. The Scud had been warped up to a kedge, that lay a hundred yards above the points of the outlet, where she had room to manœuvre in the river, which then formed the harbor of Oswego. But the total want of air prevented any such attempt, and it was soon evident that the light vessel was to be taken through the passage, under her sweeps. Not a sail was loosened, but as soon as the kedge was tripped, the heavy fall of the sweeps was heard, when the cutter, with her head up stream, began to sheer towards the centre of the current, on reaching which the efforts of the men ceased, and she drifted towards the outlet. In the narrow pass itself her movement was rapid, and in less than five minutes, the Scud was floating outside of the two low gravelly points that intercepted the waves of the lake. No anchor was let go, but the vessel continued to set off from the land, until her dark hull was seen resting on the glassy surface of the lake, fully a quarter of a mile beyond the low bluff, which formed the eastern extremity of what might be called the outer harbor, or roadstead. Here the influence of the river current ceased, and she became, virtually, stationary.

"She seems very beautiful to me, uncle," said Mabel, whose gaze had not been averted from the cutter, for a single moment, while it had thus been changing its position; "I dare say you can find faults in her appearance, and in the way she is managed, but to my ignorance both are perfect!"

"Ay—ay—she drops down with the current well enough, girl, and so would a chip. But when you come to niceties, an old tar, like myself, has no need of spectacles to find fault."

"Well, Master Cap," put in the guide, who seldom heard any thing to Jasper's prejudice, without manifesting a disposition to interfere, "I've heard old and experienced salt-water mariners confess, that the Scud is as pretty a craft as floats. I know nothing of such matters, myself, but one may have his own notions about a ship, even though they be wrong notions; and it would take more than one witness to persuade me Jasper does not keep his boat in good order."

"I do not say that the cutter is downright lubberly, Master Pathfinder, but she has faults, and great faults."

"And what are they, uncle; if he knew them, Jasper would be glad to mend them."

"What are they?—Why fifty; ay, for that matter a hundred. Very material and manifest faults."

"Do name them, sir, and Pathfinder will mention them to his friend."

"Name them? it is no easy matter to call off the stars, for the simple reason that they are so numerous. Name them, indeed!—Why, my pretty niece, Miss Magnet, what do you think of that main boom now? To my ignorant eyes, it is topped at least a foot too high; and then the pennant is foul; and—and—ay, d——e, if there is'n't a topsail gasket adrift—and, it would'n't surprise me at all, if there should prove to be a round turn in that hawser, if the kedge were to be let go, this instant! Faults, indeed. No seaman could look at her a moment without seeing that she is as full of faults, as a servant that has asked for his discharge."

"This may be very true, uncle, though I much question if Jasper knows of them. I do not think he would suffer these things, Pathfinder, if they were pointed out to him."

"Let Jasper manage his own cutter, Mabel; let him manage

his own cutter. His gifts lie that-a-way, and I'll answer for it, no one can teach him how to keep the Scud out of the hands of the Frontenackers, or their devilish Mingo friends. Who cares for round turns in kedges, and for hawsers that are topped too high, Master Cap, so long as the craft sails well, and keeps clear of the Frenchers. I will trust Jasper, against all the sea-farers of the coast, up here on the lakes—but I do not say he has any gift for the ocean, for there he has never been tried."

Cap smiled condescendingly, but he did not think it necessary to push his criticisms any farther just at that moment. His air and manner gradually became more supercilious and lofty, though he now wished to seem indifferent to any discussions on points of which one of the parties was entirely ignorant. By this time the cutter had begun to drift at the mercy of the currents of the lake, her head turning in all directions, though slowly and not in a way to attract particular attention. Just at this moment the jib was loosened and hoisted, and presently the canvass swelled towards the land, though no evidences of air were yet to be seen on the surface of the water. Slight, however, as was the impulsion, the light hull yielded, and, in another minute, the Scud was seen standing across the current of the river, with a movement so easy and moderate as to be scarcely perceptible. When out of the stream, she struck an eddy, and shot up towards the land, under the eminence where the fort stood, when Jasper dropped his kedge.

"Not lubberly done—" muttered Cap, in a sort of soliloquy—"not over-lubberly, though he should have put his helm a starboard instead of a port, for a vessel ought always to come to with her head off shore, whether she is a league from the land, or only a cable's length, since it has a careful look; and looks are something in this world."

"Jasper is a handy lad—" suddenly observed Serjeant Dunham, at his brother-in-law's elbow, "and we place great reliance on his skill in our expeditions. But come, one and all, we have but half an hour more of day-light to embark in, and the boats will be ready for us, by the time we are ready for them."

On this intimation the whole party separated, each to find

those trifles which had not been shipped already. A few taps of the drum gave the necessary signal to the soldiers, and in a minute all were in motion.

Chapter XIII

"The goblin now the fool alarms,
Hags meet to mumble o'er their charms,
The night-mare rides the dreaming ass,
And fairies trip it on the grass."
Cotton, "Night Quatrains," XVII.65–68.

THE EMBARKATION of so small a party was a matter of no great delay, or embarrassment. The whole force confided to the care of Serjeant Dunham consisted of but ten privates and two non-commissioned officers, though it was now positively known that Mr. Muir was to accompany the expedition. The Quarter Master, however, went as a volunteer, while some duty connected with his own department, as had been arranged between him and his commander, was the avowed object. To these must be added the Pathfinder and Cap, with Jasper and his subordinates, one of whom was a boy. The males of the entire party consequently consisted of less than twenty men, and a lad of fourteen. Mabel, and the wife of a common soldier, were the only females.

Serjeant Dunham carried off his command in a large batteau, and then returned for his final orders, and to see that his brother-in-law and daughter were properly attended to. Having pointed out to Cap the boat that he and Mabel were to use, he ascended the hill to seek his last interview with Lundie. The Major was met on the bastion so often mentioned. Leaving him and the serjeant together, for a short time, we will return to the beach.

It was nearly dark, when Mabel found herself in the boat that was to carry her off to the cutter. So very smooth was the surface of the lake, that it was not found necessary to bring the batteaux into the river to receive their freights, but the beach outside being totally without surf, and the water as tranquil as that of a pond, every body embarked there. As Cap had said, there was no heaving and setting, no working of vast lungs, nor any respiration of an ocean; for, on Ontario, unlike the Atlantic, gales were not agitating the element at one point, while calms prevailed at another. This the distances did not permit, and it is the usual remark of mariners, that the seas get up faster and go down sooner, on all the great lakes of the west, than on the different seas of their acquaintance. When the boat left the land, therefore, Mabel would not have known that she was afloat, on so broad a sheet of water, by any movement that is usual to such circumstances. The oars had barely time to give a dozen strokes, when the boat lay at the cutter's side.

Jasper was in readiness to receive his passengers, and, as the deck of the Scud was but two or three feet above the water, no difficulty was experienced in getting on board her. As soon as this was effected, the young man pointed out to Mabel and her companion, the accommodations prepared for their reception, and they took possession of them. The little vessel contained four apartments below, all between decks having been expressly constructed with a view to the transportation of officers and men, with their wives and families. First in rank, was what was called the after cabin, a small apartment that contained four berths, and which enjoyed the advantage of possessing small windows, for the admission of air and light. This was uniformly devoted to females, whenever any were on board, and as Mabel and her companion were alone, they had ample space and accommodations. The main cabin was larger, and lighted from above. It was now appropriated to the uses of the Quarter Master, the Serjeant, Cap, and Jasper, the Pathfinder roaming through any part of the cutter he pleased; the female apartment excepted. The corporals and common soldiers occupied the space beneath the main hatch, which had a deck for such a purpose, while the crew were berthed, as usual, in the forecastle. Although the cutter did not measure quite fifty tons, the draft of officers and men was so light, that there was ample room for all on board, there being space enough to accommodate treble the number, if necessary.

As soon as Mabel had taken possession of her own really comfortable and pretty cabin, in doing which she could not abstain from indulging in the pleasant reflection that some of Jasper's favor had been especially manifested in her behalf, she went on deck again. Here all was momentarily in motion;

the men were roving to and fro, in quest of their knapsacks and other effects, but method and habit soon reduced things to order, when the stillness on board became even imposing, for it was connected with the idea of future adventure, and ominous preparation.

Darkness was now beginning to render objects on shore indistinct, the whole of the land forming one shapeless black outline, of even, forest, summits, that was to be distinguished from the impending heavens only by the greater light of the sky. The stars, however, soon began to appear in the latter, one after another, in their usual mild, placid lustre, bringing with them that sense of quiet which ordinarily accompanies night. There was something soothing, as well as exciting in such a scene, and Mabel, who was seated on the quarter-deck sensibly felt both influences. The Pathfinder was standing near her, leaning as usual on his long rifle, and she fancied that, through the growing darkness of the hour, she could trace even stronger lines of thought than usual, in his rugged countenance.

"To you, Pathfinder, expeditions like this, can be no great novelty," she said, "though I am surprised to find how silent and thoughtful the men appear to be."

"We l'arn this, by making war ag'in Injins. Your militia are great talkers, and little doers, in gin'ral, but the soger who has often met the Mingos, l'arns to know the valu of a prudent tongue. A silent army, in the woods, is doubly strong; and a noisy one, doubly weak. If tongues made soldiers, the women of a camp would generally carry the day."

"But we are neither an army, nor in the woods. There can be no danger of Mingos, in the Scud."

"Ask Jasper, how he got to be master of this cutter, and you will find yourself answered, as to that opinion! No one is safe from a Mingo, who does not understand his very natur'; and, even then, he must act up to his own knowledge, and that closely. Ask Jasper how he got command of this very cutter!"

"And how *did* he get the command?" inquired Mabel, with an earnestness and interest that delighted her simple-minded and true-hearted companion, who was never better pleased than when he had an opportunity of saying aught in favor of a friend. "It is honorable to him, that he has reached this station, while yet so young."

"That is it—but he deserved it all, and more. A frigate would'n't have been too much to pay for so much spirit and coolness, had there been such a thing on Ontario, as there is not, howsever, or likely to be."

"But Jasper—you have not yet told me how he got the command of this schooner?"

"It is a long story, Mabel, and one your father, the sarjeant, can tell much better than I, for he was present, while I was off on a distant scoutin'. Jasper is not good at a story, I will own that; I've heard him questioned about this affair, and he never made a good tale of it, although every body knows it was a good thing. No—no—Jasper is not good at a story, as his best friends must own. The Scud had near fallen into the hands of the French and the Mingos, when Jasper saved her, in a way, that none but a quick-witted mind and a bold heart would have attempted. The Sarjeant will tell the tale better than I can, and I wish you to question him, some day, when nothing better offers. As for Jasper, himself, there will be no use in worrying the lad, since he will make a bungling matter of it, for he don't know how to give a history, at all."

Mabel determined to ask her father to repeat the incidents of the affair that very night, for it struck her young fancy that nothing better could well offer than to listen to the praises of one who was a bad historian of his own exploits.

"Will the Scud remain with us, when we reach the islands?" she asked, after a little hesitation about the propriety of the question, "or shall we be left to ourselves?"

"That's as may be. Jasper does not often keep the cutter idle, when any thing is to be done, and we may expect activity on his part. My gifts, howsever, run so little towards the water, and vessels, gin'rally, unless it be among rapids and falls, and in canoes, that I pretend to know nothing about it. We shall have all right, under Jasper, I make no doubt, who can find a trail on Ontario as well as a Delaware, can find one, on the land."

"And our own Delaware, Pathfinder—the Big Serpent—why is he not with us, to-night?"

"Your question would have been more nat'ral, had you said, 'why are *you* here, Pathfinder?'—The Sarpent is in his place, while I am not in mine. He is out, with two or three more, scouting the lake shore, and will join us down among the islands, with the tidings he may gather. The sarjeant is too good a soldier, to forget his rear, while he is facing the inimy in front. It's a thousand pities, Mabel, your father was'n't born a gin'ral, as some of the English are who come among us, for I feel sartain he would'n't leave a Frencher in the Canadas a week, could he have his own way with them."

"Shall we have enemies to face in front?" asked Mabel, smiling, and for the first time, feeling a slight apprehension about the dangers of the expedition. "Are we likely to have an engagement?"

"If we have, Mabel, there will be men enough ready and willing to stand atween you and harm. But you are a soldier's daughter, and we all know, have the spirit of one. Don't let the fear of a battle, keep your pretty eyes from sleeping."

"I do feel braver, out here in the woods, Pathfinder, than I ever felt before, amid the weaknesses of the towns, although I have always tried to remember what I owe to my dear father."

"Ay, your mother was so before you!—'You will find Mabel like her mother, no screamer, or a fainthearted girl, to trouble a man in his need, but one who would encourage her mate, and help to keep his heart up, when sorest pressed by danger'—said the sarjeant to me, before I ever laid eyes on that sweet countenance of yours, he did!"

"And why should my father have told you this, Pathfinder?" the girl demanded a little earnestly. "Perhaps he fancied you would think the better of me, if you did not believe me a silly coward, as so many of my sex love to make themselves appear."

Deception, unless it were at the expense of his enemies in the field, nay, concealment of even a thought, was so little in accordance with the Pathfinder's very nature, that he was not a little embarrassed by this simple question. To own the truth openly, he felt, by a sort of instinct for which it would have puzzled him to account, would not be proper, and to hide it agreed with neither his sense of right, nor his habits. In such a strait he involuntarily took refuge in a middle course, not revealing that which he fancied ought not to be told, nor yet absolutely concealing it.

"You must know, Mabel," he said, "that the sarjeant and I, are old friends, and have stood, side by side, or if not actually side by side, I a little in advance as became a scout, and your father with his own men, as better suited a soldier of the King, on many a hard fou't and bloody day. It's the way of us skirmishers to think little of the fight, when the rifle has done cracking; and at night around our fires, or on our marches, we talk of the things we love, just as you young women convarse about your fancies and opinions when you get together to laugh over your idees. Now it was nat'ral that the sarjeant, having such a daughter as you, should love her better than any thing else, and that he should talk of her oftener than of any thing else, while I, having neither daughter, nor sister, nor mother, nor kith nor kin, nor any thing but the Delawares to love, I nat'rally chimed in, as it were, and got to love you, Mabel, afore I ever saw you—yes I did—just by talking about you so much."

"And now you *have* seen me," returned the smiling girl, whose unmoved and natural manner proved how little she was thinking of any thing more than parental or fraternal regard, "you are beginning to see the folly of forming friendships for people before you know any thing about them, except by hearsay."

"It was'n't friendship—it is'n't friendship, Mabel, that I feel for you. I am the friend of the Delawares, and have been so from boyhood; but my feelings for them, or for the best of them, are not the same as them I got from the sarjeant for you; and, especially, now that I begin to know you better. I'm sometimes afear'd it is'n't wholesome for one who is much occupied in a very manly calling, like that of a guide, or a scout, or a soldier even, to form friendships for women—young women in particular—as they seem to me to lessen the love of enterprize, and to turn the feelings away from their gifts and nat'ral occupations."

"You, surely, do not mean, Pathfinder, that a friendship for a girl like me, would make you less bold, and more unwilling to meet the French, than you were before?"

"Not so—not so. With you in danger, for instance, I fear I might become fool hardy, but afore we became so intimate, as I may say, I loved to think of my scoutin's, and of my marches, and outlyings, and fights, and other adventures; but now my mind cares less about them; I think more of the barracks and of evenings passed in discourse, of feelings in which there are no wranglings and bloodshed, and of young women, and of their laughs, and their cheerful soft voices, their pleasant looks, and their winning ways! I sometimes tell the sarjeant, that he and his daughter will be the spoiling of one of the best and most experienced scouts on the lines!"

"Not they, Pathfinder; they will try to make that which is already so excellent, perfect. You do not know us, if you think that either wishes to see you, in the least, changed. Remain as at present, the same honest, upright, conscientious, fearless, intelligent, trustworthy guide that you are, and neither my dear father, nor myself, can ever think of you differently from what we now do."

It was too dark for Mabel to note the workings of the countenance of her listener, but her own sweet face was turned towards him, as she spoke with an energy equal to her frankness, in a way to show how little embarrassed were her thoughts, and how sincere were her words. Her countenance was a little flushed, it is true, but it was with earnestness and truth of feeling, though no nerve thrilled, no limb trembled, no pulsation quickened. In short her manner and appearance were those of a sincere-minded and frank girl, making such a declaration of good will and regard for one of the other sex, as she felt that his services and good qualities merited, without any of the emotion that invariably accompanies the consciousness of an inclination, which might lead to softer disclosures. The Pathfinder was too unpractised, however, to enter into distinctions of this kind, and his humble nature was encouraged by the directness and strength of the words he had just heard. Unwilling, if not unable to say any more, he walked away, and stood leaning on his rifle, and looking up at the stars, for quite ten minutes, in profound silence.

In the mean while, the interview on the bastion, to which we have already alluded, took place, between Lundie and the Serjeant.

"Have the men's knapsacks been examined?" demanded Major Duncan, after he had cast his eye at a written report handed to him by the serjeant, but which it was too dark to read.

"All, your honor; and all are right."

"The ammunition—arms—?"

"All in order, Major Duncan, and fit for any service."

"You have the men named in my own draft, Dunham?"

"Without an exception, sir. Better men could not be found in the regiment."

"You have need of the best of our men, serjeant. This experiment has now been tried three times; always under one of the ensigns, who have flattered me with success, but have as often failed. After so much preparation and expense, I do not like to abandon the project entirely, but this will be the last effort, and the result will mainly depend on you, and on the Pathfinder."

"You may count on us both, Major Duncan. The duty you have given us, is not above our habits and experience, and I think it will be well done—I know that the Pathfinder will not be wanting."

"On that, indeed, it will be safe to rely. He is a most extraordinary man, Dunham; one who long puzzled me, but, who, now that I understand him, commands as much of my respect as any general in His Majesty's service."

"I was in hopes, sir, that you would come to look at the proposed marriage with Mabel, as a thing I ought to wish, and forward."

"As for that, serjeant, time will show," returned Lundie, smiling; though here too, the obscurity concealed the nicer shades of expression,—"one woman is sometimes more difficult to manage than a whole regiment of men. By the way, you know that your would-be son-in-law, the Quarter Master, will be of the party, and I trust you will, at least, give him an equal chance, in the trial for your daughter's smiles."

"If respect for his rank, sir, did not cause me to do this, your honor's wish would be sufficient."

"I thank you, serjeant—we have served much together, and ought to value each other, in our several stations—Understand me, however; I ask no more for Davy Muir than 'a clear field and no favor.' In love, as in war, each man must gain his own victories. Are you certain that the rations have been properly calculated?"

"I'll answer for it, Major Duncan; but, if they were not, we cannot suffer with two such hunters as Pathfinder and the Serpent, in company."

"That will never do, Dunham," interrupted Lundie, sharply, "and it comes of your American birth, and American training! No thorough soldier ever relies on any thing but his commissary for supplies, and I beg no part of my regiment may be the first to set an example to the contrary."

"You have only to command, Major Duncan, to be obeyed; and, yet, if I might presume, sir—"

"Speak freely, serjeant; you are talking with a friend."

"I was merely about to say, that I find even the Scotch soldiers, like venison and birds, quite as well as pork, when they are difficult to be had."

"That may be very true, but likes and dislikes have nothing to do with system. An army can rely on nothing but its commissaries. The irregularity of the provincials has played the devil with the King's service, too often, to be winked at any longer."

"Gen. Braddock, your honor, might have been advised by Col. Washington—"

"Out upon your Washington!—You're all provincials together, man, and uphold each other, as if you were of a sworn confederacy."

"I believe His Majesty has no more loyal subjects than the Americans, your honor."

"In that, Dunham, I'm thinking you're right, and I have been a little too warm, perhaps. I do not consider *you* a provincial, however, serjeant, for, though born in America, a better soldier never shouldered a musket."

"And Col. Washington, your honor—"

"Well, and Col. Washington may be a useful subject too. He is the American prodigy, and I suppose I may as well give him all the credit you ask. You have no doubt of the skill of this Jasper Eau douce?"

"The boy has been tried, sir, and found equal to all that can be required of him."

"He has a French name, and has passed much of his boyhood in the French colonies—has he French blood, in his veins, serjeant?"

"Not a drop, your honor. Jasper's father was an old comrade of my own, and his mother came of an honest and loyal family, in this very province."

"How came he then so much among the French, and whence his name?—He speaks the language of the Canadas, too, I find!"

"That is easily explained, Major Duncan. The boy was left under the care of one of our mariners in the old war, and he took to the water, like a duck. Your honor knows that we have no ports on Ontario, that can be named as such, and he naturally passed most of his time on the other side of the lake, where the French have had a few vessels, these fifty years. He learned to speak their language, as a matter of course, and got his name from the Indians and Canadians, who are fond of calling men by their qualities as it might be."

"A French master, is but a poor instructor for a British sailor, notwithstanding!"

"I beg your pardon, sir; Jasper Eau douce was brought up under a real English seaman; one that had sailed under the King's Pennant, and may be called a thorough bred: that is to say, a subject born in the colonies, but none the worse at his trade, I hope, Major Duncan, for that."

"Perhaps not, serjeant; perhaps not; nor any better. This Jasper behaved well, too, when I gave him the command of the Scud; no lad could have conducted himself more loyally, or better."

"Or more bravely, Major Duncan. I am sorry to see, sir, that you have doubts as to the fidelity of Jasper."

"It is the duty of the soldier, who is entrusted with the care of a distant and important post like this, Dunham, never to relax in his vigilance. We have two of the most artful enemies, that the world has ever produced, in their several ways, to contend with; the Indians and the French; and nothing should be overlooked that can lead to injury."

"I hope your honor considers me fit to be intrusted with any particular reason that may exist for doubting Jasper, since you have seen fit to intrust me with this command."

"It is not that I doubt you, Dunham, that I hesitate to reveal all I may happen to know, but from a strong reluctance to circulate an evil report concerning one of whom I have hitherto thought well. You must think well of the Pathfinder, or you would not wish to give him your daughter?"

"For the Pathfinder's honesty I will answer with my life, sir—" returned the serjeant firmly, and not without a dignity of manner that struck his superior. "Such a man does'n't know how to be false."

"I believe you are right, Dunham, and yet this last information has unsettled all my old opinions. I have received an anonymous communication, serjeant, advising me to be on my guard against Jasper Western, or Jasper Eau douce, as he is called; who it alleges has been bought by the enemy, and giving me reason to expect that further and more precise information will soon be sent."

"Letters without signatures to them, sir, are scarcely to be regarded in war."

"Or in peace, Dunham. No one can entertain a lower opinion of the writer of an anonymous letter, in ordinary matters, than myself. The very act denotes cowardice, meanness, and baseness, and it usually is a token of falsehood, as well as of other vices. But, in matters of war, it is not exactly the same thing. Besides, several suspicious circumstances have been pointed out to me—"

"Such as is fit for an orderly to know, your honor?"

"Certainly, one in whom I confide as much, as in yourself, Dunham. It is said for instance, that your daughter and her party were permitted to escape the Iroquois, when they came in, merely to gain Jasper credit with me. I am told that the gentry at Frontenac will care more for the capture of the Scud, with Serjeant Dunham and a party of men, together with the defeat of our favorite plan, than for the capture of a girl, and the scalp of her uncle."

"I understand the hint, sir, but I do not give it credit. Jasper can hardly be true, and Pathfinder false; and, as for the last, I would as soon distrust your honor, as distrust him!"

"It would seem so, serjeant; it would indeed seem so. But Jasper is not the Pathfinder after all, and I will own, Dunham, I should put more faith in the lad, if he did'n't speak French!"

"It's no recommendation in my eyes, I assure your honor, but the boy learned it by compulsion, as it were, and ought not to be condemned too hastily, for the circumstance, by your honor's leave. If he does speak French, it's because he can't well help it."

"It's a d——d lingo, and never did any one good—at least no British subject; for I suppose the French themselves must talk together, in some language or other. I should have much more faith in this Jasper, did he know nothing of their language. This letter has made me uneasy, and were there another, to whom I could trust the cutter, I would devise some means to detain him here. I have spoken to you already of a brother-in-law, who goes with you, serjeant, and who is a sailor?"

"A real sea-faring man, your honor, and somewhat prejudiced against fresh-water. I doubt if he could be induced to risk his character on a lake, and I'm certain he never could find the station."

"The last is probably true, and, then, the man cannot know enough of this treacherous lake to be fit for the employment! You will have to be doubly vigilant, Dunham. I give you full powers, and should you detect this Jasper in any treachery, make him a sacrifice at once to offended justice."

"Being in the service of the crown, your honor, he is amenable to martial law—"

"Very true—then iron him, from his head to his heels, and send him up here, in his own cutter. That brother-in-law of yours must be able to find the way back, after he has once travelled the road."

"I make no doubt, Major Duncan, we shall be able to do all that will be necessary, should Jasper turn out as you seem to anticipate; though, I think I would risk my life on his truth."

"I like your confidence; it speaks well for the fellow, but that infernal letter!—There is such an air of truth about it—nay there is so much truth in it, touching other matters—"

"I think your honor said it wanted the name at the bottom; a great omission for an honest man to make."

"Quite right, Dunham, and no one but a rascal, and a cowardly rascal in the bargain, would write an anonymous letter, on private affairs. It *is* different, however, in war. Despatches are feigned, and artifice is generally allowed to be justifiable."

"Military, manly artifices, sir, if you will; such as ambushes, surprises, feints, false attacks, and even spies; but I never heard of a true soldier who could wish to undermine the character of an honest young man, by such means as these!"

"I have met with many strange events, and some stranger people, in the course of my experience. But fare you well, serjeant; I must detain you no longer. You are now on your guard, and I recommend to you, untiring vigilance. I think Muir means shortly to retire, and should you fully succeed in this enterprize, my influence will not be wanting, in endeavoring to put you in the vacancy, to which you have many claims."

"I humbly thank your honor," coolly returned the serjeant who had been encouraged in this manner, any time for the preceding twenty years, "and hope I shall never disgrace my station, whatever it may be. I am what nature, and Providence have made me, and I hope I'm satisfied."

"You have not forgotten the howitzer?"

"Jasper took it on board this morning, sir."

"Be wary, and do not trust that man unnecessarily. Make a confidant of Pathfinder at once; he may be of service in detecting any villainy that may be stirring. His simple honesty will favor his observation, by concealing it. *He must* be true."

"For him, sir, my own head shall answer, or even my rank in the regiment. I have seen him too often tried to doubt him."

"Of all wretched sensations, Dunham, distrust, where one is compelled to confide, is the most painful. You have bethought you of the spare flints?"

"A serjeant is a safe commander, for all such details, your honor."

"Well then, give me your hand, Dunham. God bless you, and may you be successful. Muir means to retire—by the way, let the man have an equal chance with your daughter, for it may facilitate future operations, about the promotion. One would retire more cheerfully, with such a companion as Mabel, than in cheerless widowerhood, and with nothing but oneself to love, and such a self, too, as Davy's!"

"I hope, sir, my child will make a prudent choice, and I think her mind is already pretty much made up in favor of Pathfinder. Still she shall have fair play, though disobedience is the next crime to mutiny."

"Have all the ammunition carefully examined and dried, as soon as you arrive; the damp of the lake may affect it. And now, once more farewell, serjeant. Beware of that Jasper, and consult with Muir, in any difficulty. I shall expect you to return triumphant, this day month."

"God bless, your honor—if any thing should happen to me, I trust to you, Major Duncan, to care for an old soldier's character."

"Rely on me, Dunham; you will rely on a friend. Be vigilant; remember you will be in the very jaws of the lion—pshaw of no lion, neither; but of treacherous tigers—in their very jaws and beyond support. Have the flints counted, and examined in the morning—and—farewell, Dunham, farewell."

The serjeant took the extended hand of his superior, with proper respect, and they finally parted; Lundie hastening into his own moveable abode, while the other left the fort, descended to the beach, and got into a boat.

Duncan of Lundie had said no more than the truth, when he spoke of the painful nature of distrust. Of all the feelings of the human mind, it is that which is the most treacherous in its workings, the most insidious in its approaches, and the least at the command of a generous temperament. While doubt exists, every thing may be suspected, the thoughts having no definite facts to set bounds to their wanderings, and distrust once admitted it is impossible to say to what extent conjecture may lead, or whither credulity may follow. That which had previously seemed innocent, assumes the hue of guilt, as soon as this uneasy tenant has taken possession of the thoughts, and nothing is said, or done, without being subjected to the colourings and disfigurations of jealousy and apprehension. If this is true, in ordinary affairs, it is doubly true, when any heavy responsibility, involving life or death, weighs on the unsettled mind of its subject, as in the case of the military commander, or the agent in the management of any grave political interest. It is not to be supposed, then, that

Serjeant Dunham, after he had parted from his commanding officer, was likely to forget the injunctions he had received. He thought highly of Jasper, in general, but distrust had been insinuated between his former confidence and the obligations of duty, and, as he now felt that every thing depended on his own vigilance, by the time the boat reached the side of the Scud, he was in a proper humour to let no suspicious circumstance go unheeded, or any unusual movement in the young sailor, pass without its comment. As a matter of course, he viewed things in the light suited to his peculiar mood, and his precautions, as well as his distrust, partook of the habits, opinions and education of the man.

The Scud's kedge was lifted, as soon as the boat with the serjeant, who was the last person expected, was seen to quit the shore, and the head of the cutter was cast to the eastward, by means of the sweeps. A few vigorous strokes of the latter, in which the soldiers aided, sent the light craft into the line of the current that flowed from the river, when she was suffered to drift into the offing again. As yet, there was no wind, the light and almost imperceptible air from the lake, that had existed previously to the setting of the sun having entirely failed.

All this time, an unusual quiet prevailed in the cutter. It appeared as if those on board of her felt that they were entering upon an uncertain enterprize, in the obscurity of night, and that their duty, the hour, and the manner of their departure lent a solemnity to their movements. Discipline also came in aid of these feelings. Most were silent, and those who said anything, spoke seldom and in low voices. In this manner, the cutter set slowly out into the lake, until she had got as far as the river-current would carry her, when she became stationary, waiting for the usual land breeze. An interval of half an hour followed, during the whole of which time, the Scud lay as motionless as a log, floating on the water. While the little changes just mentioned were occurring in the situation of the vessel, notwithstanding the general quiet that prevailed, all conversation had not been repressed, for Serjeant Dunham, having first ascertained that both his daughter and her female companion were on the quarter-deck, led the Pathfinder to the after-cabin, where, closing the door with great caution, and otherwise making certain he was beyond the reach of eaves-droppers, he commenced as follows.

"It is now many years, my friend, since you began to experience the hardships and dangers of the woods in my company."

"It is, sarjeant, yes it is. I sometimes fear I am too old for Mabel, who was not born until you and I had fou't the Frenchers as comrades."

"No fear on that account, Pathfinder. I was near your age, before I prevailed on the mind of her mother, and Mabel is a steady, thoughtful girl; one that will regard character, more than any thing else. A lad like Jasper Eau douce, for instance, will have no chance with her, though he is both young and comely."

"Does Jasper think of marrying?" inquired the guide, simply, but earnestly.

"I should hope not—at least not until he has satisfied every one of his fitness to possess a wife."

"Jasper is a gallant boy, and one of great gifts in his way; he may claim a wife, as well as another."

"To be frank with you, Pathfinder, I brought you here to talk about this very youngster. Major Duncan has received some information which has led him to suspect that Eau douce is false, and in the pay of the enemy; I wish to hear your opinion on the subject."

"Anan!"

"I say the Major suspects Jasper of being a traitor—a French spy—or what is worse, of being bought to betray us. He has received a letter to this effect, and has been charging me to keep an eye on the boy's movements, for he fears we shall meet with enemies when we least suspect it, and by his means."

"Duncan of Lundie has told you this, Sarjeant Dunham?"

"He has, indeed, Pathfinder; and though I have been loth to believe any thing to the injury of Jasper, I have a feeling, which tells me I ought to distrust him. Do you believe in presentiments, my friend?"

"In what, Sarjeant?"

"Presentiments—a sort of secret foreknowledge of events that are about to happen. The Scotch of our regiment are great sticklers for such things, and my opinion of Jasper is changing so fast, that I begin to fear there must be some truth in their doctrines."

"But you've been talking with Duncan of Lundie, consarning Jasper, and his words have raised misgivin's."

"Not it—not so, in the least. For, while conversing with the Major, my feelings were altogether the other way; and I endeavored to convince him, all I could, that he did the boy injustice. But there is no use in holding out against a presentiment, I find, and I fear there is something in the suspicion after all."

"I know nothing of presentiments, Sarjeant, but I have known Jasper Eau douce since he was a boy, and I have as much faith in his honesty, as I have in my own, or that of the Sarpent, himself."

"But the Serpent, Pathfinder, has his tricks and ambushes in war, as well as another!"

"Ay, them are his nat'ral gifts, and are such as belong to his people. Neither red skin nor pale face can deny natur'; but Chingachgook is not a man to feel a presentiment ag'in."

"That I believe, nor should I have thought ill of Jasper, this very morning. It seems to me, Pathfinder, since I've taken up this presentiment, that the lad does not bustle about his deck, naturally, as he used to do, but that he is silent, and moody, and thoughtful, like a man who has a load on his conscience."

"Jasper is never noisy, and he tells me noisy ships are generally ill worked ships. Master Cap agrees in this too. No—no—I will believe naught against Jasper, until I see it. Send for your brother, sarjeant, and let us question him in this matter, for to sleep with distrust of one's fri'nd in the heart, is like sleeping with lead there. I have no faith in your presentiments!"

The serjeant, although he scarce knew himself, with what object, complied, and Cap was summoned to join in the consultation. As Pathfinder was more collected than his companion, and felt so strong a conviction of the good faith of the party accused, he assumed the office of spokesman.

"We have asked you to come down, Master Cap," he commenced, "in order to inquire if you have remarked any thing out of the common way, in the movements of Eau douce, this evening."

"His movements are common enough I dare say, for fresh water, Master Pathfinder, though we should think most of his proceedings irregular, down on the coast."

"Yes, yes—we know you will never agree with the lad about the manner the cutter ought to be managed, but it is on another p'int we wish your opinion."

The Pathfinder then explained to Cap the nature of the suspicions which the Serjeant entertained, and the reasons why they had been excited, so far as the latter had been communicated by Major Duncan.

"The youngster talks French, does he?"

"They say he speaks it better than common," returned the Serjeant, gravely. "Pathfinder knows this to be true."

"I'll not gainsay it—I'll not gainsay it," answered the guide: "at least they tell me such is the fact. But this would prove nothing ag'in' a Mississagua, and least of all ag'in' one like Jasper. I speak the Mingo dialect myself, having l'arnt it while a prisoner among the reptyles, but who will say I am their fri'nd?—Not that I am an inimy, either, according to Injin notions, though I am their inimy, I will admit, agreeable to christianity."

"Ay, Pathfinder, but Jasper did not get his French as a prisoner; he took it in, in boyhood, when the mind is easily impressed, and gets its permanent notions; when nature has a presentiment, as it were, which way the character is likely to incline."

"A very just remark," added Cap, "for that is the time of life, when we all learn the catechism, and other moral improvements. The Serjeant's observation shows that he understands human nature, and I agree with him perfectly; it *is* a damnable thing for a youngster, up here, on this bit of fresh water, to talk French. If it were down on the Atlantic now, where a sea-faring man has occasion sometimes to converse with a pilot, or a linguister, in that language, I should not think so much of it, though we always look with suspicion, even there, at a shipmate who knows too much of the tongue, but up here on Ontario, I hold it to be a most suspicious circumstance."

"But Jasper must talk in French to the people on the other shore," said Pathfinder, "or hold his tongue, as there are none but French to speak to."

"You do'n't mean to tell me, Pathfinder, that France lies hereaway, on the opposite coast?" cried Cap, jerking a thumb over his shoulder, in the direction of the Canadas; "that one side of this bit of fresh water, is York, and the other France!"

"I mean to tell you this is York, and that is Upper Canada, and that English and Dutch and Indian are spoken in the first, and French and Indian in the last. Even the Mingos have got many of the French words in their dialect, and it is no improvement, neither."

"Very true, and what sort of people are the Mingos, my friend?" inquired the serjeant, touching the other on a shoulder, by way of enforcing a remark, the inherent truth of which sensibly increased its value in the eyes of the speaker—"No one knows them better than yourself, and I ask you what sort of a tribe are they?"

"Jasper is no Mingo, Sarjeant."

"He speaks French, and he might as well be, in that particular. Brother Cap, can you recollect no movement of this unfortunate young man, in the way of his calling, that would seem to denote treachery?"

"Not distinctly, serjeant, though he has gone to work wrong end fore most, half his time. It is true, that one of his hands coiled a rope against the sun, and he called it *querling* a rope, too, when I asked him what 'he was about,' but I am not certain that any thing was meant by it; though I dare say the French coil half their running rigging the wrong way, and may call it 'querling it down,' too, for that matter. Then Jasper, himself, belayed the end of the jib halyards to a stretcher in the rigging, instead of bringing them into the mast, where they belong, at least among British sailors."

"I dare say Jasper may have got some Canada notions, about working his craft, from being so much on the other side—" Pathfinder interposed—, "but catching an idee, or a word, is'n't treachery and bad faith. I sometimes get an idee from the Mingos themselves, but my heart has always been with the Delawares. No—no—Jasper is true, and the King might trust him with his crown, just as he would trust his own eldest son, who, as he is to wear it one day, ought to be the last man to wish to steal it."

"Fine talking—fine talking—" said Cap, rising to spit out of the cabin window, as is customary with men when they most feel their own great moral strength, and happen to chew tobacco—"all fine talking, Master Pathfinder, but d——d little logic. In the first place, the King's Majesty cannot lend his crown, it being contrary to the Laws of the Realm, which require him to wear it, at all times, in order that his sacred person may be known, just as the 'Silver Oar' is necessary to a sheriff's officer afloat. In the next place, it's high treason by law, for the eldest son of His Majesty ever to covet the crown, or to have a child, except in lawful wedlock, as either would derange the succession. Thus you see, friend Pathfinder, that in order to reason truly, one must get under way, as it might be, on the right tack. Law is reason, and reason is philosophy, and philosophy is a steady drag, whence it follows that crowns are regulated by law, reason and philosophy."

"I know little of all this, Master Cap, but nothing short of seeing and feeling will make me think Jasper Western a traitor."

"There you are wrong again, Pathfinder, for there is a way of proving a thing much more conclusively than by either seeing or feeling, or by both together, and that is by a circumstance."

"It may be so, in the settlements, but it is not so, here, on the lines."

"It is so in nature, which is monarch over all. Now, according to our senses, young Eau douce is this moment on deck, and by going up there, either of us might see and feel him; but, should it afterwards appear that a fact was communicated to the French at this precise moment, which fact no one but Jasper *could* communicate, why we should be bound to believe that the circumstance was true, and that our eyes and fingers deceived us. Any lawyer will tell you that."

"This is hardly right," said Pathfinder; "nor is it possible, seein' that it is ag'in fact."

"It is much more than possible, my worthy guide, it is law; absolute, King's law of the realm, and, as such to be respected and obeyed. I'd hang my own brother on such testimony; no reflections on the family, being meant, serjeant."

"God knows how far all this applies to Jasper, though I do believe Mr. Cap is right, as to the law, Pathfinder, circumstances being much stronger than the senses, on such occasions. We must all of us be watchful, and nothing suspicious should be overlooked."

"Now I, I recollect me," continued Cap, again using the window. "There was a circumstance, just after we came on board this evening, that is extremely suspicious, and which may be set down at once, as a make-weight against this lad. Jasper bent on the King's ensign with his own hands, and while he pretended to be looking at Mabel, and the soldier's wife, giving directions about showing them below, here, and all that, he got the flag Union down!"

"That might have been accident," returned the Serjeant, "for such a thing has happened to myself; besides the halyards lead to a pulley, and the flag would have come right, or not, according to the manner in which the lad hoisted it."

"A pulley!" exclaimed Cap, with strong disgust—"I wish, Serjeant Dunham, I could prevail on you to use proper terms: An ensign halyard-block is no more a pulley, than your halbert is a boarding pike. It is true that by hoisting on one part, another part would go uppermost; but I look upon that affair of the ensign, now you have mentioned your suspicions, as a circumstance, and shall bear it in mind. I trust supper is not to be overlooked, however, even if we have a hold full of traitors."

"It will be duly attended to, Brother Cap, but I shall count on you, for aid in managing the Scud, should any thing occur to induce me to arrest Jasper."

"I'll not fail you, serjeant, and in such an event you'll probably learn what this cutter can really perform, for, as yet, I fancy it is pretty much matter of guess work."

"Well, for my part," said Pathfinder, drawing a heavy sigh—"I shall cling to the hope of Jasper's innocence, and recommend plain dealing, by asking the lad, himself, without further delay, whether he is, or is not a traitor. I'll put Jasper Western ag'in all the presentiments and circumstances in the Colony."

"That will never do," rejoined the Serjeant. "The responsibility of this affair rests with me, and I request and enjoin, that nothing be said to any one, without my knowledge. We will all keep watchful eyes about us, and take proper note of circumstances."

"Ay—ay—circumstances are the things after all," returned Cap—"One circumstance is worth fifty facts. That I know to be the law of the realm. Many a man has been hanged on circumstances."

The conversation now ceased, and after a short delay, the whole party returned to the deck, each individual disposed to view the conduct of the suspected Jasper, in the manner most suited to his own habits and character.

Chapter XIV

"Even such a man, so faint, so spiritless,
So dull, so dead in look, so woe-begone,
Drew Priam's curtain in the dead of night,
And would have told him, half his Troy was burned—"

2 Henry IV, I.i.70–73.

ALL THIS TIME, matters were elsewhere passing in their usual train. Jasper, like the weather, and his vessel seemed to be waiting for the land breeze, while the soldiers accustomed to early rising had, to a man, sought their pallets, in the main hold. None remained on deck but the people of the cutter, Mr. Muir and the two females. The Quarter Master was endeavoring to render himself agreeable to Mabel, while, our heroine herself, little affected by his assiduities, which she ascribed partly to the habitual gallantry of a soldier, and partly, perhaps, to her own pretty face, was enjoying the peculiarities of a scene and situation, that, to her, were full of the charms of novelty.

The sails had been hoisted, but as yet not a breath of air was in motion, and so still and placid was the lake that not the smallest motion was perceptible in the cutter. She had drifted in the river-current to a distance a little exceeding a quarter of a mile from the land, and there she lay, beautiful in her symmetry and form, but like a fixture. Young Jasper was on the quarter-deck, near enough to hear occasionally the conversation which passed, but too diffident of his own claim, and too intent on his duties, to attempt to mingle in it. The fine blue eyes of Mabel followed his motions in curious expectation, and more than once the Quarter Master had to repeat his compliments ere she heard them, so intent was she on the little occurrences of the vessel, and, we might add, so indifferent to the eloquence of her companion. At length, even Lt. Muir became silent, and there was a deep stillness on the water. Presently an oar blade fell in a boat, beneath the fort, and the sound reached the cutter as distinctly as if it had been produced on her deck. Then came a murmur, like a sigh of the night, a fluttering of the canvass, the creaking of the boom, and the flap of the jib. These well known sounds were followed by a slight heel in the cutter, and by the bellying of all the sails.

"Here's the wind, Anderson—" called out Jasper to the oldest of his sailors—"take the helm."

This brief order was obeyed, the helm was put up, the cutter's bows fell off, and, in a few minutes, the water was heard murmuring under her head, as the Scud glanced through the lake at the rate of five miles in the hour. All this passed in profound silence, when Jasper again gave the order—"ease off the sheets a little, and keep her along the land."

It was at this instant that the party from the after cabin reappeared on the quarter-deck.

"You've no inclination, Jasper, lad, to trust yourself too near our neighbours the French," observed Muir, who took that occasion to recommence the discourse. "Well, well, your prudence will never be questioned by me, for I like the Canadas, as little as you can possibly like them yoursel'."

"I hug this shore, Mr. Muir, on account of the wind. The land breeze is always freshest close in, provided you are not so near as to make a lee of the trees. We have Mexico Bay to cross, and that, on the present course, will give us quite offing enough."

"I'm right glad it's not the Bay of Mexico," put in Cap, "which is a part of the world I would rather not visit in one of your inland craft. Does your cutter bear a weather helm, Master Oh! the deuce?"

"She is easy on her rudder, Master Cap, but likes looking up at the breeze as well as another, when in lively motion."

"I suppose you have such things as reefs, though you can hardly have occasion to use them?"

Mabel's bright eye detected the smile that gleamed, for an instant, on Jasper's handsome face, but no one else saw that momentary exhibition of surprise and contempt.

"We have reefs, and often have occasion to use them;" quietly returned the young man. "Before we get in, Master Cap, an opportunity may offer to show you the manner in which we do so, for there is easterly weather brewing, and the wind cannot chop, even on the ocean itself, more readily than it flies round on Lake Ontario."

"So much for knowing no better! I have seen the wind, on the Atlantic, fly round like a coach wheel, in a way to keep your sails shaking for an hour, and the ship would become perfectly motionless from not knowing which way to turn."

"We have no such sudden changes here, certainly," Jasper mildly answered—"though we think ourselves liable to unexpected shifts of wind. I hope, however, to carry this land breeze as far as the first islands; after which there will be less danger of our being seen and followed, by any of the look-out boats from Frontenac."

"Do you think the French keep spies out on the broad lake, Jasper?" inquired the Pathfinder.

"We know they do; one was off Oswego, during the night of Monday, last. A bark canoe came close in with the eastern point, and landed an Indian and an officer. Had you been outlying that night, as usual, we should have secured one, if not both of them."

It was too dark to betray the colour that deepened on the weather burned features of the guide, for he felt the consciousness of having lingered in the fort that night, listening to the sweet tones of Mabel's voice, as she sang ballads to her father, and gazing at a countenance that, to him, was radiant with charms. Probity, in thought and deed, being the distinguishing quality of this extraordinary man's mind, while he felt that a sort of disgrace ought to attach to his idleness, on the occasion mentioned, the last thought that could occur would be to attempt to palliate, or deny, his negligence.

"I confess it, Jasper, I confess it," he said humbly. "Had I been out that night and I now remember no sufficient reason why I was not—it might, indeed, have turned out as you say."

"It was the evening you passed with us, Pathfinder," Mabel innocently remarked; "surely one who lives so much of his time in the forest, in front of the enemy, may be excused for giving a few hours of his time to an old friend, and his daughter."

"Nay, nay, I've done little else but idle, since we reached the garrison," returned the other, sighing, "and it is well that the lad should tell me of it. The idler needs a scoldin': yes, he needs a scoldin'."

"Scolding, Pathfinder! I never dreamed of saying any thing disagreeable, and least of all would I think of rebuking you, because a solitary spy, and an Indian, or two, have escaped us! Now I know where you were, I think your absence the most natural thing in the world."

"I think nothing of it, Jasper, I think nothing of what you said, since it was desarved. We are all human, and all do wrong."

"This is unkind, Pathfinder."

"Give me your hand, lad, give me your hand. It was'n't you that gave the lesson; it was conscience."

"Well, well," interrupted Cap, "now this latter matter is settled to the satisfaction of all parties, perhaps you will tell us how it happened to be known that there were spies near us, so lately. This looks amazingly like a circumstance!"

As the mariner uttered the last sentence, he pressed a foot slyly on that of the Serjeant, and nudged the guide with his elbow, winking, at the same time, though this sign was lost in the obscurity.

"It is known, because their trail was found next day, by the Serpent, and it was that of a military boot and a moccasin. One of our hunters, moreover, saw the canoe crossing towards Frontenac next morning."

"Did the trail lead near the garrison, Jasper," Pathfinder asked in a manner so meek and subdued that it resembled the tone of a rebuked school boy. "Did the trail lead near the garrison, lad?"

"We thought not—though, of course, it did not cross the river. It was followed down to the eastern point, at the river's mouth, where what was doing in port might be seen; but it did not cross, as we could discover."

"And why did'n't you get under way, Master Jasper," Cap demanded, "and give chase. On Tuesday morning it blew a good breeze; one in which this cutter might have run nine knots."

"That may do on the ocean, Master Cap," put in Pathfinder, "but it would not do here. Water leaves no trail, and a Mingo and a Frenchman are a match for the devil, in a pursuit."

"Who wants a trail, when the chase can be seen from the

deck, as Jasper, here, said was the case with this canoe, and it mattered nothing if there were twenty of your Mingos and Frenchmen, with a good British-built bottom in their wake. I'll engage, Master Oh-the-deuce, had you given me a call, that said Tuesday morning, that we should have overhauled the blackguards."

"I dare say, Master Cap, that the advice of as old a seaman as you, might have done no harm to as young a sailor as myself, but it is a long and a hopeless chase that has a bark canoe in it."

"You would have had only to press it hard, to drive it ashore."

"Ashore, Master Cap! You do not understand our lake navigation, at all, if you suppose it an easy matter to force a bark canoe ashore. As soon as they find themselves pressed, these bubbles paddle right into the wind's eye, and before you know it, you find yourself a mile or two, dead under their lee."

"You don't wish me to believe, Master Jasper, that any one is so heedless of drowning, as to put off into this lake, in one of them egg shells, when there is any wind?"

"I have often crossed Ontario in a bark canoe, even when there has been a good deal of sea on. Well managed, they are the driest boats of which we have any knowledge."

Cap now led his brother-in-law and Pathfinder aside, when he assured him, that the admission of Jasper concerning the spies was "a circumstance," and "a strong circumstance," and as such, it deserved his deliberate investigation, while his account of the canoes was so improbable, as to wear the appearance of browbeating the listeners. Jasper spoke confidently of the character of the two individuals who had landed, and this Cap deemed pretty strong proof that he knew more about them, than was to be gathered from a mere trail. As for moccasins, he said that they were worn, in that part of the world, by white men, as well as by Indians, he had purchased a pair himself, and boots, it was notorious, did not particularly make a soldier. Although much of this logic was thrown away on the Serjeant, still it produced some effect. He thought it a little singular himself, that there should have been spies detected so near the fort, and he know nothing of it; nor did he believe that this was a branch of knowledge that fell particularly within the sphere of Jasper. It was true, that the Scud had, once or twice, been sent across the lake to land men of this character, or to bring them off; but then the part played by Jasper, to his own certain knowledge, was very secondary, the master of the cutter remaining as ignorant as any one else, of the purport of the visits of those whom he had carried to and fro, nor did he see why he, alone, of all present, should know any thing of the late visit. Pathfinder viewed the matter differently. With his habitual diffidence, he reproached himself with a neglect of duty, and that knowledge, of which the want struck him as a fault in one whose business it was to possess it, appeared a merit in the young man. He saw nothing extraordinary in Jasper's knowing the facts he had related, while he did feel it was unusual, not to say disgraceful, that he himself now heard of them for the first time.

"As for moccasins, Master Cap," he said, when a short pause invited him to speak, "they may be worn by pale faces, as well as by red skins, it is true, though they never leave the same trail on the foot of one, as on the foot of the other. Any one who is used to the woods, can tell the footstep of an Injin, from the footstep of a white man, whether it be made by a boot, or a moccasin. It will need better evidence than this, to make me believe that Jasper is false."

"You will allow, Pathfinder, that there are such things in the world, as traitors," put in Cap logically.

"I never knew an honest-minded Mingo; one that you could put faith in, if he had a temptation to deceive you. Cheatin' seems to be their gift, and I sometimes think they ought to be pitied for it, rather than parsecuted."

"Then why not believe that this Jasper may have the same weakness? A man is a man, and human nature is sometimes but a poor concern, as I know by experience; I may say we all know by experience; at least I speak for my own human nature."

This was the opening of another long and desultory conversation, in which the probability of Jasper's guilt or innocence was argued, pro and con, until both the serjeant and his brother-in-law, had nearly reasoned themselves into settled convictions, in favor of the first, while their companion grew sturdier and sturdier in his defense of the accused, and still more fixed in his opinions of his being unjustly charged with treachery. In this there was nothing out of the common course of things, for there is no more certain way of arriving at any particular notion, than by undertaking to defend it, and among the most obstinate of our opinions, may be classed those which are derived from discussions in which we affect to search for truth, while in reality we are only fortifying prejudice. By this time, the serjeant had reached a state of mind that disposed him to view every act of the young sailor with distrust, and he soon got to coincide with his relative in deeming the peculiar knowledge of Jasper, in reference to the spies, a branch of information that certainly did not come within the circle of his regular duties, as "a circumstance."

While this matter was thus discussed near the taffrail, Mabel sat silent by the companion-way; Mr. Muir having gone below, to look after his personal comforts, and Jasper standing a little aloof, with his arms crossed and his eyes wandering from the sails to the clouds, from the clouds to the dusky outline of the shore, from the shore to the lake, and from the lake back again to the sails. Our heroine, too, began to commune with her own thoughts. The excitement of the late journey, the incidents which marked the day of her arrival at the fort, the meeting with a father who was virtually a stranger to her, the novelty of her late situation in the garrison, and her present voyage, formed a vista for the mind's eye to look back through, that seemed lengthened into months. She could with difficulty believe that she had so recently left the town, with all its usages of civilized life, and she wondered, in particular, that the incidents which had occurred during the descent of the Oswego, had made so little impression on her mind. Too inexperienced to know that events, when crowded, have the effect of time, or that the quick succession of novelties that pass before us in travelling, elevate objects, in a measure, to the dignity of events, she drew upon her memory for days and dates, in order to make certain that she had known Jasper, and the Pathfinder, and her own father but little more than a fortnight. Mabel was a girl of heart, rather than of imagination, though by no means deficient in the last, and she could not easily account for the strength of her feelings in connection with those who were so lately strangers to her, for she was not sufficiently accustomed to analyze her sensations to understand the nature of the influences that have just been mentioned. As yet, however, her pure mind was free from the blight of distrust, and she had no suspicion of the views of either of her suitors, and one of the last thoughts that could have voluntarily disturbed her confidence, would have been to suppose it possible either of her companions was a traitor to his King and Country.

America, at the time of which we are writing, was remarkable for its attachment to the German family that then sat on the British throne, for, as is the fact with all provinces, the virtues and qualities that are proclaimed near the centre of power, as incense and policy, get to be a part of political faith, with the credulous and ignorant at a distance. This truth is just as apparent to-day, in connection with the prodigies of the republic, as it then was in connection with those distant rulers, whose merits it was always safe to applaud, and whose demerits it was treason to reveal. It is a consequence of this mental dependence, that public opinion is so much placed at the mercy of the designing, and the world, in the midst of its idle boasts of knowledge and improvement, is left to receive its truth, on all such points as touch the interests of the powerful and managing, through such a medium, and such a medium only, as may serve the particular views of those who pull the wires. Pressed upon by the subjects of France, who were then encircling the British colonies, with a belt of forts and settlements, that completely secured the savages for allies, it would have been difficult to say, whether the Americans loved the English more than they hated the French, and those who then lived probably would have considered the alliance which took place between the cis-Atlantic subjects, and the ancient rivals of the British crown, some twenty years later, as an event entirely without the circle of probabilities. In a word, as fashions are exaggerated in a province, so are opinions; and the loyalty, that, at London, merely formed a part of a political scheme, at New York was magnified into a faith that might almost have moved mountains. Disaffection was consequently a rare offence, and most of all, would treason that should favor France, or Frenchmen, have been odious in the eyes of the provincials. The last thing that Mabel would suspect of Jasper, was the very crime with which he now stood secretly charged, and, if others near her endured the pain of distrust, she at least was filled with the generous confidence of a woman. As yet, no whisper had reached her ear to disturb the feeling of reliance with which she had early regarded the young sailor, and her own mind would have been the last to suggest such a thought, of itself. The pictures of the past and of the present, therefore, that exhibited themselves so rapidly to her active imagination, were unclouded with a shade that might affect any in whom she felt an interest, and ere she had mused, in the manner related, a quarter of an hour, the whole scene around her was filled with unalloyed satisfaction.

The season and the night, to represent them truly, were of a nature to stimulate the sensations which youth, health and happiness are wont to associate with novelty. The weather was warm, as is not always the case in that region even in summer, while the air that came off the land, in breathing currents, brought with it the coolness and fragrance of the forest. The wind was far from being fresh, though there was enough of it to drive the Scud merrily ahead, and perhaps to keep attention alive, in the uncertainty that, more or less, accompanies darkness. Jasper, however, appeared to regard it with complacency, as was apparent by what he said in a short dialogue that now occurred between him and Mabel.

"At this rate, Eau douce," for so Mabel had also learned to style the young sailor, "we cannot be long in reaching our place of destination."

"Has your father then told you where that is, Mabel?"

"He has told me nothing; my father is too much of a soldier, and too little used to have a family around him, to talk of such matters. Is it forbidden to say whither we are bound?"

"It cannot be far, while we steer in this direction, for sixty or seventy miles will take us into the St. Lawrence, which the French might make too hot for us; and no voyage on this lake can be very long."

"So says my uncle Cap; but, to me, Jasper, Ontario and the ocean appear very much the same."

"You have then been on the ocean, while I, who pretend to be a sailor, have never yet seen salt water! You must have a great contempt for such a mariner as myself, in your heart, Mabel Dunham!"

"Then I have no such thing, in my heart, Jasper Eau douce. What right have I, a girl without experience or knowledge, to despise any; much less one like you, who are trusted by the Major and who command a vessel like this! I have never been on the ocean, though I have seen it; and, I repeat, I see no difference between this lake and the Atlantic."

"Nor, in them that sail on both? I was afraid, Mabel, your uncle has said so much against us fresh-water sailors, that you had begun to look upon us as little better than pretenders."

"Give yourself no uneasiness on that account, Jasper, for I know my uncle, and he says as many things against those who live ashore, when at York, as he now says against those who sail on fresh water. No—no—; neither my father, nor myself think any thing of such opinions! My uncle Cap, if he spoke openly, would be found to have even a worse notion of a soldier, than of a sailor who never saw the sea."

"But your father, Mabel, has a better opinion of soldiers, than of any one else; he wishes you to be the wife of a soldier."

"Jasper Eau douce!—I, the wife of a soldier!—My father wishes it?—Why should he wish any such thing—what soldier is there in the garrison that I could marry—that he could *wish me* to marry."

"One may love a calling so well, as to fancy it will cover a thousand imperfections."

"But one is not likely to love his own calling so well, as to cause him to overlook every thing else. You say my father wishes me to marry a soldier, and yet there is no soldier at Oswego, that he would be likely to give me to. I am in an awkward position, for while I am not good enough to be the wife of one of the gentlemen of the garrison, I think, even you will admit, Jasper, I am too good to be the wife of one of the common soldiers?"

As Mabel spoke thus frankly, she blushed, she knew not why, though the obscurity concealed the fact from her companion, and she laughed faintly, like one who felt that the subject, however embarrassing it might be, deserved to be treated fairly. Jasper, it would seem, viewed her position differently from herself.

"It is true, Mabel," he said, "you are not what is called a lady, in the common meaning of the word—"

"Not in any meaning, Jasper," the generous girl eagerly interrupted; "on that head, I have no vanities, I hope. Providence has made me the daughter of a serjeant, and I am content to remain in the station in which I was born."

"But all do not remain in the stations in which they were born, Mabel, for some rise above them, and some fall below them. Many serjeants have become officers; even generals; and why may not serjeants' daughters become officers' ladies?"

"In the case of Serjeant Dunham's daughter, I know no better reason than the fact that no officer is likely to wish to make her his wife," returned Mabel, laughing.

"*You* may think so, but there are some in the 55th, that know better. There is certainly one officer in that regiment, Mabel, who *does* wish to make you his wife."

Quick as the flashing lightning, the rapid thoughts of Mabel Dunham glanced over the five or six subalterns of the corps, who by age and inclinations, would be the most likely to form such a wish, and we should do injustice to her habits, perhaps, were we not to say that a lively sensation of pleasure rose momentarily in her bosom, at the thought of being raised above a station, which, whatever might be her professions of contentment, she felt that she had been too well educated to fill with perfect satisfaction. But this emotion was as transient as it was sudden, for Mabel Dunham was a girl of too much pure and womanly feeling, to view the marriage tie, through any thing so worldly as the mere advantages of station. The passing emotion, was a thrill produced by habit, while the more settled opinion which remained, was the offspring of nature and principles.

"I know no officer in the 55th, or any other regiment, who would be likely to do so foolish a thing; nor do I think I, myself, would do so foolish a thing, as to marry an officer."

"Foolish, Mabel!"

"Yes, foolish, Jasper. You know, as well as I can know, what the world would think of such matters, and I should be sorry, very sorry, to find that my husband ever regretted that he had so far yielded to a fancy for a face, or a figure, as to have married the daughter of one so much his inferior as a serjeant."

"*Your* husband, Mabel, will not be so likely to think of the father, as to think of the daughter."

The girl was talking with spirit, though feeling evidently entered into her part of the discourse, but she paused for near a minute after Jasper had made the last observation, before she uttered another word. Then she continued, in a manner less playful, and one critically attentive might have fancied in a manner that was slightly melancholy:

"Parent and child ought so to live, as not to have two hearts, or two modes of feeling and thinking. A common interest in all things, I should think as necessary to happiness, in man and wife, as between the other members of the same family. Most of all, ought neither the man nor the woman to have any unusual cause for unhappiness, the world furnishing so many of itself."

"Am I to understand, then, Mabel, you would refuse to marry an officer, merely because he was an officer?"

"Have you a right to ask such a question, Jasper?" said Mabel, smiling.

"No other right, than what a strong desire to see you happy can give, which, after all, may be very little. My anxiety has been increased, from happening to know that it is your father's intention to persuade you to marry Lt. Muir."

"My dear, dear father, can entertain no notion so ridiculous; no notion so cruel!"

"Would it then be cruel to wish you the wife of a quarter master?"

"I have told you what I think on that subject, and cannot make my words stronger. Having answered you so frankly, Jasper, I have a right to ask how you know that my father thinks of any such thing."

"That he has chosen a husband for you, I know from his own mouth; for he has told me this much, during our frequent conversations, while he has been superintending the shipment of the stores; and that Mr. Muir is to offer for you,

I know from the officer himself, who has told me as much. By putting the two things together, I have come to the opinion, mentioned."

"May not, my dear father, Jasper—" Mabel's face glowed like fire, while she spoke, though her words escaped her slowly and by a sort of involuntary impulse—"May not my dear father, have been thinking of another?—It does not follow from what you say, that Mr. Muir was in his mind."

"Is it not probable, Mabel, from all that has passed? What brings the Quarter Master here? He has never found it necessary, before, to accompany the parties that have gone below; he thinks of you for his wife, and your father has made up his own mind that you shall be so. You must see, Mabel, that Mr. Muir follows *you*."

Mabel made no answer. Her feminine instinct had indeed told her that she was an object of admiration with the Quarter Master, though she had hardly supposed to the extent that Jasper believed, and she, too, had even gathered from the discourse of her father, that he thought seriously of having her disposed of, in marriage; but, by no process of reasoning, could she ever have arrived at the inference that Lt. Muir was to be the man. She did not believe it now, though she was far from suspecting the truth. Indeed, it was her opinion that those casual remarks of her father which had struck her, had proceeded from a general wish to have her settled, rather than from any desire to see her united to any particular individual. These thoughts, however, she kept secret, for self respect and feminine reserve showed her the impropriety of making them the subject of discussion with her present companion. By way of changing the conversation, therefore, after the pause had lasted long enough to be embarrassing to both parties, she said—

"Of one thing you may be certain, Jasper, and that is all I wish to say on the subject—Lt. Muir, though he were a colonel, will never be the husband of Mabel Dunham. And now, tell me of our voyage—when will it end?"

"That is uncertain. Once afloat, we are at the mercy of the winds and waves. Pathfinder will tell you that he who begins to chase the deer in the morning, cannot tell where he will sleep at night."

"But we are not chasing a deer, nor is it morning; so Pathfinder's moral is thrown away."

"Although we are not chasing a deer, we are after that which may be as hard to catch. I can tell you no more than I have said already, for it is our duty to be close-mouthed, whether any thing depends on it, or not. I am afraid, however, I shall not keep you long enough in the Scud, to show you what she can do in fair and foul."

"I think a woman unwise who ever marries a sailor," said Mabel abruptly, and almost involuntarily.

"This is a strange opinion; why do you hold it?"

"Because a sailor's wife is certain to have a rival in his vessel. My uncle Cap, too, says, that a sailor should never marry."

"He means salt-water sailors," returned Jasper laughing. "If he thinks wives not good enough for those who sail on the ocean, he will fancy them just suited to those who sail on the lakes. I hope, Mabel, you do not take your opinions of us fresh-water mariners from all that Master Cap says?"

"Sail ho!" exclaimed the very individual of whom they were conversing—"or, boat ho! would be nearer the truth."

Jasper ran forward, and, sure enough, a small object was discernible about a hundred yards ahead of the cutter, and nearly on her lee bow. At the first glance, he saw it was a bark canoe, for though the darkness prevented hues from being distinguished, the eye that had got to be accustomed to the night, might discern forms, at some little distance; and the eye, which, like Jasper's, had long been familiar with things aquatic, could not be at a loss in discovering the outlines necessary to come to the conclusion he did.

"This may be an enemy," the young man coolly remarked, "and it may be well to overhaul him."

"He is paddling with all his might, lad," observed the Pathfinder, "and means to cross your bows and get to windward, when you might as well chase a full-grown buck on snow shoes!"

"Let her luff!—" cried Jasper, to the man at the helm—"Luff up, 'till she shakes.—There, steady and hold all that."

The helmsman complied, and, as the Scud was now dashing the water aside, merrily, a minute, or two, put the canoe so far to leeward as to render escape impracticable. Jasper now sprang to the helm, himself, and by judicious and careful handling, he got so near his chase that it was secured by a boat hook. On receiving an order, the two persons who were in the canoe, left it, and no sooner had they reached the deck of the cutter, than they were found to be Arrowhead and his wife.

Chapter XV

"What pearl is it that rich men cannot buy,
That learning is too proud to gather up;
But which the poor and the despised of all
Seek and obtain, and often find unsought?
Tell me—and I will tell thee what is truth."

Cowper, *The Task*, III.285–89.

THE MEETING with the Indian and his wife excited no surprise in the majority of those who witnessed the occurrence, but Mabel, and all who knew of the manner in which this chief had been separated from the party of Cap, simultaneously entertained suspicions, which it was far easier to feel, than to follow out, by any plausible clue, to certainty. Pathfinder, who, alone, could converse freely with the prisoners, for such they might now be considered, took Arrowhead aside, and held a long conversation with him, concerning the reasons of the latter for having deserted his charge, and the manner in which he had been since employed.

The Tuscarora met these inquiries, and he gave his answers, with the stoicism of an Indian. As respects the separation, his excuses were very simply made, and they seemed to be sufficiently plausible. When he found that the party was discovered in its place of concealment, he naturally sought his own safety, which he secured by plunging into the woods, for he made no doubt that all who could not effect this much, would be massacred on the spot. In a word, he had run away, in order to save his life.

"This is well," returned Pathfinder, affecting to believe the other's apologies; "my brother did very wisely; but his woman followed?"

"Do not the Pale Faces' women follow their husbands? Would not Pathfinder have looked back to see if one he loved was coming?"

This appeal was made to the guide, while he was in a most fortunate frame of mind to admit its force, for Mabel, and her blandishments and constancy, were getting to be images familiar to his thoughts. The Tuscarora, though he could not trace the reason, saw that his excuse was admitted, and he stood, with quiet dignity, awaiting the next inquiry.

"This is reasonable and nat'ral," returned Pathfinder in English, passing from one language to the other, insensibly to himself, as his feelings, or habit dictated, "this is nat'ral, and may be so. A woman would be likely to follow the man to whom she had plighted faith, and husband and wife are one flesh. Mabel, herself, would have been likely to follow the sarjeant, had he been present, and retreated in this manner, and no doubt, no doubt, the warm-hearted girl would have followed her husband! Your words are honest, Tuscarora," changing the language to the dialect of the other, "your words are honest, and very pleasant, and just. But, why has my brother been so long from the fort; his friends have thought of him often, but have never seen him!"

"If the doe follows the buck, ought not the buck to follow the doe!" answered the Tuscarora smiling, and laying a finger significantly on the shoulder of his interrogator. "Arrowhead's wife followed Arrowhead; it was right in Arrowhead to follow his wife. She lost her way, and they made her cook in a strange wigwam."

"I understand you, Tuscarora. The woman fell into the hands of the Mingos, and you kept upon their trail."

"Pathfinder can see a reason, as easily as he can see the moss on the trees. It is so."

"And how long have you got the woman back, and in what manner has it been done?"

"Two suns. The Dew of June was not long in coming, when her husband whispered to her the path."

"Well, well, all this seems nat'ral, and according to materimony—But, Tuscarora, how did you get that canoe, and why are you paddling towards the St. Lawrence, instead of the garrison?"

"Arrowhead can tell his own from that of another. This canoe is mine; I found it on the shore, near the fort."

"That sounds reasonable, too, for the canoe does belong to the man, and an Injin would make few words about taking it. Still, it is extr'ord'nary that we saw nothing of the fellow and his wife, for the canoe must have left the river before we did ourselves."

This idea, which passed rapidly through the mind of the guide, was now put to the Indian in the shape of a question.

"Pathfinder knows that a warrior can have shame. The father would have asked me for his daughter, and I could not give her to him. I sent the Dew of June for the canoe, and none spoke to the woman. A Tuscarora woman would not be free in speaking to strange men."

All this, too, was plausible, and in conformity with Indian character, and Indian customs. As was usual, Arrowhead had received one half of his compensation, previously to quitting the Mohawk, and his refraining to demand the residue was a proof of that conscientious consideration of mutual rights that quite as often distinguishes the morality of a savage as that of a christian. To one as upright as Pathfinder, Arrowhead had conducted himself with delicacy and propriety, though it would have been more in accordance with his own frank nature, to have met the father, and abided by the simple truth. Still, accustomed to the ways of Indians, he saw nothing out of the ordinary track of things, in the course the other had taken.

"This runs like water flowing down hill, Arrowhead," he answered, after a little reflection, "and truth obliges me to own it. It was the gift of a red skin to act in this way, though I do not think it was the gift of a Pale Face. You would not look upon the grief of the girl's father."

Arrowhead made a quiet inclination of the body, as if to assent.

"One thing more my brother will tell me," continued Pathfinder, "and there will be no cloud between his wigwam and the strong house of the Yengeese. If he can blow away this bit of fog, his friends will look at him, as he sits by his own fire, and he can look at them, as they lay aside their arms, and forget that they are warriors. Why was the head of Arrowhead's canoe, looking towards the St. Lawrence, where there are none but inimies to be found?"

"Why were the Pathfinder and his friends looking the same way?" asked the Tuscarora calmly. "A Tuscarora may look in the same direction as a Yengeese."

"Why, to own the truth, Arrowhead, we are out scouting, like;—that is sailing—in other words, we are on the King's business, and we have a right to be here, though we may not have a right to say *why* we are here."

"Arrowhead saw the big canoe, and he loves to look on the face of Eau douce. He was going towards the sun at evening, in order to seek his wigwam, but finding that the young sailor was going the other way, he turned that he might look in the same direction. Eau douce and Arrowhead were together, on the last trail."

"This may all be true, Tuscarora, and you are welcome. You shall eat of our venison, and then we must separate. The setting sun is behind us, and both of us move quick, my brother will get too far from that which he seeks, unless he turns round."

Pathfinder now returned to the others, and reported the result of his examination. He appeared himself to believe that the account of Arrowhead might be true, though he admitted that caution would be prudent with one he disliked; but his auditors, Jasper excepted, seemed less disposed to put faith in the explanations.

"This chap must be ironed at once, Brother Dunham," said Cap, as soon as Pathfinder finished his narration; "he must be turned over to the Master at Arms, if there is any such officer on fresh water, and a court martial ought to be ordered, as soon as we reach port."

"I think it wisest to detain the fellow," the serjeant answered, "but irons are unnecessary so long as he remains in the cutter. In the morning, the matter shall be inquired into."

Arrowhead was now summoned, and told the decision. The Indian listened gravely and made no objections. On the contrary, he submitted with the calm and reserved dignity with which the American Aborigines are known to yield to fate, and he stood apart, an attentive but calm observer of what was passing. Jasper caused the cutter's sails to be filled, and the Scud resumed her course.

It was now getting towards the hour to set the watch, and when it was usual to retire for the night. Most of the party went below, leaving no one on deck but Cap, the Serjeant, Jasper, and two of the crew. Arrowhead and his wife also remained, the former standing aloof in proud reserve, and the latter exhibiting, by her attitude and passiveness, the meek humility that characterizes an Indian woman.

"You will find a place for your wife below, Arrowhead, where my daughter will attend to her wants," said the Serjeant kindly, who was himself on the point of quitting the deck; "yonder is a sail, where you may sleep, yourself."

"I thank my father. The Tuscaroras are not poor. The woman will look for my blankets in the canoe."

"As you wish, my friend. We think it necessary to detain you, but not necessary to confine, or to maltreat you. Send your squaw into the canoe for the blankets, and you may follow her yourself and hand us up the paddles. As there may be some sleepy heads in the Scud, Eau douce," added the serjeant, in a lower tone, "it may be well to secure the paddles."

Jasper assented, and Arrowhead and his wife, with whom resistance appeared to be out of the question, silently complied with the directions. A few expressions of sharp rebuke passed from the Indian to his wife, while both were employed in the canoe, which the latter received with submissive quiet, immediately repairing an error she had made, by laying aside the blanket she had taken, and searching another that was more to her tyrant's mind.

"Come, bear a hand, Arrowhead," said the Serjeant, who stood at the gunwale, overlooking the movements of the two, which were proceeding too slowly for the impatience of a drowsy man, "it is getting late, and we soldiers have such a thing as reveillé. Early to bed, and early to rise."

"Arrowhead is coming—" was the answer, as the Tuscarora stepped towards the head of his canoe.

One blow of his keen knife severed the rope which held the boat, when the cutter glanced ahead, leaving the light bubble of bark, which instantly lost its way, almost stationary. So suddenly and dexterously was this manœuvre performed, that the canoe was on the lee quarter of the Scud, before the serjeant was aware of the artifice, and quite in her wake, ere he had time to announce it to his companions.

"Hard a-lee!" shouted Jasper, letting fly the jib sheet with his own hands, when the cutter came swiftly up to the breeze, with all her canvass flapping, or was running into the wind's eye, as seamen term it, until the light craft was a hundred feet to windward of her former position. Quick and dexterous as was this movement, and ready as had been the expedient, it was not quicker, or more ready, than that of the Tuscarora. With an intelligence that denoted some familiarity with vessels, he had seized his paddle, and was already skimming the water, aided by the efforts of his wife. The direction he took was south-westerly, or on a line that led him equally towards the wind and the shore, while it also kept him so far aloof from the cutter, as to avoid the danger of the latter's falling on board of him, when she filled on the other tack.

Swiftly as the Scud had shot into the wind, and far as she had forged ahead, Jasper knew it was necessary to cast her, ere she lost her way, and it was not two minutes from the time the helm had been put down, before the lively little craft was aback forward, and rapidly falling off, in order to allow her sails to fill on the opposite tack.

"He will escape!" said Jasper, the instant he caught a glimpse of the relative bearings of the cutter and the canoe. "The cunning knave is paddling dead to windward, and the Scud can never overtake him!"

"You have a canoe!" exclaimed the serjeant, manifesting the eagerness of a boy to join in the pursuit—"Let us launch it, and give chase!"

" 'Twill be useless. If Pathfinder had been on deck, there might have been a chance; but there is none now. To launch the canoe would have taken three or four minutes, and the time lost would have been sufficient for the purposes of Arrowhead."

Both Cap and the serjeant saw the truth of this, which would have been nearly self evident even to one unaccustomed to vessels. The shore was distant less than half a mile, and the canoe was already glancing into its shadows, at a rate to show that it would reach the land, ere its pursuers could probably get half the distance. The canoe itself, might have been seized, but it would have been a useless prize, for Arrowhead in the woods, would be more likely to reach the other shore without detection than if he still possessed the means to venture on the lake again, though it might be, and probably would be at greater bodily labor to himself. The helm of the Scud, was reluctantly put up again, and the cutter wore short round on her heel, coming up to her course on the other tack, as if acting on instinct. All this was done by Jasper in profound silence, his assistants understanding what was necessary, and lending their aid in a sort of mechanical imitation. While these manœuvres were in the course of execution, Cap took the Serjeant by a button and led him towards the cabin door, where he was out of ear-shot, and began to unlock his stores of thought.

"Harkee, Brother Dunham," he said with an ominous face, "this is a matter that requires mature thought, and much circumspection."

"The life of a soldier, Brother Cap, is one of constant thought and circumspection. On this frontier, were we to overlook either, our scalps might be taken from our heads in the first nap."

"But I consider this capture of Arrowhead as a circumstance—and I might add his escape as another. This Jasper Freshwater must look to it!"

"They are both circumstances truly, brother, but they tell different ways. If it is a circumstance against the lad, that the Indian has escaped, it is a circumstance in his favor, that he was first taken."

"Ay, ay, but two circumstances do not contradict each other, like two negatives. If you will follow the advice of an old seaman, serjeant, not a moment is to be lost, in taking the steps necessary, for the security of the vessel, and all on board of her. The cutter is now slipping through the water at the rate of six knots, and as the distances are so short on this bit of a pond, we may all find ourselves in a French port before morning, and in a French prison before night."

"This may be true enough; what would you advise me to do, brother?"

"In my opinion you should put this Master Freshwater under arrest, on the spot; send him below, under the charge of a sentinel, and transfer the command of the cutter to me. All this you have power to perform, the craft belonging to the army, and you being the commanding officer of the troops present."

Serjeant Dunham deliberated more than an hour on the

propriety of this proposal, for, though sufficiently prompt when his mind was really made up, he was habitually thoughtful and wary. The habit of superintending the personal police of the garrison had made him acquainted with character, and he had long been disposed to think well of Jasper. Still that subtle poison, suspicion, had entered his soul, and so much were the artifices and intrigues of the French dreaded, that, especially warned as he had been by his commander, it is not to be wondered the recollection of years of good conduct, should vanish under the influence of a distrust so keen, and seemingly so plausible. In this embarrassment, the Serjeant consulted the Quarter Master, whose opinion, as his superior, he felt bound to respect, though, at the moment, independent of his control. It is an unfortunate occurrence, for one who is in a dilemma, to ask advice of another who is desirous of standing well in his favor, the party consulted being almost certain to try to think in the manner which will be the most agreeable to the party consulting. In the present instance, it was equally unfortunate, as respects a candid consideration of the subject, that Cap, instead of the Serjeant himself, made the statement of the case, for the earnest old sailor was not backward in letting his listener perceive to which side he was desirous that the Quarter Master should lean. Lt. Muir was much too politic to offend the uncle and father of the woman he hoped and expected to win, had he really thought the case admitted of doubt, but, in the manner in which the facts were submitted to him, he was seriously inclined to think that it would be well to put the control of the Scud temporarily into the management of Cap, as a precaution against treachery. This opinion, then, decided the serjeant, who, forthwith, set about the execution of the necessary measures.

Without entering into any explanations, Serjeant Dunham simply informed Jasper that he felt it to be his duty to deprive him, temporarily, of the command of the cutter, and to confer it on his own brother-in-law. A natural and involuntary burst of surprise, which escaped the young man, was met by a quiet remark, reminding him that military service was often of a nature that required concealment, and a declaration that the present duty was of such a character that this particular arrangement had become indispensable. Although Jasper's astonishment remained undiminished—the serjeant cautiously abstaining from making any allusions to his suspicions—the young man was accustomed to obey with military submission; and he quietly acquiesced—with his own mouth directing the little crew to receive their future orders from Cap, until another change should be effected. When, however, he was told the case required that not only he, himself, but his principal assistant, who, on account of his long acquaintance with the lake, usually was termed the pilot, were to remain below, there was an alteration in his countenance and manner that denoted deep mortification, though it was so well mastered as to leave even the distrustful Cap in doubt as to its meaning. As a matter of course, however, when distrust existed, it was not long before the worst construction was put upon it.

As soon as Jasper and the pilot were below, the sentinel at the hatch received private orders to pay particular attention to both; to allow neither to come on deck again, without giving instant notice to the person who might then be in charge of the cutter, and to insist on his return below, as soon as possible. This precaution, however, was uncalled for, Jasper and his assistant, both throwing themselves silently on their pallets, which neither quitted again that night.

"And, now, Serjeant," said Cap, as soon as he found himself master of the deck, "you will just have the goodness to give me the courses and distance, that I may see the boat keeps her head the right way."

"I know nothing of either, Brother Cap," returned Dunham, not a little embarrassed at the question. "We must make the best of our way to the station among the Thousand Islands, where 'we shall land, relieve the party that is already out and get information for our future government.' That's it, nearly word for word, as it stands in the written orders."

"But you can muster a chart—something in the way of bearings and distances, that I may see the road?"

"I do not think Jasper ever had any thing of the sort to go by."

"No chart, Serjeant Dunham!"

"Not a scrap of a pen, even. Our sailors navigate this lake without any aid from maps."

"The devil they do!—They must be regular Yahoos. And do you suppose, Serjeant Dunham, that I can find one island out of a thousand, without knowing its name, or its position—without even a course, or a distance?"

"As for the *name*, Brother Cap, you need not be particular, for not one of the whole thousand *has* a name, and so a mistake can never be made on that score. As for the position, never having been there, myself, I can tell you nothing about it, nor do I think its position of any particular consequence, provided we find the spot. Perhaps one of the hands on deck can tell us the way."

"Hold on, Serjeant—hold on, a moment, if you please, Serjeant Dunham. If I am to command this craft, it must be done, if you please, without holding any councils of war with the cook and cabin boy. A ship-master is a ship-master, and he must have an opinion of his own, even if it be a wrong one. I suppose you know service well enough to understand that it is better in a commander to go wrong, than to go nowhere. At all events, the Lord High Admiral could'n't command a yawl with dignity, if he consulted the cockswain every time he wished to go ashore. No—no—if I sink, I sink; but d——e, I'll go down ship-shape and with dignity."

"But, Brother Cap, I have no wish to go down any where, unless it be to the station among the Thousand Islands, whither we are bound."

"Well, well, serjeant, rather than ask advice, that is direct, bare-faced advice, of a foremast hand, or any other than a quarter-deck officer, I would go round to the whole thousand, and examine them one by one, until we got the right haven. But, there is such a thing, as coming at an opinion, without manifesting ignorance, and I will manage to rowse all there is, out of these hands, and make them think, all the while, that I am cramming them, with my own experience. We are sometimes obliged to use the glass at sea, when there is nothing in sight, or to heave the lead, long before we strike soundings. I suppose you know in the army, serjeant, that the next thing to knowing that which is desirable, is to seem to know all about it. When a youngster, I sailed two v'y'ges with a man who navigated his ship pretty much by the latter sort of information, which sometimes answers."

"I know we are steering in the right direction, at present," returned the serjeant; "but in the course of a few hours we shall be up with a head-land, where we must feel our way, with more caution."

"Leave me to pump the man at the wheel, brother, and you shall see that I will make him suck, in a very few minutes."

Cap and the serjeant now walked aft, until they stood by the sailor who was at the helm, Cap maintaining an air of security and tranquillity, like one who was entirely confident of his own powers.

"This is a wholesome air, my lad," Cap observed, as it might be incidentally, and in the manner that a superior on board a vessel sometimes condescends to use to a favored inferior. "Of course, you have it, in this fashion, off the land, every night?"

"At this season of the year, sir," the man returned, touching his hat, out of respect to his new commander and Serjeant Dunham's connection.

"The same thing, I take it, among the Thousand Islands?— The wind will stand of course, though we shall then have land on every side of us."

"When we get further east, sir, the wind will probably shift, for there can then be no particular land breeze."

"Ay, ay—so much for your fresh water! It has always some trick that is opposed to nature. Now, down among the West-India islands, one is just as certain of having a land breeze, as he is of having a sea breeze. In that respect there is no difference, though it's quite in rule, it should be different up here, on this bit of fresh water. Of course, my lad, you know all about these said Thousand Islands?"

"Lord bless you, Master Cap, nobody knows all about them, or any thing about them. They are a puzzle to the oldest sailor on the lake, and we don't pretend to know even their names. For that matter, most of them have no more names than a child that dies before it is christened."

"Are you a Roman Catholic?—" demanded the serjeant, sharply.

"No sir, nor any thing else. I'm a generalizer about religion, never troubling that which don't trouble me."

"Hum! a generalizer; that is, no doubt, one of the new sects that afflict the country!" muttered Mr. Dunham, whose grandfather had been a New-Jersey quaker, his father a presbyterian, and who had joined the church of England, himself, after he entered the army.

"I take it, John," resumed Cap—"Your name is Jack, I believe?"

"No sir; I am called Robert."

"Ay, Robert—it's very much the same thing—Jack, or Bob—we use the two indifferently. I say, Bob, it's good holding ground, is it, down at this same station for which we are bound?"

"Bless you sir, I know no more about it, than one of the Mohawks, or a soldier of the 55th."

"Did you never anchor there?"

"Never, sir. Master Eau douce always makes fast to the shore."

"But in running in for the town, you kept the lead going, out of question, and must have tallowed as usual?"

"Tallow! and town, too! Bless you heart, Master Cap, there is no more town, than there is on your chin, and not half as much tallow."

The serjeant smiled grimly, but his brother-in-law did not detect this proof of facetiousness.

"No church tower, nor light, nor fort, ha! There is a garrison, as you call it hereaway, at least."

"Ask Serjeant Dunham, sir, if you wish to know that! All the garrison is on board the Scud."

"But, in running in, Bob, which of the channels do you think the best, the one you went last, or—or—or—ay, or the other?"

"I can't say, sir. I know nothing of either."

"You did'n't go to sleep, fellow, at the wheel did you?"

"Not at the wheel, sir, but down in the fore peak, in my berth. Eau douce sent us below, so'gers and all, with the exception of the pilot, and we know no more of the road than if we had never been over it. This he has always done, in going in and coming out, and, for the life of me, I could tell you nothing of the channel, or of the course, after we are once fairly up with the islands. No one knows any thing of either, but Jasper and the pilot."

"Here's a circumstance for you, serjeant," said Cap, leading his brother-in-law, a little aside. "There is no one on board to pump, for they all suck from ignorance, at the first stroke of the brake. How the devil am I to find the way to this station."

"Sure enough, Brother Cap; your question is more easily put than answered. Is there no such thing as figuring it out, by navigation? I thought you salt-water mariners were able to do as small a thing as that! I have often read of their discovering islands, surely."

"That you have, brother; that you have; and this discovery would be the greatest of them all, for it would not only be discovering one island, but one island out of a thousand. I might make out to pick up a single needle on this deck, old as I am, but I much doubt if I could pick one out of a haystack."

"Still, the sailors of the lake, have a method of finding the places they wish to go to."

"If I have understood you, serjeant, this station, or block house, is particularly private?"

"It is indeed; the utmost care having been taken to prevent a knowledge of its position, from reaching the enemy."

"And you expect me, a stranger on your lake, to find this place without chart, course, distance, latitude, longitude, or soundings—ay, d——e, or tallow! Allow me to ask if you think a mariner runs by his nose, like one of Pathfinder's hounds?"

"Well, brother, you may yet learn something by questioning the young man at the helm; I can hardly think that he is as ignorant as he pretends to be."

"Hum—this looks like another circumstance! For that matter, the case is getting to be so full of circumstances, that one hardly knows how to foot up the evidence. But we will soon see how much the lad knows."

Cap and the serjeant now returned to their station near the helm, and the former renewed his inquiries.

"Do you happen to know what may be the latitude and longitude of this said island, my lad?" he asked.

"The what, sir?"

"Why the latitude or the longitude; one or both; I'm not particular which, as I merely inquire in order to see how they bring up young men on this bit of fresh water."

"I'm not particular about either, myself, sir, and so I do not happen to know what you mean."

"Not what I mean!—You know what latitude is?"

"Not I, sir," returned the man, hesitating, "though I believe it is French, for the Upper Lakes."

"Whe-e-e-w," whistled Cap, drawing out his breath, like the broken stop of an organ—"Latitude, French for upper lakes! Harkee, young man; do you know what longitude means?"

"I believe I do, sir—that is five feet six, the regulation height for soldiers in the King's service."

"There's the longitude found out for you, serjeant, in the rattling of a brace block! You have some notion about a degree, and minutes, and seconds, I hope?"

"Yes sir, degree means my betters, and minutes and seconds, are for the short or long log-lines. We all know these things, as well as the salt-water people."

"D——e, Brother Dunham, if I think even Faith can get along on this lake, much as they say it can do with mountains. I'm sure character is in no security. Well, my lad, you understand the azimuth, and measuring distances, and how to box the compass."

"As for the first, sir, I can't say I do. The distances we all know, as we measure them from point to point, and as for boxing the compass, I will turn my back to no admiral in His Majesty's fleet. Nothe-nothe and by east, nothe-nothe east, nothe east and by nothe, nothe east; nothe east and by east, east nothe east, east and by nothe, east;—"

"That will do—that will do. You'll bring about a shift of wind, if you go on in this manner. I see very plainly, serjeant," walking away again, and dropping his voice, "we've nothing to hope for, from that chap. I'll stand on two hours longer, on this tack, when we'll heave-to and get the soundings; after which we will be governed by circumstances."

To this the serjeant, who, to coin a word, was very much of an idiosyncratist, made no objections, and, as the wind grew lighter, as usual with the advance of night, and there were no immediate obstacles to the navigation, he made a bed of a sail, on deck, and was soon lost in the sound sleep of a soldier. Cap continued to walk the deck, for he was one whose iron frame set fatigue at defiance, and not once that night did he close his eyes.

It was broad day-light when Serjeant Dunham awoke, and the exclamation of surprise that escaped him, as he rose to his feet, and began to look about him, was stronger than it was usual for one so drilled to suffer to be heard. He found the weather entirely changed, the view bounded by driving mist, that limited the visible horizon to a circle of about a mile in diameter, the lake raging and covered with foam, and the Scud lying to. A brief conversation with his brother-in-law, let him into the secrets of all these sudden changes.

According to the account of Master Cap, the wind had died away to a calm, about midnight, or just as he was thinking of heaving to, to sound, for islands ahead were beginning to be seen. At one A.M. it began to blow from the north east, accompanied by a drizzle, and he stood off to the northward and westward, knowing that the coast of New York lay in the opposite direction. At half past one, he stowed the staysail, reefed the mainsail, and took the bonnet off the jib. At two, he was compelled to get a second reef aft, and by half past two, he had put a balance reef in the sail, and was lying to.

"I can't say but the boat behaves well, Serjeant," the old sailor added, "but it blows forty two pounders! I had no idea there were any such currents of air, up here on this bit of fresh water, though I care not the knotting of a yarn for it, as your lake has now somewhat of a natural look, and—" spitting from his mouth, with distaste, a dash of the spray that had just wetted his face, "and if this d——d water, had a savor of salt about it, one might be comfortable."

"How long have you been heading in this direction, Brother Cap?" enquired the prudent soldier. "And at what rate may we be going through the water?"

"Why two or three hours, mayhap, and she went like a horse for the first pair of them. Oh! we've a fine offing, now, for, to own the truth, little relishing the neighborhood of them said islands, although they are to windward, I took the helm myself, and run her off free, for some league or two. We are well to leeward of them, I'll engage. I say to leeward, for, though one might wish to be well to windward of one island, or even half a dozen, when it comes to a thousand, the better way is to give it up at once, and to slide down under their lee, as fast as possible. No—no—there they are, up yonder in the drizzle, and there they may stay, for any thing Charles Cap cares!"

"As the north shore lies only some five or six leagues from us, Brother, and I know there is a large bay, in that quarter, might it not be well to consult some of the crew concerning our position, if indeed we do not call up, Jasper Eau douce, and tell him to carry us back to Oswego? It is quite impossible we should ever reach the station with this wind directly in our teeth."

"There are several serious professional reasons, serjeant, against all your propositions. In the first place, an admission of ignorance on the part of a commander, would destroy discipline—No matter, brother, I understand your shake of the head, but nothing capsizes discipline so much, as to confess ignorance. I once knew a master of a vessel who went a week on a wrong course, rather than allow he had made a mistake, and it was surprising how much he rose in the opinions of his people, just because they could not understand him."

"That may do on salt water, Brother Cap, but it will hardly do on fresh. Rather than wreck my command on the Canada shore, I shall feel it a duty to take Jasper out of arrest."

"And make a haven in Frontenac! No, serjeant, the Scud is in good hands, and will now learn something of seamanship. We have a fine offing, and no one but a madman would think of going upon a coast in a gale like this. I shall ware every watch, and then we shall be safe against all dangers, but those of the drift, which in a light low craft like this, without top hamper, will be next to nothing. Leave it all to me, serjeant, and I pledge you the character of Charles Cap, that all will go well."

Serjeant Dunham was fain to yield. He had great confidence in his connection's professional skill, and hoped that he would take such care of the cutter as would amply justify his good opinion. On the other hand, as distrust like love, "grows by what it feeds on," he entertained so much apprehension of treachery, that he was quite willing any one but Jasper should, just then, have the control of the fate of the whole party. Truth, moreover, compels us to admit another motive. The particular duty on which he was now sent, should have been confided to a commissioned officer, of right, and Major Duncan had excited a good deal of discontent among the subalterns of the garrison, by having confided it to one of the Serjeant's humble station. To return, without having even reached the point of destination, therefore, the latter felt would be a failure from which he was not likely soon to recover, and the measure would at once be the means of placing a superior in his shoes.

Chapter XVI

"Thou glorious mirror, where the Almighty's form
Glasses itself in tempests; in all time,
Calm or convulsed—in breeze, or gale, or storm,
Icing the pole, or in the torrid clime
Dark heaving;—boundless, endless and sublime—
The image of Eternity; the throne
Of the Invisible; even from out thy slime
The monsters of the deep are made; each zone
Obeys thee; thou goest forth, dread, fathomless, alone."
Byron, *Childe Harold's Pilgrimage*, IV.CLXXXIII.

As THE DAY ADVANCED, the portion of the inmates of the vessel that had the liberty of doing so, appeared on deck. As yet the sea was not very high, from which it was inferred that the cutter was still under the lee of the islands, but it was apparent to all who understood the lake, that they were about to experience one of the heavy autumnal gales of that region. Land was nowhere visible, and the horizon, on every side, exhibited that gloomy void, which lends to all views on vast bodies of water, the sublimity of mystery. The swells, or as landsmen term them, the waves, were short and curling, breaking of necessity sooner than the longer seas of the ocean, while the element itself, instead of presenting that beautiful hue, which rivals the deep tint of the southern sky, looked green and angry, though wanting in the lustre that is derived from the rays of the sun.

The soldiers were soon satisfied with the prospect, and, one by one, they disappeared, until none were left on deck but the crew, the Serjeant, Cap, Pathfinder, the Quarter Master, and Mabel. There was a shade on the brow of the latter, who had been made acquainted with the real state of things, and who had fruitlessly ventured an appeal in favor of Jasper's restoration to the command. A night's rest and a night's reflection appeared also to have confirmed the Pathfinder in his opinion of the young man's innocence, and he, too, had made a warm appeal in behalf of his friend, though with the same want of success.

Several hours passed away, the wind gradually getting to

be heavier, and the sea rising, until the motion of the cutter compelled Mabel and the Quarter Master to retreat, also. Cap wore several times, and it was now evident that the Scud was drifting into the broader and deeper parts of the lake, the seas raging down upon her in a way that none but a vessel of superior mould and build could have long ridden, and withstood. All this, however, gave Cap no uneasiness, but like the hunter that pricks his ears at the sound of the horn, or the war horse that paws and snorts with pleasure at the roll of the drum, the whole scene awakened all that was man within him, and instead of the captious, supercilious and dogmatic critic, quarrelling with trifles and exaggerating immaterial things, he began to exhibit the qualities of the hardy and experienced seaman, that he truly was. The hands soon imbibed a respect for his skill, and, though they wondered at the disappearance of their old commander and the pilot, for which no reason had been publicly given, they soon yielded an implicit and cheerful obedience to the new one.

"This bit of fresh water, after all, Brother Dunham, has some spirit, I find," cried Cap, about noon, rubbing his hands in pure satisfaction at finding himself once more wrestling with the elements. "The wind seems to be an honest old-fashioned gale, and the seas have a fanciful resemblance to those of the Gulph Stream. I like this, serjeant, I like this; and shall get to respect your lake, if it hold out twenty four hours, longer, in the fashion, in which it has begun."

"Land ho!" shouted the man who was stationed on the forecastle.

Cap hurried forward, and there, sure enough, the land was visible through the drizzle, at the distance of about half a mile, the cutter heading directly towards it. The first impulse of the old seaman was to give an order to, "stand by to ware off shore," but the cool headed soldier, restrained him.

"By going a little nearer," said the serjeant, "some of us may recognize the place. Most of us know the American shore, in this part of the lake, and it will be something gained to learn our position."

"Very true—very true; if, indeed, there is any chance of that, we will hold on. What is this, off here, a little on our weather bow?—It looks like a low head-land."

"The garrison, by Jove!" exclaimed the other, whose trained eye sooner recognized the military outlines, than the less instructed senses of his connection.

The Serjeant was not mistaken. There was the fort sure enough, though it looked dim and indistinct through the fine rain, as if it were seen in the dusk of evening, or the haze of morning. The low, sodded and verdant ramparts, the sombre palisades, now darker than ever with water, the roof of a house or two, the tall, solitary flag-staff, with its halyards blown steadily out, into a curve that appeared traced in immovable lines in the air, were all soon to be seen, though no sign of animated life could be discovered. Even the sentinel was housed, and, at first, it was believed that no eye would detect the presence of their own vessel. But the unceasing vigilance of a border garrison did not slumber. One of the look outs probably made the interesting discovery, a man or two were seen on some elevated stands, and then the entire ramparts, next the lake, were dotted with human beings.

The whole scene was one in which sublimity was singularly relieved by the picturesque. The raging of the tempest had a character of duration, that rendered it easy to imagine it might be a permanent feature of the spot. The roar of the wind was without intermission, and the raging water answered to its dull but grand strains, with hissing spray, a menacing wash, and sullen surges. The drizzle made a medium for the eye which closely resembled that of a thin mist, softening and rendering mysterious the images it revealed, while the genial feeling that is apt to accompany a gale of wind on water, contributed to aid the milder influences of the moment. The dark, interminable forest hove up out of the obscurity, grand, sombre and impressive, while the solitary, peculiar and picturesque glimpses of life that were caught in and about the fort, formed a refuge for the eye to retreat to, when oppressed with the more imposing objects of nature.

"They see us," said the Serjeant, "and think we have returned on account of the gale, and have fallen to leeward of the port. Yes, there is Major Duncan himself, on the north eastern bastion; I know him by his height, and by the officers around him!"

"Serjeant, it would be worth standing a little jeering, if we could fetch into the river, and come safely to an anchor! In that case, too, we might land this Master Oh! the deuce, and purify the boat."

"It would indeed, but poor sailor as I am, I well know it cannot be done. Nothing that sails the lake can turn to windward against this gale, and there is no anchorage outside, in weather like this."

"I know it—I see it—serjeant, and pleasant as is that sight to you landsmen, we must leave it. For myself, I am never so happy, in heavy weather, as when I am certain that the land is behind me."

The Scud had now forged so near in, that it became indispensable to lay her head off shore, again, and the necessary orders were given. The storm stay-sail was set forward, the gaff lowered, the helm put up, and the light craft, that seemed to sport with the elements like a duck, fell off a little, drew ahead swiftly, obeyed her rudder, and was soon flying away on the top of the surges, dead before the gale. While making this rapid flight, though the land still remained in view, on her larboard beam, the fort, and the groups of anxious spectators on its ramparts were swallowed up in the mist. Then followed the evolutions necessary to bring the head of the cutter up to the wind, when she again began to wallow her weary way towards the north shore.

Hours now passed, before any further change was made, the wind increasing in force, until even the dogmatical Cap fairly admitted it was blowing a thorough gale of wind. About sunset the Scud wore again, to keep her off the north shore, during the hours of darkness; and at midnight her temporary master, who by questioning the crew in an indirect manner had obtained some general knowledge of the size and shape of the lake, believed himself to be about midway between the two shores. The height and length of the seas, aided this impression, and it must be added that Cap, by this time, began to feel a respect for fresh water, that twenty four hours earlier he would have derided as impossible. Just as the night turned, the fury of the wind became so great, that he found it impossible to bear up against it, the water falling on the deck of the little craft in such masses as to cause her to shake to the centre, and, though a vessel of singularly lively qualities, to threaten to bury her beneath its weight. The people of the Scud averred that never before had they been out in such a tempest, which was true, for possessing a perfect knowledge of all the rivers and head-lands and havens, Jasper would have carried the cutter in shore, long ere this, and placed her in safety, in some secure anchorage. But, Cap still disdained to consult the young master, who continued below, determining to act like a mariner of the broad ocean.

It was one in the morning, when the storm staysail was again got on the Scud, the head of the mainsail lowered, and the cutter put before the wind. Although the canvass now exposed was merely a rag in surface, the little craft nobly justified the use of the name she bore. For eight hours did she scud, in truth, and it was almost with the velocity of the gulls that wheeled wildly over her in the tempest, apparently afraid to alight in the boiling caldron of the lake. The dawn of day brought little change, for no other horizon became visible, than the narrow circle of drizzling sky and water, already described, in which it seemed as if the elements were rioting in chaotic confusion. During this time the crew and passengers of the cutter were of necessity passive. Jasper and the pilot remained below, but, the motion of the vessel having become easier, nearly all the rest were on deck. The morning meal had been taken in silence, and eye met eye, as if their owners asked each other, in dumb show, what was to be the end of this strife in the elements. Cap, however, was perfectly composed, and his face brightened, his step grew firmer, and his whole air more assured, as the storm increased, making larger demands on his professional skill, and personal spirit. He stood on the forecastle, his arms crossed, balancing his body with a seaman's instinct, while his eyes watched the caps of the seas, as they broke and glanced past the reeling cutter, itself in such swift motion, as if they were the scud flying athwart the sky. At this sublime instant one of the hands gave the unexpected cry of "a sail!"

There was so much of the wild and solitary character of the wilderness about Ontario, that one scarcely expected to meet with a vessel on its waters. The Scud herself, to those who were in her, resembled a man threading the forest alone, and the meeting was like that of two solitary hunters beneath the broad canopy of leaves, that then covered so many millions of acres, on the continent of America. The peculiar state of the weather served to increase the romantic, almost supernatural appearance of the passage. Cap alone regarded it with practised eyes, and even he felt his iron nerves thrill under the sensations that were awakened by the wild features of the scene.

The strange vessel was about two cables' length ahead of the Scud, standing by the wind athwart her bows, and steering a course to render it probable that the latter would pass within a few yards of her. She was a full-rigged ship, and seen through the misty medium of the tempest, the most experienced eye could detect no imperfection in her gear or construction. The only canvass she had set, was a close reefed main-top-sail, and two small storm staysails, one forward and the other aft. Still the power of the wind pressed so hard upon her, as to bear her down nearly to her beam-ends, whenever the hull was not righted by the buoyancy of some wave under her lee. Her spars were all in their places, and by her motion through the water, which might have equalled four knots in the hour, it was apparent that she steered a little free.

"The fellow must know his position well," said Cap, as the cutter flew down towards the ship, with a velocity almost equalling that of the gale, "for he is standing boldly to the southward, where he expects to find anchorage or a haven. No man in his senses would run off free in that fashion, that was not driven to scudding, like ourselves, who did not perfectly understand where he was going."

"We have made an awful run, captain," returned the man to whom this remark had been addressed. "That is the French King's ship, Lee My Calm (le Montcalm) and she is standing in for the Niagara, where her owner has a garrison and a port. We've made an awful run of it!"

"Ay, bad luck to him! Frenchman like, he skulks into port, the moment he sees an English bottom."

"It might be well for us, if we could follow him," returned the man shaking his head despondingly, "for we are getting into the end of a bay, up here at the head of the lake, and it is uncertain whether we ever get out of it again!"

"Poh! man, poh!—We have plenty of sea room, and a good English hull beneath us. We are no Johnny Crapauds to hide ourselves behind a point, or a fort, on account of a puff of wind. Mind your helm, sir!"

The order was given on account of the menacing appearance of the approaching passage. The Scud was now heading directly for the forefoot of the Frenchman, and, the distance between the two vessels having diminished to a hundred yards, it was momentarily questionable if there was room to pass.

"Port, sir—port!" shouted Cap. "Port your helm and pass astern!"

The crew of the Frenchman were seen assembling to windward, and a few muskets were pointed, as if to order the people of the Scud to keep off. Gesticulations were observed, but the scene was too wild and menacing to admit of the ordinary expedients of war. The water was dripping from the muzzles of two or three light guns, on board the ship, but no one thought of loosening them for service, in such a tempest. Her black sides, as they emerged from a wave, glistened and seemed to frown, but the wind howled through her rigging, whistling the thousand notes of a ship, and the hails and cries, that escape a Frenchman with so much readiness, were inaudible.

"Let him hollow himself hoarse!" growled Cap—"This is no weather to whisper secrets in. Port, sir, port!"

The man at the helm obeyed, and the next send of the sea drove the Scud down upon the quarter of the ship, so near her that the old mariner, himself, recoiled a step, in a vague expectation that, at the next surge ahead, she would drive bows foremost into the planks of the other vessel. But this was not to be. Rising from the crouching posture she had taken, like a panther about to leap, the cutter dashed onward, and, at the next instant, she was glancing past the stern of her enemy, just clearing the end of his spanker boom, with her own lower yard.

The young Frenchman who commanded the Montcalm, leaped on the taffrail, and with that high toned courtesy which relieves even the worst acts of his countrymen, he raised his cap, and smiled a salutation as the Scud shot past.

There were *bonhommie* and good taste in this act of courtesy, when circumstances allowed of no other communications, but they were lost on Cap, who, with an instinct quite as true to his race, shook his fist menacingly and muttered to himself—

"Ay—ay—it's d——d lucky for you, I've no armament on board here, or I'd send you in to get new cabin windows fitted. Serjeant, he's a humbug."

" 'T was civil, Brother Cap," returned the other, lowering his hand from the military salute, which his pride as a soldier had induced him to return—" 't was civil, and that's as much as you can expect from a Frenchman. What he really meant by it, no one can say."

"He is not heading up to this sea without an object, neither! Well, let him run in, if he can get there; we will keep the lake, like hearty English mariners."

This sounded gloriously, but Cap eyed with envy, the glittering black mass of the Montcalm's hull, her waving top-sail, and the misty tracery of her spars, as she grew less and less distinct, and finally disappeared in the drizzle, in a form as shadowy as that of some unreal image. Gladly would he have followed in her wake, had he dared, for, to own the truth, the prospect of another stormy night in the midst of the wild waters that were raging around him, brought little consolation. Still he had too much professional pride to betray his uneasiness, and those under his care relied on his knowledge and resources, with the implicit and blind confidence, that the ignorant are apt to feel.

A few hours succeeded, and darkness came again to increase the perils of the Scud. A lull in the gale, however, had induced Cap to come by the wind once more, and throughout the night the cutter was lying-to, as before, head reaching as a matter of course, and occasionally waring to keep off the land. It is unnecessary to dwell on the incidents of this night, which resembled those of any other gale of wind. There were the pitching of the vessel, the hissing of the waters, the dashing of spray, the shocks that menaced annihilation to the little craft as she plunged into the seas, the undying howlings of the wind, and the fearful drift. The last was the most serious danger, for, though exceedingly weatherly under her canvass, and totally without top-hamper, the Scud was so light that the combing of the swells would seem, at times, to wash her down to leeward, with a velocity as great as that of the surges themselves.

During this night Cap slept soundly and for several hours. The day was just dawning, when he felt himself shaken by the shoulder, and on rousing himself he found the Pathfinder standing at his side. During the gale, the guide had appeared little on deck, for his natural modesty told him that seamen alone should interfere with the management of the vessel, and he was willing to show the same reliance on those who had charge of the Scud, as he expected those who followed through the forest, ought to manifest in his own skill. But he now thought himself justified in interfering, which he did in his own unsophisticated and peculiar manner.

"Sleep is sweet, Master Cap," he said, as soon as the eyes of the latter were fairly open, and his consciousness had sufficiently returned—"Sleep is sweet, as I know from experience, but life is sweeter still. Look about you, and say if this is exactly the moment for a commander to be off his feet."

"How now—how now—Master Pathfinder!" growled Cap, in the first moments of his awakened faculties—"Are you, too, getting on the side of the grumblers? When ashore, I admired your sagacity in running through the worst shoals, without a compass, and since we have been afloat, your meekness and submission have been as pleasant, as your confidence on your own ground; I little expected such a summons from you."

"As for myself, Master Cap, I feel I have my gifts, and I believe they'll interfere with those of no other man, but the case may be different with Mabel Dunham. She has her gifts, too, it is true, but they are not rude like ourn, but gentle, and womanish, as they ought to be. It's on her account that I speak, and not on my own."

"Ay—ay—I begin to understand. The girl is a good girl, my worthy friend, but she is a soldier's daughter and a sailor's niece, and ought not to be too taut, or too tender, in a gale. Does she show any fear?"

"Not she—not she. Mabel is a woman, but she is reasonable and silent. Not a word have I heard from her, consarning our doings, though I do think, Master Cap, she would like it better, if Jasper Eau douce were put into his proper place, and things were restored to their old situation, like. This is human natur'."

"I'll warrant it!—Girl like, and Dunham like, too. Any thing is better than an old uncle, and every body knows more than an old seaman! *This* is human natur', Master Pathfinder, and, d——e, if I'm the man to sheer a fathom, starboard or port, for all the human natur' that can be found in a minx of twenty—ay,—or—" lowering his voice a little—"for all that can be paraded in His Majesty's 55th regiment of Foot. I've not been at sea forty years, to come up on this bit of fresh water to be taught human natur'.—How this gale holds out! It blows as hard, at this moment, as if Boreas had just clapped his hand upon the bellows. And what is all this to leeward?" rubbing his eyes—"Land as sure as my name is Cap; and high land, too!"

The Pathfinder made no immediate answer, but shaking his head, he watched the expression of his companion's face, with a look of strong anxiety, in his own.

"Land, as certain as this is the Scud!—" repeated Cap—"A lee shore, and that, too, within a league of us, with as pretty a line of breakers, as one could find on the beach of all Long Island!"

"And is that encouraging, or is it disheartening?" demanded the Pathfinder.

"Ha! Encouraging—disheartening?—Why, neither. No—no—there is nothing encouraging about it; and, as for disheartening, nothing ought to dishearten a seaman. You never get disheartened, or afraid in the woods, my friend."

"I'll not say that—I'll not say that. When the danger is great, it is my gift to see it, and know it, and to try to avoid it; else would my scalp, long since, have been drying in a Mingo wigwam. On this lake, howsever, I can see no trail, and I feel it my duty to submit; though I think we ought to remember there is such a person as Mabel Dunham, on board. But here comes her father, and he will nat'rally feel for his own child."

"We are seriously situated, I believe, Brother Cap," said the serjeant, when he had reached the spot, "by what I can gather from the two hands on the forecastle. They tell me the cutter cannot carry any more sail, and her drift is so great we shall go ashore in an hour or two. I hope their fears have deceived them?"

Cap made no reply, but he gazed at the land with a rueful face, and then looked to windward, with an expression of ferocity, as if he would have gladly quarrelled with the weather.

"It may be well, brother," the serjeant continued, "to send for Jasper and consult him, as to what is to be done. There are no French here to dread, and, under all circumstances, the boy will save us from drowning if possible."

"Ay—ay—'Tis these cursed circumstances that have done all the mischief! But let the fellow come; let him come; a few well-managed questions will bring the truth out of him, I'll warrant you."

This acquiescence on the part of the dogmatical Cap was no sooner obtained, than Jasper was sent for. The young man instantly made his appearance, his whole air, countenance and mien, expressive of mortification, humility, and, as his observers fancied, rebuked deception. When he first stepped on deck, Jasper cast one hurried anxious glance around, as if curious to know the situation of the cutter, and that glance sufficed, it would seem, to let him into the secret of all her peril. At first he looked to windward, as is usual with every seaman, then he turned round the horizon, until his eye caught a view of the highlands to leeward, when the whole truth burst upon him, at once.

"I've sent for you, Master Jasper," said Cap, folding his arms, and balancing his body with the dignity of the forecastle, "in order to learn something about the haven to leeward. We take it for granted, you do not bear malice so hard, as to wish to drown us all; especially the women; and I suppose you will be man enough to help us to run the cutter into some safe berth, until this bit of a gale has done blowing?"

"I would die myself, rather than harm should come to Mabel Dunham," the young man earnestly answered.

"I knew it!—I knew it!" cried Pathfinder, clapping his hand kindly on Jasper's shoulder. "The lad is as true as the best compass that ever run a boundary, or brought a man off from a blind trail! It is a moral sin to believe otherwise."

"Humph!" ejaculated Cap, "Especially the women!—As if

they were in any particular danger. Never mind, young man; we shall understand each other, by talking like two plain seamen. Do you know of any port under our lee?"

"None. There is a large bay, at this end of the lake, but it is unknown to us all, and not easy of entrance."

"And this coast to leeward—it has nothing particular to recommend it, I suppose?"

"It is a wilderness until you reach the mouth of the Niagara, in one direction, and Frontenac in the other. North and west, they tell me there is nothing but forest and prairies, for a thousand miles."

"Thank God, then, there can be no French. Are there many savages, hereaway, on the land?"

"The Indians are to be found, in all directions, though they are nowhere very numerous. By accident, we might find a party, at any point on the shore; or, we might pass months there, without seeing one."

"We must take our chance, then, as to the blackguards—but, to be frank with you, Master Western, if this little unpleasant matter about the French had not come to pass, what would you now do with the cutter?"

"I am a much younger sailor than yourself, Master Cap," said Jasper, modestly, "and am hardly fitted to advise you."

"Ay—ay—we all know that. In a common case, perhaps not. But this is an uncommon case and a circumstance, and on this bit of fresh water it has what may be called its peculiarities, and, so, every thing considered, you may be fitted to advise even your own father. At all events, you can speak, and I can judge of your opinion, agreeably to my own experience."

"I think, sir, before two hours are over, the cutter will have to anchor."

"Anchor!—not out here in the lake?"

"No, sir; but in yonder, near the land."

"You do not mean to say, Master Oh! the deuce, you would anchor on a lee shore, in a gale of wind!"

"If I would save my vessel, that is exactly what I would do, Master Cap."

"Whe—e—e—w!—This is fresh water, with a vengeance. Harkee, young man, I've been a seafaring animal, boy and man, forty one years, and I never yet heard of such a thing. I'd throw my ground tackle overboard, before I would be guilty of so lubberly an act!"

"That is what we do, on this lake," modestly replied Jasper, "when we are hard pressed. I dare say we might do better, had we been better taught."

"That you might indeed! No; no man induces me to commit such a sin against my own bringing up. I should never dare show my face inside of Sandy Hook, again, had I committed so know-nothing an exploit. Why, Pathfinder, here, has more seamanship in him, than that comes to. You can go below, again, Master Oh! the-deuce."

Jasper quietly bowed and withdrew. Still, as he passed down the ladder, the spectators observed that he cast a lingering, anxious look at the horizon to windward, and the land to leeward, and then disappeared with concern strongly expressed in every lineament of his face.

Chapter XVII

"His still refuted quirks he still repeats;
New raised objections with new quibbles meets;
Till sinking in the quicksand he defends,
He dies disputing, and the contest ends."
Cowper, *The Progress of Error*, ll. 550–53.

As THE SOLDIER'S WIFE was sick in her berth, Mabel Dunham was the only person in the outer cabin, when Jasper returned to it; for, by an act of grace in the serjeant, he had been permitted to resume his proper place, in this part of the vessel. We should be ascribing too much simplicity of character to our heroine, if we said that she had felt no distrust of the young man, in consequence of his arrest, but we should also be doing injustice to her warmth of feelings and generosity of disposition, if we did not add that this distrust was insignificant and transient. As he now took his seat near her, his whole countenance clouded with the uneasiness he felt concerning the situation of the cutter, every thing like suspicion was banished from her mind, and she saw in him only an injured man.

"You let this affair weigh too heavily on your mind, Jasper," she said eagerly, or with that forgetfulness of self with which the youthful of her sex are wont to betray their feelings, when a strong and generous interest has obtained the ascendency—"no one, who knows you, can or does believe you guilty. Pathfinder says he will pledge his life for you."

"Then you, Mabel," returned the youth, his eyes flashing fire, "do not look upon me, as the traitor that your father seems to believe me to be?"

"My dear father is a soldier, and is obliged to act as one. My father's daughter is not, and will think of you, as she ought to think of a man who has done so much to serve her already."

"Mabel—I'm not used to talking with one like you—or, saying all I think and feel with any. I never had a sister, and my mother died when I was a child, so that I know little what your sex most likes to hear—"

Mabel would have given the world to know what lay behind the teeming word, at which Jasper hesitated, but the indefinable and controlling sense of womanly diffidence, made her suppress her womanly curiosity. She waited in silence for him to explain his own meaning.

"I wish to say, Mabel," the young man continued, after a pause which he found sufficiently embarrassing—"that I am unused to the ways and opinions of one like you, and that you must imagine all I would add."

Mabel had imagination enough to fancy any thing, but there are ideas and feelings that her sex prefer to have expressed, before they yield them all their own sympathies, and she had a vague consciousness that these of Jasper's might properly be enumerated in the class. With a readiness that belonged to her sex, therefore, she preferred changing the discourse to permitting it to proceed any further, in a manner so awkward, and so unsatisfactory.

"Tell me one thing, Jasper, and I shall be content," she said, speaking now with a firmness that denoted confidence not only in herself, but in her companion—"you do not deserve this cruel suspicion which rests upon you?"

"I do not, Mabel," answered Jasper, looking into her full blue eyes, with an openness and simplicity that might have shaken strong distrust. "As I hope for mercy, hereafter, I do not."

"I knew it—I could have sworn it—" returned the girl, warmly. "And yet my father means well—but do not let this matter disturb you, Jasper."

"There is so much more to apprehend from another quarter, just now, that I scarce think of it."

"Jasper!"

"I do not wish to alarm you, Mabel, but if your uncle could be persuaded to change his notions about handling the Scud—and, yet, he is so much older, and more experienced than I am, that he ought, perhaps, to place more reliance on his own judgment than on mine."

"Do you think the cutter is in any danger?" demanded Mabel, as quick as thought.

"I fear so—at least she would have been thought in great danger, by us of the lake; perhaps an old seaman of the ocean may have means of his own, to take care of her."

"Jasper, all agree in giving you credit for skill in managing the Scud!—You know the lake, you know the cutter—you *must* be the best judge of our real situation!"

"My concern for you, Mabel, may make me more cowardly than common; but, to be frank, I see but one method of keeping the cutter from being wrecked in the course of the next two or three hours, and that your uncle refuses to take. After all, this may be my ignorance, for, as he says, Ontario is merely fresh water."

"You cannot believe this will make any difference. Think of my dear father, Jasper!—Think of yourself, of all the lives that depend on a timely word from you to save them!"

"I think of you, Mabel, and that is more, much more, than all the rest put together—" returned the young man, with a strength of expression and an earnestness of look, that uttered infinitely more than the words themselves.

Mabel's heart beat quick, and a gleam of grateful satisfaction shot across her blushing features, but the alarm was too vivid and too serious to admit of much relief from happier thoughts. She did not attempt to repress a look of gratitude, and then she returned to the feeling that was naturally uppermost.

"My uncle's obstinacy must not be permitted to occasion this disaster. Go once more on deck, Jasper, and ask my father to come into the cabin."

While the young man was complying with this request, Mabel sat listening to the howling of the storm, and the dashing of the water against the cutter, in a dread to which she had hitherto been a stranger. Constitutionally an excellent sailor, as the term is used among passengers, she had not, hitherto, bethought her of any danger, and had passed her time since the commencement of the gale, in such womanly employments, as her situation allowed; but now alarm was seriously awakened, she did not fail to perceive, that never before had she been on the water in such a tempest. The minute or two that elapsed ere the serjeant came appeared an hour, and she scarcely breathed before she saw him and Jasper descending the ladder in company. Quick as language could express her meaning, she acquainted her father with Jasper's opinion of their situation, and intreated him, if he loved her, or had any regard for his own life, or for those of his men, to interpose with her uncle, and to induce him to yield the control of the cutter, again, to its proper commander.

"Jasper is true, father," she added earnestly, "and if false, he could have no motive in wrecking us in this distant part of the lake, at the risk of all our lives, his own included. I will pledge my own life, for his truth."

"Ay, this is well enough, for a young woman who is frightened," answered the more phlegmatick parent; "but it might not be so prudent, or excusable in one in command of an expedition. Jasper may think the chance of drowning in getting ashore, fully repaid by the chance of escaping as soon as he reaches the land."

"Serjeant Dunham!"

"Father!"

These exclamations were made simultaneously, but they were uttered in tones expressive of different feelings. In Jasper surprise was the emotion uppermost; in Mabel, reproach. The old soldier, however, was too much accustomed to deal frankly with subordinates, to heed either, and, after a moment's thought, he continued, as if neither had spoken.

"Nor is Brother Cap a man likely to submit to be taught his duty, on board a vessel."

"But, father, when all our lives are in the utmost jeopardy!"

"So much the worse. The fair weather commander is no great matter; it is when things go wrong, that the best officer shows himself in his true colours. Charley Cap will not be likely to quit the helm because the ship is in danger. Besides, Jasper Eau douce, he says your proposal, in itself, has a suspicious air about it, and sounds more like treachery than reason."

"He may think so, but let him send for the pilot, and hear his opinion. It is well known, I have not seen the man since yesterday evening."

"This does sound reasonably, and the experiment shall be tried. Follow me on deck, then, that all may be honest and above board."

Jasper obeyed, and so keen was the interest of Mabel, that she, too, ventured as far as the companion way, where her garments were sufficiently protected against the violence of the wind and her person from the spray. Here maiden modesty induced her to remain, though an absorbed witness of what was passing.

The pilot soon appeared, and there was no mistaking the look of concern that he cast around at the scene, as soon as he was in the open air. Some rumours of the situation of the Scud had found their way below, it is true, but, in this instance rumour had lessened, instead of magnifying the dangers. He was allowed a few minutes to look about him, and then the question was put as to the course that he thought it prudent to follow.

"I see no means of saving the cutter but to anchor," he answered simply, and without hesitation.

"What, out here, in the lake?" enquired Cap, as he had previously done of Jasper.

"No—but closer in; just at the outer line of the breakers."

The effect of this communication, was to leave no doubt in the mind of Cap, that there was a secret arrangement between her commander and the pilot, to cast away the Scud; most probably with the hope of effecting their escape. He consequently treated the opinion of the latter with the indifference he had manifested towards that of the former.

"I tell you, Brother Dunham," he said, in answer to the remonstrances of the serjeant against his turning a deaf ear to this double representation, "that no seaman would give such an opinion honestly. To anchor on a lee shore, in a gale of wind, would be an act of madness that I could never excuse to the underwriters, under any circumstances, as long as a rag can be set, but to anchor close to breakers would be insanity."

"His Majesty underwrites the Scud, Brother, and I am responsible for the lives of my command. These men are better acquainted with Lake Ontario than we can possibly be, and I do think their telling the same tale, entitles them to some credit."

"Uncle!" said Mabel, earnestly, but a gesture from Jasper induced the girl to restrain her feelings.

"We are drifting down upon the breakers so rapidly," said the young man, "that little need be said on the subject. Half an hour must settle the matter, one way or the other, but I warn Master Cap that the surest footed man among us, will not be able to keep his feet an instant on the deck of this low craft, should she fairly get within them. Indeed, I make little doubt that we shall fill and founder before the second line of rollers is passed!"

"And how would anchoring help the matter?" demanded Cap furiously, as if he felt that Jasper was responsible for the effects of the gale, as well as for the opinion he had just given.

"It would at least do no harm," Eau douce mildly replied. "By bringing the cutter head to sea we should lessen her drift, and even if we dragged through the breakers, it would be with the least possible danger. I hope, Master Cap, you will allow the pilot and myself to *prepare* for anchoring, since the precaution may do good, and can do no harm."

"Overhaul your ranges if you will, and get your anchors clear, with all my heart. We are now in a situation that cannot be much affected by any thing of that sort. Serjeant a word with you, aft here, if you please."

Cap led his brother-in-law out of ear-shot, and then, with more of human feeling in his voice and manner than he was apt to exhibit, he opened his heart on the subject of their real situation.

"This is a melancholy affair for poor Mabel," he said, blowing his nose, and speaking with a slight tremor—"You and I, Serjeant, are old fellows, and used to being near death, if not to actually dying. Our trades fit us for such scenes, but poor Mabel, she is an affectionate and kind-hearted girl, and I had hoped to see her comfortably settled and a mother, before my time came. Well, well; we must take the bad with the good, in every v'y'ge, and the only serious objection that an old seafaring man can with propriety make to such an event, is that it should happen on this bit of d——d fresh water."

Serjeant Dunham was a brave man, and had shown his spirit in scenes that looked much more appalling than this. But, on all such occasions, he had been able to act his part against his foes, while here he was pressed upon by an enemy whom he had no means of resisting. For himself, he cared far less, than for his daughter; feeling some of that self-reliance which seldom deserts a man of firmness, who is in vigorous health, and who has been accustomed to personal exertions, in moments of jeopardy. But, as respects Mabel, he saw no means of escape, and with a father's fondness he at once determined that, if either was doomed to perish, he and his daughter must perish together.

"Do you think this must come to pass?" he asked of Cap firmly, but with strong feeling.

"Twenty minutes will carry us into the breakers, and, look for yourself, serjeant, what chance will even the stoutest man among us have in that cauldron to leeward!"

The prospect was, indeed, little calculated to encourage hope. By this time the Scud was within a mile of the shore, on which the gale was blowing at right angles, with a violence that forbade the idea of showing any additional canvass, with a view to claw off. The small portion of the mainsail that was actually set, and which merely served to keep the head of the Scud so near the wind as to prevent the waves from breaking over her, quivered under the gusts, as if, at each moment, the stout threads which held the complicated fabric together, were about to be torn asunder. The drizzle had ceased, but the air, for a hundred feet above the surface of the lake, was filled with dazzling spray, which had an appearance not unlike that of a brilliant mist, while above all, the sun was shining gloriously, in a cloudless sky. Jasper had noted the omen, and had foretold that it announced a speedy termination to the gale, though the next hour, or two, must decide their fate. Between the cutter and the shore, the view was still more wild and appalling. The breakers extended near half a mile; while the water within their line was white with foam, the air above them was so far filled with vapor and spray, as to render the land beyond hazy and indistinct. Still it could be seen that the latter was high, not a usual thing for the shores of Ontario, and that it was covered with the verdant mantle of the interminable forest.

While the serjeant and Cap were gazing at this scene, in silence, Jasper and his people were actively engaged on the forecastle. No sooner had the young man received permission to resume his old employment, than appealing to some of the soldiers for aid, he mustered five or six assistants, and set about in earnest, the performance of a duty that had been too long delayed. On these narrow waters, anchors are never stowed in board, or cables that are intended for service unbent, and Jasper was saved much of the labor that would have been necessary in a vessel at sea. The two bowers were soon ready to be let go, ranges of the cables were overhauled, and then the party paused to look about them. No change for the better had occurred, but the cutter was falling slowly in, and each instant rendered it more certain that she could not gain an inch to windward.

One long earnest survey of the lake ended, Jasper gave new orders in a manner to prove how much he thought that the time pressed. Two kedges were got on deck, and hawsers were bent to them. The inner ends of the hawsers were bent, in their turns, to the crowns of the anchors, and every thing was got ready to throw them overboard, at the proper moment. These preparations completed, Jasper's manner changed from the excitement of exertion, to a look of calm but settled concern. He quitted the forecastle, where the seas were dashing inboard, at every plunge of the vessel, the duty just mentioned having been executed with the bodies of the crew frequently buried in the water, and walked to a drier part of the deck, aft. Here he was met by the Pathfinder, who was standing near Mabel and the Quarter Master. Most of those on board, with the exception of the individuals who have already been particularly mentioned, were below, some seeking relief from physical suffering on their pallets, and others tardily bethinking them of their sins. For the first time, most probably since her keel had dipped into the limpid waters of Ontario, the voice of prayer was heard on board the Scud.

"Jasper," commenced his friend, the guide, "I have been of no use this morning, for my gifts are of little account, as you know, in a vessel like this; but should it please God to let the sarjeant's daughter reach the shore alive, my acquaintance with the forest, may still carry her through in safety to the garrison."

" 'Tis a fearful distance thither, Pathfinder!" Mabel rejoined, the party being so near together that all which was said by one, was overheard by the others. "I am afraid none of us could live to reach the fort."

"It would be a risky path, Mabel, and a crooked one; though some of your sex have undergone even more than that, in this wilderness. But, Jasper, either you or I, or both of us must man this bark canoe; Mabel's only chance will lie in getting through the breakers in that."

"I would willingly man any thing to save Mabel," answered Jasper, with a melancholy smile, "but no human hand, Pathfinder, could carry that canoe through yonder breakers, in a gale like this. I have hopes from anchoring, after all, for once before, have we saved the Scud in an extremity nearly as great as this."

"If we are to anchor, Jasper," the serjeant enquired, " why not do it at once? Every foot we lose in drifting now, would come into the distance we shall probably drag, when the anchors are let go."

Jasper drew nearer to the Serjeant, and took his hand, pressing it earnestly, and in a way, to denote strong, almost uncontrollable feelings.

"Serjeant Dunham," he said solemnly, "you are a good man, though you have treated me harshly in this business. You love your daughter."

"That you cannot doubt, Eau douce," returned the serjeant huskily.

"Will you give her—give us all, the only chance for life, that is left."

"What would you have me do, boy; what would you have me do? I have acted according to my judgment hitherto—what would you have me do?"

"Support me against Master Cap, for five minutes, and all that man can now do, towards saving the Scud, shall be done."

The serjeant hesitated, for he was too much of a disciplinarian to fly in the face of regular orders. He disliked the appearance of vacillation too, and then he had a profound respect for his kinsman's seamanship. While he was deliberating Cap came from the post he had some time occupied, which was at the side of the man at the helm, and drew near the group.

"Master Eau-deuce," he said, as soon as near enough to be heard, "I have come to enquire if you know any spot near-by, where this cutter can be beached? The moment has arrived when we are driven to this hard alternative."

That instant of indecision on the part of Cap, secured the triumph of Jasper. Looking at the Serjeant, the young man received a nod that assured him of all he asked, and he lost not one of those moments that were getting to be so very precious.

"Shall I take the helm," he inquired of Cap, "and see if we can reach a creek that lies to leeward?"

"Do so—do so—" said the other, hemming to clear his throat, for he felt oppressed by a responsibility that weighed all the heavier on his shoulders, on account of his ignorance. "Do so, Oh-the-deuce, since, to be frank with you, I can see nothing better to be done. We must beach, or swamp."

Jasper required no more; springing aft, he soon had the tiller in his own hands. The pilot was prepared for what was to follow, and, at a sign from his young commander, the rag of sail that had so long been set was taken in. At that moment, Jasper, watching his time, put the helm up, the head of a staysail was loosened forward, and the light cutter, as if conscious she was now under the control of familiar hands, fell off, and was soon in the trough of the sea. This perilous instant was passed in safety, and, at the next moment, the little vessel appeared flying down toward the breakers, at a rate that threatened instant destruction. The distance had got to be so short, that five or six minutes sufficed for all that Jasper wished, and he put the helm down again, when the bows of the Scud came up to the wind, notwithstanding the turbulence of the waters, as gracefully as the duck varies its line of direction on the glassy pond. A sign from Jasper set all in motion on the forecastle, and a kedge was thrown from each bow. The fearful nature of the drift was now apparent even to Mabel's eyes, for the two hawsers ran out like tow-lines. As soon as they straightened to a slight strain, both anchors were let go, and cable was given to each, nearly to the better ends. It was not a difficult task to snub so light a craft, with ground tackle of a quality better than common, and in less than ten minutes from the moment when Jasper went to the helm, the Scud was riding, head to sea, with the two cables stretched ahead in lines that resembled bars of iron.

"This is not well done, Master Jasper!" angrily exclaimed

Cap, as soon as he perceived the trick that had been played him—"This is not well done, sir; I order you to cut, and to beach the cutter, without a moment's delay."

No one, however, seemed disposed to comply with this order, for so long as Eau douce saw fit to command, his own people were disposed to obey. Finding that the men remained passive, Cap, who believed they were in the utmost peril, turned fiercely to Jasper, and renewed his remonstrances.

"You did not head for your pretended creek," he added, after dealing in some objurgatory remarks that we do not deem it necessary to record, "but steered for that bluff, where every soul on board would have been drowned, had we gone ashore!"

"And you wish to cut, and put every soul ashore, at that very spot!" Jasper retorted a little drily.

"Throw a lead line over board, and ascertain the drift—" Cap now roared to the people forward. A sign from Jasper sustaining this order, it was instantly obeyed. All on deck gathered around the spot, and watched, with nearly breathless interest, the result of the experiment. The lead was no sooner on the bottom, than the line tended forward, and in about two minutes it was seen that the cutter had drifted her length, dead in towards the bluff. Jasper looked grave, for he well knew nothing would hold the vessel did she get within the vortex of the breakers, the first line of which, was appearing and disappearing about a cable's length directly under their stern.

"Traitor!" exclaimed Cap, shaking a finger at the young commander, though passion choked the rest. "You must answer for this with your life," he added after a short pause, "If I were at the head of this expedition, Serjeant, I would hang him at the end of the main-boom, lest he escape drowning."

"Moderate your feelings, brother—be more moderate, I beseech you; Jasper appears to have done all for the best, and matters may not be as bad as you believe them."

"Why did he not run for the creek, he mentioned—why has he brought us here, dead to windward of that bluff, and to a spot where even the breakers are only of half the ordinary width, as if in a hurry to drown all on board!"

"I headed for the bluff, for the precise reason that the

breakers are so narrow at this spot," answered Jasper mildly, though his gorge had risen at the language the other held.

"Do you mean to tell an old seaman like me, that this cutter could live in those breakers?"

"I do not, sir. I think she would fill and swamp, if driven into the first line of them—I am certain she would never reach the shore on her bottom, if fairly entered. I hope to keep her clear of them, altogether."

"With a drift of her length in a minute!"

"The backing of the anchors does not yet fairly tell, nor do I even hope that *they* will entirely bring her up."

"On what then do you rely? To moor a craft head and stern, by faith, hope and charity!"

"No, sir—I trust to the under-tow. I headed for the bluff, because I knew that it was stronger at that point than at any other, and because we could get nearer in with the land, without entering the breakers."

This was said with spirit, though without any particular show of resentment. Its effect on Cap was marked, the feeling that was uppermost being evidently that of surprise.

"Under-tow!" he repeated—"Who the devil ever heard of saving a vessel from going ashore by the under-tow!"

"This may never happen on the ocean, sir," Jasper answered modestly, "but we have known it to happen here."

"The lad is right, brother," put in the serjeant, "for though I do not well understand it, I have often heard the sailors of the lake speak of such a thing. We shall do well to trust to Jasper, in this strait."

Cap grumbled and swore, but as there was no remedy, he was compelled to acquiesce, Jasper being now called on to explain what he meant by the under-tow, gave this account of the matter. The water that was driven up on the shore by the gale, was necessarily compelled to find its level, by returning to the lake, by some secret channels. This could not be done on the surface, where both wind and waves were constantly urging it towards the land, and it necessarily formed a sort of lower eddy, by means of which it flowed back again, to its ancient and proper bed. This inferior current had received the name of the under-tow, and as it would necessarily act on the bottom of a vessel that drew as much water as the

Scud, Jasper trusted to the aid of this reaction to keep his cables from parting. In short, the upper and lower currents, would, in a manner, counteract each other.

Simple and ingenious as was this theory, however, as yet there was little evidence of its being reduced to practice. The drift continued, though, as the kedges and hawsers, with which the anchors were backed, took the strains, it became sensibly less. At length the man at the lead announced the joyful intelligence, that the anchors had ceased to drag, and that the vessel had brought up! At this precise moment, the first line of the breakers was about a hundred feet astern of the Scud, even appearing to approach much nearer, as the foam vanished and returned on the raging surges. Jasper sprang forward, and casting a glance over the bows, he smiled in triumph, as he pointed exultingly to the cables. Instead of resembling bars of iron in rigidity, as before, they were curving downwards, and to a seaman's senses, it was evident that the cutter rose and fell on the seas as they came in, with the ease of a ship in a tides-way, when the power of the wind is relieved by the counteracting pressure of the water.

" 'Tis the undertow!" he exclaimed with delight, fairly bounding along the deck to steady the helm, in order that the cutter might ride still easier—"Providence has placed us directly in its current, and there is no longer any danger!"

"Ay—ay, Providence is a good seaman—" growled Cap, "and often helps lubbers out of difficulty. Under tow, or upper tow, the gale has abated, and fortunately for us all, the anchors have met with good holding ground. Then this d——d fresh water has an unnatural way with it."

Men are seldom inclined to quarrel with good fortune, but it is in distress that they grow clamorous and critical. Most on board were disposed to believe that they had been saved from shipwreck by the skill and knowledge of Jasper, without regarding the opinions of Cap, whose remarks were now little heeded.

There was half an hour of uncertainty and doubt, it is true, during which period the lead was anxiously watched, and then a feeling of security came over all, and the weary slept without dreaming of instant death.

Chapter XVIII

"It is to be all made of sighs and tears;—
It is to be all made of faith and service:—
It is to be all made of fantasy,
All made of passion, and all made of wishes:
All adoration, duty, and observance,
All humbleness, all patience, and impatience,
All purity, all trial, all observance."
As You Like It, V.ii.84, 89, 94–98.

IT WAS NEAR NOON when the gale broke, and then its force abated as suddenly as its violence had arisen. In less than two hours after the wind fell, the surface of the lake, though still agitated, was no longer glittering with foam, and in double that time, the entire sheet presented the ordinary scene of disturbed water, that was unbroken by the violence of a tempest. Still the waves came rolling incessantly towards the shore, and the lines of breakers remained, though the spray had ceased to fly, the combing of the swells was more moderate, and all that there was of violence proceeded from the impulsion of wind that had abated.

As it was impossible to make head against the sea that was still up, with the light opposing air that blew from the eastward, all thoughts of getting under way that afternoon, were abandoned. Jasper, who had now quietly resumed the command of the Scud, busied himself, however, in heaving up to the anchors, which were lifted in succession. The kedges that backed them were weighed, and every thing was got in readiness for a prompt departure, as soon as the state of the weather would allow. In the mean time, they who had no concern with these duties, sought such means of amusement, as their peculiar circumstances allowed.

As is common with those who are unused to the confinement of a vessel, Mabel cast wistful eyes towards the shore, nor was it long before she expressed a wish that it were possible to land. The Pathfinder was near her at the time, and he assured her that nothing would be easier, as they had a bark canoe on deck, which was the best possible mode of conveyance to go through a surf in. After the usual doubts and misgivings, the Serjeant was appealed to. His opinion proved to be favorable, and preparations to carry the whim into effect, were immediately made.

The party that was to land, consisted of Serjeant Dunham, his daughter and the Pathfinder. Accustomed to the canoe, Mabel took her seat in the centre with great steadiness, her father was placed in the bows, while the guide assumed the office of conductor, by steering in the stern. There was little need of impelling the canoe by means of the paddle, for the rollers sent it forward, at moments, with a violence that put every effort to govern its movements at defiance. More than once, ere the shore was reached, Mabel repented of her temerity, but Pathfinder encouraged her, and really manifested so much self-possession, coolness and strength of arm, himself, that even a female might have hesitated about owning all her apprehensions. Our heroine was no coward, and while she felt the novelty of her situation, she also experienced a fair proportion of its wild delight. At moments, indeed, her heart was in her mouth, as the bubble of a boat floated on the very crest of a foaming breaker, appearing to skim the water like a swallow, and then she flushed and laughed, as, left by the glancing element, they appeared to linger behind, ashamed at having been out-done in the headlong race. A few minutes sufficed for this excitement, for, though the distance between the cutter and the land considerably exceeded a quarter of a mile, the intermediate space was passed in a very few minutes.

On landing, the Serjeant kissed his daughter kindly, for he was so much of a soldier as always to feel more at home, on terra firma, then when afloat, and taking his gun, he announced his intention to pass an hour, in quest of game.

"Pathfinder will remain near you, girl, and no doubt he will tell you some of the traditions of this part of the world, or some of his own experiences with the Mingos."

The guide laughed, promised to have a care of Mabel, and in a few minutes the father had ascended a steep acclivity, and disappeared in the forest. The others took another direction which, after a few minutes of a sharp ascent also, brought them to a small naked point on the promontory, where the eye overlooked an extensive and very peculiar panorama. Here Mabel seated herself on a fragment of fallen rock, to recover her breath and strength, while her companion, on whose sinews no personal exertion seemed to make any impression, stood at her side, leaning in his own, and not ungraceful manner on his long rifle. Several minutes passed, and neither spoke; Mabel, in particular, being lost in admiration of the view.

The position the two had obtained was sufficiently elevated, to command a wide reach of the lake, which stretched away towards the north east, in a boundless sheet, glittering beneath the rays of an afternoon's sun, and yet betraying the remains of that agitation which it had endured while tossed by the late tempest. The land set bounds to its limits, in a huge crescent, disappearing in distance towards the south-east and the north. Far as the eye could reach, nothing but forest was visible, not even a solitary sign of civilization breaking in upon the uniform and grand magnificence of nature. The gale had driven the Scud beyond the line of those posts, with which the French were then endeavoring to gird the English North American possessions, for following the channels of communications between the great lakes, their posts were on the banks of the Niagara, while our adventurers had reached a point many leagues westward of that celebrated streight. The cutter rode at single anchor, without the breakers, resembling some well imagined and accurately executed toy, that was intended rather for a glass case, than for the struggles with the elements which she had so lately gone through, while the canoe lay on the narrow beach, just out of reach of the waves that came booming upon the land, a speck upon the shingle.

"We are very far, here, from human habitations!" exclaimed Mabel, when, after a long and musing survey of the scene, its principal peculiarities forced themselves on her active and even brilliant imagination; "this is indeed being on a frontier!"

"Have they more sightly scenes than this, nearer the sea, and around their large towns?" demanded Pathfinder, with an interest he was apt to discover in such a subject.

"I will not say that; there is more to remind one of his fellow beings, there than here; less, perhaps, to remind one of God."

"Ay, Mabel, that is what my own feelings say. I am but a poor hunter I know; untaught and unlarned; but God is as near me, in this my home, as he is near the king in his royal palace."

"Who can doubt it—" returned Mabel, looking from the view up into the hard-featured but honest face of her companion, though not without surprise at the energy of his manner—"One feels nearer to God, in such a spot, I think, than when the mind is distracted by the objects of the towns."

"You say all I wish to say myself, Mabel, but in so much plainer speech, that you make me ashamed of wishing to let others know what I feel on such matters. I have coasted this lake, in s'arch of skins, afore the war, and have been here already; not at this very spot, for we landed yonder where you may see the blasted oak that stands above the cluster of hemlocks—"

"How, Pathfinder, can you remember all these trifles so accurately!"

"These are our streets and houses; our churches and palaces. Remember them, indeed! I once made an appointment with the Big Sarpent, to meet at twelve o'clock at noon, near the foot of a certain pine, at the end of six months, when neither of us was within three hundred miles of the spot. The tree stood, and stands still unless the judgment of Providence has lighted on that too, in the midst of the forest, fifty miles from any settlement, but in a most extraordinary neighborhood for beaver."

"And did you meet at that very spot and hour!"

"Does the sun rise and set? When I reached the tree, I found the Sarpent leaning against its trunk, with torn leggings and muddied moccasins. The Delaware had got into a swamp, and it worried him not a little to find his way out of it, but as the sun which comes over the eastern hills in the morning goes down behind the western at night, so was he true to time and place. No fear of Chingachgook when there is either a friend or an enemy in the case. He is equally sartain with each."

"And where is the Delaware now—why is he not with us to-day?"

"He is scouting on the Mingo trail, where I ought to have been too, but for a great human infirmity."

"You seem above, beyond, superior to all infirmity, Pathfinder—I never yet met with a man, who appeared to be so little liable to the weaknesses of nature."

"If you mean in the way of health and strength, Mabel, Providence has been kind to me; though I fancy, the open air, long hunts, or actyve scoutings, forest fare, and the sleep of a good conscience may always keep the doctors at a distance. But I'm human after all; yes, I find I'm very human in some of my feelin's!"

Mabel looked surprised, and it would be no more than delineating the character of her sex, if we added that her sweet countenance expressed a good deal of curiosity, too, though her tongue was more discreet.

"There is something bewitching in this wild life of yours, Pathfinder!" she exclaimed, the tinge of enthusiasm mantling her cheeks. "I find I'm fast getting to be a frontier girl, and am coming to love all this grand silence of the woods. The towns seem tame to me, and, as my father will probably pass the remainder of his days, here, where he has already lived so long, I begin to feel that I should be happy to continue with him, and not return to the sea-shore."

"The woods are never silent, Mabel, to such as understand their meaning. Days at a time, have I travelled them alone, without feeling the want of company, and, as for conversation, for such as can comprehend their language, there is no want of rational and instructive discourse."

"I believe you are happier when alone, Pathfinder, than when mingling with your fellow creatures."

"I will not say that—I will not say exactly that. I have seen the time, when I have thought that God was sufficient for me in the forest, and that I craved no more than his bounty and his care. But other feelin's have got uppermost, and I suppose natur' will have its way. All other creatur's mate, Mabel, and it was intended man should do so, too."

"And have you never bethought you of seeking a wife, Pathfinder, to share your fortunes," enquired the girl, with the directness and simplicity that the pure of heart and undesigning are the most apt to manifest and with that feeling of affection which is inbred in her sex. "To me, it seems, you only want a home to return to, from your wanderings, to render your life completely happy. Were I a man, it would be my delight to roam through these forests at will, or to sail over this beautiful lake!"

"I understand you, Mabel, and God bless you, for thinking of the welfare of men as humble as we are. We have our pleasures, it is true, as well as our gifts, but we might be happier; yes, I do think, we might be happier!"

"Happier!—In what way, Pathfinder?—In this pure air, with these cool and shaded forests to wander through, this lovely lake to gaze at, and sail upon, with clear consciences and abundance for all the real wants, men ought to be nothing less than as perfectly happy, as their infirmities will allow."

"Every creatur' has its gifts, Mabel, and men have theirn," answered the guide looking stealthily at his beautiful companion, whose cheeks had flushed and eyes brightened under the ardor of feelings excited by the novelty of a striking situation, "and all must obey them. Do you see yonder pigeon, that is just alightin' on the beech, here in a line with the fallen chestnut?"

"Certainly; it is the only thing stirring with life in it, besides ourselves, that is to be seen in this vast solitude."

"Not so, Mabel, not so: Providence makes nothing that lives, to live quite alone. Here is its mate, just rising on the wing; it has been feedin' near the other beech, but it will not long be separated from its companion."

"I understand you, Pathfinder," returned Mabel smiling sweetly, though as calmly as if the discourse was with her father—"But a hunter may find a mate, even in this wild region. The Indian girls are affectionate and true, I know, for such was the wife of Arrowhead to a husband who oftener frowned than smiled."

"That would never do, Mabel, and good would never come of it. Kind must cling to kind, and country to country, if one would find happiness. If, indeed, I could meet with one like you, who would consent to be a hunter's wife, and who would not scorn my ignorance and rudeness, then, indeed, would all the toil of the past appear like the sporting of the young deer, and all the future like sunshine!"

"One like me!—A girl of my years and indiscretion would hardly make a fit companion for the boldest scout and surest hunter on the lines!"

"Ah! Mabel, I fear me, that I have been improving a red skin's gifts, with a Pale face's natur'! Such a character would insure a wife, in an Injin village."

"Surely, surely, Pathfinder, you would not think of choosing one as ignorant, as frivolous, as vain, and as inexperienced as I, for your wife!" Mabel would have added, "and as young," but an instinctive feeling of delicacy repressed the words.

"And why not, Mabel? If you are ignorant of frontier usages, you know more than all of us, of pleasant anecdotes and town customs; as for frivolous, I know not what it means, but if it signifies beauty, Ah's! me; I fear it is no fault in my eyes. Vain you are not, as is seen by the kind manner in which you listen to all my idle tales about scoutings and trails, and, as for experience, that will come with years. Besides, Mabel, I fear men think little of these matters, when they are about to take wives, I do."

"Pathfinder—your words—your looks—surely all this is meant in trifling—you speak in pleasantry!"

"To me it is always agreeable to be near you, Mabel, and I should sleep sounder this blessed night, than I have done for a week past, could I think that you find such discourse as pleasant as I do."

We shall not say that Mabel Dunham had not believed herself a favorite with the guide. This her quick, feminine, sagacity had early discovered, and perhaps she had occasionally thought there had mingled with his regard and friendship, some of that manly tenderness which the ruder sex must be coarse indeed not to show, on occasions, to the gentler; but, the idea that he seriously sought her for his wife had never before crossed the mind of the spirited and ingenuous girl. Now, however, a gleam of something like the truth broke in upon her imagination, less induced by the words of her companion, perhaps, than by his manner. Looking earnestly into the rugged, honest countenance of the scout, Mabel's own features became concerned and grave, and when she spoke again, it was with a gentleness of manner that attracted him to her, even more powerfully than the words themselves were calculated to repel.

"You and I should understand each other, Pathfinder," she said, with an earnest sincerity, "nor should there be any cloud between us. You are too upright and frank to meet with any thing but sincerity and frankness in return. Surely—surely, all this means nothing—has no other connection with your feelings, than such a friendship as one of your wisdom and character would naturally feel for a girl like me?"

"I believe it's all nat'ral, Mabel; yes, I do; the Sarjeant tells me he had such feelings towards your own mother, and I think I've seen something like it, in the young people I have, from time to time, guided through the wilderness. Yes, yes—I dare say it's all nat'ral enough, and that makes it come so easy, and is a great comfort to me."

"Pathfinder, your words make me uneasy! Speak plainer, or change the subject forever. You do not—cannot mean that—you—cannot wish me to understand—" even the tongue of the spirited Mabel faultered, and she shrunk with maiden shame, from adding what she wished so earnestly to say. Rallying her courage, however, and determined to know all as soon and as plainly as possible, after a moment's hesitation she continued—"I mean, Pathfinder, that you do not wish me to understand that you seriously think of me as a wife?"

"I do, Mabel; that's it—that's just it, and you have put the matter in a much better point of view than I, with my forest gifts and frontier ways, would ever be able to do. The Sarjeant and I have concluded on the matter, if it is agreeable to you, as he thinks is likely will be the case, though I doubt my own power to please one who deserves the best husband America can produce."

Mabel's countenance changed from uneasiness to surprise, and, then by a transition still quicker, from surprise to pain.

"My father!" she exclaimed. "My dear father has thought of my becoming your wife, Pathfinder!"

"Yes, he has, Mabel; he has indeed. He has even thought such a thing might be agreeable to you, and has almost encouraged me to fancy it might be true."

"But, you, yourself—you, certainly can care nothing,

whether this singular expectation shall ever be realized or not?"

"Anan?"

"I mean, Pathfinder, that you have talked of this match more to oblige my father than any thing else; that your feelings are no way concerned, let my answer be what it may?"

The scout looked earnestly into the beautiful face of Mabel, which had flushed with the ardor and novelty of her sensations, and it was impossible to mistake the intense admiration that betrayed itself in every lineament of his ingenuous countenance.

"I have often thought myself happy, Mabel, when ranging the woods, on a successful hunt, breathing the pure air of the hills, and filled with vigor and health, but, I now feel that it has all been idleness and vanity compared with the delight it would give me to know that you thought better of me than you think of most others."

"Better of you!—I do indeed think better of you, Pathfinder, than of most others—I am not certain that I do not think better of you, than of any other; for your truth, honesty, simplicity, justice and courage are scarcely equalled by any of earth."

"Ah! Mabel!—These are sweet and encouraging words from you, and the sarjeant, a'ter all, was not as near wrong as I feared."

"Nay, Pathfinder—in the name of all that is sacred and just, do not let us misunderstand each other, in a matter of so much importance. While I esteem, respect—nay reverence you, almost as much as I reverence my own dear father, it is impossible that I should ever become your wife—that I——"

The change in her companion's countenance was so sudden and so great that the moment the effect of what she had uttered became visible in the face of the Pathfinder, Mabel arrested her own words, notwithstanding her strong desire to be explicit, the reluctance with which she could at any time cause pain being sufficient of itself to induce the pause. Neither spoke for some time, the shade of disappointment that crossed the rugged lineaments of the hunter, amounting so nearly to anguish as to frighten his companion, while the sensation of choking became so strong in the Pathfinder, that he fairly griped his throat, like one who sought physical relief for physical suffering. The convulsive manner in which his fingers worked actually struck the alarmed girl with a feeling of awe.

"Nay, Pathfinder," Mabel eagerly added, the instant she could command her voice—"I may have said more than I mean, for all things of this nature are possible, and women they say are never sure of their own minds. What I wish you to understand is, that it is not likely that you and I should ever think of each other, as man and wife ought to think of each other."

"I do not—I shall never think in that way, again, Mabel—" gasped forth the Pathfinder, who appeared to utter his words, like one just raised above the pressure of some suffocating substance. "No—no—I shall never think of you, or any one else, again, in that way."

"Pathfinder—dear Pathfinder—understand me—do not attach more meaning to my words, than I do myself. A match like that would be unwise—unnatural, perhaps—"

"Yes, unnat'ral—ag'in natur', and so I told the sarjeant, but he *would* have it otherwise."

"Pathfinder!—Oh! this is worse than I could have imagined—take my hand, excellent Pathfinder, and let me see that you do not hate me. For God's sake smile upon me again!"

"Hate you, Mabel!—Smile upon you! Ah's! me."

"Nay, give you your hand; your hardy, true and manly hand—both, both, Pathfinder, for I shall not be easy until I feel certain that we are friends again, and that all this has been a mistake."

"Mabel," said the guide, looking wistfully into the face of the generous and impetuous girl, as she held his two hard and sunburnt hands in her own pretty and delicate fingers, and laughing in his own silent and peculiar manner, while anguish gleamed over lineaments which seemed incapable of deception, even while agitated with emotions so conflicting, "Mabel, the sarjeant was wrong!"

The pent-up feelings would endure no more, and the tears rolled down the cheeks of the scout, like rain. His fingers again worked convulsively at his throat, and his breast heaved, as if it possessed a tenant of which it would be rid, by any effort, however desperate.

"Pathfinder!—Pathfinder!" Mabel almost shrieked—"any thing but this—any thing but this—Speak to me, Pathfinder—smile, again—say one kind word—any thing to prove you can forgive me."

"The sarjeant was wrong—" exclaimed the guide, laughing, amid his agony, in a way to terrify his companion by the unnatural mixture of anguish and light-heartedness. "I knowed it—I knowed it, and said it; yes, the sarjeant was wrong, a'ter all."

"We can be friends, though we cannot be man and wife," continued Mabel, almost as much disturbed as her companion, scarce knowing what she said; " we can always be friends, and always will."

"I thought the sarjeant was mistaken," resumed the Pathfinder, when a great effort had enabled him to command himself, "for I did not think my gifts were such as would please the fancy of a town bred gal. It would have been better, Mabel, had he not overpersuaded me into a different notion, and it might have been better, too, had you not been so pleasant and friendly, like; yes, it would."

"If I thought any error of mine had raised false expectations in you, Pathfinder, however unintentionally on my part, I should never forgive myself; for, believe me, I would rather endure pain in my own feelings than you should suffer."

"That's just it, Mabel; that's just it. These speeches and opinions, spoken in so soft a voice, and in a way I'm so unused to in the woods, have done the mischief. But I now see plainly, and begin to understand the difference between us better, and will strive to keep down thought, and to go abroad ag'in, as I used to do, looking for the game and the inimy. Ah's! me; Mabel, I have indeed, been on a false trail, since we met!"

"But you will now travel on the true one. In a little while you will forget all this, and think of me as a friend, who owes you her life."

"This may be the way in the towns, but I doubt if it's nat'ral to the woods. With us, when the eye sees a lovely sight, it is apt to keep it long in view, or when the mind takes in an upright and proper feeling, it is loath to part with it."

"But it is not a proper feeling that you should love me, nor am I a lovely sight. You will forget it all, when you come seriously to recollect that I am altogether unsuited to be your wife."

"So I told the sarjeant, but he would have it otherwise. I knowed you were too young and beautiful, for one of middle age like myself, and who never was comely to look at, even in youth; and then your ways have not been my ways, nor would a hunter's cabin be a fitting place for one who was edicated among chiefs, as it were. If I were younger and comelier, though, like Jasper Eau douce—"

"Never mind Jasper Eau douce——" interrupted Mabel, impatiently—" we can talk of something else."

"Jasper is a worthy lad, Mabel; ay, and a comely," returned the guileless guide, looking earnestly at the girl, as if he distrusted her judgment in speaking slightingly of his friend—"Were I only half as comely as Jasper Western, my misgivings in this affair, would not have been so great, and they might not have been so true."

"We will not talk of Jasper Western," repeated Mabel, the colour mounting to her temples—"he may be good enough in a gale, or on the lake, but he is not good enough to talk of, here."

"I fear me, Mabel, he is better than the man who is likely to be your husband, though the sarjeant says that never can take place. But the sarjeant was wrong once, and he may be wrong twice."

"And who is likely to be my husband, Pathfinder?—This is scarcely less strange, than what has just passed between us!"

"I know it is nat'ral for like to seek like, and for them that have consorted much with officers' ladies, to wish to be officers' ladies themselves. But, Mabel, I may speak plainly to you, I know, and I hope my words will not give you pain, for, now, I understand what it is to be disappointed in such feelings, I would'n't wish to cause even a Mingo sorrow, on this head. But, happiness is not always to be found in a marquee, any more than in a tent, and though the officers' quarters may look more tempting than the rest of the barracks, there is often great misery, between husband and wife, inside of their doors."

"I do not doubt it, in the least, Pathfinder, and did it rest with me to decide, I would sooner follow you to some cabin in the woods, and share your fortune, whether it might be better or worse, than go inside the door of any officer I know, with an intention of remaining there as its master's wife."

"Mabel, this is not what Lundie hopes, or Lundie thinks!"

"And what care I for Lundie?—He is Major of the 55th and may command his men to wheel and march about, as he pleases, but he cannot compel me to wed the greatest or the meanest of his mess. Besides, what can you know of Lundie's wishes on such a subject?"

"From Lundie's own mouth. The sarjeant had told him that he wished me for a son-in-law, and the Major being an old and a true friend conversed with me on the subject: He put it to me, plainly, whether it would not be more ginerous in me to let an officer succeed, than to strive to make you share a hunter's fortune. I owned the truth, I did; and that was, that I thought it might; but when he told me that the Quarter Master would be his choice, I would not abide by the conditions. No—no—Mabel; I know Davy Muir well, and though he may make you a lady, he can never make you a happy woman, or himself a gentleman. I say this honestly, I do; for I now plainly see, that the sarjeant has been wrong."

"My father has been very wrong, if he has said or done aught to cause you sorrow, Pathfinder; and so great is my respect for you, so sincere my friendship, that were it not for one—I mean that no person need fear Lt. Muir's influence with me. I would rather remain as I am, to my dying day, than become a lady at the cost of being his wife."

"I do not think you would say that which you do not feel, Mabel," returned Pathfinder, earnestly.

"Not at such a moment, on such a subject, and least of all to you. No; Lt. Muir may find wives where he can, my name shall never be on his catalogue."

"Thank you—thank you, for that, Mabel; for though there is no longer any hope for me, I could never be happy were you to take to the Quarter Master. I feared the commission might count for something, I did, and I know the man. It is not jealousy that makes me speak in this manner, but truth, for I know the man. Now, were you to fancy a desarving youth, one like Jasper Western for instance—"

"Why always mention Jasper Eau douce, Pathfinder; he can have no concern with our friendship. Let us talk of yourself, and of the manner in which you intend to pass the winter."

"Ah's! me. I'm little worth at the best, Mabel, unless it may be on a trail, or with the rifle, and less worth now that I've discovered the sarjeant's mistake. There is no need, therefore, of talking of me. It has been very pleasant to me, to be near you so long, and even to fancy that the sarjeant was right; but that is all over now. I shall go down the lake with Jasper, and then there will be business to occupy us, and that will keep useless thoughts out of the mind."

"And you will forget this—forget me—no, not forget me either, Pathfinder; but you will resume your old pursuits, and cease to think a girl of sufficient importance to disturb your peace?"

"I never know'd it afore, Mabel, but girls—as you call them, though gals is the name I've been taught to use—are of more account in this life, than I could have believed. Now, afore I knowd you, the new-born babe did not sleep more sweetly than I used to could; my head was no sooner on the root, or the stone, or mayhap on the skin, than all was lost to the senses unless it might be to go over in the night, the business of the day, in a dream, like; and there I lay till the moment came to be stirring, and the swallows were not more certain to be on the wing, with the light, than I to be afoot, at the moment I wished to be. All this seemed a gift, and might be calculated on, even in the midst of a Mingo camp; for I've been outlying, in my time, in the very villages of the vagabonds."

"And all this will return to you, Pathfinder, for one so upright and sincere will never waste his happiness on a mere fancy. You will dream again, of your hunts, of the deer you have slain, and of the beaver you have taken."

"Ah's! me, Mabel; I wish never to dream again! Before we met, I had a sort of pleasure, in following up the hounds, in fancy as it might be; and even in striking a trail of the Iroquois—nay, I've been in skrimmages, and ambushments, in thought like, and found satisfaction in it, according to my gifts; but all those things have lost their charms since I've made acquaintance with you. Now, I think no longer of any thing rude in my dreams, but the very last night we staid in the garrison, I imagined I had a cabin in a grove of sugar maples, and at the root of every tree was a Mabel Dunham, while the birds that were among the branches, sung ballads, instead of the notes that natur' gave, and even the deer stopped to listen. I tried to shoot a fa'an, but Killdeer missed fire, and the creatur' laughed in my face, as pleasantly as a young girl laughs in her merriment, and then it bounded away, looking back, as if expecting me to follow."

"No more of this, Pathfinder—we'll talk no more of these things—" said Mabel, dashing the tears from her eyes, for the simple, earnest manner in which this hardy woodsman betrayed the deep hold she had taken of his feelings, nearly proved too much for her own generous heart. "Now, let us look for my father; he cannot be distant, as I heard his gun, quite near."

"The sarjeant was wrong—yes, he was wrong, and it's of no use to attempt to make the doe consort with the wolf!"

"Here comes my dear father," interrupted Mabel; "let us look cheerful and happy, Pathfinder, as such good friends ought to look, and keep each other's secrets."

A pause succeeded; the serjeant's foot was heard crushing the dried twigs hard by, and then his form appeared shoving aside the bushes of a copse, quite near. As he issued into the open ground, the old soldier scrutinised his daughter and her companion, and speaking good-naturedly, he said—

"Mabel, child; you are young and light of foot—look for a bird I've shot, that fell just beyond the thicket of young hemlocks, on the shore; and, as Jasper is showing signs of an intention of getting under way, you need not take the trouble to clamber up this hill again, but we will meet you, on the beach, in a few minutes."

Mabel obeyed, bounding down the hill with the elastic step of youth and health. But, notwithstanding the lightness of her steps, the heart of the girl was heavy, and no sooner was she hid from observation, by the thicket, than she threw herself on the root of a tree, and wept as if her heart would break. The serjeant watched her until she disappeared, with a father's pride, and then turned to his companion, with a smile as kind and as familiar as his habits would allow him to use towards any.

"She has her mother's lightness and activity, my friend, with somewhat of her father's force," he said. "Her mother was not quite as handsome, I think myself; but the Dunhams were always thought comely, whether men or women. Well, Pathfinder, I take it for granted you've not overlooked the opportunity, but have spoken plainly to the girl? Women like frankness, in matters of this sort."

"I believe Mabel and I understand each other, at last, sarjeant," returned the other, looking another way to avoid the soldier's face.

"So much the better. Some people fancy that a little doubt and uncertainty make love all the livelier, but I am one of those who think the plainer the tongue speaks, the easier the mind will comprehend. Was Mabel surprised?"

"I fear she was, sarjeant; I fear she was taken quite by surprise—yes, I do."

"Well, well, surprises in love, are like an ambush in war, and quite as lawful; though it is not as easy to tell when a woman is surprised, as to tell when it happens to an enemy. Mabel did not run away, my worthy friend, did she?"

"No, sarjeant, Mabel did not try to escape; *that* I can say with a clear conscience."

"I hope the girl was not too willing, neither! Her mother was shy and coy for a month, at least, but frankness, after all, is a recommendation, in man or woman."

"That it is—that it is—and judgment, too."

"You are not to look for too much judgment in a young creature of twenty, Pathfinder, but let it come with experience. A mistake in you, or in me, for instance, might not be so easily overlooked, but in a girl of Mabel's years, one is not to strain at a gnat, lest they swallow a camel."

The muscles of the listener's face twitched, as the serjeant was thus delivering his sentiments, though the former had now recovered a portion of that stoicism which formed so large a part of his character, and which he had probably imbibed from long association with the Indians. His eyes rose and fell, and once a gleam shot athwart his hard features, as if he were about to indulge in his peculiar laugh, but the joyous feeling, if it really existed, was as quickly lost in a look allied to anguish. It was this unusual mixture of wild and keen mental agony, with native, simple, joyousness, that had most struck Mabel, who, in the interview just related, had a dozen times been on the point of believing that her suitor's heart was only lightly touched, as images of happiness and humour gleamed over a mind that was almost infantine in its simplicity and nature, an impression, however, that was soon driven away, by the discovery of emotions so painful and so deep, that they seemed to harrow the very soul. Indeed, in this respect, the Pathfinder was a mere child. Unpractised in the ways of the world, he had no idea of concealing a thought of any kind, and his mind received and reflected each emotion, with the pliability and readiness of that period of life. The infant scarcely yielded its wayward imagination to the passing impression, with greater facility, than this man, so simple in all his personal feelings, so stern, stoical, masculine and severe in all that touched his ordinary pursuits.

"You say true, sarjeant," Pathfinder answered—"a mistake in one like you is indeed a more serious matter."

"You will find Mabel sincere and honest in the end, give her but a little time."

"Ah's! me, Sarjeant!"

"A man of your merits, would make an impression on a rock, give him time, Pathfinder."

"Sarjeant Dunham, we are old fellow campaigners—that is, as campaigns are carried on here in the wilderness; and we have done so many kind acts to each other, that we can afford to be candid—what has caused you to believe that a girl like Mabel could ever fancy one as rude as I am?"

"What?—Why a variety of reasons, and good reasons, too, my friend. Those same acts of kindness, perhaps, and the campaigns you mention; moreover, you are my sworn and tried comrade."

"All this sounds well, so far as you and I be consarned, but they do not touch the case of your pretty da'ghter. She may think these very campaigns have destroyed the little comeliness I may once have had, and I am not quite sartain that being an old friend of her father would lead any young maiden's mind into a particular affection for a suitor. Like loves like, I tell you, sarjeant, and my gifts are not altogether the gifts of Mabel Dunham."

"These are some of your old modest qualms, Pathfinder, and will do you no credit with the girl. Women distrust men who distrust themselves, and take to men who distrust nothing. Modesty is a capital thing in a recruit, I grant you; or in a young subaltern who has just joined, for it prevents his railing at the non-commissioned officers, before he knows what to rail at; I'm not sure it is out of place in a commissary, or a parson, but it's the devil and all when it gets possession of either a real soldier, or a lover. Have as little to do with it as possible, if you would win a woman's heart. As for your doctrine that like loves like, it is as wrong as possible, in matters of this sort. If like loved like, women would love one another, and men also. No—no—like loves dislike,—" the serjeant was merely a scholar of the camp, "and you have nothing to fear from Mabel on that score. Look at Lt. Muir; the man has had five wives, already, they tell me, and there is no more modesty in him, than there is in a cat-o'-nine-tails."

"Lt. Muir will never be the husband of Mabel Dunham, let him ruffle his feathers as much as he may."

"That is a sensible remark of yours, Pathfinder, for my mind is made up that you shall be my son-in-law. If I were an officer myself, Mr. Muir might have some chance; but time has placed one door between my child and myself, and I don't intend there shall be that of a marquee, also."

"Sarjeant, we must let Mabel follow her own fancy; she is young and light of heart, and God forbid! that any wish of mine should lay the weight of a feather on a mind that is all gaiety, now, or take one note of happiness from her laughter."

"Have you conversed freely with the girl?" the serjeant demanded quickly, and with some asperity of manner.

Pathfinder was too honest to deny a truth plain as that which the answer required, and yet too honorable to betray Mabel, and expose her to the resentment of one, whom he well knew to be stern in his anger.

"We have laid open our minds," he said, "and though Mabel's is one that any man might love to look at, I find little there, sarjeant, to make me think any better of myself."

"The girl has not dared to refuse you—to refuse her father's best friend?"

Pathfinder turned his face away to conceal the look of anguish, that consciousness told him was passing athwart it, but he continued the discourse in his own quiet manly tones.

"Mabel is too kind to refuse any thing, or to utter harsh words to a dog. I have not put the question in a way to be downright refused, sarjeant."

"And did you expect my daughter to jump into your arms, before you asked her? She would not have been her mother's child had she done any such thing, nor do I think she would have been mine. The Dunhams like plain dealing, as well as the King's Majesty, but they are no jumpers. Leave me to manage this matter for you, Pathfinder, and there shall be no unnecessary delay. I'll speak to Mabel myself, this very evening, using your name as principal in the affair."

"I'd rather not—I'd rather not, sarjeant. Leave the matter to Mabel and me, and I think all will come right in the ind. Young gals be like timorsome birds; they do not over relish being hurried or spoken harshly to, nither. Leave the matter to Mabel and me."

"On one condition, I will, my friend; and that is, that you promise me, on the honor of a scout, that you will put the matter plainly to Mabel, the first suitable opportunity, and no mincing of words."

"I will ask her, sarjeant—yes I will ask her, on condition that you promise not to meddle in the affair—yes, I will promise to ask Mabel the question whether she will marry me, even though she laugh in my face, at my doing so, on that condition."

Serjeant Dunham gave the desired promise, very cheerfully, for he had completely wrought himself up into the belief that the man he so much esteemed and respected himself, must be acceptable to his daughter. He had married a woman much younger than himself, and he saw no unfitness in the respective years of the intended couple. Mabel was educated so much above him, too, that he was not aware of the difference which actually existed between the parent and child, in this respect, for it is one of the most unpleasant features in the intercourse between knowledge and ignorance, taste and unsophistication, refinement and vulgarity, that the higher qualities are often necessarily subjected to the judgments of those who have absolutely no perceptions of their existence. It followed that Serjeant Dunham was not altogether qualified to appreciate his daughter's tastes, or to form a very probable conjecture of the direction taken by those feelings which oftener depend on impulses and passion, than on reason. Still, the worthy soldier was not so wrong in his estimate of the Pathfinder's chances, as might at first, appear. Knowing, as he well did, all the sterling qualities of the man, his truth, integrity of purpose, courage, self devotion, disinterestedness, it was far from unreasonable to suppose that qualities like these, would produce a deep impression on any female heart, where there was an opportunity to acquire a knowledge of their existence, and the father erred principally in fancying that the daughter might know, as it might be, by intuition, what he himself had acquired by years of intercourse and adventure.

As Pathfinder and his military friend descended the hill to the shore of the lake, the discourse did not flag. The latter continued to endeavor to persuade the former, that his diffidence, alone, prevented complete success with Mabel, and that he had only to persevere, in order to prevail. Pathfinder was much too modest by nature, and had been too plainly, though so delicately, discouraged, in the recent interview, to believe all he heard; still, the father used so many arguments that seemed plausible, and it was so grateful to fancy that the daughter might yet be his, the reader is not to be surprised, when he is told that this unsophisticated being did not view Mabel's recent conduct in precisely the light in which he may be inclined to view it, himself. He did not credit all that the Serjeant told him, it is true, but he began to think virgin coyness, and ignorance of her own feelings might have induced Mabel to use the language she had.

"The Quarter Master is no favorite," said Pathfinder, in answer to one of his companion's remarks. "Mabel will never look on him as more than one who has had four or five wives already."

"Which is more than his share. A man may marry twice, without offence to good morals and decency, I allow, but four times is an aggravation."

"I should think even marrying once, what Master Cap calls a circumstance!" put in Pathfinder, laughing, in his quiet way, for, by this time, his spirits had recovered some of their buoyancy.

"It is, indeed, my friend, and a most solemn circumstance, too. If it were not that Mabel is to be your wife, I would advise you to remain single. But here is the girl, herself, and discretion is the word."

"Ah's! me, sarjeant, I fear you are mistaken!"

Chapter XIX

> "Thus was this place,
> A happy rural seat of various view:"
> *Paradise Lost*, IV.246–47.

Mabel was in waiting on the beach, and the canoe was soon launched. Pathfinder carried the party out through the surf, in the same skilful manner he had brought it in, and, though Mabel's colour heightened with excitement, and her heart seemed often ready to leap out of her mouth again, they reached the side of the Scud, without having received even a drop of spray.

Ontario is like a quick-tempered man, sudden to be angered, and as soon appeased. The sea had already fallen, and though the breakers bounded the shore, far as the eye could reach, it was merely in lines of brightness, that appeared and vanished, like the returning waves produced by the stone that has been dropped into a pool. The cable of the Scud was scarce seen above the water, and Jasper had already hoisted his sails, in readiness to depart, as soon as the expected breeze from the shore should fill the canvass.

It was just sunset, as the cutter's mainsail flapped, and its stem began to sever the water. The air was light and southerly, and the head of the vessel was kept looking up along the south shore, it being the intention to get to the eastward, again, as fast as possible. The night that succeeded was quiet, and the rest of those who slept, deep and tranquil.

Some difficulty occurred concerning the command of the vessel, but the matter had been finally settled by an amicable compromise. As the distrust of Jasper was far from being appeased, Cap retained a supervisory power, while the young man was allowed to work the craft, subject, at all times, to the control and interference of the old seaman. To this Jasper consented, in preference to exposing Mabel any longer to the dangers of their present situation, for, now that the violence of the elements had ceased, he well knew, that the Montcalm would be in search of them. He had the discretion, however, not to reveal his apprehensions on this head, for it happened that the very means he deemed the best to escape the enemy were those which would be most likely to awaken new suspicions of his honesty, in the minds of those who held the power to defeat his intentions. In other words, Jasper believed that the gallant young Frenchman who commanded the ship of the enemy, would quit his anchorage under the fort at Niagara, and stand up the lake, as soon as wind abated, in order to ascertain the fate of the Scud, keeping mid-way between the two shores, as the best means of commanding a broad view, and that, on his part, it would be expedient to hug one coast or the other, not only to avoid a meeting, but as affording a chance of passing without detection, by blending his sails and spars with objects on the land. He preferred the south, because it was the weather shore, and because he thought it was that which the enemy would the least expect him to take, though it necessarily led near his settlements, and in front of one of the strongest posts he held in that part of the world.

Of all this, however, Cap was happily ignorant, and the serjeant's mind was too much occupied with the details of his military trust, to enter into these niceties, which so properly belonged to another profession. No opposition was made, therefore, and, ere morning, Jasper had apparently dropped quietly into all his former authority, issuing his orders freely, and meeting with obedience without hesitation, or cavil.

The appearance of day brought all on board, on deck again, and, as is usual with adventurers on the water, the opening horizon was curiously examined, as objects started out of the obscurity, and the panorama brightened under the growing light. East, west and north, nothing was visible, but water, glittering in the rising sun, but southward stretched the endless belt of woods, that then held Ontario in a setting of forest verdure. Suddenly an opening appeared ahead, and then the massive walls of a château-looking house, with outworks, bastions, block-houses and palisadoes, frowned on a headland, that bordered the outlet of a broad stream. Just as the post became visible, a little cloud rose over it, and the white ensign of France was seen fluttering from a lofty flagstaff.

Cap gave an ejaculation as he witnessed this ungrateful

exhibition, and he cast a quick suspicious glance at his brother-in-law.

"The dirty table-cloth hung up to air, as my name is Charles Cap!" he muttered, "and we hugging this d——d shore, as if it were our wife and children, met on the return from an India v'y'ge! Harkee, Jasper, are you in search of a cargo of frogs, that you keep so near in to this New France?"

"I hug the land, sir, in hope of passing the enemy's ship without being seen, for I think she must be somewhere down here to leeward."

"Ay, ay; this sounds well, and I hope it may turn out as you say. I trust there is no under-tow, here."

"We are on a weather shore, now," said Jasper smiling; "and, I think you will admit, Master Cap, that a strong under-tow makes an easy cable. We owe all our lives to the under-tow of this very lake."

"French flummery!" growled Cap, though he did not care to be heard by Jasper. "Give me a fair, honest, English-Yankee-American tow, above board and above water, too, if I must have a tow, at all, and none of your sneaking drift that is below the surface, where one can neither see nor feel. I dare say, if the truth could be come at, that this late escape of ours was all a contrived affair."

"We have now a good opportunity, at least, to reconnoitre the enemy's post at Niagara, Brother, for such I take this fort to be," put in the Serjeant. "Let us be all eyes in passing, and remember that we are almost in face of the enemy."

This advice of the serjeant's needed nothing to enforce it, for the interest and novelty of passing a spot occupied by human beings were of themselves sufficient to attract deep attention in that scene of a vast but deserted nature. The wind was now fresh enough to urge the Scud through the water with considerable velocity, and Jasper eased her helm as she opened the river, and luffed nearly into the mouth of that noble strait, or river as it is termed. A dull, distant, heavy roar came down through the opening in the banks, swelling on the currents of the air like the deeper notes of some immense organ, and occasionally seeming to cause the earth itself to tremble.

"That sounds like surf on some long unbroken coast!" exclaimed Cap, as a swell deeper than common came to his ears.

"Ay, that is such surf as we have in this quarter of the world," Pathfinder answered. "There is no under-tow there, Master Cap, but all the water that strikes the rocks stays there, so far as going back, ag'in, is consarned. That is old Niagara that you hear, or this noble stream tumbling down a mountain!"

"No one will have the impudence to pretend that this fine broad river falls over yonder hills."

"It does, Master Cap; it does; and all for the want of stairs, or a road to come down by. This is natur' as we have it up hereaway, though I dare say you beat us down on the ocean. Ah's! me; Mabel, a pleasant hour it would be if we could walk on the shore some ten or fifteen miles up this stream, and gaze on all that God has done there!"

"You have then seen these renowned falls, Pathfinder?" the girl eagerly enquired.

"I have—yes I have, and an awful sight I witnessed at that same time. The Sarpent and I were out, scouting about the garrison there, when he told me that the traditions of his people gave an account of a mighty cataract in this neighborhood, and he asked me to vary from the line of march a little to look at the wonder. I had heard some marvels consarning the spot from the soldiers of the 60th, which is my nat'ral corps like, and not the 55th, with which I have sojourned so much of late, but there are so many terrible liars in all rigiments, that I hardly believed half they told me. Well, we went; and though we expected to be led by our ears, and to hear some of that awful roaring that we hear to-day, we were disapp'inted, for natur' was not then speaking in thunder, as she is this morning. Thus it is, in the forest, Master Cap, there being moments when God seems to be walking abroad in power, and then ag'in there is a calm over all, as if his spirit lay in quiet along the 'arth. Well, we came suddenly upon the stream, a short distance above the fall, and a young Delaware who was in our company, found a bark canoe, and he would push into the current, to reach an island that lies in the very centre of the confusion and strife. We told him of his folly, we did, and we reasoned with him on the wickedness of tempting Providence by seeking danger that led to no ind, but the youth among the Delawares are very much the same as the youth among the soldiers, risky and vain. All we could say did not change his mind, and the lad had his way. To me it seems, Mabel, that whenever a thing is really grand and potent, it has a quiet majesty about it, that is altogether unlike the frothy and flustering manner of smaller matters, and so it was with them rapids. The canoe was no sooner fairly in them, than down it went, as it might be as one sails through the air on the 'arth, and no skill of the young Delaware could resist the stream. And yet he struggled manfully for life, using the paddle to the last, like the deer that is swimming to cast the hounds. At first, he shot across the current so swiftly that we thought he would prevail, but he had miscalculated his distance, and when the truth really struck him, he turned the head up stream, and struggled in a way that was fearful to look at. I could have pitied him, even had he been a Mingo! For a few moments his efforts were so frantic that he actually prevailed over the power of the cataract; but natur' has its limits, and one faltering stroke of the paddle set him back, and then he lost ground, foot by foot, inch by inch, until he got near the spot where the river looked even and green and as if it were made of millions of threads of water, all bent over some huge rock, when he shot backward like an arrow and disappeared, the bows of the canoe tipping just enough to let us see what had become of him. I met a Mohawk, some years later, who had witnessed the whole affair, from the bed of the stream below, and he told me that the Delaware continued to paddle, in the air, until he was lost in the mists of the falls!"

"And what became of the poor wretch?" demanded Mabel, who had been strongly interested by the natural eloquence of the speaker.

"He went to the happy hunting grounds of his people, no doubt, for though he was risky and vain, he was also just and brave. Yes, he died foolishly, but the Manitou of the red skin has compassion on his creatur's as well as the God of a christian!"

A gun, at this moment, was discharged from a block-house, near the fort, and the shot, one of light weight, came whistling over the cutter's mast, an admonition to approach no nearer. Jasper was at the helm, and he kept away, smiling at the same time, as if he felt no anger at the rudeness of the salutation. The Scud was now in the current, and her outward set soon carried her far enough to leeward to avoid the danger of a repetition of the shot, and then she quietly continued her course along the land. As soon as the river was fairly opened, Jasper ascertained that the Montcalm was not at anchor in it, and a man sent aloft, came down with the report that the horizon showed no sail. The hope was now strong, that the artifice of Jasper had succeeded, and that the French commander had missed them by keeping the middle of the lake, as he steered towards its head.

All that day the wind hung to the southward, and the cutter continued her course about a league from the land, running six or eight knots an hour, in perfectly smooth water. Although the scene had one feature of monotony, the outline of unbroken forest, it was not without its interest and pleasure. Various head-lands presented themselves, and the cutter, in running from one to another, stretched across bays so deep, as almost to deserve the names of gulphs, but nowhere did the eye meet with the evidences of civilization. Rivers occasionally poured their tribute into the great reservoir of the lake, but their banks could be traced inland for miles, by the same outlines of trees, and even large bays, that lay embosomed in woods, communicating with Ontario, only by narrow outlets, appeared and disappeared, without bringing with them a single trace of a human habitation.

Of all on board, the Pathfinder viewed the scene with the most unmingled delight. His eyes feasted on the endless line of forest, and, more than once that day, notwithstanding he found it so grateful to be near Mabel, listening to her pleasant voice, and echoing, in feelings at least, her joyous laugh, did his soul pine to be wandering beneath the high arches of the maples, oaks and lindens, where his habits had induced him to fancy lasting and true joys were only to be found. Cap viewed the prospect differently. More than once, he expressed his disgust at there being no light-houses, church-towers, beacons, or roadsteds with their shipping. Such another coast, he protested, the world did not contain, and taking the serjeant aside, he gravely assured him that the region could never come to any thing, as the havens were neglected, the rivers had a deserted and useless look, and that even the breeze had a smell of the forest about it, which spoke ill of its properties.

But the humours of the different individuals in her, did not stay the speed of the Scud. When the sun was setting, she was already a hundred miles on her route towards Oswego, into which river Serjeant Dunham now thought it his duty to go, in order to receive any communications that Major Duncan might please to make. With a view to effect this purpose, Jasper continued to hug the shore all night, and though the wind began to fail him towards morning, it lasted long enough to carry the cutter up to a point that was known to be but a league or two from the fort. Here the breeze came out light at the northward, and the cutter hauled a little from the land in order to obtain a safe offing should it come on to blow, or should the weather again get to be easterly.

When the day dawned the cutter had the mouth of the Oswego well under her lee, distant about two miles, and just as the morning gun from the fort was fired, Jasper gave the order to ease off the sheets, and to bear up for his port. At that moment a cry from the forecastle drew all eyes towards the point on the eastern side of the outlet, and there, just without the range of shot from the light guns of the works, with her canvass reduced to barely enough to keep her stationary, lay the Montcalm, evidently in waiting for their appearance. To pass her was impossible, for, by filling her sails, the French ship could have intercepted them in a few minutes, and the circumstances called for a prompt decision. After a short consultation, the serjeant again changed his plan, determining to make the best of his way towards the station for which he had been originally destined, trusting to the speed of the Scud to throw the enemy so far astern, as to leave no clue to her movements.

The cutter, accordingly, hauled upon a wind, with the least possible delay, with every thing set that would draw. Guns were fired from the fort, ensigns shown, and the ramparts were again crowded. But sympathy was all the aid that Lundie could lend to his party, and the Montcalm, also firing four or five guns of defiance, and throwing abroad several of the banners of France, was soon in chase, under a cloud of canvass.

For several hours the two vessels were pressing through the water, as fast as possible, making short stretches to windward, apparently with a view to keep the port under their lee, the one to enter it, if possible, and the other to intercept it in the attempt.

At meridian, the French ship was hull down, dead to leeward, the disparity of sailing, on a wind, being very great, and some islands were near by, behind which Jasper said it would be possible for the cutter to conceal her future movements. Although Cap and the serjeant, and particularly Lt. Muir, to judge by his language, still felt a good deal of distrust of the young man, and Frontenac was not distant, this advice was followed, for time pressed, and the Quarter Master discreetly observed that Jasper could not well betray them, without running openly into the enemy's harbor, a step they could at any time prevent, since the only cruiser of force the French possessed, at the moment, was under their lee, and not in a situation to do them any immediate injury.

Left to himself, Jasper Western soon proved how much was really in him. He weathered upon the islands, passed them, and, on coming out to the eastward, kept broad away, with nothing in sight, in his wake, or to leeward. By sunset, again, the cutter was up with the first of the islands that lie in the outlet of the lake, and ere it was dark she was running through the narrow channels, on her way to the long sought station. At nine o'clock, however, Cap insisted that they should anchor, for the maze of islands became so complicated and obscure, that he feared, at every opening, the party would find themselves under the guns of a French fort. Jasper consented cheerfully, it being a part of his standing instructions to approach the station, under such circumstances as would prevent the men from obtaining any very accurate notion of its position, lest a deserter might betray the little garrison to the enemy.

The Scud was brought-to in a small retired bay, where it would have been difficult to find her by day-light and where she was perfectly concealed at night, when all but a solitary sentinel on deck sought their rest. Cap had been so harassed during the previous eight and forty hours, that his slumbers were long and deep, nor did he awake from his first nap, until the day was just beginning to dawn. His eyes were scarcely open, however, when his nautical instinct told him, that the cutter was under way. Springing up, he found the Scud threading the islands again, with no one on deck but Jasper and the pilot, unless the sentinel be excepted, who had not in the least interfered with movements that he had every reason to believe were as regular as they were necessary.

"How's this, Master Western!" demanded Cap, with sufficient fierceness for the occasion—"Are you running us into Frontenac, at last, and we all asleep below, like so many mariners waiting for the 'sentry go.' "

"This is according to orders, Master Cap, Major Duncan having commanded me never to approach the station, unless at a moment when the people were below, for he does not wish there should be more pilots in these waters, than the King has need of."

"Whe-e-e-w! A pretty job I should have made of running down among these bushes and rocks with no one on deck! Why a regular York branch could make nothing of such a channel."

"I always thought, sir," said Jasper smiling, "you would have done better, had you left the cutter in my hands, until she had safely reached her place of destination."

"We should have done it, Jasper, we should have done it, had it not been for a circumstance—these circumstances are serious matters, and no prudent man will overlook them."

"Well, sir, I hope there is now an end of them. We shall arrive in less than an hour, if the wind holds, and then you'll be safe from any circumstances that I can control."

"Humph!"

Cap was obliged to acquiesce, and as every thing around him had the appearance of Jasper's being sincere, there was not much difficulty in making up his mind to submit. It would not have been easy, indeed, for a person the most sensitive on the subject of circumstances, to fancy that the Scud was anywhere in the vicinity of a port as long established, and as well known on the frontiers, as Frontenac. The islands might not have been literally a thousand in number, but they were so numerous and small as to baffle calculation, though occasionally one of larger size than common was passed. Jasper had quitted what might have been termed the main channel, and was winding his way, with a good stiff breeze, and a favorable current, through passes that were sometimes so narrow that there appeared to be barely room sufficient for the Scud's spars to clear the trees, while at other moments, he shot across little bays, and buried the cutter again, amid rocks, forests and bushes. The water was so transparent, that there was no occasion for the lead, and being of equal depth, little risk was actually run, though Cap, with his maritime habits, was in a constant fever lest they should strike.

"I give it up!—I give it up, Pathfinder!—" the old seaman at length exclaimed, when the little vessel emerged in safety from the twentieth of these narrow inlets, through which she had been so boldly carried—"this is defying the very nature of seamanship, and sending all its laws and rules to the d——l!"

"Nay, nay, Salt-water, 'tis the parfection of the art. You perceive that Jasper never falters, but, like a hound with a true nose, he runs with his head high, as if he had a strong scent. My life on it, the lad brings us out right in the ind, as he would have done in the beginning had we given him leave."

"No pilot, no lead, no beacons, buoys or light-houses, no—"

"Trail!" interrupted Pathfinder, "for that to me, is the most mysterious part of the business. Water leaves no trail, as every one knows, and yet here is Jasper moving ahead as boldly as if he had before his eyes, the prints of moccasins on leaves, as plainly as we can see the sun in the heavens."

"D——e, if I believe there is even any compass!"

"Stand by, to haul down the jib—" called out Jasper, who merely smiled at the remarks of his companion. "Haul down—starboard your helm—starboard hard—so—melt her—gently there with the helm—touch her lightly—now jump ashore with the fast, lad—No; heave—there are some of our people ready to take it."

All this passed so quickly, as barely to allow the spectators time to note the different evolutions, ere the Scud had been thrown into the wind until her mainsail shivered, next cast a little by the use of the rudder only, and then she set bodily along side of a natural rocky quay, where she was immediately secured, by good fasts run to the shore. In a word, the station was reached, and the men of the 55th were greeted by their expecting comrades, with the satisfaction that a relief usually brings.

Mabel sprang upon the shore with a delight which she did not care to express, and her father led his men after her, with an alacrity which proved how wearied he had become of the cutter. The station, as the place was familiarly termed by the soldiers of the 55th, was indeed a spot to raise expectations of enjoyment, among those who had been cooped up so long in a vessel of the dimensions of the Scud. None of the islands were high, though all lay at a sufficient elevation above the water, to render them perfectly healthy and secure. Each had more or less of wood, and the greater number, at that distant day, were clothed with the virgin forest. The one selected by the troops for their purpose was small, containing about twenty acres of land, and by some of the accidents of the wilderness it had been partly stripped of its trees, probably centuries before the period of which we are writing, and a little grassy glade covered nearly half its surface. It was the opinion of the officer who had made the selection of this spot for a military post, that a sparkling spring near by, had early caught the attention of the Indians, and that they had long frequented this particular place, in their hunts, or when fishing for salmon, a circumstance that had kept down the second growth, and given time for the natural grasses to take root, and to gain dominion over the soil. Let the cause be what it might, the effect was to render this island far more beautiful than most of those around it, and to lend it an air of civilization that was then wanting in so much of that vast region of country.

The shores of Station Island were completely fringed with bushes, and great care had been taken to preserve them, as they answered as a screen to conceal the persons and things collected within their circle. Favored by this shelter, as well as by that of several thickets of trees, and different copses, some six or eight low huts had been erected, to be used as quarters for the officer and his men, to contain stores, and to serve the purposes of kitchen, hospital &c. These huts were built of logs, in the usual manner, had been roofed by bark brought from a distance, lest the signs of labour should attract attention, and as they had now been inhabited some months, were as comfortable as dwellings of that description usually ever get to be.

At the eastern extremity of the island, however, was a small densely wooded peninsula, with thickets of under-brush so closely matted, as nearly to prevent the possibility of seeing across it, so long as the leaves remained on the branches. Near the narrow neck that connected this acre with the rest of the island, a small block-house had been erected, with some attention to its means of resistance. The logs were bullet-proof, squared and jointed with a care to leave no defenceless points; the windows were loop-holes, the door massive and small, and the roof, like the rest of the structure was framed of hewn timber, covered properly with bark to exclude the rain. The lower apartment, as usual, contained stores and provisions; here indeed the party kept all their supplies; the second story was intended for a dwelling, as well as for the citadel, and a low garret was subdivided into two or three rooms, and could hold the pallets of some ten or fifteen persons. All the arrangements were exceedingly simple and cheap, but they were sufficient to protect the soldiers against the effects of a surprise. As the whole building was considerably less than forty feet high, its summit was concealed by the tops of the trees, except from the eyes of those who had reached the interior of the island. On that side the view was open from the upper loops, though bushes even there, more or less concealed the base of the wooden tower.

The object being purely defence, care had been taken to place the block house so near an opening in the lime-stone rock, that formed the base of the island, as to admit of a bucket's being dropped into the water, in order to obtain that great essential, in the event of a siege. In order to facilitate this operation, and to enfilade the base of the building, the upper stories projected several feet beyond the lower, in the manner usual to block houses, and pieces of wood filled the apertures cut in the log flooring which were intended as loops and traps. The communications between the different stories were by means of ladders. If we add, that these blockhouses were intended as citadels for garrisons or settlements to retreat to, in cases of attack, the general reader will obtain a sufficiently correct idea of the arrangements it is our wish to explain.

But the situation of the island itself, formed its principal merit as a military position. Lying in the midst of twenty others, it was not an easy matter to find it, since boats might pass quite near it, and, by the glimpses caught through the openings, this particular island would be taken for a part of some other. Indeed, the channels between the islands, that lay around the one we have been describing, were so narrow that it was even difficult to say which portions of the land were connected, or which separated, even as one stood in their centre, with the express desire of ascertaining the truth. The little bay in particular, that Jasper used as a harbor, was so embowered with bushes, and shut in with islands, that, the sails of the cutter being lowered, her own people, on one occasion, had searched for hours, before they could find the Scud, in their return, from an excursion among the adjacent channels, in quest of fish. In short, the place was admirably adapted, to its present uses, and its natural advantages had been as ingeniously improved as economy and the limited means of a frontier post would very well allow.

The hour that succeeded the arrival of the Scud was one of hurried excitement. The party in possession had done nothing worthy of being mentioned, and wearied with their seclusion, they were all eager to return to Oswego. The Serjeant and the officer he came to relieve, had no sooner gone through the little ceremonial of transferring the command, than the latter hurried on board the Scud, with his whole party, and Jasper, who would gladly have passed the day on the island, was required to get under way, forthwith, the wind promising a quick passage up the river, and across the lake. Before separating, however, Lt. Muir, Cap, and the Serjeant had a private conference with the ensign, who had been relieved, in which the latter was made acquainted with the suspicions that existed against the fidelity of the young sailor. Promising due caution, the officer embarked, and in less than three hours from the time when she had arrived, the cutter was again in motion.

Mabel had taken possession of a hut, and, with female readiness and skill, she made all the simple little domestic arrangements, of which the circumstances would admit, not only for her own comfort, but for that of her father. To save labor, a mess table was prepared in a hut set apart for that purpose, where all the heads of the detachment were to eat, the soldier's wife performing the necessary labor. The hut of the Serjeant, which was the best on the island, being thus freed from any of the vulgar offices of a household, admitted of such a display of womanly taste, that for the first time since her arrival on the frontier, the girl felt proud of her home. As soon as these important duties were discharged, she strolled out on the island, taking a path that led through the pretty glade, and which conducted to the only point that was not covered with bushes. Here she stood gazing at the limpid water, which lay with scarcely a ruffle on it, at her feet, musing on the novel situation in which she was placed, and permitting a pleasing and deep excitement to steal over her feelings, as she remembered the scenes through which she had so lately passed, and conjectured those which still lay veiled in the future.

"You're a beautiful fixture, in a beautiful spot, Mistress Mabel," said David Muir, suddenly appearing at her elbow, "and I'll no engage you're not just the handsomest of the two."

"I will not say, Mr. Muir, that compliments on my person are altogether unwelcome, for I should not gain credit for speaking the truth, perhaps," answered Mabel with spirit, "but I will say that if you would condescend to address to me some remarks of a different nature, I may be led to believe you think I have sufficient faculties to understand them."

"Hoot! your mind, beautiful Mabel, is polished just like the barrel of a soldier's musket, and your conversation is only too discreet and wise for a poor d——l, who has been chewing birch these four years, up here on the lines, instead of receiving it in an application that has the virtue of imparting knowledge. But you are no sorry, I take it, young lady, that you've got your pretty foot on *terra firma*, once more."

"I thought so, two hours since, Mr. Muir, but the Scud

looks so beautiful, as she sails through these vistas of trees, that I almost regret I am no longer one of her passengers."

As Mabel ceased speaking, she waved her handkerchief in return to a salutation from Jasper, who kept his eyes fastened on her form, until the white sails of the cutter had swept round a point, and were nearly lost behind its green fringe of leaves.

"There they go, and I'll no say 'joy go with them,' but may they have the luck to return safely, for without them we shall be in danger of passing the winter on this island; unless indeed we have the alternative of the castle at Quebec. Yon Jasper Eau douce is a vagrant sort of a lad, and they have reports of him in the garrison, that it pains my very heart to hear. Your worthy father, and almost-as-worthy uncle, have none of the best opinion of him."

"I am sorry to hear it, Mr. Muir; I doubt not that time will remove all their distrust."

"If time would only remove mine, pretty Mabel," rejoined the Quarter Master, in a wheedling tone, "I should feel no envy of the commander in chief. I think if I were in a condition to retire, the serjeant would just step into my shoes."

"If my dear father is worthy to step into your shoes, Mr. Muir," returned the girl, with malicious pleasure, "I'm sure that the qualification is mutual, and that you are every way worthy to step into his."

"The deuce is in the child! You would not reduce me to the rank of a non-commissioned officer, Mabel!"

"No indeed, sir, I was not thinking of the army at all, as you spoke of retiring. My thoughts were more egotistical, and I was thinking how much you reminded me of my dear father, by your experience, wisdom, and suitableness to take his place, as the head of a family."

"As its bridegroom, pretty Mabel, but not as its parent, or natural chief. I see how it is with you, loving your repartee, and brilliant with wit! Well, I like spirit in a young woman, so it be not the spirit of a scold. This Pathfinder is an extraordinair, Mabel, if truth may be said of the man."

"Truth should be said of him, or nothing. Pathfinder is my friend—my very particular friend, Mr. Muir, and no evil can be said of him, in my presence, that I shall not deny."

"I shall say nothing evil of him, I can assure you, Mabel; but, at the same time, I doubt if much good can be said in his favor."

"He is at least expert with the rifle," returned Mabel, smiling. "That *you* cannot deny."

"Let him have all the credit of his exploits in that way, if you please; but he is as illiterate as a Mohawk."

"He may not understand Latin, but his knowledge of Iroquois is greater than that of most men, and it is the more useful language of the two, in this part of the world."

"If Lundie, himself, were to call on me for an opinion which I admired most, your person, or your wit, beautiful and caustic Mabel, I should be at a loss to answer. My admiration is so nearly divided between them, that I often fancy this is the one that bears off the palm, and then the other! Ah! The late Mrs. Muir was a paragon, in that way, also!"

"The latest Mrs. Muir, did you say, sir?" asked Mabel, looking up innocently at her companion.

"Hoot—hoot!—That is some of Pathfinder's scandal. Now, I dare say, that the fellow has been trying to persuade you, Mabel, that I have had more than one wife, already."

"In that case, his time would have been thrown away, sir, as every body knows that you have been so unfortunate as to have had four."

"Only three, as sure as my name is David Muir. The fourth is pure scandal—or, rather, pretty Mabel, she is yet *in petto*, as they say at Rome, and that means, in matters of love, in the heart, my dear."

"Well, I'm glad, I'm not that fourth person, *in petto*, or in any thing else, as I should not like to be a scandal!"

"No fear of that, charming Mabel, for were you the fourth, all the others would be forgotten, and your wonderful beauty and merit would, at once, elevate you to be the first. No fear of your being the fourth in any thing."

"There is consolation in that assurance, Mr. Muir," said Mabel laughing, "whatever there may be in your other assurance, for I confess I should prefer being even a fourth-rate beauty, to being a fourth wife."

So saying she tripped away, leaving the Quarter Master to meditate on his want of success. Mabel had been induced to use her female means of defence thus freely, partly because her suitor had of late been so pointed as to stand in need of a pretty strong repulse, and partly on account of his innuendoes against Jasper and the Pathfinder. Though full of spirit and quick of intellect, she was not naturally pert, but, on the present occasion, she thought circumstances called for more than usual decision. When she left her companion, therefore, she believed she was now finally released from attentions that she thought as ill bestowed as they were certainly disagreeable. Not so, however, with David Muir. Accustomed to rebuffs, and familiar with the virtue of perseverance, he saw no reason to despair, though the half menacing, half self-satisfied manner in which he shook his head towards the retreating girl, might have betrayed designs as sinister, as they were determined. While he was thus occupied, the Pathfinder approached and got within a few feet of him, unseen.

" 'T'will never do, Quarter Master, 't'will never do," commenced the latter laughing in his noiseless way, "she is young and actyve, and none but a quick foot can overtake her. They tell me you are her suitor, if you're not her follower."

"And I hear the same of yourself, man, though the presumption would be so great, that I scarce can think it true."

"I fear you're right, I do; yes, I fear you're right!—When I consider myself; what I am; how little I know, and how rude my life has been, I altogether distrust my claim even to think a moment, of one so tutored, and gay, and light of heart, and delicate—"

"You forget handsome—" coarsely interrupted Muir.

"And handsome too, I fear," returned the meek and self-abased guide, "I might have said handsome, at once, among her other qualities, for the young fa'an just as it learns to bound, is not more pleasant to the eye of the hunter, than Mabel is lovely in mine. I do indeed fear, that all the thoughts I have harbored about her, are vain and presumptuous."

"If you think this, my friend, of your own accord, and natural modesty, as it might be, my duty to you as an old fellow campaigner compels me to say—"

"Quarter Master—" interrupted the other, regarding his

companion keenly, "you and I have lived together much behind the ramparts of forts, but very little in the open woods, or in front of the inimy."

"Garrison or tent, it all passes for part of the same campaign, you know, Pathfinder, and then my duty keeps me much within sight of the store-houses, greatly contrary to my inclinations, as ye may well suppose, having yourself the ardor of battle in your temperament. But had ye heard what Mabel has just been saying of you, ye'd no think another minute of making yourself agreeable to the saucy and uncompromising hussy."

Pathfinder looked earnestly at the lieutenant, for it was impossible he should not feel an interest in what might be Mabel's opinion, but he had too much of the innate and true feeling of a gentleman, to ask to hear what another had said of him. Muir, however, was not to be foiled by this self denial and self respect, for, believing he had a man of great truth and simplicity to deal with, he determined to practise on his credulity, as one means of getting rid of his rivalry. He therefore pursued the subject, as soon as he perceived that his companion's self denial was stronger than his curiosity.

"You ought to know her opinion, Pathfinder," he continued, "and I think every man ought to hear what his friends and acquaintances say of him, and, so, by way of proving my own regard for your character and feelings, I'll just tell you, in as few words as possible. You know that Mabel has a wicked malicious way with those eyes of hers or when she has a mind to be hard upon one's feelings?"

"To me her eyes, Lieutenant Muir, have always seemed winning and soft—though I will acknowledge that they sometimes laugh—yes, I have known them to laugh; and that right heartily, and with down-right good will."

"Well, it was just that, there. Her eyes were laughing with all their might, as it were, and in the midst of all her fun, she broke out with an exclamation to this effect—I hope 't'will no hurt your sensibility, Pathfinder?"

"I will not say, Quarter Master, I will not say—Mabel's opinion of me is of more account than that of most others."

"Then I'll no tell ye, but just keep discretion on the subject. And why should a man be telling another what his friends say of him, especially when they happen to say that which may not be pleasant to hear. I'll not add another word to this present communication."

"I cannot make you speak, Quarter Master, if you are not so minded, and perhaps it is better for me not to know Mabel's opinion, as you seem to think it is not in my favor. Ah's! me—if we could be what we wish to be, instead of being only what we are, there would be a great difference in our characters, and knowledge and appearance. One may be rude, and coarse and ignorant, and yet happy, if he does not know it, but it is hard to see our own failings, in the strongest light, just as we wish to hear the least about them."

"That's just the *rationale*, as the French say, of the matter; and so I was telling Mabel, when she ran away, and left me. You noticed the manner in which she skipped off, as you approached?"

"It was very observable—" answered Pathfinder, drawing a long breath, and clenching the barrel of his rifle, as if the fingers would bury themselves in the iron.

"It was more than observable—it was flagrant—that's just the word, and the dictionary would'n't supply a better, after an hour's search. Well, you must know, Pathfinder——for I cannot reasonably deny you the gratification of hearing this—so you must know, the minx bounded off in that manner, in preference to hearing what I had to say in your justification."

"And what could you find to say, in my behalf, Quarter Master?"

"Why, d'ye understand, my friend, I was ruled by circumstances, and no ventured indiscreetly into generalities, but was preparing to meet particulars, as it might be, with particulars. If you were thought wild, half-savage, or of a frontier formation, I could tell her, ye know, that it came of the frontier, wild and half-savage life ye'd led; and all her objections must cease at once, or there would be a sort of misunderstanding with Providence."

"And did you tell her this, Quarter Master?"

"I'll no swear to the exact words, but the idea was prevalent in my mind, ye'll understand. The girl was impatient, and would not hear the half I had to say; but away she skipped, as ye saw with your own eyes, Pathfinder, as if her opinion were fully made up, and she cared to listen no longer. I fear her mind may be said to have come to its conclusion!"

"I fear it has, indeed, Quarter Master, and her father, after all, is mistaken. Yes, yes; the sarjeant has fallen into a grievous error."

"Well, man, why need ye lament, and undo all the grand reputation ye've been so many years making? Shoulder the rifle that ye use so well, and off into the woods with ye, for there's not the female breathing that is worth a heavy heart for a minute, as I know from experience. Tak' the word of one who knows the sax, and has had two wives, that women, after all, are very much the sort of creatures we do not imagine them to be. Now, if you would really mortify Mabel, here is as glorious an occasion, as any rejected lover could desire."

"The last wish I have, Lieutenant, would be to mortify Mabel."

"Well, ye'll come to that in the end, notwithstanding; for it's human nature to desire to give unpleasant feelings to them, that give unpleasant feelings to us. But a better occasion never offered to make your friends love you, than is to be had at this very moment, and that is the certain means of causing one's enemies to envy us."

"Quarter Master, Mabel is not my inimy; and if she was, the last thing I could desire, would be to give her an uneasy moment."

"Ye say so, Pathfinder—ye say so, and I dare say, ye think so; but reason and nature are both against you, as ye'll find in the end. Ye've heard the saying of 'love me, love my dog:' well, now, that means, read backwards, 'do'n't love me, do'n't love my dog.' Now, listen to what is in your power to do. You know we occupy an exceedingly precarious and uncertain position, here, almost in the jaws of the lion, as it were?"

"Do you mean the Frenchers, by the lion, and this island as his jaws, lieutenant?"

"Metaphorically only, my friend, for the French are no lions, and this island is not a jaw—unless, indeed, it may prove to be, what I greatly fear may come true, the jaw-bone of an ass!"

Here the Quarter Master indulged in a sneering laugh, that proclaimed any thing but respect and admiration for his friend Lundie's sagacity in selecting that particular spot for his operations.

"The post is as well chosen, as any I ever put foot in," said Pathfinder, looking around him, as one surveys a position.

"I'll no deny it—I'll no deny it. Lundie is a great soldier, in a small way, and his father was a great laird, with the same qualifications. I was born on the estate, and have followed the Major so long that I've got to reverence all he says and does. That's just my weakness, ye'll know, Pathfinder. Well, this post may be the post of an ass, or of a Solomon, as men fancy, but it's most critically placed, as is apparent by all Lundie's precautions and injunctions. There are savages out, scouting through these thousand islands, and over the forest, searching for this very spot, as is known to Lundie himself, on certain information, and the greatest service you can render the 55th, is to discover their trails, and lead them off, on a false scent. Unhappily, Serjeant Dunham has taken up the notion, that the danger is to be apprehended from up stream, because Frontenac lies above us, whereas all experience tells us, that Indians come on the side that is most contrary to reason, and, consequently, are to be expected from below. Take your canoe, therefore, and go down stream, among the islands, that we may have notice if any danger approaches from that quarter. If ye should look a few miles on the main, especially on the York side, the information you'd bring in would be all the more accurate, and consequently the more valuable.

"The Big Sarpent is on the look out, in that quarter, and as he knows the station well, no doubt he will give us timely notice, should any wish to sarcumvent us, in that direction."

"He is but an Indian, after all, Pathfinder, and this is an affair that calls for the knowledge of a white man. Lundie will be eternally grateful to the man that shall help this little enterprise to come off with flying colours. To tell you the truth, my friend, he is conscious it should never have been attempted, but he has too much of the old laird's obstinacy about him, to own an error, though it be as manifest as the morning star."

The Quarter Master then continued to reason with his companion, in order to induce him to quit the island, without delay, using such arguments as first suggested themselves, sometimes contradicting himself, and not unfrequently urging at one moment a motive that at the next was directly opposed by another. The Pathfinder, simple as he was, detected these flaws in the Lieutenant's philosophy, though he was far from suspecting that they proceeded from a desire to clear the coast, of Mabel's suitor. He met bad reasons by good ones, resisted every inducement that was not legitimate, by his intimate acquaintance with his peculiar duties, and was blind, as usual, to the influence of every incentive that could not stand the test of integrity. He did not exactly suspect the secret objects of Muir, but he was far from being blind to his sophistry. The result was that the two parted, after a long dialogue, unconvinced and distrustful of each other's motives, though the distrust of the guide, like all that was connected with the man, partook of his own upright, disinterested and ingenuous nature.

A conference that took place, soon after, between Serjeant Dunham and the Lieutenant led to more consequences. When it was ended, secret orders were issued to the men, the blockhouse was taken possession of, the huts were occupied, and one accustomed to the movements of soldiers, might have detected that an expedition was in the wind. In fact, just as the sun was setting, the Serjeant who had been much occupied at what was called the harbor, came into his own hut, followed by Pathfinder and Cap, and, as he took his seat at the neat table that Mabel had prepared for him, he opened the budget of his intelligence.

"You are likely to be of some use, here, my child," the old soldier commenced, "as this tidy and well ordered supper can testify, and, I trust, when the proper moment arrives, you will show yourself to be the descendant of those who know how to face their enemies."

"You do not expect me, dear father, to play Joan of Arc, and to lead the men to battle?"

"Play whom, child—Did you ever hear of the person Mabel mentions, Pathfinder?"

"Not I, sarjeant, but what of that? I am ignorant and onedicated, and it is too great a pleasure to me to listen to her voice, and take in her words, to be particular about persons."

"I know her," said Cap, decidedly. "She sailed a privateer out of Morlaix, in the last war; and good cruises she made of them."

Mabel blushed at having inadvertently made an allusion that went beyond her father's reading, to say nothing of her uncle's dogmatism; and perhaps a little at the Pathfinder's simple ingenuous earnestness, but she did not forbear the less to smile.

"Why, father, I am not expected to fall in with the men, and help defend the island."

"And, yet, women have often done such things, in this quarter of the world, girl, as our friend, the Pathfinder, here, will tell you. But lest you should be surprised at not seeing us, when you awake in the morning, it is proper that I now tell you we intend to march in the course of this very night."

"*We*, father—and leave me and Jennie on this island alone!"

"No, my daughter, not quite as unmilitary as that. We shall leave Lt. Muir, brother Cap, Corporal McNab, and three men, to compose the garrison during our absence. Jennie will remain with you, in this hut, and brother Cap will occupy my place."

"And Mr. Muir?" said Mabel, half unconscious of what she uttered, though she foresaw a great deal of unpleasant persecution in the arrangement.

"Why, he can make love to you, if you like it, girl, for he is an amorous youth, and having already disposed of four wives, is impatient to show how much he honors their memories, by taking a fifth."

"The Quarter Master tells me," said Pathfinder, innocently, "that when a man's feelings have been harrowed by so many losses, there is no wiser way to soothe them, than by ploughing up the soil anew, in such a manner as to leave no traces of what have gone over it afore."

"Ay, that is just the difference between ploughing and harrowing," returned the Serjeant with a grim smile. "But let him tell Mabel his mind, and there will be an end of his suit. I very well know that *my* daughter will never be the wife of Lieutenant Muir."

This was said in a way that was tantamount to declaring

that no daughter of his, ever *should* become the wife of the person in question. Mabel had coloured, trembled, half laughed, and looked uneasy, but rallying her spirit, she said in a voice so cheerful as completely to conceal her agitation—

"But, father, we might better wait until Mr. Muir manifests a wish that your daughter would have him—or rather a wish to have your daughter, lest we get the fable of sour grapes thrown into our faces."

"And what is that fable, Mabel," eagerly demanded Pathfinder, who was any thing but learned in the ordinary lore of white men—"tell it to us, in your own pretty way; I dare say the sarjeant never heard it."

Mabel repeated the well known fable, and as her suitor had desired, in her own pretty way, which was a way to keep his eyes rivetted on her face, and the whole of his honest countenance covered with a smile.

"That was like a fox!" cried Pathfinder, when she had ceased, "ay, and like a Mingo, too. Cunning and cruel; that is the way with both the riptyles. As to grapes, they are sour enough in this part of the country, even to them that can get at them, though I dare say there are seasons, and times, and places, where they are sourer to them that can't. I should judge, now, my scalp is very sour in Mingo eyes."

"The sour grapes will be the other way, child, and it is Mr. Muir who will make the complaint. You would never marry that man, Mabel?"

"Not she," put in Cap, "a fellow who is only half a soldier, after all! The story of them there grapes, is quite a circumstance."

"I think little of marrying any one, dear father, and dear uncle, and would rather talk about it less, if you please. But, did I think of marrying at all, I do believe a man whose affections have already been tried by three or four wives would scarcely be my choice."

The serjeant nodded at the guide, as much as to say, you see how the land lies, and then he had sufficient consideration for his daughter's feelings to change the subject.

"Neither you, nor Mabel, brother Cap," he resumed, "can have any legal authority with the garrison I leave behind, on the island, but you may counsel and influence. Strictly speaking Corporal McNab will be the commanding officer, and I have endeavored to impress him with a sense of his dignity, lest he might give way too much to the superior rank of Lieutenant Muir, who, being a volunteer, can have no right to interfere with the duty. I wish you to sustain the corporal, brother Cap, for should the Quarter Master once break through the regulations of the expedition, he may pretend to command me, as well as McNab."

"More particularly, should Mabel really cut him adrift, while you are absent. Of course, Serjeant, you'll leave every thing that is afloat, under my care? The most d——le confusion has grown out of misunderstandings between commanders in chief, ashore and afloat."

"In one sense, brother, though, in a general way, the corporal is commander in chief. History does indeed tell us that a division of command leads to difficulties, and I shall avoid that danger. The corporal must command, but you can counsel freely, particularly in all matters relating to the boats, of which I shall leave one behind, to secure your retreat should there be occasion. I know the corporal well; he is a brave man, and a good soldier; and one that may be relied on, if the Santa Cruz can be kept from him. But then he is a Scotchman, and will be liable to the Quarter Master's influence, against which I desire both you and Mabel to be on your guard."

"But why leave us behind, dear father?—I have come thus far to be a comfort to you, and why not go farther?"

"You are a good girl, Mabel, and very like the Dunhams! But you must halt here. We shall leave the island to-morrow, before the day dawns, in order not to be seen by any prying eyes, coming from our cover, and we shall take the two largest boats, leaving you the other, and one bark canoe. We are about to go into the channel used by the French, where we shall lie in wait, perhaps a week, to intercept their supply boats that are about to pass up, on their way to Frontenac, loaded, in particular, with a heavy amount of Indian goods."

"Have you looked well to your papers, brother?" Cap anxiously demanded. "Of course, you know a capture on the high seas is piracy, unless your boat is regularily commissioned, either as a public, or a private armed cruiser."

"I have the honor to hold the colonel's appointment as Serjeant Major of the 55th," returned the other, drawing himself up with dignity, "and that will be sufficient even for the French King. If not, I have Major Duncan's written orders."

"No papers them, for a warlike cruiser."

"They must suffice, brother, as I have no other. It is of vast importance to His Majesty's interests, in this part of the world, that the boats in question should be captured and carried into Oswego. They contain the blankets, trinkets, rifles, ammunition,—in short, all the stores with which the French bribe their accursed savage allies to commit their unholy acts, setting at naught our holy religion and its precepts, the laws of humanity, and all that is sacred and dear among men. By cutting off these supplies, we shall derange their plans, and gain time on them, for the articles cannot be sent across the ocean again, this autumn."

"But, father, does not His Majesty employ Indians also?" asked Mabel, with some curiosity.

"Certainly, girl, and he has a right to employ them—God bless him! It's a very different thing, whether an Englishman or a Frenchman employs a savage, as every body can understand."

"That is plain enough, brother Dunham;—but I do not see my way so clear, in the matter of the ship's papers."

"An *English* colonel's appointment ought to satisfy any *Frenchman* of my authority; and what is more, brother, it shall."

"But I do not see the difference, father, between an Englishman's and a Frenchman's employing savages in war?"

"All the odds in the world, child, though you may not be able to see it. In the first place, an Englishman is naturally humane and considerate, while a Frenchman is naturally ferocious and timid."

"And you may add, brother, that he will dance from morning 'till night, if you'll let him."

"Very true," gravely returned the Serjeant.

"But, father, I cannot see that all this alters the case. If it be wrong in a Frenchman to hire savages to fight his enemies, it would seem to be equally wrong in an Englishman. *You* will admit this, Pathfinder."

"It's reasonable—it's reasonable, and I have never been one of them that has raised a cry ag'in the Frenchers for doing the very thing we do ourselves. Still, it is worse to consort with a Mingo, than to consort with a Delaware. If any of that just tribe were left, I should think it no sin to send them out ag'in the foe."

"And yet they scalp, and slay young and old—women and children!"

"They have their gifts, Mabel, and are not to be blamed for following them. Natur' is natur', though the different tribes have different ways of showing it. For my part, I am white, and endivor to maintain white feelings."

"This is all unintelligible to me," answered Mabel. "What is right in King George, it would seem ought to be right in King Lewis."

"The King of France's real name is Caput," observed Cap, with his mouth full of venison. "I once carried a great scholar, as a passenger, and he told me that these Lewises thirteenth, fourteenth and fifteenth were all humbugs, and that the men's real name was Caput, which is French for 'foot,' meaning that they ought to be put at the *foot* of the ladder, until ready to go up to be hanged."

"Well this does look like being given to scalping, as a nat'ral gift," Pathfinder remarked, with the air of surprise with which one receives a novel idea, "and I shall have less compunction than ever in sarving ag'in the miscreants, though I can't say I ever yet felt any worth naming."

As all parties, Mabel excepted, seemed satisfied with the course the discussion had taken, no one appeared to think it necessary to pursue the subject. The trio of men, indeed, in this particular, so much resembled the great mass of their fellow creatures, who usually judge of character equally without knowledge and without justice, that we might not have thought it necessary to record the discourse, had it not some bearing in its facts, on the incidents of the legend, and in its opinions on the motives of the characters.

Supper was no sooner ended, than the Serjeant dismissed his guests, and then held a long and confidential dialogue with his daughter. He was little addicted to giving way to the gentler emotions, but the novelty of his present situation awakened feelings that he was unused to experience. The soldier, or the sailor, so long as he acts under the immediate supervision of a superior, thinks little of the risks he runs, but the moment he feels the responsibility of command, all the hazards of his undertaking begin to associate themselves in his mind, with the chances of success or failure. While he dwells less on his own personal danger, perhaps, than when that is the principal consideration, he has more lively general perceptions of all the risks, and submits more to the influence of the feelings which doubt creates. Such was now the case with Serjeant Dunham, who, instead of looking forward to victory as certain, according to his usual habits, began to feel the possibility that he might be parting with his child, forever.

Never before had Mabel struck him as so beautiful, as she appeared that night. Possibly she never had displayed so many engaging qualities to her father, for concern on his account had begun to be active in her breast, and then her sympathies met with unusual encouragement, through those which had been stirred up in the sterner bosom of the veteran. She had never been entirely at her ease with her parent, the great superiority of her education, creating a sort of chasm which had been widened by the military severity of manner he had acquired, by dealing so long and intimately with beings who could only be kept in subjection, by an unremitted discipline. On the present occasion, however, or after they were left alone, the conversation between the father and daughter became more confidential than usual, until Mabel rejoiced to find that it was gradually becoming endearing; a state of feeling that the warm-hearted girl had silently pined for in vain, ever since her arrival.

"Then mother was about my height?" Mabel said, as she held one of her father's hands in both her own—looking up into his face with humid eyes. "I had thought her taller."

"That is the way with most children, who get a habit of thinking of their parents with respect, until they fancy them larger and more commanding than they actually are. Your mother, Mabel, was as near your height, as one woman could be to another."

"And her eyes, father?"

"Her eyes were like thine, child, too—blue, and soft, and inviting like; though hardly so laughing."

"Mine will never laugh again, dearest father, if you do not take care of yourself in this expedition."

"Thank you, Mabel—hem—thank you, child, but I must do my duty. I wish I had seen you comfortably married before we left Oswego! My mind would be easier."

"Married!—To whom, father?"

"You know the man I wish you to love. You may meet with many gayer, and many dressed in finer clothes, but with none with so true a heart, and just a mind."

"None, father?"

"I know of none; in these particulars, Pathfinder has few equals, at least."

"But I need not marry at all. You are single, and I can remain to take care of you."

"God bless you, Mabel!—I know you would, and I do not say that the feeling is not right, for I suppose it is; and yet I believe there is another, that is more so."

"What can be more right than to honor one's parents?"

"It is just as right to honor one's husband, my dear child."

"But I have no husband, father."

"Then take one, as soon as possible, that you may have a husband to honor. I cannot live forever, Mabel, but must drop off in the course of nature, ere long, if I am not carried off in the course of war. You are young, and may yet live long; and it is proper that you should have a male protector, who can see you safe through life, and take care of you in age, as you now wish to take care of me."

"And do you think, father—" said Mabel, playing with his sinewy fingers, with her own little hands, and looking down at them, as if they were subjects of intense interest, though her lips curled in a slight smile, as the words came from them—"And do you think, father, that Pathfinder is just the man to do this?—Is he not within ten or twelve years, as old as yourself?"

"What of that?—His life has been one of moderation and exercise, and years are less to be counted, girl, than constitution. Do you know another more likely to be your protector?"

Mabel did not; at least another who had expressed a desire to that effect, whatever might have been her hopes and her wishes.

"Nay, father, we are not talking of another, but of the Pathfinder," she answered evasively. "If he were younger, I think it would be more natural for me to think of him for a husband."

" 'Tis all in the constitution, I tell you, child. Pathfinder is a younger man than half our subalterns."

"He is certainly younger than one, sir—Lieutenant Muir."

Mabel's laugh was joyous and light-hearted, as if just then, she felt no care.

"That he is—young enough to be his grandson—he is younger in years too. God forbid, Mabel! that you should ever become an officer's lady, at least until you are an officer's daughter."

"There will be little fear of that, father, if I marry Pathfinder!" returned the girl, looking up archly in the serjeant's face, again.

"Not by the King's commission, perhaps, though the man is even now the friend and companion of generals. I think I could die happy, Mabel, if you were his wife."

"Father!"

" 'Tis a sad thing to go into battle, with the weight of an unprotected daughter laid upon the heart."

"I would give the world to lighten yours of its load, my dear sir!"

"It might be done—" said the serjeant, looking fondly at his child, "though I could not wish to put a burthen on yours, in order to do so."

The voice was deep and tremulous, and never before had Mabel witnessed such a show of affection in her parent. The habitual sternness of the man, lent an interest to his emotions, that they might otherwise have wanted, and the daughter's heart yearned to relieve the father's mind.

"Father, speak plainly," she cried, almost convulsively.

"Nay, Mabel, it might not be right—your wishes and mine may be very different."

"I have no wishes—know nothing of what you mean—would you speak of my future marriage?"

"If I could see you promised to Pathfinder—know that you were pledged to become his wife, let my own fate be what it might, I think I could die happy. But I will ask no pledge of you my child—I will not force you to do what you might repent. Kiss me, Mabel, and go to your bed."

Had Serjeant Dunham exacted of Mabel the pledge that he really so much desired, he would have encountered a resistance that he might have found difficult to overcome, but, by letting nature have its course, he enlisted a powerful ally on his side, and the warm-hearted, generous-minded Mabel was ready to concede to her affections, much more than she would ever have yielded to menace. At that touching moment she thought only of her parent, who was about to quit her perhaps forever, and all of that ardent love for him, which had possibly been as much fed by the imagination as by any thing else, but which had received a little check by the restrained intercourse of the last fortnight, now returned with a force that was increased by pure and intense feeling. Her father seemed all in all to her, and to render him happy, there was no proper sacrifice that she was not ready to make. One painful, rapid, almost wild gleam of thought shot across the brain of the girl, and her resolution wavered; but endeavoring to trace the foundation of the pleasing hope on which it was based, she found nothing positive to support it. Trained like a woman, to subdue her most ardent feelings, her thoughts reverted to her father, and to the blessings that awaited the child who yielded to a parent's wishes.

"Father," she said quietly, almost with a holy calm—"God blesses the dutiful daughter!"

"He will, Mabel; we have the good book for that."

"I will marry whomever you desire."

"Nay—nay, Mabel—you may have a choice of your own—"

"I have no choice—that is—none have asked me to have a choice, but Pathfinder and Mr. Muir, and between *them*, neither of us would hesitate. No, father; I will marry whomever you may choose."

"Thou knowest my choice, beloved girl; none other can make thee as happy, as the noble-hearted guide."

"Well, then, if he wish it—if he ask me again—for, father,

you would not have me offer myself, or that any one should do that office for me—" and the blood stole across the pallid cheeks of Mabel, as she spoke, for high and generous resolution had driven back the stream of life to her heart,— "no one must speak to him of it, but if he seek me again, and, knowing all that a true girl ought to tell the man she marries, and he then wishes to make me his wife, I will be his."

"Bless you, my Mabel—God in Heaven bless you, and reward you as a pious daughter deserves to be rewarded."

"Yes, father—put your mind at peace—go on this expedition with a light heart, and trust in God. For me, you will have, now, no care. In the spring—I must have a little time, father—but, in the spring, I will marry Pathfinder, if that noble hearted hunter shall then desire it."

"Mabel, he loves you, as I loved your mother. I have seen him weep like a child, when speaking of his feelings towards you."

"Yes, I believe it—I've seen enough to satisfy me, that he thinks better of me than I deserve, and, certainly the man is not living for whom I have more respect, than for Pathfinder; not even for you, dear father."

"That is as it should be, child, and the union will be blessed. May I not tell Pathfinder this?"

"I would rather you would not, father. Let it come of itself—come naturally—the man should seek the woman, and not the woman the man—" The smile that illuminated Mabel's handsome face, was angelic, as even her parent thought, though one better practised in detecting the passing emotions, as they betray themselves in the countenance, might have traced something wild and unnatural in it—"No—no—*we* must let things take their course; but, father, you have my solemn promise."

"That will do—that will do, Mabel; now kiss me—God bless and protect you, girl—you are a good daughter."

Mabel threw herself into her father's arms, it was the first time in her life, and sobbed on his bosom like an infant. The stern old soldier's heart was melted, and the tears of the two mingled. But Serjeant Dunham soon started, as if ashamed of himself, and gently forcing his daughter from him, he bade her good night, and sought his pallet. Mabel went sobbing to the rude corner that had been prepared for her reception, and in a few minutes the hut was undisturbed by any sound, save the heavy breathing of the veteran.

Chapter XX

"Wandering, I found on my ruinous walk,
By the dial stone aged and green,
One rose of the wilderness left on its stalk
To mark where a garden had been."
Campbell, "Lines Written on Visiting a
Scene in Argyleshire," ll. 10–13.

IT WAS NOT only broad day-light, when Mabel awoke, but the sun had actually been up some time. Her sleep had been tranquil, for she rested on an approving conscience, and fatigue contributed to render it sweet, and no sound of those who had been so early in motion, had interfered with her rest. Springing to her feet, and rapidly dressing herself, the girl was soon breathing the fragrance of the morning, in the open air. For the first time, she was sensibly struck with the singular beauties, as well as with the profound retirement of her present situation. The day proved to be one of those of the autumnal glory so common to a climate that is more abused than appreciated, and its influence was in every way inspiriting and genial. Mabel was benefitted by this circumstance, for, as she fancied, her heart was heavy on account of the dangers to which a father, whom she now began to love, as women love when confidence is created, was about to be exposed.

But the island seemed absolutely deserted. The previous night the bustle of the arrival, had given the spot an appearance of life that was now entirely gone, and our heroine had turned her eyes nearly around on every object in sight, before she caught a view of a single human being to remove the sense of utter solitude. Then, indeed, she beheld all who were left behind, collected in a group, around a fire which might be said to belong to the camp. The person of her uncle, to whom she was so much accustomed, reassured the girl, and she examined the remainder, with a curiosity natural to her situation. Besides Cap, and the Quarter Master, there were the corporal, the three soldiers, and the woman who was cooking. The huts were silent and empty, and the low, but tower-like summit of the block-house rose above the bushes, by which it was half concealed, in picturesque beauty. The sun was just casting its brightness into the open places of the glade, and the vault, over her head, was impending in the soft sublimity of the blue void. Not a cloud was visible, and she secretly fancied the circumstance might be taken as a harbinger of peace and security.

Perceiving that all the others were occupied with that great concern of human nature, a breakfast, Mabel walked, unobserved, towards an end of the island, where she was completely shut out of view, by the trees and bushes. Here she got a stand on the very verge of the water, by forcing aside the low branches, and stood watching the barely perceptible flow and reflow of the miniature waves that laved the shore; a sort of physical echo to the agitation that prevailed on the lake, fifty miles above her. The glimpses of natural scenery, that offered, were very soft and pleasing, and, our heroine, who had a quick and true eye for all that was lovely in nature, was not slow in selecting the more striking bits of landscape. She gazed through the different vistas formed by the openings between the islands, and thought she had never looked on aught more lovely.

While thus occupied, Mabel was suddenly alarmed by fancying that she caught a glimpse of a human form among the bushes that lined the shore of the island that lay directly before her. The distance across the water was not a hundred yards, and though she might be mistaken, and her fancy was wandering when the form passed before her sight, still she did not think she could be deceived. Aware that her sex would be no protection against a rifle bullet, should an Iroquois get a view of her, the girl instinctively drew back, taking care to conceal her person, as much as possible by the leaves, while she kept her own look rivetted on the opposite shore, vainly waiting for some time, in the expectation of the stranger. She was about to quit her post in the bushes, and hasten to her uncle in order to acquaint him of her suspicions, when she saw the branch of an alder, thrust beyond the bushes, on the other island, and waved towards her significantly, and, as she fancied, in a token of amity. This was a breathless and a trying moment, to one as inexperienced in frontier warfare as our heroine, and yet she felt the great necessity that existed for preserving her recollections, and of acting with steadiness and discretion.

It was one of the peculiarities of the exposure, to which those who dwelt on the frontiers of America were liable, to bring out the moral qualities of the women to a degree, that they must themselves, under other circumstances, have believed they were incapable of manifesting, and Mabel well knew that the borderers loved to dwell, in their legends, on the presence of mind, fortitude and spirit that their wives and sisters had displayed, under circumstances the most trying. Her emulation had been awakened by what she had heard on such subjects, and it at once struck her, that now was the moment for her to show that she was truly Serjeant Dunham's child. The motion of the branch was such as, she believed, indicated amity, and, after a moment's hesitation, she broke off a twig, fastened it to a stick, and thrusting it through an opening, waved it in return, imitating as closely as possible the manner of the other.

This dumb show lasted two or three minutes on both sides, when Mabel perceived that the bushes opposite, were cautiously pushed aside, and a human face appeared at an opening. A glance sufficed to let Mabel see that it was the countenance of a red skin, as well as of a woman. A second and a better look satisfied her, that it was the face of the Dew of June, the wife of Arrowhead. During the time she had travelled in company with this woman, Mabel had been won by the gentleness of manner, the meek simplicity and the mingled awe and affection with which she regarded her husband. Once or twice, in the course of the journey she fancied the Tuscarora had manifested towards herself an unpleasant degree of attention, and on those occasions it had struck her that his wife exhibited sorrow and mortification. As Mabel, however, had more than compensated for any pain she might, in this way, unintentionally have caused her companion, by her own kindness of manner and attentions, the woman had shown much attachment to her, and they had parted, with a deep conviction on the mind of our heroine, that, in the Dew of June, she had lost a friend.

It is useless to attempt to analyze all the ways by which the human heart is led into confidence. Such a feeling, however, had the young Tuscarora woman awakened in the breast of our heroine, and the latter, under the impression that this extraordinary visit was intended for her own good, felt every disposition to have a closer communication. She no longer hesitated about showing herself, clear of the bushes, and, was not sorry to see the Dew of June imitate her confidence, by stepping fearlessly out of her own cover. The two girls, for the Tuscarora, though married, was even younger than Mabel, now openly exchanged signs of friendship, and the latter beckoned to her friend to approach, though she knew not the manner, herself, in which this object could be effected. But, the Dew of June was not slow in letting it be seen that it was in her power, for disappearing a moment, she soon showed herself again in the end of a bark canoe, the bows of which she had drawn to the edge of the bushes, and of which the body still lay in a sort of covered creek. Mabel was about to invite her to cross, when her own name was called aloud, in the stentorian voice of her uncle. Making a hurried gesture for the Tuscarora girl to conceal herself, Mabel sprang from the bushes, and tripped up the glade towards the sound, and perceived that the whole party had just seated themselves at breakfast, Cap having barely put his appetite under sufficient restraint to summon her to join them. That this was the most favorable instant for the interview flashed on the mind of Mabel, and excusing herself on the plea of not being prepared for the meal, she bounded back to the thicket, and soon renewed her communications with the young Indian woman.

Dew of June was quick of comprehension, and with half a dozen noiseless strokes of the paddle, her canoe was concealed in the bushes of Station Island. In another minute, Mabel had her hand, and was leading her through the grove towards her own hut. Fortunately, the latter was so placed, as to be completely hidden from the sight of those at the fire, and they both entered it unseen. Hastily explaining to her guest, in the best manner she could, the necessity of quitting her for a short time, Mabel, first placing the Dew of June in her own room, with a full certainty that she would not quit it until told to do so, went to the fire, and took her seat among the rest, with all the composure it was in her power to command.

"Late come, late served, Mabel," said her uncle, between two mouthfuls of broiled salmon, for though the cookery might be very unsophisticated on that remote frontier, the viands were generally delicious; "late come, late served: it is a good rule, and keeps laggards up to their work."

"I am no laggard, uncle, for I have been stirring near an hour, and exploring our island."

"It's little you'll make o' that, Mistress Mabel," put in Muir, "that's little, by nature. Lundie, or it might be better to style him Major Duncan in this presence—" this was said in consideration of the corporal and the common men, though they were taking their meal a little apart—"it might be better to style him Major Duncan in this presence, has not added an empire to His Majesty's dominions, in getting possession of this island, which is likely to equal that of the celebrated Sancho, in revenues and profits—Sancho of whom, doubtless, Master Cap, you'll often have been reading in your leisure hours, more especially in calms, and moments of inactivity."

"I know the spot you mean, Quarter Master; Sancho's Island—coral rock, of new formation, and as bad a land fall, in a dark night and blowing weather, as a sinner could wish to keep clear of. It's a famous place for cocoa nuts and bitter water, that Sancho's Island!"

"It's no very famous for dinners," returned Muir, repressing the smile that was struggling to his lips, out of respect to Mabel, "nor do I think there'll be much to choose between its revenue, and that of this spot. In my judgment, Master Cap, this is a very unmilitary position, and I look to some calamity's befalling it, sooner or later."

"It is to be hoped not until our turn of duty is over," observed Mabel. "I have no wish to study the French language."

"We might think ourselves happy, did it not prove to be the Iroquois. I have reasoned with Major Duncan on the occupation of this position, but 'a wilfu' man maun ha' his way.' My first object, in accompanying this party, was to endeavour to make myself acceptable and useful to your beautiful niece, Master Cap; and the second was to take such an account of the stores that belong to my particular department, as shall leave no question open to controversy, concerning the manner of expenditure, when they shall have disappeared by means of the enemy."

"Do you look upon matters as so serious?" demanded Cap, actually suspending his mastication of a bit of venison, for he passed alternately, like a modern *élégant*, from fish to flesh and back again, in the interest he took in the answer. "Is the danger pressing?"

"I'll no say just that; and I'll no say, just the contrary. There is always danger in war, and there is more of it, at the advanced posts, than at the main encampment. It ought, therefore, to occasion no surprise were we to be visited by the French, at any moment."

"And what the devil, is to be done, in that case?—Six men and two women would make but a poor job, in defending such a place as this, should the enemy invade us, as no doubt Frenchmen like, they would take very good care, to come strong handed."

"That we may depend on. Some very formidable force, at the very lowest. A military disposition might be made, in defence of the island, out of all question, and according to the art of war, though we would probably fail in the force necessary to carry out the design, in any very creditable manner. In the first place, a detachment should be sent off, to the shore, with orders to annoy the enemy in landing. A strong party ought instantly to be thrown into the block-house, as the citadel, for on that all the different detachments would naturally fall back for support, as the French advanced, and an entrenched camp might be laid out around the strong-hold, as it would be very unmilitary, indeed, to let the foe get near enough to the foot of the walls to mine them. Chevaux de frise would keep the cavalry in check, and as for the artillery, redoubts should be thrown up, under cover of yon woods. Strong skirmishing parties, moreover, would be exceedingly serviceable in retarding the march of the enemy, and these different huts, if properly picketted and ditched, could be converted into very eligible positions for that object."

"Whe-e-e-w! Quarter Master. And who the d——l, is to find all the men to carry out such a plan?"

"The King, out of all question, Master Cap. It is his quarrel, and it's just he should bear the burthen o' it."

"And we are only six! This is fine talking, with a vengeance. You could be sent down to the shore, to oppose the landing, Mabel might skirmish with her tongue at least, the soldier's wife might act chevaux de frise, to entangle the cavalry, the corporal should command the entrenched camp, his three men could occupy the five huts, and I would take the block-house. Whe-e-e-w, you describe well, Lieutenant, and should have been a limner, instead of a soldier!"

"Na—I've been very literal and upright in my exposition of matters. That there is no greater force here, to carry out the plan, is a fault of His Majesty's ministers, and none of mine."

"But, should an enemy really appear," asked Mabel, with more interest than she might have shown, had she not remembered the guest in the hut; "what course ought we to pursue?"

"My advice would be to attempt to achieve that, Pretty Mabel, which rendered Xenophon so justly celebrated."

"I think you mean a retreat, though I half guess at your allusion."

"You've imagined my meaning from the possession of a strong native sense, young lady. I am aware that your worthy father has pointed out to the corporal, certain modes and methods by which he fancies this island could be held, in case the French should discover its position; but the excellent serjeant, though your father, and as good a man in his duties as ever wielded a 'spontoon, is not the great Lord Stair, or even the Duke of Marlborough. I'll no deny the serjeant's merits, in his particular sphere, though I cannot exaggerate qualities, however excellent, into those of men who may be in some trifling degree his superiors. Serjeant Dunham has taken counsel of his heart, instead of his head, in resolving to issue such orders; but, if the post fall, the blame will lie on him that ordered it to be occupied, and not on him whose duty it was to defend it. Whatever may be the determination of the latter, should the French and their allies land, a good commander never neglects the precautions necessary to effect a retreat, and I would advise Master Cap, who is the admiral of our navy, to have a boat in readiness to evacuate the island, if need comes to need. The largest boat that we have left, carries a very ample sail, and by hauling it round, here, and mooring it under those bushes, there will be a convenient place for a hurried embarkation, and then you'll perceive, Pretty Mabel, that it is scarce fifty yards before we shall be in a channel between two other islands, and hid from the sight of those who may happen to be on this."

"All that you say, is very true, Mr. Muir; but may not the French come from that quarter themselves? If it is so good for a retreat, it is equally good for an advance."

"They'll no have the sense to do so discreet a thing," returned Muir, looking furtively and a little uneasily, around him, "they'll no have sufficient discretion. Your French are a head-over-heels nation, and usually come forward in a random way; so, we may look for them, if they come at all, on the other side of the island—"

The discourse now became exceedingly desultory, touching principally, however, on the probabilities of an invasion, and the best means of meeting it.

To most of this, Mabel paid but little attention, though she felt some surprise that Lt. Muir, an officer whose character for courage stood well, should openly recommend an abandonment of what appeared to her to be doubly a duty, her father's character being connected with the defence of the island. Her mind, however, was so much occupied with her guest, that siezing the first favorable moment she left the table, and was soon in her own hut again. Carefully fastening the door, and seeing that the simple curtain was drawn before the single little window, Mabel next led the Dew of June, or June, as she was familiarly termed by those who spoke to her in English, into the outer room, making signs of affection and confidence.

"I am glad to see you, June," said Mabel, with one of her sweetest smiles, and in her own winning voice, "very glad to see you—but what has brought you, hither, and how did you discover the island?"

"Talk slow," said June, returning smile for smile, and pressing the little hand she held, with one of her own that was scarcely larger, though it had been hardened by labor—"more slow—too quick."

Mabel repeated her questions, endeavoring to repress the

impetuosity of her feelings, and she succeeded in speaking so distinctly as to be understood.

"June friend—" returned the Indian woman.

"I believe you, June; from my soul, I believe you. What has this to do with your visit?"

"Friend come to see friend," answered June, again smiling openly in the other's face.

"There is some other reason, June; else would you never run this risk, and alone. You are alone, June?"

"June wid you—no one else. June come alone—paddle canoe."

"I hope so—I think so—nay, I *know* so. You would not be treacherous with me, June?"

"What treacherous?"

"You would not betray me—would not give me to the French—to the Iroquois—to Arrowhead—" June shook her head earnestly, "—you would not sell my scalp."

Here, June passed her arm fondly around the slender waist of Mabel, and pressed her to her heart, with a tenderness and affection, that brought tears into the eyes of our heroine. It was done, in the fond caressing manner of a woman, and it was scarcely possible that it should not obtain credit for sincerity, with a young and ingenuous person of the same sex. Mabel returned the pressure, and then held the other off, at the length of her arm, looked her steadily in the face, and continued her inquiries.

"If June has something to tell her friend, let her speak plainly," she said. "My ears are open."

"June 'fraid Arrowhead kill her."

"But Arrowhead will never know it—" Mabel's blood mounted to her temples, as she said this; for she felt that she was urging a wife to be treacherous to her husband—"That is, Mabel will not tell him."

"He bury tomahawk in June's head."

"That must never be, dear June; I would rather you should say no more, than run this risk."

"Block house good place to sleep—good place to stay."

"Do you mean that I may save my life by keeping in the block-house, June? Surely, surely, Arrowhead will not hurt you for telling me that—He cannot wish me any great harm, for I never injured him."

"Arrowhead wish no harm to handsome Pale face," returned June, averting her face, and, though she always spoke in the soft, gentle, voice of an Indian girl, permitting its notes to fall so low, as to cause them to sound melancholy and timid—"Arrowhead love pale face girls."

Mabel blushed, she knew not why, and for a moment, her questions were repressed by a feeling of inherent delicacy. But it was necessary to know more, for her apprehensions had been keenly awakened, and she resumed her inquiries.

"Arrowhead can have no reason to love, or to hate *me*," she said. "Is he near you?"

"Husband always near wife, here," said June, laying her hand on her heart.

"Excellent creature!—But, tell me, June, ought I to keep in the block-house to-day—this morning—now?"

"Block-house very good—good for squaw. Block-house got no scalp."

"I fear I understand you only too well, June—Do you wish to see my father?"

"No here; gone away."

"You cannot know that, June; you see the island is full of his soldiers."

"No full; gone away—" here June held up four of her fingers—"so many red coat."

"And Pathfinder; would you not like to see the Pathfinder?—he can talk to you in the Iroquois tongue."

"Tongue gone wid him—" said June laughing—"keep tongue in his mout'."

There was something so sweet and contagious in the infantile laugh of an Indian girl, that Mabel could not refrain from joining in it, much as her fears were aroused by all that had passed.

"You appear to know, or to think you know all about us, June. But, if Pathfinder be gone, Eau douce can speak French, too. You know Eau douce; shall I run and bring *him* to talk with you?"

"Eau douce gone, too, all but heart; that there." As June said this, she laughed again, looked in different directions, as if unwilling to confuse the other, and laid her hand on Mabel's bosom.

Our heroine had often heard of the wonderful sagacity of the Indians, and of the surprising manner in which they noted all things, while they appeared to regard none, but she was scarce prepared for the direction the discourse had so singularly taken. Willing to change it, and, at the same time, truly anxious to learn how great the danger that impended over them might really be, she rose from the camp-stool, on which she had been seated, and, by assuming an attitude of less affectionate confidence, she hoped to hear more of that she really desired to learn, and to avoid allusions to that which she found so embarrassing.

"You know how much, or how little you ought to tell me, June," she said, "and I hope you love me well enough to give me the information I ought to hear. My dear uncle, too, is on the island, and you are, or ought to be, his friend, as well as mine, and both of us will remember your conduct, when we get back to Oswego."

"Maybe never get back; who know?" This was said doubtingly, or as one lays down an uncertain proposition, and not with a taunt, or a desire to alarm.

"No one knows what will happen, but God. Our lives are in his hands. Still, I think, you are to be his instrument in saving us."

This passed June's comprehension, and she only looked her ignorance, for it was evident she wished to be of use.

"Block-house very good," she repeated as soon as her countenance ceased to express uncertainty, laying strong emphasis on the two last words.

"Well, I understand this, June, and will sleep in it to-night. Of course, I am to tell my uncle, what you have said."

The Dew of June started, and she discovered a very manifest uneasiness, at the interrogatory.

"No—no—no—no—" she answered with a volubility and vehemence that was imitated from the French of the Canadas—"no good to tell Salt-water. He much talk, and long tongue. Think woods all water; understand not'ing. Tell Arrowhead, and June die."

"You do my dear uncle injustice, for he would be as little likely to betray you, as any one."

"No understand. Salt-water got tongue, but no eye, no ear, no nose—not'ing but tongue, tongue, tongue."

Although Mabel did not exactly coincide in this opinion, she saw that Cap had not the confidence of the young Indian woman, and that it was idle to expect she would consent to his being admitted to their interview.

"You appear to think you know our situation pretty well, June," Mabel continued, "have you been on the island before this visit?"

"Just come."

"How then do you know that what you say is true; my father, the Pathfinder and Eau douce may all be here within sound of my voice, if I choose to call them."

"All gone," said June positively, smiling good-humouredly at the same time.

"Nay, this is more than you *can* say certainly, not having been over the island to examine it."

"Got good eyes; see boat with men go away—see ship with Eau douce."

"Then you have been some time watching us—I think, however, you have not counted them that remain."

June laughed, held up her four fingers again, and then pointed to her two thumbs—passing a finger over the first, she repeated the words "red-coat," and touching the last, she added—"Salt-water," "Quarter Master." All this was being very accurate, and Mabel began to entertain serious doubts of the propriety of her permitting her visiter to depart without her becoming more explicit. Still it was so repugnant to her feelings to abuse the confidence this gentle and affectionate creature had evidently reposed in her, that Mabel had no sooner admitted the thought of summoning her uncle, than she rejected it, as unworthy of herself, and unjust to her friend. To aid this good resolution, too, there was the certainty that June would reveal nothing, but take refuge in a stubborn silence, if any attempt was made to coerce her.

"You think, then, June," Mabel continued, as soon as these thoughts had passed through her mind, "that I had better live in the block-house?"

"Good place for squaw. Block-house got no scalp. Logs t'ick."

"You speak confidently, June, as if you had been in it, and had measured its walls."

June laughed, and she looked knowing, though she said nothing.

"Does any one but yourself know how to find this island—have any of the Iroquois seen it?"

June looked sad, and she cast her eyes warily about her, as if distrusting a listener.

"Tuscarora everywhere—Oswego, here, Frontenac, Mohawk—everywhere. If he see June, kill her."

"But we thought that no one knew of this island, and that we had no reason to fear our enemies while on it."

"Much eye, Iroquois."

"Eyes will not always do, June—This spot is hid from ordinary sight, and few of even our own people know how to find it."

"One man can tell—Some Yengeese talk French."

Mabel felt a chill at her heart. All the suspicions against Jasper, which she had hitherto disdained entertaining crowded in a body on her thoughts, and the sensation that they brought was so sickening, that for an instant, she imagined she was about to faint. Arousing herself, and remembering her promise to her father, she arose and walked up and down the hut, for a minute, fancying that Jasper's delinquencies were naught to her, though her inmost heart yearned with the desire to think him innocent.

"I understand your meaning, June," she then said—"You wish me to know that some one has treacherously told your people where and how to find the island."

June laughed, for in her eyes artifice in war, was oftener a merit than a crime, but she was too true to her tribe, herself, to say more than the occasion required. Her object was to save Mabel, and Mabel only, and she saw no sufficient reason for "travelling out of the record," as the lawyers express it, in order to do any thing else.

"Pale face know now—" she added—"Block-house good for girls—no matter for men and warriors."

"But it is much matter with me, June, for one of these men

is my uncle, whom I love, and the others are my countrymen and friends. I must tell them what has passed."

"Then June be kill—" returned the young Indian quietly, though she spoke with concern.

"No—they shall not know that you have been here. Still, they must be on their guard, and we can all go into the block-house."

"Arrowhead know—see every thing, and June be kill. June come to tell young pale face friend, not to tell men. Every warrior watch his own scalp. June squaw, and tell squaw; no tell men."

Mabel was greatly distressed at this declaration of her wild friend, for it was now evident the young creature understood that her communication was to go no farther. She was ignorant how far these people considered the point of honor interested in her keeping the secret, and most of all, was she unable to say how far any indiscretion of her own might actually commit June, and endanger her life. All these considerations flashed on her mind, and reflection only rendered their influence more painful. June, too, manifestly viewed the matter gravely, for she began to gather up the different little articles she had dropped, in taking Mabel's hand, and was preparing to depart. To attempt detaining her, was out of the question, and to part from her, after all she had hazarded to serve her, was repugnant to all the just and kind feelings of our heroine's nature.

"June," she said eagerly, folding her arms around the gentle but uneducated being, "we are friends. From me you have nothing to fear, for no one shall know of your visit. If you could give me some signal just before the danger comes, some sign by which to know when to go into the block-house—how to take care of myself."

June paused, for she had been in earnest in her intention to depart, and then she said quietly—

"Bring June pigeon."

"A pigeon! Where shall I find a pigeon to bring you?"

"Next hut—bring old one—June go to canoe."

"I think I understand you, June—but had I not better lead you back to the bushes, lest you meet some of the men?"

"Go out first—count men—one—two—tree—four—

five—six"—here June held up her fingers and laughed—"All out of way, good—all but one, call him one side. Then sing, and fetch pigeon."

Mabel smiled at the readiness and ingenuity of the girl, and prepared to execute her requests. At the door, however, she stopped, and looked back entreatingly at the Indian woman.

"Is there no hope of your telling me more, June?" she said.

"Know all now—Block-house good—pigeon tell—Arrowhead kill."

The last words sufficed, for Mabel could not urge further communications when her companion herself told her, that the penalty of her revelations might be death by the hand of her husband. Throwing open the door, she made a sign of adieu to June, and went out of the hut. Mabel resorted to the simple expedient of the young Indian girl, to ascertain the situation of the different individuals on the island. Instead of looking about her, with the intention of recognizing faces and dresses, she merely counted them, and found that three still remained at the fire, while two had gone to the boat, one of whom was Mr. Muir. The sixth man was her uncle, and he was coolly arranging some fishing tackle, at no great distance from the fire. The woman was just entering her own hut, and this accounted for the whole party. Mabel now, affecting to have dropped something, returned nearly to the hut she had left, warbling an air, stooped as if to pick up some object from the ground, and hurried towards the hut June had mentioned. This was a dilapidated structure, and it had been converted by the soldiers of the last detachment, into a sort of store house for their live stock. Among other things, it contained a few dozen pigeons, which were regaling on a pile of wheat, that had been brought off from one of the farms plundered on the Canada shore. Mabel had not much difficulty in catching one of these pigeons, although they fluttered and flew about the hut, with a noise like that of drums, and concealing it in her dress, she stole back towards her own hut with the prize. It was empty; and without doing more than cast a glance in at the door, the eager girl hurried down to the shore. She had no difficulty in escaping observation, for the trees and bushes made a complete cover to her person. At the canoe, she found June, who took the pigeon, placed it in a basket of her own manufacturing, and repeating the words "Block-house good," she glided out of the bushes and across the narrow passage, as noiselessly as she had come. Mabel waited some time to catch a signal of leave taking or amity, after her friend had landed, but none was given. The adjacent islands, without exception, were as quiet as if no one had ever disturbed the sublime repose of nature, and nowhere could any sign or symptom be discovered, as Mabel then thought, that might denote the proximity of the sort of danger of which June had given notice.

On returning, however, from the shore, Mabel was struck with a little circumstance, that, in an ordinary situation, would have attracted no attention, but which, now that her suspicions had been aroused, did not pass before her uneasy eye, unnoticed. A small piece of red bunting, such as is used in the ensigns of ships, was fluttering at the lower branch of a small tree, fastened in a way to permit it to blow out, or to droop like a vessel's pennant.

Now that Mabel's fears were awakened, June herself could not have manifested greater quickness in analyzing facts that she believed might affect the safety of the party. She saw at a glance, that this bit of cloth could be observed from an adjacent island, that it lay so near the line between her own hut and the canoe, as to leave no doubt that June had passed near it, if not directly under it, and that it might be a signal to communicate some important fact connected with the mode of attack, to those who were probably lying in ambush near them. Tearing the little strip of bunting from the tree, Mabel hastened on, scarce knowing what duty next required. June might be false to her; but her manner, her looks, her affection, and her disposition as Mabel had known it in the journey, forbade the idea. Then came the allusion to Arrowhead's admiration of the Pale face beauties, some dim recollections of the looks of the Tuscarora, and a painful consciousness that few wives could view with kindness one who had estranged a husband's affections. None of these images were distinct and clear, but they rather gleamed over the mind of our heroine than rested in it, and they quickened her pulses, as they did her step, without bringing with them the prompt and clear decisions that usually followed her reflections. She had hurried onwards towards the hut occupied by the soldier's wife, intending to remove at once to the block-house, with the woman, though she could persuade no other to follow, when her impatient walk was interrupted by the voice of Muir.

"Whither so fast, Pretty Mabel," he cried, "and why so given to solitude?—The worthy serjeant will deride my breeding, if he hear that his daughter passes the mornings alone and unattended to, though he well knows that it is my ardent wish to be her slave and companion, from the beginning of the year to its end."

"Surely, Mr. Muir, you must have some authority here," Mabel suddenly arrested her steps to say. "One of your rank would be listened to, at least, by a corporal!"

"I don't know that—I don't know that—" interrupted Muir, with an impatience and appearance of alarm that might have excited Mabel's attention at another moment. "Command is command, discipline, discipline, and authority, authority. Your good father would be sore grieved did he find me interfering to sully, or carry off the laurels he is about to win, and I cannot command the corporal, without equally commanding the serjeant. The wisest way will be for me to remain in the obscurity of a private individual in this enterprize, and it is so that all parties, from Lundie down, understand the transaction."

"This I know, and it may be well; nor would I give my dear father any cause of complaint, but you may influence the corporal to his own good."

"I'll no say that," returned Muir, in his sly Scotch way;—"it would be far safer to promise to influence him to his injury—Mankind, pretty Mabel, have their peculiarities, and to influence a fellow being to his own good, is one of the most difficult tasks of human nature, while the opposite is just the easiest. You'll no forget this, my dear, but bear it in mind for your edification and government—but, what is that you're twisting round your slender finger, as you may be said to twist hearts?"

"It is nothing but a bit of cloth—a sort of flag—a trifle that is hardly worth our attention at this grave moment—If—"

"A trifle! it's no so trifling as ye may imagine, Mistress

Mabel," taking the bit of bunting from her, and stretching it at full length with both his arms extended, while his face grew grave, and his eye watchful. "Ye'll no ha' been finding this, Mabel Dunham, in the breakfast?"

Mabel simply acquainted him with the spot where, and the manner in which she had found the bit of cloth. While she was speaking, the eye of the Quarter Master was not quiet for a moment, glancing from the rag to the face of our heroine, then back again to the rag. That his suspicions were awakened was easy to be seen, nor was he long in letting it be known what direction they had taken.

"We are not in a part of the world, where our ensigns and gauds ought to be spread abroad to the winds, Mabel Dunham!" he said, with an ominous shake of his head.

"I thought as much myself, Mr. Muir, and brought away the little flag, lest it might be the means of betraying our presence here, to the enemy, even though nothing is intended by its display. Ought not my uncle to be made acquainted with the circumstance?"

"I no see the necessity for that, pretty Mabel, for as you justly say it is a circumstance, and circumstances sometimes worry the worthy mariner. But this flag, if flag it can be called, belongs to a seaman's craft. You may perceive that it is made of what is called bunting, and that is a description of cloth used only by vessels for such purposes, *our* colours being of silk, as you may understand, or painted canvass. It's surprisingly like the fly of the Scud's ensign! And now I recollect me, to have observed that a piece had been cut from that very flag!"

Mabel felt her heart sink, but she had sufficient self command not to attempt an answer.

"It must be looked to," Muir continued, "and, after all, I think it may be well to hold a short consultation with Master Cap, than whom a more loyal subject does not exist in the British Empire."

"I have thought the warning so serious," Mabel rejoined, "that I am about to remove to the block-house, and to take the woman with me."

"I do not see the prudence of that, Mabel. The block-house will be the first spot assailed, should there really be an attack, and it's no well provided for a siege, that must be allowed. If I might advise in so delicate a contingency, I would recommend your taking refuge in the boat, which, as you may now perceive, is most favorably placed to retreat by that channel opposite, where all in it would be hid by the islands, in one or two minutes. Water leaves no trail, as Pathfinder well expresses it, and there appear to be so many different passages, in that quarter, that escape would be more than probable. I've always been of opinion that Lundie hazarded too much, in occupying a post as far advanced, and as much exposed as this."

"It's too late to regret it now, Mr. Muir, and we have only to consult our own security."

"And the King's honor, pretty Mabel. Yes, His Majesty's arms, and his glorious name, are not to be overlooked on any occasion."

"Then I think it might be better, if we all turned our eyes towards the place that has been built to maintain them, instead of the boat," said Mabel, smiling, "and so, Mr. Muir, I am for the block-house, with a disposition to await there the return of my father, and his party. He would be sadly grieved, at finding we had fled, when he got back, successful himself, and filled with the confidence of our having been as faithful to our duties, as he has been to his own."

"Nay, nay, for Heaven's sake, do not misunderstand me, Mabel," Muir interrupted with some alarm of manner, "I am far from intimating that any but you females ought to take refuge in the boat. The duty of us men is sufficiently plain no doubt, and my resolution has been formed from the first, to stand or fall by the block-house."

"And did you imagine, Mr. Muir, that two females could row that heavy boat, in a way to escape the bark canoe of an Indian?"

"Ah! my pretty Mabel, love is seldom logical, and its fears and misgivings are apt to warp the faculties. I only saw your sweet person in possession of the means of safety, and overlooked the want of ability to use them. But you'll no be so cruel, lovely creature, as to impute to me as a fault, my intense anxiety on your own account!"

Mabel had heard enough. Her mind was too much occupied with what had passed that morning, and with her fears, to wish to linger further to listen to love speeches, that, in her most joyous and buoyant moments, she would have found unpleasant. She took a hasty leave of her companion, and was about to trip away towards the hut of the other woman, when Muir arrested the movement, by laying a hand on her arm.

"One word, Mabel," he said, "before you leave me. This little flag may, or it may not have a particular meaning; if it has, now that we are aware of its being shown, may it not be better to put it back again, while we watch vigilantly for some answer, that may betray the conspiracy; and if it mean nothing, why nothing will follow."

"This may be all right, Mr. Muir, though if the whole is accidental, the flag might be the occasion of the post's being discovered."

Mabel stayed to utter no more, but she was soon out of sight, running into the hut towards which she had been first proceeding. The Quarter Master remained on the very spot, and in the precise attitude, in which she had left him, for quite a minute, first looking at the bounding figure of the girl, and then at the bit of bunting, which he still held before him, in a way to denote indecision. His irresolution lasted but for this minute, however, for he was soon beneath the tree, where he fastened the mimic flag to a branch, again, though, from his ignorance of the precise spot from whence it had been taken by Mabel, he left it fluttering from a part of the oak, where it was still more exposed than before, to the eyes of any passengers on the river, though less in view from the island itself.

Chapter XXI

"Each one has had his supping mess,
The cheese is put into the press,
The pans and bowls clean scalded all,
Reared up against the milk house wall."
Cotton, "Evening Quatrains," ll. 33–36.

IT SEEMED STRANGE to Mabel Dunham, as she passed along, on her way to find her female companion, that others should be so composed, while she herself felt as if the responsibilities of life and death rested on her shoulders. It is true, that distrust of June's motives, mingled with her forebodings, but when she came to recall the affectionate and natural manner of the young Indian girl, and all the evidences of good faith and sincerity that she had seen in her conduct, during the familiar intercourse of their journey, she rejected the idea, with the willingness of a generous disposition, to believe the best of others. She saw, however, that she could not put her companions properly on their guard, without letting them into the secret of her conference with June, and she found herself, compelled to act cautiously and with a forethought to which she was unaccustomed, more especially in a matter of so much moment.

The soldier's wife was told to transport the necessaries into the block-house, and admonished not to be far from it, at any time, during the day. Mabel did not explain her reasons. She merely stated that she had detected some signs, in walking about the island, that induced her to apprehend that the enemy had more knowledge of its position, than had been previously believed, and that they two, at least, would do well to be in readiness to seek a refuge at the shortest notice. It was not difficult to arouse the apprehension of this person, who, though a stout-hearted Scotch woman, was ready enough to listen to any thing that confirmed her dread of Indian cruelties. As soon as Mabel believed that her companion was sufficiently frightened to render her wary, she threw out some hints touching the inexpediency of letting the soldiers know the extent of their own fears. This was done, with a view to prevent discussions and inquiries that might embarrass our heroine, she determining to render her uncle, the corporal and his men more cautious by adopting a different course. Unfortunately, the British army could not have furnished a worse person, for the particular duty that he was now required to discharge, than Corporal McNab, the individual who had been left in command, during the absence of Serjeant Dunham. On the one hand he was resolute, prompt, familiar with all the details of a soldier's life, and used to war; on the other, he was supercilious as regards the provincials, opinionated on every subject connected with the narrow limits of his professional practice, and much disposed to fancy the British empire the centre of all that is excellent in the world, and Scotland the focus of at least all moral excellence in that empire. In short, he was an epitome, though on a scale suited to his rank, of those very qualities, which were so peculiar to the servants of the crown, that were sent into the colonies, as these servants estimated themselves in comparison with the natives of the country, or, in other words he considered the American as an animal inferior to the parent stock, and viewed all his notions of military service in particular as undigested and absurd. Braddock, himself, was not less disposed to take advice from a provincial, than his humble imitator, and he had been known, on more than one occasion, to demur to the directions and orders of two or three commissioned officers of the corps, who happened to be born in America, simply for that reason; taking care, at the same time, with true Scotch wariness, to protect himself from the pains and penalties of positive disobedience. A more impracticable subject, therefore, could not well have offered for the purposes of Mabel, and yet she felt obliged to lose no time in putting her plan in execution.

"My father has left you a responsible command, corporal," she said, as soon as she could catch McNab, a little apart from the rest of the soldiers, "for should the island fall into the hands of the enemy, not only would we be captured, but the party that is now out, would in all probability, become their prisoners also."

"It needs no journey from Scotland to this place, to learn

the facts needful to be o' that way of thinking," returned McNab, drily.

"I do not doubt your understanding it, as well as myself, Mr. McNab, but I'm fearful that you veterans, accustomed as you are to dangers and battles, are a little apt to overlook some of the precautions that may be necessary in a situation, as peculiar as ours."

"They say Scotland is no conquered country, young woman, but I'm thinking there must be some mistak' in the matter, as we her children, are so drowsy headed and apt to be o'ertaken when we least expect it."

"Nay, my good friend, you mistake my meaning. In the first place, I'm not thinking of Scotland at all, but of this island; and then I am far from doubting your vigilance when you think it necessary to practise it, but my great fear is that there may be danger to which your courage will make you indifferent."

"My courage, Mistress Dunham, is doubtless of a very poor quality, being nothing but Scottish courage; your father's is yankee, and were he here amang us, we should see different preparations beyond a doubt. Well, times are getting wrang, when foreigners hold commissions and carry halberds in Scottish corps; and I no wonder that battles are lost, and campaigns go wrang end foremost."

Mabel was almost in despair, but the quiet warning of June was still too vividly impressed on her mind, to allow her to yield the matter. She changed her mode of operating, therefore, still clinging to the hope of getting the whole party within the block-house, without being compelled to betray the source whence she obtained her notices of the necessity of vigilance.

"I dare say you are right, Corporal McNab," she resumed, "for I've often heard of the heroes of your country, who have been among the first of the civilized world, if what they tell me of them is true."

"Have you read the history of Scotland, Mistress Dunham?" demanded the corporal, looking up at his pretty companion, for the first time, with something like a smile, on his hard, repulsive countenance.

"I have read a little of it, corporal, but I've heard much

more. The lady who brought me up had Scottish blood in her veins, and was fond of the subject."

"I'll warrant ye, the serjeant no troubled himself to expatiate on the renown of the country, where his regiment was raised?"

"My father has other things to think of, and the little I know, was got from the lady I have mentioned."

"She'll no be forgetting to tall ye o' Wallace?"

"Of him, I've even read a good deal."

"And o' Bruce—and the affair o' Bannockburn?"

"Of that too, as well as of Culloden Muir."

The last of these battles was then a recent event, it having actually been fought within the recollection of our heroine, whose notions of it, however, were so confused that she scarcely appreciated the effect her allusion might produce on her companion. She knew it had been a victory, and had often heard the guests of her patroness mention it with triumph; and she fancied their feelings would find a sympathetic chord in those of every British soldier. Unfortunately, McNab had fought throughout that luckless day, on the side of the Pretender, and a deep scar that garnished his face, had been left there, by the sabre of a German soldier, in the service of the House of Hanover. He fancied that his wound bled afresh, at Mabel's allusion, and it is certain that the blood rushed to his face in a torrent, as if it would pour out of his skin, at the cicatrix.

"Hoot! Hoot awa'!" he fairly shouted, "with your Cullodens and Sherrif Muirs, young woman, ye'll no be understanding the subject, at all, and will manifast not only wisdom, but modesty, in speaking o' your ain country and its many failings. King George has some loyal subjects in the colonies, na doubt, but 't will be a lang time bafore he sees or knows any guid of them."

Mabel was surprised at the corporal's heat, for she had not the smallest idea where the shoe pinched, but she was determined not to give up the point.

"I've always heard that the Scotch had two of the great qualities of soldiers," she said, "courage and circumspection, and I feel persuaded that Corporal McNab will sustain the national renown."

"Ask yer own father, Mistress Dunham; he is acquaint' with Corporal McNab, and will no be backward to point out his demerits. We have been in battle th'gither, and he is my superior officer, and has a sort o' official right to give the characters of his subordinates."

"My father thinks well of you, McNab, or he would not have left you in charge of this island, and all it contains, his own daughter included. Among other things I well know that he calculates largely on your prudence. He expects the block-house, in particular, to be strictly attended to."

"If he wishes to defend the honor of the 55th, behind logs, he ought to have remained in command himsal', for to speak frankly, it goes against a Scotsman's bluid and opinions, to be beaten out of the field, even before he is attacked. We are broad-sword men, and love to stand foot to foot with the foe. This American mode of fighting, that is getting into so much favor, will destroy the reputation of His Majesty's army, if it no destroy its spirit."

"No true soldier despises caution; even Major Duncan himself, than whom there is none braver, is celebrated for his care of his men."

"Lundie ha' his weaknesses, and is fast forgetting the broad-sword and open heaths, in his tree and rifle practice; but, Mistress Mabel, tak' the word of an old soldier, who has seen his fifty-fifth year, when he talls ye, that there is no surer method to encourage your enemy, than to seem to fear him, and, that there is no danger in this Indian warfare, that the fancies and imaginations of your Americans have not augmented and enlarged upon, until they see a savage in every bush. We Scots come from a naked region, and have no need, and less relish for covers, and so, ye'll be seeing, Mistress Dunham—"

The corporal gave a spring into the air, fell forward on his face, and rolled over on his back; the whole passing so suddenly that Mabel had scarcely heard the sharp crack of the rifle, that sent a bullet through his body. Our heroine did not shriek; did not even tremble; for the occurrence was too sudden, too awful, and too unexpected for that exhibition of weakness. On the contrary, she stepped hastily forward, with a natural impulse to aid her companion. There was just enough of life left in McNab, to betray his entire consciousness of all that had passed. His countenance had the wild look of one who had been overtaken by death, by surprise, and Mabel, in her calmer moments, fancied that it showed the tardy repentance of a wilful and obstinate sinner.

"Ye'll be getting into the block-house, as fast as possible," McNab whispered, as Mabel leaned over him to catch his dying words.

Then came over our heroine, the full consciousness of her situation, and of the necessity of exertion. She cast a rapid glance at the body at her feet, saw that it had ceased to breathe, and fled. It was but a few minutes' run to the block-house, the door of which Mabel had barely gained, when it was closed violently in her face, by Jennie, the soldier's wife, who, in blind terror, thought only of her own safety. The reports of five or six rifles were heard, while Mabel was calling out for admittance, and the additional terror they produced, prevented the woman within from undoing quickly the very fastenings she had been so expert, in applying. After a minute's delay, however, Mabel found the door reluctantly yielding to her constant pressure, and she forced her slender body through the opening, the instant it was large enough to allow of its passage. By this time, Mabel's heart ceased to beat tumultuously, and she gained sufficient self-command to act collectedly. Instead of yielding to the almost convulsive efforts of her companion, to close the door, again, she held it open long enough to ascertain that none of her own party was in sight, or likely, on the instant, to endeavor to gain admission; then she allowed the opening to be shut. Her orders and proceedings, now, became more calm and rational. But a single bar was crossed, and Jennie was directed to stand in readiness to remove even that, at an application from a friend. She then ascended the first ladder to the room above, where by means of loop-holes, she was enabled to get as good a view of the island as the surrounding bushes would allow. Admonishing her associate below to be firm and steady, she made as careful an examination of the environs as her situation permitted.

To her great surprise, Mabel could not, at first, see a living soul on the island, friend or enemy. Neither Frenchman, nor

Indian was visible, though a small straggling white cloud that was floating before the wind, told her in which quarter, she ought to look for them. The rifles had been discharged from the direction of the island whence June had come, though whether the enemy were on that island, or had actually landed on her own, Mabel could not say. Going to the loop that commanded a view of the spot, where McNab lay, her blood curdled at perceiving all three of his soldiers lying apparently lifeless at his side. These men had rushed to a common centre, at the first alarm, and had been shot down almost simultaneously, by the invisible foe, whom the corporal had affected to despise.

Neither Cap, nor Lieutenant Muir was to be seen. With a beating heart, Mabel examined every opening through the trees, and ascended even to the upper story, or garret of the block-house, where she got a full view of the whole island, so far as its covers would allow; but with no better success. She had expected to see the body of her uncle, lying on the grass, like those of the soldiers, but it was nowhere visible. Turning towards the spot where the boat lay, Mabel saw that it was still fastened to the shore, and then she supposed that, by some accident Muir had been prevented from effecting his retreat, in that quarter. In short, the island lay in the quiet of the grave, the bodies of the soldiers rendering the scene as fearful as it was extraordinary.

"For God's holy sake, Mistress Mabel," called out the woman from below, for, though her fear had got to be too ungovernable to allow her to keep silence, our heroine's superior refinement, more than the regimental station of her father, still controlled her mode of address, "For His Holy Sake! Mistress Mabel, tell me if any of our friends are living? I think I hear groans that grow fainter and fainter, and fear that they will all be tomahawked."

Mabel now remembered that one of the soldiers was this woman's husband, and she trembled at what might be the immediate effect of her sorrow, should his death become suddenly known to her. The groans, too, gave a little hope, though she feared they might come from her uncle, who lay out of view.

"We are in his holy keeping, Jennie," she answered. "We

must trust in Providence, while we neglect none of its benevolent means of protecting ourselves. Be careful with the door; on no account open it, without my directions."

"Oh! Tell me, Mistress Mabel, if you can anywhere see Sandy?—If I could only lat him know that I'm in safety, the guid man would be easier in his mind, whather free or a prisoner!"

Sandy was Jennie's husband, and he lay dead in plain view of the loop, from which our heroine was then looking.

"You no tall me if you're seeing of Sandy," the woman repeated from below, impatient at Mabel's silence.

"There are some of our people gathered about the body of McNab," was the answer, for it seemed sacrilegious in her eyes to tell a direct untruth, under the awful circumstances in which she was placed.

"Is Sandy amang them?" demanded the woman, in a voice that sounded appalling by its hoarseness and energy.

"He may be certainly—for I see, one, two, three, four, and all in the scarlet coats of the regiment."

"Sandy!" called out the woman frantically—"Why d'ye no care for yoursal', Sandy? Come hither the instant, man, and share your wife's fortunes, in weal or woe. It's no a moment for your silly discipline, and vainglorious notions of honor! Sandy!—Sandy!"

Mabel heard the bar turn, and then the door creaked on its hinges. Expectation, not to say terror, held her in suspense at the loop, and she soon beheld Jennie rushing through the bushes, in the direction of the cluster of the dead. It took the woman but an instant to reach the fatal spot. So sudden and unexpected had been the blow, that she, in her terror, did not appear to comprehend its weight. Some wild and half frantic notion of a deception troubled her fancy, and she imagined that the men were trifling with her fears. She took her husband's hand, and it was still warm, while she thought a covert smile was struggling on his lip.

"Why will ye fool life away, Sandy?" she cried, pulling at the arm. "Ye'll all be murdered by these accursed Indians, and you no takin' to the block like trusty soldiers! Awa'!—awa', and no be losing the precious moments."

In her desperate efforts, the woman pulled the body of her

husband in a way to cause the head to turn completely over, when the small hole in the temple, caused by the entrance of a rifle bullet, and a few drops of blood trickling over the skin, revealed the meaning of her husband's silence. As the horrid truth flashed, in its full extent, on her mind, the woman clasped her hands, gave a shriek that pierced the glades of every island near, and fell at length on the dead body of the soldier. Thrilling, heart-reaching, appalling as was that shriek, it was melody to the cry that followed it so quickly as to blend the sounds. The terrific war-whoop arose out of the covers of the island, and some twenty savages, horrible in their paint, and the other devices of Indian ingenuity, rushed forward, eager to secure the covetted scalps. Arrowhead was foremost, and it was his tomahawk that brained the insensible Jennie, and her reeking hair was hanging at his girdle, as a trophy, in less than two minutes after she had quitted the block-house. His companions were equally active, and McNab and his soldiers, no longer presented the quiet aspects of men who slumbered. They were left in their gore, unequivocally butchered corpses.

All this passed in much less time, than has been required to relate it, and all this did Mabel witness. She had stood riveted to the spot, gazing on the whole horrible scene, as if enchained by some charm, nor did the idea of self, or of her own danger, once obtrude itself on her thoughts. But, no sooner did she perceive the place where the men had fallen, covered with savages, exulting in the success of their surprise, than it occurred to her, that Jennie had left the block-house door unbarred. Her heart beat violently, for that defence alone stood between her and immediate death, and she sprang towards the ladder, with the intention of descending to make sure of it. Her foot had not yet reached the floor of the second story, however, when she heard the door grating on its hinges, and she gave herself up for lost. Sinking on her knees, the terrified but courageous girl endeavored to prepare herself for death, and to raise her thoughts to God. The instinct of life, however, was too strong for prayer, and while her lips moved, the jealous senses watched every sound beneath. When her ears heard the bars, which went on pivots secured to the centre of the door, turning into their fastenings, not one as she herself had directed with a view to admit her uncle should he apply, but all three, she started again to her feet, all spiritual contemplations vanishing in her actual temporal condition, and it seemed as if all her faculties were absorbed in the sense of hearing.

The thoughts are active, in a moment so fearful. At first Mabel fancied that her uncle had entered the block-house, and she was about to descend the ladder and throw herself into his arms; then the idea that it might be an Indian, who had barred the door to shut out intruders, while he plundered at leisure, arrested the movement. The profound stillness below, was unlike the bold, restless movements of Cap, and it seemed to savor more of the artifices of an enemy. If a friend, at all, it could only be her uncle, or the Quarter Master, for the horrible conviction now presented itself to our heroine, that to these two and herself were the whole party suddenly reduced, if, indeed, the two first survived. This consideration held Mabel in check, and for quite two minutes more, a breathless silence reigned in the building. During this time, the girl stood at the foot of the upper ladder, the trap which led to the lower opening on the opposite side of the floor. The eyes of Mabel were riveted on this spot, for she now began to expect to see, at each instant, the horrible sight of a savage face at the hole. This apprehension soon became so intense, that she looked about her, for a place of concealment. The procrastination of the catastrophe she now fully expected, though it were only for a moment, afforded a relief. The room contained several barrels, and behind two of these, Mabel crouched, placing her eyes at an opening by which she could still watch the trap. She made another effort to pray, but the moment was too horrible for that relief. She thought, too, that she heard a low rustling, as if one was ascending the lower ladder, with an effort at caution so great, as to betray itself by its own excess. Then followed a creaking, that she was certain came from one of the steps of the ladder, which had made the same noise, under her own light weight as she ascended. This was one of those instants, into which are compressed the sensations of years of ordinary existence. Life, death, eternity and extreme bodily pain, were all standing out in bold relief, from the plane of every-day occurrences, and she might have been taken, at that moment, for a beautiful, pallid, representation of herself, equally without motion and without vitality. But, while such was the outward appearance of the form, never had there been a time, in her brief career, when Mabel heard more acutely, saw more clearly, or felt more vividly. As yet nothing was visible at the trap, but her ears, rendered exquisitely sensitive by intense feeling, distinctly acquainted her that some one was within a few inches of the opening in the floor. Next followed the evidence of her eyes, which beheld the dark hair of an Indian rising so slowly through the passage that the movement of the head might be likened to that of the minute hand of a clock. Then came the dark skin and wild features, until the whole of the swarthy face had risen above the floor. The human countenance seldom appears to advantage when partially concealed, and Mabel imagined many additional horrors, as she first saw the black, roving eyes, and the expression of wildness, as the savage countenance was revealed, as it might be inch by inch. But, when the entire head was raised above the floor, a second and better look assured our heroine that she saw the gentle, anxious and even handsome, face of June.

Chapter XXII

"—Spectre though I be,
I am not sent to scare thee or deceive;
But in reward of thy fidelity."
Wordsworth, *Laodamia*, ll. 38–40.

IT WOULD be difficult to say which evinced the most satisfaction, when Mabel sprang to her feet, and appeared in the centre of the room, our heroine on finding that her visiter was the wife of Arrowhead, and not Arrowhead himself, or June, at discovering that her advice had been followed, and that the block-house contained the person she had so anxiously and almost hopelessly sought. They embraced each other, and the unsophisticated Tuscarora woman laughed in her sweet accents, as she held her friend at arm's length, and made certain of her presence.

"Block-house good," said the young Indian—"got no scalp."

"It is indeed good, June," Mabel answered with a shudder, veiling her eyes at the same time, as if to shut out a view of the horrors she had so lately witnessed. "Tell me, for God's sake! if you know what has become of my dear uncle?—I have looked in all directions, without being able to see him."

"No here, in block-house?" June asked, with some curiosity.

"Indeed he is not—I am quite alone in this place, Jennie, the woman, who was with me, having rushed out to join her husband, and perishing for her imprudence."

"June know—June see. Very bad. Arrowhead no feel for any wife—no feel for his own."

"Ah! June; your life, at least, is safe!"

"Don't know. Arrowhead kill me, if he knows all."

"God bless and protect you, June—he *will* bless and protect you for your humanity. Tell me what is to be done, and if my poor uncle is still living?"

"Don't know. Salt-water has boat, maybe he go on river."

"The boat is still on the shore, but neither my uncle, nor the Quarter Master is anywhere to be seen."

"No kill, or June would see. Hide away. Red man hide; no shame for pale-face."

"It is not the shame that I fear for them, but the opportunity. Your attack was awfully sudden, June!"

"Tuscarora—" returned the other, smiling with exultation at the dexterity of her husband. "Arrowhead great warrior."

"You are too good and gentle for his sort of life, June. You *cannot* be happy in such scenes!"

June's countenance grew clouded, and Mabel fancied there was some of the savage fire of a chief in her frown as she answered.

"Yengeese too greedy—take away all hunting grounds—chase Six Nation from morning to night; wicked king—wicked people. Pale Face very bad."

Mabel knew that, even in that distant day, there was much truth in this opinion, though she was too well instructed not to understand that the monarch, in this as in a thousand other cases, was blamed for acts of which he was most probably ignorant. She felt the justice of the rebuke, therefore, too much to attempt an answer, and her thoughts naturally reverted to her own situation.

"And what am I to do, June," she demanded. "It cannot be long before your people will assault this building."

"Block-house good—got no scalp."

"But they will soon discover that it has got no garrison, too, if they do not know it already. You, yourself, told me the number of people that were on the island, and doubtless you learned it from Arrowhead."

"Arrowhead know," answered June, holding up six fingers to indicate the number of the men. "All red men know. Four lose scalp already—two got 'em, yet!"

"Do not speak of it, June; the horrid thought curdles my blood. Your people cannot know that I am alone in the blockhouse, but may fancy my uncle and the Quarter Master with me, and may set fire to the building, in order to dislodge them. They tell me that fire is the great danger to such places."

"No burn block-house," said June, quietly.

"You cannot know that, my good June, and I have no means to keep them off."

"No burn block-house. Block-house good; got no scalp."

"But tell me why, June—I fear they will burn it!"

"Block-house wet—much rain—logs green—no burn easy—Red man know it—first t'ing—then no burn it, to tell Yengeese that Iroquois been here. Fader come back, miss block-house, no land. No—no—Injin too cunning—no touch any thing."

"I understand you, June, and hope your prediction may be true; for as regards my dear father, should he escape—perhaps he is already dead, or captured, June!"

"No touch fader—do'n't know where he gone. Water got no trail—red-man can't follow. No burn block-house—block-house good—got no scalp."

"Do you think it possible for me to remain here, safely, until my father returns?"

"Do'n't know—daughter tell best, when fader come back."

Mabel felt uneasy at the glance of June's dark eye, as she uttered this, for the unpleasant surmise arose, that her companion was endeavoring to discover a fact that might be useful to her own people, while it would lead to the destruction of her parent and his party. She was about to make an evasive answer, when a heavy push at the outer door, suddenly drew all her thoughts to the immediate danger.

"They come!" she exclaimed—"Perhaps, June, it is my uncle or the Quarter Master—I cannot keep out even Mr. Muir, at a moment like this."

"Why no look—plenty loop-hole—made purpose."

Mabel took the hint, and going to one of the downward loops, that had been cut through the logs, in the part that overhung the basement, she cautiously raised the little block that ordinarily filled the small hole, and caught a glance at what was passing at the door. The start and changing countenance told her companion that some of her own people were below.

"Red men," said June, lifting a finger in admonition to be prudent.

"Four, and horrible in their paint and bloody trophies. Arrowhead is among them."

June had moved to a corner, where several spare rifles were deposited, and had already taken one into her hand, when the name of her husband appeared to arrest her movements. It was but for an instant, however, for she immediately went to the loop, and was about to thrust the muzzle of the piece through it, when a feeling of natural aversion, induced Mabel to seize her arm.

"No—no—no—June," said the latter—"not against your own husband, though my life be the penalty."

"No hurt Arrowhead—" returned June, with a slight shudder—"no hurt red man at all. No fire at 'em;—only scare."

Mabel now comprehended the intention of June, and no longer opposed it. The latter thrust the muzzle of the rifle through the loop-hole, and taking care to make noise enough to attract attention, she pulled the trigger. The piece had no sooner been discharged than Mabel reproached her friend, for the very act that was intended to serve her.

"You declared it was not your intention to fire," she said, "and you may have destroyed your own husband."

"All run away, before I fire—" returned June laughing, and going to another loop to watch the movements of her friends, laughing still heartier.—"See—get cover—every warrior. Think Salt-water and Quarter Master here. Take good care, now."

"Heaven be praised! And now, June, I may hope for a little time to compose my thoughts to prayer, that I may not die like Jennie, thinking only of life and the things of the world!"

June laid aside the rifle, and came and seated herself near the box on which Mabel had sunk, under that physical reaction which accompanies joy as well as sorrow. She looked steadily in our heroine's face, and the latter thought that her countenance had an expression of severity mingled with its concern.

"Arrowhead great warrior—" said the Tuscarora's wife—"All the gals of tribe, look at him much. The pale face beauty has eyes, too."

"June!—What do these words—that look imply—what would you say?"

"Why you so 'fraid June shoot Arrowhead?"

"Would it not have been horrible, to see a wife destroy her own husband! No, June; rather would I have died myself."

"Very sure, dat all?"

"That was all, June, as God is my judge—and surely that was enough. No—no—there have been sufficient horrors to-day, without increasing them by an act like this. What other motive can you suspect?"

"Do'n't know. Poor Tuscarora gal, very foolish. Arrowhead great chief, and look all round him. Talk of pale face beauty in his sleep—Great chief like many wives."

"Can a chief possess more than one wife, June, among your people?"

"Have as many as he can keep—Great hunter marry often. Arrowhead got only June now, but he look too much, see too much—talk too much of Pale Face gal!"

Mabel was conscious of this fact, which had distressed her not a little, in the course of their journey; but it shocked her to hear this allusion, coming, as it did, from the mouth of the wife herself. She knew that habit and opinions made great differences in such matters, but, in addition to the pain and mortification she experienced at being the unwilling rival of a wife, she felt an apprehension that jealousy would be but an equivocal guarantee for her personal safety, in her present situation. A closer look at June, however, reassured her, for while it was easy to trace in the unpractised features of this unsophisticated being, the pain of blighted affections, no distrust could have tortured the earnest expression of her honest countenance, into that of treachery or hate.

"You will not betray me, June," Mabel said, pressing the other's hand, and yielding to an impulse of generous confidence. "You will not give up one of your own sex, to the tomahawk?"

"No tomahawk touch you. Arrowhead no let 'em. If June must have sister-wife—love to have you."

"No, June; my religion, my feelings, both forbid it; and, if I could be the wife of an Indian, at all, I would never take the place that is yours, in a wigwam."

June made no answer, but she looked gratified, and even grateful. She knew that few, perhaps no Indian girl, within the circle of Arrowhead's acquaintance, could compare with herself, in personal attractions, and though it might suit her husband to marry a dozen wives, she knew of no one, beside Mabel, whose influence she could really dread. So keen an interest, however, had she taken in the beauty, winning manners, kindness, and feminine gentleness of our heroine, that when jealousy came to chill these feelings, it had rather lent strength to that interest, and, under its wayward influence, had actually been one of the strongest of the incentives that had induced her to risk so much, in order to save her imaginary rival from the consequences of the attack that she so well knew was about to take place. In a word, June, with a wife's keenness of perception, had detected Arrowhead's admiration of Mabel, and instead of feeling that harrowing jealousy, that might have rendered her rival hateful, as would have been apt to be the case with a woman unaccustomed to defer to the superior rights of the lordly sex, she had studied the looks and character of the pale face beauty, until, meeting with nothing to repel her own feelings, but every thing to encourage them, she had got to entertain an admiration and love for her, which, though certainly very different, was scarcely less strong than that of her husband. Arrowhead himself had sent her to warn Mabel of the coming danger, though he was ignorant that she had stolen upon the island, in the rear of the assailants, and was now entrenched in the citadel along with the object of their joint care. On the contrary, he supposed, as his wife had said, that Cap and Muir were in the blockhouse with Mabel, and that the attempt to repel him and his companions had been made by the men.

"June sorry, the 'Lily,' " for so the Indian, in her poetical language had named our heroine, "June sorry, the Lily no marry Arrowhead. His wigwam big, and a great chief must get wives enough to fill it."

"I thank you, June, for this preference, which is not according to the notions of us white women," returned Mabel, smiling in spite of the fearful situation in which she was placed; "but I may not, probably never shall marry at all."

"Must have good husband—" said June; "marry Eau douce, if do'n't like Arrowhead."

"June!—this is not a fit subject for a girl who scarce knows if she is to live another hour, or not. I would obtain some signs of my dear uncle's being alive and safe, if possible."

"June go see."

"Can you?—will you?—would it be safe for you to be seen

on the island—Is your presence known to the warriors, and would they be pleased to find a woman on the war-path, with them?"

All this Mabel asked in rapid connection, fearing that the answer might not be as she wished. She had thought it extraordinary that June should be of the party, and, improbable as it seemed, she had fancied that the woman had covertly followed the Iroquois in her own canoe, and had got in their advance merely to give her the notice which had probably saved her life. But in all this she was mistaken, as June, in her imperfect manner, now found means to let her know.

Arrowhead, though a chief, was in disgrace with his own people, and was acting with the Iroquois, temporarily, though with a perfect understanding. He had a wigwam it is true, but was seldom in it; feigning friendship for the English, he had passed the summer ostensibly in their service, while he was in truth acting for the French, and his wife journeyed with him in his many migrations, most of the distances being passed over in canoes. In a word her presence was no secret, her husband seldom moving without her. Enough of this to embolden Mabel to wish that her friend might go out, to ascertain the fate of her uncle, did June succeed in letting the other know, and it was soon settled between them, that the Indian woman should quit the block house with that object, the moment a favorable opportunity offered.

They first examined the island, as thoroughly as their position would allow, from the different loops, and found that its conquerors were preparing for a feast, having seized upon the provisions of the English, and rifled the huts. Most of the stores were in the block-house, but enough were found outside to reward the Indians for an attack attended by so little risk. A party had already removed the dead bodies, and Mabel saw that their arms were collected in a pile, near the spot chosen for the banquet. June suggested that, by some signs she understood, the dead themselves were carried into a thicket, and either buried, or concealed from view. None of the more prominent objects on the island, however, were disturbed, it being the desire of the conquerors to lure the party of the Serjeant into an ambush, on its return. June made her companion observe a man in a tree, a look-out, as she said, to give timely notice of the approach of any boat, although the departure of the expedition being so recent, nothing but some unexpected event would be likely to bring it back so soon. There did not appear to be any design to attack the block-house immediately, but every indication, as understood by June, rather showed that it was the intention of the Indians to keep it besieged until the return of the Serjeant's party, lest the signs of an assault should give a warning to eyes as practised as those of Pathfinder. The boat, however, had been secured, and was removed to the spot where the canoes of the Indians were hid in the bushes.

June now announced her intention of joining her friends, the moment being particularly favorable for her to quit the block-house. Mabel felt some distrust as they descended the ladder, but, at the next instant, she was ashamed of the feeling as unjust to her companion, and unworthy of herself, and by the time they both stood on the ground, her confidence was restored. The process of unbarring the door was conducted with the utmost caution, and when the last bar was ready to be turned, June took her station near the spot where the opening must necessarily be. The bar was just turned free of the brackets, the door was opened merely wide enough to allow her body to pass, and June glided through the space. Mabel closed the door again, with a convulsive movement, and as the bar turned into its place, her heart beat audibly. She then felt secure, and the two other bars were turned down in a more deliberate manner. When all were fast again, she ascended to the first floor, where, alone, she could get a glimpse of what was going on without.

Long and painfully melancholy hours passed, during which Mabel had no intelligence from June. She heard the yells of the savages, for liquor had carried them beyond the bounds of precaution, occasionally caught glimpses of their mad orgies through the loops, and at all times was conscious of their fearful presence, by sounds and sights that would have chilled the blood of one who had not so lately witnessed scenes so much more terrible. Towards the middle of the day, she fancied she saw a white man on the island, though his dress and wild appearance at first made her take him for a newly arrived savage. A view of his face, although it was swarthy naturally, and much darkened by exposure, left no doubt that her conjecture was true, and she felt as if there was now one of a species more like her own present, and one to whom she might appeal for succor, in the last emergency. Mabel little knew, alas! how small was the influence exercised by the whites over their savage allies, when the latter had begun to taste of blood, or how slight, indeed, was the disposition to divert them from their cruelties.

The day seemed a month by Mabel's computation, and the only part of it that did not drag, were the minutes spent in prayer. She had recourse to this relief, from time to time, and at each effort she found her spirit firmer, her mind more tranquil, and her tendency to resignation more confirmed. She understood the reasoning of June, and believed it highly probable, that the block-house would be left unmolested, until the return of her father, in order to entice him into an ambuscade, and she felt much less apprehension of immediate danger in consequence; but the future offered little grounds of hope, and her thoughts had already begun to calculate the chances of her captivity. At such moments, Arrowhead and his offensive admiration, filled a prominent part in the background, for our heroine well knew that the Indians usually carried off to their villages, for the purposes of adoption, such captives as they did not slay, and that many instances had occurred, in which individuals of her sex had passed the remainder of their lives in the wigwams of their conquerors. Such thoughts as these, invariably drove her to her knees, and to her prayers.

While the light lasted, the situation of our heroine was sufficiently alarming, but as the shades of evening gradually gathered over the island, it became fearfully appalling. By this time, the savages had wrought themselves up to the point of fury, for they had possessed themselves of all the liquor of the English, and their outcries and gesticulations were those of men truly possessed of evil spirits. All the efforts of their French leader to restrain them, were entirely fruitless, and he had wisely withdrawn to an adjacent island, where he had a sort of bivouac, that he might keep at a safe distance from friends so apt to run into excesses. Before quitting the spot, however, this officer, at great risk to his own life, succeeded in extinguishing the fire, and in securing the ordinary means to relight it. This precaution he took, lest the Indians should burn the block-house, the preservation of which was necessary to the success of his future plans. He would gladly have removed all the arms, also, but this he found impracticable, the warriors clinging to their knives and tomahawks with the tenacity of men who regarded a point of honor, as long as a faculty was left, and to carry off the rifles, and leave behind him the very weapons that were generally used on such occasions, would have been an idle expedient. The extinguishing of the fire, proved to be the most prudent measure, for no sooner was the officer's back turned, than one of the warriors, in fact, proposed to fire the block-house. Arrowhead had also withdrawn from the group of drunkards, as soon as he found that they were losing their senses, and had taken possession of a hut, where he had thrown himself on the straw, and sought the rest that two wakeful and watchful nights rendered necessary. It followed that no one was left among the Indians to care for Mabel, if indeed any knew of her existence at all, and the proposal of the drunkard was received with yells of delight by eight or ten more, as much intoxicated and habitually as brutal as himself.

This was the fearful moment for Mabel. The Indians, in their present condition, were reckless of any rifles that the block-house might hold, though they did retain dim recollections of its containing living beings, an additional incentive to their enterprise, and they approached its base whooping and leaping like demons. As yet they were excited, not overcome by the liquor they had drunk. The first attempt was made at the door, against which they ran in a body, but the solid structure, which was built entirely of logs, defied their efforts. The rush of a hundred men, with the same object, would have been useless. This Mabel, however, did not know, and her heart seemed to leap into her mouth, as she heard the heavy shock, at each renewed effort. At length, when she found that the door resisted these assaults as if it were of stone, neither trembling, nor yielding, and only betraying its not being a part of the wall, by rattling a little on its heavy hinges, her courage revived, and she seized the first moment of a cessation, to look down through the loop, in order, if possible, to learn the extent of her danger. A silence, for which it was not easy to account, stimulated her curiosity, for nothing is so alarming to those who are conscious of the presence of imminent danger, as to be unable to trace its approach.

Mabel found that two or three of the Iroquois had been raking the embers, where they had found a few small coals, and with these they were endeavoring to light a fire. The interest with which they labored, the hope of destroying, and the force of habit enabled them to act intelligently and in unison, so long as their fell object was kept in view. A white man would have abandoned the attempt to light a fire in despair, with coals that came out of the ashes resembling sparks, but these children of the forests had many expedients that were unknown to civilization. By the aid of a few dry leaves, which they alone knew where to seek, a blaze was finally kindled, and then the addition of a few light sticks made sure of the advantage that had been obtained. When Mabel stooped down over the loop, the Indians were making a pile of brush against the door, and as she remained gazing at their proceedings, she saw the twigs ignite, the flame dart from branch to branch, until the whole pile was cracking and snapping under a bright blaze. The Indians now gave a yell of triumph and returned to their companions, well assured that the work of destruction was commenced. Mabel remained looking down, scarcely able to tear herself away from the spot, so intense and engrossing was the interest she felt in the progress of the fire. As the pile kindled throughout, however, the flames mounted, until they flashed so near her eyes, as to compel her to retreat. Just as she reached the opposite side of the room, to which she had retired in her alarm, a forked stream shot up through the loop-hole, the lid of which she had left open, and illuminated the rude apartment, with Mabel and her desolation. Our heroine now naturally enough supposed that her hour was come, for the door, the only means of retreat, had been blocked up by the brush and fire, with hellish ingenuity, and she addressed herself, as she believed for the last time, to her maker, in prayer. Her eyes were closed, and for more than a minute her spirit was abstracted, but the interests of the world too strongly divided her feelings, to be altogether suppressed, and when they involuntarily opened again, she perceived that the streak of flame was no longer flaring in the room, though the wood around the little aperture had kindled, and the blaze was slowly mounting under the impulsion of a current of air that sucked inward. A barrel of water stood in a corner, and Mabel, acting more by instinct than by reason, caught up a vessel, filled it, and pouring it on the wood, with a trembling hand, succeeded in extinguishing the fire, at that particular spot. The smoke prevented her from looking down again, for a couple of minutes, but when she did, her heart beat high with delight and hope, at finding that the pile of blazing brush had been overturned and scattered, and that water had been thrown on the logs of the door, which were still smoking, though no longer burning.

"Who is there?" said Mabel, with her mouth at the loop—"What friendly hand has a merciful Providence sent to my succour?"

A light footstep was audible below, and one of those gentle pushes at the door was heard, which just moved the massive beams on the hinges.

"Who wishes to enter?—Is it you, dear, dear, uncle?"

"Salt-water no here—St. Lawrence sweet water—" was the answer. "Open quick—want to come in."

The step of Mabel was never lighter, or her movements more quick and natural, than while she was descending the ladder and turning the bars, for all her motions were earnest and active. This time she thought only of her escape, and she opened the door with a rapidity that did not admit of caution. Her first impulse was to rush into the open air, in the blind hope of quitting the block-house, but June repulsed the attempt, and, entering, she coolly barred the door, again, before she would notice Mabel's eager efforts to embrace her.

"Bless you—bless you, June," cried our heroine, most fervently—"you are sent by Providence to be my guardian angel!"

"No hug so tight—" answered the Tuscarora woman—"Pale face women all cry, or all laugh. Let June fasten door."

Mabel became more rational, and in a few minutes the two were again in the upper room, seated as before, hand in hand, all feeling of distrust, or rivalry between them, being banished on the one side by the consciousness of favors received, and on the other by the consciousness of favors conferred.

"Now tell me, June," Mabel commenced, as soon as she had given and received one warm embrace, "have you seen or heard aught of my poor uncle?"

"Do'n't know. No one see him; no one hear him; no one know any t'ing. Salt-water run into river, I t'ink, for I no find him. Quarter Master gone, too. I look, and look, and look; but no see 'em, one t'other no where."

"Blessed be God! They must have escaped, though the means are not known to us. I thought I saw a Frenchman on the island, June?"

"Yes—French captain come, but he go away, too. Plenty of Injin, on island."

"Oh! June. June, are there no means to prevent my beloved father from falling into the hands of his enemies!"

"Do'n't no t'ink dat.—Warriors wait in ambush, and Yengeese must lose scalps."

"Surely, surely, June, you, who have done so much for the daughter, will not refuse to help the father!"

"Do'n't know fader—do'n't love fader. June help her own people, help Arrowhead—husband love scalps."

"June, this is not yourself! I cannot, will not believe that you wish to see our men murdered!"

June turned her dark eyes quietly on Mabel, and, for a moment, her look was stern, though it soon changed into one of melancholy compassion.

"Lily, Yengeese gal?" she said, as one asks a question.

"Certainly, and as a Yengeese girl, I would save my countrymen from slaughter."

"Very good—if can. June no Yengeese; June, Tuscarora—got Tuscarora husband—Tuscarora heart—Tuscarora feelings—all over Tuscarora. Lily would'n't run and tell French dat her fader was coming to gain victory?"

"Perhaps not," returned Mabel, pressing a hand on a brain that felt bewildered,—"perhaps not; but you serve me, aid me—have saved me, June! Why have you done this, if you only feel as a Tuscarora?"

"Do'n't only feel as Tuscarora—feel as gal—feel as squaw. Love pretty Lily, and put it in my bosom."

Mabel melted into tears, and she pressed the affectionate creature to her heart. It was near a minute before she could renew the discourse, but then she succeeded in speaking more calmly and with greater coherence.

"Let me know the worst, June;" she said—"To-night, your people are feasting; what do they intend to do tomorrow?"

"Don't know—afraid to see Arrowhead—afraid to ask questions—t'ink hide away, till Yengeese come back."

"Will they not attempt any thing against the block-house?—You have seen what they can threaten if they will?"

"Too much rum. Arrowhead sleep, or no dare; French captain gone away, or no dare. All go to sleep, now."

"And you think I am safe for this night, at least?"

"Too much rum—If Lily was like June, might do much for her people."

"I am like you, June, if a wish to serve my countryman, can make a resemblance with one as courageous as yourself."

"No—no—no—" muttered June, in a low voice—"no got heart, and June no let you, if had. June's moder prisoner once, and warriors got drunk; moder tomahawked 'em all. Such the way red skin women do, when people in danger, and want scalps."

"You say what is true," returned Mabel shuddering, and unconsciously dropping June's hand—"I cannot do that. I have neither the strength, the courage, nor the will to dip my hands in blood."

"T'ink that too; then stay where you be—block-house good—got no scalp."

"You believe, then, that I am safe, here, at least, until my father and his people return?"

"Know so. No one dare touch block-house in morning. Hark! All still, now—drink rum 'till head falls down, and sleep like log."

"Might I not escape?—Are there not several canoes on the island?—might I not get one, and go and give my father notice of what has happened?"

"Know how to paddle?" demanded June, glancing her eye furtively, at her companion.

"Not as well as yourself, perhaps, but enough to get out of sight before morning."

"What do then?—could'n't paddle six—ten—eight mile!"

"I do not know! I would do much to warn my father, and the excellent Pathfinder, and all the rest, of the danger they are in."

"Like Pathfinder?"

"All like him who know him—you would like him, nay love him, if you only knew his heart!"

"No like him, at all. Too good rifle—too good eye—too much shoot Iroquois, and June's people. Must get his scalp, if can."

"And I must save it, if I can, June. In this respect, then, we are opposed to each other. I will go and find a canoe the instant they are all asleep, and quit the island."

"No can—June won't let you. Call Arrowhead."

"June! You could not betray me—you would not give me up, after all you have done for me!"

"Just so—" returned June, making a backward gesture with her hand, and speaking with a warmth and earnestness Mabel had never witnessed in her before. "Call Arrowhead in loud voice. One call from wife, wake a warrior up. June no let Lily help enemy—no let Injin hurt Lily."

"I understand you, June, and feel the nature and justice of your sentiments; and, after all, it were better that I should remain here, for I have most probably overrated my strength. But, tell me one thing; if my uncle comes, in the night, and asks to be admitted, you will let me open the door of the block house that he may enter?"

"Sartain—He prisoner here, and June like prisoner, better than scalp. Scalp good for honor; prisoner good for feeling. But, Salt-Water hide so close, he do'n't know where he be himself."

Here June laughed, in her girlish mirthful way, for to her, scenes of violence were too familiar to leave impressions sufficiently deep, to change her natural character. A long and discursive dialogue now followed, in which Mabel endeavored to obtain clearer notions of her actual situation, under a faint hope that she might possibly be enabled to turn some of the facts she thus learned, to advantage. June answered all her interrogatories simply, but with a caution which showed she fully distinguished between that which was immaterial and that which might endanger the safety, or embarrass the future operations of her friends. Our heroine was incapable of making an attempt to entrap her companion, though she plainly perceived, that, could she have been guilty of the meanness, she would have found the undertaking one of extreme difficulty. June however was not required to exercise more than a discreet discrimination about what she revealed, and the substance of the information she gave, may be summed up as follows.

Arrowhead had long been in communication with the French, though this was the first occasion on which he had ever entirely thrown aside the mask. He no longer intended to trust himself among the English, for he had discovered traces of distrust, particularly in Pathfinder, and with Indian bravado, he now rather wished to blazon, than to conceal his treachery. He had led the party of warriors, in the attack on the island, subject however to the supervision of the Frenchman who has been mentioned, though June declined saying whether he had been the means of discovering the position of a place that had been thought to be so concealed from the eyes of the enemy, or not. On this point, she would say nothing, but she admitted that she and her husband had been watching the departure of the Scud, at the time they were overtaken and captured by the cutter. The French had obtained their information of the precise position of the station, but very recently, and Mabel felt a pang like that of some sharp instrument piercing her heart, when she thought that there was covert allusion of the Indian woman, which would convey the meaning that the intelligence had come from a pale face, in the employment of Duncan of Lundie. This was intimated, however, rather than said, and when Mabel had time to reflect on her companion's words, and to remember how sententious and brief her periods were, she found room to hope that she had misunderstood her, and that Jasper Western would yet come out of the affair freed from every injurious imputation.

June did not hesitate to confess that she had been sent to the island to ascertain the precise number, and the occupations of those who had been left on it, though she also betrayed in her *naïve* way, that the wish to serve Mabel, had induced her principally to consent to come. In consequence of her report, and information otherwise obtained, the enemy was aware of precisely the force that could be brought against them. They also knew the number of men that had gone with Serjeant Dunham, and were acquainted with the object he had in view, though they were ignorant of the spot where he expected to meet the French boats. It would have been a pleasant sight to witness the eager desire of each of these two sincere females to ascertain all that might be of consequence to their respective friends, and yet the native delicacy, with which each refrained from pressing the other to make revelations that would have been improper, as well as the sensitive, almost intuitive feeling with which each avoided saying aught that might prove injurious to her own nation. As respects each other, there was perfect confidence; as regarded their respective people, entire fidelity. June was quite as anxious, as Mabel could be on any other point, to know where the Serjeant had gone, and when he was expected to return, but she abstained from putting the question, with a delicacy that would have done honor to the highest civilization; nor did she once frame any other inquiry in a way to lead indirectly to a betrayal of the much desired information, on that particular point; though, when Mabel of her own accord touched on any matter that might, by possibility throw light on the subject, she listened with an intentness that almost suspended respiration.

In this manner the hours passed away, unheeded, for both were too much interested to think of rest. Nature asserted her rights, however, towards morning, and Mabel was persuaded to lie down on one of the straw beds provided for the soldiers, where she soon fell into a deep sleep. June lay near her, and a quiet reigned on the whole island, as profound as if the dominion of the forest had never been invaded by man.

When Mabel awoke, the light of the sun was streaming in through the loop-holes, and she found that the day was considerably advanced. June still lay near her, sleeping as tranquilly as if she reposed on—we will not say down, for the superior civilization of our own times repudiates the simile, but on a French mattress, and as profoundly, as if she had never experienced concern. The movements of Mabel, notwithstanding, soon awakened one so accustomed to vigilance, and then the two took a survey of what was passing around them, by means of the friendly apertures.

Chapter XXIII

"What had th' Eternal Maker need of thee
The world in his continuall course to keepe,
That dost all things deface, ne lettest see
The beautie of his worke? Indeede in sleepe
The slouthfull body that doth love to steepe
His lustless limbs, and drowne his baser mind,
Doth praise thee oft, and oft from Stygian deepe
Calles thee his goddesse, in his errour blind,
And great dame Nature's handmaide chearing every kind."

The Faerie Queene, III.iv.56.1–9.

THE TRANQUILLITY of the previous night, was not contradicted by the movements of the day. Although Mabel and June went to every loop-hole, not a sign of the presence of a living being on the island was at first to be seen, themselves excepted. There was a smothered fire on the spot where McNab and his comrades had cooked, as if the smoke that curled upwards from it, was intended as a lure to the absent, and all around the huts had been restored to former order and arrangement. Mabel started involuntarily, when her eye at length fell on a group of three men, dressed in the scarlet of the 55th, seated on the grass in lounging attitudes, as if they chatted in listless security, and her blood curdled, as on a second look she traced the bloodless faces, and glassy eyes of the dead. They were quite near the block-house, so near indeed as to have been overlooked at the first eager inquiry, and there was a mocking levity in their postures and gestures, for their limbs were stiffening in different attitudes intended to resemble life, at which the soul revolted. Still, horrible as these objects were to those near enough to discover the frightful discrepancy between their assumed and their real characters, the arrangement had been made, with an art that would have deceived a negligent observer, at the distance of a hundred yards. After carefully examining the shores of the island, June pointed out to her companion, the fourth soldier seated with his feet hanging over the water, his back fastened to a sapling, and holding a fishing-rod in his hands. The scalpless heads were covered with their caps, and all appearance of blood had been carefully washed from each countenance.

Mabel sickened at this sight, which not only did so much violence to all her notions of propriety, but which was, in itself, so revolting and so opposed to natural feeling. She withdrew to a seat, and hid her face in her apron, for several minutes, until a low call from June, again drew her to a loophole. The latter then pointed out the body of Jennie, seemingly standing in the door of a hut, leaning forward, as if to look at the group of men, her cap fluttering in the wind, and her hand grasping a broom. The distance was too great to distinguish the features, very accurately, but Mabel fancied that the jaw had been depressed, as if to distort the mouth into a sort of horrible laugh.

"June! June!" she exclaimed; "this exceeds all I have ever even heard, or imagined as possible, in the treachery and artifices of your people!"

"Tuscarora very cunning—" said June, in a way to show that she rather approved of, than condemned the uses to which the dead bodies had been applied—"Do soldier no harm now; do Iroquois, good. Got the scalps, first; now make bodies work. By and by, burn 'em."

This speech told Mabel how far she was separated from her friend, in character, and it was several minutes before she could again address her. But this temporary aversion was lost on June, who set about preparing their simple breakfast, in a way to show how insensible she was to feelings in others, that her own habits taught her to discard. Mabel ate sparingly, and her companion as if nothing had happened. Then they had leisure again for their thoughts, and for further surveys of the island. Our heroine, though devoured with a feverish desire to be always at the loops, seldom went that she did not immediately quit them in disgust, though compelled by her apprehensions to return again, in a few minutes, called by the rustling of leaves, or the sighing of the wind. It was, indeed, a solemn thing, to look out upon that deserted spot, peopled by the dead in the panoply of the living, and thrown into the attitudes and acts of careless merriment and rude enjoyment. The effect on our heroine, was much as if she had found herself an observer of the revelries of demons.

Throughout the live-long day, not an Indian, nor a Frenchman was to be seen, and night closed over the frightful but silent masquerade, with the steady and unalterable progress with which the earth obeys her laws, indifferent to the petty actors, and petty scenes, that are in daily bustle and daily occurrence on her bosom. The night was far more quiet than that which had preceded it, and Mabel slept with an increasing confidence, for she now felt satisfied that her own fate would not be decided, until the return of her father. The following day he was expected, however, and when our heroine awoke, she ran eagerly to the loops in order to ascertain the state of the weather and the aspect of the skies, as well as the condition of the island. There lounged the fearful group on the grass, the fisherman still hung over the water, seemingly intent on his sport, and the distorted countenance of Jennie glared from out the hut, in horrible contortions. But the weather had changed. The wind blew fresh from the southward, and though the air was bland, it was filled with the elements of storm.

"This grows more and more difficult to bear, June," Mabel said, when she left the window. "I could even prefer to see the enemy, than to look any longer on this fearful array of the dead."

"Hush;—here they come. June thought hear a cry, like a warrior's shout, when he take scalp."

"What mean you!—There is no more butchery! There *can* be no more."

"Salt-water!" exclaimed June laughing, as she stood peeping through a loop-hole.

"My dear uncle!—Thank God, he then lives—Oh! June—June, *you* will not let them harm *him*!"

"June poor squaw—What warrior t'ink of what she say? Arrowhead bring him, here."

By this time Mabel was at a loop, and, sure enough, there were Cap and the Quarter Master in the hands of the Indians, eight or ten of whom were conducting them to the foot of the block, for, by this capture, the enemy now well knew that there could be no man in the building. Mabel scarcely breathed until the whole party stood ranged, directly before the door, when she was rejoiced to see that the French officer was among them. A low conversation followed, in which both the white leader and Arrowhead spoke earnestly to their captives, when the Quarter Master called out to her, in a voice loud enough to be heard.

"Pretty Mabel!—Pretty Mabel!" he said—"look out of one of the loop-holes, and pity our condition. We are threatened with instant death, unless you open the door to the conquerors. Relent then, or we'll no be wearing our scalps, half an hour from this blessed moment!"

Mabel thought there were mockery and levity in this appeal, and its manner rather fortified than weakened her resolution to hold the place as long as possible.

"Speak to me, uncle," she said, with her mouth at a loop, "and tell me what I ought to do."

"Thank God!—Thank God!" ejaculated Cap, "the sound of your sweet voice, Magnet, lightens my heart of a heavy load, for I feared you had shared the fate of poor Jennie. My breast has felt the last four and twenty hours, as if a ton of kentledge had been stowed in it. You ask me what you ought to do, child, and I do not know how to advise you, though you are my own sister's daughter! The most I can say, just now, my poor girl, is most heartily to curse the day you or I ever saw this bit of fresh water—"

"But, uncle, is your life in danger—do *you* think I ought to open the door?"

"A round turn and two half-hitches make a fast belay, and I would counsel no one who is out of the hands of these devils, to unbar, or unfasten any thing, in order to fall into them. As to the Quarter Master and myself, we are both elderly men, and not of much account to mankind in general, as honest Pathfinder would say, and it can make no great odds to him, whether he balances the purser's books this year or the next; and as for myself, why, if I were on the sea-board, I should know what to do, but up here in this watery wilderness, I can only say that if I were behind that bit of a bulwark, it would take a great deal of Indian logic to rowse me out of it."

"You'll no be minding all your uncle says, Pretty Mabel," put in Muir, "for distress is obviously fast unsettling his faculties, and he is far from calculating all the necessities of the emergency. We are in the hands, here, of very considerate and gentlemanly pairsons, it must be acknowledged, and one has little occasion to apprehend disagreeable violence. The casualties that have occurred, are the common incidents of war, and can no change our sentiments of the enemy, for they are far from indicating that any injustice will be done the prisoners. I'm sure that neither Master Cap, nor myself, has any cause of complaint since we have given ourselves up to Master Arrowhead, here, who reminds me of a Roman, or a Spartan, by his virtues and moderation, but, ye'll be remembering that usages differ, and that our scalps may be lawful sacrifices to appease the manes of fallen foes, unless you save them by capitulation."

"I shall do wiser to keep within the block-house, until the fate of the island is settled," returned Mabel. "Our enemies can feel no concern on account of one like me, knowing that I can do them no harm, and I greatly prefer to remain here, as more befitting my sex and years."

"If nothing but your convenience were concerned, Mabel, we should all cheerfully acquiesce in your wishes, but these gentlemen fancy that the work will aid their operations, and they have a strong desire to possess it. To be frank with you, finding myself and your uncle in a very peculiar situation, I acknowledge that, to avert consequences, I have assumed the power that belongs to His Majesty's commission, and entered into a verbal capitulation, by which I have engaged to give up the block-house and the whole island. It is the fortune of war, and must be submitted to; so open the door, Pretty Mabel, forthwith, and confide yourself to the care of those who know how to treat beauty and virtue in distress. There's no courtier in Scotland more complaisant than this chief, or who is more familiar with the laws of decorum."

"No leave block-house," muttered June, who stood at Mabel's side, attentive to all that passed. "Block-house good; got no scalp."

Our heroine might have yielded, but for this appeal, for it began to appear to her that the wisest course would be to conciliate the enemy by concessions, instead of exasperating him by resistance. They must know, she thought, now that Muir and her uncle were in their power, that there was no man in the building, and she feared they might proceed to batter down the door, or to cut their way through the logs with axes, if she obstinately refused to give them peaceable admission, since there was no longer any reason to dread the rifle. But the words of June induced her to hesitate, and the earnest pressure of the hand, and entreating looks of her companion, strengthened a resolution that was faltering.

"No prisoner yet—" whispered June—"Let 'em make prisoner, before 'ey take prisoner. Talk big; June manage 'em."

Mabel now began to parley more resolutely with Muir, for her uncle seemed disposed to quiet his conscience by holding his tongue, and she plainly intimated that it was not her intention to yield the building.

"You forget the capitulation, Mistress Mabel," said Muir—"the honor of one of His Majesty's servants is concerned, and the honor of His Majesty through his servant. You will remember the finesse and delicacy that belong to military honor?"

"I know enough, Mr. Muir, to understand that you have no command in this expedition, and therefore can have no right to yield the block-house, and, I remember, moreover, to have heard my father say, that a prisoner loses all his authority, for the time being."

"Rank sophistry, Pretty Mabel, and treason to the king, as well as dishonoring his commission, and discrediting his name. You'll no be persevering in your intentions, when your better judgment has had leisure to reflect, and to make conclusions, on matters and circumstances."

"Ay," put in Cap—"this *is* a circumstance, and be d——d to it!"

"No mind what 'e uncle say," ejaculated June, who was occupied in a far corner of the room. "Block-house good; got no scalp."

"I shall remain as I am, Mr. Muir, until I get some tidings of my father. He will return in the course of the next ten days."

"Ah! Mabel, this artifice will no deceive the enemy, who, by means that would be unintelligible, did not our suspicions rest on an unhappy young man with too much plausibility, are familiar with all our doings and plans, and well know that the sun will not set before the worthy serjeant and his companions will be in their power. Aweel! Submission to Providence is truly a christian virtue!"

"Mr. Muir, you appear to be deceived in the strength of this work, and to fancy it weaker than it is. Do you desire to see what I can do, in the way of defence, if so disposed?"

"I dinna' mind if I do," answered the Quarter Master, who always grew Scotch, as he grew interested.

"What do you think of that, then?—Look at the loop of the upper story."

As soon as Mabel had spoken, all eyes were turned upward, and beheld the muzzle of a rifle cautiously thrust through a hole, June having resorted again to a *ruse* that had already proved so successful. The result did not disappoint expectation. No sooner did the Indians catch a sight of the fatal weapon, than they leaped aside, and, in less than a minute every man among them had sought a cover. The French officer, kept his eye on the barrel of the piece, in order to ascertain that it was not pointed in his particular direction, and he coolly took a pinch of snuff. As neither Muir, nor Cap, had any thing to apprehend from the quarter in which the others were menaced, they kept their ground.

"Be wise, my pretty Mabel, be wise," exclaimed the former, "and no be provoking a useless contention. In the name of all the Kings of Albin, who have ye closeted with you in that wooden tower, that seemeth so bloody-minded?—There is necromancy about this matter, and all our characters may be involved in the explanation!"

"What do ye think of the Pathfinder, Master Muir, for a garrison to so strong a post!" cried Mabel, resorting to an equivocation that the circumstances rendered very excusable. "What will your French and Indian companions think of the aim of Pathfinder's rifle."

"Bear gently on the unfortunate, Pretty Mabel, and do not confound the King's servants, may Heaven bless him and all his royal lineage, with the King's enemies. If Pathfinder be indeed in the block-house, let him speak, and we will hold our negotiations directly with him. He knows us as friends, and we fear no evil at his hands, and least of all to myself; for a generous mind is apt to render rivalry in a certain interest a sure ground of respect and amity; since admiration of the same woman proves a community of feeling and tastes."

The reliance on Pathfinder's friendship did not extend beyond the Quarter Master and Cap, however, for even the French officer, who had hitherto stood his ground so well, shrunk back at the sound of the terrible name. So unwilling, indeed, did this individual, a man of iron nerves, and one long accustomed to the dangers of the peculiar warfare in which he was engaged, appear to be to remain exposed to the assaults of Killdeer, whose reputation throughout all that frontier was as well established, as that of Marlborough in Europe, that he did not disdain to seek a cover, insisting that his two prisoners should follow him. Mabel was too glad to be rid of her enemies to lament the departure of her friends, though she kissed her hand to Cap, through the loop, and called out to him in the terms of affection as he moved slowly and unwillingly away.

The enemy now seemed disposed to abandon all attempts on the block-house for the present, and June, who had ascended to a trap in the roof, whence the best view was to be obtained, reported that the whole party, had assembled to eat, on a distant and sheltered part of the island, where Muir and Cap were quietly sharing in the good things that were going, as if they had no concern on their minds. This information greatly relieved Mabel, and she began to turn her thoughts, again, to the means of effecting her own escape, or at least of letting her father know of the danger that awaited him. The Serjeant was expected to return that afternoon, and she knew that a moment, gained or lost, might decide his fate.

Three or four hours flew by. The island was again buried in a profound quiet, the day was wearing away and yet Mabel had decided on nothing. June was in the basement preparing their frugal meal, and Mabel herself, had ascended to the roof, which was provided with a trap that allowed her to go out on the top of the building, whence she commanded the best view of surrounding objects that the island possessed. Still it was limited, and much obstructed by the tops of trees. The anxious girl did not dare to trust her person in sight, knowing well that the unrestrained passions of some savage, might induce him to send a bullet through her brain. She merely kept her head out of the trap, therefore, whence in the course of the afternoon she made as many surveys of the different channels about the island, as "Anne, sister Anne" took of the environs of the castle of Blue Beard.

The sun had actually set, no intelligence had been received from the boats, and Mabel ascended to the roof, to take a last look, hoping that the party would arrive in the darkness, which would at least prevent the Indians from rendering their ambuscade as fatal as it might otherwise prove, and which possibly might enable her to give some more intelligible signal, by means of fire, than it would otherwise be in her power to do. Her eye had turned carefully round the whole horizon, and she was just on the point of drawing in her person, when an object that struck her as new, caught her attention. The islands lay grouped so closely, that six or eight different channels, or passages between them were in view, and in one of the most covered, concealed in a great measure by the bushes of the shore, lay, what a second look assured her, was a bark canoe. It contained a human being beyond a question. Confident that, if an enemy, her signal could do no harm, and, if a friend, that it might do good, the eager girl waved a little flag towards the stranger, which she had prepared for her father, taking care that it should not be seen from the island.

Mabel had repeated her signal eight or ten times in vain, and she began to despair of its being noticed, when a sign was given in return, by the wave of a paddle, and the man so far discovered himself, as to let her see it was Chingachgook. Here, then, at last, was a friend; one, too, who was able, and she doubted not would be willing, to aid her! From that instant her courage and her spirits revived. The Mohican had seen her; must have recognised her, as he knew that she was of the party, and no doubt, as soon as it was sufficiently dark, he would take the steps necessary to release her. That he was aware of the presence of the enemy was apparent by the great caution he observed, and she had every reliance on his prudence and address. The principal difficulty now existed with June, for Mabel had seen too much of her fidelity to her own people, relieved as it was by sympathy for herself, to believe she would consent to a hostile Indian's entering the block-house, or indeed to her leaving it, with a view to defeat Arrowhead's plans. The half hour that succeeded the discovery of the presence of the Great Serpent, was the most painful of Mabel Dunham's life. She saw the means of effecting all she wished, as it might be within reach of her hand, and yet it eluded her grasp. She knew June's decision and coolness, notwithstanding all her gentleness and womanly feeling, and at last she came reluctantly to the conclusion that there was no other way of attaining her end, than by deceiving her tried companion and protector. It was revolting to one as sincere and natural, as pure of heart and as much disposed to ingenuousness as Mabel Dunham, to practice deception on a friend like June, but her own father's life was at stake, her companion would receive no positive injury, and she had feelings and interests directly touching herself, that would have removed greater scruples.

As soon as it was dark, Mabel's heart began to beat with violence, and she adopted and changed her plan of proceedings, at least a dozen times, in the course of a single hour. June was always the source of her greatest embarrassment, for she did not well see firstly how she was to ascertain when Chingachgook was at the door, where she doubted not he would soon appear, and, secondly, how she was to admit him, without giving the alarm to her watchful companion. Time pressed, however, for the Mohican might come and go away again, unless she was ready to receive him. It would be too hazardous to the Delaware to remain long on the island, and it became absolutely necessary to determine on some course, even at the risk of choosing one that was indiscreet. After running over various projects, in her mind, therefore, Mabel came to her companion and said with as much calmness as she could assume——

"Are you not afraid, June, now your people believe Pathfinder is in the block-house, that they will come and try to set it on fire?"

"No t'ink such t'ing. No burn block-house. Block-house good; got no scalp."

"June, we cannot know. They hid, because they believed what I told them of Pathfinder's being with us."

"Believe fear. Fear come quick; go quick. Fear make run

away; wit make come back. Fear make warrior fool, as well as young girl."

Here June laughed, as her sex is apt to laugh when any thing particularly ludicrous crosses their youthful fancies.

"I feel uneasy, June, and wish you yourself would go up again to the roof, and look out upon the island, to make certain that nothing is plotting against us; you know the signs of what your people intend to do, better than I."

"June go, Lily wish; but very well know, that Injin asleep; wait for 'e fader. Warrior eat, drink, sleep all time, when don't fight, and go on war trail. Den *never* sleep, eat, drink—never feel. Warrior sleep now."

"God send it may be so—but go up, dear June, and look well about you; danger may come when we least expect it."

June arose and prepared to ascend to the roof, but she paused with her foot on the first round of the ladder. Mabel's heart beat so violently, that she was fearful its throbs would be heard, and she fancied that some gleamings of her real intentions had crossed the mind of her friend. She was right in part; the Indian woman having actually stopped to consider whether there was any indiscretion in what she was about to do. At first, the suspicion that Mabel intended to escape flashed across her mind; then she rejected it, on the ground that the pale face had no means of getting off the island, and that the block-house was much the most secure place she could find. The next thought was, that Mabel had detected some sign of the near approach of her father. This idea lasted but an instant, for June entertained some such opinion of her companion's ability to understand symptoms of this sort, symptoms that had escaped her own sagacity, as a woman of high fashion entertains of the accomplishments of her maid. Nothing else in the same way offering, she began slowly to mount the ladder. Just as she reached the upper floor, a lucky thought suggested itself to our heroine, and by expressing it in a hurried but natural manner she gained a great advantage in executing her projected scheme.

"I will go down," she said, "and listen by the door, June, while you are on the roof, and we will thus be on our guard at the same time, above and below."

Though June thought this savored of unnecessary caution,

well knowing no one could enter the building unless aided from within, nor any serious danger menace them from the exterior, without giving sufficient warning, she attributed the proposition to Mabel's ignorance and alarm; and, as it was apparently made with frankness, it was received without distrust. By these means our heroine was enabled to descend to the door, as her friend ascended to the roof, and June felt no unusual inducement to watch her. The distance between the two, was now too great to admit of conversation, and for three or four minutes one was occupied in looking about her, as well as the darkness would allow, and the other in listening at the door, with as much intentness, as if all her senses were absorbed in the single faculty of hearing.

June discovered nothing from her elevated stand. The obscurity indeed almost forbade the hope of such a result; but it would not be easy to describe the sensation with which Mabel thought she perceived a slight and guarded push against the door. Fearful that all might not be as she wished, and anxious to let Chingachgook know that she was near, she began, though in tremulous and low notes to sing. So profound was the stillness at the moment, that the sound of the unsteady warbling ascended to the roof, and in a minute June began to descend. A slight tap at the door was heard immediately after. Mabel was bewildered, for there was no time to lose. Hope proved stronger than fear, and with unsteady hands, she commenced unbarring the door. The moccasin of June was heard on the floor above her, when only a single bar was turned. The second was released as her form reached half-way down the lower ladder.

"What you do!" exclaimed June angrily.—"Run away—mad—leave block-house? Block-house good."—The hands of both were on the last bar, and it would have been cleared from the fastenings, but for a vigorous shove from without, which jammed the wood. A short struggle ensued, though both were disinclined to violence. June would probably have prevailed, had not another and more vigorous push from without forced the bar past the trifling impediment that held it, when the door opened. The form of a man was seen to enter, and both the females rushed up the ladder, as if equally afraid of the consequences. The stranger secured the door, and, first examining the lower room with great care, he cautiously ascended the ladder. June, as soon as it became dark, had closed the loops of the principal floor, and lighted a candle. By means of this dim taper then, the two females stood in expectation, waiting to ascertain the person of their visiter, whose wary ascent of the ladder was distinctly audible though sufficiently deliberate. It would not be easy to say which was the most astonished on finding, when the stranger had got through the trap, that Pathfinder stood before them!

"God be Praised!" Mabel exclaimed, for the idea that the block-house would be impregnable with such a garrison, at once crossed her mind. "Oh! Pathfinder, what has become of my father?"

"The sarjeant is safe, as yet, and victorious, though it is not in the gift of man to say what will be the ind of it. Is not that the wife of Arrowhead, skulking in the corner, there?"

"Speak not of her reproachfully, Pathfinder; I owe her my life—my present security. Tell me what has happened to my father's party, why you are here, and I will relate all the horrible events that have passed upon this island."

"Few words will do the last, Mabel, for one used to Indian deviltries needs but little explanations on such a subject. Every thing turned out as we had hoped with the expedition, for the Sarpent was on the look out, and he met us with all the information heart could desire. We ambushed three boats, druv' the Frenchers out of them, got possession and sunk them, according to orders, in the deepest part of the channel, and the Savages of Upper Canada will fare badly for Indian goods this winter. Both powder and ball, too, will be scarcer among them, than keen hunters and actyve warriors may relish. We did not lose a man, or have even a skin barked, nor do I think the inimy suffered to speak of. In short, Mabel, it has been just such an expedition as Lundie likes; much harm to the foe, and little harm to ourselves."

"Ah! Pathfinder, I fear when Major Duncan comes to hear the whole of the sad tale, he will find reason to regret he ever undertook the affair!"

"I know what you mean—I know what you mean, but, by telling my story straight, you will understand it better. As soon as the sarjeant found himself successful, he sent me and the Sarpent off in canoes, to tell you how matters had turned out, and he is following with the two boats; which being so much heavier, cannot arrive afore morning. I parted from Chingachgook this forenoon, it being agreed that he should come up one set of channels, and I another, to see that the path was clear. I've not seen the chief since."

Mabel now explained the manner in which she had discovered the Mohican, and her expectation that he would yet come to the block-house.

"Not he—not he—A regular scout will never get behind walls, or logs, so long as he can keep the open air, and find useful employment. I should not have come myself, Mabel, but I promised the sarjeant to comfort you, and to look a'ter your safety. Ah's! me. I reconnoitred the island with a heavy heart, this forenoon, and there was a bitter hour, when I fancied you might be among the slain!"

"By what lucky accident were you prevented from paddling up boldly to the island, and from falling into the hands of the enemy?"

"By such an accident, Mabel, as Providence employs to tell the hound where to find the deer, and the deer how to throw off the hound. No—no—these artifices and deviltries with dead bodies, may deceive the soldiers of the 55th, and King's officers, but they are all lost upon men who have passed their days in the forest. I came down the channel in face of the pretended fisherman, and, though the riptyles have set up the poor wretch with art, it was not ingenious enough to take in a practysed eye. The rod was held too high, for the 55th have learned to fish at Oswego, if they never knew how afore, and then the man was too quiet for one who got neither prey nor bite. But we never come in upon a post blindly, and I have lain outside a garrison a whole night, because they had changed their sentries and their mode of standing guard. Neither the Sarpent, nor myself, would be likely to be taken in, by these contrivances, which were most probably intended for the Scotch, who are cunning enough in some particulars, though any thing but witches, when Indian sarcumventions are in the wind."

"Do you think my father and his men may yet be deceived?" said Mabel, quickly.

"Not if I can prevent it, Mabel. You say the Sarpent is on the look-out, too; so there is a double chance of our succeeding in letting him know his danger; though it is by no means sartain by which channel the party may come."

"Pathfinder—" said our heroine solemnly, for the frightful scenes she had witnessed had clothed death with unusual horrors—"Pathfinder, you have professed love for me—a wish to make me your wife?"

"I did ventur' to speak on that subject, Mabel, and the sarjeant has even lately said that you are kindly disposed; but I am not a man to parsecute the thing I love."

"Hear me, Pathfinder—I respect you—honor you—revere you—save my father from this dreadful death, and I can worship you. Here is my hand, as a solemn pledge for my faith, when you come to claim it."

"Bless you—bless you, Mabel; this is more than I desarve—more, I fear, than I shall know how to profit by, as I ought. It was not wanting, howsever, to make me sarve the sarjeant. We are old comrades, and owe each other a life—though I fear me, Mabel, being a father's comrade is not always the best recommendation with the daughter!"

"You want no other recommendation than your own acts—your courage—your fidelity—all that you do and say, Pathfinder, my reason approves, and the heart will, nay, it *shall* follow."

"This is a happiness I little expected this night, but we are in God's hands, and he will protect us, in his own way. These are sweet words, Mabel, but they were not wanting to make me do all that man can do, in the present sarcumstances; they will not lessen my endivors, neither."

"Now we understand each other, Pathfinder—" Mabel added, hoarsely, "let us not lose one of the precious moments, which may be of incalculable value. Can we not get into your canoe, and go and meet my father?"

"That is not the course I advise. I do'n't know by which channel the sarjeant will come, and there are twenty; rely on it, the Sarpent will be winding his way through them all. No—no—my advice is to remain, here. The logs of this block-house are still green, and it will not be easy to set them on fire, and I can make good the place, bating a burning, ag'in a tribe. The Iroquois nation cannot dislodge me from this fortress, so long as we can keep the flames from it. The Sarjeant is now 'camped on some island, and will not come in, until morning. If we hold the block, we can give him timely warning, by firing rifles for instance; and should he determine to attack the savages, as a man of his temper will be very likely to do, the possession of this building will be of great account in the affair. No—no—my judgment says remain, if the object be to sarve the sarjeant; though escape for our two selves, will be no very difficult matter."

"Stay—" murmured Mabel—"Stay, for God's sake, Pathfinder. Any thing, every thing, to save my father."

"Yes, that is natur'. I am glad to hear you say this, Mabel, for I own a wish to see the sarjeant fairly supported. As the matter now stands he has gained himself credit, and could he once drive off these miscreants, and make an honorable retreat, laying the huts and block in ashes, no doubt, no doubt, Lundie would remember it, and sarve him accordingly—Yes, yes, Mabel, we must not only save the sarjeant's life, but we must save his ripitation."

"No blame can rest on my father, on account of the surprise of this island?"

"There's no tellin'—there's no tellin'. Military glory is a most unsartain thing. I've seen the Delawares routed when they desarved more credit, than, at other times, when they've carried the day. A man is wrong to set his heart on success of any sort, and worst of all, on success in war. I know little of the settlements or of the notions that men hold in them, but, up hereaway, even the Indians rate a warrior's character according to his luck. The principal thing with a soldier is never to be whipt; not do I think mankind stops long to consider how the day was won, or lost. For my part, Mabel, I make it a rule when facing the inimy, to give him as good as I can send, and to try to be moderate as I can, when we get the better; as for feeling moderate, after a defeat, little need be said on that score, as a flogging is one of the most humbling things in natur'. The parsons preach about humility in the garrisons; but if humility would make christians, the King's troops ought to be saints, for they've done little, as yet, this war, but take lessons from the French, beginning at Fort du Quesne, and ending at Ty!"

"My father could not have suspected that the position of the island was known to the enemy!" resumed Mabel, whose thoughts were running on the probable effect of the recent events on the Serjeant.

"That is true; nor do I well see how the Frenchers found it out. The spot is well chosen, and it is not an easy matter even for one who has travelled the road to and from it, to find it again. There has been treachery I fear; yes, yes there must have been treachery!"

"Oh! Pathfinder, can this be!"

"Nothing is easier, Mabel, for treachery comes as nat'ral to some men as eating. Now, when I find a man all fair words, I look close to his deeds; for when the heart is right and raally intends to do good, it is generally satisfied to let the conduct speak, instead of the tongue."

"Jasper Western is not one of these," said Mabel impetuously. "No youth can be more sincere in his manner, or less apt to make the tongue act for the heart!"

"Jasper Western!—Tongue and heart are both right with that lad, depend on it, Mabel, and the notion taken up by Lundie, and the Quarter Master, and the Sarjeant, and your uncle too, is as wrong as it would be to think that the sun shone by night, and the stars shone by day. No—no—I'll answer for Eau douce's honesty, with my own scalp, or, at need, with my own rifle."

"Bless you—bless you, Pathfinder!" exclaimed Mabel extending her own hand, and pressing the iron fingers of her companion, under a state of feeling that far surpassed her own consciousness of its strength. "You are all that is generous—all that is noble; God will reward you for it."

"Ah! Mabel; I fear me if this be true, I should not covet such a wife as yourself, but would leave you to be sued for, by some gentleman of the garrison, as your desarts require!"

"We will not talk of this any more, to night—" Mabel answered in a voice so smothered, as to sound nearly choked—"We must think less of ourselves, just now, Pathfinder, and more of our friends. But I rejoice from my soul, that you believe Jasper innocent. Now, let us talk of other things—ought we not to release June?"

"I've been thinking about the woman, for it will not be safe to shut our eyes, and leave hers open, on this side of the block-house door. If we put her in the upper room, and take away the ladder, she'll be a prisoner, at least."

"I cannot treat one thus, who has saved my life. It would be better to let her depart; I think she is too much my friend to do any thing to harm me."

"You do not know the race, Mabel; you do not know the race. It's true she's not full-blooded Mingo, but she consorts with the vagabonds, and must have l'arned some of their tricks. What is that?"

"It sounds like oars—some boat is passing through the channel."

Pathfinder closed the trap that led to the lower room, to prevent June from escaping, extinguished the candle, and went hastily to a loop; Mabel looking over his shoulder, in breathless curiosity. These several movements consumed a minute or two, and by the time the eye of the scout had got a dim view of things without, two boats had swept past, and shot up to the shore, at a spot some fifty yards beyond the block, where there was a regular landing. The obscurity prevented more from being seen, and Pathfinder whispered to Mabel, that the new comers were as likely to be foes as friends, for he did not think her father could possibly have arrived so soon. A number of men were now seen to quit the boats, and then followed three hearty English cheers, leaving no further doubts of the character of the party. Pathfinder sprang to the trap, raised it, glided down the ladder, and began to unbar the door, with an earnestness that proved how critical he deemed the moment. Mabel had followed, but she rather impeded than aided his exertions, and but a single bar was turned when a heavy discharge of rifles was heard. They were still standing in breathless suspense when the war-whoop rang in all the surrounding thickets. The door now opened, and both Pathfinder and Mabel rushed into the open air. All human sounds had ceased. After listening half a minute, however, Pathfinder thought he heard a few stifled groans near the boats, but the wind blew so fresh, and the rustling of the leaves mingled so much with the murmurs of the passing air, that he was far from certain. But, Mabel was borne away by her feelings, and she rushed by him, taking the way towards the boats.

"This will not do, Mabel—" said the Scout, in an earnest but low voice, seizing her by an arm. "This will not do. Sartain death would follow, and that without sarving any one. We must return to the block."

"Father!—My poor, dear, murdered father!" said the girl wildly, though habitual caution, even at that trying moment, induced her to speak low. "Pathfinder, if you love me, let me go to my dear father!"

"This will not do, Mabel.—It is singular that no one speaks; no one returns the fire from the boats—and I have left Killdeer in the block!—But of what use would a rifle be, when no one is to be seen!"

At that moment, the quick eye of Pathfinder, which, while he held Mabel firmly in his grasp, had never ceased to roam over the dim scene, caught an indistinct view of five or six dark, crouching forms, endeavoring to steal past him, doubtless with the intention of intercepting their retreat to the block-house. Catching up Mabel, and putting her under an arm, as if she were an infant, the sinewy frame of the woodsman was exerted to the utmost, and he succeeded in entering the building. The tramp of his pursuers seemed immediately at his heels. Dropping his burthen, he turned, closed the door, and had fastened one bar, as a rush against the solid mass threatened to force it from the hinges. To secure the other bars, was the work of an instant.

Mabel now ascended to the first floor, while Pathfinder remained as a sentinel below. Our heroine was in that state in which the body exerts itself, apparently without the control of the mind. She relighted the candle mechanically, as her companion had desired, and returned with it below, where he was waiting her reappearance. No sooner was Pathfinder in possession of the light, than he examined the place carefully, to make certain no one was concealed in the fortress, ascending to each floor, in succession, after assuring himself that he left no enemy in his rear. The result was the conviction that the block-house now contained no one but Mabel and himself, June having escaped. When perfectly convinced on this material point, Pathfinder rejoined our heroine in the principal apartment, setting down the light, and examining the priming of Killdeer, before he seated himself.

"Our worst fears are realized!" said Mabel, to whom the hurry and excitement of the last five minutes, appeared to contain the emotions of a life. "My beloved father, and all his party, are slain or captured!"

"We don't know that—morning will tell us all. I do not think the affair as settled as that, or we should hear the vagabond Mingos yelling out their triumph, around the block-house. Of one thing we may be sartain; if the inimy has really got the better, he will not be long in calling upon us to surrender. The squaw will let him into the secret of our situation, and, as they well know the place cannot be fired by day-light, so long as Killdeer continues to desarve his ripitation, you may depend on it, that they will not be backward in making their attempt, while darkness helps them."

"Surely, I hear a groan!"

" 'Tis fancy, Mabel—When the mind gets to be skeary, especially a woman's mind, she often concaits things that have no reality. I've known them that imagined there was truth in dreams—"

"Nay, I am *not* deceived—there is surely one below, and in pain!"

Pathfinder was compelled to own that the quick senses of Mabel had not deceived her. He cautioned her, however, to repress her feelings, and reminded her that the savages were in the practice of resorting to every artifice, to attain their ends, and that nothing was more likely than that the groans were feigned with a view to lure them from the block-house, or, at least, to induce them to open the door.

"No—no—no—" said Mabel hurriedly—"there is no artifice in those sounds, and they come from anguish of body, if not of spirit. They are fearfully natural."

"Well, we shall soon know whether a friend is there, or not. Hide the light again, Mabel, and I will speak the person from a loop."

Not a little precaution was necessary, according to Pathfinder's judgment and experience, in performing even this simple act, for he had known the careless slain by their want of a proper attention to what might have seemed to the ignorant supererogatory means of safety. He did not place his mouth to the loop itself, but so near it that he could be heard without raising his voice, and the same precaution was observed as regards his ear.

"Who is below?" Pathfinder demanded when his arrangements were made to his mind—"Is any one in suffering? If a friend, speak boldly, and depend on our aid!"

"Pathfinder!" answered a voice that both Mabel and the person addressed, at once knew to be the Serjeant's—"Pathfinder, in the name of God, tell me what has become of my daughter?"

"Father!—I am here—unhurt—safe—and oh! that I could think the same of you!"

The ejaculation of thanksgiving that followed was distinctly audible to the two, but it was clearly mingled with a groan of pain.

"My worst forebodings are realized!" said Mabel, with a sort of desperate calmness. "Pathfinder, my father must be brought within the block, though we hazard every thing to do it."

"This is natur', and it is the law of God. But, Mabel, be calm, and endivor to be cool. All that can be effected for the sarjeant by human inventions, shall be done. I only ask you to be cool."

"I am—I am—Pathfinder. Never in my life was I more calm; more collected than at this moment. But remember how precious may be every instant; for Heaven's sake! what we do, let us do without delay."

Pathfinder was struck with the firmness of Mabel's tones, and perhaps he was a little deceived by the forced tranquillity and self-possession she had assumed. At all events, he did not deem any farther exhortations necessary, but descended forthwith, and began to unbar the door. This delicate process was conducted with the usual caution, but as he warily permitted the mass of timber to swing back on the hinges, he felt a pressure against it, that had nearly induced him to close it again. But catching a glimpse of the cause through the crack, the door was permitted to swing back, when the body of

Serjeant Dunham, which was propped against it, fell partly within the block. To draw in the legs and secure the fastenings, occupied the Pathfinder but a moment. Then there existed no obstacle to their giving their undivided care to the wounded man.

Mabel, in this trying scene, conducted herself with the sort of unnatural energy that her sex, when aroused, is apt to manifest. She got the light, administered water to the parched lips of her father, and assisted Pathfinder in forming a bed of straw, for his body, and a pillow of clothes for his head. All this was done earnestly, and almost without speaking, nor did Mabel shed a tear, until she heard the blessings of her father murmured on her head, for this tenderness and care. All this time, Mabel had merely conjectured the condition of her parent. Pathfinder, however, showed greater attention to the physical danger of the serjeant. He ascertained that a rifle ball had passed through the body of the wounded man, and he was sufficiently familiar with injuries of this nature, to be certain that the chances of his surviving the hurt, were very trifling, if any.

Chapter XXIV

"There—drink my tears, while yet they fall—
Would that my bosom's blood were balm,
And—well thou knowest—I'd shed it all
To give thy brow one minute's calm."
Moore, *Lalla Rookh*, "Paradise
and the Peri," ll. 274–77.

THE EYES of Serjeant Dunham had not ceased to follow the form of his beautiful daughter, from the moment that the light appeared. He next examined the door of the block, to ascertain its security, for he was left on the ground below, there being no available means of raising him to the upper floor. Then he sought the face of Mabel, for as life wanes fast, the affections resume their force, and we begin to value that most which we feel we are about to lose forever.

"God be praised, my child, you, at least, have escaped their murderous rifles!" he said, for he spoke with strength, and, seemingly, with no additional pain. "Give me the history of this sad business, Pathfinder."

"Ah's! me, sarjeant, it *has* been sad, as you say. That there has been treachery, and the position of the island has been betrayed, is now as sartain, in my judgment, as that we still hold the block. But——"

"Major Duncan was right," interrupted Dunham, laying a hand on the other's arm.

"Not in the sense you mean, sarjeant—no, not in that p'int of view; never. At least, not, in my opinion. I know that natur' is weak—human natur' I mean—and that we should none of us vaunt of our gifts, whether red or white; but I do not think a truer-hearted lad lives on the lines, than Jasper Western."

"Bless you—bless you for that, Pathfinder!" burst forth from Mabel's very soul, while a flood of tears gave vent to emotions that were so varied, while they were so violent. "Oh! bless you, Pathfinder, bless you; the brave should never desert the brave; the honest should sustain the honest."

The father's eyes were fastened anxiously on the face of his daughter, until the latter hid her countenance in her apron to conceal her tears, and then they turned with inquiry to the hard features of the guide. The latter merely wore their usual expression of frankness, sincerity and uprightness, and the serjeant motioned to him to proceed.

"You know the spot where the Sarpent and I left you, sarjeant," Pathfinder resumed, "and I need say nothing of all that happened afore. It is now too late to lament what is gone and passed; but I do think if I had staid with the boats, this would not have come to pass! Other men may be as good guides; I make no doubt they are; but then natur' bestows its gifts, and some must be better than other some. I dare say, poor Gilbert who took my place has suffered for his mistake."

"He fell at my elbow—" the serjeant answered in a low, melancholy tone—"we have, indeed, all suffered for our mistakes!"

"No—no—sarjeant, I meant no condemnation on you, for men were never better commanded than yourn, in this very expedition. I never beheld a prettier flanking, and the way in which you carried your own boat up ag'in their howitzer, might have teached Lundie, himself, a lesson."

The eyes of the Serjeant brightened, and his face even wore an expression of military triumph, though it was of a degree that suited the humble sphere in which he had been an actor.

" 'Twas not badly done, my friend," he said, "and we carried their log breast-work by storm!"

" 'Twas nobly done, sarjeant, though I fear, when all the truth comes to be known, it will be found that these vagabonds have got their howitzer back ag'in—Well, well, put a stout heart upon it, and try to forget all that is disagreeable, and to remember only the pleasant part of the matter. That is your truest philosophy, ay, and truest religion, too. If the inimy has got the howitzer, ag'in, they've only got what belonged to them afore, and what we could'n't help. They hav'n't got the block-house, yet, nor are they likely to get it, unless they fire it, in the dark. Well, sarjeant, the Sarpent and I separated about ten miles down the river, for we thought it wisest not to come upon even a friendly camp, without the usual caution. What has become of Chingachgook I cannot say, though Mabel tells me he is not far off, and I make no question, the noble hearted Delaware is doing his duty, although he is not now visible to our eyes. Mark my words, sarjeant; before this matter is over, we shall hear of him, at some critical time, and that in a discreet and creditable manner. Ah! the Sarpent is, indeed, a wise and virtuous chief, and any white man might covet his gifts, though his rifle is not quite as sure as Killdeer, it must be owned. Well, as I came near the island, I missed the smoke, and that put me on my guard, for I knew the men of the 55th, were not cunning enough to conceal that sign, notwithstanding all that has been told them of its danger. This made me more careful, until I came in sight of their mock fisherman, as I've just told Mabel, and then the whole of their infernal arts was as plain afore me, as if I saw it on a map. I need not tell you, sarjeant, that my first thoughts were of Mabel, and that, finding she was in the block, I came here, in order to live, or die, in her company."

The father turned a gratified look upon his child, and Mabel felt a sinking of the heart that, at such a moment, she could not have thought possible, when she wished to believe all her concern centered in the situation of her parent. As the latter held out his hand, she took it in her own, and kissed it. Then kneeling at his side, she wept as if her heart would break.

"Mabel," he said steadily—"the will of God must be done. It is useless to attempt deceiving either you, or myself; my time has come, and it is a consolation to me, to die like a soldier. Lundie will do me justice, for our good friend, Pathfinder, will tell him what has been done, and how all came to pass. You do not forget our last conversation."

"Nay, father, my time has probably come too—" exclaimed Mabel, who felt, just then, as if it would be a relief to die. "I cannot hope to escape, and Pathfinder would do well to leave us, and return to the garrison, with the sad news while he can."

"Mabel Dunham," said Pathfinder, reproachfully, though he took her hand with kindness, "I have not desarved this. I know I am wild, and uncouth, and ungainly—"

"Pathfinder!"

"Well—well—we'll forget it; you did not mean it; you could not think it. It is useless, now, to talk of escaping, for the sarjeant cannot be moved, and the block-house must be defended, cost what it will. Maybe Lundie will get the tidings of our disaster, and send a party to raise the siege."

"Pathfinder—Mabel—" said the serjeant, who had been writhing with pain, until the cold sweat stood on his forehead—"come both to my side. You understand each other, I hope?"

"Father, say nothing of that—it is all as you wish."

"Thank God. Give me your hand, Mabel—here, Pathfinder, take it. I can do no more than give you the girl in this way. I know you will make her a kind husband. Do not wait, on account of my death, but there will be a chaplain in the fort, before the season closes, and let him marry you at once. My brother, if living, will wish to go back to his vessel, and then the child will have no protector. Mabel, your husband will have been my friend, and that will be some consolation to you, I hope."

"Trust this matter to me, sarjeant," put in Pathfinder. "Leave it all on my hands, as your dying request, and depend on it, all will go as it should."

"I do—I do—I put all confidence in you, my trusty friend, and empower you to act as I could act, myself, in every particular—Mabel, child—hand me the water—you will never repent this night. Bless you, my daughter—God bless, and have you in his holy keeping!"

This tenderness was inexpressibly touching to one of Mabel's feelings, and she felt, at that moment, as if her future union with Pathfinder had received a solemnization that no ceremony of the church could render more holy. Still, a weight, as that of a mountain, lay upon her heart, and she thought it would be happiness to die. Then followed a short pause, when the serjeant, in broken sentences briefly related what had passed since he parted with Pathfinder and the Delaware. The wind had come more favorable, and, instead of encamping on an island, agreeably to the original intention, he had determined to continue on, and reach the station that night. Their approach would have been unseen, and a portion of the calamity averted, he thought, had they not grounded on the point of a neighboring island, where, no doubt the noise made by the men, in getting off the boat, gave notice of their approach, and enabled the enemy to be in readiness to receive them. They had landed without the slightest suspicion of danger, though surprised at not finding any sentinel, and had actually left their arms in the boats, with the intention of first securing their knapsacks and provisions. The fire had been so close, that notwithstanding the obscurity, it was very deadly. Every man had fallen; two or three, however, subsequently arose, and disappeared. Four or five of the soldiers had been killed outright, or so nearly so, as to survive but a few minutes, though, for some unknown reason, the enemy did not make the usual rush for the scalps. Serjeant Dunham fell with the others, and he had heard the voice of Mabel as she rushed from the block-house. This frantic appeal aroused all his parental feelings, and enabled him to crawl as far as the door of the building where he had raised himself against the logs, in the manner already mentioned.

After this simple explanation was made the serjeant was so weak as to need repose, and his companions, while they ministered to his wants, suffered some time to pass in silence. Pathfinder took the occasion, to reconnoitre from the loops and the roof, and he examined the condition of the rifles of which there were a dozen kept in the building, the soldiers having used their regimental muskets in the expedition. But, Mabel never left her father's side for an instant, and when by his breathing, she fancied he slept, she bent her knees and prayed.

The half hour that succeeded was awfully solemn and still. The moccasin of Pathfinder was barely heard over head, and occasionally the sound of the breech of a rifle fell upon the floor; for he was busied in examining the pieces, with a view to ascertain the state of their charges, and their primings. Beyond this, nothing was so loud as the breathing of the wounded man. Mabel's heart yearned to be in communication with the father she was so soon to lose, and yet she would not disturb his apparent repose. But Dunham slept not. He was in that state when the world suddenly loses its attractions, its illusions, and its power, and the unknown future fills the mind, with its conjectures, its revelations and its immensity. He had been a moral man, for one of his mode of life, but he had thought little of this all important moment.

Had the din of battle been ringing in his ears, his martial ardor might have endured to the end, but, there, in the silence of that nearly untenanted block-house, with no sound to enliven him, no appeal to keep alive factitious sentiment, no hope of victory to impel, things began to appear in their true colours, and this state of being to be estimated at its just value. He would have given treasures for religious consolation, and yet he knew not where to turn to seek it. He thought of Pathfinder, but he distrusted his knowledge. He thought of Mabel, but for the parent to appeal to the child for such succor, appeared like reversing the order of nature. Then it was that he felt the full responsibility of the parental character, and had some clear glimpses of the manner in which he himself had discharged the trust towards an orphan child. While thoughts like these were rising in his mind, Mabel, who watched the slightest change in his breathing, heard a guarded knock at the door. Supposing it might be Chingachgook, she rose, undid two of the bars, and held the third in her hand, as she asked who was there. The answer was in her uncle's voice, and he implored her to give him immediate admission. Without an instant of hesitation, she turned the bar, and Cap entered. He had barely passed the opening, when Mabel closed the door again, and secured it as before, for practice had rendered her expert, in this portion of her duties.

The sturdy seaman, when he had made sure of the state of his brother-in-law, and that Mabel as well as himself, was safe, was softened nearly to tears. His own appearance he explained, by saying that he had been carelessly guarded, under the impression that he and the Quarter Master were sleeping under the fumes of liquor, with which they had been plied, with a view to keep them quiet in the expected engagement. Muir had been left asleep, or seeming to sleep, but Cap had run into the bushes, on the alarm of the attack, and having found Pathfinder's canoe, had only succeeded, at that moment, in getting to the block-house, whither he had come with the kind intent of escaping with his niece, by water. It is scarcely necessary to say, that he changed his plan, when he ascertained the state of the serjeant, and the apparent security of his present quarters.

"If the worst comes to the worst, Master Pathfinder," he said, " we must strike, and that will entitle us to quarter. We owe it to our manhood to hold out a reasonable time, and to ourselves to haul down the ensign in season to make saving conditions. I wished Master Muir to do the same thing, when we were captured by these chaps you call vagabonds—and rightly are they named, for viler vagabonds do not walk the earth—"

"You've found out their characters!" interrupted Pathfinder, who was always as ready to chime in with abuse of the Mingos, as with the praises of his friends—"Now, had you fallen into the hands of the Delawares, you would have l'arned the difference!"

"Well, to me, they seem much of a muchness; blackguards fore and aft, always excepting our friend the Serpent, who is a gentleman, for an Injin. But, when these savages made the assault on us, killing Corporal McNab, and his men, as if they had been so many rabbits, Lt. Muir and myself took refuge in one of the holes of this here island, of which there are so many among the rocks—regular geological under-ground burrows made by the water, as the Lieutenant says,—and there we remained stowed away like two leaguers in a ship's hold, until we gave out for want of grub. A man may say that grub is the foundation of human nature. I desired the Quarter Master to make terms, for we could have defended ourselves for an hour or two in the place, bad as it was, but he declined on the ground that the knaves would'n't keep faith, if any of them were hurt, and so there was no use in asking them to. I consented to strike, on two principles; one, that we might be said to have struck already; for running below is generally thought to be giving up the ship; and the other, that we had an enemy in our stomachs that was more formidable in his attacks, than the enemy on deck. Hunger is a d——le circumstance, as any man who has lived on it eight and forty hours will acknowledge."

"Uncle!" said Mabel, in a mournful voice, and with an expostulating manner, "my poor father is sadly, sadly hurt!"

"True, Magnet, true—I will sit by him, and do my best at consolation. Are the bars well fastened, girl, for, on such an occasion, the mind should be tranquil and undisturbed."

"We are safe, I believe, from all but this heavy blow of Providence."

"Well, then, Magnet, do you go up to the deck above, and try to compose yourself, while Pathfinder runs aloft and takes a look out from the cross-trees. Your father may wish to say something to me, in private, and it may be well to leave us alone. These are solemn scenes, and inexperienced people, like myself, do not always wish what they say to be overheard."

Although the idea of her uncle's affording religious consolation by the side of a death-bed, certainly never obtruded itself on the imagination of Mabel, she thought there might be a propriety in the request, with which she was unacquainted, and she complied accordingly. Pathfinder had already ascended to the roof, to make his survey, and the brothers-in-law were left alone. Cap took a seat by the side of the serjeant, and bethought him, seriously, of the grave duty he had before him. A silence of several minutes succeeded, during which brief space, the mariner was digesting the substance of his intended discourse.

"I must say, Serjeant Dunham," Cap at length commenced in his peculiar manner, "that there has been mismanagement somewhere in this unhappy expedition, and, the present being an occasion when truth ought to be spoken, and nothing but the truth, I feel it my duty to say as much, in plain language. In short, serjeant, on this point there cannot well be two opinions, for, seaman as I am, and no soldier, I can see several errors myself, that it needs no great education to detect."

"What would you have, Brother Cap," returned the other in a feeble voice—"what is done is done; and it is now too late to remedy it."

"Very true, Brother Dunham, but not to repent of it. The good book tells us, it is never too late to repent, and I've always heard that this is the precious moment. If you've any thing on your mind, serjeant, hoist it out freely, for you know, you trust it to a friend. You were my own sister's husband, and poor little Magnet is my own sister's daughter, and living, or dead, I shall always look upon you, as a brother. It's a thousand pities that you did'n't lie off and on, with the boats, and send a canoe ahead to reconnoitre, in which case your command would have been saved, and this disaster would not have befallen us all. Well, serjeant, we are *all* mortal, that is some consolation, I make no doubt, and if you go before a little, why, we must follow. Yes, that *must* give him consolation."

"I know all this, Brother Cap, and hope I'm prepared to meet a soldier's fate. There is poor Mabel—"

"Ay, ay—that's a heavy drag, I know, but you would'n't take her with you, if you could, serjeant, and so the better way is to make as light of the separation, as you can. Mabel is a good girl, and so was her mother before her; she was *my* sister, and it shall be my care to see that her daughter gets a good husband, if our lives and scalps are spared; for I suppose no one would care about entering into a family that has no scalps."

"Brother, my child is betrothed—she will become the wife of Pathfinder."

"Well, Brother Dunham, every man has his opinions, and his manner of viewing things, and to my notion this match will be any thing but agreeable to Mabel. I have no objection to the age of the man; I'm not one of them that thinks it is necessary to be a boy to make a girl happy, but on the whole I prefer a man of about fifty for a husband; still, there ought not to be any circumstance between the parties to make them unhappy. Circumstances play the devil with materimony, and I set it down as one, that Pathfinder do'n't know as much as my niece. You've seen but little of the girl, serjeant, and have not got the run of her knowledge; but, let her pay it out freely, as she will do when she gets to be thoroughly acquainted, and you'll fall in with but few schoolmasters that can keep their luffs in her company."

"She's a good child—a dear good child—" muttered the serjeant, his eyes filling with tears—"and it is my misfortune that I have seen so little of her."

"She is, indeed, a good girl, and knows altogether too much for poor Pathfinder, who is a reasonable man and an experienced man, in his own way, but who has no more idea of the main chance than you have of spherical trigonometry, serjeant."

"Ah! Brother Cap, had Pathfinder been with us in the boats, this sad affair might not have happened!"

"That is quite likely, for his worst enemy will allow that the man is a good guide; but, serjeant, if the truth must be spoken, you have managed this expedition in a loose way, altogether; you should have hove-to off your haven, and sent in a boat to reconnoitre, as I told you before. That is a matter to be repented of, and I tell it to you, because truth, in such a case, ought to be spoken."

"My errors are dearly paid for, Brother, and poor Mabel, I fear, will be the sufferer. I think, however, that the calamity would not have happened, had there not been treason. I fear me, Brother, that Jasper Eau douce has played us false!"

"That is just my notion, for this fresh-water life, must sooner or later undermine any man's morals. Lieutenant Muir and myself talked this matter over, while we lay in a bit of a hole, out here on this island, and we both came to the conclusion that nothing short of Jasper's treachery could have brought us all into this infernal scrape. Well, serjeant, you had better compose your mind, and think of other matters, for, when a vessel is about to enter a strange port, it is more prudent to think of the anchorage inside, than to be under-running all the events that have turned up during the v'y'ge. There's the logbook expressly to note all these matters in, and what stands there, must form the column of figures that's to be footed up for, or against us. How, now, Pathfinder; is there any thing in the wind, that you come down the ladder like an Indian in the wake of a scalp?"

The guide raised a finger, for silence, and then beckoned to Cap to ascend the first ladder, and to allow Mabel to take his place, at the side of the serjeant.

"We must be prudent, and we must be bold, too," he said, in a low voice. "The riptyles are in earnest in their intention to fire the block, for they know there is now nothing to be gained by letting it stand. I hear the voice of that vagabond Arrowhead, among them, and he is urging them to set about their diviltry this very night. We must be stirring, Salt-water, and doing too. Luckily, there are four or five barrels of water in the block, and these are something towards a siege. My reckoning is wrong, too, or we shall yet reap some advantage from that honest fellow the Sarpent, being at liberty."

Cap did not wait for a second invitation, but starting up, he was soon in the upper room, with Pathfinder, while Mabel took his post at the side of her father's humble bed. Pathfinder had opened a loop, having so far concealed the light that it would not expose him to a treacherous shot, and, expecting a summons, he stood with his face near the hole, ready to answer. The stillness that succeeded, was at length broken by the voice of Muir.

"Master Pathfinder," called out the Scotchman—"a friend summons you to a parley. Come freely to one of the loops, for you've nothing to fear, so long as you are in converse with an officer of the 55th—"

"What is your will, Quarter Master—what is your will? I know the 55th, and believe it to be a brave rigiment, though I rather incline to the 60th, as my favorite, and to the Delawares more than to either. But what would you have, Quarter Master; it must be a pressing errand that brings you under the loops of a block house, at this hour of the night, with the sartainty of Killdeer's being inside of it."

"Oh! you'll no harm a friend, Pathfinder, I'm certain, and that's my security. You're a man of judgment, and have gained too great a name on this frontier for bravery, to feel the necessity of fool-hardiness to obtain a character. You'll very well understand, my good friend, there is as much credit to be gained by submitting gracefully, when resistance becomes impossible, as by obstinately holding out contrary to the rules of war. The enemy is too strong for us, my brave comrade, and I come to counsel you to give up the block, on condition of being treated as a prisoner of war."

"I thank you for this advice, Quarter Master, which is the more acceptable, as it costs nothing. But, I do not think it belongs to my gifts to yield a place like this, while food and water last."

"Well, I'd be the last, Pathfinder, to recommend any thing against so brave a resolution, did I see the means of maintaining it. But ye'll remember that Master Cap has fallen—"

"Not he—not he," roared the individual in question through another loop—"so far from that, Lieutenant, he has risen to the height of this here fortification, and has no mind to put his head of hair into the hands of such barbers, again, so long as he can help it. I look upon this block-house as a circumstance, and have no mind to throw it away."

"If that is a living voice," returned Muir, "I am glad to hear it, for we all thought the man had fallen in the late fearful confusion! But, Master Pathfinder, although ye're enjoying the society of your friend Cap, and a great pleasure do I know it to be, by the experience of two days and a night passed in a hole in the earth, we've lost that of Serjeant Dunham, who has fallen, with all the brave men he led in the late expedition. Lundie would have it so, though it would have been more discreet and becoming to send a commissioned officer in command. Dunham was a brave man, notwithstanding, and shall have justice done his memory. In short, we have all acted for the best, and that is as much as could be said in favor of Prince Eugene, the Duke of Marlborough or the Great Earl of Stair himself."

"You're wrong ag'in, Quarter Master, you're wrong ag'in," answered Pathfinder, resorting to a ruse to magnify his force. "The sarjeant is safe in the block too, where, one might say, the whole family is collected."

"Well, I rejoice to hear it, for we had certainly counted the serjeant among the slain. If pretty Mabel is in the block, still, let her not delay an instant, for Heaven's sake, in quitting it, for the enemy is about to put it to the trial by fire. Ye know the potency of that dread element, and will be acting more like the discreet and experienced warrior ye're universally allowed to be, in yielding a place you canna' defend, than in drawing down ruin on yourself and companions."

"I know the potency of fire, as you call it, Quarter Master, and am not to be told, at this late hour, that it can be used for something else, besides cooking a dinner. But, I make no doubt, you've heard of the potency of Killdeer, and the man who attempts to lay a pile of brush ag'in these logs, will get a taste of his power. As for arrows, it is not in their gift, to set this building on fire, for we've no shingles on our roof, but good solid logs and green bark, and plenty of water besides. The roof is so flat, too, as you know yourself, Quarter Master, that we can walk on it, and so no danger on that score, while water lasts. I'm peaceable enough, if let alone, but he who endivors to burn this block over my head will find the fire squinched in his own blood."

"This is idle and romantic talk, Pathfinder, and ye'll no maintain it yourself when ye come to meditate on the realities. I hope ye'll no gainsay the loyalty, or the courage of the 55th, and I feel convinced that a council of war would decide on the propriety of a surrender, forthwith. Na'—na'—Pathfinder, foolhardiness is na' mair like the bravery o' Wallace, or Bruce, than Albany on the Hudson is like the old town of Edinbro'."

"As each of us seems to have made up his mind, Quarter Master, more words are useless. If the riptyles near you, are disposed to set about their hellish job, let them begin at once. They can burn wood and I'll burn powder. If I were an Injin at the stake, I suppose I could brag as well as the rest of them, but my gifts and natur' being both white, my turn is rather for doing, than talking. You've said quite enough, considering you carry the King's commission, and should we all be consumed, none of us will bear *you* any malice."

"Pathfinder, ye'll no be exposing Mabel, pretty Mabel Dunham, to sic' a calamity!"

"Mabel Dunham is by the side of her wounded father, and God will care for the safety of a pious child. Not a hair of her head shall fall, while my arm and sight remain true, and though *you* may trust the Mingos, Master Muir, I put no faith in them. You've a knavish Tuscarora in your company there, who has art and malice enough to spoil the character of any tribe with which he consorts, though he found the Mingos ready ruined to his hands, I fear. But, enough said; let each party go to the use of his means and gifts."

Throughout this dialogue Pathfinder kept his body covered, lest a treacherous shot should be aimed at the loop, and he now directed Cap to ascend to the roof in order to be in readiness to meet the first assault. Although the latter used sufficient diligence, he found no less than ten blazing arrows sticking to the bark, while the air was filled with the yells and whoops of the enemy. A rapid discharge of rifles followed, and the bullets came pattering against the logs, in a way to show that the struggle had, indeed, seriously commenced.

These were sounds, however, that appalled neither Pathfinder, nor Cap, while Mabel was too much absorbed with her affliction to feel alarm. She had good sense enough, too, to understand the nature of the defences, and fully to appreciate their importance. As for her father, the familiar noises revived him, and it pained his child, at such a moment, to see that his glassy eye began to kindle, and that the blood returned to a cheek it had deserted, as he listened to the uproar. It was now Mabel first perceived that his reason began slightly to wander.

"Order up the light companies," he muttered—"and let the grenadiers charge!—Do they dare to attack us in our fort! Why does not the artillery open on them?"

At that instant the heavy report of a gun burst on the night, and the crash of rending wood was heard, as a heavy shot tore the logs in the room above, and the whole block shook with the force of a shell that lodged in the work. The Pathfinder narrowly escaped the passage of this formidable missile as it entered, but when it exploded, Mabel could not repress a shriek, for she supposed all over her head, whether animate, or inanimate, destroyed. To increase her horror, her father shouted in a frantic voice to—"Charge!"

"Mabel—" said Pathfinder, with his head at the trap, "this is true Mingo work, more noise than injury. The vagabonds have got the howitzer we took from the French, and have discharged it ag'in the block, but, fortunately, they have fired off the only shell we had, and there is an ind of its use for the present. There is some confusion among the stores, up in this loft, but no one is hurt. Your uncle is still on the roof, and as for myself, I've run the gauntlet of too many rifles, to be skeary about such a thing as a howitzer, and that in Injin hands."

Mabel murmured her thanks, and tried to give all her attention to her father, whose efforts to rise were only counteracted by his debility. During the few fearful minutes that succeeded, she was so much occupied with her care of the invalid, that she scarce heeded the clamour that reigned around her. Indeed, the uproar was so great, that had not her thoughts been otherwise employed, confusion of faculties, rather than alarm, would probably have been the consequence.

Cap preserved his coolness admirably. He had a profound and increasing respect for the prowess of the savages, and even for the majesty of fresh water, it is true; but his apprehensions of the former proceeded more from his dread of being scalped and tortured, than from any unmanly fear of death, and as he was now on the deck of a house, if not the deck of a ship, and knew that there was little danger of boarders, he moved about with a fearlessness, and a real exposure of his person, that Pathfinder, had he been aware of the fact, would have been the first to condemn. Instead of keeping his body covered, agreeably to the usages of Indian warfare, he was seen on every part of the roof, dashing the water right and left, with the apparent steadiness and unconcern, he would have manifested had he been a sail trimmer, exercising his art, in a battle afloat. His appearance was one of the causes of the extraordinary clamor among the assailants, who, unused to seeing their enemies so reckless, opened upon him with their tongues, like the pack that has the fox in view. Still, he appeared to possess a charmed life, for, though the bullets whistled around him on every side, and his clothes were several times torn, nothing cut his skin. When the shell passed through the logs below, the old sailor dropped his bucket, waved his hat, and gave three cheers, in which heroic act he was employed as the dangerous missile exploded. This characteristic feat probably saved his life, for, from that instant, the Indians ceased to fire at him, and even to shoot their flaming arrows at the block, having taken up the notion, simultaneously and by common consent, that the "salt water" was mad; and it was a singular effect of their magnanimity never to lift a hand against those whom they imagined devoid of reason.

The conduct of Pathfinder was very different. Every thing he did was regulated by the most exact calculation, the result of long experience and habitual thoughtfulness. His person was kept carefully out of a line with the loops, and the spot that he selected for his look out, was one that was quite removed from danger. This celebrated guide had often been known to lead forlorn hopes, he had once stood at the stake, suffering under the cruelties and taunts of savage ingenuity and savage ferocity, without quailing, and legends of his exploits, coolness and daring, were to be heard all along that extensive frontier, or, wherever men dwelt and men contended, but, on this occasion, one who did not know his history and character might have thought his exceeding care and studied attention to self preservation, proceeded from an unworthy motive. But such a judge would not have understood his subject. The Pathfinder bethought him of Mabel, and of what might possibly be the consequences to that poor girl, should any casualty befall himself, but the recollection rather quickened his intellect, than changed his customary prudence. He was in fact, one of those who was so unaccustomed to fear, that he never bethought him of the constructions others might put upon his conduct, but, while, in moments of danger, he acted with the wisdom of the serpent, it was also with the simplicity of a child.

For the first ten minutes of the assault, Pathfinder never raised the breech of his rifle from the floor, except when he changed his own position; for he well knew that the bullets of the enemy were thrown away upon the massive logs of the work, and, as he had been at the capture of the howitzer, he felt certain that the savages had no other shell than the one found in it, when the piece was taken. There existed no reason, therefore, to dread the fire of the assailants, except as a casual bullet might find a passage through a loop-hole. One or two of these accidents did occur, but the balls entered at an angle that deprived them of all chance of doing any injury, so long as the Indians kept near the block; and, if discharged from a distance, there was scarcely the probability of one in a hundred's striking the apertures. But, when Pathfinder heard the sound of moccasined feet, and the rustling of brush at the foot of the building he knew that the attempt to build a fire against the logs, was about to be renewed. He now summoned Cap from the roof, where indeed, all the danger had ceased, and directed him to stand in readiness with his water, at a hole immediately over the spot assailed.

One less trained than our hero would have been in a hurry to repel this dangerous attempt also, and might have resorted to his means prematurely. Not so with Pathfinder. His aim was not only to extinguish the fire, about which he felt little apprehension, but to give the enemy a lesson that would render him wary during the remainder of the night. In order to effect the latter purpose, it became necessary to wait until the light of the intended conflagration should direct his aim, when he well knew that a very slight effort of his skill would suffice. The Iroquois were permitted to collect their heap of dried brush, to pile it against the block, to light it, and to return to their covers, without molestation. All that Pathfinder would suffer Cap to do, was to roll a barrel filled with water, to the hole immediately over the spot, in readiness to be used at the proper instant. That moment, however, did not arrive in his judgment, until the blaze illuminated the surrounding bushes, and there had been time for his quick and practised eye to detect the forms of three or four lurking savages, who were watching the progress of the flames, with the cool indifference of men accustomed to look on human misery with apathy. Then, indeed, he spoke.

"Are you ready, Friend Cap?" he asked. "The heat begins to strike through the crevices, and, although these green logs, are not of the fiery natur' of an ill-tempered man, they may be kindled into a blaze, if one provokes them too much. Are you ready with the barrel?—See that it has the right cut, and that none of the water is wasted."

"All ready—" answered Cap, in the manner in which a seaman replies to such a demand.

"Then wait for the word. Never be over impatient, in a critical time, nor fool-risky in a battle. Wait for the word."

While the Pathfinder was giving these directions, he was also making his own preparations, for he saw it was time to act. Killdeer was deliberately raised, pointed, and discharged. The whole process occupied about half a minute, and, as the rifle was drawn in, the eye of the marksman was applied to the hole.

"There is one riptyle the less—" Pathfinder muttered to himself—"I've seen that vagabond afore, and know him to be a marciless devil. Well, well; the man acted according to his gifts, and he has been rewarded according to his gifts. One more of the knaves, and that will sarve the turn for to-night. When day-light appears, we may have hotter work."

All this time, another rifle was getting ready, and as Pathfinder ceased, a second savage fell. This, indeed, sufficed, for indisposed to wait for a third visitation from the same hand, the whole band which had been crouching in the bushes around the block, ignorant of who was, and who was not exposed to view, leaped from their covers, and fled to different places for safety.

"Now, pour away, Master Cap," said Pathfinder—"I've made my mark on the blackguards, and we shall have no more fires lighted to-night."

"Scaldings!" cried Cap, upsetting the barrel, with a care that at once, and completely extinguished the flames.

This ended the singular conflict, and the remainder of the night passed in peace. Pathfinder and Cap watched alternately, though neither can be said to have slept. Sleep, indeed, scarcely seemed necessary to them, for both were accustomed to protracted watchings, and there were seasons and times, when the former appeared to be literally insensible to the demands of hunger and thirst, and callous to the effects of fatigue.

Mabel watched by her father's pallet, and began to feel how much our happiness in this world depends even on things that are imaginary. Hitherto she had virtually lived without a father, the connection with her remaining parent being ideal rather than positive; but, now that she was about to lose him, she thought, for the moment, that the world would be a void after his death, and that she could never be acquainted with happiness again.

Chapter XXV

"There was a roaring in the wind all night;
The rain came heavily, and fell in floods;
But now the sun is rising calm and bright;
The birds are singing in the distant woods—"
Wordsworth, "Resolution and Independence," ll. 1–4.

As the light returned, Pathfinder and Cap ascended again to the roof, with a view once more to reconnoitre the state of things on the island. This part of the block house had a low battlement around it, which afforded a considerable protection to those who stood in its centre; the intention having been to enable marksmen to lie behind it, and to fire over its top. By making proper use, therefore, of these slight defences—slight as to height, though abundantly ample as far as they went—the two look-outs commanded a pretty good view of the island, its covers excepted, and of most of the channels that led to the spot.

The gale was still blowing very fresh at south, and there were places in the river where its surface looked green and angry, though the wind had hardly sweep enough to raise the water into foam. The shape of the little island was generally oval, and its greatest length was from east to west. By keeping in the channels that washed it, in consequence of their several courses, and of the direction of the gale, it would have been possible for a vessel to range past the island, on either of its principal sides, and always keep the wind very nearly abeam. These were the facts first noted by Cap, and explained to his companion, for the hopes of both now rested on the chances of relief sent from Oswego. At this instant, while they stood gazing anxiously about them, Cap cried out in his lusty, hearty, manner—

"Sail ho!"

Pathfinder turned quickly, in the direction of his companion's face, and there, sure enough, was just visible the object of the old sailor's exclamation. The elevation, enabled the two to overlook the low land of several of the adjacent islands, and the canvass of a vessel was seen through the bushes that fringed the shore of one that lay to the southward and westward. The stranger was under what seamen call low sail, but so great was the power of the wind that her white outlines were seen flying past the openings of the verdure, with the velocity of a fast travelling horse, resembling a cloud driving in the heavens.

"That cannot be Jasper," said Pathfinder in disappointment, for he did not recognise the cutter of his friend in the swift-passing object. "No—no—the lad is behind the hour, and that is some craft that the Frenchers have sent to aid their friends, the accursed Mingos."

"This time you are out in your reckoning, friend Pathfinder, if you never were before—" returned Cap, in a manner that had lost none of its dogmatism by the critical circumstances in which they were placed. "Fresh water or salt, that is the head of the Scud's mainsail, for it is cut with a smaller goar than common, and then you can see that the gaff has been fished—quite neatly done, I admit, but fished."

"I can see none of this, I confess," answered Pathfinder, to whom even the terms of his companion were Greek.

"No!—Well, I own that surprises me; for I thought *your* eyes could see any thing! Now, to me nothing is plainer than that goar and that fish, and I must say, my honest friend, that, in your place, I should apprehend that my sight was beginning to fail."

"If Jasper is truly coming, I shall apprehend but little. We can make good the block against the whole Mingo nation, for the next eight, or ten hours, and with Eau douce to cover the retreat, I shall despair of nothing. God send that the lad may not run along side of the bank, and fall into an ambushment, as befel the sarjeant!"

"Ay; there's the danger. There ought to have been signals concerted, and an anchorage ground buoyed out, and even a quarantine station, or a Lazaretto would have been useful could we have made these Minks-ho! respect the laws. If the lad fetches up, as you say, any where in the neighborhood of this island, we may look upon the cutter as lost. And, after all, Master Pathfinder; ought we not to set down this same Jasper as a secret ally of the French, rather than as a friend of our own?—I know the Serjeant views the matter in that light, and I must say this whole affair looks like treason!"

"We shall soon know, we shall soon know, Master Cap, for there, indeed, comes the cutter, clear of the other island, and five minutes must settle the matter. It would be no more than fair, howsever, if we could give the boy some sign in the way of warning. It is not right that he should fall into the trap, without a notice that it has been laid."

Anxiety and suspense, notwithstanding, prevented either from attempting to make any signal. It was not easy, truly, to see how it could be done, for the Scud came foaming through the channel, on the weather side of the island, at a rate that scarce admitted of the necessary time. Nor was any one visible on her deck, to make signs to; even her helm seemed deserted, though her course was as steady as her progress was rapid.

Cap stood in silent admiration of a spectacle so unusual. But as the Scud drew nearer, his practised eye detected the helm in play, by means of tiller ropes, though the person who steered was concealed. As the cutter had weather-boards of some little height, the mystery was explained, no doubt remaining that her people lay behind the latter, in order to be protected from the rifles of the enemy. As this fact showed that no force, beyond that of the small crew, could be on board, Pathfinder received his companion's explanation with an ominous shake of the head.

"This proves that the Sarpent has not reached Oswego," he said, "and that we are not to expect succor from the garrison. I hope Lundie has not taken it into his head to displace the lad, for Jasper Western would be a host of himself, in such a strait. We three, Master Cap, ought to make a manful warfare—you, as a seaman, to keep up the intercourse with the cutter, Jasper as a laker, who knows all that is necessary to be done on the water, and I with gifts that are as good as any among the Mingos, let me be what I may, in other particulars. I say, we ought to make a manful fight, in Mabel's behalf."

"That we ought—and that we will—" answered Cap, heartily, for he began to have more confidence in the security of his scalp, now that he saw the sun again; "I set down the arrival of the Scud as one circumstance, and the chances of Oh! the deuce's honesty as another. This Jasper is a young man of prudence, you find, for he keeps a good offing, and seems determined to know how matters stand on the island, before he ventures to bring up."

"I have it! I have it!—" exclaimed Pathfinder with exultation—"There lies the canoe of the Sarpent, on the cutter's deck, and the chief has got on board, and no doubt has given a true account of our condition, for, unlike a Mingo, a Delaware is sartain to get a story right, or to hold his tongue."

Pathfinder's disposition to think well of the Delawares, and to think ill of the Mingos, must, by this time, be very apparent to the reader. Of the veracity of the former he entertained the highest respect, while of the latter he thought, as the more observant and intelligent classes of this country are getting pretty generally to think of certain scribblers among ourselves, who are known to have been so long in the habits of mendacity, that it is thought they can no longer tell the truth, even when they seriously make the effort.

"That canoe may belong to the cutter," said the captious seaman—"Oh! the Deuce had one on board, when we sailed."

"Very true, friend Cap; but, if you know your sails and masts, by your goars and fishes, I know my canoes and my paths, by frontier knowledge. If you can see new cloth in a sail, I can see new bark in a canoe. That is the boat of the Sarpent, and the noble fellow has struck off for the garrison, as soon as he found the block besieged, has fallen in with the Scud, and, after telling his story, has brought the cutter down here to see what can be done. The Lord grant that Jasper Western be still on board her!"

"Yes—yes—it might not be amiss, for traitor or loyal, the lad has a handy way with him in a gale, it must be owned."

"And in coming over water-falls!" said Pathfinder, nudging the ribs of his companion, with an elbow, and laughing in his silent, but hearty manner. "We will give the boy his due, though he scalps us all with his own hand!"

The Scud was now so near, that Cap made no reply. The scene, just at that instant, was so peculiar that it merits a particular description; which may also aid the reader in forming a more accurate notion of the picture we wish to draw.

The gale was still blowing violently. Many of the smaller trees bowed their tops, as if ready to descend to the earth, while the rushing of the wind through the branches of the groves, resembled the roar of distant chariots. The air was filled with leaves, which, at that late season, were readily driven from their stems, and flew from island to island, like flights of birds. With this exception, the spot seemed silent as the grave. That the savages still remained, was to be inferred from the fact that their canoes, together with the boats of the 55th, lay in a group, in the little cove, that had been selected as a harbour. Otherwise, not a sign of their presence was to be detected. Though taken entirely by surprise by the cutter, the sudden return of which was altogether unlooked for, so uniform and inbred, were their habits of caution, while on the war-path, that, the instant an alarm was given, every man had taken to his cover, with the instinct and cunning of a fox seeking his hole. The same stillness reigned in the block-house, for though Pathfinder and Cap could command a view of the channel, they took the precaution necessary to lie concealed. The unusual absence of any thing like animal life on board the Scud, too, was still more remarkable. As the Indians witnessed her apparently undirected movements, a feeling of awe gained a footing among them, and some of the boldest of their party, began to distrust the issue of an expedition that had commenced so prosperously. Even Arrowhead, accustomed as he was, to intercourse with the whites on both sides of the lakes, fancied there was something ominous in the appearance of this unmanned vessel, and he would gladly, at that moment, have been landed again on the main.

In the mean time, the progress of the cutter was steady and rapid. She held her way mid-channel, now inclining to the gusts, and now rising again, like the philosopher that bends to the calamities of life to resume his erect attitude as they pass away, but always piling the water beneath her bows, in foam. Although she was under so very short canvass, her velocity was great, and there could not have elapsed ten minutes between the time when her sails were first seen glancing past the trees and bushes, in the distance, and the moment when she was abreast of the block-house. Cap and Pathfinder leaned forward, as the cutter came beneath their eyrie, eager to get a better view of her deck, when to the delight of both, Jasper Eau douce, sprang upon his feet, and gave three hearty cheers. Regardless of all risk, Cap leaped upon the rampart of logs, and returned the greeting cheer for cheer. Happily, the policy of the enemy saved the latter, for they still lay quiet, not a rifle being discharged. On the other hand, Pathfinder kept in view the useful, utterly disregarding the more dramatic part of warfare. The moment he beheld his friend Jasper, he called out to him with Stentorian lungs—

"Stand by us, lad, and the day's our own! Give 'em a grist in yonder bushes, and you'll put 'em up like partridges."

Part of this reached Jasper's ears, but most was borne off to leeward, on the wings of the wind. By the time this was said, the Scud had driven past, and in the next moment she was hid from view by the grove in which the block-house was partially concealed.

Two anxious minutes succeeded, but, at the expiration of that brief space, the sails were again gleaming through the trees, Jasper having wore, jibed, and hauled up under the lee of the island, on the other tack. The wind was free enough, as has been already explained, to admit of this manœuvre, and the cutter catching the current under her lee bow, was breasted up to her course, in a way that showed she would come out to windward of the island again, without any difficulty. This whole evolution was made with the greatest facility, not a sheet being touched, the sails trimming themselves, the rudder alone, controlling the admirable machine. The object appeared to be a reconnoissance. When, however, the Scud had made the circuit of the entire island, and had again got her weatherly position, in the channel by which she had first approached, her helm was put down, and she tacked. The noise of the mainsail flapping when it filled, close reefed as it was, sounded like the report of a gun, and Cap trembled lest the seams should open.

"His Majesty gives good canvass, it must be owned," muttered the old seaman, "and it must be owned, too, that boy handles his boat, as if he were thoroughly bred! D——e, Master Pathfinder, if I believe, after all that has been reported in the matter, that this Mister Oh! the Deuce got his trade on this bit of fresh water."

"He did; yes he did. He never saw the ocean, and has come by his calling altogether, up here on Ontario. I have often thought he has a nat'ral gift, in the way of schooners and sloops, and have respected him accordingly. As for treason, and lying, and black hearted vices, friend Cap, Jasper Western is as free as the most virtuousest of the Delaware warriors, and if you crave to see a truly honest man, you must go among that tribe to discover him."

"There he comes round!" exclaimed the delighted Cap, the Scud at this moment filling on her original tack, "and now we shall see what the boy would be at; he cannot mean to keep running up and down these passages, like a girl footing it through a country dance!"

The Scud now kept so much away, that, for a moment, the two observers on the block-house, feared Jasper meant to come to, and the savages, in their lairs, gleamed out upon her, with a sort of exultation that the crouching tiger may be supposed to feel, as he sees his unconscious victim approach his bed. But Jasper had no such intention. Familiar with the shore, and acquainted with the depth of water on every part of the island, he well knew that the Scud might be run against the bank with impunity, and he ventured fearlessly so near, that as he passed through the little cove, he swept the two boats of the soldiers from their fastenings, and forced them out into the channel, towing them with the cutter. As all the canoes were fastened to the two Dunham boats, by this bold and successful attempt the savages were at once deprived of the means of quitting the island, unless by swimming, and they appeared to be instantly aware of the very important fact. Rising in a body, they filled the air with yells, and poured in a harmless fire. While up, in this unguarded manner, two rifles were discharged by their adversaries. One came from the summit of the block, and an Iroquois fell dead in his tracks, shot through the brain. The other came from the Scud. The last was the piece of the Delaware, but, less true than that of his friend, it only maimed an enemy for life. The people of the Scud shouted, and the savages, sank again, to a man, as if it might be into the earth.

"That was the Sarpent's voice," said Pathfinder, as soon as the second piece was discharged. "I know the crack of his rifle, as well as I do that of Killdeer. 'Tis a good barrel, though not sartain death. Well—well—with Chingachgook and Jasper on the water, and you and I in the block, friend Cap, it will be hard, if we do'n't teach these Mingo scamps the rationality of a fight!"

All this time, the Scud was in motion. As soon as she had reached the end of the island, Jasper sent his prizes adrift, and they went down before the wind, until they stranded on a point, more than a mile to leeward. He then wore, and came stemming the current again, through the other passage. Those on the summit of the block, could now perceive that something was in agitation on the deck of the Scud, and to their great delight, just as the cutter came abreast of the principal cover, or the spot where most of the enemy lay, the howitzer, which composed her sole armament, was unmasked, and a shower of case shot was sent hissing into the bushes. A bevy of quail would not have risen quicker than this unexpected discharge of iron hail, put up the Iroquois, when a second savage fell by a messenger sent from Killdeer, and another went limping away, by a visit from the rifle of Chingachgook. New covers were immediately found, however, and each party seemed to prepare for the renewal of the strife, in another form. But, the appearance of June bearing a white flag, and accompanied by the French officer and Muir, stayed the hands of all, and was the forerunner of another parley.

The negotiation that followed was held beneath the blockhouse, and so near it, as at once to put those who were uncovered completely at the mercy of Pathfinder's unerring aim. Jasper anchored directly abeam, and the howitzer, too, was kept trained upon the negotiators, so that the besieged and their friends, with the exception of the man who held the match, had no hesitation about exposing their persons. Chingachgook, alone, lay in ambush, more, however, from habit, than distrust.

"You've triumphed, Pathfinder," called out the Quarter Master, "and Capt. Sanglier has come himself to offer terms. You'll no be denying a brave enemy an honorable retreat, when he has fought ye fairly, and done all the credit he could to king and country. Ye are too loyal a subject yourself, to visit loyalty and fidelity with a heavy judgment. I am authorized to offer, on the part of the enemy, an evacuation of the island, a mutual exchange of prisoners, and a restoration of scalps. In the absence of baggage and artillery, little more can be done."

As the conversation was necessarily carried on in a high key, both on account of the wind, and on account of the distance, all that was said was heard equally by those in the block, and those in the cutter.

"What do you say to that, Jasper?" called out Pathfinder. "You hear the tarms; shall we let the vagabonds go, or shall we mark them, as they mark their sheep, in the settlements, that we may know them, ag'in?"

"What has befallen Mabel Dunham?" demanded the young man, with a frown on his handsome face, that was visible even to those in the block—"If a hair of her head has been touched, it will go hard with the whole Iroquois tribe!"

"Nay—nay, she is safe below, nursing a dying parent, as becomes her sex. We owe no grudge on account of the Sarjeant's hurt, which comes of lawful warfare; and, as for Mabel—"

"She is here—" exclaimed the girl herself, who had mounted to the roof, the moment she found the direction things were taking. "She is here, and, in the name of our holy religion, and of that God whom we profess to worship in common, let there be no more bloodshed! Enough has been spilt already, and if these men will go away, Pathfinder—if they will depart peaceably, Jasper—oh! do not detain one of them. My poor father is approaching his end, and it were better that he should draw his last breath, in peace with the world. Go—go—Frenchmen and Indians; we are no longer your enemies, and will harm none of you."

"Tut—tut—Magnet," put in Cap, "this sounds religious, perhaps, or like a book of poetry, but it does not sound like common sense. The enemy is just ready to strike; Jasper is anchored, with his broadside to bear, and no doubt with springs on his cable; Pathfinder's eye and hand are as true as the needle, and we shall get prize-money, head-money, and honor, in the bargain, if you will not interfere, for the next half-hour."

"Well," said Pathfinder, "I incline to Mabel's way of thinking. There *has* been enough blood shed to answer our purposes, and to sarve the King, and as for honor, in that meaning, it will do better for young ensigns and recruits, than for cool headed, obsarvant, Christian men. There is honor in doing what's right, and unhonor in doing what's wrong; and I think it wrong to take the life, even of a Mingo, without a useful ind in view, I do; and right to hear reason at all times. So, Lieutenant Muir, let us know what your friends the Frenchers and Injins have to say for themselves."

"My friends!" said Muir, starting—"You'll no be calling the King's enemies my friends, Pathfinder, because the fortune of war has thrown me into their hands? Some of the greatest warriors, both of ancient and modern times, have been prisoners of war, and yon is Master Cap, who can testify whether we did not do all that men could devise to escape the calamity?"

"Ay—ay—" drily answered Cap—"escape is the proper word. We ran below and hid ourselves, and so discreetly, that we might have remained in the hole to this hour, had it not been for the necessity of re-stowing the bread lockers. You burrowed on that occasion, Quarter Master, as handily as a fox; and how the d——l, you knew so well where to find the spot is a matter of wonder to me. A regular skulk on board ship, does not tail aft more readily, when the jib is to be stowed, than you went into that same hole!"

"And did ye no follow! There are moments in a man's life, when reason ascends to instinct—"

"And men descend into holes," interrupted Cap, laughing in his boisterous way, while Pathfinder chimed in, in his peculiar manner. Even Jasper, though still filled with concern for Mabel, was obliged to smile. "They say the d——l would'n't make a sailor, if he did'n't look aloft, and now it seems he'll not make a soldier, if he does'n't look below!"

This burst of merriment, though it was any thing but agreeable to Muir, contributed largely towards keeping the peace. Cap fancied he had said a thing much better than common, and that disposed him to yield his own opinion on the main point, so long as he got the good opinion of his companions on his novel claim to be a wit. After a short discussion, all the savages on the island, were collected in a body, without arms, at the distance of a hundred yards from the block, and under the gun of the Scud, while Pathfinder descended to the door of the block-house, and settled the terms, on which the island was to be finally evacuated, by the enemy. Considering all the circumstances, the conditions were not very discreditable to either party. The Indians were compelled to give up all their arms, even to their knives and tomahawks, as a measure of precaution, their force being still quadruple that of their foes. The French officer, Monsieur Sanglier, as he was rightly styled, or chose to call himself, remonstrated against this act, as one likely to reflect more discredit on his command, than any other part of the affair, but, Pathfinder, who had witnessed one or two Indian massacres, and knew how valueless pledges became when put in opposition to interest, where a savage was concerned, was obdurate. The second stipulation was of nearly the same importance. It compelled Capt. Sanglier to give up all his prisoners, who had been kept well guarded, in the very hole, or cave, in which Cap and Muir had taken refuge. When these men were produced, four of them were found to be unhurt; they had fallen merely to save their lives, a common artifice in that species of warfare, and of the remainder, two were so slightly injured as not to be unfit for service. As they brought their muskets with them, this addition to his force, immediately put Pathfinder at his ease; for having collected all the arms of the enemy in the block-house, he directed these men to take possession of the building, stationing a regular sentinel at the door. The remainder of the soldiers were dead, the badly wounded having been instantly dispatched, in order to obtain the much coveted scalps.

As soon as Jasper was made acquainted with the terms, and the preliminaries had been so far observed as to render it safe for him to be absent, he got the Scud under way, and running down to the point where the boats had stranded, he took them in tow again, and, making a few stretches, brought them into the leeward passage. Here all the savages instantly embarked, when Jasper took the boats in tow, a third time, and running off before the wind, he soon set them adrift, quite a mile to leeward of the island. The Indians were furnished with but a single oar in each boat to steer with; the young sailor well knowing, that, by keeping before the wind, they would land on the shores of Canada, in the course of the morning.

Capt. Sanglier, Arrowhead and June alone remained, when this disposition had been made of the rest of the party; the former having certain papers to draw up and sign with Lieutenant Muir, who, in his eyes, possessed the virtues which are attached to a commission, and the latter preferring, for reasons of his own, not to depart in company with his late friends, the Iroquois. Canoes were retained, for the departure of these three, when the proper moment should arrive.

In the mean time, or while the Scud was running down with the boats in tow, Pathfinder and Cap aided by proper assistants, busied themselves with preparing a breakfast; most of the party not having eaten for four and twenty hours. The brief space that passed in this manner, before the Scud came to, again, was little interrupted by discourse, though Pathfinder found leisure to pay a visit to the serjeant, to say a few friendly words to Mabel, and to give such directions as he thought might smooth the passage of the dying man. As for Mabel, herself, he insisted on her taking some light refreshment, and there no longer existing any motive for keeping it there, he had the guard removed from the block, in order that the daughter might have no impediment to her attentions to her father. These little arrangements completed, our hero returned to the fire, around which he found all the remainder of the party assembled, including Jasper.

Chapter XXVI

"You saw but sorrow in its waning form,
A working sea remaining from a storm;
When now the weary waves roll o'er the deep,
And faintly murmur ere they fall asleep—"
Dryden, *Aureng-Zebe,* IV.i.197–200.

MEN ACCUSTOMED to a warfare, like that we have been describing, are not apt to be much under the influence of tender feelings, while still in the field. Notwithstanding their habits, however, more than one heart was with Mabel in the block, while the incidents we are about to relate were in the course of occurrence, and even the indispensable meal was less relished by the hardiest of the soldiers, than it might have been had not the serjeant been so near his end.

As Pathfinder returned from the block, he was met by Muir, who led him aside in order to hold a private discourse. The manner of the Quarter Master had that air of supererogatory courtesy about it, which almost invariably denotes artifice, for while physiognomy, and phrenology are but lame sciences, at the best, and perhaps lead to as many false as right conclusions, we hold that there is no more infallible evidence of insincerity of purpose, short of overt acts, than a face that smiles when there is no occasion, and the tongue that is out of measure smooth. Muir had much of this manner in common, mingled with an apparent frankness, that his Scottish intonation of voice, Scottish accent, and Scottish modes of expression were singularly adapted to sustain. He owed his preferment, indeed, to a long exercised deference to Lundie and his family, for, while the Major himself was much too acute to be the dupe of one so much his inferior in real talents and attainments, most persons are accustomed to make liberal concessions to the flatterer, even while they distrust his truth, and are perfectly aware of his motive. On the present occasion, the contest in skill, was between two men as completely the opposites of each other, in all the leading essentials of character, as very well could be. Pathfinder was as simple, as the Quarter Master was practised; he was as sincere as the other was false, and as direct as the last was tortuous. Both were cool and calculating, and both were brave, though in different modes and degrees; Muir never exposing his person except for effect, while the guide included fear among the rational passions, or as a sensation to be deferred to only when good might come of it.

"My dearest friend," Muir commenced, "for ye'll be dearer to us all, by seventy and seven fold, after your late conduct than ever ye were, ye've just established yourself, in this late transaction! It's true, that they'll no be making ye a commissioned officer, for that species of prefairment is not much in your line, nor much in your wishes, I'm thinking; but, as a guide, and a counsellor, and a loyal subject, and an expert marksman, yer' renown may be said to be full. I doubt if the commander in chief will carry away with him from America, as much credit as will fall to yer' share, and ye ought just to sit down in content, and enjoy yerself for the remainder of yer' days. Get married, man, without delay, and look to your precious happiness, for ye've no occasion to look any longer to your glory. Tak' Mabel Dunham, o' Heaven's sake, to yer bosom, and ye'll have both a bonny bride, and a bonny reputation."

"Why, Quarter Master, this is a new piece of advice to come from your mouth!—They've told me I had a rival in you!"

"And ye had, man, and a formidable one too, I can tell ye! One that has never yet courted in vain, and yet one that has courted five times. Lundie twits me with four; and I deny the charge; but he little thinks the truth would outdo even his own arithmetic! Yes, yes; ye had a rival, Pathfinder, but ye've one no langer in me. Ye've my hearty wishes for yer' success with Mabel, and were the honest serjeant likely to survive, ye might rely on my good word with him, too, for a certainty."

"I feel your friendship, Quarter Master, I feel your friendship, though I have no great need of any favor with Sarjeant Dunham, who has long been my friend. I believe we may look upon the matter to be as sartain as most things in war time, for, Mabel and her father consenting, the whole 55th, could'n't very well put a stop to it. Ah's! me; the poor father will scarcely live to see what his heart has so long been set upon!"

"But he'll have the consolation of knowing it will come to pass, in dying. Oh! it's a great relief, Pathfinder, for the parting spirit to feel certain that the beloved ones left behind, will be well provided for, after its departure. All the Mistress Muirs have duly expressed that sentiment, with their dying breaths."

"All your wives, Quarter Master, have been likely to feel this consolation?"

"Out upon ye, man—I'd no thought ye such a wag! Well—well—pleasant words make no heart-burnings between auld fri'nds. If I cannot espouse Mabel, ye'll no object to my esteeming her, and speaking well of her, and of yoursal' too, on all suitable occasions, and in all companies. But, Pathfinder, ye'll easily understan' that a poor deevil, who loses such a bride, will probably stand in need of some consolation?"

"Quite likely—quite likely, Quarter Master," returned the simple-minded guide; "I know the loss of Mabel would be heavy to be borne, by myself. It may bear hard on your feelings to see us married, but the death of the sarjeant will be likely to put it off, and you'll have time to think more manfully of it, you will."

"I'll bear up against it—yes, I'll bear up against it, though my heart strings crack, and ye might help me, man, by giving me something to do. Ye'll understand that this expedition has been of a varry peculiar nature, for, here am I, bearing the King's commission, just a volunteer, as it might be; while a mere orderly has had the command. I've submitted for various reasons, though my blood has boiled to be in authority, while ye war' battling for the honor of the country, and His Majesty's rights—"

"Quarter Master," interrupted the guide, "you fell so early into the inimy's hands, that your conscience ought to be easily satisfied on that score, so, take my advice, and say nothing about it."

"That's just my opinion, Pathfinder; we'll all say nothing about it. Serjeant Dunham is *hors de combat*—"

"Anan!" said the guide.

"Why the serjeant can command no longer, and it will hardly do to leave a corporal at the head of a victorious party, like this, for the flower that will bloom in a garden will die on the heath, and I was just thinking I would claim the authority that belongs to one who holds a lieutenant's commission. As for the men, they'll no dare to raise any objactions, and as for yoursal', my dear friend, now that ye've so much honor, and Mabel, and the consciousness of having done yer' duty, which is more precious than all, I expect to find an ally, rather than one to oppose the plan."

"As for commanding the soldiers of the 55th, lieutenant, it is your right, I suppose, and no one here, will be likely to gainsay it; though you've been a prisoner of war, and there are men who might stand out ag'in giving up their authority to a prisoner released by their own deeds. Still, no one here, will be likely to say any thing hostyle to your wishes."

"That's just it, Pathfinder; and when I come to draw up the report of our success against the boats, and the defence of the block, together with the general operations, including the capitulation, ye'll no find any omission of your claims and merits."

"Tut, for my claims and merits, Quarter Master! Lundie knows what I am, in the forest, and what I am in the fort, and the general knows better than he. No fear of me; tell your own story, only taking care to do justice by Mabel's father, who, in one sense, is the commanding officer, at this very moment."

Muir expressed his entire satisfaction with this arrangement, as well as his determination to do justice by all, when the two went to the group that was assembled round the fire. Here the Quarter Master began, for the first time since leaving Oswego, to assume some of the authority that might properly be supposed to belong to his rank. Taking the remaining corporal aside, he distinctly told that functionary, that he must in future be regarded as one holding the King's commission, and directed him to acquaint his subordinates with the new state of things. This change in the dynasty was effected without any of the usual symptoms of a revolution, for as all well understood the Lieutenant's legal claims to command, no one felt disposed to dispute his orders. For reasons best known to themselves, Lundie and the Quarter Master had, originally, made a different disposition, and now for reasons of his own, the latter had seen fit to change it. This was reasoning enough for soldiers, though the hurt received by Serjeant Dunham would have sufficiently explained the circumstance, had any explanation been required.

All this time Capt. Sanglier was looking after his own breakfast, with the resignation of a philosopher, the coolness of a veteran, the ingenuity and science of a Frenchman and the voracity of an ostrich. This person had now been in the colony some thirty years, having left France in some such situation in his own army, as Muir filled in the 55th. An iron constitution, perfect obduracy of feeling, a certain address well suited to manage savages, and an indomitable courage, had early pointed him out to the Commander in chief, as a suitable agent to be employed in directing the military operations of his Indian allies. In this capacity, then, he had risen to the titular rank of captain, and, with his promotion, had acquired a portion of the habits and opinions of his associates, with a facility and an adaptation of self that are thought, in this part of the world, to be peculiar to his countrymen. He had often led parties of the Iroquois in their predatory expeditions, and his conduct on such occasions, exhibited the contradictory results of both alleviating the misery produced by this species of warfare, and of augmenting it, by the broader views and greater resources of civilization. In other words, he planned enterprises that, in their importance and consequences much exceeded the usual policy of the Indians, and then stepped in to lessen some of the evils of his own creating. In short, he was an adventurer whom circumstances had thrown into a situation, where the callous qualities of men of his class, might readily show themselves, for good or for evil, and he was not of a character to baffle fortune, by any ill timed squeamishness on the score of early impressions, or to trifle with her liberality, by unnecessarily provoking her frowns through wanton cruelty. Still, as his name was unavoidably connected with many of the excesses committed by his parties, he was generally considered in the American Provinces, a wretch who delighted in bloodshed, and who found his greatest happiness in tormenting the helpless and the innocent, and the name of Sanglier, which was a soubriquet of his own adopting, or of Flint Heart, as he was usually termed on the borders, had got to be as terrible to the women and children of that part of the country, as those of Butler and Brandt became at a later day.

The meeting between Pathfinder and Sanglier bore some resemblance to that celebrated interview between Wellington and Blucher, which has been so often and graphically told. It took place at the fire, and the parties stood earnestly regarding each other for more than a minute without speaking. Each felt that in the other, he saw a formidable foe, and each felt, while he ought to treat the other with the manly liberality due to a warrior, that there was little in common between them, in the way of character, as well as of interests. One served for money and preferment, the other because his life had been cast in the wilderness, and the land of his birth needed his arm and experience. The desire of rising above his present situation, never disturbed the tranquillity of Pathfinder, nor had he ever known an ambitious thought, as ambition usually betrays itself, until he became acquainted with Mabel. Since then, indeed, distrust of himself, reverence for her, and the wish to place her in a situation above that which he then filled, had caused him some uneasy moments, but the directness and simplicity of his character had early afforded the required relief, and he soon came to feel, that the woman who would not hesitate to accept him for her husband, would not scruple to share his fortunes, however humble. He respected Sanglier as a brave warrior, and he had far too much of that liberality which is the result of practical knowledge, to believe half of what he had heard to his prejudice; for the most bigotted and illiberal on every subject, are usually those who know nothing about it; but he could not approve of his selfishness, cold blooded calculations, and least of all, the manner in which he forgot his "white gifts" to adopt those that were purely "red." On the other hand, Pathfinder was a riddle to Capt. Sanglier. The latter could not comprehend the other's motives. He had often heard of his disinterestedness, justice and truth; and, in several instances, they had led him into grave errors, on that principle by which a frank and open-mouthed diplomatist is said to keep his secrets better than one that is close-mouthed and wily.

After the two heroes had gazed at each other, in the manner mentioned, Mons. Sanglier touched his cap, for the rudeness of a border life had not entirely destroyed the courtesy of manner he had acquired in youth, nor extinguished that appearance of *bonhommie* which seems inbred in a Frenchman.

"Monsieur le Pathfindair," he said, with a very decided accent, though with a friendly smile. "*Un militaire* honour *le courage, et la loyauté*. You speak Iroquois?"

"Ay, I understand the language of the riptyles, and can get along with it, if there's occasion," returned the literal and truth-telling guide; "but it's neither a tongue, nor a tribe to my taste. Wherever you find the Mingo blood, in my opinion, Master Flinty-heart, you find a knave. Well, I've seen you afore, though it was in battle, and I must say, it was always in the van. You must know most of our bullets by sight?"

"Nevvair, sair, your own. *Une balle* from your honorable hand, be sairtaine deat'. You kill my best warrior, on some island."

"That may be—that may be—though, I dare say, if the truth was known, they would turn out to be great rascals. No offence to you, Master Flinty-heart, but you keep desperate evil company."

"Yes, sair—" returned the Frenchman, who, bent on saying that which was courteous himself, and comprehending with difficulty, was disposed to think he received a compliment—"you, too good. But, *un brave* always *comme ça*. What that mean—ha!—What that *jeune homme* do?"

The hand and eye of Capt. Sanglier directed the look of Pathfinder to the opposite side of the fire, where Jasper, just at that moment, had been rudely seized by two of the soldiers, who were binding his arms, under the directions of Muir.

"What does that mean, indeed," cried the guide, stepping forward, and shoving the two subordinates aside with a power of muscle that would not be denied. "Who has the heart to do this to Jasper Eau douce; and who the boldness to do it afore my eyes?"

"It is by my orders, Pathfinder," answered the Quarter Master, "and I command it on my own responsibility. Ye'll no tak' on yourself, to dispute the legality of orders given by one who bears the King's commission, to the King's soldiers!"

"I'd dispute the King's words, if they came from the King's own mouth, did he say that Jasper desarves this! Has not the lad just saved all our scalps?—Taken us from defeat, and given us victory? No—no—Lieutenant; if this is the first use that you make of your authority, I for one, will not respect it."

"This savors a little of insubordination," answered Muir; "but we can bear much from Pathfinder. It is true, this Jasper has *seemed* to serve us, in this affair, but we ought not to overlook past transactions. Did not Major Duncan himself denounce him to Serjeant Dunham before we left the post; have we not seen sufficient with our own eyes, to make sure of having been betrayed, and is it not natural and almost necessary to believe that this young man has been the traitor. Ah! Pathfinder, ye'll no be makin' yourself a great statesman or a great captain, if ye put too much faith in appearances. Lord Bless me!—Lord Bless me!—If I do not believe, could the truth be come at, as you often say yourself, Pathfinder, that hypocrisy is a more common vice than even envy, and that's the bane o' human nature!"

Capt. Sanglier shrugged his shoulders; then he looked earnestly from Jasper towards the Quarter Master and from the Quarter Master towards Jasper.

"I care not for your envy, or your hypocrisy or even for your human natur'," returned Pathfinder—"Jasper Eau douce is my friend—Jasper Eau douce is a brave lad, and an honest lad, and a loyal lad, and no man of the 55th shall lay hands on him, short of Lundie's own orders, while I'm in the way to prevent it. You may have authority over your soldiers, but you have none over Jasper or me, Master Muir."

"Bon—" ejaculated Sanglier, the sound partaking equally of the energies of the throat and of the nose.

"Will ye no hearken to reason, Pathfinder. Ye'll no be forgetting our suspicions and judgments, and here is another circumstance to augment and aggravate them all. Ye can see this little bit of bunting—well where should it be found, but by Mabel Dunham on the branch of a tree, on this very island, just an hour or so, before the attack of the enemy, and if ye'll be at the trouble to look at the fly of the Scud's ensign ye'll just see, that the cloth has been cut from out it. Circumstantial evidence was never stronger."

"Ma foi——c'est un peu fort, ceci—" growled Sanglier, between his teeth.

"Talk to me of no ensigns, and signals, when I know the heart—" continued Pathfinder. "Jasper has the gift of honesty, and it is too rare a gift to be trifled with, like a Mingo's conscience. No—no—off hands, or we shall see, which can make the stoutest battle, you and your men of the 55th, or the Sarpent, here, and Killdeer, with Jasper and his crew. You overrate your force, Lieutenant Muir, as much as you underrate Eau douce's truth."

"Très bon!"

"Well, if I must speak plainly, Pathfinder, I e'en must. Capt. Sanglier, here, and Arrowhead, this brave Tuscarora, have both informed me that this unfortunate boy is the traitor. After such testimony, you can no longer refuse my right to arrest him, as well as the necessity of the act."

"Scélérat—" muttered the Frenchman.

"Capt. Sanglier is a brave soldier, and will not gainsay the conduct of an honest sailor," put in Jasper. "Is there any traitor, here, Capt. Flinty-heart?"

"Ay," added Muir, "lat him speak out, then, since ye wish it, unhappy youth, that the truth may be known. I only hope that ye may escape the last punishment when a court will be sitting on yer misdeeds. How is it, Captain; do ye, or do ye not see a traitor amang us?"

"Oui—yes, sair—*bien sûr."*

"Too much lie—" said Arrowhead, in a voice of thunder, striking the breast of Muir, with the back of his own hand, in a sort of ungovernable gesture. "Where, my warriors?—Where Yengeese scalp? Too much lie."

Muir wanted not for personal courage, nor for a certain sense of personal honor. The violence which had been intended only for a gesture, he mistook for a blow, for conscience was suddenly aroused within him, and he stepped back a pace, extending a hand towards a gun. His face was livid with rage, and his countenance expressed the fell intent of his heart. But Arrowhead was too quick for him. With a wild glare of the eye, the Tuscarora looked about him, then thrusting a hand beneath his own girdle, drew forth a concealed knife, and in the twinkling of an eye buried it in the body of the Quarter Master to the handle. As the latter fell at his feet, gazing into his face with the vacant stare of one surprised by death, Sanglier took a pinch of snuff, and said in a calm voice—

"Voilà l'affaire finie—mais—" shrugging his shoulders, *"ce n'est qu'un scélérat de moins."*

The act was too sudden to be prevented, and when Arrowhead, uttering a yell, bounded into the bushes, the white men were too confounded to follow. Chingachgook, however, was more collected, and the bushes had scarcely closed on the passing body of the Tuscarora, than they were again opened by that of the Delaware, in full pursuit.

Jasper Western spoke French fluently, and the words and manner of Sanglier struck him.

"Speak, Monsieur," he cried in English—"*am* I the traitor?"

"Le voilà—" answered the cool Frenchman. "Là-dat is our *espion*—our *agent*—our friend—*Ma foi—c'etait un grand scélérat! Voici—*"

While speaking, Sanglier bent over the dead body, and thrust a hand into a pocket of the Quarter Master, out of which he drew a purse. Emptying the contents on the ground, several double Louis rolled towards the soldiers, who were not slow in picking them up. Casting the purse from him, in contempt, the soldier of fortune turned towards the soup he had been preparing with so much care, and finding it to his liking, he began to break his fast, with an air of indifference that the most stoical Indian warrior might have envied.

Chapter XXVII

"The only amaranthine flower on Earth
Is virtue; th' only lasting treasure, Truth."
Cowper, *The Task*, III.268–69.

THE READER must imagine some of the occurrences, that followed the sudden death of Muir. While his body was in the hands of his soldiers, who laid it decently aside, and covered it with a great coat, Chingachgook silently resumed his place at the fire, and both Sanglier and Pathfinder remarked that he carried a fresh and bleeding scalp at his girdle. No one asked any questions, and the former, although perfectly satisfied that Arrowhead had fallen, manifested neither curiosity nor feeling. He continued calmly eating his soup, as if the meal had been tranquil as usual. There was something of pride, and of an assumed indifference to fate, imitated from the Indians, in all this, but there was more that really resulted from practice, habitual self-command, and constitutional hardihood. With Pathfinder, the case was a little different in feeling, though much the same in appearance. He disliked Muir, whose smooth-tongued courtesy was little in accordance with his own frank and ingenuous nature, but he had been shocked at his unexpected and violent death, though accustomed to similar scenes, and he had been surprised at the exposure of his treachery. With a view to ascertain the extent of the latter, as soon as the body was removed, he began to question the captain on the subject. The latter having no particular motive for secrecy, now that his agent was dead, in the course of the breakfast revealed the following circumstances, which will serve to clear up some of the minor incidents of our tale.

Soon after the 55th appeared on the frontiers, Muir had volunteered his services to the enemy. In making his offers, he boasted of his intimacy with Lundie, and of the means it afforded of furnishing more accurate and important information than usual. His terms had been accepted, and Mons. Sanglier, had several interviews with him, in the vicinity of the fort at Oswego, and had actually passed one entire night secreted in the garrison. Arrowhead, however, was the usual channel of communication, and the anonymous letter to Major Duncan had been originally written by Muir, transmitted to Frontenac, copied and sent back by the Tuscarora, who was returning from that errand when captured by the Scud. It is scarcely necessary to add, that Jasper was to be sacrificed, in order to conceal the Quarter Master's treason, and that the position of the island had been betrayed to the enemy by the latter. An extraordinary compensation, that which was found in his purse, had induced him to accompany the party under Serjeant Dunham, in order to give the signals that were to bring on the attack. The disposition of Muir towards the sex was a natural weakness, and he would have married Mabel, or any one else who would accept his hand, but his admiration of her was in a great degree feigned, in order that he might have an excuse for accompanying the party, without sharing in the responsibility of its defeat, or incurring the risk of having no other strong and seemingly sufficient motive. Much of this was known to Capt. Sanglier, particularly the part in connection with Mabel, and he did not fail to let his auditors into the whole secret, frequently laughing, in a sarcastic manner, as he revealed the different expedients of the luckless Quarter Master.

"*Touchez-la,*" said the cold blooded partisan, holding out his sinewy hand to Pathfinder, when he ended his explanations—"You be *honnête*, and dat is *beaucoup*. We tak' de spy, as we tak' *la médicine*, for de good, mais, *je les déteste! Touchez-la.*"

"I'll shake your hand, captain, I will, for you're a lawful and nat'ral inimy," returned Pathfinder, "and a manful one; but the body of the Quarter Master shall never disgrace English ground. I did intend to carry it back to Lundie, that he might play his bagpipes over it, but, now, it shall lie here, on the spot where he acted his villainy, and have his own treason for a headstone. Capt. Flinty-heart, I suppose this consorting with traitors is a part of a soldier's regular business, but, I tell you honestly, it is not to my liking, and I'd rather it should be you, than I, who had this affair on his conscience. What an awful sinner!—to plot, right and left, ag'in country, friends and the Lord!—Jasper, boy, a word with you, aside, for a single minute."

Pathfinder now led the young man apart, and squeezing his hand, with the tears in his own eyes, he continued—

"You know me, Eau douce, and I know you," he said, "and this news has not changed my opinion of you, in any manner. I never believed their tales, though it looked solemn at one minute, I will own; yes, it did look solemn; and it made me feel solemn, too. I never suspected you for a minute, for I know your gifts do'n't lie that-a-way, but, I must own I did n't suspect the Quarter Master, neither."

"And he holding His Majesty's commission, Pathfinder!"

"It isn't so much that, Jasper Western; it isn't so much that. He held a commission from God to act right, and to deal fairly with his fellow creatur's, and he has failed awfully in his duty!"

"To think of his pretending love for one like Mabel, too, when he felt none!"

"That was bad, sartainly; the fellow must have had Mingo blood in his veins. The man that deals unfairly by a woman can be but a mongrel, lad, for the Lord has made them helpless on purpose that we may gain their love by kindness and sarvice. Here is the sarjeant, poor man, on his dying bed; he has given me his daughter for a wife, and Mabel, dear girl, she has consented to it, and it makes me feel that I have two welfares to look after, two natur's to care for, and two hearts to gladden. Ah's! me, Jasper; I sometimes feel that I'm not good enough for that sweet child!"

Eau douce had nearly gasped for breath, when he first heard this intelligence, and, though he succeeded in suppressing any other outward sign of agitation, his cheek was blanched nearly to the paleness of death. Still, he found means to answer, not only with firmness, but with energy—

"Say not so, Pathfinder; you are good enough for a Queen."

"Ay, ay, boy, according to your idees of my goodness; that is to say—I can kill a deer, or even a Mingo at need, with any man on the lines; or I can follow a forest path with as true an eye, or, read the stars, when others do not understand them. No doubt, no doubt, Mabel will have venison enough, and fish enough, and pigeons enough; but will she have knowledge enough, and will she have idees enough, and pleasant conversation enough, when life comes to drag a little, and each of us begins to pass for our true valu!"

"If you pass for your value, Pathfinder, the greatest lady in the land, would be happy with you. On that head, you have no reason to feel afraid."

"Now, Jasper, I dare to say *you* think so—nay, I *know* you do; for it is nat'ral and according to friendship, for people to look over favorably at them they love. Yes, yes; if I had to marry you, boy, I should give myself no consarn about being well looked upon, for you have always shown a disposition to see me and all I do with friendly eyes. But a young gal, after all, must wish to marry a man that is nearer to her own age and fancies, than to have one old enough to be her father, and rude enough to frighten her. I wonder, Jasper, that Mabel never took a fancy to you, now, rather than setting her mind on me!"

"Take a fancy to me, Pathfinder!" returned the young man, endeavoring to clear his voice without betraying himself—"What is there about me, to please such a girl as Mabel Dunham? I have all that you find fault with in yourself, with none of that excellence that makes even the generals respect you."

"Well—well—it's all chance, say what we will about it. Here have I journeyed and guided through the woods, female after female, and consorted with them in the garrisons, and never have I ever felt an inclination for any, until I saw Mabel Dunham. It's true the poor sarjeant first set me to thinking about his daughter, but after we got a little acquainted like, I'd no need of being spoken to, to think of her night and day. I'm tough, Jasper; yes, I'm very tough; and I'm risolute, enough, as you all know; and yet I do think it would quite break me down, now, to lose Mabel Dunham!"

"We will talk no more of it, Pathfinder," said Jasper, returning his friend's squeeze of the hand, and moving back towards the fire, though slowly and in the manner of one who cared little where he went; "we will talk no more of it. You are worthy of Mabel, and Mabel is worthy of you—you like Mabel, and Mabel likes you—her father has chosen you for her husband, and no one has a right to interfere. As for the Quarter Master, his feigning love for Mabel, is worse even than his treason to the king!"

By this time, they were so near the fire, that it was necessary to change the conversation. Luckily, at that instant, Cap, who had been in the block in company with his dying brother-in-law, and who knew nothing of what had passed since the capitulation, now appeared, walking with a meditative and melancholy air towards the group. Much of that hearty dogmatism, that imparted even to his ordinary air and demeanor, an appearance of something like contempt for all around him, had disappeared, and he seemed thoughtful, if not meek.

"This death, gentlemen," he said, when he had got sufficiently near, "is a melancholy business, make the best of it. Now, here is Serjeant Dunham, a very good soldier, I make no question, about to slip his cable, and yet he holds on to the better end of it, as if he was determined it should never run out of the hawse-hole, and all because he loves his daughter, it seems to me. For my part, when a friend is really under the necessity of making a long journey, I always wish him well and happily off."

"You would n't kill the sarjeant afore his time," Pathfinder reproachfully answered. "Life is sweet, even to the aged, and, for that matter, I've known some that seemed to set more store by it, when it got to be of the least valu."

Nothing had been farther from Cap's real thoughts, than the wish to hasten his brother-in-law's end. He had found himself embarrassed with the duties of smoothing a death-bed, and all he had meant was to express a sincere desire that the serjeant were happily rid of doubt and suffering. A little shocked, therefore, at the interpretation that had been put on his words, he rejoined with some of the asperity of the man, though rebuked by a consciousness of not having done his own wishes justice.

"You are too old and too sensible a person, Pathfinder," he said, "to fetch a man up with a surge, when he is paying out his ideas in distress, as it might be. Serjeant Dunham is both my brother-in-law, and my friend—that is to say, as intimate a friend, as a soldier well can be with a sea-faring man, and I respect and honor him accordingly. I make no doubt, moreover, that he has lived such a life as becomes a man, and there can be no great harm, after all, in wishing any one well berthed in heaven. Well! We are mortal the best of us, that, you'll not deny; and it ought to be a lesson not to feel pride in our strength and beauty. Where is the Quarter Master, Pathfinder?—It is proper he should come and have a parting word with the poor serjeant, who is only going a little before us."

"You have spoken more truth, Master Cap, than you've been knowing to, all this time; in which there is no great wonder, howsever, mankind as often telling biting truths, when they least mean it, as at any other time. You might have gone farther, notwithstanding, and said that we are mortal, the *worst* of us, which is quite as true, and a good deal more wholesome than saying that we are mortal, the *best* of us. As for the Quarter Master's coming to speak a parting word to the sarjeant, it is quite out of the question, seeing that he has gone ahead, and that too with little parting notice to himself, or any one else."

"You are not quite as clear as common, in your language, Pathfinder. I know that we ought all to have solemn thoughts, on these occasions, but I see no use in speaking in parables."

"If my words are not plain, the idee is. In short, Master Cap, while Sarjeant Dunham has been preparing himself for a long journey, like a conscientious and honest man as he is, deliberately and slowly, the Quarter Master has started, in a hurry, afore him; and, although it is a matter on which it does not become me to be very positive, I give it as my opinion that they travel such different roads, that they will never meet."

"Explain yourself, my friend," said the bewildered seaman, looking around him in search of Muir, whose absence began to excite his distrust. "I see nothing of the Quarter Master, but I think him too much of a man to run away, now that the victory is gained. If the fight were ahead, instead of in our wake, the case would be altered."

"There lies all that is left of him, beneath that great-coat," returned the guide, who then briefly related the manner of the Lieutenant's death. "The Tuscarora was as venomous in his blow, as a rattler, though he failed to give the warning," continued Pathfinder. "I've seen many a desperate fight, and several of these sudden outbreaks of savage temper, but never, before, did I see a human soul quit the body more unexpectedly, or at a worse moment, for the hopes of the dying man. His breath was stopped with the lie on his lips, and the spirit might be said to have passed away in the very ardor of wickedness!"

Cap listened with a gaping mouth, and he gave two or three violent hems, as the other concluded, like one who distrusted his own respiration.

"This is an uncertain and uncomfortable life of yours, Master Pathfinder, what between the fresh water and the savages," he said, "and the sooner I get quit of it, the higher will be my opinion of myself. Now you mention it, I will say that the man ran for that berth in the rocks, when the enemy first bore down upon us, with a sort of instinct that I thought surprising in an officer, but I was in too great a hurry to follow, to log the whole matter accurately. God bless me—God bless me! A traitor do you say, and ready to sell his country, and to a bloody Frenchman too?"

"To sell any thing—country, soul, body, Mabel and all our scalps; and no ways particular, I'll engage, as to the purchaser. The countrymen of Capt. Flinty-heart, here, were the paymasters this time."

"Just like 'em; ever ready to buy, when they can't thrash, and to run when they can do neither."

Mons. Sanglier lifted his cap with ironical gravity, and acknowledged the compliment with an expression of polite contempt that was altogether lost on its insensible subject. But Pathfinder had too much native courtesy, and was far too just-minded, to allow the attack to go unnoticed—

"Well—well—" he interposed, "to my mind there is no great difference atween an Englishman and a Frenchman, a'ter all. They talk different tongues, and live under different kings I will allow, but both are human, and feel like human beings, when there is occasion for it. If a Frenchman is sometimes skeary, so is an Englishman; and as for running away, why a man will now and then do it, as well as a horse, let him come of what people he may."

Capt. Flinty-heart, as Pathfinder called him, made another obeisance, but this time the smile was friendly, and not ironical, for he felt that the intention was good, whatever might have been the mode of expressing it. Too philosophical, however, to heed what a man like Cap might say, or think, he finished his breakfast without allowing his attention to be again diverted from that important pursuit.

"My business, here, was principally with the Quarter Master," Cap continued, as soon as he had done regarding the Frenchman's pantomine; "the serjeant must be near his end, and I have thought he might wish to say something to his successor in authority, before he finally departed. It is too late, it would seem, and, as you say, Pathfinder, the Lieutenant has truly gone before."

"That he has, though on a different path. As for authority, I suppose the corporal has now a right to command what's left of the 55th, though a small and worried, not to say frightened, party it is. But, if any thing needs to be done, the chances are greatly in favor of my being called on to do it. I suppose, howsever, we have only to bury our dead, and set fire to the block and the huts, for they stand in the inimy's territory, by position if not by law, and must not be left for their convenience. Our using them again, is out of the question, for now the Frenchers know where the island is to be found, it would be like thrusting the hand into a wolf trap, with our eyes wide open. This part of the work, the Sarpent and I will see to, for we are as practysed in retreats, as in advances."

"All that is very well, my good friend; and now for my poor brother-in-law: though he is a soldier, we cannot let him slip, without a word of consolation, and a leave-taking, in my judgment. This has been an unlucky affair, on every tack, though I suppose it is what one had a right to expect, considering the state of the times, and the nature of the navigation. We must make the best of it, and try to help the worthy man to unmoor, without straining his messengers. Death is a circumstance, after all, Master Pathfinder, and one of a very general character, too, seeing that we must all submit to it, sooner or later."

"You say truth, you say truth, and for that reason I hold it to be wise to be always ready. I've often thought, Salt-water, that he is happiest who has the least to leave behind him, when the summons comes. Now, here am I, a hunter, and a scout, and a guide, although I do not own a foot of land on 'arth, yet do I enjoy and possess more than the great Albany Patroon. With the heavens over my head, to keep me in mind of the last great hunt, and the dried leaves beneath my feet, I tramp over the ground as freely as if I was its lord and owner, and what more need heart desire? I do not say, that I love nothing, that belongs to 'arth; for I do, though not much, unless it might be Mabel Dunham, that I can't carry with me. I have some pups, at the higher fort, that I valu, considerable, though they are too noisy for warfare, and so we are compelled to live separate for a while; and, then, I think it would grieve me to part with Killdeer, but I see no reason why we should not be buried in the same grave, for we are as near as can be of the same length, six feet to a hair's breadth; but, 'bating these, and a pipe that the Sarpent gave me, and a few tokens received from travellers, all of which might be put in a pouch, and laid under my head, when the order comes to march, I shall be ready at a minute's warning; and, let me tell you, Master Cap, that's what I call a circumstance, too!"

" 'Tis just so with me," answered the sailor, as the two walked towards the block, too much occupied with their respective morality to remember, at the moment, the melancholy errand they were on—"that's just my way, of feeling and reasoning. How often have I felt, when near shipwreck, the relief of not owning the craft! 'If she goes,' I have said to myself, 'why my life goes with her, but not my property, and there's great comfort in that.' I've discovered, in the course of boxing about the world, from the Horn to Cape North, not to speak of this run on a bit of fresh water, that if a man has a few dollars, and puts them in a chest, under lock and key, he is pretty certain to fasten up his heart in the same till, and so I carry pretty much all I own, in a belt round my body, in order, as I say, to keep the vitals in the right place. D——e,

Pathfinder, if I think a man without a heart, any better than a fish with a hole in his air bag."

"I don't know how that may be, Master Cap, but a man without a conscience is but a poor creatur', take my word for it, as any one will discover who has to do with a Mingo. I trouble myself but little with dollars, or half-joes, for these are the favoryte coin in this part of the world, but I can easily believe, by what I've seen of mankind, that if a man *has* a chest filled with either, he may be said to lock up his heart in the same box. I once hunted for two summers, during the last peace, and I collected so much peltry that I found my right feelings giving way to a craving after property, and if I have consarn in marrying Mabel, it is that I may get to love such things too well, in order to make her comfortable."

"You're a philosopher, that's clear, Pathfinder, and I don't know but you're a christian!"

"I should be out of humour with the man that gainsayed the last, Master Cap. I have not been christianized by the Moravians, like so many of the Delawares, it is true, but I hold to Christianity and white gifts. With me, it is as oncreditable for a white man not to be a Christian, as it is for a red skin not to believe in his happy hunting grounds; indeed, after allowing for difference in traditions, and some variations about the manner in which the spirit will be occupied after death, I hold that a good Delaware is a good Christian, though he never saw a Moravian, and a good Christian a good Delaware, so far as natur' is consarned. The Sarpent and I talk these matters over, often, for he has a hankerin' after christianity—"

"The d——l he has!" interrupted Cap. "And what does he intend to do in a church, with all the scalps he takes."

"Don't run away with a false idee, friend Cap; don't run away, with a false idee. These things are only skin deep and all depend on edication and nat'ral gifts. Look around you, at mankind, and tell me why you see a red warrior here, a black one there, and white armies in another place? All this, and a great deal more of the same kind, that I could point out, has been ordered for some 'special purpose, and it is not for us to fly in the face of facts, and deny their truth. No—

no—each colour has its gifts, and its laws, and its traditions; and one is not to condemn another because he does not exactly comprehend it."

"You must have read a great deal, Pathfinder, to see things as clear as this," returned Cap, who was not a little mystified by his companion's simple creed—"It's all as plain as day to me, now, though I must say I never fell in with these opinions before. What denomination do you belong to, my friend?"

"Anan?"

"What sect do you hold out for?—What particular church do you fetch up in?"

"Look about you, and judge for yourself. I'm in church now; I eat in church, drink in church, sleep in church. The 'arth is the temple of the Lord, and I wait on him hourly, daily, without ceasing, I humbly hope. No—no—I'll not deny my blood and colour, but am Christian born, and shall die in the same faith. The Moravians tried me hard, and one of the King's chaplains has had his say, too, though that's a class no ways strenuous on such matters, and a missionary sent from Rome talked much with me, as I guided him through the forest, during the last peace, but I've had one answer for them all—I'm a christian, already, and want to be neither Moravian, nor Churchman, nor Papist. No—no—I'll not deny my birth and blood."

"I think a word from you might lighten the serjeant over the shoals of death, Master Pathfinder. He has no one with him but poor Mabel, and she, you know, besides being his daughter, is but a girl and a child after all."

"Mabel is feeble in body, friend Cap, but in matters of this natur', I doubt if she may not be stronger than most men. But Sarjeant Dunham is my friend, and he is your brother-in-law, so, now the press of fighting and maintaining our rights is over, it is fitting we should both go and witness his departure. I've stood by many a dying man, Master Cap," continued Pathfinder, who had a besetting propensity to enlarge on his experience, stopping and holding his companion by a button—"I've stood by many a dying man's side, and seen his last gasp, and heard his last breath, for when the hurry and tumult of the battle is over, it is good to bethink us of the misfortunate, and it is remarkable to witness how differently human natur' feels at such solemn moments. Some go their way, as stupid and ignorant, as if God had never given them reason and an accountable state, while others quit us rejoicing, like men who leave heavy burthens behind them. I think that the mind sees clearly at such moments, my friend, and that past deeds stand thick before the recollection."

"I'll engage they do, Pathfinder. I have witnessed something of this myself, and hope I'm the better man for it. I remember once that I thought my own time had come, and the log was overhauled with a diligence I did not think myself capable of, until that moment. I've not been a very great sinner, friend Pathfinder; that is to say, never on a large scale; though, I dare say, if the truth were spoken, a considerable amount of small matters might be raked up against me, as well as against another man; but, then I've never committed piracy, nor high treason, nor arson, nor any of them sort of things. As to smuggling, and the like of that, why I'm a seafaring man, and I suppose all callings have their weak spots. I dare say, your trade is not altogether without blemish, honorable and useful as it seems to be?"

"Many of the scouts and guides are desperate knaves, and like the Quarter Master, here, some of them take pay of both sides. I hope I'm not one of them, though all occupations lead to temptation. Thrice have I been sorely tried in my life, and once yielded a little, though I hope it was not in a matter to disturb a man's conscience, in his last moments. The first time was, when I found in the woods, a pack of skins that I knowed belonged to a Frencher who was hunting on our side of the lines, where he had no business to be; twenty six as handsome beavers, as ever gladdened human eyes! Well, that was a tight temptation, for I thought the law would have been almost with me, although it was in peace times. But, then I remembered that such laws was'n't made for us hunters, and bethought me that the poor man might have built great expectations for the next winter, on the sale of his skins, and I left them where they lay. Most of our people said I did wrong, but the manner in which I slept that night, convinced me that I had done right. The next trial, was when I found the rifle that is sartainly the only one in this part of the world that can be calculated on as surely as Killdeer, and knowed that by taking it, or even hiding it, I might at once rise to be the first shot in all these parts. I was then young, and by no means as expart as I have since got to be, and youth is ambitious and striving; but, God be praised! I mastered that feeling, and, friend Cap, what is almost as good, I mastered my rival in as fair a shooting match as was ever witnessed in a garrison; he with his piece, and I with Killdeer, and before the General, in person, too!" Here Pathfinder stopped to laugh, his triumph still glittering in his eyes, and glowing on his sunburnt and browned cheek.—"Well, the next conflict with the devil, was the hardest of them all, and that was when I came suddenly, upon a camp of six Mingos, asleep in the woods, with their guns and horns piled in a way that enabled me to get possession of them without waking a miscreant of them all. What an opportunity that would have been for the Sarpent, who would have despatched them one after another with his knife, and had their six scalps at his girdle, in about the time it takes me to tell you the story. Oh! He's a valiant warrior, that Chingachgook, and as honest as he's brave, and as good as he's honest."

"And what may *you* have done in this matter, Master Pathfinder," demanded Cap, who began to be interested in the result—"It seems to me, you had made either a very lucky, or a very unlucky landfall."

" 'Twas lucky, and 'twas unlucky, if you can understand that. 'Twas unlucky, for it proved a desperate trial, and yet 'twas lucky, all things considered, in the ind. I did not touch a hair of their heads, for a white man has no nat'ral gifts to take scalps, nor did I even make sure of one of their rifles. I distrusted myself, knowing that a Mingo is no favorite, in my own eyes."

"As for the scalps, I think you were right enough, my worthy friend, but as for the armament and the stores, they would have been condemned by any prize-court in Christendom!"

"That they would—that they would, but then the Mingos would have gone clear, seeing that a white man can no more attack an unarmed, than a sleeping, inimy. No—no—I did myself, and my colour, and my religion, too, greater justice.

I waited 'till their nap was over, and they well on their war-path ag'in, and by ambushing them here, and flanking them, there, I peppered the blackguards so intrinsically, like," Pathfinder occasionally caught a fine word from his associates, and used it a little vaguely—"that only one ever got back to his village; and he came into his wigwam limping. Luckily as it turned out, the Great Delaware had only halted to jerk some venison, and was following on my trail, and when he got up, he had five of the scoundrels' scalps hanging where they ought to be; so you see nothing was lost by doing right, either in the way of honor or in that of profit."

Cap grunted an assent, though the distinctions in his companion's morality, it must be owned, were not exactly clear to his understanding. The two had occasionally moved towards the block, as they conversed, and then stopped again, as some matter of more interest than common, brought them to a halt. They were now so near the building, however, that neither thought of pursuing the subject any further, but each prepared himself for the final scene with Serjeant Dunham.

Chapter XXVIII

"Thou barraine ground, whom winter's wrath hath wasted,
Art made a mirror to behold my plight:
Whilome thy fresh spring flowr'd; and after hasted
Thy summer prowde, with daffodillies dight;
And now is come thy winter's stormy state,
Thy mantle mar'd wherein thou maskedst late."

Spenser, *The Shepheardes Calender,*
"Januarye," ll. 19–24.

ALTHOUGH THE SOLDIER may regard danger, and even death, with indifference, in the tumult of battle, when the passage of the soul is delayed to moments of tranquility and reflection, the change commonly brings with it the usual train of solemn reflection; of regrets for the past, and of doubts and anticipations for the future. Many a man has died with an heroic expression on his lips, but with heaviness and distrust at his heart; for, whatever may be the varieties of our religious creeds—let us depend on the mediation of Christ, the dogmas of Mahomet, or the elaborated allegories of the East, there is a conviction common to all men, that death is but the stepping-stone between this and a more elevated state of being. Serjeant Dunham was a brave man, but he was departing for a country in which resolution could avail him nothing, and, as he felt himself gradually loosened from the grasp of the world, his thoughts and feelings took the natural direction; for, if it be true that death is the great leveller, in nothing is it more true, than that it reduces all to the same views of the vanity of life.

Pathfinder, though a man of quaint and peculiar habits and opinions, was always thoughtful and disposed to view the things around him, with a shade of philosophy as well as with seriousness. In him, therefore, the scene in the block house awakened no very novel feelings; but the case was different with Cap. Rude, opinionated, dogmatical and boisterous, the old sailor was little accustomed to view even death, with any approach to the gravity that its importance demands, and, notwithstanding all that had passed, and his real regard for his brother-in-law, he now entered the room of the dying man, with much of that callous unconcern which was the fruit of long training in a school, that, while it gives so many lessons in the sublimest truths, generally wastes its admonitions on scholars who are little disposed to profit by them.

The first proof that Cap gave of his not entering as fully as those around him, into the solemnity of the moment, was by commencing a narration of the events which had just led to the deaths of Muir and Arrowhead. "Both tripped their anchors in a hurry, brother Dunham," he concluded, "and you have the consolation of knowing that others have gone before you, in the great journey, and they, too, men, whom you've no particular reason to love; which to me, were I placed in your situation, would be a source of very great satisfaction. My mother always said, Master Pathfinder, that dying people's spirits should not be damped, but that they ought to be encouraged by all proper and prudent means, and this news will give the poor fellow a great lift, if he feels towards them savages, any way as I feel myself."

June arose, at this intelligence, and stole from the block-house with a noiseless step. Dunham listened with a vacant stare, for life had already lost so many of its ties that he had really forgotten Arrowhead, and cared nothing for Muir; but he inquired, in a feeble voice, for Eau douce. The young man was immediately summoned, and soon made his appearance. The serjeant gazed at him kindly, and the expression of his eyes, was that of regret for the injury he had done him, in thought. The party in the block-house now consisted of Pathfinder, Cap, Mabel, Jasper, and the dying man. With the exception of the daughter, all stood around the serjeant's pallet, in attendance on his last moments. Mabel kneeled at his side, now pressing a clammy hand to her heart, now applying moisture to the parched lips of her father.

"Your case will shortly be ourn, sarjeant," said Pathfinder, who could hardly be said to be awestruck by the scene, for he had witnessed the approach and victories of death too often for that, but who felt the full difference between his triumphs in the excitement of battle, and in the quiet of the domestic circle; "and I make no question we shall meet ag'in, hereafter. Arrowhead has gone his way 'tis true, but it can never be the way of a just Indian. You've seen the last of him; for his path cannot be the path of the just. Reason is ag'in the thought, in his case, as it is also, in my judgment, ag'in it, too, in the case of Lieutenant Muir. You have done your duty in life, and when a man does that, he may start on the longest journey, with a light heart, and an actyve foot."

"I hope so, my friend—I've tried to do my duty."

"Ay—ay—" put in Cap; "intention is half the battle, and though you would have done better had you hove-to in the offing, and sent a craft in to feel how the land lay, things might have turned out differently, no one, here, doubts that you meant all for the best, and, no one anywhere else, I should think, from what I've seen of this world, and read of t'other."

"I did—yes—I meant all for the best."

"Father!—Oh! my beloved father!"

"Magnet is taken aback by this blow, Master Pathfinder, and can say, or do, but little to carry her father over the shoals, so we must try all the harder to serve him a friendly turn ourselves."

"Did you speak, Mabel?" Dunham asked, turning his eyes in the direction of his daughter, for he was already too feeble to turn his body.

"Yes, Father; rely on nothing you have done yourself for mercy and salvation; trust altogether in the blessed mediation of the son of God!"

"The chaplain has told us something like this, brother—the dear child may be right."

"Ay—ay—that's doctrine, out of doubt. He will be our judge, and keeps the log-book of our acts, and will foot them all up, at the last day, and then say who has done well, and who has done ill. I do believe Mabel is right, but then you need not be concerned, as no doubt the account has been fairly kept."

"Uncle!—Dearest Father!—This is a vain illusion—Oh! Place all your trust in the mediation of our holy redeemer! Have you not often felt your own insufficiency to effect your own wishes in the commonest things, and how can you imagine yourself, by your own acts, equal to raising a frail and sinful nature sufficiently to be received into the presence of perfect purity? There is no hope for any, but in the mediation of Christ!"

"This is what the Moravians used to tell us," said Pathfinder to Cap, in a low voice; "Mabel is right."

"Right enough, friend Pathfinder, in the distances, but wrong in the course. I'm afraid the child will get the serjeant adrift, at the very moment when we had him in the best of the water, and in the plainest part of the channel."

"Leave it to Mabel—leave it to Mabel. She knows better than any of us, and can do no harm."

"I have heard this before—" Dunham at length replied—"Ah! Mabel; it is strange for the parent to lean on the child, at a moment like this!"

"Put your trust in God, father—lean on his holy and compassionate son. Pray, dearest, dearest, father—pray for his omnipotent support."

"I am not used to prayer—brother—Pathfinder—Jasper—can you help me to words?"

Cap scarce knew what prayer meant, and he had no answer to give. Pathfinder prayed often, daily if not hourly—but it was mentally, in his own simple modes of thinking, and without the aid of words at all. In this strait, therefore, he was as useless as the mariner, and had no reply to make. As for Jasper Eau douce, though he would gladly have endeavored to move a mountain, to relieve Mabel, this was asking assistance it exceeded his power to give, and he shrunk back with the shame, that is only too apt to overcome the young and vigorous, when called on to perform an act that tacitly confesses their real weakness and dependence on a superior power.

"Father—" said Mabel, wiping her eyes, and endeavoring to compose features that were pallid, and actually quivering with emotion—"*I* will pray with you—*for* you—for *myself*, for us *all*. The petition of the feeblest and humblest is never unheeded."

There was something sublime, as well as much that was supremely touching in this act of filial piety. The quiet, but earnest manner in which this young creature prepared herself to perform this duty, the self-abandonment with which she forgot her sex's timidity and sex's shame, in order to sustain her parent at that trying moment, the loftiness of purpose with which she directed all her powers to the immense object before her, with a woman's devotion, and a woman's superiority to trifles, when her affections make the appeals, and the holy calm into which her grief was compressed, rendered her, for the moment, an object of something very like awe and veneration to her companions.

Mabel had been religiously and reasonably educated; equally without exaggeration and without self-sufficiency. Her reliance on God, was cheerful and full of hope, while it was of the humblest and most dependant nature. She had been accustomed from childhood, to address herself to the Deity, in prayer;—taking example from the divine mandate of Christ himself, who commanded his followers to abstain from 'vain repetitions' and who has left behind him a petition that is unequalled for sublimity and sententiousness, as if expressly to rebuke the disposition of man to set up his own loose and random thoughts as the most acceptable sacrifice. The sect in which she had been reared, has furnished to its followers some of the most beautiful compositions of the language, as a suitable vehicle for its adoration and solicitations. Accustomed to this mode of public and even private prayer, the mind of our heroine had naturally fallen into its train of lofty thought, her taste had become improved by its study, and her language elevated and enriched by its phrases. In short, Mabel, in this respect, was an instance of the influence of familiarity with propriety of thought, fitness of language, and decorum of manner, on the habits and expressions of even those who might be supposed not to be always so susceptible of receiving high impressions of this nature. When she kneeled at the bedside of her father, the very reverence of her attitude and manner, prepared the spectators for what was to come, and as her affectionate heart prompted her tongue, and memory came in aid of both, the petition and praises that she offered up, were of a character that might have worthily led the spirits of any. Although the words were not slavishly borrowed, the expressions partook of the simple dignity of the liturgy to which she had been accustomed, and were probably as worthy of the being to whom they were addressed as they could well be made by human powers. They produced their full impression on the hearers, for it is worthy of remark that, notwithstanding the pernicious effects of a false taste when long submitted to, real sublimity and beauty are so closely allied to nature, that they generally find an echo in every heart.

But when our heroine came to touch upon the situation of the dying man, she became the most truly persuasive, for then she was the most truly zealous and natural. The beauty of the language was preserved, but it was sustained by the simple power of love, and her words were warmed by a holy zeal that approached to the grandeur of true eloquence. We might record some of her expressions, but doubt the propriety of subjecting such sacred themes to a too familiar analysis, and refrain.

The effect of this singular but solemn scene, was different on the different individuals present. Dunham himself, was soon lost in the subject of the prayer, and he felt some such relief as one who finds himself staggering on the edge of a precipice, under a burthen difficult to be borne, might be supposed to experience, when he unexpectedly feels the weight removed, in order to be placed on the shoulders of another, better able to sustain it. Cap was surprised, as well as awed, though the effects on his mind were not very deep, or very lasting. He wondered a little at his own sensations, and had his doubts whether they were as manly and heroic as they ought to be, but he was far too sensible of the influence of truth, humility, religious submission and human dependency, to think of interposing with any of his crude objections. Jasper knelt opposite to Mabel, covered his face, and followed her words, with an earnest wish to aid her prayer with his own, though it may be questioned if his thoughts did not dwell quite as much on the soft, gentle accents of the petitioner, as on the subject of her petitions.

The effect on Pathfinder was striking and visible; visible because he stood erect, also opposite to Mabel, and the workings of his countenance, as usual, betrayed the workings of the spirit within. He leaned on his rifle, and, at moments, the sinewy fingers grasped the barrel, with a force that seemed to compress the weapon, while, once or twice, as Mabel's language rose, in intimate association with her thoughts, he lifted his eyes to the floor above him, as if he expected to find some visible evidence of the presence of the dread being, to whom the words were addressed. Then again, his feelings reverted to the fair creature who was thus pouring out her spirit in fervent but calm petitions in behalf of a dying parent; for Mabel's cheek was no longer pallid, but was flushed with a holy enthusiasm, while her blue eyes were upturned in the light, in a way to resemble a picture by Guido. At these moments, all the honest and manly attachment of Pathfinder, glowed in his ingenuous features, and his gaze at our heroine was such as the fondest parent might fasten on the child of his love.

Serjeant Dunham laid his hand feebly, on the head of Mabel, as she ceased praying, and buried her face in his blanket.

"Bless you—my beloved child—bless you—" he rather whispered than uttered aloud—"this is truly consolation—Would that I, too, could pray!"

"Father, you know the Lord's prayer—you taught it to me yourself, while I was yet an infant."

The serjeant's face gleamed with a smile, for he *did* remember to have discharged that portion at least, of the paternal duty, and the consciousness of it gave him inconceivable gratification at that solemn moment. He was then silent for several minutes, and all present believed that he was communing with God.

"Mabel—my child—" he at length uttered, in a voice that seemed to be reviving—"Mabel—I'm quitting you—" The spirit, at its great and final passage, appears ever to consider the body as nothing—"I'm quitting you, my child—where is your hand?"

"Here, dearest Father—here are both—oh! take both."

"Pathfinder—" added the serjeant, feeling on the opposite side of the bed, where Jasper still knelt, getting one of the hands of the young man, by mistake—"Take it—I leave you as her father—as you and she may please—bless you—bless you, both—"

At that awful instant no one would rudely apprise the serjeant of his mistake, and he died a minute or two later, holding Jasper's and Mabel's hands covered by both his own. Our heroine was ignorant of the fact, until an exclamation of Cap's announced the death of her father, when raising her face, she saw the eyes of Jasper riveted on her own, and felt the warm pressure of his hand. But a single feeling was predominant, at that instant, and Mabel withdrew to weep, scarcely conscious of what had occurred. The Pathfinder took the arm of Eau douce, and left the block.

The two friends walked in silence past the fire, along the glade, and nearly reached the opposite shore of the island, in profound silence. Here they stopped, and Pathfinder spoke.

" 'Tis all over, Jasper," he said; " 'tis all over. Ah's, me! Poor Sarjeant Dunham has finished his march, and that, too, by the hand of a venomous Mingo. Well, we never know what is to happen, and his luck may be your'n, or mine, to-morrow, or next day!"

"And, Mabel?—What is to become of Mabel, Pathfinder?"

"You heard the sarjeant's dying words—he left his child in my care, Jasper, and it is a most solemn trust, it is; yes, it is a most solemn trust!"

"It's a trust, Pathfinder, of which any man would be glad to relieve you—" returned the youth with a bitter smile.

"I've often thought it has fallen into wrong hands. I'm not consaited, Jasper; I'm not consaited, I do think I'm not; but if Mabel Dunham is willing to overlook all my imperfections and ignorances like, I should be wrong to gainsay it, on account of any sartainty I may have myself about my own want of merit."

"No one will blame you, Pathfinder, for marrying Mabel Dunham, any more than they will blame you for wearing a precious jewel in your bosom, that a friend had fairly given you."

"Do you think they'll blame Mabel, lad?—I've had my misgivings about that, too; for all persons may not be as disposed to look at me with the same eyes as you, and the sarjeant's daughter—" Jasper Eau douce started, as a man flinches at sudden bodily pain, but he otherwise maintained his self-command—"and mankind is envious and ill-natured, more particularly in and about the garrisons. I sometimes wish, Jasper, that Mabel could have taken a fancy to you, I do; and that you had taken a fancy to her, for, it often seems to me that one like you, after all, might make her happier, than I ever can!"

"We will not talk about this, Pathfinder—" interrupted Jasper hoarsely, and impatiently—"You will be Mabel's husband, and it is not right to speak of any one else, in that character. As for me, I shall take Master Cap's advice, and try and make a man of myself, by seeing what is to be done on the salt-water."

"You, Jasper Western!—You quit the lakes, the forests, and the lines, and this, too, for the towns and wasty ways of the settlements, and a little difference in the taste of the water. Have'n't we the salt licks, if salt is necessary to you, and ought n't man to be satisfied with what contents the other creatur's of God. I counted on you, Jasper; I counted on you, I did—and thought, now, that Mabel and I intend to dwell in a cabin of our own, that some day you might be tempted to choose a companion too, and come and settle in our neighborhood. There is a beautiful spot, about fifty miles west of the garrison, that I had chosen in my mind, for my own place of abode, and there is an excellent harbor, about ten leagues this side of it, where you could run in and out, with the cutter, at any leisure minute, and I'd even fancied you and your wife in possession of the one place, and Mabel and I in possession of t'other. We should be just a healthy hunt apart, and if the Lord does intend any of his creatur's to be happy on 'arth, none could be happier than we four!"

"You forget, my friend," answered Jasper, taking the guide's hand, and forcing a friendly smile—"that I have no fourth person to love and cherish; and I much doubt if I ever shall love any other, as I love you and Mabel."

"Thank'ee, boy; I thank you, with all my heart—but what you call love for Mabel, is only friendship like, and a very different thing from what I feel. Now, instead of sleeping, as sound as natur' at midnight, as I used to could, I dream nightly of Mabel Dunham. The young does sport before me, and when I raise Killdeer, in order to take a little venison, the animals look back, and it seems as if they all had Mabel's sweet countenance, laughing in my face, and looking as if they said, 'shoot me, if you dare!' Then I hear her soft voices calling out among the birds as they sing; and no later than the last nap I took, I bethought me, in fancy, of going over the Niagara, holding Mabel in my arms, rather than part from her. The bitterest moments I've ever known, were them in which the devil, or some Mingo conjurer, perhaps, has just put into my head to fancy in dreams that Mabel is lost to me, by some unaccountable calamity; either by changefulness, or by violence."

"Oh! Pathfinder, if you think this so bitter in a dream, what must it be to one who feels it in reality, and knows it all to be true—true—true. So true, as to leave no hope; to leave nothing but despair!"

These words burst from Jasper, as a fluid pours from the vessel that has been suddenly broken. They were uttered involuntarily, almost unconsciously, but with a truth and feeling that carried with them the instant conviction of their deep sincerity. Pathfinder started, gazed at his friend for quite a minute, like one bewildered, and then it was, that, in despite of all his simplicity, the truth gleamed upon him. All know how corroborating proofs crowd upon the mind, as soon as it catches a direct clue to any hitherto unsuspected fact; how rapidly the thoughts flow, and premises tend to their just conclusions, under such circumstances. Our hero was so confiding by nature, so just, and so much disposed to imagine that all his friends wished him the same happiness as he wished them, that, until this unfortunate moment, a suspicion of Jasper's attachment for Mabel had never been awakened in his bosom. He was, however, now too experienced in the emotions that characterize the passion, and the burst of feeling in his companion, was too violent and too natural, to leave any further doubt on the subject. The feeling that first followed this change of opinion was one of deep humility and exquisite pain. He bethought him of Jasper's youth, his higher claims to personal appearance, and all the general probabilities that such a suitor would be more agreeable to Mabel, than he could possibly be, himself. Then the noble rectitude of mind, for which the man was so distinguished, asserted its power. It was sustained by his rebuked manner of thinking of himself, and all that habitual deference for the rights and feelings of others, which appeared to be inbred in his very nature. Taking the arm of Jasper, he led him to a log, where he compelled the young man to seat himself, by a sort of irresistible exercise of his iron muscles, and where he placed himself at his side.

The instant his feelings had found vent, Eau douce was both alarmed at, and ashamed of their violence. He would have given all he possessed on earth, could the last three minutes be recalled, but he was too frank by disposition, and too much accustomed to deal ingenuously by his friend, to think a moment, of attempting further concealment, or of any evasion of the explanation that he knew was about to be demanded. Even while he trembled in anticipation of what was about to follow, he never contemplated equivocation.

"Jasper," Pathfinder commenced, in a tone so solemn as to thrill on every nerve in his listener's body, "this *has* surprised me! You have kinder feelings towards Mabel, than I had thought, and, unless my own mistaken vanity and consait have cruelly deceived me, I pity you, boy, from my soul, I do! Yes, I think, I know how to pity any one, who has set his heart on a creatur' like Mabel, unless he sees a prospect of her regarding him, as he regards her. This matter must be cleared up, Eau douce, as the Delawares say, until there shall not be a cloud atween us."

"What clearing up can it want, Pathfinder? I love Mabel Dunham, and Mabel Dunham does not love me—She prefers you for a husband, and the wisest thing I can do, is to go off at once, to the salt-water and, to try to forget you both."

"Forget me, Jasper! —that would be a punishment I don't desarve. But, how do you know that Mabel prefars *me*?—how do you know it, lad; to me it seems impossible, like!"

"Is she not to marry you, and would Mabel marry a man she does not love?"

"She has been hard urged by the sarjeant, she has; and a dutiful child may have found it difficult to withstand the wishes of a dying parent. Have you ever told Mabel, that you prefarred her, Jasper; that you bore her these feelings?"

"Never—Pathfinder—I would not do you that wrong!"

"I believe you, lad, I do believe you; and I think you would now go off to the salt-water and let the secret die with you. But this must not be. Mabel shall hear all, and she shall have her own way, if my heart breaks in the trial, she shall. No words have ever passed atween you then, Jasper?"

"Nothing of account—nothing direct. Still, I will own all my foolishness, Pathfinder, for I ought to own it to a generous friend like you, and there will be an end of it. You know how young people understand each other, or think they understand each other, without always speaking out, in plain speech, and get to know each other's thoughts, or to think they know them, by means of a hundred little ways?"

"Not I, Jasper, not I," truly answered the guide, for, sooth to say, his advances had never been met with any of that sweet and precious encouragement that silently marks the course of sympathy united to passion. "Not I, Jasper—I know nothing of all this. Mabel has always treated me fairly, and said what she has had to say, in speech as plain as tongue could tell it."

"You have had the pleasure of hearing her say that she loved you, Pathfinder!"

"Why, no, Jasper, not just that, in words. She has told me that we never could—never ought to be married—that *she* was not good enough for *me*, though she *did* say that she honored me, and respected me. But, then, the sarjeant said it was always so with the youthful and timid; that her mother did so, and said so afore her, and that I ought to be satisfied if she would consent, on any tarms, to marry me; and, therefore, I have concluded that all was right, I have."

In spite of all his friendship for the successful wooer, in spite of all his honest, sincere wishes for his happiness, we should be unfaithful chroniclers did we not own that Jasper felt his heart bound with an uncontrollable feeling of delight, at this admission. It was not that he saw, or felt, any hope connected with the circumstance, but it was grateful to the jealous covetousness of unlimited love, thus to learn that no other ears had heard the sweet confessions that were denied his own.

"Tell me more of this manner of talking without the use of the tongue—" continued Pathfinder, whose countenance was getting to be grave, and who now questioned his companion, like one that seemed to anticipate evil in the reply. "I can, and have conversed with Chingachgook, and with his son Uncas, too, in that mode, afore the latter fell, but I did n't know that young gals practysed this art, and least of all, Mabel Dunham!"

" 'Tis nothing, Pathfinder—I mean only a look, or a smile, or a glance of the eye, or the trembling of an arm, or a hand, when the young woman has had occasion to touch me; and because I have been weak enough to tremble even at Mabel's breath, or her brushing me with her clothes, my vain thoughts have misled me. I never spoke plainly to Mabel, myself, and now there is no reason for it, since there is clearly no hope."

"Jasper," returned Pathfinder simply, but with a dignity that precluded farther remarks at the moment, "we will talk of the sarjeant's funeral, and of our own departure from this island; after these things are disposed of, it will be time enough to say more of the sarjeant's daughter. This matter must be looked into, for the father left me the care of his child."

Jasper was glad enough to change the subject, and the friends separated, each charged with the duty most peculiar to his own station, and habits.

That afternoon all the dead were interred, the grave of Serjeant Dunham being dug in the centre of the glade, beneath the shade of a huge elm. Mabel wept bitterly at the ceremony, and she found relief in thus disburthening her sorrow. The night passed tranquilly, as did the whole of the following day, Jasper declaring that the gale was too severe to venture on the lake. This circumstance, detained Capt. Sanglier also, who did not quit the island until the morning of the third day after the death of Dunham, when the weather had moderated, and the wind had become fair. Then, indeed, he departed, after taking leave of the Pathfinder, in the manner of one who believed he was in company of a distinguished character, for the last time. The two separated, like those who respect one another, while each felt that the other was an enigma to himself.

Chapter XXIX

"Playful she turned that he might see
The passing smile her cheek put on;
But when she marked how mournfully
His eyes met hers, that smile was gone,—"
Moore, *Lalla Rookh*,
"The Fire-Worshippers," ll. 269–72.

THE OCCURRENCES of the last few days had been too exciting, and had made too many demands on the fortitude of our heroine to leave her in the helplessness of grief. She mourned for her father, and she occasionally shuddered, as she recalled the sudden death of Jennie, and all the horrible scenes she had witnessed, but, on the whole, she had aroused herself, and was no longer in the deep depression that usually accompanies grief. Perhaps the overwhelming, almost stupefying sorrow that crushed poor June, and left her for nearly twenty four hours in a state of stupor, assisted Mabel in conquering her own feelings, for she had felt called on to administer consolation to the young Indian woman. This she had done, in the quiet, soothing, insinuating way, in which her sex usually exerts its influence, on such occasions.

The morning of the third day, was set for that on which the Scud was to sail. Jasper had made all his preparations; the different effects were embarked, and Mabel had taken leave of June, a painful and affectionate parting. In a word, all was ready, and every soul had left the island but the Indian woman, Pathfinder, Jasper and our heroine. The former had gone into a thicket to weep, and the three last were approaching the spot where three canoes lay; one of which was the property of June, and the other two were in waiting to carry the others off to the Scud. Pathfinder led the way, but, when he drew near the shore, instead of taking the direction to the boats, he motioned to his companions to follow, and proceeded to a fallen tree, that lay on the margin of the glade, and out of view of those in the cutter. Seating himself on the trunk, he signed to Mabel to take her place on one side of him, and to Jasper to occupy the other.

"Sit down here, Mabel; sit down there, Eau douce," he

commenced, as soon as he had taken his own seat; "I've something that lies heavy on my mind, and now is the time to take it off, if it's ever to be done. Sit down, Mabel, and let me lighten my heart, if not my conscience, while I've the strength to do it."

The pause that succeeded, lasted two or three minutes, and both the young people wondered what was to come next, the idea that Pathfinder could have any weight on his conscience, seeming equally improbable to each.

"Mabel," our hero at length resumed, " we must talk plainly to each other, afore we join your uncle in the cutter, where the Salt-water has slept every night since the last rally; for he says it's the only place in which a man can be sure of keeping the hair on his head, he does—Ah's! me; what have I to do with these follies and sayings, now! I try to be pleasant, and to feel light-hearted, but the power of man can't make water run upstream. Mabel, you know that the sarjeant, afore he left us, had settled it atween us two, that we were to become man and wife, and that we were to live together, and to love one another as long as the Lord was pleased to keep us both on 'arth, yes, and afterwards, too?"

Mabel's cheeks had regained a little of their ancient bloom, in the fresh air of the morning, but at this unlooked for address they blanched again, nearly to the pallid hue which grief had imprinted there. Still she looked kindly, though seriously, at Pathfinder, and even endeavored to force a smile.

"Very true, my excellent friend—" she answered—"this was my poor father's wish, and I feel certain that a whole life devoted to your welfare and comforts could scarcely repay you for all you have done for us."

"I fear me, Mabel, that man and wife needs be bound together by a stronger tie than such feelings, I do. You have done nothing for me, or nothing of any account, and yet my very heart yearns toward you, it does, and therefore it seems likely that these feelings come from something besides saving scalps and guiding through woods."

Mabel's cheeks had begun to glow again; and, though she struggled hard to smile, her voice trembled a little, as she answered.

"Had we not better postpone this conversation, Pathfinder," she said; "we are not alone, and nothing is so unpleasant to a listener, they say, as family matters in which he feels no interest."

"It's because we are not alone, Mabel—or rather because Jasper is with us, that I wish to talk of this matter. The sarjeant believed I might make a suitable companion for you, and though I had misgivings about it—yes, I had many misgivings—he finally persuaded me into the idee, and things came round atween us, as you know. But when you promised your father to marry me, Mabel, and gave me your hand so modestly, but so prettily, there was one circumstance, as your uncle calls it, that you did'n't know, and I've thought it right to tell you what it is, afore matters are finally settled. I've often taken a poor deer for my dinner, when good venison was not to be found, but it's in natur' not to take up with the worst, when the best may be had."

"You speak in a way, Pathfinder, that is difficult to be understood. If this conversation is really necessary, I trust you will be more plain."

"Well, then, Mabel, I've been thinking it was quite likely when you gave in to the sarjeant's wishes, that you did not know the natur' of Jasper Western's feelings towards you?"

"Pathfinder!"—and Mabel's cheek now paled to the livid hue of death; then it flushed to the tint of crimson, and her whole form shuddered. Pathfinder, however, was too intent on his own object to notice this agitation, and Eau douce had hid his face in his hands, in time to shut out its view.

"I've been talking with the lad, and, on comparing his dreams with my dreams, his feelings with my feelings and his wishes with my wishes, I fear we think too much alike consarning you, for both of us to be very happy."

"Pathfinder—you forget—you should remember that we are betrothed!" said Mabel huskily, and in a voice so low, that it required acute attention in the listeners, to catch the syllables. Indeed, the last word was not quite intelligible to the guide, and he confessed his ignorance by the usual——

"Anan?"

"You forget that we are to be married; and such allusions are improper, as well as painful."

"Every thing is proper that is right, Mabel, and every thing is right that leads to justice, and fair dealing; though it *is painful* enough, as you say, as I find on trial, I do. Now, Mabel, had you known that Eau douce thinks of you in this way, maybe you never would have consented to be married to one as old and as uncomely as I am!"

"Why this cruel trial, Pathfinder—To what can all this lead—Jasper Western thinks no such thing—he says nothing—he feels nothing—"

"Mabel!" burst from out of the young man's lips, in a way to betray the uncontrollable nature of his emotions, though he uttered not another syllable.

Mabel buried her face in both her hands, and the two sat, like a pair of guilty beings, suddenly detected in the commission of some crime that involved the happiness of a common patron. At that instant, perhaps, Jasper himself was inclined to deny his passion, through an extreme unwillingness to injure his friend, while Mabel, on whom this positive announcement of a fact, that she had rather unconsciously hoped than believed, came so unexpectedly, felt her mind momentarily bewildered, and she scarce knew whether to weep, or to rejoice. Still she was the first to speak, since Eau douce could utter naught that would be disingenuous, or that would pain his friend.

"Pathfinder," she said—"you talk wildly;—why mention this, at all?"

"Well, Mabel, if I talk wildly, I *am* half wild, you know; by natur', I fear, as well as by habits—" as he said this he endeavored to laugh in his usual noiseless way, but the effect produced a strange and discordant sound, and it appeared nearly to choke him. "Yes, I *must* be wild; I'll not attempt to deny it."

"Dearest Pathfinder!—my best, almost my only friend! you *cannot*, *do not* think I intended to say that!" interrupted Mabel, almost breathless in her haste to relieve his mortification—"If courage, truth, nobleness of soul and conduct, unyielding principles and a hundred other excellent qualities can render any man respectable, esteemed, or beloved, your claims are inferior to those of no other human being."

"What tender and bewitching voices they have, Jasper!" resumed the guide, now laughing freely and naturally—"Yes, natur' seems to have made them on purpose, to sing in our ears, when the music of the woods is silent! But we must come to a right understanding; we must. I ask you ag'in, Mabel, if you had known that Jasper Western loves you as well as I do, or better perhaps, though that is scarce possible; that in his dreams, he sees your face in the water of the lake; that he talks to you, and of you, in his sleep; fancies all that is beautiful, like Mabel Dunham, and all that is good and virtuous; believes he never knowed happiness until he knowed you; could kiss the ground on which you have trod, and forgets all the joys of his calling, to think of you and of the delight of gazing at your beauty, and in listening to your voice, would you then have consented to marry me?"

Mabel could not have answered this question, if she would, but, though her face was buried in her hands, the tint of the rushing blood was visible between the openings, and the suffusion seemed to impart itself to her very fingers. Still nature asserted her power, for there was a single instant when the astonished, almost terrified girl stole a glance at Jasper, as if disputing Pathfinder's history of his feelings, read the truth of all he said in that furtive look, and instantly concealed her face again, as if she would hide it from observation, forever.

"Take time to think, Mabel," the guide continued, "for it is a solemn thing to accept one man for a husband, while the thoughts and wishes lead to another. Jasper and I have talked this matter over, freely and like old friends, and though I always knowed that we viewed most things pretty much alike, I could'n't have thought that we regarded any particular object with the very same eyes, as it might be, until we opened our minds to each other, about you. Now, Jasper owns that the very first time he beheld you, he thought you the sweetest and winningest creatur' he had ever met; that your voice sounded like murmuring water in his ears; that he fancied his sails were your garments, fluttering in the wind; that your laugh, haunted him in his sleep, and that, ag'in and ag'in, has he started up affrighted, because he has fancied some one wanted to force you out of the Scud, where he imagined you had taken up your abode. Nay, the lad has even acknowledged that he weeps often, at the thought that you are likely to spend your days with another, and not with him."

"Jasper!"

"It's solemn truth, Mabel, and it's right you should know it. Now stand up, and choose atween us. I do believe Eau douce loves you as well as I do myself; he has tried to persuade me that he loves you better, but that I will not allow, for I do not think it possible, but I will own the boy loves you, heart and soul, and he has a good right to be heard. The sarjeant left me your protector, and not your tyrant. I told him that I would be a father to you, as well as a husband, and it seems to me no feeling father would deny his child this small privilege. Stand up, Mabel, therefore, and speak your thoughts as freely, as if I were the sarjeant himself, seeking your good, and nothing else."

Mabel dropped her hands, arose, and stood face to face, with her two suitors, though the flush that was on her cheeks was feverish, the evidence of excitement, rather than of shame.

"What would you have, Pathfinder?—" she asked. "Have I not already promised my poor father to do all you desire?"

"Then I desire this. Here I stand, a man of the forest, and of little larning, though I fear with an ambition beyond my desarts, and I'll do my endivors to do justice to both sides. In the first place, it is allowed that so far as feelings in your behalf are consarned, we love you just the same; Jasper thinks his feelings *must* be the strongest, but this I cannot say, in honesty, for it does n't seem to me that it *can* be true; else I would frankly and freely confess it, I would. So in this particular, Mabel, we are here afore you, on equal tarms. As for myself, being the oldest, I'll first say what little can be produced in my favor, as well as ag'in it. As a hunter, I do think there is no man near the lines that can outdo me. If venison, or bear's meat, or even birds and fish should ever be scarce in our cabin, it would be more likely to be owing to natur' and Providence, than to any fault of mine. In short, it does seem to me, that the woman who depended on me, would never be likely to want for food. But, I'm fearful ignorant! It's true, I speak several tongues, such as they be, while I'm very far from being expart at my own. Then, my years are greater than your own, Mabel, and the circumstance that I was so long the sarjeant's comrade, can be no great merit in your eyes. I wish, too, I was more comely, I do; but we are all as natur' made us, and the last thing that a man ought to lament, except on very special occasions, is his looks. When all is remembered, age, looks, larning and habits, Mabel, conscience tells me I ought to confess that I'm altogether unfit for you, if not downright unworthy, and I would give up the hope, this minute, I would, if I did n't feel something pulling at my heart strings which seems hard to undo."

"Pathfinder!—Noble, generous Pathfinder—" cried our heroine, seizing his hand, and kissing it with a species of holy reverence—"you do yourself injustice—you forget my poor father and your promise—you do not know *me*!"

"Now, here's Jasper," continued the guide, without allowing the girl's caresses to win him from his purpose; "with *him*, the case is different. In the way of providing, as in that of loving, there's not much to choose atween us, for the lad is frugal, industrious and careful. Then he is quite a scholar—knows the tongue of the Frenchers—reads many books, and some, I know, that you like to read yourself—can understand you at all times, which, perhaps, is more than I can say for myself."

"What of all this—" interrupted Mabel, impatiently—"why speak of it now—why speak of it, at all!"

"Then the lad has a manner of letting his thoughts be known, that I fear I can never equal. If there's any thing on 'arth that would make my tongue bold and persuading, Mabel, I do think it's yourself, and, yet, in our late conversations, Jasper has outdone me, even on this point, in a way to make me ashamed of myself. He has told me how simple you were, and how true-hearted, and kind-hearted; and how you looked down upon vanities, for though you might be the wife of more than one officer, as he thinks, that you cling to feeling, and would rather be true to yourself, and natur', than a colonel's lady. He fairly made my blood warm, he did, when he spoke of your having beauty without seeming ever to have looked upon it, and the manner in which you moved about like a young fa'an, so nat'ral and graceful like, without knowing it; and the truth and justice of your idees, and the warmth and generosity of your heart—"

"Jasper!" interrupted Mabel, giving way to feelings that had gathered an ungovernable force by being so long pent, and falling into the young man's willing arms, weeping like a child, and almost as helpless. "Jasper!—Jasper!—Why have you kept this from me!"

The answer of Eau douce was not very intelligible, nor was the murmured dialogue that followed remarkable for coherency. But the language of affection is easily understood. The hour that succeeded passed like a very few minutes of ordinary life, so far as a computation of time was concerned, and when Mabel recollected herself, and bethought her of the existence of others, her uncle was pacing the cutter's deck, in great impatience, and wondering why Jasper should be losing so much of a favorable wind. Her first thought was of him, who was so likely to feel the recent betrayal of her real emotions.

"Oh! Jasper!" she exclaimed like one suddenly self convicted—"the Pathfinder!"

Eau douce fairly trembled, not with unmanly apprehension, but with the painful consciousness of the pang he had given his friend, and he looked in all directions, in the expectation of seeing his person. But Pathfinder had withdrawn, with a tact and a delicacy, that might have done credit to the sensibility and breeding of a courtier. For several minutes the two lovers sate, silently waiting his return, uncertain what propriety required, under circumstances so marked, and so peculiar. At length they beheld their friend advancing slowly towards them, with a thoughtful and even pensive air.

"I now understand what you meant, Jasper, by speaking without a tongue, and hearing without an ear," he said, when close enough to the tree to be heard,—"Yes, I understand it, now, I do, and a very pleasant sort of discourse it is, when one can hold it with Mabel Dunham. Ah's me!—I told the sarjeant I was'n't fit for her; that I was too old, too ignorant, and too wild like, but he *would* have it, otherwise."

Jasper and Mabel sate, resembling Milton's picture of our first parents, when the consciousness of sin first laid its leaden weight on their souls. Neither spoke; neither even moved; though both at that moment, fancied they could part with their new-found happiness, in order to restore their friend to his peace of mind. Jasper was pale as death, but, in Mabel, maiden modesty had caused the blood to mantle on her cheeks, until their bloom was heightened to a richness that was scarce equalled in her hours of light-hearted buoyancy and joy. As the feeling which in her sex, always accompanies the security of love returned, threw its softness and tenderness over her countenance, she was singularly beautiful. Pathfinder gazed at her, with an intentness he did not endeavor to conceal, and then he fairly laughed, in his own way, and with a sort of wild exultation as men that are untutored are wont to express their delight. This momentary indulgence, however, was expiated by the pang that followed the sudden consciousness that this glorious young creature was lost to him, forever. It required a full minute, for this simple-minded being to recover from the shock of this conviction, and then he resumed his dignity of manner, speaking with gravity, almost with solemnity.

"I have always known, Mabel Dunham, that men have their gifts," he said, "but I'd forgotten that it did not belong to mine, to please the young, and beautiful, and l'arned. I hope the mistake has been no very heavy sin, and if it was, I've been heavily punished for it, I have. Nay, Mabel, I know what you'd say, but it's unnecessary. I *feel* it all, and that is as good as if I *heard* it all. I've had a bitter hour, Mabel. I've had a very bitter hour, lad—"

"Hour!" echoed Mabel, as the other first used the word, the tell-tale blood, which had begun to ebb towards her heart, rushing again tumultuously to her very temples—"surely not an hour, Pathfinder!"

"Hour!" exclaimed Jasper, at the same instant—"no—no—my worthy friend, it is not ten minutes, since you left us!"

"Well, it may be so, though to me it has seemed to be a day. I begin to think, howsever, that the happy count time by minutes, and the miserable count it by months. But we will talk no more of this; it is all over now, and many words about it, will make you no happier, while they will only tell me what I've lost, and quite likely how much I desarved to lose her—no—no—Mabel, 'tis useless to interrupt me; I admit it all, and your gainsaying it, though it be so well meant, cannot change my mind. Well, Jasper, she is yourn, and though it's hard to think it, I do believe you'll make her happier than I could, for your gifts are better suited to do so, though I would have strived hard to do as much, if I know myself I would. I ought to have known better than to believe the sarjeant, and I ought to have put faith in what Mabel told me at the head of the lake, for reason and judgment might have shown me its truth; but it is so pleasant to think what we wish, and mankind so easily over-persuade us, when we over-persuade ourselves! But, what's the use in talking of it, as I said afore. It's true, Mabel seemed to be consenting, though it all came from a wish to please her father, and from being skeary about the savages—"

"Pathfinder!"

"I understand you, Mabel, and bear no hard feelings, I don't. I sometimes think I should like to live in your neighborhood, that I might look at your happiness, but, on the whole, it's better I should quit the 55th altogether, and go back to the 60th, which is my natyve rigiment, as it might be. It would have been better, perhaps, had I never left it, though my sarvices were much wanted, in this quarter, and I'd been with some of the 55th, years agone, Sarjeant Dunham for instance, when he was in another corps. Still, Jasper, I do not regret that I've known you—"

"And me, Pathfinder—" impetuously interrupted Mabel—"do you regret having known *me*?—Could I think so, I should never be at peace with myself!"

"You, Mabel—" returned the guide, taking the hand of our heroine, and looking up into her countenance with guileless simplicity, but earnest affection, "how could I be sorry that a ray of the sun came across the gloom of a cheerless day; that light has broken in upon darkness, though it remained so short a time? I do not flatter myself with being able to march quite as light-hearted, as I once used to could, or to sleep as sound, for some time to come, but I shall always remember how near I was to being undesarvedly happy, I shall. So far from blaming you, Mabel, I only blame myself for being so vain, as to think it possible I could please such a creatur', for, sartainly, you told me how it was, when we talked it over, on the mountain, and I ought to have believed you, then, for I do suppose it's nat'ral that young women should know their own minds better than their fathers. Ah's me! It's settled now, and nothing remains but for me to take leave of you, that you may depart; I feel that Master Cap, must be impatient, and there is danger of his coming on shore to look for us, all."

"To take leave!" exclaimed Mabel.

"Leave!" echoed Jasper, "you do not mean to quit us, my friend?"

" 'Tis best, Mabel—'tis altogether best, Eau douce, and it's wisest. I could live and die in your company, if I only followed feeling; but if I follow reason, I shall quit you, here. You will go back to Oswego and become man and wife, as soon as you arrive, for, all that is determined with Master Cap, who hankers after the sea ag'in, and who knows what is to happen; while, I shall return to the wilderness, and my Maker. Come Mabel," continued Pathfinder, rising and drawing nearer to our heroine, with grave decorum. "Kiss me. Jasper will not grudge me one kiss; then we'll part."

"Oh! Pathfinder—" exclaimed Mabel falling into the arms of the guide, and kissing his cheeks, again and again, with a freedom and warmth she had been far from manifesting while held to the bosom of Jasper—"God bless you, dearest Pathfinder—you will come to us, hereafter—we shall see you again—when old, you will come to our dwelling, and let me be a daughter to you?"

"Yes—that's it—" returned the guide, almost gasping for breath—"I'll try to think of it, in that way. You're more befitting to be my daughter, than to be my wife, you are. Farewell, Jasper. Now we'll go to the canoe—it's time you were on board."

The manner in which Pathfinder led the way to the shore, was solemn and calm. As soon as he reached the canoe, he again took Mabel, by the hands, held her at the length of his own arms, and gazed wistfully into her face, until the unbidden tears rolled out of the fountains of feeling, and trickled down his rugged cheeks, in streams.

"Bless me, Pathfinder?" said Mabel, kneeling reverently at his feet. "Oh! at least bless me, before we part."

That untutored, but noble-minded being, did as she desired, and aiding her to enter the canoe, seemed to tear himself away, as one snaps a strong and obstinate cord. Before he retired, however, he took Jasper by the arm, and led him a little aside, when he spoke as follows.

"You're kind of heart, and gentle by natur', Jasper, but we are both rough and wild in comparison with that dear creatur'. Be careful of her, and never show the roughness of man's natur' to her soft disposition. You'll get to understand her, in time, and the Lord who governs the lake and the forest, alike, who looks upon virtue with a smile, and upon vice with a frown, keep you happy, and worthy to be so!"

Pathfinder made a sign for his friend to depart, and he stood leaning on his rifle, until the canoe had reached the side of the Scud. Mabel wept as if her heart would break, nor did her eyes once turn from the open spot in the glade, where the form of the Pathfinder was to be seen, until the cutter had passed a point that completely shut out the island. When last in view, the sinewy frame of this extraordinary man was as motionless, as if it were a statue set up in that solitary place, to commemorate the scenes of which it had so lately been the site and the witness.

Chapter XXX

"Oh! let me only breathe the air,
The blessed air that's breathed by thee;
And whether on its wings it bear
Healing or death, 'tis sweet to me!"
Moore, *Lalla Rookh*,
"Paradise and the Peri," ll. 250–53.

PATHFINDER was accustomed to solitude, but, when the Scud had actually disappeared, he was almost overcome with a sense of his loneliness. Never before had he been conscious of his isolated condition in the world, for his feelings had gradually been accustoming themselves to the blandishments and wants of social life, particularly as the last were connected with the domestic affections. Now, all had vanished, as it might be, in one moment, and he was left equally without companions and without hope. Even Chingachgook had left him, though it was but temporarily; still his presence was missed at the precise instant which might be termed the most critical in our hero's life.

Pathfinder stood leaning on his rifle, in the attitude described in the last chapter, a long time after the Scud had disappeared. The rigidity of his limbs seemed permanent, and none but a man accustomed to put his muscles to the severest proof, could have maintained that posture, with its marble-like inflexibility, for so great a length of time. At length he moved away from the spot, motion of the body being preceded by a sigh that seemed to heave up from the very depths of his bosom.

It was a peculiarity of this extraordinary being, that his senses and his limbs, for all practical purposes, were never at fault, let the mind be preoccupied with other interests as much as it might. On the present occasion, neither of these great auxiliaries failed him, but, though his thoughts were exclusively occupied with Mabel, her beauty, her preference of Jasper, her tears and her departure, he moved in a direct line to the spot where June still remained, which was the grave of her husband. The conversation that followed, passed in the language of the Tuscaroras, which Pathfinder spoke fluently, but, as that tongue is understood only by the extremely learned, we shall translate it freely into the English, preserving, as far as possible, the tone of thought of each interlocutor, as well as the peculiarities of manner.

June had suffered her hair to fall about her face, had taken a seat on a stone that had been dug from the excavation made by the grave, and was hanging over the spot that contained the body of Arrowhead, unconscious of the presence of any other. She believed, indeed, that all had left the island but herself, and the tread of the guide's moccasined foot was too noiseless, rudely to undeceive her.

Pathfinder stood gazing at the woman, for several minutes, in mute attention. The contemplation of her grief, the recollection of her irreparable loss, and the view of her desolation produced a healthful influence on his own feelings; his reason telling him how much deeper lay the sources of grief, in a young wife, who was suddenly and violently deprived of her husband, than in himself.

"Dew of June," he said, solemnly, but with an earnestness that denoted the strength of his sympathy—"you are not alone in your sorrow. Turn, and let your eyes look upon a friend."

"June has no longer any friend!" the woman answered. "Arrowhead has gone to the happy hunting grounds, and there is no one left to care for June. The Tuscaroras would chase her from their wigwams; the Iroquois are hateful in her eyes, and she could not look at them. No—leave June to starve over the grave of her husband."

"This will never do—this will never do. 'Tis ag'in reason and right. You believe in Manitou, June?"

"He has hid his face from June, because he is angry. He has left her alone, to die."

"Listen to one, who has had a long acquaintance with red natur', though he has a white birth, and white gifts. When the Manitou of a pale face wishes to produce good in a pale face heart, he strikes it with grief, for it is in our sorrows, June, that we look with the truest eyes into ourselves, and with the farthest sighted eyes too, as respects right. The Great Spirit wishes you well, and he has taken away the chief, lest you should be led astray, by his wily tongue, and get to be a

Mingo in your disposition, as you were already in your company."

"Arrowhead was a great chief!" returned the woman proudly.

"He had his merits, he had; and he had his demerits, too. But, June, you're not desarted, nor will you be soon. Let your grief out—let it out, according to natur', and when the proper time comes, I shall have more to say to you."

Pathfinder now went to his own canoe, and he left the island. In the course of the day, June heard the crack of his rifle, once or twice, and as the sun was setting, he reappeared bringing her birds ready cooked, and of a delicacy and flavor that might have tempted the appetite of an epicure. This species of intercourse lasted a month, June obstinately refusing to abandon the grave of her husband, all that time, though she still accepted the friendly offerings of her protector. Occasionally they met and conversed, Pathfinder sounding the state of the woman's feelings, but the interviews were short, and far from frequent. June slept in one of the huts, and she laid down her head in security, for she was conscious of the protection of a friend, though Pathfinder invariably retired at night, to an adjacent island, where he had built himself a hut.

At the end of the month, however, the season was getting to be too far advanced to render her situation pleasant to June. The trees had lost their leaves, and the nights were becoming cold and wintry. It was time to depart.

At this moment Chingachgook reappeared. He had a long and confidential interview on the island, with his friend. June witnessed their movements, and she saw that her guardian was distressed. Stealing to his side, she endeavored to soothe his sorrow, with a woman's gentleness, and with a woman's instinct.

"Thank you, June—thank you—" he said—"'Tis well meant, though it's useless. But it is time to quit this place. To-morrow, we shall depart. You will go with us, for now you've got to feel reason."

June assented in the meek manner of an Indian woman, and she withdrew to pass the remainder of her time, near the grave of Arrowhead. Regardless of the hour and the season, the young widow did not pillow her head during the whole of that autumnal night. She sat near the spot that held the remains of her husband, and prayed, in the manner of her people, for his success on the endless path on which he had so lately gone, and for their reunion in the land of the just. Humble and degraded as she would have seemed in the eyes of the sophisticated and unreflecting, the image of God was on her soul, and it vindicated its divine origin by aspirations and feelings that would have surprised those, who feigning more, feel less.

In the morning all three departed; Pathfinder earnest and intelligent in all he did, the Great Serpent silent and imitative, and June meek, resigned, but sorrowful. They went in two canoes, that of the woman being abandoned. Chingachgook led the way, and Pathfinder followed, the course being up stream. Two days they paddled westward, and as many nights they encamped on islands. Fortunately the weather became mild, and when they reached the lake, it was found smooth, and glassy as a pond. It was the Indian summer, and the calms, and almost the blandness of June, slept in the hazy atmosphere.

On the morning of the third day, they passed the mouth of the Oswego, where the fort and the sleeping ensign invited them in vain to enter. Without casting a look aside, Chingachgook paddled past the dark water of the river, and Pathfinder still followed, in silent industry. The ramparts were crowded with spectators, but, Lundie, who knew the persons of his old friends, refused to allow them to be even hailed.

It was noon, when Chingachgook entered a little bay, where the Scud lay at anchor, in a sort of road-stead. A small, ancient clearing was on the shore, and near the margin of the lake was a log dwelling, recently and completely though rudely fitted up. There was an air of frontier comfort, and of frontier abundance around the place, though it was necessarily wild and solitary. Jasper stood on the shore, and, when Pathfinder landed, he was the first to take him by the hand. The meeting was simple, but very cordial. No questions were asked, it being apparent that Chingachgook had made the necessary explanations. Pathfinder never squeezed his friend's hand more cordially, than in this interview, and he even laughed cordially in his face, as he told him how happy and well he appeared.

"Where is she, Jasper?—where is she," the guide at length whispered, for, at first, he had seemed to be afraid to trust himself with the question.

"She is waiting for us in the house, my dear friend, where you see that June has already hastened before us."

"June may use a lighter step, to meet Mabel, but she cannot carry a lighter heart. And so, lad, you found the chaplain at the garrison, and all was soon settled?"

"We were married within a week after we left you, and Master Cap departed next day—You have forgotten to enquire about your friend, Salt-water—"

"Not I—not I. The Sarpent has told me all that, and then I love so much to hear of Mabel, and her happiness, I do. Did the child smile, or did she weep, when the ceremony was over?"

"She did both, my friend; but——"

"Yes, that's their natur'; tearful and cheerful! Ah's me! they are very pleasant to us of the woods, and I do believe, I should think all right, whatever Mabel might do. And do you think, Jasper, that she thought of me, at all, on that joyful occasion?"

"I know she did, Pathfinder; and she thinks of you, and talks of you daily, almost hourly. None love you as we do!"

"I know few love me better, than yourself, Jasper. Chingachgook is perhaps now the only creatur', of whom I can say that. Well, there's no use in putting it off, any longer; it must be done, and may as well be done at once; so, Jasper, lead the way, and I'll endivor to look upon her sweet countenance once more."

Jasper did lead the way, and they were soon in the presence of Mabel. The latter met her late suitor, with a bright blush, and her limbs trembled so, she could hardly stand. Still her manner was affectionate and frank. During the hour of Pathfinder's visit, for it lasted no longer, though he ate in the dwelling of his friends, one who was expert in tracing the workings of the human mind, might have seen a faithful index to the feelings of Mabel, in her manner to Pathfinder and her husband. With the latter she still had a little of the reserve that usually accompanies young wedlock; but the tones of her voice were kinder even than common, the glance of her eye was tender, and she seldom looked at him without the glow that tinged her cheek betraying the existence of feelings that habit and time had not yet soothed into absolute tranquillity. With Pathfinder all was earnest, sincere, even anxious, but the tones never trembled, the eye never fell, and if the cheek flushed it was with the emotions that are connected with concern.

At length the moment came, when Pathfinder must go his way. Chingachgook had already abandoned the canoes, and was posted on the margin of the woods, where a path led into the forest. Here he calmly waited to be joined by his friend. As soon as the latter was aware of this fact he rose in a solemn manner, and took his leave.

"I've sometimes thought that my own fate has been a little hard," he said, "but that of this woman, Mabel, has shamed me into reason—"

"June remains, and lives with me," eagerly interrupted our heroine.

"So I comprehend it. If any body can bring her back from her grief, and make her wish to live, you can do it, Mabel, though I've misgivings about even your success. The poor creatur' is without a tribe, as well as without a husband, and it's not easy to reconcile the feelings to both losses. Ah's me!—What have I to do, with other people's miseries, and marriages, as if I had n't affliction enough of my own. Don't speak to me, Mabel—don't speak to me, Jasper—let me go my way, in peace and like a man. I've seen your happiness, and that is a great deal, and I shall be able to bear my own sorrow, all the better for it. No—I'll never kiss you ag'in, Mabel: I'll never kiss you ag'in—Here's my hand, Jasper—squeeze it, boy, squeeze it; no fear of its giving way, for it's the hand of a man—And, now, Mabel do you take it,—nay, you must not do this—" preventing Mabel from kissing it, and bathing it with her tears—"you must not do this—"

"Pathfinder—" asked Mabel; "when shall we see you, again?"

"I've thought of that too; yes I've thought of that, I have.

If the time should ever come when I can look upon you altogether as a sister, Mabel, or a child—it might be better to say a child, since you're young enough to be my daughter—depend on it, I'll come back, for it would lighten my very heart to witness your gladness. But if I cannot—Farewell—farewell—the sarjeant was wrong—yes, the sarjeant was wrong."

This was the last the Pathfinder ever uttered to the ears of Jasper Western and Mabel Dunham. He turned away, as if the words choked him, and was quickly at the side of his friend. As soon as the latter saw him approach, he shouldered his own burthen, and glided in among the trees, without waiting to be spoken to. Mabel, her husband and June, all watched the form of the Pathfinder, in the hope of receiving a parting gesture, or a stolen glance of the eye, but he did not look back. Once or twice, they thought they saw his head shake, as one trembles in bitterness of spirit, and a toss of the hand was given, as if he knew that he was watched, but a tread whose vigor no sorrow could enfeeble, soon bore him out of view, and he was lost in the depths of the forest.

Neither Jasper nor his wife ever beheld the Pathfinder again. They remained for another year on the banks of Ontario, and then the pressing solicitations of Cap, induced them to join him in New-York, where Jasper eventually became a successful and respected merchant. Thrice Mabel received valuable presents of furs, at intervals of years, and her feelings told her whence they came, though no name accompanied the gifts. Later in life still, when the mother of several youths, she had occasion to visit the interior, and found herself on the banks of the Mohawk, accompanied by her sons, the eldest of whom was capable of being her protector. On that occasion, she observed a man, in a singular guise, watching her, in the distance, with an intentness, that induced her to inquire into his pursuits and character. She was told he was the most renowned hunter of that portion of the State—it was after the revolution—a being of great purity of character, and of as marked peculiarities, and that he was known in that region of country, by the name of the Leatherstocking. Further than this, Mrs. Western could not ascertain, though the distant glimpse and singular deportment of this unknown hunter, gave her a sleepless night, and cast a shade of melancholy over her still lovely face, that lasted many a day.

As for June, the double loss of husband and tribe produced the effect that Pathfinder had foreseen. She died in the cottage of Mabel, on the shores of the lake, and Jasper conveyed her body to the island, where he interred it by the side of that of Arrowhead.

Lundie, lived to marry his ancient love, and retired a war-worn and battered veteran, but his name has been rendered illustrious in our own time, by the deeds of a younger brother, who succeeded to his territorial title, which, however, was shortly after merged in one earned by his valor on the ocean.

THE DEERSLAYER

or, The First War-Path

Preface

THIS BOOK has not been written, without many misgivings as to its probable reception. To carry one and the same character through five several works would seem to be a wilful over drawing on the good nature of the public, and many persons may very reasonably suppose it an act, of itself, that ought to invite a rebuke. To this natural objection, the author can only say that, if he has committed a grave fault on this occasion, his readers are in some measure answerable for it. The favorable manner in which the more advanced career, and the death of Leather Stocking were received, has created, in the mind of the author at least, a sort of necessity for giving some account of his younger days. In short the pictures, of his life, such as they are, were already so complete as to excite some little desire to see the 'study,' from which they have all been drawn.

"The Leather-Stocking Tales," form now something like a drama in five acts; complete as to material and design, though quite probably very incomplete as to execution. Such as they are, the reading world has them before it. Their author hopes, should it decide that this particular act, the last in execution, though the first in the order of perusal, is not the best of the series, it will also come to the conclusion that it is not absolutely the worst. More than once, he has been tempted to burn his manuscript, and to turn to some other subject, though he has met with an encouragement, in the course of his labors, of a character so singular, as to be worth mentioning. An anonymous letter from England, has reached him, written as he thinks by a lady, in which he is urged to do almost the very thing he had already more than half executed; a request that he has been willing enough to construe into a sign that his attempt will be partially forgiven, if not altogether commended.

Little need be said concerning the characters and scenery of this Tale. The former are fictitious, as a matter of course; but the latter is as true to nature, as an intimate knowledge of the present appearance of the region described, and such probable conjectures concerning its ancient state as could be furnished by the imagination, enabled the writer to render it. The lake, mountains, valley and forests, are all believed to be sufficiently exact, while the river, rock and shoal are faithful transcripts from nature. Even the points exist, a little altered by civilization, but so nearly answering to the descriptions, as to be easily recognised by all who are familiar with the scenery of the particular region in question.

As to the accuracy of the incidents, of this Tale, in whole or in part, it is the intention of the author to stand on his rights, and say no more than he deems to be necessary. In the great struggle for veracity, that is carrying on between History and Fiction, the latter has so often the best of it, that he is quite willing to refer the reader to his own researches, by way of settling this particular point. Should it appear on inquiry, that any professed historian, the public documents, or even the local traditions, contradict the statements of this book, the writer is ready to admit that the circumstance has entirely escaped his observation, and to confess his ignorance. On the other hand, should it be found that the annals of America do not contain a syllable, in opposition to what has been now laid before the world, as he firmly believes investigation will show to be the case, he shall claim for his legend just as much authority as it deserves.

There is a respectable class of novel-readers—respectable for numbers, quite as much as for every thing else—who have often been likened to the man that "sings when he reads, and reads when he sings." These persons are exceedingly imaginative in all matters of fact, and as literal as a school boy's translation, in every thing that relates to poetry. For the benefit of all such persons, it is explicitly stated, that Judith Hutter is Judith Hutter, and not Judith any one else; and, generally, that wherever a coincidence may occur in a christian name, or in the color of hair, nothing more is meant than can properly be inferred from a coincidence in a christian name, or in the color of hair. Long experience has taught the writer, that this portion of his readers is much the most difficult to please, and he would respectfully suggest, for the benefit of both parties, that they try the experiment of reading works of the imagination as if they were intended for matters of fact. Such a plan might possibly enable them to believe in the possibility of fiction.

There is another class of readers—less important certainly, in a republican country, inasmuch as it is materially in the minority—which is addicted to taking things as they are offered, and of understanding them as they are meant. These persons are advised to commence at chapter first, and to read consecutively, just as far as the occupation may prove agreeable to themselves, and not a page beyond it. Should any of this class reach the end of the book, and fancy the time spent in the perusal not entirely thrown away, the circumstance will afford its author sincere gratification.

Preface to The Leather-Stocking Tales

THIS SERIES of Stories, which has obtained the name of "The Leather-Stocking Tales," has been written in a very desultory and inartificial manner. The order in which the several books appeared was essentially different from that in which they would have been presented to the world, had the regular course of their incidents been consulted. In "The Pioneers," the first of the series written, the Leather-Stocking is represented as already old, and driven from his early haunts in the forest, by the sound of the axe, and the smoke of the settler. "The Last of the Mohicans," the next book in the order of publication, carried the readers back to a much earlier period in the history of our hero, representing him as middle-aged, and in the fullest vigor of manhood. In "The Prairie," his career terminates, and he is laid in his grave. There, it was originally the intention to leave him, in the expectation that, as in the case of the human mass, he would soon be forgotten. But a latent regard for this character induced the author to resuscitate him in "The Pathfinder," a book that was not long after succeeded by "The Deerslayer," thus completing the series as it now exists.

While the five books that have been written were originally published in the order just mentioned, that of the incidents, insomuch as they are connected with the career of their principal character, is, as has been stated, very different. Taking the life of the Leather-Stocking as a guide, "The Deerslayer" should have been the opening book, for in that work he is seen just emerging into manhood; to be succeeded by "The Last of the Mohicans," "The Pathfinder," "The Pioneers," and "The Prairie." This arrangement embraces the order of events, though far from being that in which the books at first appeared. "The Pioneers" was published in 1823; "The Deerslayer" in 1841; making the interval between them eighteen years. Whether these progressive years have had a tendency to lessen the value of the last-named book, by lessening the native fire of its author, or of adding somewhat in the way of improved taste and a more matured judgment, is for others to decide.

If anything from the pen of the writer of these romances is at all to outlive himself, it is, unquestionably, the series of "The Leather-Stocking Tales." To say this, is not to predict a very lasting reputation for the series itself, but simply to express the belief it will outlast any, or all, of the works from the same hand.

It is undeniable that the desultory manner in which "The Leather-Stocking Tales" were written, has, in a measure, impaired their harmony, and otherwise lessened their interest. This is proved by the fate of the two books last published, though probably the two most worthy an enlightened and cultivated reader's notice. If the facts could be ascertained, it is probable the result would show that of all those (in America, in particular) who have read the three first books of the series, not one in ten has a knowledge of the existence even of the two last. Several causes have tended to produce this result. The long interval of time between the appearance of "The Prairie" and that of "The Pathfinder," was itself a reason why the later books of the series should be overlooked. There was no longer novelty to attract attention, and the interest was materially impaired by the manner in which events were necessarily anticipated, in laying the last of the series first before the world. With the generation that is now coming on the stage this fault will be partially removed by the edition contained in the present work, in which the several tales will be arranged solely in reference to their connexion with each other.

The author has often been asked if he had any original in his mind, for the character of Leather-Stocking. In a physical sense, different individuals known to the writer in early life, certainly presented themselves as models, through his recollections; but in a moral sense this man of the forest is purely a creation. The idea of delineating a character that possessed little of civilization but its highest principles as they are exhibited in the uneducated, and all of savage life that is not incompatible with these great rules of conduct, is perhaps natural to the situation in which Natty was placed. He is too proud of his origin to sink into the condition of the wild

Indian, and too much a man of the woods not to imbibe as much as was at all desirable, from his friends and companions. In a moral point of view it was the intention to illustrate the effect of seed scattered by the way side. To use his own language, his "gifts" were "white gifts," and he was not disposed to bring on them discredit. On the other hand, removed from nearly all the temptations of civilized life, placed in the best associations of that which is deemed savage, and favorably disposed by nature to improve such advantages, it appeared to the writer that his hero was a fit subject to represent the better qualities of both conditions, without pushing either to extremes.

There was no violent stretch of the imagination, perhaps, in supposing one of civilized associations in childhood, retaining many of his earliest lessons amid the scenes of the forest. Had these early impressions, however, not been sustained by continued, though casual connexion with men of his own color, if not of his own caste, all our information goes to show he would soon have lost every trace of his origin. It is believed that sufficient attention was paid to the particular circumstances in which this individual was placed, to justify the picture of his qualities that has been drawn. The Delawares early attracted the attention of the missionaries, and were a tribe unusually influenced by their precepts and example. In many instances they became Christians, and cases occurred in which their subsequent lives gave proof of the efficacy of the great moral changes that had taken place within them.

A leading character in a work of fiction has a fair right to the aid which can be obtained from a poetical view of the subject. It is in this view, rather than in one more strictly circumstantial, that Leather-Stocking has been drawn. The imagination has no great task in portraying to itself a being removed from the every-day inducements to err, which abound in civilized life, while he retains the best and simplest of his early impressions; who sees God in the forest; hears him in the winds; bows to him in the firmament that o'ercanopies all; submits to his sway in a humble belief of his justice and mercy; in a word, a being who finds the impress of the Deity in all the works of nature, without any of the blots produced by the expedients, and passion, and mistakes of man. This is the most that has been attempted in the character of Leather-Stocking. Had this been done without any of the drawbacks of humanity, the picture would have been, in all probability, more pleasing than just. In order to preserve the *vrai-semblable*, therefore, traits derived from the prejudices, tastes, and even the weaknesses of his youth, have been mixed up with these higher qualities and longings, in a way, it is hoped, to represent a reasonable picture of human nature, without offering to the spectator a "monster of goodness."

It has been objected to these books that they give a more favorable picture of the red man than he deserves. The writer apprehends that much of this objection arises from the habits of those who have made it. One of his critics, on the appearance of the first work in which Indian character was portrayed, objected that its "characters were Indians of the school of Heckewelder, rather than of the school of nature." These words quite probably contain the substance of the true answer to the objection. Heckewelder was an ardent, benevolent missionary, bent on the good of the red man, and seeing in him one who had the soul, reason, and characteristics of a fellow-being. The critic is understood to have been a very distinguished agent of the government, one very familiar with Indians, as they are seen at the councils to treat for the sale of their lands, where little or none of their domestic qualities come in play, and where, indeed, their evil passions are known to have the fullest scope. As just would it be to draw conclusions of the general state of American society from the scenes of the capital, as to suppose that the negotiating of one of these treaties is a fair picture of Indian life.

It is the privilege of all writers of fiction, more particularly when their works aspire to the elevation of romances, to present the *beau-idéal* of their characters to the reader. This it is which constitutes poetry, and to suppose that the red man is to be represented only in the squalid misery or in the degraded moral state that certainly more or less belongs to his condition, is, we apprehend, taking a very narrow view of an author's privileges. Such criticism would have deprived the world of even Homer.

Preface to The Deerslayer

As has been stated in the preface to the series of the Leather-Stocking Tales, "The Deerslayer" is properly the first in the order of reading, though the last in that of publication. In this book the hero is represented as just arriving at manhood, with the freshness of feeling that belongs to that interesting period of life, and with the power to please that properly characterizes youth. As a consequence, he is loved; and, what denotes the real waywardness of humanity, more than it corresponds with theories and moral propositions, perhaps, he is loved by one full of art, vanity, and weakness, and loved principally for his sincerity, his modesty, and his unerring truth and probity. The preference he gives to the high qualities named, over beauty, delirious passion, and sin, it is hoped, will offer a lesson that can injure none. This portion of the book is intentionally kept down, though it is thought to be sufficiently distinct to convey its moral.

The intention has been to put the sisters in strong contrast; one admirable in person, clever, filled with the pride of beauty, erring, and fallen; the other, barely provided with sufficient capacity to know good from evil, instinct, notwithstanding, with the virtues of woman, reverencing and loving God, and yielding only to the weakness of her sex, in admiring personal attractions in one too coarse and unobservant to distinguish or to understand her quiet, gentle feeling in his favor.

As for the scene of this tale, it is intended for, and believed to be a close description of the Otsego, prior to the year 1760, when the first rude settlement was commenced on its banks, at that time only an insignificant clearing near the outlet, with a small hut of squared logs, for the temporary dwelling of the Deputy Superintendent of Indian affairs. The recollections of the writer carry him back distinctly to a time when nine tenths of the shores of this lake were in the virgin forest, a peculiarity that was owing to the circumstance of the roads running through the first range of valleys removed from the water side. The woods and the mountains have ever formed a principal source of beauty with this charming sheet of water, enough of the former remaining to this day to relieve the open grounds from monotony and tameness.

In most respects the descriptions of scenery in the tale are reasonably accurate. The rock appointed for the rendezvous between the Deerslayer and his friend the Delaware still remains, bearing the name of the Otsego Rock. The shoal on which Hutter is represented as having built his "castle" is a little misplaced, lying, in fact, nearer to the northern end of the lake, as well as to the eastern shore, than is stated in this book. Such a shoal, however, exists, surrounded on all sides by deep water. In the dryest seasons a few rocks are seen above the surface of the lake, and rushes, at most periods of the year, mark its locality. In a word, in all but precise position, even this feature of the book is accurate. The same is true of the several points introduced, of the bays, of the river, of the mountains and all the other accessories of the place.

The legend is purely fiction, no authority existing for any of its facts, characters, or other peculiarities, beyond that which was thought necessary to secure the semblance of reality. Truth compels us to admit that the book has attracted very little notice, and that if its merits are to be computed by its popularity, the care that has been bestowed on this edition might as well be spared. Such, at least, has been its fate in America; whether it has met with better success in any other country we have no means of knowing.

Chapter I

"There is a pleasure in the pathless woods,
There is a rapture on the lonely shore,
There is society where none intrudes,
By the deep sea, and music in its roar:
I love not man the less, but nature more,
From these our interviews, in which I steal
From all I may be, or have been before,
To mingle with the universe, and feel
What I can ne'er express, yet cannot all conceal."

Byron, *Childe Harold's Pilgrimage*, IV.clxxviii.

ON THE HUMAN IMAGINATION, events produce the effects of time. Thus, he who has travelled far and seen much is apt to fancy that he has lived long; and the history that most abounds in important incidents, soonest assumes the aspect of antiquity. In no other way can we account for the venerable air that is already gathering around American annals. When the mind reverts to the earliest days of colonial history, the period seems remote and obscure, the thousand changes that thicken along the links of recollections, throwing back the origin of the nation to a day so distant as seemingly to reach the mists of time; and yet four lives of ordinary duration would suffice to transmit, from mouth to mouth, in the form of tradition, all that civilized man has achieved within the limits of the republic. Although New-York, alone, possesses a population materially exceeding that of either of the four smallest kingdoms of Europe, or materially exceeding that of the entire Swiss Confederation, it is little more than two centuries since the Dutch commenced their settlement, rescuing the region from the savage state. Thus, what seems venerable by an accumulation of changes, is reduced to familiarity when we come seriously to consider it solely in connection with time.

This glance into the perspective of the past, will prepare the reader to look at the pictures we are about to sketch, with less surprise than he might otherwise feel, and a few additional explanations may carry him back in imagination, to the precise condition of society that we desire to delineate. It is matter of history that the settlements on the eastern shores of the Hudson, such as Claverack, Kinderhook, and even Poughkeepsie, were not regarded as safe from Indian incursions a century since, and there is still standing on the banks of the same river, and within musket shot of the wharves of Albany, a residence of a younger branch* of the van Rensselaers, that has loop-holes constructed for defence against the same crafty enemy, although it dates from a period scarcely so distant. Other similar memorials of the infancy of the country are to be found, scattered through what is now deemed the very centre of American civilization, affording the plainest proofs that all we possess of security from invasion and hostile violence, is the growth of but little more than the time that is frequently filled by a single human life.

The incidents of this tale occurred between the years 1740 and 1745, when the settled portions of the Colony of New-York were confined to the four Atlantic counties, a narrow belt of country on each side of the Hudson, extending from its mouth to the falls near its head, and to a few advanced "neighborhoods" on the Mohawk and the Schoharie. Broad belts of the virgin wilderness, not only reached the shores of the first river, but they even crossed it, stretching away into New England, and affording forest cover to the noiseless moccasin of the native warrior, as he trod the secret and bloody war-path. A bird's eye view of the whole region east of the Mississippi, must then have offered one vast expanse of woods, relieved by a comparatively narrow fringe of cultivation along the sea, dotted by the glittering surfaces of lakes, and intersected by the waving lines of rivers. In such a vast picture of solemn solitude, the district of country we design to paint, sinks into insignificance, though we feel encouraged to proceed by the conviction that, with slight and immaterial distinctions, he who succeeds in giving an accurate idea of any portion of this wild region, must necessarily convey a tolerably correct notion of the whole.

Whatever may be the changes produced by man, the eternal round of the seasons is unbroken. Summer and winter, seed time and harvest, return in their stated order, with a sublime

*It is no more than justice to say that the Greenbush Van Rensselaers claim to be the oldest branch of that ancient and respectable family.

precision, affording to man one of the noblest of all the occasions he enjoys of proving the high powers of his far reaching mind, in compassing the laws that control their exact uniformity, and in calculating their never ending revolutions. Centuries of summer suns had warmed the tops of the same noble oaks and pines, sending their heats even to the tenacious roots, when voices were heard calling to each other, in the depths of a forest, of which the leafy surface lay bathed in the brilliant light of a cloudless day in June, while the trunks of the trees rose in gloomy grandeur in the shades beneath. The calls were in different tones, evidently proceeding from two men who had lost their way, and were searching in different directions for their path. At length a shout proclaimed success, and presently a man of gigantic mould broke out of the tangled labyrinth of a small swamp, emerging into an opening that appeared to have been formed partly by the ravages of the wind, and partly by those of fire. This little area, which afforded a good view of the sky, although it was pretty well filled with dead trees, lay on the side of one of the high hills, or low mountains, into which nearly the whole surface of the adjacent country was broken.

"Here is room to breathe in!" exclaimed the liberated forester, as soon as he found himself under a clear sky, shaking his huge frame like a mastiff that has just escaped from a snow bank; "Hurrah! Deerslayer; here is day-light, at last, and yonder is the lake, itself."

These words were scarcely uttered when the second forester dashed aside the bushes of the swamp, and appeared in the area. After making a hurried adjustment of his arms and disordered dress, he joined his companion, who had already begun his dispositions for a halt.

"Do you know this spot?" demanded the one called Deerslayer, "or do you shout at the sight of the sun?"

"Both, lad, both; I know the spot, and am not sorry to see so useful a friend as the sun. Now we have got the p'ints of the compass in our minds, once more, and 'twill be our own faults if we let any thing turn them topsy turvy, ag'in, as has just happened. My name is not Hurry Harry, if this be not the very spot where the land-hunters 'camped the last summer, and passed a week. See, yonder are the dead bushes of their bower, and here is the spring. Much as I like the sun, boy, I've no occasion for it to tell me it is noon; this stomach of mine is as good a timepiece as is to be found in the colony, and it already p'ints to half past twelve. So open the wallet, lad, and let us wind up for another six hours' run."

At this suggestion both set themselves about making the preparations necessary for their usual frugal, but hearty, meal. We will profit by this pause in the discourse to give the reader some idea of the appearance of the men, each of whom is destined to enact no insignificant part in our legend. It would not have been easy to find a more noble specimen of vigorous manhood, than was offered in the person of him who called himself Hurry Harry. His real name was Henry March, but the frontiermen having caught the practice of giving *sobriquets*, from the Indians, the appellation of Hurry was far oftener applied to him than his proper designation, and not unfrequently he was termed Hurry Skurry, a nick-name he had obtained from a dashing, reckless, off-hand manner, and a physical restlessness that kept him so constantly on the move, as to cause him to be known along the whole line of scattered habitations that lay between the province and the Canadas. The stature of Hurry Harry exceeded six feet four, and being unusually well proportioned, his strength fully realized the idea created by his gigantic frame. The face did no discredit to the rest of the man, for it was both good-humoured and handsome. His air was free, and though his manner necessarily partook of the rudeness of a border life, the grandeur that pervaded so noble a physique prevented it from becoming altogether vulgar.

Deerslayer, as Hurry called his companion, was a very different person in appearance, as well as in character. In stature, he stood about six feet in his moccasins, but his frame was comparatively light and slender, showing muscles, however, that promised unusual agility, if not unusual strength. His face would have had little to recommend it except youth, were it not for an expression that seldom failed to win upon those who had leisure to examine it, and to yield to the feeling of confidence it created. This expression was simply that of guileless truth, sustained by an earnestness of purpose, and a sincerity of feeling, that rendered it remarkable. At times this air of integrity seemed to be so simple as to awaken the suspicion of a want of the usual means to discriminate between artifice and truth, but few came in serious contact with the man, without losing this distrust in respect for his opinions and motives.

Both these frontiermen were still young, Hurry having reached the age of six or eight and twenty, while Deerslayer was several years his junior. Their attire needs no particular description, though it may be well to add that it was composed in no small degree of dressed deer skin, and had the usual signs of belonging to those who passed their time between the skirts of civilized society and the boundless forests. There was, notwithstanding, some attention to smartness and the picturesque in the arrangements of Deerslayer's dress, more particularly to the part connected with his arms and accoutrements. His rifle was in perfect condition, the handle of his hunting knife was neatly carved, his powder horn was ornamented with suitable devices lightly cut into the material, and his shot-pouch was decorated with wampum. On the other hand, Hurry Harry, either from constitutional recklessness, or from a secret consciousness how little his appearance required artificial aids, wore every thing in a careless, slovenly manner, as if he felt a noble scorn for the trifling accessories of dress and ornaments. Perhaps the peculiar effect of his fine form and great stature was increased, rather than lessened, by this unstudied and disdainful air of indifference.

"Come, Deerslayer, fall to, and prove that you have a Delaware stomach, as you say you have had a Delaware edication," cried Hurry, setting the example, by opening his mouth to receive a slice of cold venison steak, that would have made an entire meal for a European peasant. "Fall to, lad, and prove your manhood, on this poor devil of a doe, with your teeth, as you've already done with your rifle."

"Nay—nay, Hurry, there's little manhood in killing a doe, and that, too, out of season; though there might be some, in bringing down a painter, or a catamount," returned the other disposing himself to comply. "The Delawares have given me my name, not so much on account of a bold heart, as on account of a quick eye, and an actyve foot. There may not be any cowardyce, in overcoming a deer, but sartain it is, there's no great valour."

"The Delawares, themselves, are no heroes," muttered Hurry through his teeth, the mouth being too full to permit it to be fairly opened, "or, they would never have allowed them loping vagabonds, the Mingos, to make them women."

"That matter is not rightly understood—has never been rightly explained," said Deerslayer earnestly, for he was as zealous a friend, as his companion was dangerous as an enemy. "The Mengwe fill the woods with their lies, and misconstruct words and treaties. I have now lived ten years with the Delawares, and know them to be as manful as any other nation, when the proper time to strike comes."

"Harkee, Master Deerslayer, since we are on the subject, we may as well open our minds to each other in a man to man way; answer me one question; you have had so much luck among the game as to have gotten a title, it would seem, but did you ever hit any thing human, or intelligible: did you ever pull trigger on an inimy that was capable of pulling one upon you?"

This question produced a singular collision between mortification and correct feeling, in the bosom of the youth, that was easily to be traced in the workings of his ingenuous countenance. The struggle was short, however, uprightness of heart soon getting the better of false pride, and frontier boastfulness.

"To own the truth, I never did," answered Deerslayer, "seeing that a fitting occasion never offered. The Delawares have been peaceable since my sojourn with 'em, and I hold it to be onlawful to take the life of man, except in open and ginerous warfare."

"What!—Did you never find a fellow thieving among your traps and skins, and do the law on him, with your own hands, by way of saving the magistrates trouble, in the settlements, and the rogue himself the costs of the suit?"

"I am no trapper, Hurry," returned the young man proudly. "I live by the rifle, a we'pon at which I will not turn my back on any man of my years, atween the Hudson and the St. Lawrence. I never offer a skin, that has not a hole in its head, besides them which natur' made to see with, or to breathe through."

"Ay—ay—this is all very well, in the animal way, though it makes but a poor figure along side of scalps and and-bushes. Shooting an Indian from an and-bush is acting up to his own principles, and now we have what you call a lawful war, on our hands, the sooner you wipe that disgrace off your character, the sounder will be your sleep; if it only come from knowing there is one inimy the less prowling in the woods. I shall not frequent your society long, friend Natty, unless you look higher than four footed beasts to practyse your rifle on."

"Our journey is nearly ended you say, Master March, and we can part to-night, if you see occasion. I have a fri'nd waiting for me, who will think it no disgrace to consart with a fellow creatur' that has never yet slain his kind."

"I wish I knew what has brought that skulking Delaware into this part of the country, so early in the season"—muttered Hurry to himself, in a way to show equally distrust, and a recklessness of its betrayal. "Where did you say, the young chief was to give you the meeting?"

"At a small round rock, near the foot of the lake, where they tell me the tribes are given to resorting to make their treaties, and to bury their hatchets. This rock have I often heard the Delawares mention, though lake and rock are equally strangers to me. The country is claimed by both Mingos and Mohicans, and is a sort of common territory to fish and hunt through, in times of peace, though what it may become in war-time, the Lord only knows!"

"Common territory!" exclaimed Hurry, laughing aloud. "I should like to know what Floating Tom Hutter would say to that? He claims the lake as his own property, in vartue of fifteen years' possession, and will not be likely to give it up to either Mingo or Delaware, without a battle for it."

"And what will the Colony say to such a quarrel—all this country must have some owner, the gentry pushing their cravings into the wilderness, even where they never dare to ventur' in their own parsons to look at the land they own."

"That may do in other quarters of the colony, Deerslayer, but it will not do here. Not a human being, the Lord excepted, owns a foot of s'ile, in this part of the country. Pen was never put to paper, consarning either hill or valley, hereaway, as I've heard old Tom say, time and ag'in, and so he claims the best right to it of any man breathing; and what Tom claims, he'll be very likely to maintain."

"By what I've heard you say, Hurry, this Floating Tom must be an oncommon mortal; neither Mingo, Delaware, nor Pale Face. His possession, too, has been long, by your tell, and altogether beyond frontier endurance. What's the man's history and human natur'?"

"Why as to old Tom's human natur' it is not much like other men's human natur', but more like a muskrat's human natur', seeing that he takes more to the ways of that animal than to the ways of any other fellow creatur'. Some think he was a free liver on the salt-water in his youth, and a companion of a sartain Kidd, who was hanged for piracy, long afore you and I were born, or acquainted, and that he came up into these regions, thinking that the King's cruisers could never cross the mountains, and that he might enjoy the plunder peaceably in the woods."

"There he was wrong, Hurry; very wrong. A man can enjoy plunder *peaceably* no where."

"That's much as his turn of mind may happen to be. I've known them that never could enjoy it at all, unless it was in the midst of a jollification, and them ag'in that enjoyed it best in a corner. Some men have no peace if they don't find plunder, and some if they do. Human natur' is crooked in these matters. Old Tom seems to belong to neither set, as he enjoys his, if plunder he has really got, with his darters, in a very quiet and comfortable way, and wishes for no more."

"Ay, he has darters, too; I've heard the Delawares, who've hunted this-a-way, tell their histories of these young women. Is there no mother, Hurry?"

"There was *once*, as in reason; but she has now been dead and sunk these two good years."

"Anan?" said Deerslayer, looking up at his companion in a little surprise.

"Dead and sunk, I say, and I hope that's good English. The old fellow lowered his wife into the lake, by way of seeing the last of her, as I can testify, being an eye-witness of the ceremony; but whether Tom did it to save digging, which is no easy job among roots, or out of a consait that water washes away sin sooner than 'arth, is more than I can say."

"Was the poor woman oncommon wicked, that her husband should take so much pains with her body?"

"Not onreasonable; though she had her faults. I consider Judith Hutter to have been as graceful, and about as likely to make a good ind, as any woman who had lived so long beyond the sound of church bells, and I conclude old Tom sunk her as much by way of *saving* pains, as by way of *taking* it. There was a little steel in her temper, it's true, and as old Hutter is pretty much flint, they struck out sparks once and awhile, but, on the whole, they might be said to live amicable like. When they did kindle, the listeners got some such insights into their past lives, as one gets into the darker parts of the woods, when a stray gleam of sunshine finds its way down to the roots of the trees. But Judith I shall always esteem, as it's recommend enough to one woman to be the mother of such a creatur' as her darter, Judith Hutter!"

"Ay, Judith was the name the Delawares mentioned, though it was pronounced after a fashion of their own. From their discourse I do not think the girl would much please my fancy."

"Thy fancy!" exclaimed March, taking fire equally at the indifference and at the presumption of his companion, "what the devil have you to do with a fancy, and that too consarning one like Judith? You are but a boy—a sapling that has scarce got root—Judith has had *men* among her suitors, ever since she was fifteen; which is now near five years; and will not be apt to cast even a look upon a half grown creatur' like you!"

"It is June, and there is not a cloud atween us and the sun, Hurry, so all this heat is not wanted," answered the other, altogether undisturbed; "any one may have a fancy, and a squirrel has a right to make up his mind touching a catamount."

"Ay, but it might not be wise, always, to let the catamount know it," growled March. "But you're young and thoughtless, and I'll overlook your ignorance. Come, Deerslayer," he added, with a good-natured laugh, after pausing a moment to reflect, "come, Deerslayer, we are sworn fri'nds, and will not quarrel about a light-minded, jilting jade, just because she happens to be handsome; more especially as you have never seen her. Judith is only for a man whose teeth show the full marks, and it's foolish to be afeard of a boy. What *did* the Delawares say of the hussy; for, an Indian, after all, has his notions of womankind, as well as a white man?"

"They said she was fair to look on, and pleasant of speech; but over-given to admirers, and light-minded."

"They are devils incarnate! After all, what schoolmaster is a match for an Indian, in looking into natur'? Some people think they are only good on a trail, or the war-path, but I say that they are philosophers, and understand a man, as well as they understand a beaver, and a woman as well as they understand either. Now that's Judith's character to a riband! To own the truth to you, Deerslayer, I should have married the gal two years since, if it had not been for two particular things, one of which was this very light-mindedness."

"And what may have been the other?" demanded the hunter, who continued to eat like one that took very little interest in the subject.

"T' other was an insartainty about her having *me*. The hussy is handsome, and she knows it. Boy, not a tree that is growing in these hills is straighter, or waves in the wind with an easier bend, nor did you ever see the doe that bounded with a more nat'ral motion. If that was all, every tongue would sound her praises; but she has such failings that I find it hard to overlook them, and sometimes I swear I'll never visit the lake ag'in."

"Which is the reason that you always come back? Nothing is ever made more sure by swearing about it."

"Ah, Deerslayer, you are a novelty in these partic'lars; keeping as true to edication as if you had never left the settlements. With me the case is different, and I never want to clinch an idee, that I do not feel a wish to swear about it. If you know'd all that I know consarning Judith, you'd find a justification for a little cussing. Now, the officers sometimes stray over to the lake, from the forts on the Mohawk, to fish and hunt, and then the creatur' seems beside herself! You can see it in the manner in which she wears her finery, and the airs she gives herself with the gallants."

"That is unseemly in a poor man's darter," returned Deerslayer gravely, "the officers are all gentry, and can only look on such as Judith with evil intentions."

"There's the unsartainty, and the damper! I have my misgivings about a particular captain, and Jude has no one to blame but her own folly, if I'm wrong. On the whole, I wish to look upon her as modest and becoming, and yet the clouds that drive among these hills are not more unsartain. Not a dozen white men have ever laid eyes upon her, since she was a child, and yet her airs, with two or three of these officers, are extinguishers!"

"I would think no more of such a woman, but turn my mind altogether to the forest; *that* will not deceive you, being ordered and ruled by a hand that never wavers."

"If you know'd Judith, you would see how much easier it is to say this, than it would be to do it. Could I bring my mind to be easy about the officers, I would carry the gal off to the Mohawk by force, make her marry me in spite of her whiffling, and leave old Tom to the care of Hetty, his other child, who, if she be not as handsome, or as quick-witted as her sister, is much the most dutiful."

"Is there another bird in the same nest?" asked Deerslayer, raising his eyes with a species of half-awakened curiosity—"The Delawares spoke to me only of one."

"That's nat'ral enough, when Judith Hutter and Hetty Hutter are in question. Hetty is only comely, while her sister, I tell thee, boy, is such another as is not to be found atween this and the sea; Judith is as full of wit, and talk, and cunning, as an old Indian orator, while poor Hetty, is at the best but 'compass meant us.' "

"Anan?" inquired, again, the Deerslayer.

"Why, what the officers call, 'compass meant us,' which I understand to signify that she means always to go in the right direction, but sometimes does'nt know how. 'Compass' for the p'int, and 'meant us' for the intention. No, poor Hetty, is what I call on the varge of ignorance, and sometimes she stumbles on one side of the line, and sometimes on t'other."

"Them are beings that the Lord has in his 'special care," said Deerslayer, solemnly, "for he looks carefully to all who fall short of their proper share of reason. The Redskins honor and respect them who are so gifted, knowing that the Evil Spirit delights more to dwell in an artful body, than in one that has no cunning to work upon."

"I'll answer for it, then, that he will not remain long with poor Hetty—for the child is just 'compass meant us,' as I have told you. Old Tom has a feeling for the gal, and so has Judith, quick witted and glorious as she is herself; else would I not answer for her being altogether safe among the sort of men that sometimes meet on the lake shore."

"I thought this water an onknown and little frequented sheet," observed the Deerslayer, evidently uneasy at the idea of being too near the world.

"It's all that, lad, the eyes of twenty white men never having been laid on it; still, twenty true bred frontiermen—hunters, and trappers, and scouts, and the like,—can do a deal of mischief if they try. 'Twould be an awful thing to me, Deerslayer, did I find Judith married, after an absence of six months!"

"Have you the gal's faith, to incourage you to hope otherwise?"

"Not at all. I know not how it is—I'm good-looking, boy; that much I can see in any spring on which the sun shines—and yet I could never get the hussy to a promise, or even a cordial willing smile, though she will laugh by the hour. If she *has* dared to marry in my absence, she'll be like to know the pleasures of widowhood, afore she is twenty!"

"You would not harm the man she had chosen, Hurry, simply because she found him more to her liking than yourself?"

"Why not? If an inimy crosses my path, will I not beat him out of it! Look at me—am I a man like to let any sneaking, crawling, skin-trader, get the better of me in a matter that touches me as near as the kindness of Judith Hutter? Besides, when we live beyond law, we must be our own judges and executioners. And if a man *should* be found dead in the woods, who is there to say who slew him, even admitting that the Colony took the matter in hand, and made a stir about it?"

"If that man should be Judith Hutter's husband, after what

has passed, I might tell enough, at least, to put the Colony on the trail."

"You!—Half-grown, venison hunting bantling! You, dare to think of informing against Hurry-Harry in so much as a matter touching a mink, or a woodchuck!"

"I would dare to speak truth, Hurry, consarning you, or any man that ever lived."

March looked at his companion, for a moment, in silent amazement; then seizing him by the throat, with both hands, he shook his comparatively slight frame, with a violence that menaced the dislocation of some of the bones. Nor was this done jocularly, for anger flashed from the giant's eyes, and there were certain signs, that seemed to threaten much more earnestness than the occasion would appear to call for. Whatever might be the real intention of March, and it is probable there was none settled in his mind, it is certain that he was unusually aroused, and most men who found themselves throttled by one of a mould so gigantic, in such a mood, and in a solitude so deep and helpless, would have felt intimidated, and tempted to yield even the right. Not so, however, with Deerslayer. His countenance remained unmoved; his hand did not shake, and his answer was given in a voice that did not resort to the artifice of louder tones, even, by way of proving its owner's resolution.

"You may shake, Hurry, until you bring down the mountain," he said quietly, "but nothing beside truth will you shake from me. It is probable that Judith Hutter has no husband to slay, and you may never have a chance to way lay one, else would I tell her of your threat, in the first conversation I held with the gal."

March released his gripe, and sat regarding the other, in silent astonishment.

"I thought we had been friends," he at length added—"but you've got the last secret of mine, that will ever enter your ears."

"I want none, if they are to be like this. I know we live in the woods, Hurry, and are thought to be beyond human laws—and perhaps we are so, in fact, whatever it may be in right—but there is a law, and a law maker, that rule across the whole continent. He that flies in the face of either, need not call me fri'nd."

"Damme, Deerslayer, if I do not believe you are, at heart, a Moravian, and no fair minded, plain dealing hunter, as you've pretended to be!"

"Fair minded or not, Hurry, you will find me as plain-dealing in deeds, as I am in words. But this giving way to sudden anger is foolish, and proves how little you have sojourned with the red men. Judith Hutter no doubt is still single, and you spoke but as the tongue ran, and not as the heart felt. There's my hand, and we will say and think no more about it."

Hurry seemed more surprised than ever; then he burst forth in a loud good-natured laugh, which brought tears to his eyes. After this, he accepted the offered hand, and the parties became friends.

" 'Twould have been foolish to quarrel about an idee," March cried, as he resumed his meal, "and more like lawyers in the towns, than like sensible men in the woods. They tell me, Deerslayer, much ill blood grows out of idees, among the people in the lower counties, and that they sometimes get to extremities upon them."

"That do they—that do they, and about other matters that might better be left to take care of themselves. I have heard the Moravians say that there are lands in which men quarrel even consarning their religion, and if they can get their tempers up on such a subject, Hurry, the Lord have marcy on 'em. Howsever, there is no occasion for our following their example, and more especially about a husband that this Judith Hutter may never see, or never wish to see. For my part, I feel more cur'osity about the feeble-witted sister, than about your beauty. There's something that comes close to a man's feelin's, when he meets with a fellow creatur' that has all the outward show of an accountable mortal, and who fails of being what he seems, only through a lack of reason. This is bad enough in a man, but when it comes to a woman, and she a young, and may-be a winning creatur', it touches all the pitiful thoughts his natur' has. God knows, Hurry, that such poor things be defenceless enough with all their wits about 'em; but it's a cruel fortun' when that great protector and guide fails 'em."

"Harkee, Deerslayer, you know what the hunters, and trappers, and peltry-men in general be, and their best friends will not deny that they are head-strong and given to having their own way without much bethinking 'em of other people's rights, or feelin's, and yet I don't think the man is to be found, in all this region, who would harm Hetty Hutter, if he could; no, not even a red skin."

"Therein, fri'nd Hurry, you do the Delawares at least, and all their allied tribes only justice, for a red skin looks upon a being thus struck by God's power, as especially under his care. I rejoice to hear what you say, howsever, I rejoice to hear it, but as the sun is beginning to turn towards the a'ternoon's sky, had we not better strike the trail ag'in, and make forward that we may get an opportunity of seeing these wonderful sisters."

Harry March giving a cheerful assent, the remnants of the meal were soon collected; then the travellers shouldered their packs, resumed their arms, and quitting the little area of light, they again plunged into the deep shadows of the forest.

Chapter II

"Thou'rt passing from the lake's green side,
 And the hunter's hearth away;
For the time of flowers, for the summer's pride,
 Daughter! Thou canst not stay."

Mrs. Hemans, "Edith. A Tale of the Woods," ll. 191–94.

OUR TWO ADVENTURERS had not far to go. Hurry knew the direction, as soon as he had found the open spot and the spring, and he now led on with the confident step of a man assured of his object. The forest was dark, as a matter of course, but it was no longer obstructed by under brush, and the footing was firm and dry. After proceeding near a mile, March stopped, and began to cast about him with an inquiring look, examining the different objects with care, and occasionally turning his eyes on the trunks of the fallen trees, with which the ground was well sprinkled, as is usually the case in an American wood, especially in those parts of the country where timber has not yet become valuable.

"*This* must be the place, Deerslayer," March at length observed—"Here is a beech by the side of a hemlock, with three pines at hand, and yonder is a white birch with a broken top; and yet I see no rock, nor any of the branches bent down, as I told you would be the case."

"Broken branches are onskilful land-marks, as the least exper'enced know that branches don't often break of themselves," returned the other, "and they also lead to suspicion and discoveries. The Delawares never trust to broken branches, unless it is in friendly times, and on an open trail. As for the beeches, and pines, and hemlocks, why, they are to be seen on all sides of us, not only by two and threes, but by forties, and fifties and hundreds."

"Very true, Deerslayer, but you never calcilate on positions?—Here is a beech and a hemlock—"

"Yes, and there is another beech and a hemlock, as loving as two brothers, or, for that matter, more loving than some brothers; and yonder are others, for neither tree is a rarity in these woods. I fear me, Hurry, you are better at trapping beaver and shooting bears, than at leading on a blindish sort of a trail—ha! There's what you wish to find, a'ter all!"

"Now, Deerslayer, this is one of your Delaware pretensions, for, hang me if I see any thing but these trees, which do seem to start up around us, in a most onaccountable and perplexing manner."

"Look this-a-way, Hurry—here in a line with the black oak—don't you see the crooked sapling that is hooked up in the branches of the bass-wood, near it?—now, that sapling was once snow-ridden and got the bend by its weight, but it never straightened itself, and fastened itself in among the bass-wood branches, in the way you see. The hand of man did that act of kindness for it."

"That hand was mine!" exclaimed Hurry. "I found the slender young thing bent to the airth, like an unfortunate creatur' borne down by misfortune, and stuck it up where you see it. After all, Deerslayer, I must allow you're getting to have an oncommon good eye for the woods!"

" 'Tis improving, Hurry—'tis improving, I will acknowledge, but 'tis still only a child's eye compared to some I know. There's Tamenund, now, though a man so old, that few remember when he was in his prime, Tamenund lets nothing escape his look, which is more like the scent of a hound, than the sight of an eye. Then Uncas,* the father of Chingachgook, and the lawful chief of the Mohicans, is another that it is almost hopeless to pass unseen. I'm improving, I will allow; I'm improving but far from being parfect, as yet."

"And who is this Chingachgook, of whom you talk so much, Deerslayer?" asked Hurry, as he moved off in the direction of the righted sapling—"a loping red skin, at the best, I make no question."

"Not so, Hurry, but the best of loping red-skins, as you call 'em. If he had his rights, he would be a great chief; but, as it is, he is only a brave and just minded Delaware; respected, and even obeyed in some things 'tis true, but of a fallen race, and belonging to a fallen people. Ah! Harry March, 'twould warm the heart within you, to sit in their

*Lest the similarity of the names should produce confusion, it may be well to say that the Uncas here mentioned is the grandfather of him who plays so conspicuous a part in the Last of the Mohicans.

lodges of a winter's night, and listen to the traditions of the ancient greatness and power of the Mohicans!"

"Harkee, fri'nd Nathaniel," said Hurry, stopping short to face his companion, in order that his words might carry greater weight with them, "if a man believed all that other people choose to say in their own favor, he might get an oversized opinion of them, and an undersized opinion of himself. These red-skins are notable boasters, and I set down more than half of their traditions, as pure talk."

"There is truth in what you say, Hurry; I'll not deny it, for I've seen it, and believe it. They *do* boast, but then that is a gift from natur', and it's sinful to withstand nat'ral gifts. See; this is the spot you come to find."

This remark cut short the discourse, and both the men now gave all their attention to the object immediately before them. Deerslayer pointed out to his companion the trunk of a huge linden, or bass-wood, as it is termed in the language of the country, which had filled its time, and fallen by its own weight. This tree, like so many millions of its brethren, lay where it had fallen, and was mouldering under the slow but certain influence of the seasons. The decay, however, had attacked its centre, even while it stood erect, in the pride of vegetation, hollowing out its heart, as disease sometimes destroys the vitals of animal life, even while a fair exterior is presented to the observer. As the trunk lay stretched for near a hundred feet along the earth, the quick eye of the hunter detected this peculiarity, and, from this, and other circumstances, he knew it to be the tree of which March was in search.

"Ay, here we have what we want," cried Hurry, looking in at the larger end of the linden; "every thing is as snug as if it had been left in an old woman's cupboard. Come, lend me a hand, Deerslayer, and we'll be afloat in half an hour."

At this call the hunter joined his companion, and the two went to work deliberately and regularly, like men accustomed to the sort of thing in which they were employed. In the first place, Hurry removed some pieces of bark that lay before the large opening in the tree, and which the other declared to be disposed in a way that would have been more likely to attract attention, than to conceal the cover, had any straggler passed that way. The two, then, drew out a bark canoe, containing its seats, paddles, and other appliances, even to fishing lines and rods. This vessel was by no means small, but such was its comparative lightness, and so gigantic was the strength of Hurry, that the latter shouldered it with seeming ease, declining all assistance even in the act of raising it to the awkward position in which he was obliged to hold it.

"Lead ahead, Deerslayer," said March, "and open the bushes; the rest I can do for myself."

The other obeyed, and the men left the spot, Deerslayer clearing the way for his companion, and inclining to the right, or to the left, as the latter directed. In about ten minutes, they both broke suddenly into the brilliant light of the sun, on a low gravelly point, that was washed by water, on quite half of its outline.

An exclamation of surprise broke from the lips of Deerslayer, an exclamation that was low and guardedly made, however, for his habits were much more thoughtful and regulated than those of the reckless Hurry, when on reaching the margin of the lake he beheld the view that unexpectedly met his gaze. It was, in truth, sufficiently striking to merit a brief description. On a level with the point lay a broad sheet of water, so placid and limpid, that it resembled a bed of the pure mountain atmosphere, compressed into a setting of hills and woods. Its length was about three leagues, while its breadth was irregular, expanding to half a league, or even more, opposite to the point, and contracting to less than half that distance more to the southward. Of course its margin was irregular, being indented by bays, and broken by many projecting, low, points. At its northern, or nearest end, it was bounded by an isolated mountain, lower land falling off, east and west, gracefully relieving the sweep of the outline. Still the character of the country was mountainous; high hills, or low mountains, rising abruptly from the water, on quite nine tenths of its circuit. The exceptions, indeed, only served a little to vary the scene, and even beyond the parts of the shore that were comparatively low, the back-ground was high, though more distant.

But the most striking peculiarities of this scene, were its solemn solitude, and sweet repose. On all sides, wherever the eye turned, nothing met it, but the mirror-like surface of the lake, the placid void of heaven, and the dense setting of wood. So rich and fleecy were the outlines of the forest, that scarce an opening could be seen, the whole visible earth, from the rounded mountain-top, to the water's edge, presenting one unvaried hue of unbroken verdure. As if vegetation were not satisfied with a triumph so complete, the trees overhung the lake, itself, shooting out towards the light, and there were miles along its eastern shore, where a boat might have pulled beneath the branches, of dark, Rembrandt-looking hem-locks, "quivering aspens," and melancholy pines. In a word, the hand of man had never yet defaced, or deformed any part of this native scene, which lay bathed in the sun-light, a glorious picture of affluent forest grandeur, softened by the balminess of June, and relieved by the beautiful variety afforded by the presence of so broad an expanse of water.

"This is grand!—'Tis solemn!—'Tis an edication of itself, to look upon!" exclaimed Deerslayer, as he stood leaning on his rifle, and gazing to the right and left, north and south, above and beneath, in whichever direction his eye could wander. "Not a tree disturbed, even by red skin hand, as I can discover, but every thing left in the ordering of the Lord, to live and die according to his own designs and laws! Hurry, your Judith ought to be a moral and well disposed young woman, if she has passed half the time you mention, in the centre of a spot so favored."

"That's a naked truth, and yet the gal has her vagaries. *All* her time has not been passed here, howsever, old Tom having the custom, afore I know'd him, of going to spend the winters, in the neighborhood of the settlers, or under the guns of the forts. No—no—Jude has caught more than is for her good, from the settlers, and especially from the gallantifying officers."

"If she has—if she has, Hurry, this is a school to set her mind right, ag'in. But what is this I see off here, abreast of us, that seems too small for an island, and too large for a boat, though it stands in the midst of the water."

"Why that is what these gallanting gentry from the forts, call Muskrat Castle, and old Tom, himself, will grin at the name, though it bears so hard on his own natur' and character. 'Tis the stationary house, there being two; this which never moves, and the other that floats, being sometimes in one part of the lake, and sometimes in another. The last goes by the name of the Ark, though what may be the meaning of the word, is more than I can tell you."

"It must come from the missionaries, Hurry, whom I have heard speak and read of such a thing. They say that the 'arth was once covered with water, and that Noah with his children, was saved from drowning by building a vessel called an Ark, in which he embarked in season. Some of the Delawares believe this tradition, and some deny it; but, it behoves you and me, as white men born, to put our faith in its truth. Do you see any thing of this ark?"

"Tis down south, no doubt, or anchored in some of the bays. But the canoe is ready, and fifteen minutes will carry two such paddles as your'n and mine, to the castle."

At this suggestion, Deerslayer helped his companion to place the different articles in the canoe, which was already afloat. This was no sooner done, than the two frontiermen embarked, and by a vigorous push sent the light bark some eight or ten rods from the shore. Hurry now took the seat in the stern, while Deerslayer placed himself forward, and by leisurely but steady strokes of the paddles, the canoe glided across the placid sheet, towards the extraordinary looking structure, that the former had styled Muskrat Castle. Several times the men ceased paddling, and looked about them at the scene, as new glimpses opened from behind points, enabling them to see farther down the lake, or to get broader views of the wooded mountains. The only changes, however, were in the new forms of the hills, the varying curvature of the bays, and the wider reaches of the valley south, the whole earth apparently being clothed in a gala dress of leaves.

"This *is* a sight to warm the heart!" exclaimed Deerslayer, when they had thus stopped for the fourth or fifth time. "The lake seems made to let us get an insight into the noble forests; and land and water, alike, stand in the beauty of God's Providence! Do you say, Hurry, that there is no man who calls himself lawful owner of all these glories?"

"None but the King, lad. He may pretend to some right of that natur', but he is so far away that his claim will never trouble old Tom Hutter, who has got possession, and is like to keep it as long as his life lasts. Tom is no squatter, not being on land, I call him a floater."

"I in*vy* that man!—I know it's wrong, and I strive ag'in the feelin', but I in*vy* that man! Do'n't think, Hurry, that I'm consarting any plan to put myself in his moccasins, for such a thought does not harbor in my mind, but I can't help a little in*vy*. 'Tis a nat'ral feelin', and the best of us are but nat'ral, a'ter all, and give way to such feelin's, at times."

"You've only to marry Hetty to inherit half the estate," cried Hurry, laughing. "The gal is comely; nay, if it was n't for her sister's beauty, she would be even handsome; and then her wits are so small that you may easily convart her into one of your own way of thinking in all things. Do *you* take Hetty off the old fellow's hands, and *I'll* engage he'll give you an interest in every deer you can knock over, within five miles of his lake."

"Does game abound?" suddenly demanded the other, who paid but little attention to March's raillery.

"It has the country to itself. Scarce a trigger is pulled on it, and as for the trappers, this is not a region they greatly frequent. I ought not to be so much here, myself, but Jude pulls one way, while the beaver pulls another. More than a hundred Spanish dollars has that creatur' cost me, the two last seasons; and yet I could not forego the wish to look upon her face, once more."

"Do the red-men often visit this lake, Hurry?" continued Deerslayer, pursuing his own train of thought.

"Why, they come and go; sometimes in parties, and sometimes singly. The country seems to belong to no native tribe in particular, and so it has fallen into the hands of the Hutter tribe. The old man tells me that some sharp ones have been wheedling the Mohawks for an Indian deed, in order to git a title out of the Colony, but nothing has come of it, seeing that no one heavy enough for such a trade, has yet meddled with the matter. The hunters have a good life lease, still, of this wilderness."

"So much the better—so much the better, Hurry. If I was King of England the man that fell one of these trees without good occasion for the timber, should be banished to a desarted and forlorn region, in which no four footed animal ever trod. Right glad am I that Chingachgook app'inted our meeting on this lake, for, hitherto, eye of mine never looked on such a glorious spectacle!"

"That's because you've kept so much among the Delawares, in whose country there are no lakes. Now, further north, and farther west, these bits of water abound, and you're young, and may yet live to see 'em. But, though there be other lakes, Deerslayer, there's no other Judith Hutter."

At this remark his companion smiled, and then he dropped his paddle into the water, as if, in consideration of a lover's haste. Both now pulled vigorously until they got within a hundred yards of the "castle," as Hurry familiarly called the house of Hutter, when they again ceased paddling, the admirer of Judith restraining his impatience the more readily, as he perceived that the building was untenanted, at the moment. This new pause was to enable Deerslayer to survey the singular edifice, which was of a construction so novel as to merit a particular description.

Muskrat Castle, as the house had been facetiously named by some waggish officer, stood in the open lake, at a distance of fully a quarter of a mile from the nearest shore. On every other side the water extended much farther, the precise position being distant about two miles from the northern end of the sheet, and near, if not quite a mile from its eastern shore. As there was not the smallest appearance of any island, but the house stood on piles with the water flowing beneath it, and Deerslayer had already discovered that the lake was of a great depth, he was fain to ask an explanation of this singular circumstance. Hurry solved the difficulty by telling him that on this spot alone, a long narrow shoal, which extended for a few hundred yards in a north and south direction, rose within six or eight feet of the surface of the lake, and that Hutter had driven piles into it, and placed his habitation on them, for the purpose of security.

"The old fellow was burnt out three times, atween the Indians and the hunters, and in one affray with the red skins he lost his only son; since which time he has taken to the water for safety. No one can attack him, here, without coming in a boat, and the plunder and scalps would scarce be worth the trouble of digging out canoes. Then, it's by no means sartain which would whip, in such a skrimmage, for, old Tom is well supplied with arms and ammunition, and the castle, as you may see, is a tight breast-work, ag'in light shot."

Deerslayer had some theoretical knowledge of frontier warfare, though he had never yet been called on to raise his hand, in anger, against a fellow creature. He saw that Hurry did not over-rate the strength of this position, in a military point of view, since it would not be easy to attack it, without exposing the assailants to the fire of the besieged. A good deal of art had also been manifested in the disposition of the timber, of which the building was constructed, and which afforded a protection much greater than was usual to the ordinary log cabins of the frontier. The sides and ends were composed of the trunks of large pines, cut about nine feet long, and placed upright, instead of being laid horizontally, as was the practice of the country. These logs were squared on three sides, and had large tennons on each end. Massive sills were secured on the heads of the piles, with suitable grooves dug out of their upper surfaces, which had been squared for the purpose, and the lower tennons of the upright pieces were placed in these grooves, giving them a secure fastening below. Plates had been laid on the upper ends of the upright logs and were kept in their places, by a similar contrivance; the several corners of the structure being well fastened by scarfing and pinning the sills, and plates. The floors were made of smaller logs, similarly squared, and the roof was composed of light poles, firmly united, and well covered with bark. The effect of this ingenious arrangement was to give its owner a house that could be approached only by water, the sides of which were composed of logs, closely wedged together, which were two feet thick in their thinnest parts and which could be separated only by a deliberate and laborious use of human hands, or by the slow operation of time. The outer surface of the building was rude and uneven, the logs being of unequal sizes, but the squared surfaces within, gave both the sides and floors as uniform an appearance as was desired either for use, or show. The chimney was not the least singular portion of the castle, as Hurry made his companion observe, while he explained the process by which it had been made. The material was a stiff clay, properly worked, which had been put together in a mould of sticks, and suffered to harden a foot or two, at a time, commencing at the bottom. When the entire chimney had thus been raised, and had been properly bound in with outward props, a brisk fire was kindled, and kept going until it was burned to something like a brick red. This had not been an easy operation, nor had it succeeded entirely, but by dint of filling the cracks with fresh clay, a safe fire-place and chimney had been obtained in the end. This part of the work stood on the log floor, secured beneath by an extra pile. There were a few other peculiarities about this dwelling, which will better appear in the course of the narrative.

"Old Tom is full of contrivances," added Hurry, "and he set his heart on the success of his chimney, which threatened, more than once, to give out altogether, but parseverance will even overcome smoke; and now he has a comfortable cabin of it, though it did promise, at one time, to be a chinky sort of a flue to carry flames and fire."

"You seem to know the whole history of the castle, Hurry, chimney and sides," said Deerslayer, smiling. "Is love so overcoming that it causes a man to study the story of his sweetheart's habitation?"

"Partly that, lad, and partly eye sight," returned the good natured giant, laughing. "There was a large gang of us, in at the lake, the summer the old fellow built, and we helped him along with the job. I raised no small part of the weight of them uprights with my own shoulders, and the axes flew, I can inform you, Master Natty, while we were beeing it among the trees ashore. The old devil is no way stingy about food, and as we had often eat at his hearth, we thought we would just house him comfortably, afore we went in to Albany with our skins. Yes, many is the meal I've swallowed in Tom Hutter's cabins, and, Hetty, though so weak in the way of wits, has a wonderful particular way about a frying pan, or a grid-iron!"

While the parties were thus discoursing, the canoe had been gradually drawing nearer to the 'castle', and was now so close, as to require but a single stroke of a paddle to reach the landing. This was at a floored platform in front of the entrance, that might have been some twenty feet square.

"Old Tom calls this sort of a wharf, his door-yard," observed Hurry, as he fastened the canoe, after he and his companion had left it, "and the gallants from the forts have named it the 'castle court,' though what a 'court' can have to do here, is more than I can tell you, seeing that there is no law. 'Tis as I supposed; not a soul within, but the whole family is off on a v'y'ge of discovery!"

While Hurry was bustling about the 'door yard', examining the fishing spears, rods, nets and other similar appliances of a frontier cabin, Deerslayer, whose manner was altogether more rebuked and quiet, entered the building, with a curiosity that was not usually exhibited by one so long trained in Indian habits. The interior of the 'castle' was as faultlessly neat, as its exterior was novel. The entire space, some twenty feet by forty, was subdivided into several small sleeping rooms, the apartment into which he first entered serving equally for the ordinary uses of its inmates, and for a kitchen. The furniture was of the strange mixture that it is not uncommon to find in the remotely situated log tenements of the interior. Most of it was rude and to the last degree rustic, but there was a clock, with a handsome case of dark wood, in a corner, and two or three chairs, with a table and bureau, that had evidently come from some dwelling of more than usual pretension. The clock was industriously ticking, but its leaden-looking hands did no discredit to their dull aspect, for they pointed to the hour of eleven, though the sun plainly showed it was some time past the turn of the day. There was also a dark, massive chest. The kitchen utensils were of the simplest kind, and far from numerous, but every article was in its place, and showed the nicest care in its condition.

After Deerslayer had cast a look about him, in the outer room, he raised a wooden latch, and entered a narrow passage that divided the inner end of the house, into two equal parts. Frontier usages being no way scrupulous, and his curiosity being strongly excited, the young man now opened a door, and found himself in a bed-room. A single glance sufficed to show that the apartment belonged to females. The bed was of the feathers of wild geese, and filled nearly to overflowing, but it lay in a rude bunk, raised only a foot from the floor. On one side of it were arranged on pegs, various dresses of a quality much superior to what one would expect to meet in such a place, with ribbons and other similar articles to correspond. Pretty shoes, with handsome silver buckles, such as were then worn by females in easy circumstances, were not wanting, and no less than six fans of gay colours, were placed, half open, in a way to catch the eye by their conceits and hues. Even the pillow on this side of the bed, was covered with finer linen than its companion, and it was ornamented with a small ruffle. A cap, coquettishly decorated with ribbons, hung above it, and a pair of long gloves, such as were rarely used in those days by persons of the laboring classes, were pinned ostentatiously to it, as if with an intention to exhibit them there, if they could not be shown on the owner's arms.

All this Deerslayer saw, and noted with a degree of minuteness that would have done credit to the habitual observation of his friends the Delawares. Nor did he fail to perceive the distinction that existed between the appearances on the different sides of the bed, the head of which stood against the wall. On that opposite to the one just described, every thing was homely, and uninviting except through its perfect neatness. The few garments that were hanging from the pegs, were of the coarsest materials, and of the commonest forms, while nothing seemed made for show. Of ribbons there was not one, nor was there either cap, or kerchief, beyond those which Hutter's daughters might be fairly entitled to wear.

It was now several years since Deerslayer had been in a spot especially devoted to the uses of females of his own colour and race. The sight brought back to his mind a rush of childish recollections, and he lingered in the room with a tenderness of feeling to which he had long been a stranger. He bethought him of his mother, whose homely vestments he remembered to have seen hanging on pegs, like those which he felt must belong to Hetty Hutter, and he bethought him of a sister whose incipient and native taste for finery had exhibited itself somewhat in the manner of that of Judith, though necessarily in a lesser degree. These little resemblances opened a long hidden vein of sensations, and as he quitted the room, it was with a saddened mien. He looked no farther, but returned slowly and thoughtfully towards the "door-yard."

"Old Tom has taken to a new calling, and has been trying his hand at the traps," cried Hurry, who had been coolly examining the borderer's implements. "If that is his humour, and you're disposed to remain in these parts, we can make an oncommon comfortable season of it, for while the old man and I out-knowledge the beaver, you can fish and knock down the deer, to keep body and soul together. We always give the poorest hunters half a share, but one as actyve and sartain as yourself, might expect a full one."

"Thank'ee, Hurry; thank'ee, with all my heart, but I do a little beavering for myself, as occasions offer. 'Tis true the Delawares call me Deerslayer, but it's not so much because I'm pretty fatal with the venison, as because that while I kill so many bucks and does, I've never yet taken the life of a fellow creatur'. They say their traditions do not tell of another who had shed so much blood of animals, that had not shed the blood of man."

"I hope they don't account you chicken-hearted, lad? A faint-hearted man is like a no-tailed beaver."

"I don't believe, Hurry, that they account me as out-of-the-way timoursome, even though they may not account me as out-of-the-way brave. But I'm not quarrelsome, and that goes a great way towards keeping blood off the hands, among the hunters and red-skins, and then, Harry March, it keeps blood off the conscience, too."

"Well, for my part, I account game, a red skin, and a Frenchman, as pretty much the same thing; though I'm as onquarrelsome a man, too, as there is in all the colonies. I despise a quarreller, as I do a cur dog, but one has no need to be over scrupulsome, when it's the right time to show the flint."

"I look upon him as the most of a man, who acts nearest the right, Hurry. But this is a glorious spot, and my eyes never aweary looking at it!"

" 'Tis your first acquaintance with a lake, and these idees come over us all, at such times. Lakes have a general character, as I say, being pretty much water, and land, and points, and bays."

As this definition by no means met the feelings that were uppermost in the mind of the young hunter, he made no immediate answer, but stood gazing at the dark hills and the glassy water, in silent enjoyment.

"Have the governor's, or the King's people given this lake a name?" he suddenly asked, as if struck with a new idea. "If they've not begun to blaze their trees, and set up their compasses, and line off their maps, it's likely they've not bethought them to disturb natur' with a name."

"They've not got to that yet, and the last time I went in with skins, one of the king's surveyors was questioning me consarning all the region, hereabouts. He had heard that there was a lake, in this quarter, and had got some general notions about it, such as that there was water and hills, but how much of either, he know'd no more than you know of the Mohawk tongue. I did'nt open the trap any wider than was necessary, giving him but poor encouragement in the way of farms and clearings. In short, I left on his mind some such opinion of this country, as a man gets of a spring of dirty water, with a path to it that is so muddy that one mires afore he sets out. He told me they had'n't got the spot down, yet, on their maps, though I conclude that is a mistake, for he showed me his parchment, and there is a lake down on it, where there is no lake in fact, and which is about fifty miles from the place where it ought to be, if they meant it for this. I don't think my account will encourage him to mark down another, by way of improvement."

Here Hurry laughed heartily, such tricks being particularly grateful to a set of men who dreaded the approaches of civilization as a curtailment of their own lawless empire. The egregious errors that existed in the maps of the day, all of which were made in Europe, were, moreover, a standing topic of ridicule among them, for, if they had not science enough to make any better themselves, they had sufficient local information to detect the gross blunders contained in those that existed. Any one who will take the trouble to compare these unanswerable evidences of the topographical skill of our fathers a century since, with the more accurate sketches of our own times, will at once perceive that the men of the woods had sufficient justification for all their criticism on this branch of the skill of the colonial governments, which did not at all hesitate to place a river, or a lake, a degree or two out of the way, even though they lay within a day's march of the inhabited parts of the country.

"I'm glad it has no name," resumed Deerslayer, "or, at least, no pale face name, for their christenings always foretel waste and destruction. No doubt, howsever, the red skins have their modes of knowing it, and the hunters and trappers, too, they are likely to call the place by something reasonable and resembling?"

"As for the tribes, each has its own tongue, and its own way of calling things, and they treat this part of the world just as they treat all the others. Among ourselves we've got to calling the place the 'Glimmerglass,' seeing that its whole basin is so often fringed with pines cast upward from its face, as if it would throw back the hills that hang over it."

"There is one outlet I know, for all lakes have outlets, and the rock at which I am to meet Chingachgook, stands near an outlet. Has *that* no Colony name, yet?"

"In that particular, they've got the advantage of us. Having one end, and that the biggest, in their own keeping, they've given it a name, which has found its way up to its source; names nat'rally working up stream. No doubt, Deerslayer, you've seen the Susquehannah, down in the Delaware country?"

"That have I, and hunted along its banks a hundred times."

"That and this are the same in fact, and I suppose the same in sound. I am glad they've been compelled to keep the red men's name, for it would be too hard to rob them of both land and names!"

Deerslayer made no answer, but he stood leaning on his rifle, gazing at the view which so much delighted him. The reader is not to suppose, however, that it was the picturesque alone, which so strongly attracted his attention. The spot was very lovely, of a truth, and it was then seen in one of its most favorable moments, the surface of the lake being as smooth as glass, and limpid as pure air, throwing back the mountains, clothed in dark pines, along the whole of its eastern boundary, the points thrusting forward their trees even to nearly horizontal lines, while the bays were seen glittering through an occasional arch beneath, left by a vault fretted with branches and leaves. It was the air of deep repose, the solitudes that spoke of scenes and forests untouched by the hands of man, the reign of nature, in a word, that gave so much pure delight to one of his habits and turn of mind. Still, he felt, though it was unconsciously, like a poet also. He found a pleasure in studying this large, and, to him, unusual opening into the mysteries and forms of the woods, as one is gratified in getting broader views of any subject that has long occupied his thoughts. He was not insensible to the innate loveliness of such a landscape, either, but felt a portion of that soothing of the spirit which is a common attendant of a scene so thoroughly pervaded by the holy calm of nature.

Chapter III

"Come, shall we go and kill us venison?
And yet it irks me, the poor dappled fools,—
Being native burghers of this desert city,—
Should, in their own confines, with forked heads
Have their round haunches gored."

As You Like It, II.i.21–25.

HURRY HARRY thought more of the beauties of Judith Hutter, than of those of the Glimmerglass, and its accompanying scenery. As soon as he had taken a sufficiently intimate survey of Floating Tom's implements, therefore, he summoned his companion to the canoe, that they might go down the lake in quest of the family. Previously to embarking, however, Hurry carefully examined the whole of the northern end of the water, with an indifferent ship's glass, that formed a part of Hutter's effects. In this scrutiny no part of the shore was overlooked, the bays and points, in particular, being subjected to a closer inquiry than the rest of the wooded boundary.

" 'Tis as I thought," said Hurry, laying aside the glass—"The old fellow is drifting about the south end, this fine weather, and has left the castle to defend itself. Well, now we know that he is not up this-a-way, 'twill be but a small matter to paddle down, and hunt him up in his hiding place."

"Does Master Hutter think it necessary to burrow on this lake?" inquired Deerslayer, as he followed his companion into the canoe. "To my eye, it is such a solitude as one might open his whole soul in, and fear no one to disarrange his thoughts, or his worship."

"You forget your friends the Mingos, and all the French savages. Is there a spot on 'arth, Deerslayer, to which them disquiet rogues don't go? Where is the lake, or even the deer lick, that the blackguards don't find out, and having found out, don't, sooner or later, discolour its water with blood."

"I hear no good character of 'em, sartainly, friend Hurry, though I've never been called on, yet, to meet them, or any other mortal, on the warpath. I dare to say that such a lovely spot as this, would not be likely to be overlooked by such plunderers, for, though I've not been in the way of quarrelling with them tribes myself, the Delawares give me such an account of 'em that I've pretty much set 'em down in my own mind, as thorough miscreants."

"You may do that with a safe conscience, or, for that matter, any other savage you may happen to meet."

Here Deerslayer protested, and as they went paddling down the lake, a hot discussion was maintained concerning the respective merits of the pale-faces and the redskins. Hurry had all the prejudices and antipathies of a white hunter, who generally regards the Indian as a sort of natural competitor, and not unfrequently as a natural enemy. As a matter of course, he was loud, clamorous, dogmatical and not very argumentative. Deerslayer, on the other hand, manifested a very different temper, proving by the moderation of his language, the fairness of his views, and the simplicity of his distinctions, that he possessed every disposition to hear reason, a strong, innate desire to do justice, and an ingenuousness that was singularly indisposed to have recourse to sophisms to maintain an argument, or to defend a prejudice. Still he was not altogether free from the influence of the latter feeling. This tyrant of the human mind, which rushes on its prey through a thousand avenues, almost as soon as men begin to think and feel, and which seldom relinquishes its iron sway until they cease to do either, had made some impression on even the just propensities of this individual, who probably offered in these particulars, a fair specimen of what absence from bad example, the want of temptation to go wrong, and native good feeling can render youth.

"You will allow, Deerslayer, that a Mingo is more than half devil," cried Hurry, following up the discussion with an animation that touched closely on ferocity, "though you want to overpersuade me that the Delaware tribe is pretty much made up of angels. Now, I gainsay that proposal consarning white men, even. All white men are not faultless, and therefore all Indians *ca'nt* be faultless. And so your argument is out at the elbow, in the start. But, this is what I call reason. Here's three colours on 'arth; white, black and red. White is the highest colour, and therefore the best man; black comes next, and is put to live in the neighborhood of the white man, as tolerable and fit to be made use of; and red comes last, which shows that those that made 'em never expected an Indian to be accounted as more than half human."

"God made all three, alike, Hurry—"

"Alike! Do you call a nigger like a white man, or me like an Indian?"

"You go off at half-cock, and do'n't hear me out. God made us all, white, black and red, and no doubt had his own wise intentions in colouring us differently. Still he made us, in the main, much the same in feelin's; though I'll not deny that he gave each race its gifts. A white man's gifts are christianized, while a red skin's are more for the wilderness. Thus it would be a great offence for a white man to scalp the dead, whereas it's a signal vartue in an Indian. Then, ag'in, a white man cannot amboosh women and children in war, while a red skin may. 'Tis *cruel* work I'll allow, but for them it's *lawful* work, while for *us* it would be a grievous sin."

"That depends on your inimy. As for scalping, or even skinning a savage, I look upon them, pretty much the same as cutting off the ears of wolves for the bounty, or stripping a bear of its hide. And, then, you're out significantly, as to taking the poll of a red skin in hand, seeing that the very Colony has offered a bounty for the job, all the same as it pays for wolves' ears, and crows' heads."

"Ay, and a bad business it is, Hurry. Even the Indians, themselves, cry shame on it, seeing it's ag'in a white man's gifts. I do not pretend that all that white men do is properly christianized and according to the lights given them; for then they would be what they *ought* to be, which we know they are not; but I will maintain that tradition, and use, and colour, and laws, make such a difference in races as to amount to gifts. I do not deny that there are tribes among the Indians that are nat'rally pervarse and wicked, as there are nations among the whites. Now, I account the Mingos as belonging to the first, and the Frenchers, in the Canadas, to the last. In a state of lawful warfare, such as we have lately got into, it is a duty to keep down all compassionate feelin's, so far as life goes, ag'in either; but when it comes to scalps, it's a very different matter."

"Just hearken to reason, if you please, Deerslayer, and tell me if the colony can make an onlawful law? Is'n't an onlawful law more ag'in natur', than scalpin' a savage? A law can no more be onlawful, than truth can be a lie."

"That *sounds* reasonable, but it has a most onreasonable bearing, Hurry. Laws don't all come from the same quarter. God has given us his'n, and some come from the colony, and other some from the King and parliament. When the colony's laws, or even the king's laws, run ag'in the laws of God, they get to be onlawful, and ought not to be obeyed. I hold to a white man's respecting white laws, so long as they do not cross the track of a law comin' from a higher authority, and for a red man to obey his own red-skin usages, under the same privilege. But, 'tis useless talking, as each man will think for himself, and have his say agreeable to his thoughts. Let us keep a good look-out for your friend, Floating Tom, lest we pass him, as he lies hidden under this bushy shore."

Deerslayer had not named the borders of the lake amiss. Along their whole length the smaller trees overhung the water, with their branches often dipping in the transparent element. The banks were steep, even from the narrow strand, and, as vegetation invariably struggles toward the light, the effect was precisely that at which the lover of the picturesque would have aimed, had the ordering of this glorious setting of forest been submitted to his control. The points, and bays, too, were sufficiently numerous to render the outline broken and diversified. As the canoe kept close along the western side of the lake, with a view, as Hurry had explained to his companion, of reconnoitring for enemies before he trusted himself too openly in sight, the expectations of the two adventurers were kept constantly on the stretch, as neither could foretel what the next turning of a point might reveal. Their progress was swift, the gigantic strength of Hurry enabling him to play with the light bark as if it had been a feather, while the skill of his companion almost equalized their usefulness, notwithstanding the disparity in natural means.

Each time the canoe passed a point, Hurry turned a look behind him, expecting to see the "Ark" anchored, or beached, in the bay. He was fated to be disappointed, however, and they had got within a mile of the southern end of the lake, or a distance of quite two leagues from the 'castle', which was now hidden from view by half a dozen intervening projections of the land, when he suddenly ceased paddling, as if uncertain in what direction next to steer.

"It is possible that the old chap has dropped into the river," said Hurry, often looking carefully along the whole of the eastern shore, which was about a mile distant, and open to his scrutiny for more than half its length; "for he has taken to trapping considerable of late, and, barring flood-wood, he might drop down it, a mile or so, though he would have a most scratching time in getting back again!"

"Where is this outlet?" asked Deerslayer. "I see no opening in the banks, or the trees, that looks as if it would let a river like the Susquehannah run through it."

"Ay, Deerslayer, rivers are like human mortals; having small beginnings, and ending with broad shoulders, and wide mouths. You don't see the outlet, because it passes atween high steep banks, and the pines, and hemlocks, and basswoods hang over it, as a roof hangs over a house. If old Tom is not in the ' 'Rat's Cove', he must have burrowed in the river; we'll look for him first in the Cove, and then we'll cross to the outlet."

As they proceeded Hurry explained that there was a shallow bay, formed by a long low point, that had gotten the name of the " 'Rat's Cove" from the circumstance of its being a favorite haunt of the muskrat, and which offered so complete a cover for the 'ark' that its owner was fond of lying in it, whenever he found it convenient.

"As a man never knows who may be his visiters, in this part of the country," continued Hurry, "it's a great advantage to get a good look at 'em, before they come too near. Now, it's war, such caution is more than commonly useful, since a Canada man, or a Mingo might get into his hut afore he invited 'em. But, Hutter is a first rate look-outer, and can pretty much scent danger, as a hound scents the deer."

"I should think the castle so open, that it would be sartan to draw inimies, if any happened to find the lake, a thing onlikely enough I will allow, as it's off the trail of the forts and settlements."

"Why, Deerslayer, I've got to believe that a man meets with

inimies easier than he meets with fri'nds. It's skearful to think for how many causes one gets to be your inimy, and for how few your fri'nd. Some take up the hatchet because you do n't think just as they think, other some because you run ahead of 'em in the same idees, and I once know'd a vagabond that quarrelled with a fri'nd because he did n't think him handsome. Now, you're no monument in the way of beauty, yourself, Deerslayer, and yet you would n't be so onreasonable as to become my inimy for just saying so."

"I'm as the Lord made me, and I wish to be accounted no better, nor any worse. Good looks I may not have, that is to say to a degree that the light minded and vain crave, but I hope I'm not altogether without some ricommend in the way of good conduct. There's few nobler looking men to be seen than yourself, Hurry, and I know that I am not to expect any to turn their eyes on me, when such a one as you can be gazed on; but I do not know that a hunter is less expart with the rifle, or less to be relied on for food, because he does'n't wish to stop at every shining spring he may meet to study his own countenance in the water."

Here Hurry burst into a fit of loud laughter, for, while he was too reckless to care much about his own manifest physical superiority, he was well aware of it, and, like most men who derive an advantage from the accidents of birth or nature, he was apt to think complacently on the subject whenever it happened to cross his mind.

"No—no—Deerslayer, you're no beauty, as you will own yourself if you'll look over the side of the canoe," he cried. "Jude will say *that* to your face, if you start her, for a parter tongue is not to be found in any gal's head, in or out of the settlements, if you provoke her to use it. My advice to you, is never to aggravate Judith; though you may tell any thing to Hetty, and she'll take it as meek as a lamb. No, Jude will be just as like as not to tell you her opinion consarning your looks."

"And if she does, Hurry, she will tell me no more than you have said already"—

"You're not thick'ning up about a small remark, I hope, Deerslayer, when no harm is meant. You are *not* a beauty, as you must know, and why should'n't fri'nds tell each other these little trifles? If you *was* handsome, or ever like to be, I'd be one of the first to tell you of it, and that ought to content you. Now, if Jude was to tell me that I'm as ugly as a sinner, I'd take it as a sort of obligation, and try not to believe her."

"It's easy for them that natur' has favored, to jest about such matters, Hurry, though it is sometimes hard for others. I'll not deny but I've had my cravings towards good looks; yes I have; but then I've always been able to get them down by considering how many I've known with fair outsides, who have had nothing to boast of inwardly. I'll not deny, Hurry, that I often wish I'd been created more comely to the eye, and more like such a one as yourself, in them particulars, but then I get the feelin' under by remembering how much better off I am in a great many respects, than some fellow mortals. I might have been born lame, and onfit even for a squirrel hunt; or, blind, which would have made me a burthen on myself, as well as on my fri'nds, or, without hearing, which would have totally onqualified me for ever campaigning, or scouting, which I look forward to, as part of a man's duty in troublesome times. Yes—yes; it's not pleasant, I will allow, to see them that's more comely, and more sought a'ter, and honored than yourself; but it may all be borne, if a man looks the evil in the face, and don't mistake his gifts and his obligations."

Hurry, in the main, was a good hearted, as well as good-natured fellow, and the self abasement of his companion completely got the better of the passing feeling of personal vanity. He regretted the allusion he had made to the other's appearance, and endeavored to express as much, though it was done in the uncouth manner that belonged to the habits and opinions of the frontier.

"I meant no harm, Deerslayer," he answered in a deprecating manner, "and hope you'll forget what I've said. If you're not downright handsome, you've a sartain look that says plainer than any words, that all's right within. Then you set no valie by looks, and so will the sooner forgive any little slight to your appearance. I will not say that Jude will greatly admire you, for that might be to raise hopes that would only breed disapp'intment, but there's Hetty, now, would be just as likely to find satisfaction in looking at *you*, as in looking at any other man. Then you're altogether too grave and considerate like, to care much about Judith—for, though the gal *is* oncommon, she is so general in her admiration that a man need not be exalted because she happens to smile. I sometimes think the hussy loves herself better than she does any thing else breathin'!"

"If she did, Hurry, she'd do no more, I'm afeard, than most queens on their thrones, and ladies in the towns," answered Deerslayer, smiling, and turning back towards his companion, with every trace of feeling banished from his honest-looking and frank countenance. "I never yet know'd even a Delaware of whom you might not say that much. But here is the end of the long p'int, you mentioned, and the 'Rat's Cove, can't be far off."

This point, instead of thrusting itself forward, like all the others, ran in a line with the main shore of the lake, which here swept within it, in a deep and retired bay, circling round south, again, at the distance of a quarter of a mile, and crossed the valley, forming the southern termination of the water. In this bay, Hurry felt almost certain of finding the Ark, since, anchored behind the trees that covered the narrow strip of the point, it might have lain concealed from prying eyes an entire summer. So complete, indeed, was the cover, in this spot, that a boat hauled close to the beach within the point, and near the bottom of the bay, could by possibility be seen from only one direction, and that was from a densely wooded shore, within the sweep of the water, where strangers would be little apt to go.

"We shall soon see the Ark," said Hurry, as the canoe glided round the extremity of the point, where the water was so deep as actually to appear black; "he loves to burrow up among the rushes, and we shall be in his nest, in five minutes, although the old fellow may be off among the traps himself."

March proved a false prophet. The canoe completely doubled the point, so as to enable the two travellers to command a view of the whole cove, or bay, for it was more properly the last, and no object, but those that nature had placed there, became visible. The placid water swept round in a graceful curve, the rushes bent gently towards its surface, and the trees over-hung it as usual, but all lay in the soothing and sublime solitude of a wilderness. The scene was such as a poet, or an artist would have delighted in, but it had no charm for Hurry Harry, who was burning with impatience to get a sight of his light-minded beauty.

The motion of the canoe had been attended with little, or no noise, the frontier-men from habit getting accustomed to caution in most of their movements, and it now lay on the glassy water, appearing to float in air, partaking of the breathing stillness that seemed to pervade the entire scene. At this instant, a dry stick was heard cracking on the narrow strip of land that concealed the bay from the open lake. Both the adventurers started, and each extended a hand towards his rifle, the weapon never being out of reach of the arm.

" 'Twas too heavy, for any light creatur'," whispered Hurry, "and it sounded like the tread of a man!"

"Not so—not so—" returned Deerslayer—" 'twas, as you say, too heavy for one, but it was too light for the other. Put your paddle in the water, and send the canoe in to that log; I'll land and cut off the creatur's retreat up the p'int, be it a Mingo, or be it only a muskrat."

As Hurry complied, Deerslayer was soon on the shore, advancing into the thicket with a moccasined foot, and a caution that prevented the least noise. In a minute he was in the centre of the narrow strip of land, and moving slowly down towards its end, the bushes rendering extreme watchfulness necessary. Just as he reached the centre of the thicket, the dried twigs cracked again, and the noise was repeated, at short intervals, as if some creature having life, walked slowly towards the point. Hurry heard these sounds also, and pushing the canoe off into the bay, he seized his rifle to watch the result. A breathless minute succeeded, after which a noble buck walked out of the thicket, proceeded with a stately step to the sandy extremity of the point, and began to slake his thirst from the water of the lake. Hurry hesitated an instant, and then raising his rifle hastily to his shoulder, he took sight and fired. The effect of this sudden interruption of the solemn stillness of such a scene, was not its least striking peculiarity. The report of the weapon, had the usual sharp, short sound of the rifle, but, when a few moments of silence had succeeded the sudden crack, during which the noise was floating in air across the water, it reached the rocks of the opposite mountain, where the vibrations accumulated, and were rolled from cavity to cavity, for miles along the hills, seeming to awaken the sleeping thunders of the woods. The buck merely shook his head at the report of the rifle and the whistling of the bullet, for never before had he come in contact with man; but the echoes of the hills awakened his distrust, and leaping forward, with his four legs drawn under his body, he fell at once into deep water, and began to swim towards the foot of the lake. Hurry shouted and dashed forward in chase, and for one or two minutes the water foamed around the pursuer and the pursued. The former was dashing past the point, when Deerslayer appeared on the sand and signed to him to return.

" 'Twas inconsiderate to pull a trigger, afore we had re-conn'itred the shore, and made sartain that no inimies harbored near it," said the latter, as his companion slowly and reluctantly complied. "This much I have l'arned from the Delawares, in the way of schooling and traditions, even though I've never yet been on a war-path. And, moreover, venison can hardly be called in season now, and we do not want for food. They call me Deerslayer, I'll own, and perhaps I desarve the name, in the way of understanding the creatur's habits, as well as for some sartainty in the aim, but they can't accuse me of killing an animal when there is no occasion for the meat, or the skin. I may be a slayer, it's true, but I'm no slaughterer."

" 'Twas an awful mistake to miss that buck!" exclaimed Hurry, doffing his cap and running his fingers through his handsome but matted curls, as if he would loosen his tangled ideas by the process. "I've not done so onhandy a thing since I was fifteen."

"Never lament it, as the creatur's death could have done neither of us any good, and might have done us harm. Them echoes are more awful in my ears, than your mistake, Hurry, for they sound like the voice of natur' calling out ag'in a wasteful and onthinking action."

"You'll hear plenty of such calls, if you tarry long in this quarter of the world, lad," returned the other laughing. "The echoes repeat pretty much all that is said or done on the Glimmerglass, in this calm summer weather. If a paddle falls you hear of it sometimes, ag'in and ag'in, as if the hills were mocking your clumsiness, and a laugh, or a whistle, comes out of them pines, when they're in the humour to speak, in a way to make you believe they can r'ally convarse."

"So much the more reason for being prudent and silent. I do not think the inimy can have found their way into these hills yet, for I do'nt know what they are to gain by it, but all the Delawares tell me that, as courage is a warrior's first vartue, so is prudence his second. One such call from the mountains, is enough to let a whole tribe into the secret of our arrival."

"If it does no other good, it will warn old Tom to put the pot over, and let him know visiters are at hand. Come, lad; get into the canoe, and we will hunt the ark up, while there is yet day."

Deerslayer complied, and the canoe left the spot. Its head was turned diagonally across the lake, pointing towards the south-eastern curvature of the sheet. In that direction, the distance to the shore, or to the termination of the lake, on the course the two were now steering, was not quite a mile, and, their progress being always swift, it was fast lessening under the skilful, but easy sweeps of the paddles. When about half way across, a slight noise drew the eyes of the men towards the nearest land, and they saw that the buck was just emerging from the lake and wading towards the beach. In a minute, the noble animal shook the water from his flanks, gazed upward at the covering of trees, and, bounding against the bank, plunged into the forest.

"That creatur' goes off with gratitude in his heart," said Deerslayer, "for natur' tells him he has escaped a great danger. You ought to have some of the same feelin's, Hurry, to think your eye was'n't true, or that your hand was onsteady, when no good could come of a shot that was intended onmeaningly rather than in reason."

"I deny the eye and the hand," cried March with some heat. "You've got a little character, down among the Delawares, there, for quickness and sartainty, at a deer, but I should like to see you behind one of them pines, and a full painted Mingo behind another, each with a cock'd rifle and astriving for the chance! Them's the situations, Nathaniel, to try the sight and the hand, for they begin with trying the narves. I never look upon killing a creatur' as an explite, but killing a savage is. The time will come to try your hand, now we've got to blows ag'in, and we shall soon know what a ven'son repitation can do in the field. I deny that either hand or eye was onsteady; it was all a miscaculation on the buck, which stood still when he ought to have kept in motion, and so I shot ahead of him."

"Have it your own way, Hurry; all I contend for is, that it's lucky. I dare say I shall not pull upon a human mortal, as steadily, or with as light a heart, as I pull upon a deer—"

"Who's talking of mortals, or of human beings at all, Deerslayer? I put the matter to you on the suppersition of an Injin. I dare say any man would have his feelin's when it got to be life, or death, ag'in another human mortal, but there would be no such scruples in regard to an Injin, nothing but the chance of his hitting you, or the chance of you hitting him."

"I look upon the red men to be quite as human as we are ourselves, Hurry. They have their gifts, and their religion, it's true, but that makes no difference in the end, when each will be judged according to his deeds, and not according to his skin."

"That's downright missionary, and will find little favor, up in this part of the country where the Moravians don't congergate. Now, skin makes the man. This is reason; else how are people to judge of each other. The skin is put on, over all, in order that when a creatur', or a mortal, is fairly seen, you may know at once what to make of him. You know a bear from a hog by his skin, and a grey squirrel from a black."

"True, Hurry," said the other looking back and smiling, "nevertheless they are both squirrels."

"Who denies it?—But you'll not say that a red man and a white man are both Injins?"

"No; but I *do* say they are both men. Men of different races and colours, and having different gifts and traditions, but, in the main, with the same natur's. Both have souls and both will be held accountable for their deeds in this life."

Hurry was one of those theorists who believed in the inferiority of all of the human race, who were not white. His notions on the subject were not very clear, nor were his definitions at all well settled, but his opinions were none the less dogmatical, or fierce. His conscience accused him of sundry lawless acts against the Indians, and he had found it an exceedingly easy mode of quieting it, by putting the whole family of red men, incontinently, without the category of human rights. Nothing angered him sooner, than to deny his proposition, more especially if the denial were accompanied by a show of plausible argument, and he did not listen to his companion's remarks, with much composure, of either manner, or feeling.

"You're a boy, Deerslayer, mislead and misconsaited by Delaware arts, and Missionary ignorance," he exclaimed, with his usual indifference to the forms of speech, when excited. "*You* may account yourself as a red skin's brother, but *I* hold 'em all to be animals, with nothing human about 'em but cunning. *That* they have, I'll allow; but so has a fox, or even a bear. I'm older than you, and have lived longer in the woods—or, for that matter, have lived always there,—and am not to be told what an Injin is, or what he is not. If you wish to be considered a savage you've only to say so, and I'll name you as such to Judith and the old man, and then we'll see how you'll like your welcome."

Here, Hurry's imagination did his temper some service, since, by conjuring up the reception his semi aquatic acquaintance would be likely to bestow on one thus introduced, he burst into a hearty fit of laughter. Deerslayer too well knew the uselessness of attempting to convince such a being of any thing against his prejudices, to feel a desire to undertake the task, and he was not sorry that the approach of the canoe to the south eastern curve of the lake, gave a new direction to his ideas. They were now, indeed, quite near to the place that March had pointed out for the position of the outlet, and both began to look for it, with a curiosity that was increased by the expectation of finding the Ark.

It may strike the reader as a little singular that the place where a stream of any size passed through banks that had an elevation of some twenty feet, should be a matter of doubt with men, who could not now have been more than two hundred yards distant from the precise spot. It will be recollected, however, that the trees and bushes, here as elsewhere, fairly overhung the water, making such a fringe to the lake, as to conceal any little variations from its general outline.

"I've not been down at this end of the lake, these two summers," said Hurry, standing up in the canoe the better to look about him.—"Ay—There's the rock, showing its chin above the water, and I know that the river begins in its neighborhood."

The men now plied the paddles, again, and they were presently within a few yards of the rock, floating towards it, though their efforts were suspended. This rock was not large, being merely some five or six feet high, only half of which elevation rose above the lake. The incessant washing of the water, for centuries, had so rounded its summit, that it resembled a large bee-hive in shape, its form being more than usually regular and even. Hurry remarked as they floated slowly past, that this rock was well known to all the Indians in that part of the country, and that they were in the practice of using it as a mark to designate their place of meeting, when separated by their hunts and marches.

"And here is the river, Deerslayer," he continued, "though so shut in by trees and bushes, as to look more like an and-bush, than the outlet of such a sheet as the Glimmerglass."

Hurry had not badly described the place, which did truly seem to be a stream lying in ambush. The high banks might have been a hundred feet asunder, but on the western side a small bit of low land, extended so far forward, as to diminish the breadth of the stream to half that width. As the bushes hung in the water beneath, and pines that had the stature of church steeples, rose in tall columns above, all inclining towards the light until their branches intermingled, the eye, at a little distance, could not easily detect any opening in the shore to mark the egress of the water. In the forest above, no traces of this outlet were to be seen from the lake, the whole presenting the same connected and seemingly interminable carpet of leaves. As the canoe slowly advanced, sucked in by the current, it entered beneath an arch of trees, through which the light from the heavens struggled, by casual openings, faintly relieving the gloom beneath.

"This is a nat'ral and-bush," half-whispered Hurry, as if he felt that the place was devoted to secrecy and watchfulness, "and, depend on it, old Tom has burrowed with the Ark, somewhere in this quarter. We will drop down with the current, a short distance, and ferret him out."

"This seems no place for a vessel of any size," returned the other, "and it appears to me that we shall have hardly room enough for the canoe."

Hurry laughed at this suggestion, and, as it soon appeared with reason, for the fringe of bushes immediately on the shore of the lake was no sooner passed, than the adventurers found themselves in a narrow stream, of a sufficient depth of limpid water, with a strong current, and a canopy of leaves, upheld by arches composed of the limbs of hoary trees. Bushes lined the shores, as usual, but they left sufficient space between them to admit the passage of any thing that did not exceed twenty feet in width, and to allow of a perspective ahead of eight or ten times that distance.

Neither of our two adventurers used his paddle except to keep the light bark in the centre of the current, but both watched each turning of the stream, of which there were two or three within the first hundred yards, with jealous vigilance. Turn after turn, however, was passed, and the canoe had dropped down with the current some little distance, when Hurry caught a bush, and arrested its movement, so suddenly and silently as to denote some unusual motive for the act. Deerslayer laid his hand on the stock of his rifle, as soon as he noted this proceeding, but it was quite as much with a hunter's habit, as from any feeling of alarm.

"There the old fellow is!" whispered Hurry, pointing with a finger, and laughing heartily, though he carefully avoided making a noise. " 'Ratting it away, just as I supposed, up to his knees in the mud and water, looking to the traps and the bait. But, for the life of me, I can see nothing of the Ark, though I'll bet every skin I take this season, Jude is'n't trusting her pretty little feet in the neighborhood of that black mud. The gal's more likely to be braiding her hair, by the side of some spring, where she can see her own good looks, and collect scornful feelings ag'in us men."

"You over-judge young women, yes you do, Hurry, who as often bethink them of their failings as they do of their perfections. I dare to say, this Judith now, is no such admirer of herself, and no such scorner of our sex, as you seem to think; and that she is quite as likely to be sarving her father in the house, wherever that may be, as he is to be sarving her among the traps."

"It's a pleasure to hear truth from a man's tongue, if it be only once in a girl's life," cried a pleasant, rich, and yet soft female voice so near the canoe, as to make both the listeners start. "As for you, Master Hurry, fair words are so apt to choak you, that I no longer expect to hear them from your mouth, the last you uttered sticking in your throat and coming near to death. But I'm glad to see you keep better society than formerly, and that they who know how to esteem and treat women, are not ashamed to journey in your company."

As this was said, a singularly handsome and youthful female face was thrust through an opening in the leaves, within reach of Deerslayer's paddle. Its owner smiled graciously on the young man, and the frown that she then cast on Hurry, though simulated and pettish, had the effect to render her beauty more striking, by exhibiting the play of an expressive but capricious countenance; one that seemed to change from the soft to the severe, the mirthful to the reproving, with facility and indifference.

A second look explained the nature of the surprise. Unwittingly the men had dropped along side of the Ark, which had been purposely concealed in bushes, cut and arranged for the purpose, and Judith Hutter had merely pushed aside the leaves that lay before a window, in order to show her face, and speak to them.

Chapter IV

"And that timid fawn starts not with fear
When I steal to her secret bower,
And that young May violet to me is dear,
And I visit the silent streamlet near,
To look on the lovely flower."
Bryant, "An Indian Story," ll. 11–15.

THE ARK, as the floating habitation of the Hutters was generally called, was a very simple contrivance. A large flat, or scow, composed the buoyant part of the vessel, and, in its centre, occupying the whole of its breadth and about two thirds of its length, stood a low fabric, resembling the castle in construction, though made of materials so light as barely to be bulletproof. As the sides of the scow were a little higher than usual, and the interior of the cabin had no more elevation than was necessary for comfort, this unusual addition had neither a very clumsy, nor a very obtrusive appearance. It was, in short, little more than a modern canal boat, though more rudely constructed, of greater breadth than common, and bearing about it the signs of the wilderness, in its bark-covered posts and roof. The scow, however, had been put together with some skill, being comparatively light, for its strength, and sufficiently manageable. The cabin was divided into two apartments, one of which served for a parlor, and the sleeping-room of the father, and the other was appropriated to the uses of the daughters. A very simple arrangement sufficed for the kitchen, which was in one end of the scow, and removed from the cabin, standing in the open air; the Ark being altogether a summer habitation.

The 'and-bush', as Hurry in his ignorance of English termed it, is quite as easily explained. In many parts of the lake and river, where the banks were steep and high, the smaller trees, and larger bushes, as has been already mentioned, fairly overhung the stream, their branches not unfrequently dipping into the water. In some instances they grew out in nearly horizontal lines, for thirty or forty feet. The water being uniformly deepest near the shores, where the banks were highest and the nearest to a perpendicular, Hutter had found no difficulty in letting the Ark drop under one of these covers, where it had been anchored with a view to conceal its position, security requiring some such precautions, in his view of the case. Once beneath the trees and bushes, a few stones fastened to the ends of the branches had caused them to bend sufficiently to dip into the river, and a few severed bushes, properly disposed, did the rest. The reader has seen that this cover was so complete, as to deceive two men accustomed to the woods, and who were actually in search of those it concealed, a circumstance that will be easily understood by those who are familiar with the matted and wild luxuriance of a virgin American forest, more especially in a rich soil.

The discovery of the Ark produced very different effects on our two adventurers. As soon as the canoe could be got round to the proper opening, Hurry leaped on board, and in a minute was closely engaged in a gay, and a sort of recriminating discourse with Judith, apparently forgetful of the existence of all the rest of the world. Not so with Deerslayer. He entered the Ark with a slow, cautious step, examining every arrangement of the cover, with curious and scrutinizing eyes. It is true, he cast one admiring glance at Judith, which was extorted by her brilliant and singular beauty, but even this could detain him but a single instant from the indulgence of his interest in Hutter's contrivances. Step by step did he look into the construction of the singular abode, investigate its fastenings and strength, ascertain its means of defence, and make every inquiry that would be likely to occur to one whose thoughts dwelt principally on such expedients. Nor was the cover neglected. Of this he examined the whole minutely, his commendation escaping him more than once in audible comments. Frontier usages admitting of this familiarity, he passed through the rooms, as he had previously done at the 'Castle', and opening a door issued into the end of the scow opposite to that where he had left Hurry and Judith. Here he found the other sister, employed at some coarse needle-work, seated beneath the leafy canopy of the cover.

As Deerslayer's examination was by this time ended, he dropped the butt of his rifle, and, leaning on the barrel, with both hands, he turned towards the girl with an interest the singular beauty of her sister had not awakened. He had gathered from Hurry's remarks that Hetty was considered to have less intellect than ordinarily falls to the share of human beings, and his education among Indians had taught him to treat those who were thus afflicted by Providence, with more than common tenderness. Nor was there any thing in Hetty Hutter's appearance, as so often happens, to weaken the interest her situation excited. An idiot she could not properly be termed, her mind being just enough enfeebled to lose most of those traits that are connected with the more artful qualities, and to retain its ingenuousness and love of truth. It had often been remarked of this girl, by the few who had seen her, and who possessed sufficient knowledge to discriminate, that her perception of the right seemed almost intuitive, while her aversion to the wrong formed so distinctive a feature of her mind, as to surround her with an atmosphere of pure morality; peculiarities that are not infrequent with persons who are termed feeble-minded; as if God had forbidden the evil spirits to invade a precinct so defenceless, with the benign purpose of extending a direct protection to those, who had been left without the usual aids of humanity. Her person, too, was agreeable, having a strong resemblance to that of her sister's, of which it was a subdued and humble copy. If it had none of the brilliancy of Judith's, the calm, quiet, almost holy expression of her meek countenance, seldom failed to win on the observer, and few noted it long, that did not begin to feel a deep and lasting interest in the girl. She had no colour, in common, nor was her simple mind apt to present images that caused her cheek to brighten, though she retained a modesty so innate, that it almost raised her to the unsuspecting purity of a being superior to human infirmities. Guileless, innocent, and without distrust, equally by nature and from her mode of life, providence had, nevertheless, shielded her from harm, by a halo of moral light, as it is said 'to temper the wind to the shorn lamb.'

"You are Hetty Hutter," said Deerslayer, in the way one puts a question, unconsciously to himself assuming a kindness of tone and manner that were singularly adapted to win the confidence of her he addressed. "Hurry Harry has told me of you, and I know you must be the child?"

"Yes, I'm Hetty Hutter," returned the girl in a low, sweet

voice, which nature, aided by some education, had preserved from vulgarity of tone and utterance—"I'm Hetty; Judith Hutter's sister; and Thomas Hutter's youngest daughter."

"I know your history, then, for Hurry Harry talks considerable, and he is free of speech when he can find other people's consarns to dwell on. You pass most of your life on the lake, Hetty."

"Certainly. Mother is dead; father is gone a-trapping, and Judith and I stay at home. What's *your* name?"

"That's a question more easily asked than it is answered, young woman, seeing that I'm so young, and yet have borne more names than some of the greatest chiefs in all America."

"But you've *got* a name—you don't throw away one name, before you come honestly by another?"

"I hope not, gal—I hope not. My names have come nat'rally, and I suppose the one I bear now, will be of no great lasting, since the Delawares seldom settle on a man's ra'al title, until such time as he has an opportunity of showing his true natur', in the council, or on the warpath; which has never behappened me; seeing firstly, because I'm not born a red skin and have no right to sit in *their* councillings, and am much too humble to be called on for opinions from the great of my own colour; and, secondly, because this is the first war that has befallen in my time, and no inimy has yet inroaded far enough into the colony, to be reached by an arm even longer than mine."

"Tell me your names," added Hetty, looking up at him, artlessly, "and maybe I'll tell you your character."

"There is some truth in that, I'll not deny, though it often fails. Men are deceived in other men's characters, and frequently give 'em names they by no means desarve. You can see the truth of this in the Mingo names, which in their own tongue signify the same things as the Delaware names—at least, so they tell me, for I know little of that tribe unless it be by report,—and no one can say they are as honest, or as upright a nation. I put no great dependence, therefore, on names."

"Tell me *all* your names," repeated the girl, earnestly, for her mind was too simple to separate things from professions, and she *did* attach importance to a name; "I want to know what to think of you."

"Well, sartain; I've no objection, and you shall hear them all. In the first place, then, I'm christian, and white born, like yourself, and my parents had a name that came down from father to son, as is a part of their gifts. My father was called Bumppo, and I was named after him, of course, the given name being Nathaniel, or, Natty, as most people saw fit to tarm it.—"

"Yes—yes—Natty—and Hetty—" interrupted the girl quickly, and looking up from her work, again, with a smile—"You are Natty, and I'm Hetty—though you are Bumppo and I'm Hutter. Bumppo is'n't as pretty as Hutter, is it?"

"Why that's as people fancy. Bumppo has no lofty sound, I admit, and yet men have bumped through the world with it. I did not go by this name, howsever, very long, for the Delawares soon found out, or thought they found out, that I was not given to lying, and they called me, firstly, Straight-tongue."

"That's a *good* name," interrupted Hetty, again, earnestly and in a positive manner. "Do'n't tell me there's no virtue in names!"

"I do not say *that*, for, perhaps, I desarved to be so called, lies being no favorites with me, as they are with some. After a while they found out that I was quick of foot, and then they called me 'The Pigeon,' which you know has a swift wing, and flies in a direct line."

"*That* was a *pretty* name!" exclaimed Hetty: "pigeons are pretty birds!"

"Most things that God has created are pretty in their way, my good gal, though they get to be deformed by mankind, so as to change their natur's, as well as their appearances. From carrying messages, and striking blind trails, I got at last to following the hunters, when it was thought I was quicker and surer at finding the game than most lads, and then they called me the 'Lap-ear,' as they said I partook of the sagacity of a hound."

"That's not so pretty—" answered Hetty. "I hope you did'n't keep *that* name long."

"Not after I was rich enough to buy a rifle," returned the other, betraying a little pride through his usually quiet and subdued manner. "*Then* it was seen I could keep a wigwam in ven'son, and, in time, I got the name of 'Deerslayer,' which is that I now bear; homely as some will think it, who set more valie on the scalp of a fellow mortal, than on the horns of a buck."

"Well, Deerslayer, I'm not one of them," answered Hetty, simply. "Judith likes soldiers, and flaring coats, and fine feathers, but they're all nought to me. *She* says the officers are great, and gay, and of soft speech, but they make me shudder, for their business is to kill their fellow creatures. I like your calling better, and your last name is a very good one—better than Natty Bumppo."

"This is nat'ral in one of your turn of mind, Hetty, and much as I should have expected. They tell me your sister is handsome—uncommon, for a mortal, and beauty is apt to seek admiration."

"Did you never see Judith?" demanded the girl, with quick earnestness. "If you never have, go, at once, and look at her. Even Hurry Harry is'n't more pleasant to look at, though *she* is a woman and *he* is a man."

Deerslayer regarded the girl, for a moment, with concern. Her pale face had flushed a little, and her eye usually so mild and serene, brightened as she spoke, in the way to betray the inward impulses.

"Ay, Hurry Harry," he muttered to himself, as he walked through the cabin towards the other end of the boat, "this comes of good looks, if a light tongue has had no consarn in it. It's easy to see which way that poor creatur's feelin's are leanin', whatever may be the case with your Jude's."

But an interruption was put to the gallantry of Hurry, the coquetry of his mistress, the thoughts of Deerslayer and the gentle feelings of Hetty, by the sudden appearance of the canoe of the Ark's owner, in the narrow opening among the bushes, that served as a sort of moat to his position. It would seem that Hutter, or Floating Tom, as he was familiarly called by all the hunters who knew his habits, recognised the canoe of Hurry, for he expressed no surprise at finding him in the scow. On the contrary, his reception was such as to denote not only gratification, but a pleasure mingled with a little disappointment at his not having made his appearance some days sooner.

"I look'd for you last week," he said, in a half grumbling, half welcoming manner, "and was disappointed uncommonly, that you did'n't arrive. There came a runner through to warn all the trappers and hunters that the Colony and the Canadas were again in trouble, and I felt lonesome up in these mountains, with three scalps to see to, and only one pair of hands to protect them."

"That's reasonable," returned March, "and 't'was feelin' like a parent. No doubt if I had two such darters as Judith and Hetty, my exper'ence would tell the same story, though in gin'ral I am just as well satisfied with having the nearest neighbor fifty miles off, as when he is within call."

"Notwithstanding, you did'n't choose to come into the wilderness alone, now you knew that the Canada savages are likely to be stirring—" returned Hutter, giving a sort of distrustful and, at the same time, enquiring glance at Deerslayer.

"Why should I— They say a bad companion on a journey helps to shorten the path, and this young man I account to be a reasonably good one. This is Deerslayer, old Tom, a noted hunter among the Delawares, and christian born, and christian edicated too, like you and me. The lad is not parfect, perhaps, but there's worse men in the country that he came from, and it's likely he'll find some that's no better, in this part of the world. Should we have occasion to defend our traps and the territory, he'll be useful in feeding us all, for he's a reg'lar dealer in ven'son."

"Young man, you are welcome," growled Tom, thrusting a hard bony hand towards the youth, as a pledge of his sincerity; "in such times a white face is a friend's, and I count on you as a support. Children sometimes make a stout heart feeble, and these two daughters of mine give me more concern than all my traps, and skins, and rights in the country."

"That's nat'ral!" cried Hurry. "Yes, Deerslayer, you and I do'n't know it yet by exper'ence, but, on the whole, I consider that as nat'ral. If we *had* darters, it's more than probable we should have some such feelin's, and I honor the man that owns 'em. As for Judith, old man, I enlist, at once, as her soldier, and here is Deerslayer to help you to take care of Hetty."

"Many thanks to you, Master March," returned the beauty, in a full rich voice, and with an accuracy of intonation and utterance, that she shared in common with her sister, and which showed that she had been better taught than her father's life and appearance would give reason to expect; "many thanks to you; but Judith Hutter has the spirit and the experience that will make her depend more on herself, than on good-looking rovers like you. Should there be need to face the savages, do you land with my father, instead of burrowing in the huts, under the show of defending us females, and—"

"Girl—girl—" interrupted the father, "quiet that glib tongue of thine, and hear the truth. There are savages on the lake shore, already, and no man can say how near to us they may be at this very moment, or when we may hear more from them!"

"If this be true, Master Hutter," said Hurry, whose change of countenance denoted how serious he deemed the information, though it did not denote any unmanly alarm— "if this be true, your Ark is in a most misfortinate position for, though the cover did deceive Deerslayer and myself, it would hardly be overlooked by a full-blooded Injin, who was out seriously, in s'arch of scalps!"

"I think as you do, Hurry, and wish, with all my heart, we lay any where else, at this moment, than in this narrow, crooked, stream, which has many advantages to hide in, but which is almost fatal, to them that are discovered. The savages are near us, moreover, and the difficulty is, to get out of the river, without being shot down like deer standing at a 'lick.' "

"Are you sartain, Master Hutter, that the red skins you dread are ra'al Canadas?" asked Deerslayer, in a modest, but earnest manner. "Have you seen any, and can you describe their paint?"

"I have fallen in with the signs of their being in the neighborhood, but have seen none of 'em. I was down stream, a mile or so, looking to my traps, when I struck a fresh trail, crossing the corner of a swamp, and moving northward. The man had not passed an hour, and I know'd it for an Indian footstep by the size of the foot, and the in-toe, even before I found a worn moccasin, which its owner had dropped as useless. For that matter, I found the spot, where he halted to make a new one, which was only a few yards from the place where he had dropped the old one."

"That does'n't look much like a red skin on the war path!" returned the other shaking his head. "An exper'enced warrior, at least, would have burned, or buried, or sunk in the river, such signs of his passage, and your trail is, quite likely, a peaceable trail. But the moccasin may greatly relieve my mind, if you bethought you of bringing it off. I've come here to meet a young chief, myself, and his course would be much in the direction you've mentioned. The trail may have been his'n."

"Hurry Harry, you're well acquainted with this young man, I hope, who has meetings with savages in a part of the country where he has never been before?" demanded Hutter, in a tone, and in a manner, that sufficiently indicated the motive of the question; these rude beings seldom hesitating, on the score of delicacy, to betray their feelings. "Treachery is an Indian virtue, and the whites that live much in their tribes, soon catch their ways and practices."

"True,—true as the gospel, Old Tom, but not personable to Deerslayer, who's a young man of truth, if he has no other riccommend. I'll answer for his *honesty*, whatever I may do for his valor in battle."

"I should like to know his errand in this strange quarter of the country?"

"That is soon told, Master Hutter," said the young man, with the composure of one who kept a clean conscience; "I think, moreover, you've a *right* to ask it. The father of two such darters, who occupies a lake, after your fashion, has just the same right to inquire into a stranger's business in his neighborhood, as the Colony would have to demand the reason why the Frenchers put more rijiments than common, along the lines. No—no—I'll not deny your right to know why a stranger comes into your habitation, or country, in times as serious as these."

"If such is your way of thinking, friend, let me hear your story, without more words."

"'Tis soon told, as I said afore, and shall be honestly told. I'm a young man, and as yet have never been on a war path, but, no sooner did the news come among the Delawares, that wampum and a hatchet was about to be sent in to the tribe, than they wished me to go out among the people of my own colour, and get the exact state of things for 'em. This I did, and, after delivering my talk to the chiefs, on my return, I met an officer of the crown, on the Schoharie, who had messages to send to some of the fri'ndly tribes that live farther west. This was thought a good occasion for Chingachgook, a young chief who has never struck a foe, and myself, to go on our first war path in company, and an app'intment was made for us, by an old Delaware, to meet at the rock near the foot of this lake. I'll not deny that Chingachgook has *another* object in view, but it has no consarn with any here, and is his secret and not mine; therefore I'll say no more about it.—"

" 'Tis something about a young woman," interrupted Judith hastily, then laughing at her own impetuosity, and even having the grace to colour a little, at the manner in which she had betrayed her readiness to impute such a motive. "If 'tis neither war, nor a hunt, it must be love."

"Ay, it comes easy for the young and handsome, who hear so much of them feelin's, to suppose that they lie at the bottom of most proceedin's; but, on that head, I say nothin'. Chingachgook is to meet me at the rock, an hour afore sunset to-morrow evening, after which we shall go our way together, molesting none but the king's inimies, who are lawfully our own. Knowing Hurry of old, who once trapped in our hunting grounds, and falling in with him on the Schoharie, just as he was on the p'int of starting for his summer ha'nts, we agreed to journey in company; not so much from fear of the Mingos, as from good fellowship, and, as he says, to shorten a long road."

"And you think the trail I saw may have been that of your friend, ahead of his time?" said Hutter.

"That's my idee, which may be wrong, but which may be right. If I saw the moccasin, howsever, I could tell, in a minute, whether it is made in the Delaware fashion, or not."

"Here it is, then," said the quick witted Judith, who had already gone to the canoe in quest of it. "Tell us what it says; friend or enemy. You look honest, and *I* believe all you say, whatever father may think."

"That's the way with you, Jude; forever finding out friends, where I distrust foes," grumbled Tom: "but, speak out, young man, and tell us what you think of the moccasin."

"That's not Delaware made," returned Deerslayer, examining the worn and rejected covering for the foot with a cautious eye. "I'm too young on a war-path to be positive, but I should say that moccasin has a northern look, and comes from beyond the Great Lakes."

"If such is the case, we ought not to lie here a minute longer than is necessary," said Hutter, glancing through the leaves of his cover, as if he already distrusted the presence of an enemy, on the opposite shore of the narrow and sinuous stream. "It wants but an hour, or so, of night, and to move in the dark, will be impossible, without making a noise that would betray us. Did you hear the echo of a piece, in the mountains, half an hour since?"

"Yes, old man, and heard the piece itself," answered Hurry, who now felt the indiscretion of which he had been guilty, "for the last was fired from my own shoulder."

"I feared it came from the French Indians; still, it may put them on the look-out, and be a means of discovering us. You did wrong to fire, in war-time, unless there was good occasion."

"So I begin to think myself, uncle Tom; and yet, if a man can't trust himself to let off his rifle in a wilderness that is a thousand miles square, lest some inimy should hear it, where's the use in carrying one!"

Hutter now held a long consultation with his two guests, in which the parties came to a true understanding of their situation. He explained the difficulty that would exist in attempting to get the Ark out of so swift, and narrow a stream in the dark, without making a noise that could not fail to attract Indian ears. Any strollers in their vicinity, would keep near the river, or the lake, but the former had swampy shores, in many places, and was both so crooked, and so fringed with bushes, that it was quite possible to move by day-light without incurring much danger of being seen. More was to be apprehended, perhaps, from the ear than from the eye, especially as long as they were in the short, straitened, and canopied reaches of the stream.

"I never drop down into this cover, which is handy to my traps, and safer than the lake from curious eyes, without providing the means of getting out ag'in," continued this singular being, "and that is easier done by a pull than a push. My anchor is now lying above the suction, in the open lake, and here is a line, you see, to haul us up to it. Without some such help, a single pair of hands would make heavy work, in forcing a scow, like this, up stream. I have a sort of a crab too, that lightens the pull on occasion. Jude can use the oar astarn, as well as myself, and when we fear no enimy, to get out of the river gives us but little trouble."

"What should we gain, Master Hutter, by changing the position?" asked Deerslayer, with a good deal of earnestness. "This is a safe cover, and a stout defence might be made from the inside of this cabin. I've never fou't, unless in the way of traditions, but it seems to me, we might beat off twenty Mingos, with palisades like these afore us."

"Ay—ay; you've never fought, except in traditions, that's plain enough, young man! Did you ever see as broad a sheet of water as this above us, before you came in upon it, with Hurry?"

"I can't say that I ever did," Deerslayer answered, modestly. "Youth is the time to l'arn, and I'm far from wishing to raise my voice in council, afore it is justified by exper'ence."

"Well, then, I'll teach you the disadvantage of fighting in this position, and the advantage of taking to the open lake. Here, you may see, the savages will know where to aim every shot, and it would be too much to hope that *some* would not find their way through the crevices of the logs. Now, on the other hand, *we* should have nothing but a forest to aim at. Then we are not safe from fire, here, the bark of this roof being little better than so much kindling wood. The Castle, too, might be entered and ransacked, in my absence, and all my possessions overrun and destroyed. Once in the lake, we can be attacked only in boats, or on rafts, shall have a fair chance with the enemy, and can protect the Castle with the Ark. Do you understand this reasoning, youngster?"

"It sounds well—yes, it has a rational sound, and I'll not gainsay it."

"Well, old Tom," cried Hurry, "if we are to move, the sooner we make a beginning, the sooner we shall know whether we are to have our scalps for night-caps, or not."

As this proposition was self-evident, no one denied its justice. The three men, after a short preliminary explanation, now set about their preparations to move the Ark in earnest. The slight fastenings were quickly loosened, and by hauling on the line, the heavy craft slowly emerged from the covers. It was no sooner free from the incumbrance of the branches, than it swung into the stream, sheering quite close to the western shore by the force of the current. Not a soul on board, heard the rustling of the branches as the cabin came against the bushes and trees of the western bank, without a feeling of uneasiness, for no one knew at what moment, or in what place, a secret and murderous enemy might unmask himself. Perhaps the gloomy light, that still struggled through the impending canopy of leaves, or found its way through the narrow, riband-like opening which seemed to mark, in the air above, the course of the river that flowed beneath, aided in augmenting the appearance of the danger, for it was little more than sufficient to render objects visible, without giving up all their outlines at a glance. Although the sun had not absolutely set, it had withdrawn its direct rays from the valley, and the hues of evening were beginning to gather around objects that stood uncovered, rendering those within the shadows of the woods, still more sombre and gloomy.

No interruption followed the movement, however, and, as the men continued to haul on the line, the Ark passed steadily ahead, the great breadth of the scow preventing its sinking into the water, and from offering much resistance to the progress of the swift element beneath its bottom. Hutter, too, had adopted a precaution, suggested by experience, which might have done credit to a seaman, and which completely prevented any of the annoyances and obstacles which, otherwise, would have attended the short turns of the river. As the Ark descended, heavy stones, attached to the line, were dropped in the centre of the stream, forming local anchors, each of which was kept from dragging by the assistance of those above it, until the uppermost of all was reached, which got its 'backing' from the anchor, or grapnel, that lay well out in the lake. In consequence of this expedient, the Ark floated clear of the incumbrances of the shore, against which it would otherwise have been unavoidably hauled at every turn, producing embarrassments that Hutter, single-handed, would have found it very difficult to overcome.

Favored by this foresight, and stimulated by the apprehensions of discovery, Floating Tom and his two athletic companions hauled the Ark ahead, with quite as much rapidity as comported with the strength of the line. At every turn in the stream a stone was raised from the bottom, when the direction of the scow changed to one that pointed towards the stone that lay above. In this manner, with the channel buoyed out for him, as a sailor might term it, did Hutter move forward, occasionally urging his friends in a low and guarded voice, to increase their exertions, and, then, as occasions offered, warning them against efforts that might, at particular moments, endanger all by too much zeal. In spite of their long familiarity with the woods, the gloomy character of the shaded river added to the uneasiness that each felt, and when the Ark reached the first bend in the Susquehannah, and the eye caught a glimpse of the broader expanse of the lake, all felt a relief, that perhaps none would have been willing to confess. Here the last stone was raised from the bottom, and the line led directly towards the grapnel, which, as Hutter had explained, was dropped above the suction of the current.

"Thank God!" ejaculated Hurry, "*there* is day-light, and we shall soon have a chance of *seeing* our inimies, if we are to *feel* 'em."

"That is more than you, or any man can say," growled Hutter. "There is no spot so likely to harbor a party, as the shore around the outlet, and the moment we clear these trees, and get into open water will be the most trying time, since it will leave the enemy a cover, while it puts us out of one. Judith, girl; do you and Hetty leave the oar to take care of itself, and go within the cabin, and be mindful not to show your faces at a window, for they who will look at them, won't stop to praise their beauty. And, now Hurry, we'll step into this outer room, ourselves, and haul through the door, where we shall all be safe from a surprise at least. Friend Deerslayer, as the current is lighter, and the line has all the strain on it that is prudent, do you keep moving from window to window, taking care not to let your head be seen, if you set any value on your life. No one knows, when or where, we shall hear from our neighbors."

Deerslayer complied, with a sensation that had nothing in common with fear, but which had all the interest of a perfectly novel and a most exciting situation. For the first time in his life, he was in the vicinity of enemies, or had good reason to think so, and that too, under all the thrilling circumstances of Indian surprises, and Indian artifices. As he took his stand at a window, the Ark was just passing through the narrowest part of the stream, a point where the water first entered what was properly termed the river, and where the trees fairly interlocked over-head, causing the current to rush into an arch of verdure, a feature as appropriate and peculiar to the country, perhaps, as that of Switzerland, where the rivers come rushing literally from chambers of ice.

The Ark was in the act of passing the last curve of this leafy entrance, as Deerslayer, having examined all that could be seen of the eastern bank of the river, crossed the room to look from the opposite window at the western. His arrival at this aperture was most opportune, for he had no sooner placed his eye at a crack, than a sight met his gaze that might well have alarmed a sentinel so young and inexperienced. A sapling overhung the water, in nearly half a circle, having first grown towards the light, and then been pressed down into this form by the weight of the snows; a circumstance of common occurrence in the American woods. On this tree no less than six Indians had already appeared, others standing ready to follow them as they left room, each evidently bent on running out on the trunk, and dropping on the roof of the Ark, as it passed beneath. This would have been an exploit of no great difficulty, the inclination of the tree admitting of an easy passage, the adjoining branches offering ample support for the hands, and the fall being too trifling to be apprehended. When Deerslayer first saw this party, it was just unmasking itself, by ascending the part of the tree nearest to the earth, or that which was much the most difficult to overcome, and his knowledge of Indian habits told him, at once, that they were all in their war paint, and belonged to a hostile tribe.

"Pull, Hurry," he cried; "pull for your life, and as you love Judith Hutter. Pull, man, pull!"

This call was made to one that the young man knew had the strength of a giant. It was so earnest and solemn, that both Hutter and March felt it was not idly given, and they applied all their force to the line simultaneously, and at a most critical moment. The scow redoubled its motion, and seemed to glide from under the tree, as if conscious of the danger that was impending over head. Perceiving that they were discovered, the Indians uttered the fearful war-whoop, and running forward on the tree leaped desperately towards their fancied prize. There were six on the tree and each made the effort. All but their leader fell into the river, more or less distant from the Ark, as they came sooner or later to the leaping place. The chief who had taken the dangerous post in advance, having an earlier opportunity than the others, struck the scow just within the stern. The fall proving so much greater than he had anticipated, he was slightly stunned, and for a moment he remained half bent and unconscious of his situation. At this instant, Judith rushed from her cabin, her beauty heightened by the excitement that produced the bold act, which flushed her cheek to crimson, and throwing all her strength into the effort, she pushed the intruder over the edge of the scow, headlong into the river. This decided feat was no sooner accomplished than the woman resumed her sway; Judith looked over the stern to ascertain what had become of the man, and the expression of her eyes softened to concern; next, her cheek crimsoned between shame and surprise at her own temerity, and then she laughed in her own merry and sweet manner. All this occupied less than a minute, when the arm of Deerslayer was thrown around her waist, and she was dragged swiftly within the protection of the cabin. This retreat was not effected too soon. Scarcely were the two in safety, when the forest was filled with yells, and bullets began to patter against the logs.

The Ark being in swift motion, all this while, it was beyond the danger of pursuit by the time these little events had occurred, and the savages, as soon as the first burst of their anger had subsided, ceased firing, with the consciousness that they were expending their ammunition in vain. When the scow came up over her grapnel, Hutter tripped the latter in a way not to impede the motion, and being now beyond the influence of the current, the vessel continued to drift ahead, until fairly in the open lake, though still near enough to the land to render exposure to a rifle-bullet dangerous. Hutter and March got out two small sweeps, and covered by the cabin, they soon urged the Ark far enough from the shore, to leave no inducement to their enemies to make any further attempt to injure them.

Chapter V

> "Why, let the strucken deer go weep,
> The hart ungalled play:
> For some must watch, while some must sleep;
> Thus runs the world away."
>
> *Hamlet*, III.ii.271–74.

ANOTHER CONSULTATION took place, in the forward part of the scow, at which both Judith and Hetty were present. As no danger could now approach unseen, immediate uneasiness had given place to the concern which attended the conviction that enemies were, in considerable force, on the shores of the lake, and that they might be sure no practicable means of accomplishing their own destruction would be neglected. As a matter of course, Hutter felt these truths the deepest, his daughters having an habitual reliance on his resources, and knowing too little to appreciate fully all the risks they ran, while his male companions were at liberty to quit him at any moment they saw fit. His first remark showed that he had an eye to the latter circumstance, and might have betrayed to a keen observer, the apprehension that was, just then, uppermost.

"We've a great advantage over the Iroquois, or the enemy, whoever they are, in being afloat," he said. "There's not a canoe on the lake, that I don't know where it's hid, and now yours is here, Hurry, there are but three more on the land, and they're so snug in hollow logs, that I don't believe the Indians could find them, let them try ever so long."

"There's no telling that—no one can say that," put in Deerslayer. "A hound is not more sartain on the scent, than a red-skin when he expects to get any thing by it. Let this party see scalps afore 'em, or plunder, or honor, accordin' to their idees of what honor is, and 't'will be a tight log that hides a canoe from their eyes."

"You're right, Deerslayer," cried Harry March; "you're downright gospel in this matter, and I rej'ice that my bunch of bark is safe enough, here, within reach of my arm. I calcilate they'll be at all the rest of the canoes, afore to-morrow night, if they are in ra'al 'arnest to smoke you out, old Tom, and we may as well overhaul our paddles for a pull."

Hutter made no immediate reply. He looked about him in silence for quite a minute, examining the sky, the lake, and the belt of forest which enclosed it, as it might be hermetically, like one consulting their signs. Nor did he find any alarming symptoms. The boundless woods were sleeping in the deep repose of nature, the heavens were placid, but still luminous with the light of the retreating sun, while the lake looked more lovely and calm than it had before done that day. It was a scene altogether soothing, and of a character to lull the passions into a species of holy calm. How far this effect was produced, however, on the party in the Ark must appear in the progress of our narrative.

"Judith," called out the father, when he had taken this close but short survey of the omens, "night is at hand; find our friends food; a long march gives a sharp appetite."

"We're not starving, Master Hutter," March observed, "for we filled up just as we reached the lake, and for one, I prefar the company of Jude, even to her supper. This quiet evening is very agreeable to sit by her side."

"Natur' is natur'," objected Hutter, "and must be fed. Judith, see to the meal, and take your sister to help you. I've a little discourse to hold with you, friends," he continued, as soon as his daughters were out of hearing, "and wish the girls away. You see my situation, and I should like to hear your opinions concerning what is best to be done. Three times have I been burnt out, already, but that was on the shore, and I've considered myself as pretty safe, ever since I got the castle built, and the Ark afloat. My other accidents, however, happened in peaceable times, being nothing more than such flurries as a man must meet with, in the woods; but this matter looks serious, and your ideas would greatly relieve my mind."

"It's my notion, old Tom, that you, and your huts, and your traps, and your whole possessions, hereaway, are in desperate j'iparday," returned the matter-of-fact Hurry, who saw no use in concealment; "accordin' to my idees of valie, they're altogether not worth half as much to-day, as they was yesterday, nor would I give more for 'em, taking the pay in skins."

"Then I've children!—" continued the father, making the allusion in a way that it might have puzzled even an indifferent observer to say was intended as a bait, or as an exclamation of paternal concern. "Daughters, as you know, Hurry, and good girls too, I may say, though I *am* their father."

"A man may say any thing, Master Hutter, particularily when pressed by time and circumstances. You've darters, as you say, and one of them has'n't her equal on the frontiers, for good-looks, whatever she may have for good behaviour. As for poor Hetty, she's Hetty Hutter, and that's as much as one can say about the poor thing. Give me Jude, if her conduct was only equal to her looks."

"I see, Harry March, I can only count on you as a fair weather friend, and I suppose that your companion will be of the same way of thinking—" returned the other, with a slight show of pride, that was not altogether without dignity, "well; I must depend on Providence, which will not turn a deaf ear, perhaps, to a father's prayers."

"If you've understood Hurry, here, to mean that he intends to desart you," said Deerslayer, with an earnest simplicity that gave double assurance of its truth, "I *think* you do him injustice, as I *know* you do me in supposing I would follow him, was he so ontrue-hearted as to leave a family of his own colour in such a strait as this. I've come on this lake, Master Hutter, to rende'vous a fri'nd, and I only wish he was here, himself, as I make no doubt he will be, at sunset to-morrow, when you'd have another rifle to aid you—an inexper'enced one, I'll allow, like my own, but one that has proved true so often ag'in the game, big and little, that I'll answer for its sarvice ag'in mortals."

"May I depend on *you* to stand by me and my daughters, then, Deerslayer?" demanded the old man with a father's anxiety in his countenance.

"That may you, Floating Tom, if that's your name, and as a brother would stand by a sister, a husband his wife, or a suitor his sweetheart. In this strait, you may count on me, through all advarsities, and I think Hurry does discredit to his natur', and wishes, if you can't count on him."

"Not he," cried Judith thrusting her handsome face out of the door, "his nature is hurry, as well as his name, and he'll hurry off, as soon as he thinks his fine figure in danger. Neither 'old Tom,' nor his 'gals', will depend much on Master March, now they know him, but *you* they will rely on, Deerslayer; for your honest face, and as honest heart, tell us that what you promise you will perform."

This was said as much, perhaps, in affected scorn for Hurry as in sincerity; still it was not said without feeling. The fine face of Judith sufficiently proved the latter circumstance; and if the conscious March fancied that he had never seen in it, a stronger display of contempt—a feeling in which the beauty was apt to indulge—than while she was looking at him, it certainly seldom exhibited more of womanly softness and sensibility than when her speaking blue eyes were turned on his travelling companion.

"Leave us, Judith," Hutter ordered sternly, before either of the young men could reply. "Leave us, and do not return until you come with the venison and fish. The girl has been spoilt by the flattery of the officers who sometimes find their way up here, Master March, and you'll not think any harm of her silly words."

"You never said truer syllable, old Tom," retorted Hurry, who smarted under Judith's observations—"The devil-tongued youngsters of the garrisons, have proved her undoing! I scarce know Jude any longer, and shall soon take to admiring her sister, who is getting to be much more to my fancy."

"I'm glad to hear this, Harry, and look upon it as a sign that you're coming to your right senses. Hetty would make a much safer and more rational companion than Jude, and would be much the most likely to listen to your suit, as the officers have, I greatly fear, unsettled her sister's mind."

"No man need a safer wife than Hetty," said Hurry, laughing, "though I'll not answer for her being of the most rational. But, no matter; Deerslayer has not misconceived me when he told you I should be found at my post. I'll not quit *you*, uncle Tom, just now, whatever may be my feelin's and intentions respecting your eldest darter."

Hurry had a respectable reputation for prowess among his associates, and Hutter heard this pledge with a satisfaction that was not concealed. Even the great personal strength of such an aid, became of moment in moving the Ark, as well as in the species of hand to hand conflicts that were not unfrequent in the woods, and no commander, who was hard pressed, could feel more joy at hearing of the arrival of reinforcements, than this borderer experienced at being told this important auxiliary was not about to quit him. A minute before, Hutter would have been well content to compromise his danger, by entering into a compact to act only on the defensive, but no sooner did he feel some security on this point, than the restlessness of man induced him to think of the means of carrying the war into the enemy's country.

"High prices are offered for scalps on both sides," he observed with a grim smile, as if he felt the force of the inducement, at the very time he wished to affect a superiority to earning money by means that the ordinary feelings of those who aspire to be civilized men repudiated, even while they were adopted. "It is'nt right, perhaps, to take gold for human blood, and yet when mankind is busy in killing one another, there can be no great harm in adding a little bit of skin to the plunder. What's your sentiments, Hurry, touching these p'ints."

"That you've made a vast mistake, old man, in calling savage blood, human blood, at all. I think no more of a red skin's scalp, than I do of a pair of wolf's ears; and would just as lief finger money for the one, as for the other. With *white* people 'tis different, for they've a nat'ral avarsion to being scalped, whereas your Indian shaves his head in readiness for the knife, and leaves a lock of hair, by way of braggadocia, that one can lay hold of, in the bargain."

"That's manly, however, and I felt, from the first, that we had only to get you on our side, to have you heart and hand," returned Tom, losing all his reserve, as he gained a renewed confidence in the dispositions of his companions. "Something more may turn up from this inroad of the red skins, than they have bargained for. Deerslayer, I conclude you're of Hurry's way of thinking, and look upon money 'arned in this way, as being as likely to pass, as money 'arned in trapping, or hunting."

"I've no such feelin', nor any wish to harbor it, not I," returned the other. "My gifts are not scalper's gifts, but such as belong to my religion and colour. I'll stand by you, old man, in the Ark, or in the castle, the canoe, or the woods, but I'll not unhumanize my natur' by falling into ways that God intended for another race. If you and Hurry have got any thoughts that lean towards the colony's gold, go by yourselves in s'arch of it, and leave the females to my care. Much as I must differ from you both, on all gifts that do not properly belong to a white man, we shall agree that it is the duty of the strong to take care of the weak, especially when the last belong to them that natur' intended man to protect and console by his gentleness and strength."

"Hurry Harry, that is a lesson you might learn and practise on to some advantage," said the sweet but spirited voice of Judith, from the cabin, a proof that she had overheard all that had hitherto been said.

"No more of this, Jude!" called out the father angrily. "Move further off; we are about to talk of matters unfit for a woman to listen to."

Hutter did not take any steps, however, to ascertain whether he was obeyed or not, but, dropping his voice a little, he pursued the discourse.

"The young man is right, Hurry," he said, "and we can leave the children in his care. Now, my idea is just this, and I think you'll agree that it is rational and correct. There's a large party of these savages on the shore, and, though I didn't tell it before the girls, for they're womanish and apt to be troublesome when any thing like real work is to be done, there's women among 'em. This I know from moccasin prints, and 'tis likely they are hunters, after all, who have been out so long that they know nothing of the war, or of the bounties—"

"In which case, old Tom, why was their first salute an attempt to cut all our throats?"

"We don't know that their design was so bloody. It's natural and easy for an Indian to fall into ambushes and surprises, and no doubt they wished to get on board the Ark first, and to make their conditions afterwards. That a disap-p'inted savage should fire at us, is in rule, and I think nothing of that. Besides, how often have they burned me out, and robbed my traps—ay, and pulled trigger on me,—in the most peaceful times?"

"The blackguards will do such things, I must allow, and we

pay 'em off pretty much in their own c'ine. Women would not be on the war-path, sartainly, and so far there's reason in your idee."

"Nor would a hunter be in his war-paint," returned Deerslayer. "I saw the Mingos, and *know* that they are out on the trail of mortal men, and not for beaver, or deer."

"There you have it ag'in, old fellow," said Hurry. "In the way of an eye, now, I'd as soon trust this young man as trust the oldest settler in the colony; and if he says paint, why paint it was."

"Then a hunting party and a war-party have met, for women must have been with 'em. It's only a few days since the runner went through with the tidings of the troubles, and it may be that warriors have come out to call in their women and children, and to get an early blow."

"That would stand the courts and is just the truth," cried Hurry. "You've got it now, old Tom, and I should like to hear what you mean to make out of it?"

"The bounty—" returned the other, looking up at his attentive companion, in a cool, sullen, manner, in which, however, heartless cupidity, and indifference to the means, were far more conspicuous than any feelings of animosity, or revenge. "If there's women, there's children, and big and little have scalps; the Colony pays for all alike."

"More shame to it, that it should do so," interrupted Deerslayer; "more shame to it that it do'n't understand its gifts, and pay greater attention to the will of God."

"Hearken to reason, lad, and do'n't cry out afore you understand a case," returned the unmoved Hurry. "The savages scalp—your fr'inds the Delawares, or Mohicans, whichever they may be, among the rest—and why should'n't we scalp? I will own it would be ag'in right for you and I, now, to go into the settlements and bring out scalps, but it's a very different matter as consarns Indians. A man should'n't take scalps, if he is'n't ready to be scalped, himself, on fitting occasions. One good turn desarves another, all the world over. That's reason, and I believe it to be good religion."

"Ay, Master Hurry," again interrupted the rich voice of Judith—"is it religion to say that one *bad* turn deserves another."

"I'll never reason ag'in you, Judy, for you beat me with beauty, if you can'n't with sense. Here's the Canadas paying their Injins for scalps, and why not we pay—"

"*Our* Indians!" exclaimed the girl, laughing with a sort of melancholy merriment. "Father—Father!—Think no more of this, and listen to the advice of Deerslayer, who *has* a conscience, which is more than I can say, or think, of Harry March."

Hutter now rose, and entering the cabin, he compelled his daughters to go into the adjoining room, when he secured both the doors and returned. Then he and Hurry pursued the subject, but, as the purport of all that was material in this discourse will appear in the narrative, it need not be related here, in detail. The reader, however, can have no difficulty in comprehending the morality that presided over their conference. It was in truth that, which, in some form or other, rules most of the acts of men, and in which the controlling principle is that one wrong will justify another. Their enemies paid for scalps, and this was sufficient to justify the colony for retaliating. It is true, the French used the same argument, a circumstance, as Hurry took occasion to observe in answer to one of Deerslayer's objections, that proved its truth, as mortal enemies would not be likely to have recourse to the same reason, unless it were a good one. But, neither Hutter, nor Hurry was a man likely to stick at trifles, in matters connected with the rights of the aborigines, since it is one of the consequences of aggression that it hardens the conscience, as the only means of quieting it. In the most peaceable state of the country, a species of warfare was carried on between the Indians, especially those of the Canadas, and men of their caste, and the moment an actual and recognised warfare existed, it was regarded as the means of lawfully revenging a thousand wrongs, real and imaginary. Then, again, there was some truth, and a good deal of expediency in the principle of retaliation, of which they both availed themselves, in particular to answer the objections of their juster minded and more scrupulous companion.

"You must fight a man with his own we'pons, Deerslayer," cried Hurry, in his uncouth dialect, and in his dogmatical manner of disposing of all moral propositions—"If he's f'erce, you must be f'ercer; if he's stout of heart, you must be stouter. This is the way to get the better of christian, or savage; by keepin' up to this trail, you'll get soonest to the ind of your journey."

"That's not Moravian doctrine, which teaches that all are to be judged according to their talents, or l'arning; the Injin like an Injin, and the white-man like a white-man. Some of their teachers say that if you're struck on the cheek, it's a duty to turn the other side of the face, and take another blow, instead of seeking revenge, whereby I understand—"

"That's enough!" shouted Hurry. "That's all I want to prove a man's doctrine! How long would it take to kick a man through the colony—in at one ind, and out at the other—on that principle?"

"Do'n't mistake me, March," returned the young hunter, with dignity. "I do'n't understand by this any more than that it's *best* to do this, if *possible*. Revenge is an Injin gift, and forgiveness a white-man's. That's all. Overlook all you *can*, is what's meant, and not *revenge* all you can. As for kicking, Master Hurry—" Deerslayer's sun burnt cheek flushed, as he continued—"into the colony, or out of the colony, that's neither here nor there, seeing no one proposes it, and no one would be likely to put up with it. What I wish to say is that a red skin's scalping, do'n't justify a pale face's scalping."

"Do as you're done by, Deerslayer; that's even the christian parsons' doctrine."

"No, Hurry, I've asked the Moravians consarning that, and it's altogether different. 'Do as you *would* be done by,' they tell me is the *true* saying, while men practyse the *false*. They think all the colonies wrong that offer bounties for scalps, and believe no blessing will follow the measures. Above all things they forbid revenge."

"*That* for your Moravians!" cried March, snapping his fingers. "They're the next thing to quakers, and if you'd believe all they tell you, not even a 'rat would be skinned, out of marcy. Who ever heard of marcy on a muskrat!"

The disdainful manner of Hurry prevented a reply, and he and the old man resumed the discussion of their plans in a more quiet and confidential manner. This conference lasted until Judith appeared, bearing the simple but savory supper.

March observed, with a little surprise, that she placed the choicest bits before Deerslayer, and that in the little nameless attentions it was in her power to bestow, she quite obviously manifested a desire to let it be seen that she deemed him the honored guest. Accustomed, however, to the waywardness and coquetry of the beauty, this discovery gave him little concern, and he ate with an appetite that was in no degree disturbed by any moral causes. The easily digested food of the forests offering the fewest possible obstacles to the gratification of this great animal indulgence, Deerslayer, notwithstanding the hearty meal both had taken in the woods, was in no manner behind his companions in doing justice to the viands.

An hour later the scene had greatly changed. The lake was still placid and glassy, but the gloom of the hour had succeeded to the soft twilight of a summer evening, and all within the dark setting of the woods lay in the quiet repose of night. The forests gave up no song, or cry, or even murmur, but looked down from the hills on the lovely basin they encircled in solemn stillness, and the only sound that was audible was the regular dip of the sweeps, at which Hurry and Deerslayer lazily pushed, impelling the Ark towards the Castle. Hutter had withdrawn to the stern of the scow, in order to steer, but finding that the young men kept even strokes, and held the desired course by their own skill, he had permitted the oar to drag in the water, taken a seat on the end of the vessel and lighted his pipe. He had not been thus placed many minutes, ere Hetty came stealthily out of the cabin, or house, as they usually termed that part of the Ark, and placed herself at his feet, on a little bench that she had brought with her. As this movement was by no means unusual in his feeble minded child, the old man paid no other attention to it, than to lay his hand kindly on her head, in an affectionate and approving manner, an act of grace that the girl received in meek silence.

After a pause of several minutes, Hetty began to sing. Her voice was low and tremulous, but it was earnest and solemn. The words and the tune were of the simplest form, the first being a hymn that she had been taught by her mother, and the last one of those natural melodies that find favor with all classes, in every age, coming from, and being addressed to, the feelings. Hutter never listened to this simple strain without finding his heart and manner softened, facts that his daughter well knew, and by which she had often profited, through the sort of holy instinct that enlightens the weak of mind, more especially in their aims toward good.

Hetty's low, sweet, tones had not been raised many moments, when the dip of the oars ceased, and the holy strain arose singly, on the breathing silence of that wilderness. As if she gathered courage with her theme, her powers appeared to increase as she proceeded, and, though nothing vulgar or noisy mingled in her melody, its strength and melancholy tenderness grew on the ear, until the air was filled with this simple homage of a soul that seemed almost spotless. That the men forward were not indifferent to this touching interruption was proved by their inaction, nor did their oars again dip until the last of the sweet sounds had actually died among the remarkable echoes, which, at that witching hour would waft, even the lowest modulations of the human voice, more than a mile. Hutter was much affected, for, rude as he was by early habits, and even ruthless as he had got to be by long exposure to the practices of the wilderness, his nature was of that fearful mixture of good and evil, that so generally enters into the moral composition of man.

"You are sad to-night, child," said the father, whose manner and language usually assumed some of the gentleness and elevation of the civilized life he had led in youth, when he thus communed with this particular child. "We have just escaped from enemies, and ought rather to rejoice."

"You can never do it, father!" said Hetty, in a low remonstrating manner, taking his hard knotty hand into both her own—"You have talked long with Harry March, but neither of you have the heart to do it!"

"This is going beyond your means, foolish child; you must have been naughty enough to have listened, or you could know nothing of our talk."

"Why should you and Hurry kill people—especially women and children?"

"Peace, girl, peace. We are at war, and must do to our enemies as our enemies would do to us."

"That's not it, father!—I heard Deerslayer say how it was. You must do to your enemies, as you *wish* your enemies would do to you. No one wishes his enemies to kill him."

"We kill our enemies in war, girl, lest they should kill us. One side or the other must begin, and them that begin first are most apt to get the victory. You know nothing about these things, poor Hetty, and had best say nothing."

"*Judith* says it is wrong, father; and Judith has sense, though I have none."

"Jude understands better than to talk to me of these matters, for she has sense, as you say, and knows I'll not bear it. Which would you prefer, Hetty; to have your own scalp taken and sold to the French, or that we should kill our enemies, and keep them from harming us?"

"That's not it, father! Don't kill them, nor let them kill us. Sell your skins, and get more if you can, but don't sell human blood."

"Come, come, child; let us talk of matters you understand. Are you glad to see our old friend March back, again?—You like Hurry, and must know that one day he may be your brother—if not something nearer."

"That ca'n't be, father—" returned the girl, after a considerable pause. "Hurry has had one father and one mother, and people never have two."

"So much for your weak mind, Hetty. When Jude marries, her husband's father will be her father, and her husband's sister, her sister. If she should marry Hurry, then he will be your brother."

"Judith will never have Hurry," returned the girl mildly; but positively. "Judith don't like Hurry."

"That's more than you can know, Hetty. Harry March is the handsomest, and the strongest, and the boldest young man that ever visits the lake, and as Jude is the greatest beauty, I don't see why they should'n't come together. He has as much as promised that he will enter into this job with me, on condition that I'll consent."

Hetty began to move her body back and forth, and otherwise to express mental agitation, but she made no answer for more than a minute. Her father, accustomed to her manner, and suspecting no immediate cause of concern, continued to smoke with the apparent phlegm which would seem to belong to that particular species of enjoyment.

"Hurry *is* handsome, father—" said Hetty with a simple emphasis that she might have hesitated about using had her mind been more alive to the inferences of others.

"I told you so, child," muttered old Hutter, without removing the pipe from between his teeth. "He's the likeliest youth in these parts, and Jude is the likeliest young woman I've met with since her poor mother was in her best days."

"Is it wicked to be ugly, father?"

"One might be guilty of worse things—but you're by no means ugly, though not as comely as Jude."

"Is Judith any happier for being so handsome?"

"She may be, child; and she may not be. But talk of other matters now, for you hardly understand these, poor Hetty. How do you like our new acquaintance, Deerslayer?"

"He is'n't handsome, father. Hurry is far handsomer than Deerslayer."

"That's true, but they say he is a noted hunter. His fame had reached me before I ever saw him, and I did hope he would prove to be as stout a warrior, as he is dexterous with the deer. All men are not alike, howsever, child, and it takes time, as I know by experience, to give a man a true wilderness heart."

"Have I got a wilderness heart, father?—and, Hurry, is *his* heart true wilderness?"

"You sometimes ask queer questions, Hetty! Your heart is good, child, and fitter for the settlements than for the woods, while your reason is fitter for the woods than for the settlements."

"Why has Judith more reason than I, father?"

"Heaven help thee, child!—This is more than I can answer. God gives sense, and appearance, and all these things, and he grants them as he seeth fit. Dost thou wish for more sense?"

"Not I. The little I have troubles me, for when I think the

hardest, then I feel the unhappiest. I do'n't believe thinking is good for me, though I *do* wish I was as handsome as Judith!"

"Why so, poor child?—Thy sister's beauty may cause her trouble, as it caused her mother before her. It's no advantage, Hetty, to be so marked for any thing, as to become an object of envy, or to be sought after more than others."

"Mother was good, if she *was* handsome," returned the girl, the tears starting to her eyes, as usually happened when she adverted to her deceased parent.

Old Hutter, if not equally affected, was moody and silent at this allusion to his wife. He continued smoking, without appearing disposed to make any answer, until his simple-minded daughter repeated her remark in a way to show that she felt uneasiness, lest he might be inclined to deny her assertion. Then he knocked the ashes out of his pipe, and laying his hand in a sort of rough kindness on the girl's head, he made her a reply.

"Thy mother was too good for this world," he said, "though others might not think so. Her good looks did not befriend her, and you have no occasion to mourn that you are not as much like her as your sister. Think less of beauty, child, and more of your duty, and you'll be as happy on this lake, as you could be in the King's palace."

"I know it, father; but Hurry says beauty is every thing in a young woman."

Hutter made an ejaculation expressive of dissatisfaction, and went forward, passing through the house in order to do so. Hetty's simple betrayal of her weakness in behalf of March gave him uneasiness on a subject concerning which he had never felt before, and he determined to come to an explanation at once with his visiter, for directness of speech, and decision in conduct, were two of the best qualities of this rude being, in whom the seeds of a better education seemed to be constantly struggling upward, to be choked by the fruits of a life, in which his hard struggles for subsistence and security, had steeled his feelings and indurated his nature. When he reached the forward end of the scow, he manifested an intention to relieve Deerslayer at the oar, directing the latter to take his own place aft. By these changes, the old man and Hurry were again left alone, while the young hunter was transferred to the other end of the Ark.

Hetty had disappeared when Deerslayer reached his new post, and for some little time he directed the course of the slow-moving craft by himself. It was not long, however, before Judith came out of the cabins, as if disposed to do the honors of the place to a stranger engaged in the service of her family. The star-light was sufficient to permit objects to be plainly distinguished, when near at hand, and the bright eyes of the girl had an expression of kindness in them, when they met those of the youth, that the latter was easily enabled to discern. Her rich hair shaded her spirited and yet soft countenance, even at that hour rendering it the more beautiful, as the rose is loveliest when reposing amid the shadows and contrasts of its native foliage. Little ceremony is used in the intercourse, of the woods, and Judith had acquired a readiness of address, by the admiration, that she so generally excited, which, if it did not amount to forwardness, certainly in no degree lent to her charms the aid of that retiring modesty on which poets love to dwell.

"I thought I should have killed myself with laughing, Deerslayer," the beauty abruptly, but coquettishly commenced, " when I saw that Indian dive into the river! He was a good-looking savage, too—" the girl always dwelt on personal beauty as a sort of merit—"And yet one coul'n't stop to consider whether his paint would stand water!"

"And I thought they would have killed you with their we'pons, Judith," returned Deerslayer, "for it was an awful risk for a female to run, in the face of a dozen Mingos!"

"Did *that* make *you* come out of the cabin, in spite of their rifles too?" asked the girl, with more real interest than she would have cared to betray, though with an indifference of manner that was the result of a good deal of practice, united to native readiness.

"Men are'n't apt to see females in danger, and not come to their assistance. Even a Mingo knows that."

This sentiment was uttered with as much simplicity of manner as of feeling, and Judith rewarded it, with a smile so sweet that even Deerslayer, who had imbibed a prejudice against the girl, in consequence of Hurry's suspicions of her levity, felt its charm, notwithstanding half its winning influence was lost in the feeble light. It at once created a sort of confidence between them, and the discourse was continued on the part of the hunter without the lively consciousness of the character of this coquette of the wilderness, with which it had certainly commenced.

"You are a man of deeds and not of words, I see plainly, Deerslayer," continued the beauty, taking her seat near the spot where the other stood, "and I foresee we shall be very good friends. Hurry-Harry has a tongue, and giant as he is, he talks more than he performs."

"March is your fri'nd, Judith; and fri'nds should be tender of each other, when apart."

"We all know what Hurry's friendship comes to. Let him have his own way in every thing, and he's the best fellow in the colony; but, 'head him off', as you say of the deer, and he is master of every thing near him, but himself. Hurry is no favorite of mine, Deerslayer, and I dare say, if the truth was known, and his conversation about me repeated, it would be found that he thinks no better of me, than I own I do of him."

The latter part of this speech was uttered not without uneasiness. Had the girl's companion been more sophisticated, he might have observed the averted face, the manner in which the pretty little foot was agitated, and other signs that, for some reason unexplained, the opinions of March were not quite as much matter of indifference to her as she thought fit to pretend. Whether this was no more than the ordinary working of female vanity, feeling keenly even where it affected not to feel at all, or whether it proceeded from that deeply seated consciousness of right and wrong, which God himself has implanted in our breasts that we may know good from evil, will be made more apparent to the reader, as we proceed in the tale. Deerslayer felt embarrassed. He well remembered the cruel imputations left by March's distrust, and, while he did not wish to injure his associate's suit by exciting resentment against him, his tongue was one that literally knew no guile. To answer without saying more or less than he wished, was consequently a delicate duty.

"March has his say of all things in natur', whether of fri'nd, or foe," slowly and cautiously rejoined the hunter. "He's one of them that speak as they feel, while the tongue's a-going, and that's sometimes different from what they'd speak if they took time to consider. Give me a Delaware, Judith, for one that reflects and rumernates on his idees. Inmity has made 'em thoughtful, and a loose tongue is no riccommend at their Council Fires."

"I dare say March's tongue goes free enough when it gets on the subject of Judith Hutter and her sister," said the girl, rousing herself as if in careless disdain. "Young women's good names are a pleasant matter of discourse with some that would'n't dare to be so open mouthed, if there was a brother in the way. Master March may find it pleasant to traduce us, but, sooner or later, he'll repent!"

"Nay, Judith, this is taking the matter up too much in 'arnest. Hurry has never whispered a syllable ag'in the good-name of Hetty, to begin with—"

"I see how it is—I see how it is—" impetuously interrupted Judith. "*I* am the one he sees fit to scorch with his withering tongue!—Hetty, indeed!—Poor Hetty—" she continued, her voice sinking into low husky tones, that seemed nearly to stifle her in the utterance—"*She* is beyond and above his slanderous malice! Poor Hetty! If God has created her feeble-minded, the weakness lies altogether on the side of errors which she seems to know nothing about. The earth never held a purer being than Hetty Hutter, Deerslayer!"

"I can believe it—yes I can believe *that*, Judith, and I hope 'arnestly that the same can be said of her handsome sister."

There was a soothing sincerity in the voice of Deerslayer, which touched the girl's feelings, nor did the allusion to her beauty lessen the effect with one who only knew too well the power of her personal charms. Nevertheless, the still, small voice of conscience was not hushed, and it prompted the answer which she made, after giving herself time to reflect.

"I dare say Hurry had some of his vile hints about the people of the garrisons—" she added. "He knows they are gentlemen, and can never forgive any one for being what he feels he can never become himself."

"Not in the sense of a King's officer, Judith, sartainly, for March has no turn that-a-way, but in the sense of reality, why may not a beaver-hunter be as respectable as a governor. Since you speak of it, yourself, I'll not deny that he *did* complain of one as humble as you, being so much in the company of scarlet coats and silken sashes. But 'twas jealousy that brought it out of him, and I do think that he mourned over his own thoughts, as a mother would have mourned over her child."

Perhaps Deerslayer was not aware of the full meaning that his earnest language conveyed. It is certain he did not see the colour that crimsoned the whole of Judith's fine face, nor detect the uncontrollable distress that, immediately after, changed its hue to a deadly paleness. A minute or two elapsed in profound stillness, the splash of the water seeming to occupy all the avenues of sound, and then Judith arose, and grasped the hand of the hunter, almost convulsively, with one of her own.

"Deerslayer," she said hurriedly—"I'm glad the ice is broke between us. They say that sudden friendships lead to long enmities, but I do not believe it will turn out so with us. I know not how it is—but, you are the first man I ever met, who did not seem to wish to flatter—to wish my ruin—to be an enemy in disguise—never mind; say nothing to Hurry, and another time we'll talk together, again."

As the girl released her grasp, she vanished in the house leaving the astonished young man standing at the steering-oar, as motionless as one of the pines on the hills. So abstracted indeed had his thoughts become, that he was hailed by Hutter to keep the scow's head in the right direction, before he remembered his actual situation.

Chapter VI

"So spake th' apostate Angel, though in pain,
Vaunting aloud, but racked with deep despair:"

Paradise Lost, I.125–26.

SHORTLY AFTER the disappearance of Judith, a light southerly air arose, and Hutter set a large square sail, that had once been the flying top-sail of an Albany sloop, but which, having become threadbare in catching the breezes of Tappan, had been condemned and sold. He had a light tough spar of tamarack that he could raise on occasion, and with a little contrivance, his duck was spread to the wind in a sufficiently professional manner. The effect on the Ark was such as to supersede the necessity of rowing, and, in about two hours, the Castle was seen, in the darkness, rising out of the black water, at the distance of a hundred yards. The sail was then lowered, and by slow degrees the scow drifted up to the building, and was secured.

No one had visited the house, since Hurry and his companion left it. The place was found in the quiet of midnight, a sort of type of the solitude of a wilderness. As an enemy was known to be near, Hutter directed his daughters to abstain from the use of lights, luxuries in which they seldom indulged during the warm months, lest they might prove beacons to direct their foes where they might be found.

"In open day-light, I should'n't fear a host of savages, behind these stout logs, and they without any cover to skulk into," added Hutter, when he had explained to his guests the reason why he forbade the use of lights, "for I've three or four trusty weapons always loaded, and Killdeer, in particular, is a piece that never misses. But it's a different thing at night. A canoe might get upon us unseen, in the dark, and the savages have so many cunning ways of attacking, that I look upon it as bad enough to deal with 'em, under a bright sun. I built this dwelling, in order to have 'em at arm's length, in case we should ever get to blows, again. Some people think it's too open and exposed, but I'm for anchoring out here, clear of underbrush and thickets, as the surest means of making a safe berth."

"You was once a sailor, they tell me, old Tom?" said Hurry, in his abrupt manner, struck by one or two expressions that the other had just used; "and some people believe you could give us strange accounts of inimies and ship wrecks, if you'd a mind to come out with all you know?"

"There are people in this world, Hurry," returned the other evasively, " who live on other men's thoughts, and some such often find their way into the woods. What I've been, or what I've seen in youth, is of less matter now, than what the savages are. It's of more account to find out what will happen in the next twenty four hours, than to talk over what happened twenty four years since."

"That's judgment, Deerslayer; yes, that's sound judgment. Here's Judith and Hetty to take care on, to say nothing of our own top-knots; and for my part I can sleep as well in the dark, as I could under a noon day sun. To me it's no great matter whether there is light, or not, to see to shut my eyes by."

As Deerslayer seldom thought it necessary to answer his companion's peculiar vein of humour, and Hutter was evidently indisposed to dwell longer on the subject, its discussion ceased with this remark. The latter had something more on his mind, however, than recollections. His daughters had no sooner left them, with an expressed intention of going to bed, than he invited his two companions to follow him again into the scow. Here the old man opened his project, keeping back the portions that he had reserved for execution by Hurry and himself.

"The great object for people posted like ourselves, is to command the water," he commenced. "So long as there is no other craft on the lake, a bark canoe is as good as a man-of-war, since the castle will not be easily taken by swimming. Now, there are but five canoes remaining in these parts, two of which are mine, and one is Hurry's. These three we have with us, here, one being fastened in the canoe-dock beneath the house, and the other two being along side the scow. The other canoes are housed on the shore, in hollow logs, and the savages, who are such venomous enemies, will leave no likely place unexamined in the morning, if they're serious in s'arch of bounties"—

"Now, friend Hutter," interrupted Hurry, "the Indian do'n't live that can find a canoe that is suitably wintered. I've done something at this business before now, and Deerslayer, here, knows that I am one that can hide a craft in such a way that I can't find it myself."

"Very true, Hurry," put in the person to whom the appeal had been made, "but you overlook the sarcumstance that if you couldn't see the trail of the man who did the job, *I could*. I'm of Master Hutter's mind that it's far wiser to mistrust a savage's ingenuerty, than to build any great expectations on his want of eye-sight. If these two canoes can be got off to the castle, therefore, the sooner it's done the better."

"Will you be of the party that's to do it?" demanded Hutter, in a way to show that the proposal both surprised and pleased him.

"Sartain. I'm ready to enlist in any interprise that's not ag'in a white man's lawful gifts. Natur' orders us to defend our lives, and the lives of others too, when there's occasion and oppertunity. I'll follow you, Floating Tom, into the Mingo camp on such an ar'n'd, and will strive to do my duty, should we come to blows, though, never having been tried in battle, I don't like to promise more than I may be able to perform. We all know our wishes, but none know their might 'till put to the proof."

"That's modest and suitable, lad," exclaimed Hurry. "You've never yet heard the crack of an angry rifle, and let me tell you, 'tis as different from the persuasion of one of your venison speeches, as the laugh of Judith Hutter, in her best humour, is from the scolding of a Dutch housekeeper on the Mohawk. I do'n't expect you'll prove much of a warrior, Deerslayer, though your equal with the bucks, and the does, do'n't exist in all these parts. As for the ra'al sarvice, howsever, you'll turn out rather rearward, according to my consait."

"We'll see, Hurry, we'll see," returned the other meekly, and so far as human eye could discover not at all disturbed by these expressed doubts concerning his conduct on a point on which men are uniformly sensitive, precisely in the degree that they feel the consciousness of demerit,—"having never been tried, I'll wait to know, before I form any opinion myself, and then there'll be sartainty instead of bragging. I've heard of them that was valiant afore the fight, who did little in it, and of them that waited to know their own tempers, and found that they were'n't as bad as some expected, when put to the proof."

"At any rate we know you can use a paddle, young man," said Hutter, "and that's all we shall ask of you to-night. Let us waste no more time, but get into the canoe, and *do* in place of talking."

As Hutter led the way in the execution of his project, the boat was soon ready, with Hurry and Deerslayer at the paddles. Before the old man embarked himself, however, he held a conference of several minutes with Judith, entering the house for that purpose; then, returning, he took his place in the canoe, which left the side of the Ark at the next instant.

Had there been a temple reared to God, in that solitary wilderness, its clock would have told the hour of midnight as the party set forth on their expedition. The darkness had increased, though the night was still clear, and the light of the stars sufficed for all the purposes of the adventurers. Hutter alone knew the places where the canoes were hid, and he directed the course, while his two athletic companions raised and dipped their paddles with proper caution, lest the sound should be carried to the ears of their enemies, across that sheet of placid water, in the stillness of deep night. But the bark was too light to require any extraordinary efforts, and, skill supplying the place of strength, in about half an hour, they were approaching the shore, at a point near a league from the Castle.

"Lay on your paddles, men," said Hutter, in a low voice; "and let us look about us for a moment. We must now be all eyes and ears, for these vermin have noses like blood hounds."

The shores of the lake were examined closely, in order to discover any glimmering of light that might have been left in a camp, and the men strained their eyes, in the obscurity, to see if some thread of smoke was not still stealing along the mountain-side, as it arose from the dying embers of a fire. Nothing unusual could be traced, and as the position was at some distance from the outlet, or the spot where the savages had been met, it was thought safe to land. The paddles were plied, again, and the bows of the canoe ground up on the gravelly beach, with a gentle motion, and a sound barely audible. Hutter and Hurry immediately landed, the former carrying his own and his friend's rifle, leaving Deerslayer in charge of the canoe.

The hollow log lay at a little distance up the side of the mountain, and the old man led the way towards it, using so much caution as to stop at every third or fourth step to listen if any tread betrayed the presence of a foe. The same death like stillness, however, reigned on the midnight scene, and the desired place was reached without an occurrence to induce alarm.

"This is it," whispered Hutter, laying a foot on the trunk of a fallen linden—"hand me the paddles first, and draw the boat out with care, for the wretches may have left it for a bait, after all."

"Keep my rifle handy, butt towards me, old fellow," answered March—"If they attack me loaded, I shall want to unload the piece at 'em, at least. And feel if the pan is full."

"All's right—" muttered the other. "Move slow when you get your load, and let me lead the way."

The canoe was drawn out of the log with the utmost care, raised by Hurry to his shoulder, and the two began to return to the shore, moving but a step at a time, lest they should tumble down the steep declivity. The distance was not great, but the descent was extremely difficult, and towards the end of their little journey, Deerslayer was obliged to land and meet them, in order to aid in lifting the canoe through the bushes. With his assistance, the task was successfully accomplished, and the light craft soon floated by the side of the other canoe. This was no sooner done, than all three turned anxiously toward the forest and the mountain, as if expecting an enemy to break out of the one, or to come rushing down the other. Still the silence was unbroken, and they all embarked with the caution that had been used in coming ashore.

Hutter now steered broad off towards the centre of the lake. Having got a sufficient distance from the shore, he cast his prize loose, knowing that it would drift slowly up the lake, before the light southerly air, and intending to find it on his return. Thus relieved of his tow, the old man held his way down the lake, steering towards the very point, where Hurry had made his fruitless attempt on the life of the deer. As the distance from this point to the outlet was less than a mile, it was like entering an enemy's country, and redoubled caution became necessary. They reached the extremity of the point, however, and landed in safety, on the little gravelly beach already mentioned. Unlike the last place at which they had gone ashore, here was no acclivity to ascend, the mountains looming up in the darkness quite a quarter of a mile further west, leaving a margin of level ground between them and the strand. The point itself, though long, and covered with tall trees, was nearly flat, and, for some distance, only a few yards in width. Hutter and Hurry landed as before, leaving their companion in charge of the boat.

In this instance the dead tree that contained the canoe of which they had come in quest, lay about half way between the extremity of this narrow slip of land, and the place where it joined the main shore; and, knowing that there was water so near him on his left, the old man led the way along the eastern side of the belt, with some confidence, walking boldly though still with caution. He had landed at the point expressly to get a glimpse into the bay, and to make certain that the coast was clear; otherwise he would have come ashore directly abreast of the hollow tree. There was no difficulty in finding the latter, from which the canoe was drawn as before, and, instead of carrying it down to the place where Deerslayer lay, it was launched at the nearest favorable spot. As soon as it was in the water, Hurry entered it, and paddled down to the point, whither Hutter also proceeded following the beach. As the three men had now in their possession all the boats on the lake, their confidence was greatly increased, and there was no longer the same feverish desire to quit the shore, or the same necessity for extreme caution. Their position on the extremity of the long, narrow bit of land added to the feeling of security, as it permitted an enemy to approach in only one direction, that in their front, and under circumstances that would render discovery, with their habitual vigilance, almost certain. The three now landed together, and stood grouped in consultation on the gravelly point.

"We've fairly tree'd the scamps," said Hurry, chuckling at their success, "and if they wish to visit the castle, let 'em wade or swim! Old Tom, that idee of your'n, in burrowing out in the lake was high proof, and carries a fine bead. There be men who would think the land safer than the water, but after all reason shows it is'n't; the beavers, and 'rats, and other l'arned creatur's, taking to the last, when hard pressed. I call our position, now, entrenched, and set the Canadas at defiance."

"Let us paddle along this south shore," said Hutter, "and see if there's no signs of an encampment—but, first, let me have a better look into the bay, for no one has been far enough round the inner shore of the point, to make sure of that quarter, yet."

As Hutter ceased speaking all three moved in the direction he had named. Scarce had they fairly opened the bottom of the bay, when a general start proved that their eyes had lighted on a common object, at the same instant. It was no more than a dying brand, giving out its flickering and failing light, but at that hour, and in that place, it was at once as conspicuous as "a good deed in a naughty world." There was not a shadow of doubt that this fire had been kindled at an encampment of the Indians. The situation, sheltered from observation on all sides but one, and even on that except for a very short distance, proved that more care had been taken to conceal the spot, than would be used for ordinary purposes, and Hutter, who knew that a spring was near at hand, as well as one of the best fishing stations on the lake, immediately inferred that this encampment contained the women and children of the party.

"That's not a warrior's encampment," he growled to Hurry, "and there's a bounty enough sleeping round that fire to make a heavy division of head-money. Send the lad to the canoes, for there'll come no good of him in such an onset, and let us take the matter in hand, at once, like men."

"There's judgment in your notion, old Tom, and I like it to the back-bone. Deerslayer, do you get into the canoe, lad, and paddle off into the lake, with the spare one, and set it adrift, as we did with the other; after which you can float along shore, as near as you can get to the head of the bay, keeping outside the point, howsever, and outside the rushes too. You can hear us when we want you, and if there's any delay I'll call like a loon—yes, that'll do it—the call of a loon shall be the signal. If you hear rifles, and feel like sogering, why you may close in, and see if you can make the same hand with the savages that you do with the deer."

"If my wishes could be followed, this matter would not be undertaken, Hurry—"

"Quite true—no body denies it, boy; but your wishes *ca'n't* be followed, and that inds the matter. So just canoe yourself off into the middle of the lake, and by the time you get back, there'll be movements in that camp!"

The young man set about complying with great reluctance and a heavy heart. He knew the prejudices of the frontier men too well, however, to attempt a remonstrance. The latter, indeed, under the circumstances, might prove dangerous, as it would certainly prove useless. He paddled the canoes, therefore, silently and with the former caution to a spot near the centre of the placid sheet of water, and set the boat just recovered adrift, to float towards the castle, before the light southerly air. This expedient had been adopted, in both cases, under the certainty that the drift could not carry the light barks more than a league or two before the return of light, when they might easily be overtaken. In order to prevent any wandering savage from using them, by swimming off and getting possession, a possible but scarcely a probable event, all the paddles were retained.

No sooner had he set the recovered canoe adrift, than Deerslayer turned the bows of his own towards the point on the shore that had been indicated by Hurry. So light was the movement of the little craft, and so steady the sweep of its master's arm, that ten minutes had not elapsed ere it was again approaching the land, having in that brief time passed over fully half a mile of distance. As soon as Deerslayer's eye caught a glimpse of the rushes, of which there were many growing in the water a hundred feet from the shore, he arrested the motion of the canoe, and anchored his boat by holding fast to the delicate but tenacious stem of one of the drooping plants. Here he remained, awaiting with an intensity of suspense that can be easily imagined, the result of the hazardous enterprise.

It would be difficult to convey to the minds of those who have never witnessed it, the sublimity that characterizes the silence of a solitude as deep as that which now reigned over the Glimmerglass. In the present instance, this sublimity was increased by the gloom of night, which threw its shadowy and fantastic forms around the lake, the forest, and the hills. It is not easy, indeed, to conceive of any place more favorable to heighten these natural impressions than that Deerslayer now occupied. The size of the lake brought all within the reach of human senses, while it displayed so much of the imposing scene at a single view, giving up, as it might be, at a glance, a sufficiency to produce the deepest impressions. As has been said, this was the first lake Deerslayer had ever seen. Hitherto his experience had been limited to the courses of rivers and smaller streams, and never before had he seen so much of that wilderness, which he so well loved, spread before his gaze. Accustomed to the forest, however, his mind was capable of portraying all its hidden mysteries, as he looked upon its leafy surface. This was also the first time he had been on a trail, when human lives depended on the issue. His ears had often drunk in the traditions of frontier warfare, but he had never yet been confronted with an enemy.

The reader will readily understand, therefore, how intense must have been the expectation of the young man, as he sat in his solitary canoe, endeavoring to catch the smallest sound that might denote the course of things on the shore. His training had been perfect, so far as theory could go, and his self-possession, notwithstanding the high excitement that was the fruit of novelty, would have done credit to a veteran. The visible evidences of the existence of the camp, or of the fire, could not be detected from the spot where the canoe lay, and he was compelled to depend on the sense of hearing alone. He did not feel impatient, for the lessons he had heard, taught him the virtue of patience, and most of all inculcated the necessity of wariness in conducting any covert assault on the Indians. Once he thought he heard the cracking of a dried twig, but expectation was so intense it might mislead him. In this manner, minute after minute passed, until the whole time since he left his companions was extended to quite an hour. Deerslayer knew not whether to rejoice in, or to mourn over this cautious delay, for if it augured security to his associates, it foretold destruction to the feeble and innocent.

It might have been an hour and a half after his companions and he had parted, when Deerslayer was aroused by a sound that filled him equally with concern and surprise. The quavering call of a loon arose from the opposite side of the lake; evidently at no great distance from its outlet. There was no mistaking the note of this bird, which is so familiar to all who know the sounds of the American lakes. Shrill, tremulous, loud and sufficiently prolonged, it seems the very cry of warning. It is often raised also, at night, an exception to the habits of most of the other feathered inmates of the wilderness, a circumstance which had induced Hurry to select it as his own signal. There had been sufficient time certainly for the two adventurers to make their way by land, from the point where they had been left, to that whence the call had come, but it was not probable that they would adopt such a course. Had the camp been deserted, they would have summoned Deerslayer to the shore, and did it prove to be peopled, there could be no sufficient motive for circling it, in order to re-embark at so great a distance. Should he obey the signal, and be drawn away from the landing, the lives of those who depended on him might be the forfeit, and should he neglect the call, on the supposition that it had been really made, the consequences might be equally disastrous, though from a different cause. In this indecision, he waited, trusting that the call, whether feigned or natural, would be speedily renewed. Nor was he mistaken. A very few minutes elapsed before the same shrill, warning cry was repeated, and from the same part of the lake. This time, being on the alert, his senses were not deceived. Although he had often heard admirable imitations of this bird, and was no mean adept himself in raising its notes, he felt satisfied that Hurry, to whose efforts in that way he had attended, could never so completely and closely follow nature. He determined, therefore, to disregard that cry, and to wait for one less perfect, and nearer at hand.

Deerslayer had hardly come to this determination, when the profound stillness of night and solitude was broken by a cry so startling, as to drive all recollection of the more melancholy call of the loon, from the listener's mind. It was a shriek of agony, that came either from one of the female sex, or from a boy so young as not yet to have attained a manly voice. This appeal could not be mistaken. Heart rending terror—if not writhing agony—was in the sounds, and the anguish that had awakened them was as sudden as it was fearful. The young man released his hold of the rush, and dashed his paddle into the water; to do, he knew not what—to steer, he know not whither. A very few moments, however, removed his indecision. The breaking of branches, the cracking of dried sticks, and the fall of feet were distinctly audible, the sounds appearing to approach the water, though in a direction that led diagonally towards the shore, and a little farther north than the spot that Deerslayer had been ordered to keep near. Following this clue, the young man urged the canoe ahead, paying but little attention to the manner in which he might betray its presence. He had reached a part of the shore, where its immediate bank was tolerably high and quite steep. Men were evidently threshing through the bushes and trees, on the summit of this bank, following the line of the shore, as if those who fled sought a favorable place for descending. Just at this instant, five or six rifles flashed, and the opposite hills gave back, as usual, the sharp reports, in prolonged, rolling echoes. One or two shrieks, like those which escape the bravest when suddenly overcome by unexpected anguish and alarm, followed, and then the threshing among the bushes was renewed, in a way to show that man was grappling with man.

"Slippery devil!" shouted Hurry, with the fury of disappointment, "his skin's greased! I sha'n't grapple!—Take *that* for your cunning!"

The words were followed by the fall of some heavy object among the smaller trees that fringed the bank, appearing to Deerslayer as if his gigantic associate had hurled an enemy from him, in this unceremonious manner. Again the flight and pursuit were renewed, and then the young man saw a human form break down the hill, and rush several yards into the water. At this critical moment the canoe was just near enough to the spot to allow this movement, which was accompanied by no little noise, to be seen, and feeling that there he must take in his companions, if anywhere, Deerslayer urged the canoe forward, to the rescue. His paddle had not been raised twice, when the voice of Hurry was heard filling the air with imprecations, and he rolled on the narrow beach, literally loaded down with enemies. While prostrate, and almost smothered with his foes, the athletic frontier-man gave his loon-call, in a manner that would have excited laughter, under circumstances less terrific. The figure in the water seemed suddenly to repent his own flight, and rushed to the shore to aid his companion, but was met and immediately overpowered, by half a dozen fresh pursuers who, just then, came leaping down the bank.

"Let up—you painted riptyles—let up!" cried Hurry, too hard pressed to be particular about the terms he used—"is'n't it enough that I'm withed like a saw-log, that ye must choke, too?"

This speech satisfied Deerslayer that his friends were prisoners, and that to land would be to share their fate. He was already within a hundred feet of the shore, when a few timely strokes of the paddle, not only arrested his advance, but forced him off to six or eight times that distance from his enemies. Luckily for him, all of the Indians had dropped their rifles in the pursuit, or this retreat might not have been effected with impunity; though no one had noted the canoe in the first confusion of the *mêlée*.

"Keep off the land, lad," called out Hutter—"The girls depend only on you, now; you will want all your caution to escape these savages. Keep off, and God prosper you, as you aid my children!"

There was little sympathy in general, between Hutter and the young man, but the bodily and mental anguish with which this appeal was made, served at the moment, to conceal from the latter all the former's faults. He saw only the father in his sufferings, and resolved at once to give a pledge of fidelity to his interests, and to be faithful to his word.

"Put your heart at ease, Master Hutter," he called out;—"The gals shall be look'd to, as well as the castle. The inimy has got the shore, 'tis no use to deny, but he has'n't got the water. Providence has the charge of all, and no one can say what will come of it; but, if good will can serve you and your'n, depend on that much. My exper'ence is small, but my will is good."

"Ay—ay, Deerslayer—" returned Hurry, in his stentorian

voice, which was losing some of its heartiness, notwithstanding—"Ay—ay—Deerslayer, you *mean* well enough, but what can you *do*. You're no great matter in the best of times, and such a person is not likely to turn out a miracle in the worst. If there's one savage on this lake shore, there's forty, and that's an army you a'nt the man to overcome. The best way, in my judgment, will be to make a straight course to the castle, get the gals into the canoe, with a few eatables, then strike off for the corner of the lake where we came in, and take the best trail for the Mohawk. These devils won't know where to look for you, for some hours, and if they did, and went off hot in the pursuit, they must turn either the foot, or the head, of the lake to get at you. That's my judgment in the matter, and if old Tom, here, wishes to make his last will and testament in a manner favorable to his darters he'll say the same."

"Twill never do, young man," rejoined Hutter. "The enemy has scouts out, at this moment, looking for canoes, and you'll be seen and taken. Trust to the castle, and above all things, keep clear of the land. Hold out a week, and parties from the garrisons will drive the savages off."

"T'won't be four and twenty hours, old fellow, afore these foxes will be rafting off, to storm your castle," interrupted Hurry, with more of the heat of argument, than might be expected from a man who was bound and a captive, and about whom nothing could be called free but his opinions and his tongue. "Your advice has a stout sound, but it will have a fatal tarmination. If you, or I, was in the house, we might hold out a few days, but remember that this lad has never seen an inimy afore to-night, and is what you yourself called settlement-conscienced; though, for my part I think the consciences in the settlements pretty much the same as they are out here in the woods. These savages are making signs, Deerslayer, for me to incourage you to come ashore with the canoe, but that I'll never do, as it's ag'in reason and natur'. As for old Tom and myself, whether they'll scalp us to-night, keep us for the torture by fire, or carry us to Canada, is more than any one knows, but the Devil that advises them how to act. I've such a big and bushy head, that it's quite likely they'll indivor to get two scalps off it, for this bounty is a tempting thing, or old Tom and I would'n't be in this scrape. Ay—there they go with their signs ag'in, but if I advise you to land, may they eat me as well as roast me. No—no—Deerslayer, do you keep off where you are, and after daylight, on no account, come within two hundred yards—"

This injunction of Hurry's was stopped by a hand's being rudely slapped against his mouth, the certain sign that some one in the party understood English sufficiently, to have at length detected the drift of his discourse. Immediately after the whole group entered the forest, Hutter and Hurry apparently making no resistance to the movement. Just as the sounds of the cracking bushes were ceasing, however, the voice of the father was again heard.

"As you're true to my children, God prosper you, young man!" were the words that reached Deerslayer's ears; after which he found himself left to follow the dictates of his own discretion.

Several minutes elapsed, in death-like stillness, after the party on the shore had disappeared in the woods. Owing to the distance, rather more than two hundred yards, and the obscurity, Deerslayer had been able barely to distinguish the group, and to see it retiring, but even this dim connection with human forms, gave an animation to the scene, that was strongly in contrast to the absolute solitude that remained. Although the young man leaned forward to listen, holding his breath and condensing every faculty in the single sense of hearing, not another sound reached his ears, to denote the vicinity of human beings. It seemed as if a silence that had never been broken, reigned on the spot again, and, for an instant, even that piercing shriek which had so lately broken the stillness of the forest, or the execrations of March, would have been a relief to the feeling of desertion, to which it gave rise.

This paralysis of mind and body, however, could not last long in one constituted mentally and physically, like Deerslayer. Dropping his paddle into the water, he turned the head of the canoe, and proceeded slowly, as one walks who thinks intently, towards the centre of the lake When he believed himself to have reached a point in a line with that where he had set the last canoe adrift, he changed his direction northward, keeping the light air as nearly on his back as possible. After paddling a quarter of a mile in this direction, a dark object became visible on the lake, a little to the right, and turning on one side for the purpose, he had soon secured his last prize to his own boat. Deerslayer now examined the heavens, the course of the air, and the position of the two canoes. Finding nothing in either to induce a change of plan, he lay down and prepared to catch a few hours' sleep, that the morrow might find him equal to its exigencies.

Although the hardy and the tired sleep profoundly, even in scenes of danger, it was some time before Deerslayer lost his recollection. His mind dwelt on what had passed, and his half conscious faculties kept figuring the events of the night, in a sort of waking dream. Suddenly he was up and alert, for he fancied he heard the preconcerted signal of Hurry, summoning him to the shore. But all was still as the grave, again. The canoes were slowly drifting northward, the 'thoughtful stars' were glimmering in their mild glory, over his head, and the forest bound sheet of water, lay embedded between its mountains, as calm and melancholy, as if never troubled by the winds, or brightened by a noon-day sun. Once more the loon raised his tremulous cry, near the foot of the lake, and the mystery of the alarm was explained. Deerslayer adjusted his hard pillow, stretched his form in the bottom of the canoe, and slept.

Chapter VII

"Clear, placid Leman! Thy contrasted lake
With the wild world I dwelt in, is a thing
Which warns me, with its stillness, to forsake
Earth's troubled waters for a purer spring.
This quiet sail is as a noiseless wing
To waft me from distraction: once I lov'd
Torn ocean's roar, but thy soft murmuring
Sounds sweet as if a sister's voice reproved,
That I with stern delights should ere have been so mov'd."
Byron, *Childe Harold's Pilgrimage*, III.lxxxv.

DAY HAD FAIRLY dawned, before the young man, whom we have left in the situation described in the last chapter, again opened his eyes. This was no sooner done, than he started up, and looked about him with the eagerness of one who suddenly felt the importance of accurately ascertaining his precise position. His rest had been deep and undisturbed, and when he awoke it was with a clearness of intellect, and a readiness of resources that were much needed at that particular moment. The sun had not risen, it is true, but the vault of heaven was rich with the winning softness that 'brings and shuts the day', while the whole air was filled with the carols of birds, the hymns of the feathered tribe. These sounds first told Deerslayer the risks he run. The air, for wind it could scarce be called, was still light it is true, but it had increased a little in the course of the night, and, as the canoes were mere feathers on the water, they had drifted twice the expected distance, and what was still more dangerous, had approached so near the base of the mountain that here rose precipitously from the eastern shore, as to render the carols of the birds plainly audible. This was not the worst. The third canoe had taken the same direction, and was slowly drifting towards a point where it must inevitably touch, unless turned aside by a shift of wind, or human hands. In other respects, nothing presented itself to attract attention, or to awaken alarm. The Castle stood on its shoal, nearly abreast of the canoes, for the drift had amounted to miles, in the course of the night, and the Ark lay fastened to its piles, as both had been left so many hours before.

As a matter of course, Deerslayer's attention was first given to the canoe ahead. It was already quite near the point, and a very few strokes of the paddle sufficed to tell him that it must touch before he could possibly overtake it. Just at this moment, too, the wind inopportunely freshened, rendering the drift of the light craft much more rapid and certain. Feeling the impossibility of preventing a contact with the land, the young man wisely determined not to heat himself with unnecessary exertions, but, first looking to the priming of his piece, he proceeded slowly and warily towards the point, taking care to make a little circuit, that he might be exposed on only one side, as he approached.

The canoe adrift, being directed by no such intelligence, pursued its proper way, and grounded on a small sunken rock, at the distance of three or four yards from the shore. Just at that moment, Deerslayer had got abreast of the point, and turned the bows of his own boat to the land; first casting loose his tow, that his movements might be unencumbered. The canoe hung an instant on the rock, then it rose a hair's breadth on an almost imperceptible swell of the water, swung round, floated clear, and reached the strand. All this the young man noted, but it neither quickened his pulses, nor hastened his hand. If any one had been lying in wait for the arrival of the waif, he must be seen, and the utmost caution in approaching the shore became indispensable. If no one was in ambush, hurry was unnecessary. The point being nearly diagonally opposite to the Indian encampment, he hoped the last, though the former was not only possible, but probable; for the savages were prompt in adopting all the expedients of their particular modes of warfare, and quite likely had many scouts searching the shores for craft to carry them off to the castle. As a glance at the lake from any height, or projection, would expose the smallest object on its surface, there was little hope that either of the canoes could pass unseen, and Indian sagacity needed no instruction to tell which way a boat, or a log, would drift, when the direction of the wind was known.

As Deerslayer drew nearer and nearer to the land, the

stroke of his paddle grew slower, his eye became more watchful, and his ears and nostrils almost dilated with the effort to detect any lurking danger. 'Twas a trying moment for a novice, nor was there the encouragement which even the timid sometimes feel, when conscious of being observed and commended. He was entirely alone, thrown on his own resources, and was cheered by no friendly eye, emboldened by no encouraging voice. Notwithstanding all these circumstances, the most experienced veteran in forest warfare could not have behaved better. Equally free from recklessness and hesitation, his advance was marked by a sort of philosophical prudence, that appeared to render him superior to all motions but those which were best calculated to effect his purpose. Such was the commencement of a career in forest exploits, that afterwards rendered this man, in his way, and under the limits of his habits and opportunities, as renowned as many a hero whose name has adorned the pages of works more celebrated than legends simple as ours can ever become.

When about a hundred yards from the shore, Deerslayer rose in the canoe, gave three or four vigorous strokes with the paddle, sufficient of themselves to impel the bark to land, and then quickly laying aside the instrument of labor, he seized that of war. He was in the very act of raising the rifle, when a sharp report, was followed by the buzz of a bullet that passed so near his body, as to cause him involuntarily to start. The next instant Deerslayer staggered, and fell his whole length in the bottom of the canoe. A yell—it came from a single voice—followed, and an Indian leaped from the bushes, upon the open area of the point, bounding towards the canoe. This was the moment the young man desired. He rose on the instant, and levelled his own rifle, at his uncovered foe; but his finger hesitated about pulling the trigger on one whom he held at such a disadvantage. This little delay, probably saved the life of the Indian, who bounded back into the cover, as swiftly as he had broken out of it. In the mean time Deerslayer had been swiftly approaching the land, and his own canoe reached the point just as his enemy disappeared. As its movements had not been directed, it touched the shore a few yards from the other boat, and though the rifle of his foe had to be loaded, there was not time to secure his prize, and to carry it beyond danger, before he would be exposed to another shot. Under the circumstances, therefore, he did not pause an instant, but dashed into the woods and sought a cover.

On the immediate point there was a small open area, partly in native grass, and partly beach, but a dense fringe of bushes lined its upper side. This narrow belt of dwarf vegetation passed, one issued immediately into the high, and gloomy vaults of the forest. The land was tolerably level for a few hundred feet, and then it rose precipitously in a mountain side. The trees were tall, large, and so free from underbrush, that they resembled vast columns, irregularly scattered, upholding a dome of leaves. Although they stood tolerably close together, for their ages and size, the eye could penetrate to considerable distances, and bodies of men, even, might have engaged beneath their cover, with concert and intelligence.

Deerslayer knew that his adversary must be employed in reloading, unless he had fled. The former proved to be the case, for the young man had no sooner placed himself behind a tree, than he caught a glimpse of the arm of the Indian, his body being concealed by an oak, in the very act of forcing the leathered bullet home. Nothing would have been easier than to spring forward and decide the affair by a close assault on his unprepared foe, but every feeling of Deerslayer revolted at such a step, although his own life had just been attempted from a cover. He was as yet unpractised in the ruthless expedients of savage warfare, of which he knew nothing except by tradition and theory, and it struck him as an unfair advantage to assail an unarmed foe. His colour had heightened, his eye frowned, his lips were compressed, and all his energies were collected and ready, but, instead of advancing to fire, he dropped his rifle to the usual position of a sportsman in readiness to catch his aim, and muttered to himself, unconscious that he was speaking—

"No—no—that may be red-skin warfare, but it's not a christian's gifts. Let the miscreant charge, and then we'll take it out like men; for the canoe he *must* not and *shall* not have. No—no; let him have time to load, and then God will take care of the right!"

All this time the Indian had been so intent on his own

movements, that he was even ignorant that his enemy was in the wood. His only apprehension was that the canoe would be recovered and carried away, before he might be in readiness to prevent it. He had sought the cover from habit, but was within a few feet of the fringe of bushes, and could be at the margin of the forest, in readiness to fire in a moment. The distance between him and his enemy was about fifty yards, and the trees were so arranged by nature that the line of sight was not interrupted, except by the particular tree behind which each party stood.

His rifle was no sooner loaded, than the savage glanced around him, and advanced, incautiously as regarded the real, but stealthily as respected the fancied position of his enemy, until he was fairly exposed. Then Deerslayer stepped from behind his own cover, and hailed him.

"This-a-way, red-skin; this-a-way, if you're looking for me," he called out. "I'm young in war, but not so young as to stand on an open beach to be shot down like an owl by day-light. It rests on yourself whether it's peace, or war, atween us, for my gifts are white gifts, and I'm not one of them that thinks it valiant to slay human mortals singly, in the woods."

The savage was a good deal startled by this sudden discovery of the danger he run. He had a little knowledge of English, however, and caught the drift of the other's meaning. He was also too well schooled to betray alarm, but dropping the butt of his rifle to the earth, with an air of confidence, he made a gesture of lofty courtesy. All this was done with the ease and self possession of one accustomed to consider no man his superior. In the midst of this consummate acting, however, the volcano that raged within, caused his eyes to glare, and his nostrils to dilate, like those of some wild beast, that is suddenly prevented from taking the fatal leap.

"Two canoe," he said, in the deep guttural tones of his race, holding up the number of fingers he mentioned, by way of preventing mistakes—"one for you—one for me."

"No—no—Mingo, that will never do. You own neither; and neither shall you have, as long as I can prevent it. I know it's war atween your people and mine, but that's no reason why human mortals should slay each other, like savage creatur's, that meet in the woods; go your way then, and leave me to go mine. The world is large enough for us both, and when we meet fairly in battle, why the Lord will order the fate of each of us."

"Good!" exclaimed the Indian—"My brother, missionary—great talk; all about Manitou."

"Not so—not so, warrior. I'm not good enough for the Moravians, and am too good for most of the other vagabonds that preach about in the woods. No—no—I'm only a hunter as yet, though afore the peace is made, 'tis like enough there'll be occasion to strike a blow at some of your people. Still I wish it to be done in fair fight, and not in a quarrel about the ownership of a miserable canoe."

"Good! My brother very young—but, he very wise. Little warrior, great talker. Chief, sometime, in council."

"I don't know this, nor do I say it, Injin," returned Deerslayer, colouring a little at the ill concealed sarcasm of the other's manner. "I look forward to a life in the woods, and I only hope it may be a peaceable one. All young men must go on the war path when there's occasion, but war is'n't needfully massacre. I've seen enough of the last, this very night, to know that providence frowns on it, and I now invite you to go your own way, while I go mine; and hope that we may part fri'nds."

"Good! My brother has two scalp—gray hair under t' other. Old wisdom, young tongue."

Here the savage advanced with confidence, his hand extended, his face smiling, and his whole bearing denoting amity and respect. Deerslayer met his offered friendship in a proper spirit, and they shook hands cordially, each endeavoring to assure the other of his sincerity and desire to be at peace.

"All have his own," said the Indian—"my canoe, mine; your canoe, your'n. Go look; if your'n, you keep; if mine, my keep."

"That's just, red-skin, though you must be wrong in thinking the canoe your property. Howsever, seein' is believin', and we'll go down to the shore, where you may look with your own eyes, for it's likely you'll object to trustin' altogether to mine."

The Indian uttered his favorite exclamation of "good!" and then they walked, side by side, towards the shore. There was no apparent distrust in the manner of either, the Indian moving in advance, as if he wished to show his companion that he did not fear turning his back to him. As they reached the open ground, the former pointed towards Deerslayer's boat, and said emphatically—

"No mine—Pale face canoe—*this* red man's. No want other man's canoe—want his own."

"You're wrong, red-skin, you're altogether wrong. This canoe was left in old Hutter's keeping, and is his'n according to all law, red or white, 'till its owner comes to claim it. Here's the seats and the stitching of the bark to speak for themselves—no man ever know'd an Injin to turn off such work."

"Good—my brother little ole, big wisdom. Injin no make him. White man's work."

"I'm glad you think so, for holding out to the contrary might have made ill blood atween us. Every one having a right to take possession of his own, I'll just shove the canoe out of reach of dispute, at once, as the quickest way of settling difficulties."

While Deerslayer was speaking he put a foot against the end of the light boat, and giving a vigorous shove, he sent it out into the lake, a hundred feet or more, where, taking the true current, it would necessarily float past the point, and be in no further danger of coming ashore. The savage started at this ready and decided expedient, and his companion saw that he cast a hurried and fierce glance at his own canoe, or that which contained the paddles. The change of manner, however, was but momentary, and then the Iroquois resumed his air of friendliness, and a smile of satisfaction.

"Good," he repeated with stronger emphasis than ever. "Young head, old mind. Know how to settle quarrel. Farewell, brother. He go to house in water—muskrat house—Injin go to camp; tell chief no find canoe."

Deerslayer was not sorry to hear this proposal, for he felt anxious to join the females, and he took the offered hand of the Indian very willingly. The parting words were friendly, and while the red man walked calmly towards the wood, with his rifle in the hollow of his arm, without once looking back in uneasiness or distrust, the white man moved towards the remaining canoe, carrying his piece in the same pacific manner it is true, but keeping his eyes fastened on the movements of the other. This distrust, however, seemed to be altogether uncalled for, and, as if ashamed to have entertained it, the young man averted his look, and stepped carelessly up to his boat. Here he began to push the canoe from the shore, and to make his other preparations for departing. He might have been thus employed a minute, when happening to turn his face towards the land, his quick and certain eye told him at a glance, the imminent jeopardy in which his life was placed. The black, ferocious eyes of the savage were glaring on him, like those of the crouching tiger, through a small opening in the bushes, and the muzzle of his rifle seemed already to be opening in a line with his own body.

Then, indeed, the long practice of Deerslayer as a hunter, did him good service. Accustomed to fire with the deer on the bound, and often when the precise position of the animal's body, had in a manner to be guessed at, he used the same expedients here. To cock and poise his rifle were the acts of a single moment, and a single motion; then, aiming almost without sighting, he fired into the bushes where he knew a body ought to be, in order to sustain the appalling countenance which alone was visible. There was not time to raise the piece any higher, or to take a more deliberate aim. So rapid were his movements that both parties discharged their pieces at the same instant, the concussions mingling in one report. The mountains, indeed, gave back but a single echo. Deerslayer dropped his piece, and stood, with head erect, steady as one of the pines in the calm of a June morning, watching the result; while the savage gave the yell that has become historical for its appalling influence, leaped through the bushes, and came bounding across the open ground, flourishing a tomahawk. Still, Deerslayer moved not, but stood with his unloaded rifle fallen against his shoulder, while with a hunter's habits, his hands were mechanically feeling for the powder horn and charger. When about forty feet from his enemy, the savage hurled his keen weapon, but it was with an eye so vacant, and a hand so unsteady and feeble, that the young man caught it by the handle, as it was flying past him. At that instant, the Indian staggered and fell, his whole length on the ground.

"I know'd it—I knowed it!" exclaimed Deerslayer, who was already preparing to force a fresh bullet into his rifle—"I know'd it must come to this, as soon as I had got the range from the creatur's eyes. A man sights suddenly, and fires quick, when his own life's in danger; yes, I know'd it would come to this. I was about the hundredth part of a second too quick for him, or it might have been bad for me! The riptyle's bullet has just grazed my side, but say what you will, for or ag'in 'em, a red-skin is by no means as sartain with powder and ball, as a white man. Their gifts don't seem to lie that-a-way. Even Chingachgook, great as he is in other matters, is not downright deadly with the rifle."

By this time the piece was reloaded, and Deerslayer, after tossing the tomahawk into the canoe, advanced to his victim, and stood over him, leaning on his rifle, in melancholy attention. It was the first instance in which he had seen a man fall in battle, it was the first fellow creature against whom he had ever seriously raised his own hand. The sensations were novel; and regret, with the freshness of our better feelings, mingled with his triumph. The Indian was not dead, though shot directly through the body. He lay on his back motionless, but his eyes, now full of consciousness, watched each action of his victor, as the fallen bird regards the fowler, jealous of every movement. The man probably expected the fatal blow, which was to precede the loss of his scalp; or, perhaps he anticipated that this latter act of cruelty would precede his death. Deerslayer read his thoughts, and he found a melancholy satisfaction in relieving the apprehensions of the helpless savage.

"No—no—red-skin," he said. "You've nothing more to fear from me. I am of a christian stock, and scalping is not of my gifts—I'll just make sartain of your rifle, and then come back and do you what sarvice I can. Though here I can't stay much longer, as the crack of three rifles will be apt to bring more of your devils upon me."

The close of this was said in a sort of a soliloquy, as the young man went in quest of the fallen rifle. The piece was found where its owner had dropped it, and was immediately put into the canoe. Laying his own rifle at its side, Deerslayer then returned and stood over the Indian, again.

"All inmity atween you and me's at an ind, red-skin," he said, "and you may set your heart at rest, on the score of the scalp, or any further injury. My gifts are white, as I've told you, and I hope my conduct will be white also."

Could looks have conveyed all they meant, it is probable Deerslayer's innocent vanity on the subject of colour, would have been rebuked a little, but he comprehended the gratitude that was expressed in the eyes of the dying savage, without, in the least, detecting the bitter sarcasm that struggled with the better feeling.

"Water—" ejaculated the thirsty and unfortunate creature—"give poor Injin water—"

"Ay, water you shall have, if you drink the lake dry. I'll just carry you down to it, that you may take your fill. This is the way, they tell me, with all wounded people—water is their greatest comfort and delight."

So saying, Deerslayer raised the Indian in his arms and carried him to the lake. Here he first helped him to take an attitude in which he could appease his burning thirst; after which he seated himself on a stone, and took the head of his wounded adversary in his own lap, and endeavored to soothe his anguish, in the best manner he could.

"It would be sinful in me to tell you your time had'n't come, warrior," he commenced, "and, therefore, I'll not say it. You're passed the middle age, already, and considerin' the sort of lives ye lead, your days have been pretty well filled. The principal thing now, is to look forward to what comes next. Neither red skin nor pale face, on the whole, calculates much on sleepin' forever, but both expect to live in another world. Each has his gifts, and will be judged by 'em, and I suppose you've thought these matters over enough, not to stand in need of sarmons when the trial comes. You'll find your happy hunting grounds, if you've been a just Injin, and if an onjust, you'll meet your desarts in another way. I've my own idees about these things, but you're too old and exper'enced to need any explanations from one as young as I."

"Good!" ejaculated the Indian, whose voice retained its depth, even as life ebbed away. "Young head—ole wisdom."

"It's sometimes a consolation when the ind comes to know that them we've harmed, or *tried* to harm, forgive us. I suppose natur' seeks this relief, by way of getting a pardon on 'arth, as we never can know whether *He* pardons, who is all in all, 'till judgment itself comes. It's soothing to know that *any* pardon, at such times, and that I conclude is the secret. Now, as for myself, I overlook altogether your designs ag'in my life; first, because no harm came of 'em; next, because it's your gifts, and natur' and trainin', and I ought not to have trusted you, at all; and, finally and chiefly, because I can bear no ill will to a dying man, whether heathen or christian. So put your heart at ease, so far as I'm consarned; you know best what other matters ought to trouble you, or what ought to give you satisfaction in so trying a moment."

It is probable that the Indian had some of the fearful glimpses of the unknown state of being, which God, in mercy, seems, at times, to afford to all the human race, but they were necessarily in conformity with his habits and prejudices. Like most of his people, and like too many of our own, he thought more of dying in a way to gain applause among those he left, than to secure a better state of existence, hereafter. While Deerslayer was speaking, his mind was a little bewildered, though he felt that the intention was good; and when he had done, a regret passed over his spirit that none of his own tribe were present to witness his stoicism, under extreme bodily suffering, and the firmness with which he met his end. With the high, innate courtesy that so often distinguishes the Indian warrior, before he becomes corrupted by too much intercourse with the worst class of the white men, he endeavored to express his thankfulness for the other's good intentions, and to let him understand that they were appreciated.

"Good!" he repeated, for this was an English word much used by savages—"good—young head; young *heart*, too. *Old* heart tough; no shed tear. Hear Indian when he die, and no want to lie—what he call him?"

"Deerslayer is the name I bear now, though the Delawares

have said that when I get back from this war-path, I shall bear a more manly title, provided I can 'arn one."

"That good name for boy—poor name for warrior. Get better quick. No fear *there*—" the savage had strength sufficient, under the strong excitement he felt, to raise a hand and tap the young man on his breast—"eye, sartain—finger, lightening—aim, death. Great warrior, soon—No Deerslayer—Hawkeye—Hawkeye—Hawkeye—Shake hand."

Deerslayer—or Hawkeye as the youth was then first named, for in after years he bore the appellation throughout all that region—Deerslayer took the hand of the savage, whose last breath was drawn in that attitude, gazing in admiration at the countenance of a stranger, who had shewn so much readiness, skill and firmness, in a scene that was equally trying and novel. When the reader remembers it is the highest gratification an Indian can receive to see his enemy betray weakness, he will be better able to appreciate the conduct which had extorted so great a concession, at such a moment.

"His spirit has fled!" said Deerslayer, in a suppressed, melancholy, voice. "Ah's, me!—Well, to this we must all come, sooner or later; and he is happiest, let his skin be of what colour it may, who is best fitted to meet it. Here lies the body of, no doubt, a brave warrior, and the soul is already flying towards its heaven, or hell, whether that be a happy hunting ground, or a place scant of game, regions of glory according to Moravian doctrine, or flames of fire! So it happens, too, as regards other matters! Here have old Hutter and Hurry Harry got themselves into difficulty, if they have'n't got themselves into torment and death, and all for a bounty that luck offers to me in what many would think a lawful and suitable manner. But not a farthing of such money shall cross my hand. White I was born, and white will I die; clinging to colour to the last, even though the King's Majesty, his governors, and all his councils, both at home and in the colonies, forget from what they come, and where they hope to go, and all for a little advantage in warfare. No—no—warrior; hand of mine shall never molest your scalp, and so your soul may rest in peace on the p'int of making a decent appearance, when the body comes to join it, in your own land of spirits."

Deerslayer arose as soon as he had spoken. Then he placed

the body of the dead man, in a sitting posture, with its back against the little rock, taking the necessary care to prevent it from falling, or in any way settling into an attitude that might be thought unseemly by the sensitive, though wild, notions of a savage. When this duty was performed, the young man stood gazing at the grim countenance of his fallen foe, in a sort of melancholy abstraction. As was his practice, however, a habit gained by living so much alone in the forest, he then began, to give utterance to his thoughts, and feelings aloud.

"I did'n't wish your life, red-skin," he said, "but you left me no choice atween killing, or being killed. Each party acted according to his gifts, I suppose, and blame can light on neither. You were treacherous, according to your natur' in war, and I was a little oversightful, as I'm apt to be in trusting others. Well, this is my first battle with a human mortal, though it's not likely to be the last. I have fou't most of the creatur's of the forest, such as bears, wolves, painters and catamounts, but this is the beginning with red-skins. If I was Injin born, now, I might tell of this, or carry in the scalp, and boast of the expl'ite afore the whole tribe; or, if my inimy had only been even a bear, 'twould have been nat'ral and proper to let every body know what had happened; but I do'n't well see how I'm to let even Chingachgook into this secret, so long as it can be done only by boasting with a white tongue. And why should I wish to boast of it, a'ter all? It's slaying a human, although he was a savage; and how do I know that he was a just Injin; and that he has not been taken away suddenly, to any thing but happy hunting grounds. When it's onsartain whether good, or evil, has been done, the wisest way is not to be boastful—still, I *should* like Chingachgook to know that I have'n't discredited the Delawares, or my training!"

Part of this was uttered aloud, while part was merely muttered between the speaker's teeth; his more confident opinions enjoying the first advantage, while his doubts were expressed in the latter mode. Soliloquy and reflections received a startling interruption, however, by the sudden appearance of a second Indian on the lake shore, a few hundred yards from the point. This man, evidently another scout, who had probably been drawn to the place by the reports of the rifles, broke out of the forest with so little caution that Deerslayer caught a view of his person, before he was himself discovered. When the latter event did occur, as was the case a moment later, the savage gave a loud yell, which was answered by a dozen voices from different parts of the mountain-side. There was no longer any time for delay, and, in another minute the boat was quitting the shore under long and steady sweeps of the paddle.

As soon as Deerslayer believed himself to be at a safe distance, he ceased his efforts, permitting the little bark to drift, while he leisurely took a survey of the state of things. The canoe first sent adrift was floating before the air, quite a quarter of a mile above him, and a little nearer to the shore than he wished, now that he knew more of the savages were so near at hand. The canoe shoved from the point was within a few yards of him, he having directed his own course towards it, on quitting the land. The dead Indian lay in grim quiet, where he had left him, the warrior who had shown himself from the forest had already vanished, and the woods themselves were as silent, and seemingly as deserted, as the day they came fresh from the hands of their great creator. This profound stillness, however, lasted but a moment. When time had been given to the scouts of the enemy to reconnoitre, they burst out of the thicket, upon the naked point, filling the air with yells of fury, at discovering the death of their companion. These cries were immediately succeeded by shouts of delight, when they reached the body, and clustered eagerly around it. Deerslayer was a sufficient adept in the usages of the natives, to understand the reason of the change. The yell was the customary lamentation at the loss of a warrior, the shout a sign of rejoicing that the conqueror had not been able to secure the scalp; the trophy, without which a victory was never considered complete. The distance at which the canoes lay, probably prevented any attempts to injure the conqueror, the American Indian, like the panther of his own woods, seldom making any effort against his foe, unless tolerably certain it is under circumstances that may be expected to prove effective.

As the young man had no longer any motive to remain near the point, he prepared to collect his canoes, in order to tow them off to the castle. That nearest was soon in tow, when he proceeded in quest of the other, which was, all this time, floating up the lake. The eye of Deerslayer was no sooner fastened on this last boat, than it struck him that it was nearer to the shore than it would have been, had it merely followed the course of the gentle current of air. He began to suspect the influence of some unseen current in the water, and he quickened his exertions, in order to regain possession of it, before it could drift in to a dangerous proximity to the woods. On getting nearer, he thought that the canoe had a perceptible motion through the water, and, as it lay broadside to the air, that this motion was taking it towards the land. A few vigorous strokes of the paddle carried him still nearer, when the mystery was explained. Something was evidently in motion on the off side of the canoe, or that which was furthest from himself, and closer scrutiny, showed that it was a naked human arm. An Indian was lying in the bottom of the canoe, and was propelling it slowly, but certainly, to the shore, using his hand as a paddle. Deerslayer understood the whole artifice at a glance. A savage had swam off to the boat, while he was occupied with his enemy on the point, got possession, and was using these means to urge it to the shore.

Satisfied that the man in the canoe could have no arms, Deerslayer did not hesitate to dash close along side of the retiring boat, without deeming it necessary to raise his own rifle. As soon as the wash of the water, which he made in approaching, became audible to the prostrate savage, the latter sprang to his feet, and uttered an exclamation that proved how completely he was taken by surprise.

"If you've enj'yed yourself enough in that canoe, red-skin," Deerslayer coolly observed, stopping his own career in sufficient time to prevent an absolute collision between the two boats—"if you've enj'yed yourself enough in that canoe, you'll do a prudent act by taking to the lake ag'in. I'm reasonable in these matters, and do'n't crave your blood, though there's them about, that would look upon you more as a due-bill for the bounty, than a human mortal. Take to the lake, this minute, afore we get to hot words."

The savage was one of those who did not understand a

word of English, and he was indebted to the gestures of Deerslayer, and to the expression of an eye that did not often deceive, for an imperfect comprehension of his meaning. Perhaps, too, the sight of the rifle that lay so near the hand of the white man quickened his decision. At all events, he crouched like a tiger about to take his leap, uttered a yell, and the next instant his naked body disappeared in the water. When he rose to take breath, it was at a distance of several yards from the canoe, and the hasty glance he threw behind him, denoted how much he feared the arrival of a fatal messenger from the rifle of his foe. But the young man made no indication of any hostile intention. Deliberately securing the canoe to the others, he began to paddle from the shore, and by the time the Indian reached the land, and had shaken himself, like a spaniel on quitting the water, his dreaded enemy was already beyond rifle shot, on his way to the castle. As was so much his practice, Deerslayer did not fail to soliloquize on what had just occurred while steadily pursuing his course, towards the point of destination.

"Well—well—" he commenced, "'twould have been wrong to kill a human mortal without an object. Scalps are of no account with me, and life is sweet, and ought not to be taken marcilessly, by them that have white gifts. The savage was a Mingo, it's true, and I make no doubt he is, and will be, as long as he lives, a ra'al riptyle and vagabond, but that's no reason I should forget my gifts and colour. No—no—let him go; if ever we meet ag'in, rifle in hand, why then t'will be seen which has the stoutest heart and the quickest eye.—Hawkeye! That's not a bad name for a warrior, sounding much more manful and valiant than Deerslayer! 'Twould'n't be a bad title to begin with, and it has been fairly 'arned. If 'twas Chingachgook, now, he might go home and boast of his deeds, and the chiefs would name him Hawkeye, in a minute, but it do'n't become white blood to brag and 'tis'n't easy to see how the matter can be known, unless I do. Well—well—every thing is in the hands of Providence; this affair as well as another; and I'll trust to that for getting my desarts in all things."

Having thus betrayed what might be termed his weak spot, the young man continued to paddle in silence, making his way diligently, and as fast as his tows would allow him, towards the castle. By this time the sun had not only risen, but it had appeared over the eastern mountains, and was shedding a flood of glorious light on this, as yet, unchristened sheet of water. The whole scene was radiant with beauty, and no one unaccustomed to the ordinary history of the woods, would fancy it had so lately witnessed incidents so ruthless and barbarous. As he approached the building of old Hutter, Deerslayer thought, or rather *felt*, that its appearance was in singular harmony with all the rest of the scene. Although nothing had been consulted but strength and security, the rude massive logs, covered with their rough bark, the projecting roof, and the form would contribute to render the building picturesque in almost any situation, while its actual position added novelty and piquancy to its other points of interest.

When Deerslayer drew nearer to the castle, however, objects of interest presented themselves, that at once eclipsed any beauties that might have distinguished the scenery of the lake, and the site of the singular edifice. Judith and Hetty stood on the platform, awaiting his approach with manifest anxiety, the former, from time to time, taking a survey of his person and of the canoes, through the old ship's spy glass that has been already mentioned. Never probably did this girl seem more brilliantly beautiful than at that moment; the flush of anxiety and alarm increasing her colour to its richest tints, while the softness of her eyes, a charm that even poor Hetty shared with her, was deepened by intense concern. Such at least, without pausing, or pretending, to analyze motives, or to draw any other very nice distinctions between cause and effect, were the opinions of the young man as his canoes reached the side of the Ark, where he carefully fastened all three, before he put his foot on the platform.

Chapter VIII

"His words are bonds, his oaths are oracles;
His love sincere, his thoughts immaculate;
His tears pure messengers sent from his heart;
His heart as far from fraud, as heaven from earth."

Two Gentlemen of Verona, II.vii.75–78.

NEITHER OF the girls spoke, as Deerslayer stood before them alone, his countenance betraying all the apprehension he felt on account of the two absent members of their party.

"Father!" Judith at length exclaimed, succeeding in uttering the word, as it might be, by a desperate effort.

"He's met with misfortune, and there's no use in concealing it," answered Deerslayer, in his direct and simple-minded manner. "He and Hurry are in Mingo hands, and Heaven only knows what's to be the tarmination. I've got all the canoes safe, and that's a consolation, since the vagabonds will have to swim for it, or raft off, to come near this place. At sunset we'll be reinforced by Chingachgook, if I can manage to get him into a canoe, and then, I think, we two can answer for the ark and the castle, 'till some of the officers in the garrisons, hear of this war-path, which sooner or later must be the case, when we may look for succour, from that quarter, if from no other."

"The officers!" exclaimed Judith, impatiently, her colour deepening, and her eye expressing a lively but passing emotion. "Who thinks, or speaks of the heartless gallants, now?—We are sufficient of ourselves, to defend the castle;—but what of my father—and of poor Hurry Harry?"

"'Tis natural you should feel this consarn for your own parent, Judith, and I suppose it's equally so that you should feel it for Hurry Harry too."

Deerslayer, then, commenced a succinct but clear narrative of all that occurred during the night, in no manner concealing what had befallen his two companions, or his own opinion of what might prove to be the consequences. The girls listened with profound attention, but neither betrayed that feminine apprehension and concern, which would have followed such a communication, when made to those who were less accustomed to the hazards and incidents of a frontier life. To the surprise of Deerslayer, Judith seemed the most distressed, Hetty listening eagerly, but appearing to brood over the facts in melancholy silence, rather than betraying any outward signs of feeling. The former's agitation, the young man did not fail to attribute to the interest she felt in Hurry, quite as much as to her filial love, while Hetty's apparent indifference was ascribed to that mental darkness which, in a measure, obscured her intellect, and which possibly prevented her from foreseeing all the consequences. Little was said, however, by either, Judith and her sister busying themselves in making their preparations for the morning meal, as they who habitually attend to such matters, toil on mechanically even in the midst of suffering and sorrow. The plain but nutritious breakfast was taken by all three, in sombre silence. The girls ate little, but Deerslayer gave proof of possessing one material requisite of a good soldier, that of preserving his appetite in the midst of the most alarming and embarrassing circumstances. The meal was nearly ended before a syllable was uttered; then, however, Judith spoke in the convulsive and hurried manner in which feeling breaks through restraint, after the latter has become more painful than even the betrayal of emotions.

"Father would have relished this fish!" she exclaimed; "he says the salmon of the lakes is almost as good as the salmon of the sea."

"Your father has been acquainted with the sea, they tell me, Judith," returned the young man, who could not forbear throwing a glance of inquiry at the girl, for, in common with all who knew Hutter he had some curiosity on the subject of his early history. "Hurry Harry tells he was once a sailor."

Judith first looked perplexed; then influenced by feelings that were novel to her, in more ways than one, she became suddenly communicative, and seemingly much interested in the discourse.

"If Hurry knows any thing of father's history, I would he had told it to me!" she cried. "Sometimes I think too, he was once a sailor, and then again I think he was not. If that chest were open, or if it could speak, it might let us into his whole history. But its fastenings are too strong to be broken like pack-thread."

Deerslayer turned to the chest in question, and for the first time examined it closely. Although discolored, and bearing proofs of having received much ill treatment, he saw that it was of materials and workmanship altogether superior to any thing of the same sort he had ever before beheld. The wood was dark, rich, and had once been highly polished, though the treatment it had received left little gloss on its surface, and various scratches and indentations proved the rough collisions that it had encountered with substances still harder than itself. The corners were firmly bound with steel, elaborately and richly wrought, while the locks, of which it had no less than three, and the hinges were of a fashion and workmanship that would have attracted attention even in a warehouse of curious furniture. This chest was quite large, and when Deerslayer arose, and endeavored to raise an end by its massive handle, he found that the weight fully corresponded with the external appearance.

"Did you never see that chest opened, Judith," the young man demanded with frontier freedom, for delicacy on such subjects was little felt among the people on the verge of civilization, in that age, even if it be to-day.

"Never. Father has never opened it in my presence, if he ever opens it at all. No one here, has ever seen its lid raised, unless it be father; nor do I even know that he has ever seen it."

"Now, you're wrong, Judith," Hetty quietly answered. "Father *has* raised the lid, and *I've* seen him do it."

A feeling of manliness kept the mouth of Deerslayer shut, for, while he would not have hesitated about going far beyond what would be thought the bounds of propriety, in questioning the elder sister, he had just scruples about taking what might be thought, an advantage of the feeble intellect of the younger. Judith, being under no such restraint, however turned quickly to the last speaker, and continued the discourse.

"When and where did you ever see that chest opened, Hetty?"

"Here, and, again and again. Father often opens it, when *you* are away, though he don't in the least mind my being by, and seeing all he does, as well as hearing all he says."

"And what is it that he does, and what does he say?"

"That I cannot tell *you*, Judith—" returned the other in a low, but resolute voice—"*Father's* secrets, are not *my* secrets."

"Secrets!—This is stranger still, Deerslayer; that father should tell them to Hetty, and not tell them to me!"

"There's good reason for that, Judith, though you're not to know it. Father's not here to answer for himself, and I'll say no more about it."

Judith and Deerslayer looked surprised, and, for a minute, the first seemed pained. But, suddenly recollecting herself, she turned away from her sister, as if in pity for her weakness, and addressed the young man.

"You've told but half your story," she said, "breaking off at the place where you went to sleep in the canoe—or, rather, where you rose to listen to the cry of the loon. We heard the call of the loons too, and thought their cries might bring a storm, though we are little used to tempests on this lake, at this season of the year."

"The winds blow, and the tempests howl as God pleases; sometimes at one season, and sometimes at another," answered Deerslayer; "and the loons speak accordin' to their natur'. Better would it be, if men were as honest and frank. After I rose to listen to the birds, finding it could not be Hurry's signal, I lay down and slept. When the day dawned, I was up and stirring as usual, and then I went in chase of the two canoes, lest the Mingos should lay hands on 'em."

"You have not told us all, Deerslayer," said Judith, earnestly—"We heard rifles, under the eastern mountain; the echoes were full and long, and came so soon after the reports that the pieces must have been fired on, or quite near to the shore. Our ears are used to these signs, and are not to be deceived."

"They've done their duty, gal, this time; yes, they've done their duty. Rifles have been sighted, this morning, ay, and triggers pulled too, though not as often as they might have been. One warrior has gone to his happy hunting grounds, and that's the whole of it. A man of white blood, and white gifts, is not to be expected to boast of his expl'ites, and to flourish scalps."

Judith listened almost breathlessly, and, when Deerslayer, in his quiet, modest, manner, seemed disposed to quit the subject, she rose, and, crossing the room, took a seat by his side. The manner of the girl had nothing forward about it, though it betrayed the quick instinct of a female's affection, and the sympathizing kindness of a woman's heart. She even took the hard hand of the hunter, and pressed it in both her own, unconsciously to herself perhaps, while she looked earnestly and even reproachfully into his sun burned face.

"You have been fighting the savages, Deerslayer, singly and by yourself!" she said. "In your wish to take care of us—of Hetty—of me, perhaps—you've fought the enemy bravely, with no eye to encourage your deeds, or to witness your fall, had it pleased Providence to suffer so great a calamity!"

"I've fou't, Judith; yes I *have* fou't the inimy, and that, too, for the first time in my life. These things must be, and they bring with 'em a mix'd feelin' of sorrow and triumph. Human natur' is a fightin' natur', I suppose, as all nations and colours kill in battle, and we must be true to our rights and gifts. What has yet been done is no great matter, but, should Chingachgook come to the rock this evening, as is agreed atween us, and I get him off it, onbeknown to the savages, or if known to them, ag'in their wishes and designs, then may we all look to something like warfare, afore the Mingos shall get possession of either the castle, or the Ark, or yourselves."

"Who is this Chingachgook; from what place does he come, and *why* does he come *here*?"

"The questions are nat'ral, and right, I suppose, though the youth has a great name, already, in his own part of the country. Chingachgook is a Mohican by blood, consorting with the Delawares by usage, as is the case with most of his tribe; which has long been broken up by the increase of our colour. He is of the family of the great chiefs; Uncas, his father, having been the considerablest warrior and counsellor of his people. Even old Tamenund honors Chingachgook, though he is thought to be yet too young to lead in war; and then the nation is so dispersed and diminished, that chieftainship among 'em has got to be little more than a name. Well, this war having commenced in 'arnest, the Delaware and I rendezvous'd an app'intment to meet this evening, at sunset, on the rendezvous-rock, at the foot of this very lake, intending to come out on our first hostile expedition ag'in the Mingos. *Why* we come exactly this-a-way, is our own secret, but thoughtful young men, on a warpath, as you may suppose, do nothing without a calculation, and a design."

"A Delaware can have no unfriendly intentions towards us," said Judith, after a moment's hesitation, "and we know you to be friendly."

"Treachery is the last crime I hope to be accused of," returned Deerslayer, hurt at the gleam of distrust that had shot through Judith's mind; "and, least of all, treachery to my own colour."

"No one suspects *you*, Deerslayer," the girl impetuously cried—"No—no—your honest countenance would be a sufficient surety, for the truth of a thousand hearts! If all men had as honest tongues, and no more promised what they did not mean to perform, there would be less wrong done in the world, and fine feathers and scarlet cloaks would not be thought excuses for baseness and deception!"

The girl spoke with strong, nay even with convulsed feeling, and her fine eyes, usually so soft and alluring, flashed fire as she concluded. Deerslayer could not but observe this extraordinary emotion, but, with the tact of a courtier, he avoided not only any allusion to the circumstance, but succeeded in concealing the effect of his discovery on himself. Judith gradually grew calm, again, and, as she was obviously anxious to appear to advantage in the eyes of the young man, she was soon able to renew the conversation as composedly as if nothing had occurred to disturb her.

"I have no right to look into your secrets, or the secrets of your friends, Deerslayer," she continued, "and am ready to take all you say on trust. If we can really get another male ally to join us, at this trying moment, it will aid us much, and I am not without hopes that when the savages find we are able to keep the lake, they will offer to give up their prisoners in exchange for skins, or at least for the keg of powder that we have in the house."

The young man had the words "scalps" and "bounty" on his lips, but a reluctance to alarm the feelings of the daughters, prevented him from making the allusion he had intended to the probable fate of their father. Still, so little was he practised in the arts of deception, that his expressive countenance was, of itself, understood by the quick witted Judith, whose intelligence had been sharpened by the risks and habits of her forest life.

"I understand what you mean," she continued, hurriedly, "and what you would say, but for the fear of hurting me—*us*—I mean; for Hetty loves her father quite as well as I do. But this is not as we think of Indians. They never scalp an unhurt prisoner, but would rather take him away alive; unless, indeed, the fierce wish for torturing should get the mastery of them. I fear nothing for my father's scalp, and little for his life. Could they steal on us, in the night, we should all probably suffer in this way, but men taken in open strife are seldom injured; not, at least, until the time of torture comes."

"That's tradition I'll allow, and it's accordin' to practise—but, Judith, do you know the ar'n'd on which your father and Hurry went ag'in the savages?"

"I do; and a cruel errand it was! But, what will you have? Men will be men, and some even that flaunt in their gold and silver, and carry the king's commission in their pockets, are not guiltless of equal cruelty—" Judith's eye again flashed, but, by a desperate struggle, she resumed her composure. "I get warm, when I think of all the wrong that men do," she added, affecting to smile, an effort in which she only succeeded indifferently well—"All this is silly. What is done, is done, and it cannot be mended by complaints. But the Indians think so little of the shedding of blood, and value men so much for the boldness of their undertakings, that did they know the business on which their prisoners came, they would be more likely to honor, than to injure them for it."

"For a time, Judith; yes, I allow *that* for a time. But, when that feelin' dies away, then will come the love of revenge. We must indivour, Chingachgook and I, we must indivour to see what we can do to get Hurry and your father, free; for the Mingos will no doubt, hover about this lake some days, in order to make the most of their success."

"You think this Delaware can be depended on, Deerslayer?" demanded the girl, thoughtfully.

"As much as I can myself. You say you do not suspect *me*, Judith?"

"You!" taking his hand again, and pressing it between her own with a warmth that might have awakened the vanity of one less simple-minded, and more disposed to dwell on his own good qualities, "I would as soon suspect a brother! I have known you but a day, Deerslayer, but it has awakened the confidence of a year. Your name, however, is not unknown to me, for the gallants of the garrisons frequently speak of the lessons you have given them in hunting, and all proclaim your honesty."

"Do they ever talk of the shooting, gal?—" inquired the other eagerly, after, however, laughing, in a silent but heart-felt manner—"Do they ever talk of the shooting? I want to hear nothing about my own, for, if that is'n't sartified to, by this time, in all these parts, there's little use in being skilful and sure; but what do the officers say of their own—yes, what do they say of their own! Arms, as they call it, is their trade, and yet there's some among 'em that know very little how to use 'em!"

"Such, I hope, will not be the case with your friend Chingachgook, as you call him—what is the English of his Indian name?"

"Big Sarpent.—So called for his wisdom and cunning. Uncas is his ra'al name—all his family being called Uncas; until they get a title that has been 'arned by deeds."

"If he has all this wisdom, we may expect a useful friend in him, unless his own business, in this part of the country, should prevent him from serving us?"

"I see no great harm in telling you his ar'n'd, a'ter all, and, as you may find means to help us, I will let you and Hetty into the whole matter, trusting that you'll keep the secret as if it was your own. You must know that Chingachgook is a comely Injin, and is much look'd upon and admired by the young women of his tribe, both on account of his family, and on account of himself. Now, there is a chief that has a darter called Wah-ta!-Wah, which is intarpreted into Hist-oh!-Hist, in the English tongue; the rarest gal among the Delawares, and the one most sought a'ter and craved for a wife, by all the young warriors of the nation. Well, Chingachgook, among others took a fancy to Wah-ta!-Wah, and Wah-ta!-Wah took a fancy to him." Here Deerslayer paused an instant, for, as he got thus far in his tale, Hetty Hutter arose, approached, and stood attentive, at his knee, as a child draws near to listen to the legends of its mother. "Yes, he fancied *her*, and she fancied *him*," resumed Deerslayer, casting a friendly and approving glance at the innocent and interested girl, "and when that is the case, and all the elders are agreed, it does not often happen that the young couple keep apart. Chingachgook could'n't well carry off such a prize without making inimies among them that wanted her as much as he did himself. A sartain Briarthorn, as we call him in English, or Yocommon as he is tarmed in Injin, took it most to heart, and we mistrust him of having a hand in all that followed. Wah-ta!-Wah went with her father and mother, two moons ago, to fish for salmon, on the western streams, where, it is agreed by all in these parts, that fish most abounds, and while thus empl'y'd the gal vanished. For several weeks we could get no tidings of her, but, here, ten days since, a runner that came through the Delaware country brought us a message, by which we l'arn that Wah-ta!-Wah was stolen from her people—we think, but do not know it, by Briarthorn's sarcumventions—and that she was now with the inimy, who had adopted her, and who wanted her to marry a young Mingo chief. The message said, that the party intended to hunt and forage through this region, for a month or two, afore it went back into the Canadas, and that if we could contrive to get on a scout in this quarter, something might turn up, that would lead to our getting the maiden off."

"And how does that concern *you*, Deerslayer?" demanded Judith, a little anxiously.

"It consarns me, as all things that touches a fri'nd consarn a fri'nd. I'm here as Chingachgook's aid and helper, and if we can get the young maiden he likes back ag'in, it will give me almost as much pleasure, as if I'd got back my own sweetheart."

"And where, then, *is your* sweet-heart, Deerslayer?"

"She's in the forest, Judith—hanging from the boughs of

the trees, in a soft rain—in the dew on the open grass—the clouds that float about in the blue heavens—the birds that sing in the woods—the sweet springs where I slake my thirst—and in all the other glorious gifts that come from God's Providence."

"You mean that—as yet—you've never loved one of my sex, but love best your haunts, and your own manner of life."

"That's it—that's just it. I am white—have a white heart, and can't, in reason, love a red skinned maiden, who must have a red-skin heart and feelin's. No—no—I'm sound enough, in them partic'lars, and hope to remain so; at least, 'till this war is over. I find my time too much taken up with Chingachgook's affair, to wish to have one of my own, on my hands, afore that is settled."

"The girl that finally wins you, Deerslayer, will at least, win an *honest* heart; one without treachery or guile, and that will be a victory, that most of her sex ought to envy."

As Judith uttered this, her beautiful face had a resentful frown on it, while a bitter smile lingered around a mouth that no derangement of the muscles could render any thing but handsome. Her companion observed the change, and, though little skilled in the workings of the female heart, he had sufficient native delicacy to understand that it might be well to drop the subject.

As the hour when Chingachgook was expected, still remained distant, Deerslayer had time enough to examine into the state of the defences, and to make such additional arrangements as were in his power, and the exigency of the moment seemed to require. The experience and foresight of Hutter had left little to be done, in these particulars; still several precautions suggested themselves to the young man, who may be said to have studied the art of frontier warfare, through the traditions and legends of the people among whom he had so long lived. The distance between the castle and the nearest point on the shore, prevented any apprehensions on the subject of rifle bullets thrown from the land. The house was within musket shot, in one sense, it was true, but aim was entirely out of the question, and even Judith professed a perfect disregard of any danger from that source. So long then as the party remained in possession of the fortress, they were safe; unless their assailants could find the means to come off and carry it, by fire, or storm; or, by some of the devices of Indian cunning and Indian treachery. Against the first source of danger Hutter had made ample provision, and the building itself, the bark roof excepted, was not very combustible. The floor was scuttled in several places, and buckets provided with ropes, were in daily use, in readiness for any such emergency. One of the girls could easily extinguish any fire that might be lighted, provided it had not time to make much headway. Judith, who appeared to understand all her father's schemes of defence, and who had the spirit to take no unimportant share in the execution of them, explained all these details to the young man, who was thus saved much time and labor in making his investigations.

Little was to be apprehended during the day. In possession of the canoes, and of the Ark, no other vessel was to be found on the lake. Nevertheless, Deerslayer well knew that a raft was soon made, and as dead trees were to be found in abundance, near the water, did the savages seriously contemplate the risks of an assault, it would not be a very difficult matter to find the necessary means. The celebrated American axe, a tool that is quite unrivalled in its way, was then not very extensively known, and the savages were far from expert in the use of its hatchet-like substitute; still, they had sufficient practice in crossing streams by this mode, to render it certain they would construct a raft, should they deem it expedient to expose themselves to the risks of an assault. The death of their warrior might prove a sufficient incentive, or it might act as a caution, but Deerslayer thought it more than possible that the succeeding night would bring matters to a crisis, and in this precise way. This impression caused him to wish ardently for the presence and succour of his Mohican friend, and to look forward to the approach of sunset with an increasing anxiety.

As the day advanced, the party in the castle matured their plans, and made their preparations. Judith was active, and seemed to find a pleasure in consulting and advising with her new acquaintance, whose indifference to danger, manly devotion to herself and sister, guilelessness of manner and truth of feeling had won rapidly on both her imagination and her affections. Although the hours appeared long in some respects to Deerslayer, Judith did not find them so, and when the sun began to descend towards the pine-clad summits of the western hills, she felt and expressed her surprise that the day should so soon be drawing to a close. On the other hand, Hetty was moody and silent. She was never loquacious, or if she occasionally became communicative, it was under the influence of some temporary excitement, that served to arouse her unsophisticated mind; but, for hours at a time, in the course of this all-important day, she seemed to have absolutely lost the use of her tongue. Nor did apprehension on account of their father, materially affect the manner of either sister. Neither appeared seriously to dread any evil greater than captivity, and, once or twice, when Hetty did speak, she intimated the expectation that Hutter would find the means to liberate himself. Although Judith was less sanguine on this head, she too betrayed the hope that propositions for a ransom would come, when the Indians discovered that the castle set their expedients and artifices at defiance. Deerslayer, however, treated these passing suggestions, as the ill digested fancies of girls, making his own arrangements as steadily, and brooding over the future as seriously, as if they had never fallen from their lips.

At length the hour arrived, when it became necessary to proceed to the place of rendezvous appointed with the Mohican; or Delaware, as Chingachgook was more commonly called. As the plan had been matured by Deerslayer, and fully communicated to his companions, all three set about its execution, in concert, and intelligently. Hetty passed into the ark, and fastening two of the canoes together, she entered one, and paddled up to a sort of gate-way in the palisadoes that surrounded the building, through which she carried both; securing them beneath the house by chains that were fastened within the building. These palisadoes were trunks of trees, driven firmly into the mud, and served the double purpose of a small enclosure that was intended to be used in this very manner, and to keep any enemy that might approach in boats at arm's length. Canoes thus *docked* were, in a measure, hid from sight, and as the gate was properly barred and fastened, it would not be an easy task to remove them, even in the event of their being seen. Previously however to closing the gate, Judith also entered within the enclosure with the third canoe, leaving Deerslayer busy in securing the door and windows, inside the building, over her head. As every thing was massive and strong, and small saplings were used as bars, it would have been the work of an hour or two, to break into the building, when Deerslayer had ended his task, even allowing the assailants the use of any tools but the axe, and to be unresisted. This attention to security, arose from Hutter's having been robbed, once or twice, by the lawless whites of the frontiers, during some of his many absences from home.

As soon as all was fast, in the inside of the dwelling, Deerslayer appeared at a trap, from which he descended into the canoe of Judith. When this was done, he fastened the door, with a massive staple, and stout padlock. Hetty was then received in the canoe, which was shoved outside of the palisadoes. The next precaution was to fasten the gate, and the keys were carried into the Ark. The three were now fastened out of the dwelling, which could only be entered by violence, or by following the course taken by the young man in quitting it.

The glass had been brought outside, as a preliminary step, and Deerslayer next took a careful survey of the entire shore of the lake, as far as his own position would allow. Not a living thing was visible, a few birds excepted, and even the last fluttered about in the shade of the trees, as if unwilling to encounter the heat of a sultry afternoon. All the nearest points, in particular, were subjected to a severe scrutiny, in order to make certain that no raft was in preparation, the result every where giving the same picture of calm solitude. A few words will explain the greatest embarrassment belonging to the situation of our party. Exposed themselves, to the observation of any watchful eyes, the movements of their enemies were concealed by the drapery of a dense forest. While the imagination would be very apt to people the latter, with more warriors than it really contained, their own weakness must be too apparent to all who might choose to cast a glance in their direction.

"Nothing is stirring, howsever," exclaimed Deerslayer, as he finally lowered the glass, and prepared to enter the Ark, "If the vagabonds do harbor mischief in their minds, they are too cunning to let it be seen; it's true, a raft may be in preparation in the woods, but it has not yet been brought down to the lake. They can't guess that we are about to quit the castle, and, if they did, they've no means of knowing where we intend to go."

"This is so true, Deerslayer," returned Judith, "that now all is ready, we may proceed, at once, boldly, and without the fear of being followed. Else we shall be behind our time."

"No—no—the matter needs management—for, though the savages are in the dark as to Chingachgook and the rock, they've eyes and legs, and will see in what direction we steer, and will be sartain to follow us. I shall strive to baffle 'em, hows'ever, by heading the scow in all manner of ways, first in one quarter, and then in another, until they get to be a-leg-weary, and well tired of tramping a'ter us."

So far as it was in his power, Deerslayer was as good as his word. In less than five minutes after this speech was made, the whole party was in the Ark, and in motion. There was a gentle breeze from the north, and boldly hoisting the sail, the young man laid the head of the unwieldy craft in such a direction as, after making a liberal but necessary allowance for lee-way, would have brought it ashore a couple of miles down the lake, and on its eastern side. The sailing of the Ark was never very swift, though; floating as it did on the surface, it was not difficult to get it in motion, or to urge it along, over the water, at the rate of some three or four miles in the hour. The distance between the Castle and the Rock was a little more than two leagues. Knowing the punctuality of an Indian, Deerslayer had made his calculations closely, and had given himself a little more time than was necessary to reach the place of rendezvous, with a view to delay, or to press his arrival, as might prove most expedient. When he hoisted the sail, the sun lay above the western hills, at an elevation that promised rather more than two hours of day, and a few minutes satisfied him that the progress of the scow was such as to equal his expectations.

It was a glorious June afternoon, and never did that solitary sheet of water seem less like an arena of strife and bloodshed. The light air scarce descended as low as the bed of the lake, hovering over it, as if unwilling to disturb its deep tranquility, or to ruffle its mirror-like surface. Even the forests appeared to be slumbering in the sun, and a few piles of fleecy clouds had lain for hours along the northern horizon, like fixtures in the atmosphere, placed there purely to embellish the scene. A few aquatic fowls occasionally skimmed along the water, and a single raven was visible, sailing high above the trees, and keeping a watchful eye on the forest beneath him, in order to detect any thing having life that the mysterious woods might offer as prey.

The reader will probably have observed, that, amidst the frankness and abruptness of manner, which marked the frontier habits of Judith, her language was superior to that used by her male companions, her own father included. This difference extended as well to pronunciation, as to the choice of words and phrases. Perhaps nothing so soon betrays the education and association as the modes of speech, and few accomplishments so much aid the charm of female beauty as a graceful and even utterance, while nothing so soon produces the disenchantment that necessarily follows a discrepancy between appearance and manner, as a mean intonation of voice, or a vulgar use of words. Judith and her sister were marked exceptions to all the girls of their class, along that whole frontier, the officers of the nearest garrison having often flattered the former with the belief that few ladies of the towns acquitted themselves better than herself, in this important particular. This was far from being literally true, but it was sufficiently near the fact to give birth to the compliment. The girls were indebted to their mother for this proficiency, having acquired from her, in childhood, an advantage that no subsequent study or labor can give without a drawback, if neglected beyond the earlier periods of life. Who that mother was, or, rather, had been, no one but Hutter knew. She had now been dead two summers, and, as was stated by Hurry, she had been buried in the lake, whether in indulgence of a prejudice, or from a reluctance to take the trouble to dig her grave, had frequently been a matter of discussion between the rude beings of that region. Judith had never visited the spot, but Hetty was present at the interment, and she often paddled a canoe, about sunset, or by the light of the moon, to the place, and gazed down into the limpid water, in the hope of being able to catch a glimpse of a form that she had so tenderly loved, from infancy to the sad hour of their parting.

"Must we reach the rock, exactly at the moment the sun sets?" Judith demanded of the young man, as they stood near each other, Deerslayer holding the steering-oar, and she working with a needle at some ornament of dress, that much exceeded her station in life, and was altogether a novelty in the woods. "Will a few minutes, sooner or later, alter the matter; it will be very hazardous to remain long as near the shore as that Rock!"

"That's it—Judith;—that's the very difficulty! The Rock's within p'int blank for a shot-gun, and 'twill never do to hover about it too close, and too long. When you have to deal with an Injin, you must calculate and manage, for a red natur' dearly likes sarcumvention. Now, you see, Judith, that I do not steer towards the rock at all, but here to the eastward of it, whereby the savages will be tramping off in that direction, and get their legs awearied, and all for no advantage!"

"You think, then, they see us, and watch our movements, Deerslayer? I was in hopes they might have fallen back into the woods, and left us to ourselves, for a few hours."

"That's altogether a woman's consait. There's no let-up in an Injin's watchfulness when he's fairly on a war path, and eyes are on us at this minute, 'though the lake presarves us. We must draw near the rock on a calculation, and indivour to get the miscreants on a false scent. The Mingos have good noses, they tell me, but a white man's reason ought always to equalize their instinct."

Judith now entered into a desultory discourse with Deerslayer, in which the girl betrayed her growing interest in the young man; an interest that his simplicity of mind, and her decision of character, sustained as it was by the consciousness awakened by the consideration her personal charms so universally produced, rendered her less anxious to conceal than might otherwise have been the case. She was scarcely forward in her manner, though there was sometimes a freedom in her glances, that it required all the aids of her exceeding beauty to prevent from awakening suspicions unfavorable to her discretion, if not to her morals. With Deerslayer, however, these glances were rendered less obnoxious to so unpleasant a construction, for she seldom looked at him, without discovering much of the sincerity and nature that accompany the purest emotions of woman. It was a little remarkable that, as his captivity lengthened neither of the girls manifested any great concern for her father, but, as has been said already, their habits gave them confidence, and they looked forward to his liberation, by means of a ransom, with a confidence that might, in a great degree, account for their apparent indifference. Once before Hutter had been in the hands of the Iroquois, and a few skins had readily effected his release. This event, however, unknown to the sisters, had occurred in a time of peace between England and France, and when the savages were restrained, instead of being encouraged to commit their excesses, by the policy of the different colonial governments.

While Judith was loquacious and caressing in her manner, Hetty remained thoughtful and silent. Once, indeed, she drew near to Deerslayer, and questioned him a little closely, as to his intentions, as well as concerning the mode of effecting his purpose, but her wish to converse went no farther. As soon as her simple queries were answered—and answered they all were, in the fullest and kindest manner—she withdrew to her seat, and continued to work on a coarse garment that she was making for her father, sometimes humming a low melancholy air, and frequently sighing.

In this manner the time passed away, and when the sun was beginning to glow behind the fringe of pines that bounded the western hill, or about twenty minutes before it actually set, the Ark was nearly as low as the point where Hutter and Hurry had been made prisoners. By sheering first to one side of the lake, and then to the other, Deerslayer managed to create an uncertainty as to his object, and, doubtless, the savages, who were unquestionably watching his movements, were led to believe that his aim was to communicate with them, at or near this spot, and would hasten in that direction, in order to be in readiness to profit by circumstances. This artifice was well managed, since the sweep of the bay, the curvature of the lake, and the low marshy land that intervened would probably allow the Ark to reach the rock, before its pursuers, if really collected near the point, could have time to make the circuit that would be required to get there by land. With a view to aid this deception, Deerslayer stood as near the western shore, as was at all prudent, and, then, causing Judith and Hetty to enter the house, or cabin, and crouching himself so as to conceal his person by the frame of the scow, he suddenly threw the head of the latter round, and began to make the best of his way towards the outlet. Favored by an increase in the wind, the progress of the Ark was such as to promise the complete success of this plan, though the crab-like movement of the craft compelled the helmsman to keep its head looking in a direction very different from that in which it was actually moving.

Chapter IX

"Yet art thou prodigal of smiles—
Smiles, sweeter than thy frowns are stern:
Earth sends from all her thousand isles,
A shout at thy return.
The glory that comes down from thee
Bathes, in deep joy, the land and sea."
Bryant, "The Firmament," ll. 19–24.

IT MAY ASSIST the reader in understanding the events we are about to record, if he has a rapidly sketched picture of the scene, placed before his eyes at a single view. It will be remembered that the lake was an irregularly shaped basin, of an outline that, in the main, was oval, but with bays and points to relieve its formality and ornament its shores. The surface of this beautiful sheet of water was now glittering like a gem, in the last rays of the evening sun, and the setting of the whole, hills clothed in the richest forest verdure, was lighted up with a sort of radiant smile, that is best described in the beautiful lines we have placed at the head of this chapter. As the banks, with few exceptions, rose abruptly from the water, even where the mountain did not immediately bound the view, there was a nearly unbroken fringe of leaves overhanging the placid lake, the trees starting out of the acclivities, inclining to the light, until, in many instances they extended their long limbs and straight trunks some forty or fifty feet beyond the line of the perpendicular. In these cases we allude only to the giants of the forest, pines of a hundred or a hundred and fifty feet in height, for of the smaller growth, very many inclined so far as to steep their lower branches in the water.

In the position in which the Ark had now got, the castle was concealed from view by the projection of a point, as indeed was the northern extremity of the lake itself. A respectable mountain, forest clad, and rounded, like all the rest, limited the view in that direction, stretching immediately across the whole of the fair scene, with the exception of a deep bay that passed its western end, lengthening the basin, for more than a mile. The manner in which the water flowed out of the lake, beneath the leafy arches of the trees that lined the sides of the stream, has already been mentioned, and it has also been said that the rock, which was a favorite place of rendezvous throughout all that region, and where Deerslayer now expected to meet his friend, stood near this outlet, and at no great distance from the shore. It was a large, isolated stone that rested on the bottom of the lake, apparently left there when the waters tore away the earth from around it, in forcing for themselves a passage down the river, and which had obtained its shape from the action of the elements, during the slow progress of centuries. The height of this rock could scarcely equal six feet, and, as has been said, its shape was not unlike that which is usually given to bee-hives, or to a hay-cock. The latter, indeed, gives the best idea not only of its form, but of its dimensions. It stood, and still stands, for we are writing of real scenes, within fifty feet of the bank, and in water that was only two feet in depth, though there were seasons in which its rounded apex, if such a term can properly be used, was covered by the lake. Many of the trees stretched so far forward, as almost to blend the rock with the shore, when seen from a little distance, and one tall pine in particular overhung it in a way to form a noble and appropriate canopy to a seat that had held many a forest chieftain, during the long succession of unknown ages, in which America, and all it contained, had existed apart, in mysterious solitude, a world by itself; equally without a familiar history, and without an origin that the annals of man can reach.

When distant some two or three hundred feet from the shore, Deerslayer took in his sail. He dropped his grapnel, as soon as he found the Ark had drifted in a line that was directly to windward of the rock. The motion of the scow was then checked, when it was brought head to wind, by the action of the breeze. As soon as this was done, Deerslayer "paid out line," and suffered the vessel to "set down" upon the rock, as fast as the light air could force it to leeward. Floating entirely on the surface, this was soon effected, and the young man checked the drift when he was told that the stern of the scow was within fifteen or eighteen feet of the desired spot.

In executing this manoeuvre, Deerslayer had proceeded promptly, for, while he did not in the least doubt that he was both watched and followed by the foe, he believed he had distracted their movements, by the apparent uncertainty of his own, and he knew they could have no means of ascertaining that the rock was his aim, unless indeed one of their prisoners had betrayed him; a chance so improbable in itself, as to give him no concern. Notwithstanding the celerity and decision of his movements, he did not, however, venture so near the shore without taking due precautions to effect a retreat, in the event of its becoming necessary. He held the line in his hand, and Judith was stationed at a loop, on the side of the cabin next the shore, where she could watch the beach and the rock, and give timely notice of the approach of either friend or foe. Hetty was also placed on watch, but it was to keep the trees over head in view, lest some enemy might ascend one, and, by completely commanding the interior of the scow render the defences of the hut, or cabin, useless.

The sun had disappeared from the lake and valley, when Deerslayer checked the Ark, in the manner mentioned. Still it wanted a few minutes to the true sun-set, and he knew Indian punctuality too well to anticipate any unmanly haste in his friend. The great question was, whether, surrounded by enemies as he was known to be, he had escaped their toils. The occurrences of the last twenty-four hours must be a secret to him, and like himself, Chingachgook was yet young on a warpath. It was true, he came prepared to encounter the party that withheld his promised bride, but he had no means of ascertaining the extent of the danger he run, or the precise positions occupied by either friends, or foes. In a word, the trained sagacity, and untiring caution of an Indian were all he had to rely on, amid the critical risks he unavoidably ran.

"Is the rock empty, Judith?" enquired Deerslayer, as soon as he had checked the drift of the Ark, deeming it imprudent to venture unnecessarily near the shore. "Is any thing to be seen of the Delaware chief?"

"Nothing, Deerslayer. Neither rock, shore, trees, nor lake, seems to have ever held a human form."

"Keep close, Judith—keep close, Hetty—a rifle has a prying eye, a nimble foot, and a desperate fatal tongue. Keep close then, but keep up actyve looks, and be on the alart. 'T would grieve me to the heart, did any harm befal either of you."

"And *you*, Deerslayer—" exclaimed Judith, turning her handsome face from the loop, to bestow a gracious and grateful look on the young man—"do *you* 'keep close', and have a proper care that the savages do not catch a glimpse of you! A bullet might be as fatal to *you*, as to one of us; and the blow that you felt, would be felt by us all."

"No fear of me, Judith—no fear of me, my good gal. Do not look this-a-way, although you look so pleasant and comely, but keep your eyes on the rock, and the shore, and the—"

Deerslayer was interrupted by a slight exclamation from the girl, who, in obedience to his hurried gestures, as much as in obedience to his words, had immediately bent her looks again, in the opposite direction.

"What is't?—What is't, Judith?" he hastily demanded—"Is any thing to be seen?"

"There is a man on the rock!—An Indian warrior, in his paint—and armed!"

"Where does he wear his hawk's feather?" eagerly added Deerslayer, relaxing his hold of the line, in readiness to drift nearer to the place of rendezvous. "Is it fast to the war-lock, or does he carry it above the left ear?"

"'Tis as you say, above the left ear; he smiles, too, and mutters the word 'Mohican.'"

"God be praised, 'tis the Sarpent, at last!" exclaimed the young man, suffering the line to slip through his hands, until hearing a light bound, in the other end of the craft, he instantly checked the rope, and began to haul it in, again, under the assurance that his object was effected.

At that moment the door of the cabin was opened hastily, and, a warrior, darting through the little room, stood at Deerslayer's side, simply uttering the exclamation "hughh!" At the next instant, Judith and Hetty shrieked, and the air was filled with the yell of twenty savages, who came leaping through the branches, down the bank, some actually falling headlong into the water, in their haste.

"Pull, Deerslayer," cried Judith, hastily barring the door, in order to prevent an inroad by the passage through which the Delaware had just entered; "pull, for life and death—the lake is full of savages, wading after us!"

The young men—for Chingachgook immediately came to his friend's assistance—needed no second bidding, but they applied themselves to their task in a way that showed how urgent they deemed the occasion. The great difficulty was in suddenly overcoming the *vis inertia* of so large a mass, for, once in motion, it was easy to cause the scow to skim the water, with all the necessary speed.

"Pull, Deerslayer, for Heaven's sake!" cried Judith, again at the loop—"These wretches rush into the water like hounds following their prey! Ah—the scow moves! and now, the water deepens, to the arm-pits of the foremost, but they reach forward, and will seize the Ark!"

A slight scream, and then a joyous laugh followed from the girl; the first produced by a desperate effort of their pursuers, and the last by its failure; the scow, which had now got fairly in motion gliding ahead into deep water, with a velocity that set the designs of their enemies at nought. As the two men were prevented by the position of the cabin, from seeing what passed astern, they were compelled to enquire of the girls, into the state of the chase.

"What now, Judith?—What next?—Do the Mingos still follow, or are we quit of 'em, for the present," demanded Deerslayer when he felt the rope yielding as if the scow was going fast ahead, and heard the scream and the laugh of the girl, almost in the same breath.

"They have vanished!—One—the last—is just burying himself in the bushes of the bank—There, he has disappeared in the shadows of the trees! You have got your friend, and we are all safe!"

The two men now made another great effort, pulled the Ark up swiftly to the grapnel, tripped it, and when the scow had shot some distance, and lost its way, they let the anchor drop again. Then, for the first time since their meeting, they ceased their efforts. As the floating house now lay several hundred feet from the shore, and offered a complete protection against bullets, there was no longer any danger, or any motive for immediate exertion.

The manner in which the two friends now recognised each other, was highly characteristic. Chingachgook, a noble, tall, handsome and athletic young Indian warrior, first examined his rifle, with care, opening the pan to make sure that the priming was not wet, and, assured of this important fact, he next cast furtive but observant glances around him, at the strange habitation, and at the two girls. Still he spoke not, and most of all, did he avoid the betrayal of a womanish curiosity, by asking questions.

"Judith and Hetty—" said Deerslayer, with an untaught, natural courtesy—"this is the Mohican chief of whom you've heard me speak; Chingachgook as he is called; which signifies Big Sarpent; so named for his wisdom and prudence, and cunning, and my 'arliest and latest fri'nd. I know'd it must be he, by the hawk's feather, over the left ear, most other warriors wearing 'em on the war-lock."

As Deerslayer ceased speaking, he laughed heartily, excited more perhaps by the delight of having got his friend safe at his side, under circumstances so trying, than by any conceit that happened to cross his fancy, and exhibiting this outbreaking of feeling in a manner that was a little remarkable, since his merriment was not accompanied by any noise. Although Chingachgook both understood and spoke English, he was unwilling to communicate his thoughts in it, like most Indians, and when he had met Judith's cordial shake of the hand, and Hetty's milder salute, in the courteous manner that became a chief, he turned away, apparently to await the moment when it might suit his friend to enter into an explanation of his future intentions, and to give a narrative of what had passed since their separation. The other understood his meaning, and discovered his own mode of reasoning in the matter, by addressing the girls.

"This wind will soon die away altogether, now the sun is down," he said, "and there is no need for rowing ag'in it. In half an hour, or so, it will either be a flat calm, or the air will come off from the south shore, when we will begin our journey back ag'in to the castle; in the mean while, the Delaware and I will talk over matters, and get correct idees of each other's notions, consarning the course we ought to take."

No one opposed this proposition, and the girls withdrew

into the cabin to prepare the evening meal, while the two young men took their seats on the head of the scow and began to converse. The dialogue was in the language of the Delawares. As that dialect, however, is but little understood, even by the learned, we shall, not only on this, but on all subsequent occasions, render such parts, as it may be necessary to give closely, into liberal English; preserving, as far as possible, the idioms and peculiarities of the respective speakers, by way of presenting the pictures in the most graphic forms to the minds of the readers.

It is unnecessary to enter into the details first related by Deerslayer, who gave a brief narrative of the facts that are already familiar to those who have read our pages. In relating these events, however, it may be well to say that the speaker touched only on the outlines, more particularly abstaining from saying any thing about his encounter with, and victory over the Iroquois, as well as to his own exertions in behalf of the two deserted young women. When Deerslayer ended, the Delaware took up the narrative, in turn, speaking sententiously and with grave dignity. His account was both clear and short, nor was it embellished by any incidents that did not directly concern the history of his departure from the villages of his people, and his arrival in the valley of the Susquehannah. On reaching the latter, which was at a point only half a mile south of the outlet, he had soon struck a trail, which gave him notice of the probable vicinity of enemies. Being prepared for such an occurrence, the object of the expedition calling him directly into the neighborhood of the party of Iroquois that was known to be out, he considered the discovery as fortunate, rather than the reverse, and took the usual precautions to turn it to account. First following the river to its source, and ascertaining the position of the rock, he met another trail, and had actually been hovering for hours on the flanks of his enemies, watching equally for an opportunity to meet his mistress, and to take a scalp; and it may be questioned which he most ardently desired. He kept near the lake, and occasionally he ventured to some spot, where he could get a view of what was passing on its surface. The Ark had been seen and watched, from the moment it hove in sight, though the young chief was necessarily ignorant that it was to be the instrument of his effecting the desired junction with his friend. The uncertainty of its movements, and the fact that it was unquestionably managed by white men, soon led him to conjecture the truth, however, and he held himself in readiness to get on board whenever a suitable occasion might offer. As the sun drew near the horizon he repaired to the rock, where, on emerging from the forest, he was gratified in finding the Ark lying, apparently in readiness to receive him. The manner of his appearance, and of his entrance into the craft is known.

Although Chingachgook had been closely watching his enemies for hours, their sudden and close pursuit, as he reached the scow, was as much a matter of surprise to himself, as it had been to his friend. He could only account for it, by the fact of their being more numerous than he had at first supposed, and by their having out parties of the existence of which he was ignorant. Their regular, and permanent encampment, if the word permanent can be applied to the residence of a party that intended to remain out, in all probability, but a few weeks, was not far from the spot where Hutter and Hurry had fallen into their hands, and, as a matter of course, near a spring.

"Well, Sarpent," asked Deerslayer, when the other had ended his brief but spirited narrative, speaking always in the Delaware tongue, which for the reader's convenience only we render into the peculiar vernacular of the speaker—"Well, Sarpent, as you've been scouting around these Mingos, have you any thing to tell us of their captyves, the father of these young women, and of another, who, I somewhat conclude, is the lovyer of one of 'em."

"Chingachgook has seen them. An old man, and a young warrior—the falling hemlock and the tall pine."

"You're not so much out, Delaware; you're not so much out. Old Hutter is decaying, of a sartainty, though many solid blocks might be hewn out of his trunk yet, and, as for Hurry Harry, so far as heighth, and strength and comliness go, he may be called the pride of the human forest. Were the men bound, or, in any manner, suffering torture? I ask on account of the young women, who, I dare to say, would be glad to know."

"It is not so, Deerslayer. The Mingos are too many to cage their game. Some watch; some sleep; some scout; some hunt. The pale faces are treated like brothers to-day; to-morrow they will lose their scalps."

"Yes, that's red natur', and must be submitted to! Judith and Hetty, here's comforting tidings for you, the Delaware telling me that neither your father nor Hurry Harry is in suffering, but, bating the loss of liberty, as well off, as we are ourselves. Of course they are kept in the camp; otherwise they do much as they please."

"I rejoice to hear this, Deerslayer," returned Judith, "and now we are joined by your friend, I make no manner of question that we shall find an opportunity to ransom the prisoners. If there are any women in the camp, I have articles of dress that will catch their eyes, and, should the worst come to the worst, we can open the great chest, which, I think will be found to hold things that may tempt the chiefs."

"Judith," said the young man, looking up at her, with a smile, and an expression of earnest curiosity, that, spite of the growing obscurity did not escape the watchful looks of the girl, "can you find it in your heart, to part with your own finery, to release prisoners; even though one be your own father, and the other is your sworn suitor and lovyer?"

The flush on the face of the girl arose in part from resentment, but more perhaps from a gentler and a novel feeling, that, with the capricious waywardness of taste, had been rapidly rendering her more sensitive to the good opinion of the youth who questioned her, than to that of any other person. Suppressing the angry sensation, with instinctive quickness, she answered with a readiness and truth, that caused her sister to draw near to listen, though the obtuse intellect of the latter was far from comprehending the workings of a heart as treacherous, as uncertain, and as impetuous in its feelings, as that of the spoiled and flattered beauty.

"Deerslayer," answered Judith, after a moment's pause, "I shall be honest with *you*. I confess, that the time *has* been when what you call finery, was to me the dearest thing on earth; but I begin to feel differently. Though Hurry Harry is nought to me nor ever can be, I would give all I own to set him free. If I would do this, for blustering, bullying, talking

Hurry, who has nothing but good looks to recommend him, you may judge what I would do for my own father."

"This sounds well, and is according to woman's gifts. Ah's, me! The same feelin's is to be found among the young women of the Delawares. I've known 'em, often and often, sacrifice their vanity to their hearts. 'Tis as it should be—'tis as it should be I suppose, in both colours. Woman was created for the feelin's, and is pretty much ruled by feelin'."

"Would the savages let father go, if Judith and I give them all our best things?" demanded Hetty, in her innocent, mild, manner.

"Their women might interfere, good Hetty; yes, their women might interfere with such an ind in view. But, tell me, Sarpent, how is it as to squaws among the knaves; have they many of their own women in the camp?"

The Delaware heard, and understood all that passed, though with Indian gravity and finesse he had sat, with averted face, seemingly inattentive to a discourse in which he had no direct concern. Thus appealed to, however, he answered his friend in his ordinary sententious manner.

"Six—" he said, holding up all the fingers of one hand, and the thumb of the other, "beside *this*." The last number denoted his betrothed, whom, with the poetry and truth of nature, he described by laying his hand on his own heart.

"Did you see her, chief—did you get a glimpse of her pleasant countenance, or come close enough to her ear, to sing in it the song she loves to hear?"

"No, Deerslayer—the trees were too many, and leaves covered their boughs like clouds hiding the heavens, in a storm. But"—and the young warrior turned his dark face towards his friend, with a smile on it that illuminated its fierce-looking paint, and naturally stern lineaments, with a bright gleam of human feeling, "Chingachgook heard the laugh of Wah-ta!-Wah, and knew it from the laugh of the women of the Iroquois. It sounded in his ears, like the chirp of the wren."

"Ay, trust a lovyer's ear for that, and a Delaware's ear for all sounds that are ever heard in the woods. I know not why it is so, Judith, but when young men—and I dares to say it may be all the same with young women, too—but when they get to have kind feelin's towards each other, it's wonderful how pleasant the laugh, or the speech becomes, to the other person. I've seen grim warriors listening to the chattering and the laughing of young gals, as if it was church music, such as is heard in the old Dutch church that stands in the great street of Albany, where I've been, more than once, with peltry and game."

"And *you*, Deerslayer," said Judith quickly, and with more sensibility than marked her usually light and thoughtless manner,—"have *you* never felt how pleasant it is to listen to the laugh of the girl you love?"

"Lord bless you gal!—Why I've never lived enough among my own colour to drop into them sort of feelin's,—no never! I dares to say, they are nat'ral and right, but to me there's no music so sweet as the sighing of the wind in the tree tops, and the rippling of a stream from a full, sparkling, natyve fountain of pure forest water—unless, indeed," he continued, dropping his head for an instant in a thoughtful manner—"unless indeed it be the open mouth of a sartain hound, when I'm on the track of a fat buck—As for unsartain dogs, I care little for their cries, seein' they are as likely to speak when the deer is not in sight, as when it is."

Judith walked slowly and pensively away, nor was there any of her ordinary calculating coquetry, in the light tremulous sigh, that, unconsciously to herself, arose to her lips. On the other hand Hetty listened with guileless attention, though it struck her simple mind as singular that the young man should prefer the melody of the woods, to the songs of girls, or even to the laugh of innocence and joy. Accustomed, however, to defer, in most things, to her sister, she soon followed Judith into the cabin, where she took a seat, and remained pondering intensely over some occurrence, or resolution, or opinion—which was a secret to all but herself. Left alone, Deerslayer and his friend resumed their discourse.

"Has the young pale-face hunter been long on this lake?" demanded the Delaware, after courteously waiting for the other to speak first.

"Only since yesterday noon, Sarpent, though that has been long enough to see and do much."

The gaze that the Indian fastened on his companion was so

keen that it seemed to mock the gathering darkness of the night. As the other furtively returned his look, he saw the two black eyes glistening on him, like the balls of the panther, or those of the penned wolf. He understood the meaning of this glowing gaze, and answered evasively, as he fancied would best become the modesty of a white man's gifts.

"Tis as you suspect, Sarpent; yes, 'tis somewhat that-a-way. I *have* fell in with the inimy, and I suppose it may be said I've fou't them, too."

An exclamation of delight and exultation escaped the Indian, and then laying his hand eagerly on the arm of his friend, he asked if there were any scalps taken.

"That I *will* maintain in the face of all the Delaware tribe, old Tamenund, and your own father, the great Uncas, as well as the rest, is ag'in white gifts! *My* scalp is on my head, as you can see, Sarpent, and that was the only scalp that was in danger, when one side was altogether Christian and white."

"Did no warrior fall?—Deerslayer did not get his name, by being slow of sight, or clumsy with the rifle!"

"In that particular, chief, you're nearer reason, and therefore nearer being right. I may say one Mingo fell."

"A chief!" demanded the other with startling vehemence.

"Nay, that's more than I know, or can say. He was artful, and treacherous, and stout-hearted, and may well have gained popularity enough with his people to be named to that rank. The man fou't well, though his eye was'n't quick enough for one who had had his schooling in your company, Delaware."

"My brother and friend struck the body?"

"That was uncalled for, seeing that the Mingo died in my arms. The truth may as well be said, at once; he fou't like a man of red gifts, and I fou't like a man with gifts of my own colour. God gave me the victory; I coul'n't fly in the face of his Providence by forgetting my birth and natur'. White he made me, and white I shall live and die."

"Good! Deerslayer is a pale face, and has pale-face hands. A Delaware will look for the scalp, and hang it on a pole, and sing a song in his honour, when we go back to our people. The glory belongs to the tribe; it must not be lost."

"This is easy talking, but 'twill not be as easy doing. The Mingo's body is in the hands of his fri'nds, and, no doubt, is hid in some hole, where Delaware cunning will never be able to get at the scalp."

The young man then gave his friend a succinct, but clear account, of the event of the morning, concealing nothing of any moment, and yet touching on every thing modestly and with a careful attention to avoid the Indian habit of boasting. Chingachgook again expressed his satisfaction at the honour won by his friend, and then both arose, the hour having arrived when it became prudent to move the ark further from the land.

It was quite dark, the heavens having become clouded, and the stars hid. The north wind had ceased, as was usual, with the setting of the sun, and a light air arose from the south. This change favouring the design of Deerslayer, he lifted his grapnel, and the scow immediately and quite perceptibly began to drift more into the lake. The sail was set, when the motion of the craft increased to a rate not much less than two miles in the hour. As this superseded the necessity of rowing—an occupation that an Indian would not be likely to desire—Deerslayer, Chingachgook and Judith seated themselves in the stern of the scow, where the first governed its movements by holding the oar. Here they discoursed on their future movements, and on the means that ought to be used in order to effect the liberation of their friends.

In this dialogue Judith held a material part; the Delaware readily understanding all she said, while his own replies and remarks, both of which were few and pithy, were occasionally rendered into English by his friend. Judith rose greatly in the estimation of her companions, in the half hour that followed. Prompt of resolution and firm of purpose, her suggestions and expedients partook of her spirit and sagacity, both of which were of a character to find favour with men of the frontier. The events that had occurred since their meeting, as well as her isolated and dependent situation, induced the girl to feel towards Deerslayer like the friend of a year, instead of an acquaintance of a day; and so completely had she been won by his guileless truth of character and of feeling—pure novelties in our sex, as respected her own experience—that his peculiarities excited her curiosity, and created a confidence that had never been awakened by any other man. Hitherto she had been compelled to stand on the defensive, in her intercourse with men,—with what success was best known to herself; but here had she been suddenly thrown into the society, and under the protection of a youth, who evidently as little contemplated evil towards herself, as if he had been her brother. The freshness of his integrity, the poetry and truth of his feelings, and even the quaintness of his forms of speech, all had their influence, and aided in awakening an interest that she found as pure as it was sudden and deep. Hurry's fine face and manly form had never compensated for his boisterous and vulgar tone; and her intercourse with the officers had prepared her to make comparisons under which even his great natural advantages suffered. But this very intercourse with the officers who occasionally came upon the lake to fish and hunt, had an effect in producing her present sentiments towards the young stranger. With them, while her vanity had been gratified, and her self-love strongly awakened, she had many causes deeply to regret the acquaintance—if not to mourn over it, in secret sorrow—for it was impossible for one of her quick intellect not to perceive how hollow was the association between superior and inferior, and that she was regarded as the plaything of an idle hour, rather than as an equal and a friend, by even the best intentioned and least designing of her scarlet-clad admirers. Deerslayer, on the other hand, had a window in his breast, through which the light of his honesty was ever shining; and even his indifference to charms that so rarely failed to produce a sensation, piqued the pride of the girl, and gave him an interest that another, seemingly more favoured by nature, might have failed to excite.

In this manner half an hour passed, during which time the ark had been slowly stealing over the water, the darkness thickening around it; though it was easy to see that the gloom of the forest at the southern end of the lake, was getting to be distant, while the mountains that lined the sides of the beautiful basin were overshadowing it, nearly from side to side. There was, indeed, a narrow stripe of water, in the centre of the lake, where the dim light that was still shed from the heavens fell upon its surface, in a line extending north and south; and along this faint track—a sort of inverted milky-way, in which the obscurity was not quite as dense as in other places—the scow held her course, he who steered well knowing that it led in the direction he wished to go. The reader is not to suppose, however, that any difficulty could exist as to the course. This would have been determined by that of the air, had it not been possible to distinguish the mountains, as well as by the dim opening to the south, which marked the position of the valley in that quarter, above the plain of tall trees, by a sort of lessened obscurity; the difference between the darkness of the forest, and that of the night, as seen only in the air. The peculiarities at length caught the attention of Judith and the Deerslayer, and the conversation ceased, to allow each to gaze at the solemn stillness and deep repose of nature.

"Tis a gloomy night—" observed the girl, after a pause of several minutes—"I hope we may be able to find the castle."

"Little fear of our missing *that*, if we keep this path, in the middle of the lake," returned the young man. "Natur' has made us a road here, and, dim as it is, there'll be little difficulty in following it."

"Do you hear nothing, Deerslayer?—It seemed as if the water was stirring quite near us!"

"Sartainly something *did* move the water, oncommon like; it must have been a fish. Them creatur's prey upon each other like men, and animals on the land; one has leaped into the air, and fallen hard, back into his own element. 'Tis of little use, Judith, for any to strive to get out of their elements, since it's natur' to stay in 'em, and natur' will have its way. Ha! *That* sounds like a paddle, used with more than common caution!"

At this moment the Delaware bent forward, and pointed significantly into the boundary of gloom, as if some object had suddenly caught his eye. Both Deerslayer and Judith followed the direction of his gesture, and each got a view of a canoe at the same instant. The glimpse of this startling neighbor was dim, and to eyes less practised, it might have been uncertain; though to those in the Ark, the object was evidently a canoe, with a single individual in it; the latter, standing erect, and paddling. How many lay concealed in its bottom, of course could not be known. Flight, by means of oars, from a bark canoe impelled by vigorous and skilful hands, was utterly impracticable, and each of the men seized his rifle, in expectation of a conflict.

"I can easily bring down the paddler," whispered Deerslayer, "but we'll first hail him, and ask his ar'n'd." Then raising his voice, he continued in a solemn manner—"hold! If ye come nearer, I must fire, though contrary to my wishes, and then sartain death will follow. Stop paddling, and answer."

"Fire, and slay a poor, defenceless, girl," returned a soft tremulous female voice. "And God will never forgive you! Go your way, Deerslayer, and let me go mine."

"Hetty!" exclaimed the young man and Judith in a breath; and the former sprang instantly to the spot where he had left the canoe they had been towing. It was gone, and he understood the whole affair. As for the fugitive, frightened at the menace, she ceased paddling, and remained dimly visible, resembling a spectral outline of a human form, standing on the water. At the next moment, the sail was lowered, to prevent the Ark from passing the spot where the canoe lay. This last expedient, however, was not taken in time, for the momentum of so heavy a craft, and the impulsion of the air, soon set her by, bringing Hetty directly to windward, though still visible, as the change in the positions of the two boats, now placed her in that species of milky way which has been mentioned.

"What can this mean, Judith?" demanded Deerslayer—"Why has your sister taken the canoe, and left us?"

"You know she is feeble-minded, poor girl!—and she has her own ideas of what ought to be done. She loves her father more than most children love their parents—and—then—"

"Then, what, gal?—This is a trying moment; one in which truth must be spoken!"

Judith felt a generous and womanly regret at betraying her sister, and she hesitated ere she spoke again. But once more urged by Deerslayer, and conscious herself of all the risks the whole party was running by the indiscretion of Hetty, she could refrain no longer.

"Then, I fear, poor, weak-minded, Hetty has not been altogether able to see all the vanity, and rudeness and folly, that lie hid behind the handsome face and fine form of Hurry

Harry. She talks of him, in her sleep, and sometimes betrays the inclination, in her waking moments."

"You think, Judith, that your sister is now bent on some mad scheme to serve her father and Hurry, which will, in all likelihood, give them riptyles the Mingos, the mastership of a canoe?"

"Such, I fear, will turn out to be the fact, Deerslayer: Poor Hetty has hardly sufficient cunning to outwit a savage."

All this while, the canoe, with the form of Hetty, erect in one end of it, was dimly perceptible, though the greater drift of the Ark, rendered it, at each instant, less and less distinct. It was evident no time was to be lost, lest it should altogether disappear. The rifles were now laid aside, as useless, the two men seizing the oars, and sweeping the head of the scow round, in the direction of the canoe. Judith, accustomed to the office, flew to the other end of the Ark, and placed herself at what might be called the helm. Hetty took the alarm, at these preparations, which could not be made without noise, and started off like a bird, that had been suddenly put up by the approach of unexpected danger.

As Deerslayer and his companion rowed with the energy of those who felt the necessity of straining every nerve, and Hetty's strength was impaired by a nervous desire to escape, the chase would have quickly terminated in the capture of the fugitive, had not the girl made several short and unlooked-for deviations in her course. These turnings gave her time, and they had also the effect of gradually bringing both canoe and Ark within the deeper gloom, cast by the shadows from the hills. They also gradually increased the distance between the fugitive and her pursuers, until Judith called out to her companions to cease rowing, for she had completely lost sight of the canoe.

When this mortifying announcement was made, Hetty was actually so near as to understand every syllable her sister uttered, though the latter had used the precaution of speaking as low as circumstances would allow her to do, and to make herself heard. Hetty stopped paddling at the same moment, and waited the result with an impatience that was breathless, equally from her late exertions, and her desire to land. A dead silence immediately fell on the lake, during which the three in the Ark were using their senses differently, in order to detect the position of the canoe. Judith bent forward to listen, in the hope of catching some sound that might betray the direction in which her sister was stealing away, while her two companions brought their eyes, as near as possible, to a level with the water, in order to detect any object that might be floating on its surface. All was vain, however, for neither sound, nor sight, rewarded their efforts. All this time Hetty, who had not the cunning to sink into the canoe, stood erect, a finger pressed on her lips, gazing in the direction in which the voices had last been heard, resembling a statue of profound and timid attention. Her ingenuity had barely sufficed to enable her to seize the canoe and to quit the Ark, in the noiseless manner related, and then it appeared to be momentarily exhausted. Even the doublings of the canoe had been as much the consequence of an uncertain hand, and of nervous agitation, as of any craftiness, or calculation.

The pause continued several minutes, during which Deerslayer and the Delaware conferred together, in the language of the latter. Then the oars dipped, again, and the Ark moved away, rowing with as little noise as possible. It steered westward, a little southerly, or in the direction of the encampment of the enemy. Having reached a point, at no great distance from the shore, and where the obscurity was intense, on account of the proximity of the land, it lay there near an hour, in waiting for the expected approach of Hetty, who, it was thought, would make the best of her way, to that spot, as soon as she believed herself released from the danger of pursuit. No success rewarded this little blockade, however, neither appearance nor sound denoting the passage of the canoe. Disappointed at this failure, and conscious of the importance of getting possession of the fortress, before it could be seized by the enemy, Deerslayer now took his way towards the castle, with the apprehension that all his foresight in securing the canoes would be defeated, by this unguarded and alarming movement on the part of the feeble minded Hetty.

Chapter X

> "—But who in this wild wood
> May credit give to either eye, or ear?
> From rocky precipice or hollow cave,
> 'Midst the confused sound of rustling leaves,
> And creaking boughs, and cries of nightly birds,
> Returning seeming answer!"
>
> Joanna Baillie, *Rayner: A Tragedy*, II.i.3–4, 6–9.

FEAR, as much as calculation, had induced Hetty to cease paddling, when she found that her pursuers did not know in which direction to proceed. She remained stationary until the Ark had pulled in near the encampment, as has been related in the preceding chapter, when she resumed the paddle, and with cautious strokes made the best of her way towards the western shore. In order to avoid her pursuers, however, who, she rightly suspected, would soon be rowing along that shore themselves, the head of the canoe was pointed so far north, as to bring her to land on a point that thrust itself into the lake, at the distance of near a league from the outlet. Nor was this altogether the result of a desire to escape, for, feeble minded as she was, Hetty Hutter had a good deal of that instinctive caution which so often keeps those whom God has thus visited from harm. She was perfectly aware of the importance of keeping the canoes from falling into the hands of the Iroquois, and long familiarity with the lake had suggested one of the simplest expedients, by which this great object could be rendered compatible with her own purpose.

The point in question, was the first projection that offered on that side of the lake, where a canoe, if set adrift with a southerly air would float clear of the land, and where it would be no great violation of probabilities to suppose it might even hit the castle; the latter lying above it, almost in a direct line with the wind. Such then was Hetty's intention, and she landed on the extremity of the gravelly point, beneath an overhanging oak, with the express intention of shoving the canoe off from the shore, in order that it might drift up towards her father's insulated abode. She knew, too, from the logs that occasionally floated about the lake, that did it miss the castle, and its appendages, the wind would be likely to change before the canoe could reach the northern extremity of the lake, and that Deerslayer might have an opportunity of regaining it, in the morning, when no doubt he would be earnestly sweeping the surface of the water, and the whole of its wooded shores, with the glass. In all this, too, Hetty was less governed by any chain of reasoning, than by her habits, the latter often supplying the defects of mind, in human beings, as they perform the same office for animals of the inferior classes.

The girl was quite an hour finding her way to the point, the distance and the obscurity equally detaining her, but she was no sooner on the gravelly beach, than she prepared to set the canoe adrift, in the manner mentioned. While in the act of pushing it from her, she heard low voices, that seemed to come from among the trees behind her. Startled at this unexpected danger, Hetty was on the point of springing into the canoe again, in order to seek safety in flight, when she thought she recognised the tones of Judith's melodious voice. Bending forward, so as to catch the sounds more directly, they evidently came from the water, and then she understood that the Ark was approaching from the south, and so close in with the western shore, as necessarily to cause it to pass the point, within twenty yards of the spot where she stood. Here, then, was all she could desire; the canoe was shoved off into the lake, leaving its late occupant alone on the narrow strand.

When this act of self-devotion was performed, Hetty did not retire. The foliage of the overhanging trees and bushes would have almost concealed her person, had there been light, but in that obscurity, it was utterly impossible to discover any object thus shaded, at the distance of a few feet. Flight, too, was perfectly easy, as twenty steps would effectually bury her in the forest. She remained, therefore, watching with intense anxiety the result of her expedient, intending to call the attention of the others to the canoe, with her voice, should they appear to pass without observing it. The Ark approached under its sail, again, Deerslayer standing in its bow, with Judith near him, and the Delaware at the helm. It would seem that, in the bay below, it had got too close to the shore, in the lingering hope of intercepting Hetty, for, as it came nearer, the latter distinctly heard the directions that the young man forward, gave to his companion aft, in order to clear the point.

"Lay her head more off the shore, Delaware," said Deerslayer for the third time, speaking in English that his fair companion might understand his words—"Lay her head well off shore. We have got embayed here, and needs keep the mast clear of the trees. Judith, there's a canoe!"

The last words were uttered with great earnestness, and Deerslayer's hand was on his rifle, ere they were fairly out of his mouth. But the truth flashed on the mind of the quick-witted girl, and she instantly told her companion that the boat *must* be that in which her sister had fled.

"Keep the scow straight, Delaware; steer as straight as your bullet flies when sent ag'in a buck—There,—I have it."

The canoe was seized, and immediately secured again to the side of the Ark. At the next moment the sail was lowered, and the motion of the Ark arrested, by means of the oars.

"Hetty!" called out Judith, concern, even affection betraying itself in her tones. "Are you within hearing, sister—for God's sake answer, and let me hear the sound of your voice, again! Hetty!—dear Hetty."

"I'm here, Judith—here on the shore, where it will be useless to follow me, as I will hide in the woods."

"Oh! Hetty what is't you do! Remember 'tis drawing near midnight, and that the woods are filled with savages and wild beasts!"

"Neither will harm a poor half-witted girl, Judith. God is as much with me, here, as he would be in the Ark or in the hut. I am going to help my father, and poor Hurry Harry, who will be tortured and slain, unless some one cares for them."

"We all care for them, and intend to-morrow to send them a flag of truce, to buy their ransom. Come back then, sister; trust to us, who have better heads than you, and who will do all we can for father."

"I know your head is better than mine, Judith, for mine is very weak, to be sure; but, I must go to father and poor Hurry. Do you and Deerslayer keep the castle, sister; leave me in the hands of God."

"God is with us all, Hetty—in the castle, or on the shore—father as well as ourselves, and it is sinful not to trust to his goodness. You can do nothing in the dark; will lose your way in the forest, and perish for want of food."

"God will not let that happen to a poor child that goes to serve her father, sister. I must try and find the savages."

"Come back for this night only; in the morning, we will put you ashore, and leave you to do as you may think right."

"You *say* so, Judith, and you *think* so; but you would not. Your heart would soften, and you'd see tomahawks and scalping knives, in the air. Besides, I've got a thing to tell the Indian chief that will answer all our wishes, and I'm afraid I may forget it, if I don't tell it to him at once. You'll see that he will let father go, as soon as he hears it!"

"Poor Hetty! What can *you* say to a ferocious savage that will be likely to change his bloody purpose!"

"That which will frighten him, and make him let father go—" returned the simple minded girl, positively. "You'll see, sister; you'll see, how soon it will bring him to, like a gentle child!"

"Will you tell *me*, Hetty, what you intend to say?" asked Deerslayer. "I know the savages well, and can form some idee how far fair words will be likely, or not, to work on their bloody natur's. If it's not suited to the gifts of a red skin, twill be of no use; for reason goes by gifts, as well as conduct."

"Well, then," answered Hetty, dropping her voice to a low, confidential, tone, for the stillness of the night, and the nearness of the Ark, permitted her to do this, and still to be heard—"Well, then, Deerslayer, as you seem a good and honest young man I will tell *you*. I mean not to say a word to any of the savages until I get face to face with their head chief, let them plague me with as many questions as they please—no—I'll answer none of them, unless it be to tell them to lead me to their wisest man—Then, Deerslayer, I'll tell him that God will not forgive murder, and thefts; and that if father and Hurry did go after the scalps of the Iroquois, he must return good for evil, for so the bible commands, else he will go into everlasting punishment. When he hears this, and feels it to be true, as feel it he must, how long will it be before he sends father, and Hurry, and me to the shore, opposite the castle, telling us all three to go our way in peace?"

The last question was put in a triumphant manner, and then the simple minded girl laughed at the impression she never doubted that her project had made on her auditors. Deerslayer was dumb-founded at this proof of guileless feebleness of mind, but Judith had suddenly bethought her of a means of counteracting this wild project, by acting on the very feelings that had given it birth. Without adverting to the closing question, or the laugh, therefore, she hurriedly called to her sister by name, as one suddenly impressed with the importance of what she had to say. But no answer was given to the call.

By the snapping of twigs, and the rustling of leaves, Hetty had evidently quitted the shore, and was already burying herself in the forest. To follow would have been bootless, since the darkness, as well as the dense cover that the woods every where offered, would have rendered her capture next to impossible, and there was also the never ceasing danger of falling into the hands of their enemies. After a short and melancholy discussion, therefore, the sail was again set, and the Ark pursued its course towards its habitual moorings, Deerslayer silently felicitating himself on the recovery of the canoe, and brooding over his plans for the morrow. The wind rose as the party quitted the point, and in less than an hour they reached the castle. Here all was found, as it had been left, and the reverse of the ceremonies had to be taken, in entering the building, that had been used on quitting it. Judith occupied a solitary bed that night, bedewing the pillow with her tears, as she thought of the innocent and hitherto neglected creature, who had been her companion, from childhood, and bitter regrets came over her mind, from more causes than one, as the weary hours passed away, making it nearly morning before she lost her recollection in sleep. Deerslayer and the Delaware took their rest in the Ark, where we shall leave them enjoying the deep sleep of the honest, the healthful and fearless, to return to the girl we have last seen in the midst of the forest.

When Hetty left the shore, she took her way unhesitatingly

into the woods, with a nervous apprehension of being followed. Luckily, this course was the best she could have hit on to effect her own purpose, since it was the only one that led her from the point. The night was so intensely dark, beneath the branches of the trees, that her progress was very slow, and the direction she went altogether a matter of chance, after the first few yards. The formation of the ground, however, did not permit her to deviate far from the line in which she desired to proceed. On one hand it was soon bounded by the acclivity of the hill, while the lake, on the other, served as a guide. For two hours did this single-hearted and simple-minded girl toil through the mazes of the forest, sometimes finding herself on the brow of the bank that bounded the water, and at others struggling up an ascent that warned her to go no farther in that direction, since it necessarily ran at right angles to the course on which she wished to proceed. Her feet often slid from beneath her, and she got many falls, though none to do her injury; but, by the end of the period mentioned, she had become so weary as to want strength to go any farther. Rest was indispensable, and she set about preparing a bed, with the readiness and coolness of one to whom the wilderness presented no unnecessary terrors. She knew that wild beasts roamed through all the adjacent forest, but animals that preyed on the human species were rare, and of dangerous serpents there were literally none. These facts had been taught her by her father, and whatever her feeble mind received at all, it received so confidingly as to leave her no uneasiness from any doubts, or scepticism. To her the sublimity of the solitude in which she was placed, was soothing, rather than appalling, and she gathered a bed of leaves, with as much indifference to the circumstances that would have driven the thoughts of sleep entirely from the minds of most of her sex, as if she had been preparing her place of nightly rest, beneath the paternal roof.

As soon as Hetty had collected a sufficient number of the dried leaves to protect her person from the damps of the ground, she kneeled beside the humble pile, clasped her raised hands in an attitude of deep devotion, and in a soft, low, but audible voice repeated the Lord's Prayer. This was followed by those simple and devout verses, so familiar to children, in which she recommended her soul to God, should it be called away to another state of existence, ere the return of morning. This duty done, she lay down and disposed herself to sleep. The attire of the girl, though suited to the season, was sufficiently warm for all ordinary purposes, but the forest is ever cool, and the nights of that elevated region of country, have always a freshness about them, that renders clothing more necessary than is commonly the case in the summers of a low latitude. This had been foreseen by Hetty, who had brought with her, a coarse heavy mantle, which, when laid over her body, answered all the useful purposes of a blanket. Thus protected, she dropped asleep, in a few minutes, as tranquilly as if watched over by the guardian care of that mother, who had so recently been taken from her forever, affording in this particular, a most striking contrast between her own humble couch, and the sleepless pillow of her sister.

Hour passed after hour, in a tranquility as undisturbed and a rest as sweet, as if angels, expressly commissioned for that object, watched around the bed of Hetty Hutter. Not once did her soft eyes open, until the grey of the dawn came struggling through the tops of the trees, falling on their lids, and, united to the freshness of a summer's morning, giving the usual summons to awake. Ordinarily, Hetty was up ere the rays of the sun tipped the summits of the mountains, but on this occasion her fatigue had been so great, and her rest was so profound, that the customary warnings failed of their effect. The girl murmured in her sleep, threw an arm forward, smiled as gently as an infant in its cradle, but still slumbered. In making this unconscious gesture, her hand fell on some object that was warm, and in the half unconscious state in which she lay, she connected the circumstance with her habits. At the next moment, a rude attack was made on her side, as if a rooting animal were thrusting its snout beneath, with a desire to force her position, and then, uttering the name of "Judith" she awoke. As the startled girl arose to a sitting attitude she perceived that some dark object sprang from her, scattering the leaves and snapping the fallen twigs in its haste. Opening her eyes, and recovering from the first confusion and astonishment of her situation, Hetty perceived a cub, of the common American brown bear, balancing itself on its hinder legs, and still looking towards her, as if doubtful whether it would be safe to trust itself near her person again. The first impulse of Hetty, who had been mistress of several of these cubs, was to run and seize the little creature as a prize, but a loud growl warned her of the danger of such a procedure. Recoiling a few steps, the girl looked hurriedly round, and perceived the dam, watching her movements, with fiery eyes, at no great distance. A hollow tree, that had once been the home of bees, having recently fallen, the mother with two more cubs, was feasting on the dainty food that this accident had placed within her reach; while the first kept a jealous eye on the situation of its truant and reckless young.

It would exceed all the means of human knowledge to pretend to analyze the influences that govern the acts of the lower animals. On this occasion, the dam, though proverbially fierce when its young is thought to be in danger, manifested no intention to attack the girl. It quitted the honey, and advanced to a place within twenty feet of her, where it raised itself on its hind legs, and balanced its body in a sort of angry, growling discontent, but approached no nearer. Happily, Hetty did not fly. On the contrary, though not without terror, she knelt with her face towards the animal, and with clasped hands and uplifted eyes, repeated the prayer of the previous night. This act of devotion was not the result of alarm, but it was a duty she never neglected to perform ere she slept, and when the return of consciousness awoke her to the business of the day. As the girl arose from her knees, the bear dropped on its feet again, and collecting its cubs around her, permitted them to draw their natural sustenance. Hetty was delighted with this proof of tenderness in an animal that has but a very indifferent reputation for the gentler feelings, and as a cub would quit its mother to frisk and leap about in wantonness, she felt a strong desire again to catch it up in her arms, and play with it. But admonished by the growl, she had self command sufficient not to put this dangerous project in execution, and recollecting her errand among the hills, she tore herself away from the group, and proceeded on her course, along the margin of the lake, of which she now caught glimpses again through the trees. To her surprise, though not to her alarm, the family of bears arose and followed her steps, keeping a short distance behind her; apparently watching every movement as if they had a near interest in all she did.

In this manner, escorted by the dam and cubs, the girl proceeded nearly a mile, thrice the distance she had been able to achieve in the darkness, during the same period of time. She then reached a brook that had dug a channel for itself into the earth, and went brawling into the lake, between steep and high banks, covered with trees. Here, Hetty performed her ablutions; then drinking of the pure mountain water, she went her way, refreshed and lighter of heart, still attended by her singular companions. Her course now lay along a broad and nearly level terrace, which stretched from the top of the bank that bounded the water, to a low acclivity that rose to a second and irregular platform above. This was at a part of the valley where the mountains ran obliquely, forming the commencement of a plain that spread between the hills, southward of the sheet of water. Hetty knew, by this circumstance, that she was getting near to the encampment, and had she not, the bears would have given her warning of the vicinity of human beings. Snuffing the air, the dam refused to follow any further, though the girl looked back and invited her to come by childish signs, and even by direct appeals made in her own sweet voice. It was while making her way slowly through some bushes, in this manner, with averted face and eyes riveted on the immovable animals, that the girl suddenly found her steps arrested by a human hand, that was laid lightly on her shoulder.

"Where go?—" said a soft female voice, speaking hurriedly, and in concern. "Indian—red-man—savage—wicked warrior—thataway."

This unexpected salutation alarmed the girl no more than the presence of the fierce inhabitants of the woods. It took her a little by surprise, it is true, but she was in a measure prepared for some such meeting, and the creature who stopped her, was as little likely to excite terror as any who ever appeared in the guise of an Indian. It was a girl, not much older than herself, whose smile was sunny as Judith's in her brightest moments, whose voice was melody itself, and whose accents and manner had all the rebuked gentleness that characterizes the sex among a people, who habitually treat their women as the attendants and servitors of the warriors. Beauty among the women of the aboriginal Americans, before they have become exposed to the hardships of wives and mothers, is by no means uncommon. In this particular, the original owners of the country were not unlike their more civilized successors, *nature* appearing to have bestowed that delicacy of mien and outline that forms so great a charm in the youthful female, but of which they are so early deprived; and that, too, as much by the habits of domestic life, as from any other cause.

The girl who had so suddenly arrested the steps of Hetty was dressed in a calico mantle that effectually protected all the upper part of her person, while a short petticoat of blue cloth edged with gold lace, that fell no lower than her knees, leggings of the same, and moccasins of deer-skin, completed her attire. Her hair fell in long dark braids down her shoulders and back, and was parted above a low smooth forehead, in a way to soften the expression of eyes that were full of archness and natural feeling. Her face was oval, with delicate features, the teeth were even and white, while the mouth expressed a melancholy tenderness, as if it wore this peculiar meaning in intuitive perception of the fate of a being who was doomed from birth to endure a woman's sufferings, relieved by a woman's affections. Her voice, as has been already intimated, was soft as the sighing of the night air, a characteristic of the females of her race, but which was so conspicuous in herself as to have produced for her the name of Wah-ta!-Wah; which rendered into English means Hist-oh!-Hist.

In a word, this was the betrothed of Chingachgook, who having succeeded in lulling their suspicions, was permitted to wander around the encampment of her captors. This indulgence was in accordance with the general policy of the red man, who well knew, moreover, that her trail could have been easily followed in the event of flight. It will also be remembered that the Iroquois, or Hurons, as it would be better to call them, were entirely ignorant of the proximity of her lover, a fact, indeed, that she did not know herself.

It is not easy to say which manifested the most self-possession at this unexpected meeting; the pale face, or the red-girl. But, though a little surprised, Wah-ta!-Wah was the most willing to speak, and far the readier in foreseeing consequences, as well as in devising means to avert them. Her father, during her childhood, had been much employed as a warrior by the authorities of the Colony, and dwelling for several years near the forts, she had caught a knowledge of the English tongue, which she spoke in the usual, abbreviated manner of an Indian, but fluently, and without any of the ordinary reluctance of her people.

"Where go?—" repeated Wah-ta!-Wah, returning the smile of Hetty, in her own gentle, winning, manner—"*wicked* warrior that-a-way—*good* warrior, far off."

"What's your name?" asked Hetty, with the simplicity of a child.

"Wah-ta!-Wah. I no Mingo—good Delaware—Yengeese friend. Mingo cruel, and love scalp, for blood—Delaware love him, for honor. Come here, where no eyes."

Wah-ta!-Wah now led her companion towards the lake, descending the bank so as to place its overhanging trees and bushes between them, and any probable observers. Nor did she stop until they were both seated, side by side, on a fallen log, one end of which actually lay buried in the water.

"*Why* you come for?" the young Indian eagerly inquired—"*Where* you come for?"

Hetty told her tale in her own simple and truth-loving manner. She explained the situation of her father, and stated her desire to serve him, and if possible to procure his release.

"Why your fader come to Mingo 'camp in night?" asked the Indian girl, with a directness, which if not borrowed from the other, partook largely of its sincerity. "He know it wartime, and he no boy—he no want beard—no want to be told Iroquois carry tomahawk, and knife, and rifle. Why he come night time, seize *me* by hair, and try to scalp, Delaware girl?"

"You!" said Hetty, almost sickening with horror—"Did he seize *you*—did he try to scalp *you*?"

"Why no? Delaware scalp sell for much as Mingo scalp. Governor no tell difference. Wicked t'ing for pale face to scalp. No his gifts, as the good Deerslayer alway tell me."

"And do *you* know the Deerslayer?" said Hetty, coloring

with delight and surprise; forgetting her regrets, at the moment, in the influence of this new feeling. "I know him, too. He is now in the Ark, with Judith and a Delaware who is called the Big Serpent. A bold and handsome warrior is this Serpent, too!"

Spite of the rich deep colour that nature had bestowed on the Indian beauty, the tell-tale blood deepened on her cheeks, until the blush gave new animation and intelligence to her jet-black eyes. Raising a finger in an attitude of warning, she dropped her voice, already so soft and sweet, nearly to a whisper, as she continued the discourse.

"Chingachgook!" returned the Delaware girl, sighing out the harsh name, in sounds so softly guttural, as to cause it to reach the ear in melody—"His father, Uncas—great chief of the Mahicanni—next to old Tamenund!—More as warrior, not so much gray hair, and less at Council Fire. *You* know Serpent?"

"He joined us last evening, and was in the Ark with me, for two or three hours before I left it. I'm afraid, Hist—" Hetty could not pronounce the Indian name of her new friend, but having heard Deerslayer give her this familiar appellation, she used it without any of the ceremony of civilized life—"I'm afraid Hist, he has come after scalps, as well as my poor father and Hurry Harry."

"Why he should'n't—ha? Chingachgook red warrior—very red—scalp make his honor—Be sure he take him."

"Then," said Hetty, earnestly, "he will be as wicked as any other. God will not pardon in a red-man, what he will not pardon in a white man."

"No true—" returned the Delaware girl, with a warmth, that nearly amounted to passion. "No true, I tell you! The Manitou smile and pleased when he see young warrior come back from the war path, with two, ten, hundred scalp on a pole! Chingachgook father take scalp—grandfather take scalp—all old chief take scalp, and Chingachgook take as many scalp as he can carry, himself!"

"Then, Hist, his sleep, of nights, must be terrible to think of! No one can be cruel, and hope to be forgiven."

"No cruel—plenty forgiven—" returned Wah-ta!-Wah, stamping her little foot on the stony strand, and shaking her head in a way to show how completely feminine feeling, in one of its aspects, had gotten the better of feminine feeling in another. "I tell you, Serpent brave; he go home, this time, with four,—yes—*two* scalp."

"And is that his errand, here?—Did he really come all this distance, across mountain, and valley, rivers and lakes, to torment his fellow creatures, and do so wicked a thing?"

This question at once appeased the growing ire of the half-offended Indian beauty. It completely got the better of the prejudices of education, and turned all her thoughts to a gentler and more feminine channel. At first, she looked around her, suspiciously, as if distrusting eaves-droppers; then she gazed wistfully into the face of her attentive companion; after which this exhibition of girlish coquetry and womanly feeling, terminated by her covering her face with both her hands, and laughing in a strain that might well be termed the melody of the woods. Dread of discovery, however, soon put a stop to this *naïve* exhibition of feeling, and removing her hands, this creature of impulses, gazed again wistfully into the face of her companion, as if inquiring how far she might trust a stranger with her secret. Although Hetty had no claims to her sister's extraordinary beauty, many thought her countenance the most winning of the two. It expressed all the undisguised sincerity of her character, and it was totally free from any of the unpleasant physical accompaniments, that so frequently attend mental imbecility. It is true that one accustomed to closer observations than common, might have detected the proofs of her feebleness of intellect in the language of her sometimes vacant eyes, but they were signs that attracted sympathy by their total want of guile, rather than by any other feeling. The effect on Hist, to use the English and more familiar translation of the name, was favorable, and yielding to an impulse of tenderness, she threw her arms around Hetty, and embraced her with an outpouring emotion, so natural that it was only equalled by its warmth.

"*You* good—" whispered the young Indian—"you good, I know; it so long since Wah-ta!-Wah have a friend—a sister—any body to speak her heart to! You Hist friend; do'n't I say trut'?"

"I never had a friend," answered Hetty, returning the warm

embrace with unfeigned earnestness. "I've a sister, but no friend. Judith loves me, and I love Judith; but that's natural, and as we are taught in the bible—but I *should* like to have a *friend*! I'll be your friend, with all my heart, for I like your voice and your smile, and your way of thinking in every thing, except about the scalps—"

"No t'ink more of him—no say more of scalp—" interrupted Hist, soothingly—"You pale face, I red skin; we bring up different fashion. Deerslayer and Chingachgook great friend, and no the same colour, Hist and—what your name, pretty pale face?"

"I am called Hetty, though when they spell the name in the bible, they always spell it, Esther."

"What that make?—no good, no harm. No need to spell name at all—Moravian try to make Wah-ta!-Wah spell, but no won't let him. No good for Delaware girl to know too much—know more than warrior some time; that great shame. My name Wah-ta!-Wah—that say Hist in your tongue; you call him, Hist—I call him, Hetty."

These preliminaries settled to their mutual satisfaction, the two girls began to discourse of their several hopes and projects. Hetty made her new friend more fully acquainted with her intentions in behalf of her father, and, to one in the least addicted to prying into the affairs, Hist would have betrayed her own feelings and expectations in connection with the young warrior of her own tribe. Enough was revealed on both sides, however, to let each party get a tolerable insight into the views of the other, though enough still remained in mental reservation, to give rise to the following questions and answers, with which the interview in effect closed. As the quickest witted, Hist was the first with her interrogatories. Folding an arm about the waist of Hetty, she bent her head so as to look up playfully into the face of the other, and, laughing, as if her meaning were to be extracted from her looks, she spoke more plainly.

"Hetty got broder, as well as fader?—" she said—"Why no talk of broder, as well as fader?"

"I have no brother, Hist. I had one once, they say, but he is dead many a year, and lies buried in the lake, by the side of my mother."

"No got broder—got a young warrior—Love him, almost as much as fader, eh? Very handsome, and brave-looking; fit to be chief, if he *good* as he *seem* to be."

"It's wicked to love any man as well as I love my father, and so I strive not to do it, Hist," returned the conscientious Hetty, who knew not how to conceal an emotion, by an approach to an untruth as venial as an evasion, though powerfully tempted by female shame to err, "though I sometimes think wickedness will get the better of me, if Hurry comes so often to the lake. I *must* tell you the truth, dear Hist, because you ask me, but I should fall down and die in the woods, if he knew it!"

"Why he no ask you, himself?—Brave looking—why not bold speaking? Young warrior ought to ask young girl, no make young girl speak first. Mingo girls too shame for *that*."

This was said indignantly, and with the generous warmth a young female of spirit would be apt to feel, at what she deemed an invasion of her sex's most valued privilege. It had little influence on the simple-minded, but also just-minded Hetty, who, though inherently feminine in all her impulses, was much more alive to the workings of her own heart, than to any of the usages with which convention has protected the sensitiveness of her sex.

"Ask me *what*?" the startled girl demanded, with a suddenness that proved how completely her fears had been aroused. "Ask me, if I like him as well as I do my own father! Oh! I hope he will never put such a question to *me*, for I should have to answer, and that would *kill* me!"

"No—no—no kill, *quite*—almost," returned the other, laughing in spite of herself. "Make blush come—make shame come, too: but he no stay great while; then feel happier than ever. Young warrior must tell young girl he want to make wife, else never can live in his wigwam."

"Hurry do'n't want to marry me—No body will ever want to marry me, Hist."

"How you can know? P'raps every body want to marry you, and by-and-bye, tongue say what heart feel. Why nobody want to marry you?"

"I am not full witted, they say. Father often tells me this; and so does Judith, sometimes, when she is vexed; but I should'n't so much mind them, as I did mother. *She* said so *once*; and then she cried as if her heart would break; and, so, I *know* I'm not full witted."

Hist gazed at the gentle, simple, girl, for quite a minute without speaking, and then the truth appeared to flash all at once on the mind of the young Indian maid. Pity, reverence and tenderness seemed struggling together in her breast, and then rising, suddenly, she indicated a wish to her companion that she would accompany her to the camp, which was situated at no great distance. This unexpected change from the precautions that Hist had previously manifested a desire to use, in order to prevent being seen, to an open exposure of the person of her friend, arose from the perfect conviction that no Indian would harm a being whom the Great Spirit had disarmed, by depriving it of its strongest defence, reason. In this respect, nearly all unsophisticated nations resemble each other, appearing to offer spontaneously, by a feeling creditable to human nature, that protection by their own forbearance, which has been withheld by the inscrutable wisdom of Providence. Wah-ta!-Wah, indeed, knew that, in many tribes, the mentally imbecile and the mad, were held in a species of religious reverence, receiving from these untutored inhabitants of the forest respect and honors, instead of the contumely and neglect that it is their fortune to meet with, among the more pretending and sophisticated.

Hetty accompanied her new friend without apprehension, or reluctance. It was her wish to reach the camp, and, sustained by her motives, she felt no more concern for the consequences, than did her companion herself, now the latter was apprized of the character of the protection that the pale face maiden carried with her. Still, as they proceeded slowly along a shore that was tangled with overhanging bushes, Hetty continued the discourse, assuming the office of interrogating, which the other had instantly dropped, as soon as she ascertained the character of the mind to which her questions had been addressed.

"But *you* are not half-witted," said Hetty, "and there's no reason why the Serpent should not marry *you*."

"Hist prisoner, and Mingo got big ear. No speak of Chingachgook when they by. Promise Hist that, good Hetty."

"I know—I know—" returned Hetty, half-whispering, in her eagerness to let the other see she understood the necessity of caution. "I know—Deerslayer and the Serpent mean to get you away from the Iroquois, and you wish me not to tell the secret."

"How you know?" said Hist, hastily, vexed at the moment, that the other was not even more feeble minded than was actually the case. "How you know? Better not talk of any but fader and Hurry—Mingo understand *dat*; he no understand *t'udder*. Promise you no talk about what you no understand."

"But I *do* understand this, Hist, and so I *must* talk about it. Deerslayer as good as told father all about it, in my presence, and as nobody told me not to listen, I overheard it all, as I did Hurry and father's discourse about the scalps."

"Very bad for pale faces to talk about scalps, and very bad for young woman to hear! Now you love Hist, I know, Hetty, and so, among Injins, when love hardest never talk most."

"That's not the way among white people, who talk most about them they love best. I suppose it's because I'm only half-witted that I don't see the reason why it should be so different among red people."

"That what Deerslayer call gift. One gift to talk; t'udder gift to hold tongue. Hold tongue your gift, among Mingos. If Sarpent want to see Hist, so Hetty want to see Hurry. Good girl never tell secret of friend."

Hetty understood this appeal, and she promised the Delaware girl not to make any allusion to the presence of Chingachgook, or to the motive of his visit to the lake.

"Maybe he get off Hurry and fader, as well as Hist, if let him have his way," whispered Wah-ta!-Wah to her companion, in a confiding flattering way, just as they got near enough to the encampment to hear the voices of several of their own sex, who were apparently occupied in the usual toils of women of their class. "T'ink of dat, Hetty, and put two, twenty finger on mouth. No get friend free without Sarpent do it."

A better expedient could not have been adopted, to secure the silence and discretion of Hetty, than that which was now presented to her mind. As the liberation of her father and the young frontier man was the great object of her adventure, she felt the connection between it and the services of the Delaware, and with an innocent laugh, she nodded her head, and in the same suppressed manner, promised a due attention to the wishes of her friend. Thus assured, Hist tarried no longer, but immediately and openly led the way into the encampment of her captors.

Chapter XI

—"The great King of Kings
Hath in the table of his law commanded,
That thou shalt do no murder.
Take heed; for he holds vengeance in his hand,
To hurl upon their heads that break his law."
Richard III, I.iv.195–97, 199–200.

THAT THE PARTY to which Hist compulsorily belonged was not one that was regularly on the war path, was evident by the presence of females. It was a small fragment of a tribe that had been hunting and fishing within the English limits, where it was found by the commencement of hostilities, and, after passing the winter and spring by living on what was strictly the property of its enemies, it chose to strike a hostile blow before it finally retired. There was also deep Indian sagacity in the manoeuvre which had led them so far into the territory of their foes. When the runner arrived who announced the breaking out of hostilities between the English and French—a struggle that was certain to carry with it all the tribes that dwelt within the influence of the respective belligerents—this particular party of the Iroquois were posted on the shores of the Oneida, a lake that lies some fifty miles nearer to their own frontier than that which is the scene of our tale. To have fled in a direct line for the Canadas would have exposed them to the dangers of a direct pursuit, and the chiefs had determined to adopt the expedient of penetrating deeper into a region that had now become dangerous, in the hope of being able to retire in the rear of their pursuers, instead of having them on their trail. The presence of the women had induced the attempt at this *ruse*, the strength of these feebler members of the party being unequal to the effort of escaping from the pursuit of warriors. When the reader remembers the vast extent of the American wilderness, at that early day, he will perceive that it was possible for even a tribe to remain months undiscovered in particular portions of it; nor was the danger of encountering a foe, the usual precautions being observed, as great in the woods, as it is on the high seas, in a time of active warfare.

The encampment being temporary, it offered to the eye no more than the rude protection of a bivouac, relieved in some slight degree by the ingenious expedients which suggested themselves to the readiness of those who passed their lives amid similar scenes. One fire, that had been kindled against the roots of a living oak, sufficed for the whole party; the weather being too mild to require it for any purpose but cooking. Scattered around this centre of attraction, were some fifteen or twenty low huts, or perhaps kennels would be a better word, into which their different owners crept at night, and which were also intended to meet the exigencies of a storm. These little huts were made of the branches of trees, put together with some ingenuity, and they were uniformly topped with bark that had been stripped from fallen trees; of which every virgin forest possesses hundreds, in all stages of decay. Of furniture they had next to none. Cooking utensils of the simplest sort were lying near the fire, a few articles of clothing were to be seen in, or around the huts, rifles, horns, and pouches leaned against the trees, or were suspended from the lower branches, and the carcases of two or three deer were stretched to view on the same natural shambles.

As the encampment was in the midst of a dense wood, the eye could not take in its *tout ensemble* at a glance, but hut after hut started out of the gloomy picture, as one gazed about him in quest of objects. There was no centre, unless the fire might be so considered, no open area where the possessors of this rude village might congregate, but all was dark, covert and cunning, like its owners. A few children strayed, from hut to hut, giving the spot a little of the air of domestic life, and the suppressed laugh, and low voices of the women occasionally broke in upon the deep stillness of the sombre forest. As for the men, they either ate, slept, or examined their arms. They conversed but little, and then usually apart, or in groups withdrawn from the females, whilst an air of untiring, innate, watchfulness and apprehension of danger seemed to be blended even with their slumbers.

As the two girls came near the encampment, Hetty uttered a slight exclamation, on catching a view of the person of her father. He was seated on the ground, with his back to a tree, and Hurry stood near him, indolently whittling a twig. Apparently they were as much at liberty as any others in, or about the camp, and one unaccustomed to Indian usages would have mistaken them for visiters, instead of supposing them to be captives. Wah-ta!-Wah led her new friend quite near them, and then modestly withdrew, that her own presence might be no restraint on her feelings. But Hetty was not sufficiently familiar with caresses, or outward demonstrations of fondness, to indulge in any outbreaking of feeling. She merely approached and stood at her father's side without speaking, resembling a silent statue of filial affection. The old man expressed neither alarm, nor surprise, at her sudden appearance. In these particulars, he had caught the stoicism of the Indians, well knowing that there was no more certain mode of securing their respect than by imitating their self-command. Nor did the savages themselves betray the least sign of surprise at this sudden appearance of a stranger among them. In a word, this arrival produced much less visible sensation, though occurring under circumstances so peculiar, than would be seen in a village of higher pretensions to civilization, did an ordinary traveller drive up to the door of its principal inn. Still a few warriors collected, and it was evident by the manner in which they glanced at Hetty as they conversed together, that she was the subject of their discourse, and probable that the reasons of her unlooked-for appearance were matters of discussion. This phlegm of manner is characteristic of the North American Indian—some say of his white successor also—but, in this case much should be attributed to the peculiar situation in which the party was placed. The force in the Ark, the presence of Chingachgook excepted, was well known, no tribe or body of troops was believed to be near, and vigilant eyes were posted round the entire lake, watching, day and night, the slightest movement of those whom it would not be exaggerated now to term the besieged.

Hutter was inwardly much moved by the conduct of Hetty, though he affected so much indifference of manner. He recollected her gentle appeal to him, before he left the Ark, and misfortune rendered that of weight, which might have been forgotten amid the triumph of success. Then he knew the simple, single-hearted fidelity of his child, and understood why she had come, and the total disregard of self that reigned in all her acts.

"This is not well, Hetty," he said, deprecating the consequences to the girl herself, more than any other evil. "These are fierce Iroquois, and are as little apt to forget an injury, as a favor."

"Tell me, father—" returned the girl, looking furtively about her, as if fearful of being overheard, "did God let you do the cruel errand on which you came? I want much to know this, that I may speak to the Indians plainly, if he did not."

"You should not have come hither, Hetty; these brutes will not understand your nature, or your intentions!"

"How was it, father; neither you, nor Hurry, seems to have any thing that looks like scalps."

"If that will set your mind at peace, child, I can answer you, no. I had caught the young creatur' who came here with you, but her screeches soon brought down upon me a troop of the wild cats, that was too much for any single christian to withstand. If that will do you any good, we are as innocent of having taken a scalp, this time, as I make no doubt we shall also be innocent of receiving the bounty."

"Thank god for that, father! Now I can speak boldly to the Iroquois, and with an easy conscience. I hope Hurry, too, has not been able to harm any of the Indians?"

"Why, as to that matter, Hetty," returned the individual in question, "you've put it pretty much in the natyve character of the religious truth. Hurry has not been *able*, and that is the long and short of it. I've seen many squalls, old fellow, both on land and on the water, but never did I feel one as lively and as snappish as that which come down upon us, night afore last, in the shape of an Indian hurrah-boys! Why, Hetty, you're no great matter at a reason, or an idee that lies a little deeper than common, but you're human, and have some human notions—now, I'll just ask you to look at them circumstances. Here was old Tom, your father, and myself, bent on a legal operation, as is to be seen in the words of the law and the proclomation; thinking no harm; when we were set upon by critturs that were more like a pack of hungry wolves, than mortal savages even, and there they had us tethered like two sheep, in less time than it has taken me to tell you the story."

"You are free, now, Hurry," returned Hetty, glancing timidly at the fine unfettered limbs of the young giant—"You have no cords, or withes, to pain your arms, or legs, now."

"Not I, Hetty. Natur' is natur', and freedom is natur', too. My limbs have a free look, but that's pretty much the amount of it, sin' I can't use them in the way I should like. Even these trees have eyes; ay, and tongues too; for was the old man, here, or I, to start one single rod beyond our gaol limits, sarvice would be put on the bail afore we could 'gird up our loins' for a race, and, like as not, four or five rifle bullets would be travelling arter us, carrying so many invitations to curb our impatience. There is'n't a gaol in the colony as tight as this, we are now in; for I've tried the vartues of two or three on 'em, and I know the mater'als they are made of, as well as the men that made 'em; takin' down being the next step in schoolin', to puttin' up, in all such fabrications."

Lest the reader should get an exaggerated opinion of Hurry's demerits, from this boastful and indiscreet revelation, it may be well to say that his offences were confined to assaults and batteries, for several of which he had been imprisoned, when, as he has just said, he often escaped by demonstrating the flimsiness of the constructions in which he was confined, by opening for himself doors, in spots where the architects had neglected to place them. But Hetty had no knowledge of gaols, and little of the nature of crimes, beyond what her unadulterated and almost instinctive perceptions of right and wrong taught her, and this sally of the rude being who had spoken, was lost upon her. She understood his general meaning, however, and answered in reference to that alone.

"It's so best, Hurry," she said. "It is best father and you should be quiet and peaceable, 'till I have spoken to the Iroquois, when all will be well and happy. I don't wish either of you to follow, but leave me to myself. As soon as all is settled, and you are at liberty to go back to the castle, I will come and let you know it."

Hetty spoke with so much simple earnestness, seemed so confident of success, and wore so high an air of moral feeling and truth, that both the listeners felt more disposed to attach an importance to her mediation, than might otherwise have happened. When she manifested an intention to quit them, therefore, they offered no obstacle, though they saw she was about to join the group of chiefs who were consulting apart, seemingly on the manner and motive of her own sudden appearance.

When Hist—for so we love best, to call her—quitted her companion, she strayed near one or two of the elder warriors, who had shown her most kindness in her captivity, the principal man of whom, had even offered to adopt her as his child, if she would consent to become a Huron. In taking this direction, the shrewd girl did so to invite inquiry. She was too well trained in the habits of her people, to obtrude the opinions of one of her sex and years on men and warriors, but nature had furnished a tact and ingenuity that enabled her to attract the attention she desired, without wounding the pride of those to whom it was her duty to defer, and respect. Even her affected indifference stimulated curiosity, and Hetty had hardly reached the side of her father, before the Delaware girl was brought within the circle of the warriors, by a secret but significant gesture. Here she was questioned as to the person of her companion, and the motives that had brought her to the camp. This was all that Hist desired. She explained the manner in which she had detected the weakness of Hetty's reason, rather exaggerating than lessening the deficiency in her intellect, and then she related, in general terms, the object of the girl in venturing among her enemies. The effect was all that the speaker expected, her account investing the person and character of their visiter with a sacredness and respect, that she well knew would prove her protection. As soon as her own purpose was attained, Hist withdrew to a distance, where, with female consideration, and a sisterly tenderness she set about the preparation of a meal, to be offered to her new friend, as soon as the latter might be at liberty to partake of it. While thus occupied, however, the ready girl in no degree relaxed in her watchfulness, noting every change of countenance among the chiefs, every movement of Hetty's, and the smallest occurrence that could be likely to affect her own interests, or that of her new friend.

As Hetty approached the chiefs, they opened their little circle, with an ease and deference of manner, that would have done credit to men of more courtly origin. A fallen tree lay near, and the oldest of the warriors made a quiet sign for the girl to be seated on it, taking his place at her side, with the gentleness of a father. The others arranged themselves around the two, with grave dignity, and then the girl, who had sufficient observation to perceive that such a course was expected of her, began to reveal the object of her visit. The moment she opened her mouth to speak, however, the old chief gave a gentle sign for her to forbear, said a few words to one of his juniors, and then waited in silent patience until the latter had summoned Hist to the party. This interruption proceeded from the chief's having discovered that there existed a necessity for an interpreter, few of the Hurons present understanding the English language, and they but imperfectly.

Wah-ta!-Wah was not sorry to be called upon to be present at the interview, and least of all in the character in which she was now wanted. She was aware of the hazards she run in attempting to deceive one or two of the party, but was none the less resolved to use every means that offered, and to practice every artifice that an Indian education could supply, to conceal the facts of the vicinity of her betrothed, and of the errand on which he had come. One unpractised in the expedients and opinions of savage life, would not have suspected the readiness of invention, the wariness of action, the high resolution, the noble impulses, the deep self-devotion, and the feminine disregard of self when the affections were concerned, that lay concealed beneath the demure looks, the mild eyes, and the sunny smiles of this young Indian beauty. As she approached them, the grim old warriors regarded her with pleasure, for they had a secret pride in the hope of engrafting so rare a scion on the stock of their own nation; adoption being as regularly practised, and as distinctly recognized among the tribes of America, as it ever had been among those nations that submit to the sway of the Civil Law.

As soon as Hist was seated by the side of Hetty, the old chief desired her to ask "the fair young pale-face" what had brought her among the Iroquois, and what they could do to serve her.

"Tell them, Hist, who I am—Thomas Hutter's youngest daughter; Thomas Hutter, the oldest of their two prisoners; he who owns the castle and the Ark, and who has the best right to be thought the owner of these hills, and that lake, since he has dwelt so long, and trapped so long, and fished so long, among them—They'll know whom you mean by Thomas Hutter, if you tell them, *that*. And then tell them that I've come here to convince them they ought not to harm father, and Hurry, but let them go, in peace, and to treat them as brethren, rather than as enemies. Now tell them all this plainly, Hist, and fear nothing for yourself, or me. God will protect us."

Wah-ta!-Wah did as the other desired, taking care to render the words of her friend as literally as possible into the Iroquois tongue, a language she used with a readiness almost equal to that with which she spoke her own. The chiefs heard this opening explanation, with grave decorum, the two who had a little knowledge of English, intimating their satisfaction with the interpreter, by furtive but significant glances of the eyes.

"And, now, Hist," continued Hetty, as soon as it was intimated to her that she might proceed, "and, now, Hist, I wish you to tell these red men, word for word, what I am about to say. Tell them first, that father and Hurry came here with an intention to take as many scalps as they could, for the wicked governor and the province have offered money for scalps, whether of warriors, or women, men or children, and the love of gold was too strong for their hearts to withstand it. Tell them this, dear Hist, just as you have heard it from me, word for word."

Wah-ta!-Wah hesitated about rendering this speech as literally as had been desired, but detecting the intelligence of those who understood English, and apprehending even a greater knowledge than they actually possessed she found herself compelled to comply. Contrary to what a civilized man would have expected, the admission of the motives and of the errands of their prisoners, produced no visible effect, on either the countenances or the feelings of the listeners. They probably considered the act meritorious, and that which neither of them would have hesitated to perform in his own person, he would not be apt to censure in another.

"And, now, Hist," resumed Hetty, as soon as she perceived that her first speeches were understood by the chiefs, "you can tell them more. They know that father and Hurry did not succeed, and therefore they can bear them no grudge for any harm that has been done. If they had slain their children and wives, it would not alter the matter, and I'm not certain that what I am about to tell them would not have more weight had there been mischief done. But ask them first, Hist, if they know there is a God, who reigns over the whole earth, and is ruler and chief of all who live, let them be red, or white, or what color they may?"

Wah-ta!-Wah looked a little surprised at this question, for the idea of the Great Spirit is seldom long absent from the mind of an Indian girl. She put the question, as literally as possible, however, and received a grave answer in the affirmative.

"This is right," continued Hetty, "and my duty will now be light. This Great Spirit, as you call our God, has caused a book to be written, that we call a bible, and in this book have been set down all his commandments, and his holy will and pleasure, and the rules by which all men are to live, and directions how to govern the thoughts even, and the wishes, and the will. Here, this is one of these holy books, and you must tell the chiefs what I am about to read to them, from its sacred pages."

As Hetty concluded, she reverently unrolled a small English bible from its envelope of coarse calico, treating the volume with the sort of external respect that a Romanist would be apt to show to a religious relic. As she slowly proceeded in her task the grim warriors watched each movement with riveted eyes, and when they saw the little volume appear a slight expression of surprise escaped one or two of them. But Hetty held it out towards them, in triumph as if she expected the sight would produce a visible miracle, and then, without betraying either surprise or mortification at the Stoicism of the Indian, she turned eagerly to her new friend, in order to renew the discourse.

"This is the sacred volume, Hist," she said—"and these words, and lines, and verses, and chapters, all came from God."

"Why Great Spirit no send book to Injin, too?" demanded Hist, with the directness of a mind that was totally unsophisticated.

"Why?" answered Hetty, a little bewildered by a question so unexpected. "Why?—Ah! you know the Indians don't know how to read."

If Hist was not satisfied with this explanation, she did not deem the point of sufficient importance to be pressed. Simply bending her body, in a gentle admission of the truth of what she heard, she sat patiently awaiting the further arguments of the pale-face enthusiast.

"You can tell these chiefs that throughout this book, men are ordered to forgive their enemies; to treat them as they would brethren; and never to injure their fellow creatures, more especially on account of revenge, or any evil passions. Do you think you can tell them this, so that they will understand it, Hist?"

"Tell him well enough, but he no very easy to understand."

Hist then conveyed the ideas of Hetty, in the best manner she could, to the attentive Indians, who heard her words, with some such surprise as an American of our own times would be apt to betray at a suggestion that the great modern, but vacillating ruler of things human, public opinion, might be wrong. One or two of their number, however, having met with missionaries, said a few words in explanation, and then the group gave all its attention to the communications that were to follow. Before Hetty resumed she enquired earnestly of Hist if the chiefs had understood her, and receiving an evasive answer, was fain to be satisfied.

"I will now read to the warriors some of the verses that it is good for them to know," continued the girl, whose manner grew more solemn and earnest as she proceeded—"and they will remember that they are the very words of the Great Spirit. First, then, ye are commanded to *'love thy neighbor as thyself.'* Tell them *that*, dear Hist."

"Neighbor, for Injin, no mean pale face," answered the Delaware girl, with more decision than she had hitherto thought it necessary to use. "Neighbor mean Iroquois for Iroquois, Mohican for Mohican. Pale face for pale face. No need tell chief any thing else."

"You forget, Hist, these are the words of the Great Spirit, and the chiefs must obey them as well as others. Here is another commandment—*'Whosoever shall smite thee on the right cheek, turn to him the other also.'*"

"What that mean?" demanded Hist, with the quickness of lightning.

Hetty explained that it was an order not to resent injuries, but rather to submit to receive fresh wrongs from the offender.

"And hear this, too, Hist," she added. "*'Love your enemies, bless them that curse you, do* good *to them that hate you, and pray for them which despitefully use you and persecute you.'*"

By this time Hetty had become excited; her eye gleamed with the earnestness of her feelings, her cheeks flushed, and her voice, usually so low and modulated, became stronger and more impressive. With the bible she had been early made familiar by her mother, and she now turned from passage to passage, with surprising rapidity, taking care to cull such verses as taught the sublime lessons of christian charity and christian forgiveness. To translate half she said, in her pious earnestness, Wah-ta!-Wah would have found impracticable, had she made the effort, but wonder held her tongue tied, equally with the chiefs, and the young, simple-minded enthusiast had fairly become exhausted with her own efforts, before the other opened her mouth, again, to utter a syllable. Then, indeed, the Delaware girl gave a brief translation of the substance of what had been both read and said, confining herself to one or two of the more striking of the verses, those that had struck her own imagination as the most paradoxical, and which certainly would have been the most applicable to the case, could the uninstructed minds of the listeners embrace the great moral truths they conveyed.

It will be scarcely necessary to tell the reader the effect that such novel duties would be likely to produce among a group of Indian warriors, with whom it was a species of religious principle never to forget a benefit, or to forgive an injury. Fortunately, the previous explanations of Hist had prepared the minds of the Hurons for something extravagant, and most of that which to them seemed inconsistent and paradoxical, was accounted for by the fact that the speaker possessed a mind that was constituted differently from those of most of the human race. Still there were one or two old men who had heard similar doctrines from the missionaries, and these felt a desire to occupy an idle moment by pursuing a subject that they found so curious.

"This is the Good Book of the pale faces," observed one of these chiefs, taking the volume from the unresisting hands of Hetty, who gazed anxiously at his face, while he turned the leaves, as if she expected to witness some visible results from the circumstance. "This is the law by which my white brethren professes to live?"

Hist, to whom this question was addressed, if it might be considered as addressed to any one, in particular, answered simply in the affirmative; adding that both the French of the Canadas, and the Yengeese of the British provinces equally admitted its authority, and affected to revere its principles.

"Tell my young sister," said the Huron, looking directly at Hist, "that I will open my mouth and say a few words."

"The Iroquois chief go to speak—My pale face friend listen," said Hist.

"I rejoice to hear it!" exclaimed Hetty. "God has touched his heart, and he will now let father and Hurry go."

"This is the pale face law," resumed the chief. "It tells him to do good to them, that hurt him, and when his brother asks him for his rifle to give him the powder horn, too. Such is the pale face law?"

"Not so—not so—" answered Hetty earnestly, when these words had been interpreted—"There is not a word about rifles in the whole book, and powder and bullets give offence to the Great Spirit."

"Why then does the pale face use them? If he is ordered to *give* double to him that asks only for one thing, why does he *take* double from the poor Indian who ask for *no* thing. He comes from beyond the rising sun, with this book in his hand, and he teaches the red man to read it, but why does he forget himself all it says? When the Indian gives, he is never satisfied; and now he offers gold for the scalps of our women and children, though he calls us beasts if we take the scalp of a warrior killed in open war. My name is Rivenoak."

When Hetty had got this formidable question fairly presented to her mind in the translation, and Hist did her duty with more than usual readiness on this occasion, it scarcely need be said that she was sorely perplexed. Abler heads than that of this poor girl have frequently been puzzled by questions of a similar drift, and it is not surprising that with all her own earnestness and sincerity she did not know what answer to make.

"What shall I tell them, Hist," she asked imploringly—"I *know* that all I have read from the book is true, and yet it would'n't seem so, would it, by the conduct of those to whom the book was given?"

"Give 'em pale-face reason," returned Hist, ironically—"that always good for one side; though he bad for t'other."

"No—no—Hist there can't be two sides to truth—and yet it does seem strange! I'm certain I have read the verses right, and no one would be so wicked as to print the word of God wrong. *That* can never be, Hist."

"Well, to poor Injin girl, it seem every thing *can* be to pale faces," returned the other, coolly. "One time 'ey say white, and one time 'ey say black. Why *never can be*?"

Hetty was more and more embarrassed, until overcome with the apprehension that she had failed in her object, and that the lives of her father and Hurry would be the forfeit of some blunder of her own, she burst into tears. From that moment the manner of Hist lost all its irony and cool indifference, and she became the fond caressing friend, again. Throwing her arms around the afflicted girl, she attempted to soothe her sorrows, by the scarcely ever failing remedy of female sympathy.

"Stop cry—no cry—" she said, wiping the tears from the face of Hetty, as she would have performed the same office for a child, and stopping to press her occasionally to her own warm bosom with the affection of a sister. "Why you so trouble? You no make he book, if he be wrong, and you no make he pale face if he wicked. There wicked red man, and wicked white man—no colour all good—no colour all wicked. Chiefs know *that* well enough."

Hetty soon recovered from this sudden burst of grief, and then her mind reverted to the purpose of her visit, with all its single-hearted earnestness. Perceiving that the grim looking chiefs were still standing around her in grave attention, she hoped that another effort to convince them of the right might be successful.

"Listen, Hist," she said, struggling to suppress her sobs, and to speak distinctly—"Tell the chiefs that it matters not what the wicked do—right is right—The words of The Great Spirit are the words of The Great Spirit—and no one can go harmless for doing an evil act, because another has done it before him. *'Render good for evil,'* says this book, and that is the law for the red man as well as for the white man."

"Never hear such law among Delaware, or among Iroquois—" answered Hist soothingly. "No good to tell chiefs any such laws as *dat*. Tell 'em somet'ing they believe."

Hist was about to proceed, notwithstanding, when a tap on the shoulder, from the finger of the oldest chief caused her to look up. She then perceived that one of the warriors had left the group, and was already returning to it with Hutter and Hurry. Understanding that the two last were to become parties in the inquiry, she became mute, with the unhesitating obedience of an Indian woman. In a few seconds the prisoners stood face to face with the principal men of the captors.

"Daughter," said the senior chief to the young Delaware, "ask this grey beard why he came into our camp?"

The question was put by Hist, in her own imperfect English, but in a way that was easy to be understood. Hutter was too stern and obdurate by nature, to shrink from the consequences of any of his acts, and he was also too familiar with the opinions of the savages not to understand that nothing was to be gained by equivocation or an unmanly dread of their anger. Without hesitating, therefore, he avowed the purpose with which he had landed, merely justifying it by the fact that the government of the province had bid high for scalps. This frank avowal was received by the Iroquois, with evident satisfaction, not so much, however, on account of the advantage it gave them in a moral point of view, as by its proving that they had captured a man worthy of occupying their thoughts and of becoming a subject of their revenge. Hurry, when interrogated, confessed the truth, though he would have been more disposed to concealment than his sterner companion, did the circumstances very well admit of its adoption. But he had tact enough to discover that equivocation would be useless, at that moment, and he made a merit of necessity by imitating a frankness, which, in the case of Hutter, was the offspring of habits of indifference acting on a disposition that was always ruthless, and reckless of personal consequences.

As soon as the chiefs had received the answers to their questions, they walked away, in silence, like men who deemed the matter disposed of, all Hetty's dogmas being thrown away on beings trained in violence, from infancy to manhood. Hetty and Hist were now left alone with Hutter and Hurry, no visible restraint being placed on the movements of either; though all four, in fact, were vigilantly and unceasingly watched. As respects the men, care was had to prevent them from getting possession of any of the rifles, that lay scattered about, their own included; and there all open manifestations of watchfulness ceased. But they, who were so experienced in Indian practices, knew too well how great was the distance between appearances and reality, to become the dupes of this seeming carelessness. Although both thought incessantly of the means of escape, and this without concert, each was aware of the uselessness of attempting any project of the sort that was not deeply laid, and promptly executed. They had been long enough in the encampment, and were sufficiently observant to have ascertained that Hist, also, was a sort of captive, and, presuming on the circumstance, Hutter spoke in her presence, more openly than he might otherwise have thought it prudent to do; inducing Hurry to be equally unguarded by his example.

"I'll not blame you, Hetty, for coming on this errand, which was well meant if not very wisely planned," commenced the father, seating himself by the side of his daughter, and taking her hand; a sign of affection that this rude being was accustomed to manifest to this particular child. "But preaching, and the bible, are not the means to turn an Indian from his ways. Has Deerslayer sent any message; or has he any scheme by which he thinks to get us free?"

"Ay, that's the substance of it!" put in Hurry. "If you can help us, gal, to half a mile of freedom, or even a good start of a short quarter, I'll answer for the rest. Perhaps the old man may want a little more, but for one of my height and years *that* will meet all objections."

Hetty looked distressed, turning her eyes from one to the other, but she had no answer to give to the question of the reckless Hurry.

"Father," she said, "neither Deerslayer, nor Judith knew of my coming, until I had left the Ark. They are afraid the Iroquois will make a raft, and try to get off to the hut, and think more of defending *that*, than of coming to aid you."

"No—no—no—" said Hist hurriedly, though in a low voice, and with her face bent towards the earth, in order to conceal from those whom she knew to be watching them the fact of her speaking at all. "No—no—no—Deerslayer different man. He no t'ink of defending 'self, with friend in danger. Help one another, and all get to hut."

"This sounds well, old Tom," said Hurry, winking and laughing, though he too used the precaution to speak low—"Give me a ready witted squaw for a fri'nd, and though I'll not downright defy an Iroquois, I think I would defy the devil."

"No talk loud," said Hist. "Some Iroquois got Yengeese tongue, and all got Yengeese ear."

"Have we a friend in you, young woman?" enquired Hutter with an increasing interest in the conference. "If so, you may calculate on a solid reward, and nothing will be easier than to send you to your own tribe, if we can once fairly get you off with us to the castle. Give us the Ark and the canoes, and we can command the lake, spite of all the savages in the Canadas. Nothing but artillery could drive us out of the castle, if we can get back to it."

" 'S'pose 'ey come ashore to take scalp?" retorted Hist, with cool irony, at which the girl appeared to be more expert than is common for her sex.

"Ay—ay—that was a mistake; but there is little use in lamentations, and less still, young woman, in flings."

"Father," said Hetty, "Judith thinks of breaking open the big chest, in hopes of finding something in *that* which may buy your freedom of the savages."

A dark look came over Hutter at the announcement of this fact, and he muttered his dissatisfaction in a way to render it intelligible enough.

"What for no break open chest?" put in Hist. "Life sweeter than old chest—scalp sweeter than old chest. If no tell darter to break him open, Wah-ta!-Wah no help him to run away."

"Ye know not what ye ask—ye are but silly girls, and the wisest way for ye both is to speak of what ye understand and to speak of nothing else. I little like this cold neglect of the savages, Hurry; it's a proof that they think of something serious, and if we are to do any thing, we must do it soon. Can we count on this young woman, think you?"

"Listen—" said Hist quickly, and with an earnestness that proved how much her feelings were concerned—"Wah-ta!-Wah no Iroquois—All over Delaware—got Delaware heart—Delaware feeling. She prisoner, too. One prisoner help t'udder prisoner. No good to talk more, now. Darter stay with fader—Wah-ta!-Wah come and see friend—all look right—*Then* tell what he do."

This was said in a low voice, but distinctly, and in a manner to make an impression. As soon as it was uttered the girl arose, and left the group, walking composedly towards the hut she occupied, as if she had no further interest in what might pass between the pale-faces.

Chapter XII

"She speaks much of her father; says she hears,
There's tricks i' the world; and hems, and beats her breast;
Spurns enviously at straws; speaks things in doubt,
That carry but half sense; her speech is nothing,
Yet the unshaped use of it doth move
The hearers to collection;—"

Hamlet, IV.v.4–9.

WE LEFT THE OCCUPANTS of the castle and the ark, buried in sleep. Once, or twice, in the course of the night, it is true, Deerslayer, or the Delaware, arose and looked out upon the tranquil lake; when, finding all safe, each returned to his pallet, and slept like a man who was not easily deprived of his natural rest. At the first signs of the dawn, the former arose, however, and made his personal arrangements for the day; though his companion, whose nights had not been tranquil, or without disturbances, of late, continued on his blanket, until the sun had fairly risen. Judith too, was later than common, that morning, for the earlier hours of the night had brought her little of either refreshment, or sleep. But ere the sun had shown himself over the eastern hills, these too were up and afoot, even the tardy in that region seldom remaining on their pallets, after the appearance of the great luminary.

Chingachgook was in the act of arranging his forest toilet, when Deerslayer entered the cabin of the Ark and threw him a few coarse but light summer vestments that belonged to Hutter.

"Judith hath given me them for your use, chief," said the latter, as he cast the jacket and trousers at the feet of the Indian, "for it's ag'in all prudence and caution to be seen in your war dress and paint. Wash off all them fiery streaks from your cheeks, put on these garments, and here is a hat, such as it is, that will give you an awful oncivilized sort of civilization, as the missionaries call it. Remember that Hist is at hand, and what we do for the maiden, must be done while we are doing for others. I know it's ag'in your gifts and your natur' to wear clothes, unless they are cut and carried in a red man's fashion, but make a vartue of necessity, and put these on, at once, even if they do rise a little in your throat."

Chingachgook, or the Serpent, eyed the vestments with strong disgust; but he saw the usefulness of the disguise, if not its absolute necessity. Should the Iroquois discover a red-man, in or about the Castle, it might, indeed, place them more on their guard, and give their suspicions a direction towards their female captive. Any thing was better than a failure as it regarded his betrothed, and, after turning the different garments round and round, examining them with a species of grave irony, affecting to draw them on in a way that defeated itself, and otherwise manifesting the reluctance of a young savage to confine his limbs in the usual appliances of civilized life, the chief submitted to the directions of his companion, and finally stood forth, so far as the eye could detect, a red man in colour alone. Little was to be apprehended from this last peculiarity, however, the distance from the shore, and the want of glasses preventing any very close scrutiny, and Deerslayer, himself, though of a brighter and fresher tint, had a countenance that was burnt by the sun to a hue scarcely less red than that of his Mohican companion. The awkwardness of the Delaware in his new attire, caused his friend to smile, more than once that day, but he carefully abstained from the use of any of those jokes, which would have been bandied among white men on such an occasion, the habits of a chief, the dignity of a warrior on his first path, and the gravity of the circumstances in which they were placed, uniting to render so much levity out of season.

The meeting at the morning meal of the three islanders, if we may use the term, was silent, grave and thoughtful. Judith showed by her looks that she had passed an unquiet night, while the two men had the future before them, with its unseen and unknown events. A few words of courtesy passed between Deerslayer and the girl, in the course of the breakfast, but no allusion was made to their situation. At length Judith, whose heart was full, and whose novel feelings disposed her to entertain sentiments more gentle and tender than common, introduced the subject, and this in a way to show how much of her thoughts it had occupied, in the course of the last sleepless night.

"It would be dreadful, Deerslayer," the girl abruptly exclaimed, "should any thing serious befall my father and Hetty! We cannot remain quietly here, and leave them in the hands of the Iroquois, without bethinking us of some means of serving them."

"I'm ready, Judith, to sarve them, and all others who are in trouble, could the way to do it be p'inted out. It's no trifling matter to fall into red-skin hands, when men set out on an ar'n'd like that which took Hutter and Hurry ashore; that I know as well as another, and I would'n't wish my worst inimy in such a strait, much less them with whom I've journeyed, and eat, and slept. Have you any scheme, that you would like to have the Sarpent and me, indivour to carry out?"

"I know of no other means to release the prisoners, than by bribing the Iroquois. They are not proof against presents, and we might offer enough, perhaps, to make them think it better to carry away what to them will be rich gifts, than to carry away poor prisoners; if, indeed, they should carry them away at all!"

"This is well enough, Judith; yes, it's well enough, if the inimy is to be bought and we can find articles to make the purchase with. Your father has a convenient lodge, and it is most cunningly placed, though it does'n't seem overstock'd with riches that will be likely to buy his ransom. There's the piece he calls Killdeer, might count for something, and I understand there's a keg of powder about, which might be a make weight, sartain; and yet two able bodied men are not to be bought off for a trifle—besides—"

"Besides what?" demanded Judith impatiently, observing that the other hesitated to proceed, probably from a reluctance to distress her.

"Why, Judith, the Frenchers offer bounties as well as our own side, and the price of two scalps would purchase a keg of powder, and a rifle; though I'll not say one of the latter altogether as good as Killdeer, there, which your father va'nts as oncommon, and onequalled, like. But fair powder, and a pretty sartain rifle; then the red men are not the expartest in fire arms, and don't always know the difference atwixt that which is ra'al, and that which is seeming."

"This is horrible!" muttered the girl, struck by the homely

manner in which her companion was accustomed to state his facts. "But you overlook my own clothes, Deerslayer, and they, I think, might go far with the women of the Iroquois."

"No doubt they would; no doubt they would, Judith," returned the other, looking at her keenly, as if he would ascertain whether she were really capable of making such a sacrifice. "But, are you sartain, gal, you could find it in your heart, to part with your own finery for such a purpose? Many is the man who has thought he was valiant 'till danger stared him in the face; I've known them, too, that consaited they were kind and ready to give away all they had to the poor, when they've been listening to other people's hard heartedness; but whose fists have clench'd as tight as the riven hickory when it came to downright offerings of their own. Besides, Judith, you're handsome—oncommon in that way, one might obsarve and do no harm to the truth—and they that have beauty, like to have that which will adorn it. Are you sartain you could find it in your heart to part with your own finery?"

The soothing allusion to the personal charms of the girl, was well timed, to counteract the effect produced by the distrust that the young man expressed of Judith's devotion to her filial duties. Had another said as much as Deerslayer, the compliment would most probably have been overlooked in the indignation awakened by the doubts, but even the unpolished sincerity, that so often made this simple minded hunter bare his thoughts, had a charm for the girl; and, while she colored, and, for an instant her eyes flashed fire, she could not find it in her heart to be really angry with one whose very soul seemed truth and manly kindness. Look her reproaches she did, but conquering the desire to retort, she succeeded in answering in a mild and friendly manner.

"You must keep all your favorable opinions, for the Delaware girls, Deerslayer, if you seriously think thus of those of your own colour," she said, affecting to laugh. "But, *try* me; if you find that I regret either ribband or feather, silk or muslin, then may you think what you please of my heart, and say what you think."

"That's justice!—The rarest thing to find on 'arth, is a

truly just man. So says Tamenund, the wisest prophet of the Delawares, and so all must think, that have occasion to see, and talk and act among mankind. I love a just man, Sarpent. His eyes are never covered with darkness towards his inimies, while they are all sunshine and brightness toward his fri'nds. He uses the reason that God has given him, and he uses it with a feelin' of his being ordered to look at, and to consider things as they *are*, and not as he *wants* them to be. It's easy enough to find men who *call* themselves just, but it's wonderful oncommon to find them that are the very thing, in fact. How often have I seen Indians, gal, who believed they were lookin' into a matter agreeable to the will of the Great Spirit, when, in truth, they were only striving to act up to their own will and pleasure, and this, half the time, with a temptation to go wrong that could no more be seen by themselves, than the stream that runs in the next valley, can be seen by us through yonder mountain; though any looker on might have discovered it, as plainly as we can discover the parch that are swimming around this hut!"

"Very true, Deerslayer," rejoined Judith, losing every trace of displeasure in a bright smile—"very true, and I hope to see you act on this love of justice, in all matters in which I am concerned. Above all, I hope you will judge for yourself, and not believe every evil story that a prating idler, like Hurry Harry, may have to tell, that goes to touch the good name of any young woman, who may not happen to have the same opinion of his face and person that the blustering gallant has of himself."

"Hurry Harry's idees do not pass for gospel with me, Judith; but even worse than he may have eyes and ears," returned the other gravely.

"Enough of this!" exclaimed Judith, with flashing eye and a flush that mounted to her temples, "and more of my father and his ransom. 'Tis as you say, Deerslayer; the Indians will not be likely to give up their prisoners, without a heavier bribe than my clothes can offer, and father's rifle and powder. There is the chest—"

"Ay, there is the chist, as you say, Judith, and when the question gets to be between a secret and a scalp, I should think most men would prefar keeping the last. Did your father ever give you any downright commands consarning that chist?"

"Never. He has always appeared to think its locks, and its steel bands, and its strength, its best protection."

"'Tis a rare chist, and altogether of curious build," returned Deerslayer, rising and approaching the thing in question, on which he seated himself, with a view to examine it with greater ease. "Chingachgook, this is no wood that comes of any forest that you or I have ever trailed through! 'Tis'n't the black walnut, and yet it's quite as comely, if not more so, did the smoke and the treatment give it fair play."

The Delaware drew near, felt of the wood, examined its grain, endeavored to indent the surface with a nail, and passed his hand curiously over the steel bands, the heavy padlocks, and the other novel peculiarities of the massive box.

"No—nothing like this grows in these regions—" resumed Deerslayer. "I've seen all the oaks, both the maples, the elms, the bass woods, all the walnuts, the butternuts, and every tree that has a substance and colour, wrought into some form or other, but never have I before seen such a wood as this! Judith, the chist itself, would buy your father's freedom, or Iroquois cur'osity is'n't as strong as red skin cur'osity, in general; especially in the matter of woods."

"The purchase might be cheaper made, perhaps, Deerslayer. The chest is full, and it would be better to part with half than to part with the whole. Besides, father—I know not why—but, father values that chest highly."

"He would seem to prize what it holds more than the chist, itself, judging by the manner in which he treats the outside, and secures the inside. Here are three locks, Judith; is there no key?"

"I've never seen one; and yet key there must be, since Hetty told us, *she* had often seen the chest opened."

"Keys no more lie in the air, or float on the water, than humans, gal; if there is a key, there must be a place in which it is kept."

"That is true, and it might not be difficult to find it, did we dare to search!"

"This is for you, Judith; it is altogether for you. The chist is your'n, or your father's; and Hutter is your father, not mine. Cur'osity is a woman's, and not a man's failing, and there you have got all the reasons before you. If the chist has articles for ransom, it seems to me they would be wisely used in redeeming their owner's life, or even in saving his scalp; but that is a matter for your judgment, and not for ourn. When the lawful owner of a trap, or a buck, or a canoe, is'n't present, his next of kin becomes his riprisentyve by all the laws of the woods. We therefore leave you to say whether the chist shall, or shall not be opened."

"I hope you do not believe I can hesitate, when my father's life's in danger, Deerslayer!"

"Why, it's pretty much putting a scolding ag'in tears and mourning. It's not onreasonable to foretell that old Tom may find fault with what you've done, when he sees himself, once more, in his hut, here, but there's nothing unusual in men's falling out with what has been done for their own good; I dare to say that even the moon would seem a different thing from what it now does, could we look at it from the other side."

"Deerslayer, if we can find the key, I will authorize you to open the chest, and to take such things from it, as you may think will buy father's ransom."

"First find the key, gal; we'll talk of the rest a'terwards. Sarpent, you've eyes like a fly, and a judgment that's seldom out; can you help us, in calculating where Floating Tom would be apt to keep the key of a chist that he holds to be as private as this."

The Delaware had taken no part in the discourse, until he was thus directly appealed to, when he quitted the chest, which had continued to attract his attention, and cast about him for the place in which a key would be likely to be concealed, under such circumstances. As Judith and Deerslayer were not idle, the while, the whole three were soon engaged in an anxious and spirited search. As it was certain that the desired key was not to be found in any of the common drawers, or closets, of which there were several in the building, none looked there, but all turned their enquiries to those places that struck them as ingenious hiding places, and more likely to be used for such a purpose. In this manner the outer room was thoroughly but fruitlessly examined, when they entered the sleeping apartment of Hutter. This part of the rude building was better furnished than the rest of the structure, containing several articles that had been especially devoted to the service of the deceased wife, of its owner, but as Judith had all the rest of the keys, it was soon rummaged, without bringing to light the particular key desired.

They now entered the bed room of the daughters. Chingachgook was immediately struck with the contrast between the articles, and the arrangement, of that side of the room that might be called Judith's and that which more properly belonged to Hetty. A slight exclamation escaped him, and pointing in each direction he alluded to the fact in a low voice, speaking to his friend in the Delaware tongue.

"Tis as you think, Sarpent," answered Deerslayer, whose remarks we always translate into English, preserving as much as possible of the peculiar phraseology and manner of the man, "'Tis just so, as any one may see, and 'tis all founded in natur'. One sister loves finery, some say overmuch; while t'other is as meek and lowly as God ever created goodness and truth. Yet, after all, I dare say that Judith has her vartues, and Hetty has her failin's."

"And the 'Feeble-Mind' has seen the chist opened?" inquired Chingachgook, with curiosity in his glance.

"Sartain; that much I've heard from her own lips; and, for that matter, so have you. It seems her father does'n't misgive *her* discretion, though he does that of his eldest darter."

"Then, the key is hid only from the 'Wild Rose'?" for so Chingachgook had begun gallantly to term Judith, in his private discourse with his friend.

"That's it! That's just it! One he trusts, and the other he does'n't. There's red and white in that, Sarpent, all tribes and nations agreeing in trusting some, and refusing to trust other some. It depends on character and judgment."

"Where could a key be put, so little likely to be found by the Wild Rose, as among coarse clothes?"

Deerslayer started, and turning to his friend, with admiration expressed in every lineament of his face, he fairly laughed, in his silent but hearty manner, at the ingenuity and readiness of the conjecture.

"Your name's well bestowed, Sarpent—yes, 'tis well bestowed! Sure enough, where would a lover of finery be so little likely to s'arch, as among garments as coarse and onseemly as these of poor Hetty's. I dares to say, Judith's delicate fingers have'n't touched a bit of cloth as rough and oncomely as that petticoat, now, since she first made acquaintance with the officers! Yet, who knows? The key may be as likely to be on the same peg, as in any other place. Take down the garment, Delaware, and let us see if you are ra'ally a prophet."

Chingachgook did as desired, but no key was found. A coarse pocket, apparently empty, hung on the adjoining peg, and this was next examined. By this time, the attention of Judith was called in that direction, and she spoke hurriedly and like one who wished to save unnecessary trouble.

"Those are only the clothes of poor Hetty, dear simple girl!" she said, "nothing we seek, would be likely to be there."

The words were hardly out of the handsome mouth of the speaker, when Chingachgook drew the desired key from the pocket. Judith was too quick of apprehension, not to understand the reason a hiding place so simple and exposed, had been used. The blood rushed to her face, as much with resentment perhaps, as with shame, and she bit her lip, though she continued silent. Deerslayer and his friend now discovered the delicacy of men of native refinement, neither smiling or even by a glance betraying how completely he understood the motives and ingenuity of this clever artifice. The former, who had taken the key from the Indian, led the way into the adjoining room, and applying it to a lock ascertained that the right instrument had actually been found. There were three pad-locks, each of which however was easily opened by this single key. Deerslayer removed them all, loosened the hasps, raised the lid a little to make certain it was loose, and then he drew back from the chest, several feet, signing to his friend to follow.

"This is a family chist, Judith," he said, "and 'tis like to hold family secrets. The Sarpent and I will go into the Ark, and look to the canoes, and paddles, and oars, while you can examine it by yourself, and find out whether any thing that will be a make weight in a ransom, is, or is not, among the articles. When you've got through, give us a call, and we'll all sit in council, together, touching the valie of the articles."

"Stop, Deerslayer," exclaimed the girl, as he was about to withdraw. "Not a single thing will I touch—I will not even raise the lid—unless you are present. Father and Hetty have seen fit to keep the inside of this chest a secret from me, and I am much too proud to pry into their hidden treasures, unless it were for their own good. But, on no account, will I open the chest alone. Stay with me, then; I want witnesses of what I do."

"I rather think, Sarpent, that the gal is right! Confidence and reliance beget security, but suspicion is like to make us all wary. Judith has a right to ask us to be present, and should the chist hold any of Master Hutter's secrets, they will fall into the keeping of two as close mouthed young men as are to be found. We *will* stay with you, Judith—but, first let us take a look at the lake and the shore, for this chist will not be emptied in a minute."

The two men now went out on the platform, and Deerslayer swept the shore with the glass, while the Indian gravely turned his eye on the water and the woods, in quest of any sign that might betray the machinations of their enemies. Nothing was visible, and assured of their temporary security, the three collected around the chest, again, with the avowed object of opening it.

Judith had held this chest, and its unknown contents, in a species of reverence as long as she could remember. Neither her father, nor her mother, ever mentioned it, in her presence, and there appeared to be a silent convention, that in naming the different objects that occasionally stood near it, or even lay on its lid, care should be had to avoid any allusion to the chest itself. Habit had rendered this so easy, and so much a matter of course, that it was only quite recently the girl had began even to muse on the singularity of the circumstance. But there had never been sufficient intimacy between Hutter and his eldest daughter to invite confidence. At times he was kind, but in general, with her more especially, he was stern and morose. Least of all had his authority been exercised in a way to embolden his child to venture on the liberty she was about to take, without many misgivings of the consequences, although the liberty proceeded from a desire to serve himself. Then Judith was not altogether free from a little superstition, on the subject of this chest, which had stood a sort of tabooed relic before her eyes, from childhood to the present hour. Nevertheless the time had come when it would seem that this mystery was to be explained, and that under circumstances, too, which left her very little choice in the matter.

Finding that both her companions were watching her movements, in grave silence, Judith placed a hand on the lid, and endeavored to raise it. Her strength, however, was insufficient, and it appeared to the girl, who was fully aware that all the fastenings were removed, that she was resisted in an unhallowed attempt by some supernatural power.

"I cannot raise the lid, Deerslayer!" she said—"Had we not better give up the attempt, and find some other means of releasing the prisoners?"

"Not so—Judith; not so, gal. No means are as sartain and easy, as a good bribe," answered the other. "As for the lid, 'tis held by nothing but its own weight, which is prodigious for so small a piece of wood, loaded with iron as it is."

As Deerslayer spoke, he applied his own strength to the effort, and succeeded in raising the lid against the timbers of the house, where he took care to secure it, by a sufficient prop. Judith fairly trembled, as she cast her first glance at the interior, and she felt a temporary relief in discovering that a piece of canvass, that was carefully tucked in, around the edges, effectually concealed all beneath it. The chest was apparently well stored, however, the canvass lying within an inch of the lid.

"Here's a full cargo," said Deerslayer, eyeing the arrangement, "and we had needs go to work leisurely, and at our ease. Sarpent, bring some stools, while I spread this blanket on the floor, and then we'll begin work orderly, and in comfort."

The Delaware complied, Deerslayer civilly placed a stool for Judith, took one himself, and commenced the removal of the canvas covering. This was done deliberately, and in as cautious a manner, as if it were believed that fabrics of a delicate construction lay hidden beneath. When the canvass was removed, the first articles that came in view were some of the habiliments of the male sex. They were of fine materials, and, according to the fashions of the age, were gay in colours, and rich in ornaments. One coat in particular was of scarlet, and had button holes worked in gold thread. Still it was not military, but was part of the attire of a civilian of condition, at a period when social rank was rigidly respected in dress. Chingachgook could not refrain from an exclamation of pleasure, as soon as Deerslayer opened this coat, and held it up to view, for, notwithstanding all his trained self-command, the splendor of the vestment was too much for the philosophy of an Indian. Deerslayer turned quickly, and he regarded his friend with momentary displeasure, as this burst of weakness escaped him, and then he soliloquized as was his practice, whenever any strong feeling suddenly got the ascendant.

"'Tis his gift!—yes, 'tis the gift of a redskin to love finery, and he is not to be blamed. This is an extr'ornary garment, too, and extr'ornary things get up extr'ornary feelin's. I think this will do, Judith, for the Indian heart is hardly to be found in all America, that can withstand, colours like these, and glitter like that. If this coat was ever made for your father, you've come honestly by the taste for finery, you have."

"That coat was never made for father," answered the girl, quickly—"it is much too long, while father is short and square."

"Cloth was plenty if it was, and glitter cheap," answered Deerslayer, with his silent, joyous laugh. "Sarpent, this garment was made for a man of your size, and I should like to see it on your shoulders."

Chingachgook, nothing loth, submitted to the trial, throwing aside the coarse and thread bare jacket of Hutter, to deck his person in a coat that was originally intended for a gentleman. The transformation was ludicrous, but as men are seldom struck with incongruities in their own appearance, any more than in their own conduct, the Delaware studied this change in a common glass, by which Hutter was in the habit of shaving, with grave interest. At that moment he thought of Hist, and we owe it to truth, to say, though it may militate a little against the stern character of a warrior to avow it, that he wished he could be seen by her, in his present improved aspect.

"Off with it, Sarpent—off with it," resumed the inflexible Deerslayer. "Such garments as little become you, as they would become me. Your gifts are for paint, and hawk's feathers, and blankets, and wampum, and mine are for doublets of skins, tough leggings, and sarviceable moccasins. I say moccasins, Judith, for though white, living as I do in the woods, it's necessary to take to some of the prac*ty*ces of the woods, for comfort's sake, and cheapness."

"I see no reason, Deerslayer, why one man may not wear a scarlet coat, as well as another," returned the girl. "I wish I could see *you* in this handsome garment."

"See me in a coat fit for a Lord!—Well, Judith, if you wait till that day, you'll wait until you see me beyond reason and memory. No—no—gal, my gifts are my gifts, and I'll live and die in 'em, though I never bring down another deer, or spear another salmon. What have I done that you should wish to see *me* in such a flaunting coat, Judith."

"Because I think, Deerslayer, that the false-tongued and false-hearted young gallants of the garrisons, ought not alone to appear in fine feathers, but that truth and honesty have *their* claims to be honored and exalted."

"And what exaltification—" the reader will have remarked that Deerslayer had not very critically studied his dictionary—"and what exaltification would it be to me, Judith, to be bedizzened and bescarleted like a Mingo chief that has just got his presents up from Quebec? No—no—I'm well as I am; and if not, I can be no better. Lay the coat down on the blanket, Sarpent, and let us look farther into the chist."

The tempting garment, one surely that was never intended for Hutter, was laid aside, and the examination proceeded. The male attire, all of which corresponded with the coat in quality, was soon exhausted, and then succeeded female. A beautiful dress of brocade, a little the worse from negligent treatment, followed, and this time open exclamations of delight escaped the lips of Judith. Much as the girl had been addicted to dress, and favorable as had been her opportunities of seeing some little pretension in that way, among the wives of the different commandants, and other ladies of the forts, never before had she beheld a tissue, or tints, to equal those that were now so unexpectedly placed before her eyes. Her rapture was almost childish, nor would she allow the enquiry to proceed, until she had attired her person in a robe so unsuited to her habits and her abode. With this end, she withdrew into her own room, where with hands practised in such offices, she soon got rid of her own neat gown of linen, and stood forth in the gay tints of the brocade. The dress happened to fit the fine, full, person of Judith, and certainly it had never adorned a being, better qualified by natural gifts, to do credit to its really rich hues and fine texture. When she returned, both Deerslayer and Chingachgook, who had passed the brief time of her absence, in taking a second look at the male garments, arose in surprise, each permitting exclamations of wonder and pleasure to escape him, in a way so unequivocal as to add new lustre to the eyes of Judith, by flushing her cheeks with a glow of triumph. Affecting, however, not to notice the impression she had made, the girl seated herself with the stateliness of a queen, desiring that the chest might be looked into, further.

"I do'n't know a better way to treat with the Mingos, gal," cried Deerslayer, "than to send you ashore, as you be, and to tell 'em that a queen has arrived among 'em! They'll give up old Hutter, and Hurry, and Hetty, too, at such a spectacle!"

"I thought your tongue too honest to flatter, Deerslayer," returned the girl, gratified at this admiration more than she would have cared to own. "One of the chief reasons of my respect for you, was your love for truth."

"And 'tis truth, and solemn truth, Judith, and nothing else. Never did eyes of mine gaze on as glorious a lookin' creatur', as you be yourself, at this very moment! I've seen beauties in my time too; both white and red; and them that was renowned and talk'd of, far and near; but never have I beheld one that could hold any comparison with what you are at this blessed instant, Judith; never."

The glance of delight which the girl bestowed on the frank-speaking hunter, in no degree lessened the effect of her charms, and as the humid eyes blended with it a look of sensibility, perhaps Judith never appeared more truly lovely, than at what the young man had called that "blessed instant." He shook his head, held it suspended a moment over the open chest, like one in doubt, and then proceeded with the examination.

Several of the minor articles of female dress came next, all of a quality to correspond with the gown. These were laid at Judith's feet, in silence, as if she had a natural claim to their possession. One or two, such as gloves, and lace, the girl caught up, and appended to her already rich attire in affected playfulness, but with the real design of decorating her person as far as circumstances would allow. When these two remarkable suits, male and female they might be termed, were removed, another canvass covering separated the remainder of the articles from the part of the chest which they had occupied. As soon as Deerslayer perceived this arrangement, he paused, doubtful of the propriety of proceeding any further.

"Every man has his secrets, I suppose," he said, "and all men have a right to their enj'yment. We've got low enough in this chist, in my judgment to answer our wants, and it seems to me we should do well by going no farther; and by letting Master Hutter have to himself, and his own feelin's, all that's beneath this cover."

"Do you mean, Deerslayer, to offer these clothes to the Iroquois, as ransom?" demanded Judith, quickly.

"Sartain. What are we prying into another man's chist for, but to sarve its owner, in the best way we can. This coat, alone, would be very apt to gain over the head chief of the riptyles, and if his wife or darter should happen to be out with him, that there gownd would soften the heart of any woman that is to be found atween Albany and Montreal. I do not see that we want a larger stock in trade than them two articles."

"To you it may seem so, Deerslayer," returned the disappointed girl, "but of what use could a dress like this be to any Indian woman? She could not wear it among the branches of the trees, the dirt and smoke of the wigwam would soon soil it, and how would a pair of red arms appear, thrust through these short, laced sleeves!"

"All very true, gal, and you might go on and say, it is altogether out of time, and place and season, in this region at all. What is it to us how the finery is treated, so long as it answers our wishes? I do not see that your father can make any use of such clothes, and it's lucky he has things that are of no valie to himself, that will bear a high price with others. We can make no better trade for him, than to offer these duds for his liberty. We'll throw in the light frivol'ties, and get Hurry off in the bargain."

"Then you think, Deerslayer, that Thomas Hutter has no one in his family—no child—no daughter, to whom this dress may be thought becoming, and whom you could wish to see in it, once and awhile, even though it should be at long intervals, and only in playfulness?"

"I understand you, Judith—yes, I now understand your meaning, and I think I can say, your wishes. That you are as glorious, in that dress, as the sun when it rises, or sets, in a soft October day, I'm ready to allow, and that you greatly become it, is a good deal more sartain than that it becomes you. There's gifts in clothes, as well as in other things. Now I do not think that a warrior on his first path, ought to lay on the same awful paints as a chief that has had his virtue tried, and knows from exper'ence he will not disgrace his pretensions. So it is with all of us, red or white. You are Thomas Hutter's darter, and that gownd was made for the child of some governor, or a lady of high station, and it was intended to be worn among fine furniture, and in rich company. In my eyes, Judith, a modest maiden never looks more becoming, than when becomingly clad, and nothing is suitable that is out of character. Besides, gal, if there's a creatur' in the colony that can afford to do without finery, and to trust to her own good looks, and sweet countenance, it's yourself."

"I'll take off the rubbish this instant, Deerslayer," cried the girl, springing up to leave the room, "and never do I wish to see it on any human being, again."

"So it is with 'em, all, Sarpent," said the other, turning to his friend and laughing, as soon as the beauty had disappeared. "They like finery, but they like their natyve charms most of all. I'm glad the gal has consented to lay aside her furbelows, howsever, for it's ag'in reason for one of her class to wear 'em; and then she *is* handsome enough, as I call it, to go alone. Hist would show oncommon likely, too, in such a gownd, Delaware!"

"Wah-ta!-Wah is a red skin girl, Deerslayer," returned the

Indian, "like the young of the pigeon, she is to be known by her own feathers. I should pass by without knowing her, were she dressed in such a skin. It's wisest always to be so clad that our friends need not ask us for our names. The 'Wild Rose' is very pleasant, but she is no sweeter for so many colours."

"That's it!—that's natur', and the true foundation for love and protection. When a man stoops to pick a wild strawberry, he does not expect to find a melon; and when he wishes to gather a melon, he's disapp'inted if it proves to be a squash; though squashes *be* often brighter to the eye than melons. That's it, and it means, stick to your gifts, and your gifts will stick to you."

The two men had now a little discussion together, touching the propriety of penetrating any farther into the chest of Hutter, when Judith re-appeared, divested of her robes, and in her own simple, linen frock again.

"Thank you, Judith," said Deerslayer, taking her kindly by the hand—"for I know it went a little ag'in the nat'ral cravings of woman, to lay aside so much finery, as it might be in a lump. But you're more pleasing to the eye as you stand, you be, than if you had a crown on your head, and jewels dangling from your hair. The question now is, whether to lift this covering, to see what will be ra'ally the best bargain we can make for Master Hutter, for we must do as we think *he* would be willing to do, did he stand here in our places."

Judith looked very happy. Accustomed as she was to adulation, the homely homage of Deerslayer had given her more true satisfaction, than she had ever yet received from the tongue of man. It was not the terms in which this admiration had been expressed, for *they* were simple enough, that produced so strong an impression; nor yet their novelty, or their warmth of manner, nor any of those peculiarities that usually give value to praise; but the unflinching truth of the speaker, that carried his words so directly to the heart of the listener. This is one of the great advantages of plain dealing and frankness. The habitual and wily flatterer may succeed until his practises recoil on himself, and like other sweets his aliment cloys by its excess; but he who deals honestly, though he often necessarily offends, possesses a power of praising that no quality but sincerity can bestow, since his words go directly to the heart, finding their support in the understanding. Thus it was with Deerslayer and Judith. So soon and so deeply did this simple hunter impress those who knew him, with a conviction of his unbending honesty, that all he uttered in commendation was as certain to please, as all he uttered in the way of rebuke was as certain to rankle and excite enmity, where his character had not awakened a respect and affection, that in another sense rendered it painful. In after life, when the career of this untutored being brought him in contact with officers of rank, and others entrusted with the care of the interests of the state, this same influence was exerted on a wider field, even generals listening to his commendations with a glow of pleasure, that it was not always in the power of their official superiors to awaken. Perhaps Judith was the first individual of his own colour, who fairly submitted to this natural consequence of truth and fair-dealing, on the part of Deerslayer. She had actually pined for his praise, and she had now received it, and that in the form which was most agreeable to her weaknesses and habits of thought. The result will appear in the course of the narrative.

"If we knew all that chest holds, Deerslayer," returned the girl, when she had a little recovered from the immediate effect produced by his commendations of her personal appearance, "we could better determine on the course we ought to take."

"That's not onreasonable, gal, though it's more a pale-face than a red-skin gift to be prying into other people's secrets."

"Curiosity is natural, and it is expected that all human beings, should have human failings. Whenever I've been at the garrisons, I've found that most, in and about them, had a longing to learn their neighbor's secrets."

"Yes, and sometimes to fancy them, when they could'n't find 'em out! That's the difference atween an Indian gentleman, and a white gentleman. The Sarpent, here, would turn his head aside, if he found himself onknowingly lookin' into another chief's wigwam, whereas, in the settlements while all pretend to be great people, most prove they've got betters, by the manner in which they talk of their consarns. I'll be bound, Judith, you would'n't get the Sarpent, there, to confess there was another in the tribe so much greater than himself, as to become the subject of his idees, and to empl'y his tongue in conversations about his movements, and ways, and food, and all the other little matters that occupy a man when he's not empl'y'd in his greater duties. He who does this, is but little better than a blackguard, in the grain, and them that encourages him, is pretty much of the same kidney, let them wear coats as fine as they may, or of what dye they please."

"But this is not another man's wigwam; it belongs to my father, these are his things, and they are wanted in his service."

"That's true, gal; that's true, and it carries weight with it. Well, when all is before us, we may, indeed, best judge, which to offer for the ransom, and which to withhold."

Judith was not altogether as disinterested in her feelings, as she affected to be. She remembered that the curiosity of Hetty had been indulged, in connection with this chest, while her own had been disregarded, and she was not sorry to possess an opportunity of being placed on a level with her less gifted sister, in this one particular. It appearing to be admitted all round, that the enquiry into the contents of the chest ought to be renewed, Deerslayer proceeded to remove the second covering of canvass.

The articles that lay uppermost, when the curtain was again raised on the secrets of the chest, were a pair of pistols, curiously inlaid with silver. Their value would have been considerable, in one of the towns, though as weapons, in the woods, they were a species of arms seldom employed; never, indeed, unless it might be by some officer from Europe, who visited the colonies, as many were then wont to do, so much impressed with the superiority of the usages of London, as to fancy they were not to be laid aside on the frontiers of America. What occurred on the discovery of these weapons, will appear, in the succeeding chapter.

Chapter XIII

"An oaken, broken, elbow-chair;
A caudle-cup without an ear;
A battered, shattered ash bedstead;
A box of deal without a lid;
A pair of tongs, but out of joint;
A back-sword poker, without point;
A dish which might good meat afford once;
An Ovid, and an old Concordance."
Thomas Sheridan, "A True and Faithful Inventory of the Goods belonging to Dr. Swift," ll. 1–6, 13–14.

NO SOONER did Deerslayer raise the pistols, than he turned to the Delaware and held them up, for his admiration.

"Child gun," said the Serpent, smiling, while he handled one of the instruments as if it had been a toy.

"Not it, Sarpent; not it—t'was made for a man and would satisfy a giant, if rightly used. But stop; white men are remarkable for their carelessness in putting away fire arms, in chists and corners. Let me look if care has been given to these."

As Deerslayer spoke, he took the weapon from the hand of his friend, and opened the pan. The last was filled with priming, caked like a bit of cinder, by time, moisture and compression. An application of the ramrod showed that both the pistols were charged, although Judith could testify that they had probably lain for years in the chest. It is not easy to portray the surprise of the Indian, at this discovery, for he was in the practice of renewing his priming daily, and of looking to the contents of his piece, at other short intervals.

"This is white neglect," said Deerslayer, shaking his head, "and scarce a season goes by, that some one, in the settlements does n't suffer from it. It's extr'ornary too, Judith—yes, it's downright extr'ornary that the owner shall fire his piece at a deer, or some other game, or perhaps at an inimy, and twice out of three times he'll miss; but let him catch an accident with one of these forgotten charges, and he makes it sartain death to a child, or a brother, or a fri'nd! Well, we shall do a good turn to the owner if we fire these pistols for him, and as they're novelties to you and me, Sarpent, we'll try our hands at a mark. Freshen that priming, and I'll do the same with this, and then we'll see who is the best man with a pistol; as for the rifle, that's long been settled atween us."

Deerslayer laughed heartily, at his own conceit, and, in a minute or two, they were both standing on the platform, selecting some object in the Ark for their target. Judith was led by curiosity to their side.

"Stand back, gal, stand a little back; these we'pons have been long loaded," said Deerslayer, "and some accident may happen in the discharge."

"Then *you* shall not fire them! Give them both to the Delaware; or it would be better to unload them, without firing."

"That's ag'in usage—and some people say, ag'in manhood; though I hold to no such silly doctrine. We must fire 'em, Judith; yes, we must fire 'em; though I foresee that neither will have any great reason to boast of his skill."

Judith, in the main, was a girl of great personal spirit, and her habits prevented her from feeling any of the terror that is apt to come over her sex, at the report of fire arms. She had discharged many a rifle, and had even been known to kill a deer, under circumstances that were favorable to the effort. She submitted therefore, falling a little back by the side of Deerslayer, giving the Indian the front of the platform to himself. Chingachgook raised the weapon several times, endeavored to steady it by using both hands, changed his attitude, from one that was awkward, to another still more so, and finally drew the trigger with a sort of desperate indifference, without having, in reality, secured any aim at all. The consequence was, that instead of hitting the knot which had been selected for the mark, he missed the ark altogether; the bullet skipping along the water, like a stone that was thrown by hand.

"Well done—Sarpent—well done—" cried Deerslayer laughing, with his noiseless glee, "you've hit the lake, and that's an expl'ite for some men! I know'd it, and as much as said it, here, to Judith; for your short we'pons do'n't belong to red skin gifts. You've hit the lake, and that's better than only hitting the air! Now, stand back and let us see what white gifts can do with a white we'pon. A pistol is'n't a rifle, but colour is colour."

The aim of Deerslayer was both quick and steady, and the report followed almost as soon as the weapon rose. Still the pistol hung fire, as it is termed, and fragments of it flew in a dozen directions, some falling on the roof of the castle, others in the Ark, and one in the water. Judith screamed, and when the two men turned anxiously towards the girl, she was as pale as death, trembling in every limb.

"She's wownded—yes, the poor gal's wownded—Sarpent, though one could'n't foresee it, standing where she did. We'll lead her in to a seat, and we must do the best for her, that our knowledge and skill can afford."

Judith allowed herself to be supported to a seat, swallowed a mouthful of the water that the Delaware offered her in a gourd, and, after a violent fit of trembling, that seemed ready to shake her fine frame to dissolution, she burst into tears.

"The pain must be borne, poor Judith—yes, it must be borne," said Deerslayer, soothingly, "though I am far from wishing you not to weep; for weeping often lightens galish feelin's. Where can she be hurt, Sarpent?—I see no signs of blood, nor any rent of skin, or garments?"

"I am uninjured, Deerslayer—" stammered the girl, through her tears. "It's fright—nothing more, I do assure you, and, God be praised! no one, I find, has been harmed by the accident."

"This is extr'ornary!" exclaimed the unsuspecting and simple minded hunter—"I thought, Judith, you'd been above settlement weaknesses, and that you was a gal not to be frightened by the sound of a bursting we'pon—No—I didn't think you so skeary! *Hetty* might well have been startled; but you've too much judgment and reason to be frightened when the danger's all over. They're pleasant to the eye, chief, and changeful, but very unsartain in their feelin's!"

Shame kept Judith silent. There had been no acting in her agitation, but all had fairly proceeded from sudden and uncontrollable alarm—an alarm that she found almost as inexplicable to herself, as it proved to be to her companions. Wiping away the traces of tears, however, she smiled again, and was soon able to join in the laugh at her own folly.

"And you, Deerslayer," she at length succeeded in saying—"are you, indeed, altogether unhurt? It seems almost miraculous that a pistol should have burst in your hand, and you escape without the loss of a limb, if not of life!"

"Such wonders ar'n't oncommon, at all, among worn out arms. The first rifle they gave me play'd the same trick, and yet I liv'd through it, though not as onharmless as I've got out of this affair. Thomas Hutter is master of one pistol less than he was this morning, but, as it happened in trying to sarve him, there's no ground of complaint. Now, draw near, and let us look farther into the inside of the chist."

Judith, by this time, had so far gotten the better of her agitation as to resume her seat, and the examination went on. The next article that offered was enveloped in cloth, and on opening it, it proved to be one of the mathematical instruments that were then in use among seamen, possessing the usual ornaments and fastenings in brass. Deerslayer and Chingachgook expressed their admiration and surprise at the appearance of the unknown instrument, which was bright and glittering, having apparently been well cared for.

"This goes beyond the surveyors, Judith!" Deerslayer exclaimed, after turning the instrument several times in his hands. "I've seen all their tools often, and wicked and heartless enough are they, for they never come into the forest but to lead the way to waste and destruction; but none of them have as designing a look as this! I fear me, after all, that Thomas Hutter has journeyed into the wilderness with no fair intentions towards its happiness. Did you ever see any of the cravings of a surveyor about your father, gal?"

"He is no surveyor, Deerslayer, nor does he know the use of that instrument, though he seems to own it. Do you suppose that Thomas Hutter ever wore that coat? It is as much too large for him, as this instrument is beyond his learning."

"That's it—that must be it, Sarpent, and the old fellow, by some onknown means, has fallen heir to another man's goods! They say he has been a mariner, and no doubt this chist, and all it holds—ha! What have we here?—This far out does the brass and black wood of the tool!"

Deerslayer had opened a small bag, from which he was taking, one by one, the pieces of a set of chess-men. They were of ivory, much larger than common, and exquisitely wrought. Each piece represented the character, or thing after which it is named; the knights being mounted, the castles stood on elephants, and even the pawns possessed the heads and busts of men. The set was not complete, and a few fractures betrayed bad usage; but all that was left had been carefully put away and preserved. Even Judith expressed wonder, as these novel objects were placed before her eyes, and Chingachgook fairly forgot his Indian dignity in admiration and delight. The latter took up each piece, and examined it with never tiring satisfaction, pointing out to the girl, the more ingenious and striking portions of the workmanship. But the elephants gave him the greatest pleasure. The "Hugh's!" that he uttered, as he passed his fingers over their trunks, and ears, and tails, were very distinct, nor did he fail to note the pawns, which were armed as archers. This exhibition lasted several minutes, during which time Judith and the Indian had all the rapture to themselves. Deerslayer sate silent, thoughtful, and even gloomy, though his eyes followed each movement of the two principal actors, noting every new peculiarity about the pieces as they were held up to view. Not an exclamation of pleasure, nor a word of condemnation passed his lips. At length his companions observed his silence, and, then, for the first time since the chess men had been discovered, did he speak.

"Judith," he asked earnestly, but with a concern that amounted almost to tenderness of manner, "did your parents ever talk to you of religion?"

The girl coloured, and the flashes of crimson that passed over her beautiful countenance were like the wayward tints of a Neapolitan sky in November. Deerslayer had given her so strong a taste for truth, however, that she did not waver in her answer, replying simply and with sincerity.

"My *mother* did often," she said, "my father *never*. I thought it made my mother sorrowful to speak of our prayers and duties, but my father has never opened his mouth on such matters, before or since her death."

"That I can believe—that I can believe. He has no God—no such God as it becomes a man of white skin to worship, or even a red-skin. Them things are idols!"

Judith started, and for a moment she seemed seriously hurt. Then she reflected, and in the end she laughed. "And you think, Deerslayer, that these ivory toys are my father's Gods? I have heard of idols, and know what they are."

"Them are idols!" repeated the other, positively. "Why should your father keep 'em, if he does'n't worship 'em."

"Would he keep his gods in a bag, and locked up in a chest? No—no—Deerslayer; my poor father carries his God with him, wherever he goes, and that is in his own cravings. These things may really be idols—I think they are myself, from what I have heard and read of idolatry, but they have come from some distant country, and like all the other articles, have fallen into Thomas Hutter's hands, when he was a sailor."

"I'm glad of it—I am downright glad to hear it, Judith, for I do not think I could have mustered the resolution to strive to help a white idolater out of his difficulties! The old man is of my colour and nation and I wish to sarve him, but as one who denied all his gifts, in the way of religion, it would have come hard to do so. That animal seems to give you great satisfaction, Sarpent, though it's an idolatrous beast at the best."

"It is an elephant," interrupted Judith. "I've often seen pictures of such animals, at the garrisons, and mother had a book in which there was a printed account of the creature. Father burnt that with all the other books, for he said Mother loved reading too well. This was not long before mother died, and I've sometimes thought that the loss hastened her end."

This was said equally without levity and without any very deep feeling. It was said without levity, for Judith was saddened by her recollections, and yet she had been too much accustomed to live for self, and for the indulgence of her own vanities, to feel her mother's wrongs very keenly. It required extraordinary circumstances to awaken a proper sense of her situation, and to stimulate the better feelings of this beautiful, but misguided girl, and those circumstances had not yet occurred in her brief existence.

"Elephant, or no elephant, t'is an idol," returned the hunter, "and not fit to remain in christian keeping."

"Good for Iroquois!" said Chingachgook, parting with one of the castles with reluctance, as his friend took it from him to replace it in the bag—"Elephon buy whole tribe—Buy Delaware, almost!"

"Ay, that it would, as any one who comperhends red-skin natur' must know," answered Deerslayer, "but the man that passes false money, Sarpent, is as bad as he who makes it. Did you ever know a just Injin that would'n't scorn to sell a 'coon skin, for the true marten, or to pass off a mink for a beaver. I know that a few of these idols, perhaps *one* of them elephants, would go far towards buying Thomas Hutter's liberty, but it goes ag'in conscience to pass such counterfeit money. Perhaps no Injin tribe, hereaway, is downright idolators but there's some that come so near it, that white gifts ought to be particular about encouraging them in their mistake."

"If idolatry is a *gift*, Deerslayer, and *gifts* are what you seem to think them, idolatry in such people can hardly be a sin," said Judith with more smartness than discrimination.

"God grants no such gifts to any of his creatur's, Judith," returned the hunter, seriously. "*He* must be adored, under some name or other, and not creatur's of brass or ivory. It matters not whether the Father of All is called God, or Manitou, Deity or Great Spirit, he is none the less our common maker and master; nor does it count for much whether the souls of the just go to Paradise, or Happy Hunting Grounds, since He may send each his own way, as suits his own pleasure and wisdom; but it curdles my blood, when I find human mortals so bound up in darkness and consait, as to fashion the 'arth, or wood, or bones, things made by their own hands, into motionless, senseless iffigies, and then fall down afore them, and worship 'em as a Deity!"

"After all, Deerslayer, these pieces of ivory may not be idols, at all. I remember, now, to have seen one of the officers, at the garrison, with a set of fox and geese made in some such a design as these, and here is something hard, wrapped in cloth, that may belong to your idols."

Deerslayer took the bundle the girl gave him, and unrolling it, he found the board within. Like the pieces it was large, rich, and inlaid with ebony and ivory. Putting the whole in conjunction, the hunter, though not without many misgivings, slowly came over to Judith's opinion, and finally admitted that the fancied idols must be merely the curiously carved men of some unknown game. Judith had the tact to use her victory with great moderation, nor did she once, even in the most indirect manner, allude to the ludicrous mistake of her companion.

This discovery of the uses of the extraordinary-looking little images, settled the affair of the proposed ransom. It was agreed generally, and all understood the weaknesses and tastes of Indians, that nothing could be more likely to tempt the cupidity of the Iroquois, than the elephants, in particular. Luckily the whole of the castles were among the pieces, and these four tower-bearing animals it was finally determined should be the ransom offered. The remainder of the men, and, indeed, all the rest of the articles in the chest, were to be kept out of view, and to be resorted to only as a last appeal. As soon as these preliminaries were settled, every thing but those intended for the bribe was carefully replaced in the chest, all the covers were 'tucked in', as they had been found, and it was quite possible, could Hutter have been put in possession of the castle again, that he might have passed the remainder of his days in it, without even suspecting the invasion that had been made on the privacy of the chest. The rent pistol would have been the most likely to reveal the secret, but this was placed by the side of its fellow, and all were pressed down as before, some half a dozen packages in the bottom of the chest not having been opened at all. When this was done, the lid was lowered, the padlocks replaced, and the key turned. The latter was then replaced in the pocket from which it had been taken.

More than an hour was consumed in settling the course proper to be pursued, and in returning every thing to its place. The pauses to converse were frequent, and Judith, who experienced a lively pleasure in the open, undisguised admiration, with which Deerslayer's honest eyes gazed at her handsome face, found the means to prolong the interview, with a dexterity that seems to be innate in female coquetry. Deerslayer, indeed, appeared to be the first who was conscious of the time that had been thus wasted, and to call the attention of his companions to the necessity of doing something towards putting the plan of ransoming into execution. Chingachgook had remained in Hutter's bed room, where the elephants were laid, to feast his eyes with the images of animals so wonderful, and so novel. Perhaps an instinct told him that his presence would not be as acceptable to his companions, as this holding himself aloof, for Judith had not much reserve in the manifestations of her preferences, and the Delaware had not got so far as one betrothed without acquiring some knowledge of the symptoms of the master passion.

"Well, Judith," said Deerslayer, rising, after the interview had lasted much longer than even he himself suspected, "t'is pleasant convarsing with you, and settling all these matters, but duty calls us another way. All this time, Hurry and your father, not to say Hetty—"

The word was cut short in the speaker's mouth, for, at that critical moment, a light step was heard on the platform, or 'court-yard', a human figure darkened the door-way, and the person last mentioned stood before him. The low exclamation that escaped Deerslayer and the slight scream of Judith were hardly uttered, when an Indian youth, between the ages of fifteen and seventeen, stood beside her. These two entrances had been made with moccasined feet, and consequently almost without noise, but, unexpected and stealthy as they were, they had not the effect to disturb Deerslayer's self possession. His first measure was to speak rapidly in Delaware to his friend, cautioning him to keep out of sight, while he stood on his guard; the second was to step to the door to ascertain the extent of the danger. No one else, however, had come, and a simple contrivance, in the shape of a raft, that lay floating at the side of the Ark, at once explained the means that had been used in bringing Hetty off. Two dead and dry, and consequently buoyant, logs of pine were bound together with pins and withes and a little platform of riven chestnut had been rudely placed on their surfaces. Here Hetty had been seated, on a billet of wood, while the young Iroquois had rowed the primitive, and slow-moving, but perfectly safe, craft, from the shore. As soon as Deerslayer had taken a close survey of this raft, and satisfied himself nothing else was near, he shook his head, and muttered in his soliloquizing way—

"This comes of prying into another man's chist! Had we been watchful, and keen eyed, such a surprise could never have happened, and, getting this much from a boy, teaches us what we may expect when the old warriors set themselves fairly about their sarcumventions. It opens the way, howsever, to a treaty for the ransom, and I will hear what Hetty has to say."

Judith, as soon as her surprise and alarm had a little abated, discovered a proper share of affectionate joy, at the return of her sister. She folded her to her bosom, and kissed her, as had been her wont in the days of their childhood and innocence. Hetty herself was less affected, for to her there was no surprise, and her nerves were sustained by the purity and holiness of her purpose. At her sister's request she took a seat, and entered into an account of her adventures since they had parted. Her tale commenced just as Deerslayer returned, and he also became an attentive listener, while the young Iroquois stood near the door, seemingly as indifferent to what was passing, as one of its posts.

The narrative of the girl was sufficiently clear, until she reached the time where we left her in the camp, after the interview with the chiefs, and, at the moment when Hist quitted her, in the abrupt manner already related. The sequel of the story may be told in her own language.

"When I read the texts to the chiefs, Judith, you could not have seen that they made any changes on their minds," she said, "but if seed is planted, it *will* grow. God planted the seeds of all these trees—"

"Ay that did he—that did he—" muttered Deerslayer—"and a goodly harvest has followed."

"God planted the seeds of all these trees," continued Hetty, after a moment's pause, "and you see to what a height and shade they have grown! So it is with the bible. You may read a verse this year, and forget it, and it will come back to you a year hence, when you least expect to remember it."

"And did you find any thing of this, among the savages, poor Hetty."

"Yes, Judith, and sooner, and more fully than I had even hoped. I did not stay long with father and Hurry, but went to get my breakfast with Hist. As soon as we had done, the chiefs came to us, and *then* we found the fruits of the seed that had been planted. They said what I had read from the good book was right—it *must* be right—it sounded *right*; like a sweet bird singing in their ears; and they told me to come back and say as much to the great warrior who had slain one of their braves; and to tell it to you, and to say how happy they should be to come to church here, in the castle, or to come out in the sun, and hear me read more of the sacred volume—and to tell you that they wish you would lend them some canoes that they can bring father and Hurry, and their women to the castle, that we might all sit on the platform there, and listen to the singing of the Pale Face Manitou. There, Judith; did you ever know of any thing that so plainly shows the power of the bible, as *that*!"

"If it were true 't would be a miracle, indeed, Hetty. But all this is no more than Indian cunning and Indian treachery, striving to get the better of us by management, when they find it is not to be done by force."

"Do you doubt the bible, sister, that you judge the savages so harshly!"

"I do not doubt the bible, poor Hetty, but I much doubt an Indian and an Iroquois. What do you say to this visit, Deerslayer?"

"First let me talk a little with Hetty," returned the party appealed to; "Was the raft made a'ter you had got your breakfast, gal, and did you walk from the camp to the shore opposite to us, here?"

"Oh! no, Deerslayer. The raft was ready made and in the water—could that have been by a miracle, Judith!"

"Yes—yes—an Indian miracle—" rejoined the hunter—"They're expart enough in them sort of miracles. And you found the raft ready made to your hands, and in the water, and in waiting like for its cargo?"

"It was all as you say. The raft was near the camp, and the Indians put me on it, and had ropes of bark, and they dragged me to the place opposite to the castle, and then they told that young man to row me off, here."

"And the woods are full of the vagabonds, waiting to know what is to be the upshot of the miracle. We comperhend this affair, now, Judith, but I'll first get rid of this young Canada blood sucker, and then we'll settle our own course. Do you and Hetty leave us together, first bringing me the elephants, which the Sarpent is admiring, for 'twill never do to let this loping deer be alone a minute, or he'll borrow a canoe without asking."

Judith did as desired, first bringing the pieces, and retiring with her sister into their own room. Deerslayer had acquired some knowledge of most of the Indian dialects of that region, and he knew enough of the Iroquois to hold a dialogue in the language. Beckoning to the lad, therefore, he caused him to take a seat on the chest, when he placed two of the castles suddenly before him. Up to that moment, this youthful savage had not expressed a single intelligible emotion, or fancy. There were many things, in and about the place, that were novelties to him, but he had maintained his self-command with philosophical composure. It is true, Deerslayer had detected his dark eye scanning the defences and the arms, but the scrutiny had been made with such an air of innocence, in such a gaping, indolent, boyish manner, that no one but a man who had himself been taught in a similar school, would have even suspected his object. The instant, however, the eyes of the savage fell upon the wrought ivory, and the images of the wonderful, unknown, beasts, surprise and admiration got the mastery of him. The manner in which the natives of the South Sea Islands first beheld the toys of civilized life has been often described, but the reader is not to confound it with the manner of an American Indian, under similar circumstances. In this particular case, the young Iroquois or Huron, permitted an exclamation of rapture to escape him, and then he checked himself like one who had been guilty of an indecorum. After this, his eyes ceased to wander, but became riveted on the elephants, one of which, after a short hesitation, he even presumed to handle. Deerslayer did not interrupt him for quite ten minutes, knowing that the lad was taking such note of the curiosities, as would enable him to give the most minute and accurate description of their appearance, to his seniors, on his return. When he thought sufficient time had been allowed to produce the desired effect, the hunter laid a finger on the naked knee of the youth and drew his attention to himself.

"Listen—" he said—"I want to talk with my young friend from the Canadas. Let him forget that wonder for a minute."

"Where t'other pale brother?" demanded the boy, looking up and letting the idea that had been most prominent in his mind, previously to the introduction of the chess men, escape him involuntarily.

"He sleeps,—or if he is'n't fairly asleep, he is in the room, where the men do sleep—" returned Deerslayer. "How did my young friend know there was another?"

"See him from the shore. Iroquois have got long eyes—see beyond the clouds—see the bottom of the Great Spring!"

"Well, the Iroquois are welcome. Two pale faces are prisoners in the camp of your fathers, boy."

The lad nodded, treating the circumstance with great apparent indifference; though a moment after, he laughed as if exulting in the superior address of his own tribe.

"Can you tell me, boy, what your chiefs intend to do with these captives, or have'n't they yet made up their minds?"

The lad looked, a moment, at the hunter with a little surprise. Then he coolly put the end of his fore finger on his own head, just above the left ear, and passed it round his crown with an accuracy and readiness that showed how well he had been drilled in the peculiar art of his race.

"When—" demanded Deerslayer, whose gorge rose at this cool demonstration of indifference to human life. "And why not take them to your wigwams?"

"Road too long, and full of pale faces. Wigwam full, and scalps sell high. Small scalp, much gold."

"Well that explains it—yes, that does explain it. There's no need of being any plainer. Now, you know, lad, that the oldest of your prisoners, is the father of these two young women, and the other is the suitor of one of them. The gals nat'rally wish to save the scalps of such fri'nds, and they will give them two ivory creatur's, as ransom. One for each scalp. Go back and tell this to your chiefs, and bring me the answer before the sun sets."

The boy entered zealously into this project, and with a sincerity that left no doubt of his executing his commission with intelligence and promptitude. For a moment he forgot his love of honor, and all his clannish hostility to the British and their Indians, in his wish to have such a treasure in his tribe, and Deerslayer was satisfied with the impression he had made. It is true the lad proposed to carry one of the elephants with him, as a specimen of the other, but to this his brother negotiator was too sagacious to consent; well knowing that it might never reach its destination if confided to such hands. This little difficulty was soon arranged, and the boy prepared to depart. As he stood on the platform, ready to step aboard of the raft, he hesitated, and turned short with a proposal to borrow a canoe, as the means most likely to shorten the negotiations. Deerslayer quietly refused the request, and, after lingering a little longer, the boy rowed slowly away from the castle, taking the direction of a thicket on the shore, that lay less than half a mile distant. Deerslayer seated himself on a stool, and watched the progress of the ambassador, sometimes closely scanning the whole line of shore, as far as eye could reach, and then placing an elbow on a knee, he remained a long time with his chin resting on the hand.

During the interview between Deerslayer and the lad, a different scene took place in the adjoining room. Hetty had enquired for the Delaware, and being told why and where he remained concealed, she joined him. The reception which Chingachgook gave his visiter was respectful and gentle. He understood her character, and, no doubt, his disposition to be kind to such a being was increased by the hope of learning some tidings of his betrothed. As soon as the girl entered, she took a seat, and invited the Indian to place himself near her; then she continued silent, as if she thought it decorous for him to question her, before she consented to speak on the subject she had on her mind. But, as Chingachgook did not understand this feeling, he remained respectfully attentive to any thing she might be pleased to tell him.

"You are Chingachgook,—the Great Serpent of the Delawares, ar'n't you?" the girl at length commenced, in her own simple way losing her self-command in the desire to proceed, but anxious first to make sure of the individual.

"Chingachgook," returned the Delaware with grave dignity. "That say Great Sarpent, in Deerslayer tongue."

"Well, that is my tongue. Deerslayer, and father, and Judith, and I, and poor Hurry Harry—do you know Henry March, Great Serpent? I know you do'n't, however, or *he* would have spoken of *you*, too."

"Did any tongue name Chingachgook, Drooping-Lily"? for so the chief had named poor Hetty. "Was his name sung by a little bird among Iroquois?"

Hetty did not answer at first, but, with that indescribable feeling that awakens sympathy and intelligence among the youthful and unpractised of her sex, she hung her head, and the blood suffused her cheek ere she found her tongue. It would have exceeded her stock of intelligence to explain this embarrassment, but, though poor Hetty could not reason, on every emergency, she could always feel. The colour slowly receded from her cheeks, and the girl looked up archly at the Indian, smiling with the innocence of a child, mingled with the interest of a woman.

"My sister, the Drooping Lily hear such bird!" Chingachgook added, and this with a gentleness of tone and manner that would have astonished those who sometimes heard the discordant cries that often came from the same throat; these transitions from the harsh and guttural, to the soft and melodious not being infrequent in ordinary Indian dialogues. "My sister's ears were open—has she lost her tongue?"

"You *are* Chingachgook—you *must* be; for there is no other red man here, and she thought Chingachgook would come."

"Chin—gach—gook—" pronouncing the name slowly, and dwelling on each syllable—"Great Sarpent, Yengeese* tongue."

"Chin—gach—gook—" repeated Hetty, in the same deliberate manner. "Yes, so Hist called it, and you *must* be the chief."

*It is singular there should be any question concerning the origin of the well known *sobriquet* of "Yankees." Nearly all the old writers, who speak of the Indians first known to the Colonists, make them pronounce the word "English," as "Yengeese." Even at this day, it is a provincialism of New England to say "*En*glish" instead of "*In*glish" and there is a close conformity of sound between "*En*glish" and "Yengeese," more especially if the latter word, as was probably the case, be pronounced short. The transition from "Yengeese," thus pronounced, to "Yankees" is quite easy. If the former is pronounced "Yangis" it is almost identical with "Yankees," and Indian words have seldom been spelt as they are pronounced. Thus the scene of this tale is spelt "Ot*se*go," and is properly pronounced "Ot*sa*go." The liquids of the Indians would easily convert "En" into "Yen."

"Wah—ta!—Wah—" added the Delaware.

"Wah—ta!—Wah, or Hist—oh!—Hist. I think Hist prettier than Wah, and so I call her Hist."

"Wah! very sweet in Delaware ears!"

"You make it sound differently from me. But, never mind; I *did* hear the bird you speak of sing, Great Serpent."

"Will my sister say words of song. What she sing most—how she look—often she laugh?"

"She sang Chin—gach—gook oftener than any thing else; and she laughed heartily, when I told how the Iroquois waded into the water after us, and could'n't catch us. I hope these logs have'n't ears, Serpent!"

"No fear logs; fear sister next room—No fear Iroquois; Deerslayer stuff his eyes and ears, with strange beast."

"I understand you, Serpent, and I understood Hist. Sometimes I think I'm not half as feeble minded as they say I am. Now, do you look up at the roof, and I'll tell you all. But you frighten me you look so eager, when I speak of Hist."

The Indian controlled his looks, and affected to comply with the simple request of the girl.

"Hist told me to say, in a very low voice, that you must'n't trust the Iroquois in any thing. They are more artful than any Indians she knows. Then she says that there is a large bright star that comes over the hill, about an hour after dark,—(Hist had pointed out the planet Jupiter, without knowing it)—and just as that star comes in sight, she will be on the point, where I landed last night, and that you must come for her, in a canoe."

"Good—Chingachgook understand well enough, now; but he understand better if my sister sing him, ag'in."

Hetty repeated her words, more fully explaining what star was meant, and mentioning the part of the point where he was to venture ashore. She now proceeded in her own unsophisticated way to relate her intercourse with the Indian maid, and to repeat several of her expressions and opinions that gave great delight to the heart of her betrothed. She particularly renewed her injunctions to be on their guard against treachery, a warning that was scarcely needed, however, as addressed to men as wary as those to whom it was sent. She also explained, with sufficient clearness, for on all such subjects the mind of the girl seldom failed her, the present state of the enemy, and the movements they had made since morning. Hist had been on the raft with her, until it quitted the shore, and was now somewhere in the woods, opposite to the castle, and did not intend to return to the camp, until night approached; when she hoped to be able to slip away from her companions, as they followed the shore on their way home, and conceal herself on the point. No one appeared to suspect the presence of Chingachgook, though it was necessarily known that an Indian had entered the Ark, the previous night, and it was suspected that he had since appeared in, and about the castle, in the dress of a pale-face. Still some little doubt existed on the latter point, for, as this was the season when white men might be expected to arrive, there was some fear that the garrison of the castle was increasing by these ordinary means. All this had Hist communicated to Hetty while the Indians were dragging them along shore, the distance, which exceeded six miles, affording abundance of time.

"Hist do'n't know, herself, whether they suspect her, or not; or, whether they suspect *you*, but she hopes neither is the case. And now, Serpent, since I have told you so much from your betrothed," continued Hetty, unconsciously taking one of the Indian's hands, and playing with the fingers, as a child is often seen to play with those of a parent, "you must let me tell you something from myself. When you marry Hist, you must be kind to her, and smile on her, as you do now on me, and not look cross as some of the chiefs do at their squaws. Will you promise this?"

"Always good to Wah!—too tender to twist hard; else she break."

"Yes, and smile, too; you do'n't know how much a girl craves smiles from them she loves. Father scarce smiled on me once, while I was with him—and, Hurry—yes—Hurry talked loud and laughed, but I do'n't think *he* smiled once either. You know the difference between a smile and a laugh?"

"Laugh, best. Hear Wah! laugh, think bird sing!"

"I know that; her laugh *is* pleasant, but *you* must smile. And then, Serpent, you must'n't make her carry burthens and hoe corn, as so many Indians do; but treat her more as the pale faces treat their wives."

"Wah-ta!-Wah no pale face—got red skin; red heart, red feelin's. All red; no pale. *Must* carry papoose."

"Every woman is willing to carry her child," said Hetty smiling, "and there is no harm in *that*. But you must love Hist, and be gentle, and good to her; for she is gentle and good herself."

Chingachgook gravely bowed, and then he seemed to think this part of the subject might be dismissed. Before there was time for Hetty to resume her communications, the voice of Deerslayer was heard calling on his friend, in the outer room. At this summons the Serpent arose to obey, and Hetty joined her sister.

Chapter XIV

> " 'A stranger animal,' cries one,
> 'Sure never liv'd beneath the sun;
> A lizard's body lean and long,
> A fish's head, a serpent's tongue,
> Its foot, with triple claw disjoined;
> And what a length of tail behind!' "
> James Merrick, "The Chameleon," ll. 21–26.

THE FIRST ACT of the Delaware, on rejoining his friend, was to proceed gravely to disencumber himself of his civilized attire, and to stand forth an Indian warrior again. The protest of Deerslayer was met by his communicating the fact that the presence of an Indian in the hut, was known to the Iroquois, and that maintaining the disguise would be more likely to direct suspicions to his real object, than if he came out openly as a member of a hostile tribe. When the latter understood the truth, and was told that he had been deceived in supposing the chief had succeeded in entering the Ark undiscovered, he cheerfully consented to the change, since further attempt at concealment was useless. A gentler feeling than the one avowed, however, lay at the bottom of the Indian's desire to appear as a son of the forest. He had been told that Hist was on the opposite shore, and nature so far triumphed over all distinctions of habit, and tribes and people, as to reduce this young savage warrior to the level of a feeling which would have been found in the most refined inhabitant of a town, under similar circumstances. There was a mild satisfaction in believing that she he loved could see him, and as he walked out on the platform in his scanty, native attire, an Apollo of the wilderness, a hundred of the tender fancies that fleet through lovers' brains, beset his imagination and softened his heart.

All this was lost on Deerslayer, who was no great adept in the mysteries of Cupid, but whose mind was far more occupied with the concerns that forced themselves on his attention, than with any of the truant fancies of love. He soon recalled his companion, therefore, to a sense of their actual condition, by summoning him to a sort of council of war, in which they were to settle their future course. In the dialogue that followed, the parties mutually made each other acquainted with what had passed in their several interviews. Chingachgook was told the history of the treaty about the ransom, and Deerslayer heard the whole of Hetty's communications. The latter listened with generous interest to his friend's hopes, and promised cheerfully all the assistance he could lend.

"Tis our main ar'n'd, Sarpent, as you know, this battling for the castle and old Hutter's darters, coming in as a sort of accident. Yes—yes—I'll be act*yve* in helping little Hist, who's not only one of the best and handsomest maidens of the tribe, but the *very* best and handsomest. I've always encouraged you, chief, in that liking, and it's proper, too, that a great and ancient race like your'n shouldn't come to an end. If a woman of red skin and red gifts could get to be near enough to me to wish her for a wife, I'd s'arch for just such another, but that can *never* be; no, that can *never* be. I'm glad Hetty has met with Hist, howsever, for though the first is a little short of wit and understanding, the last has enough for both. Yes, Sarpent—" laughing heartily—"put 'em together, and two smarter gals is'n't to be found in all York Colony!"

"I will go to the Iroquois camp," returned the Delaware, gravely. "No one knows Chingachgook but Wah!, and a treaty for lives and scalps should be made by a chief! Give me the strange beasts, and let me take a canoe."

Deerslayer dropped his head, and played with the end of a fish-pole in the water, as he sate dangling his legs over the edge of the platform, like a man who was lost in thought, by the sudden occurrence of a novel idea. Instead of directly answering the proposal of his friend, he began to soliloquize, a circumstance however that in no manner rendered his words more true, as he was remarkable for saying what he thought, whether the remarks were addressed to himself, or to any one else.

"Yes—yes—" he said—"this must be what they call love! I've heard say that it sometimes upsets reason altogether, leaving a young man as helpless, as to calculation and caution, as a brute beast. To think that the Sarpent should be so lost to reason, and cunning, and wisdom! We must, sartainly, manage to get Hist off, and have 'em married as soon as we get back to the tribe, or this war will be of no more use to the chief, than a hunt a little oncommon extr'ornary. Yes—yes—he'll never be the man he was, till this matter is off his mind, and he comes to his senses like all the rest of mankind. Sarpent, you can't be in airnest, and therefore I shall say but little to your offer. But you're a chief, and will soon be sent out on the war-path at head of the parties, and I'll just ask if you'd think of putting your forces into the inimy's hands, afore the battle is fou't?"

"Wah!" ejaculated the Indian.

"Ay—Wah!—I know well enough it's Wah!, and altogether Wah!—Ra'ally, Sarpent, I'm consarned and mortified about you! I never heard so weak an idee come from a chief, and he, too, one that's already got a name for being wise, young and inexper'enced as he is. Canoe you sha'n't have, so long as the v'ice of fri'ndship and warning can count for any thing."

"My pale-face friend is right. A cloud came over the face of Chingachgook, and weakness got into his mind, while his eyes were dim. My brother has a good memory for good deeds, and a weak memory for bad. He will forget."

"Yes, that's easy enough. Say no more about it chief, but if another of them clouds blow near you, do your endivours to get out of its way. Clouds are bad enough in the weather, but when they come to the reason, it gets to be serious. Now, sit down by me here, and let us calculate our movements a little, for we shall soon either have a truce and a peace, or we shall come to an ac*tyve*, and bloody war. You see the vagabonds can make logs sarve their turn, as well as the best raftsmen on the rivers, and it would be no great expl'ite for them to invade us in a body. I've been thinking of the wisdom of putting all old Tom's stores into the Ark, of barring and locking up the Castle, and of taking to the Ark, altogether. That is moveable, and by keeping the sail up, and shifting places, we might worry through a great many nights, without them Canada wolves finding a way into our sheep fold!"

Chingachgook listened to this plan, with approbation. Did the negotiation fail, there was now little hope that the night would pass without an assault, and the enemy had sagacity enough to understand that, in carrying the castle, they would probably become masters of all it contained, the offered ransom included, and still retain the advantages they had hitherto gained. Some precaution of the sort appeared to be absolutely necessary, for now the numbers of the Iroquois were known, a night attack could scarcely be successfully met. It would be impossible to prevent the enemy from getting possession of the canoes and the Ark, and the latter itself would be a hold in which the assailants would be as effectually protected against bullets as were those in the building. For a few minutes, both the men thought of sinking the Ark, in the shallow water, of bringing the canoes into the house, and of depending altogether on the castle for protection. But reflection satisfied them that, in the end, this expedient would fail. It was so easy to collect logs on the shore, and to construct a raft of almost any size, that it was certain the Iroquois, now they had turned their attention to such means, would resort to them seriously, so long as there was the certainty of success by perseverance. After deliberating maturely, and placing all the considerations fairly before them, the two young beginners in the art of forest warfare, settled down into the opinion that the Ark offered the only available means of security. This decision was no sooner come to, than it was communicated to Judith. The girl had no serious objection to make, and all four set about the measures necessary to carrying the plan into execution.

The reader will readily understand that Floating Tom's worldly goods were of no great amount. A couple of beds, some wearing apparel, the arms and ammunition, a few cooking utensils, with the mysterious and but half examined chest formed the principal items. These were all soon removed, the Ark having been hauled on the eastern side of the building, so that the transfer could be made without being seen from the shore. It was thought unnecessary to disturb the heavier and coarser articles of furniture, as they were not required in the Ark, and were of but little value in themselves. As great caution was necessary in removing the different objects, most of which were passed out of a window with a view to conceal what was going on, it required two or three hours before all could be effected. By the expiration of that time, the raft made its appearance, moving from the shore. Deerslayer immediately had recourse to the glass, by the aid of which he perceived that two warriors were on it, though they appeared to be unarmed. The progress of the raft was slow, a circumstance that formed one of the great advantages that would be possessed by the scow, in any future collision between them, the movements of the latter being comparatively swift and light. As there was time to make the dispositions for the reception of the two dangerous visiters, every thing was prepared for them, long before they had got near enough to be hailed. The Serpent, and the girls retired into the building, where the former stood near the door, well provided with rifles, while Judith watched the proceedings without through a loop. As for Deerslayer, he had brought a stool to the edge of the platform, at the point towards which the raft was advancing, and taken his seat with his rifle leaning carelessly between his legs.

As the raft drew nearer, every means possessed by the party in the castle was resorted to, in order to ascertain if their visiters had any fire arms. Neither Deerslayer nor Chingachgook could discover any, but Judith, unwilling to trust to simple eye-sight, thrust the glass through the loop, and directed it towards the hemlock boughs that lay between the two logs of the raft, forming a sort of flooring, as well as a seat for the use of the rowers. When the heavy moving craft was within fifty feet of him, Deerslayer hailed the Hurons, directing them to cease rowing, it not being his intention to permit them to land. Compliance, of course, was necessary, and the two grim-looking warriors instantly quitted their seats, though the raft continued slowly to approach, until it had driven in much nearer to the platform.

"Are ye chiefs?" demanded Deerslayer with dignity—"Are ye chiefs?—Or have the Mingos sent me warriors without names, on such an ar'n'd? If so, the sooner ye go back, the sooner them will be likely to come that a warrior can talk with."

"Hugh!" exclaimed the elder of the two on the raft, rolling his glowing eyes over the different objects that were visible in and about the Castle, with a keenness that showed how little escaped him. "My brother is very proud, but Rivenoak (we use the literal translation of the term, writing as we do in English) is a name to make a Delaware turn pale."

"That's true, or it's a lie, Rivenoak, as it may be; but I am not likely to turn pale, seeing that I was born pale. What's your ar'n'd, and why do you come among light bark canoes, on logs that are not even dug out?"

"The Iroquois are not ducks, to walk on water! Let the pale faces give them a canoe, and they'll come in a canoe."

"That's more rational, than likely to come to pass. We have but four canoes, and being four persons that's only one for each of us. We thank you for the offer, howsever, though we ask leave not to accept it. You are welcome, Iroquois, on your logs."

"Thanks—My young pale face warrior—he has got a name—how do the chiefs call him?"

Deerslayer hesitated a moment, and a gleam of pride and human weakness came over him. He smiled, muttered between his teeth, and then looking up proudly, he said—

"Mingo, like all who are young and actyve, I've been known by different names, at different times. One of your warriors whose spirit started for the Happy Grounds of your people, as lately as yesterday morning, thought I desarved to be known by the name of Hawkeye, and this because my sight happened to be quicker than his own, when it got to be life or death, atween us."

Chingachgook, who was attentively listening to all that passed, heard and understood this proof of passing weakness in his friend, and on a future occasion he questioned him more closely concerning the transaction on the point, where Deerslayer had first taken human life. When he had got the whole truth, he did not fail to communicate it to the tribe, from which time the young hunter was universally known among the Delawares, by an appellation so honorably earned. As this, however, was a period posterior to all the incidents of this tale, we shall continue to call the young hunter by the name under which he has been first introduced to the reader. Nor was the Iroquois less struck with the vaunt of the white man. He knew of the death of his comrade, and had no difficulty in understanding the allusion, the intercourse between the conqueror and his victim on that occasion, having been seen by several savages on the shore of the lake, who had been stationed at different points just within the margin of bushes to watch the drifting canoes, and who had not time to reach the scene of action, ere the victor had retired. The effect on this rude being of the forest, was an exclamation of surprise; then such a smile of courtesy, and wave of the hand, succeeded, as would have done credit to Asiatic diplomacy. The two Iroquois spoke to each other, in low tones, and both drew near the end of the raft that was closest to the platform.

"My brother, Hawkeye, has sent a message to the Hurons," resumed Rivenoak, "and it has made their hearts very glad. They hear he has images of beasts with two tails! Will he show them to his friends."

"Inimies would be truer," returned Deerslayer, "but sound is n't sense, and does little harm. Here is one of the images; I toss it to you under faith of treaties. If it's not returned, the rifle will settle the p'int atween us."

The Iroquois seemed to acquiesce in the conditions, and Deerslayer arose and prepared to toss one of the elephants to the raft, both parties using all the precaution that was necessary to prevent its loss. As practice renders men expert in such things, the little piece of ivory was soon successfully transferred from one hand to the other, and then followed another scene on the raft, in which astonishment and delight got the mastery of Indian stoicism. These two grim old warriors manifested even more feeling, as they examined the curiously wrought chess-man, than had been betrayed by the boy; for, in the case of the latter, recent schooling had interposed its influence; while the men, like all who are sustained by well established characters, were not ashamed to let some of their emotions be discovered. For a few minutes they apparently lost the consciousness of their situation, in the intense scrutiny they bestowed on a material so fine, work so highly wrought, and an animal so extraordinary. The lip of the moose is, perhaps, the nearest approach to the trunk of the elephant that is to be found in the American forest, but this resemblance was far from being sufficiently striking to bring the new creature within the range of their habits and ideas, and the more they studied the image, the greater was their astonishment. Nor did these children of the forest mistake the structure on the back of the elephant for a part of the animal. They were familiar with horses and oxen, and had seen towers in the Canadas, and found nothing surprising in creatures of burthen. Still, by a very natural association, they supposed the carving meant to represent, that the animal they saw, was of a strength sufficient to carry a fort on its back; a circumstance that, in no degree, lessened their wonder.

"Has my pale face brother any more such beasts?" at last the senior of the Iroquois asked, in a sort of petitioning manner.

"There's more where them came from, Mingo," was the answer; "one is enough, howsever, to buy off fifty scalps."

"One of my prisoners is a great warrior—tall as a pine—strong as the moose—active as a deer—fierce as the panther! Some day he'll be a great chief, and lead the army of King George!"

"Tut—tut—Mingo; Hurry Harry is Hurry Harry, and you'll never make more than a corporal of him, if you do that. He's tall enough, of a sartainty; but that's of no use, as he only hits his head ag'in the branches as he goes through the forest. He's strong too, but a strong body is'n't a strong head, and the king's generals are not chosen for their sinews; he's swift, if you will, but a rifle bullet is swifter; and as for f'erceness, it's no great ricommend to a soldier; they that think they feel the stoutest, often givin' out at the pinch. No—no—you'll niver make Hurry's scalp pass for more than a good head of curly hair, and a rattle pate beneath it!"

"My old prisoner very wise—king of the lake—great warrior, wise counsellor!"

"Well, there's them that might gainsay all this, too, Mingo. A very wise man would'n't be apt to be taken in so foolish a manner as befel Master Hutter, and if he gives good counsel, he must have listened to very bad, in that affair. There's only one king of this lake, and he's a long way off, and is'n't likely ever to see it. Floating Tom is some such king of this region, as the wolf that prowls through the woods, is king of the forest. A beast with two tails is well worth two such scalps!"

"But my brother has another beast?—He will give two—" holding up as many fingers—"for old father?"

"Floating Tom is no father of mine, but he'll fare none the

worse for that. As for giving two beasts for his scalp, and each beast with two tails, it is quite beyond reason. Think yourself well off, Mingo, if you make a much worse trade."

By this time the self-command of Rivenoak had got the better of his wonder, and he began to fall back on his usual habits of cunning, in order to drive the best bargain he could. It would be useless to relate more than the substance of the desultory dialogue that followed, in which the Indian manifested no little management, in endeavoring to recover the ground lost under the influence of surprise. He even affected to doubt whether any original for the image of the beast existed, and asserted that the oldest Indian had never heard a tradition of any such animal. Little did either of them imagine, at the time, that long ere a century elapsed, the progress of civilization would bring even much more extraordinary and rare animals into that region, as curiosities to be gazed at by the curious, and that the particular beast, about which the disputants contended, would be seen laving its sides, and swimming in the very sheet of water, on which they had met.* As is not uncommon on such occasions, one of the parties got a little warm, in the course of the discussion, for Deerslayer met all the arguments and prevarication of his subtle opponent, with his own cool directness of manner, and unmoved love of truth. What an elephant was he knew little better than the savage, but he perfectly understood that the carved pieces of ivory must have some such value in the eyes of an Iroquois, as a bag of gold, or a package of beaver skins would in those of a trader. Under the circumstances, therefore, he felt it to be prudent not to concede too much at first, since there existed a nearly unconquerable obstacle to making the transfers, even after the contracting parties had actually agreed upon the terms. Keeping this difficulty in view, he held the extra chess-men in reserve, as a means of smoothing any difficulty in the moment of need.

At length the savage pretended that further negotiation was useless, since he could not be so unjust to his tribe as to part with the honor and emoluments of two excellent, full grown,

*The Otsego is a favorite place for the caravan keepers to let their elephants bathe. The writer has seen two at a time, since the publication of this book, swimming about in company.

male, scalps for a consideration so trifling as a toy like that he had seen, and he prepared to take his departure. Both parties now felt as men are wont to feel, when a bargain that each is anxious to conclude, is on the eve of being broken off, in consequence of too much pertinacity in the way of management. The effect of the disappointment was very different, however, on the respective individuals. Deerslayer was mortified, and filled with regret, for he not only felt for the prisoners, but he also felt deeply for the two girls. The conclusion of the treaty, therefore, left him melancholy and full of regret. With the savage, his defeat produced the desire of revenge. In a moment of excitement, he had loudly announced his intention to say no more, and he felt equally enraged with himself and with his cool opponent, that he had permitted a pale face to manifest more indifference and self-command than an Indian chief. When he began to urge his raft away from the platform, his countenance lowered, and his eye glowed, even while he affected a smile of amity and a gesture of courtesy, at parting.

It took some little time to overcome the *vis inertiæ* of the logs, and while this was being done by the silent Indian, Rivenoak stalked over the hemlock boughs that lay between the logs, in sullen ferocity, eyeing keenly the while, the hut, the platform, and the person of his late disputant. Once he spoke in low, quick tones to his companion, and he stirred the boughs with his feet, like an animal that is restive. At that moment, the watchfulness of Deerslayer had a little abated, for he sat musing on the means of renewing the negotiation without giving too much advantage to the other side. It was perhaps fortunate for him that the keen and bright eyes of Judith were as vigilant as ever. At the instant when the young man was least on his guard, and his enemy was the most on the alert, she called out, in a warning voice, to the former, most opportunely, giving the alarm.

"Be on your guard, Deerslayer," the girl cried—"I see rifles with the glass, beneath the hemlock brush, and the Iroquois is loosening them with his feet!"

It would seem that the enemy had carried their artifices so far as to employ an agent who understood English. The previous dialogue had taken place in his own language, but it was evident, by the sudden manner in which his feet ceased their treacherous occupation, and in which the countenance of Rivenoak changed from sullen ferocity to a smile of courtesy, that the call of the girl was understood. Signing to his companion to cease his efforts to set the logs in motion, he advanced to the end of the raft which was nearest to the platform, and spoke.

"Why should Rivenoak and his brother leave any cloud between them," he said. "They are both wise, both brave, and both generous; they ought to part friends. One beast shall be the price of one prisoner."

"And, Mingo," answered the other, delighted to renew the negotiations on almost any terms, and determined to clinch the bargain if possible by a little extra liberality, "you'll see that a pale face knows how to pay a full price, when he trades with an open heart, and an open hand. Keep the beast that you had forgotten to give back to me, as you was about to start, and which I forgot to ask for, on account of consarn at parting in anger. Show it to your chiefs. When you bring us our fri'nds, two more shall be added to it—and—" hesitating a moment in distrust of the expediency of so great a concession; then, deciding in its favor—"and, if we see them afore the sun sets, we may find a fourth to make up an even number."

This settled the matter. Every gleam of discontent vanished from the dark countenance of the Iroquois, and he smiled as graciously, if not as sweetly, as Judith Hutter, herself. The piece already in his possession was again examined, and an ejaculation of pleasure, showed how much he was pleased with this unexpected termination of the affair. In point of fact, both he and Deerslayer had momentarily forgotten what had become of the subject of their discussion, in the warmth of their feelings, but such had not been the case with Rivenoak's companion. This man retained the piece, and had fully made up his mind, were it claimed under such circumstances as to render its return necessary, to drop it in the lake, trusting to his being able to find it, again, at some future day. This desperate expedient, however, was no longer necessary, and after repeating the terms of agreement, and professing to understand them, the two Indians finally took their departure, moving slowly towards the shore.

"Can any faith be put in such wretches?" asked Judith, when she and Hetty had come out on the platform, and were standing at the side of Deerslayer, watching the dull movement of the logs. "Will they not rather keep the toy they have, and send us off some bloody proofs of their getting the better of us in cunning, by way of boasting? I've heard of acts as bad as this."

"No doubt—Judith; no manner of doubt, if it was'n't for Indian natur'. But I'm no judge of a red skin, if that two tail'd beast does'n't set the whole tribe in some such stir, as a stick raises in a beehive! Now, there's the Sarpent; a man with narves like flint, and no more cur'osity in every day consarns, than is befitting prudence; why he was so overcome with the sight of the creatur', carved as it is in bone, that I felt ashamed for him! That's just their gifts, howsever, and one can't well quarrel with a man for his gifts, when they are lawful. Chingachgook will soon get over his weakness, and remember that he's a chief, and that he comes of a great stock, and has a renowned name to support and uphold; but, as for yonder scamps, there'll be no peace among 'em, until they think they've got possession of every thing of the natur' of that bit of carved bone, that's to be found among Thomas Hutter's stores!"

"They only know of the elephants, and can have no hopes about the other things."

"That's true, Judith; still, covetousness is a craving feelin'! They'll say, if the pale faces have these cur'ous beasts with two tails, who knows but they've got some with three, or, for that matter, with four! That's what the schoolmasters call nat'ral arithmetic, and t'will be sartain to beset the feelin's of savages. They'll never be easy, till the truth is known."

"Do you think, Deerslayer," inquired Hetty, in her simple and innocent manner, "that the Iroquois wo'n't let father and Hurry go?—I read to them several of the very best verses in the whole bible, and you see what they have done, already."

The hunter, as he always did, listened kindly and even affectionately to Hetty's remarks; then he mused a moment in silence. There was something like a flush on his cheek, as he answered, after quite a minute had passed.

"I do'n't know whether a white man ought to be ashamed,

or not, to own he can't read, but such is my case, Judith. You are skilful, I find, in all such matters, while I have only studied the hand of God, as it is seen in the hills and the valleys, the mountain-tops, the streams, the forests and the springs. Much l'arning may be got in this way, as well as out of books; and, yet, I sometimes think it is a white man's gift to read! When I hear from the mouths of the Moravians, the words of which Hetty speaks, they raise a longing in my mind, and I then think I *will* know how to read 'em myself; but the game in summer, and the traditions, and lessons in war, and other matters, have always kept me behind hand."

"Shall I teach you, Deerslayer?" asked Hetty, earnestly. "I'm weak-minded, they say, but I can read as well as Judith. It might save your life to know how to read the bible to the savages, and it will certainly save your soul; for mother told me *that*, again and again!"

"Thankee, Hetty—yes, thankee, with all my heart. These are like to be too stirring times for much idleness, but, after it's peace, and I come to see you ag'in on this lake, then I'll give myself up to it, as if 'twas pleasure and profit, in a single business. Perhaps I ought to be ashamed, Judith, that 'tis so; but truth is truth. As for these Iroquois, tis'n't very likely they'll forget a beast with two tails, on account of a varse or two from the bible. I rather expect they'll give up the prisoners, and trust to some sarcumvention, or other, to get 'em back, ag'in, with us and all in the castle and the Ark, in the bargain. Howsever, we must humour the vagabonds, first to get your father and Hurry out of their hands, and next to keep the peace atween us, until such time as the Sarpent there, can make out to get off his betrothed wife. If there's any sudden outbreakin' of anger and ferocity, the Indians will send off all their women and children to the camp, at once, whereas, by keeping 'em calm and trustful, we may manage to meet Hist, at the spot she has mentioned. Rather than have the bargain fall through, now, I'd throw in half a dozen of them effigy bow-and-arrow men, such as we've in plenty in the chist."

Judith cheerfully assented, for she would have resigned even the flowered brocade, rather than not redeem her father and please Deerslayer.

The prospects of success were now so encouraging, as to raise the spirits of all in the castle, though a due watchfulness, of the movements of the enemy was maintained. Hour passed after hour, notwithstanding, and the sun had once more begun to fall towards the summits of the western hills, and yet no signs were seen of the return of the raft. By dint of sweeping the shore with the glass, Deerslayer at length discovered a place in the dense and dark woods, where he entertained no doubt, the Iroquois were assembled in considerable numbers. It was near the thicket whence the raft had issued, and a little rill that trickled into the lake, announced the vicinity of a spring. Here, then, the savages were probably holding their consultation, and the decision was to be made that went to settle the question of life or death for the prisoners. There was one ground for hope in spite of the delay, however, that Deerslayer did not fail to place before his anxious companions. It was far more probable that the Indians had left their prisoners in the camp, than that they had encumbered themselves by causing them to follow through the woods, a party that was out on a merely temporary excursion. If such was the fact, it required considerable time to send a messenger the necessary distance, and to bring the two white men to the spot where they were to embark. Encouraged by these reflections, a new stock of patience was gathered, and the declension of the sun was viewed with less alarm.

The result justified Deerslayer's conjecture. Not long before the sun had finally disappeared, the two logs were seen coming out of the thicket, again, and, as it drew near, Judith announced that her father and Hurry, both of them pinioned, lay on the bushes in the centre. As before, the two Indians were rowing. The latter seemed to be conscious that the lateness of the hour demanded unusual exertions, and contrary to the habits of their people, who are ever averse to toil, they labored hard at the rude substitutes for oars. In consequence of this diligence, the raft occupied its old station, in about half the time that had been taken in the previous visits.

Even after the conditions were so well understood, and matters had proceeded so far, the actual transfer of the prisoners was not a duty to be executed without difficulty. The Iroquois were compelled to place great reliance on the good faith of their foes, though it was reluctantly given; and was yielded to necessity rather than to confidence. As soon as Hutter and Hurry should be released, the party in the castle numbered two to one, as opposed to those on the raft, and escape by flight was out of the question, as the former had three bark canoes, to say nothing of the defences of the house and the Ark. All this was understood by both parties, and it is probable the arrangement never could have been completed, had not the honest countenance and manner of Deerslayer wrought their usual effect on Rivenoak.

"My brother knows I put faith in *him*—" said the latter, as he advanced with Hutter, whose legs had been released to enable the old man to ascend to the platform. "One scalp—one more beast."

"Stop—Mingo—" interrupted the hunter—"keep your prisoner a moment. I have to go and seek the means of payment."

This excuse, however, though true in part, was principally a fetch. Deerslayer left the platform, and entering the house, he directed Judith to collect all the arms, and to conceal them in her own room. He then spoke earnestly to the Delaware, who stood on guard as before, near the entrance of the building, put the three remaining castles in his pocket, and returned.

"You are welcome back, to your old abode, Master Hutter," said Deerslayer, as he helped the other up on the platform, slily passing into the hand of Rivenoak, at the same time, another of the castles. "You'll find your darters right glad to see you, and here's Hetty come herself, to say as much in her own behalf."

Here the hunter stopped speaking and broke out into a hearty fit of his silent and peculiar laughter. Hurry's legs were just released, and he had been placed on his feet. So tightly had the ligatures been drawn, that the use of his limbs was not immediately recovered, and the young giant presented, in good sooth, a very helpless and a somewhat ludicrous picture. It was this unusual spectacle, particularly the bewildered countenance, that excited the merriment of Deerslayer.

"You look like a girdled pine in a clearin', Hurry Harry, that is rocking in a gale," said Deerslayer, checking his unseasonable mirth, more from delicacy to the others, than from any respect to the liberated captive. "I'm glad, howsever, to see that you have'n't had your hair dressed by any of the Iroquois barbers, in your late visit to their camp."

"Harkee, Deerslayer," returned the other a little fiercely, "it will be prudent for you to deal less in mirth, and more in friendship, on this occasion. Act like a christian, for once, and not like a laughing gal, in a country school, when the master's back is turned, and just tell me whether there's any feet, or not, at the end of these legs of mine. I think I can see them, but as for feelin' they might as well be down on the banks of the Mohawk, as be where they seem to be."

"You've come off whole, Hurry, and that's not a little," answered the other, secretly passing to the Indian the remainder of the stipulated ransom, and making an earnest sign, at the same moment, for him to commence his retreat. "You've come off whole, feet and all, and are only a little numb, from a tight fit of the withes. Natur'll soon set the blood in motion, and then you may begin to dance, to celebrate what I call a most wonderful and onexpected deliverance from a den of wolves."

Deerslayer released the arms of his friends, as each landed, and the two were now stamping and limping about on the platform, growling and uttering denunciations, as they endeavored to help the returning circulation. They had been tethered too long, however, to regain the use of their limbs in a moment, and the Indians being quite as diligent on their return, as on their advance, the raft was fully a hundred yards from the castle, when Hurry, turning accidentally in that direction, discovered how fast it was getting beyond the reach of his vengeance. By this time, he could move with tolerable facility, though still numb and awkward. Without considering his own situation, however, he seized the rifle that leaned against the shoulder of Deerslayer, and attempted to cock and present it. The young hunter was too quick for him. Seizing the piece he wrenched it from the hands of the giant, not, however, until it had gone off in the struggle, when pointed directly upward. It is probable that Deerslayer could have prevailed in such a contest, on account of the condition of Hurry's limbs, but the instant the gun went off, the latter yielded, and stumped towards the house, raising his legs at each step, quite a foot from the ground, from an uncertainty of the actual position of his feet. But he had been anticipated by Judith. The whole stock of Hutter's arms, which had been left in the building, as a resource in the event of a sudden outbreaking of hostilities, had been removed, and were already secreted, agreeably to Deerslayer's directions. In consequence of this precaution, no means offered by which March could put his designs in execution.

Disappointed in his vengeance, Hurry seated himself, and like Hutter, for half an hour, he was too much occupied in endeavoring to restore the circulation, and in regaining the use of his limbs, to indulge in any other reflections. By the end of this time the raft had disappeared, and night was beginning to throw her shadows once more over the whole silvan scene. Before darkness had completely set in, and while the girls were preparing the evening meal, Deerslayer related to Hutter an outline of events that had taken place, and gave him a history of the means he had adopted for the security of his children and property.

Chapter XV

"As long as Edwarde rules thys lande,
Ne quiet you wylle know;
Your sonnes and husbandes shall be slayne,
And brookes with blowde shall flowe.

You leave youre goode and lawfulle kynge
Whenne ynne aduersitye
Like mee, untoe the true cause stycke,
And for the true cause dye."
Chatterton, "Bristowe Tragedie," ll. 357–64.

THE CALM OF EVENING was again in singular contrast to, while its gathering gloom was in as singular unison with, the passions of men. The sun was set, and the rays of the retiring luminary ceased to gild the edges of the few clouds that had sufficient openings to admit the passage of its fading light. The canopy overhead was heavy and dense, promising another night of darkness, but the surface of the lake was scarcely disturbed by a ripple. There was a little air, though it scarce deserved to be termed wind. Still, being damp and heavy it had a certain force. The party in the castle were as gloomy and silent as the scene. The two ransomed prisoners felt humbled and dishonored, but their humility partook of the rancor of revenge. They were far more disposed to remember the indignity with which they had been treated during the last few hours of their captivity, than to feel grateful for the previous indulgence. Then that keensighted monitor conscience, by reminding them of the retributive justice of all they had endured, goaded them, rather to turn the tables on their enemies, than to accuse themselves. As for the others, they were thoughtful equally from regret and joy. Deerslayer and Judith felt most of the former sensation, though from very different causes, while Hetty for the moment was perfectly happy. The Delaware had also lively pictures of felicity in the prospect of so soon regaining his betrothed. Under such circumstances, and in this mood, all were taking the evening meal.

"Old Tom!" cried Hurry, bursting into a fit of boisterous laughter, "you look'd amazin'ly like a tethered bear, as you was stretched on them hemlock boughs, and I only wonder you did n't growl, more. Well, it's over, and syth's and lamentations won't mend the matter! There's the blackguard Rivenoak, he that brought us off, has an oncommon scalp, and I'd give as much for it myself, as the colony. Yes, I feel as rich as the governor, in these matters now, and will lay down with 'em, doubloon for doubloon. Judith, darling, did you mourn for me much, when I was in the hands of the Philipsteins."

The last were a family of German descent on the Mohawk, to whom Hurry had a great antipathy, and whom he had confounded with the enemies of Judea.

"Our tears have raised the lake, Harry March, as you might have seen by the shore!" returned Judith, with a feigned levity she was far from feeling. "That Hetty and I should have grieved for father was to be expected, but we fairly rained tears for you."

"We *were* sorry for poor Hurry, as well as for father, Judith!" put in her innocent and unconscious sister.

"True, girl, true; but we feel sorrow for every body that's in trouble, you know," returned the other in a quick, admonitory manner and a low tone. "Nevertheless, we are glad to see you, Master March, and out of the hands of the Philipsteins, too."

"Yes, they're a bad set, and so is the other brood of 'em, down on the river. It's a wonderment to me, how you got us off, Deerslayer, and I forgive you the interference that prevented my doin' justice on that vagabond, for this small sarvice. Let us into the secret, that we may do you the same good turn, at need. Was it by lying, or by coaxing?"

"By neither, Hurry, but by buying. We paid a ransom for you both, and that, too, at a price so high, you had well be on your guard ag'in another cap*ty*vement, lest our stock of goods should'n't hold out."

"A ransom!—Old Tom has paid the fiddler, then, for nothing of mine would have bought off the hair, much less the skin. I didn't think men as keen set as them vagabonds, would let a fellow up so easy, when they had him fairly at a close hug, and floored. But money is money and somehow it's unnat'ral hard to withstand. Injin or White man, 'tis pretty much the same. It must be owned, Judith, there's a considerable of human natur' in mankind ginirally, arter all!"

Hutter now rose, and signing to Deerslayer, he led him to an inner room, where, in answer to his questions he first learned the price that had been paid for his release. The old man expressed neither resentment nor surprise at the inroad that had been made on his chest, though he did manifest some curiosity to know how far the investigation of its contents had been carried. He also inquired where the key had been found. The habitual frankness of Deerslayer prevented any prevarication, and the conference soon terminated by the return of the two to the outer room, or that which served for the double purpose of parlor and kitchen.

"I wonder if it's peace or war, between us and the savages!" exclaimed Hurry, just as Deerslayer, who had paused for a single instant, listened attentively, and was passing through the outer door without stopping. "This givin' up captives has a friendly look, and when men have traded together, on a fair and honorable footing, they ought to part fri'nds, for that occasion, at least. Come back, Deerslayer, and let us have your judgment, for I'm beginnin' to think more of you, since your late behaviour, than I used to do."

"There's an answer to your question, Hurry, since you're in such haste to come, ag'in, to blows."

As Deerslayer spoke, he threw on the table, on which the other was reclining with one elbow, a sort of miniature faggot, composed of a dozen sticks bound tightly together with a deerskin thong. March seized it eagerly, and holding it close to a blazing knot of pine that lay on the hearth, and which gave out all the light there was in the room, ascertained that the ends of the several sticks had been dipped in blood.

"If this is'n't plain English," said the reckless frontier man, "it's plain Injin! Here's what they call a dicliration of war, down at York, Judith. How did you come by this defiance, Deerslayer?"

"Fairly enough. It lay, not a minut' since, in what you call Floatin' Tom's door yard."

"How came it there? It never fell from the clouds, Judith, as little toads sometimes do, and then it don't rain. You must prove where it come from, Deerslayer, or we shall suspect some design to skear them that would have lost their wits long ago, if fear could drive 'em away."

Deerslayer had approached a window, and cast a glance out of it, on the dark aspect of the lake. As if satisfied with what he beheld, he drew near Hurry, and took the bundle of sticks into his own hand, examining it attentively.

"Yes, this is an Indian dicliration of war, sure enough," he said, "and it's a proof how little you're suited to be on the path it has travelled, Harry March, that it has got here, and you never the wiser, as to the means. The savages may have left the scalp on your head, but they must have taken off the *ears*; else you'd have heard the stirring of the water made by the lad as he come off, ag'in, on his two logs. His ar'n'd was to throw these sticks at our door, as much as to say, we've struck the war post, since the trade, and the next thing will be to strike *you*."

"The prowling wolves! But hand me that rifle Judith, and I'll send an answer back to the vagabonds, through their messenger."

"Not while I stand by, Master March," coolly put in Deerslayer, motioning for the other to forbear. "Faith is faith, whether given to a redskin, or to a christian. The lad lighted a knot, and came off fairly, under its blaze, to give us this warning, and no man, here, should harm him, while empl'yed on such an ar'n'd. There's no use in words, for the lad is too cunning to leave the knot burning, now his business is done, and the night is already too dark for a rifle to have any sartainty."

"That may be true enough, as to a gun, but there's virtue still in a canoe," answered Hurry passing towards the door, with enormous strides, carrying a rifle in his hands. "The being doesn't live that shall stop me from following, and bringing back that riptyle's scalp. The more on 'em, that you crush in the egg, the fewer they'll be to dart at you in the woods!"

Judith trembled like the aspen, she scarce knew why herself, though there was the prospect of a scene of violence; for, if Hurry was fierce and overbearing in the consciousness of his vast strength, Deerslayer had about him the calm determination that promises greater perseverance, and a resolution more likely to effect its object. It was the stern, resolute eye of the latter, rather than the noisy vehemence of the first, that excited her apprehensions. Hurry soon reached the spot where the canoe was fastened, but not before Deerslayer had spoken in a quick, earnest voice to the Serpent in Delaware. The latter had been the first, in truth, to hear the sounds of the oars, and he had gone upon the platform, in jealous watchfulness. The light satisfied him that a message was coming, and when the boy cast his bundle of sticks at his feet, it neither moved his anger, nor induced surprise. He merely stood at watch, rifle in hand, to make certain that no treachery lay behind the defiance. As Deerslayer now called to him, he stepped into the canoe, and quick as thought removed the paddles. Hurry was furious when he found that he was deprived of the means of proceeding. He first approached the Indian with loud menaces, and even Deerslayer stood aghast at the probable consequences. March shook his sledge-hammer fists, and flourished his arms, as he drew near the Indian, and all expected he would attempt to fell the Delaware to the earth; one of them, at least, was well aware that such an experiment would be followed by immediate bloodshed. But even Hurry was awed by the stern composure of the chief, and he, too, knew that such a man was not to be outraged with impunity; he, therefore, turned to vent his rage on Deerslayer, where he foresaw no consequences so terrible. What might have been the result of this second demonstration if completed, is unknown, since it was never made.

"Hurry," said a gentle, soothing voice at his elbow—"it's wicked to be so angry, and God will not overlook it. The Iroquois treated you well, and they did n't take *your* scalp, though you and father wanted to take *theirs*."

The influence of mildness on passion is well known. Hetty, too, had earned a sort of consideration, that had never before been enjoyed by her, through the self-devotion and decision of her recent conduct. Perhaps her established mental imbecility, by removing all distrust of a wish to control, aided her influence. Let the cause be as questionable as it might, the effect was sufficiently certain. Instead of throttling his old fellow traveller, Hurry turned to the girl, and poured out a portion of his discontent, if none of his anger, on her attentive ears.

"'Tis too bad, Hetty!" he exclaimed; "as bad as a county gaol, or a lack of beaver, to get a creatur' into your very trap, and then to see it get off. As much as six first quality skins, in valie, has paddled off on them clumsy logs, when twenty strokes of a well turned paddle, would overtake 'em. I say in valie, for as to the boy in the way of natur', he is only a boy, and is worth neither more nor less than one. Deerslayer, you've been ontrue to your fri'nds in letting such a chance slip through my fingers, as well as your own."

The answer was given quietly, but with a voice as steady as a fearless nature, and the consciousness of rectitude could make it.

"I should have been ontrue to the right, had I done otherwise—" returned the Deerslayer, steadily, "and neither you, nor any other man has authority to demand that much of me. The lad came on a lawful business, and the meanest red-skin that roams the woods, would be ashamed of not respecting his ar'n'd. But he's now far beyond your reach, Master March, and there's little use in talking, like a couple of women, of what can no longer be helped."

So saying, Deerslayer turned away, like one resolved to waste no more words on the subject, while Hutter pulled Hurry by the sleeve, and led him into the Ark. There they sat long, in private conference. In the mean time, the Indian and his friend, had their secret consultation, for, though it wanted some three or four hours to the rising of the star, the former could not abstain from canvassing his scheme, and from opening his heart to the other. Judith, too, yielded to her softer feelings, and listened to the whole of Hetty's artless narrative of what occurred after she had landed. The woods had few terrors for either of these girls, educated as they had been, and accustomed as they were to look out daily at their rich expanse, or to wander beneath their dark shades, but the elder sister felt that she would have hesitated about thus venturing alone into an Iroquois camp. Concerning Hist, Hetty was not very communicative. She spoke of her kindness, and gentleness and of the meeting in the forest, but the secret of Chingachgook was guarded with a shrewdness and fidelity, that many a sharper witted girl might have failed to display.

At length the several conferences were broken up by the reappearance of Hutter on the platform. Here he assembled the whole party, and communicated as much of his intentions as he deemed expedient. Of the arrangement made by Deerslayer, to abandon the castle during the night, and to take refuge in the Ark he entirely approved. It struck him, as it had the others, as the only effectual means of escaping destruction. Now that the savages had turned their attention to the construction of rafts, no doubt could exist of their at least making an attempt to carry the building, and the message of the bloody sticks sufficiently showed their confidence in their own success. In short, the old man viewed the night as critical, and he called on all to get ready as soon as possible, in order to abandon the dwelling, temporarily, at least, if not forever.

These communications made, every thing proceeded promptly and with intelligence. The castle was secured in the manner already described, the canoes were withdrawn from the dock, and fastened to the Ark, by the side of the other, the few necessaries that had been left in the house, were transferred to the cabin, the fire was extinguished, and all embarked.

The vicinity of the hills, with their drapery of pines, had the effect to render nights that were obscure, darker than common, on the lake. As usual, however, a belt of comparative light was stretched through the centre of the sheet, while it was within the shadows of the mountains that the gloom rested most heavily on the water. The island, or castle, stood in this belt of comparative light, but still the night was so dark, as to cover the departure of the Ark. At the distance of an observer on the shore, her movements could not be seen at all, more particularly as a back ground of dark hillside filled up the perspective of every view that was taken diagonally, or directly across the water. The prevalent winds on the lakes of that region are west, but owing to the avenues formed by the mountains, it is frequently impossible to tell the true direction of the currents, as they often vary, within short distances, and brief differences of time. This is truer in light, fluctuating puffs of air, than in steady breezes, though the squalls of even the latter, are familiarly known to be uncertain and baffling in all mountainous regions and narrow waters. On the present occasion, Hutter himself, as he shoved the Ark from her berth, at the side of the platform, was at a loss to pronounce which way the wind blew. In common, this difficulty was solved by the clouds, which, floating high above the hill tops, as a matter of course obeyed the true currents, but now the whole vault of heaven seemed a mass of gloomy wall. Not an opening of any sort was visible, and Chingachgook was already trembling lest the non-appearance of the star might prevent his betrothed from being punctual to her appointment. Under these circumstances, Hutter hoisted his sail, seemingly with the sole intention of getting away from the castle, as it might be dangerous to remain much longer in its vicinity. The air soon filled the cloth; and when the scow was got under command, and the sail was properly trimmed, it was found that the direction was southerly, inclining towards the eastern shore. No better course offering for the purposes of the party, the singular craft was suffered to skim the surface of the water in this direction for more than an hour, when a change in the currents of the air drove them over towards the camp.

Deerslayer watched all the movements of Hutter and Hurry, with jealous attention. At first, he did not know whether to ascribe the course they held to accident, or to design, but he now began to suspect the latter. Familiar as Hutter was with the lake, it was easy to deceive one who had little practice on the water, and let his intentions be what they might, it was evident, ere two hours had elapsed, that the Ark had got over sufficient space to be within a hundred rods of the shore, directly abreast of the known position of the camp. For a considerable time previously to reaching this point, Hurry, who had some knowledge of the Algonquin languages, had been in close conference with the Indian, and the result was now announced by the latter to Deerslayer, who had been a cold, not to say distrusted, looker-on of all that passed.

"My old father, and my young brother, the Big Pine,—" for so the Delaware had named March, "want to see Huron scalps at their belts," said Chingachgook to his friend. "There is room for some on the girdle of the Serpent, and his people will look for them when he goes back to his village. Their eyes must not be left long in a fog, but they must see what they look for. I know that my brother has a white hand; he will not strike even the dead. He will wait for us; when we come back he will not hide his face from shame for his friend. The Great Serpent of the Mohicans, must be worthy to go on the warpath with Hawkeye."

"Ay—ay—Sarpent, I see how it is; that name's to stick, and in time, I shall get to be known by it," returned Deerslayer. "Well, if such honors will come, the humblest of us all must be willing to abide by 'em. As for you looking for scalps, it belongs to your gifts, and I see no harm in it. Be marciful, Sarpent, howsever; be marciful, I beseech of you. It surely can do no harm to a red skin's honor to show a little marcy. As for the old man, the father of two young women who might ripen better feelin's in his heart, and Harry March, here, who, pine as he is, might better bear the fruit of a more christianized tree, as for *them* two, I leave 'em in the hands of the white man's god. Was'n't it for the bloody sticks no man should go ag'in the Mingos this night, seein' that it would dishonor our faith and characters; but them that crave blood, can't complain if blood is shed at their call. Still, Sarpent, you can be *marciful.* Do'n't begin your career with the wails of women, and the cries of children. Bear yourself so that Hist will smile, and not weep, when she meets you. Go, then; and the Manitou presarve you."

"My brother will stay here with the scow. Wah! will soon be standing on the shore waiting, and Chingachgook must hasten."

The Indian then joined his two coadventurers, and first lowering the sail, they all three entered a canoe, and left the side of the Ark. Neither Hutter nor March spoke to Deerslayer concerning their object, or the probable length of their absence. All this had been confided to the Indian, who had acquitted himself of the trust with characteristic brevity. As soon as the canoe was out of sight, and that occurred ere the paddles had given a dozen strokes, Deerslayer made the best dispositions he could to keep the Ark as nearly stationary as possible, and then he sat down in the end of the scow, to chew the cud of his own bitter reflections. It was not long, however, before he was joined by Judith, who now sought every occasion to be near him, managing her attack on his affections, with the address that was suggested by native coquetry aided by no little practice, but which received much of its most dangerous power, from the touch of feeling that threw around her manner, voice, accents, thoughts and acts the indescribable witchery of natural tenderness. Leaving the young hunter exposed to these dangerous assailants, it has become our more immediate business to follow the party in the canoe, to the shore.

The controlling influence that led Hutter and Hurry to repeat their experiment against the camp was precisely that which had induced the first attempt, a little heightened, perhaps, by the desire of revenge. But, neither of these two rude beings, so ruthless in all things that touched the rights and interests of the red man, though possessing veins of human feeling on other matters, was much actuated by any other desire than a heartless longing for profit. Hurry had felt angered at his sufferings, when first liberated, it is true, but that emotion soon disappeared in the habitual love of gold, which he sought with the reckless avidity of a needy spendthrift, rather than with the ceaseless longings of a miser. In short, the motive that urged them both so soon to go against the Hurons was an habitual contempt of their enemy, acting on the unceasing cupidity of prodigality. The additional chances of success, however, had their place in the formation of the second enterprise. It was known that a large portion of the warriors—perhaps all—were encamped for the night, abreast of the castle, and it was hoped that the scalps of helpless victims would be the consequence. To confess the truth, Hutter in particular—he who had just left two daughters behind him—expected to find few besides women and children in the camp. This fact had been but slightly alluded to, in his communications with Hurry, and with Chingachgook it had been kept entirely out of view. If the Indian thought of it at all, it was known only to himself.

Hutter steered the canoe; Hurry had manfully taken his post in the bows, and Chingachgook stood in the centre. We say stood, for all three were so skilled in the management of that species of frail bark, as to be able to keep erect positions, in the midst of the darkness. The approach to the shore was made with great caution, and the landing effected in safety. The three now prepared their arms, and began their tiger-like approach upon the camp. The Indian was on the lead, his two companions treading in his footsteps, with a stealthy cautiousness of manner, that rendered their progress almost literally noiseless. Occasionally a dried twig snapped under the heavy weight of the gigantic Hurry, or the blundering clumsiness of the old man, but, had the Indian walked on air his step could not have seemed lighter. The great object was first to discover the position of the fire, which was known to be the centre of the whole encampment. At length the keen eye of Chingachgook caught a glimpse of this important guide. It was glimmering at a distance, among the trunks of trees. There was no blaze, but merely a single smouldering brand, as suited the hour; the savages usually retiring and rising with the revolutions of the sun.

As soon as a view was obtained of this beacon, the progress of the adventurers became swifter and more certain. In a few minutes they got to the edge of the circle of little huts. Here they stopped to survey their ground, and to concert their movements. The darkness was so deep, as to render it difficult to distinguish any thing but the glowing brand, the trunks of the nearest trees, and the endless canopy of leaves that veiled the clouded heaven. It was ascertained, however, that a hut was quite near, and Chingachgook attempted to reconnoitre its interior. The manner in which the Indian approached the place that was supposed to contain enemies, resembled the wily advances of the cat on the bird. As he drew near he stooped to his hands and knees, for the entrance was so low as to require this attitude, even as a convenience. Before trusting his head inside, however, he listened long to catch the breathings of sleepers. No sound was audible, and this human Serpent thrust his head in at the door, or opening, as another serpent would have peered in at the nest. Nothing rewarded the hazardous experiment, for, after feeling cautiously with a hand, the place was found to be empty.

The Delaware proceeded in the same guarded manner to

one or two more of the huts, finding all in the same situation. He then returned to his companions, and informed them, that the Hurons had deserted their camp. A little further enquiry corroborated this fact, and it only remained to return to the canoe. The different manner in which the adventurers bore the disappointment, is worthy of a passing remark. The chief, who had landed solely with the hope of acquiring renown, stood stationary, leaning against a tree waiting the pleasure of his companions. He was mortified, and a little surprised it is true, but he bore all with dignity, falling back for support on the sweeter expectations that still lay in reserve for that evening. It was true, he could not now hope to meet his mistress with the proofs of his daring and skill on his person, but he might still hope to meet her; and the warrior, who was zealous in the search, might always hope to be honored. On the other hand, Hutter and Hurry, who had chiefly been instigated by the basest of all human motives, the thirst of gain, could scarce control their feelings. They went prowling among the huts, as if they expected to find some forgotten child, or careless sleeper, and, again and again, did they vent their spite on the insensible huts, several of which were actually torn to pieces, and scattered about the place. Nay, they even quarrelled with each other, and fierce reproaches passed between them. It is possible some serious consequences might have occurred, had not the Delaware interfered to remind them of the danger of being so unguarded, and of the necessity of returning to the Ark. This checked the dispute, and in a few minutes they were paddling sullenly back to the spot where they hoped to find that vessel.

It has been said that Judith took her place at the side of Deerslayer, soon after the adventurers departed. For a short time the girl was silent, and the hunter was ignorant which of the sisters had approached him; but he soon recognised the rich full spirited voice of the elder, as her feelings escaped in words.

"This is a terrible life for women, Deerslayer!" she exclaimed. "Would to Heaven, I could see an end of it!"

"The life is well enough, Judith," was the answer, "being pretty much as it is used, or abused. What would you wish to see in its place?"

"I should be a thousand times happier to live nearer to civilized beings—where there are farms and churches, and houses built as it might be by christian hands; and where my sleep at night would be sweet and tranquil! A dwelling near one of the forts, would be far better than this dreary place where we live!"

"Nay, Judith, I can't agree too lightly in the truth of all this. If forts are good to keep off inimies, they sometimes hold inimies of their own. I do'n't think twould be for your good, or the good of Hetty to live near one, and if I *must* say what I think, I'm afeard you are a little too near, as it is." Deerslayer went on, in his own steady, earnest, manner, for the darkness concealed the tints that coloured the cheeks of the girl almost to the brightness of crimson, while her own great efforts suppressed the sounds of the breathing that nearly choked her—"As for farms, they have their uses, and there's them that like to pass their lives on 'em, but what comfort can a man look for in a clearin', that he can't find in double quantities in the forest? If air, and room, and light are a little craved, the wind-rows, and the streams will furnish 'em, or here are the lakes for such as have bigger longings in that way; but where are you to find your shades, and laughing springs, and leaping brooks, and vinerable trees, a thousand years old, in a clearin'? You do'n't find *them*, but you find their disabled trunks, marking the 'arth like head-stones in a grave yard. It seems to me that the people who live in such places, must be always thinkin' of their own inds, and of univarsal decay; and that, too, not of the decay that is brought about by time and natur', but the decay that follows waste and violence. Then as to churches, they are good, I suppose, else would'n't good men uphold 'em. But they are not altogether necessary. They call 'em the temples of the Lord, but, Judith, the whole 'arth is a temple of the Lord's, to such as have the right minds. Neither forts nor churches make people happier of themselves. Moreover, all is contradiction in the settlements, while all is concord in the woods. Forts and churches almost always go together, and yet they're downright contradictions; churches being for peace, and forts for war. No—no—give me the strong places of the wilderness, which is the trees, and the churches, too, which are arbors raised by the hand of natur'."

"Woman is not made for scenes like these, Deerslayer; scenes of which we shall have no end, as long as this war lasts."

"If you mean women of white colour, I rather think you're not far from the truth, gal; but as for the females of the red men, such visitations are quite in character. Nothing would make Hist, now, the bargained wife of yonder Delaware, happier than to know that he is at this moment prowling around his nat'ral inimies, striving after a scalp."

"Surely, surely, Deerslayer, she cannot be a woman, and not feel concern when she thinks the man she loves is in danger!"

"She does'n't think of the danger, Judith, but of the honor, and when the heart is desperately set on such feelin's, why there is little room to crowd in fear. Hist is a kind, gentle, laughin', pleasant creatur', but she loves honor, as well as any Delaware gal I ever know'd. She's to meet the Sarpent an hour hence, on the p'int where Hetty landed, and no doubt she has her anxiety about it, like any other woman; but she'd be all the happier did she know that her lovyer was at this moment way-laying a Mingo for his scalp."

"If you really believe this, Deerslayer, no wonder you lay so much stress on gifts. Certain am I, that no white girl could feel any thing but misery while she believed her betrothed in danger of his life! Nor do I suppose, even you, unmoved and calm as you ever seem to be, could be at peace, if you believed *your* Hist, in danger."

"That's a different matter—tis altogether a different matter, Judith. Woman is too weak and gentle to be intended to run such risks, and man *must* feel for her. Yes, I rather think that's as much red natur', as it's white. But I have no Hist, nor am I like to have, for I hold it wrong to mix colours, any way except in friendship, and sarvices."

"In that you act and feel as a white man should! As for Hurry Harry, I do think it would be all the same to him, whether his wife were a squaw, or a governor's daughter, provided she was a little comely, and could help to keep his craving stomach full!"

"You do March injustice, Judith; yes, you do. The poor fellow dotes on *you*, and when a man has ra'ally set his heart on such a creatur', it is'n't a Mingo, or even a Delaware gal, that'll be likely to unsettle his mind. You may laugh at such men as Hurry, and I, for we're rough, and unteached in the way of books and other knowledge, but we've our good p'ints, as well as our bad ones. An honest heart is not to be despised, gal, even though it be not varsed in all the niceties that please a female fancy."

"*You*, Deerslayer!—And *do* you—*can* you, for an instant, suppose I place *you*, by the side of Harry March? No—no. I am not as far gone in dulness as that. No one—man or woman, could think of naming your honest heart, manly nature, and simple truth, with the boisterous selfishness, greedy avarice, and overbearing ferocity of Henry March. The very best that can be said of him, is to be found in his name of Hurry Skurry, which if it means no great harm, means no great good. Even my father, following his feelings with the other, as he is doing, at this moment, well knows the difference between you. This I *know*, for he has said as much to me, in plain language."

Judith was a girl of quick sensibilities, and of impetuous feelings, and, being under few of the restraints that curtail the manifestations of maiden emotions, among those who are educated in the habits of civilized life, she sometimes betrayed the latter with a freedom that was so purely natural, as to place it as far above the wiles of coquetry, as it was superior to its heartlessness. She had now even taken one of the hard hands of the hunter, and pressed it between both her own, with a warmth and earnestness that proved how sincere was her language. It was perhaps, fortunate that she was checked by the very excess of her feelings since the same power might have urged her on to avow *all* that her father had said, the old man not having been satisfied with making a comparison favorable to Deerslayer, as between the hunter and Hurry, but having actually, in his blunt rough way, briefly advised his daughter to cast off the latter entirely, and to think of the former as a husband. Judith would not willingly have said this to any other man, but there was so much confidence awakened by the guileless simplicity of Deerslayer, that one of her nature found it a constant temptation to overstep the bounds of habit. She went no farther, however, immediately relinquishing the hand, and falling back on a reserve that was more suited to her sex, and, indeed, to her natural modesty.

"Thankee, Judith, thank'ee, with all my heart," returned the hunter, whose humility prevented him from placing any flattering interpretation on either the conduct, or the language of the girl. "Thankee, as much as if it all was true. Harry's sightly—yes, he's as sightly as the tallest pine of these mountains, and the Sarpent has named him accordingly; howsever, some fancy good looks, and some fancy good conduct, only. Hurry has one advantage, and it depends on himself whether, he'll have the t'other or—Hark! That's your father's voice, gal, and he speaks like a man who's riled, at something."

"God save us from any more of these horrible scenes!" exclaimed Judith, bending her face to her knees, and endeavoring to exclude the discordant sounds, by applying her hands to her ears. "I sometimes wish I had no father!"

This was bitterly said, and the repinings which extorted the words, were bitterly felt. It is impossible to say what might next have escaped her, had not a gentle, low, voice, spoken at her elbow.

"Judith, I ought to have read a chapter to father and Hurry!" said the innocent, but terrified speaker, "and *that* would have kept them from going again on such an errand. Do you call to them, Deerslayer, and tell them I want them, and that it will be good for them both, if they'll return, and hearken to my words."

"Ahs! me—poor Hetty, you little know the cravin's for gold and revenge, if you believe they are so easily turned aside from their longin's! But this is an oncommon business, in more ways than one, Judith! I hear your father and Hurry, growling like bears, and yet no noise comes from the mouth of the young chief. There's an ind of secrecy, and yet his whoop, which ought to ring in the mountains, accordin' to rule, in such sarcumstances, is silent!"

"Justice may have alighted on him, and his death have saved the lives of the innocent!"

"Not it—not it—the Sarpent is not the one to suffer, if *that's* to be the law. Sartainly there has been no onset, and 'tis most likely that the camp's deserted, and the men are coming back disapp'inted. That accounts for the growls of Hurry and the silence of the Sarpent."

Just at this instant a fall of a paddle was heard in the canoe, for vexation had made March reckless, and Deerslayer felt convinced that his conjecture was true. The sail being down, the Ark had not drifted far, and ere many minutes, he heard Chingachgook, in a low quiet tone directing Hutter how to steer, in order to reach it. In less time than it takes to tell the fact, the canoe touched the scow, and the adventurers entered the latter. Neither Hutter nor Hurry spoke of what had occurred. But the Delaware in passing his friend merely uttered the words "fires out," which if not literally true, sufficiently explained the truth to his listener.

It was now a question as to the course to be steered. A short surly conference was held, when Hutter decided that the wisest way would be to keep in motion, as the means most likely to defeat any attempt at a surprise, announcing his own and March's intention to requite themselves for the loss of sleep, during their captivity, by lying down. As the air still baffled and continued light, it was finally determined to sail before it, let it come in what direction it might, so long as it did not blow the Ark upon the strand. This point settled, the released prisoners helped to hoist the sail, and then they threw themselves on two of the pallets, leaving Deerslayer and his friend to look after the movements of the craft. As neither of the latter was disposed to sleep, on account of the appointment with Hist, this arrangement was acceptable to all parties. That Judith and Hetty remained up also, in no manner impaired the agreeable features of this change.

For some time the scow rather drifted than sailed along the western shore, following a light southerly current of the air. The progress was slow, not exceeding a couple of miles in the hour, but the two men perceived that it was not only carrying them towards the point they desired to reach, but at a rate that was quite as fast as the hour yet rendered necessary. But little was said the while, even by the girls, and that little had more reference to the rescue of Hist, than to any other subject. The Indian was calm, to the eye, but as minute after minute passed, his feelings became more and more excited, until they reached a state that might have satisfied the demands of even the most exacting mistress. Deerslayer kept the craft, as much in the bays as was prudent, for the double purpose of sailing within the shadows of the woods, and of detecting any signs of an encampment they might pass on the shore. In this manner they doubled one low point, and were already in the bay that was terminated north, by the goal at which they aimed. The latter was still a quarter of a mile distant, when Chingachgook came silently to the side of his friend and pointed to a place directly ahead. A small fire was glimmering just within the verge of the bushes that lined the shore, on the southern side of the point, leaving no doubt that the Indians had suddenly removed their camp to the very place, or at least to the very projection of land, where Hist had given them the rendezvous!

Chapter XVI

"I hear thee babbling to the vale
Of sunshine and of flowers,
But unto me thou bring'st a tale
Of visionary hours."
Wordsworth, "To the Cuckoo," ll. 9–12.

THE DISCOVERY mentioned at the close of the preceding chapter, was of great moment in the eyes of Deerslayer and his friend. In the first place, there was the danger, almost the certainty, that Hutter and Hurry would make a fresh attempt on this camp should they awake and ascertain its position. Then there was the increased risk of landing to bring off Hist, and there were the general uncertainty and additional hazards that must follow from the circumstance that their enemies had begun to change their position. As the Delaware was aware that the hour was near when he ought to repair to the rendezvous, he no longer thought of trophies torn from his foes, and one of the first things arranged between him and his associate, was to permit the two others to sleep on, lest they should disturb the execution of their plans, by substituting some of their own. The Ark moved slowly, and it would have taken fully a quarter of an hour to reach the point, at the rate at which they were going, thus affording time for a little forethought. The Indians, in the wish to conceal their fire from those who were thought to be still in the Castle, had placed it so near the southern side of the point, as to render it extremely difficult to shut it in by the bushes, though Deerslayer varied the direction of the scow, both to the right and to the left, in the hope of being able to effect that object.

"There's one advantage, Judith, in finding that fire so near the water," he said, while executing these little manoeuvres, "since it shows the Mingos believe we are in the hut, and our coming on 'em, from this quarter, will be an onlooked for event. But 'tis lucky Harry March and your father are asleep, else we should have 'em prowling after scalps ag'in. Ha! There—The bushes are beginning to shut in the fire—and now it can't be seen at all!"

Deerslayer waited a little to make certain that he had at last gained the desired position, when he gave the signal agreed on, and Chingachgook let go the grapnel, and lowered the sail.

The situation in which the Ark now lay had its advantages, and its disadvantages. The fire had been hid by sheering towards the shore, and the latter was nearer perhaps than was desirable. Still, the water was known to be very deep further off in the lake, and anchoring in deep water, under the circumstances in which the party was placed, was to be avoided if possible. It was also believed no raft could be within miles, and, though the trees in the darkness appeared almost to overhang the scow, it would not be easy to get off to her, without using a boat. The intense darkness that prevailed so close in with the forest, too, served as an effectual screen, and so long as care was had not to make a noise, there was little, or no danger of being detected. All these things Deerslayer pointed out to Judith, instructing her as to the course she was to follow in the event of an alarm, for it was thought to the last degree inexpedient to arouse the sleepers, unless it might be in the greatest emergency.

"And now, Judith, as we understand one another, it is time the Sarpent and I had taken to the canoe," the hunter concluded. "The star has not risen yet, it's true; but it soon must, though none of us are likely to be any the wiser for it, to-night, on account of the clouds. Howsever, Hist has a ready mind, and she's one of them that does'n't always need to have a thing afore her, to see it. I'll warrant you she'll not be either two minutes, or two feet out of the way, unless them jealous vagabonds, the Mingos, have taken the alarm, and put her as a stool pigeon to catch us; or have hid her away, in order to prepare her mind for a Huron instead of a Mohican husband."

"Deerslayer—" interrupted the girl earnestly—"This is a most dangerous service; why do *you* go on it, at all!"

"Anan!—Why you know, gal, we go to bring off Hist, the Sarpent's betrothed—The maid he means to marry, as soon as we get back to the tribe."

"That is all right for the Indian—but *you* do not mean to marry Hist;—*you* are not betrothed, and why should *two* risk their lives and liberties, to do that which one can just as well perform?"

"Ah!—now I understand you, Judith—yes, now I begin to take the idee. You think as Hist is the Sarpent's betrothed, as they call it, and not mine, it's altogether his affair; and as one man can paddle a canoe, he ought to be left to go after his gal alone! But you forget this is our ar'n'd here, on the lake, and it would not tell well to forget an ar'n'd just at the pinch. Then, if love does count for so much with some people, particularly with young women, fri'ndship counts for something, too, with other some. I dares to say, the Delaware can paddle a canoe by himself, and can bring off Hist, by himself, and perhaps he would like that quite as well, as to have me with him, but he could'n't sarcumvent sarcumventions, or stir up an ambushment, or fight with the savages and get his sweetheart off at the same time, as well by himself as if he had a fri'nd with him to depend on, even if that fri'nd is no better than myself. No—no—Judith, you would'n't desart one that counted on *you*, at such a moment, and you can't, in reason, expect me to do it."

"I fear—I believe you are right, Deerslayer, yet I wish you were not to go! Promise me one thing, at least, and that is not to trust yourself among the savages, or to do anything more than to save the girl. That will be enough for once, and with that you ought to be satisfied."

"Lord bless you! gal; one would think it was Hetty that's talking, and not the quick witted, and wonderful Judith Hutter! But fright makes the wise, silly, and the strong, weak. Yes, I've seen proofs of that, time and ag'in! Well, it's kind, and soft hearted in you, Judith, to feel this consarn for a fellow creatur', and I shall always say that you are kind and of true feelin's, let them that invy your good looks, tell as many idle stories of you as they may."

"Deerslayer!" hastily said the girl, interrupting him, though nearly choked by her emotions—"do you believe all you hear about a poor, motherless, girl? Is the foul tongue of Hurry Harry to blast my life!"

"Not it, Judith—not it. I've told Hurry it was'n't manful to backbite them he could'n't win by fair means, and that even an Indian is always tender, touching a young woman's good name."

"If I had a brother, he would'n't dare to do it!" exclaimed Judith, with eyes flashing fire. "But, finding me without any protector but an old man, whose ears are getting to be as dull as his feelings, he has his way as he pleases!"

"Not exactly that, Judith; no, not exactly that, neither! *No* man, brother or stranger, would stand by and see as fair a gal as yourself hunted down, without saying a word in her behalf. Hurry's in 'arnest in wanting to make you his wife, and the little he does let out, ag'in you, comes more from jealousy, like, than from any thing else. Smile on him when he awakes, and squeeze his hand only half as hard as you squeezed mine a bit ago, and my life on it, the poor fellow will forget every thing but your comeliness. Hot words do'n't always come from the heart, but oftener from the stomach, than any where else. Try him, Judith, when he wakes, and see the vartue of a smile."

Deerslayer laughed, in his own manner, as he concluded, and then he intimated to the patient looking, but really impatient Chingachgook, his readiness to proceed. As the young man entered the canoe, the girl stood immovable as stone, lost in the musings that the language and manner of the other were likely to produce. The simplicity of the hunter had completely put her at fault, for, in her narrow sphere, Judith was an expert manager of the other sex, though in the present instance she was far more actuated by impulses, in all she had said and done, than by calculation. We shall not deny that some of Judith's reflections were bitter, though the sequel of the tale must be referred to, in order to explain how merited, or how keen were her sufferings.

Chingachgook, and his pale face friend set forth on their hazardous and delicate enterprise, with a coolness and method that would have done credit to men who were on their twentieth, instead of being on their first war-path. As suited his relation to the pretty fugitive in whose service they were engaged, the Indian took his place in the head of the canoe, while Deerslayer guided its movements in the stern. By this arrangement the former would be the first to land, and of course the first to meet his mistress. The latter had taken his post, without comment, but in secret influenced by the reflection that one who had so much at stake as the Indian, might not possibly guide the canoe with the same steadiness and intelligence, as another who had more command of his feelings. From the instant they left the side of the Ark, the movements of the two adventurers were like the manoeuvres of highly drilled soldiers, who for the first time were called on to meet the enemy in the field. As yet, Chingachgook had never fired a shot in anger, and the *debût* of his companion in warfare is known to the reader. It is true the Indian had been hanging about his enemy's camp for a few hours, on his first arrival, and he had even once entered it, as related in the last chapter, but no consequences had followed either experiment. Now, it was certain that an important result was to be effected, or a mortifying failure was to ensue. The rescue, or the continued captivity of Hist depended on their enterprise. In a word, it was virtually the maiden expedition of these two ambitious young forest soldiers, and while one of them set forth, impelled by sentiments that usually carry men so far, both had all their feelings of pride and manhood enlisted in their success.

Instead of steering in a direct line to the point, then distant from the Ark less than a quarter of a mile, Deerslayer laid the head of his canoe diagonally towards the centre of the lake, with a view to obtain a position, from which he might approach the shore, having his enemies in his front only. The spot where Hetty had landed, and where Hist had promised to meet them, moreover, was on the upper side of the projection rather than on the lower, and to reach it, would have required the adventurers to double nearly the whole point, close in with the shore, had not this preliminary step been taken. So well was the necessity for this measure understood, that Chingachgook quietly paddled on, although it was adopted without consulting him, and apparently was taking him in a direction nearly opposite to that one might think he most wished to go. A few minutes sufficed, however, to carry the canoe the necessary distance, when both the young men ceased paddling as it were by instinctive consent, and the boat became stationary.

The darkness increased rather than diminished, but it was

still possible, from the place where the adventurers lay, to distinguish the outlines of the mountains. In vain did the Delaware turn his head eastward, to catch a glimpse of the promised star; for, notwithstanding the clouds broke a little, near the horizon, in that quarter of the heavens, the curtain continued so far drawn as effectually to conceal all behind it. In front, as was known by the formation of land above and behind it, lay the point, at a distance of about a thousand feet. No signs of the castle could be seen, nor could any movement in that quarter of the lake reach the ear. The latter circumstance might have been equally owing to the distance, which was several miles, or to the fact that nothing was in motion. As for the Ark, though scarcely farther from the canoe than the point, it lay so completely buried in the shadows of the shore, that it would not have been visible even had there been many degrees more of light than actually existed.

The adventurers now held a conference in low voices, consulting together as to the probable time. Deerslayer thought it wanted yet some minutes to the rising of the star, while the impatience of the chief caused him to fancy the night further advanced, and to believe that his betrothed was already waiting his appearance on the shore. As might have been expected, the opinion of the latter prevailed, and his friend disposed himself to steer for the place of rendezvous. The utmost skill and precaution now became necessary in the management of the canoe. The paddles were lifted, and returned to the water in a noiseless manner, and when within a hundred yards of the beach, Chingachgook took in his, altogether, laying his hand on his rifle in its stead. As they got still more within the belt of darkness that girded the woods, it was seen that they were steering too far north, and the course was altered accordingly. The canoe now seemed to move by instinct, so cautious and deliberate were all its motions. Still it continued to advance, until its bows grated on the gravel of the beach, at the precise spot where Hetty had landed, and whence her voice had issued, the previous night, as the Ark was passing. There was, as usual, a narrow strand, but bushes fringed the woods, and in most places overhung the water.

Chingachgook stepped upon the beach, and cautiously examined it, for some distance, on each side of the canoe. In order to do this, he was often obliged to wade to his knees in the lake, but no Hist rewarded his search. When he returned he found his friend, also on the shore. They now conferred in whispers, the Indian apprehending that they must have mistaken the place of rendezvous. But Deerslayer thought it more probable they had mistaken the hour. While he was yet speaking, he grasped the arm of the Delaware, caused him to turn his head in the direction of the lake, and pointed towards the summits of the eastern mountains. The clouds had broken a little, apparently behind rather than above the hills, and the selected star was glittering among the branches of a pine. This was every way a flattering omen, and the young men leaned on their rifles, listening intently for the sound of approaching footsteps. Voices they often heard, and mingled with them were the suppressed cries of children, and the low but sweet laugh of Indian women. As the native Americans are habitually cautious, and seldom break out in loud conversation, the adventurers knew by these facts, that they must be very near the encampment. It was easy to perceive that there was a fire within the woods, by the manner in which some of the upper branches of the trees were illuminated, but it was not possible, where they stood, to ascertain exactly how near it was to themselves. Once or twice, it seemed as if stragglers from around the fire, were approaching the place of rendezvous, but these sounds were either altogether illusion, or those who had drawn near, returned again without coming to the shore. A quarter of an hour was passed in this state of intense expectation and anxiety, when Deerslayer proposed that they should circle the point in the canoe, and by getting a position close in, where the camp could be seen, reconnoitre the Indians, and thus enable themselves to form some plausible conjectures for the non-appearance of Hist. The Delaware, however, resolutely refused to quit the spot, plausibly enough offering as a reason, the disappointment of the girl, should she arrive in his absence. Deerslayer felt for his friend's concern, and offered to make the circuit of the point, by himself, leaving the latter concealed in the bushes to await the occurrence of any fortunate event that might favor his views. With this understanding, then, the parties separated.

As soon as Deerslayer was at his post again, in the stern of the canoe, he left the shore with the same precautions, and in the same noiseless manner, as he had approached it. On this occasion he did not go far from the land, the bushes affording a sufficient cover, by keeping as close in as possible. Indeed, it would not have been easy to devise any means more favorable to reconnoitring round an Indian camp, than those afforded by the actual state of things. The formation of the point permitted the place to be circled on three of its sides, and the progress of the boat was so noiseless, as to remove any apprehensions from an alarm through sound. The most practised and guarded foot might stir a bunch of leaves, or snap a dried stick, in the dark, but a bark canoe could be made to float over the surface of smooth water, almost with the instinctive readiness, and certainly with the noiseless movements of an aquatic bird.

Deerslayer had got nearly in a line between the camp and the Ark, before he caught a glimpse of the fire. This came upon him suddenly, and a little unexpectedly, at first causing an alarm, lest he had incautiously ventured within the circle of light it cast. But, perceiving at a second glance, that he was certainly safe from detection, so long as the Indians kept near the centre of the illumination, he brought the canoe to a state of rest, in the most favorable position he could find, and commenced his observations.

We have written much, but in vain, concerning this extraordinary being, if the reader require now to be told, that, untutored as he was in the learning of the world, and simple as he ever showed himself to be in all matters touching the subtleties of conventional taste, he was a man of strong, native, poetical feeling. He loved the woods for their freshness, their sublime solitudes, their vastness, and the impress that they every where bore of the divine hand of their creator. He rarely moved through them, without pausing to dwell on some peculiar beauty that gave him pleasure, though seldom attempting to investigate the causes, and never did a day pass without his communing in spirit, and this too without the aid of forms, or language, with the infinite source of all he saw, felt, and beheld. Thus constituted in a moral sense, and of a steadiness that no danger could appal, or any crisis disturb, it is not surprising that the hunter felt a pleasure at looking on the scene he now beheld, that momentarily caused him to forget the object of his visit. This will more fully appear when we describe it.

The canoe lay in front of a natural vista, not only through the bushes that lined the shore, but of the trees also, that afforded a clear view of the camp. It was by means of this same opening that the light had been first seen from the Ark. In consequence of their recent change of ground, the Indians had not yet retired to their huts, but had been delayed by their preparations, which included lodging as well as food. A large fire had been made, as much to answer the purpose of torches, as for the uses of their simple cookery, and at this precise moment it was blazing high and bright, having recently received a large supply of dried brush. The effect was to illuminate the arches of the forest, and to render the whole area occupied by the camp as light as if hundreds of tapers were burning. Most of the toil had ceased and even the hungriest child had satisfied its appetite. In a word, the time was that moment of relaxation, and general indolence which is apt to succeed a hearty meal, and when the labors of the day have ended. The hunters and the fishermen had been equally successful, and food, that one great requisite of savage life, being abundant, every other care appeared to have subsided in the sense of enjoyment dependant on this all important fact.

Deerslayer saw at a glance that many of the warriors were absent. His acquaintance Rivenoak, however, was present, being seated in the foreground of a picture that Salvator Rosa would have delighted to draw, his swarthy features illuminated as much by pleasure, as by the torch-like flame, while he showed another of the tribe, one of the elephants that had caused so much sensation among his people. A boy was looking over his shoulder, in dull curiosity, completing the group. More in the back-ground eight or ten warriors lay half recumbent on the ground, or sat with their backs inclining against trees, so many types of indolent repose. Their arms were near them, sometimes leaning against the same trees as themselves, or were lying across their bodies in careless preparation. But the group that most attracted the attention of Deerslayer was that composed of the women and children. All the females appeared to be collected together, and, almost as a matter of course, their young were near them. The former laughed and chatted, in their rebuked and quiet manner, though one who knew the habits of the people might have detected that every thing was not going on in its usual train. Most of the young women seemed to be light hearted enough; but one old hag was seated apart, with a watchful, soured aspect, which the hunter at once knew betokened that some duty of an unpleasant character had been assigned her by the chiefs. What that duty was he had no means of knowing, but he felt satisfied it must be, in some measure, connected with her own sex, the aged among the women generally being chosen for such offices, and for no other.

As a matter of course, Deerslayer looked eagerly and anxiously for the form of Hist. She was nowhere visible, though the light penetrated to considerable distances, in all directions around the fire. Once, or twice, he started, as he thought he recognised her laugh, but his ears were deceived by the soft melody that is so common to the Indian female voice. At length the old woman spoke loud and angrily, and then he caught a glimpse of one or two dark figures, in the back ground of trees, which turned as if obedient to the rebuke, and walked more within the circle of the light. A young warrior's form first came fairly into view; then followed two youthful females, one of whom proved to be the Delaware girl. Deerslayer now comprehended it all. Hist was watched, possibly by her young companion, certainly by the old woman. The youth was probably some suitor of either hers, or her companion's, but even his discretion was distrusted under the influence of his admiration. The known vicinity of those who might be supposed to be her friends, and the arrival of a strange red-man on the lake, had induced more than the usual care, and the girl had not been able to slip away from those who watched her, in order to keep her appointment. Deerslayer traced her uneasiness, by her attempting, once or twice, to look up through the branches of the trees, as if endeavoring to get glimpses of the star she had herself named, as the sign for meeting. All was vain, however, and after strolling about the camp, a little longer, in affected indifference, the two girls quitted their male escort, and took seats among their own sex. As soon as this was done, the old sentinel changed her place to one more agreeable to herself, a certain proof that she had hitherto been exclusively on watch.

Deerslayer now felt greatly at a loss how to proceed. He well knew that Chingachgook could never be persuaded to return to the Ark, without making some desperate effort for the recovery of his mistress, and his own generous feelings well disposed him to aid in such an undertaking. He thought he saw the signs of an intention among the females to retire for the night, and should he remain, and the fire continue to give out its light, he might discover the particular hut, or arbor under which Hist reposed; a circumstance that would be of infinite use, in their future proceedings. Should he remain however, much longer where he was, there was great danger that the impatience of his friend, would drive him into some act of imprudence. At each instant, indeed, he expected to see the swarthy form of the Delaware, appearing in the back-ground, like the tiger prowling around the fold. Taking all things into consideration, therefore, he came to the conclusion it would be better to rejoin his friend, and endeavor to temper his impetuosity by some of his own coolness and discretion. It required but a minute or two to put this plan in execution, the canoe returning to the strand some ten or fifteen minutes after it had left it.

Contrary to his expectations, perhaps, Deerslayer found the Indian at his post, from which he had not stirred, fearful that his betrothed might arrive during his absence. A conference followed, in which Chingachgook was made acquainted with the state of things in the camp. When Hist named the point as the place of meeting, it was with the expectation of making her escape from the old position, and of repairing to a spot that she expected to find without any occupants, but the sudden change of localities had disconcerted all her plans. A much greater degree of vigilance than had been previously required, was now necessary, and the circumstance that an aged woman was on watch, also denoted some special grounds of alarm. All these considerations, and many more that will readily suggest themselves to the reader, were briefly discussed, before the young men came to any decision. The occasion, however, being one that required acts instead of words, the course to be pursued was soon chosen.

Disposing of the canoe in such a manner that Hist must see it, should she come to the place of meeting, previously to their return, the young men looked to their arms, and prepared to enter the wood. The whole projection into the lake contained about two acres of land, and the part that formed the point, and on which the camp was placed, did not compose a surface of more than half that size. It was principally covered with oaks, which, as is usual in the American forests, grew to a great height without throwing out a branch, and then arched in a dense and rich foliage. Beneath, except the fringe of thick bushes along the shore, there was very little underbrush; though, in consequence of their shape, the trees were closer together than is common in regions where the axe has been freely used, resembling tall, straight, rustic columns, upholding the usual canopy of leaves. The surface of the land was tolerably even, but it had a small rise near its centre, which divided it into a northern and southern half. On the latter the Hurons had built their fire, profiting by the formation to conceal it from their enemies, who it will be remembered were supposed to be in the castle, which bore northerly. A brook also came brawling down the sides of the adjacent hills, and found its way into the lake on the southern side of the point. It had cut for itself a deep passage through some of the higher portions of the ground, and, in later days, when this spot has become subjected to the uses of civilization, by its windings and shaded banks, it has become no mean accessory in contributing to the beauty of the place. This brook lay west of the encampment, and its waters found their way into the great reservoir of that region on the same side, and quite near to the spot chosen for the fire. All these peculiarities, so far as circumstances allowed, had been noted by Deerslayer, and explained to his friend.

The reader will understand that the little rise in the ground, that lay behind the Indian encampment, greatly favored the secret advance of the two adventurers. It prevented the light of the fire diffusing itself on the ground directly in the rear, although the land fell away towards the water so as to leave what might be termed the left, or eastern flank of the position, unprotected by this covering. We have said 'unprotected,' though that is not properly the word, since the knoll behind the huts and the fire, offered a cover for those who were now stealthily approaching, rather than any protection to the Indians. Deerslayer did not break through the fringe of bushes immediately abreast of the canoe, which might have brought him too suddenly within the influence of the light, since the hillock did not extend to the water, but he followed the beach northerly until he had got nearly on the opposite side of the tongue of land, which brought him under the shelter of the low acclivity, and consequently more in shadow.

As soon as the friends emerged from the bushes, they stopped to reconnoitre. The fire was still blazing, behind the little ridge, casting its light upward, into the tops of the trees, producing an effect that was more pleasing than advantageous. Still the glare had its uses, for, while the back ground was in obscurity, the fore-ground was in strong light; exposing the savages and concealing their foes. Profiting by the latter circumstance, the young men advanced cautiously towards the ridge, Deerslayer in front, for he insisted on this arrangement, lest the Delaware should be led by his feelings into some indiscretion. It required but a moment to reach the foot of the little ascent, and then commenced the most critical part of the enterprise. Moving with exceeding caution, and trailing his rifle, both to keep its barrel out of view and in readiness for service, the hunter put foot before foot, until he had got sufficiently high to overlook the summit, his own head being alone brought into the light. Chingachgook was at his side, and both paused to take another close examination of the camp. In order, however, to protect themselves against any straggler in the rear, they placed their bodies against the trunk of an oak, standing on the side next the fire.

The view that Deerslayer now obtained of the camp, was exactly the reverse of that he had perceived from the water. The dim figures which he had formerly discovered must have been on the summit of the ridge, a few feet in advance of the spot where he was now posted. The fire was still blazing brightly, and around it were seated on logs, thirteen warriors, which accounted for all whom he had seen from the canoe.

They were conversing, with much earnestness among themselves, the image of the elephant passing from hand to hand. The first burst of savage wonder had abated, and the question now under discussion, was the probable existence, the history and habits of so extraordinary an animal. We have not leisure to record the opinions of these rude men on a subject so peculiar to their lives and experience, but little is hazarded in saying that they were quite as plausible, and far more ingenious, than half the conjectures that precede the demonstrations of science. However much they may have been at fault as to their conclusions and inferences, it is certain that they discussed the questions with a zealous and most undivided attention. For the time being, all else was forgotten, and our adventurers could not have approached at a more fortunate instant.

The females were collected near each other, much as Deerslayer had last seen them, nearly in a line between the place where he now stood and the fire. The distance from the oak against which the young men leaned, and the warriors, was about thirty yards; the women may have been half that number of yards nigher. The latter, indeed, were so near as to make the utmost circumspection, as to motion and noise, indispensable. Although they conversed in their low, soft, voices, it was possible, in the profound stillness of the woods, even to catch passages of the discourse, and the light hearted laugh that escaped the girls, might occasionally have reached the canoe. Deerslayer felt the tremor that passed through the frame of his friend, when the latter first caught the sweet sounds that issued from the plump, pretty lips of Hist. He even laid a hand on the shoulder of the Indian, as a sort of admonition to command himself. As the conversation grew more earnest each leaned forward to listen.

"The Hurons have more curious beasts than that!" said one of the girls, contemptuously, for, like the men, they conversed of the elephant and his qualities. "The Delawares will think this creature wonderful, but to-morrow, no Huron tongue will talk of it. Our young men will find him, if the animal dares to come near our wigwams!"

This was in fact addressed to Wah-ta!-Wah, though she

who spoke uttered her words with an assumed diffidence and humility, that prevented her looking at the other.

"The Delawares are so far from letting such creatures come into their country," returned Hist, "that no one has even seen their images there! *Their* young men would frighten away the *images*, as well as the *beasts*."

"The Delaware young men!—the nation is women; even the deer walk when they hear their hunters coming! Who has ever heard the name of a young Delaware warrior?"

This was said in good humour, and with a laugh; but it was also said, bitingly. That Hist so felt it, was apparent by the spirit betrayed in her answer.

"Who has ever heard the name of a young Delaware!" she repeated earnestly. "Tamenund, himself, though now as old as the pines on the hill, or as the eagles in the air, was once young; his name was heard from the great salt lake, to the sweet waters of the west. What is the family of Uncas? Where is another as great, though the pale faces have ploughed up its graves, and trodden on its bones? Do the eagles fly as high, is the deer as swift, or the panther as brave? Is there no young warrior of that race? Let the Huron maidens open their eyes wider, and they may see one called Chingachgook, who is as stately as a young ash, and as tough as the hickory."

As the girl used her figurative language, and told her companions to "open their eyes, and they would see" the Delaware, Deerslayer thrust his fingers into the side of his friend, and indulged in a fit of his hearty, but silent laughter. The other smiled, but the language of the speaker was so flattering, and the tones of her voice too sweet for him to be led away, by any accidental coincidence, however ludicrous. The speech of Hist produced a retort, and the dispute, though conducted in good humour, and without any of the coarse violence of tone and gesture that often impairs the charms of the sex, in what is called civilized life, grew warm and slightly clamorous. In the midst of this scene, the Delaware caused his friend to stoop, so as completely to conceal himself, and then he made a noise so closely resembling the little chirrup of the smallest species of the American squirrel, that, Deerslayer himself, though he had heard the imitation a hundred times, actually thought it came from one of the little animals, skipping about, over his head. The sound is so familiar in the woods, that none of the Hurons paid it the least attention. Hist, however, instantly ceased talking, and sate motionless. Still, she had sufficient self-command to abstain from turning her head. She had heard the signal, by which her lover so often called her from the wigwam, to a stolen interview, and it came over her senses and her heart, as the serenade affects the maiden in the land of song.

From that moment, Chingachgook felt certain that his presence was known. This was effecting much, and he could now hope for a bolder line of conduct on the part of his mistress, than she might dare to adopt under an uncertainty of his situation. It left no doubt of her endeavoring to aid him in his effort to release her. Deerslayer arose, as soon as the signal was given, and though he had never held that sweet communion which is known only to lovers, he was not slow to detect the great change that had come over the manner of the girl. She still affected to dispute, though it was no longer with spirit and ingenuity, but what she said was uttered more as a lure to draw her antagonists on to an easy conquest, than with any hopes of succeeding herself. Once or twice, it is true, her native readiness suggested a retort, or an argument that raised a laugh, and gave her a momentary advantage; but these little rallies, the offspring of mother wit, served the better to conceal her real feelings, and to give to the triumph of the other party, a more natural air than it might have possessed without them. At length the disputants became wearied, and they rose in a body, as if about to separate. It was now that Hist, for the first time, ventured to turn her face in the direction whence the signal had come. In doing this, her movements were natural but guarded, and she stretched her arms and yawned, as if overcome with a desire to sleep. The chirrup was again heard, and the girl felt satisfied as to the position of her lover, though the strong light in which she herself was placed, and the comparative darkness in which the adventurers stood, prevented her from seeing their heads, the only portions of their forms that appeared above the ridge at all. The tree against which they were posted, had a dark shadow cast upon it, by the intervention of an enormous pine that grew between it and the fire, a circumstance which alone would have rendered objects within its cloud invisible at any distance. This Deerslayer well knew, and it was one of the reasons why he had selected this particular tree.

The moment was near when it became necessary for Hist to act. She was to sleep in a small hut, or bower, that had been built near the spot where she stood, and her companion was the aged hag, already mentioned. Once within the hut, with this sleepless old woman stretched across the entrance, as was her nightly practice, the hope of escape was nearly destroyed, and she might, at any moment, be summoned to her bed. Luckily, at this instant, one of the warriors called to the old woman by name, and bade her bring him water to drink. There was a delicious spring on the northern side of the point, and the hag took a gourd from a branch, and, summoning Hist to her side, she moved towards the summit of the ridge, intending to descend and cross the point to the natural fountain. All this was seen and understood by the adventurers, and they fell back into the obscurity, concealing their persons by trees, until the two females had passed them. In walking, Hist was held tightly by the hand. As she moved by the tree, that hid Chingachgook and his friend, the former felt for his tomahawk, with the intention to bury it in the brain of the woman. But the other saw the hazard of such a measure, since a single scream might bring all the warriors upon them, and he was averse to the act on the considerations of humanity. His hand, therefore, prevented the blow. Still as the two moved past, the chirrup was repeated, and the Huron woman stopped and faced the tree whence the sounds seemed to proceed, standing at the moment, within six feet of her enemies. She expressed her surprise that a squirrel should be in motion at so late an hour, and said it boded evil. Hist answered that she had heard the same squirrel three times, within the last twenty minutes, and that she supposed it was waiting to obtain some of the crumbs left from the late supper. This explanation appeared satisfactory, and they moved towards the spring, the men following stealthily and closely. The gourd was filled, and the old woman was hurrying back, her hand still grasping the wrist of the girl, when she was suddenly seized so violently by the throat, as to cause her to release her captive, and to prevent her making any other sound than a sort of gurgling, suffocating noise. The Serpent passed his arm round the waist of his mistress and darted through the bushes with her, on the north side of the point. Here he immediately turned along the beach, and ran towards the canoe. A more direct course could have been taken, but it might have led to a discovery of the place of embarking.

Deerslayer kept playing on the throat of the old woman like the keys of an organ, occasionally allowing her to breathe, and then compressing his fingers again, nearly to strangling. The brief intervals for breath, however, were well improved, and the hag succeeded in getting out a screech or two that served to alarm the camp. The tramp of the warriors, as they sprung from the fire, was plainly audible, and, at the next moment three or four of them appeared on the top of the ridge, drawn against the back ground of light, resembling the dense shadows of the phantasmagoria. It was now quite time for the hunter to retreat. Tripping up the heels of his captive, and giving her throat a parting squeeze, quite as much in resentment at her indomitable efforts to sound the alarm, as from any policy, he left her on her back, and moved towards the bushes, his rifle at a poise, and his head over his shoulders, like a lion at bay.

Chapter XVII

"There, ye wise saints, behold your light, your star,
Ye *would* be dupes and victims and ye *are*.
Is it enough? or, must I, while a thrill
Lives in your sapient bosoms, cheat you still?"
Thomas Moore, *Lalla Rookh*, "The Veiled Prophet
of Khorassan," ll. 1954–57.

THE FIRE, the canoe, and the spring, near which Deerslayer commenced his retreat, would have stood in the angles of a triangle of tolerably equal sides. The distance from the fire to the boat was a little less than the distance from the fire to the spring, while the distance from the spring to the boat, was about equal to that between the two points first named. This, however, was in straight lines, a means of escape to which the fugitives could not resort. They were obliged to have recourse to a *détour* in order to get the cover of the bushes, and to follow the curvature of the beach. Under these disadvantages, then, the hunter commenced his retreat, disadvantages that he felt to be so much the greater from his knowledge of the habits of all Indians, who rarely fail in cases of sudden alarms, more especially when in the midst of cover, immediately to throw out flankers, with a view to meet their foes at all points, and if possible to turn their rear. That some such course was now adopted he believed from the tramp of feet, which not only came up the ascent, as related, but were also heard, under the first impulse, diverging not only towards the hill in the rear, but towards the extremity of the point, in a direction opposite to that he was about to take himself. Promptitude, consequently became a matter of the last importance, as the parties might meet on the strand, before the fugitive could reach the canoe.

Notwithstanding the pressing nature of the emergency, Deerslayer hesitated a single instant, ere he plunged into the bushes that lined the shore. His feelings had been awakened by the whole scene, and a sternness of purpose had come over him, to which he was ordinarily a stranger. Four dark figures loomed on the ridge, drawn against the brightness of the fire, and an enemy might have been sacrificed at a glance. The

Indians had paused to gaze into the gloom, in search of the screeching hag, and with many a man less given to reflection than the hunter, the death of one of them would have been certain. Luckily he was more prudent. Although the rifle dropped a little towards the foremost of his pursuers, he did not aim or fire, but disappeared in the cover. To gain the beach, and to follow it round to the place where Chingachgook was already in the canoe, with Hist, anxiously waiting his appearance, occupied but a moment. Laying his rifle in the bottom of the canoe, Deerslayer stooped to give the latter a vigorous shove from the shore, when a powerful Indian leaped through the bushes, alighting like a panther on his back. Every thing was now suspended by a hair; a false step ruining all. With a generosity that would have rendered a Roman illustrious throughout all time, but which, in the career of one so simple and humble, would have been forever lost to the world but for this unpretending legend, Deerslayer threw all his force into a desperate effort, shoved the canoe off with a power that sent it a hundred feet from the shore, as it might be in an instant, and fell forward into the lake, himself, face downward; his assailant necessarily following him.

Although the water was deep within a few yards of the beach, it was not more than breast high, as close in, as the spot where the two combatants fell. Still this was quite sufficient to destroy one who had sunk, under the great disadvantages in which Deerslayer was placed. His hands were free, however, and the savage was compelled to relinquish his hug, to keep his own face above the surface. For half a minute there was a desperate struggle, like the floundering of an alligator that has just seized some powerful prey, and then both stood erect, grasping each other's arms, in order to prevent the use of the deadly knife, in the darkness. What might have been the issue of this severe personal struggle cannot be known, for half a dozen savages came leaping into the water to the aid of their friend, and, Deerslayer yielded himself a prisoner, with a dignity that was as remarkable as his self-devotion.

To quit the lake and lead their new captive to the fire, occupied the Indians but another minute. So much engaged were they all with the struggle and its consequences, that the canoe was unseen, though it still lay so near the shore as to render every syllable that was uttered, perfectly intelligible to the Delaware and his betrothed; and the whole party left the spot, some continuing the pursuit after Hist, along the beach, though most proceeded to the light. Here Deerslayer's antagonist so far recovered his breath and his recollection, for he had been throttled nearly to strangulation, as to relate the manner in which the girl had got off. It was now too late to assail the other fugitives, for no sooner was his friend led into the bushes, than the Delaware placed his paddle into the water, and the light canoe glided noiselessly away, holding its course towards the centre of the lake, until safe from shot, after which it sought the Ark.

When Deerslayer reached the fire, he found himself surrounded by no less than eight grim savages, among whom was his old acquaintance Rivenoak. As soon as the latter caught a glimpse of the captive's countenance, he spoke apart to his companions, and a low, but general exclamation of pleasure and surprise escaped them. They knew that the conqueror of their late friend, he who had fallen on the opposite side of the lake, was in their hands, and subject to their mercy, or vengeance. There was no little admiration mingled in the ferocious looks that were thrown on the prisoner; an admiration that was as much excited by his present composure, as by his past deeds. This scene may be said to have been the commencement of the great and terrible reputation that Deerslayer, or Hawkeye, as he was afterwards called, enjoyed among all the tribes of New York and Canada; a reputation that was certainly more limited in its territorial and numerical extent, than those which are possessed in civilized life, but which was compensated for what it wanted in these particulars, perhaps, by its greater justice, and the total absence of mystification and management.

The arms of Deerslayer were not pinioned, and he was left the free use of his hands, his knife having been first removed. The only precaution that was taken to secure his person was untiring watchfulness, and a strong rope of bark that passed from ancle to ancle, not so much to prevent his walking, as to place an obstacle in the way of his attempting to escape by any sudden leap. Even this extra provision against flight was not made, until the captive had been brought to the light, and his character ascertained. It was, in fact, a compliment to his prowess, and he felt proud of the distinction. That he might be bound when the warriors slept he thought probable, but to be bound in the moment of capture, showed that he was already, and thus early, attaining a name. While the young Indians were fastening the rope, he wondered if Chingachgook would have been treated in the same manner, had he too fallen into the hands of the enemy. Nor did the reputation of the young pale face rest altogether on his success in the previous combat, or in his discriminating and cool manner of managing the late negotiation, for it had received a great accession by the occurrences of the night. Ignorant of the movements of the Ark, and of the accident that had brought their fire into view, the Iroquois attributed the discovery of their new camp to the vigilance of so shrewd a foe. The manner in which he ventured upon the point, the abstraction or escape of Hist, and most of all the self-devotion of the prisoner, united to the readiness with which he had sent the canoe adrift, were so many important links in the chain of facts, on which his growing fame was founded. Many of these circumstances had been seen, some had been explained, and all were understood.

While this admiration, and these honors were so unreservedly bestowed on Deerslayer, he did not escape some of the penalties of his situation. He was permitted to seat himself on the end of a log, near the fire, in order to dry his clothes, his late adversary standing opposite, now holding articles of his own scanty vestments to the heat, and now feeling his throat, on which the marks of his enemy's fingers were still quite visible. The rest of the warriors consulted together, near at hand, all those who had been out having returned to report that no signs of any other prowlers near the camp were to be found. In this state of things, the old woman, whose name was Shebear, in plain English, approached Deerslayer, with her fists clenched and her eyes flashing fire. Hitherto, she had been occupied with screaming, an employment at which she had played her part with no small degree of success, but having succeeded in effectually alarming all within reach of a pair of lungs that had been strengthened by long practice, she next turned her attention to the injuries her own person had sustained in the struggle. These were in no manner material, though they were of a nature to arouse all the fury of a woman who had long ceased to attract by means of the gentler qualities, and who was much disposed to revenge the hardships she had so long endured, as the neglected wife and mother of savages, on all who came within her power. If Deerslayer had not permanently injured her, he had temporarily caused her to suffer, and she was not a person to overlook a wrong of this nature, on account of its motive.

"Skunk of the pale-faces—" commenced this exasperated and semi-poetic fury, shaking her fist under the nose of the impassable hunter, "you are not even a woman. Your friends the Delawares are only women, and you are their sheep. Your own people will not own you, and no tribe of red *men* would have you in their wigwams; you skulk among petticoated warriors. *You* slay our brave friend who has left us?—No—his great soul scorned to fight you, and left his body rather than have the shame of slaying *you*! But the blood that you spilt when the spirit was not looking on, has not sunk into the ground. It must be buried in your groans. What music do I hear? Those are not the wailings of a red man!—no red warrior groans so much like a hog. They come from a pale face throat—a Yengeese bosom, and sound as pleasant as girls singing—Dog—skunk—wood-chuck—mink—hedge-hog—pig—toad—spider—yengee—"

Here the old woman having expended her breath, and exhausted her epithets, was fain to pause a moment, though both her fists were shook in the prisoner's face, and the whole of her wrinkled countenance was filled with fierce resentment. Deerslayer looked upon these impotent attempts to arouse him, as indifferently as a gentleman in our own state of society, regards the vituperative terms of a blackguard: the one party feeling that the tongue of an old woman could never injure a warrior, and the other knowing that mendacity and vulgarity can only permanently affect those who resort to their use; but he was spared any further attack at present, by the interposition of Rivenoak, who shoved aside the hag, bidding her quit the spot, and prepared to take his seat at the side of his prisoner. The old woman withdrew, but the hunter well understood that he was to be the subject of all her means of annoyance, if not of positive injury, so long as he remained in the power of his enemies, for nothing rankles so deeply as the consciousness that an attempt to irritate has been met by contempt, a feeling that is usually the most passive of any that is harbored in the human breast. Rivenoak quietly took the seat we have mentioned, and, after a short pause, he commenced a dialogue, which we translate as usual, for the benefit of those readers who have not studied the North American languages.

"My paleface friend is very welcome," said the Indian, with a familiar nod, and a smile so covert that it required all Deerslayer's vigilance to detect, and not a little of his philosophy to detect unmoved—"he is welcome. The Hurons keep a hot fire to dry the white man's clothes by."

"I thank you, Huron—or Mingo, as I most like to call you—" returned the other—"I thank you for the welcome, and I thank you for the fire. Each is good in its way, and the last is very good, when one has been in a spring as cold as the Glimmerglass. Even Huron warmth may be pleasant, at such a time, to a man with a Delaware heart."

"The paleface—but my brother has a name? So great a warrior would not have lived without a name?"

"Mingo," said the hunter, a little of the weakness of human nature exhibiting itself in the glance of his eye, and the colour on his cheek—"Mingo, *your* brave, called me Hawkeye, I suppose on account of a quick and sartain aim, when he was lying with his head in my lap, afore his spirit started for the Happy Hunting Grounds."

"Tis a good name! The hawk is sure of his blow. Hawkeye is not a woman; why does he live with the Delawares?"

"I understand you, Mingo, but we look on all that as a sarcumvention of some of your subtle devils, and deny the charge. Providence placed me among the Delawares young, and, 'bating what christian usages demand of my colour and gifts, I hope to live and die in their tribe. Still I do not mean to throw away altogether, my nat*yve* rights, and shall strive to do a pale face's duty, in red skin society."

"Good; a Huron is a red skin, as well as a Delaware. Hawkeye is more of a Huron than of a woman."

"I suppose you know, Mingo, your own meaning; if you do'n't I make no question t'is well known to Satan. But if you wish to get any thing out of me, speak plainer, for bargains can not be made blindfolded, or tongue tied."

"Good; Hawkeye has not a forked tongue, and he likes to say what he thinks. He is an acquaintance of the Muskrat;" this was the name by which all the Indians designated Hutter—"and has lived in his wigwam. But he is not a friend. He wants no scalps, like a miserable Indian, but fights like a stout-hearted pale face. The Muskrat is neither white, nor red. Neither a beast nor a fish. He is a water snake; sometimes in the spring and sometimes on the land. He looks for scalps, like an out-cast. Hawkeye can go back and tell him how he has outwitted the Hurons, how he has escaped, and when his eyes are in a fog, when he ca'n't see as far as from his cabin to the shore, then Hawkeye can open the door for the Hurons. And how will the plunder be divided? Why, Hawkeye, will carry away the most, and the Hurons will take what he may choose to leave behind him. The scalps can go to Canada, for a pale-face has no satisfaction in *them*."

"Well, well, Rivenoak—for so I hear 'em tarm you—This is plain English, enough, though spoken in Iroquois. I understand all you mean, now, and must say it out-devils even Mingo deviltry! No doubt, twould be easy enough to go back and tell the Muskrat, that I had got away from you, and gain some credit, too, by the expl'ite."

"Good. That is what I want the paleface to do."

"Yes—yes—That's plain enough. I know what you want me to do, without more words. When inside the house, and eating the Muskrat's bread, and laughing and talking with his pretty darters, I might put his eyes into so thick a fog, that he could'n't even see the door, much less the land."

"Good! Hawkeye should have been born a Huron! His blood is not more than half white!"

"There you're out, Huron; yes, there you're as much out, as if you mistook a wolf for a catamount. I'm white in blood, heart, natur' and gifts, though a little red skin in feelin's and habits. But when old Hutter's eyes are well be-fogged, and his pretty darters perhaps in a deep sleep, and Hurry Harry, the Great Pine as you Indians tarm him, is dreaming of any thing but mischief, and all suppose Hawkeye is acting as a faithful sentinel, all I have to do is to set a torch somewhere in sight for a signal, open the door, and let in the Hurons, to knock 'em all on the head."

"Surely my brother is mistaken; he *cannot* be white! He is worthy to be a great chief among the Hurons!"

"That is true enough, I dares to say, if he could do all this. Now, harkee, Huron, and for once hear a few honest words from the mouth of a plain man. I am christian born, and them that come of such a stock, and that listen to the words that were spoken to their fathers, and will be spoken to their children, until 'arth, and all it holds perishes, can never lend themselves to such wickedness. Sarcumventions in war, may be, and *are*, lawful; but sarcumventions, and deceit, and treachery, among fri'nds are fit only for the pale-face devils. I know that there are white men enough, to give you this wrong idee of our natur', but such are ontrue to their blood and gifts, and ought to be, if they are not, out casts and vagabonds. No upright pale-face could do what you wish, and to be as plain with you as I wish to be, in my judgment, no upright Delaware either. With a Mingo it may be different."

The Huron listened to this rebuke with obvious disgust, but he had his ends in view, and was too wily to lose all chance of effecting them, by a precipitate avowal of resentment. Affecting to smile, he seemed to listen eagerly, and he then pondered on what he had heard.

"Does Hawkeye love the Muskrat," he abruptly demanded. "Or does he love his daughters?"

"Neither, Mingo. Old Tom is not a man to gain my love, and, as for the darters, they are comely enough to gain the liking of any young man, but there's reason ag'in any very great love for either. Hetty is a good soul, but natur' has laid a heavy hand on her mind, poor thing!"

"And the Wild Rose!" exclaimed the Huron—for the fame of Judith's beauty had spread among those who could travel the wilderness, as well as the highway, by means of old eagles' nests, rocks, and riven trees, known to them by report and tradition, as well as among the white borderers, "And the

Wild Rose; is she not sweet enough to be put in the bosom of my brother?"

Deerslayer had far too much of the innate gentleman to insinuate aught against the fair fame of one who, by nature and position was so helpless, and as he did not choose to utter an untruth, he preferred being silent. The Huron mistook the motive, and supposed that disappointed affection lay at the bottom of his reserve. Still bent on corrupting, or bribing his captive, in order to obtain possession of the treasures with which his imagination filled the Castle, he persevered in his attack.

"Hawkeye is talking with a friend," he continued. "He knows that Rivenoak is a man of his word, for they have traded together, and trade opens the soul. My friend has come here, on account of a little string held by a girl, that can pull the whole body of the sternest warrior?"

"You are nearer the truth, now, Huron, than you've been afore, since we began to talk. This is true. But one end of that string was not fast to my heart, nor did the Wild Rose hold the other."

"This is wonderful! Does my brother love in his head, and not in his heart? And can the Feeble Mind pull so hard against so stout a warrior?"

"There it is ag'in; sometimes right, and sometimes wrong! The string you mean, is fast to the heart of a great Delaware; one of Mohican stock in fact, living among the Delawares since the disparsion of his own people, and of the family of Uncas—Chingachgook by name, or Great Sarpent. He has come here, led by the string, and I've followed, or rather come afore, for I got here first, pulled by nothing stronger than fri'ndship; which is strong enough for such as are not niggardly of their feelin's, and are willing to live a little for their fellow creatur's, as well as for themselves."

"But a string has two ends—one is fast to the mind of a Mohican; and the other?"—

"Why the other was here close to the fire, half an hour since. Wah-ta!-Wah held it in her hand, if she did'n't hold it to her heart."

"I understand what you mean, my brother," returned the Indian gravely, for the first time catching a direct clue to the adventures of the evening. "The Great Serpent, being strongest, pulled the hardest, and Hist was forced to leave us."

"I do'n't think there was much pulling about it," answered the other, laughing, always in his silent manner, with as much heartiness as if he were not a captive, and in danger of torture or death—"I do'n't think there was much pulling about it; no I do'n't. Lord help you, Huron! He likes the gal, and the gal likes him, and it surpassed Huron sarcumventions to keep two young people apart, where there was so strong a feelin' to bring 'em together."

"And Hawkeye and Chingachgook came into our camp on this errand, only?"

"That's a question that'll answer itself, Mingo! Yes, if a question could talk it would answer itself, to your parfect satisfaction. For what else should we come? And yet, it is'n't exactly so, neither; for we did'n't come into your camp at all, but only as far as that pine, there, that you see on the other side of the ridge, where we stood watching your movements, and conduct, as long as we liked. When we were ready, the Sarpent gave his signal, and then all went just as it should, down to the moment when yonder vagabond leaped upon my back. Sartain; we come for that, and for no other purpose, and we got what we come for; there's no use in pretending otherwise. Hist is off with a man who's the next thing to her husband, and come what will to me, *that's* one good thing detarmined."

"What sign, or signal, told the young maiden that her lover was nigh?" asked the Huron with more curiosity than it was usual for him to betray.

Deerslayer laughed again, and seem'd to enjoy the success of the exploit, with as much glee, as if he had not been its victim.

"Your squirrels are great gadabouts, Mingo," he cried still laughing—"yes, they're sartainly, great gadabouts! When other folk's squirrels are at home and asleep, yourn keep in motion among the trees, and chirrup and sing, in a way that even a Delaware gal can understand their musick! Well, there's four legged squirrels, and there's two legged squirrels, and give me the last, when there's a good tight string atween two hearts. If one brings 'em together, t'other tells when to pull hardest!"

The Huron look'd vexed, though he succeeded in suppressing any violent exhibition of resentment. He now quitted his prisoner, and joining the rest of the warriors, he communicated the substance of what he had learned. As in his own case, admiration was mingled with anger, at the boldness and success of their enemies. Three or four of them ascended the little acclivity and gazed at the tree where it was understood the adventurers had posted themselves, and one even descended to it, and examined for foot prints around its roots, in order to make sure that the statement was true. The result confirmed the story of the captive, and they all returned to the fire, with increased wonder and respect. The messenger who had arrived with some communication from the party above, while the two adventurers were watching the camp, was now despatched with some answer, and doubtless bore with him the intelligence of all that had happened.

Down to this moment, the young Indian who had been seen walking in company with Hist and another female, had made no advances to any communication with Deerslayer. He had held himself aloof from his friends even, passing near the bevy of younger women, who were clustering together, apart as usual, and conversed in low tones on the subject of the escape of their late companion. Perhaps it would be true to say, that these last were pleased as well as vexed at what had just occurred. Their female sympathies were with the lovers, while their pride was bound up in the success of their own tribe. It is possible too, that the superior personal advantages of Hist, rendered her dangerous to some of the younger part of the group, and they were not sorry to find she was no longer in the way of their own ascendency. On the whole, however, the better feeling was most prevalent, for neither the wild condition in which they lived, the clannish prejudices of tribes, nor their hard fortunes as Indian women, could entirely conquer the inextinguishable leaning of their sex to the affections. One of the girls even laughed at the disconsolate look of the swain who might fancy himself deserted, a circumstance that seemed suddenly to arouse his energies, and induce him to move towards the log, on which the prisoner was still seated, drying his clothes.

"This is Catamount!" said the Indian, striking his hand boastfully on his naked breast, as he uttered the words in a manner to show how much weight he expected them to carry.

"This is Hawkeye—" quietly returned Deerslayer, adopting the name by which he knew he would be known in future, among all the tribes of the Iroquois. "My sight is keen—is my brother's leap long?"

"From here to the Delaware villages. Hawkeye has stolen my wife—he must bring her back, or his scalp will hang on a pole, and dry in my wigwam."

"Hawkeye has stolen nothing, Huron. He does'n't come of a thieving breed, nor has he thieving gifts. Your wife, as you call Wah-ta!-Wah, will never be the wife of any red skin of the Canadas; her mind is in the cabin of a Delaware, and her body has gone to find it. The catamount is actyve I know, but its legs can't keep pace with a woman's wishes."

"The Serpent of the Delawares is a dog—he is a poor bull-pout, that keeps in the water; he is afraid to stand on the hard earth, like a brave Indian!"

"Well, well, Huron, that's pretty impudent, considering it's not an hour since the Sarpent stood within a hundred feet of you, and would have tried the toughness of your skin with a rifle bullet, when I pointed you out to him, had'n't I laid the weight of a little judgment on his hand. You may take in timersome gals in the settlements, with your catamount whine, but the ears of a man can tell truth from ontruth."

"Hist laughs at him! She sees he is lame, and a poor hunter, and he has never been on a war path. She will take a man for a husband, and not a fish."

"How do you know that, Catamount; how do you know that," returned Deerslayer laughing. "She has gone into the lake, you see, and may be she prefars a trout to a mongrel cat. As for war paths, neither the Sarpent nor I, have much exper'ence, we are ready to own, but if you do n't call this one, you must tarm it, what the gals in the settlements tarm it, the high road to matrimony. Take my advice Catamount, and s'arch for a wife among the Huron women; you'll never get one, with a willing mind, from among the Delawares."

Catamount's hand felt for his tomahawk, and when the fingers reached the handle, they worked convulsively, as if their owner hesitated between policy and resentment. At this critical moment Rivenoak approached, and by a gesture of authority, induced the young man to retire, assuming his former position, himself, on the log, at the side of Deerslayer. Here he continued silent for a little time, maintaining the grave reserve of an Indian chief.

"Hawkeye is right—" the Iroquois at length began; "his sight is so strong that he can see truth in a dark night, and our eyes have been blinded. He is an owl, darkness hiding nothing from him. He ought not to strike his friends. He is right."

"I'm glad you think so, Mingo," returned the other, "for a traitor, in my judgment, is worse than a coward. I care as little for the Muskrat, as one pale face ought to care for another, but I care too much for him, to ambush him in the way you wished. In short, according to my idees, any sarcumventions, except open-war sarcumventions, are ag'in both law, and what we whites call 'gospel', too."

"My pale-face brother is right; he is no Indian, to forget his Manitou and his colour. The Hurons know that they have a great warrior for their prisoner, and they will treat him as one. If he is to be tortured, his torments shall be such as no common man can bear; if he is to be treated as a friend, it will be the friendship of chiefs."

As the Huron uttered this extraordinary assurance of consideration, his eye furtively glanced at the countenance of his listener, in order to discover how he stood the compliment, though his gravity and apparent sincerity would have prevented any man but one practised in artifices, from detecting his motives. Deerslayer belonged to the class of the unsuspicious, and acquainted with the Indian notions of what constitutes respect, in matters connected with the treatment of captives, he felt his blood chill at the announcement, even while he maintained an aspect so steeled that his quick sighted enemy could discover in it, no signs of weakness.

"God has put me in your hands, Huron," the captive at length answered, "and I suppose you will act your will on me. I shall not boast of what I can do, under torment, for I've never been tried, and no man can say 'till he has been; but I'll do my endivours not to disgrace the people among whom I got my training. Howsever, I wish you now to bear witness that I'm altogether of white blood, and, in a nat'ral way of white gifts too; so, should I be overcome and forget myself, I hope you'll lay the fault where it properly belongs, and, in no manner put it on the Delawares, or their allies and friends the Mohicans. We're all created with more or less weakness, and I'm afeard it's a pale face's to give in, under great bodily torment, when a red skin will sing his songs, and boast of his deeds in the very teeth of his foes."

"We shall see. Hawkeye has a good countenance, and he is tough—But why should he be tormented, when the Hurons love him?—He is not born their enemy, and the death of one warrior will not cast a cloud between them forever."

"So much the better, Huron; so much the better. Still I do'n't wish to owe any thing to a mistake about each other's meaning. It is so much the better that you bear no malice for the loss of a warrior who fell in war, and yet it is ontrue that there is no inmity—lawful inmity I mean—atween us. So far as I have red skin feelin's at all, I've Delaware feelin's, and I leave you to judge for yourself how far they are likely to be fri'ndly to the Mingos"—

Deerslayer ceased, for a sort of spectre stood before him, that put a stop to his words, and, indeed, caused him for a moment to doubt the fidelity of his boasted vision. Hetty Hutter was standing at the side of the fire as quietly as if she belonged to the tribe.

As the hunter and the Indian sat watching the emotions that were betrayed in each other's countenance, the girl had approached unnoticed, doubtless ascending from the beach on the southern side of the point, or that next to the spot where the Ark had anchored, and had advanced to the fire with the fearlessness that belonged to her simplicity, and which was certainly justified by the treatment formerly received from the Indians. As soon as Rivenoak perceived the girl, she was recognised, and calling to two or three of the younger warriors, the chief sent them out to reconnoitre, lest her appearance should be the forerunner of another attack. He then motioned to Hetty to draw near.

"I hope your visit is a sign that the Sarpent and Hist are in safety, Hetty," said Deerslayer, as soon as the girl had complied with the Huron's request. "I do'n't think you'd come ashore ag'in, on the ar'n'd that brought you here afore."

"Judith told me to come this time, Deerslayer," Hetty replied, "she paddled me ashore herself, in a canoe as soon as the Serpent had shown her Hist, and told his story. How handsome Hist is to-night, Deerslayer, and how much happier she looks than when she was with the Hurons!"

"That's natur' gal; yes, that may be set down as human natur'. She's with her betrothed, and no longer fears a Mingo husband. In my judgment, Judith, herself, would lose most of her beauty if she thought she was to bestow it all on a Mingo! Content is a great fortifier of good looks, and I'll warrant you, Hist is contented enough, now she is out of the hands of these miscreants, and with her chosen warrior! Did you say that Judith told you to come ashore—why should your sister do that?"

"She bid me come to see you, and to try and persuade the savages to take more elephants to let you off, but I've brought the bible with me—*that* will do more than all the elephants in father's chest!"

"And your father, good little Hetty—and Hurry; did they know of your ar'n'd?"

"Not they. Both are asleep, and Judith and the Serpent thought it best they should not be woke, lest they might want to come again after scalps, when Hist had told them how few warriors, and how many women and children there were in the camp. Judith would give me no peace, 'till I had come ashore to see what had happened to *you.*"

"Well, that's remarkable as consarns Judith! Why should she feel so much unsartainty about me?—Ah—I see how it is, now; yes, I see into the whole matter, now. You must understand, Hetty, that your sister is oneasy lest Harry March should wake, and come blundering here into the hands of the inimy ag'in, under some idee that, being a travelling comrade, he ought to help me in this matter! Hurry is a blunderer, I will allow, but I do n't think he'd risk as much for my sake, as he would for his own."

"Judith do n't care for Hurry, though Hurry cares for her," replied Hetty innocently, but quite positively.

"I've heard you say as much as that afore; yes, I've heard that from you, afore, gal, and yet it is n't true. One don't live in a tribe, not to see something of the way in which liking works in a woman's heart. Though no way given to marrying myself, I've been a looker on among the Delawares, and this is a matter in which pale-face and red skin gifts are all as one as the same. When the feelin' begins, the young woman is thoughtful, and has no eyes or ears onless for the warrior that has taken her fancy; then follows melancholy and sighing, and such sort of actions; after which, especially if matters don't come to plain discourse, she often flies round to back biting and fault finding, blaming the youth for the very things she likes best in him. Some young creatur's are forward in this way of showing their love, and I'm of opinion, Judith is one of 'em. Now, I've heard her as much as deny that Hurry was good-looking, and the young woman who could do *that*, must be far gone indeed!"

"The young woman who liked Hurry would own that he is handsome. *I* think Hurry *very* handsome, Deerslayer, and I'm sure every body must think so, that has eyes. Judith do n't like Harry March, and that's the reason she finds fault with him."

"Well—well—my good little Hetty, have it your own way. If we should talk from now 'till winter, each would think as at present, and there's no use in words. I must believe that Judith is much wrapped up in Hurry, and that, sooner or later, she'll have him; and this, too, all the more from the manner in which she abuses him; and I dare to say, you think just the contrary. But mind what I now tell you, gal, and pretend not to know it—" continued this being, who was so obtuse on a point on which men are usually quick enough to make discoveries, and so acute in matters that would baffle the observation of much the greater portion of mankind, "I see how it is, with them vagabonds. Rivenoak has left us, you see, and is talking yonder with his young men, and though too far to be *heard*, I can *see* what he is telling them. Their orders is to watch your movements, and to find where the canoe is to meet you, to take you back to the Ark, and then to seize all and what they can. I'm sorry Judith sent you, for I suppose she wants you to go back ag'in."

"All that's settled, Deerslayer," returned the girl, in a low, confidential and meaning manner, "and you may trust me to out-wit the best Indian of them all. I know I am feeble minded, but I've got *some* sense, and you'll see how I'll use it, in getting back, when my errand is done!"

"Ahs! me, poor girl; I'm afeard all that's easier said than done. They're a venomous set of riptyles and their p'ison's none the milder, for the loss of Hist. Well, I'm glad the Sarpent was the one to get off with the gal, for now there'll be two happy at least, whereas had *he* fallen into the hands of the Mingos, there'd been two miserable, and another far from feelin' as a man likes to feel."

"Now you put me in mind of a part of my errand, that I had almost forgotten, Deerslayer. Judith told me to ask you, what you thought the Hurons would do with you, if you could'n't be bought off, and what *she* had best do to serve you. Yes, this was the most important part of the errand—what *she* had best do, in order to serve you?"

"That's as *you* think, Hetty; but it's no matter. Young women are apt to lay most stress on what most touches their feelin's; but no matter; have it your own way, so you be but careful not to let the vagabonds get the mastery of a canoe. When you get back to the Ark, tell 'em to keep close, and to keep moving too, most especially at night. Many hours can't go by, without the troops on the river hearing of this party, and then your fri'nds may look for relief. 'Tis but a day's march from the nearest garrison, and true soldiers will never lie idle with the foe in their neighborhood. This is my advice, and you may say to your father and Hurry, that scalp-hunting will be a poor business now, as the Mingos are up and awake, and nothing can save 'em, 'till the troops come, except keeping a good belt of water atween 'em and the savages."

"What shall I tell Judith about you, Deerslayer; I know she will send me back again, if I don't bring her the truth about *you*."

"Then tell her the *truth*. I see no reason Judith Hutter

should n't hear the *truth* about me, as well as a *lie*. I'm a captyve in Indian hands, and Providence only knows what will come of it! Harkee, Hetty—" dropping his voice and speaking still more confidentially, "you *are* a little weak minded, it must be allowed, but you know something of Injins. Here I am in their hands, after having slain one of their stoutest warriors, and they've been endivouring to work upon me through fear of consequences, to betray your father, and all in the Ark. I understand the blackguards as well as if they'd told it all out plainly, with their tongues. They hold up avarice afore me, on one side, and fear on t'other, and think honesty will give way, atween 'em both. But let your father and Hurry know, 'tis all useless; as for the Sarpent, *he* knows it already."

"But what shall I tell *Judith*?—She will certainly send me back, if I don't satisfy her mind."

"Well, tell Judith the same. No doubt the savages will try the torments, to make me give in, and to revenge the loss of their warrior, but I must hold out ag'in nat'ral weakness in the best manner I can. You may tell Judith to feel no consarn on my account—it will come hard I know, seeing that a white man's gifts don't run to boasting and singing under torment, for he generally feels smallest when he suffers most—but you may tell her not to have any consarn. I think I shall make out to stand it, and she may rely on this, let me give in, as much as I may, and prove completely that I am white, by wailings, and howlings, and even tears, yet I'll never fall so far as to betray my fri'nds. When it gets to burning holes in the flesh, with heated ramrods, and to hacking the body, and tearing the hair out by the roots, natur' may get the upperhand, so far as groans, and complaints are consarned, but there the triumph of the vagabonds will ind; nothing short of god's abandoning him to the devils, can make an honest man ontrue to his colour and duty."

Hetty listened with great attention, and her mild but speaking countenance manifested a strong sympathy in the anticipated agony of the supposititious sufferer. At first she seemed at a loss how to act; then, taking a hand of Deerslayer's she affectionately recommended to him to borrow her bible, and to read it, while the savages were inflicting their torments.

When the other honestly admitted that it exceeded his power to read, she even volunteered to remain with him, and to perform this holy office in person. The offer was gently declined, and Rivenoak being about to join them, Deerslayer requested the girl to leave him, first enjoining her again, to tell those in the Ark to have full confidence in his fidelity. Hetty now walked away, and approached the group of females, with as much confidence and self-possession, as if she were a native of the tribe. On the other hand the Huron resumed his seat by the side of his prisoner, the one continuing to ask questions with all the wily ingenuity of a practised Indian counsellor, and the other baffling him by the very means that are known to be the most efficacious in defeating the finesse of the more pretending diplomacy of civilisation, or by confining his answers to the truth, and the truth only.

Chapter XVIII

"Thus died she; never more on her
Shall sorrow light, or shame. She was not made
Through years or moons the inner weight to bear,
Which colder hearts endure till they are laid
By age in earth; her days and pleasures were
Brief but delightful—such as had not stayed
Long with her destiny; but she sleeps well
By the sea shore whereon she loved to dwell."

Byron, *Don Juan*, IV.lxxi.

THE YOUNG MEN who had been sent out to reconnoitre, on the sudden appearance of Hetty, soon returned to report their want of success in making any discovery. One of them had even been along the beach as far as the spot opposite to the Ark, but the darkness completely concealed that vessel from his notice. Others had examined in different directions, and every where the stillness of night was added to the silence and solitude of the woods. It was consequently believed that the girl had come alone, as on her former visit, and on some similar errand. The Iroquois were ignorant that the Ark had left the Castle, and there were movements projected, if not in the course of actual execution by this time, which also greatly added to the sense of security. A watch was set therefore, and all but the sentinels disposed themselves to sleep.

Sufficient care was had to the safe keeping of the captive, without inflicting on him any unnecessary suffering, and, as for Hetty, she was permitted to find a place among the Indian girls, in the best manner she could. She did not find the friendly offices of Hist, though her character not only bestowed impunity from pain and captivity, but it procured for her a consideration and an attention that placed her, on the score of comfort quite on a level with the wild but gentle beings around her. She was supplied with a skin, and made her own bed on a pile of boughs a little apart from the huts. Here she was soon in a profound sleep, like all around her.

There were now thirteen men in the party, and three kept watch at a time. One remained in shadow, not far from the fire, however. His duty was to guard the captive, to take care that the fire neither blazed up so as to illuminate the spot, nor yet became wholly extinguished, and to keep an eye generally on the state of the camp. Another passed from one beach to the other, crossing the base of the point, while the third kept moving slowly around the strand on its outer extremity, to prevent a repetition of the surprise that had already taken place that night. This arrangement was far from being usual among savages, who ordinarily rely more on the secrecy of their movements, than on vigilance of this nature, but it had been called for by the peculiarity of the circumstances in which the Hurons were now placed. Their position was known to their foes, and it could not easily be changed at an hour, which demanded rest. Perhaps, too, they placed most of their confidence on the knowledge of what they believed to be passing higher up the lake, and which, it was thought, would fully occupy the whole of the pale-faces, who were at liberty, with their solitary Indian ally. It was also probable Rivenoak was aware, that, in holding his captive, he had in his own hands the most dangerous of all his enemies.

The precision with which those, accustomed to watchfulness, or lives of disturbed rest, sleep, is not the least of the phenomena of our mysterious being. The head is no sooner on the pillow, than consciousness is lost, and yet, at a necessary hour, the mind appears to arouse the body, as promptly as if it had stood sentinel over it the while. There can be no doubt that they who are thus roused, awake by the influence of thought over matter, though the mode in which this influence is exercised must remain hidden from our curiosity, until it shall be explained, should that hour ever arrive, by the entire enlightenment of the soul, on the subject of all human mysteries. Thus it was with Hetty Hutter. Feeble as the immaterial portion of her existence was thought to be, it was sufficiently active to cause her to open her eyes at midnight. At that hour she awoke, and leaving her bed of skin and boughs, she walked innocently and openly to the embers of the fire, stirring the latter, as the coolness of the night and the woods, in connection with an exceedingly unsophisticated bed, had a little chilled her. As the flame shot up, it lighted the swarthy countenance of the Huron on watch, whose dark eyes glistened under its light, like the balls of the panther that is pursued to his den with burning brands. But Hetty felt no fear, and she approached the spot where the Indian stood. Her movements were so natural, and so perfectly devoid of any of the stealthiness of cunning, or deception, that he imagined she had merely arisen on account of the coolness of the night, a common occurrence in a bivouac, and the one of all others, perhaps, the least likely to excite suspicion. Hetty spoke to him, but he understood no English. She then gazed near a minute at the sleeping captive, and moved slowly away, in a sad and melancholy manner.

The girl took no pains to conceal her movements. Any ingenious expedient of this nature quite likely exceeded her powers; still her step was habitually light, and scarcely audible. As she took the direction of the extremity of the point, or the place where she had landed in her first adventure, and where Hist had embarked, the sentinel saw her light form gradually disappear in the gloom without uneasiness, or changing his own position. He knew that others were on the look-out, and he did not believe that one who had twice come into the camp voluntarily, and had already left it openly, would take refuge in flight. In short, the conduct of the girl excited no more attention than that of any person of feeble intellect would excite in civilized society, while her person met with more consideration and respect.

Hetty certainly had no very distinct notions of the localities, but she found her way to the beach, which she reached on the same side of the point as that on which the camp had been made. By following the margin of the water, taking a northern direction, she soon encountered the Indian, who paced the strand as sentinel. This was a young warrior, and when he heard her light tread coming along the gravel, he approached swiftly, though with any thing but menace in his manner. The darkness was so intense that it was not easy to discover forms, within the shadows of the woods, at the distance of twenty feet, and quite impossible to distinguish persons until near enough to touch them. The young Huron manifested disappointment when he found whom he had met, for truth to say, he was expecting his favorite, who had promised to relieve the *ennui* of a midnight watch with her presence. This man was also ignorant of English, but he was at no loss to understand why the girl should be up at that hour. Such things were usual in an Indian village and camp, where sleep is as irregular as the meals. Then poor Hetty's known imbecility, as in most things connected with the savages, stood her friend on this occasion. Vexed at his disappointment, and impatient of the presence of one he thought an intruder, the young warrior signed for the girl to move forward, holding the direction of the beach. Hetty complied, but as she walked away, she spoke aloud in English, in her usual, soft, tones, which the stillness of the night made audible at some little distance.

"If you took me for a Huron girl, warrior," she said, "I do n't wonder you are so little pleased. I am Hetty Hutter, Thomas Hutter's daughter, and have never met any man at night, for mother always said it was wrong, and modest young women should never do it—modest young women of the pale-faces, I mean, for customs are different in different parts of the world, I know. No—no—I'm Hetty Hutter, and would n't meet even Hurry Harry, though he should fall down on his knees and ask me! Mother said it was wrong."

By the time Hetty had said this, she reached the place where the canoes had come ashore, and owing to the curvature of the land and the bushes, would have been completely hid from the sight of the sentinel, had it been broad day. But another footstep had caught the lover's ear, and he was already nearly beyond the sound of the girl's silvery voice. Still Hetty, bent only on her own thoughts and purposes, continued to speak, though the gentleness of her tones prevented the sounds from penetrating far into the woods. On the water they were more widely diffused.

"Here I am, Judith," she added, "and there is no one near me. The Huron on watch has gone to meet his sweetheart, who is an Indian girl, you know, and never had a christian mother to tell her how wrong it is to meet a man at night.—"

Hetty's voice was hushed by a "hist!," that came from the water, and then she caught a dim view of the canoe, which approached noiselessly, and soon grated on the shingle with its bow. The moment the weight of Hetty was felt in the light craft, the canoe withdrew stern foremost, as if possessed of life and volition, until it was a hundred yards from the shore. Then it turned, and making a wide sweep, as much to prolong the passage as to get beyond the sound of voices, it held its way towards the Ark. For several minutes nothing was uttered, but believing herself to be in a favorable position to confer with her sister, Judith, who alone sat in the stern, managing the canoe with a skill little short of that of a man, began a discourse, which she had been burning to commence ever since they quitted the point.

"Here we are safe, Hetty," she said, "and may talk without the fear of being overheard. You must speak low, however, for sounds are heard far on the water, in a still night. I was so close to the point, some of the time, while you were on it that I heard the voices of the warriors, and I heard your shoes on the gravel of the beach, even before you spoke."

"I do n't believe, Judith, the Hurons know I have left them!"

"Quite likely they do not, for a lover makes a poor sentry, unless it be to watch for his sweetheart!—But, tell me, Hetty, did you see, and speak with Deerslayer?"

"Oh! yes—There he was seated near the fire, with his legs tied, though they left his arms free, to move them as he pleased."

"Well, what did he tell you, child? Speak, quick; I am dying to know what message he sent me."

"What did he tell me?—Why, what do you think, Judith; he told me that he could n't read! Only think of that; a white man, and not know how to read his bible, even! He never could have had a mother, sister!"

"Never mind *that*, Hetty. All men can't read; though mother knew so much, and taught us so much, father knows very little about books, and he can barely read the bible, you know."

"Oh! I never thought fathers *could* read much, but *mothers* ought all to read, else how can they teach their children. Depend on it, Judith, Deerslayer could never have had a mother, else he would know how to read."

"Did you tell him *I* sent you ashore, Hetty, and how much concern I felt for his misfortune?" asked the other, impatiently.

"I believe I did, Judith; but you know I am feeble-minded, and I may have forgotten. I *did* tell him you brought me ashore. And he told me a great deal that I was to say to you, which I remember well, for it made my blood run cold to hear him. He told me to say that his friends—I suppose you are one of them, sister?"

"How can you torment me thus, Hetty! Certainly, I am one of the truest friends he has on earth."

"Torment you! yes, now I remember all about it. I am glad you used that word, Judith, for it brings it all back to my mind. Well he said he might be *tormented* by the savages, but he would try to bear it as becomes a christian white-man, and that no one need be afeard—why does Deerslayer call it afeard, when mother always taught us to say afraid?"

"Never mind, dear Hetty, never mind *that*, now," cried the other, almost gasping for breath. "Did Deerslayer really tell you that he thought the savages would put him to the torture? Recollect now well, Hetty, for this is a most awful and serious thing."

"Yes he did, and I remembered it, by your speaking about my tormenting you. Oh! I felt very sorry for him, and Deerslayer took all so quietly and without noise! Deerslayer is not as handsome as Hurry Harry, Judith, but he is more quiet."

"He's worth a million Hurry's! Yes, he's worth all the young men who ever came upon the lake put together," said Judith, with an energy and positiveness that caused her sister to wonder. "He is *true*. There is no lie about Deerslayer. *You*, Hetty, may not know what a merit it is in a man to have truth, but when you get—no—I hope you will never know it. Why should one like you, be ever made to learn the hard lesson to distrust and hate!"

Judith bowed her face, dark as it was, and unseen as she must have been, by any eye but that of omniscience, between her hands, and groaned. This sudden paroxysm of feeling, however, lasted but for a moment, and she continued more calmly, still speaking frankly to her sister, whose intelligence, and whose discretion in any thing that related to herself, she did not in the least distrust. Her voice, however, was low and husky, instead of having its former clearness and animation.

"It is a hard thing to fear truth, Hetty," she said, "and yet do I more dread Deerslayer's truth, than any enemy! One cannot tamper with such truth—so much honesty—such obstinate uprightness! But we are not altogether unequal, sister—Deerslayer and I? He is not altogether my superior?"

It was not usual for Judith so far to demean herself, as to appeal to Hetty's judgment. Nor did she often address her by the title of sister, a distinction that is commonly given by the junior to the senior, even where there is perfect equality in all other respects. As trifling departures from habitual deportment oftener strike the imagination than more important changes, Hetty perceived the circumstances, and wondered at them in her own simple way.

Her ambition was a little quickened, and the answer was as much out of the usual course of things, as the question, the poor girl attempting to refine beyond her strength.

"Superior, Judith!" she repeated with pride. "In what *can* Deerslayer be *your* superior?—Are you not mother's child, and does he know how to read, and was n't mother before any woman in all this part of the world? I should think so far from supposing himself *your* superior, he would hardly believe himself *mine*. You are handsome and he is ugly"—

"No, not ugly, Hetty—" interrupted Judith—"Only plain. But his honest face has a look in it, that is far better than beauty. In my eyes Deerslayer is handsomer than Hurry Harry."

"Judith Hutter! You frighten me. Hurry is the handsomest mortal in the world—even handsomer than you are yourself, because a man's good looks, you know, are always better than a woman's good looks."

This little innocent touch of natural taste did not please the elder sister at the moment, and she did not scruple to betray it.

"Hetty, you now speak foolishly, and had better say no more, on this subject," she answered. "Hurry is not the handsomest mortal in the world, by many, and there are officers in the garrisons—" Judith stammered at the words—"there are officers in the garrisons, near us, far comelier than he. But, why do you think me the equal of Deerslayer—speak of *that*, for I do not like to hear you show so much admiration of a man like Hurry Harry, who has neither feelings, manners, nor conscience. *You* are too good for *him*, and he ought to be told it, at once."

"*I!* Judith how you forget! Why *I* am not beautiful, and am feeble minded."

"You are *good*, Hetty, and that is more than can be said of Henry March. He may have a *face*, and a *body*, but he has no *heart*. But enough of this for the present. Tell me what raises me to an equality with Deerslayer."

"To think of you asking me this, Judith! He can n't read, and you can. He do n't know how to talk, but speaks worse than Hurry even;—for, sister, Harry does n't always pronounce his words right! Did you ever notice *that*?"

"Certainly. He is as coarse in speech, as in every thing else. But, I fear you flatter me, Hetty, when you think I can be justly called the equal of a man like Deerslayer. It is true, I have been better taught; in one sense am more comely; and perhaps might look higher, but then his truth—his truth—makes a fearful difference between us! Well, I will talk no more of this, and we will bethink us of the means of getting him out of the hands of the Hurons. We have father's chest in the Ark, Hetty, and might try the temptation of more elephants; though I fear such baubles will not buy the liberty of a man like Deerslayer. I am afraid Father and Hurry will not be as willing to ransom Deerslayer, as Deerslayer was to ransom them!"

"Why not, Judith? Hurry and Deerslayer are friends, and friends should always help one another."

"Alas! poor Hetty, you little know mankind! Seeming friends are often more to be dreaded than open enemies, particularly by females. But you'll have to land in the morning, and try again what can be done for Deerslayer. Tortured he *shall* not be, while Judith Hutter lives, and can find means to prevent it."

The conversation now grew desultory, and was drawn out, until the elder sister had extracted from the younger, every fact that the feeble faculties of the latter permitted her to retain, and to communicate. When Judith was satisfied—though, she could never be said to be satisfied whose feelings seemed to be so interwoven with all that related to the subject as to have excited a nearly inappeasable curiosity—but, when

Judith could think of no more questions to ask, without resorting to repetition, the canoe was paddled towards the scow. The intense darkness of the night, and the deep shadows which the hills and forest cast upon the water, rendered it difficult to find the vessel, anchored, as it had been, as close to the shore as a regard to safety rendered prudent. Judith was expert in the management of a bark canoe, the lightness of which demanded skill rather than strength, and she forced her own little vessel swiftly over the water, the moment she had ended her conference with Hetty, and had come to the determination to return. Still no Ark was seen. Several times the sisters fancied they saw it, looming up in the obscurity, like a low black rock, but on each occasion it was found to be either an optical illusion, or some swell of the foliage on the shore. After a search that lasted half an hour, the girls were forced to the unwelcome conviction that the Ark had departed.

Most young women would have felt the awkwardness of their situation, in a physical sense, under the circumstances in which the sisters were left, more than any apprehensions of a different nature. Not so with Judith, however; and even Hetty felt more concern about the motives that might have influenced her father and Hurry, than any fears for her own safety.

"It cannot be, Hetty," said Judith, when a thorough search had satisfied them both that no Ark was to be found, "it cannot be that the Indians have rafted, or swam off, and surprised our friends as they slept?"

"I do n't believe that Hist and Chingachgook would sleep, until they had told each other all they had to say, after so long a separation, do you sister?"

"Perhaps not, child. There was much to keep them awake, but one Indian may have been surprised even when not asleep, especially as his thoughts may have been on other things. Still we should have heard a noise, for in a night like this, an oath of Hurry Harry's would have echoed in the eastern hills like a clap of thunder."

"Hurry *is* sinful and thoughtless about his words, Judith," Hetty meekly and sorrowfully answered.

"No—no; 'tis impossible the Ark could be taken and I not

hear the noise. It is not an hour since I left it, and the whole time I have been attentive to the smallest sound. And, yet, it is not easy to believe a father would willingly abandon his children!"

"Perhaps Father has thought us in our cabin, asleep, Judith, and has moved away to go home. You know, we often move the Ark in the night."

"This is true, Hetty, and it must be as you suppose. There is a little more southern air than there was, and they have gone up the lake.—"

Judith stopped, for, as the last word was on her tongue, the scene was suddenly lighted, though only for a single instant, by a flash. The crack of a rifle succeeded, and then followed the roll of the echo along the eastern mountains. Almost at the same moment, a piercing female cry arose in the air in a prolonged shriek. The awful stillness that succeeded was, if possible, more appalling than the fierce and sudden interruption of the deep silence of midnight. Resolute as she was both by nature and habit, Judith scarce breathed, while poor Hetty hid her face and trembled.

"That was a woman's cry, Hetty," said the former solemnly, "and it was a cry of anguish! If the Ark has moved from this spot, it can only have gone north with this air, and the gun and shriek came from the point. Can any thing have befallen Hist!"

"Let us go and see, Judith; she may want our assistance, for besides herself, there are none but men in the Ark."

It was not a moment for hesitation, and ere Judith had ceased speaking her paddle was in the water. The distance to the point, in a direct line was not great, and the impulses under which the girls worked were too exciting to allow them to waste the precious moments in useless precautions. They paddled incautiously for them, but the same excitement kept others from noting their movements. Presently a glare of light caught the eye of Judith through an opening in the bushes, and steering by it she so directed the canoe as to keep it visible, while she got as near the land as was either prudent or necessary.

The scene that was now presented to the observation of the girls, was within the woods, on the side of the acclivity, so often mentioned, and in plain view from the boat. Here all in the camp were collected, some six or eight carrying torches of fat-pine, which cast a strong but funereal light on all beneath the arches of the forest. With her back supported against a tree, and sustained on one side by the young sentinel whose remissness had suffered Hetty to escape, sate the female whose expected visit had produced his delinquency. By the glare of the torch that was held near her face, it was evident that she was in the agonies of death, while the blood that trickled from her bared bosom betrayed the nature of the injury she had received. The pungent, peculiar smell of gunpowder, too, was still quite perceptible in the heavy, damp, night air. There could be no question that she had been shot. Judith understood it all, at a glance. The streak of light had appeared on the water, a short distance from the point, and either the rifle had been discharged from a canoe hovering near the land, or it had been fired from the Ark, in passing. An incautious exclamation, or laugh, may have produced the assault, for it was barely possible that the aim had been assisted by any other agent than sound. As to the effect, that was soon still more apparent, the head of the victim dropping, and the body sinking in death. Then all the torches but one were extinguished, a measure of prudence, and the melancholy train that bore the body to the camp, was just to be distinguished by the glimmering light that remained.

Judith sighed heavily and shuddered, as her paddle again dipped, and the canoe moved cautiously around the point. A sight had afflicted her senses, and now haunted her imagination, that was still harder to be borne, than even the untimely fate, and passing agony of the deceased girl. She had seen, under the strong glare of all the torches, the erect form of Deerslayer, standing, with commiseration, and as she thought with shame, depicted on his countenance, near the dying female. He betrayed neither fear, nor backwardness, *himself*, but it was apparent by the glances cast at him by the warriors, that fierce passions were struggling in *their* bosoms. All this seemed to be unheeded by the captive, but it remained impressed on the memory of Judith throughout the night.

No canoe was met hovering near the point. A stillness and darkness, as complete as if the silence of the forest had never been disturbed, or the sun had never shone on that retired region, now reigned on the point, and on the gloomy water, the slumbering woods, and even the murky sky. No more could be done, therefore, than to seek a place of safety, and this was only to be found in the centre of the lake. Paddling, in silence to that spot, the canoe was suffered to drift northerly, while the girls sought such repose as their situation and feelings would permit.

Chapter XIX

> "Stand to your arms, and guard the door—all's lost
> Unless that fearful bell be silenced soon.
> The officer hath miss'd his path, or purpose,
> Or met some unforeseen and hideous obstacle.
> Anselmo, with thy company proceed
> Straight to the tower; the rest remain with me."
>
> Byron, *Marino Faliero*, IV.ii.230–35.

THE CONJECTURE of Judith Hutter, concerning the manner in which the Indian girl had met her death, was accurate in the main. After sleeping several hours, her father and March awoke. This occurred a few minutes after she had left the Ark to go in quest of her sister, and when of course Chingachgook and his betrothed were on board. From the Delaware the old man learned the position of the camp, and the recent events, as well as the absence of his daughters. The latter gave him no concern, for he relied greatly on the sagacity of the elder, and the known impunity with which the younger passed among the savages. Long familiarity with danger, too, had blunted his sensibilities. Nor did he seem much to regret the captivity of Deerslayer, for, while he knew how material his aid might be in a defence, the difference in their views on the morality of the woods, had not left much sympathy between them. He would have rejoiced to know the position of the camp before it had been alarmed by the escape of Hist, but it would be too hazardous now to venture to land, and he reluctantly relinquished for the night, the ruthless designs that cupidity and revenge had excited him to entertain. In this mood Hutter took a seat in the head of the scow, where he was quickly joined by Hurry, leaving the Serpent and Hist in quiet possession of the other extremity of the vessel.

"Deerslayer has shown himself a boy, in going among the savages at this hour, and letting himself fall into their hands like a deer that tumbles into a pit," growled the old man, perceiving as usual the mote in his neighbor's eyes, while he overlooked the beam in his own; "if he is left to pay for his stupidity with his own flesh, he can blame no one but himself."

"That's the way of the world, old Tom," returned Hurry. "Every man must meet his own debts, and answer for his own sins. I'm amazed, howsever, that a lad as skilful and watchful as Deerslayer, should have been caught in such a trap! Did n't he know any better than to go prowling about a Huron camp, at midnight, with no place to retreat to, but a lake; or did he think himself a buck, that by taking to the water could throw off the scent and swim himself out of difficulty. I had a better opinion of the boy's judgment, I'll own; but we must overlook a little ignorance in a raw hand. I say, Master Hutter, do you happen to know what has become of the gals—I see no signs of Judith, or Hetty, though I've been through the Ark, and looked into all its living creatur's."

Hutter briefly explained the manner in which his daughters had taken to the canoe, as it had been related by the Delaware, as well as the return of Judith after landing her sister, and her second departure.

"This comes of a smooth tongue, Floating Tom," exclaimed Hurry, grating his teeth in pure resentment—"This comes of a smooth tongue, and a silly gal's inclinations, and you had best look into the matter! You and I were both prisoners—" Hurry could recal that circumstance *now*—"you and I were both prisoners and yet Judith never stirred an inch to do us any sarvice! She is bewitched with this lank-looking Deerslayer, and he, and she, and you, and all of us, had best look to it. I am not a man to put up with such a wrong quietly, and I say, all the parties had best look to it! Let's up kedge, old fellow, and move nearer to this p'int, and see how matters are getting on."

Hutter had no objections to this movement, and the Ark was got under way, in the usual manner; care being taken to make no noise. The wind was passing northward, and the sail soon swept the scow so far up the lake, as to render the dark outlines of the trees that clothed the point, dimly visible. Floating Tom steered, and he sailed along as near the land, as the depth of the water, and the overhanging branches would allow. It was impossible to distinguish any thing that stood within the shadows of the shore, but the forms of the sail and of the hut, were discerned by the young sentinel on the beach, who has already been mentioned. In the moment of sudden surprise, a deep Indian exclamation escaped him. In that spirit of recklessness and ferocity that formed the essence of Hurry's character, this man dropped his rifle and fired. The ball was sped by accident, or by that overruling providence which decides the fates of all, and the girl fell. Then followed the scene with the torches, which has just been described.

At the precise moment when Hurry committed this act of unthinking cruelty, the canoe of Judith was within a hundred feet of the spot from which the Ark had so lately moved. Her own course has been described, and it has now become our office to follow that of her father and his companions. The shriek announced the effects of the random shot of March, and it also proclaimed that the victim was a woman. Hurry himself was startled at these unlooked for consequences, and for a moment he was sorely disturbed by conflicting sensations. At first he laughed, in reckless and rude-minded exultation; and then conscience, that monitor planted in our breasts by God, and which receives its more general growth from the training bestowed in the tillage of childhood, shot a pang to his heart. For a minute, the mind of this creature equally of civilization and of barbarism, was a sort of chaos as to feeling, not knowing what to think of its own act; and then the obstinacy and pride of one of his habits, interposed to assert their usual ascendency. He struck the butt of his rifle on the bottom of the scow, with a species of defiance, and began to whistle a low air with an affectation of indifference. All this time the Ark was in motion, and it was already opening the bay above the point, and was consequently quitting the land.

Hurry's companions did not view his conduct with the same indulgence, as that with which he appeared disposed to regard it himself. Hutter growled out his dissatisfaction, for the act led to no advantage, while it threatened to render the warfare more vindictive than ever, and none censure motiveless departures from the right, more severely than the mercenary and unprincipled. Still he commanded himself, the captivity of Deerslayer rendering the arm of the offender of double consequence to him at that moment. Chingachgook arose, and for a single instant the ancient animosity of tribes was forgotten, in a feeling of colour; but he recollected himself in season to prevent any of the fierce consequences that, for a passing moment, he certainly meditated. Not so with Hist. Rushing through the hut, or cabin, the girl stood at the side of Hurry, almost as soon as his rifle touched the bottom of the scow, and with a fearlessness that did credit to her heart, she poured out her reproaches with the generous warmth of a woman.

"What for you shoot?" she said. "What Huron gal do, dat you kill him? What you t'ink Manitou *say*? What you t'ink Manitou, *feel*? What Iroquois *do*? No get honour—no get camp—no get prisoner—no get battle—no get scalp—no get not'ing at all! Blood come after blood! How you feel, your wife killed? Who pity you, when tear come for moder, or sister? You big as great pine—Huron gal little slender birch—why you fall on her and crush her! You t'ink Huron forget it? No; red skin never forget! Never forget friend; never forget enemy. Red man Manitou in *dat*. Why you so wicked, great paleface?"

Hurry had never been so daunted as by this close and warm attack of the Indian girl. It is true that she had a powerful ally in his conscience, and while she spoke earnestly, it was in tones so feminine as to deprive him of any pretext for unmanly anger. The softness of her voice added to the weight of her remonstrance, by lending to the latter an air of purity and truth. Like most vulgar minded men, he had only regarded the Indians through the medium of their coarser and fiercer characteristics. It had never struck him that the affections are human, that even high principles—modified by habits and prejudices, but not the less elevated within their circle—can exist in the savage state, and that the warrior who is most ruthless in the field, can submit to the softest and gentlest influences, in the moments of domestic quiet. In a word, it was the habit of his mind to regard all Indians as being only a slight degree removed from the wild beasts that roamed the woods, and to feel disposed to treat them accordingly, whenever interest or caprice supplied a motive, or an impulse. Still, though daunted by these reproaches, the handsome barbarian could hardly be said to be penitent. He was too much rebuked by conscience to suffer an outbreak of temper to escape him, and perhaps he felt that he had already committed an act that might justly bring his manhood in question. Instead of resenting, or answering the simple but natural appeal of Hist, he walked away, like one who disdained entering into a controversy with a woman.

In the mean while, the Ark swept onward, and by the time the scene with the torches, was enacting beneath the trees, it had reached the open lake, Floating Tom causing it to sheer further from the land, with a sort of instinctive dread of retaliation. An hour now passed in gloomy silence, no one appearing disposed to break it. Hist had retired to her pallet, and Chingachgook lay sleeping in the forward part of the scow. Hutter and Hurry alone remained awake, the former at the steering oar, while the latter brooded over his own conduct, with the stubbornness of one little given to a confession of his errors, and the secret goadings of the worm that never dies. This was at the moment when Judith and Hetty reached the centre of the lake, and had lain down to endeavor to sleep, in their drifting canoe.

The night was calm, though so much obscured by clouds. The season was not one of storms, and those which did occur in the month of June, on that embedded water, though frequently violent were always of short continuance. Nevertheless, there was the usual current of heavy, damp night air, which, passing over the summits of the trees, scarcely appeared to descend as low as the surface of the glassy lake, but kept moving a short distance above it, saturated with the humidity that constantly arose from the woods, and apparently never proceeding far in any one direction. The currents were influenced by the formation of the hills, as a matter of course, a circumstance that rendered even fresh breezes baffling, and which reduced the feebler efforts of the night air to be a sort of capricious and fickle sighings of the woods. Several times the head of the Ark pointed east, and once it was actually turned towards the south, again; but, on the whole, it worked its way north; Hutter making always a fair wind, if wind it could be called, his principal motive appearing to be a wish to keep in motion, in order to defeat any treacherous design of his enemies. He, now, felt some little concern about his daughters, and perhaps as much about the canoe; but, on the whole, this uncertainty did not much disturb him, as he had the reliance already mentioned on the intelligence of Judith.

It was the season of the shortest nights, and it was not long before the deep obscurity which precedes the day began to yield to the returning light. If any earthly scene could be presented to the senses of man that might soothe his passions and temper his ferocity, it was that which grew upon the eyes of Hutter and Hurry, as the hours advanced, changing night to morning. There were the usual soft tints of the sky, in which neither the gloom of darkness nor the brilliancy of the sun prevails, and under which objects appear more unearthly and we might add holy, than at any other portion of the twenty four hours. The beautiful and soothing calm of even tide has been extolled by a thousand poets, and yet it does not bring with it, the far-reaching and sublime thoughts of the half hour that precedes the rising of a summer sun. In the one case the panorama is gradually hid from the sight, while in the other, its objects start out from the unfolding picture, first dim and misty; then marked in, in solemn back ground; next seen in the witchery of an *increasing*, a thing as different as possible from the *decreasing* twilight, and finally mellow, distinct and luminous, as the rays of the great centre of light diffuse themselves in the atmosphere. The hymns of birds, too, have no moral counterpart in the retreat to the roost, or the flight to the nest, and these invariably accompany the advent of the day, until the appearance of the sun itself—

"Bathes in deep joy, the land and sea."

All this, however, Hutter and Hurry witnessed without experiencing any of that calm delight, which the spectacle is wont to bring, when the thoughts are just, and the aspirations pure. They not only witnessed it, but they witnessed it under circumstances that had a tendency to increase its power, and to heighten its charms. Only one solitary object became visible in the returning light, that had received its form or uses from human taste, or human desires which as often deform as beautify a landscape. This was the castle, all the rest being native, and fresh from the hand of God. That singular residence, too, was in keeping with the natural objects of the view, starting out from the gloom, quaint, picturesque, and ornamental. Nevertheless the whole was lost on the observers, who knew no feeling of poetry, had lost their sense of natural devotion in lives of obdurate and narrow selfishness, and had little other sympathy with nature, than that which originated with her lowest wants.

As soon as the light was sufficiently strong to allow of a distinct view of the lake, and more particularly of its shores, Hutter turned the head of the Ark directly towards the castle, with the avowed intention of taking possession, for the day at least, as the place most favorable for meeting his daughters, and for carrying on his operations against the Indians. By this time, Chingachgook was up, and Hist was heard stirring among the furniture of the kitchen. The place for which they steered was distant only a mile, and the air was sufficiently favorable to permit it to be reached by means of the sail. At this moment, too, to render the appearances generally auspicious, the canoe of Judith was seen floating northward in the broadest part of the lake; having actually passed the scow in the darkness, in obedience to no other power than that of the elements. Hutter got his glass, and took a long and anxious survey, to ascertain if his daughters were in the light craft, or not, and a slight exclamation like that of joy escaped him, as he caught a glimpse of what he rightly conceived to be a part of Judith's dress above the top of the canoe. At the next instant the girl arose, and was seen gazing about her, like one assuring herself of her situation. A minute later, Hetty was seen on her knees, in the other end of the canoe, repeating the prayers that had been taught her, in childhood, by a misguided but repentant mother. As Hutter laid down the glass, still drawn to its focus, the Serpent raised it to his eye, and turned it towards the canoe. It was the first time he had ever used such an instrument, and Hist understood by his "hugh!," the expression of his face, and his entire mien, that something wonderful had excited his admiration. It is well known that the American Indians, more particularly those of superior characters and stations, singularly maintain their self-possession and stoicism, in the midst of the flood of marvels that present themselves in their occasional visits to the abodes of civilization, and Chingachgook had imbibed enough of this impassibility to suppress any very undignified manifestation of surprise. With Hist, however, no such law was binding, and when her lover managed to bring the glass in a line with a canoe, and her eye was applied to the smaller end, the girl started back in alarm; then she clapped her hands with delight, and a laugh, the usual attendant of untutored admiration, followed. A few minutes sufficed to enable this quick witted girl to manage the instrument for herself, and she directed it at every prominent object that struck her fancy. Finding a rest in one of the windows, she and the Delaware first surveyed the lake; then the shores, the hills, and, finally, the castle attracted their attention. After a long steady gaze at the latter, Hist took away her eye, and spoke to her lover in a low earnest manner. Chingachgook immediately placed his eye to the glass, and his look even exceeded that of his betrothed in length and intensity. Again they spoke together, confidentially, appearing to compare opinions, after which the glass was laid aside, and the young warrior quitted the cabin to join Hutter and Hurry.

The Ark was slowly but steadily advancing, and the castle was materially within half a mile, when Chingachgook joined the two white men in the stern of the scow. His manner was calm, but it was evident to the others, who were familiar with the habits of the Indians, that he had something to communicate. Hurry was generally prompt to speak and, according to custom, he took the lead on this occasion.

"Out with it, red-skin," he cried, in his usual rough manner. "Have you discovered a chip-munk in a tree, or is there a salmon-trout swimming under the bottom of the scow? You find what a pale-face can do in the way of eyes, now, Sarpent, and must n't wonder that they can see the land of the Indians from afar off."

"No good to go to Castle," put in Chingachgook with emphasis, the moment the other gave him an opportunity of speaking. "Huron there."

"The devil he is!—If this should turn out to be true, Floating Tom, a pretty trap were we about to pull down on our heads! Huron, there!—Well, this may be so; but no signs can I see of any thing, near or about the old hut, but logs, water, and bark—bating two or three windows, and one door."

Hutter called for the glass, and took a careful survey of the spot, before he ventured an opinion, at all; then he somewhat cavalierly expressed his dissent from that given by the Indian.

"You've got this glass wrong end foremost, Delaware," continued Hurry. "Neither the old man, nor I can see any trail in the lake."

"No trail—water make no trail," said Hist, eagerly. "Stop boat—no go too near. Huron there!"

"Ay, that's it!—Stick to the same tale, and more people will believe you. I hope Sarpent, you and your gal will agree in telling the same story arter marriage, as well as you do now. 'Huron, there!'—Whereabouts is he to be seen—in the padlock, or the chains, or the logs. There is n't a gaol in the colony that has a more lock up look about it, than old Tom's *chientè*, and, I know something about gaols from exper'ence."

"No see moccasin—" said Hist, impatiently—"why no *look*—and see him."

"Give me the glass, Harry," interrupted Hutter, "and lower the sail. It is seldom that an Indian woman meddles, and when she does, there is generally a cause for it. There *is*, truly, a moccasin floating against one of the piles, and it may, or may not be a sign that the castle has n't escaped visitors, in our absence. Moccasins are no rarities, however, for I wear 'em myself; and Deerslayer wears 'em, and you wear 'em, March, and, for that matter so does Hetty, quite as often as she wears shoes, though I never yet saw Judith trust her pretty foot in a moccasin."

Hurry had lowered the sail, and by this time the Ark was within two hundred yards of the castle, setting in, nearer and nearer, each moment, but at a rate too slow to excite any uneasiness. Each now took the glass in turn, and the castle, and every thing near it, was subjected to a scrutiny still more rigid than ever. There the moccasin lay, beyond a question, floating so lightly, and preserving its form so well, that it was scarcely wet. It had caught by a piece of the rough bark of one of the piles, on the exterior of the water-palisade that formed the dock already mentioned, which circumstance alone prevented it from drifting away before the air. There were many modes, however, of accounting for the presence of the moccasin, without supposing it to have been dropped by an enemy. It might have fallen from the platform, even while Hutter was in possession of the place, and drifted to the spot where it was now seen, remaining unnoticed until detected by the acute vision of Hist. It might have drifted from a distance, up or down the lake, and accidentally become attached to the pile, or palisade. It might have been thrown from a window, and alighted in that particular place; or it might certainly have fallen from a scout, or an assailant, during the past night, who was obliged to abandon it, to the lake, in the deep obscurity which then prevailed.

All these conjectures passed from Hutter to Hurry, the former appearing disposed to regard the omen as a little sinister, while the latter treated it with his usual reckless disdain. As for the Indian, he was of opinion that the moccasin should be viewed as one would regard a trail in the woods, which might, or might not, equally, prove to be threatening. Hist, however, had something available to propose. She declared her readiness to take a canoe, to proceed to the palisade and bring away the moccasin, when its ornaments would show whether it came from the Canadas or not. Both the white men were disposed to accept this offer, but the Delaware interfered to prevent the risk. If such a service was to be undertaken, it best became a warrior to expose himself in its execution, and he gave his refusal to let his betrothed proceed, much in the quiet but brief manner in which an Indian husband issues his commands.

"Well then, Delaware, go yourself if you're so tender of your squaw," put in the unceremonious Hurry. "That moccasin must be had, or Floating Tom will keep off, here, at arm's length, till the hearth cools in his cabin. It's but a little deerskin, a'ter all, and cut this-a-way or that-a-way, it's not a skear-crow to frighten true hunters from their game. What say you, Sarpent, shall you or I canoe it?"

"Let red man go.—Better eyes than pale-face—know Huron trick better, too."

"That I'll gainsay, to the hour of my death! A white man's eyes, and a white man's nose, and for that matter his sight and ears are all better than an Injin's when fairly tried. Time and ag'in have I put that to the proof, and what is proved is sartain. Still I suppose the poorest vagabond going, whether

Delaware or Huron, can find his way to yonder hut and back ag'in, and so, Sarpent, use your paddle and welcome."

Chingachgook was already in the canoe, and he dipped the implement the other named into the water, just as Hurry's limber tongue ceased. Wah-ta!-Wah saw the departure of her warrior on this occasion, with the submissive silence of an Indian girl, but with most of the misgivings and apprehensions of her sex. Throughout the whole of the past night, and down to the moment, when they used the glass together in the hut, Chingachgook had manifested as much manly tenderness towards his betrothed, as one of the most refined sentiment could have shown under similar circumstances, but now every sign of weakness was lost in an appearance of stern resolution. Although Hist timidly endeavored to catch his eye, as the canoe left the side of the Ark, the pride of a warrior would not permit him to meet her fond and anxious looks. The canoe departed and not a wandering glance rewarded her solicitude.

Nor were the Delaware's care and gravity misplaced, under the impressions with which he proceeded on this enterprise. If the enemy had really gained possession of the building, he was obliged to put himself under the very muzzles of their rifles, as it were, and this too without the protection of any of that cover, which forms so essential an ally in Indian warfare. It is scarcely possible to conceive of a service more dangerous, and had the Serpent been fortified by the experience of ten more years, or had his friend the Deerslayer been present, it would never have been attempted; the advantages in no degree compensating for the risk. But the pride of an Indian chief was acted on by the rivalry of colour, and it is not unlikely that the presence of the very creature from whom his ideas of manhood prevented his receiving a single glance, overflowing as he was with the love she so well merited, had no small influence on his determination.

Chingachgook paddled steadily towards the palisades, keeping his eyes on the different loops of the building. Each instant he expected to see the muzzle of a rifle protruded, or to hear its sharp crack; but he succeeded in reaching the piles in safety. Here he was, in a measure, protected, having the heads of the palisades between him and the hut, and the chances of any attempt on his life while thus covered, were greatly diminished. The canoe had reached the piles with its head inclining northward, and at a short distance from the moccasin. Instead of turning to pick up the latter, the Delaware slowly made the circuit of the whole building, deliberately examining every object that should betray the presence of enemies, or the commission of violence. Not a single sign could he discover, however, to confirm the suspicions that had been awakened. The stillness of desertion pervaded the building; not a fastening was displaced, not a window had been broken. The door looked as secure as at the hour when it was closed by Hutter, and even the gate of the dock had all the customary fastenings. In short, the most wary and jealous eye could detect no other evidence of the visit of enemies, than that which was connected with the appearance of the floating moccasin.

The Delaware was now greatly at a loss how to proceed. At one moment, as he came round in front of the castle, he was on the point of stepping up on the platform, and of applying his eye to one of the loops, with a view of taking a direct personal inspection of the state of things within; but he hesitated. Though of little experience in such matters, himself, he had heard so much of Indian artifices through traditions, had listened with such breathless interest to the narration of the escapes of the elder warriors, and, in short, was so well schooled in the theory of his calling, that it was almost as impossible for him to make any gross blunder on such an occasion, as it was for a well grounded scholar, who had commenced correctly, to fail in solving his problem in mathematics. Relinquishing the momentary intention to land, the chief slowly pursued his course round the palisades. As he approached the moccasin, having now nearly completed the circuit of the building, he threw the ominous article into the canoe, by a dexterous and almost imperceptible movement of his paddle. He was now ready to depart, but retreat was even more dangerous than the approach, as the eye could no longer be riveted on the loops. If there was really any one in the castle, the motive of the Delaware in reconnoitring must be understood, and it was the wisest way, however perilous it might be, to retire with an air of confidence, as if all distrust were terminated by the examination. Such, accordingly, was the course adopted by the Indian, who paddled deliberately away, taking the direction of the Ark, suffering no nervous impulse to quicken the motions of his arms, or to induce him to turn even a furtive glance behind him.

No tender wife, reared in the refinements of the highest civilization, ever met a husband on his return from the field, with more of sensibility in her countenance, than Hist discovered, as she saw the Great Serpent of the Delawares, step, unharmed, into the Ark. Still she repressed her emotion, though the joy that sparkled in her dark eyes, and the smile that lighted her pretty mouth, spoke a language that her betrothed could understand.

"Well, Sarpent," cried Hurry, always the first to speak, "what news from the muskrats? Did they shew their teeth, as you surrounded their dwelling?"

"I no like him—" sententiously returned the Delaware. "Too still. So still, can see silence!"

"That's downright Injin—as if any thing could make less noise than nothing! If you've no better reason than this to give, old Tom had better hoist his sail, and go and get his breakfast under his own roof. What has become of the moccasin?"

"Here," returned Chingachgook, holding up his prize for the general inspection.

The moccasin was examined, and Hist confidently pronounced it to be Huron, by the manner in which the porcupine's quills were arranged on its front. Hutter and the Delaware, too, were decidedly of the same opinion. Admitting all this, however, it did not necessarily follow that its owners were in the castle. The moccasin might have drifted from a distance, or it might have fallen from the foot of some scout, who had quitted the place when his errand was accomplished. In short it explained nothing, while it awakened so much distrust.

Under the circumstances, Hutter and Hurry were not men to be long deterred from proceeding by proofs as slight as that of the moccasin. They hoisted the sail again, and the Ark was soon in motion, heading towards the castle. The wind, or air continued light, and the movement was sufficiently slow, to allow of a deliberate survey of the building, as the scow approached. The same death-like silence reigned, and it was difficult to fancy that any thing possessing animal life could be in or around the place. Unlike the Serpent, whose imagination had acted through his traditions, until he was ready to perceive an artificial, in a natural stillness, the others saw nothing to apprehend in a tranquility that, in truth, merely denoted the repose of inanimate objects. The accessories of the scene, too, were soothing and calm, rather than exciting. The day had not yet advanced so far as to bring the sun above the horizon, but the heavens, the atmosphere, and the woods and lake were all seen under that softened light which immediately precedes his appearance, and which perhaps is the most witching period of the four and twenty hours. It is the moment, when every thing is distinct, even the atmosphere seeming to possess a liquid lucidity; the hues appearing gray and softened, with the outlines of objects defined, and the perspective just as moral truths, that are presented in their simplicity, without the meretricious aids of ornament, or glitter. In a word, it is the moment when the senses seem to recover their powers, in the simplest and most accurate forms, like the mind emerging from the obscurity of doubts, into the tranquility and peace of demonstration. Most of the influence that such a scene is apt to produce on those who are properly constituted in a moral sense, was lost on Hutter and Hurry; but both the Delawares, though too much accustomed to witness the loveliness of morning-tide, to stop to analyze their feelings, were equally sensible of the beauties of the hour, though it was probably in a way unknown to themselves. It disposed the young warrior to peace, and never had he felt less longings for the glory of the combat, than when he joined Hist in the cabin, the instant the scow rubbed against the side of the platform. From the indulgence of such gentle emotions, however, he was aroused by a rude summons from Hurry, who called on him to come forth, and help to take in the sail, and to secure the Ark.

Chingachgook obeyed, and by the time he had reached the head of the scow, Hurry was on the platform, stamping his feet, like one glad to touch what, by comparison, might be called *terra firma*, and proclaiming his indifference to the whole Huron tribe, in his customary noisy, dogmatical, manner. Hutter had hauled a canoe up to the head of the scow, and was already about to undo the fastenings of the gate, in order to enter within the 'dock.' March had no other motive in landing than a senseless bravado, and having shaken the door, in a manner to put its solidity to the proof, he joined Hutter in the canoe, and began to aid him in opening the gate. The reader will remember that this mode of entrance was rendered necessary by the manner in which the owner of this singular residence habitually secured it, whenever it was left empty; more particularly at moments when danger was apprehended. Hutter had placed a line in the Delaware's hand, on entering the canoe, intimating that the other was to fasten the Ark to the platform and to lower the sail. Instead of following these directions, however, Chingachgook left the sail standing, and throwing the bight of the rope over the head of a pile, he permitted the Ark to drift round, until it lay against the defences, in a position where it could be entered only by means of a boat, or by passing along the summits of the palisades; the latter being an exploit that required some command of the feet, and which was not to be attempted in the face of a resolute enemy.

In consequence of this change in the position of the scow, which was effected before Hutter had succeeded in opening the gate of his dock, the Ark and the Castle, lay, as sailors would express it, yard-arm and yard-arm, kept asunder some ten or twelve feet, by means of the piles. As the scow pressed close against the latter, their tops formed a species of breast work, that rose to the height of a man's head, covering in a certain degree, the parts of the scow that were not protected by the cabin. The Delaware surveyed this arrangement with great satisfaction, and, as the canoe of Hutter passed through the gate, into the dock, he thought that he might defend his position against any garrison in the castle, for a sufficient time, could he but have had the helping arm of his friend Deerslayer. As it was, he felt comparatively secure, and no longer suffered the keen apprehensions he had lately experienced in behalf of Hist.

A single shove sent the canoe from the gate, to the trap beneath the castle. Here Hutter found all fast, neither pad lock nor chain, nor bar, having been molested. The key was produced, the locks removed, the chain loosened, and the trap pushed upward. Hurry now thrust his head in at the opening; the arms followed, and the colossal legs rose without any apparent effort. At the next instant, his heavy foot was heard stamping in the passage above; that which separated the chambers of the father and daughters, and into which the trap opened. He then gave a shout of triumph.

"Come on, old Tom," the reckless woodsman called out from within the building—"here's your tenement, safe and sound; ay, and as empty as a nut that has passed half an hour in the paws of a squirrel! The Delaware brags of being able to *see* silence; let him come here, and he may *feel* it, in the bargain."

"Any silence where you are, Hurry Harry," returned Hutter, thrusting his head in at the hole, as he uttered the last word, which instantly caused his voice to sound smothered to those without—"Any silence where you are, ought to be both seen and felt, for it's unlike any other silence."

"Come—come—old fellow; hoist yourself up, and we'll open doors and windows and let in the fresh air to brighten up matters. Few words in troublesome times, make men the best fri'nds. Your darter Judith, is what I call a misbehaving young woman, and the hold of the whole family on me is so much weakened by her late conduct, that it would n't take a speech as long as the ten commandments to send me off to the river, leaving you and your traps, your Ark and your children, your man servants and your maid servants, your oxen and your asses, to fight this battle with the Iroquois, by yourselves. Open that window, Floating Tom, and I'll blunder through and do the same job to the front door."

A moment of silence succeeded, and a noise like that produced by the fall of a heavy body followed. A deep execration from Hurry succeeded, and then the whole interior of the building seemed alive. The noises that now so suddenly, and we may add so unexpectedly even to the Delaware, broke the stillness within, could not be mistaken. They resembled those that would be produced by a struggle between tigers in a cage. Once or twice the Indian yell was given, but it seemed smothered, and as if it proceeded from exhausted or compressed throats, and, in a single instance, a deep and another shockingly revolting execration came from the throat of Hurry. It appeared as if bodies were constantly thrown upon the floor with violence, as often rising to renew the struggle. Chingachgook felt greatly at a loss what to do. He had all the arms in the Ark, Hutter and Hurry having proceeded without their rifles, but there was no means of using them, or of passing them to the hands of their owners. The combatants, were literally caged, rendering it almost as impossible under the circumstances to get out, as to get into the building. Then there was Hist to embarrass his movements, and to cripple his efforts. With a view to relieve himself from this disadvantage, he told the girl to take the remaining canoe, and to join Hutter's daughters, who were incautiously but deliberately approaching, in order to save herself, and to warn the others of their danger. But the girl positively and firmly refused to comply. At that moment, no human power, short of an exercise of superior physical force, could have induced her to quit the Ark. The exigency of the moment did not admit of delay, and the Delaware seeing no possibility of serving his friends, cut the line and by a strong shove forced the scow some twenty feet clear of the piles. Here he took the sweeps and succeeded in getting a short distance to windward, if any direction could be thus termed in so light an air, but neither the time, nor his skill at the oars, allowed the distance to be great. When he ceased rowing, the Ark might have been a hundred yards from the platform, and half that distance to the southward of it, the sail being lowered. Judith and Hetty had now discovered that something was wrong, and were stationary a thousand feet farther north.

All this while the furious struggle continued within the house. In scenes like these, events thicken in less time than they can be related. From the moment when the first fall was heard within the building to that when the Delaware ceased his awkward attempts to row, it might have been three or four minutes, but it had evidently served to weaken the combatants. The oaths and execrations of Hurry were no longer heard, and even the struggles had lost some of their force and fury. Nevertheless they still continued with unabated perseverance. At this instant the door flew open, and the fight was transfered to the platform, the light and the open air.

A Huron had undone the fastenings of the door, and three or four of his tribe rushed after him upon the narrow space, as if glad to escape from some terrible scene within. The body of another followed, pitched headlong through the door, with terrific violence. Then March appeared, raging like a lion at bay, and for an instant free'd from his numerous enemies. Hutter was already a captive and bound. There was now a pause in the struggle, which resembled a lull in a tempest. The necessity of breathing was common to all, and the combatants stood watching each other, like mastiffs that have been driven from their holds, and are waiting for a favorable opportunity of renewing them. We shall profit by this pause to relate the manner in which the Indians had obtained possession of the castle, and this the more willingly because it may be necessary to explain to the reader why a conflict which had been so close and fierce, should have also been so comparatively bloodless.

Rivenoak and his companion, particularly the latter who had appeared to be a subordinate and occupied solely with his raft, had made the closest observations in their visits to the castle. Even the boy had brought away minute and valuable information. By these means the Hurons obtained a general idea of the manner in which the place was constructed and secured, as well as of details that enabled them to act intelligently in the dark. Notwithstanding the care that Hutter had taken to drop the Ark on the east side of the building when he was in the act of transferring the furniture from the former to the latter, he had been watched in a way to render the precaution useless. Scouts were on the look-out on the eastern, as well as on the western, shore of the lake, and the whole proceeding had been noted. As soon as it was dark, rafts like that already described, approached from both shores to reconnoitre, and the Ark had passed within fifty feet of one of them, without its being discovered; the men it held lying at their length on the logs, so as to blend themselves and their slow moving machine with the water. When these two sets of adventurers drew near the castle they encountered each other, and after communicating their respective observations, they unhesitatingly approached the building. As had been expected, it was found empty. The rafts were immediately sent for a reinforcement to the shore, and two of the savages remained to profit by their situation. These men succeeded in getting on the roof, and by removing some of the bark, in entering what might be termed the garret. Here they were found by their companions. Hatchets now opened a hole through the squared logs of the upper floor, through which no less than eight of the most athletic of the Indians dropped into the rooms beneath. Here they were left, well supplied with arms and provisions, either to stand a siege, or to make a sortie, as the case might require. The night was passed in sleep, as is usual with Indians in a state of inactivity. The returning day brought them a view of the approach of the Ark through the loops, the only manner in which light and air were now admitted, the windows being closed most effectually with plank, rudely fashioned to fit. As soon as it was ascertained that the two white men were about to enter by the trap, the chief who directed the proceedings of the Hurons took his measures accordingly. He removed all the arms from his own people, even to the knives, in distrust of savage ferocity when awakened by personal injuries, and he hid them where they could not be found, without a search. Ropes of bark were then prepared, and taking their stations in the three different rooms, they all waited for the signal to fall upon their intended captives. As soon as the party had entered the building, men without replaced the bark of the roof, removed every sign of their visit, with care, and then departed for the shore. It was one of these who had dropped his moccasin, which he had not been able to find, again, in the dark. Had the death of the girl been known, it is probable nothing could have saved the lives of Hurry and Hutter, but that event occurred after the ambush was laid, and at a distance of several miles from the encampment near the castle. Such were the means that had been employed to produce the state of things we shall continue to describe.

Chapter XX

"Now all is done that man can do,
And all is done in vain!
My love! my native land, adieu
For I must cross the main,
My dear,
For I must cross the main."
Robert Burns, "It was a' for
our Rightfu' King," ll. 7–12.

IN THE LAST CHAPTER we left the combatants breathing in their narrow lists. Accustomed to the rude sports of wrestling, and jumping, then so common in America, more especially on the frontiers, Hurry possessed an advantage, in addition to his prodigious strength, that had rendered the struggle less unequal than it might otherwise appear to be. This alone had enabled him to hold out so long, against so many enemies, for the Indian is by no means remarkable for his skill, or force, in athletic exercises. As yet, no one had been seriously hurt, though several of the savages had received severe falls, and he, in particular, who had been thrown bodily upon the platform, might be said to be temporarily *hors de combat*. Some of the rest were limping, and March himself had not entirely escaped from bruises, though want of breath was the principal loss that both sides wished to repair.

Under circumstances like those in which the parties were placed, a truce, let it come from what cause it might, could not well be of long continuance. The arena was too confined, and the distrust of treachery, too great, to admit of this. Contrary to what might be expected, in his situation, Hurry was the first to recommence hostilities. Whether this proceeded from policy, an idea that he might gain some advantage by making a sudden and unexpected assault or was the fruit of irritation and his undying hatred of an Indian, it is impossible to say. His onset was furious, however, and at first it carried all before it. He seized the nearest Huron by the waist, raised him entirely from the platform, and hurled him into the water, as if he had been a child. In half a minute, two more were at his side, one of whom received a grave injury by falling on the friend who had just preceded him. But four enemies remained, and, in a hand to hand conflict, in which no arms were used but those which nature had furnished, Hurry believed himself fully able to cope with that number of red-skins.

"Hurrah! Old Tom," he shouted—"The rascals are taking to the lake, and I'll soon have 'em all swimming!" As these words were uttered a violent kick in the face sent back the injured Indian, who had caught at the edge of the platform and was endeavoring to raise himself to its level, helplessly and hopelessly into the water. When the affray was over, his dark body was seen, through the limpid element of the Glimmerglass, lying, with outstretched arms, extended on the bottom of the shoal on which the Castle stood, clinging to the sands and weeds, as if life were to be retained by this frenzied grasp of death. A blow sent into the pit of another's stomach doubled him up like a worm that had been trodden on, and but two able bodied foes remained to be dealt with. One of these, however, was not only the largest and strongest, of the Hurons, but he was also the most experienced of their warriors present, and that one whose sinews were the best strung in fights, and by marches on the warpath. This man fully appreciated the gigantic strength of his opponent, and had carefully husbanded his own. He was also equipped in the best manner for such a conflict, standing in nothing but his breech-cloth, the model of a naked and beautiful statue of agility and strength. To grasp him required additional dexterity and unusual force. Still Hurry did not hesitate, but the kick that had actually destroyed one fellow creature was no sooner given, than he closed in with this formidable antagonist, endeavoring to force him into the water, also. The struggle that succeeded was truly frightful. So fierce did it immediately become, and so quick and changeful were the evolutions of the athletæ, that the remaining savage had no chance for interfering, had he possessed the desire; but wonder and apprehension held him spell bound. He was an inexperienced youth, and his blood curdled as he witnessed the fell strife of human passions, exhibited too, in an unaccustomed form.

Hurry first attempted to throw his antagonist. With this

view he seized him by the throat, and an arm, and tripped with the quickness and force of an American borderer. The effect was frustrated by the agile movements of the Huron, who had clothes to grasp by, and whose feet avoided the attempt with a nimbleness equal to that with which it was made. Then followed a sort of *mêlée*, if such a term can be applied to a struggle between two, in which no efforts were distinctly visible, the limbs and bodies of the combatants assuming so many attitudes and contortions, as to defeat observation. This confused but fierce rally lasted less than a minute, however; when, Hurry, furious at having his strength baffled by the agility and nakedness of his foe, made a desperate effort, which sent the Huron from him, hurling his body violently against the logs of the hut. The concussion was so great as momentarily to confuse the latter's faculties. The pain, too, extorted a deep groan; an unusual concession to agony, to escape a red man in the heat of battle. Still he rushed forward again, to meet his enemy, conscious that his safety rested on his resolution. Hurry now seized the other by the waist, raised him bodily from the platform, and fell with his own great weight on the form beneath. This additional shock so far stunned the sufferer, that his gigantic white opponent now had him completely at his mercy. Passing his hands round the throat of his victim, he compressed them with the strength of a vice, fairly doubling the head of the Huron over the edge of the platform, until the chin was uppermost, with the infernal strength he expended. An instant sufficed to show the consequences. The eyes of the sufferer seemed to start forward, his tongue protruded, and his nostrils dilated nearly to splitting. At this instant a rope of bark, having an eye, was passed dexterously within the two arms of Hurry, the end threaded the eye, forming a noose, and his elbows were drawn together behind his back, with a power that all his gigantic strength could not resist. Reluctantly, even under such circumstances, did the exasperated borderer see his hands drawn from their deadly grasp, for all the evil passions were then in the ascendant. Almost at the same instant, a similar fastening secured his ancles, and his body was rolled to the centre of the platform as helplessly, and as cavalierly, as if it were a log of wood. His rescued antagonist, however, did not rise, for while he began again to breathe, his head still hung helplessly over the edge of the logs, and it was thought at first that his neck was dislocated. He recovered gradually only, and it was hours before he could walk. Some fancied that neither his body, nor his mind, ever totally recovered from this near approach to death.

Hurry owed his defeat and capture to the intensity with which he had concentrated all his powers, on his fallen foe. While thus occupied, the two Indians he had hurled into the water mounted to the heads of the piles, along which they passed, and joined their companion on the platform. The latter had so far rallied his faculties as to have gotten the ropes, which were in readiness for use as the others appeared, and they were applied in the manner related, as Hurry lay pressing his enemy down with his whole weight, intent only on the horrible office of strangling him. Thus were the tables turned, in a single moment; he who had been so near achieving a victory that would have been renowned for ages, by means of traditions, throughout all that region, lying, helpless, bound and a captive. So fearful had been the efforts of the pale face, and so prodigious the strength he exhibited, that even as he lay, tethered like a sheep before them, they regarded him with respect, and not without dread. The helpless body of their stoutest warrior was still stretched on the platform, and, as they cast their eyes towards the lake, in quest of the comrade that had been hurled into it so unceremoniously, and of whom they had lost sight in the confusion of the fray, they perceived his lifeless form clinging to the grass on the bottom, as already described. These several circumstances contributed to render the victory of the Hurons almost as astounding to themselves, as a defeat.

Chingachgook, and his betrothed, witnessed the whole of this struggle from the Ark. When the three Hurons were about to pass the cords around the arms of the prostrate Hurry, the Delaware sought his rifle, but, before he could use it, the white man was bound, and the mischief was done. He might still bring down an enemy, but to obtain the scalp was impossible, and the young chief, who would so freely risk his own life, to obtain such a trophy, hesitated about taking that of a foe, without such an object in view. A glance at Hist, and the recollection of what might follow, checked any transient wish for revenge. The reader has been told that Chingachgook could scarcely be said to know how to manage the oars of the Ark at all, however expert he might be in the use of the paddle. Perhaps there is no manual labor, at which men are so bungling and awkward, as in their first attempts to pull an oar, even the experienced mariner, or boat man, breaking down in his efforts to figure with the celebrated rullock of the gondolier. In short it is, temporarily, an impracticable thing for a new beginner to succeed with a single oar, but, in this case, it was necesary to handle two, at the same time, and those of great size. Sweeps, or large oars, however, are sooner rendered of use by the raw hand, than lighter implements, and this was the reason that the Delaware had succeeded in moving the Ark as well as he did, in a first trial. That trial, notwithstanding, sufficed to produce distrust, and he was fully aware of the critical situation in which Hist and himself were now placed, should the Hurons take to the canoe that was still lying beneath the trap, and come against them. At one moment he thought of putting Hist into the canoe in his own possession, and of taking to the eastern mountain, in the hope of reaching the Delaware villages by direct flight. But many considerations suggested themselves to put a stop to this indiscreet step. It was almost certain that scouts watched the lake on both sides, and no canoe could possibly approach the shore without being seen from the hills. Then a trail could not be concealed from Indian eyes, and the strength of Hist was unequal to a flight sufficiently sustained, to outstrip the pursuit of trained warriors. This was a part of America in which the Indians did not know the use of horses, and every thing would depend on the physical energies of the fugitives. Last, but far from being least, were the thoughts connected with the situation of Deerslayer, a friend who was not to be deserted in his extremity.

Hist, in some particulars, reasoned, and even felt, differently, though she arrived at the same conclusions. Her own danger disturbed her less than her concern for the two sisters, in whose behalf her womanly sympathies were now strongly enlisted. The canoe of the girls, by the time the struggle on the platform had ceased, was within three hundred yards of the castle, and here Judith ceased paddling, the evidences of strife first becoming apparent to the eyes. She and Hetty were standing erect, anxiously endeavoring to ascertain what had occurred, but unable to satisfy their doubts from the circumstance that the building, in a great measure, concealed the scene of action.

The parties in the Ark, and in the canoe, were indebted to the ferocity of Hurry's attack for their momentary security. In any ordinary case, the girls would have been immediately captured, a measure easy of execution now the savages had a canoe, were it not for the rude check the audacity of the Hurons had received, in the recent struggle. It required some little time to recover from the effects of this violent scene, and this so much the more, because the principal man of the party, in the way of personal prowess at least, had been so great a sufferer. Still it was of the last importance that Judith and her sister should seek immediate refuge in the Ark, where the defences offered a temporary shelter at least, and the first step was to devise the means of inducing them to do so. Hist showed herself in the stern of the scow, and made many gestures and signs, in vain, in order to induce the girls to make a circuit to avoid the Castle, and to approach the Ark from the eastward. But these signs were distrusted or misunderstood. It is probable Judith was not yet sufficiently aware of the real state of things to put full confidence in either party. Instead of doing as desired, she rather kept more aloof, paddling slowly back to the north, or into the broadest part of the lake, where she could command the widest view, and had the fairest field for flight before her. At this instant the sun appeared above the pines of the eastern range of mountains and a light southerly breeze arose, as was usual enough, at that season and hour.

Chingachgook lost no time in hoisting the sail. Whatever might be in reserve for him, there could be no question that it was every way desirable to get the Ark at such a distance from the castle, as to reduce his enemies to the necessity of approaching the former in the canoe, which the chances of war had so inopportunely for his wishes and security, thrown into their hands. The appearance of the opening duck seemed first to arouse the Hurons from their apathy, and by the time the head of the scow had fallen off before the wind, which it did unfortunately in the wrong direction, bringing it within a few yards of the platform, Hist found it necessary to warn her lover of the importance of covering his person against the rifles of his foes. This was a danger to be avoided under all circumstances, and so much the more, because the Delaware found that Hist would not take to the cover herself, so long as he remained exposed. Accordingly, Chingachgook abandoned the scow to its own movements, forced Hist into the cabin, the doors of which he immediately secured, and then he looked about him for the rifles.

The situation of the parties was now so singular as to merit a particular description. The Ark was within sixty yards of the castle, a little to the southward, or to windward of it, with its sail full, and the steering oar abandoned. The latter, fortunately, was loose, so that it produced no great influence on the crab like movements of the unwieldy craft. The sail being set, as sailors term it, flying, or having no braces, the air forced the yard forward, though both sheets were fast. The effect was threefold on a boat with a bottom that was perfectly flat, and which drew merely some three or four inches of water. It pressed the head slowly round to leeward, it forced the whole fabric bodily in the same direction at the same time, and the water that unavoidably gathered under the lee, gave the scow also a forward movement. All these changes were exceedingly slow, however, for the wind was not only light, but it was baffling as usual, and twice or thrice the sail shook. Once it was absolutely taken aback.

Had there been any keel to the Ark, it would inevitably have run foul of the platform, bows on, when it is probable nothing could have prevented the Hurons from carrying it; more particularly as the sail would have enabled them to approach under cover. As it was, the scow wore slowly round, barely clearing that part of the building. The piles projecting several feet, *they* were not cleared, but the head of the slow moving craft caught between two of them, by one of its square corners, and hung. At this moment the Delaware was vigilantly watching through a loop, for an opportunity to fire, while the Hurons kept within the building, similarly occupied. The exhausted warrior reclined against the hut, there having been no time to remove him, and Hurry lay, almost as helpless as a log, tethered like a sheep on its way to the slaughter, near the middle of the platform. Chingachgook could have slain the first, at any moment, but his scalp would have been safe, and the young chief disdained to strike a blow that could lead to neither honor nor advantage.

"Run out one of the poles, Sarpent, if Sarpent you be," said Hurry, amid the groans that the tightness of the ligatures was beginning to extort from him—"run out one of the poles, and shove the head of the scow off, and you'll drift clear of us—and, when you've done that good turn for *yourself*, just finish this gagging blackguard for *me*."

The appeal of Hurry, however, had no other effect, than to draw the attention of Hist to his situation. This quick witted creature comprehended it at a glance. His ancles were bound with several turns of stout bark rope, and his arms, above the elbows, were similarly secured behind his back; barely leaving him a little play of the hands and wrists. Putting her mouth near a loop she said in a low but distinct voice—

"Why you do n't roll here, and fall in scow? Chingachgook shoot Huron, if he chace!"

"By the Lord, gal, that's a judgematical thought, and it shall be tried, if the starn of your scow will come a little nearer. Put a bed at the bottom, for me to fall on."

This was said at a happy moment, for, tired of waiting, all the Indians made a rapid discharge of their rifles, almost simultaneously, injuring no one; though several bullets passed through the loops. Hist had heard part of Hurry's words, but most of what he said was lost in the sharp reports of the fire arms. She undid the bar of the door that led to the stern of the scow, but did not dare to expose her person. All this time, the head of the Ark hung, but by a gradually decreasing hold as the other end swung slowly round, nearer and nearer to the platform. Hurry, who now lay with his face towards the Ark, occasionally writhing and turning over like one in pain, evolutions he had performed ever since he was secured, watched every change, and, at last, he saw that the whole vessel was free, and was beginning to grate slowly along the sides of the piles. The attempt was desperate, but it seemed to be the only chance for escaping torture and death, and it suited the reckless daring of the man's character. Waiting to the last moment, in order that the stern of the scow might fairly rub against the platform, he began to writhe again, as if in intolerable suffering, execrating all Indians in general, and the Hurons in particular, and then he suddenly and rapidly rolled over and over, taking the direction of the stern of the scow. Unfortunately, Hurry's shoulders required more space to revolve in than his feet, and, by the time he reached the edge of the platform his direction had so far changed as to carry him clear of the Ark altogether, and the rapidity of his revolutions and the emergency admitting of no delay, he fell into the water. At this instant, Chingachgook, by an understanding with his betrothed drew the fire of the Hurons, again, not a man of whom saw the manner in which one, whom they knew to be effectually tethered, had disappeared. But Hist's feelings were strongly interested in the success of so bold a scheme, and she watched the movements of Hurry, as the cat watches the mouse. The moment he was in motion she foresaw the consequences, and this the more readily, as the scow was now beginning to move with some steadiness, and she bethought her of the means of saving him. With a sort of instinctive readiness, she opened the door, at the very moment the rifles were ringing in her ears, and, protected by the intervening cabin, she stepped into the stern of the scow, in time to witness the fall of Hurry into the lake. Her foot was unconsciously placed on the end of one of the sheets of the sail, which was fastened aft, and catching up all the spare rope, with the awkwardness, but also with the generous resolution, of a woman, she threw it in the direction of the helpless Hurry. The line fell on the head and body of the sinking man, and he not only succeeded in grasping separate parts of it with his hands, but he actually got a portion of it between his teeth. Hurry was an expert swimmer, and, tethered as he was, he resorted to the very expedient that philosophy and reflection would have suggested. He had fallen on his back, and instead of floundering and drowning himself by desperate efforts to walk on the water, he permitted his body to sink as low as possible, and was already submerged, with the exception of his face, when the line reached him. In this situation he might possibly have remained until rescued by the Hurons, using his hands as fishes use their fins, had he received no other succour, but the movement of the Ark soon tightened the rope, and of course he was dragged gently ahead, holding even pace with the scow. The motion aided in keeping his face above the surface of the water, and it would have been possible for one accustomed to endurance, to have been towed a mile in this singular but simple manner.

It has been said that the Hurons did not observe the sudden disappearance of Hurry. In his present situation, he was not only hid from view, by the platform, but, as the Ark drew slowly ahead, impelled by a sail that was now filled, he received the same friendly service from the piles. The Hurons, indeed, were too intent on endeavoring to slay their Delaware foe, by sending a bullet through some one of the loops or crevices of the cabin, to bethink them at all, of one whom they fancied so thoroughly tied. Their great concern was the manner in which the Ark rubbed past the piles, although its motion was lessened at least one half by the friction, and they passed into the northern end of the castle, in order to catch opportunities of firing through the loops of that part of the building. Chingachgook was similarly occupied, and remained as ignorant as his enemies, of the situation of Hurry. As the Ark grated along, the rifles sent their little clouds of smoke from one cover to the other, but the eyes and movements of the opposing parties were too quick to permit any injury to be done. At length one side had the mortification, and the other the pleasure of seeing the scow swing clear of the piles altogether, when it immediately moved away, with a materially accelerated motion, towards the north.

Chingachgook now first learned from Hist, the critical condition of Hurry. To have exposed either of their persons in the stern of the scow, would have been certain death, but, fortunately, the sheet to which the man clung, led forward to the foot of the sail. The Delaware found means to unloosen it from the cleet aft, and Hist, who was already forward for that purpose, immediately began to pull upon the line. At this moment Hurry was towing fifty or sixty feet astern, with nothing but his face above water. As he was dragged out clear of the castle and the piles, he was first perceived by the Hurons, who raised a hideous yell, and commenced a fire on, what may very well be termed, the floating mass. It was at the same instant, that Hist began to pull upon the line forward, a circumstance that probably saved Hurry's life, aided by his own self-possession and border readiness. The first bullet struck the water directly on the spot, where the broad chest of the young giant was visible through the pure element, and might have pierced his heart, had the angle at which it was fired, been less acute. Instead of penetrating the lake, however, it glanced from its smooth surface, rose, and actually buried itself in the logs of the cabin, near the spot at which Chingachgook had shown himself the minute before, while clearing the line from the cleet. A second, and a third, and a fourth bullet followed, all meeting with the same resistance from the surface of the water, though Hurry sensibly felt the violence of the blows they struck upon the lake so immediately above, and so near his breast. Discovering their mistake, the Hurons now changed their plan, and aimed at the uncovered face, but, by this time Hist was pulling on the line, the target advanced, and the deadly missiles still fell upon the water. In another moment the body was dragged past the end of the scow, and became concealed. As for the Delaware and Hist they worked perfectly covered by the cabin, and in less time than it requires to tell it, they had hauled the huge frame of Hurry to the place they occupied. Chingachgook stood in readiness with his keen knife, and bending over the side of the scow, he soon severed the bark that bound the limbs of the borderer. To raise him high enough to reach the edge of the boat, and to aid him in entering were less easy tasks, as Hurry's arms were still nearly useless, but both were done in time, when the liberated man staggered forward, and fell exhausted and helpless, into the bottom of the scow. Here we shall leave him to recover his strength and the due circulation of his blood, while we proceed with the narrative of events that crowd upon us too fast to admit of any postponement.

The moment the Hurons lost sight of the body of Hurry, they gave a common yell of disappointment, and three of the most active of their number ran to the trap and entered the canoe. It required some little delay, however, to embark with their weapons, to find the paddles and, if we may use a phrase so purely technical, "to get out of dock." By this time Hurry was in the scow, and the Delaware had his rifles, again, in readiness. As the Ark necessarily sailed before the wind, it had got by this time quite two hundred yards from the castle, and was sliding away each instant, farther and farther, though with a motion so easy as scarcely to stir the water. The canoe of the girls was quite a quarter of a mile distant from the Ark, obviously keeping aloof, in ignorance of what had occurred, and in apprehension of the consequences of venturing too near. They had taken the direction of the eastern shore, endeavoring at the same time to get to windward of the Ark, and in a manner between the two parties, as if distrusting which was to be considered a friend, and which an enemy. The girls, from long habit, used the paddles with great dexterity, and Judith, in particular, had often sportively gained races, in trials of speed with the youths that occasionally visited the lake.

When the three Hurons emerged from behind the palisades, and found themselves on the open lake, and under the necessity of advancing unprotected on the Ark, if they persevered in the original design, their ardor sensibly cooled. In a bark canoe, they were totally without cover, and Indian discretion was entirely opposed to such a sacrifice of life as would most probably follow any attempt to assault an enemy, entrenched as effectually as the Delaware. Instead of following the Ark therefore, these three warriors inclined towards the eastern shore, keeping at a safe distance from the rifles of Chingachgook. But this manœuvre rendered the position of the girls exceedingly critical. It threatened to place them if not between two fires, at least between two dangers, or what they conceived to be dangers, and, instead of permitting the Hurons to enclose her, in what she fancied a sort of net, Judith immediately commenced her retreat, in a southern direction, at no very great distance from the shore. She did not dare to land; if such an expedient were to be resorted to at all, she could only venture on it, in the last extremity. At first the Indians paid little or no attention to the other canoe, for, fully apprised of its contents, they deemed its capture of comparatively little moment, while the Ark, with its imaginary treasures, the persons of the Delaware and of Hurry, and its means of movement on a large scale, was before them. But this Ark had its dangers as well as its temptations, and after wasting near an hour, in vacillating evolutions, always at a safe distance from the rifle, the Hurons seemed suddenly to take their resolution, and began to display it by giving eager chase to the girls.

When this last design was adopted, the circumstances of all parties, as connected with their relative positions, were materially changed. The Ark had sailed and drifted quite half a mile, and was nearly that distance due north of the castle. As soon as the Delaware perceived that the girls avoided him, unable to manage his unwieldy craft, and knowing that flight from a bark canoe, in the event of pursuit, would be a useless expedient if attempted, he had lowered his sail, in the hope it might induce the sisters to change their plan, and to seek refuge in the scow. This demonstration produced no other effect than to keep the Ark nearer to the scene of action, and to enable those in her to become witnesses of the chase. The canoe of Judith was about a quarter of a mile south of that of the Hurons, a little nearer to the east shore, and about the same distance to the southward of the castle, as it was from the hostile canoe, a circumstance which necessarily put the last nearly abreast of Hutter's fortress. With the several parties thus situated the chase commenced.

At the moment when the Hurons so suddenly changed their mode of attack their canoe was not in the best, possible, racing trim. There were but two paddles, and the third man was so much extra and useless cargo. Then the difference in weight, between the sisters and the other two men, more especially in vessels so extremely light, almost neutralized any difference that might proceed from the greater strength of the Hurons, and rendered the trial of speed far from being as unequal, as it might seem. Judith did not commence her exertions, until the near approach of the other canoe, rendered the object of the movement certain, and then she exhorted Hetty to aid her with her utmost skill and strength.

"Why should we run, Judith?" asked the simple minded girl. "The Hurons have never harmed *me*, nor do I think they ever will."

"That may be true as to you, Hetty, but it will prove very

different with me. Kneel down and say your prayer, and then rise, and do your utmost to help escape. Think of me, dear girl, too, as you pray."

Judith gave these directions from a mixed feeling; first because she knew that her sister ever sought the support of her great ally in trouble, and next because a sensation of feebleness and dependance suddenly came over her own proud spirit, in that moment of apparent desertion and trial. The prayer was quickly said, however, and the canoe was soon in rapid motion. Still, neither party resorted to their greatest exertions from the outset, both knowing that the chase was likely to be arduous and long. Like two vessels of war that are preparing for an encounter, they seemed desirous of first ascertaining their respective rates of speed, in order that they might know how to graduate their exertions, previously to the great effort. A few minutes sufficed to show the Hurons that the girls were expert, and that it would require all their skill and energies to overtake them.

Judith had inclined towards the eastern shore, at the commencement of the chase, with a vague determination of landing and flying to the woods, as a last resort, but as she approached the land, the certainty that scouts must be watching her movements, made her reluctance to adopt such an expedient unconquerable. Then she was still fresh, and had sanguine hopes of being able to tire out her pursuers. With such feelings she gave a sweep with her paddle, and sheered off from the fringe of dark hemlocks beneath the shades of which she was so near entering, and held her way, again, more towards the centre of the lake. This seemed the instant favorable for the Hurons to make their push, as it gave them the entire breadth of the sheet to do it in; and this too in the widest part, as soon as they had got between the fugitives and the land. The canoes now flew, Judith making up for what she wanted in strength, by her great dexterity and self command. For half a mile the Indians gained no material advantage, but the continuance of so great exertions for so many minutes sensibly affected all concerned. Here the Indians resorted to an expedient that enabled them to give one of their party time to breathe, by shifting their paddles from hand to hand, and this too without sensibly relaxing their efforts.

Judith occasionally looked behind her, and she saw this expedient practised. It caused her immediately to distrust the result, since her powers of endurance were not likely to hold out against those of men who had the means of relieving each other. Still she persevered, allowing no very visible consequences immediately to follow the change.

As yet the Indians had not been able to get nearer to the girls, than two hundred yards, though they were what seamen would term 'in their wake'; or in a direct line behind them, passing over the same track of water. This made the pursuit what is technically called a "stern chase", which is proverbially a "long chase": the meaning of which is that, in consequence of the relative positions of the parties, no change becomes apparent except that which is a direct gain in the nearest possible approach. "Long" as this species of chase is admitted to be, however, Judith was enabled to perceive that the Hurons were sensibly drawing nearer and nearer, before she had gained the centre of the lake. She was not a girl to despair, but there was an instant when she thought of yielding, with the wish of being carried to the camp where she knew the Deerslayer to be a captive; but the considerations connected with the means she hoped to be able to employ, in order to procure his release, immediately interposed, in order to stimulate her to renewed exertions. Had there been any one there to note the progress of the two canoes, he would have seen that of Judith flying swiftly away from its pursuers, as the girl gave it freshly impelled speed, while her mind was thus dwelling on her own ardent and generous schemes. So material, indeed, was the difference in the rate of going between the two canoes, for the next five minutes, that the Hurons began to be convinced all their powers must be exerted, or they would suffer the disgrace of being baffled by women. Making a furious effort, under the mortification of such a conviction, one of the strongest of their party broke his paddle at the very moment when he had taken it from the hand of a comrade, to relieve him. This at once decided the matter, a canoe containing three men and having but one paddle, being utterly unable to overtake fugitives like the daughters of Thomas Hutter.

"There, Judith!" exclaimed Hetty, who saw the accident—

"I hope, now, you will own, that praying is useful! The Hurons have broke a paddle, and they never *can* overtake us."

"I never denied it, poor Hetty, and sometimes wish, in bitterness of spirit, that I had prayed more myself, and thought less of my beauty! As you say, we are now safe and need only go a little south, and take breath."

This was done; the enemy giving up the pursuit, as suddenly as a ship that has lost an important spar, the instant the accident occurred. Instead of following Judith's canoe, which was now lightly skimming over the water towards the south, the Hurons turned their bows towards the castle, where they soon arrived and landed. The girls, fearful that some spare paddles might be found in, or about the buildings, continued on, nor did they stop, until so distant from their enemies as to give them every chance of escape, should the chase be renewed. It would seem that the savages meditated no such design, but at the end of an hour their canoe, filled with men, was seen quitting the castle, and steering towards the shore. The girls were without food, and they now drew nearer to the buildings and the Ark, having finally made up their minds, from its manoeuvres, that the latter contained friends.

Notwithstanding the seeming desertion of the castle, Judith approached it with extreme caution. The Ark was now quite a mile to the northward, but sweeping up towards the buildings, and this, too, with a regularity of motion that satisfied Judith a white man was at the oars. When within a hundred yards of the building, the girls began to encircle it, in order to make sure that it was empty. No canoe was nigh, and this emboldened them, to draw nearer and nearer, until they had gone round the piles, and reached the platform.

"Do you go into the house, Hetty," said Judith, "and see that the savages are gone. They will not harm you, and if any of them are still here, you can give me the alarm. I do not think they will fire on a poor defenceless girl, and I at least may escape, until I shall be ready to go among them of my own accord."

Hetty did as desired, Judith retiring a few yards from the platform, the instant her sister landed, in readiness for flight. But the last was unnecessary, not a minute elapsing before Hetty returned to communicate that all was safe.

"I've been in all the rooms, Judith," said the latter earnestly, "and they are empty, except father's; he is in his own chamber, sleeping, though not as quietly as we could wish."

"Has any thing happened to father?" demanded Judith, as her foot touched the platform; speaking quick, for her nerves were in a state to be easily alarmed.

Hetty seemed concerned, and she looked furtively about her, as if unwilling any one but a child should hear what she had to communicate, and even that *she* should learn it abruptly.

"You know how it is with father, sometimes, Judith," she said, "When overtaken with liquor he does n't always know what he says, or does, and he seems to be overtaken with liquor, now."

"That is strange!—Would the savages have drunk with him, and then leave him behind? But tis a grievous sight to a child, Hetty, to witness such a failing in a parent, and we will not go near him 'till he wakes."

A groan from the inner room, however, changed this resolution, and the girls ventured near a parent, whom it was no unusual thing for them to find in a condition that lowers a man to the level of brutes. He was seated, reclining in a corner of the narrow room, with his shoulders supported by the angle, and his head fallen heavily on his chest. Judith moved forward, with a sudden impulse, and removed a canvass cap that was forced so low on his head as to conceal his face, and indeed all but his shoulders. The instant this obstacle was taken away, the quivering and raw flesh, the bared veins and muscles, and all the other disgusting signs of mortality, as they are revealed by tearing away the skin, showed he had been scalped, though still living.

Chapter XXI

> "Lightly they'll talk of the spirit that's gone,
> And o'er his cold ashes upbraid him;
> But nothing he'll reck, if they'll let him sleep on,
> In the grave where a Briton has laid him."
> Charles Wolfe, "The Burial of Sir John Moore," vi.

THE READER must imagine the horror that daughters would experience, at unexpectedly beholding the shocking spectacle that was placed before the eyes of Judith and Esther, as related in the close of the last chapter. We shall pass over the first emotions, the first acts of filial piety, and proceed with the narrative, by imagining rather than relating most of the revolting features of the scene. The mutilated and ragged head was bound up, the unseemly blood was wiped from the face of the sufferer, the other appliances required by appearances and care were resorted to, and there was time to enquire into the more serious circumstances of the case. The facts were never known until years later, in all their details, simple as they were, but they may as well be related here, as it can be done in a few words. In the struggle with the Hurons, Hutter had been stabbed by the knife of the old warrior, who had used the discretion to remove the arms of every one but himself. Being hard pushed by his sturdy foe, his knife had settled the matter. This occurred just as the door was opened, and Hurry burst out upon the platform, as has been previously related. This was the secret of neither party's having appeared in the subsequent struggle; Hutter having been literally disabled, and his conqueror being ashamed to be seen with the traces of blood about him, after having used so many injunctions to convince his young warriors of the necessity of taking their prisoners alive. When the three Hurons returned from the chase, and it was determined to abandon the castle, and join the party on the land, Hutter was simply scalped, to secure the usual trophy, and was left to die by inches, as has been done in a thousand similar instances, by the ruthless warriors of this part of the American continent. Had the injury of Hutter been confined to his head, he might have recovered, however, for it was the blow of the knife that proved mortal.

There are moments of vivid consciousness, when the stern justice of God stands forth in colours so prominent, as to defy any attempts to veil them from the sight, however unpleasant they may appear, or however anxious we may be to avoid recognising it. Such was now the fact with Judith and Hetty, who both perceived the decrees of a retributive Providence, in the manner of their father's suffering, as a punishment for his own recent attempts on the Iroquois. This was seen and felt by Judith with the keenness of perception and sensibility that were suited to her character, while the impression made on the simpler mind of her sister was perhaps less lively, though it might well have proved more lasting.

"Oh! Judith—" exclaimed the weak minded girl, as soon as their first care had been bestowed on the sufferer—"Father went for scalps, himself, and now where is his own? The bible might have foretold this dreadful punishment!"

"Hush—Hetty—hush, poor sister—He opens his eyes; he may hear and understand you. 'Tis as you say and think, but 'tis too dreadful to speak of!"

"Water—" ejaculated Hutter, as it might be by a desperate effort, that rendered his voice frightfully deep and strong, for one as near death as he evidently was—"Water—foolish girls—will you let me die of thirst."

Water was brought and administered to the sufferer; the first he had tasted in hours of physical anguish. It had the double effect of clearing his throat, and of momentarily reviving his sinking system. His eyes opened with that anxious, distended gaze, which is apt to accompany the passage of a soul surprised by death, and he seemed disposed to speak.

"Father—" said Judith, inexpressibly pained by his deplorable situation, and this so much the more from her ignorance of what remedies ought to be applied—"Father, can we do any thing for you?—Can Hetty and I relieve your pain?"

"Father!"—slowly repeated the old man. "No—Judith—no—Hetty—I'm no father. *She* was your mother, but I'm no father. Look in the chest—'Tis all there—give me more water."

The girls complied, and Judith, whose early recollections

extended farther back than her sister's, and who, on every account, had more distinct impressions of the past, felt an uncontrollable impulse of joy, as she heard these words. There had never been much sympathy between her reputed father and herself, and suspicions of this very truth had often glanced across her mind, in consequence of dialogues she had overheard between Hutter and her mother. It might be going too far to say she had never loved him, but it is not so to add, that she rejoiced it was no longer a duty. With Hetty the feeling was different. Incapable of making all the distinctions of her sister, her very nature was full of affection, and she *had* loved her reputed parent, though far less tenderly than the real parent, and it grieved her, now, to hear him declare he was not naturally entitled to that love. She felt a double grief, as if his death and his words together, were twice depriving her of parents. Yielding to her feelings, the poor girl went aside and wept.

The very opposite emotions of the two girls, kept both silent for a long time. Judith gave water to the sufferer frequently, but she forbore to urge him with questions, in some measure out of consideration for his condition, but, if truth must be said, quite as much, lest something he should add, in the way of explanation, might disturb her pleasing belief that she was not Thomas Hutter's child. At length Hetty dried her tears, and came and seated herself on a stool by the side of the dying man, who had been placed at his length on the floor, with his head supported by some coarse vestments that had been left in the house.

"Father—" she said—"you will let me *call* you father, though you say you are not one—Father shall I read the bible to you—mother always said the bible was good for people in trouble. She was often in trouble herself, and then she made me read the bible to her—for Judith was n't as fond of the bible as I am—and it always did her good. Many is the time I've known mother begin to listen with the tears streaming from her eyes, and end with smiles and gladness. Oh! father, you do n't know how much good the bible can do, for you've never tried it—Now, I'll read a chapter, and it will soften your heart, as it softened the hearts of the Hurons."

While poor Hetty had so much reverence for, and faith in,

the virtues of the bible, her intellect was too shallow to enable her fully to appreciate its beauties, or to fathom its profound, and sometimes mysterious wisdom. That instinctive sense of right, which appeared to shield her from the commission of wrong, and even cast a mantle of moral loveliness and truth around her character, could not penetrate abstrusities, or trace the nice affinities between cause and effect, beyond their more obvious and indisputable connection, though she seldom failed to see all the latter, and to defer to all their just consequences. In a word, she was one of those who feel and act correctly, without being able to give a logical reason for it, even admitting revelation as her authority. Her selections from the bible, therefore, were commonly distinguished by the simplicity of her own mind, and were oftener marked for containing images of known and palpable things, than for any of the higher cast of moral truths with which the pages of that wonderful book abound—wonderful, and unequalled, even without referring to its divine origin, as a work replete with the profoundest philosophy, expressed in the noblest language. Her mother, with a connection that will probably strike the reader, had been fond of the book of Job, and Hetty had, in a great measure, learned to read by the frequent lessons she had received from the different chapters of this venerable and sublime poem—now believed to be the oldest book in the world. On this occasion the poor girl was submissive to her training, and she turned to that well known part of the sacred volume, with the readiness with which the practised counsel would cite his authorities from the stores of legal wisdom. In selecting the particular chapter, she was influenced by the caption, and she chose that which stands in our English version as *"Job excuseth his desire of death."* This she read steadily, from beginning to end, in a sweet, low and plaintive voice; hoping devoutly that the allegorical and abstruse sentences might convey to the heart of the sufferer the consolation he needed. It is another peculiarity of the comprehensive wisdom of the bible, that scarce a chapter, unless it be strictly narration, can be turned to, that does not contain some searching truth that is applicable to the condition of every human heart, as well as to the temporal state of its owner, either through the workings of that heart, or even in a still more direct form. In this instance, the very opening sentence—*"Is there not an appointed time to man on earth?"* was startling, and as Hetty proceeded, Hutter applied, or fancied he could apply many aphorisms and figures to his own worldly and mental condition. As life is ebbing fast, the mind clings eagerly to hope when it is not absolutely crushed by despair. The solemn words *"I have sinned; what shall I do unto thee, O thou preserver of men? Why hast thou set me as a mark against thee, so that I am a burden to myself,"* struck Hutter more perceptibly than the others, and, though too obscure for one of his blunted feelings and obtuse mind either to feel or to comprehend in their fullest extent, they had a directness of application to his own state that caused him to wince under them.

"Do n't you feel better now, father?" asked Hetty, closing the volume. "Mother was always better when she had read the bible."

"Water—" returned Hutter—"give me water, Judith. I wonder if my tongue will always be so hot! Hetty, is n't there something in the bible about cooling the tongue of a man who was burning in Hell fire?"

Judith turned away shocked, but Hetty eagerly sought the passage, which she read aloud to the conscience stricken victim of his own avaricious longings.

"That's it—poor Hetty—yes—that's it. My tongue wants cooling, *now*—what will it be *here after*!"

This appeal silenced even the confiding Hetty, for she had no answer ready for a confession so fraught with despair. Water, so long as it could relieve the sufferer, it was in the power of the sisters to give, and, from time to time, it was offered to the lips of the sufferer, as he asked for it. Even Judith prayed. As for Hetty, as soon as she found that her efforts to make her father listen to her texts were no longer rewarded with success, she knelt at his side, and devoutly repeated the words which the Saviour has left behind him, as a model for human petitions. This she continued to do, at intervals, as long as it seemed to her that the act could benefit the dying man. Hutter, however, lingered longer than the girls had believed possible, when they first found him. At times he spoke intelligibly, though his lips oftener moved in utterance of sounds that carried no distinct impressions to the mind. Judith listened intently, and she heard the words—"husband"—"death"—"pirate"—"law"—"scalps"—and several others of similar import, though there was no sentence to tell the precise connection in which they were used. Still they were sufficiently expressive to be understood by one whose ears had not escaped all the rumours that had been circulated to her reputed father's discredit, and whose comprehension was as quick, as her faculties were attentive.

During the whole of the painful hour that succeeded, neither of the sisters bethought her sufficiently of the Hurons, to dread their return. It seemed as if their desolation and grief placed them above the danger of such an interruption, and when the sound of oars was at length heard, even Judith, who alone had any reason to apprehend the enemy, did not start, but at once understood that the Ark was near. She went upon the platform fearlessly, for should it turn out that Hurry was not there, and that the Hurons were masters of the scow also, escape was impossible. Then she had the sort of confidence that is inspired by extreme misery. But there was no cause for any new alarm, Chingachgook, Hist, and Hurry all standing in the open part of the scow, cautiously examining the building to make certain of the absence of the enemy. They, too, had seen the departure of the Hurons, as well as the approach of the canoe of the girls to the castle, and presuming on the latter fact, March had swept the scow up to the platform. A word sufficed to explain that there was nothing to be apprehended, and the Ark was soon moored in her old berth.

Judith said not a word concerning the condition of her father, but Hurry knew her too well, not to understand that something was more than usually wrong. He led the way, though with less of his confident bold manner than usual, into the house, and penetrating to the inner room, found Hutter lying on his back, with Hetty sitting at his side, fanning him with pious care. The events of the morning had sensibly changed the manner of Hurry. Notwithstanding his skill as a swimmer, and the readiness with which he had adopted the only expedient that could possibly save him, the helplessness of being in the water, bound hand and foot, had produced some such effect on him, as the near approach of punishment is known to produce on most criminals, leaving a vivid impression of the horrors of death upon his mind, and this too in connection with a picture of bodily helplessness; the daring of this man being far more the offspring of vast physical powers, than of the energy of the will, or even of natural spirit. Such heroes invariably lose a large portion of their courage with the failure of their strength, and, though Hurry was now unfettered and as vigorous as ever events were too recent to permit the recollection of his late deplorable condition to be at all weakened. Had he lived a century, the occurrences of the few momentous minutes during which he was in the lake, would have produced a chastening effect on his character, if not always on his manner.

Hurry was not only shocked when he found his late associate in this desperate situation, but he was greatly surprised. During the struggle in the building, he had been far too much occupied himself, to learn what had befallen his comrade, and, as no deadly weapon had been used in his particular case, but every effort had been made to capture him without injury, he naturally believed that Hutter had been overcome, while he owed his own escape to his great bodily strength, and to a fortunate concurrence of extraordinary circumstances. Death, in the silence and solemnity of a chamber, was a novelty to him. Though accustomed to scenes of violence, he had been unused to sit by the bedside, and watch the slow beating of the pulse, as it gradually grew weaker and weaker. Notwithstanding the change in his feelings, the manners of a life could not be altogether cast aside in a moment, and the unexpected scene extorted a characteristic speech from the borderer.

"How now! old Tom," he said, "have the vagabonds got you at an advantage, where you're not only down, but are likely to be kept down! I thought you a captyve it's true, but never supposed you so hard run as this!"

Hutter opened his glassy eyes, and stared wildly at the speaker. A flood of confused recollections rushed on his wavering mind, at the sight of his late comrade. It was evident that he struggled with his own images, and knew not the real from the unreal.

"Who are you?" he asked in a husky whisper, his failing

strength refusing to aid him in a louder effort of his voice. "Who are you?—You look like the mate of 'The Snow'—he was a giant, too, and near overcoming us."

"I'm your mate, Floating Tom, and your comrade, but have nothing to do with any snow. It's summer now, and Harry March always quits the hills, as soon after the frosts set in, as is convenient."

"I know you—Hurry Skurry—I'll sell you a scalp!—a sound one, and of a full grown man—What'll you give?"

"Poor Tom! That scalp business has n't turned out at all profitable, and I've pretty much concluded to give it up; and to follow a less bloody calling."

"Have you got any scalp? Mine's gone—How does it feel to have a scalp?—I know how it feels to lose one—Fire and flames about the brain—and, a wrenching at the heart—no—no—kill *first*, Hurry, and scalp, *afterwards*."

"What does the old fellow mean, Judith? He talks like one that is getting tired of the business as well as myself. Why have you bound up his head; or, have the savages tomahawked him about the brains."

"They have done that for *him*, which you and he, Harry March, would have so gladly done for *them*. His skin and hair have been torn from his head to gain money from the governor of Canada, as you would have torn theirs from the heads of the Hurons, to gain money from the governor of York."

Judith spoke with a strong effort to appear composed, but it was neither in her nature, nor in the feeling of the moment to speak altogether without bitterness. The strength of her emphasis, indeed, as well as her manner caused Hetty to look up reproachfully.

"These are high words to come from Thomas Hutter's darter, as Thomas Hutter lies dying before her eyes," retorted Hurry.

"God be praised for that!—whatever reproach it may bring on my poor mother, I am *not* Thomas Hutter's daughter."

"Not Thomas Hutter's darter!—Don't disown the old fellow in his last moments, Judith, for *that's* a sin the Lord will never overlook. If you're not Thomas Hutter's darter, whose darter be you?"

This question rebuked the rebellious spirit of Judith, for, in getting rid of a parent, whom she felt it was a relief to find she might own she had never loved, she overlooked the important circumstance that no substitute was ready to supply his place.

"I cannot tell you, Harry, who my father was," she answered more mildly; "I hope he was an honest man, at least."

"Which is more than you think was the case, with old Hutter? Well, Judith, I'll not deny that hard stories were in circulation consarning Floating Tom, but who is there that does n't get a scratch, when an inimy holds the rake? There's them that say hard things of *me*, and even *you*, beauty as you be, do n't always escape."

This was said with a view to set up a species of community of character between the parties, and, as the politicians are wont to express it, with ulterior intentions. What might have been the consequences with one of Judith's known spirit, as well as her assured antipathy to the speaker, it is not easy to say, for, just then, Hutter gave unequivocal signs that his last moment was nigh. Judith and Hetty had stood by the dying bed of their mother, and neither needed a monitor to warn them of the crisis, and every sign of resentment vanished from the face of the first. Hutter opened his eyes, and even tried to feel about him with his hands, a sign that sight was failing. A minute later, his breathing grew ghastly; a pause totally without respiration followed; and, then, succeeded the last, long drawn sigh, on which the spirit is supposed to quit the body. This sudden termination of the life of one who had hitherto filled so important a place in the narrow scene on which he had been an actor, put an end to all discussion.

The day passed by without further interruption, the Hurons, though possessed of a canoe, appearing so far satisfied with their success as to have relinquished all immediate designs on the castle. It would not have been a safe undertaking, indeed, to approach it under the rifles of those it was now known to contain, and it is probable that the truce was more owing to this circumstance than to any other. In the mean while the preparations were made for the interment of Hutter. To bury him on the land was impracticable, and it was Hetty's wish that his body should lie by the side of that of her mother, in the lake. She had it in her power to quote one of his speeches, in which he himself had called the lake the "family burying ground," and luckily this was done without the knowledge of her sister, who would have opposed the plan, had she known it, with unconquerable disgust. But Judith had not meddled with the arrangement, and every necessary disposition was made without her privity or advice.

The hour chosen for the rude ceremony, was just as the sun was setting, and a moment and a scene more suited to paying the last offices to one of calm and pure spirit could not have been chosen. There are a mystery and a solemn dignity in death, that dispose the living to regard the remains of even a malefactor with a certain degree of reverence. All wordly distinctions have ceased; it is thought that the veil has been removed, and that the character and destiny of the departed are now as much beyond human opinions, as they are beyond human ken. In nothing is death more truly a leveller than in this, since, while it may be impossible absolutely to confound the great with the low, the worthy with the unworthy, the mind feels it to be arrogant to assume a right to judge of those who are believed to be standing at the judgment seat of God. When Judith was told that all was ready, she went upon the platform, passive to the request of her sister, and then she first took heed of the arrangement. The body was in the scow, enveloped in a sheet, and quite a hundred weight of stones, that had been taken from the fire place, were enclosed with it, in order that it might sink. No other preparation seemed to be thought necessary, though Hetty carried her bible beneath her arm.

When all were on board the Ark, the singular habitation of the man whose body it now bore to its final abode, was set in motion. Hurry was at the oars. In his powerful hands, indeed, they seemed little more than a pair of sculls, which were wielded without effort, and, as he was expert in their use, the Delaware remained a passive spectator of the proceedings. The progress of the Ark had something of the stately solemnity of a funeral procession, the dip of the oars being measured, and the movement slow and steady. The wash of the water, as the blades rose and fell, kept time with the efforts of Hurry, and might have been likened to the measured tread of mourners. Then the tranquil scene was in beautiful accordance with a rite that ever associates with itself the idea of God. At that instant, the lake had not even a single ripple, on its glassy surface, and the broad panorama of woods seemed to look down on the holy tranquillity of the hour and ceremony in melancholy stillness. Judith was affected to tears, and even Hurry, though he hardly knew why, was troubled. Hetty preserved the outward signs of tranquillity, but her inward grief greatly surpassed that of her sister, since her affectionate heart loved more from habit and long association, than from the usual connections of sentiment and taste. She was sustained by religious hope, however, which in her simple mind usually occupied the space that worldly feelings filled in that of Judith, and she was not without an expectation of witnessing some open manifestation of divine power, on an occasion so solemn. Still she was neither mystical nor exaggerated; her mental imbecility denying both. Nevertheless her thoughts had generally so much of the purity of a better world about them that it was easy for her to forget earth altogether, and to think only of heaven. Hist was serious, attentive and interested, for she had often seen the interments of the pale-faces, though never one that promised to be as peculiar as this; while the Delaware, though grave, and also observant, in his demeanor was stoical and calm.

Hetty acted as pilot, directing Hurry how to proceed, to find that spot in the lake, which she was in the habit of terming "mother's grave." The reader will remember that the castle stood near the southern extremity of a shoal that extended near half a mile northerly, and it was at the farthest end of this shallow water that Floating Tom had seen fit to deposit the remains of his wife and child. His own were now in the course of being placed at their side. Hetty had marks on the land by which she usually found the spot, although the position of the buildings, the general direction of the shoal, and the beautiful transparency of the water all aided her, the latter even allowing the bottom to be seen. By these means the girl was enabled to note their progress, and at the proper time, she approached March, whispering—

"Now, Hurry you can stop rowing. We have passed the stone on the bottom, and mother's grave is near."

March ceased his efforts, immediately dropping the kedge,

and taking the warp in his hand, in order to check the scow. The Ark turned slowly round, under this restraint, and when it was quite stationary, Hetty was seen at its stern, pointing into the water, the tears streaming from her eyes, in ungovernable natural feeling. Judith had been present at the interment of her mother, but she had never visited the spot since. This neglect proceeded from no indifference to the memory of the deceased, for she had loved her *mother*, and, bitterly, bitterly had she found occasion to mourn her loss, but she was averse to the contemplation of death, and there had been passages in her own life since the day of that interment, which increased this feeling, and rendered her if possible still more reluctant to approach the spot that contained the remains of one whose severe lessons of female morality and propriety had been deepened and rendered doubly impressive by remorse for her own failings. With Hetty, the case had been very different. To her simple and innocent mind the remembrance of her mother, brought no other feeling than one of gentle sorrow; a grief that is so often termed luxurious, even, because it associates with itself the images of excellence, and the purity of a better state of existence. For an entire summer, she had been in the habit of repairing to the place after nightfall, and carefully anchoring her canoe so as not to disturb the body, she would sit and hold fancied conversations with the deceased, sing sweet hymns to the evening air, and repeat the orisons that the being who now slumbered below, had taught her in infancy. Hetty had passed her happiest hours in this indirect communion with the spirit of her mother, the wildness of Indian traditions, and Indian opinions, unconsciously to herself, mingling with the christian lore received in childhood. Once she had even been so far influenced by the former, as to have bethought her of performing some of those physical rites at her mother's grave, which the red men are known to observe, but the passing feeling had been obscured by the steady, though mild, light of christianity, which never ceased to burn in her gentle bosom. Now, her emotions were merely the natural outpourings of a daughter that wept for a mother whose love was indelibly impressed on the heart, and whose lessons had been too earnestly taught to be easily forgotten by one who had so little temptation to err.

There was no other priest than nature, at that wild and singular funeral rite. March cast his eyes below, and through the transparent medium of the clear water, which was almost as pure as air, he saw what Hetty was accustomed to call "mother's grave." It was a low straggling mound of earth, fashioned by no spade, out of a corner of which gleamed a bit of the white cloth, that formed the shroud of the dead. The body had been lowered to the bottom, and Hutter brought earth from the shore and let it fall upon it, until all was concealed. In this state the place had remained, until the movement of the waters revealed the solitary sign of the uses of the spot, that has just been mentioned. Even the most rude and brawling are chastened by the ceremonies of a funeral. March felt no desire to indulge his voice in any of its coarse outbreakings, and was disposed to complete the office he had undertaken in decent sobriety. Perhaps he reflected on the retribution that had alighted on his late comrade, and bethought him of the frightful jeopardy in which his own life had so lately been placed. He signified to Judith that all was ready, received her directions to proceed, and with no other assistant than his own vast strength, raised the body and bore it to the end of the scow. Two parts of a rope were passed beneath the legs and shoulders, as they are placed beneath coffins, and then the corpse was slowly lowered beneath the surface of the lake.

"Not *there*—Harry March—no, not *there*," said Judith, shuddering involuntarily—"do not lower it, quite so near the spot where mother lies!"

"Why, not, Judith?" asked Hetty, earnestly—"They lived together in life, and should lie together in death."

"No—no—Harry March; further off—further off—Poor Hetty, you know not what you say.—Leave me to order this."

"I know I am weak minded, Judith, and that you are clever—but, surely a husband should be placed near a wife. Mother always said that this was the way they bury in christian church yards!"

This little controversy was conducted earnestly, but in smothered voices, as if the speakers feared that the dead might overhear them. Judith could not contend with her sister, at such a moment, but a significant gesture from her, induced March to lower the body, at a little distance from that of his wife, when he withdrew the cords, and the act was performed.

"There's an end of Floating Tom!" exclaimed Hurry, bending over the scow, and gazing through the water at the body. "He was a brave companion on a scout, and a notable hand with traps. Do n't weep, Judith, do n't be overcome Hetty, for the righteousest of us all must die; and when the time comes, lamentations and tears can't bring the dead to life. Your father will be a loss to you, no doubt; most fathers are a loss, especially to onmarried darters; but there's a way to cure that evil, and you're both too young and handsome to live long without finding it out. When it's agreeable to hear what an honest and onpretending man has to say, Judith, I should like to talk a little with you, apart."

Judith had scarce attended to this rude attempt of Hurry's at consolation, although she necessarily understood its general drift, and had a tolerably accurate notion of its manner. She was weeping at the recollection of her mother's early tenderness, and painful images of long forgotten lessons and neglected precepts were crowding her mind. The words of Hurry, however, recalled her to the present time, and abrupt and unseasonable as was their import, they did not produce those signs of distaste that one might have expected from the girl's character. On the contrary, she appeared to be struck with some sudden idea, gazed intently for a moment at the young man, dried her eyes, and led the way to the other end of the scow, signifying her wish for him to follow. Here she took a seat and motioned for March to place himself at her side. The decision and earnestness with which all this was done, a little intimidated her companion, and Judith found it necessary to open the subject herself.

"You wish to speak to me of marriage, Harry March," she said, "and I have come here, over the grave of my parents, as it might be—no—no—over the grave of my poor, dear—dear, mother, to hear what you have to say."

"This is oncommon, and you have a skearful way with you, this evening, Judith," answered Hurry, more disturbed than he would have cared to own, "but truth is truth, and it shall come out, let what will follow. You well know, gal, that I've long thought you the comeliest young woman my eyes ever beheld, and that I've made no secret of that fact, either here on the lake, out among the hunters and trappers, or in the settlements."

"Yes—yes, I've heard this before, and I suppose it to be true," answered Judith with a sort of feverish impatience.

"When a young man holds such language of any particular young woman, it's reasonable to calculate he sets store by her."

"True—true, Hurry—all this you've told me, again and again."

"Well, if it's agreeable, I should think a woman coul'n't hear it too often. They all tell me this is the way with your sex, that nothing pleases them more than to repeat over and over, for the hundredth time, how much you like 'em, unless it be to talk to 'em of their good looks!"

"No doubt—we like both, on most occasions, but this is an uncommon moment, Hurry, and vain words should not be too freely used. I would rather hear you speak plainly."

"You shall have your own way, Judith, and I some suspect you always will. I've often told you that I not only like you better than any other young woman going, or, for that matter, better than *all* the young women going, but you must have obsarved, Judith, that I've never asked you, in up and down tarms, to marry me."

"I have observed both," returned the girl, a smile struggling about her beautiful mouth, in spite of the singular and engrossing intentness which caused her cheeks to flush and lighted her eyes with a brilliancy that was almost dazzling—"I have observed both, and have thought the last remarkable for a man of Harry March's decision and fearlessness."

"There's been a reason, gal, and it's one that troubles me even now—nay, do n't flush up so, and look fiery like, for there are thoughts which will stick long in any man's mind, as there be words that will stick in his throat—but, then, ag'in, there's feelin's that will get the better of 'em all, and to these feelin's I find I must submit. You've no longer a father, or a mother, Judith, and it's morally unpossible that you and Hetty could live here, alone, allowing it was peace and the Iroquois was quiet; but, as matters stand, not only would you starve, but you'd both be prisoners, or scalped, afore a week was out. It's time to think of a change and a husband, and, if you'll accept of me, all that's past shall be forgotten, and there's an end on't."

Judith had difficulty in repressing her impatience until this rude declaration and offer were made, which she evidently wished to hear, and which she now listened to with a willingness that might well have excited hope. She hardly allowed the young man to conclude, so eager was she to bring him to the point, and so ready to answer.

"There—Hurry—that's enough—" she said, raising a hand as if to stop him—"I understand you as well, as if you were to talk a month. You prefer me to other girls, and you wish me to become your wife."

"You put it in better words than I can do, Judith, and I wish you to fancy them said, just as you most like to hear 'em."

"They're plain enough, Harry, and 'tis fitting they should be so. This is no place to trifle or deceive in. Now, listen to my answer, which shall be, in every tittle, as sincere as your offer. There is a reason, March, why I should never—"

"I suppose I understand you, Judith, but if I'm willing to overlook that reason, it's no one's consarn but mine—Now, do n't brighten up like the sky at sundown, for no offence is meant, and none should be taken."

"I do not brighten up, and will *not* take offence," said Judith, struggling to repress her indignation, in a way she had never found it necessary to exert before. "There is a reason why I should not, *cannot*, ever be your wife, Hurry, that you seem to overlook, and which it is my duty now to tell you, as plainly as you have asked me to consent to become so. I do not, and I am certain that I never shall, love you well enough to marry you. No man can wish for a wife who does not prefer him to all other men, and when I tell you this frankly, I suppose you yourself will thank me for my sincerity."

"Ah! Judith, them flaunting, gay, scarlet-coated officers of the garrisons, have done all this mischief!"

"Hush, March; do not calumniate a daughter over her mother's grave! Do not, when I only wish to treat you fairly, give me reason to call for evil on your head in bitterness of heart! Do not forget that I am a woman, and that you are a man; and that I have neither father, nor brother, to revenge your words!"

"Well, there is something in the last, and I'll say no more. Take time, Judith, and think better on this."

"I want no time—my mind has long been made up, and I have only waited for you to speak plainly, to answer plainly. We now understand each other, and there is no use in saying any more."

The impetuous earnestness of the girl awed the young man, for never before had he seen her so serious and determined. In most of their previous interviews she had met his advances with evasion, or sarcasm, but these Hurry had mistaken for female coquetry, and had supposed might easily be converted into consent. The struggle had been with himself, about offering, nor had he ever seriously believed it possible that Judith would refuse to become the wife of the handsomest man on all that frontier. Now that the refusal came, and that in terms so decided, as to put all cavilling out of the question, if not absolutely dumbfounded, he was so much mortified and surprised, as to feel no wish to attempt to change her resolution.

"The Glimmerglass has now no great call for me," he exclaimed, after a minute's silence. "Old Tom is gone, the Hurons are as plenty on the shore, as pigeons in the woods, and altogether it is getting to be an onsuitable place."

"Then leave it. You see it is surrounded by dangers, and there is no reason why you should risk your life for others. Nor do I know that you can be of any service to us. Go, tonight; we'll never accuse you of having done any thing forgetful, or unmanly."

"If I do go, 'twill be with a heavy heart on your account, Judith; I would rather take you with me."

"That is not to be spoken of any longer, March; but, I will land you in one of the canoes, as soon as it is dark and you can strike a trail for the nearest garrison. When you reach the fort, if you send a party—"

Judith smothered the words, for she felt that it was humiliating to be thus exposing herself to the comments and reflections of one who was not disposed to view her conduct in connection with all in those garrisons, with an eye of favor. Hurry however, caught the idea, and, without perverting it, as the girl dreaded, he answered to the purpose.

"I understand *what* you would say, and *why* you do n't say it," he replied. "If I get safe to the fort, a party shall start on the trail of these vagabonds, and I'll come with it, myself, for I should like to see you, and Hetty, in a place of safety, before we part forever."

"Ah, Harry March, had you always spoken thus, felt thus, my feelings towards you might have been different!"

"Is it too late, now, Judith? I'm rough and a woodsman, but we all change under different treatment from what we have been used to."

"It *is* too late, March. I can never feel towards you, or any other man but *one*, as you would wish to have me. There, I've said enough, surely, and you will question me no further. As soon as it is dark, I, or the Delaware will put you on the shore. You will make the best of your way to the Mohawk, and the nearest garrison, and send all you can to our assistance. And, Hurry, we are now friends, and I may trust in you, may I not?"

"Sartain, Judith; though our fri'ndship would have been all the warmer, could you look upon me, as I look upon you."

Judith hesitated, and some powerful emotion was struggling within her. Then, as if determined to look down all weaknesses, and accomplish her purposes, at every hazard, she spoke more plainly.

"You will find a captain of the name of Warley at the nearest post," she said, pale as death, and even trembling as she spoke; "I think it likely he will wish to head the party, but I would greatly prefer it should be another. If Captain Warley *can* be kept back, 't would make me very happy!"

"That's easier said than done, Judith, for these officers do pretty much as they please. The Major will order, and captains, and lieutenants, and ensigns must obey. I know the officer you mean, a red faced, gay, oh! be joyful sort of a gentleman, who swallows madeira enough to drown the Mohawk, and yet a pleasant talker. All the gals in the valley admire him, and they say he admires all the gals. I do n't wonder he is your dislike, Judith, for he's a very gin'ral lover, if he is n't a gin'ral officer."

Judith did not answer, though her frame shook, and her colour changed from pale to crimson, and from crimson back again to the hue of death.

"Alas! my poor mother!" she ejaculated mentally instead of uttering it aloud, " we are over thy grave, but little dost thou know how much thy lessons have been forgotten; thy care neglected; thy love defeated!"

As this goading of the worm that never dies was felt, she arose and signified to Hurry, that she had no more to communicate.

Chapter XXII

"—That point
In misery, which makes the oppressed man
Regardless of his own life, makes him too
Lord of the oppressor's.—"
Coleridge, *Remorse*, V.i.201–04.

ALL THIS TIME Hetty had remained seated in the head of the scow, looking sorrowfully into the water which held the body of her mother, as well as that of the man whom she had been taught to consider her father. Hist stood near her in gentle quiet, but had no consolation to offer in words. The habits of her people taught her reserve in this respect, and the habits of her sex induced her to wait patiently for a moment when she might manifest some soothing sympathy by means of acts, rather than of speech. Chingachgook held himself a little aloof, in grave reserve, looking like a warrior, but feeling like a man.

Judith joined her sister with an air of dignity and solemnity it was not her practice to show, and, though the gleamings of anguish were still visible on her beautiful face, when she spoke it was firmly and without tremor. At that instant Hist and the Delaware withdrew, moving towards Hurry, in the other end of the boat.

"Sister," said Judith kindly, "I have much to say to you; we will get into this canoe, and paddle off to a distance from the Ark—The secrets of two orphans ought not to be heard by every ear."

"Certainly, Judith, by the ears of their parents? Let Hurry lift the grapnel and move away with the Ark, and leave us here, near the graves of father and mother, to say what we may have to say."

"Father!" repeated Judith slowly, the blood for the first time since her parting with March mounting to her cheeks—"He was no father of ours, Hetty! *That* we had from his own mouth, and in his dying moments."

"Are you glad, Judith, to find you had no father! He took care of us, and fed us, and clothed us, and loved us; a father could have done no more. I do'n't understand why he was'n't a father."

"Never mind, dear child, but let us do as you have said. It may be well to remain here, and let the Ark move a little away. Do you prepare the canoe, and I will tell Hurry and the Indians our wishes."

This was soon and simply done, the Ark moving, with measured strokes of the sweeps a hundred yards from the spot, leaving the girls floating, seemingly in air, above the place of the dead; so buoyant was the light vessel that held them, and so limpid the element by which it was sustained.

"The death of Thomas Hutter," Judith commenced, after a short pause had prepared her sister to receive her communications, "has altered all our prospects, Hetty. If he was *not* our father, we are *sisters*, and must feel alike and live together."

"How do I know, Judith, that you would n't be as glad to find I am not your sister, as you are in finding that Thomas Hutter, as you call him, was not your father. I am only half witted, and few people like to have half-witted relations; and then I'm not handsome—at least, not as handsome as you—and you may wish a handsomer sister."

"No—no—Hetty. *You* and you only are my sister—my heart, and my love for you tell me that—and mother was my mother—of that too am I glad, and proud; for she was a mother to be proud of—but father was not father!"

"Hush, Judith! His spirit may be near; it would grieve it to hear his children talking so, and that, too, over his very grave. Children should never grieve parents, mother often told me, and especially when they are dead!"

"Poor Hetty! They are happily removed beyond all cares on our account. Nothing that *I* can do or say, will cause mother any sorrow *now*—there is some consolation in that, at least!—and nothing *you* can say or do will make her smile, as she used to smile on your good conduct when living."

"You do n't know that, Judith. Spirits can see, and mother may see as well as any spirit. She always told us that God saw all we did, and that we should do nothing to offend *him*; and now *she* has left us, I strive to do nothing that can displease *her*. Think how her spirit would mourn and feel sorrow,

Judith, did it see either of us doing what is not right; and spirits *may* see, after all; especially the spirits of parents that feel anxious about their children."

"Hetty—Hetty—you know not what you say!" murmured Judith, almost livid with emotion—"The dead *cannot* see, and know nothing of what passes, here! But, we will not talk of this any longer. The bodies of Mother and Thomas Hutter lie together in the lake, and we will hope that the spirits of both are with God. That we, the children of one of them, remain on earth is certain; it is now proper to know what we are to do in future."

"If we are not Thomas Hutter's children, Judith, no one will dispute our right to his property. We have the castle and the Ark, and the canoes, and the woods, and the lakes, the same as when he was living, and what can prevent us from staying here, and passing our lives just as we ever have done."

"No—no—poor sister—this can no longer be. Two girls would not be safe here, even should these Hurons fail in getting us into their power. Even father had as much as he could sometimes do, to keep peace upon the lake, and we should fail altogether. We must quit this spot, Hetty, and remove into the settlements."

"I am sorry you think so, Judith," returned Hetty, dropping her head on her bosom, and looking thoughtfully down at the spot where the funeral pile of her mother could just be seen. "I am *very* sorry to hear it. I would rather stay here, where, if I was n't born, I've passed my life. I do n't like the settlements—they are full of wickedness and heart burnings, while God dwells unoffended in these hills! I love the trees, and the mountains, and the lake, and the springs; all that his bounty has given us, and it would grieve me sorely, Judith, to be forced to quit them. You are handsome, and not at all half-witted, and one day you will marry, and then you will have a husband, and I a brother to take care of us, if women can't really take care of themselves in such a place as this."

"Ah! if this *could* be so, Hetty, then, indeed, I could *now* be a thousand times happier in these woods, than in the settlements. *Once*, I did not feel thus, but *now* I do. Yet where is the man to turn this beautiful place into such a garden of Eden, for us?"

"Harry March loves you, sister," returned poor Hetty, unconsciously picking the bark off the canoe as she spoke. "He would be glad to be your husband, I'm sure, and a stouter and a braver youth is not to be met with the whole country round."

"Harry March and I understand each other, and no more need be said about *him*. There is one—but no matter. It is all in the hands of providence, and we must shortly come to some conclusion about our future manner of living. Remain here—that is, remain here, alone, we cannot—and perhaps no occasion will ever offer for remaining in the manner you think of. It is time, too, Hetty, we should learn all we can concerning our relations and family. It is not probable we are altogether without relations, and they may be glad to see us. The old chest is now our property, and we have a right to look into it, and learn all we can by what it holds. Mother was so very different from Thomas Hutter, that, now I know we are not his children, I burn with a desire to know whose children we can be. There are papers in that chest, I am certain, and those papers may tell us all about our parents and natural friends."

"Well, Judith, you know best, for you are cleverer than common, mother always said, and I am only half-witted. Now father and mother are dead, I do n't much care for any relation but you, and do n't think I could love them I never saw, as well as I ought. If you do n't like to marry Hurry, I do n't see who you can choose for a husband, and then I fear we shall have to quit the lake, after all."

"What do you think of Deerslayer, Hetty?" asked Judith, bending forward like her unsophisticated sister, and endeavoring to conceal her embarrassment in a similar manner.—"Would he not make a brother-in-law to your liking?"

"Deerslayer!" repeated the other, looking up in unfeigned surprise. "Why, Judith, Deerslayer is n't, in the least, comely, and is altogether unfit for one like you!"

"He is not ill-looking, Hetty, and beauty in a man is not of much matter."

"Do you think so, Judith?—I know that beauty is of no great matter, in man or woman, in the eyes of God, for mother has often told me so, when she thought I might have been sorry I was not as handsome as you, though she need n't have been uneasy on that account, for I never coveted any thing that is yours, sister;—but, tell me so she did—still, beauty is very pleasant to the eye, in both! I think, if I were a man, I should pine more for good looks, than I do as a girl. A handsome man is a more pleasing sight, than a handsome woman."

"Poor child!—You scarce know what you say, or what you mean! Beauty in our sex *is* something, but in men, it passes for little. To be sure, a man ought to be tall, but others are tall, as well as Hurry; and active—and I think I know those that are more active;—and strong; well, he has n't all the strength in the world—and brave—I am certain I can name a youth who is braver!"

"This is strange, Judith!—I did n't think the earth held a handsomer, or a stronger, or a more active or a braver man than Hurry Harry! I'm sure, *I* never met his equal, in either of these things."

"Well—well—Hetty—say no more of this. I dislike to hear *you* talking in this manner. Tis not suitable to your innocence, and truth, and warm-hearted sincerity—. Let Harry March go. He quits us to-night, and no regret of mine will follow him, unless it be that he has staid so long, and to so little purpose."

"Ah! Judith; that is what I've long feared—and I did *so* hope he might be my brother-in-law!"

"Never mind it now. Let us talk of our poor mother—and of Thomas Hutter."

"Speak kindly then, sister, for you can't be quite certain that spirits do n't both hear and see. If father was n't father, he was good to us, and gave us food and shelter. We can't put any stones over their graves, here in the water, to tell people all this, and so we ought to say it with our tongues."

"They will care little for that, girl. 'Tis a great consolation to know, Hetty, that if mother ever did commit any heavy fault when young, she lived sincerely to repent of it; no doubt her sins were forgiven her."

"Tis n't right, Judith, for children to talk of their parents' sins. We had better talk of our own."

"Talk of your sins, Hetty!—If there ever was a creature on earth without sin, it is you! I wish I could say, or think the same of myself; but we shall see. No one knows what changes affection for a good husband, can make in a woman's heart. I do n't think, child, I have even now the same love for finery I once had."

"It would be a pity, Judith, if you did think of clothes, over your parents' graves! We will never quit this spot, if you say so, and will let Hurry go where he pleases."

"I am willing enough to consent to the last, but cannot answer for the first, Hetty. We must live, in future, as becomes respectable young women, and cannot remain here, to be the talk and jest of all the rude and foul tongu'd trappers and hunters that may come upon the lake. Let Hurry go by himself, and then I'll find the means to see Deerslayer, when the future shall be soon settled. Come, girl, the sun has set, and the Ark is drifting away from us; let us paddle up to the scow, and consult with our friends. This night I shall look into the chest, and to-morrow shall determine what we are to do. As for the Hurons, now we can use our stores without fear of Thomas Hutter, they will be easily bought off. Let me get Deerslayer once out of their hands, and a single hour shall bring things to an understanding."

Judith spoke with decision, and she spoke with authority, a habit she had long practised towards her feeble-minded sister. But, while thus accustomed to have her way, by the aid of manner and a readier command of words, Hetty occasionally checked her impetuous feelings and hasty acts by the aid of those simple moral truths, that were so deeply engrafted in all her own thoughts and feelings; shining through both, with a mild and beautiful lustre, that threw a sort of holy halo around so much of what she both said and did. On the present occasion, this healthful ascendancy of the girl of weak intellect, over her of a capacity that, in other situations, might have become brilliant and admired, was exhibited in the usual simple and earnest manner.

"You forget, Judith, what has brought us here," she said reproachfully. "This is mother's grave, and we have just laid the body of father by her side. We have done wrong to talk so much of ourselves at such a spot, and ought now to pray

God to forgive us, and ask *him* to teach us where we are to go, and what we are to do."

Judith involuntarily laid aside her paddle, while Hetty dropped on her knees, and was soon lost in her devout but simple petitions. Her sister did not pray. This she had long ceased to do directly, though anguish of spirit frequently wrung from her mental and hasty appeals to the great source of benevolence for support, if not for a change of spirit. Still she never beheld Hetty on her knees, that a feeling of tender recollection, as well as of profound regret at the deadness of her own heart, did not come over her. Thus had she herself done in childhood, and even down to the hour of her ill fated visits to the garrisons, and she would willingly have given worlds, at such moments, to be able to exchange her present sensations, for the confiding faith, those pure aspirations, and the gentle hope that shone through every lineament and movement of her, otherwise, less favored sister. All she could do, however, was to drop her head to her bosom, and assume in her attitude some of that devotion in which her stubborn spirit refused to unite.

When Hetty rose from her knees, her countenance had a glow and serenity that rendered a face that was always agreeable, positively handsome. Her mind was at peace, and her conscience acquitted her, of a neglect of duty.

"Now, you may go, if you want to, Judith," she said, "for God has been kind to me, and lifted a burden off my heart. Mother had many such burdens, she used to tell me, and she always took them off in this way. Tis the only way, sister, such things can be done. You may raise a stone, or a log, with your hands; but the heart *must* be lightened by prayer. I do n't think you pray as often as you used to do, when younger, Judith!"

"Never mind—never mind, child—" answered the other huskily—" 'tis no matter, now. Mother is gone, and Thomas Hutter is gone, and the time has come when we must think and act for ourselves."

As the canoe moved slowly away from the place, under the gentle impulsion of the elder sister's paddle, the younger sat musing, as was her wont, whenever her mind was perplexed by any idea more abstract and difficult of comprehension than common.

"I do n't know what you mean by 'future', Judith," she at length, suddenly observed. "Mother used to call Heaven the future, but you seem to think it means next week, or to-morrow!"

"It means both, dear sister—every thing that is yet to come, whether in this world or another. It is a solemn word, Hetty, and most so, I fear, to them that think the least about it. Mother's future is eternity; ours may yet mean what will happen while we live in this world—Is not that a canoe just passing behind the castle—here, more in the direction of the point, I mean; it is hid, now; but certainly I saw a canoe stealing behind the logs!"

"I've seen it some time," Hetty quietly answered, for the Indians had few terrors for her, "but I did n't think it right to talk about such things over mother's grave! The canoe came from the camp, Judith, and was paddled by a single man. He seemed to be Deerslayer, and no Iroquois."

"Deerslayer!" returned the other, with much of her native impetuosity—"That cannot be! Deerslayer is a prisoner, and I have been thinking of the means of setting him free. Why did you fancy it Deerslayer, child?"

"You can look for yourself, sister, for there comes the canoe in sight, again, on this side of the hut."

Sure enough, the light boat had passed the building, and was now steadily advancing towards the Ark; the persons on board of which were already collecting in the head of the scow, to receive their visiter. A single glance sufficed to assure Judith that her sister was right, and that Deerslayer was alone in the canoe. His approach was so calm and leisurely, however, as to fill her with wonder, since a man who had effected his escape from enemies, by either artifice or violence, would not be apt to move with the steadiness and deliberation with which his paddle swept the water. By this time the day was fairly departing, and objects were already seen dimly under the shores. In the broad lake, however, the light still lingered, and around the immediate scene of the present incidents, which was less shaded than most of the sheet, being in its broadest part, it cast a glow that bore some faint resemblance to the warm tints of an Italian or Grecian sunset. The logs of the hut and Ark had a sort of purple hue, blended with the growing obscurity, and the bark of the hunter's boat was losing its distinctness in colours richer, but more mellowed, than those it showed under a bright sun. As the two canoes approached each other—for Judith and her sister had plied their paddles so as to intercept the unexpected visiter ere he reached the Ark—even Deerslayer's sun-burned countenance wore a brighter aspect than common, under the pleasing tints that seemed to dance in the atmosphere. Judith fancied that delight at meeting her had some share in this unusual and agreeable expression. She was not aware that her own beauty appeared to more advantage than common, from the same natural cause, nor did she understand, what it would have given her so much pleasure to know, that the young man actually thought her, as she drew nearer, the loveliest creature of her sex, his eyes had ever dwelt on.

"Welcome—welcome, Deerslayer!" exclaimed the girl, as the canoes floated at each other's side; "we have had a melancholy—a frightful day—but your return is, at least, one misfortune the less! Have the Hurons become more human, and let you go; or have you escaped from the wretches, by your own courage and skill?"

"Neither, Judith—neither one nor t'other. The Mingos are Mingos still, and will live and die Mingos; it is not likely their natur's will ever undergo much improvement. Well! They've *their* gifts, and we've our'n, Judith, and it does'n't much become either to speak ill of what the Lord has created; though, if the truth must be said, I find it a sore trial to think kindly, or to talk kindly of them vagabonds. As for outwitting them, that might have been done, and it *was* done, too, atween the Sarpent, yonder, and me, when we were on the trail of Hist—" here the hunter stopped to laugh in his own silent fashion—"but it's no easy matter to sarcumvent the sarcumvented. Even the fa'ans get to know the tricks of the hunters afore a single season is over, and an Indian whose eyes have once been opened by a sarcumvention never shuts them ag'in in precisely the same spot. I've known whites to do that, but never a red skin. What they l'arn comes by practice, and not by books, and of all schoolmasters exper'ence gives lessons that are the longest remembered."

"All this is true, Deerslayer, but if you have not escaped from the savages, how came you here?"

"That's a nat'ral question, and charmingly put. You *are* wonderful handsome this evening, Judith, or, Wild Rose, as the Sarpent calls you, and I may as well say it, since I honestly think it! You may well call them Mingos, savages too, for savage enough do they feel, and savage enough will they act, if you once give them an opportunity. They feel their loss here, in the late skrimmage, to their hearts' cores, and are ready to revenge it on any creatur' of English blood that may fall in their way. Nor, for that matter do I much think they would stand at taking their satisfaction out of a Dutch man."

"They have killed father; that ought to satisfy their wicked cravings for blood," observed Hetty reproachfully.

"I know it, gal—I know the whole story—partly from what I've seen from the shore, since they brought me up from the point, and partly from their threats ag'in myself, and their other discourse. Well, life is unsartain at the best, and we all depend on the breath of our nostrils for it, from day to day. If you've lost a staunch fri'nd, as I make no doubt you have, Providence will raise up new ones in his stead, and since our acquaintance has begun in this oncommon manner, I shall take it as a hint that it will be a part of my duty in futur', should the occasion offer, to see you do n't suffer for want of food in the wigwam. I can't bring the dead to life, but as to feeding the living, there's few on all this frontier can outdo me, though I say it in the way of pity and consolation, like, and in no particular, in the way of boasting."

"We understand you, Deerslayer," returned Judith, hastily, "and take all that falls from your lips, as it is meant, in kindness and friendship. Would to Heaven all men had tongues as true, and hearts as honest!"

"In that respect men *do* differ, of a sartainty, Judith. I've known them that was n't to be trusted any farther than you can see them; and others ag'in whose messages, sent with a small piece of wampum, perhaps, might just as much be depended on, as if the whole business was finished afore your face. Yes, Judith, you never said truer word, than when you said some men might be depended on, and other some might not."

"You are an unaccountable being, Deerslayer," returned the girl, not a little puzzled with the childish simplicity of character that the hunter so often betrayed—a simplicity so striking that it frequently appeared to place him nearly on a level with the fatuity of poor Hetty, though always relieved by the beautiful moral truth that shone through all that this unfortunate girl both said and did—"You are a most unaccountable man, and I often do not know how to understand you. But never mind, just now; you have forgotten to tell us by what means you are here."

"I!—Oh! That's not very onaccountable, if I am myself, Judith. I'm out on furlough."

"Furlough!—That word has a meaning among the soldiers that I understand; but I cannot tell what it signifies when used by a prisoner."

"It means just the same. You're right enough; the soldiers do use it, and just in the same way as I use it. A furlough is when a man has leave to quit a camp, or a garrison for a sartain specified time; at the end of which he is to come back and shoulder his musket, or submit to his torments, just as he may happen to be a soldier, or a captyve. Being the last, I must take the chances of a prisoner."

"Have the Hurons suffered you to quit them in this manner, without watch or guard."

"Sartain—I woul'n't have come in any other manner, unless indeed it had been by a bold rising, or a sarcumvention."

"What pledge have they that you will ever return?"

"My word," answered the hunter simply. "Yes, I own I gave 'em *that*, and big fools would they have been to let me come without it! Why in that case, I should n't have been obliged to go back and ondergo any deviltries their fury may invent, but might have shouldered my rifle, and made the best of my way to the Delaware villages. But, Lord! Judith, they know'd this, just as well as you and I do, and would no more let me come away, without a promise to go back, than they would let the wolves dig up the bones of their fathers!"

"Is it possible you mean to do this act of extraordinary self-destruction and recklessness?"

"Anan!"

"I ask if it can be possible that you expect to be able to put yourself again in the power of such ruthless enemies, by keeping your word."

Deerslayer looked at his fair questioner for a moment, with stern displeasure. Then the expression of his honest and guileless face suddenly changed, lighting as by a quick illumination of thought, after which he laughed in his ordinary manner.

"I did n't understand you, at first, Judith; no, I did n't! You believe that Chingachgook and Hurry Harry won't suffer it; but you do n't know mankind thoroughly yet, I see. The Delaware would be the last man on 'arth to offer any objections to what he knows is a duty, and, as for March, he does n't care enough about any creatur' but himself to spend many words on such a subject. If he did, 'twould make no great difference howsever; but not he, for he thinks more of his gains than of even his own word. As for my promises, or your'n, Judith, or any body else's, they give him no consarn. Don't be under any oneasiness, therefore, gal; I shall be allowed to go back according to the furlough; and if difficulties was made, I've not been brought up, and edicated as one may say, in the woods, without knowing how to look 'em down."

Judith made no answer for some little time. All her feelings as a woman, and as a woman who, for the first time in her life was beginning to submit to that sentiment which has so much influence on the happiness or misery of her sex, revolted at the cruel fate that she fancied Deerslayer was drawing down upon himself, while the sense of right, which God has implanted in every human breast, told her to admire an integrity as indomitable and as unpretending as that which the other so unconsciously displayed. Argument, she felt would be useless, nor was she, at that moment, disposed to lessen the dignity and high principle that were so striking in the intentions of the hunter, by any attempt to turn him from his purpose. That something might yet occur to supersede the necessity for this self immolation she tried to hope, and then she proceeded to ascertain the facts in order that her own conduct might be regulated by her knowledge of circumstances.

"When is your furlough out, Deerslayer," she asked, after

both canoes were heading towards the Ark, and moving, with scarcely a perceptible effort of the paddles, through the water.

"To-morrow noon; not a minute afore; and you may depend on it, Judith, I shan't quit what I call christian company, to go and give myself up to them vagabonds, an instant sooner than is downright necessary. They begin to fear a visit from the garrisons, and would n't lengthen the time a moment, and it's pretty well understood atween us, that, should I fail in my ar'n'd, the torments are to take place when the sun begins to fall, that they may strike upon their home trail as soon as it is dark."

This was said solemnly, as if the thought of what was believed to be in reserve duly weighed on the prisoner's mind, and yet so simply, and without a parade of suffering, as rather to repel than to invite any open manifestations of sympathy.

"Are they bent on revenging their losses?" Judith asked faintly, her own high spirit yielding to the influence of the other's quiet but dignified integrity of purpose.

"Downright, if I can judge of Indian inclinations, by the symptoms. They think howsever I do n't suspect their designs, I do believe, but one that has lived so long among men of red skin gifts, is no more likely to be misled in Injin feelin's, than a true hunter is like to lose his trail, or a stanch hound his scent. My own judgment is greatly ag'in my own escape, for I see the women are a good deal enraged on behalf of Hist, though I say it, perhaps, that should n't say it, seein' that I had a considerable hand myself in getting the gal off. Then there was a cruel murder in their camp last night, and that shot might just as well have been fired into my breast. Howsever, come what will, the Sarpent and his wife will be safe, and that is some happiness in any case."

"Oh! Deerslayer, they will think better of this, since they have given you until to-morrow noon to make up your mind!"

"I judge not, Judith; yes, I judge not. An Injin is an Injin, gal, and it's pretty much hopeless to think of swarving him, when he's got the scent and follows it with his nose in the air. The Delawares, now, are a half christianized tribe—not that I think such sort of christians much better than your whole blooded onbelievers—but, nevertheless, what good half christianizing can do to a man, some among 'em have got, and yet revenge clings to their hearts like the wild creepers here to the tree! Then, I slew one of the best and boldest of their warriors, they say, and it *is* too much to expect that they should captivate the man who did this deed, in the very same scouting on which it was performed, and they take no account of the matter. Had a month, or so, gone by, their feelin's would have been softened down, and we might have met in a more friendly way, but it is, as it is. Judith, this is talking of nothing but myself, and my own consarns, when you have had trouble enough, and may want to consult a fri'nd a little about your own matters. Is the old man laid in the water, where I should think his body would like to rest?"

"It is, Deerslayer," answered Judith, almost inaudibly. "That duty has just been performed. You are right in thinking that I wish to consult a friend; and that friend is yourself. Hurry Harry is about to leave us; when he is gone, and we have got a little over the feelings of this solemn office, I hope you will give me an hour alone. Hetty and I are at a loss what to do."

"That's quite nat'ral, coming as things have, suddenly and fearfully. But here's the Ark, and we'll say more of this, when there is a better opportunity."

Chapter XXIII

"The winde is great upon the highest hilles;
The quiet life is in the dale below;
Who tread on ice shall slide against their willes;
They want not cares, that curious arts should know;
Who lives at ease and can content him so,
Is perfect wise, and sets us all to schoole:
Who hates this lore may well be called a foole."

Thomas Churchyard, "Shore's Wife," xlvii.

THE MEETING between Deerslayer and his friends in the Ark was grave and anxious. The two Indians, in particular, read in his manner that he was not a successful fugitive, and a few sententious words sufficed to let them comprehend the nature of what their friend had termed his 'furlough.' Chingachgook immediately became thoughtful, while Hist, as usual, had no better mode of expressing her sympathy than by those little attentions which mark the affectionate manner of woman.

In a few minutes, however, something like a general plan for the proceedings of the night was adopted, and to the eye of an uninstructed observer things would be thought to move in their ordinary train. It was now getting to be dark, and it was decided to sweep the Ark up to the castle, and secure it in its ordinary berth. This decision was come to, in some measure on account of the fact that all the canoes were again in the possession of their proper owners, but principally, from the security that was created by the representations of Deerslayer. He had examined the state of things among the Hurons, and felt satisfied that they meditated no further hostilities during the night, the loss they had met having indisposed them to further exertions for the moment. Then, he had a proposition to make; the object of his visit; and, if this were accepted, the war would at once terminate between the parties; and it was improbable that the Hurons would anticipate the failure of a project on which their chiefs had apparently set their hearts, by having recourse to violence previously to the return of their messenger.

As soon as the Ark was properly secured, the different members of the party occupied themselves in their several peculiar manners, haste in council, or in decision, no more characterizing the proceedings of these border whites, than it did those of their red neighbors. The women busied themselves in preparations for the evening meal, sad and silent, but ever attentive to the first wants of nature. Hurry set about repairing his moccasins, by the light of a blazing knot; Chingachgook seated himself in gloomy thought, while Deerslayer proceeded, in a manner equally free from affectation and concern, to examine 'Killdeer', the rifle of Hutter that has been already mentioned, and which subsequently became so celebrated, in the hands of the individual who was now making a survey of its merits. The piece was a little longer than usual, and had evidently been turned out from the work shops of some manufacturer of a superior order. It had a few silver ornaments, though, on the whole, it would have been deemed a plain piece by most frontier men, its great merit consisting in the accuracy of its bore, the perfection of the details, and the excellence of the metal. Again and again did the hunter apply the breech to his shoulder, and glance his eye along the sights, and as often did he poise his body and raise the weapon slowly, as if about to catch an aim at a deer, in order to try the weight, and to ascertain its fitness for quick and accurate firing. All this was done, by the aid of Hurry's torch, simply, but with an earnestness and abstraction that would have been found touching by any spectator who happened to know the real situation of the man.

" 'Tis a glorious we'pon, Hurry!" Deerslayer at length exclaimed, "and it may be thought a pity that it has fallen into the hands of women. The hunters have told me of its expl'ites, and by all I have heard, I should set it down as sartain death in exper'enced hands. Hearken to the tick of this lock—a wolf trap has'n't a livelier spring; pan and cock speak together, like two singing masters undertaking a psalm in meetin'. I never *did* see so true a bore, Hurry, that's sartain!"

"Ay, Old Tom used to give the piece a character, though he was n't the man to particularize the ra'al natur' of any sort of fire arms, in practise," returned March, passing the deer's thongs through the moccasin with the coolness of a cobbler.

"He was no marksman, that we must all allow; but he had his good p'ints, as well as his bad ones. I have had hopes that Judith might consait the idee of giving Killdeer to me."

"There's no saying what young women may do, that's a truth, Hurry, and I suppose you're as likely to own the rifle as another. Still, when things are so very near perfection, it's a pity not to reach it entirely."

"What do you mean by that?—Would not that piece look as well on my shoulder, as on any man's?"

"As for looks, I say nothing, You are both good-looking, and might make what is called a good-looking couple. But the true p'int is as to conduct. More deer would fall in one day, by that piece, in some man's hands, than would fall in a week in your'n, Hurry! I've seen you try; yes, remember the buck t'other day."

"That buck was out of season, and who wishes to kill venison out of season. I was merely trying to frighten the creatur', and I think you will own that he was pretty well skeared, at any rate."

"Well, well, have it as you say. But this is a lordly piece, and would make a steady hand and quick eye the King of the Woods!"

"Then keep it, Deerslayer, and become King of the Woods," said Judith, earnestly, who had heard the conversation, and whose eye was never long averted from the honest countenance of the hunter. "It can never be in better hands than it is, at this moment, and there I hope it will remain these fifty years."

"Judith you can't be in 'arnest!" exclaimed Deerslayer; taken so much by surprise, as to betray more emotion than it was usual for him to manifest on ordinary occasions. "Such a gift would be fit for a ra'al King to make; yes, and for a ra'al King to receive."

"I never was more in earnest, in my life, Deerslayer, and I am as much in earnest in the wish as in the gift."

"Well, gal, well; we'll find time to talk of this ag'in. You must n't be down hearted, Hurry, for Judith is a sprightly young woman, and she has a quick reason; she knows that the credit of her father's rifle is safer in my hands, than it can possibly be in yourn; and, therefore, you must n't be down hearted. In other matters, more to your liking, too, you'll find she'll give you the preference."

Hurry growled out his dissatisfaction, but he was too intent on quitting the lake, and in making his preparations, to waste his breath on a subject of this nature. Shortly after, the supper was ready, and it was eaten in silence, as is so much the habit of those who consider the table as merely a place of animal refreshment. On this occasion, however, sadness and thought contributed their share to the general desire not to converse, for Deerslayer was so far an exception to the usages of men of his cast, as not only to wish to hold discourse on such occasions, but as often to create a similar desire in his companions.

The meal ended, and the humble preparations removed, the whole party assembled on the platform to hear the expected intelligence from Deerslayer on the subject of his visit. It had been evident he was in no haste to make his communication, but the feelings of Judith would no longer admit of delay. Stools were brought from the Ark and the hut, and the whole six placed themselves in a circle, near the door, watching each other's countenances, as best they could, by the scanty means that were furnished by a lovely star-light night. Along the shores, beneath the mountains, lay the usual body of gloom, but in the broad lake no shadow was cast, and a thousand mimic stars were dancing in the limpid element, that was just stirred enough by the evening air to set them all in motion.

"Now, Deerslayer," commenced Judith, whose impatience resisted further restraint—"now, Deerslayer, tell us all the Hurons have to say, and the reason why they have sent you on parole, to make us some offer."

"Furlough, Judith; furlough is the word; and it carries the same meaning with a capt*yve* at large, as it does with a soldier who has leave to quit his colors. In both cases the word is past to come back, and now I remember to have heard that's the ra'al signification; 'furlough' meaning a 'word' passed for the doing of any thing of the like. Parole I rather think is Dutch, and has something to do with the tattoos of the garrisons. But this makes no great difference, since the vartue of a pledge lies in the idee, and not in the word. Well, then, if the message must be given, it must; and perhaps there is no use in putting it off. Hurry will soon be wanting to set out on his journey to the river, and the stars rise and set, just as if they cared for neither Injin nor message. Ah's! me; 'Tis n't a pleasant, and I know it's a useless ar'n'd, but it must be told."

"Harkee, Deerslayer," put in Hurry, a little authoritatively—"You're a sensible man in a hunt, and as good a fellow on a march, as a sixty-miler-a-day could wish to meet with, but you're oncommon slow about messages; especially them that you think won't be likely to be well received. When a thing is to be told, why tell it; and do n't hang back like a Yankee lawyer pretending he can't understand a Dutchman's English, just to get a double fee out of him."

"I understand you, Hurry, and well are you named to-night, seeing you've no time to lose. But let us come at once to the p'int, seeing that's the object of this council—for council it may be called, though women have seats among us. The simple fact is this. When the party came back from the castle, the Mingos held a council, and bitter thoughts were uppermost, as was plain to be seen by their gloomy faces. No one likes to be beaten, and a red skin, as little as a pale face. Well, when they had smoked upon it, and made their speeches, and their council fire had burnt low, the matter came out. It seems the elders among 'em consaited I was a man to be trusted on a furlough—They're wonderful observant, them Mingos; *that* their worst inimies must allow—but they consaited I was such a man; and it is n't often—" added the hunter, with a pleasing consciousness that his previous life justified this implicit reliance on his good faith—"it is'n't often they consait any thing so good of a pale face; but so they did with me, and, therefore, they did n't hesitate to speak their minds, which is just this:—You see the state of things. The lake, and all on it, they fancy, lie at their marcy. Thomas Hutter is deceased, and, as for Hurry, they've got the idee he has been near enough to death to-day, not to wish to take another look at him, this summer. Therefore, they account all your forces as reduced to Chingachgook and the two young women, and, while they know the Delaware to be of a high race, and a born warrior, they know he's now on his first war path. As for the gals, of course they set them down much as they do women in gin'ral."

"You mean that they despise us!" interrupted Judith, with eyes that flashed so brightly as to be observed by all present.

"That will be seen in the ind. They hold that all on the lake lies at their marcy, and, therefore, they send by me this belt of wampum," showing the article in question to the Delaware, as he spoke, "with these words. 'Tell the Sarpent, they say, that he has done well for a beginner; he may now strike across the mountains, for his own villages, and no one shall look for his trail. If he has found a scalp, let him take it with him, for the Huron braves have hearts, and can feel for a young warrior who does n't wish to go home empty-handed. If he is nimble, he is welcome to lead out a party in pursuit. Hist, howsever, must go back to the Hurons, for, when she left them in the night, she carried away, by mistake, that which does n't belong to her—'"

"That *can't* be true!" said Hetty earnestly. "Hist is no such girl, but one that gives every body his due—"

How much more she would have said, in remonstrance, cannot be known, inasmuch as Hist, partly laughing, and partly hiding her face in shame, past her own hand across the speaker's mouth, in a way to check the words.

"You do n't understand Mingo messages, poor Hetty—" resumed Deerslayer, "which seldom mean what lies exactly uppermost. Hist has brought away with her the inclinations of a young Huron, and they want her back again, that the poor young man may find them where he last saw them! The Sarpent they say is too promising a young warrior not to find as many wives as he wants, but this one he cannot have. That's their meaning, and nothing else, as I understand it."

"They are very obliging and thoughtful, in supposing a young woman can forget all her own inclinations in order to let this unhappy youth find his!" said Judith, ironically; though her manner became more bitter as she proceeded. "I suppose a woman is a woman, let her colour be white, or red, and your chiefs know little of a woman's heart, Deerslayer, if they think it can ever forgive when wronged, or ever forget when it fairly loves."

"I suppose that's pretty much the truth, with some women,

Judith, though I've known them that could do both. The next message is to you. They say the Muskrat, as they called your father, has dove to the bottom of the lake; that he will never come up again, and that his young will soon be in want of wigwams if not of food. The Huron huts they think, are better than the huts of York, and they wish you to come and try them. Your colour is white, they own, but they think young women who've lived so long in the woods, would lose their way in the clearin's. A great warrior among them, has lately lost his wife, and he would be glad to put the Wild Rose on her bench at his fireside. As for the Feeble Mind, she will always be honored and taken care of by red warriors. Your father's goods they think ought to go to enrich the tribe, but your own property, which is to include every thing of a female natur', will go like that of all wives, into the wigwam of the husband. Moreover, they've lost a young maiden by violence, lately, and 'twill take two pale faces to fill her seat."

"And do *you* bring such a message to *me*!" exclaimed Judith, though the tone in which the words were uttered, had more in it of sorrow than of anger. "Am I a girl to be an Indian's slave?"

"If you wish my honest thoughts on this p'int, Judith, I shall answer that I do n't think you'll, willingly, ever become any man's slave; red-skin or white. You're not to think hard, howsever, of my bringing the message, as near as I could, in the very words in which it was given to me. Them was the conditions on which I got my furlough, and a bargain is a bargain, though it is made with a vagabond. I've told you what *they've* said, but I've not yet told you what I think you ought, one and all, to answer."

"Ay; let's hear that, Deerslayer," put in Hurry. "My cur'osity is up on that consideration, and I should like, right well, to hear your idees of the reasonableness of the reply. For my part, though, my own mind is pretty much settled, on the p'int of my own answer, which shall be made known as soon as necessary."

"And so is mine, Hurry, on all the different heads, and on no one is it more sartainly settled than on yourn. If I was you, I should say—'Deerslayer, tell them scamps, they don't know Harry March! He is human; and having a white skin, he has also a white natur', which natur' won't let him desart females of his own race and gifts, in their greatest need. So set me down as one that will refuse to come into your treaty, though you should smoke a hogshead of tobacco over it.'"

March was a little embarrassed at this rebuke, which was uttered with sufficient warmth of manner, and with a point that left no doubt of the meaning. Had Judith encouraged him, he would not have hesitated about remaining to defend her and her sister, but under the circumstances, a feeling of resentment rather urged him to abandon them. At all events, there was not a sufficiency of chivalry in Hurry Harry to induce him to hazard the safety of his own person, unless he could see a direct connection between the probable consequences and his own interests. It is no wonder, therefore, that his answer partook equally of his intention, and of the reliance he so boastingly placed on his gigantic strength, which if it did not always make him courageous, usually made him impudent, as respects those with whom he conversed.

"Fair words make long friendships, Master Deerslayer," he said a little menacingly. "You're but a stripling and, you know by exper'ence, what you are in the hands of a man. As you're not me, but only a go between, sent by the savages to us christians, you may tell your emply'ers that they do know Harry March, which is a proof of their sense, as well as his. He's human enough to follow human natur', and that tells him to see the folly of one man's fighting a whole tribe. If females desart him, they must expect to be desarted *by* him, whether they're of his own gifts, or another man's gifts. Should Judith see fit to change her mind, she's welcome to my company to the river, and Hetty with her; but should n't she come to this conclusion, I start as soon as I think the enemy's scouts are beginning to nestle themselves in among the brush and leaves, for the night."

"Judith will *not* change her mind, and she does not ask your company, Master March," returned the girl, with spirit.

"That p'int's settled, then," resumed Deerslayer, unmoved by the other's warmth. "Hurry Harry must act for himself, and do that which will be most likely to suit his own fancy. The course he means to take will give him an easy race, if it don't give him an easy conscience. Next comes the question with Hist—what say you gal?—Will you desart your duty, too, and go back to the Mingos and take a Huron husband, and all not for the love of the man you're to marry, but for the love of your own scalp?"

"Why you talk so to Hist!" demanded the girl half-offended. "You t'ink a red-skin girl made like captain's lady, to laugh and joke with any officer that come."

"What I think, Hist, is neither here nor there, in this matter. I must carry back your answer, and in order to do so it is necessary that you should send it. A faithful messenger gives his ar'n'd, word for word."

Hist no longer hesitated to speak her mind fully. In the excitement she rose from her bench, and naturally recurring to that language in which she expressed herself the most readily, she delivered her thoughts and intentions, beautifully and with dignity, in the tongue of her own people.

"Tell the Hurons, Deerslayer," she said, "that they are as ignorant as moles; they do n't know the wolf from the dog. Among my people, the rose dies on the stem where it budded, the tears of the child fall on the graves of its parents; the corn grows where the seed has been planted. The Delaware girls are not messengers to be sent, like belts of wampum, from tribe to tribe. They are honeysuckles, that are sweetest in their own woods; their own young men carry them away in their bosoms, because they are fragrant; they are sweetest when plucked from their native stems. Even the robin and the martin come back, year after year, to their old nests; shall a woman be less true hearted than a bird? Set the pine in the clay and it will turn yellow; the willow will not flourish on the hill; the tamarack is healthiest in the swamp; the tribes of the sea love best to hear the winds that blow over the salt water. As for a Huron youth, what is he to a maiden of the Lenni Lenape. He may be fleet, but her eyes do not follow him in the race; they look back towards the lodges of the Delawares. He may sing a sweet song for the girls of Canada, but there is no music for Wah, but in the tongue she has listened to from childhood. Were the Huron born of the people that once owned the shores of the salt lake, it would be in vain, unless he were of the family of Uncas. The young pine will rise to be as high as any of its fathers. Wah-ta!-Wah has but one heart, and it can love but one husband."

Deerslayer listened to this characteristic message, which was given with an earnestness suited to the feelings from which it sprung, with undisguised delight, meeting the ardent eloquence of the girl, as she concluded, with one of his own heart-felt, silent, and peculiar fits of laughter.

"That's worth all the wampum in the woods!" he exclaimed. "You don't understand it, I suppose, Judith, but if you'll look into your feelin's, and fancy that an inimy had sent to tell you to give up the man of your ch'ice, and to take up with another that was n't the man of your ch'ice, you'll get the substance of it, I'll warrant! Give me a woman for ra'al eloquence, if they'll only make up their minds to speak what they *feel*. By speakin', I do n't mean chatterin', howsever; for most of them will do *that* by the hour; but comin' out with their honest, deepest, feelin's in proper words. And now, Judith, having got the answer of a red skin girl, it is fit I should get that of a pale face, if, indeed, a countenance that is as blooming as your'n can in any wise, so be tarmed. You are well named the Wild Rose, and so far as colour goes, Hetty ought to be called the Honeysuckle."

"Did this language come from one of the garrison gallants, I should deride it, Deerslayer, but coming from *you*, I know it can be depended on," returned Judith, deeply gratified by his unmeditated and characteristic compliments. "It is too soon, however, to ask my answer; the Great Serpent has not yet spoken."

"The Sarpent! Lord; I could carry back his speech without hearing a word of it! I did n't think of putting the question to him at all, I will allow; though 'twould be hardly right either, seeing that truth is truth, and I'm bound to tell these Mingos the fact and nothing else. So, Chingachgook, let us hear *your* mind on this matter—are you inclined to strike across the hills towards your village, to give up Hist to a Huron, and to tell the chiefs at home, that, if they're actyve and successful, they may possibly get *on* the end of the Iroquois trail some two or three days a'ter the inimy has got *off* of it?"

Like his betrothed, the young chief arose, that his answer might be given with due distinctness and dignity. Hist had spoken with her hands crossed upon her bosom, as if to suppress the emotions within, but the warrior stretched an arm before him with a calm energy that aided in giving emphasis to his expressions.

"Wampum should be sent for wampum," he said; "a message must be answered by a message. Hear what the Great Serpent of the Delawares has to say to the pretended wolves from the great lakes, that are howling through our woods. They are no wolves; they are dogs that have come to get their tails and ears cropped by the hands of the Delawares. They are good at stealing young women; bad at keeping them. Chingachgook takes his own where he finds it; he asks leave of no cur from the Canadas. If he has a tender feeling in his heart, it is no business of the Hurons. He tells it to her who most likes to know it; he will not bellow it in the forest, for the ears of those that only understand yells of terror. What passes in his lodge is not for the chiefs of his own people to know; still less for Mingo rogues—"

"Call 'em vagabonds, Sarpent—" interrupted Deerslayer, unable to restrain his delight—"yes, just call 'em up-and-down vagabonds, which is a word easily intarpreted, and the most hateful of all to their ears, it's so true. Never fear me; I'll give 'em your message, syllable for syllable, sneer for sneer, idee for idee, scorn for scorn, and they desarve no better at your hands—only call 'em vagabonds, once or twice, and that will set the sap mounting in 'em, from their lowest roots to the uppermost branches!"

"Still less for Mingo vagabonds," resumed Chingachgook, quite willingly complying with his friend's request. "Tell the Huron dogs to howl louder, if they wish a Delaware to find them in the woods, where they burrow like foxes, instead of hunting like warriors. When they had a Delaware maiden in their camp, there was a reason for hunting them up; now they will be forgotten unless they make a noise. Chingachgook do n't like the trouble of going to his villages for more warriors; he can strike their run-a-way trail; unless they hide it under ground, he will follow it to Canada alone. He will keep Wah-ta!-Wah with him to cook his game; they two will be Delawares enough to scare all the Hurons back to their own country."

"That's a grand despatch, as the officers call them things!" cried Deerslayer; "twill set all the Huron blood in motion; most particularily that part where he tells 'em Hist, too, will keep on their heels, 'till they're fairly driven out of the country. Ahs! me; big words arn't always big deeds, notwithstanding! The Lord send that we be able to be only one half as good as we promise to be! And now, Judith, it's your turn to speak, for them miscreants will expect an answer from each person, poor Hetty, perhaps, excepted."

"And why not Hetty, Deerslayer? She often speaks to the purpose; the Indians may respect her words, for they feel for people in her condition."

"That is true, Judith, and quick-thoughted in you. The red-skins *do* respect misfortunes of all kinds, and Hetty's in particular. So, Hetty, if you have any thing to say, I'll carry it to the Hurons as faithfully as if it was spoken by a schoolmaster, or a missionary."

The girl hesitated a moment, and then she answered in her own gentle, soft, tones, as earnestly as any who had preceded her.

"The Hurons can't understand the difference between white people and themselves," she said, "or they would n't ask Judith and me to go and live in their villages. God has given one country to the red men and another to us. He meant us to live apart. Then mother always said that we should never dwell with any but christians, if possible, and *that* is a reason why we can't go. This lake is ours, and we wo'n't leave it. Father and Mother's graves are in it, and even the worst Indians love to stay near the graves of their fathers. I will come and see them, again, if they wish me to, and read more out of the bible to them, but I can't quit father's and mother's graves."

"That will do—that will do, Hetty, just as well as if you sent 'em a message twice as long," interrupted the hunter. "I'll tell 'em all you've said, and all you mean, and I'll answer for it, that they'll be easily satisfied. Now, Judith, your turn comes next, and then this part of my ar'n'd will be tarminated, for the night."

Judith manifested a reluctance to give her reply, that had awakened a little curiosity in the messenger. Judging from her known spirit, he had never supposed the girl would be less true to her feelings and principles than Hist, or Hetty, and yet there was a visible wavering of purpose that rendered him slightly uneasy. Even now when directly required to speak, she seemed to hesitate, nor did she open her lips, until the profound silence told her how anxiously her words were expected. Then indeed, she spoke, but it was doubtingly and with reluctance.

"Tell me first—tell *us*, first, Deerslayer," she commenced, repeating the words merely to change the emphasis—"what effect will our answers have on *your* fate? If you are to be the sacrifice of our spirit, it would have been better had we all been more wary as to the language we use. What, then, are likely to be the consequences to yourself?"

"Lord, Judith, you might as well ask me which way the wind will blow next week, or what will be the age of the next deer that will be shot! I can only say that their faces look a little dark upon me, but it does n't thunder every time a black cloud rises, nor does every puff of wind blow up rain. That's a question, therefore, much more easily put than answered."

"So is this message of the Iroquois to me," answered Judith rising, as if she had determined on her own course for the present. "My answer shall be given, Deerslayer, after you and I have talked together alone, when the others have laid themselves down for the night."

There was a decision in the manner of the girl, that disposed Deerslayer to comply, and this he did the more readily as the delay could produce no material consequences, one way or the other. The meeting now broke up, Hurry announcing his resolution to leave them speedily. During the hour that was suffered to intervene, in order that the darkness might deepen, before the frontier-man took his departure, the different individuals occupied themselves in their customary modes, the hunter, in particular, passing most of the time in making further enquiries into the perfection of the rifle already mentioned.

The hour of nine soon arrived, however, and then it had been determined that Hurry should commence his journey. Instead of making his adieus frankly, and in a generous spirit, the little he thought it necessary to say was uttered sullenly and in coldness. Resentment at what he considered Judith's obstinacy, was blended with mortification at the career he had run, since reaching the lake, and, as is usual with the vulgar and narrow-minded, he was more disposed to reproach others with his failures, than to censure himself. Judith gave him her hand, but it was quite as much in gladness, as with regret, while the two Delawares were not sorry to find he was leaving them. Of the whole party, Hetty alone betrayed any real feeling. Bashfulness, and the timidity of her sex and character, kept even her aloof, so that Hurry entered the canoe, where Deerslayer was already waiting for him, before she ventured near enough to be observed. Then, indeed, the girl came into the Ark, and approached its end, just as the little bark was turning from it, with a movement so light and steady as to be almost imperceptible. An impulse of feeling now overcame her timidity, and Hetty spoke.

"Good bye, Hurry—" she called out, in her sweet voice—"good bye, dear Hurry. Take care of yourself in the woods, and do n't stop once, 'till you reach the garrison. The leaves on the trees are scarcely plentier than the Hurons round the lake, and they'll not treat a strong man like you, as kindly as they treat me."

The ascendency which March had obtained over this feeble-minded, but right-thinking, and right-feeling girl, arose from a law of nature. Her senses had been captivated by his personal advantages, and her moral communications with him had never been sufficiently intimate to counteract an effect that must have been otherwise lessened, even with one whose mind was as obtuse as her own. Hetty's instinct of right, if such a term can be applied to one who seemed taught by some kind spirit how to steer her course with unerring accuracy, between good and evil, would have revolted at Hurry's character, on a thousand points, had there been opportunities to enlighten her, but while he conversed and trifled with her sister, at a distance from herself, his perfection of form and feature had been left to produce their influence on her simple imagination, and naturally tender feelings, without suffering by the alloy of his opinions and coarseness. It is true, she found him rough and rude; but her father was that, and most of the other men she had seen, and that which she believed to belong to all of the sex, struck her less unfavorably in Hurry's character, than it might otherwise have done. Still, it was not absolutely love that Hetty felt for Hurry, nor do we wish so to portray it, but merely that awakening sensibility and admiration, which, under more propitious circumstances, and always supposing no untoward revelations of character on the part of the young man, had supervened to prevent it, might soon have ripened into that engrossing feeling. She felt for him an incipient tenderness, but scarcely any passion. Perhaps the nearest approach to the latter, that Hetty had manifested, was to be seen in the sensitiveness which had caused her to detect March's predilection for her sister, for, among Judith's many admirers, this was the only instance in which the dull mind of the girl had been quickened into an observation of the circumstances.

Hurry received so little sympathy at his departure, that the gentle tones of Hetty, as she thus called after him, sounded soothingly. He checked the canoe, and with one sweep of his powerful arm brought it back to the side of the Ark. This was more than Hetty, whose courage had risen with the departure of her hero, expected, and she now shrunk timidly back at this unexpected return.

"You're a good gal, Hetty, and I can't quit you without shaking hands," said March kindly. "Judith, a'ter all, is n't worth as much as you, though she may be a trifle better looking. As to wits, if honesty and fair dealing with a young man is a sign of sense in a young woman, you're worth a dozen Judiths; ay, and for that matter, most young women of my acquaintance."

"Don't say any thing against Judith, Harry," returned Hetty imploringly. "Father's gone, and mother's gone, and nobody's left but Judith and me, and it is n't right for sisters to speak evil, or to hear evil of each other. Father's in the lake, and so is mother, and we should all fear God, for we do n't know when we may be in the lake, too."

"That sounds reasonable, child, as does most you say. Well, if we ever meet ag'in, Hetty, you'll find a fri'nd in me, let your sister do what she may. I was no great fri'nd of your mother I'll allow, for we did n't think alike on most p'ints, but then your father, Old Tom, and I, fitted each other as remarkably as a buckskin garment will fit any reasonable-built man. I've always been unanimous of opinion that Old Floating Tom Hutter, at the bottom, was a good fellow, and will maintain that ag'in all inimies for his sake, as well as for your'n."

"Good bye, Hurry," said Hetty, who now wanted to hasten the young man off, as ardently as she had wished to keep him only the moment before, though she could give no clearer account of the latter than of the former feeling; "good bye, Hurry; take care of yourself in the woods; do n't halt 'till you reach the garrison. I'll read a chapter in the bible for you, before I go to bed, and think of you in my prayers."

This was touching a point on which March had no sympathies, and without more words, he shook the girl cordially by the hand, and re-entered the canoe. In another minute the two adventurers were a hundred feet from the Ark, and half a dozen had not elapsed before they were completely lost to view. Hetty sighed deeply, and rejoined her sister and Hist.

For some time Deerslayer and his companion paddled ahead in silence. It had been determined to land Hurry at the precise point where he is represented, in the commencement of our tale, as having embarked, not only as a place little likely to be watched by the Hurons, but because he was sufficiently familiar with the signs of the woods, at that spot, to thread his way through them in the dark. Thither, then, the light craft proceeded, being urged as diligently, and as swiftly, as two vigorous and skilful canoe-men could force their little vessel through, or rather *over*, the water. Less than a quarter of an hour sufficed for the object, and, at the end of that time, being within the shadows of the shore, and quite near the point they sought, each ceased his efforts in order to make their parting communications out of ear shot of any straggler who might happen to be in the neighborhood.

"You will do well to persuade the officers at the garrison to lead out a party ag'in these vagabonds, as soon as you git in, Hurry," Deerslayer commenced; "and you'll do better if you volunteer to guide it up yourself. You know the paths, and the shape of the lake, and the natur' of the land, and can do it better than a common, gin'ralizing scout. Strike at the Huron camp first, and follow the signs that will then show themselves. A few looks at the hut and the Ark will satisfy you, as to the state of the Delaware and the women, and, at any rate, there'll be a fine opportunity to fall on the Mingo trail, and to make a mark on the memories of the blackguards that they'll be apt to carry with 'em a long time. It won't be likely to make much difference with me, since *that* matter will be detarmined afore to-morrow's sun has set, but it may make a great change in Judith and Hetty's hopes and prospects!"

"And as for yourself, Nathaniel," Hurry enquired with more interest than he was accustomed to betray in the welfare of others—"And, as for yourself, what do you think is likely to turn up?"

"The Lord, in his wisdom, only can tell, Henry March! The clouds look black and threatening, and I keep my mind in a state to meet the worst. Vengeful feelin's are uppermost in the hearts of the Mingos, and any little disapp'intment about the plunder, or the prisoners, or Hist, may make the torments sartain. The Lord, in his wisdom, can only detarmine my fate, or yourn!"

"This is a black business, and ought to be put a stop to in some way or other—" answered Hurry, confounding the distinctions between right and wrong, as is usual with selfish and vulgar men. "I heartily wish old Hutter and I had scalped every creatur' in their camp, the night we first landed with that capital object! Had you not held back, Deerslayer, it might have been done, and then you would n't have found yourself, at the last moment, in the desperate condition you mention."

"Twould have been better had you said, you wished you had never attempted to do what it little becomes any white man's gifts to undertake; in which case, not only might we have kept from coming to blows, but Thomas Hutter would now have been living, and the hearts of the savages would be less given to vengeance. The death of that young woman, too, was oncalled for, Henry March, and leaves a heavy load on our names if not on our consciences!"

This was so apparent, and it seemed so obvious to Hurry himself, at the moment, that he dashed his paddle into the water, and began to urge the canoe towards the shore, as if bent only on running away from his own lively remorse. His companion humoured this feverish desire for change, and, in a minute or two, the bows of the boat grated lightly on the shingle of the beach. To land, shoulder his pack and rifle, and to get ready for his march occupied Hurry but an instant, and with a growling adieu, he had already commenced his march, when a sudden twinge of feeling brought him to a dead stop, and immediately after to the other's side.

"You cannot mean to give yourself up ag'in to them murdering savages, Deerslayer!" he said, quite as much in angry remonstrance, as with generous feeling. "Twould be the act of a madman or a fool!"

"There's them that thinks it madness to keep their words, and there's them that don't, Hurry Harry. You may be one of the first, but I'm one of the last. No red skin breathing shall have it in his power to say, that a Mingo minds his word more than a man of white blood and white gifts, in any thing that consarns me. I'm out on a furlough, and if I've strength and reason, I'll go in on a furlough afore noon to-morrow!"

"What's an Injin, or a word passed, or a furlough taken from creatur's like them, that have neither souls, nor reason!"

"If they've got neither souls nor reason, you and I have both, Henry March, and one is accountable for the other. This furlough is not, as you seem to think, a matter altogether atween me and the Mingos, seeing it is a solemn bargain made atween me and God. He who thinks that he can say what he pleases, in his distress, and that twill all pass for nothing, because 'tis uttered in the forest, and into red men's ears, knows little of his situation, and hopes, and wants. The woods are but the ears of the Almighty, the air is his breath, and the light of the sun is little more than a glance of his eye. Farewell, Harry; we may not meet ag'in, but I would wish you never to treat a furlough, or any other solemn thing, that your christian God has been called on to witness, as a duty so light that it may be forgotten according to the wants of the body, or even accordin' to the cravings of the spirit."

March was now glad again to escape. It was quite impossible that he could enter into the sentiments that ennobled his companion, and he broke away from both with an impatience that caused him secretly to curse the folly that could induce a man to rush, as it were, on his own destruction. Deerslayer, on the contrary, manifested no such excitement. Sustained by his principles, inflexible in the purpose of acting up to them, and superior to any unmanly apprehension, he regarded all before him, as a matter of course, and no more thought of making any unworthy attempt to avoid it, than a Mussulman thinks of counteracting the decrees of Providence. He stood calmly on the shore, listening to the reckless tread with which Hurry betrayed his progress through the bushes, shook his head in dissatisfaction at the want of caution, and then stepped quietly into his canoe. Before he dropped the paddle again into the water, the young man gazed about him, at the scene presented by the star-lit night. This was the spot where he had first laid his eyes on the beautiful sheet of water on which he floated. If it was then glorious in the bright light of a summer's noon-tide, it was now sad and melancholy under the shadows of night. The mountains rose around it like black barriers to exclude the outer world, and the gleams of pale light that rested on the broader parts of the basin, were no bad symbols of the faintness of the hopes that were so dimly visible in his own future. Sighing heavily, he pushed the canoe from the land, and took his way, back, with steady diligence towards the Ark and the castle.

Chapter XXIV

"Thy secret pleasure turns to open shame;
Thy private feasting to a public fast;
Thy smoothing titles to a ragged name;
Thy sugar'd tongue to bitter worm wood taste:
Thy violent vanities can never last."

Shakespeare, *Rape of Lucrece*, ll. 890–94.

JUDITH WAS WAITING the return of Deerslayer on the platform, with stifled impatience, when the latter reached the hut. Hist and Hetty were both in a deep sleep, on the bed usually occupied by the two daughters of the house, and the Delaware was stretched on the floor of the adjoining room, his rifle at his side, and a blanket over him, already dreaming of the events of the last few days. There was a lamp burning in the Ark, for the family was accustomed to indulge in this luxury on extraordinary occasions, and possessed the means, the vessel being of a form and material to render it probable it had once been an occupant of the chest.

As soon as the girl got a glimpse of the canoe, she ceased her hurried walk up and down the platform, and stood ready to receive the young man, whose return she had now been anxiously expecting for some time. She helped him to fasten the canoe, and by aiding in the other little similar employments, manifested her desire to reach a moment of liberty as soon as possible. When this was done, in answer to an inquiry of his, she informed him of the manner in which their companions had disposed of themselves. He listened attentively, for the manner of the girl was so earnest and impressive as to apprise him that she had something on her mind of more than common concern.

"And now, Deerslayer," Judith continued, "you see I have lighted the lamp, and put it in the cabin of the Ark. That is never done with us, unless on great occasions, and I consider this night as the most important of my life. Will you follow me and see what I have to show you—hear what I have to say."

The hunter was a little surprised, but, making no objections, both were soon in the scow, and in the room that contained the light. Here two stools were placed at the side of the chest, with the lamp on another, and a table near by to receive the different articles as they might be brought to view. This arrangement had its rise in the feverish impatience of the girl, which could brook no delay that it was in her power to obviate. Even all the padlocks were removed, and it only remained to raise the heavy lid, again, to expose all the treasures of this long secreted hoard.

"I see, in part, what all this means," observed Deerslayer—"yes, I see through it, in part. But why is not Hetty present; now, Thomas Hutter is gone, she is one of the owners of these cur'osities, and ought to see them opened and handled."

"Hetty sleeps—" answered Judith, huskily. "Happily for her, fine clothes and riches have no charms. Besides she has this night given her share of all that the chest may hold, to me, that I may do with it as I please."

"Is poor Hetty composs enough for that, Judith?" demanded the just-minded young man. "It's a good rule, and a righteous one, never to take when them that give don't know the valie of their gifts; and such as god has visited heavily in their wits, ought to be dealt with as carefully as children that have n't yet come to their understandings."

Judith was hurt at this rebuke, coming from the person it did, but she would have felt it far more keenly had not her conscience fully acquitted her of any unjust intentions towards her feeble-minded but confiding sister. It was not a moment, however, to betray any of her usual mountings of the spirit, and she smothered the passing sensation in the desire to come to the great object she had in view.

"Hetty will not be wronged," she mildly answered; "she even knows not only what I am about to do, Deerslayer, but *why* I do it. So take your seat, raise the lid of the chest, and this time we will go to the bottom. I shall be disappointed if something is not found to tell us more of the history of Thomas Hutter and my mother."

"Why Thomas Hutter, Judith, and not your father? The dead ought to meet with as much reverence as the living!"

"I have long suspected that Thomas Hutter was not *my* father, though I did think he might have been Hetty's, but now we know he was the father of neither. He acknowledged that much in his dying moments. I am old enough to remember better things than we have seen on this lake, though they are so faintly impressed on my memory, that the earlier part of my life seems like a dream."

"Dreams are but miserable guides when one has to detarmine about realities, Judith," returned the other, admonishingly. "Fancy nothing, and hope nothing on their account, though I've known chiefs that thought 'em useful."

"I expect nothing for the future, from them, my good friend, but cannot help remembering what has been. This is idle, however, when half an hour of examination may tell us all, or even more than I want to know."

Deerslayer, who comprehended the girl's impatience, now took his seat, and proceeded once more to bring to light the different articles that the chest contained. As a matter of course, all that had been previously examined were found where they had been last deposited, and they excited much less interest, or comment, than when formerly exposed to view. Even Judith laid aside the rich brocade with an air of indifference, for she had a far higher aim before her than the indulgence of vanity, and was impatient to come at the still hidden, or rather unknown, treasures.

"All these we have seen before," she said, "and will not stop to open. The bundle under your hand, Deerslayer, is a fresh one; that we will look into. God send it may contain something to tell poor Hetty and myself, who we really are!"

"Ay, if some bundles could speak, they might tell wonderful secrets," returned the young man deliberately undoing the folds of another piece of course canvass, in order to come at the contents of the roll that lay on his knees: "though this doesn't seem to be one of that family, seeing 'tis neither more nor less than a sort of flag, though of what nation, it passes my l'arnin' to say."

"That flag must have some meaning to it—" Judith hurriedly interposed. "Open it wider, Deerslayer, that we may see the colours."

"Well, I pity the ensign that has to shoulder this cloth, and to parade it about on the field. Why 'tis large enough, Judith, to make a dozen of them colours the King's officers set so much store by. These can be no ensign's colours, but a gin'ral's!"

"A ship might carry it, Deerslayer, and ships I know do use such things. Have you never heard any fearful stories about Thomas Hutter's having once been concerned with the people they call buccaneers?"

"*Buck-ah-near!* Not I—not I—I never heard him mentioned as good at a buck far off, or near by. Hurry Harry did till me something about its being supposed that he had formerly, in some way or other, dealings with sartain sea robbers, but, Lord, Judith, it can't surely give you any satisfaction to make out that ag'in your mother's own husband, though he isn't your father."

"Any thing will give me satisfaction that tells me who I am, and helps to explain the dreams of childhood. My mother's husband! Yes, he must have been that, though why a woman like *her*, should have chosen a man like *him*, is more than mortal reason can explain. You never saw mother, Deerslayer, and can't feel the vast, vast difference there was between them!"

"Such things *do* happen, howsever;—yes, they *do* happen; though why providence lets them come to pass, is more than I understand. I've knew the f'ercest warriors with the gentlest wives of any in the tribe, and awful scolds fall to the lot of Injins fit to be missionaries."

"That was not it, Deerslayer; that was not it. Oh! if it should prove that—no; I can not wish she should not have been his wife at all. *That* no daughter can wish for her own mother! Go on, now, and let us see what the square looking bundle holds."

Deerslayer complied, and he found that it contained a small trunk of pretty workmanship, but fastened. The next point was to find a key; but, search proving ineffectual, it was determined to force the lock. This Deerslayer soon effected by the aid of an iron instrument, and it was found that the interior was nearly filled with papers. Many were letters; some fragments of manuscripts, memorandums, accounts, and other similar documents. The hawk does not pounce upon the chicken with a more sudden swoop, than Judith sprang forward to seize this mine of hitherto concealed knowledge. Her education, as the reader will have perceived, was far superior to her situation in life, and her eye glanced over page after page of the letters, with a readiness that her schooling supplied, and with an avidity that found its origin in her feelings. At first, it was evident that the girl was gratified; and we may add with reason, for the letters written by females, in innocence and affection, were of a character to cause her to feel proud of those with whom she had every reason to think she was closely connected by the ties of blood. It does not come within the scope of our plan to give more of these epistles, however, than a general idea of their contents, and this will best be done by describing the effect they produced on the manner, appearance, and feeling of her who was so eagerly perusing them.

It has been said, already, that Judith was much gratified with the letters that first met her eye. They contained the correspondence of an affectionate and intelligent mother, to an absent daughter, with such allusions to the answers, as served, in a great measure, to fill up the vacuum left by the replies. They were not without admonitions and warnings, however, and Judith felt the blood mounting to her temples, and a cold shudder succeeding, as she read one in which the propriety of the daughter's indulging in as much intimacy, as had evidently been described in one of the daughter's own letters, with an officer "who came from Europe, and who could hardly be supposed to wish to form an honorable connection in America," was rather coldly commented on by the mother. What rendered it singular, was the fact that the signatures had been carefully cut from every one of these letters, and wherever a name occurred in the body of the epistles, it had been erased with so much diligence as to render it impossible to read it. They had all been enclosed in envelopes, according to the fashion of the age, and not an address either was to be found. Still the letters themselves had been religiously preserved, and Judith thought she could discover traces of tears remaining on several. She now remembered to have seen the little trunk in her mother's keeping, previously to her death, and she supposed it had first been deposited in the chest, along with the other forgotten, or concealed objects, when the letters could no longer contribute to that parent's grief or happiness.

Next came another bundle, and these were filled with the protestations of love, written with passion certainly, but also with that deceit which men so often think it justifiable to use to the other sex. Judith had shed tears abundantly over the first packet, but now she felt a sentiment of indignation and pride better sustaining her. Her hand shook, however, and cold shivers again passed through her frame, as she discovered a few points of strong resemblance between these letters and some it had been her own fate to receive. Once, indeed, she laid the packet down, bowed her head to her knees, and seemed nearly convulsed. All this time Deerslayer sat a silent, but attentive observer of every thing that passed. As Judith read a letter, she put it into his hands to hold, until she could peruse the next; but this served in no degree to enlighten her companion, as he was totally unable to read. Nevertheless he was not entirely at fault, in discovering the passions that were contending in the bosom of the fair creature by his side, and, as occasional sentences escaped her in murmurs, he was nearer the truth, in his divinations, or conjectures, than the girl would have been pleased at discovering.

Judith had commenced with the earliest letters, luckily for a ready comprehension of the tale they told, for they were carefully arranged in chronological order, and to any one who would take the trouble to peruse them, would have revealed a sad history of gratified passion, coldness, and finally of aversion. As she obtained the clue to their import, her impatience would not admit of delay, and she soon got to glancing her eyes over a page, by way of coming at the truth, in the briefest manner possible. By adopting this expedient, one to which all who are eager to arrive at results, without encumbering themselves with details, are so apt to resort, Judith made a rapid progress in these melancholy revelations of her mother's failing and punishment. She saw that the period of her own birth was distinctly referred to, and even learned that the homely name she bore, was given her by the father, of whose person she retained so faint an impression as to resemble a dream. This name was not obliterated from the text of the letters, but stood as if nothing was to be gained by erasing it. Hetty's birth was mentioned once, and in that instance the name was the mother's, but ere this period was reached came the signs of coldness, shadowing forth the desertion that was so soon to follow. It was in this stage of the correspondence that her mother had recourse to the plan of copying her own epistles. They were but few, but were eloquent with the feelings of blighted affection, and contrition. Judith sobbed over them, until again and again she felt compelled to lay them aside from sheer physical in a inability to see; her eyes being literally obscured with tears. Still she returned to the task, with increasing interest, and finally succeeded in reaching the end of the latest communication that had probably ever passed between her parents.

All this occupied fully an hour, for near a hundred letters were glanced at, and some twenty had been closely read. The truth now shone clear upon the acute mind of Judith, so far as her own birth and that of Hetty, were concerned. She sickened at the conviction, and for the moment the rest of the world seemed to be cut off from her, and she had now additional reasons for wishing to pass the remainder of her life on the lake, where she had already seen so many bright and so many sorrowing days.

There yet remained more letters to examine. Judith found these were a correspondence between her mother and Thomas Hovey. The originals of both parties were carefully arranged, letter and answer, side by side; and they told the early history of the connection between the ill-assorted pair far more plainly than Judith wished to learn it. Her mother made the advances towards a marriage, to the surprise, not to say horror of her daughter, and she actually found a relief when she discovered traces of what struck her as insanity—or a morbid desperation, bordering on that dire calamity—in the earlier letters of that ill-fated woman. The answers of Hovey were coarse and illiterate, though they manifested a sufficient desire to obtain the hand of a woman of singular personal attractions, and whose great error he was willing to overlook for the advantage of possessing one, every way so much his superior, and, who, it also appeared was not altogether destitute of money. The remainder of this part of the correspondence was brief, and it was soon confined to a few communications on business, in which the miserable wife hastened the absent husband in his preparations to abandon a world, which there was a sufficient reason to think was as dangerous to one of the parties, as it was disagreeable to the other. But a sincere expression had escaped her mother, by which Judith could get a clue to the motives that had induced her to marry Hovey, or Hutter, and this she found was that feeling of resentment which so often tempts the injured to inflict wrongs on themselves, by way of heaping coals on the heads of those through whom they have suffered. Judith had enough of the spirit of that mother, to comprehend this sentiment, and for a moment did she see the exceeding folly which permitted such revengeful feelings to get the ascendancy.

There, what may be called the historical part of the papers ceased. Among the loose fragments, however, was an old newspaper that contained a proclamation offering a reward for the apprehension of certain free-booters by name, among which was that of Thomas Hovey. The attention of the girl was drawn to the proclamation and to this particular name, by the circumstance that black lines had been drawn under both, in ink. Nothing else was found among the papers that could lead to a discovery of either the name or the place of residence of the wife of Hutter. All the dates, signatures, and addresses, had been cut from the letters, and wherever a word occurred in the body of the communications, that might furnish a clue, it was scrupulously erased. Thus Judith found all her hopes of ascertaining who her parents were, defeated, and she was obliged to fall back on her own resources and habits for every thing connected with the future. Her recollection of her mother's manners, conversation, and sufferings filled up many a gap in the historical facts she had now discovered, and the truth, in its outlines, stood sufficiently distinct before her, to take away all desire, indeed, to possess any more details. Throwing herself back in her seat, she simply desired her companion to finish the examination of the other articles in the chest, as it might yet contain something of importance.

"I'll do it, Judith; I'll do it," returned the patient Deerslayer, "but if there's many more letters to read, we shall see the sun ag'in, afore you've got through with the reading of them! Two good hours have you been looking at them bits of papers!"

"They tell me of my parents, Deerslayer, and have settled my plans for life. A girl may be excused who reads about her *own* father and mother, and that too for the first time in her life. I am sorry to have kept you waiting."

"Never mind me, gal, never mind me. It matters little whether I sleep or watch; but, though you be pleasant to look at, and are so handsome, Judith, it is not altogether agreeable to sit so long to behold you shedding tears. I know that tears do n't kill, and that some people are better for shedding a few, now and then, especially women, but I'd rather see you smile, any time, Judith, than see you weep."

This gallant speech was rewarded with a sweet, though a melancholy smile, and then the girl again desired her companion to finish the examination of the chest. The search necessarily continued some time, during which Judith collected her thoughts, and regained her composure. She took no part in the search, leaving every thing to the young man, looking listlessly, herself, at the different articles that came uppermost. Nothing further of much interest, or value, however, was found. A sword or two, such as were then worn by gentlemen, some buckles of silver, or so richly plated as to appear silver, and a few handsome articles of female dress composed the principal discoveries. It struck both Judith and the Deerslayer notwithstanding, that some of these things might be made useful in effecting a negotiation with the Iroquois, though the latter saw a difficulty in the way that was not so apparent to the former. The conversation was first renewed in connection with this point.

"And now, Deerslayer," said Judith, " we may talk of yourself, and of the means of getting you out of the hands of the Hurons. Any part, or all of what you have seen in the chest will be cheerfully given by me and Hetty, to set you at liberty."

"Well, that's ginerous—yes, 'tis downright free-hearted, and free-handed, and ginerous. This is the way with women; when they take up a fri'ndship, they do nothing by halves, but are as willing to part with their property, as if it had no valie in their eyes. Howsever, while I thank you both, just as much as if the bargain was made, and Rivenoak, or any of the other vagabonds, was here to accept and close the treaty, there's two principal reasons why it can never come to pass, which may be as well told at once, in order no onlikely expectations may be raised in you, or any onjustifiable hopes in me."

"What reason *can* there be, if Hetty and I are willing to part with the trifles for your sake, and the savages are willing to receive them?"

"That's it, Judith—you've got the idees, but they're a little out of their places, as if a hound should take the back'ard instead of the leading scent. That the Mingos will be willing to receive them things, or any more like 'em, you may have to offer is probable enough, but whether they'll pay valie for 'em, is quite another matter. Ask yourself, Judith, if any one should send you a message to say that, for such or such a price, you and Hetty might have that chist and all it holds, whether you'd think it worth your while to waste many words on the bargain?"

"But this chest and all it holds, are already ours; there is no reason why we should purchase what is already our own."

"Just so the Mingos caculate! They say the chist is theirn, already; or, as good as theirn, and they'll not thank anybody for the key."

"I understand you, Deerslayer; surely we are yet in possession of the lake, and we can keep possession of it, until Hurry sends troops to drive off the enemy. This we may certainly do, provided you will stay with us, instead of going back and giving yourself up a prisoner, again, as you now seem determined on".

"That Hurry Harry should talk in thisaway, is nat'ral, and according to the gifts of the man. He knows no better, and, therefore, he is little likely to feel, or to act any better; but, Judith, I put it to your heart and conscience—would you, *could* you think of me as favorably, as I hope and believe you now do, was I to forget my furlough and not go back to the camp?"

"To think *more* favorably of you than I now do, Deerslayer, would not be easy; but I might continue to think *as* favorably—at least it seems so—I hope I could, for, a world would n't tempt me to let you do any thing that might change my real opinion of you."

"Then do n't try to entice me to overlook my furlough, gal!—A furlough is a sacred thing among warriors and men that carry their lives in their hands, as we of the forests do, and what a grievous disapp'intment would it be to old Tamenund, and to Uncas, the father of the Sarpent, and to my other fri'nds in the tribe, if I was so to disgrace myself, on my very first war-path? This you will pairceive, moreover, Judith, is without laying any stress on nat'ral gifts, and a white man's duties, to say nothing of conscience. The last is king with me, and I try never to dispute his orders."

"I believe you are right, Deerslayer," returned the girl, after a little reflection and in a saddened voice: "a man like *you*, ought not to act, as the selfish and dishonest would be apt to act; *you* must, indeed, go back. We will talk no more of this, then. Should I persuade you to any thing for which you would be sorry hereafter, my own regret would not be less than yours. You shall not have it to say, Judith—I scarce know by what name to call myself, now!"

"And why not?—Why not, gal? Children take the names of their parents, nat'rally, and by a sort of gift, like, and why should n't you and Hetty do, as others have done afore ye? Hutter was the old man's name, and Hutter should be the name of his darters;—at least until you are given away in lawful and holy wedlock."

"I am Judith, and Judith only," returned the girl positively—"until the law gives me a right to another name. Never will I use that of Thomas Hutter again; nor, with my consent, shall Hetty! Hutter was not even his own name, I find, but had he a thousand rights to it, it would give none to me. *He* was not my father, thank heaven; though I may have no reason to be proud of him that *was*!"

"This is strange!" said Deerslayer, looking steadily at the excited girl, anxious to know more, but unwilling to inquire into matters that did not properly concern him; "yes, this is very strange and oncommon! Thomas Hutter was n't Thomas Hutter, and his darters were n't his darters! Who, then, could Thomas Hutter be, and who are his darters?"

"Did you never hear any thing whispered against the

former life of this person, Deerslayer?" demanded Judith—"Passing, as I did, for his child, such reports reached even me."

"I'll not deny it, Judith; no, I'll not deny it. Sartain things have been said, as I've told you, but I'm not very credible as to reports. Young as I am, I've lived long enough to l'arn there's two sorts of characters in the world—them that is 'arned by deeds, and them that is 'arned by tongues, and so I prefar to see and judge for myself, instead of letting every jaw that chooses to wag become my judgment. Hurry Harry spoke pretty plainly of the whole family, as we journeyed this-a-way, and he did hint something consarning Thomas Hutter's having been a free-liver on the water, in his younger days. By free-liver, I mean that he made free to live on other men's goods."

"He told you he was a pirate—there is no need of mincing matters between friends. Read that, Deerslayer, and you will see that he told you no more than the truth. This Thomas Hovey was the Thomas Hutter you knew, as is seen by these letters."

As Judith spoke, with a flushed cheek and eyes dazzling with the brilliancy of excitement, she held the newspaper towards her companion, pointing to the proclamation of a Colonial Governor, already mentioned.

"Bless you, Judith!" answered the other laughing, "you might as well ask me to print that—or, for that matter to write it. My edication has been altogether in the woods; the only book I read, or care about reading, is the one which God has opened afore all his creatur's in the noble forests, broad lakes, rolling rivers, blue skies, and the winds and tempests, and sunshine, and other glorious marvels of the land! This book I can read, and I find it full of wisdom and knowledge."

"I crave your pardon, Deerslayer," said Judith, earnestly, more abashed than was her wont, in finding that she had inadvertently made an appeal that might wound her companion's pride. "I had forgotten your manner of life, and least of all did I wish to hurt your feelings."

"Hurt my feelin's?—Why should it hurt my feelin's to ask me to read, when I can't read. I'm a hunter—and I may now begin to say a warrior, and no missionary, and therefore books and papers are of no account with such as I—No, no—Judith," and here the young man laughed cordially, "not even for wads, seeing that your true deerkiller always uses the hide of a fa'a'n, if he's got one, or some other bit of leather suitably prepared. There's some that *do* say, all that stands in print is true, in which case I'll own an unl'arned man must be somewhat of a loser; nevertheless, it can't be truer than that which God has printed with his own hand, in the sky, and the woods, and the rivers, and the springs."

"Well, then, Hutter, or Hovey, was a pirate, and being no father of mine, I cannot wish to call him one. His name shall no longer be my name."

"If you dislike the name of that man, there's the name of your mother, Judith. Hern may sarve you just as good a turn."

"I do not know it. I've look'd through those papers, Deerslayer, in the hope of finding some hint, by which I might discover who my mother was, but there is no more trace of the past, in that respect, than the bird leaves in the air."

"That's both oncommon, and onreasonable. Parents are bound to give their offspring a name, even though they give 'em nothing else. Now I come of a humble stock, though we have white gifts and a white natur', but we are not so poorly off, as to have no name. Bumppo we are called, and I've heard it said—" a touch of human vanity glowing on his cheek, "that the time has been when the Bumppos had more standing and note among mankind, than they have just now."

"They never deserved them more, Deerslayer, and the name is a good one; either Hetty, or myself, would a thousand times rather be called Hetty Bumppo, or Judith Bumppo, than to be called Hetty or Judith Hutter."

"That's a moral impossible," returned the hunter, good-humouredly, "onless one of you should so far demean herself as to marry me."

Judith could not refrain from smiling, when she found how simply and naturally the conversation had come round to the very point at which she had aimed to bring it. Although far from unfeminine or forward, either in her feelings, or her habits, the girl was goaded by a sense of wrongs not altogether merited, incited by the hopelessness of a future that seemed to contain no resting place, and still more influenced by feelings that were as novel to her, as they proved to be active and engrossing. The opening was too good, therefore, to be neglected, though she came to the subject with much of the indirectness and perhaps, justifiable, address of a woman.

"I do not think Hetty will ever marry, Deerslayer," she said, "and if your name is to be borne by either of us, it must be borne by me."

"There's been handsome women too, they tell me, among the Bumppos, Judith, afore now, and should you take up with the name, oncommon as you be, in this particular, them that knows the family won't be altogether surprised."

"This is not talking as becomes either of us, Deerslayer, for whatever is said on such a subject, between man and woman, should be said seriously, and in sincerity of heart. Forgetting the shame that ought to keep girls silent, until spoken to, in most cases, I will deal with you as frankly as I know one of your generous nature will most like to be dealt by. Can you—do you think, Deerslayer, that you could be happy with such a wife as a woman like myself would make?"

"A woman like you, Judith! But where's the sense in trifling about such a thing?—A woman like you, that is handsome enough to be a captain's lady, and fine enough, and so far as I know edicated enough, would be little apt to think of becoming my wife. I suppose young gals that feel themselves to be smart, and know themselves to be handsome, find a sartain satisfaction in passing their jokes ag'in them that's neither, like a poor Delaware hunter."

This was said good naturedly, but not without a betrayal of feeling which showed that some thing like mortified sensibility was blended with the reply. Nothing could have occurred more likely to awaken all Judith's generous regrets, or to aid her in her purpose, by adding the stimulant of a disinterested desire to atone, to her other impulses, and cloaking all under a guise so winning and natural, as greatly to lessen the unpleasant feature of a forwardness unbecoming the sex.

"You do me injustice if you suppose I have any such thought, or wish," she answered, earnestly. "Never was I more serious in my life, or more willing to abide by any agreement, that we may make to-night. I have had many suitors, Deerslayer—nay, scarce an unmarried trapper or hunter has been in at the Lake these four years, who has not offered to take me away with him, and I fear some that were married, too—"

"Ay, I'll warrant that!" interrupted the other—"I'll warrant all that! Take 'em as a body, Judith, 'arth don't hold a set of men more given to theirselves, and less given to God and the law."

"Not one of them would I—could I listen to; happily for myself perhaps, has it been that such was the case. There have been well looking youths among them too, as you may have seen in your acquaintance, Henry March."

"Yes, Harry is sightly to the eye, though, to my idees, less so to the judgment. I thought, at first, you meant to have him, Judith, I did; but afore he went, it was easy enough to verify that the same lodge would n't be big enough for you both."

"You have done me justice in that at least, Deerslayer. Hurry is a man I could never marry, though he were ten times more comely to the eye, and a hundred times more stout of heart, than he really is."

"Why not, Judith, why not? I own I'm cur'ous to know why a youth like Hurry should n't find favor with a maiden like you?"

"Then you shall know, Deerslayer," returned the girl, gladly availing herself of the opportunity of indirectly extolling the qualities which had so strongly interested her in her listener; hoping by these means covertly to approach the subject nearest her heart. "In the first place, looks in a man are of no importance with a woman, provided he is manly, and not disfigured, or deformed."

"There I can't altogether agree with you," returned the other thoughtfully, for he had a very humble opinion of his own personal appearance; "I have noticed that the comeliest warriors commonly get the best-looking maidens of the tribe, for wives, and the Sarpent, yonder, who is sometimes wonderful in his paint, is a gineral favorite with all the Delaware young women, though he takes to Hist, himself, as if she was the only beauty on 'arth!"

"It may be so with Indians; but it is different with white girls. So long as a young man has a straight and manly frame, that promises to make him able to protect a woman, and to keep want from the door, it is all they ask of the figure. Giants like Hurry may do for grenadiers, but are of little account as lovers. Then as to the face, an honest look, one that answers for the heart within, is of more value than any shape or colour, or eyes, or teeth, or trifles like them. The last may do for girls, but who thinks of them at all, in a hunter, or a warrior, or a husband?—If there are women so silly, Judith is not among them."

"Well, this is wonderful! I always thought that handsome liked handsome, as riches love riches!"

"It may be so with you men, Deerslayer, but it is not always so with us women. We like stout-hearted men, but we wish to see them modest; sure on a hunt, or the war-path, ready to die for the right, and unwilling to yield to the wrong. Above all we wish for honesty—tongues that are not used to say what the mind does not mean, and hearts that feel a little for others, as well as for themselves. A true-hearted girl could die for such a husband! while the boaster, and the double-tongued suitor gets to be as hateful to the sight, as he is to the mind."

Judith spoke bitterly, and with her usual force, but her listener was too much struck with the novelty of the sensations he experienced to advert to her manner. There was something so soothing to the humility of a man of his temperament, to hear qualities that he could not but know he possessed himself, thus highly extolled by the loveliest female he had ever beheld, that, for the moment, his faculties seemed suspended in a natural and excusable pride. Then it was that the idea of the possibility of such a creature as Judith becoming his companion for life, first crossed his mind. The image was so pleasant, and so novel, that he continued completely absorbed by it, for more than a minute, totally regardless of the beautiful reality that was seated before him, watching the expression of his upright and truth-telling countenance with a keenness that gave her a very fair, if not an absolutely accurate clue to his thoughts. Never before had so pleasing a vision floated before the mind's eye of the young hunter, but, accustomed most to practical things, and little addicted to submitting to the power of his imagination, even while possessed of so much true poetical feeling in connection with natural objects in particular, he soon recovered his reason, and smiled at his own weakness, as the fancied picture faded from his mental sight, and left him the simple, untaught, but highly moral being he was, seated in the Ark of Thomas Hutter, at midnight, with the lovely countenance of its late owner's reputed daughter, beaming on him with anxious scrutiny, by the light of the solitary lamp.

"You're wonderful handsome, and enticing, and pleasing to look on, Judith!" he exclaimed, in his simplicity, as fact resumed its ascendency over fancy. "Wonderful! I do n't remember ever to have seen so beautiful a gal, even among the Delawares; and I'm not astonished that Hurry Harry went away soured as well as disapp'inted!"

"Would you have had me, Deerslayer, become the wife of such a man as Henry March?"

"There's that which is in his favor, and there's that which is ag'in him. To my taste, Hurry would n't make the best of husbands, but I fear that the tastes of most young women, hereaway, would n't be so hard upon him."

"No—no—Judith without a name, would never consent to be called Judith March! Any thing would be better than *that*."

"Judith Bumppo would n't sound as well, gal; and there's many names that would fall short of March, in pleasing the ear."

"Ah! Deerslayer, the pleasantness of the sound, in such cases, does n't come through the ear, but through the heart. Every thing is agreeable, when the heart is satisfied. Were Natty Bumppo, Henry March, and Henry March, Natty Bumppo, I might think the name of March better than it is; or were he, you, I should fancy the name of Bumppo, horrible!"

"That's just it—yes, that's the reason of the matter. Now, I'm nat'rally avarse to sarpents, and I hate even the word, which, the missionaries tell me, comes from human natur', on account of a sartain sarpent at the creation of the 'arth, that outwitted the first woman; yet, ever since Chingachgook has 'arned the title he bears, why the sound is as pleasant to my ears as the whistle of the whip-poor-will, of a calm evening, it is. The feelin's make all the difference in the world, Judith, in the natur' of sounds; ay, even in that of looks, too."

"This is so true, Deerslayer, that I am surprised you should think it remarkable a girl, who may have some comeliness herself, should not think it necessary that her husband should have the same advantage; or, what you fancy an advantage. To me, looks in a man are nothing, provided his countenance be as honest as his heart."

"Yes, honesty is a great advantage, in the long run; and they that are the most apt to forget it, in the beginning, are the most apt to l'arn it in the ind. Nevertheless, there's more, Judith, that look to present profit, than to the benefit that is to come after a time. One they think a sartainty, and the other an onsartainty. I'm glad, howsever, that *you* look at the thing in its true light, and not in the way in which so many is apt to deceive themselves."

"I do thus look at it, Deerslayer," returned the girl with emphasis, still shrinking, with a woman's sensitiveness, from a direct offer of her hand, "and can say, from the bottom of my heart, that I would rather trust my happiness to a man whose truth and feelings may be depended on, than to a false-tongued and false hearted wretch, that had chests of gold, and houses and lands—yes though he were even seated on a throne!"

"These are brave words, Judith; yes, they're downright brave words, but do you think that the feelin's would keep 'em company, did the ch'ice actually lie afore you? If a gay gallant in a scarlet coat stood on one side, with his head smelling like a deer's foot, his face smooth and blooming as your own, his hands as white and soft as if god had n't bestowed 'em that man might live by the sweat of his brow, and his step as lofty as dancing teachers and a light heart could make it; and on the other side, stood one that has passed his days in the open air, 'till his forehead is as red as his cheek; had cut his way through swamps and bushes till his hand was as rugged as the oaks he slept under; had trodden on the scent of game 'till his step was as stealthy as the catamount's, and had no other pleasant odour about him, than such as natur' gives in the free air, and the forest—now, if both these men stood here, as suitors for your feelin's, which do you think would win your favor?"

Judith's fine face flushed, for the picture that her companion had so simply drawn of a gay officer of the garrisons had once been particularly grateful to her imagination, though experience and disappointment had not only chilled all her affections, but given them a backward current, and the passing image had a momentary influence on her feelings; but the mounting colour was succeeded by a paleness so deadly, as to make her appear ghastly.

"As God is my judge," the girl solemnly answered, "did both these men stand before me, as I may say one of them does, my choice, if I know my own heart, would be the latter. I have no wish for a husband who is any way better than myself."

"This is pleasant to listen to, and might lead a young man in time, to forget his own onworthiness, Judith! Howsever, you hardly think all that you say. A man like me is too rude and ignorant for one that has had such a mother to teach her. Vanity is nat'ral, I do believe, but vanity like that, would surpass reason."

"Then you do not know of what a woman's heart is capable! Rude *you* are not, Deerslayer, nor can one be called ignorant that has studied what is before his eyes as closely as you have done. When the affections are concerned, all things appear in their pleasantest colors, and trifles are overlooked, or are forgotten. When the heart feels sunshine, nothing is gloomy, even dull looking objects, seeming gay and bright, and so it would be between you and the woman who should love you, even though your wife might happen, in some matters, to possess what the world calls the advantage over you."

"Judith, you come of people altogether above mine, in the world, and onequal matches, like onequal fri'ndships can't often tarminate kindly. I speak of this matter altogether as a fanciful thing, since it's not very likely that *you*, at least, would be apt to treat it as a matter that can ever come to pass."

Judith fastened her deep blue eyes on the open, frank countenance of her companion, as if she would read his soul. Nothing there betrayed any covert meaning, and she was obliged to admit to herself, that he regarded the conversation as argumentative, rather than positive, and that he was still without any active suspicion that her feelings were seriously involved in the issue. At first, she felt offended; then she saw the injustice of making the self-abasement and modesty of the hunter a charge against him, and this novel difficulty gave a piquancy to the state of affairs that rather increased her interest in the young man. At that critical instant, a change of plan flashed on her mind, and with a readiness of invention that is peculiar to the quick-witted and ingenious, she adopted a scheme by which she hoped effectually to bind him to her person. This scheme partook equally of her fertility of invention, and of the decision and boldness of her character. That the conversation might not terminate too abruptly, however, or any suspicion of her design exist, she answered the last remark of Deerslayer, as earnestly and as truly, as if her original intention remained unaltered.

"I, certainly, have no reason to boast of parentage, after what I have seen this night," said the girl, in a saddened voice. "I had a mother, it is true; but of her name even, I am ignorant—and, as for my father, it is better, perhaps, that I should never know who he was, lest I speak too bitterly of him!"

"Judith," said Deerslayer, taking her hand kindly, and with a manly sincerity that went directly to the girl's heart, " 'tis better to say no more to-night. Sleep on what you've seen and felt; in the morning things that now look gloomy, may look more che'rful. Above all, never do any thing in bitterness, or because you feel as if you'd like to take revenge on yourself, for other people's backslidings. All that has been said, or done, atween us, this night, is your secret, and shall never be talked of by me, even with the Sarpent, and you may be sartain if he can't get it out of me no man can. If your parents have been faulty, let the darter be less so; remember that you're young, and the youthful may always hope for better times; that you're more quick-witted than usual, and such gin'rally get the better of difficulties, and that, as for beauty, you're oncommon, which is an advantage with all. It is time to get a little rest, for to-morrow is like to prove a trying day to some of us."

Deerslayer arose as he spoke, and Judith had no choice but to comply. The chest was closed and secured, and they parted in silence, she to take her place by the side of Hist and Hetty, and he to seek a blanket on the floor of the cabin he was in. It was not five minutes ere the young man was in a deep sleep, but the girl continued awake for a long time. She scarce knew whether to lament, or to rejoice, at having failed in making herself understood. On the one hand, were her womanly sensibilities spared; on the other was the disappointment of defeated, or at least of delayed expectations, and the uncertainty of a future that looked so dark. Then came the new resolution, and the bold project for the morrow, and when drowsiness finally shut her eyes, they closed on a scene of success and happiness, that was pictured by the fancy, under the influence of a sanguine temperament, and a happy invention.

Chapter XXV

"But, mother, now a shade has past,
  Athwart my brightest visions here,
A cloud of darkest gloom has wrapt,
  The remnant of my brief career!
No song, no echo can I win,
The sparkling fount has died within."
  Margaret Davidson, "To my Mother," ll. 7–12.

HIST AND HETTY arose with the return of light, leaving Judith still buried in sleep. It took but a minute for the first to complete her toilet. Her long coal-black hair was soon adjusted in a simple knot, the calico dress belted tight to her slender waist, and her little feet concealed in their gaudily ornamented moccasins. When attired, she left her companion employed in household affairs, and went herself on the platform to breathe the pure air of the morning. Here she found Chingachgook studying the shores of the lake, the mountains and the heavens, with the sagacity of a man of the woods, and the gravity of an Indian.

The meeting between the two lovers was simple, but affectionate. The chief showed a manly kindness, equally removed from boyish weakness and haste, while the girl betrayed, in her smile and half averted looks, the bashful tenderness of her sex. Neither spoke, unless it were with the eyes, though each understood the other as fully as if a vocabulary of words and protestations had been poured out. Hist seldom appeared to more advantage, than at that moment, for just from her rest and ablutions, there was a freshness about her youthful form and face, that the toils of the wood do not always permit to be exhibited, by even the juvenile and pretty. Then Judith had not only imparted some of her own skill in the toilet, during their short intercourse, but she had actually bestowed a few well selected ornaments from her own stores, that contributed not a little to set off the natural graces of the Indian maid. All this the lover saw and felt, and for a moment his countenance was illuminated with a look of pleasure, but it soon grew grave, again, and became saddened and anxious. The stools used the previous night were still standing on the platform; placing two against the walls of the hut, he seated himself on one, making a gesture to his companion to take the other. This done, he continued thoughtful and silent, for quite a minute, maintaining the reflecting dignity of one born to take his seat at the Council Fire, while Hist was furtively watching the expression of his face, patient and submissive as became a woman of her people. Then the young warrior stretched his arm before him, as if to point out the glories of the scene at that witching hour, when the whole panorama, as usual, was adorned by the mellow distinctness of early morning, sweeping with his hand slowly over lake, hills and heavens. The girl followed the movement with pleased wonder, smiling as each new beauty met her gaze.

"Hugh!" exclaimed the chief, in admiration of a scene so unusual even to him, for this was the first lake he had ever beheld—"this is the country of the Manitou! It is too good for Mingos, Hist; but the curs of that tribe are howling in packs through the woods. They think that the Delawares are asleep, over the mountains."

"All but one of them is, Chingachgook. There is one here; and he is of the blood of Uncas!"

"What is one warrior against a tribe?—The path to our villages is very long and crooked, and we shall travel it under a cloudy sky. I am afraid, too, Honeysuckle of the Hills, that we shall travel it alone!"

Hist understood the allusion, and it made her sad; though it sounded sweet to her ears to be compared, by the warrior she so loved, to the most fragrant, and the pleasantest of all the wild-flowers of her native woods. Still she continued silent, as became her when the allusion was to a grave interest that men could best control, though it exceeded the power of education to conceal the smile that gratified feeling brought to her pretty mouth.

"When the sun is thus," continued the Delaware, pointing to the zenith, by simply casting upward a hand and finger, by a play of the wrist, "the great hunter of our tribe, will go back to the Hurons, to be treated like a bear, that they roast and skin, even on full stomachs."

"The Great Spirit may soften their hearts, and not suffer them to be so bloody minded. I have lived among the

Hurons, and know them. They have hearts, and will not forget their own children, should they fall into the hands of the Delawares."

"A wolf is forever howling; a hog will always eat. They have lost warriors; even their women will call out for vengeance. The pale face has the eyes of an eagle, and can see into a Mingo's heart; he looks for no mercy. There is a cloud over his spirit, though it is not before his face."

A long, thoughtful pause succeeded, during which Hist stealthily took the hand of the chief, as if seeking his support, though she scarce ventured to raise her eyes to a countenance that was now literally becoming terrible, under the conflicting passions, and stern resolution that were struggling in the breast of its owner.

"What will the Son of Uncas do?" the girl at length timidly asked. "He is a chief, and is already celebrated in council, though so young; what does his heart tell him is wisest; does the head, too, speak the same words as the heart?"

"What does Wah-ta!-Wah say, at a moment when my dearest friend is in such danger. The smallest birds sing the sweetest; it is always pleasant, to hearken to their songs. I wish I could hear the Wren of the Woods in my difficulty; its note would reach deeper than the ear."

Again Hist experienced the profound gratification that the language of praise can always awaken, when uttered by those we love. The 'Honeysuckle of the Hills' was a term often applied to the girl, by the young men of the Delawares, though it never sounded so sweet in her ears, as from the lips of Chingachgook; but the latter alone had ever styled her the Wren of the Woods. With him, however, it had got to be a familiar phrase, and it was past expression pleasant to the listener, since it conveyed to her mind the idea that her advice and sentiments were as acceptable to her future husband, as the tones of her voice and modes of conveying them were agreeable; uniting the two things most prized by an Indian girl, as coming from her betrothed, admiration for a valued physical advantage, with respect for her opinion. She pressed the hand she held, between both her own, and answered—

"Wah-ta!-Wah says that neither she nor the Great Serpent could ever laugh, again, or ever sleep without dreaming of the Hurons, should the Deerslayer die under a Mingo tomahawk, and they do nothing to save him. She would rather go back, and start on her long path alone, than let such a dark cloud pass before her happiness."

"Good! The husband and the wife will have but one heart; they will see with the same eyes, and feel with the same feelings."

What further was said, need not be related here. That the conversation was of Deerslayer, and his hopes, has been seen already, but the decision that was come to, will better appear in the course of the narrative. The youthful pair were yet conversing when the sun appeared above the tops of the pines, and the light of a brilliant American day streamed down into the valley, bathing "in deep joy" the lake, the forests and the mountain sides. Just at this instant Deerslayer came out of the cabin of the Ark, and stepped upon the platform. His first look was at the cloudless heavens, then his rapid glance took in the entire panorama of land and water, when he had leisure for a friendly nod at his friends, and a cheerful smile for Hist.

"Well," he said, in his usual, composed manner, and pleasant voice, "he that sees the sun set in the west, and wakes 'arly enough in the morning will be sartain to find him coming back ag'in in the east, like a buck that is hunted round his ha'nt. I dare say, now, Hist, you've beheld this, time and ag'in, and yet it never entered into your galish mind to ask the reason?"

Both Chingachgook and his betrothed looked up at the luminary, with an air that betokened sudden wonder, and then they gazed at each other, as if to seek the solution of the difficulty. Familiarity deadens the sensibilities, even as connected with the gravest natural phenomena, and never before had these simple beings thought of enquiring into a movement that was of daily occurrence, however puzzling it might appear on investigation. When the subject was thus suddenly started, it struck both alike, and at the same instant, with some such force, as any new and brilliant proposition in the natural sciences would strike the scholar. Chingachgook alone saw fit to answer.

"The pale-faces know every thing," he said; "can they tell us why the sun hides his face, when he goes back, at night."

"Ay, that is downright red-skin l'arnin'," returned the other, laughing, though he was not altogether insensible to the pleasure of proving the superiority of his race, by solving the difficulty, which he set about doing, in his own peculiar manner. "Harkee, Sarpent," he continued more gravely, though too simply for affectation; "this is easierly explained than an Indian brain may fancy. The sun, while he seems to keep travelling in the heavens, never budges, but it is the 'arth that turns round, and any one can understand, if he is placed on the side of a mill-wheel, for instance, when it's in motion, that he must some times see the heavens, while he is at other times under water. There's no great secret in that; but plain natur'; the difficulty being in setting the 'arth in motion."

"How does my brother know that the earth turns round?" demanded the Indian. "Can he see it?"

"Well, that's been a puzzler, I will own, Delaware, for I've often tried, but never could fairly make it out. Sometimes I've consaited that I could; and then ag'in, I've been obliged to own it an onpossibility. Howsever, turn it does, as all my people say, and you ought to believe 'em, since they can foretel eclipses, and other prodigies, that used to fill the tribes with terror, according to your own traditions of such things."

"Good. This is true; no red-man will deny it. When a wheel turns, my eyes can see it—they do not see the earth turn."

"Ay, that's what I call sense obstinacy! Seeing is believing, they say, and what they can't see, some men won't in the least give credit to. Nevertheless, chief, that is n't quite as good reason as it may at first seem. You believe in the Great Spirit, I know, and yet, I conclude, it would puzzle you to show where you see him!"

"Chingachgook can see Him every where—every where in *good* things—the Evil Spirit in *bad*. Here, in the lake; there, in the forest; yonder, in the clouds; in Hist, in the Son of Uncas, in Tamenund, in Deerslayer. The Evil Spirit is in the Mingos. That I see; I do not see the earth turn round."

"I do n't wonder they call you the Sarpent, Delaware; no, I do n't! There's always a meaning in your words, and there's often a meaning in your countenance, too! Notwithstanding, your answers does n't quite meet my idee. That God is observable in all nat'ral objects is allowable, but then he is not parceptible in the way I mean. *You* know there is a Great Spirit by his works, and the pale faces know that the 'arth turns round by its works. This is the reason of the matter, though how it is to be explained, is more than I can exactly tell you. This I know; all my people consait that fact, and what all the pale-faces consait, is very likely to be true."

"When the sun is in the top of that pine to-morrow, where will my brother Deerslayer be?"

The hunter started, and he looked intently, though totally without alarm, at his friend. Then he signed for him to follow, and led the way into the Ark, where he might pursue the subject unheard by those, whose feelings he feared might get the mastery over their reason. Here he stopped, and pursued the conversation in a more confidential tone.

" 'Twas a little onreasonable in you, Sarpent," he said, "to bring up such a subject afore Hist, and when the young women of my own colour might overhear what was said. Yes, 'twas a little more onreasonable than most things that you do. No matter; Hist did n't comprehind, and the other did n't hear. Howsever, the question is easier put than answered. No mortal can say where he will be when the sun rises to-morrow. I will ask you the same question, Sarpent, and should like to hear what answer you can give."

"Chingachgook will be with his friend Deerslayer—If he be in the land of spirits, the Great Serpent will crawl at his side; if beneath yonder sun, its warmth and light shall fall on both."

"I understand you Delaware," returned the other, touched with the simple self-devotion of his friend. "Such language is as plain in one tongue as in another. It comes from the heart, and goes to the heart, too. 'Tis well to think so, and it may be well to *say* so, for that matter, but it would not be well to *do* so, Sarpent. You are no longer alone in life, for though you have the lodges to change, and other ceremonies to go through, afore Hist becomes your lawful wife, yet are you as good as married, in all that bears on the feelin's, and joy, and misery. No—no—Hist must not be desarted, because a cloud is passing atween you and me, a little onexpectedly and a little darker than we may have looked for."

"Hist is a daughter of the Mohicans. She knows how to

obey her husband. Where he goes, she will follow. *Both* will be with the Great Hunter of the Delawares, when the sun shall be in the pine to-morrow."

"The Lord bless and protect you!—Chief; this is downright madness. Can either, or both of you, alter a Mingo natur'. Will your grand looks, or Hist's tears and beauty, change a wolf into a squirrel, or make a catamount as innocent as a fa'an? No—Sarpent, you will think better of this matter, and leave me in the hands of God. A'ter all, it's by no means sartain that the scamps design the torments, for they may yet be pitiful, and bethink them of the wickedness of such a course—though it *is* but a hopeless expectation to look forward to a Mingo's turning aside from evil, and letting marcy get uppermost in his heart—Nevertheless, no one knows to a sartainty what will happen, and young creatur's, like Hist, an't to be risked on onsartainties. This marrying is altogether a different undertaking from what some young men fancy. Now, if you was single, or as good as single, Delaware, I should expect you to be act*yve* and stirring about the camp of the vagabonds, from sunrise to sunset, sarcumventing and contriving, as restless as a hound off the scent, and doing all manner of things to help me, and to distract the inimy, but two are oftener feebler than one, and we must take things as they are, and not as we want 'em to be."

"Listen, Deerslayer," returned the Indian with an emphasis so decided as to show how much he was in earnest. "If Chingachgook was in the hands of the Hurons, what would my pale-face brother do? Sneak off to the Delaware villages, and say to the chiefs, and old men, and young warriors—'see, here is Wah-ta!-Wah; she is safe, but a little tired; and here is the Son of Uncas, not as tired as the Honeysuckle, being stronger, but just as safe.' Would he do this?"

"Well, that's oncommon ingen'ous; it's cunning enough for a Mingo, himself! The Lord only knows what put it into your head to ask such a question. What would I do?—Why, in the first place, Hist would n't be likely to be in my company at all, for she would stay as near you as possible, and therefore all that part about *her* could n't be said, without talking nonsense. As for her being tired, that would fall through, too, if she did n't go, and no part of your speech would be likely to come from me; so, you see, Sarpent, reason is ag'in you, and you may as well give it up, since to hold out ag'in reason, is no way becoming a chief of your character and repitation."

"My brother is not himself; he forgets that he is talking to one who has sat at the Council Fire of his nation," returned the other kindly. "When men speak, they should say that which does not go in at one side of the head and out at the other. Their words should n't be feathers, so light that a wind which does not ruffle the water, can blow them away. He has not answered my question; when a chief puts a question, his friend should not talk of other things."

"I understand you, Delaware; I understand well enough what you mean, and truth won't allow me to say otherwise. Still it's not as easy to answer as you seem to think, for this plain reason. You wish me to say what I would do if I had a betrothed as you have, here, on the lake, and a fri'nd yonder in the Huron camp, in danger of the torments. That's it, is n't it?"

The Indian bowed his head silently, and always with unmoved gravity, though his eye twinkled at the sight of the other's embarrassment.

"Well, I never had a betrothed—never had the kind of feelin's toward any young woman, that you have towards Hist, though the Lord knows my feelin's are kind enough towards 'em all!—still my heart, as they call it, in such matters, is n't touched, and therefore I can't say what I would do. A fri'nd pulls strong, that I know by exper'ence, Sarpent, but, by all that I've seen and heard consarning love, I'm led to think that a betrothed pulls stronger."

"True; but the betrothed of Chingachgook does not pull towards the lodges of the Delawares; she pulls towards the camp of the Hurons."

"She's a noble gal, for all her little feet, and hands that an't bigger than a child's, and a voice that is as pleasant as a mocker's; she's a noble gal, and like the stock of her sires! Well, what is it, Sarpent; for I conclude she has n't changed her mind, and means to give herself up, and turn Huron wife. What is it you want?"

"Wah-ta!-Wah will never live in the wigwam of an Iroquois," answered the Delaware drily. "She has little feet, but they can carry her to the villages of her people; she has small hands, too, but her mind is large. My brother will see what we can do, when the time shall come, rather than let him die under Mingo torments."

"Attempt nothing heedlessly, Delaware," said the other earnestly; "I suppose you must and will have your way; and, on the whole it's right you should, for you'd neither be happy, unless something was undertaken. But attempt nothing heedlessly—I did n't expect you'd quit the lake, while my matter remained in unsartainty, but remember, Sarpent, that no torments that Mingo ingenuity can invent, no ta'ntings, and revilings; no burnings, and roastings, and nail-tearings, nor any other onhuman contrivances can so soon break down my spirit, as to find that you and Hist, have fallen into the power of the inimy, in striving to do something for my good."

"The Delawares are prudent. The Deerslayer will not find them running into a strange camp, with their eyes shut."

Here the dialogue terminated. Hetty announced that the breakfast was ready, and the whole party was soon seated around the simple board, in the usual primitive manner of borderers. Judith was the last to take her seat, pale, silent, and betraying in her countenance that she had passed a painful, if not a sleepless, night. At this meal scarce a syllable was exchanged, all the females manifesting want of appetities, though the two men were unchanged in this particular. It was early when the party arose, and there still remained several hours before it would be necessary for the prisoner to leave his friends. The knowledge of this circumstance, and the interest all felt in his welfare, induced the whole to assemble on the platform again, in the desire to be near the expected victim, to listen to his discourse, and if possible to show their interest in him, by anticipating his wishes. Deerslayer, himself, so far as human eyes could penetrate, was wholly unmoved, conversing cheerfully and naturally, though he avoided any direct allusions to the expected and great event of the day. If any evidence could be discovered of his thought's reverting to that painful subject at all, it was in the manner in which he spoke of death and the last great change.

"Grieve not, Hetty," he said, for it was while consoling this simple-minded girl for the loss of her parents that he thus betrayed his feelings, "since God has app'inted that all must die. Your parents, or them you fancied your parents, which is the same thing, have gone afore you; this is only in the order of natur', my good gal, for the aged go first, and the young follow. But one that had a mother like your'n, Hetty, can be at no loss to hope the best, as to how matters will turn out in another world. The Delaware, here, and Hist, believe in happy hunting grounds, and have idees befitting their notions and gifts, as red skins, but we who are of white blood hold altogether to a different doctrine. Still, I rather conclude our heaven is their land of spirits, and that the path which leads to it will be travelled by all colours alike. 'Tis onpossible for the wicked to enter on it, I will allow, but fri'nds can scarce be separated, though they are not of the same race on 'arth. Keep up your spirits, poor Hetty, and look forward to the day when you will meet your mother ag'in, and that without pain, or sorrowing."

"I do expect to see mother," returned the truth-telling and simple girl, "but what will become of father?"

"That's a non-plusser, Delaware," said the hunter, in the Indian dialect—"yes, that is a down-right non-plusser! The Muskrat was not a saint on 'arth, and it's fair to guess he'll not be much of one, here after! Howsever, Hetty," dropping into the English by an easy transition, "howsever, Hetty, we must all hope for the best. That is wisest, and it is much the easiest to the mind, if one can only do it. I ricommend to you, trusting to God, and putting down all misgivings and faint-hearted feelin's. It's wonderful, Judith, how different people have different notions about the futur', some fancying one change, and some fancying another. I've known white teachers that have thought all was spirit, hereafter, and them, ag'in, that believed the body will be transported to another world, much as the red-skins themselves imagine, and that we shall walk about, in the flesh, and know each other, and talk together, and be fri'nds there, as we've been fri'nds here."

"Which of these opinions is most pleasing to *you*, Deerslayer?" asked the girl, willing to indulge his melancholy mood, and far from being free from its influence herself. "Would it be disagreeable to think that you should meet all who are now on this platform in another world? Or have you known enough of us here, to be glad to see us no more."

"The last would make death a bitter portion; yes it would. It's eight good years since the Sarpent and I began to hunt together, and the thought that we were never to meet ag'in, would be a hard thought to me. He looks forward to the time when he shall chase a sort of spirit-deer, in company, on plains where there's no thorns, or brambles, or marshes, or other hardships to overcome, whereas I can't fall into all these notions, seeing that they appear to be ag'in reason. Spirits can't eat, nor have they any use for clothes, and deer can only rightfully be chased to be slain, or slain, unless it be for the venison, or the hides. Now, I find it hard to suppose that blessed spirits can be put to chasing game, without an object, tormenting the dumb animals just for the pleasure and agreeableness of their own amusements. I never, yet, pulled a trigger on buck or doe, Judith, unless when food or clothes was wanting."

"The recollection of which, Deerslayer, must now be a great consolation to you."

"It is the thought of such things, my fri'nds, that enables a man to keep his furlough. It might be done without it, I own; for the worst red skins, sometimes do their duty in this matter; but it makes that which might otherwise be hard, easy, if not altogether to our liking. Nothing truly makes a bolder heart, than a light conscience."

Judith turned paler than ever, but she struggled for self-command, and succeeded in obtaining it. The conflict had been severe, however, and it left her so little disposed to speak, that Hetty pursued the subject. This was done in the simple manner natural to the girl.

"It would be cruel to kill the poor deer," she said, "in this world, or any other, when you do n't want their venison, or their skins. No good white-man, and no good red man would do it. But it's wicked for a christian to talk about chasing any thing in heaven. Such things are not done before the face of God, and the missionary that teaches these doctrines, can't be a true missionary. He must be a wolf in sheep's clothing. I suppose you know what a sheep is, Deerslayer."

"That I do, gal, and a useful creatur' it is, to such as like cloths better than skins, for winter garments. I understand the natur' of sheep, though I've had but little to do with 'em, and the natur' of wolves too, and can take the idee of a wolf in the fleece of a sheep, though I think it would be like to prove a hot jacket for such a beast, in the warm months!"

"And sin, and hypocrisy are hot jackets, as *they* will find, who put them on," returned Hetty, positively, "so the wolf would be no worse off than the sinner. Spirits do n't hunt, nor trap, nor fish, nor do any thing that vain men undertake, since they've none of the longings of this world to feed. Oh! Mother told me all that, years ago, and I don't wish to hear it denied."

"Well, my good Hetty, in that case you'd better not broach your doctrine to Hist, when she and you are alone, and the young Delaware maiden is inclined to talk religion. It's her fixed idee, I know, that the good warriors do nothing but hunt, and fish in the other world, though I do n't believe that she fancies any of them are brought down to trapping, which is no empl'yment for a brave. But of hunting and fishing, accordin' to her notion, they've their fill, and that, too, over the most agreeablest hunting grounds, and among game that is never out of season, and which is just actyve and instinctyve enough to give a pleasure to death. So I would n't ricommend it to you to start Hist on that idee."

"Hist can't be so wicked as to believe any such thing," returned the other, earnestly. "No Indian hunts after he is dead."

"No wicked Indian, I grant you; no wicked Indian, sartainly. He is obliged to carry the ammunition, and to look on without sharing in the sport, and to cook, and to light the fires, and to do every thing that is n't manful. Now, mind; I do n't tell you these are my idees, but they are Hist's idees, and, therefore, for the sake of peace the less you say to her ag'in 'em, the better."

"And what are your ideas of the fate of an Indian, in the other world?" demanded Judith, who had just found her voice.

"Ah! gal, any thing but that! I am too christianized to expect any thing so fanciful, as hunting and fishing after death, nor do I believe there is one Manitou for the red skin and another for a pale face. You find different colours on 'arth, as any one may see, but you do n't find different natur's. Different gifts, but only one natur'."

"In what is a gift different from a nature? Is not nature itself a gift from God?"

"Sartain; that's quick-thoughted, and creditable, Judith, though the main idee is wrong. A natur' is the creatur' itself; its wishes, wants, idees and feelin's, as all are born in him. This natur' never can be changed, in the main, though it may undergo some increase, or lessening. Now, gifts come of sarcumstances. Thus, if you put a man in a town, he gets town gifts; in a settlement, settlement gifts; in a forest, gifts of the woods. A soldier has soldierly gifts, and a missionary preaching gifts. All these increase and strengthen, until they get to fortify natur', as it might be, and excuse a thousand acts and idees. Still the creatur' is the same at the bottom; just as a man who is clad in regimentals is the same as the man that is clad in skins. The garments make a change to the eye, and some change in the conduct, perhaps; but none in the man. Herein lies the apology for gifts; seein' that you expect different conduct from one in silks and satins, from one in homespun; though the Lord, who did n't make the dresses, but who made the creatur's themselves, looks only at his own work. This is n't ra'al missionary doctrine, but it's as near it, as a man of white colour need be. Ah's! me; little did I think to be talking of such matters, to-day, but it's one of our weaknesses never to know what will come to pass. Step into the Ark with me, Judith, for a minute; I wish to convarse with you."

Judith complied with a willingness she could scarce conceal. Following the hunter into the cabin, she took a seat on a stool, while the young man brought Killdeer, the rifle she had given him, out of a corner, and placed himself on another, with the weapon laid upon his knees. After turning the piece round and round, and examining its lock and its breech with a sort of affectionate assiduity, he laid it down and proceeded to the subject which had induced him to desire the interview.

"I understand you, Judith, to say that you gave me this rifle," he said. "I agreed to take it, because a young woman can have no particular use for fire-arms. The we'pon has a great name, and it desarves it, and ought of right to be carried by some known and sure hand, for the best repitation may be lost by careless and thoughtless handling."

"Can it be in better hands than those in which it is now, Deerslayer. Thomas Hutter seldom missed with it; with you it must turn out to be—"

"Sartain death!" interrupted the hunter, laughing. "I once know'd a beaver-man that had a piece he called by that very name, but 'twas all boastfulness, for I've seen Delawares that were as true with arrows, at a short range. Howsever, I'll not deny my gifts—for *this* is a gift, Judith, and not natur'—but, I'll not deny my gifts, and therefore allow that the rifle could n't well be in better hands than it is at present. But, how long will it be likely to remain there? Atween us, the truth may be said, though I should n't like to have it known to the Sarpent and Hist; but, to *you* the truth may be spoken, since *your* feelin's will not be as likely to be tormented by it, as those of them that have known me longer and better. How long am I like to own this rifle or any other? That is a serious question for our thoughts to rest on, and should that happen which is so likely to happen, Killdeer would be without an owner."

Judith listened with apparent composure, though the conflict within came near overpowering her. Appreciating the singular character of her companion, however, she succeeded in appearing calm, though, had not his attention been drawn exclusively to the rifle, a man of his keenness of observation could scarce have failed to detect the agony of mind with which the girl had hearkened to his words. Her great self-command, notwithstanding, enabled her to pursue the subject in a way still to deceive him.

"What would you have me do with the weapon," she asked—"should that which you seem to expect, take place?"

"That's just what I wanted to speak to you about, Judith; that's just it. There's Chingachgook, now, though far from being parfect sartainty, with a rifle—for few red skins ever get to be *that*—though far from being parfect sartainty, he is respectable, and is coming on. Nevertheless, he is my fri'nd, and all the better fri'nd, perhaps, because there never can be any hard feelin's atween us, touchin' our gifts, his'n bein' red, and mine bein' altogether white. Now, I should like to leave

Killdeer to the Sarpent, should any thing happen to keep me from doing credit and honor to your precious gift, Judith."

"Leave it to whom you please, Deerslayer. The rifle is your own, to do with as you please. Chingachgook shall have it, should you never return to claim it, if that be your wish."

"Has Hetty been consulted in this matter?—Property goes from the parent to the children, and not to one child, in partic'lar!"

"If you place your right on that of the law, Deerslayer, I fear none of us can claim to be the owner. Thomas Hutter was no more the father of Esther, than he was the father of Judith. Judith and Esther we are truly, having no other name!"

"There may be law in that, but there's no great reason, gal. Accordin' to the custom of families, the goods are your'n, and there's no one here to gainsay it. If Hetty would only say that she is willing, my mind would be quite at ease in the matter. It's true, Judith, that your sister has neither your beauty, nor your wit; but we should be the tenderest of the rights and welfare of the most weak-minded."

The girl made no answer but placing herself at a window, she summoned her sister to her side. When the question was put to Hetty, that simple-minded and affectionate creature cheerfully assented to the proposal to confer on Deerslayer a full right of ownership to the much-coveted rifle. The latter now seemed perfectly happy, for the time being at least, and after again examining and re-examining his prize, he expressed a determination to put its merits to a practical test, before he left the spot. No boy could have been more eager to exhibit the qualities of his trumpet, or his cross-bow, than this simple forester was to prove those of his rifle. Returning to the platform, he first took the Delaware aside, and informed him that this celebrated piece was to become his property, in the event of any thing serious befalling himself.

"This is a new reason why you should be wary, Sarpent, and not run into any oncalculated danger," the hunter added, "for, it will be a victory of itself, to a tribe to own such a piece as this! The Mingos will turn green with envy, and, what is more, they will not ventur' heedlessly near a village where it is known to be kept. So, look well to it, Delaware, and remember that you've now to watch over a thing that has all the valie of a creatur', without its failin's. Hist may be, and should be precious to you, but Killdeer will have the love and veneration of your whole people."

"One rifle like another, Deerslayer," returned the Indian, in English, the language used by the other, a little hurt at his friend's lowering his betrothed to the level of a gun. "All kill; all wood and iron. Wife dear to heart; rifle good to shoot."

"And what is a man in the woods without something to shoot with?—a miserable trapper, or a forlorn broom and basket maker, at the best. Such a man may hoe corn, and keep soul and body together, but he can never know the savory morsels of venison, or tell a bear's ham from a hog's. Come, my fri'nd, such another occasion may never offer ag'in, and I feel a strong craving for a trial with this celebrated piece. You shall bring out your own rifle, and I will just sight Killdeer in a careless way, in order that we may know a few of its secret vartues."

As this proposition served to relieve the thoughts of the whole party, by giving them a new direction, while it was likely to produce no unpleasant results, every one was willing to enter into it; the girls bringing forth the fire-arms with an alacrity, bordering on cheerfulness. Hutter's armory was well supplied, possessing several rifles, all of which were habitually kept loaded, in readiness to meet any sudden demand for their use. On the present occasion, it only remained to freshen the primings, and each piece was in a state for service. This was soon done, as all assisted in it, the females being as expert in this part of the system of defence, as their male companions.

"Now, Sarpent, we'll begin in a humble way, using Old Tom's commoners first, and coming to your we'pon and Killdeer as the winding up observations," said Deerslayer, delighted to be again, weapon in hand, ready to display his skill. "Here's birds in abundance, some in, and some over the lake, and they keep at just a good range, hovering round the hut. Speak your mind, Delaware, and p'int out the creatur' you wish to alarm. Here's a diver nearest in, off to the eastward, and that's a creatur' that buries itself at the flash, and will be like enough to try both piece and powder."

Chingachgook was a man of few words. No sooner was the bird pointed out to him, than he took his aim and fired. The duck dove at the flash, as had been expected, and the bullet skipped harmlessly along the surface of the lake, first striking the water within a few inches of the spot where the bird had so lately swam. Deerslayer laughed, cordially and naturally, but, at the same time, he threw himself into an attitude of preparation, and stood keenly watching the sheet of placid water. Presently a dark spot appeared, and then the duck arose to breathe, and shook its wings. While in this act, a bullet passed directly through its breast, actually turning it over lifeless, on its back. At the next moment, Deerslayer stood with the breech of his rifle on the platform, as tranquil as if nothing had happened, though laughing in his own peculiar manner.

"There's no great trial of the pieces in that!" he said, as if anxious to prevent a false impression of his own merit. "No, that proof's neither for, nor ag'in the rifles, seeing it was all quickness of hand and eye. I took the bird at a disadvantage, or he might have got under, again, afore the bullet reached him. But the Sarpent is too wise to mind such tricks, having long been used to them. Do you remember the time, chief, when you thought yourself sartain of the wild-goose, and I took him out of your very eyes, as it might be with a little smoke! Howsever, such things pass for nothing, atween fri'nds, and young folk will have their fun, Judith. Ay; here's just the bird we want, for it's as good for the fire, as it is for the aim, and nothing should be lost that can be turned to just account. There, further north, Delaware."

The latter looked in the required direction, and he soon saw a large black duck floating in stately repose on the water. At that distant day, when so few men were present to derange the harmony of the wilderness, all the smaller lakes with which the interior of New York so abounds, were places of resort for the migratory aquatic birds, and this sheet like the others had once been much frequented by all the varieties of the duck, by the goose, the gull, and the loon. On the appearance of Hutter, the spot was comparatively deserted for other sheets, more retired and remote, though some of each species continued to resort thither, as indeed they do to the present hour. At that instant, a hundred birds were visible from the castle, sleeping on the water, or laving their feathers in the limpid element, though no other offered so favorable a mark as that Deerslayer had just pointed out to his friend. Chingachgook as usual, spared his words, and proceeded to execution. This time his aim was more careful than before, and his success in proportion. The bird had a wing crippled, and fluttered along the water screaming, materially increasing its distance from its enemies.

"That bird must be put out of pain," exclaimed Deerslayer, the moment the animal endeavored to rise on the wing, "and this is the rifle and the eye to do it."

The duck was still floundering along, when the fatal bullet overtook it, severing the head from the neck as neatly as if it had been done with an axe. Hist had indulged in a low cry of delight at the success of the young Indian, but now she affected to frown and resent the greater skill of his friend. The chief, on the contrary, uttered the usual exclamation of pleasure, and his smile proved how much he admired, and how little he envied.

"Never mind the gal, Sarpent, never mind Hist's feelin's, which will neither choke, nor drown, slay nor beautify," said Deerslayer, laughing. " 'Tis nat'ral for women to enter into their husband's victories and defeats, and you are as good as man and wife, so far as prejudyce and fri'ndship go. Here is a bird over head that will put the pieces, to the proof. I challenge you to an upward aim, with a flying target. That's a ra'al proof, and one that needs sartain rifles, as well as sartain eyes."

The species of eagle that frequents the water, and lives on fish, was also present, and one was hovering at a considerable height above the hut, greedily watching for an opportunity to make a swoop; its hungry young elevating their heads from a nest that was in sight, in the naked summit of a dead pine. Chingachgook silently turned a new piece against this bird, and after carefully watching his time, fired. A wider circuit than common, denoted that the messenger had passed through the air, at no great distance from the bird though it missed its object. Deerslayer, whose aim was not more true than it was quick, fired as soon as it was certain his friend had missed, and the deep swoop that followed left it momentarily doubtful whether the eagle was hit or not. The marksman himself, however, proclaimed his own want of success, calling on his friend to seize another rifle, for he saw signs on the part of the bird of an intention to quit the spot.

"I made him wink, Sarpent, I do think his feathers were ruffled, but no blood has yet been drawn, nor is that old piece fit for so nice and quick a sight. Quick, Delaware, you've now a better rifle, and, Judith, bring out Killdeer, for this is the occasion to try his merits, if he has 'em."

A general movement followed, each of the competitors got ready, and the girls stood in eager expectation of the result. The eagle had made a wide circuit after his low swoop, and fanning his way upward, once more hovered nearly over the hut, at a distance even greater than before. Chingachgook gazed at him, and then expressed his opinion of the impossibility of striking a bird at that great height, and while he was so nearly perpendicular, as to the range. But a low murmur from Hist, produced a sudden impulse and he fired. The result showed how well he had calculated, the eagle not even varying his flight, sailing round and round in his airy circle, and looking down, as if in contempt, at his foes.

"Now, Judith," cried Deerslayer, laughing, with glistening and delighted eyes, " we'll see if Killdeer is n't Killeagle, too! Give me room Sarpent, and watch the reason of the aim, for by reason any thing may be l'arned."

A careful sight followed, and was repeated again and again, the bird continuing to rise higher and higher. Then followed the flash and the report. The swift messenger sped upward, and, at the next instant, the bird turned on its side, and came swooping down, now struggling with one wing and then with the other, sometimes whirling in a circuit, next fanning desperately as if conscious of its injury, until, having described several complete circles around the spot, it fell heavily into the end of the Ark. On examining the body, it was found that the bullet had pierced it about half way between one of its wings and the breast-bone.

Chapter XXVI

"Upon two stony tables, spread before her,
She lean'd her bosom, more than stony hard,
There slept th' impartial judge, and strict restorer
Of wrong, or right, with pain or with reward;
There hung the score of all our debts, the card
Where good, and bad, and life, and death, were painted;
Was never heart of mortal so untainted,
But when the roll was read, with thousand terrors fainted."

Giles Fletcher, *Christ's Victory in Heaven*, I.xv.

"We've done an unthoughtful thing, Sarpent—yes, Judith, we've done an unthoughtful thing in taking life with an object no better than vanity!" exclaimed Deerslayer, when the Delaware held up the enormous bird, by its wings, and exhibited the dying eyes riveted on its enemies with the gaze that the helpless ever fasten on their destroyers. "Twas more becomin' two boys to gratify their feelin's, in this onthoughtful manner, than two warriors on a war path, even though it be their first. Ah's! me; well, as a punishment I'll quit you at once, and when I find myself alone with them bloody-minded Mingos, it's more than like I'll have occasion to remember that life is sweet, even to the beasts of the woods and the fowls of the air. There, Judith; there's Killdeer; take him back, ag'in, and keep him for some hand that's more desarving to own such a piece."

"I know of none as deserving as your own, Deerslayer," answered the girl in haste; "none but yours shall keep the rifle."

"If it depended on skill, you might be right enough, gal, but we should know *when* to use fire-arms, as well as *how* to use 'em. I have n't l'arnt the first duty yet, it seems; so keep the piece till I have. The sight of a dyin' and distressed creatur', even though it be only a bird, brings wholesome thoughts to a man who don't know how soon his own time may come, and who *is* pretty sartain that it will come afore the sun sets; I'd give back all my vain feelin's, and rej'icin's in hand and eye, if that poor eagle was only on its nest ag'in, with its young, praisin' the Lord, for any thing that we can know about the matter, for health and strength!"

The listeners were confounded with this proof of sudden repentance in the hunter, and that too for an indulgence so very common, that men seldom stop to weigh its consequences, or the physical suffering it may bring on the unoffending and helpless. The Delaware understood what was said, though he scarce understood the feelings which had prompted the words, and by way of disposing of the difficulty, he drew his keen knife, and severed the head of the sufferer from its body.

"What a thing is power!" continued the hunter, "and what a thing it is, to have it, and not to know how to use it. It's no wonder, Judith, that the great so often fail of their duties, when even the little and the humble find it so hard to do what's right, and not to do what's wrong. Then, how one evil acts brings others a'ter it! Now, wasn't it for this furlough of mine, which must soon take me back to the Mingos, I'd find this creatur's nest, if I travelled the woods a forthnight—though an eagle's nest is soon found by them that understands the bird's natur',—but I'd travel a forthnight rather than not find it, just to put the young, too, out of their pain."

"I'm glad to hear you say this, Deerslayer," observed Hetty, "and God will be more apt to remember your sorrow for what you've done, than the wickedness itself. I thought how wicked it was to kill harmless birds, while you were shooting, and meant to tell you so; but, I do n't know how it happened,—I was so curious to see if you *could* hit an eagle at so great a height, that I forgot altogether to speak, 'till the mischief was done."

"That's it; that's just it, my good Hetty. We can all see our faults and mistakes when it's too late to help them! Howsever, I'm glad you did n't speak, for I do n't think a word or two would have stopped me, just at that moment, and so the sin stands in its nakedness, and not aggravated by any unheeded calls to forbear. Well, well, bitter thoughts are hard to be borne at all times, but there's times when they're harder than at others."

Little did Deerslayer know, while thus indulging in feelings that were natural to the man, and so strictly in accordance with his own unsophisticated and just principles, that, in the course of the inscrutable providence, which so uniformly and yet so mysteriously covers all events with its mantle, the very fault he was disposed so severely to censure, was to be made the means of determining his own earthly fate. The mode and the moment in which he was to feel the influence of this interference, it would be premature to relate, but both will appear in the course of the succeeding chapters. As for the young man, he now slowly left the Ark, like one sorrowing for his misdeeds, and seated himself in silence on the platform. By this time the sun had ascended to some height, and its appearance, taken in connection with his present feelings, induced him to prepare to depart. The Delaware got the canoe ready for his friend, as soon as apprised of his intention, while Hist busied herself in making the few arrangements that were thought necessary to his comfort. All this was done without ostentation, but in a way that left Deerslayer fully acquainted with, and equally disposed to appreciate, the motive. When all was ready, both returned to the side of Judith and Hetty, neither of whom had moved from the spot where the young hunter sat.

"The best fri'nds must often part," the last began, when he saw the whole party grouped around him—"yes, fri'ndship can't alter the ways of Providence, and let our feelin's be as they may, we must part. I've often thought there's moments when our words dwell longer on the mind than common, and when advice is remembered, just because the mouth that gives it, is n't likely to give it ag'in. No one knows what will happen in this world, and therefore it may be well, when fri'nds separate under a likelihood that the parting may be long, to say a few words in kindness, as a sort of keepsakes. If all but one will go into the Ark, I'll talk to each in turn, and what is more, I'll listen to what you may have to say back ag'in, for it's a poor counsellor that won't take as well as give."

As the meaning of the speaker was understood, the two Indians immediately withdrew as desired, leaving the sisters, however, still standing at the young man's side. A look of Deerslayer's induced Judith to explain.

"You can advise Hetty as you land," she said hastily, "for I intend that she shall accompany you to the shore."

"Is this wise, Judith? It's true, that under common sarcumstances a feeble-mind is a great protection among redskins, but when their feelin's are up, and they're bent on revenge, it's hard to say what may come to pass. Besides—"

"What were you about to say, Deerslayer?" asked Judith, whose gentleness of voice and manner amounted nearly to tenderness, though she struggled hard to keep her emotions and apprehensions in subjection.

"Why, simply that there are sights and doin's that one even as little gifted with reason and memory as Hetty here, might better not witness. So, Judith, you would do well to let me land alone, and to keep your sister back."

"Never fear for me, Deerslayer," put in Hetty, who comprehended enough of the discourse to know its general drift, "I'm feeble minded, and that they say is an excuse for going any where; and what that won't excuse, will be overlooked on account of the bible I always carry. It is wonderful, Judith, how all sorts of men; the trappers as well as the hunters; redmen as well as white; Mingos as well as Delawares do reverence and fear the bible!"

"I think you have not the least ground to fear any injury, Hetty," answered the sister, "and therefore I shall insist on your going to the Huron camp with our friend. Your being there can do no harm, not even to yourself, and may do great good to Deerslayer."

"This is not a moment, Judith, to dispute, and so have the matter your own way," returned the young man. "Get yourself ready, Hetty, and go into the canoe, for I've a few parting words to say to your sister, which can do you no good."

Judith and her companion, continued silent, until Hetty had so far complied, as to leave them alone, when Deerslayer took up the subject, as if it had been interrupted by some ordinary occurrence, and in a very matter of fact way.

"Words spoken at parting, and which may be the last we ever hear from a fri'nd are not soon forgotten," he repeated, "and so, Judith, I intend to speak to you like a brother, seein' I'm not old enough to be your father. In the first place, I wish to caution you ag'in your inimies, of which two may be said to ha'nt your very footsteps, and to beset your ways. The first is oncommon good-looks, which is as dangerous a foe to some young women, as a whole tribe of Mingos could prove, and which calls for great watchfulness—not to admire and praise—but to distrust and sarcumvent. Yes, good looks may be sarcumvented, and fairly outwitted, too. In order to do this you've only to remember that they melt like the snows, and, when once gone, they never come back ag'in. The seasons come and go, Judith, and if we have winter, with storms and frosts, and spring with chills and leafless trees, we have summer with its sun and glorious skies, and fall with its fruits, and a garment thrown over the forest, that no beauty of the town could rummage out of all the shops in America. 'Arth is in an etarnal round, the goodness of God, bringing back the pleasant when we've had enough of the onpleasant. But it's not so with good looks. *They* are lent for a short time in youth, to be used and not abused, and, as I never met with a young woman to whom providence has been as bountiful, as it has to you, Judith, in this partic'lar, I warn you, as it might be with my dyin' breath, to beware of the inimy—fri'nd, or inimy, as we deal with the gift."

It was so grateful to Judith to hear these unequivocal admissions of her personal charms, that much would have been forgiven to the man, who made them, let him be who he might. But, at that moment, and from a far better feeling, it would not have been easy for Deerslayer seriously to offend her, and she listened with a patience, which, had it been foretold only a week earlier, it would have excited her indignation to hear.

"I understand your meaning, Deerslayer," returned the girl, with a meekness and humility that a little surprised her listener, "and hope to be able to profit by it. But, you have mentioned only one of the enemies I have to fear; who, or what is the other."

"The other is givin' way afore your own good sense and judgment, I find, Judith; yes, he's not as dangerous as I supposed. Howsever, havin' opened the subject, it will be as well to end it honestly. The first inimy you have to be watchful of, as I've already told you, Judith, is oncommon good-looks, and the next is an oncommon knowledge of the sarcumstance. If the first is bad, the last does n't, in any way, mend the matter, so far as safety and peace of mind are consarned."

How much longer the young man would have gone on in his simple and unsuspecting, but well intentioned manner, it might not be easy to say, had he not been interrupted by his listener's bursting into tears, and giving way to an outbreak of feeling, which was so much the more violent from the fact that it had been with so much difficulty suppressed. At first her sobs were so violent and uncontrollable that Deerslayer was a little appalled, and he was abundantly repentant from the instant that he discovered how much greater was the effect produced by his words, than he had anticipated. Even the austere and exacting are usually appeased by the signs of contrition, but the nature of Deerslayer did not require proofs of intense feelings so strong in order to bring him down to a level with the regrets felt by the girl herself. He arose, as if an adder had stung him, and the accents of the mother that soothes her child were scarcely more gentle and winning than the tones of his voice, as he now expressed his contrition at having gone so far.

"It was well meant, Judith," he said, "but it was not intended to hurt your feelin's so much. I have overdone the advice, I see; yes, I've overdone it, and I crave your pardon for the same. Fri'ndship's an awful thing! Sometimes it chides us for not having done enough; and then, ag'in it speaks in strong words for havin' done too much. Howsever, I acknowledge I've overdone the matter, and as I've a ra'al and strong regard for you, I rej'ice to say it, inasmuch as it proves how much better you are, than my own vanity, and consaits had made you out to be."

Judith now removed her hands from her face, her tears had ceased, and she unveiled a countenance so winning with the smile which rendered it even radiant, that the young man gazed at her, for a moment, with speechless delight.

"Say no more, Deerslayer," she hastily interposed; "it pains me to hear you find fault with yourself. I know my own weakness, all the better, now I see that you have discovered it; the lesson, bitter as I have found it for a moment, shall not be forgotten. We will not talk any longer, of these things, for I do not feel myself brave enough for the undertaking, and I should not like the Delaware, or Hist, or even Hetty, to notice my weakness. Farewell, Deerslayer; may God bless and protect you as your honest heart deserves blessings and protection, and as I must think he will."

Judith had so far regained the superiority that properly belonged to her better education, high spirit, and surpassing personal advantages, as to preserve the ascendancy she had thus accidentally obtained, and effectually prevented any return to the subject that was as singularly interrupted, as it had been singularly introduced. The young man permitted her to have every thing her own way, and when she pressed his hard hand in both her own, he made no resistance, but submitted to the homage as quietly, and with quite as matter of course a manner, as a sovereign would have received a similar tribute from a subject, or the mistress from her suitor. Feeling had flushed the face and illuminated the whole countenance of the girl, and her beauty was never more resplendant than when she cast a parting glance at the youth. That glance was filled with anxiety, interest and gentle pity. At the next instant, she darted into the hut and was seen no more, though she spoke to Hist from a window, to inform her that their friend expected her appearance.

"You know enough of red skin natur', and red skin usages, Wah-ta!-Wah, to see the condition I am in on account of this furlough," commenced the hunter in Delaware, as soon as the patient and submissive girl of that people had moved quietly to his side; "you will therefore best onderstand how onlikely I am ever to talk with you ag'in. I've but little to say; but that little comes from long livin' among your people, and from havin' obsarved and noted their usages. The life of a woman is hard at the best, but I must own, though I'm not opinionated in favor of my own colour, that it is harder among the red men than it is among the pale faces. This is a p'int on which christians may well boast, if boasting can be set down for christianity in any manner or form, which I rather think it cannot. Howsever, all women have their trials. Red women have their'n in what I should call the nat'ral way, while white women take 'em innoculated like. Bear your burthen, Hist, becomingly, and remember if it be a little toilsome, how much lighter it is than that of most Indian women. I know the Sarpent well—what I call cordially—and he will never be a tyrant to any thing he loves, though he will expect to be treated himself like a Mohican Chief. There will be cloudy days in your lodge I suppose, for they happen under all usages, and among all people, but, by keepin' the windows of the heart open there will always be room for the sun-shine to enter. You come of a great stock yourself, and so does Chingachgook. It's not very likely that either will ever forget the sarcumstance, and do any thing to disgrace your forefathers. Nevertheless, likin' is a tender plant, and never thrives long when watered with tears. Let the 'arth around your married happiness be moistened by the dews of kindness."

"My pale brother is very wise; Wah will keep in her mind all that his wisdom tells her."

"That's judicious and womanly, Hist. Care in listening, and stout-heartedness in holding to good counsel, is a wife's great protection. And, now, ask the Sarpent to come and speak with me, for a moment, and carry away with you all my best wishes and prayers. I shall think of you Hist, and of your intended husband, let what may come to pass, and always wish you well, here and hereafter, whether the last is to be according to Indian idees, or christian doctrines."

Hist shed no tear at parting. She was sustained by the high resolution of one who had decided on her course, but her dark eyes were luminous with the feelings that glowed within, and her pretty countenance beamed with an expression of determination that was in marked and singular contrast to its ordinary gentleness. It was but a minute ere the Delaware advanced to the side of his friend with the light, noiseless tread of an Indian.

"Come, this-a-way, Sarpent, here more out of sight of the women," commenced the Deerslayer, "for I've several things to say that must n't so much as be suspected, much less overheard. *You* know too well the natur' of furloughs and Mingos to have any doubts or misgivin's consarnin' what is like to happen, when I get back to the camp. On them two p'ints therefore, a few words will go a great way. In the first place, chief, I wish to say a little about Hist, and the manner in which you red men treat your wives. I suppose it's accordin' to the gifts of your people that the women should work, and the men hunt; but there's such a thing as moderation in all matters. As for huntin', I see no good reason why any limits need to be set to *that*, but Hist comes of too good a stock to toil like a common drudge. One of your means and standin' need never want for corn, or potatoes, or any thing that the fields yield; therefore, I hope the hoe will never be put into the hands of any wife of yourn. You know I am not quite a beggar, and all I own, whether in ammunition, skins, arms, or calicoes, I give to Hist, should I not come back to claim them by the end of the season. This will set the maiden up, and will buy labor for her, for a long time to come. I suppose I need n't tell you to love the young woman, for that you do already, and whomsoever the man ra'ally loves, he'll be likely enough to cherish. Nevertheless, it can do no harm to say that kind words never rankle, while bitter words do. I know you're a man, Sarpent, that is less apt to talk in his own lodge, than to speak at the Council Fire; but forgetful moments may overtake us all, and the practyse of kind doin', and kind talkin', is a wonderful advantage in keepin' peace in a cabin, as well as on a hunt."

"My ears are open," returned the Delaware gravely; "the words of my brother have entered so far that they never can fall out again. They are like rings, that have no end, and cannot drop. Let him speak on; the song of the wren and the voice of a friend never tire."

"I will speak a little longer, chief, but you will excuse it for the sake of old companionship, should I now talk about myself. If the worst comes to the worst, it's not likely there'll be much left of me but ashes, so a grave would be useless, and a sort of vanity. On that score I'm no way partic'lar, though it might be well enough to take a look at the remains of the pile, and should any bones, or pieces be found, 'twould be more decent to gather them together, and bury them, than to let them lie for the wolves to gnaw at, and howl over. These matters can make no great difference in the ind, but men of white blood and christian feelin's have rather a gift for graves."

"It shall be done as my brother says," returned the Indian, gravely. "If his mind is full, let him empty it in the bosom of a friend."

"I thank you, Sarpent; my mind's easy enough; yes, it's tolerable easy. Idees will come uppermost that I'm not apt to think about in common, it's true, but by striving ag'in some, and lettin' other some out, all will come right, in the long run. There's one thing, howsever, chief, that *does* seem to me to be *on*reasonable, and ag'in natur', though the missionaries say it's true, and bein' of my religion and colour I feel bound to believe them. They say an Injin may torment and tortur' the body to his heart's content, and scalp, and cut, and tear, and burn, and consume all his inventions and deviltries, until nothin' is left but ashes, and they shall be scattered to the four winds of heaven, yet when the trumpet of God shall sound, all will come together ag'in, and the man will stand forth in his flesh, the same creatur' as to looks, if not as to feelin's, that he was afore he was harmed!"

"The missionaries are good men—mean well," returned the Delaware courteously; "they are not great medicines. They think all they say, Deerslayer; that is no reason why warriors and orators should be all ears. When Chingachgook shall see the father of Tamenund standing in his scalp, and paint, and war lock, then will he believe the missionaries."

"Seein' *is* believin', of a sartainty; ahs! me—and some of us may see these things sooner than we thought. I comprehind your meanin' about Tamenund's father, Sarpent, and the idee's a close idee. Tamenund is now an elderly man, say eighty every day of it, and his father was scalped, and tormented, and burnt, when the present prophet was a youngster. Yes, if one could see *that* come to pass, there would n't be much difficulty in yieldin' faith to all that the missionaries say. Howsever, I am not ag'in the opinion now, for you must know, Sarpent, that the great principle of christianity is to believe *without* seeing, and a man should always act up to his religion and principles, let them be what they may."

"That is strange for a wise nation!" said the Delaware with emphasis. "The red man looks hard, that he may *see* and understand."

"Yes, that's plauserble, and is agreeable to mortal pride, but it's not as deep as it seems. If we could understand *all* we see, Sarpent, there might be not only sense, but safety, in refusin' to give faith to any *one* thing that we might find oncomprehensible; but when there's so many things, about which, it may be said, we know nothin' at all, why, there's little use, and no reason, in bein' difficult touchin' any one in partic'lar. For my part, Delaware, all my thoughts have n't been on the game, when outlyin' in the hunts and scoutin's, of our youth. Many's the hour I've passed, pleasantly enough too, in what is tarmed conterplation by my people. On such occasions the mind is actyve, though the body seems lazy and listless. An open spot on a mountain side, where a wide look can be had at the heavens and the 'arth, is a most judicious place for a man to get a just idee of the power of the Manitou, and of his own littleness. At such times, there is n't any great disposition to find fault with little difficulties, in the way of comperhension, as there are so many big ones to hide them. Believin' comes easy enough to me, at such times, and, if the Lord made man first out of 'arth, as they tell me it is written in the bible; then turns him into dust, at death; I see no great difficulty in the way to bringin' him back in the body, though ashes be the only substance left. These things lie beyond our understandin', though they may and do lie so close to our feelin's. But, of all the doctrines, Sarpent, that which disturbs me, and disconsarts my mind the most, is the one which teaches us to think that a pale face goes to one heaven, and a red skin to another; it may separate in death, them which lived much together, and loved each other well, in life!"

"Do the missionaries teach their white brethren to think it is so?" demanded the Indian, with serious earnestness. "The Delawares believe that good men and brave warriors will hunt together in the same pleasant woods, let them belong to whatever tribe they may; that all the unjust Indians and cowards, will have to sneak in with the dogs and the wolves, to get venison for their lodges."

"Tis wonderful how many consaits mankind have consarnin' happiness and misery, here after!" exclaimed the hunter, borne away by the power of his own thoughts. "Some believe in burnin's and flames, and some think punishment is to eat with the wolves and dogs. Then, ag'in, some fancy heaven to be only the carryin' out of their own 'arthly longin's, while others fancy it all gold and shinin' lights! Well, I've an idee of my own, in that matter, which is just this, Sarpent. Whenever I've done wrong, I've ginirally found 'twas owin' to some blindness of the mind, which hid the right from view, and when sight has returned, then has come sorrow and repentance. Now, I consait that, after death, when the body is laid aside, or, if used at all, is purified and without its longin's, the spirit sees all things in their ra'al lights and never becomes blind to truth and justice. Such bein' the case, all that has been done in life, is beheld as plainly as the sun is seen at noon; the good brings joy, while the evil brings sorrow. There's nothin' onreasonable in that, but it's agreeable to every man's exper'ence."

"I thought the pale faces believed *all* men were wicked; who then could ever find the white man's heaven?"

"That's ingen'ous, but it falls short of the missionary teachin's. You'll be christianized one day, I make no doubt, and then 'twill all come plain enough. You must know, Sarpent, that there's been a great deed of salvation done, that, by God's help, enables all men to find a pardon for their wickednesses, and *that* is the essence of the white man's religion. I can't stop to talk this matter over with you any longer, for Hetty's in the canoe, and the furlough takes me away, but the time will come I hope, when you'll *feel* these things; for, after all, they must be *felt* rather than reasoned about. Ah's! me; well, Delaware, there's my hand; you know it's that of a fri'nd, and will shake it as such, though it never has done you one half the good its owner wishes it had."

The Indian took the offered hand, and returned its pressure warmly. Then falling back on his acquired stoicism of manner, which so many mistake for constitutional indifference, he drew up in reserve, and prepared to part from his friend with dignity. Deerslayer, however, was more natural, nor would he have at all cared about giving way to his feelings, had not the recent conduct and language of Judith given him some secret, though ill defined apprehensions of a scene. He was too humble to imagine the truth concerning the actual feelings of that beautiful girl, while he was too observant not to have noted the struggle she had maintained with herself, and which had so often led her to the very verge of discovery. That something extraordinary was concealed in her breast, he thought obvious enough, and, through a sentiment of manly delicacy that would have done credit to the highest human refinement, he shrunk from any exposure of her secret that might subsequently cause regret to the girl, herself. He, therefore, determined to depart, now, and that without any further manifestations of feeling either from himself, or from others.

"God bless you! Sarpent—God bless you!" cried the hunter, as the canoe left the side of the platform. "Your Manitou and my God, only know when and where we shall meet agin; I shall count it a great blessing, and a full reward for any little good I may have done on 'arth, if we shall be permitted to know each other, and to consort together, hereafter, as we have so long done in these pleasant woods afore us!"

Chingachgook waved his hand. Drawing the light blanket he wore over his head, as a Roman would conceal his grief in his robes, he slowly withdrew into the Ark, in order to indulge his sorrow and his musings, alone. Deerslayer did not speak again, until the canoe was half-way to the shore. Then he suddenly ceased paddling, at an interruption that came from the mild, musical voice of Hetty.

"Why do *you* go back to the Hurons, Deerslayer?" demanded the girl. "They say *I* am feeble-minded, and such they never harm, but you have as much sense as Hurry Harry; and more too, Judith thinks, though I don't see how that can well be."

"Ah! Hetty, afore we land I must convarse a little with you child, and that too on matters touching your own welfare, principally. Stop paddling—or, rather, that the Mingos need n't think we are plotting and contriving, and so treat us accordingly, just dip your paddle lightly, and give the canoe a little motion and no more. That's just the idee and the movement; I see you're ready enough at an appearance, and might be made useful at a sarcumvention if it was lawful now to use one—that's just the idee and the movement! Ah's! me. Desait and a false tongue are evil things, and altogether onbecoming our colour, Hetty, but it *is* a pleasure and a satisfaction to outdo the contrivances of a red-skin in the strife of lawful warfare. My path has been short, and is like soon to have an end, but I can see that the wanderings of a warrior ar n't altogether among brambles and difficulties. There's a bright side to a war-path, as well as to most other things, if we'll only have the wisdom to see it, and the ginerosity to own it."

"And why should your war path, as you call it, come so near to an end, Deerslayer?"

"Because, my good girl, my furlough comes so near to an end. They're likely to have pretty much the same tarmination, as regards time, one following on the heels of the other, as a matter of course."

"I don't understand your meaning, Deerslayer—" returned the girl, looking a little bewildered. "Mother always said people ought to speak more plainly to me than to most other persons, because I'm feeble-minded. Those that are feeble minded, don't understand as easily, as those that have sense."

"Well then, Hetty, the simple truth is this. You know that I'm now a capt*yve* to the Hurons, and capt*yves* can't do, in all things, as they please—"

"But how can you be a captive," eagerly interrupted the girl—"when you are out here on the lake, in father's best canoe, and the Indians are in the woods with no canoe at all? *That* can't be true, Deerslayer!"

"I wish with all my heart and soul, Hetty, that you was right, and that I was wrong, instead of your bein' all wrong, and I bein' only too near the truth. Free as I seem to your eyes, gal, I'm bound hand and foot in ra'ality."

"Well it *is* a great misfortune not to have sense! Now, I can't see, or understand that you are a captive, or bound in any manner. If you are bound, with what are your hands and feet fastened?"

"With a furlough, gal; that's a thong that binds tighter than any chain. One *may* be broken, but the other can't. Ropes and chains allow of knives, and desait, and contrivances; but a furlough can be neither cut, slipped nor sarcumvented."

"What sort of a thing is a furlough, then, if it be stronger than hemp or iron? I never saw a furlough."

"I hope you may never feel one, gal; the tie is altogether in the feelin's, in these matters, and therefore is to be felt and not seen. You can understand what it is to give a promise, I dare to say, good little Hetty?"

"Certainly. A promise is to say you will do a thing, and

that binds you to be as good as your word. Mother always kept her promises to me, and then she said it would be wicked if I did n't keep my promises to her, and to every body else."

"You have had a good mother, in some matters, child, whatever she may have been in other some. That is a promise, and as you say it must be kept. Now, I fell into the hands of the Mingos last night, and they let me come off to see my fri'nds and send messages in to my own colour, if any such feel consarn on my account, on condition that I shall be back, when the sun is up to-day, and take whatever their revenge and hatred can contrive, in the way of torments, in satisfaction for the life of a warrior that fell by my rifle, as well as for that of the young woman shot by Hurry, and other disap-p'intments met with on and about this lake. What is called a promise atween mother and darter, or even atween strangers in the settlements is called a furlough when given by one soldier to another, on a warpath. And now I suppose you understand my situation, Hetty."

The girl made no answer for some time, but she ceased paddling altogether, as if the novel idea distracted her mind too much to admit of other employment. Then she resumed the dialogue earnestly and with solicitude.

"Do you think the Hurons will have the heart to do what you say, Deerslayer?" she asked. "I have found them kind and harmless."

"That's true enough as consarns one like you, Hetty, but it's a very different affair, when it comes to an open inimy, and he too the owner of a pretty sartain rifle. I don't say that they bear me special malice on account of any expl'ites already performed, for that would be bragging, as it might be, on the varge of the grave, but it's no vanity to believe that they know one of their bravest and cunnin'est chiefs fell by my hands. Such bein' the case, the tribe would reproach them if they failed to send the spirit of a pale face to keep the company of the spirit of their red brother; always supposin' that he can catch it. I look for no marcy, Hetty, at their hands; and my principal sorrow is that such a calamity should befal me on my first war-path: that it would come sooner or later, every soldier counts on and expects."

"The Hurons shall *not* harm you, Deerslayer," cried the girl, much excited—" 'Tis wicked as well as cruel; I have the bible, here, to tell them so. Do you think I would stand by and see you tormented?"

"I hope not, my good Hetty, I hope not; and, therefore, when the moment comes, I expect you will move off, and not be a witness of what you can't help, while it would grieve you. But, I have n't stopped the paddles to talk of my own afflictions and difficulties, but to speak a little plainly to you, gal, consarnin' your own matters."

"What can you have to say to me, Deerslayer! Since mother died, few talk to me of such things."

"So much the worse, poor gal; yes, 'tis so much the worse, for one of your state of mind needs frequent talking to, in order to escape the snares and desaits of this wicked world. You have n't forgotten Hurry Harry, gal, so soon, I calculate?"

"I!—I forget Henry March!" exclaimed Hetty, starting. "Why should I forget him, Deerslayer, when he is our friend, and only left us last night. Then, the large bright star that mother loved so much to gaze at, was just over the top of yonder tall pine on the mountain, as Hurry got into the canoe; and when you landed him on the point, near the east bay, it was n't more than the length of Judith's handsomest ribbon above it."

"And how can you know how long I was gone, or how far I went to land Hurry, seein' you were not with us, and the distance was so great, to say nothing of the night?"

"Oh! I know when it was, well enough," returned Hetty positively—"There's more ways than one for counting time and distance. When the mind is engaged, it is better than any clock. Mine is feeble, I know, but it goes true enough, in all that touches poor Hurry Harry. Judith will never marry March, Deerslayer."

"That's the p'int, Hetty; that's the very p'int I want to come to. I suppose you know, that it's nat'ral for young people to have kind feelin's for one another, more especially when one happens to be a youth and t'other a maiden. Now, one of your years and mind, gal, that has neither father nor mother, and who lives in a wilderness frequented by hunters and trappers, needs be on her guard against evils she little dreams of."

"What harm can it be to think well of a fellow creature," returned Hetty simply, though the conscious blood was stealing to her cheeks in spite of a spirit so pure that it scarce knew why it prompted the blush, "the bible tells us to 'love them who despitefully use' us, and why should n't we like them that do not."

"Ah! Hetty, the love of the missionaries is n't the sort of likin' I mean. Answer me one thing, child; do you believe yourself to have mind enough to become a wife, and a mother?"

"That's not a proper question to ask a young woman, Deerslayer, and I'll not answer it," returned the girl, in a reproving manner—much as a parent rebukes a child for an act of indiscretion. "If you have any thing to say about Hurry, I'll hear *that*—but you must not speak evil of him; he is absent, and 'tis unkind to talk evil of the absent."

"Your mother has given you so many good lessons, Hetty, that my fears for you, are not as great as they were. Nevertheless, a young woman without parents, in your state of mind, and who is not without beauty, must always be in danger in such a lawless region as this. I would say nothin' amiss of Hurry, who, in the main, is not a bad man for one of his callin', but you ought to know one thing, which it may not be altogether pleasant to tell you, but which must be said. March has a desperate likin' for your sister Judith."

"Well, what of that? Every body admires Judith, she's so handsome, and Hurry has told me, again and again, how much he wishes to marry her. But that will never come to pass, for Judith don't like Hurry. She likes another, and talks about him in her sleep; though you need not ask me who he is, for all the gold in King George's crown, and all the jewels too, would n't tempt me to tell you his name. If sisters can't keep each other's secrets, who can?"

"Sartainly, I do not wish you to tell me, Hetty, nor would it be any advantage to a dyin' man to know. What the tongue says when the mind's asleep, neither head nor heart is answerable for."

"I wish I knew why Judith talks so much in her sleep, about

officers, and honest hearts, and false tongues, but I suppose she don't like to tell me, as I'm feeble minded. Is n't it odd, Deerslayer, that Judith don't like Hurry—he, who is the bravest looking youth that ever comes upon the lake, and is as handsome as she is herself. Father always said they would be the comeliest couple in the country, though mother did n't fancy March any more than Judith. There's no telling what will happen, they say, until things actually come to pass."

"Ahs! me—well, poor Hetty, 'tis of no great use to talk to them that can't understand you, and so I'll say no more about what I did wish to speak of, though it lay heavy on my mind. Put the paddle in motion, ag'in, gal, and we'll push for the shore, for the sun is nearly up, and my furlough is almost out."

The canoe now glided ahead, holding its way towards the point where Deerslayer well knew that his enemies expected him, and where he now began to be afraid he might not arrive in season to redeem his plighted faith. Hetty perceiving his impatience, without very clearly comprehending its cause, however, seconded his efforts, in a way that soon rendered their timely return no longer a matter of doubt. Then, and then only, did the young man suffer his exertions to flag, and Hetty began, again, to prattle in her simple confiding manner, though nothing farther was uttered that it may be thought necessary to relate.

Chapter XXVII

"Thou hast been busy, Death, this day, and yet
But half thy work is done! The gates of hell
Are thronged, yet twice ten thousand spirits more
Who from their warm and healthful tenements
Fear no divorce, must, ere the sun go down,
Enter the world of woe!"—
Southey, *Roderick, the Last of the Goths*, XXIV, 1–6.

ONE EXPERIENCED in the signs of the heavens, would have seen that the sun wanted but two or three minutes of the zenith, when Deerslayer landed on the point, where the Hurons were now encamped, nearly abreast of the castle. This spot was similar to the one already described, with the exception that the surface of the land was less broken, and less crowded with trees. Owing to these two circumstances, it was all the better suited to the purpose for which it had been selected, the space beneath the branches bearing some resemblance to a densely wooded lawn. Favoured by its position and its spring, it had been much resorted to by savages and hunters, and the natural grasses had succeeded their fires, leaving an appearance of sward in places, a very unusual accompaniment of the virgin forest. Nor was the margin of water fringed with bushes, as on so much of its shore, but the eye penetrated the woods immediately on reaching the strand, commanding nearly the whole area of the projection.

If it was a point of honor with the Indian warrior to redeem his word, when pledged to return and meet his death at a given hour, so was it a point of characteristic pride to show no womanish impatience, but to reappear as nearly as possible at the appointed moment. It was well not to exceed the grace accorded by the generosity of the enemy, but it was better to meet it to a minute. Something of this dramatic effect mingles with most of the graver usages of the American aborigines, and no doubt, like the prevalence of a similar feeling among people more sophisticated and refined, may be referred to a principle of nature. We all love the wonderful, and when it comes attended by chivalrous self-devotion and a rigid regard to honor, it presents itself to our admiration in a shape doubly attractive. As respects Deerslayer, though he took a pride in showing his white blood, by often deviating from the usages of the red men, he frequently dropped into their customs, and oftener into their feelings, unconsciously to himself, in consequence of having no other arbiters to appeal to, than their judgments and tastes. On the present occasion, he would have abstained from betraying a feverish haste by a too speedy return, since it would have contained a tacit admission that the time asked for, was more than had been wanted; but, on the other hand, had the idea occurred to him, he would have quickened his movements a little, in order to avoid the dramatic appearance of returning at the precise instant set as the utmost limit of his absence. Still, accident had interfered to defeat the last intention, for when the young man put his foot on the point, and advanced with a steady tread towards the group of chiefs that was seated in grave array on a fallen tree, the oldest of their number cast his eye upward, at an opening in the trees, and pointed out to his companions the startling fact that the sun was just entering a space that was known to mark the zenith. A common, but low exclamation of surprise and admiration, escaped every mouth, and the grim warriors looked at each other, some with envy and disappointment, some with astonishment at the precise accuracy of their victim, and others with a more generous and liberal feeling. The American Indian always deemed his moral victories the noblest, prizing the groans and yielding of his victim under torture, more than the trophy of his scalp; and the trophy itself more than his life. To slay, and not to bring off the proof of victory, indeed, was scarcely deemed honorable, even these rude and fierce tenants of the forest, like their more nurtured brethren of the court and the camp, having set up for themselves imaginary and arbitrary points of honor, to supplant the conclusions of the right, and the decisions of reason.

The Hurons had been divided in their opinions concerning the probability of their captive's return. Most among them, indeed, had not expected it possible for a pale-face to come back voluntarily, and meet the known penalties of an Indian torture; but a few of the seniors expected better things from one who had already shown himself so singularly cool, brave and upright. The party had come to its decision, however, less in the expectation of finding the pledge redeemed, than in the hope of disgracing the Delawares by casting into their teeth the delinquency of one bred in their villages. They would have greatly preferred that Chingachgook should be their prisoner, and prove the traitor, but the pale-face scion of the hated stock was no bad substitute, for their purposes, failing in their designs against the ancient stem. With a view to render their triumph as signal as possible, in the event of the hour's passing without the reappearance of the hunter, all the warriors and scouts of the party had been called in, and the whole band, men, women and children, was now assembled at this single point, to be a witness of the expected scene. As the castle was in plain view, and by no means distant, it was easily watched by day-light, and, it being thought that its inmates were now limited to Hurry, the Delaware and the two girls, no apprehensions were felt, of their being able to escape unseen. A large raft having a breast-work of logs, had been prepared, and was in actual readiness to be used against either Ark or Castle, as occasion might require, so soon as the fate of Deerslayer was determined, the seniors of the party having come to the opinion that it was getting to be hazardous to delay their departure for Canada, beyond the coming night. In short, the band waited merely to dispose of this single affair, ere it brought matters with those in the Castle to a crisis, and prepared to commence its retreat towards the distant waters of Ontario.

It was an imposing scene, into which Deerslayer now found himself advancing. All the older warriors were seated on the trunk of the fallen tree, waiting his approach with grave decorum. On the right, stood the young men, armed, while the left was occupied by the women and children. In the centre was an open space of considerable extent, always canopied by leaves, but from which the underbrush, dead wood, and other obstacles had been carefully removed. The more open area had probably been much used by former parties, for this was the place where the appearance of a sward was the most decided. The arches of the woods, even at high noon, cast their sombre shadows on the spot, which the brilliant rays of the sun that struggled through the leaves contributed to mellow, and, if such an expression can be used, to illuminate. It was probably from a similar scene that the mind of man first got its idea of the effects of gothic tracery and churchly hues, this temple of nature producing some such effect, so far as light and shadow were concerned, as the well known offspring of human invention.

As was not unusual among the tribes and wandering bands of the Aborigines, two chiefs shared, in nearly equal degrees, the principal and primitive authority that was wielded over these children of the forest. There were several who might claim the distinction of being chief men, but the two in question were so much superior to all the rest in influence, that, when they agreed, no one disputed their mandates, and when they were divided the band hesitated, like men who had lost their governing principle of action. It was also in conformity with practice, perhaps we might add in conformity with nature, that one of the chiefs was indebted to his mind for his influence, whereas the other owed his distinction altogether to qualities that were physical. One was a senior, well known for eloquence in debate, wisdom in council, and prudence in measures; while his great competitor, if not his rival, was a brave distinguished in war, notorious for ferocity, and remarkable, in the way of intellect, for nothing but the cunning and expedients of the war path. The first was Rivenoak, who has already been introduced to the reader, while the last was called le Panthère, in the language of the Canadas, or the Panther, to resort to the vernacular of the English colonies. The appellation of the fighting chief was supposed to indicate the qualities of the warrior, agreeably to a practice of the red man's nomenclature, ferocity, cunning and treachery being, perhaps, the distinctive features of his character. The title had been received from the French, and was prized so much the more from that circumstance, the Indian submitting profoundly to the greater intelligence of his pale face allies, in most things of this nature. How well the *sobriquet* was merited, will be seen in the sequel.

Rivenoak and the Panther sat side by side awaiting the approach of their prisoner, as Deerslayer put his moccasined foot on the strand, nor did either move, or utter a syllable, until the young man had advanced into the centre of the area, and proclaimed his presence with his voice. This was done firmly, though in the simple manner that marked the character of the individual.

"Here I am, Mingos," he said, in the dialect of the Delawares, a language that most present understood, "here I am, and there is the sun. One is not more true to the laws of natur', than the other has proved true to his word. I am your prisoner; do with me what you please. My business with man and 'arth is settled; nothing remains now but to meet the white man's God, accordin' to a white man's duties and gifts."

A murmur of approbation escaped even the women at this address, and, for an instant there was a strong and pretty general desire to adopt into the tribe, one who owned so brave a spirit. Still there were dissenters from this wish, among the principal of whom might be classed the Panther, and his sister, le Sumach, so called from the number of her children, who was the widow of le Loup Cervier, now known to have fallen by the hand of the captive. Native ferocity held one in subjection, while the corroding passion of revenge prevented the other from admitting any gentler feeling at the moment. Not so with Rivenoak. This chief arose, stretched his arm before him, in a gesture of courtesy, and paid his compliments with an ease and dignity that a prince might have envied. As, in that band, his wisdom and eloquence were confessedly without rivals, he knew that on himself would properly fall the duty of first replying to the speech of the pale-face.

"Pale-face, you are honest," said the Huron orator. "My people are happy in having captured a man, and not a skulking fox. We now know you; we shall treat you like a brave. If you have slain one of our warriors, and helped to kill others, you have a life of your own ready to give away in return. Some of my young men thought that the blood of a pale face was too thin; that it would refuse to run under the Huron knife. You will show them it is not so; your heart is stout, as well as your body. It is a pleasure to make such a prisoner; should my warriors say that the death of le Loup Cervier ought not to be forgotten, and that he cannot travel towards the land of spirits alone, that his enemy must be sent to overtake him, they will remember that he fell by the hand of a brave, and send you after him with such signs of our friendship as shall not make him ashamed to keep your company. I have spoken; you know what I have said."

"True enough, Mingo, all true as the gospel," returned the simple minded hunter, "you *have* spoken, and I *do* know not only what you have *said*, but, what is still more important, what you *mean*. I dare to say your warrior the Lynx, was a stout-hearted brave, and worthy of your fri'ndship and respect, but I do not feel unworthy to keep his company, without any passport from your hands. Nevertheless, here I am, ready to receive judgment from your council, if, indeed, the matter was not detarmined among you, afore I got back."

"My old men would not sit in council over a pale face until they saw him among them," answered Rivenoak, looking around him a little ironically; "they said it would be like sitting in council over the winds; they go where they will, and come back as they see fit, and not otherwise. There was one voice that spoke in your favor, Deerslayer, but it was alone, like the song of the wren whose mate has been struck by the hawk."

"I thank that voice whosever it may have been, Mingo, and will say it was as true a voice, as the rest were lying voices. A furlough is as binding on a pale-face, if he be honest, as it is on a red skin, and was it not so, I would never bring disgrace on the Delawares, among whom I may be said to have received my edication. But words are useless, and lead to braggin' feelin's; here I am; act your will on me."

Rivenoak made a sign of acquiescence, and then a short conference was privately held among the chiefs. As soon as the latter ended, three or four young men fell back from among the armed group, and disappeared. Then it was signified to the prisoner that he was at liberty to go at large on the point, until a council was held concerning his fate. There was more of seeming, than of real confidence, however, in this apparent liberality, inasmuch as the young men mentioned, already formed a line of sentinels across the breadth of the point, inland, and escape from any other part was out of the question. Even the canoe was removed beyond this line of sentinels, to a spot where it was considered safe from any sudden attempt. These precautions did not proceed from a failure of confidence, but from the circumstance that the prisoner had now complied with all the required conditions of his parole, and it would have been considered a commendable and honorable exploit to escape from his foes. So nice, indeed, were the distinctions drawn by the savages, in cases of this nature, that they often gave their victims a chance to evade the torture, deeming it as creditable to the captors to overtake, or to out wit a fugitive, when his exertions were supposed to be quickened by the extreme jeopardy of his situation, as it was for him to get clear from so much extraordinary vigilance.

Nor was Deerslayer unconscious of, or forgetful, of his rights, and of his opportunities. Could he now have seen any probable opening for an escape, the attempt would not have been delayed a minute. But the case seem'd desperate. He was aware of the line of sentinels, and felt the difficulty of breaking through it, unharmed. The lake offered no advantages, as the canoe would have given his foes the greatest facilities for overtaking him; else would he have found it no difficult task to swim as far as the castle. As he walked about the point, he even examined the spot to ascertain if it offered no place of concealment, but its openness, its size, and the hundred watchful glances that were turned towards him, even while those who made them affected not to see him, prevented any such expedient from succeeding. The dread and disgrace of failure had no influence on Deerslayer, who deemed it even a point of honor to reason and feel like a white man, rather than as an Indian, and who felt it a sort of duty, to do all he could, that did not involve a dereliction from principle, in order to save his life. Still he hesitated about making the effort, for he also felt that he ought to see the chance of success before he committed himself.

In the mean time the business of the camp appeared to proceed in its regular train. The chiefs consulted apart, admitting no one but the Sumach to their councils, for she, the widow of the fallen warrior, had an exclusive right to be heard on such an occasion. The young men strolled about in indolent listlessness, awaiting the result with Indian patience, while the females prepared the feast that was to celebrate the termination of the affair, whether it proved fortunate, or otherwise, for our hero. No one betrayed feeling, and an indifferent observer, beyond the extreme watchfulness of the sentinels, would have detected no extraordinary movement or sensation to denote the real state of things. Two or three old women put their heads together, and it appeared unfavorably to the prospects of Deerslayer, by their scowling looks, and angry gestures; but a group of Indian girls were evidently animated by a different impulse, as was apparent by stolen glances that expressed pity and regret. In this condition of the camp, an hour soon glided away.

Suspense is perhaps the feeling of all others that is most difficult to be supported. When Deerslayer landed, he fully expected in the course of a few minutes to undergo the tortures of an Indian revenge, and he was prepared to meet his fate, manfully; but, the delay proved far more trying than the nearer approach of suffering, and the intended victim began seriously to meditate some desperate effort at escape, as it might be from sheer anxiety to terminate the scene, when he was suddenly summoned, to appear once more in front of his judges, who had already arranged the band in its former order, in readiness to receive him.

"Killer of the Deer," commenced Rivenoak, as soon as his captive stood before him, "my aged men have listened to wise words; they are ready to speak. You are a man whose fathers came from beyond the rising sun; we are children of the setting sun; we turn our faces towards the Great Sweet Lakes, when we look towards our villages. It may be a wide country and full of riches towards the morning, but it is very pleasant towards the evening. We love most to look in that direction. When we gaze at the east, we feel afraid, canoe after canoe bringing more and more of your people in the track of the sun, as if their land was so full as to run over. The red men are few already; they have need of help. One of our best lodges has lately been emptied, by the death of its master; it will be a long time before his son can grow big enough to sit in his place. There is his widow; she will want venison to feed her and her children, for her sons are yet like the young of the robin, before they quit the nest. By your hand has this great calamity befallen her. She has two duties; one to le Loup Cervier, and one to his children. Scalp for scalp, life for life, blood for blood, is one law; to feed her young, another. We know you, Killer of the Deer. You are honest; when you say a thing, it is so. You have but one tongue, and that is not forked, like a snake's. Your head is never hid in the grass; all can see it. What you say, that will you do. You are just. When you have done wrong, it is your wish to do right, again, as soon as you can. Here is the Sumach; she is alone in her wigwam, with children crying around her for food—yonder is a rifle; it is loaded and ready to be fired. Take the gun, go forth and shoot a deer; bring the venison and lay it before the widow of Le Loup Cervier, feed her children; call yourself her husband. After which, your heart will no longer be Delaware, but Huron; le Sumach's ears will not hear the cries of her children; my people will count the proper number of warriors."

"I fear'd this, Rivenoak," answered Deerslayer, when the other had ceased speaking—"yes, I did dread that it would come to this. Howsever, the truth is soon told, and that will put an end to all expectations on this head. Mingo, I'm white and christian born; 't would ill become me to take a wife, under red-skin forms, from among heathen. That which I wouln't do, in peaceable times, and under a bright sun, still less would I do behind clouds, in order to save my life. I may never marry; most likely Providence in putting me, up here, in the woods, has intended I should live single, and without a lodge of my own; but should such a thing come to pass, none but a woman of my own colour and gifts shall darken the door of my wigwam. As for feeding the young of your dead warrior, I would do that cheerfully, could it be done without discredit; but it cannot, seeing that I can never live in a Huron village. Your own young men must find the Sumach in venison, and the next time she marries, let her take a husband whose legs are not long enough to overrun territory that do n't belong to him. We fou't a fair battle, and he fell; in this, there is nothin' but what a brave expects, and should be ready to meet. As for getting a Mingo heart, as well might you expect to see gray hairs on a boy, or the blackberry growing on the pine. No—no—Huron; my gifts are white so far as wives are consarned; it is Delaware, in all things touchin' Injins."

These words were scarcely out of the mouth of Deerslayer, before a common murmur betrayed the dissatisfaction with which they had been heard. The aged women, in particular, were loud in their expressions of disgust, and the gentle Sumach, herself, a woman quite old enough to be our hero's mother, was not the least pacific in her denunciations. But all the other manifestations of disappointment and discontent were thrown into the back-ground, by the fierce resentment of the Panther. This grim chief had thought it a degradation to permit his sister to become the wife of a pale face of the Yengeese, at all, and had only given a reluctant consent to the arrangement—one by no means unusual among the Indians, however—at the earnest solicitations of the bereaved widow; and it goaded him to the quick to find his condescension slighted, the honor he had with so much regret been persuaded to accord, contemned. The animal from which he got his name, does not glare on his intended prey, with more frightful ferocity, than his eyes gleamed on the captive, nor was his arm backward in seconding the fierce resentment that almost consumed his breast.

"Dog of the pale faces!" he exclaimed in Iroquois, "go yell among the curs of your own evil hunting grounds!"

The denunciation was accompanied by an appropriate action. Even while speaking his arm was lifted, and the tomahawk hurled. Luckily the loud tones of the speaker had drawn the eye of Deerslayer towards him, else would that moment have probably closed his career. So great was the dexterity with which this dangerous weapon was thrown, and so deadly the intent, that it would have riven the scull of the prisoner, had he not stretched forth an arm, and caught the handle in one of its turns, with a readiness quite as remarkable, as the skill with which the missile had been hurled. The projectile force was so great, notwithstanding, that when Deerslayer's arm was arrested, his hand was raised above and behind his own head, and in the very attitude necessary to return the attack. It is not certain whether the circumstance of finding himself unexpectedly in this menacing posture and armed, tempted the young man to retaliate, or whether sudden resentment overcame his forbearance and prudence. His eye kindled, however, and a small red spot appeared on each cheek, while he cast all his energy into the effort of his arm, and threw back the weapon at his assailant. The unexpectedness of this blow contributed to its success, the Panther neither raising an arm, nor bending his head to avoid it. The keen little axe struck the victim in a perpendicular line with the nose, directly between the eyes, literally braining him on the spot. Sallying forward, as the serpent darts at its enemy even while receiving its own death wound, this man of powerful frame, fell his length into the open area formed by the circle, quivering in death. A common rush to his relief left the captive, for a single instant, quite without the crowd, and, willing to make one desperate effort for life, he bounded off, with the activity of a deer. There was but a breathless instant, when the whole band, old and young, women and children, abandoning the lifeless body of the Panther, where it lay, raised the yell of alarm and followed in pursuit.

Sudden as had been the event which induced Deerslayer to make this desperate trial of speed, his mind was not wholly unprepared for the fearful emergency. In the course of the past hour, he had pondered well on the chances of such an experiment, and had shrewdly calculated all the details of success and failure. At the first leap, therefore, his body was completely under the direction of an intelligence that turned all its efforts to the best account, and prevented every thing like hesitation or indecision at the important instant of the start. To this alone was he indebted for the first great advantage, that of getting through the line of sentinels unharmed. The manner in which this was done, though sufficiently simple, merits a description.

Although the shores of the point were not fringed with bushes, as was the case with most of the others on the lake, it was owing altogether to the circumstance that the spot had been so much used by hunters and fishermen. This fringe commenced on what might be termed the main land, and was as dense as usual, extending in long lines both north and south. In the latter direction, then, Deerslayer held his way, and, as the sentinels were a little without the commencement of this thicket, before the alarm was clearly communicated to them, the fugitive had gained its cover. To run among the bushes, however, was out of the question, and Deerslayer held his way, for some forty or fifty yards, in the water, which was barely knee deep, offering as great an obstacle to the speed of his pursuers, as it did to his own. As soon as a favorable spot presented, he darted through the line of bushes, and issued into the open woods.

Several rifles were discharged at Deerslayer while in the water, and more followed as he came out into the comparative exposure of the clear forest. But the direction of his line of flight, which partially crossed that of the fire, the haste with which the weapons had been aimed, and the general confusion that prevailed in the camp prevented any harm from being done. Bullets whistled past him, and many cut twigs from the branches at his side, but not one touched even his dress. The delay caused by these fruitless attempts was of great service to the fugitive, who had gained more than a hundred yards on even the leading men of the Hurons, ere something like concert and order had entered into the chase. To think of following with rifles in hand, was out of the question, and after emptying their pieces in vague hopes of wounding their captive, the best runners of the Indians threw them aside, calling out to the women and boys to recover and load them, again, as soon as possible.

Deerslayer knew too well the desperate nature of the struggle in which he was engaged to lose one of the precious moments. He also knew that his only hope was to run in a straight line, for as soon as he began to turn, or double, the greater number of his pursuers would put escape out of the question. He held his way therefore, in a diagonal direction up the acclivity, which was neither very high nor very steep, in this part of the mountain, but which was sufficiently toilsome for one contending for life, to render it painfully oppressive. There, however, he slackened his speed, to recover breath, proceeding even at a quick walk, or a slow trot, along the more difficult parts of the way. The Hurons were whooping and leaping behind him, but this he disregarded, well knowing they must overcome the difficulties he had surmounted, ere they could reach the elevation to which he had attained. The summit of the first hill was now quite near him, and he saw, by the formation of the land, that a deep glen intervened, before the base of a second hill could be reached.

Walking deliberately to the summit, he glanced eagerly about him, in every direction, in quest of a cover. None offered in the ground, but a fallen tree lay near him, and desperate circumstances required desperate remedies. This tree lay in a line parallel to the glen, at the brow of the hill. To leap on it, and then to force his person as close as possible, under its lower side, took but a moment. Previously to disappearing from his pursuers, however, Deerslayer stood on the height, and gave a cry of triumph, as if exulting at the sight of the descent that lay before him. In the next instant he was stretched beneath the tree.

No sooner was this expedient adopted, than the young man ascertained how desperate had been his own efforts, by the violence of the pulsations in his frame. He could hear his heart beat, and his breathing was like the action of a bellows, in quick motion. Breath was gained, however, and the heart soon ceased to throb, as if about to break through its confinement. The footsteps of those who toiled up the opposite side of the acclivity were now audible, and presently voices and treads announced the arrival of the pursuers. The foremost shouted as they reached the height; then, fearful that their enemy would escape under favor of the descent, each leaped upon the fallen tree, and plunged into the ravine, trusting to get a sight of the pursued, ere he reached the bottom. In this manner, Huron followed Huron, until Natty began to hope the whole had passed. Others succeeded, however, until quite forty had leaped over the tree, and then he counted them, as the surest mode of ascertaining how many could be behind. Presently all were in the bottom of the glen, quite a hundred feet below him, and some had even ascended part of the opposite hill, when it became evident an inquiry was making, as to the direction he had taken. This was the critical moment, and one of nerves less steady, or of a training that had been neglected, would have seized it to rise, and fly. Not so with Deerslayer. He still lay quiet, watching with jealous vigilance every movement below, and fast regaining his breath.

The Hurons now resembled a pack of hounds, at fault. Little was said, but each man ran about, examining the dead leaves, as the hound hunts for the lost scent. The great number of moccasins that had passed made the examination difficult, though the in-toe of an Indian was easily to be distinguished from the freer and wider step of a white man. Believing that no more pursuers remained behind, and hoping to steal away unseen, Deerslayer suddenly threw himself over the tree, and fell on the upper side. This achievement appeared to be effected successfully, and hope beat high in the bosom of the fugitive. Rising to his hands and feet, after a moment lost in listening to the sounds in the glen, in order to ascertain if he had been seen, the young man next scrambled to the top of the hill, a distance of only ten yards, in the expectation of getting its brow between him and his pursuers, and himself so far under cover. Even this was effected, and he rose to his feet, walking swiftly but steadily along the summit, in a direction opposite to that in which he had first fled. The nature of the calls in the glen, however, soon made him uneasy, and he sprang upon the summit, again, in order to reconnoitre. No sooner did he reach the height than he was seen, and the chase renewed. As it was better footing, on the level ground, Deerslayer now avoided the side hill, holding his flight along the ridge; while the Hurons, judging from the general formation of the land, saw that the ridge would soon melt into the hollow, and kept to the latter, as the easiest mode of heading the fugitive. A few, at the same time, turned south, with a view to prevent his escaping in that direction, while some crossed his trail towards the water, in order to prevent his retreat by the lake, running southerly.

The situation of Deerslayer was now more critical than it ever had been. He was virtually surrounded on three sides, having the lake on the fourth. But he had pondered well on all the chances, and took his measures with coolness, even while at the top of his speed. As is generally the case, with the vigorous border men, he could outrun any single Indian among his pursuers, who were principally formidable to him, on account of their numbers, and the advantages they possessed in position, and he would not have hesitated to break off, in a straight line, at any spot, could he have got the whole band again, fairly behind him. But no such chance did, or indeed could now offer, and when he found that he was descending towards the glen, by the melting away of the ridge, he turned short, at right angles to his previous course, and went down the declivity with tremendous velocity, holding his way towards the shore. Some of his pursuers, came panting up the hill, in direct chase, while most still kept on, in the ravine, intending to head him at its termination.

Deerslayer had now a different, though a desperate project in view. Abandoning all thoughts of escape by the woods, he made the best of his way towards the canoe. He knew where it lay; could it be reached, he had only to run the gauntlet of a few rifles, and success would be certain. None of the warriors had kept their weapons, which would have retarded their speed, and the risk would come either from the uncertain hands of the women, or from those of some well grown boy; though most of the latter were already out in hot pursuit. Every thing seemed propitious to the execution of this plan, and the course being a continued descent, the young man went over the ground at a rate that promised a speedy termination to his toil.

As Deerslayer approached the point, several women, and children were passed, but, though the former endeavoured to cast dried branches between his legs, the terror inspired by his bold retaliation on the redoubted Panther, was so great, that none dared come near enough seriously to molest him. He went by all triumphantly, and reached the fringe of bushes. Plunging through these, our hero found himself once more in the lake, and within fifty feet of the canoe. Here he ceased to run, for he well understood that his breath was now all important to him. He even stooped, as he advanced, and cooled his parched mouth, by scooping water up in his hand, to drink. Still the moments pressed, and he soon stood at the side of the canoe. The first glance told him that the paddles had been removed! This was a sore disappointment, after all his efforts, and, for a single moment, he thought of turning, and of facing his foes by walking with dignity into the centre of the camp, again. But an infernal yell, such as the American savage alone can raise, proclaimed the quick approach of the nearest of his pursuers, and the instinct of life triumphed. Preparing himself duly, and giving a right direction to its bows, he ran off into the water bearing the canoe before him, threw all his strength and skill into a last effort, and cast himself forward so as to fall into the bottom of the light craft, without materially impeding its way. Here he remained on his back, both to regain his breath, and to cover his person from the deadly rifle. The lightness, which was such an advantage in paddling the canoe, now operated unfavorably. The material was so like a feather, that the boat had no momentum, else would the impulse in that smooth and placid sheet have impelled it to a distance from the shore, that would have rendered paddling with the hands safe. Could such a point once be reached, Deerslayer thought he might get far enough out to attract the attention of Chingachgook and Judith, who would not fail to come to his relief, with other canoes, a circumstance that promised every thing. As the young man lay in the bottom of the canoe, he watched its movements, by studying the tops of the trees on the mountainside, and judged of his distance by the time and the motions. Voices on the shore were now numerous, and he heard something said about manning the raft, which, fortunately for the fugitive, lay at a considerable distance, on the other side of the point.

Perhaps the situation of Deerslayer had not been more critical that day, than it was at this moment. It certainly had not been one half as tantalizing. He lay perfectly quiet, for two or three minutes, trusting to the single sense of hearing, confident that the noise in the lake would reach his ears, did any one venture to approach by swimming. Once or twice, he fancied that the element was stirred by the cautious movement of an arm, and then he perceived it was the wash of the water on the pebbles of the strand; for, in mimicry of the ocean, it is seldom that those little lakes are so totally tranquil, as not to possess a slight heaving and setting on their shores. Suddenly all the voices ceased, and a death like stillness pervaded the spot: A quietness as profound as if all lay in the repose of inanimate life. By this time, the canoe had drifted so far as to render nothing visible to Deerslayer, as he lay on his back, except the blue void of space, and a few of those brighter rays, that proceed from the effulgence of the sun, marking his proximity. It was not possible to endure this uncertainty long. The young man well knew that the profound stillness foreboded evil, the savages never being so silent, as when about to strike a blow, resembling the stealthy foot of the panther ere he takes his leap. He took out a knife, and was about to cut a hole through the bark, in order to get a view of the shore, when he paused from a dread of being seen, in the operation, which would direct the enemy where to aim their bullets. At this instant a rifle *was* fired, and the ball pierced both sides of the canoe, within eighteen inches of the spot where his head lay. This was close work, but our hero had too lately gone through that which was closer to be appalled. He lay still half a minute longer, and then he saw the summit of an oak coming slowly within his narrow horizon.

Unable to account for this change, Deerslayer could restrain his impatience no longer. Hitching his body along, with the utmost caution, he got his eye at the bullet hole, and fortunately commanded a very tolerable view of the point. The canoe, by one of those imperceptible impulses that so often decide the fate of men as well as the course of things, had inclined southerly, and was slowly drifting down the lake. It was lucky that Deerslayer had given it a shove sufficiently vigorous to send it past the end of the point, ere it took this inclination, or it must have gone ashore again. As it was, it drifted so near it, as to bring the tops of two or three trees within the range of the young man's view, as has been mentioned, and, indeed, to come in quite as close proximity with the extremity of the point, as was at all safe. The distance could not much have exceeded a hundred feet, though fortunately a light current of air, from the south west, began to set it slowly off shore.

Deerslayer now felt the urgent necessity of resorting to some expedient to get farther from his foes, and if possible to apprise his friends of his situation. The distance rendered the last difficult, while the proximity to the point rendered the first indispensable. As was usual in such craft, a large, round, smooth stone, was in each end of the canoe, for the double purpose of seats and ballast; one of these was within reach of his feet. This stone he contrived to get so far between his legs, as to reach it with his hands, and then he managed to roll it to the side of its fellow in the bows, where the two served to keep the trim of the light boat, while he worked his own body as far aft as possible. Before quitting the shore, and as soon as he perceived that the paddles were gone, Deerslayer had thrown a bit of dead branch into the canoe, and this was within reach of his arm. Removing the cap he wore, he put it on the end of this stick, and just let it appear over the edge of the canoe, as far as possible from his own person. This *ruse* was scarcely adopted, before the young man had a proof how much he had underrated the intelligence of his enemies. In contempt of an artifice so shallow and common place, a bullet was fired directly through another part of the canoe, which actually rased his skin. He dropped the cap, and instantly raised it immediately over his head, as a safeguard. It would seem that this second artifice was unseen, or what was more probable, the Hurons feeling certain of recovering their captive, wished to take him alive.

Deerslayer lay passive a few minutes longer, his eye at the bullet hole, however, and much did he rejoice at seeing that he was drifting, gradually, farther and farther, from the shore. When he looked upward, the tree-tops had disappeared, but he soon found that the canoe was slowly turning, so as to prevent his getting a view of any thing at his peep-hole, but of the two extremities of the lake. He now bethought him of the stick, which was crooked, and offered some facilities for rowing, without the necessity of rising. The experiment succeeded on trial, better even than he had hoped, though his great embarrassment was to keep the canoe straight. That his present manoeuvre was seen, soon became apparent by the clamor on the shore, and a bullet entering the stern of the canoe, traversed its length whistling between the arms of our hero, and passed out at the head. This satisfied the fugitive that he was getting away with tolerable speed, and induced him to increase his efforts. He was making a stronger push than common, when another messenger from the point, broke the stick out-board, and at once deprived him of his oar. As the sound of voices seemed to grow more and more distant, however, Deerslayer determined to leave all to the drift, until he believed himself beyond the reach of bullets. This was nervous work, but it was the wisest of all the expedients that offered, and the young man was encouraged to persevere in it, by the circumstance that he felt his face fanned by the air, a proof that there was a little more wind.

Chapter XXVIII

"Nor widows' tears, nor tender orphans' cries
Can stop th' invader's force;
Nor swelling seas, nor threatening skies,
Prevent the pirate's course:
Their lives to selfish ends decreed
Through blood and rapine they proceed;
No anxious thoughts of ill repute,
Suspend the impetuous and unjust pursuit;
But power and wealth obtain'd, guilty and great,
Their fellow creatures' fears they raise, or urge their hate."
Congreve, "Pindaric Ode," ii.

BY THIS TIME, Deerslayer had been twenty minutes in the the canoe, and he began to grow a little impatient for some signs of relief from his friends. The position of the boat still prevented his seeing in any direction, unless it were up or down the lake, and, though he knew that his line of sight must pass within a hundred yards of the castle, it, in fact, passed that distance to the westward of the buildings. The profound stillness troubled him also, for he knew not whether to ascribe it to the increasing space between him and the Indians, or to some new artifice. At length, wearied with fruitless watchfulness, the young man turned himself on his back, closed his eyes, and awaited the result in determined acquiescence. If the savages could so completely control their thirst for revenge, he was resolved to be as calm as themselves, and to trust his fate to the interposition of the currents and air.

Some additional ten minutes may have passed in this quiescent manner, on both sides, when Deerslayer thought he heard a slight noise, like a low rubbing against the bottom of his canoe. He opened his eyes of course, in expectation of seeing the face or arm of an Indian rising from the water, and found that a canopy of leaves was impending directly over his head. Starting to his feet, the first object that met his eye was Rivenoak, who had so far aided the slow progress of the boat, as to draw it on the point, the grating on the strand being the sound that had first given our hero the alarm. The change in the drift of the canoe, had been altogether owing to the baffling nature of the light currents of the air, aided by some eddies in the water.

"Come," said the Huron with a quiet gesture of authority, to order his prisoner to land, "my young friend has sailed about till he is tired; he will forget how to run again, unless he uses his legs."

"You've the best of it, Huron," returned Deerslayer, stepping steadily from the canoe, and passively following his leader to the open area of the point; "Providence has helped you in an onexpected manner. I'm your prisoner ag'in, and I hope you'll allow that I'm as good at breaking gaol, as I am at keeping furloughs."

"My young friend is a Moose!" exclaimed the Huron. "His legs are very long; they have given my young men trouble. But he is not a fish; he cannot find his way in the lake. We did not shoot him; fish are taken in nets, and not killed by bullets. When he turns Moose, again, he will be treated like a Moose."

"Ay, have your talk, Rivenoak; make the most of your advantage. 'Tis your right, I suppose, and I know it is your gift. On that p'int there'll be no words atween us, for all men must and ought to follow their gifts. Howsever, when your women begin to ta'nt and abuse me, as I suppose will soon happen, let 'em remember that if a pale face struggles for life so long as it's lawful and manful, he knows how to loosen his hold on it, decently, when he feels that the time has come. I'm your capt*yve*; work your will on me."

"My brother has had a long run on the hills, and a pleasant sail on the water," returned Rivenoak, more mildly, smiling, at the same time, in a way that his listener knew denoted pacific intentions. "He has seen the woods; he has seen the water. Which does he like best? Perhaps, he has seen enough, to change his mind, and make him hear reason."

"Speak out, Huron. Something is in your thoughts, and the sooner it is said, the sooner you'll get my answer."

"That is straight! There is no turning in the talk of my pale face friend, though he is a fox in running. I will speak to him; his ears are now open wider than before, and his eyes are not shut. The Sumach is poorer than ever. Once she had a brother and a husband. She had children, too. The time came and the husband started for the Happy Hunting Grounds, without saying farewell; he left her alone with his children. This he could not help, or he would not have done it; le Loup Cervier was a good husband. It was pleasant to see the venison, and wild ducks, and geese, and bear's meat, that hung in his lodge, in winter. It is now gone; it will not keep in warm weather. Who shall bring it back again? Some thought the brother would not forget his sister, and that, next winter, he would see that the lodge should not be empty. We thought this; but the Panther yelled, and followed the husband on the path of death. They are now trying which shall first reach the Happy Hunting Grounds. Some think the Lynx can run fastest, and some think the Panther can jump the farthest. The Sumach thinks both will travel so fast and so far that neither will ever come back. Who shall feed her and her young? The man who told her husband and her brother to quit her lodge, that there might be room for him to come into it. He is a great hunter, and we know that the woman will never want."

"Ay, Huron this is soon settled, accordin' to your notions, but it goes sorely ag'in the grain of a white man's feelin's. I've heard of men's saving their lives this-a-way, and I've know'd them that would prefar death to such a sort of captivity. For my part, I do not seek my end, nor do I seek matrimony."

"The pale face will think of this, while my people get ready for the council. He will be told what will happen. Let him remember how hard it is to lose a husband and a brother. Go; when we want him, the name of Deerslayer will be called."

This conversation had been held with no one near but the speakers. Of all the band that had so lately thronged the place, Rivenoak alone was visible. The rest seemed to have totally abandoned the spot. Even the furniture, clothes, arms, and other property of the camp had entirely disappeared, and the place bore no other proofs of the crowd that had so lately occupied it, than the traces of their fires and resting places, and the trodden earth, that still showed the marks of their feet. So sudden and unexpected a change caused Deerslayer a good deal of surprise and some uneasiness, for he had never known it to occur, in the course of his experience among the

Delawares. He suspected, however, and rightly, that a change of encampment was intended, and that the mystery of the movement was resorted to, in order to work on his apprehensions.

Rivenoak walked up the vista of trees, as soon as he ceased speaking, leaving Deerslayer by himself. The chief disappeared behind the covers of the forest, and one unpractised in such scenes might have believed the prisoner left to the dictates of his own judgment. But the young man, while he felt a little amazement at the dramatic aspect of things, knew his enemies too well to fancy himself at liberty, or a free agent. Still, he was ignorant how far the Hurons meant to carry their artifices, and he determined to bring the question, as soon as practicable, to the proof. Affecting an indifference he was far from feeling, he strolled about the area, gradually getting nearer and nearer to the spot where he had landed, when he suddenly quickened his pace, though carefully avoiding all appearance of flight, and pushing aside the bushes, he stepped upon the beach. The canoe was gone, nor could he see any traces of it, after walking to the northern and southern verges of the point, and examining the shores in both directions. It was evidently removed beyond his reach and knowledge, and under circumstances to show that such had been the intention of the savages.

Deerslayer now better understood his actual situation. He was a prisoner on the narrow tongue of land, vigilantly watched beyond a question, and with no other means of escape than that of swimming. He, again, thought of this last expedient, but the certainty that the canoe would be sent in chase, and the desperate nature of the chances of success deterred him from the undertaking. While on the strand, he came to a spot where the bushes had been cut, and thrust into a small pile. Removing a few of the upper branches, he found beneath them the dead body of the Panther. He knew that it was kept until the savages might find a place to inter it, where it would be beyond the reach of the scalping knife. He gazed wistfully towards the castle, but there all seemed to be silent and desolate, and a feeling of loneliness and desertion came over him to increase the gloom of the moment.

"God's will be done!" murmured the young man, as he

walked sorrowfully away from the beach, entering again beneath the arches of the wood. "God's will be done, on 'arth as it is in heaven! I did hope that my days would not be numbered so soon, but it matters little a'ter all. A few more winters, and a few more summers, and 'twould have been over, accordin' to natur'. Ah's! me, the young and act*yv*e seldom think death possible, till he grins in their faces, and tells 'em the hour is come!"

While this soliloquy was being pronounced, the hunter advanced into the area, where to his surprise he saw Hetty alone, evidently awaiting his return. The girl carried the bible under her arm, and her face, over which a shadow of gentle melancholy was usually thrown, now seemed sad, and downcast. Moving nearer, Deerslayer spoke.

"Poor Hetty," he said, "times have been so troublesome, of late, that I'd altogether forgotten you; we meet, as it might be to mourn over what is to happen. I wonder what has become of Chingachgook and Wah!"

"Why did you kill the Huron, Deerslayer?—" returned the girl reproachfully. "Don't you know your commandments, which say 'Thou shalt not kill!' They tell me you have now slain the woman's husband and brother!"

"It's true, my good Hetty—'tis gospel truth, and I'll not deny what has come to pass. But, you must remember, gal, that many things are lawful in war, which would be onlawful in peace. The husband was shot in open fight—or, open so far as I was consarned, while he had a better cover than common—and the brother brought his end on himself, by casting his tomahawk at an unarmed prisoner. Did you witness that deed, gal?"

"I saw it, and was sorry it happened, Deerslayer, for I hoped you would n't have returned blow for blow, but good for evil."

"Ah, Hetty, that may do among the Missionaries, but 'twould make an onsartain life in the woods! The Panther craved my blood, and he was foolish enough to throw arms into my hands, at the very moment he was striving a'ter it. 'Twould have been ag'in natur' not to raise a hand in such a trial, and 'twould have done discredit to my training and gifts. No—no—I'm as willing to give every man his own, as another, and so I hope you'll testify to them that will be likely to question you as to what you've seen this day."

"Deerslayer, do you mean to marry Sumach, now she has neither husband nor brother to feed her?"

"Are such your idees of matrimony, Hetty! Ought the young to wive with the old—the pale face with the red skin—the christian with the heathen? It's ag'in reason and natur', and so you'll see, if you think of it a moment."

"I've always heard mother say," returned Hetty, averting her face more from a feminine instinct, than from any consciousness of wrong, "that people should never marry, until they loved each other better than brothers and sisters, and I suppose that is what you mean. Sumach *is* old, and you *are* young!"

"Ay and she's red, and I'm white. Beside, Hetty, suppose you was a wife, now, having married some young man of your own years, and state, and colour—Hurry Harry, for instance—" Deerslayer selected this example, simply from the circumstance that he was the only young man known to both—"and that he had fallen on a war path, would you wish to take to your bosom, for a husband, the man that slew him?"

"Oh! no, no, no—" returned the girl shuddering—"*That* would be wicked as well as heartless! No christian girl could, or would do *that*! I never shall be the wife of Hurry, I know, but were he my husband no man should ever be it, again, after his death!"

"I thought it would get to this, Hetty, when you come to understand sarcumstances. 'Tis a moral impossibility that I should ever marry Sumach, and, though Injin weddin's have no priests and not much religion, a white man who knows his gifts and duties can't profit by that, and so make his escape at the fitting time. I do think, death would be more nat'ral like, and welcome, than wedlock with this woman."

"Don't say it too loud," interrupted Hetty impatiently; "I suppose she will not like to hear it. I'm sure Hurry would rather marry even me than suffer torments, though I *am* feeble minded; and I am sure it would kill me to think he'd prefer death to being my husband."

"Ay, gal, you an't Sumach, but a comely young Christian,

with a good heart, pleasant smile, and kind eye. Hurry might be proud to get you, and that, too, not in misery and sorrow, but in his best and happiest days. Howsever, take my advice, and never talk to Hurry about these things; he's only a borderer, at the best."

"I would n't tell him, for the world!" exclaimed the girl, looking about her, like one affrighted, and blushing, she knew not why. "Mother always said young women should n't be forward, and speak their minds before they're asked; Oh! I never forget what mother told me. Tis a pity Hurry is so handsome, Deerslayer; I do think fewer girls would like him then, and he would sooner know his own mind."

"Poor gal, poor gal, it's plain enough how it is, but the Lord will bear in mind one of your simple heart, and kind feelin's! We'll talk no more of these things; if you had reason, you'd be sorrowful at having let others so much into your secret. Tell me, Hetty, what has become of all the Hurons, and why they let you roam about the p'int, as if you, too, was a prisoner?"

"I'm no prisoner, Deerslayer, but a free girl, and go when and where I please. Nobody dare hurt *me*! If they did, God would be angry, as I can show them in the bible. No—no—Hetty Hutter is not afraid; *she's* in good hands. The Hurons are up yonder in the woods, and keep a good watch on us both, I'll answer for it, since all the women and children are on the look-out. Some are burying the body of the poor girl who was shot, so that the enemy and the wild beasts can't find it. I told 'em that father and mother lay in the lake, but I would n't let them know, in what part of it, for Judith and I don't want any of their heathenish company, in our burying ground."

"Ahs! me;—Well, it *is* an awful despatch to be standing here, alive and angry, and with the feelin's up and ferocious, one hour, and then to be carried away at the next, and put out of sight of mankind in a hole in the 'arth! No one knows what will happen to him on a warpath, that's sartain."

Here the stirring of leaves and the cracking of dried twigs interrupted the discourse, and apprised Deerslayer of the approach of his enemies. The Hurons closed around the spot that had been prepared for the coming scene, and in the centre of which the intended victim now stood, in a circle, the armed men being so distributed, among the feebler members of the band, that there was no safe opening through which the prisoner could break. But the latter no longer contemplated flight, the recent trial having satisfied him of his inability to escape when pursued so closely by numbers. On the contrary, all his energies were aroused, in order to meet his expected fate, with a calmness that should do credit to his colour and his manhood; one equally removed from recreant alarm, and savage boasting.

When Rivenoak re-appeared in the circle, he occupied his old place at the head of the area. Several of the elder warriors stood near him, but, now that the brother of Sumach had fallen, there was no longer any recognised chief present, whose influence and authority offered a dangerous rivalry to his own. Nevertheless, it is well known that little which could be called monarchical, or despotic entered into the politics of the North American tribes, although the first colonists, bringing with them to this hemisphere, the notions and opinions of their own countries, often dignified the chief men of those primitive nations, with the titles of kings and princes. Hereditary influence did certainly exist, but there is much reason to believe it existed rather as a consequence of hereditary merit and acquired qualifications, than as a birth-right. Rivenoak, however, had not even this claim, having risen to consideration purely by the force of talents, sagacity, and, as Bacon expresses it, in relation to all distinguished statesmen, "by a union of great and mean qualities;" a truth of which the career of the profound Englishman himself furnishes so apt an illustration. Next to arms, eloquence offers the great avenue to popular favor, whether it be in civilized or savage life, and Rivenoak had succeeded, as so many have succeeded, before him, quite as much by rendering fallacies acceptable to his listeners, as by any profound or learned expositions of truth, or the accuracy of his logic. Nevertheless, he had influence; and was far from being altogether without just claims to its possession. Like most men who reason more than they feel, the Huron was not addicted to the indulgence of the more ferocious passions of his people: he had been commonly found on the side of mercy, in all the scenes of vindictive torture and revenge that had occurred in his tribe, since his own attainment to power. On the present occasion, he was reluctant to proceed to extremities, although the provocation was so great. Still it exceeded his ingenuity to see how that alternative could well be avoided. Sumach resented her rejection more than she did the deaths of her husband and brother, and there was little probability that the woman would pardon a man who had so unequivocally preferred death to her embraces. Without her forgiveness, there was scarce a hope that the tribe could be induced to overlook its loss, and even to Rivenoak, himself, much as he was disposed to pardon, the fate of our hero now appeared to be almost hopelessly sealed.

When the whole band was arrayed around the captive, a grave silence, so much the more threatening from its profound quiet, pervaded the place. Deerslayer perceived that the women and boys had been preparing splinters of the fat pine roots, which he well knew were to be stuck into his flesh, and set in flames, while two or three of the young men held the thongs of bark with which he was to be bound. The smoke of a distant fire announced that the burning brands were in preparation, and several of the elder warriors passed their fingers over the edges of their tomahawks, as if to prove their keenness and temper. Even the knives seemed loosened in their sheathes, impatient for the bloody and merciless work to begin.

"Killer of the Deer," recommenced Rivenoak, certainly without any signs of sympathy or pity in his manner, though with calmness and dignity, "Killer of the Deer, it is time that my people knew their minds. The sun is no longer over our heads; tired of waiting on the Hurons, he has begun to fall near the pines on this side of the valley. He is travelling fast towards the country of our French fathers; it is to warn his children that their lodges are empty, and that they ought to be at home. The roaming wolf has his den, and he goes to it, when he wishes to see his young. The Iroquois are not poorer than the wolves. They have villages, and wigwams, and fields of corn; the Good Spirits will be tired of watching them alone. My people must go back, and see to their own business. There will be joy in the lodges when they hear our whoop from the forest! It will be a sorrowful whoop; when it is understood, grief will come after it. There will be one scalp-whoop, but there will be only one. We have the fur of the Muskrat; his body is among the fishes. Deerslayer must say whether another scalp shall be on our pole. Two lodges are empty; a scalp, living or dead, is wanted at each door."

"Then take 'em dead, Huron," firmly, but altogether without dramatic boasting, returned the captive. "My hour is come, I do suppose, and what must be, must. If you are bent on the tortur', I'll do my indivours to bear up ag'in it, though no man can say how far his natur' will stand pain, until he's been tried."

"The pale face cur begins to put his tail between his legs!" cried a young and garrulous savage, who bore the appropriate title of the Corbeau Rouge; a *sobriquet* he had gained from the French, by his facility in making unseasonable noises, and an undue tendency to hear his own voice; "he is no warrior; he has killed the Loup Cervier when looking behind him not to see the flash of his own rifle. He grunts like a hog, already; when the Huron women begin to torment him, he will cry like the young of the catamount. He is a Delaware woman, dressed in the skin of a Yengeese!"

"Have your say, young man; have your say," returned Deerslayer, unmoved; "you know no better, and I can overlook it. Talking may aggravate women, but can hardly make knives sharper, fire hotter, or rifles more sartain."

Rivenoak now interposed, reproving the Red Crow for his premature interference, and then directing the proper persons to bind the captive. This expedient was adopted, not from any apprehensions that he would escape, or from any necessity, that was yet apparent, of his being unable to endure the torture with his limbs free, but from an ingenious design of making him feel his helplessness, and of gradually sapping his resolution, by undermining it, as it might be, little by little. Deerslayer offered no resistance. He submitted his arms and legs, freely if not cheerfully, to the ligaments of bark, which were bound around them, by order of the chief, in a way to produce as little pain as possible. These directions were secret, and given in the hope that the captive would finally save himself from any serious bodily suffering, by consenting to take the Sumach for a wife. As soon as the body of Deerslayer was withed in bark sufficiently to create a lively sense of helplessness, he was literally carried to a young tree, and bound against it, in a way that effectually prevented him from moving, as well as from falling. The hands were laid flat against the legs, and thongs were passed over all, in a way nearly to incorporate the prisoner with the tree. His cap was then removed, and he was left half-standing, half-sustained by his bonds, to face the coming scene, in the best manner he could.

Previously to proceeding to any thing like extremities, it was the wish of Rivenoak to put his captive's resolution to the proof, by renewing the attempt at a compromise. This could be effected only in one manner, the acquiescence of the Sumach being indispensably necessary to a compromise of her right to be revenged. With this view, then, the woman was next desired to advance, and to look to her own interests; no agent being considered as efficient as the principal, herself, in this negotiation. The Indian females, when girls, are usually mild, and submissive, with musical tones, pleasant voices, and merry laughs, but toil and suffering generally deprive them of most of these advantages, by the time they have reached an age which the Sumach had long before passed. To render their voices harsh, it would seem to require active, malignant, passions, though, when excited, their screams can rise to a sufficiently conspicuous degree of discordancy, to assert their claim to possess this distinctive peculiarity of the sex. The Sumach was not altogether without feminine attraction, however, and had so recently been deemed handsome in her tribe, as not to have yet learned the full influence that time and exposure produce on man, as well as on woman. By an arrangement of Rivenoak's, some of the women around her, had been employing the time in endeavoring to persuade the bereaved widow, that there was still a hope Deerslayer might be prevailed on to enter her wigwam, in preference to entering the world of spirits, and this, too, with a success that previous symptoms scarcely justified. All this was the result of a resolution on the part of the chief to leave no proper means unemployed, in order to get transferred to his own nation the greatest hunter that was then thought to exist in all that region, as well as a husband for a woman who he felt would be likely to be troublesome, were any of her claims to the attention and care of the tribe overlooked.

In conformity with this scheme, the Sumach had been secretly advised to advance into the circle, and to make her appeal to the prisoner's sense of justice, before the band had recourse to the last experiment. The woman, nothing loth, consented, for there was some such attraction in becoming the wife of a noted hunter, among the females of the tribes, as is experienced by the sex, in more refined life, when they bestow their hands on the affluent. As the duties of a mother were thought to be paramount to all other considerations, the widow felt none of that embarrassment, in preferring her claims, to which even a female fortune hunter among ourselves, might be liable. When she stood forth, before the whole party, therefore, the children that she led by the hands, fully justified all she did.

"You see me before you, cruel pale face," the woman commenced; "your spirit must tell you my errand. I have found *you*; I cannot find le Loup Cervier, nor the Panther; I have looked for them, in the lake, in the woods, in the clouds. I cannot say where they have gone."

"No man knows, good Sumach, no man knows," interposed the captive. "When the spirit leaves the body, it passes into a world beyond our knowledge, and the wisest way, for them that are left behind, is to hope for the best. No doubt both your warriors, have gone to the Happy Hunting Grounds, and at the proper time you will see 'em ag'in, in their improved state. The wife and sister of braves, must have looked forward to some such tarmination of their 'arthly careers."

"Cruel pale-face, what had my warriors done that you should slay them! They were the best hunters, and the boldest young men of their tribe; the Great Spirit intended that they should live until they withered like the branches of the hemlock, and fell of their own weight—"

"Nay—nay—good Sumach," interrupted Deerslayer, whose love of truth was too indomitable to listen to such hyperbole, with patience, even though it came from the torn breast of a widow—"Nay—nay, good Sumach, this is a little out-doing red skin privileges. Young man was neither, any more than you can be called a young woman, and as to the Great Spirit's intending that they should fall otherwise than they did, that's a grievous mistake, inasmuch as what the Great Spirit intends, is sartain to come to pass. Then, ag'in, it's plain enough neither of your fri'nds did me any harm; I raised my hand ag'in 'em on account of what they were *striving* to do, rather than what they did. This is nat'ral law, 'to do lest you should be done by.' "

"It is so. Sumach has but one tongue; she can tell but one story. The Pale face struck the Hurons lest the Hurons should strike him. The Hurons are a just nation; they will forget it. The chiefs will shut their eyes and pretend not to have seen it; the young men will believe the Panther and the Lynx have gone to far off hunts, and the Sumach, will take her children by the hand, and go into the lodge of the pale face and say—'See; these are *your* children; they are also mine—feed us, and we will live with you.' "

"The tarms are onadmissable, woman, and though I feel for your losses, which must be hard to bear, the tarms cannot be accepted. As to givin' you ven'son, in case we lived near enough together, that would be no great expl'ite; but as for becomin' your husband, and the father of your children, to be honest with you, I feel no callin' that-a-way."

"Look at this boy, cruel pale face; he has no father to teach him to kill the deer, or to take scalps. See this girl; what young man will come to look for a wife in a lodge that has no head? There are more among my people in the Canadas, and the Killer of Deer will find as many mouths to feed, as his heart can wish for."

"I tell you, woman," exclaimed Deerslayer, whose imagination was far from seconding the appeal of the widow, and who began to grow restive under the vivid pictures she was drawing, "all this is nothing to me. People and kindred must take care of their own fatherless, leaving them that have no children to their own loneliness. As for me, I have no offspring, and I want no wife. Now, go away Sumach; leave me in the hands of your chiefs, for my colour, and gifts, and natur' itself cry out ag'in the idee of taking you for a wife."

It is unnecessary to expatiate on the effect of this downright refusal of the woman's proposals. If there was any thing like tenderness in her bosom—and no woman was probably ever entirely without that feminine quality—it all disappeared at this plain announcement. Fury, rage, mortified pride, and a volcano of wrath burst out, at one explosion, converting her into a sort of maniac, as it might be at the touch of a magician's wand. Without deigning a reply in words, she made the arches of the forest ring with screams, and then flew forward at her victim, seizing him by the hair, which she appeared resolute to draw out by the roots. It was some time before her grasp could be loosened. Fortunately for the prisoner her rage was blind, since his total helplessness left him entirely at her mercy. Had it been better directed it might have proved fatal before any relief could have been offered. As it was, she did succeed in wrenching out two or three handsful of hair, before the young men could tear her away from her victim.

The insult that had been offered to the Sumach was deemed an insult to the whole tribe; not so much, however, on account of any respect that was felt for the woman, as on account of the honor of the Huron nation. Sumach, herself, was generally considered to be as acid as the berry from which she derived her name, and now that her great supporters, her husband and brother, were both gone, few cared about concealing their aversion. Nevertheless, it had become a point of honor to punish the pale face who disdained a Huron woman, and more particularly one who coolly preferred death to relieving the tribe from the support of a widow and her children. The young men showed an impatience to begin to torture, that Rivenoak understood, and, as his older associates manifested no disposition to permit any longer delay, he was compelled to give the signal, for the infernal work to proceed.

Chapter XXIX

"The ugly bear now minded not the stake,
Nor how the cruel mastiffs do him tear,
The stag lay still unroused from the brake,
The foamy boar feared not the hunter's spear:
All thing was still in desert, bush, and briar:"
Thomas Sackville, "The Complaint of
Henry Duke of Buckingham," lxxxi.

IT WAS one of the common expedients of the savages, on such occasions, to put the nerves of their victims to the severest proofs. On the other hand, it was a matter of Indian pride to betray no yielding to terror, or pain, but for the prisoner to provoke his enemies to such acts of violence as would soonest produce death. Many a warrior had been known to bring his own sufferings to a more speedy termination, by taunting reproaches and reviling language, when he found that his physical system was giving way under the agony of sufferings produced by a hellish ingenuity that might well eclipse all that has been said of the infernal devices of religious persecution. This happy expedient of taking refuge from the ferocity of his foes, in their passions, was denied Deerslayer however, by his peculiar notions of the duty of a white man, and he had stoutly made up his mind to endure every thing, in preference to disgracing his colour.

No sooner did the young men understand that they were at liberty to commence, than some of the boldest and most forward among them sprang into the arena, tomahawk in hand. Here they prepared to throw that dangerous weapon, the object being to strike the tree as near as possible to the victim's head, without absolutely hitting him. This was so hazardous an experiment, that none but those who were known to be exceedingly expert with the weapon, were allowed to enter the lists, at all, lest an early death might interfere with the expected entertainment. In the truest hands it was seldom that the captive escaped injury in these trials, and it often happened that death followed, even when the blow was not premeditated. In the particular case of our hero, Rivenoak and the older warriors were apprehensive that the example of the Panther's fate might prove a motive with some fiery spirit suddenly to sacrifice his conqueror, when the temptation of effecting it in precisely the same manner, and possibly with the identical weapon with which the warrior had fallen, offered. This circumstance of itself, rendered the ordeal of the tomahawk doubly critical for the Deerslayer.

It would seem, however, that all who now entered, what we shall call the lists, were more disposed to exhibit their own dexterity, than to resent the deaths of their comrades. Each prepared himself for the trial, with the feelings of rivalry, rather than with the desire for vengeance, and, for the first few minutes, the prisoner had little more connection with the result, than grew out of the interest that necessarily attached itself to a living target. The young men were eager, instead of being fierce, and Rivenoak thought he still saw signs of being able to save the life of the captive, when the vanity of the young men had been gratified; always admitting, that it was not sacrificed to the delicate experiments that were about to be made.

The first youth who presented himself, for the trial, was called The Raven, having as yet had no opportunity of obtaining a more warlike *sobriquet*. He was remarkable for high pretension, rather than for skill, or exploits, and those who knew his character thought the captive in imminent danger, when he took his stand, and poised the tomahawk. Nevertheless, the young man was good natured, and no thought was uppermost in his mind, other than the desire to make a better cast, than any of his fellows. Deerslayer got an inkling of this warrior's want of reputation, by the injunctions that he had received from the seniors, who, indeed, would have objected to his appearing in the arena, at all, but for an influence derived from his father; an aged warrior of great merit, who was then in the lodges of the tribe. Still, our hero maintained an appearance of self-possession. He had made up his mind that his hour was come, and it would have been a mercy, instead of a calamity, to fall by the unsteadiness of the first hand that was raised against him. After a suitable number of flourishes, and gesticulations that promised much more than he could perform, the Raven let the tomahawk quit his hand. The weapon whirled through the air, with the usual evolutions, cut a chip from the sapling to which the prisoner was bound, within a few inches of his cheek, and stuck in a large oak that grew several yards behind him. This was decidedly a bad effort, and a common sneer proclaimed as much, to the great mortification of the young man. On the other hand, there was a general but suppressed murmur of admiration, at the steadiness with which the captive stood the trial. The head was the only part he could move, and this had been purposely left free, that the tormentors might have the amusement, and the tormented endure the shame, of his dodging, and otherwise attempting to avoid the blows. Deerslayer disappointed these hopes, by a command of nerve that rendered his whole body as immovable as the tree to which he was bound. Nor did he even adopt the natural and usual expedient of shutting his eyes, the firmest and oldest warrior of the red-men never having more disdainfully denied himself this advantage, under similar circumstances.

The Raven had no sooner made his unsuccessful and puerile effort, than he was succeeded by le Daim-Mose, or the Moose; a middle aged warrior, who was particularly skilful in the use of the tomahawk, and from whose attempt the spectators confidently looked for gratification. This man had none of the good nature of the Raven, but he would gladly have sacrificed the captive to his hatred of the pale faces generally, were it not for the greater interest he felt in his own success as one particularly skilled in the use of this weapon. He took his stand quietly, but with an air of confidence, poised his little axe but a single instant, advanced a foot with a quick motion, and threw. Deerslayer saw the keen instrument whirling towards him, and believed all was over; still, he was not touched. The tomahawk had actually bound the head of the captive to the tree, by carrying before it some of his hair, having buried itself deep beneath the soft bark. A general yell expressed the delight of the spectators, and the Moose felt his heart soften a little towards the prisoner, whose steadiness of nerve alone, enabled him to give this evidence of his consummate skill.

Le Daim-Mose was succeeded by the Bounding Boy, or *le Garçon qui Bondi* who came leaping into the circle, like a hound, or a goat, at play. This was one of those elastic youths, whose muscles seemed always in motion, and who either affected, or who from habit was actually unable, to move in any other manner, than by showing the antics just mentioned. Nevertheless, he was both brave and skilful, and had gained the respect of his people, by deeds in war, as well as success in the hunts. A far nobler name would long since have fallen to his share, had not a French-man of rank inadvertently given him this *sobriquet*, which he religiously preserved as coming from his Great Father, who lived beyond the Wide Salt Lake. The Bounding Boy skipped about in front of the captive, menacing him with his tomahawk, now on one side and now on another, and then again in front, in the vain hope of being able to extort some sign of fear by this parade of danger. At length Deerslayer's patience became exhausted by all this mummery, and he spoke for the first time, since the trial had actually commenced.

"Throw away, Huron," he cried, "or your tomahawk will forget its ar'n'd. Why do you keep loping about like a fa'a'n that's showing its dam how well it can skip, when you're a warrior grown, yourself, and a warrior grown defies you and all your silly antiks. Throw, or the Huron gals will laugh in your face."

Although not intended to produce such an effect, the last words aroused the "Bounding" warrior to fury. The same nervous excitability which rendered him so active in his person, made it difficult to repress his feelings, and the words were scarcely past the lips of the speaker, than the tomahawk left the hand of the Indian. Nor was it cast without ill-will, and a fierce determination to slay. Had the intention been less deadly, the danger might have been greater. The aim was uncertain, and the weapon glanced near the cheek of the captive, slightly cutting the shoulder in its evolutions. This was the first instance in which any other object, than that of terrifying the prisoner, and of displaying skill had been manifested, and the Bounding Boy was immediately led from the arena, and was warmly rebuked for his intemperate haste, which had come so near defeating all the hopes of the band.

To this irritable person succeeded several other young warriors, who not only hurled the tomahawk, but who cast the knife, a far more dangerous experiment, with reckless indifference; yet they always manifested a skill that prevented any injury to the captive. Several times Deerslayer was grazed, but in no instance did he receive what might be termed a wound. The unflinching firmness with which he faced his assailants, more especially in the sort of rally with which this trial terminated, excited a profound respect in the spectators, and when the chiefs announced that the prisoner had well withstood the trials of the knife and the tomahawk, there was not a single individual in the band who really felt any hostility towards him, with the exception of Sumach and the Bounding Boy. These two discontented spirits got together, it is true, feeding each other's ire, but, as yet, their malignant feelings were confined very much to themselves, though there existed the danger that the others, ere long, could not fail to be excited by their own efforts, into that demoniacal state which usually accompanied all similar scenes among the red men.

Rivenoak now told his people that the pale face had proved himself to be a man. He might live with the Delawares, but he had not been made woman, with that tribe. He wished to know whether it was the desire of the Hurons to proceed any further. Even the gentlest of the females, however, had received too much satisfaction in the late trials, to forego their expectations of a gratifying exhibition, and there was but one voice, in the request to proceed. The politic chief, who had some such desire to receive so celebrated a hunter into his tribe, as a European Minister has to devise a new and available means of taxation, sought every plausible means of arresting the trial in season, for, he well knew, if permitted to go far enough to arouse the more ferocious passions of the tormentors, it would be as easy to dam the waters of the great lakes of his own region, as to attempt to arrest them in their bloody career. He therefore called four or five of the best marksmen to him, and bid them put the captive to the proof of the rifle, while, at the same time he cautioned them touching the necessity of their maintaining their own credit, by the closest attention to the manner of exhibiting their skill.

When Deerslayer saw the chosen warriors step into the circle, with their arms prepared for service, he felt some such relief, as the miserable sufferer, who has long endured the agonies of disease, feels at the certain approach of death. Any trifling variance in the aim of this formidable weapon, would prove fatal; since, the head being the target, or rather the point it was desired to graze without injuring, an inch or two of difference in the line of projection, must at once determine the question of life or death.

In the torture by the rifle there was none of the latitude permitted that appeared in the case of even Gessler's apple, a hair's breadth being, in fact, the utmost limits that an expert marksman would allow himself on an occasion like this. Victims were frequently shot through the head by too eager, or unskilful hands, and it often occurred that, exasperated by the fortitude and taunts of the prisoner, death was dealt intentionally, in a moment of ungovernable irritation. All this Deerslayer well knew, for it was in relating the traditions of such scenes, as well as of the battles and victories of their people, that the old men beguiled the long winter evenings, in their cabins. He now fully expected the end of his career, and experienced a sort of melancholy pleasure in the idea that he was to fall by a weapon as much beloved as the rifle. A slight interruption, however, took place before the business was allowed to proceed.

Hetty Hutter witnessed all that passed, and the scene at first had pressed upon her feeble mind in a way to paralyze it entirely; but, by this time, she had rallied, and was growing indignant at the unmerited suffering the Indians were inflicting on her friend. Though timid, and shy as the young of the deer, on so many occasions, this right-feeling girl was always intrepid in the cause of humanity; the lessons of her mother, and the impulses of her own heart,—perhaps we might say the promptings of that unseen and pure spirit that seemed ever to watch over and direct her actions—uniting to keep down the apprehensions of woman, and to impel her to be bold and resolute. She now appeared in the circle, gentle, feminine, even bashful in mien, as usual, but earnest in her words and countenance, speaking like one who knew herself to be sustained by the high authority of God.

"Why do you torment Deerslayer, red-men?" she asked—"What has he done that you trifle with his life; who has given you the right to be his judges? Suppose one of your knives, or tomahawks had hit him; what Indian among you all could cure the wound you would make. Besides, in harming Deerslayer, you injure your own friend; when father and Hurry Harry came after your scalps, he refused to be of the party, and staid in the canoe by himself. You are tormenting a good friend, in tormenting this young man!"

The Hurons listened with grave attention, and one among them, who understood English, translated what had been said into their native tongue. As soon as Rivenoak was made acquainted with the purport of her address he answered it in his own dialect; the interpreter conveying it to the girl in English.

"My daughter is very welcome to speak," said the stern old orator, using gentle intonations and smiling as kindly as if addressing a child—"The Hurons are glad to hear her voice; they listen to what she says. The Great Spirit often speaks to men with such tongues. This time, her eyes have not been open wide enough, to see all that has happened. Deerslayer did not come for our scalps; that is true; why did he not come? Here they are; on our heads; the war-locks are ready to be taken hold of; a bold enemy ought to stretch out his hand to seize them. The Iroquois are too great a nation to punish men that take scalps. What they do themselves, they like to see others do. Let my daughter look around her and count my warriors. Had I as many hands as four warriors, their fingers would be fewer than my people, when they came into your hunting grounds. Now, a whole hand is missing. Where are the fingers? Two have been cut off by this pale face; my Hurons wish to see if he did this by means of a stout heart, or by treachery. Like a skulking fox, or like a leaping panther."

"You know yourself, Huron, how one of them fell. I saw it, and you all saw it, too. 'Twas too bloody to look at; but it was not Deerslayer's fault. Your warrior sought his life, and he defended himself. I do n't know whether this good book says that it was right, but all men will do that. Come, if you want to know which of you, can shoot best, give Deerslayer a rifle, and then you will find how much more expert he is, than any of your warriors; yes, than *all* of them together!"

Could one have looked upon such a scene with indifference, he would have been amused at the gravity with which the savages listened to the translation of this unusual request. No taunt, no smile mingled with their surprise, for Hetty had a character and a manner too saintly to subject her infirmity to the mockings of the rude and ferocious. On the contrary, she was answered with respectful attention.

"My daughter does not always talk, like a chief at a Council Fire," returned Rivenoak, "or she would not have said this. Two of my warriors have fallen by the blows of our prisoner; their grave is too small to hold a third. The Hurons do not like to crowd their dead. If there is another spirit about to set out for the far off world, it must not be the spirit of a Huron; it must be the spirit of a pale face. Go, daughter, and sit by Sumach, who is in grief; let the Huron warriors show how well they can shoot; let the pale face show how little he cares for their bullets."

Hetty's mind was unequal to a sustained discussion, and accustomed to defer to the directions of her seniors she did as told, seating herself passively on a log, by the side of the Sumach, and averting her face from the painful scene that was occurring within the circle.

The warriors, as soon as this interruption had ceased, resumed their places, and again prepared to exhibit their skill. As there was a double object in view, that of putting the constancy of the captive to the proof, and that of showing how steady were the hands of the marksmen, under circumstances of excitement, the distance was small, and, in one sense, safe. But in diminishing the distance taken by the tormentors, the trial to the nerves of the captive was essentially increased. The face of Deerslayer, indeed, was just removed sufficiently from the ends of the guns to escape the effects of the flash, and his steady eye was enabled to look directly into their muzzles, as it might be, in anticipation of the fatal messenger that was to issue from each. The cunning Hurons well knew this fact, and scarce one levelled his piece without first causing it to point as near as possible at the forehead of the prisoner, in the hope that his fortitude would fail him, and that the band would enjoy the triumph of seeing a victim quail under their ingenious cruelty. Nevertheless each of the competitors was still careful not to injure, the disgrace of striking prematurely, being second only to that of failing altogether in attaining the object. Shot after shot was made; all the bullets coming in close proximity to the Deerslayer's head, without touching it. Still no one could detect even the twitching of a muscle on the part of the captive, or the slightest winking of an eye. This indomitable resolution, which so much exceeded every thing of its kind that any present had before witnessed, might be referred to three distinct causes. The first was resignation to his fate, blended with natural steadiness of deportment; for our hero had calmly made up his mind that he must die, and preferred this mode to any other; the second was his great familiarity with this particular weapon, which deprived it of all the terror that is usually connected with the mere form of the danger; and the third was this familiarity carried out in practice, to a degree so nice as to enable the intended victim to tell, within an inch, the precise spot where each bullet must strike, for he calculated its range by looking in at the bore of the piece. So exact was Deerslayer's estimation of the line of fire, that his pride of feeling finally got the better of his resignation, and when five or six had discharged their bullets into the tree, he could not refrain from expressing his contempt at their want of hand and eye.

"You may call this shooting, Mingos!" he exclaimed, "but we've squaws among the Delawares, and I have known Dutch gals on the Mohawk, that could outdo your greatest indivours. Ondo these arms of mine, put a rifle into my hands, and I'll pin the thinnest warlock in your party, to any tree you can show me, and this at a hundred yards—ay, or at two hundred if the objects can be seen, nineteen shots in twenty; or, for that matter twenty in twenty, if the piece is creditable and trusty!"

A low menacing murmur followed this cool taunt. The ire of the warriors kindled at listening to such a reproach from one, who so far disdained their efforts as to refuse even to wink, when a rifle was discharged as near his face as could be done without burning it. Rivenoak perceived that the moment was critical, and, still retaining his hope of adopting so noted a hunter into his tribe, the politic old chief interposed in time, probably to prevent an immediate resort to that portion of the torture, which must necessarily have produced death through extreme bodily suffering, if in no other manner. Moving into the centre of the irritated groupe, he addressed them with his usual wily logic, and plausible manner, at once suppressing the fierce movement that had commenced.

"I see how it is," he said. "We have been like the pale faces when they fasten their doors at night, out of fear of the red men. They use so many bars that the fire comes and burns them, before they can get out. We have bound the Deerslayer too tight: the thongs keep his limbs from shaking and his eyes from shutting. Loosen him; let us see what his own body is really made of."

It is often the case when we are thwarted in a cherished scheme, that any expedient, however unlikely to succeed, is gladly resorted to in preference to a total abandonment of the project. So it was with the Hurons. The proposal of the chief found instant favor, and several hands were immediately at work, cutting and tearing the ropes of bark from the body of our hero. In half a minute Deerslayer stood as free from bonds, as when, an hour before he had commenced his flight on the side of the mountain. Some little time was necessary that he should recover the use of his limbs, the circulation of the blood having been checked by the tightness of the ligatures, and this was accorded to him by the politic Rivenoak, under the pretence that his body would be more likely to submit to apprehension, if its true tone were restored; though really with a view to give time to the fierce passions which had been awakened in the bosoms of his young men, to subside. This *ruse* succeeded, and Deerslayer by rubbing his limbs, stamping his feet, and moving about, soon regained the circulation, recovering all his physical powers, as effectually as if nothing had occurred to disturb them.

It is seldom men think of death in the pride of their health and strength. So it was with Deerslayer. Having been helplessly bound and, as he had every reason to suppose, so lately on the very verge of the other world, to find himself so unexpectedly liberated, in possession of his strength and with a full command of limb, acted on him like a sudden restoration to life, reanimating hopes that he had once absolutely abandoned. From that instant all his plans changed. In this, he simply obeyed a law of nature; for while we have wished to represent our hero as being resigned to his fate, it has been far from our intention to represent him as anxious to die. From the instant that his buoyancy of feeling revived, his thoughts were keenly bent on the various projects that presented themselves as modes of evading the designs of his enemies, and he again became, the quick witted, ingenious and determined woodsman, alive to all his own powers and resources. The change was so great, that his mind resumed its elasticity, and no longer thinking of submission, it dwelt only on the devices of the sort of warfare in which he was engaged.

As soon as Deerslayer was released, the band divided itself in a circle around him, in order to hedge him in, and the desire to break down his spirit grew in them, precisely as they saw proofs of the difficulty there would be in subduing it. The honor of the band was now involved in the issue, and even the sex lost all its sympathy with suffering, in the desire to save the reputation of the tribe. The voices of the girls, soft and melodious as nature had made them, were heard mingling with the menaces of the men, and the wrongs of Sumach suddenly assumed the character of injuries inflicted on every Huron female. Yielding to this rising tumult, the men drew back a little, signifying to the females, that they left the captive, for a time, in their hands, it being a common practice on such occasions, for the women to endeavor to throw the victim into a rage, by their taunts and revilings, and then to turn him suddenly over to the men, in a state of mind that was little favorable to resisting the agony of bodily suffering. Nor was this party without the proper instruments for effecting such a purpose. Sumach had a notoriety as a scold, and one or two crones, like the She Bear, had come out with the party, most probably as the conservators of its decency and moral discipline; such things occurring in savage as well as in civilized life. It is unnecessary to repeat all that ferocity and ignorance could invent for such a purpose, the only difference between this outbreaking of feminine anger, and a similar scene among ourselves, consisting in the figures of speech and the epithets, the Huron women calling their prisoner by the names of the lower and least respected animals that were known to themselves.

But Deerslayer's mind was too much occupied, to permit him to be disturbed by the abuse of excited hags, and their rage necessarily increasing with his indifference, as his indifference increased with their rage, the furies soon rendered themselves impotent by their own excesses. Perceiving that the attempt was a complete failure, the warriors interfered to put a stop to this scene, and this so much the more, because preparations were now seriously making for the commencement of the real tortures, or that which would put the fortitude of the sufferer to the test of severe bodily pain. A sudden and unlooked for announcement, that proceeded from one of the look-outs, a boy ten or twelve years old, however, put a momentary check to the whole proceedings. As this interruption has a close connection with the *dénouement* of our story, it shall be given in a separate chapter.

Chapter XXX

"So deem'st thou—so each mortal deems
Of that which is from that which seems;
But other harvest here
Than that which peasant's scythe demands,
Was gather'd in by sterner hands,
With bayonet, blade, and spear."
Scott, "The Field of Waterloo," V.1–6.

IT EXCEEDED Deerslayer's power to ascertain what had produced the sudden pause in the movements of his enemies, until the fact was revealed in the due course of events. He perceived that much agitation prevailed among the women in particular, while the warriors rested on their arms, in a sort of dignified expectation. It was plain no alarm was excited, though it was not equally apparent that a friendly occurrence produced the delay. Rivenoak was evidently apprised of all, and by a gesture of his arm he appeared to direct the circle to remain unbroken, and for each person to await the issue in the situation he, or she, then occupied. It required but a minute or two, to bring an explanation of this singular and mysterious pause, which was soon terminated by the appearance of Judith on the exterior of the line of bodies, and her ready admission within its circle.

If Deerslayer was startled by this unexpected arrival, well knowing that the quick witted girl could claim none of that exemption from the penalties of captivity, that was so cheerfully accorded to her feebler minded sister, he was equally astonished at the guise in which she came. All her ordinary forest attire, neat and becoming as this usually was, had been laid aside for the brocade that has been already mentioned, and which had once before wrought so great and magical an effect in her appearance. Nor was this all. Accustomed to see the ladies of the garrison, in the formal, gala attire of the day, and familiar with the more critical niceties of these matters, the girl had managed to complete her dress, in a way to leave nothing strikingly defective in its details, or even to betray an incongruity that would have been detected by one practised in the mysteries of the toilet. Head, feet, arms, hands, bust, and drapery, were all in harmony, as female attire was then deemed attractive and harmonious, and the end she aimed at, that of imposing on the uninstructed senses of the savages, by causing them to believe their guest was a woman of rank and importance, might well have succeeded with those whose habits had taught them to discriminate between persons. Judith, in addition to her rare native beauty, had a singular grace of person, and her mother had imparted enough of her own deportment, to prevent any striking or offensive vulgarity of manner; so that, sooth to say, the gorgeous dress might have been worse bestowed in nearly every particular. Had it been displayed in a capital, a thousand might have worn it, before one could have been found to do more credit to its gay colours, glossy satins, and rich laces, than the beautiful creature whose person it now aided to adorn.

The effect of such an apparition had not been miscalculated. The instant Judith found herself within the circle, she was, in a degree, compensated for the fearful personal risk she ran, by the unequivocal sensation of surprise and admiration produced by her appearance. The grim old warriors uttered their favorite exclamation "hugh!" The younger men were still more sensibly overcome, and even the women were not backward in letting open manifestations of pleasure escape them. It was seldom that these untutored children of the forest had ever seen any white female above the commonest sort, and, as to dress, never before had so much splendor shone before their eyes. The gayest uniforms of both French and English seemed dull compared with the lustre of the brocade, and while the rare personal beauty of the wearer added to the effect produced by its hues, the attire did not fail to adorn that beauty in a way which surpassed even the hopes of its wearer. Deerslayer himself was astounded, and this quite as much by the brilliant picture the girl presented, as at the indifference to consequences with which she had braved the danger of the step she had taken. Under such circumstances, all waited for the visiter to explain her object, which to most of the spectators seemed as inexplicable as her appearance.

"Which of these warriors is the principal chief?" demanded Judith of Deerslayer, as soon as she found it was expected that she should open the communications; "my errand is too important to be delivered to any of inferior rank. First explain to the Hurons, what I say; then give an answer to the question I have put."

Deerslayer quietly complied, his auditors greedily listening to the interpretation of the first words that fell from so extraordinary a vision. The demand seemed perfectly in character for one who had every appearance of an exalted rank, herself. Rivenoak gave an appropriate reply, by presenting himself before his fair visiter in a way to leave no doubt that he was entitled to all the consideration he claimed.

"I can believe this, Huron," resumed Judith, enacting her assumed part, with a steadiness and dignity that did credit to her powers of imitation, for she strove to impart to her manner the condescending courtesy she had once observed in the wife of a general officer, at a similar though a more amicable scene: "I can believe you to be the principal person of this party; I see in your countenance the marks of thought and reflection. To you, then, I must make my communication."

"Let the Flower of the Woods speak," returned the old chief courteously, as soon as her address had been translated so that all might understand it—"If her words are as pleasant as her looks, they will never quit my ears; I shall hear them long after the winter of Canada has killed all the flowers, and frozen all the speeches of summer."

This admiration was grateful to one constituted like Judith, and contributed to aid her self-possession, quite as much as it fed her vanity. Smiling involuntarily, or in spite of her wish to seem reserved, she proceeded in her plot.

"Now, Huron," she continued, "listen to my words. Your eyes tell you that I am no common woman. I will not say I am queen of this country; *she* is afar off, in a distant land; but under our gracious monarchs, there are many degrees of rank; one of these I fill. What that rank is precisely, it is unnecessary for me to say, since you would not understand it. For that information you must trust your eyes. You *see* what I am; you must *feel* that in listening to my words, you listen to one who can be your friend, or your enemy, as you treat her."

This was well uttered, with a due attention to manner, and a steadiness of tone, that was really surprising, considering all the circumstances of the case. It was well, though simply rendered into the Indian dialect too, and it was received with a respect and gravity that augured favourably for the girl's success. But Indian thought is not easily traced to its sources. Judith waited with anxiety to hear the answer, filled with hope even while she doubted. Rivenoak was a ready speaker, and he answered as promptly as comported with the notions of Indian decorum; that peculiar people seeming to think a short delay respectful, inasmuch as it manifests that the words already heard, have been duly weighed.

"My daughter is handsomer than the wild roses of Ontario; her voice is pleasant to the ear as the song of the wren," answered the cautious and wily chief, who of all the band, stood alone in not being fully imposed on by the magnificent and unusual appearance of Judith; but who distrusted even while he wondered: "the humming bird is not much larger than the bee; yet its feathers are as gay as the tail of the peacock. The Great Spirit sometimes puts very bright clothes on very little animals. Still He covers the Moose with coarse hair. These things are beyond the understanding of poor Indians, who can only comprehend what they see and hear. No doubt my daughter has a very large wigwam, somewhere about the lake; the Hurons have not found it, on account of their ignorance?"

"I have told you, chief, that it would be useless to state my rank and residence, in as much as you would not comprehend them. You must trust to your eyes for this knowledge; what red man is there who cannot see? This blanket that I wear, is not the blanket of a common squaw; these ornaments are such as the wives and daughters of chiefs only appear in. Now, listen and hear why I have come alone, among your people, and hearken to the errand that has brought me here. The Yengeese have young men, as well as the Hurons; and plenty of them, too; this you well know."

"The Yengeese are as plenty as the leaves on the trees! This every Huron knows, and feels."

"I understand you, chief. Had I brought a party with me, it might have caused trouble. My young men and your young men, would have looked angrily at each other; especially had my young men seen that pale face bound for the torture. He is a great hunter, and is much loved by all the garrisons, far and near. There would have been blows about him, and the trail of the Iroquois back to the Canadas would have been marked with blood."

"There is so much blood on it, now," returned the chief, gloomily, "that it blinds our eyes. My young men see that it is all Huron."

"No doubt; and more Huron blood would be spilt had I come surrounded with pale faces. I have heard of Rivenoak, and have thought it would be better to send him back in peace to his village, that he might leave his women and children behind him; if he then wished to come for our scalps, we would meet him. He loves animals made of ivory, and little rifles. See; I have brought some with me to show him. I am his friend. When he has packed up these things among his goods, he will start for his village, before any of my young men can overtake him, and then he will show his people in Canada what riches they can come to seek, now that our great fathers, across the Salt Lake, have sent each other the war hatchet. I will lead back with me, this great hunter, of whom I have need to keep my house in venison."

Judith, who was sufficiently familiar with Indian phraseology, endeavored to express her ideas in the sententious manner common to those people, and she succeeded even beyond her own expectations. Deerslayer did her full justice in the translation, and this so much the more readily, since the girl carefully abstained from uttering any direct untruth; a homage she paid to the young man's known aversion to falsehood, which he deemed a meanness altogether unworthy of a white man's gifts. The offering of the two remaining elephants, and of the pistols already mentioned, one of which was all the worse for the recent accident, produced a lively sensation among the Hurons, generally, though Rivenoak received it coldly, notwithstanding the delight with which he had first discovered the probable existence of a creature with two tails. In a word, this cool and sagacious savage was not so easily imposed on, as his followers, and with a sentiment of honor, that half the civilized world would have deemed supererogatory, he declined the acceptance of a bribe that he felt no disposition to earn by a compliance with the donor's wishes.

"Let my daughter keep her two-tailed hog, to eat, when venison is scarce," he drily answered, "and the little gun, which has two muzzles. The Hurons will kill deer when they are hungry, and they have long rifles to fight with. This hunter cannot quit my young men now; they wish to know if he is as stout hearted, as he boasts himself to be."

"That I deny, Huron—" interrupted Deerslayer, with warmth—"Yes, that I down right deny, as ag'in truth and reason. No man has heard me *boast*, and no man shall, though ye flay me alive, and then roast the quivering flesh, with your own infarnal devices and cruelties! I may be humble, and misfortunate, and your prisoner; but I'm no boaster, by my very gifts."

"My young pale-face *boasts* he is *no* boaster," returned the crafty chief: "he *must* be right. I hear a strange bird singing. It has very rich feathers. No Huron ever before saw such feathers! They will be ashamed to go back to their village, and tell their people that they let their prisoner go on account of the song of this strange bird and not be able to give the *name* of the bird. They do not know how to say whether it is a wren, or a cat bird. This would be a great disgrace; my young men would not be allowed to travel in the woods, without taking their mothers with them, to tell them the names of the birds!"

"You can ask my name of your prisoner," returned the girl. "It is Judith; and there is a great deal of the history of Judith in the Pale face's best book, the bible. If I am a bird of fine feathers, I have also my name."

"No," answered the wily Huron, betraying the artifice he had so long practised, by speaking in English, with tolerable accuracy, "I not ask prisoner. He tired; he want rest. I ask my daughter, with feeble mind. She speak truth. Come here, daughter; you answer. *Your* name, Hetty?"

"Yes, that's what they call me," returned the girl, "though it's written Esther in the bible."

"He write *him* in bible, too! All write in bible. No matter—what *her* name?"

"That's Judith, and it's so written in the bible, though father sometimes called her Jude. That's my sister Judith, Thomas Hutter's daughter—Thomas Hutter, whom you called the Muskrat; though he was *no* muskrat, but a man like yourselves—he lived in a house on the water, and that was enough for *you*!"

A smile of triumph gleamed on the hard wrinkled countenance of the chief, when he found how completely his appeal to the truth-loving Hetty had succeeded. As for Judith, herself, the moment her sister was questioned, she saw that all was lost; for no sign, or even intreaty could have induced the right feeling girl to utter a falsehood. To attempt to impose a daughter of the Muskrat on the savages, as a princess, or a great lady, she knew would be idle, and she saw her bold and ingenious expedient for liberating the captive fail, through one of the simplest and most natural causes that could be imagined. She turned her eye on Deerslayer, therefore, as if imploring him to interfere, to save them both.

"It will not do, Judith," said the young man, in answer to this appeal, which he understood, though he saw its uselessness; "it will not do. Twas a bold idee, and fit for a general's lady, but yonder Mingo—" Rivenoak had withdrawn to a little distance, and was out of ear-shot—"but yonder Mingo, is an oncommon man, and not to be deceived by any unnat'ral sarcumvention. Things must come afore him, in their right order, to draw a cloud afore *his* eyes! Twas too much to attempt making him fancy that a queen, or a great lady, lived in these mountains, and no doubt he thinks the fine clothes you wear, is some of the plunder of your own father—or, at least, of him who once passed for your father; as quite likely it was, if all they say is true."

"At all events, Deerslayer, my presence here, will save you for a time. They will hardly attempt torturing you before my face!"

"Why not, Judith? Do you think they will treat a woman of the pale faces, more tenderly than they treat their own? It's true that your sex will most likely save you from the torments, but it will not save your liberty, and may not save your scalp. I wish you had n't come, my good Judith; it can do no good to me, while it may do great harm to yourself."

"I can share your fate," the girl answered with generous enthusiasm. "They shall not injure you, while I stand by, if in my power to prevent it—besides—"

"Besides, what, Judith? What means have you to stop Injin cruelties, or to avart Injin deviltries?"

"None, perhaps, Deerslayer," answered the girl, with firmness, "but I can suffer with my friends—die with them if necessary."

"Ah! Judith—suffer you may; but die you will not, until the Lord's time shall come. It's little likely that one of your sex and beauty will meet with a harder fate than to become the wife of a chief, if, indeed your white inclinations can stoop to match with an Injin. 'Twould have been better had you staid in the Ark, or the castle, but what has been done, is done. You was about to say something, when you stopped at 'besides'?"

"It might not be safe to mention it here, Deerslayer," the girl hurriedly answered, moving past him carelessly, that she might speak in a lower tone; "half an hour, is all in all to us. None of your friends are idle."

The hunter replied merely by a grateful look. Then he turned towards his enemies, as if ready again to face their torments. A short consultation had passed among the elders of the band, and by this time they also were prepared with their decision. The merciful purpose of Rivenoak had been much weakened by the artifice of Judith, which, failing of its real object, was likely to produce results the very opposite of those she had anticipated. This was natural; the feeling being aided by the resentment of an Indian, who found how near he had been to becoming the dupe of an inexperienced girl. By this time, Judith's real character was fully understood, the wide spread reputation of her beauty contributing to the exposure. As for the unusual attire, it was confounded with the profound mystery of the animals with two tails, and, for the moment lost its influence.

When Rivenoak, therefore, faced the captive again, it was with an altered countenance. He had abandoned the wish of saving him, and was no longer disposed to retard the more serious part of the torture. This change of sentiment was, in effect, communicated to the young men, who were already eagerly engaged in making their preparations for the contemplated scene. Fragments of dried wood were rapidly collected, near the sapling, the splinters which it was intended to thrust into the flesh of the victim, previously to lighting, were all collected, and the thongs were already produced that were again to bind him to the tree. All this was done in profound silence, Judith watching every movement with breathless expectation, while Deerslayer himself, stood seemingly as unmoved, as one of the pines of the hills. When the warriors advanced to bind him, however, the young man glanced at Judith, as if to enquire whether resistance or submission were most advisable. By a significant gesture she counselled the last, and, in a minute, he was once more fastened to the tree, a helpless object of any insult, or wrong, that might be offered. So eagerly did every one now act, that nothing was said. The fire was immediately lighted in the pile, and the end of all was anxiously expected.

It was not the intention of the Hurons absolutely to destroy the life of their victim by means of fire. They designed merely to put his physical fortitude to the severest proofs it could endure, short of that extremity. In the end, they fully intended to carry his scalp with them into their village, but it was their wish first to break down his resolution, and to reduce him to the level of a complaining sufferer. With this view, the pile of brush and branches had been placed at a proper distance, or, one at which it was thought the heat would soon become intolerable, though it might not be immediately dangerous. As often happened, however, on these occasions, this distance had been miscalculated, and the flames began to wave their forked tongues in a proximity to the face of the victim, that would have proved fatal, in another instant, had not Hetty rushed through the crowd, armed with a stick, and scattered the blazing pile, in a dozen directions. More than one hand was raised to strike this presumptuous intruder to the earth, but the chiefs prevented the blows, by reminding their irritated followers of the state of her mind. Hetty, herself, was insensible to the risk she ran, but, as soon as she had performed this bold act, she stood looking about her, in frowning resentment, as if to rebuke the crowd of attentive savages, for their cruelty.

"God bless you, dearest sister, for that brave and ready act!" murmured Judith, herself unnerved so much as to be incapable of exertion—"Heaven, itself, has sent you on its holy errand."

"Twas well meant, Judith—" rejoined the victim—"twas excellently meant, and 'twas timely; though it may prove ontimely in the ind! What is to come to pass, must come to pass soon, or 'twill quickly be too late. Had I drawn in one mouthful of that flame in breathing, the power of man could not save my life, and you see that, this time, they've so bound my forehead, as not to leave my head the smallest chance. Twas well meant, but it might have been more marciful to let the flames act their part."

"Cruel, heartless Hurons!" exclaimed the still indignant Hetty—"Would you burn a man and a christian, as you would burn a log of wood! Do you never read your bibles?—Or do you think God will forget such things?"

A gesture from Rivenoak caused the scattered brands to be collected. Fresh wood was brought, even the women and children busying themselves eagerly, in the gathering of dried sticks. The flame was just kindling a second time, when an *Indian* female pushed through the circle, advanced to the heap, and with her foot dashed aside the lighted twigs, in time to prevent the conflagration. A yell followed this second disappointment, but when the offender turned, towards the circle, and presented the countenance of Hist, it was succeeded by a common exclamation of pleasure and surprise. For a minute, all thought of pursuing the business in hand was forgotten. Young and old crowded around the girl, in haste to demand an explanation of her sudden and unlooked-for return. It was at this critical instant that Hist spoke to Judith in a low voice, placed some small object unseen in her hand, and then turned to meet the salutations of the Huron girls, with whom she was personally a great favorite. Judith recovered her self-possession, and acted promptly. The small, keen edged knife, that Hist had given to the other, was passed by the latter into the hands of Hetty, as the safest and least suspected medium of transferring it to Deerslayer. But the feeble intellect of the last, defeated the well-grounded hopes of all three. Instead of first cutting loose the hands of the victim, and then concealing the knife in his clothes, in readiness for action, at the most available instant, she went to work herself, with earnestness and simplicity, to cut the thongs that bound his head, that he might not again be in danger of inhaling flames. Of course this deliberate procedure was seen, and the hands of Hetty were arrested, ere she had more than liberated the upper portion of the captive's body, not including his arms, below the elbows. This discovery at once pointed distrust towards Hist, and to Judith's surprise, when questioned on the subject, that spirited girl was not disposed to deny her agency in what had passed.

"Why should I not help the Deerslayer?" the girl demanded, in the tones of a firm minded woman. "He is the brother of a Delaware chief; my heart is all Delaware. Come forth, miserable Briarthorn, and wash the Iroquois paint from your face; stand before the Hurons, the crow that you are. You would eat the carrion of your own dead, rather than starve. Put him face to face with Deerslayer, chiefs and warriors; I will show you how great a knave you have been keeping in your tribe."

This bold language, uttered in their own dialect, and with a manner full of confidence, produced a deep sensation among the Hurons. Treachery is always liable to distrust, and though the recreant Briarthorn had endeavoured to serve the enemy well, his exertions and assiduities had gained for him little more than toleration. His wish to obtain Hist for a wife, had first induced him to betray her, and his own people, but serious rivals to his first project had risen up among his new friends, weakening still more their sympathies with treason. In a word, Briarthorn had been barely permitted to remain in the Huron encampment, where he was as closely and as jealously watched as Hist, herself, seldom appearing before the chiefs, and sedulously keeping out of view of Deerslayer, who, until this moment, was ignorant even of his presence. Thus summoned, however, it was impossible to remain in the back ground. "Wash the Iroquois paint from his face," he did not, for when he stood in the centre of the circle, he was so disguised in these new colours, that at first, the hunter did not recognise him. He assumed an air of defiance, notwithstanding, and haughtily demanded what any could say against "Briarthorn."

"Ask yourself that," continued Hist with spirit, though her manner grew less concentrated, and there was a slight air of abstraction that became observable to Deerslayer and Judith, if to no others—"Ask that of your own heart, sneaking wood-chuck of the Delawares; come not here with the face of an innocent man. Go look into the spring; see the colours of your enemies on your lying skin; then come back and boast how you run from your tribe and took the blanket of the French for your covering! Paint yourself as bright as the humming bird, you will still be black as the crow!"

Hist had been so uniformly gentle, while living with the Hurons, that they now listened to her language with surprise. As for the delinquent, his blood boiled in his veins, and it was well for the pretty speaker that it was not in his power to execute the revenge he burned to inflict on her, in spite of his pretended love.

"Who wishes Briarthorn?" he sternly asked—"If this pale face is tired of life, if afraid of Indian torments, speak, Rivenoak; I will send him after the warriors we have lost."

"No, chiefs—no, Rivenoak—" eagerly interrupted Hist—"Deerslayer fears nothing; least of all a crow! Unbind him—cut his withes, place him face to face with this cawing bird; then let us see which is tired of life!"

Hist made a forward movement, as if to take a knife from a young man, and perform the office she had mentioned in person, but an aged warrior interposed, at a sign from Rivenoak. This chief watched all the girl did with distrust, for, even while speaking in her most boastful language, and in the steadiest manner, there was an air of uncertainty and expectation about her, that could not escape so close an observer. She acted well; but two or three of the old men were equally satisfied that it was merely acting. Her proposal to release Deerslayer, therefore, was rejected, and the disappointed Hist found herself driven back from the sapling, at the very moment she fancied herself about to be successful. At the same time, the circle, which had got to be crowded and confused, was enlarged, and brought once more into order. Rivenoak now announced the intention of the old men again to proceed, the delay having continued long enough, and leading to no result.

"Stop Huron—stay chiefs!—" exclaimed Judith, scarce knowing what she said, or why she interposed, unless to obtain time. "For God's sake, a single minute longer—"

The words were cut short, by another and a still more extraordinary interruption. A young Indian came bounding through the Huron ranks, leaping into the very centre of the circle, in a way to denote the utmost confidence, or a temerity bordering on fool-hardiness. Five or six sentinels were still watching the lake at different and distant points, and it was the first impression of Rivenoak that one of these had come in, with tidings of import. Still the movements of the stranger were so rapid, and his war dress, which scarcely left him more drapery than an antique statue, had so little distinguishing about it, that, at the first moment, it was impossible to ascertain whether he were friend or foe. Three leaps carried this warrior to the side of Deerslayer, whose withes were cut, in the twinkling of an eye, with a quickness and precision that left the prisoner perfect master of his limbs. Not till this was effected, did the stranger bestow a glance on any other object; then he turned and showed the astonished Hurons, the noble brow, fine person, and eagle-eye, of a young warrior, in the paint and panoply of a Delaware. He held a rifle in each hand, the butts of both, resting on the earth, while from one dangled its proper pouch and horn. This was Killdeer which, even as he looked boldly and in defiance at the crowd around him, he suffered to fall back into the hands of its proper owner. The presence of two armed men, though it was in their midst, startled the Hurons. Their rifles were scattered about against the different trees, and their only weapons were their knives and tomahawks. Still they had too much self-possession to betray fear. It was little likely that so small a force would assail so strong a band, and each man expected some extraordinary proposition to succeed so decisive a step. The stranger did not seem disposed to disappoint them; he prepared to speak.

"Hurons," he said, "this earth is very big. The Great Lakes are big, too; there is room beyond them for the Iroquois; there is room for the Delawares on this side. I am Chingachgook the Son of Uncas; the kinsman of Tamenund. This is my betrothed; that pale face is my friend. My heart was heavy, when I missed him; I followed him to your camp, to see that no harm happened to him. All the Delaware girls are waiting for Wah; they wonder that she stays away so long. Come, let us say farewell, and go on our path."

"Hurons, this is your mortal enemy, the Great Serpent of them you hate!" cried Briarthorn. "If he escape, blood will be in your moccasin prints, from this spot to the Canadas. *I* am *all* Huron!"

As the last words were uttered, the traitor cast his knife at the naked breast of the Delaware. A quick movement of the arm, on the part of Hist, who stood near, turned aside the blow, the dangerous weapon burying its point in a pine. At the next instant, a similar weapon glanced from the hand of the Serpent, and quivered in the recreant's heart. A minute had scarcely elapsed from the moment in which Chingachgook bounded into the circle, and that in which Briarthorn fell, like a log, dead in his tracks. The rapidity of events had prevented the Hurons from acting; but this catastrophe permitted no farther delay. A common exclamation followed, and the whole party was in motion. At this instant a sound unusual to the woods was heard, and every Huron, male and female, paused to listen, with ears erect and faces filled with expectation. The sound was regular and heavy, as if the earth were struck with beetles. Objects became visible among the trees of the back ground, and a body of troops, was seen advancing with measured tread. They came upon the charge, the scarlet of the King's livery shining among the bright green foliage of the forest.

The scene that followed is not easily described. It was one in which wild confusion, despair, and frenzied efforts, were so blended, as to destroy the unity and distinctness of the action. A general yell burst from the enclosed Hurons; it was succeeded by the hearty cheers of England. Still not a musket or rifle was fired, though that steady, measured, tramp continued, and the bayonet was seen gleaming in advance of a line that counted nearly sixty men. The Hurons were taken at a fearful disadvantage. On three sides was the water, while their formidable and trained foes, cut them off from flight, on the fourth. Each warrior rushed for his arms, and then all on the point, man, woman and child, eagerly sought the covers. In this scene of confusion and dismay, however, nothing could surpass the discretion and coolness of Deerslayer. His first care was to place Judith and Hist, behind trees, and he looked for Hetty; but she had been hurried away in the crowd of Huron women. This effected, he threw himself on a flank of the retiring Hurons, who were inclining off towards the southern margin of the point, in the hope of escaping through the water. Deerslayer watched his opportunity, and finding two of his recent tormentors in a range, his rifle first broke the silence of the terrific scene. The bullet brought down both at one discharge. This drew a general fire from the Hurons, and the rifle and war cry of the Serpent were heard in the clamor. Still the trained men returned no answering volley, the whoop and piece of Hurry alone being heard on their side, if we except, the short, prompt word of authority, and that heavy, measured and menacing tread. Presently, however, the shrieks, groans, and denunciations that usually accompany the use of the bayonet followed. That terrible and deadly weapon was glutted in vengeance. The scene that succeeded was one of those, of which so many have occurred in our own times, in which neither age nor sex forms an exemption to the lot of a savage warfare.

Chapter XXXI

"The flower that smiles to-day
  To-morrow dies;
All that we wish to stay,
  Tempts and then flies:
What is this world's delight?—
Lightning that mocks the night,
Brief even as bright."
    Shelley, "Mutability," ll. 1–7.

THE PICTURE next presented, by the point of land that the unfortunate Hurons had selected for their last place of encampment, need scarcely be laid before the eyes of the reader. Happily for the more tender-minded and the more timid, the trunks of the trees, the leaves, and the smoke had concealed much of that which passed, and night shortly after drew its veil over the lake, and the whole of that seemingly interminable wilderness; which may be said to have then stretched, with few and immaterial interruptions, from the banks of the Hudson to the shores of the Pacific Ocean. Our business carries us into the following day, when light returned upon the earth, as sunny and as smiling, as if nothing extraordinary had occurred.

When the sun rose on the following morning, every sign of hostility and alarm had vanished from the basin of the Glimmerglass. The frightful event of the preceding evening had left no impression on the placid sheet, and the untiring hours pursued their course in the placid order prescribed by the powerful hand that set them in motion. The birds were again skimming the water, or were seen poised on the wing, high above the tops of the tallest pines of the mountains, ready to make their swoops, in obedience to the irresistable law of their natures. In a word, nothing was changed, but the air of movement and life that prevailed in and around the castle. Here, indeed, was an alteration that must have struck the least observant eye. A sentinel, who wore the light infantry uniform of a royal regiment, paced the platform with measured tread, and some twenty more of the same corps, lounged about the place, or were seated in the ark. Their arms were stacked under the eye of their comrade on post. Two officers stood examining the shore, with the ship's glass so often mentioned. Their looks were directed to that fatal point, where scarlet coats were still to be seen gliding among the trees, and where the magnifying power of the instrument also showed spades at work, and the sad duty of interment going on. Several of the common men bore proofs on their persons, that their enemies had not been overcome entirely without resistance, and the youngest of the two officers on the platform, wore an arm in a sling. His companion, who commanded the party, had been more fortunate. He it was who used the glass, in making the reconnoissances in which the two were engaged.

A serjeant approached to make a report. He addressed the senior of these officers, as Capt. Warley, while the other was alluded to as Mr.—which was equivalent to Ensign—Thornton. The former it will at once be seen was the officer who had been named with so much feeling, in the parting dialogue between Judith and Hurry. He was, in truth, the very individual with whom the scandal of the garrisons, had most freely connected the name of this beautiful but indiscreet girl. He was a hard featured, red faced, man, of about five and thirty; but of a military carriage, and with an air of fashion that might easily impose on the imagination of one as ignorant of the world, as Judith.

"Craig is covering us with benedictions," observed this person to his young ensign, with an air of indifference as he shut the glass, and handed it to his servant; "to say the truth, not without reason; it is certainly more agreeable to be here in attendance on Miss Judith Hutter, than to be burying Indians, on a point of the lake, however romantic the position, or brilliant the victory. By the way, Wright—is Davis still living?"

"He died about ten minutes since, your honor," returned the sergeant to whom this question was addressed. "I knew how it would be, as soon as I found the bullet had touched the stomach. I never knew a man who could hold out long, if he had a hole in his stomach."

"No; it is rather inconvenient for carrying away any thing very nourishing," observed Warley gaping. "This being up two nights *de suite*, Arthur, plays the devil with a man's faculties! I'm as stupid, as one of those Dutch parsons on the Mohawk—I hope your arm is not painful, my dear boy?"

"It draws a few grimaces from me, sir, as I suppose you see," answered the youth, laughing at the very moment, his countenance was a little awry with pain. "But it may be borne. I suppose Graham can spare a few minutes, soon, to look at my hurt."

"She is a lovely creature, this Judith Hutter, after all, Thornton; and it shall not be my fault if she is not seen and admired in the Parks!" resumed Warley, who thought little of his companion's wound—"your arm, eh! Quite true—Go into the ark, serjeant, and tell Dr. Graham I desire he would look at Mr. Thornton's injury, as soon as he has done with the poor fellow with the broken leg. A lovely creature! and she looked like a queen in that brocade dress in which we met her. I find all changed here; father and mother both gone, the sister dying, if not dead, and none of the family left, but the beauty! This has been a lucky expedition all round, and promises to terminate better than Indian skirmishes in general."

"Am I to suppose, sir, that you are about to desert your colours, in the great corps of bachelors, and close the campaign with matrimony?"

"I, Tom Warley, turn Benedict! Faith, my dear boy, you little know the corps you speak of, if you fancy any such thing. I do suppose there *are* women in the colonies, that a captain of Light Infantry need not disdain; but they are not to be found up here, on a mountain lake; or even down on the Dutch river where we are posted. It is true, my uncle, the general, once did me the favor to choose a wife for me in Yorkshire; but she had no beauty, and I would not marry a princess, unless she were handsome."

"If handsome, you would marry a beggar?"

"Ay, these are the notions of an ensign! Love in a cottage—doors—and windows—the old story, for the hundredth time. The twenty —th do n't *marry*. We are not a marrying corps, my dear boy. There's the Colonel, Old Sir Edwin ——, now; though a full General he has never thought of a wife; and when a man gets as high as a Lieutenant General, without matrimony, he is pretty safe. Then the

Lieutenant Colonel is *confirmed*, as I tell my cousin the Bishop. The Major is a widower, having tried matrimony, for twelve months in his youth, and we look upon him, now, as one of our most certain men. Out of ten captains, but one is in the dilemma, and he, poor devil, is always kept at regimental head quarters, as a sort of *memento mori*, to the young men as they join. As for the subalterns, not one has ever yet had the audacity to speak of introducing a wife into the regiment. But your arm is troublesome, and we'll go ourselves and see what has become of Graham."

The Surgeon who had accompanied the party, was employed very differently from what the captain supposed. When the assault was over, and the dead and wounded were collected, poor Hetty had been found among the latter. A rifle bullet had passed through her body, inflicting an injury that was known at a glance, to be mortal. How this wound was received, no one knew; it was probably one of those casualties that ever accompany scenes like that related in the previous chapter.

The Sumach, all the elderly women, and some of the Huron girls, had fallen by the bayonet, either in the confusion of the *mêlée*, or from the difficulty of distinguishing the sexes, when the dress was so simple. Much the greater portion of the warriors suffered on the spot. A few had escaped, however, and two or three had been taken unharmed. As for the wounded, the bayonet saved the surgeon much trouble. Rivenoak had escaped with life and limb, but was injured and a prisoner. As Captain Warley, and his ensign, went into the Ark, they passed him, seated, in dignified silence, in one end of the scow, his head and leg bound, but betraying no visible sign of despondency or despair. That he mourned the loss of his tribe, is certain; still he did it in a manner that best became a warrior and a chief.

The two soldiers found their surgeon in the principal room of the Ark. He was just quitting the pallet of Hetty, with an expression of sorrowful regret, on his hard, pock-marked Scottish features, that it was not usual to see there. All his assiduity had been useless, and he was compelled, reluctantly to abandon the expectation of seeing the girl survive many hours. Dr. Graham was accustomed to death-bed scenes, and ordinarily they produced but little impression on him. In all that relates to religion, his was one of those minds which, in consequence of reasoning much on material things, logically and consecutively, and overlooking the total want of premises which such a theory must ever possess, through its want of a primary agent, had become sceptical; leaving a vague opinion concerning the origin of things, that, with high pretentions to philosophy, failed in the first of all philosophical principles, a cause. To him religious dependence appeared a weakness, but when he found one gentle and young like Hetty, with a mind beneath the level of her race, sustained at such a moment by these pious sentiments, and that, too, in a way that many a sturdy warrior, and reputed hero might have looked upon with envy, he found himself affected by the sight, to a degree that he would have been ashamed to confess. Edinburgh and Aberdeen, then as now, supplied no small portion of the medical men of the British service, and Dr. Graham, as indeed his name and countenance equally indicated, was by birth, a North Briton.

"Here is an extraordinary exhibition for a forest, and one but half-gifted with reason," he observed with a decided Scotch accent, as Warley and the ensign entered; "I just hope, gentlemen, that when we three shall be called on to quit the twenty —th, we may be found as resigned to go on the half pay of another existence, as this poor demented chiel!"

"Is there no hope that she can survive the hurt?" demanded Warley, turning his eyes towards the pallid Judith, on whose cheeks, however, two large spots of red had settled, as soon as he came into the cabin.

"No more than there is for Chairlie Stuart! Approach and judge for yourselves, gentlemen; ye'll see faith exemplified in an exceeding and wonderful manner. There is a sort of *arbitrium* between life and death, in actual conflict in the poor girl's mind, that renders her an interesting study to a philosopher. Mr. Thornton, I'm at your service, now; we can just look at the arm, in the next room, while we speculate as much as we please on the operations and sinuosities of the human mind."

The surgeon and ensign retired, and Warley had an opportunity of looking about him, more at leisure, and with a better understanding of the nature and feelings of the group collected in the cabin. Poor Hetty had been placed on her own simple bed, and was reclining in a half seated attitude, with the approaches of death on her countenance, though they were singularly dimmed by the lustre of an expression, in which all the intelligence of her entire being appeared to be concentrated. Judith and Hist were near her, the former seated in deep grief; the latter standing, in readiness to offer any of the gentle attentions of feminine care. Deerslayer stood at the end of the pallet, leaning on Killdeer, unharmed in person, all the fine martial ardor that had so lately glowed in his countenance, having given place to the usual look of honesty and benevolence, qualities of which the expression was now softened by manly regret and pity. The Serpent was in the back-ground of the picture, erect, and motionless as a statue; but so observant that not a look of the eye, escaped his own keen glances. Hurry completed the group, being seated on a stool near the door, like one who felt himself out of place in such a scene, but who was ashamed to quit it, unbidden.

"Who is that, in scarlet?" asked Hetty, as soon as the Captain's uniform caught her eye. "Tell me, Judith, is it the friend of Hurry?"

" 'Tis the officer who commands the troops, that have rescued us all from the hands of the Hurons," was the low answer of the sister.

"Am I rescued, too!—I thought they said I was shot, and about to die. Mother is dead; and so is father; but you are living, Judith, and so is Hurry. I was afraid Hurry would be killed, when I heard him shouting among the soldiers."

"Never mind—never mind, dear Hetty—" interrupted Judith, sensitively alive to the preservation of her sister's secret, more, perhaps at such a moment, than at any other. "Hurry is well, and Deerslayer is well, and the Delaware is well, too."

"How came they to shoot a poor girl like me, and let so many men go unharmed? I did n't know that the Hurons were so wicked, Judith!"

" 'Twas an accident, poor Hetty; a sad—sad—accident it has been! No one would willingly have injured *you*."

"I'm glad of that!—I thought it strange; I am feeble

minded, and the red men have never harmed me before. I should be sorry to think that they had changed their minds. I am glad too, Judith, that they haven't hurt Hurry. Deerslayer, I don't think God will suffer any one to harm. It was very fortunate the soldiers came as they did though, for fire *will* burn!"

"It was, indeed fortunate, my sister; God's holy name be forever blessed for the mercy!"

"I dare say, Judith, you know some of the officers; you used to know so many!"

Judith made no reply; she hid her face in her hands and groaned. Hetty gazed at her in wonder; but naturally supposing her own situation was the cause of this grief, she kindly offered to console her sister.

"Don't mind me, dear Judith," said the affectionate and pure-hearted creature—"I don't suffer; if I do die, why father and mother are both dead, and what happens to *them*, may well happen to *me*. You know I am of less account than any of the family; therefore few will think of me after I'm in the lake."

"No—no—no—poor, dear, dear Hetty!" exclaimed Judith, in an uncontrollable burst of sorrow, "I, at least, will ever think of you; and gladly, oh! how gladly would I exchange places with you, to be the pure, excellent, sinless creature you are!"

Until now, Captain Warley had stood leaning against the door of the cabin; when this outbreak of feeling, and perchance of penitence, however, escaped the beautiful girl, he walked slowly and thoughtfully away; even passing the ensign, then suffering under the surgeon's care, without noticing him.

"I have got my bible here, Judith," returned her sister, in a voice of triumph. "It's true, I can't read any longer, there's something the matter with my eyes—*you* look dim and distant—and so does Hurry, now I look at him—well, I never could have believed that Henry March would have so dull a look!—What can be the reason, Judith, that I see so badly, to-day? I, who mother always said, had the best eyes in the whole family. Yes, that was it: my mind was feeble—what people call half-witted—but my eyes were *so* good!"

Again Judith groaned; this time no feeling of self, no retrospect of the past caused the pain. It was the pure, heartfelt sorrow of sisterly love, heightened by a sense of the meek humility and perfect truth of the being before her. At that moment, she would gladly have given up her own life to save that of Hetty. As the last, however, was beyond the reach of human power, she felt there was nothing left her but sorrow. At this moment Warley returned to the cabin, drawn by a secret impulse he could not withstand, though he felt, just then, as if he would gladly abandon the American continent for ever, were it practicable. Instead of pausing at the door, he now advanced so near the pallet of the sufferer as to come more plainly within her gaze. Hetty could still distinguish large objects, and her look soon fastened on him.

"Are you the officer that came with Hurry?" she asked—"If you are, we ought all to thank you, for, though I am hurt, the rest have saved their lives. Did Harry March tell you, where to find us, and how much need there was for your services?"

"The news of the party reached us by means of a friendly runner," returned the Captain, glad to relieve his feelings by this appearance of a friendly communication, "and I was immediately sent out to cut it off. It was fortunate, certainly, that we met Hurry Harry, as you call him, for he acted as a guide, and it was not less fortunate, that we heard a firing, which I now understand was merely a shooting at the mark, for it not only quickened our march, but called us to the right side of the lake. The Delaware saw us on the shore, with the glass it would seem, and he and Hist, as I find his squaw is named, did us excellent service. It was really altogether, a fortunate concurrence of circumstances, Judith?"

"Talk not to me of any thing fortunate, sir," returned the girl huskily, again concealing her face. "To me the world is full of misery. I wish never to hear of marks, or rifles, or soldiers, or *men*, again!"

"Do you know my sister?" asked Hetty, ere the rebuked soldier had time to rally for an answer. "How came you to know that her name is Judith? You are right, for that *is* her name; and I am Hetty, Thomas Hutter's daughters."

"For heaven's sake, dearest sister,—for *my* sake, beloved Hetty," interposed Judith, imploringly, "say no more of this!"

Hetty looked surprised, but accustomed to comply, she ceased her awkward and painful interrogations of Warley, bending her eyes towards the bible which she still held between her hands, as one would cling to a casket of precious stones, in a shipwreck, or a conflagration. Her mind now adverted to the future, losing sight, in a great measure, of the scenes of the past.

"We shall not long be parted, Judith," she said; "when *you* die, you must be brought and be buried in the lake, by the side of mother too."

"Would to God, Hetty, that I lay there, at this moment!"

"No, that cannot be, Judith; people must die before they have any right to be buried. 'Twould be wicked to bury you, or for you to bury yourself, while living. Once I thought of burying myself; God kept me from that sin."

"You!—You, Hetty Hutter, think of such an act!" exclaimed Judith, looking up in uncontrollable surprise, for she well knew nothing passed the lips of her conscientious sister, that was not religiously true.

"Yes, I did, Judith, but God has forgotten—no he *forgets* nothing—but he has *forgiven* it," returned the dying girl, with the subdued manner of a repentant child. "'Twas after mother's death; I felt I had lost the best friend I had on earth, if not the *only* friend. 'Tis true, you and father were kind to me, Judith, but I was so feeble-minded, I knew I should only give you trouble; and then you were so often ashamed of such a sister and daughter, and 'tis hard to live in a world where all look upon you as below them. I thought then, if I could bury myself by the side of mother, I should be happier in the lake, than in the hut."

"Forgive me—pardon me, dearest Hetty—on my bended knees, I beg you to pardon me, sweet sister, if any word, or act of mine drove you to so maddening and cruel a thought!"

"Get up, Judith—kneel to God; do n't kneel to me. Just so I felt when mother was dying! I remembered every thing I had said and done to vex her, and could have kissed her feet for forgiveness. I think it must be so with all dying people;

though, now I think of it, I don't remember to have had such feelings on account of father."

Judith arose, hid her face in her apron, and wept. A long pause—one of more than two hours succeeded, during which Warley entered and left the cabin several times; apparently uneasy when absent, and yet unable to remain. He issued various orders, which his men proceeded to execute, and there was an air of movement in the party, more especially as Mr. Craig, the lieutenant, had got through the unpleasant duty of burying the dead, and had sent for instructions from the shore, desiring to know what he was to do with his detachment. During this interval Hetty slept a little, and Deerslayer and Chingachgook left the Ark to confer together. But, at the end of the time mentioned, the Surgeon passed upon the platform, and with a degree of feeling his comrades had never before observed in one of his habits, he announced that the patient was rapidly drawing near her end. On receiving this intelligence the group collected again, curiosity to witness such a death—or a better feeling—drawing to the spot, men who had so lately been actors in a scene seemingly of so much greater interest and moment. By this time, Judith had got to be inactive through grief, and Hist alone was performing the little offices of feminine attention that are so appropriate to the sick bed. Hetty herself, had undergone no other apparent change, than the general failing that indicated the near approach of dissolution. All that she possessed of mind was as clear as ever, and, in some respects, her intellect perhaps was more than usually active.

"Don't grieve for me so much, Judith," said the gentle sufferer, after a pause in her remarks—"I shall soon see mother—I think I see her *now*; her face is just as sweet and smiling as it used to be! Perhaps when I'm dead, God will give me all my mind, and I shall become a more fitting companion for mother, than I ever was before."

"You will be an angel in heaven, Hetty," sobbed the sister; "no spirit there will be more worthy of its holy residence!"

"I don't understand it quite; still, I know it must be all true; I've read it in the bible. How dark it's becoming! Can it be night so soon? I can hardly see you at all—where is Hist?"

"I here, poor girl—Why you no see me."

"I do see you; but I could n't tell whether 'twas you, or Judith. I believe I shan't see you much longer, Hist."

"Sorry for that, poor Hetty. Never mind—pale face got a heaven for girls as well as for warrior."

"Where's the Serpent—let me speak to him—Give me his hand—so—I feel it. Delaware you will love and cherish this young Indian woman—I know how fond she is of *you*; you must be fond of *her*. Don't treat her as some of your people treat their wives; be a real husband to her. Now, bring Deerslayer near me; give me *his* hand."

This request was complied with, and the hunter stood by the side of the pallet, submitting to the wishes of the girl, with the docility of a child.

"I feel, Deerslayer," she resumed—"though I could n't tell why—but I feel that you and I are not going to part for ever. 'Tis a strange feeling!—I never had it before—I wonder what it comes from!"

" 'Tis God encouraging you in extremity, Hetty; as such it ought to be harbored and respected. Yes, we *shall* meet ag'in, though it may be a long time, first, and in a far distant land."

"Do you mean to be buried in the lake, too? If so, that may account for the feeling."

" 'Tis little likely, gal; 'tis little likely—but there's a region for christian souls, where there's no lakes, nor woods, they say; though why there should be none of the *last*, is more than I can account for; seeing that pleasantness and peace is the object in view. My grave will be found in the forest, most likely, but I hope my spirit will not be far from yourn."

"So it must be, then. I am too weak-minded to understand these things, but I *feel* that you and I will meet again.—Sister, where are you?—I can't see, now, any thing but darkness—it must be night, surely!"

"Oh! Hetty, I am here—at your side—these are my arms that are around you," sobbed Judith. "Speak, dearest; is there any thing you wish to say, or have done, in this awful moment."

By this time Hetty's sight had entirely failed her. Nevertheless death approached with less than usual of its horrors, as if in tenderness to one of her half endowed faculties. She was pale as a corpse, but her breathing was easy and unbroken, while her voice, though lowered almost to a whisper, remained clear and distinct. When her sister put this question, however, a blush diffused itself over the features of the dying girl, so faint however as to be nearly imperceptible; resembling that hue of the rose which is thought to portray the tint of modesty, rather than the dye of the flower in its richer bloom. No one but Judith detected this exposure of feeling, one of the gentle expressions of womanly sensibility even in death. On her however, it was not lost, nor did she conceal from herself the cause.

"Hurry is here, dearest Hetty—" whispered the sister, with her face so near the sufferer, as to keep the words from other ears. "Shall I tell him to come and receive your good wishes?"

A gentle pressure of the hand answered in the affirmative. Then Hurry was brought to the side of the pallet. It is probable that this handsome, but rude woodsman had never before found himself so awkwardly placed, though the inclination which Hetty felt for him—a sort of secret yielding to the instincts of nature, rather than any unbecoming impulse of an ill regulated imagination—was too pure and unobtrusive to have created the slightest suspicion of the circumstance in his mind. He allowed Judith to put his hard colossal hand between those of Hetty, and stood waiting the result in awkward silence.

"This is Hurry, dearest," whispered Judith, bending over her sister, ashamed to utter the words so as to be audible to herself. "Speak to him, and let him go."

"What shall I say, Judith?"

"Nay, whatever your own pure spirit teaches, my love. Trust to that, and you need fear nothing."

"Good bye, Hurry—" murmured the girl, with a gentle pressure of his hand—"I wish you would try and be more like Deerslayer."

These words were uttered with difficulty; a faint flush succeeded them for a single instant. Then the hand was relinquished, and Hetty turned her face aside, as if done with the world. The mysterious feeling that bound her to the young man, a sentiment so gentle as to be almost imperceptible to herself, and which could never have existed at all, had her reason possessed more command over her senses, was forever lost in thoughts of a more elevated, though scarcely of a purer character.

"Of what are you thinking, my sweet sister?" whispered Judith—"Tell me, that I may aid you, at this moment."

"Mother—I see Mother, now, and bright beings around her in the lake. Why is n't father there?—It's odd, that I can see mother, when I can't see *you*!—Farewell, Judith."

The last words were uttered after a pause, and her sister had hung over her some time, in anxious watchfulness, before she perceived that the gentle spirit had departed. Thus died Hetty Hutter, one of those mysterious links between the material and immaterial world, which, while they appear to be deprived of so much that is esteemed and necessary for this state of being, draw so near to, and offer so beautiful an illustration of the truth, purity, and simplicity of another.

Chapter XXXII

"A baron's chylde to be begylde! it were a cursed dede:
To be felàwe with an outlàwe! Almighty God forbede!
Yea, better were, the pore squyère alone to forest yede,
Then ye sholde say another day, that by my cursed dede
Ye were betrayed: wherefore, good mayde, the best rede that I can,
Is, that I to the grene wode go, alone, a banyshed man."

Thomas Percy, "Notbrowne Mayde," ll. 265–76
from *Reliques of Ancient English Poetry*, Vol. II.

THE DAY that followed, proved to be melancholy, though one of much activity. The soldiers, who had so lately been employed in interring their victims, were now called on to bury their own dead. The scene of the morning had left a saddened feeling on all the gentlemen of the party, and the rest felt the influence of a similar sensation, in a variety of ways, and from many causes. Hour dragged on after hour, until evening arrived, and then came the last melancholy offices in honor of poor Hetty Hutter. Her body was laid in the lake, by the side of that of the mother she had so loved and reverenced, the surgeon, though actually an unbeliever, so far complying with the received decencies of life, as to read the funeral service over her grave, as he had previously done over those of the other *christian* slain! It mattered not;—that all seeing eye which reads the heart, could not fail to discriminate between the living and the dead, and the gentle soul of the unfortunate girl, was already far removed beyond the errors, or deceptions, of any human ritual. These simple rites, however, were not wholly wanting in suitable accompaniments. The tears of Judith and Hist were shed freely, and Deerslayer gazed upon the limpid water, that now flowed over one whose spirit was even purer than its own mountain springs, with glistening eyes. Even the Delaware turned aside to conceal his weakness, while the common men gazed on the ceremony with wondering eyes and chastened feelings.

The business of the day closed with this pious office. By order of the commanding officer, all retired early to rest, for it was intended to begin the march homeward, with the return of light. One party, indeed, bearing the wounded, the prisoners, and the trophies, had left the castle in the middle of the day, under the guidance of Hurry, intending to reach the fort by shorter marches. It had been landed on the point, so often mentioned, or that described in our opening pages, and, when the sun set, was already encamped on the brow of the long, broken, and ridgy hills, that fell away towards the valley of the Mohawk. The departure of this detachment had greatly simplified the duty of the succeeding day, disencumbering its march of its baggage and wounded, and otherwise leaving him who had issued the order greater liberty of action.

Judith held no communications with any but Hist, after the death of her sister, until she retired for the night. Her sorrow had been respected, and both the females had been left with the body, unintruded on, to the last moment. The rattling of the drum broke the silence of that tranquil water, and the echoes of the tattoo were heard among the mountains, so soon after the ceremony was over, as to preclude the danger of interruption. That star which had been the guide of Hist, rose on a scene as silent as if the quiet of nature had never yet been disturbed, by the labors or passions of man. One solitary sentinel, with his relief, paced the platform throughout the night, and morning was ushered in, as usual, by the martial beat of the reveillé.

Military precision succeeded to the desultory proceedings of border men, and when a hasty and frugal breakfast was taken, the party began its movement towards the shore, with a regularity and order, that prevented noise or confusion. Of all the officers, Warley alone remained. Craig headed the detachment in advance, Thornton was with the wounded, and Graham accompanied his patients as a matter of course. Even the chest of Hutter, with all the more valuable of his effects, was borne away, leaving nothing behind that was worth the labor of a removal. Judith was not sorry to see that the captain respected her feelings, and that he occupied himself entirely with the duty of his command, leaving her to her own discretion and feelings. It was understood by all, that the place was to be totally abandoned; but beyond this no explanations were asked or given.

The soldiers embarked in the Ark, with the captain at their

head. He had enquired of Judith in what way she chose to proceed, and understanding her wish to remain with Hist to the last moment, he neither molested her with requests, nor offended her with advice. There was but one safe and familiar trail to the Mohawk, and on that, at the proper hour, he doubted not that they should meet in amity, if not in renewed intercourse.

When all were on board, the sweeps were manned, and the Ark moved in its sluggish manner towards the distant point. Deerslayer and Chingachgook, now lifted two of the canoes from the water, and placed them in the castle. The windows and door were then barred, and the house was left by means of the trap, in the manner already described. On quitting the palisades, Hist was seen in the remaining canoe, where the Delaware immediately joined her, and paddled away, leaving Judith standing alone on the platform. Owing to this prompt proceeding, Deerslayer found himself alone with the beautiful and still weeping mourner. Too simple to suspect any thing, the young man swept the light boat round, and received its mistress in it, when he followed the course already taken by his friend.

The direction to the point, led diagonally past, and at no great distance from, the graves of the dead. As the canoe glided by, Judith, for the first time that morning spoke to her companion. She said but little; merely uttering a simple request to stop, for a minute or two, ere she left the place.

"I may never see this spot again, Deerslayer," she said, "and it contains the bodies of my mother and sister! Is it not possible, think you, that the innocence of one of these beings, may answer in the eyes of God, for the salvation of both?"

"I do n't understand it so, Judith, though I'm no missionary, and am but poorly taught. Each spirit answers for its own backslidings, though a hearty repentance will satisfy God's laws."

"Then *must* my poor poor mother be in heaven!—Bitterly—bitterly—has she repented of her sins, and surely her sufferings in this life, ought to count as something against her sufferings in the next!"

"All this goes beyond me, Judith—I strive to do right, here, as the surest means of keeping all right, hereafter. Hetty was oncommon, as all that know'd her must allow, and her soul was as fit to consart with angels the hour it left its body, as that of any saint in the bible!"

"I do believe you only do her justice! Alas!—Alas!—that there should be so great differences between those who were nursed at the same breast, slept in the same bed, and dwelt under the same roof! But, no matter—move the canoe, a little farther east, Deerslayer—the sun so dazzles my eyes that I cannot see the graves. This is Hetty's, on the right of mother's?"

"Sartain—you ask'd that of us, and all are glad to do as you wish, Judith, when you do that which is right."

The girl gazed at him near a minute, in silent attention; then she turned her eyes backward, at the castle.

"This lake will soon be entirely deserted," she said—"and this, too, at a moment when it will be a more secure dwelling place than ever. What has so lately happened will prevent the Iroquois from venturing again to visit it, for a long time to come."

"That it will!—yes, that may be set down as sartain. I do not mean to pass this-a-way, ag'in, so long as the war lasts, for, to my mind no Huron moccasin will leave its print on the leaves of this forest, until their traditions have forgotten to tell their young men of their disgrace and rout."

"And do you so delight in violence and bloodshed?—I had thought better of *you*, Deerslayer—believed you one, who could find his happiness in a quiet domestic home, with an attached and loving wife, ready to study your wishes, and healthy and dutiful children, anxious to follow in your footsteps, and to become as honest and just as yourself."

"Lord, Judith, what a tongue you're mistress of! Speech and looks go hand in hand, like, and what one can't do, the other is pretty sartain to perform! Such a gal, in a month, might spoil the stoutest warrior in the colony."

"And am I then so mistaken?—Do you really love war, Deerslayer, better than the hearth, and the affections?"

"I understand your meaning, gal; yes, I do understand what you mean, I believe, though I do n't think you altogether understand *me*. Warrior I may now call myself, I suppose, for I've both fou't and conquered, which is sufficient for the name; neither will I deny that I've feelin's for the callin', which is both manful and honorable, when carried on accordin' to nat'ral gifts, but I've no relish for blood. Youth is youth, howsever, and a Mingo is a Mingo. If the young men of this region stood by, and suffered the vagabonds to overrun the land, why, we might as well all turn Frenchers at once, and give up country and kin. I'm no fire eater, Judith, or one that likes fightin' for fightin's sake, but I can see no great difference atween *givin' up territory afore a war, out of a dread of war, and givin' it up a'ter a war, because we can't help it, onless it be that the last is the most manful and honorable.*"

"No woman would ever wish to see her husband, or brother, stand by, and submit to insult and wrong, Deerslayer, however she might mourn the necessity of his running into the dangers of battle. But, you've done enough already, in clearing this region of the Hurons; since to you is principally owing the credit of our late victory. Now, listen to me patiently, and answer me with that native honesty, which it is as pleasant to regard in one of your sex, as it is unusual to meet with."

Judith paused, for now that she was on the very point of explaining herself, native modesty asserted its power, notwithstanding the encouragement and confidence she derived from the great simplicity of her companion's character. Her cheeks, which had so lately been pale, flushed, and her eyes lighted with some of their former brilliancy. Feeling gave expression to her countenance and softness to her voice, rendering her who was always beautiful, trebly seductive and winning.

"Deerslayer," she said, after a considerable pause, "this is not a moment for affectation, deception, or a want of frankness of any sort. Here, over my mother's grave, and over the grave of truth-loving, truth-telling Hetty, every thing like unfair dealing seems to be out of place. I will, therefore, speak to you without any reserve, and without any dread of being misunderstood. You are not an acquaintance of a week, but it appears to me as if I had known you for years. So much, and so much that is important has taken place, within that short time, that the sorrows, and dangers, and escapes of a whole life have been crowded into a few days, and they who have suffered and acted together in such scenes, ought not to feel like strangers. I know that what I am about to say might be misunderstood by most men, but I hope for a generous construction of my course from you. We are not here, dwelling among the arts and deceptions of the settlements, but young people who have no occasion to deceive each other, in any manner or form.—I hope I make myself understood?"

"Sartain, Judith; few convarse better than yourself, and none more agreeable, like. Your words are as pleasant as your looks."

"It is the manner in which you have so often praised those looks, that gives me courage to proceed—Still, Deerslayer, it is not easy, for one of my sex and years to forget all her lessons of infancy, all her habits, and her natural diffidence, and say openly what her heart feels!"

"Why not, Judith? Why should n't women as well as men deal fairly and honestly by their fellow creatur's? I see no reason why you should not speak as plainly as myself, when there is any thing ra'ally important to be said."

This indomitable diffidence, which still prevented the young man from suspecting the truth, would have completely discouraged the girl, had not her whole soul, as well as her whole heart, been set upon making a desperate effort to rescue herself from a future that she dreaded with a horror as vivid, as the distinctness with which she fancied she foresaw it. This motive, however, raised her above all common considerations, and she persevered even to her own surprise, if not to her great confusion.

"I will—I *must* deal as plainly with you, as I would with poor, dear Hetty, were that sweet child living!" she continued, turning pale, instead of blushing, the high resolution by which she was prompted reversing the effect that such a procedure would ordinarily produce on one of her sex; "yes, I will smother all other feelings, in the one that is now uppermost! You love the woods and the life that we pass, here, in the wilderness, away from the dwellings and towns of the whites."

"As I loved my parents, Judith, when they was living! This very spot, would be all creation to me, could this war be fairly over, once; and the settlers kept at a distance."

"Why quit it then?—It has no owner—at least none who can claim a better right than mine, and *that* I freely give to you. Were it a kingdom, Deerslayer, I think I should delight to say the same. Let us then return to it, after we have seen the priest at the fort, and never quit it again, until God calls us away to that world where we shall find the spirits of my poor mother and sister."

A long, thoughtful pause succeeded; Judith here covered her face with both her hands, after forcing herself to utter so plain a proposal, and Deerslayer musing equally in sorrow and surprise, on the meaning of the language he had just heard. At length the hunter broke the silence, speaking in a tone that was softened to gentleness by his desire not to offend.

"You have n't thought well of this, Judith—" he said—"no, your feelin's are awakened by all that has lately happened, and believin' yourself to be without kindred in the world, you are in too great haste to find some to fill the places of them that's lost."

"Were I living in a crowd of friends, Deerslayer, I should still think, as I now think—say as I now say," returned Judith, speaking with her hands still shading her lovely face.

"Thank you, gal—thank you, from the bottom of my heart. Howsever, I am not one to take advantage of a weak moment, when you're forgetful of your own great advantages, and fancy 'arth and all it holds, is in this little canoe. No—no—Judith 'twould be onginerous in me; what you've offered can never come to pass!"

"It all may be, and that without leaving cause of repentance to any—" answered Judith, with an impetuosity of feeling and manner, that at once unveiled her eyes. "We can cause the soldiers to leave our goods on the road, till we return, when they can easily be brought back to the house; the lake will be no more visited by the enemy, this war at least; all your skins may be readily sold at the garrison; there *you* can buy the few necessaries we shall want, for I wish never to see the spot, again; and Deerslayer," added the girl smiling with a sweetness and nature that the young man found it hard to resist—"as a proof how wholly I am and wish to be yours,—how completely I desire to be nothing but your wife, the very first fire that we kindle, after our return, shall be lighted with the brocade dress, and fed by every article I have that you may think unfit for the woman you wish to live with!"

"Ah's! me—you're a winning and a lovely creatur', Judith; yes, you *are* all that, and no one can deny it, and speak truth. These pictur's are pleasant to the thoughts, but they mightn't prove so happy as you now think 'em. Forget it all, therefore, and let us paddle after the Sarpent and Hist, as if nothing had been said on the subject."

Judith was deeply mortified, and, what is more, she was profoundly grieved. Still there was a steadiness and quiet in the manner of Deerslayer that completely smothered her hopes, and told her that for once, her exceeding beauty had failed to excite the admiration and homage it was wont to receive. Women are said seldom to forgive those who slight their advances, but this high spirited and impetuous girl entertained no shadow of resentment, then or ever, against the fair dealing and ingenuous hunter. At the moment, the prevailing feeling was the wish to be certain that there was no misunderstanding. After another painful pause, therefore, she brought the matter to an issue by a question too direct to admit of equivocation.

"God forbid, that we lay up regrets, in after life, through any want of sincerity now," she said. "I hope we understand each other, at least. You will not accept me for a wife, Deerslayer?"

" 'Tis better for both that I should n't take advantage of your own forgetfulness, Judith. We can never marry."

"You do not love me,—cannot find it in your heart, perhaps, to esteem me, Deerslayer!"

"Every thing in the way of fri'ndship, Judith—every thing, even to sarvices and life itself. Yes, I'd risk as much for you, at this moment, as I would risk in behalf of Hist, and that is sayin' as much as I can say of any darter of woman. I do not think I feel towards either—mind I say *either*, Judith—as if I wished to quit father and mother—if father and mother was livin', which, howsever, neither is—but if both was livin', I do not feel towards any woman as if I wish'd to quit 'em in order to cleave unto *her*."

"This is enough!" answered Judith, in a rebuked and

smothered voice—"I understand all that you mean. Marry you cannot without loving, and that love you do not feel for me. Make no answer, if I am right, for I shall understand your silence—*That* will be painful enough of itself."

Deerslayer obeyed her, and he made no reply. For more than a minute, the girl riveted her bright eyes on him, as if to read his soul, while he sat playing with the water, like a corrected school boy. Then Judith, herself, dropped the end of her paddle, and urged the canoe away from the spot, with a movement as reluctant as the feelings which controlled it. Deerslayer quietly aided the effort, however, and they were soon on the trackless line taken by the Delaware.

In their way to the point, not another syllable was exchanged between Deerslayer and his fair companion. As Judith sat in the bow of the canoe, her back was turned towards him, else it is probable the expression of her countenance might have induced him to venture some soothing terms of friendship and regard. Contrary to what would have been expected, resentment was still absent, though the colour frequently changed, from the deep flush of mortification to the paleness of disappointment. Sorrow, deep, heart-felt sorrow, however, was the predominant emotion, and this was betrayed in a manner not to be mistaken.

As neither labored hard at the paddle, the ark had already arrived and the soldiers had disembarked, before the canoe of the two loiterers reached the point. Chingachgook had preceded it, and was already some distance in the wood, at a spot, where the two trails, that to the garrison, and that to the villages of the Delawares separated. The soldiers, too, had taken up their line of march, first setting the Ark adrift again, with a reckless disregard of its fate. All this Judith saw, but she heeded it not. The Glimmerglass had no longer any charms for her, and when she put her foot on the strand, she immediately proceeded on the trail of the soldiers, without casting a single glance behind her. Even Hist was passed unnoticed, that modest young creature shrinking from the averted face of Judith, as if guilty herself of some wrong doing.

"Wait you here, Sarpent," said Deerslayer as he followed in the footsteps of the dejected beauty, while passing his friend—"I will just see Judith among her party, and come and j'ine you."

A hundred yards had hid the couple from those in front, as well as those in their rear, when Judith turned, and spoke.

"This will do, Deerslayer," she said sadly—"I understand your kindness but shall not need it. In a few minutes I shall reach the soldiers. As you cannot go with me on the journey of life, I do not wish you to go further on this. But, stop—before we part, I would ask you a single question. And I require of you, as you fear God, and reverence the truth, not to deceive me in your answer. I know you do not love another and I can see but one reason why you cannot, *will* not love me. Tell me then, Deerslayer,—" The girl paused, the words she was about to utter seeming to choke her. Then rallying all her resolution, with a face that flushed and paled at every breath she drew, she continued.

"Tell me then, Deerslayer, if any thing light of me, that Henry March has said may not have influenced your feelings?"

Truth was the Deerslayer's polar star. He ever kept it in view, and it was nearly impossible for him to avoid uttering it, even when prudence demanded silence. Judith read his answer in his countenance, and with a heart nearly broken by the consciousness of undue erring, she signed to him an adieu, and buried herself in the woods. For some time Deerslayer was irresolute as to his course; but, in the end, he retraced his steps, and joined the Delaware. That night the three 'camped on the head waters of their own river, and the succeeding evening they entered the village of the tribe, Chingachgook and his betrothed in triumph; their companion honored and admired, but in a sorrow that it required months of activity to remove.

The war that then had its rise was stirring and bloody. The Delaware chief rose among his people, until his name was never mentioned without eulogiums, while another Uncas, the last of his race, was added to the long line of warriors who bore that distinguishing appellation. As for the Deerslayer, under the *sobriquet* of Hawkeye, he made his fame spread far and near, until the crack of his rifle became as terrible to the ears of the Mingos, as the thunders of the

Manitou. His services were soon required by the officers of the crown, and he especially attached himself, in the field, to one in particular, with whose after life, he had a close and important connection.

Fifteen years had passed away, ere it was in the power of the Deerslayer to revisit the Glimmerglass. A peace had intervened, and it was on the eve of another and still more important war, when he and his constant friend, Chingachgook, were hastening to the forts to join their allies. A stripling accompanied them, for Hist already slumbered beneath the pines of the Delawares, and the three survivors had now become inseparable. They reached the lake just as the sun was setting. Here all was unchanged. The river still rushed through its bower of trees; the little rock was washing away, by the slow action of the waves, in the course of centuries, the mountains stood in their native dress, dark, rich and mysterious, while the sheet glistened in its solitude, a beautiful gem of the forest.

The following morning, the youth discovered one of the canoes drifted on the shore, in a state of decay. A little labor put it in a state for service, and they all embarked, with a desire to examine the place. All the points were passed, and Chingachgook pointed out to his son, the spot where the Hurons had first encamped, and the point whence he had succeeded in stealing his bride. Here they even landed, but all traces of the former visit had disappeared. Next they proceeded to the scene of the battle, and there they found a few of the signs that linger around such localities. Wild beasts had disinterred many of the bodies, and human bones were bleaching in the rains of summer. Uncas regarded all with reverence and pity, though traditions were already rousing his young mind to the ambition and sternness of a warrior.

From the point, the canoe took its way toward the shoal, where the remains of the castle were still visible, a picturesque ruin. The storms of winter had long since unroofed the house, and decay had eaten into the logs. All the fastenings were untouched, but the seasons rioted in the place, as if in mockery at the attempt to exclude them. The palisades were rotting, as were the piles, and it was evident that a few more recurrences of winter, a few more gales and tempests, would sweep all into the lake, and blot the building from the face of that magnificent solitude. The graves could not be found. Either the elements had obliterated their traces, or time had caused those who looked for them, to forget their position.

The Ark was discovered stranded on the eastern shore, where it had long before been driven with the prevalent northwest winds. It lay on the sandy extremity of a long low point, that is situated about two miles from the outlet, and which is itself fast disappearing before the action of the elements. The scow was filled with water, the cabin unroofed, and the logs were decaying. Some of its coarser furniture still remained, and the heart of Deerslayer beat quick, as he found a ribband of Judith's fluttering from a log. It recalled all her beauty, and we may add all her failings. Although the girl had never touched his heart, the Hawkeye, for so we ought now to call him, still retained a kind and sincere interest in her welfare. He tore away the ribband, and knotted it to the stock of Killdeer, which had been the gift of the girl herself.

A few miles farther up the lake, another of the canoes was discovered, and on the point where the party finally landed, were found those which had been left there upon the shore. That in which the present navigation was made, and the one discovered on the eastern shore, had dropped through the decayed floor of the castle, drifted past the falling palisades, and had been thrown as waifs upon the beach.

From all these signs, it was probable the lake had not been visited, since the occurrence of the final scene of our tale. Accident, or tradition, had rendered it again, a spot sacred to nature, the frequent wars, and the feeble population of the colonies, still confining the settlements within narrow boundaries. Chingachgook and his friend left the spot with melancholy feelings. It had been the region of their First War Path, and it carried back the minds of both to scenes of tenderness, as well as to hours of triumph. They held their way towards the Mohawk in silence, however, to rush into new adventures, as stirring and as remarkable as those which had attended their opening careers, on this lovely lake. At a later day, they returned to the place, where the Indian found a grave.

Time and circumstances have drawn an impenetrable

mystery around all else connected with the Hutters. They lived, erred, died, and are forgotten. None connected have felt sufficient interest in the disgraced and disgracing to withdraw the veil, and a century is about to erase even the recollection of their names. The history of crime is ever revolting, and it is fortunate that few love to dwell on its incidents. The sins of the family have long since been arraigned at the judgment seat of God, or are registered for the terrible settlement of the last great day.

The same fate attended Judith. When Hawkeye reached the garrison on the Mohawk he enquired anxiously after that lovely but misguided creature. None knew her—even her person was no longer remembered. Other officers had, again and again, succeeded the Warleys and Craigs and Grahams, though an old sergeant of the garrison, who had lately come from England, was enabled to tell our hero, that Sir Robert Warley lived on his paternal estates, and that there was a lady of rare beauty in the Lodge, who had great influence over him, though she did not bear his name. Whether this was Judith relapsed into her early failing, or some other victim of the soldier's, Hawkeye never knew, nor would it be pleasant or profitable to inquire. We live in a world of transgressions and selfishness, and no pictures that represent us otherwise can be true, though, happily, for human nature, gleamings of that pure spirit in whose likeness man has been fashioned, are to be seen relieving its deformities, and mitigating if not excusing its crimes.

Chronology

1789 Born James Cooper to William Cooper and Elizabeth Fenimore Cooper, both of Quaker ancestry, September 15 in Burlington, N. J., the twelfth of thirteen children. Four brothers (Richard, b. 1775, Isaac, b. 1781, William, b. 1785, and Samuel, b. 1787) and two sisters (Hannah, b. 1777, and Anne, b. 1784) survive childhood.

1790–91 Family moves to Lake Otsego, in upper New York State, where father has acquired a large tract of land formerly owned by Col. George Croghan and has established the wilderness settlement to be known as Cooperstown.

1791–1800 Otsego is made a county, and Cooper's father, a Federalist squire with firm convictions about the relationship between property and political power, begins term as first judge of the Court of Common Pleas for Otsego County, and is elected to Congress in 1795 and 1799. Cooper attends public school in Cooperstown (except for the winters of 1796–97 and 1798–99, when he is enrolled in school in Burlington, N. J.). Reported to have been venturesome, athletic, and an enthusiastic reader. Sister Hannah says her brothers are "very wild" and "show plainly that they have been bred in the Woods." Hannah dies when she falls from a horse September 10, 1800. (Cooper later wrote that she was "a sort of second mother to me. From her I received many of my earliest lessons. . . . A lapse of forty years has not removed the pain with which I allude to the subject at all.")

1801–02 Becomes a boarding student in the home of father's friend, Rev. Thomas Ellison, rector of St. Peter's Church, Albany, N.Y., where he is drilled in Latin and forced to memorize long passages of Virgil. After Ellison dies in April 1802, goes to New Haven to be tutored for Yale College.

1803 Matriculates at Yale in February. (One of his professors, Benjamin Silliman, recalled twenty-five years later that the young Cooper was a "fine sparkling beautiful boy of alluring person and interesting manners.") Career at Yale marred by inattention to studies and a series of pranks (family tradition says that he tied a donkey in a professor's chair and stuffed a rag impregnated with gunpowder into the keyhole of another student's door and set it afire). Dismissed from Yale in junior year, returns to Cooperstown, and continues education with tutor, the Reverend William Neill, who regards him as rather wayward, disinclined to study, and addicted to novel-reading.

1806–07 To prepare for a naval career, serves as sailor-before-the-mast on the merchant vessel *Stirling*. Sails October 1806 to the Isle of Wight, London, Spain, then London again before returning home September 1807. On this voyage meets Edward R. Meyers, an apprentice seaman (whose biography he would write in 1843).

1808–09 Receives midshipman's warrant January 1, 1808. Serves in the bomb ketch *Vesuvius* from March to July. Stationed at Fort Oswego, a frontier outpost on Lake Ontario, August 22, 1808, to October 1809 to apprehend smugglers during the 1808 embargo. In November, requests transfer to the sloop *Wasp 18*, anchored in New York, under Lieutenant James Lawrence, and is assigned task of recruiting sailors. Meets fellow recruiter William Branford Shubrick (later Rear Admiral), who becomes his most intimate friend. Judge Cooper dies December 22 of pneumonia (contracted after being struck from behind by a political opponent). Cooper willed $50,000 as his share of the legacy and a remainder interest with his brothers and sister in the $750,000 estate.

1810 Meets Susan Augusta De Lancey, eighteen, daughter of a prominent Westchester County family that had supported the Loyalist cause during the war. "I loved her like a man," Cooper writes to his brother Richard, "and told her of it like a sailor." Requests a year's furlough to settle affairs following father's death, and a year later resigns from the navy.

1811–13 On New Year's Day, 1811, marries Susan De Lancey at her home in Mamaroneck, N.Y.; in April begins farming in a small way in New Rochelle. First child, Elizabeth, born September 27. Buys a farm, which he names Fenimore, on the western shore of Lake Otsego about a mile from

Cooperstown, hoping to establish residence there permanently. Oldest brother, Richard, dies March 6, 1813. Second daughter, Susan Augusta, born April 17, 1813. Elizabeth dies July 13th, 1813, soon after the move to Fenimore.

1814 Family lives in small frame house while permanent stone manor house is built. Cooper, a gentleman farmer and one of the founders of the county agricultural society, is active in the militia and the local Episcopal church.

1815–17 Two more daughters are born: Caroline Martha, June 26, 1815, and Anne Charlotte, May 14, 1817. Family moves back to Westchester County, autumn, 1817, because Mrs. Cooper wishes to be near her family and also because Cooper faces increasing financial difficulties caused by the depression following the War of 1812, claims against estate, and personal debts.

1818 Builds home on De Lancey land, Scarsdale, N.Y., and names farm Angevine. Attempts to retrieve family fortune in speculative ventures. Becomes active in local Clintonian Republican politics. Two brothers die: William, to whom he was most attached, and Isaac, who had been most like his father. Mother, who has been living in the family residence, Otsego Hall, dies in December.

1819 With associate Charles Thomas Dering, invests in Sag Harbor whaler *The Union*, April 15 (Cooper owns the ship and two-thirds of the outfit); frequently sails on it. June 15, daughter Maria Frances is born. Appointed quartermaster, with rank of colonel, in New York State militia, July 1819. Last remaining brother, Samuel, dies.

1820 Writes first novel, *Precaution*, an imitation of a class of popular British novels, reportedly on challenge from wife. Its publication in November brings him into New York City literary and artistic circles. Begins to frequent the bookshop of Charles Wiley, and to write reviews for Wiley's *Literary and Scientific Repository*, meeting friends—among them Fitz-Greene Halleck and William Dunlap—in a back room he later christens "The Den."

1821 First son, Fenimore, born October 23. Second novel, *The Spy*, published December 22, is an immediate and resounding success. Translated into French and published in Paris.

1822 Quarrels with De Lancey family, and moves with wife and children from Westchester County to New York City, to be near publishers and to improve daughters' opportunities for schooling. Founds the Bread and Cheese, a lunch club often referred to as "the Cooper Club," whose informal membership would include merchants, painters, poets, journalists, and army and navy officers. Though his earnings are improved, Cooper's financial difficulties are not fully resolved.

1823 3500 copies of *The Pioneers* sold on the morning of publication (February 1). English edition published by Murray is the first of Cooper's works not to be pirated. Becomes interested in journalism; writes account of a horse race for the New York *Patriot*. April, becomes a member of the American Philosophical Society. Moves to 3 Beach Street, New York City, in May. In July, the house at Fenimore burns to the ground. Son Fenimore dies August 5. In autumn, household goods inventoried (but not sold) by Sheriff of New York. Has "bilious attack" from which he continues to suffer for several years.

1824 Publishes first sea romance, *The Pilot*, in January, an attempt in part to show the nautical inaccuracies in Sir Walter Scott's *The Pirate*. Paul Fenimore Cooper born February 5. Writes account of the celebration at Castle Garden in honor of General Lafayette for the New York *American*. Moves family in May to 345 Greenwich Street, New York City. In August, receives honorary M.A. from Columbia College. Accompanies four English noblemen (including Edward Stanley, Earl of Derby and future prime minister of England) on a sight-seeing trip to Saratoga, Ballston, Lake George, Ticonderoga, and Lake Champlain. In a cavern in Glen Falls with Stanley, decides to write *The Last of the Mohicans*. ("I must place one of my old Indians here.")

1825 Publishes *Lionel Lincoln*, the first of his commercial failures. Forms close friendship with Samuel F. B. Morse, artist (and future inventor of the telegraph).

1826 *The Last of the Mohicans*, published in February, receives enthusiastic press and becomes the best known of his novels on both sides of the Atlantic. Formally adds Fenimore to his name in fulfillment of pledge to his mother. Receives silver medal in May from the Corporation of the City of New York. Attends a farewell banquet in his honor given by the Bread and Cheese. In June, the family (including sixteen-year-old nephew William) sails for Europe for Cooper's health, the children's education, and, as Cooper confesses, "perhaps . . . a little pleasure concealed in the bottom of the cup"; European residence will extend to seven years. Carries with him unfinished manuscript of *The Prairie* and a nominal commission as U.S. Consul for Lyons, France. Following a brief visit to England, family settles in Paris, July 22, and after a few weeks in the Hotel Montmorency, moves to the Hotel Jumilhac, 12 Rue St. Maur, in the Faubourg St. Germain, where Cooper is courted by Parisian society. "The people," he writes to a friend, "seem to think it marvelous that an American can write." Visits Lafayette, who becomes his closest European friend, at his home, La Grange. November, Sir Walter Scott visits to enlist his help to change the American copyright laws and secure revenue from his American imprints.

1827 Publishes *The Prairie* (April, London; May, Philadelphia). Works on *The Red Rover* and, at Lafayette's suggestion, begins work on *Notions of the Americans*, intended to describe American institutions and the American character and to correct misconceptions about the United States current in England. Translations of works into French are paid for and published by Goddelin. June 1 to November 16, family lives in a thirty-room walled-in villa in St. Ouèn, on the Seine, four miles from Paris. Health improves in the country air. *The Red Rover* published November in Paris and London, and January in Philadelphia.

1828–29 February, visits London with wife, son Paul, and nephew William to finish *Notions* and see it through the press and is astonished by the warmth of his reception in literary and political, mainly Whig, circles. Finishes the book May 17. Returns to Paris June 9, via Holland and Belgium. July 28, family settles in Berne, Switzerland, where Cooper works on *The Wept of Wish-ton-Wish* and makes notes on his Swiss travels. Takes excursions to many parts of the country. Resigns as Consul of Lyons September 8, and leaves for Italy in October. Resides at Palazzo Ricasoli in Florence, November 25 to May 11, 1829. (Later writes of Italy: ". . . it is the only region of the earth that I truly love.") Mingles widely in Florentine society and comes to know members of the Bonaparte family. Among American expatriates, is especially attracted to young American sculptor Horatio Greenough, from whom he commissions a work. (". . . of all the arts that of statuary is perhaps the one we most want, since it is more openly and visibly connected with the taste of the people.") February, sets out alone to Paris to arrange for the printing of *The Wept of Wish-ton-Wish*, but after negotiations in Marseilles, the work is set and printed in Florence. *Notions of the Americans* published in England June 1828, and in America two months later. In July 1829, family travels from Leghorn to Naples in a chartered felucca, and in August settles in a chateau called "Tasso's house" in Sorrento, where Cooper writes most of *The Water-Witch*. December, family settles in Rome for a stay of several months. Goes riding on the campagna. ("Rome is only to be seen at leisure, and I think, it is only to be seen well, on horseback.")

1830 Reads Jefferson's letters and writes to a friend: "Have we not had a false idea of that man? I own he begins to appear to me, to be the greatest man, we ever had." Coopers leave Rome in mid-April, travel slowly north, pausing ten days in Venice, and arrive late in May in Dresden, where Cooper supervises the printing of *The Water-Witch*. August, returns to Paris (". . . the revolution which was consummated in Paris . . . induced me to come post haste . . ."). Through Lafayette, a prime mover in the events of the July revolution, follows closely the course of the new monarchy of Louis Philippe, to whom he is presented. Interests himself also in revolutionary movements in Belgium, Italy, and particularly Poland, whose struggle with Russia he actively supports.

1831 Decides to stay at least another year in Europe so daughters can finish their education, and in April takes large, unfurnished flat at 59 St. Dominique in the Faubourg St. Germain. Undertakes to revise and write new prefaces to his previously published works for Colburn and Bentley, who pay him £50 per title. Receives additional money from European translations of his works. No longer encumbered by debts, expects to earn $20,000 during the year. September, tours Belgium and the Rhine with wife, Paul, and Frances. Sends nephew William, who has been ill, to Le Havre in the hope that sea air may cure him. William dies of consumption October 1. *The Bravo*, first novel in a European trilogy chronicling the decline of feudalism and the rise of popular institutions, published October 15. At Lafayette's urging, enters the "Finance Controversy" (provoked by an article in the *Revue Brittanique* on the French national budget that claims monarchy is less expensive than the American republic) by writing a "Letter to General Lafayette," dated November 25 (published in English by Baudry in December, and in French translation in the *Revue des Deux Mondes* in January), citing official records to prove the republic is less expensive.

1832 Letter becomes focus of debate in the January session of the Chamber of Deputies, and further exchanges of letters are published. Cooper suspects, incorrectly, that the American minister to France, William C. Rives, has taken a view contrary to his. Goes less into society; spends much time with Samuel Morse after he comes to Paris in September, visiting galleries, viewing and discussing art. Writes to William Dunlap: "I have cut all Kings & Princes, go to no great Officers and jog on this way from the beginning to the end of the month." Considers visiting America to decide whether family should ever return permanently. Feels "heart-sick" about unfavorable American criticism of his political actions in Europe and of *The Bravo*. Cholera epidemic breaks out in Paris in April. Morse returns to America in July. *The Heidenmauer*, second volume in European trilogy, published (London, July; Philadelphia, Sept.). Between July and October the Coopers travel in Belgium, the Rhineland, and Switzerland for Mrs. Cooper's health and a long-deferred vacation. On return to Paris, works on *The Headsman*. Arranges for Bentley's publication of William Dunlap's *History of the American Theatre*. Becomes increasingly restive as European attacks on his republicanism are published in America together with adverse reviews of his books. Resents what he calls "this slavish dependence on foreign opinion" and determines to abandon writing after *The Headsman*.

1833 June 15, goes to London to supervise the printing of *The Headsman*, last volume of the European trilogy (published London, Sept.; Philadelphia, Oct.). Soon after returning to Paris at the end of July, family leaves for America, stopping en route for a few weeks in England. Arrives in New York November 5, and moves family temporarily into a house on Bleecker Street rented for them by Samuel Morse. Sensing a chill in homecoming reception, Cooper declines testimonial dinner in his honor proposed by the Bread and Cheese. Enters speculative cotton market with James de Peyster Ogden and makes tour of Washington, Baltimore, and Philadelphia in December for business reasons and to observe firsthand the effects of five years of Jacksonian democracy. Concludes that country has changed but not improved and that there is "a vast expansion of mediocrity." Writes a friend that "were it not for my family, I should return to Europe, and pass the remainder of my life there."

1834 Spring, family moves to townhouse at 4 St. Marks Place. Publication, in June, of *A Letter to His Countrymen* (arguing that American "practice of deferring to foreign opinion is dangerous to the institutions of the country") increases unpopularity and provokes widespread attacks in the Whig press. After seventeen years' absence, revisits Cooperstown in June; October, purchases the family seat, Otsego Hall, and sets about renovating it for possible permanent occupancy. "My pen is used up—or rather it is thrown away," he writes a correspondent. "This is not a country for literature, at least not yet." Resumes the writing of *The Monikins*, allegorical satire on England, France, and America begun in Paris in 1832. Writes the first of a series of political articles in December—dealing mainly with the payment of the French debt, the differences between American constitutional government and the French system, and the functions of the three branches of government in America—for the New York *Evening Post* under the pseudonym "A.B.C."

1835 Sends manuscript chapter of *The Bravo* to Princess Victoria (later Queen of England) when asked for autograph.

The Monikins, published July, fails with critics and public. Family spends summer in Cooperstown, winter in New York City.

1836 Family leaves house at St. Marks Place in May and moves the remainder of their furniture to Cooperstown. Cooper goes to Philadelphia in July to see *Sketches of Switzerland* through the press (a practice he will continue with many of his future works). Part I published May, Part II, October.

1837 Becomes involved in a misunderstanding with townspeople over public use of Three Mile Point, a picnic ground on Lake Otsego owned by the Cooper family for which Cooper is trustee. After users damage the property, Cooper publishes No Trespass Notice, offending those who assumed the Point was public property. Local excitement subsides after Cooper sends two letters to the *Freeman's Journal* explaining the situation. Some county newspaper editors disregard explanation and publish articles attacking him. When offending newspapers refuse to retract statements, Cooper sues for libel. (Before these suits come to trial, publishes *Home as Found*, a novel of social criticism, in which a fictionalized version of the incident caricatures a newspaper editor. Major New York Whig editors now join in the quarrel against Cooper, justifying their attacks by maintaining that he put himself into the book and has thus made himself a legitimate target. Cooper begins suits against them. Though eventually winning most of these suits, it is at the cost of much time, energy, and popularity. Awarded $400 in damages in May 1839, writes to a correspondent, "We shall bring the press, again, under the subjection of the law. When one considers the characters, talents, motives and consistency of those who control it, as a body, he is lost in wonder that any community should have so long submitted to a tyranny so low and vulgar. When it is rebuked thoroughly, it may again become useful.") Travel books drawn from his European letters and journals are published under the general title *Gleanings in Europe*. (*France*: London, Jan., Phila., Mar.; *England*: London, May, Phila., Sept.; and *Italy*, published as *Excursions in Italy* in London, Feb. 28, 1838, Phila., May 1838.)

1838 Publishes *The American Democrat* (Cooperstown, Apr.), *Chronicles of Cooperstown, Homeward Bound* (London, May; Phila., August) and its sequel *Home as Found* (Nov.). Attacked in Whig press for his condescending portrayal of American manners. Meanwhile, works on *History of the Navy of the United States of America*, a project contemplated for more than a decade. December, goes with wife and four daughters to Philadelphia to research and see the work through the press. Stays until May 1839.

1839 Begins friendship with historian George Bancroft. *History of the Navy*, published May, sells well until it is attacked in the press by partisans of Commodore Oliver Hazard Perry for its account of the controversial Battle of Lake Erie. Defends account in letters to the *Freeman's Journal* and sues his critics (particularly William A. Duer). Suits for libel continue to occupy much of his time for the next several years. Writes *The Pathfinder* and goes to Philadelphia in December to see it through the press.

1840 *The Pathfinder* published (London, Feb.; Phila., March). It is well received, and Balzac writes an admiring tribute to Cooper's work. Goes again to Philadelphia to see *Mercedes of Castile* (his "Columbus book") through the press in October, taking a cruise during this time with old friend Commodore Shubrick on the *Macedonian*. The work is published November in Philadelphia, and a month later in London.

1841 Continues to purchase old family property. June, tries once again, unsuccessfully, to interest publishers in a "sea story all ships and no men." August, delivers the commencement address at Geneva College, where son Paul is a student, on the thesis "Public Opinion is a Despot in a Democracy." Travels to Philadelphia in June, and again in August to see works through the press. *The Deerslayer* and a short version of *The History of the Navy* published in September.

1842 Addresses a series of letters to "Brother Jonathan" (begun Dec. 1841), defending *Homeward Bound* and *Home as Found* as fictions. ("When a work *professes* to be fiction, the reader is bound to consider all those parts fiction, which cannot be proved otherwise.") Wins judgments in court in libel suits against William Leete Stone of the *Commercial Advertiser* (for the William A. Duer articles on the Battle of Lake Erie) and against Thurlow Weed and Horace Greeley (for articles on Three Mile Point). Large audience attends the Duer-Stone trial and Cooper speaks eloquently for himself. Publishes *The Two Admirals* (May) and *The Wing-and-Wing* (*Jack O'Lantern* in England, Nov.). Persuaded by editor Rufus Wilmot Griswold to write for *Graham's Magazine*, agrees to do a series of brief biographies of naval officers, for the first time receiving pay for serial publication (sketches appear between 1842–45, beginning with "Richard Somers," October).

1843 Becomes engrossed with the *Somers* mutiny case and the proceedings against Capt. Alexander Slidell Mackenzie, on whose orders one midshipman and two crew members, presumed mutineers, had been executed at sea, the midshipman being the son of the Secretary of War in Tyler's cabinet. Writes eighty-page review of the case (published as an annex to the *Proceedings* of the naval court martial in 1844). *Autobiography of a Pocket Handkerchief* (or *Le Mouchoir*) serialized in *Graham's* January through April. After thirty-six years hears from old shipmate, Edward (Ned) Meyers, and brings him for five-month stay in Cooperstown. Writes Ned's biography, using his own words as much as possible. Journeys with John Pendleton Kennedy and William Gilmore Simms to Philadelphia. Publishes *The Battle of Lake Erie* (June), *Wyandotté* (London, Aug.; Phila., Sept.), *Ned Myers, or a Life Before the Mast* (Nov.). Income from writings begins to diminish seriously because of cheap reprints from abroad and difficult economic conditions at home.

1844 Writes in January to William Gilmore Simms, "We serve a hard master, my dear Sir, in writing for America." *Afloat and Ashore* published by Cooper himself in America and by Bentley in London, June. Second part, entitled *Miles Wallingford*, published October (Sept. in England, with title *Lucy Hardinge*). Begins work on the anti-rent (or Littlepage) trilogy, tracing the history of four generations of a landed New York family which culminates in conflict between tenants and landlords.

1845 First two volumes of the trilogy, *Satanstoe* (June) and *The Chainbearer* (Nov.), published and criticized on the grounds that Cooper is too partial to the interests of landed proprietors. John Pendleton Kennedy family visits Otsego in August. Attends Annual Diocesan Convention of the Protestant Episcopal Church in September, to consider the charge against Bishop Benjamin Tredwell Onderdonk of "immorality and impurity." Convinced of the truth of the charges, speaks at the convention, offering a solution to the tangled procedural system, but without success.

1846 Final volume of the anti-rent trilogy, *The Redskins* (*Ravensnest* in England), published July. *The Lives of Distinguished Naval Officers*, originally serialized in *Graham's*, published in two volumes in Philadelphia, March and May. *Jack Tier* serialized in *Graham's* and Bentley's *Miscellany*, November 1846–March 1848, under title "The Islets of the Gulf" (published March 1848; English title, *Captain Spike*).

1847 Begins a series of trips in June to Michigan in connection with unfortunate land investments and is impressed with the unspoiled country. August, publishes *The Crater*. ("It is a remarkable book, and ought to make a noise.") October, goes again to Detroit on business.

1848 Enters debate concerning the circumstances of General Nathaniel Woodhull's death during the American Revolution, writing several letters to the *Home Journal*, February–June. Writes letters on the new French republic in March and April for the Albany *Argus*. June and October, travels to Michigan. Publishes *The Oak Openings; or the Bee Hunter*, set in frontier Michigan, in August.

1849 Writes a long appreciative letter to Louis Legrand Nobel about Thomas Cole: "As an artist, I consider Mr. Cole one of the very first geniuses of the age." Daughter Caroline Martha marries Henry Frederick Phinney in Cooperstown, February 8. Though Cooper has quarreled with members of the groom's family and is unhappy about the match, he writes his daughter: ". . . your happiness will be the first consideration . . . Under no circumstances must there be coldness, alienation, or indifference. You are my dearly beloved child . . ." Publishes *The Sea Lions*, April, which does well in America but fails in England. The success of the collected edition of Washington Irving's writings encourages G. P. Putnam to begin issuing a uniform edition of Cooper, extending only to eleven volumes. Spends most of the time from October through April at the Globe Hotel, New York City, mainly to be close to the publishing center. Works on *The Ways of the Hour* and renews old acquaintances.

1850 Last novel, *The Ways of the Hour*, published in April. Cooper's only play, *Upside Down, or, Philosophy in Petticoats*, a satire on socialism, is performed June 18–21 at Burton's Chambers Street Theatre, New York, featuring actor-producer William E. Burton. Works on a projected third volume of his *History of the Navy*. July, travels to Niagara and Michigan with wife and daughter Charlotte. Goes to New York City in November to consult Dr. John Wakefield Francis about health problems: sharp pains in heels, with other symptoms, such as numbness of hands and feet. Daughter Maria Francis marries cousin Richard Cooper, December 10, in Cooperstown.

1851 Works on a history of greater New York, *The Towns of Manhattan* (unfinished, though he dictates a chapter in August after he is too ill to hold a pen). Writes to friend that he has lost twenty-two pounds. Continues to suffer from ailments, and in March goes to New York on business, and also to consult doctor. Consents to receive sacraments of the Protestant Episcopal Church. With great effort, travels the short distance to Christ Church, July 27, to be confirmed by Bishop De Lancey (his wife's brother). Sends introduction and eight chapters of *The Towns of Manhattan* to Putnam in July. Handwriting fails, and he dictates letters and work in progress to wife and daughters. Condition worsens, though he feels little pain. Dies at 1:30 P.M., September 14, 1851, in Otsego Hall. Buried in the family plot in Cooperstown.

Note on the Texts

This volume contains the last two of James Fenimore Cooper's five Leatherstocking Tales: *The Pathfinder* (1840) and *The Deerslayer* (1841). A companion volume contains *The Pioneers* (1823), *The Last of the Mohicans* (1826), and *The Prairie* (1827). The texts reprinted here are those established for *The Writings of James Fenimore Cooper* under the general editorship of James Franklin Beard, with James P. Elliott as textual editor, and published by the State University of New York Press, Albany (hereafter referred to as the SUNY edition): *The Pathfinder* (1981) and *The Deerslayer* (page proofs). These texts were prepared according to the standards established by—and they have received the official approval of—the Center for Editions of American Authors (or its successor, the Center for Scholarly Editions) of the Modern Language Association of America (see *The Center for Scholarly Editions: An Introductory Statement*, 1977). The aim of the SUNY edition is to establish a text that as nearly as possible represents the author's final intentions. In selecting their copy-text, the editors give priority to the holograph manuscript, in whole or part, when it exists; when it does not survive, preference goes next to proofs corrected in the author's hand, or, if these do not exist, to the editions Cooper is known to have supervised or revised. Though circumstances beyond his control frequently defeated his intentions, Cooper was a painstaking reviser who corrected compositorial errors, rewrote sentences and phrases, altered punctuation and spelling (his own punctuation and spelling were not always consistent), sharpened diction, and in particular resisted the attempts of editors, compositors, and amanuenses to normalize dialect expression (e.g. " 'arth" to "earth," "ag'in" to "again," "Injin" to "Indian").

Cooper's decision to return to Leatherstocking some thirteen years after he had recounted his death and burial in *The Prairie* must be credited in part to a suggestion from his English publisher, Richard Bentley. In a letter of April 6, 1839, Bentley proposed that the novelist "undertake a naval story on your own inland Seas." Cooper readily complied. By June he was at work on what he described to Bentley as his "nautico-lake-savage romance," *The Pathfinder*. On October 19 he reported to his wife from Philadelphia, where he had gone to be near his American publisher, that the first volume was being printed but that the second was not yet written. He finished the novel in December, and the printing was completed in January 1840. To protect the British copyright, the English edition, published by Richard Bentley February 24, 1840, preceded the American edition, published March 14 in Philadelphia by Lea and Blanchard.

Fortunately, the holograph manuscript of *The Pathfinder: or, The Inland Sea* survives and is now in the University of Virginia Library. It serves as the copy-text for the SUNY edition. The first American edition was set from Cooper's manuscript and is the first authorial edition. Cooper made many alterations in the proofs of the first edition to simplify expression, clarify meaning, improve diction, add information, correct names, and, as was habitual with him, increase and refine dialect forms. The manuscript (which was needed to protect the British copyright) and proof sheets were then sent on to Bentley. Bentley, following Cooper's explicit instructions, set the English edition from the Lea and Blanchard proofs. In the rush to complete the work, Cooper made corrections in the proof sheets of the introduction sent to England that he apparently failed to make in the American edition. The introduction in the English edition, therefore, is authoritative. The second authorial edition appeared in Putnam's Author's Revised Edition in 1851. Though Cooper apologized in the preface to that edition for the many errors remaining in the first edition, most of them the result of compositorial misreadings, this second edition retained most of the first edition's misreadings and introduced nearly two hundred non-authorial readings. Cooper restored forty-nine manuscript words or phrases, and corrected dialect forms: for example, "real" becomes "raal," "concerning" becomes "consarning," "girls" becomes "gals." He also added a new preface, as he had done for other works in this edition. As a result, the text of *The Pathfinder*, like that of the other Leatherstocking Tales, did not achieve an approximation of what would have been Cooper's final intentions during his lifetime. The SUNY textual editor, Richard Dilworth Rust, collated all the relevant documents and determined which variants were intended by Cooper, and which were caused by compositorial misreading or editorial intervention. The intended emendations were then inserted into the copy-text.

Presumably Cooper was well into the composition of *The Deerslayer: or, The First War-Path* on November 10, 1840, when he wrote to Richard Bentley proposing terms for the novel, which, he indicated, "will contain the *early* life of Leatherstocking—a period that is only wanted to fill up his career." At the end of January 1841, he informed Bentley that the work was nearly half finished and that he was considering several alternative titles: " 'Judith and Esther, or, the Girls of the Glimmerglass.'—'Wah!-Ta-Wah!, or, Hist!-Oh!-Hist!' 'The Deerslayer, or a Legend of the Glimmerglass.' &c &c. In some respects I prefer the last—" By early July, Bentley had received the manuscript and duplicate proof sheets, together with Cooper's request that the novel be published as early in September as possible. Lea and Blanchard published *The Deerslayer* in Philadelphia on August 27, 1841; Richard Bentley brought out the British edition on September 7. (In this case, Bentley seems not to have had any problem in maintaining the British copyright.)

The copy-text for *The Deerslayer* is the corrected holograph manuscript, now in the Pierpont Morgan Library, from which the first American edition was set. Because of Cooper's overcrowded and interlineated manuscript, the compositors at Lea and Blanchard made a number of significant misreadings that Cooper, despite his careful proofreading, failed to correct. Though no page proofs of the Lea and Blanchard edition are known to survive, it is clear from Cooper's correspondence that he made revisions that were incorporated into that text. The Lea and Blanchard edition of 1841 is therefore the first authorial edition. The second is the Putnam's Author's Revised Edition of 1850. *The Deerslayer* was the first of the Leatherstocking Tales to appear in this edition, and Cooper wrote for it a general "Preface to the Leather-Stocking Tales." This preface has been included in the SUNY edition. As with the other Leatherstocking Tales in the Putnam series, the revisions were not extensive and were limited mainly to correcting grammatical errors, tightening style, and, as always, insisting on the preservation of dialect forms. The SUNY textual editors, Lance Schachterle, Kent P. Ljungquist, and James A. Kilby, collated all the relevant documents and determined which variants were intended by Cooper.

The standards for American English continue to fluctuate and in some ways were conspicuously different in earlier periods from what they are now. In nineteenth-century writings, for example, a word might be spelled in more than one way, even in the same work, and such variations might be carried into print. Commas were sometimes used expressively to suggest the movements of voice, and capitals were sometimes meant to give significances to a word beyond those it might have in its uncapitalized form. Since modernization would remove such effects, this volume preserves the spelling, punctuation, capitalization, and wording of the SUNY edition, which strives to be as faithful to Cooper's usage as surviving evidence permits.

This volume offers the reader the results of the most detailed scholarly effort thus far made to establish the texts of *The Pathfinder* and *The Deerslayer*. The present edition is concerned only with representing the *texts* of these editions; it does not attempt to reproduce features of the typographic design—such as the display capitalization of chapter openings. Epigraphs from Shakespeare have been keyed by the SUNY editors to *The Riverside Shakespeare*, ed. G. Blakemore Evans (Boston: Houghton Mifflin, 1974); other epigraphs are keyed to unspecified "standard editions," "first editions," or "early American editions" available to Cooper at the time he wrote the Tales. The texts in this volume follow exactly the SUNY *The Pathfinder* (first printing) and *The Deerslayer* (page proofs), except for the following errors: 87.4, woiuld; 96.17, hand.; 122.33, trip it."; 122.34, serjeant; 135.10, deceived.; 151.30, 'Put; 153.4, to the; 157.15, Amerians; 215.11, thik; 219.17, companion-way. Mr. Muir; 279.18, Better; 279.24, serjeant; 279.31, is; 280.25, you hardy; 293.2, where; 325.30, solutide; 334.36, Eau-douce; 372.20, civilization.; 380.13, *rúse*; 392.13–15, Mabel—" said the Scout, in an earnest but low voice, seizing her by an arm.——"This will not do. Sartain; 433.24, hyprocisy; 435.11, *Violà*; 451.6, fully at. (These errors in the SUNY edition will be corrected in future printings.)

Notes

In the notes below, the numbers refer to page and line of this volume (the line count includes chapter headings). No note is made for material included in a standard desk-reference book. Notes at the foot of the page are Cooper's own. For additional textual and explanatory notes, see the relevant volumes in the SUNY edition.

THE PATHFINDER

5.1 Preface] Added in the Author's Revised Edition, 1851.

10.21 Tuscaroras] Originally from North Carolina and linguistically related to the Mohawks, the Tuscaroras suffered from the white settlers' unfair trading practices and enslavement of their children. Subsequently decimated in warfare with the whites, they were driven north early in the eighteenth century, taking refuge with the Iroquois and later becoming the Sixth Nation of their Confederacy.

21.1–2 Prophet . . . Delawares] Tamenund. See *The Last of the Mohicans*, 811.3.

24.19 kid and can] A kid was a small tub in which sailors received their food; a can was a small or moderate-sized vessel used as a drinking cup.

37.25 Fort Stanwix] A colonial outpost near the site of present-day Rome, N.Y., which controlled the main route from the Hudson to Lake Ontario. Established originally by the French, it fell into disrepair and was rebuilt by the English in 1758. During the Revolution it was known as Fort Schuyler.

57.22–23 That . . . again."] Chapter XXXII in *The Last of the Mohicans* (death of Cora).

79.5 Ty!"] Ticonderoga.

99.35 sarvice . . . officer] Major Oliver Effingham. See *The Pioneers*.

111.22 Oswego] Established on Lake Ontario in 1722 by the English, Oswego had orginally served as a vital trading post for the Albany fur trade.

122.35 Thousand Islands] A group of more than 1500 islands in the St. Lawrence where it issues from Lake Ontario.

180.23 Powles . . . first rate] Paulus Hook, as it was known in the eighteenth century, is a low point of land protruding into the Hudson River at what is now Jersey City, N.J., and was the location of a British fort captured during the Revolution. A piragua (or, in the French adaptation from the

Spanish, pirogue) was a dugout canoe used by the Caribs in British Guiana. A "first rate" is a warship deemed superior in size and armament.

220.12–13 German . . . throne] Hanover was from 1692 to 1806 an electorate of the Holy Roman Empire. The house of Hanover secured the British succession, by virtue of the Act of Settlement of 1701, in favor of the electress Sophia (1630–1714), granddaughter of James I of Great Britain, who married Ernest Augustus, Duke of Hanover (1629–98), in 1658. Sophia's son, the elector George Louis (1660–1727), became George I, inaugurating a 123-year-long personal union between Great Britain and Hanover.

316.22 the Santa Cruz] St. Croix rum from the Virgin Islands.

318.16 Caput] The direct descendants of Hugh Capet, crowned in 987, ruled continuously until 1328 and the death of Charles IV. Cap's "Lewises" reigned in the sixteenth and seventeenth centuries. "Kaput" is German for "finished" or "vanquished."

348.8–11 "She'll . . . Muir."] Sir William Wallace (1272?–1305) drove the English out of Scotland in 1297, but was defeated the following year and ultimately executed. His compatriot, the eighth Robert de Bruce (1274–1329), was crowned King at Scone in 1306. Recognized by the Scottish clergy in 1310, his defeat of a larger English force at Bannockburn in 1314 completed the liberation of Scotland and led to acceptance by the Pope in 1323 and a peace treaty with England in 1328. At Culloden Moor, in Invernesshire, on April 16, 1746, the Hanoverian forces under the Duke of Cumberland defeated the Highland clans led by the Young Pretender, Prince Charles Edward Stuart (1720–88), widely known as Bonnie Prince Charlie, bringing to an end the Jacobite uprising of 1745.

382.4 castle . . . Beard] In Charles Perrault's version of the Blue Beard story (first translated into English in 1729), Blue Beard's wife, threatened with imminent death because she disobeyed her husband's orders and discovered his secret, stations her sister on the castle tower to watch for rescue by her brothers. Periodically she calls to "Anne, sister Anne" for word that her brothers are in sight.

407.17–18 Prince . . . himself."] Francois Eugene de Savoie-Carignan (1663–1736), Prince of Savoy, and John Churchill (1650–1722), first Duke of Marlborough, commanded the Austrian and English forces that defeated the French and Bavarians at the battle of Blenheim (August 13, 1704), during the War of the Spanish Succession. John Dalrymple (1673–1747), second Earl of Stair, was an aide-de-camp to Marlborough.

431.1–5 name . . . day.] The name Sanglier means "wild boar." John Butler (1728–94), Loyalist, soldier, and Indian agent, formed a group called Butler's Rangers, drawn from Loyalists in Niagara, to harass Continental settlements. He was held responsible for the atrocities committed by his Indian allies following the capitulation of Fort Forty, in the Wyoming Valley of Pennsylvania, on July 4, 1778. His son, Captain Walter N. Butler (d. 1781), led his father's Rangers in the attack on Cherry Valley, New York (November 11, 1778). He was blamed for the massacre committed there by his Iroquois allies under the famous Mohawk chief, Joseph Brant (Thayendanegea). Cooper probably had the younger Butler in mind.

THE DEERSLAYER

485.1 Preface] This preface appeared in the first edition.

489.1–2 Preface . . . Tales] Written for the collected edition in 1850, where for the first time the Tales were arranged according to the age of Leatherstocking.

492.15 One . . . critics] Lewis Cass, writing in *North American Review*, April 1828.

493.1 Preface . . . Deerslayer] Written for the 1850 edition.

496.6–7 residence . . . Rensselaers] The earliest home of the Van Rensselaer family, built as a fort on the east side of the Hudson at Greenbush, underwent reconstructions, but the ground floor retained many of the early loopholes.

508.4 a Moravian] Deerslayer had been educated by the Moravians, who carried on a mission among the Delawares. A reformed church founded by the followers of John Huss in 1457, sixty years before Luther's Reformation, the Moravians emigrated to America in the mid-eighteenth century and founded a colony at Bethlehem, Pennsylvania.

582.18 "a good . . . world."] *The Merchant of Venice*, V.i.90–91: Portia: "How far that little candle throws his beams! / So shines a good deed in a naughty world."

712.25 Yengeese*] This is the only footnote that appeared in the first edition.

759.30 Salvator Rosa] Salvator Rosa (1615–73) was an Italian painter of the Neapolitan school whose landscapes were much admired in Cooper's day. Sir Joshua Reynolds spoke of his art as having "the sort of dignity which belongs to savage and uncultivated nature."

LIBRARY OF CONGRESS CATALOGING IN PUBLICATION DATA

Cooper, James Fenimore, 1789–1851.
The Leatherstocking tales.

(The Library of America; 26–27)
Edited by Blake Nevius.
Contents: v.1. The pioneers, or The sources of the Susquehanna. The last of the Mohicans. The prairie.—v.2. The Pathfinder, or The inland sea. The Deerslayer, or The first war-path.
1. United States—History—Colonial period, ca. 1600–1775—Fiction. I. Nevius, Blake, 1916– II. Title: The Leatherstocking Tales. III. Title: The pioneers. IV. Title: The last of the Mohicans. V. Title: The prairie. VI. Title: The Pathfinder. VII. Title: The Deerslayer. VIII. Series: The Library of America.
PS1402 1985 813′.2 84–25060
ISBN 0–940450–20–8 (v.1)
ISBN 0–940450–21–6 (v.2)

This book is set in 10 point Linotron Galliard, a face designed for photocomposition by Matthew Carter and based on the sixteenth-century face Granjon. The paper is Olin Nyalite and conforms to guidelines adopted by the Committee on Book Longevity of the Council on Library Resources. The binding material is Brillianta, a 100% rayon cloth made by Van Heek-Scholco Textielfabrieken, Holland. Composition by Haddon Craftsmen, Inc. and The Clarinda Company. Printing and binding by R. R. Donnelley & Sons Company. Designed by Bruce Campbell.